HOLT

Elements of
LITERATURE

First Course

Kylene Beers

Carol Jago

Deborah Appleman

Leila Christenbury

Sara Kajder

Linda Rief

HOLT, RINEHART AND **WINSTON**

Program Authors

Kylene Beers is the senior program author for *Elements of Literature*. A former middle school teacher, she is now Senior Reading Advisor to Secondary Schools for Teachers College Reading and Writing Project at Columbia University. She is the author of *When Kids Can't Read: What Teachers Can Do* and co-editor (with Linda Rief and Robert E. Probst) of *Adolescent Literacy: Turning Promise into Practice*. The former editor of the National Council of Teachers of English (NCTE) literacy journal *Voices from the Middle*, Dr. Beers assumed the NCTE presidency in 2008. With articles in *English Journal, Journal of Adolescent and Adult Literacy, School Library Journal, Middle Matters,* and *Voices from the Middle,* she speaks both nationally and internationally as a recognized authority on struggling readers. Dr. Beers has served on the review boards of *English Journal, The ALAN Review,* the Special Interest Group on Adolescent Literature of the International Reading Association, and the Assembly on Literature for Adolescents of the NCTE. She is the 2001 recipient of the Richard W. Halley Award given by NCTE for outstanding contributions to middle school literacy.

Carol Jago is a teacher with thirty-two years of experience at Santa Monica High School in California. The author of nine books on education, she continues to share her experiences as a writer and as a speaker at conferences and seminars across the country. Her wide and varied experience in standards assessment and secondary education in general has made her a sought-after speaker. As an author, Ms. Jago also works closely with Heinemann Publishers and with the National Council of Teachers of English. Her longtime association with NCTE led to her June 2007 election to a four-year term on the council's board. During that term she will serve for one year as president of the council. She is also active with the California Association of Teachers of English (CATE) and has edited CATE's scholarly journal *California English* since 1996. Ms. Jago served on the planning committees for the 2009 NAEP Reading Framework and the 2011 NAEP Writing Framework.

Deborah Appleman is professor and chair of educational studies and director of the Summer Writing Program at Carleton College in Northfield, Minnesota. Dr. Appleman's primary research interests include adolescent response to literature, multicultural literature, and the teaching of literary theory in high school. With a team of classroom teachers, she co-edited *Braided Lives,* a multicultural literature anthology. In addition to many articles and book chapters, she is the author of

Linda Rief, Alfred Tatum, Kylene Beers, Patrick Schwarz, and Carol Jago

III

PROGRAM AUTHORS continued

Critical Encounters in High School English: Teaching Literary Theory to Adolescents and co-author of *Teaching Literature to Adolescents.* Her most recent book, *Reading for Themselves,* explores the use of extracurricular book clubs to encourage adolescents to read for pleasure. Dr. Appleman was a high school English teacher, working in both urban and suburban schools. She is a frequent national speaker and consultant and continues to work weekly in high schools with students and teachers.

Leila Christenbury is a former high school English teacher and currently professor of English education at Virginia Commonwealth University, Richmond. The former editor of *English Journal,* she is the author of ten books, including *Writing on Demand, Making the Journey,* and *Retracing the Journey: Teaching and Learning in an American High School.* Past president of the National Council of Teachers of English, Dr. Christenbury is also a former member of the steering committee of the National Assessment of Educational Progress (NAEP). A recipient of the Rewey Belle Inglis Award for Outstanding Woman in English Teaching, Dr. Christenbury is a frequent speaker on issues of English teaching and learning and has been interviewed and quoted on CNN and in the *New York Times, USA Today, Washington Post, Chicago Tribune,* and *US News & World Report.*

Sara Kajder, author of *Bringing the Outside In: Visual Ways to Engage Reluctant Readers* and *The Tech-Savvy English Classroom,* is an assistant professor at Virginia Polytechnic Institute and State University (Virginia Tech). She has served as co-chair of NCTE's Conference on English Education (CEE) Technology Commission and of the Society for Information Technology and Teacher Education (SITE) English Education Committee. Dr. Kajder is the recipient of the first SITE National Technology Leadership Fellowship in English Education; she is a former English and language arts teacher for high school and middle school.

Linda Rief has been a classroom teacher for twenty-five years. She is author of *The Writer's-Reader's Notebook, Inside the Writer's-Reader's Notebook, Seeking Diversity, 100 Quickwrites,* and *Vision and Voice* as well as the co-author (with Kylene Beers and Robert E. Probst) of *Adolescent Literacy: Turning Promise into Practice.* Ms. Rief has written numerous chapters and journal articles, and she co-edited the first five years of *Voices from the Middle.* During the summer she teaches graduate courses at the University of New Hampshire and Northeastern University. She is a national and international consultant on adolescent literacy issues.

Leila Christenbury, Héctor Rivera, Sara Kajder, Eric Cooper, and Deborah Appleman

Program Consultants

Mabel Rivera, Harvey Daniels, Margaret McKeown, and Isabel Beck

Isabel L. Beck is professor of education and senior scientist at the University of Pittsburgh. Dr. Beck has conducted extensive research on vocabulary and comprehension and has published well over one hundred articles and several books, including *Improving Comprehension with Questioning the Author* (with Margaret McKeown) and *Bringing Words to Life: Robust Vocabulary Instruction* (with Margaret McKeown and Linda Kucan). Dr. Beck's numerous national awards include the Oscar S. Causey Award for outstanding research from the National Reading Conference and the William S. Gray Award from the International Reading Association for lifetime contributions to the field of reading research and practice.

Margaret G. McKeown is a senior scientist at the University of Pittsburgh's Learning Research and Development Center. Her research in reading comprehension and vocabulary has been published extensively in outlets for both research and practitioner audiences. Recognition of her work includes the International Reading Association's (IRA) Dissertation of the Year Award and a National Academy of Education Spencer Fellowship. Before her career in research, Dr. McKeown taught elementary school.

Amy Benjamin is a veteran teacher, literacy coach, consultant, and researcher in secondary-level literacy instruction. She has been recognized for excellence in teaching from the New York State English Council, Union College, and Tufts University. Ms. Benjamin is the author of several books about reading comprehension, writing instruction, grammar, and differentiation. Her most recent book (with Tom Oliva) is *Engaging Grammar: Practical Advice for Real Classrooms,* published by the National Council of Teachers of English. Ms. Benjamin has had a long association and leadership role with the NCTE's Assembly for the Teaching of English Grammar (ATEG).

Eric Cooper is the president of the National Urban Alliance for Effective Education (NUA) and co-founder of the Urban Partnership for Literacy with the IRA. He currently works with the NCTE to support improvements in urban education and collaborates with the Council of the Great City Schools. In line with his educational mission to support the improvement of education for urban and minority students, Dr. Cooper writes, lectures, and produces educational documentaries and talk shows to provide advocacy for children who live in disadvantaged circumstances.

Harvey Daniels is a former college professor and classroom teacher, working in urban and suburban Chicago schools. Known for his pioneering work on student book clubs, Dr. Daniels is author and co-author of many books, including *Literature Circles: Voice and Choice in Book Clubs and Reading Groups* and *Best Practice: Today's Standards for Teaching and Learning in America's Schools.*

Ben Garcia is associate director of education at the Skirball Cultural Center in Los Angeles, California, where he oversees school programs and teacher professional development. He is a board member of the Museum Educators of Southern California and presents regularly at conferences in the area of visual arts integration across curricula. Prior to the Skirball, he worked with classroom teachers for six years in the *Art and Language Arts* program at the J. Paul Getty Museum. Recent publications include *Art and Science: A Curriculum for K–12 Teachers* and *Neoclassicism and the Enlightenment: A Curriculum for Middle and High School Teachers.*

PROGRAM CONSULTANTS continued

Judith L. Irvin taught middle school for several years before entering her career as a university professor. She now teaches courses in curriculum and instructional leadership and literacy at Florida State University. Dr. Irvin's many publications include *Reading and the High School Student: Strategies to Enhance Literacy* and *Integrating Literacy and Learning in the Content Area Classroom*. Her latest book, *Taking Action: A Leadership Model for Improving Adolescent Literacy,* is the result of a Carnegie-funded project and is published by the Association for Supervision and Curriculum Development.

Victoria Ramirez is the interim education director at the Museum of Fine Arts, Houston, Texas, where she plans and implements programs, resources, and publications for teachers and serves as liaison to local school districts and teacher organizations. She also chairs the Texas Art Education Association's museum division. Dr. Ramirez earned a doctoral degree in curriculum and instruction from the College of Education at the University of Houston and an M.A.T. in museum education from George Washington University. A former art history instructor at Houston Community College, Dr. Ramirez currently teaches education courses at the University of Houston.

Héctor H. Rivera is an assistant professor at Southern Methodist University, School of Education and Human Development. Dr. Rivera is also the director of the SMU Professional Development/ESL Supplemental Certification Program for Math and Science Teachers of At-Risk Middle and High School LEP Newcomer Adolescents. This federally funded program develops, delivers, and evaluates professional development for educators who work with at-risk newcomer adolescent students. Dr. Rivera is also collaborating on school reform projects in Guatemala and with the Institute of Arctic Education in Greenland.

Mabel Rivera is a research assistant professor at the Texas Institute for Measurement, Evaluation, and Statistics at the University of Houston. Her current research interests include the education of and prevention of reading difficulties in English-language learners. In addition, Dr. Rivera is involved in local and national service activities for preparing school personnel to teach students with special needs.

Robin Scarcella is a professor at the University of California at Irvine, where she also directs the Program in Academic English/English as a Second Language. She has a Ph.D. in linguistics from

Amy Benjamin, Ben Garcia, Robin Scarcella, and Judith Irvin

the University of Southern California and an M.A. degree in education-second language acquisition from Stanford University. She has taught all grade levels. She has been active in shaping policies affecting language assessment, instruction, and teacher professional development. In the last four years, she has spoken to over ten thousand teachers and administrators. She has written over thirty scholarly articles that appear in such journals as the *TESOL Quarterly* and *Brain and Language*. Her most recent publication is *Accelerating Academic English: A Focus on the English Learner*.

Patrick Schwarz is professor of special education and chair of the Diversity in Learning and Development department for National-Louis University, Chicago, Illinois. He is author of *From Disability to Possibility* and *You're Welcome* (co-written with Paula Kluth), texts that have inspired teachers worldwide to reconceptualize inclusion to help all children. Other books co-written with Paula

Kluth include *Just Give Him the Whale* and *Inclusion Bootcamp*. Dr. Schwarz also presents and consults worldwide through Creative Culture Consulting.

Alfred W. Tatum is an associate professor in the Department of Curriculum and Instruction at the University of Illinois at Chicago (UIC), where he earned his Ph.D. He also serves as the director of the UIC Reading Clinic. He began his career as an eighth-grade teacher, later becoming a reading specialist. Dr. Tatum has written more than twenty-five articles, chapters, and monographs and is the author of *Teaching Reading to Black Adolescent Males: Closing the Achievement Gap*. His work focuses on the literacy development of African American adolescent males, particularly the impact of texts on their lives.

UNIT INTRODUCTION WRITERS ON WRITING

UNIT 1 FICTION AND NONFICTION

Gary Paulsen

"As surely as my lead dog Cookie pulled me from the bottom of a lake after I fell through the ice, books are the reason I survived my miserable childhood."

UNIT 2 SHORT STORIES

Gary Soto

"Short stories may be short, but the impressions, I hope, last a long time in the reader."

UNIT 3 NONFICTION

Kathleen Krull

"I'm intrigued by the shape of a life—the arc, the story."

UNIT 4 POETRY

Pat Mora

"Poetry connects me with me, and me with you. Poetry connects us."

UNIT 5 DRAMA

Allan Knee

"I love playwriting, pain or no pain. I see life in terms of drama, conflict, and resolution."

UNIT 6 MYTHS, FOLK TALES, AND LEGENDS

Jane Yolen

"And I thought: What if this story is about something other than what it pretends to be?"

Critical Reviewers

Dee Ambrose-Stahl
Ligonier Valley High School
Ligonier, Pennsylvania

Melinda Bogart
Switzerland Point Middle School
St. Augustine, Florida

Abigayl Brown
Valley Stream Memorial
    Junior High School
Valley Stream, New York

Kim Brown
Buckeye Valley Middle School
Delaware, Ohio

Kathryn Abbey Chwalisz
Glenridge Middle School
Orlando, Florida

Parniece Crawford
Lockhart Middle School
Orlando, Florida

Chrissy Cuenca
Winston Park K-8 Center
Miami, Florida

Heather Dick
Amherst Junior High School
Amherst, Ohio

Sabrina R. Dorsey
General Ray Davis Middle School
Stockbridge, Georgia

Gloria Feather
Independence Middle School
Pittsburgh, Pennsylvania

Lisa Anne Flowers
Olympia High School
Orlando, Florida

Sandi Green
Swanson Middle School
Arlington, Virginia

Bobbi Ann Hammill
Elderton High School
Elderton, Pennsylvania

Pat Harris
Bryant Middle School
Bryant, Arkansas

Clifford Hartline
Harrison Middle School
Grand Rapids, Michigan

Carolyn Matthews
Memphis City Schools
Memphis, Tennessee

Patricia Mentgen
John P. Freeman Optional School
Memphis, Tennessee

Jennifer Nzeza
Booker Middle School
Sarasota, Florida

Marcia Rosen
Independence Middle School
Pittsburgh, Pennsylvania

Shahara M. Ruth
Tucker Middle School
Tucker, Georgia

Donna Scheidt
Highland Middle School
Highland, Indiana

Patricia Sherman
Baldwin Middle School
Baldwin, New York

Laura Jeannine Simon
Princeton Community
    Middle School
Cincinnati, Ohio

Jennifer Warford
Boone County Schools
Florence, Kentucky

FIELD-TEST PARTICIPANTS

Brandi Anzaldua
North Richland Middle School
North Richland Hills, Texas

Lisa Archibald
Pasco Middle School
Dade City, Florida

Julie Bruce-Magee
Kathleen & Tim Harney
    Middle School
Las Vegas, Nevada

Contents in Brief

Fiction and Nonfiction

COLLECTION **1** Forms of Prose

"Every one of us gets through the tough times because somebody is there, standing in the gap to close it for us." —**Oprah Winfrey**

What Do You Think? How do you manage through tough times?

Skills Focus

Literary Skills Understand and analyze forms of prose; understand conflict; understand plot structure.

Reading Skills Compare and contrast; set a purpose for reading; activate prior knowledge; identify and understand chronological organization/order.

Informational Skills Take notes, and make outlines; summarize and organize information from one or more sources by taking notes, outlining ideas, or making charts; understand how to summarize; summarize an article; summarize the main ideas.

Vocabulary Skills Use context clues in words, sentences, and paragraphs to decode new vocabulary; understand denotation and connotation; identify synonyms.

Writing Skills Write comparison-contrast essay; choose a topic to write about; decide on a purpose for writing; plan writing by targeting an audience; identify similarities and differences; include important details; organize writing by block order; organize writing by point-by-point order.

Short Stories

COLLECTION 2 Plot and Setting

"You gain strength, courage, and confidence by every experience in which you really stop to look fear in the face." —**Eleanor Roosevelt**

What Do You Think? How might confronting a difficult situation help you become a stronger person?

Skills Focus

Literary Skills Understand and analyze plot and setting; understand conflict; understand suspense and foreshadowing.

Reading Skills Make predictions from a text; understand how to summarize; summarize a text; describe mental images that text descriptions evoke; visualize.

Informational Skills Understand the structure and purpose of a newspaper article; analyze newspapers; understand the structure and purpose of a textbook; analyze textbooks; understand the structure and purpose of an instructional manual; analyze instructional manuals; understand the structure and purpose of signs; analyze signs.

Vocabulary Skills Use context clues in words, sentences, and paragraphs to decode new vocabulary.

Writing Skills Write narratives; narrate a sequence of events; pace the presentation of actions.

Short Stories

COLLECTION 3 Character

"Be who you are and say what you feel, because those who matter don't mind and those who mind don't matter."

—Dr. Seuss (Theodor Seuss Geisel)

What Do You Think? How do other people help you discover something within yourself?

Skills Focus

Literary Skills Understand and analyze characterization.

Reading Skills Make inferences from a text; make connections from a text; understand how character affects plot.

Informational Skills Identify and understand comparison-contrast organization/text structure.

Vocabulary Skills Identify and understand etymology/word origins/roots; identify and use Greek, Latin, and Anglo-Saxon roots and affixes to understand vocabulary; use context clues in words, sentences, and paragraphs to understand vocabulary.

Writing Skills Write persuasive essays or articles; support persuasive arguments with reasons and evidence; address potential objections; include a call to action.

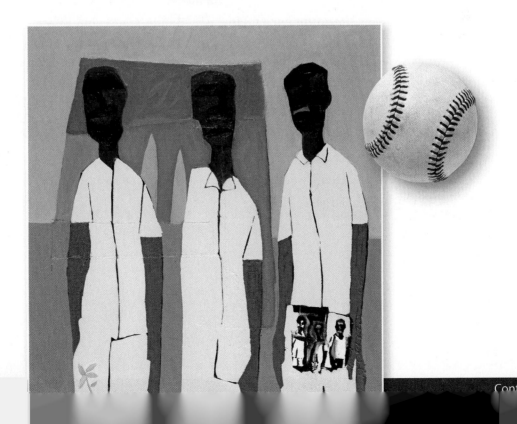

UNIT 2
Short Stories

COLLECTION **4** Theme and Point of View

"If you live in my heart, you live rent free." —**Irish proverb**

What Do You Think? What makes us care about certain people? Why do we connect with some people and not with others?

Skills Focus

Literary Skills Understand theme; understand point of view.

Reading Skills Find the theme; identify and understand cause and effect; make predictions from a text.

Informational Skills Identify and trace the development of the author's argument in a text; evaluate an argument; evaluate and judge the author's evidence; analyze the appropriateness of evidence; identify stereotypes and bias.

Vocabulary Skills Understand word analogies; identify and use Latin roots and affixes to understand vocabulary; understand idioms.

Writing Skills Write autobiographical narratives; include the meaning of the experience; include thoughts and feelings.

Nonfiction

COLLECTION **5** Elements of Nonfiction

"You cannot control what happens to you, but you can control your attitude toward what happens to you." —**Brian Tracy**

What Do You Think? How do our attitudes influence the changes and challenges we face in life?

Skills Focus

Literary Skills Analyze forms of prose; analyze an author's perspective; analyze subjective and objective points of view.

Reading Skills Identify the main idea; organize information; analyze facts and opinions; determine the author's purpose.

Informational Skills Understand an author's purpose and perspective; evaluate the author's point of view or perspective in a text.

Vocabulary Skills Clarify word meanings through definitions; use context clues in words, sentences, and paragraphs to decode new vocabulary.

Writing Skills Write a response to literature; choose a topic to write about; include a statement of thesis/main idea; decide on a purpose for writing; plan writing by targeting an audience; support ideas/theses with relevant evidence.

Nonfiction

COLLECTION 6 Reading for Life

"There is an art of reading, as well as an art of thinking, and an art of writing." —Benjamin Disraeli

What Do You Think? How can reading help you make decisions or solve problems?

> **Skills Focus**
>
> **Informational Skills** Analyze consumer documents; analyze workplace documents; analyze public documents/informational materials; follow technical directions and steps in a process.
>
> **Reading Skills** Skim and scan; preview a text; interpret and use graphic sources of information; use reading strategies to clarify meanings.
>
> **Writing Skills** Create print and nonprint multimedia presentations; choose a topic to write about; decide on a purpose for writing; plan writing by organizing ideas and information.

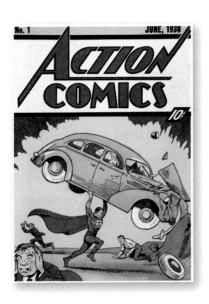

Poetry

Writers on Writing .... PAT MORA 642

COLLECTION **7** Elements of Poetry

"Poetry is when an emotion has found its thought and the thought has found words."
—**Robert Frost**

What Do You Think? What kinds of experiences and feelings would you write about in a poem?

Skills Focus

Literary Skills Understand and analyze forms of poetry; understand and analyze elements of poetry; understand and analyze sounds of poetry, such as rhythm, rhyme, alliteration, and onomatopoeia; understand tone; understand imagery.

Reading Skills Read a poem; re-read to enhance comprehension of text; use questioning to improve comprehension.

Vocabulary Skills Identify metaphors and similes; identify and interpret figurative language; analyze figurative meanings of phrases.

Writing Skills Write descriptive essays; describe a place; include importance of subject.

Drama

COLLECTION **8** Elements of Drama

*"In a good play, each detail falls into useful place. And you know
that the shortest line, the smallest stage movement, has an end in
view, and is not being used to trick us."* **—Lillian Hellman**

What Do You Think? What characteristics of drama make it
so much like real life?

Skills Focus

Literary Skills Analyze elements of drama.
Reading Skills Visualize; determine the author's purpose; adjust reading rate based on purposes for reading.
Informational Skills Identify and trace the development of an author's argument in text; identify and
evaluate the use of accurate supporting citations and evidence in a text.
Vocabulary Skills Use context clues in words, sentences, and paragraphs to decode new vocabulary; clarify
word meanings through definitions.
Writing Skills Write a how-to explanation; choose a topic to write about; decide on a purpose for writing; plan
writing by targeting an audience; include important details.

Myths, Folk Tales, and Legends

COLLECTION **9** Greek Myths and World Folk Tales

"Lonely as they were, by themselves, early people looked inside themselves and expressed a longing to discover; to explain who they were, why they were, and from what and where they came."

—Virginia Hamilton

What Do You Think? What truths about life do myths and folk tales reveal?

Skills Focus

Literary Skills Understand and analyze elements of myths; understand and analyze elements of folk tales.

Reading Skills Make predictions from a text; summarize a text; make generalizations from a text; draw conclusions; understand characters; understand conflict; read a graphic story.

Informational Skills Understand an author's purpose and perspective.

Vocabulary Skills Identify and use Greek and Latin roots and affixes to understand vocabulary; identify and correctly use multiple-meaning words; use prefixes to interpret and create words; use suffixes to interpret and create words; use context clues in words, sentences, and paragraphs to decode new vocabulary.

Writing Skills Write research papers; select a research strategy; use a variety of sources in writing; evaluate appropriateness of sources; paraphrase sources; integrate quotations into writing; cite sources correctly.

Literary Selections

Comparing Texts

Informational Text Focus

Selections by Alternative Themes

Selections are listed here in alternative theme groupings.

SELECTIONS BY ALTERNATIVE THEMES continued

Skills, Workshops, and Features

SKILLS

LITERARY FOCUS ESSAYS BY LINDA RIEF

READING FOCUS ESSAYS BY KYLENE BEERS

LITERARY SKILLS

INFORMATIONAL TEXT SKILLS

READING SKILLS FOR LITERARY TEXTS

READING SKILLS FOR INFORMATIONAL TEXTS

SKILLS, WORKSHOPS, AND FEATURES continued

WORKSHOPS
WRITING WORKSHOPS

PREPARING FOR TIMED WRITING

LISTENING AND SPEAKING WORKSHOPS

FEATURES
ANALYZING VISUALS

SKILLS, WORKSHOPS, AND FEATURES continued

Why Be a Reader/Writer?

by **Kylene Beers**

Not Just a FAD

Years ago there was a popular gag gift called the Pet Rock. This plain, ordinary rock came in a cardboard box with a book that explained the rock's care and feeding and the tricks it could do. For instance, people put their Pet Rocks on a table, said "Sit," and then laughed at the silliness of the joke. Eventually, the jokes got stale, and the Pet Rocks were released into the wilds of our backyards.

Pet Rocks—like yo-yos and scooters—were a fad. Most of us have fun getting swept up in one fad or another, but eventually we get bored and move on to other things. Fads come and go because they aren't meaningful.

We—the authors and editors of this book—hope that reading and writing aren't just a fad that you'll eventually set aside. However, without meaningful reasons to keep reading and writing, you will get bored—and you'll move on. So, what meaningful reasons are there for reading and writing?

Some people will tell you it's all about getting good grades or passing required tests, **BUT** someday you won't be in school. No one will grade you, and no one will test you on how well you read or write. Others will tell you that you need to read and write so you can graduate from high school, go to college, or get the job you want. **NOW**, these things are certainly important, but they happen as a result of being a reader and a writer—they are the effects, not the reason.

From Me to **YOU**

I think the real reason you should read and write is to discover more about yourself and to learn more about your world. Why? Because no matter your age, you're trying to find out how you fit into the world and to understand what's going on in your life.

* *Sometimes that means reading about the experiences of someone else, whether an imaginary or real person; reading about other places, down the street or on the other side of the world; or reading about other times, from Roman times to future eras.*

* *Then, after you read, even though you may not realize it now, you will usually want to share your ideas about what you've read—to communicate with someone else. One way to do that is to write: in a journal, song lyrics, letters, e-mails, or on a Web site. Writing lets you explore your thoughts about what you've read and share them with others—a close friend; a brother or sister; a pen pal across town, in another state, on another continent (and maybe someday, in a faraway galaxy)!*

This Is **NOW**

By now, you've learned some important ideas about reading and writing. This year, you'll learn even more about being an active reader and a skillful writer. If you look carefully at the questions and activities in this book, you'll see that we repeatedly ask what *you* think: how what *you* have read or written changes what *you* understand about *yourself* and *your* world.

We want you to make good grades, pass tests, go to college, and end up with the job you want. But we want much more than that for you.

We want you to hold on to reading and writing much longer than people held on to Pet Rocks or yo-yos or scooters. Let yourself think and feel and care as you read and write this year, and you'll discover, I predict, your meaningful reason to be a reader and a writer.

Kylene Beers

Senior Author, *Elements of Literature*

How to Use Your Textbook

Getting to know a new textbook is like getting to know a new video game. In each case, you have to figure out how the game or book is structured and what the rules are. Knowing how your book is structured, you can be successful from the start.

Writers on Writing

If you think about the authors of the selections in your book, you may think they are a rare breed, like astronauts or underwater explorers. **Writers on Writing** introduces you to authors whose stories, poems, plays, or articles began with experiences that were transformed by the authors' words.

Collection Opener

What is the focus of each collection, or section of the book? What does the image suggest about what the collection will cover? On the right, you'll see a bold heading, such as "Plot and Setting" or "Character." This lists the **literary skills** you will study in the collection. Below this heading is the **Informational Text Focus** for the collection. This lists skills you might use when reading a newspaper, Web site, or other informational text. Keep the **What Do You Think?** question in mind as you go through the collection. Your answers may surprise even you.

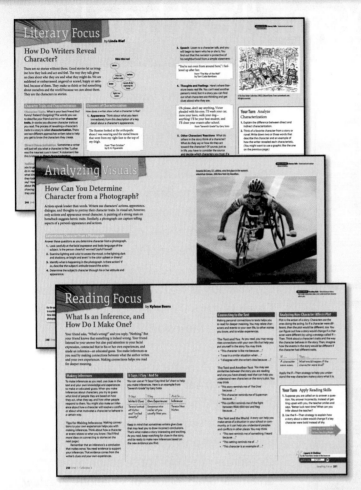

Literary Focus

Like a set of rules or a map, the **Literary Focus** shows you how literary elements work in stories and poems, helping you navigate through selections more easily. The Literary Focus will help you get to your destination—understanding and enjoying the selection.

Analyzing Visuals

Visuals are all around you: murals on buildings, magazine ads, or video game graphics. Because you see images daily, you probably know quite a bit about analyzing them. **Analyzing Visuals** helps you apply these skills so you better understand the literary elements that drive the selections.

Reading Focus

Your mind is working all the time as you read, even if you're not aware of it. Still, all readers—even very good ones—sometimes don't understand what they have read. **Reading Focus** gives you the skills to help you improve your reading.

Reading Model

You tend to do things more quickly and easily if you have a model to follow. The **Reading Model** shows you the literary and reading skills that you will use in the collection so that you can learn them more quickly and easily.

Wrap Up

Think of **Wrap Up** as a bridge that gives you a chance to practice the skills on which the collection will focus. Wrap Up also introduces you to the collection's **Academic Vocabulary:** the language of school, business, and standardized tests. To be successful in school, you'll need to understand and use its language.

How to Use Your Textbook

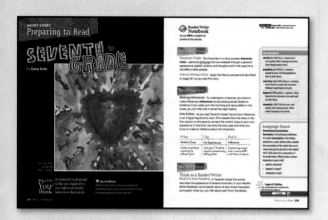

Literary Selection Pages
Preparing to Read

If you have ever done something complicated, you know that things go more smoothly with some preparation. It's the same with reading. The **Preparing to Read** page gives you a boost by presenting the literary, reading, and writing skills you'll learn about and use as you read the selection. The list of **Vocabulary** words defines words you need to know for reading the selection as well as other texts. **Language Coach** explains the inner workings of English—like a look at the inside of a clock.

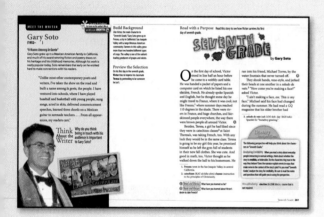

Selection

Meet the Writer gives you all kinds of interesting tidbits about the authors who wrote the selections in this book. **Build Background** provides information you sometimes need when a selection deals with unfamiliar times, places, or situations. **Preview the Selection** presents the selection's main character, like a movie trailer that hints at what is to come. **Read with a Purpose** helps you set a goal for your reading. It helps you answer the question, "What's the point of this selection?"

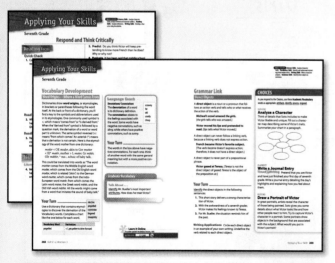

Applying Your Skills

If you have a special talent or hobby, you know that you have to practice to master it. In **Applying Your Skills,** you will apply the reading, literary, vocabulary, and language skills that are described on the Preparing to Read page and that you practiced as you read the selection. These activities give you a chance to check on how you are mastering these skills.

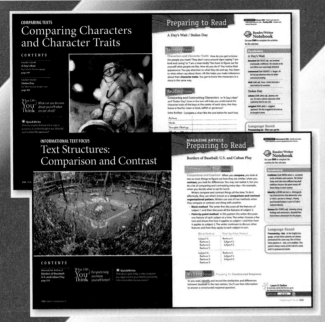

Comparing Texts

You probably compare people, places, and things all the time, such as a favorite singer's new songs with her older ones. In **Comparing Texts,** you will compare different works—sometimes by the same author, sometimes by different authors—that have something in common.

Informational Text Focus

If you've ever read a Web site or followed a technical manual, you've read informational text. The skills you use in this type of reading are different from the ones you use for literary text. **Informational Text Focus** helps you gain the skills that will enable you to be a more successful reader in daily life and on standardized tests.

Preparing for Standardized Tests

Do you dread test-taking time? Do you struggle over reading the passage and then choosing the correct answer? **Preparing for Standardized Tests** can reduce your "guesses" and give you the practice you need to feel more confident during testing.

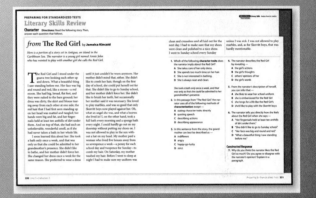

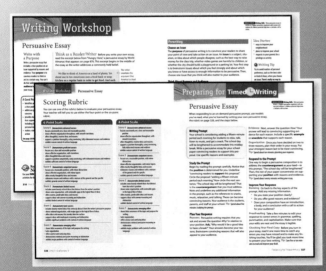

Writing Workshop

Does a blank piece of paper send shivers up your spine? The **Writing Workshop** will help you tackle the page by showing you step-by-step how to develop an effective piece of writing. Models, annotations, graphic organizers, and charts take the "What now?" out of writing for different purposes and audiences.

Preparing for Timed Writing

What's your idea of a nightmare? Maybe it's trying to respond to a writing prompt. **Preparing for Timed Writing** helps you practice for on-demand, or timed, writing so that you can realize your dreams of success.

Fiction and Nonfiction
Writers on Writing

Gary Paulsen on Fiction and Nonfiction The writer and outdoorsman Gary Paulsen has written more than a hundred fiction and nonfiction books. He draws from his own real-life adventures to tell stories about young people facing challenges.

"I write what I know—personal inspection at zero altitude. Every book I've written has pieces of me and my life in it whether it's been labeled fiction or nonfiction. I write from my life, from what I see and hear and smell and taste.

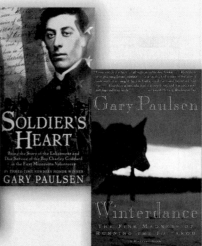

Writing is so much a part of the way I live that I would be lost without the discipline and routine. I write every day, and it gives me balance and focus. I wake up, usually at 4:30, with the sole purpose of sitting down to write with a cup of hot tea and a laptop or a pad of paper.

Sometimes I'm lucky and the living part of life gets folded into the writing part, like with my novels *Dogsong, Harris and Me,* and *How Angel Peterson Got His Name.* I took experiences that I had and turned them into fiction—adding and subtracting bits to make the stories more exciting or funnier or more dramatic.

I've spent a great deal of time in the outdoors, but not with the specific goal of writing about it. I did later publish these stories as nonfiction in *Woodsong, Guts,* and *Caught by the Sea.* I'll be honest, though, and tell you that I enjoyed writing about these times as much as, if not more than, I enjoyed living through them.

I have also written works of historical fiction, such as *Nightjohn, Soldier's Heart,* and *The Legend of Bass Reeves.* I hadn't expected to find characters for my own books when I started reading history. The character of Sarny in *Nightjohn* came when I stumbled across slave narratives while doing research in the National Archives. I discovered Charley Goddard from *Soldier's Heart* while reading a book about the Minnesota First Volunteers. *The Legend of Bass Reeves* is based on the true story of Bass, a runaway slave who became a federal marshal. I'd read Bass's name and bits and pieces of his life story in history books, but I never got a full picture of his life. I could not shake these historical figures until I tried to figure out on paper what their lives must have been like.

I personally want just two things. I want to write, and I want as many young readers as possible to see what I write because books saved my life. As surely as my lead dog Cookie pulled me from the bottom of a lake after I fell through the ice, books are the reason I survived my miserable childhood. As certainly as my sloop *Scallywag* has safely taken me through storms and huge seas, books have sustained me as an adult.

I have been writing for over thirty years, trying to make words come together in the loops and whorls of the story dance. It is still a wonder for me—what books are and how they become part of a reader's mind and soul. "

Think as a Writer

As a writer, what does Paulsen see as the similarities and differences between fiction and nonfiction? Where does he get his inspiration for each?

(left) Elijah Wood and (right) Sean Astin from the *Lord of the Rings* movie series.

Forms of Prose

INFORMATIONAL TEXT FOCUS
Note Taking, Outlining, and Summarizing

"Every one of us gets through
the tough times because
somebody is there, standing
in the gap to close it for us."

—Oprah Winfrey

What Do
You
Think?
How do you
manage through
tough times?

AN EPIC MOTION PICTURE TRILOGY
COMING SOON FROM NEW LINE CINEMA
J.R.R.
TOLKIEN

THE LORD OF THE RINGS
—— PART TWO ——
The Two Towers

Learn It Online
Use the interactive graphic organizers online to help
you in this collection.

go.hrw.com   L7-3   **Go**

Literary Focus

by **Linda Rief**

What Are the Forms of Prose?

You might think of prose as everything that isn't poetry. In fact, you've been speaking prose all your life. You also read prose every day—in your textbooks, in novels, in magazines and newspapers, and on the Web. There are many types of prose, as this organizer shows. Prose is generally divided into fiction and nonfiction.

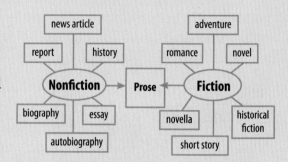

Prose: Some Types of Fiction

Short Story It's just what it sounds like: A **short story** is a short work of fiction in which a few characters move through a series of events (the **plot**). They work through a conflict, which leads to a **climax,** or a high point, and a **resolution,** or an ending—happy or not. You will study these elements of a short story in depth in Unit 2.

> Antonio Cruz and Felix Vargas were both seventeen years old. They were so together in friendship that they felt themselves to be brothers. They had known each other since childhood, growing up on the Lower East Side of Manhattan in the same tenement building on Fifth Street between Avenue A and Avenue B.
>
> from "Amigo Brothers"
> by Piri Thomas

Novel If you find yourself looking at one hundred pages or more, the work is a **novel.** In a novel you meet characters, explore many themes, encounter many conflicts, and probably see subplots (other, less important plots) unfold within the larger plot. There may be several settings.

Novella If a work is longer than twenty pages but shorter than one hundred pages, it is a **novella,** which is simply a short novel.

> Mama's back was to me. She was dipping flour from a near-empty canister, while my older brother, Stacey, built a fire in the huge iron-bellied stove.
>
> from *Song of the Trees*
> by Mildred D. Taylor

Folk Tale A **folk tale** is a story with no known author that has been passed on from one generation to another by word of mouth. Folk tales usually teach a lesson and often contain fantastic elements or events that could not happen in the world as we know it. These stories tend to travel, so similar characters and plots are found in the folk tales of several cultures.

> There was once a rich man whose wife lay sick, and when she felt her end drawing near, she called to her only daughter to come near her bed.
>
> from "Aschenputtel," German folk tale retold by Jakob and Wilhelm Grimm

Prose: Some Types of Nonfiction

Essay and Article Essays and articles are short pieces of prose that discuss a limited topic. Some people write short personal essays about simple things, such as eating an ice-cream cone or taking a dog for a walk. Others write long essays about complex topics, such as freedom, respect, and justice. People write articles for different purposes—to explain something, to persuade, to deliver information, or even to make you laugh.

> On Christmas Eve I saw that my mother had outdone herself in creating a strange menu. She was pulling black veins out of the backs of fleshy prawns. The kitchen was littered with appalling mounds of raw food. . . .
>
> from "Fish Cheeks"
> by Amy Tan

Some nonfiction topics are too complex to be covered in the short format of an essay. Biographies and autobiographies are examples of longer types of nonfiction.

Biography If you wanted to know the whole story of a person's life, you'd read a book-length biography. A **biography** is the story of a real person's life, written by another person.

Autobiography An **autobiography** is the story of a person's life, written by that person.

> After Laos became a Communist country in 1975, my family, along with many others, fled in fear of persecution.
>
> from "An Unforgettable Journey" by Maijue Xiong

Elements of Fiction and Nonfiction

Elements of Fiction	• **Characters** are the imaginary people or animals in a story.
	• **Plot** is the series of events in a story.
	• **Setting** is the time and place in which a story is set. This may or may not be made up.
	• **Point of view** is the vantage point from which a story is told. In **first-person point of view,** one of the characters, using the personal pronoun *I,* is telling a story. In **third-person,** or **omniscient, point of view,** the narrator knows everything about the characters and their problems.
	• Many works of fiction convey a **theme,** which is a universal message about life.
Elements of Nonfiction	• Nonfiction is about **real people, events, or ideas.**
	• It is told from the **point of view,** or **perspective,** of the author.
	• It presents **facts** and **ideas.**
	• It may mention the **historical context** of the subject—information about the society and culture of the time.

Your Turn Analyze Forms of Prose

Decide whether each description of a written work is an example of fiction or nonfiction.

1. an article supporting a proposed law
2. a story about a princess and a frog falling in love
3. a story about an imaginary character set during the Civil War

Learn It Online
Try the *PowerNotes* version of this lesson on:

go.hrw.com	L7-5	Go

Analyzing Visuals

How Can Visuals Help You Compare Fiction and Nonfiction?

Why is knowing the difference between fiction and nonfiction important? It helps you anticipate what you'll find in a text. Once you know you are reading a short story, for example, you'll be expecting characters, conflict, and a theme—you won't be looking for the personal opinions or factual accuracy that you'd expect to find in an autobiography.

Works of **fiction** are imaginary. **Nonfiction** deals with real people, places, and events, without ever changing any facts. Looking at the differences between a work of art, which comes from the artist's imagination, and a photograph—in this case an image from nature—can help you think about the differences between fiction and nonfiction.

1. What do you focus on first when you look at *The Enchanted Owl*?

2. What words would you use to describe this owl?

The Enchanted Owl (1960) by Kenojuak Ashevak. Stonecut in red, blue, and black on laid paper. Printed by Eegyvudluk Pootoogook. ©National Gallery of Canada, Ottawa. Reproduced by permission of Dorset Fine Arts.

3. What do you notice first when you look at this photograph?

4. What other details do you see as you study the owl?

5. What words would you use to describe the owl?

Comparing the Art and the Photograph

Answer these questions as you compare the artwork and the photograph:

1. What characteristics do both owls share? Find at least three.

2. In what ways are the owls different?

3. Which of the owl's natural characteristics does the artist emphasize?

Your Turn   Talk About Fiction and Nonfiction

Now that you've studied both owls, consider this: How is the piece of art like **fiction**? How is the nature photograph like **nonfiction**?

Reading Focus

by **Kylene Beers**

What Skills Move You Forward with Prose?

Reading is like riding a bicycle: You've got to do many things to get where you want to go. Skilled bikers know how to balance, shift gears, and use hand brakes as they ride. Skilled readers also multitask. As a skilled reader, you set a purpose for reading, compare and contrast events and characters, make connections with your prior knowledge, and notice time order.

Comparing and Contrasting

When you compare, you look for similarities, or likenesses. When you contrast, you look for differences. You compare and contrast things every day. For instance, you might compare and contrast the features of your cat to a friend's cat. When you read, you might compare the traits of two important characters or a confrontation at the beginning of a story to a confrontation at the end.

Venn Diagram A **Venn diagram** helps you recognize similarities and differences. The one below compares and contrasts two stories in Collection 1. In the space where the circles overlap, note how the stories are alike. Where there is no overlap, note differences.

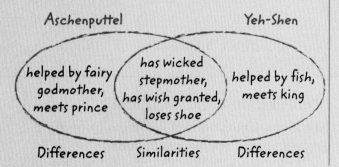

Aschenputtel · Yeh-Shen

helped by fairy godmother, meets prince

has wicked stepmother, has wish granted, loses shoe

helped by fish, meets king

Differences · Similarities · Differences

Setting a Purpose for Reading

When you read an article about your favorite actor, you read it differently than you read directions for installing a computer program because you have a **purpose,** or reason, for reading. When you read directions, your purpose is to understand how to complete a task. You'll read directions more slowly than you would a magazine article because you must understand every step in the directions.

How to Set a Purpose Before you read, you need to choose a purpose for reading. Previewing a text will help you set a purpose. Look at a text's title, headings, and illustrations. They often reveal reasons for reading it. See the chart below for purposes you might set for reading various forms of prose.

Form of Prose	Purpose for Reading
Short story	to be entertained
Autobiography	to learn about a person
News editorial	to make a decision on an issue
Technical directions	to complete a task

Activating Prior Knowledge

When you read a text on an unfamiliar topic, you can increase your comprehension by using your prior knowledge. When you **activate prior knowledge,** you recall what you already know to help you understand something new. Your knowledge can come from your own experience or from other information you've heard or read.

A Model for Activating Prior Knowledge

Read the paragraph below. Then, see how one reader might activate prior knowledge.

> Dinner threw me deeper into despair. My relatives licked the ends of their chopsticks and reached across the table, dipping them into the dozen or so plates of food. Robert and his family waited patiently for platters to be passed to them.

← Dinner seems like a strange time to be upset.

← I really like Chinese food, but I don't know how to use chopsticks.

When I'm eating at someone's house, I sometimes worry about my table manners.

Chronological Order

Most narrative texts, true or fictional, are written in **chronological order.** Writers are using chronological order if they put events in **sequence,** or the order in which they actually happened. "An Unforgettable Journey," an autobiography in this collection, is written in chronological order. It begins with "I was born in a small village" and goes on to relate important events in the writer's life as they happened in time, one after the other.

Words That Signal Chronological Order

first	then
next	after
during	later
while	last
meanwhile	finally

All of these words are clues that events are written in chronological order.

Your Turn Apply Reading Skills

1. Write a sentence that compares and contrasts fiction and nonfiction.

2. What purpose would you set if you were going to read a biography? Why?

3. If you were reading an essay about holiday family dinners, what prior knowledge might help you understand the essay?

4. Why would you expect an autobiography to be written in chronological order?

Now go to the Skills in Action: Reading Model.

Learn It Online
Need help understanding comparison and contrast? Check out the interactive Reading Workshop on:

go.hrw.com   L7-9   Go

Read with a Purpose Read the following personal essay to discover the lesson Amy Tan learns from her mother.

Fish Cheeks

by **Amy Tan**

I fell in love with the minister's son the winter I turned fourteen. He was not Chinese, but as white as Mary in the manger. For Christmas I prayed for this blond-haired boy, Robert, and a slim new American nose.

When I found out that my parents had invited the minister's family over for Christmas Eve dinner, I cried. What would Robert think of our shabby *Chinese* Christmas? What would he think of our noisy *Chinese* relatives who lacked proper American manners? What terrible disappointment would he feel upon seeing not a roasted turkey and sweet potatoes but *Chinese* food?

On Christmas Eve I saw that my mother had outdone herself in creating a strange menu. She was pulling black veins out of the backs of fleshy prawns. The kitchen was littered with appalling mounds of raw food: a slimy rock cod with bulging fish eyes that pleaded not to be thrown into a pan of hot oil. Tofu, which looked like stacked wedges of rubbery white sponges. A bowl soaking dried fungus back to life. A plate of squid, their backs crisscrossed with knife markings so they resembled bicycle tires.

And then they arrived—the minister's family and all my relatives in a clamor of doorbells and rumpled Christmas packages. Robert grunted hello, and I pretended he was not worthy of existence.

Analyzing Visuals

Viewing and Interpreting
Compare and contrast these
foods to those Tan mentions.
Which might you find on
Tan's dinner menu?

Redfish Still Life (2002) by
Diana Ong (1940–   ).
Computer graphics.

Dinner threw me deeper into despair. My relatives licked the
ends of their chopsticks and reached across the table, dipping
them into the dozen or so plates of food. Robert and his family
waited patiently for platters to be passed to them. My relatives
murmured with pleasure when my mother brought out the
whole steamed fish. Robert grimaced. Then my father poked his
chopsticks just below the fish eye and plucked out the soft meat.
"Amy, your favorite," he said, offering me the tender fish cheek.
I wanted to disappear.

At the end of the meal my father leaned back and belched
loudly, thanking my mother for her fine cooking. "It's a polite
Chinese custom to show you are satisfied," explained my father
to our astonished guests. Robert was looking down at his plate
with a reddened face. The minister managed to muster up a
quiet burp. I was stunned into silence for the rest of the night.

After everyone had gone, my mother said to me, "You want
to be the same as American girls on the outside." She handed
me an early gift. It was a miniskirt in beige tweed. "But inside

Reading Focus

Comparing and Contrasting
Tan contrasts Robert's family with
her own. Notice how the two
families act differently during
the meal.

Literary Focus

Essay Notice the comical details
and images in this passage.
Writers of personal essays often
include elements of humor.

Reading Focus

Setting a Purpose for Reading
By setting a purpose before you read, you know to look for the lesson Tan learns from her mother.

you must always be Chinese. You must be proud you are different. Your only shame is to have shame."

And even though I didn't agree with her then, I knew that she understood how much I had suffered during the evening's dinner. It wasn't until many years later—long after I had gotten over my crush on Robert—that I was able to fully appreciate her lesson and the true purpose behind our particular menu. For Christmas Eve that year, she had chosen all my favorite foods.

Read with a Purpose Explain the lesson Tan learns from her mother in your own words.

MEET THE WRITER

Amy Tan
(1952–   )

Accepting Who She Is

Amy Tan spent her childhood in Oakland, California, where her parents had settled after leaving China. "I was the only Chinese girl in class from third grade on. . . . When I was a teenager, I rejected everything Chinese."

When she was fifteen, her father and brother died from brain tumors. After these losses, Amy's mother revealed a secret: Amy had three half sisters still living in China. These upheavals changed her identity, and suddenly her Chinese heritage became important to her.

A Journey to Success

Tan's writing career began when she and a partner started a business. Later, under a pseudonym (a made-up name), she wrote booklets for corporations. Finally, she decided to write fiction under her own name. She became a success with the publication of her first novel, *The Joy Luck Club*, which was a national bestseller that was inspired by her mother. Tan now embraces the Chinese culture she once tried to reject.

Think About the Writer Why do you think Tan used a pseudonym, or pen name, when she started her career?

Wrap Up

Into Action: Charting Sequence

Fill out the sequence chart below to organize the events in "Fish Cheeks." Add more boxes as needed.

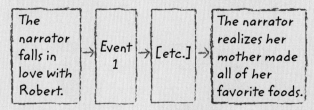

Talk About . . .

1. How do you think Robert and his family reacted to Christmas Eve dinner at the Tans' house? With a partner, discuss your ideas. Use details from the essay to support your response. Try to use each Academic Vocabulary word listed at the right at least once in your discussion.

Write About . . .

Use the underlined Academic Vocabulary words in your answers to the following questions about "Fish Cheeks."

2. Discuss the <u>significance</u> of the title of the essay. How does the title relate to the events Tan describes?

3. What <u>impact</u> did Tan's use of humor have on you? How did you react to the descriptions of her embarrassing moments? Explain.

4. <u>Interpret</u> the following statement: Amy's mother tells her that Amy can be an American girl on the outside but must always be Chinese on the inside. Do you think this is possible? Is it a good idea? Explain your answer.

Writing Focus

Think as a Reader/Writer

The Writing Focus activities on the Preparing to Read pages in Collection 1 guide you to understand ways in which each writer creates suspenseful plots and memorable settings. On the Applying Your Skills pages, you will have the opportunity to practice using those techniques in your own writing.

Academic Vocabulary for Collection 1

Talking and Writing About Forms of Prose

Academic Vocabulary is the language you use to write and talk about literature. Use these words to discuss the prose you read in this collection. The words are underlined in the collection.

interpret (ihn TUR priht) *v.*: decide on the meaning of something. *Years later Tan came to interpret the reason behind her mother's menu.*

impact (IHM pakt) *n.*: powerful effect. *Tan's vivid images have a strong impact on readers.*

insight (IHN syt) *n.*: power to understand. *Tan gives readers insight into the experience of adjusting to the customs of two cultures.*

significance (sihg NIHF uh kuhns) *n.*: importance; meaning. *The food Tan's mother served had special significance.*

Your Turn

Copy the Academic Vocabulary words into your *Reader/Writer Notebook*. Then, use each word in a sentence about "Fish Cheeks." Practice using these Academic Vocabulary words as you talk and write about the selections in this collection.

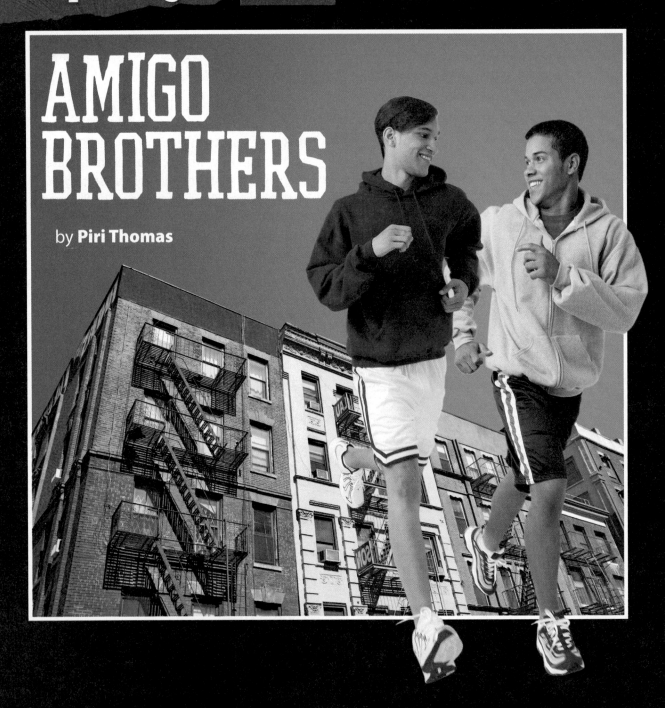

AMIGO BROTHERS

by **Piri Thomas**

What Do **You** **Think**

Can you rely on friendship during a competition? Which is more important, winning or friendship?

 QuickWrite

What advice would you give two friends competing against each other? Create a list titled "Rules for Competing Against a Friend."

Reader/Writer
Notebook

Use your **RWN** to complete the
activities for this selection.

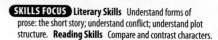

Literary Focus

The Short Story A short work of fiction, usually around five to twenty pages, is called a **short story.** (Sometimes a story that's even shorter is called a **short-short story.**) Short stories pack a lot of punch into a few pages. We meet the **main characters,** get involved in their **conflicts** or **problems,** sort out the **complications,** and move speedily to a **climax** and a **resolution.** A good short story can convey an important message in a brief format.

Reading Focus

Comparing and Contrasting Piri Thomas contrasts the two best friends: "Antonio was fair, lean, and lanky, while Felix was dark, short, and husky." A **comparison** points out similarities between things; a **contrast** points out differences. After you read the story, go back over it and use a Venn diagram like the one below to help identify ways in which Felix and Antonio are alike and different. Write their likenesses in the space where the circles overlap.

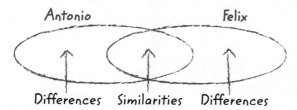

Writing Focus

Think as a Reader/Writer

Find It in Your Reading Piri Thomas uses **vivid verbs**—colorful verbs that help you picture actions clearly—to help you visualize the action in this story. Here are a few of the vivid verbs used in "Amigo Brothers": *blasting, blared,* and *roaring.* Make a list of other vivid verbs you notice as you read.

Vocabulary

bouts (bowts) *n.:* matches; contests. *Both boxers had won many bouts.*

pensively (PEHN sihv lee) *adv.:* thoughtfully. *Felix nodded pensively as he rested.*

torrent (TAWR uhnt) *n.:* flood; rush. *A torrent of emotion left him close to tears.*

dispelled (dihs PEHLD) *v.:* driven away. *All doubt was dispelled the moment Tony made up his mind.*

frenzied (FREHN zeed) *adj.:* wild; out of control. *The audience's reaction was as frenzied as the battle in the ring.*

Language Coach

Suffixes Many English words are made up of various word parts. For example, a **suffix** is one or more letters or syllables added to the end of a word or word part to create a new word. Adding a suffix to a word also changes its part of speech. *Pensive* is an adjective that means "thoughtful." The suffix *–ly* means "in a certain way." How does adding *–ly* to *pensive* change its meaning? What part of speech is *pensively*?

Learn It Online
To preview this story, watch the video introduction on:

| go.hrw.com | L7-15 | **Go** |

Piri Thomas
(1928–   )

A Survivor from the Mean Streets

Like Antonio and Felix in "Amigo Brothers," Piri Thomas grew up in a rough neighborhood in New York City. Unfortunately, he wasn't as lucky as Antonio and Felix—he didn't have a sport like boxing to help him escape the lures of drugs and crime. As a result, Thomas spent time in prison.

Rising Above

While in prison, Thomas discovered that he could write, and after his release, he published an autobiography called *Down These Mean Streets* (1967). Thomas has worked for many years to help drug addicts give up their addictions and start new lives. He says of the kind of Hispanic neighborhood in which he grew up:

> "I believe love is the barrio's greatest strength. The proof is on the faces of the children who, against heavy odds, can still smile with amazing grace as they struggle to survive and rise above the mean streets."

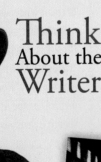

Think About the Writer

Thomas feels strongly about the community in which he was raised. What makes your community strong?

PIRI THOMAS

THIRTIETH ANNIVERSARY EDITION

DOWN THESE MEAN STREETS

Build Background

Boxing matches consist of three-minute rounds. Fighters are given one minute to rest between rounds. If a fighter is knocked down, he or she is given ten seconds to get up and continue fighting. If the fighter cannot get up, he or she is considered knocked out, or down for the count. If neither fighter gets knocked out after fighting a specified number of rounds, judges determine the winner.

Preview the Selection

This story is about two friends (*amigos* in Spanish), **Antonio** and **Felix,** living on the Lower East Side of New York City. Like many boys from the Lower East Side, Antonio and Felix dream of building a better life by winning the New York Golden Gloves, a tournament started in 1927 by Paul Gallico, a newspaper writer. This tournament marks an amateur's entry into the world of big-time boxing.

AMIGO BROTHERS

by **Piri Thomas**

Antonio Cruz and Felix Vargas were both seventeen years old. They were so together in friendship that they felt themselves to be brothers. They had known each other since childhood, growing up on the Lower East Side of Manhattan in the same tenement[1] building on Fifth Street between Avenue A and Avenue B.

Antonio was fair, lean, and lanky, while Felix was dark, short, and husky. Antonio's hair was always falling over his eyes, while Felix wore his black hair in a natural Afro style. **A**

Each youngster had a dream of someday becoming lightweight champion of the world. Every chance they had, the boys worked out, sometimes at the Boys' Club on 10th Street and Avenue A and sometimes at the pro's gym on 14th Street. Early morning sunrises would find them running along the East River Drive, wrapped in sweat shirts, short towels around their necks, and handkerchiefs Apache style around their foreheads. **B**

While some youngsters were into street negatives, Antonio and Felix slept, ate, rapped, and dreamt positive. Between them, they had a collection of *Fight* magazines second to none, plus a scrapbook filled with torn tickets to every boxing match they had ever attended, and some clippings of their own. If asked a question about any given fighter, they would immediately zip out from their memory banks divisions, weights, records of fights, knockouts, technical knockouts, and draws or losses.

Each had fought many bouts representing their community and had won two gold-plated medals plus a silver and bronze medallion. The difference was in their style. Antonio's lean form and long reach made him the better boxer, while Felix's short and muscular frame made him the better slugger. Whenever they had met in the ring for sparring sessions,[2] it had always been hot and heavy.

---

1. **tenement:** apartment. Tenement buildings are often cheaply built and poorly maintained.

2. **sparring sessions:** practice matches in which boxers use light punches.

A **Reading Focus** **Compare and Contrast** How are the boys similar? How are they different?

B **Literary Focus** **Short Story** What internal emotional conflicts might confront two boys with the same dream?

Vocabulary **bouts** (bowts) *n.*: matches; contests.

Now, after a series of elimination bouts, they had been informed that they were to meet each other in the division finals that were scheduled for the seventh of August, two weeks away—the winner to represent the Boys' Club in the Golden Gloves Championship Tournament. **C**

The two boys continued to run together along the East River Drive. But even when joking with each other, they both sensed a wall rising between them.

One morning less than a week before their bout, they met as usual for their daily workout. They fooled around with a few jabs at the air, slapped skin, and then took off, running lightly along the dirty East River's edge.

Antonio glanced at Felix, who kept his eyes purposely straight ahead, pausing from time to time to do some fancy leg work while throwing one-twos followed by uppercuts to an imaginary jaw. Antonio then beat the air with a barrage of body blows and short devastating lefts with an overhead jaw-breaking right.

After a mile or so, Felix puffed and said, "Let's stop a while, bro. I think we both got something to say to each other."

Antonio nodded. It was not natural to be acting as though nothing unusual was happening when two ace-boon buddies were going to be blasting each other within a few short days.

They rested their elbows on the railing separating them from the river. Antonio wiped his face with his short towel. The sunrise was now creating day.

Felix leaned heavily on the river's railing and stared across to the shores of Brooklyn. Finally, he broke the silence.

"Man. I don't know how to come out with it."

Antonio helped. "It's about our fight, right?"

"Yeah, right." Felix's eyes squinted at the rising orange sun.

"I've been thinking about it too, panin.[3] In fact, since we found out it was going to be me and you, I've been awake at night, pulling punches on you, trying not to hurt you."

"Same here. It ain't natural not to think about the fight. I mean, we both are cheverote[4] fighters and we both want to win. But only one of us can win. There ain't no draws in the eliminations." **D**

Felix tapped Antonio gently on the shoulder. "I don't mean to sound like I'm bragging, bro. But I wanna win, fair and square."

Antonio nodded quietly. "Yeah. We both know that in the ring the better man wins. Friend or no friend, brother or no . . ."

Felix finished it for him. "Brother. Tony, let's promise something right here. OK?"

"If it's fair, hermano,[5] I'm for it." Antonio admired the courage of a tugboat pulling

---

3. **panin** (pah NEEN): Puerto Rican Spanish slang for "pal" or "buddy."
4. **cheverote** (cheh vuh ROH tay): Puerto Rican Spanish slang for "the greatest."
5. **hermano** (ehr MAH noh): Spanish for "brother."

C [Read and Discuss] Knowing what you do about Felix and Antonio, what do you think they might feel about having the opportunity to fight in the Golden Gloves Championship Tournament?

D [Literary Focus] Short Story What inner struggle does each boy face?

Right Hook—Left Hook: The Boxing Controversy

Doctors have expressed deep concern about boxing injuries such as those received by the former heavyweight champion Muhammad Ali. Ali suffers from Parkinson's disease, an illness probably caused by the hits he took in the ring. The symptoms of Parkinson's disease range from unclear speech to difficulty walking. In 1984, the American Medical Association (AMA) supported a complete ban on boxing.

However, the sport remains popular. Supporters believe that training young people to box teaches them self-control. Supporters also point out the benefits of fighting according to a set of rules. Some doctors disagree with the AMA's position and believe boxing produces few injuries because all the major muscle groups are used.

Ask Yourself
Where do you stand on this issue?

---

a barge five times its welterweight size.

"It's fair, Tony. When we get into the ring, it's gotta be like we never met. We gotta be like two heavy strangers that want the same thing and only one can have it. You understand, don't cha?"

"Sí, I know." Tony smiled. "No pulling punches. We go all the way."

"Yeah, that's right. Listen, Tony. Don't you think it's a good idea if we don't see each other until the day of the fight? I'm going to stay with my Aunt Lucy in the Bronx. I can use Gleason's Gym for working out. My manager says he got some sparring partners with more or less your style."

Tony scratched his nose pensively. "Yeah, it would be better for our heads." He held out his hand, palm upward. "Deal?"

"Deal." Felix lightly slapped open skin. **E**

"Ready for some more running?" Tony asked lamely.

"Naw, bro. Let's cut it here. You go on. I kinda like to get things together in my head."

"You ain't worried, are you?" Tony asked.

"No way, man." Felix laughed out loud. "I got too much smarts for that. I just think it's cooler if we split right here. After the fight, we can get it together again like nothing ever happened."

The amigo brothers were not ashamed to hug each other tightly.

"Guess you're right. Watch yourself, Felix. I hear there's some pretty heavy dudes up in the Bronx. Suavecito,[6] OK?"

"OK. You watch yourself too, sabe?"[7]

---

6. **suavecito** (swah vay SEE toh): Puerto Rican Spanish slang for "cool."

7. **sabe** (SAH bay): Spanish for "you know."

E  **Read and Discuss** What is happening between the boys now?

Vocabulary **pensively** (PEHN sihv lee) *adv.*: thoughtfully.

Tony jogged away. Felix watched his friend disappear from view, throwing rights and lefts. Both fighters had a lot of psyching up to do before the big fight. **F**

The days in training passed much too slowly. Although they kept out of each other's way, they were aware of each other's progress via the ghetto grapevine.

The evening before the big fight, Tony made his way to the roof of his tenement. In the quiet early dark, he peered over the ledge. Six stories below, the lights of the city blinked and the sounds of cars mingled with the curses and the laughter of children in the street. He tried not to think of Felix, feeling he had succeeded in psyching his mind. But only in the ring would he really know. To spare Felix hurt, he would have to knock him out, early and quick.

Up in the South Bronx, Felix decided to take in a movie in an effort to keep Antonio's face away from his fists. The flick was *The Champion* with Kirk Douglas, the third time Felix was seeing it.

The champion was getting beaten, his face being pounded into raw, wet hamburger. His eyes were cut, jagged, bleeding, one eye swollen, the other almost shut. He was saved only by the sound of the bell.

Felix became the champ and Tony the challenger.

The movie audience was going out of its head, roaring in blood lust at the butchery going on. The champ hunched his shoulders, grunting and sniffing red blood back into his broken nose. The challenger, confident that he had the championship in the bag, threw a left. The champ countered with a dynamite right that exploded into the challenger's brains.

Felix's right arm felt the shock. Antonio's face, superimposed on the screen, was shattered and split apart by the awesome force of the killer blow. Felix saw himself in the ring, blasting Antonio against the ropes. The champ had to be forcibly restrained. The challenger was allowed to crumble slowly to the canvas, a broken bloody mess.

When Felix finally left the theater, he had figured out how to psych himself for tomorrow's fight. It was Felix the Champion vs. Antonio the Challenger. **G**

He walked up some dark streets, deserted except for small pockets of wary-looking kids wearing gang colors. Despite the fact that he was Puerto Rican like them, they eyed him as a stranger to their turf. Felix did a fast shuffle, bobbing and weaving, while letting loose a torrent of blows that would demolish whatever got in its way. It seemed to impress the brothers, who went about their own business.

Finding no takers, Felix decided to split to his aunt's. Walking the streets had not relaxed him; neither had the fight flick. All it had done was to stir him up. He let himself quietly into his Aunt Lucy's apartment and went straight to bed, falling into a fitful sleep with sounds of the gong for Round One.

Antonio was passing some heavy time on his rooftop. How would the fight

F **Read and Discuss** How does the boys' decision to train separately add to what you know about Antonio and Felix?

G **Literary Focus** Short Story What does this scene in the movie theater contribute to the story's plot?

Vocabulary torrent (TAWR uhnt) *n*.: flood; rush.

20 Unit 1 • Collection 1

tomorrow affect his relationship with Felix? After all, fighting was like any other profession. Friendship had nothing to do with it. A gnawing doubt crept in. He cut negative thinking real quick by doing some speedy fancy dance steps, bobbing and weaving like mercury. The night air was blurred with perpetual motions of left hooks and right crosses. Felix, his amigo brother, was not going to be Felix at all in the ring. Just an opponent with another face. Antonio went to sleep, hearing the opening bell for the first round. Like his friend in the South Bronx, he prayed for victory via a quick clean knockout in the first round. **H**

> Antonio went to sleep, hearing the opening bell for the first round.

Large posters plastered all over the walls of local shops announced the fight between Antonio Cruz and Felix Vargas as the main bout.

The fight had created great interest in the neighborhood. Antonio and Felix were well liked and respected. Each had his own loyal following. Betting fever was high and ranged from a bottle of Coke to cold hard cash on the line.

Antonio's fans bet with unbridled faith in his boxing skills. On the other side, Felix's admirers bet on his dynamite-packed fists. **I**

Felix had returned to his apartment early in the morning of August 7th and stayed there, hoping to avoid seeing Antonio. He turned the radio on to salsa[8] music sounds and then tried to read while waiting for word from his manager. **J**

The fight was scheduled to take place in Tompkins Square Park. It had been decided that the gymnasium of the Boys' Club was not large enough to hold all the people who were sure to attend. In Tompkins Square Park, everyone who wanted could view the fight, whether from ringside or window fire escapes or tenement rooftops. The morning of the fight Tompkins Square was a beehive of activity with numerous workers setting up the ring, the seats, and the guest speakers' stand. The scheduled bouts began shortly after noon and the park had begun filling up even earlier.

The local junior high school across from Tompkins Square Park served as the dressing room for all the fighters. Each was given a separate classroom with desk tops, covered with mats, serving as resting tables. Antonio thought he caught a glimpse of Felix waving to him from a room at the far end of the corridor. He waved back just in case it had been him.

The fighters changed from their street clothes into fighting gear. Antonio wore white trunks, black socks, and black shoes.

---

8. **salsa** (SAHL sah): Latin American dance music, usually played at a fast tempo.

H [Read and Discuss] What is going on with the boys now?

I [Reading Focus] Compare and Contrast Identify the phrase that signals the use of contrast in this paragraph.

J [Literary Focus] Short Story Has Felix completely resolved the conflict he feels about fighting Antonio? How do you know?

Felix wore sky-blue trunks, red socks, and white boxing shoes. They had dressing gowns to match their fighting trunks with their names neatly stitched on the back.

The loudspeakers blared into the open windows of the school. There were speeches by dignitaries, community leaders, and great boxers of yesteryear. Some were well prepared; some improvised on the spot. They all carried the same message of great pleasure and honor at being part of such a historic event. This great day was in the tradition of champions emerging from the streets of the Lower East Side. **Ⓚ**

Interwoven with the speeches were the sounds of the other boxing events. After the sixth bout, Felix was much relieved when his trainer, Charlie, said, "Time change. Quick knockout. This is it. We're on."

Waiting time was over. Felix was escorted from the classroom by a dozen fans in white T-shirts with the word "Felix" across their fronts.

Antonio was escorted down a different stairwell and guided through a roped-off path.

As the two climbed into the ring, the crowd exploded with a roar. Antonio and Felix both bowed gracefully and then raised their arms in acknowledgment.

Antonio tried to be cool, but even as the roar was in its first birth, he turned slowly to meet Felix's eyes looking directly into his. Felix nodded his head and Antonio responded. And both as one, just as quickly, turned away to face his own corner.

Ⓚ **Read and Discuss** What picture is the author painting for you in this paragraph?

Bong—bong—bong. The roar turned to stillness.

"Ladies and Gentlemen, Señores y Señoras."

The announcer spoke slowly, pleased at his bilingual efforts.

"Now the moment we have all been waiting for—the main event between two fine young Puerto Rican fighters, products of our Lower East Side."

"Loisaida,"[9] called out a member of the audience.

"In this corner, weighing 134 pounds, Felix Vargas. And in this corner, weighing 133 pounds, Antonio Cruz. The winner will represent the Boys' Club in the tournament of champions, the Golden Gloves. There will be no draw. May the best man win."

The cheering of the crowd shook the window panes of the old buildings surrounding Tompkins Square Park. At the center of the ring, the referee was giving instructions to the youngsters.

"Keep your punches up. No low blows. No punching on the back of the head. Keep your heads up. Understand? Let's have a clean fight. Now shake hands and come out fighting."

Both youngsters touched gloves and nodded. They turned and danced quickly to their corners. Their head towels and dressing gowns were lifted neatly from their shoulders by their trainers' nimble fingers. Antonio crossed himself. Felix did the same.

BONG! BONG! ROUND ONE. Felix and Antonio turned and faced each other

9. **Loisaida** (loy SY dah): Puerto Rican English dialect for "Lower East Side."

Analyzing Visuals

Viewing and Interpreting
How do the photos of these two boys help you connect to the characters?

squarely in a fighting pose. Felix wasted no time. He came in fast, head low, half-hunched toward his right shoulder, and lashed out with a straight left. He missed a right cross as Antonio slipped the punch and countered with one-two-three lefts that snapped Felix's head back, sending a mild shock coursing through him. If Felix had any small doubt about their friendship affecting their fight, it was being neatly dispelled. **Ⓛ**

Antonio danced, a joy to behold. His left hand was like a piston pumping jabs one right after another with seeming ease. Felix bobbed and weaved and never stopped boring in. He knew that at long range he was at a disadvantage. Antonio had too much reach on him. Only by coming in close could Felix hope to achieve the dreamed-of knockout.

Antonio knew the dynamite that was stored in his amigo brother's fist. He ducked a short right and missed a left hook. Felix trapped him against the ropes just long enough to pour some punishing rights and lefts to Antonio's hard midsection. Antonio slipped away from Felix, crashing two lefts to his head, which set Felix's right ear to ringing.

Bong! Both amigos froze a punch well on its way, sending up a roar of approval for good sportsmanship.

Felix walked briskly back to his corner. His right ear had not stopped ringing. Antonio gracefully danced his way toward his stool none the worse, except for glowing glove burns showing angry red against the whiteness of his midribs.

"Watch that right, Tony." His trainer talked into his ear. "Remember Felix always goes to the body. He'll want you to drop your hands for his overhand left or right. Got it?"

Antonio nodded, spraying water out between his teeth. He felt better as his sore midsection was being firmly rubbed.

Felix's corner was also busy.

"You gotta get in there, fella." Felix's trainer poured water over his curly Afro locks. "Get in there or he's gonna chop you up from way back." **Ⓜ**

Bong! Bong! Round Two. Felix was off his stool and rushed Antonio like a bull, sending a hard right to his head. Beads of water exploded from Antonio's long hair.

Antonio, hurt, sent back a blurring barrage of lefts and rights that only meant pain to Felix, who returned with a short left to the head followed by a looping right to the body. Antonio countered with his own flurry, forcing Felix to give ground. But not for long.

Felix bobbed and weaved, bobbed and weaved, occasionally punching his two gloves together.

Antonio waited for the rush that was sure to come. Felix closed in and feinted with his left shoulder and threw a right instead. Lights suddenly exploded inside Felix's head as Antonio slipped the blow and hit him with a pistonlike left, catching him flush on the point of his chin.

Bedlam broke loose as Felix's legs momentarily buckled. He fought off a series

---

Ⓛ **Literary Focus** Short Story How has the conflict between the two friends changed?

Ⓜ **Read and Discuss** What do you learn from the advice of the two trainers?

Vocabulary **dispelled** (dihs PEHLD) *v.:* driven away.

of rights and lefts and came back with a strong right that taught Antonio respect.

Antonio danced in carefully. He knew Felix had the habit of playing possum when hurt, to sucker an opponent within reach of the powerful bombs he carried in each fist.

A right to the head slowed Antonio's pretty dancing. He answered with his own left at Felix's right eye that began puffing up within three seconds.

Antonio, a bit too eager, moved in too close, and Felix had him entangled into a rip-roaring, punching toe-to-toe slugfest that brought the whole Tompkins Square Park screaming to its feet.

Rights to the body. Lefts to the head. Neither fighter was giving an inch. Suddenly a short right caught Antonio squarely on the chin. His long legs turned to jelly and his arms flailed out desperately. Felix, grunting like a bull, threw wild punches from every direction. Antonio, groggy, bobbed and weaved, evading most of the blows. Suddenly his head cleared. His left flashed out hard and straight, catching Felix on the bridge of his nose. **N**

Felix lashed back with a haymaker, right off the ghetto streets. At the same instant, his eye caught another left hook from Antonio. Felix swung out, trying to clear the pain. Only the frenzied screaming of those along ringside let him know that he had dropped Antonio. Fighting off the growing haze, Antonio struggled to his feet, got up, ducked, and threw a smashing right that dropped Felix flat on his back.

Felix got up as fast as he could in his own corner, groggy but still game. He didn't even hear the count. In a fog, he heard the roaring of the crowd, who seemed to have gone insane. His head cleared to hear the bell sound at the end of the round. He was glad. His trainer sat him down on the stool. **O**

N **Reading Focus** **Compare and Contrast** Compare and contrast the boys' fighting styles. How are they alike and different?

O **Read and Discuss** How is the match going so far?

Vocabulary **frenzied** (FREHN zeed) *adj.*: wild; out of control.

Analyzing Visuals **Viewing and Interpreting** What moment in the story might this photograph depict?

25

In his corner, Antonio was doing what all fighters do when they are hurt. They sit and smile at everyone.

The referee signaled the ring doctor to check the fighters out. He did so and then gave his OK. The cold-water sponges brought clarity to both amigo brothers. They were rubbed until their circulation ran free.

Bong! Round Three—the final round. Up to now it had been tic-tac-toe, pretty much even. But everyone knew there could be no draw and that this round would decide the winner.

This time, to Felix's surprise, it was Antonio who came out fast, charging across the ring. Felix braced himself but couldn't ward off the barrage of punches. Antonio drove Felix hard against the ropes.

The crowd ate it up. Thus far the two had fought with mucho corazón.[10] Felix tapped his gloves and commenced his attack anew. Antonio, throwing boxer's caution to the winds, jumped in to meet him.

Both pounded away. Neither gave an inch and neither fell to the canvas. Felix's left eye was tightly closed. Claret-red blood poured from Antonio's nose. They fought toe-to-toe.

---

10. **mucho corazón** (MOO choh koh rah SOHN): Spanish for "a lot of heart."

> No matter what the decision, they knew they would always be champions to each other.

The sounds of their blows were loud in contrast to the silence of a crowd gone completely mute. The referee was stunned by their savagery.

Bong! Bong! Bong! The bell sounded over and over again. Felix and Antonio were past hearing. Their blows continued to pound on each other like hailstones.

Finally the referee and the two trainers pried Felix and Antonio apart. Cold water was poured over them to bring them back to their senses. **P**

They looked around and then rushed toward each other. A cry of alarm surged through Tompkins Square Park. Was this a fight to the death instead of a boxing match?

The fear soon gave way to wave upon wave of cheering as the two amigos embraced.

No matter what the decision, they knew they would always be champions to each other.

BONG! BONG! BONG! "Ladies and Gentlemen. Señores and Señoras. The winner and representative to the Golden Gloves Tournament of Champions is . . ."

The announcer turned to point to the winner and found himself alone. Arm in arm the champions had already left the ring. **Q**

P **Read and Discuss** How does Round Three reflect the boys' fears of fighting their best fight?

Q **Literary Focus** Short Story How do the boys resolve their conflict?

Applying Your Skills

SKILLS FOCUS Literary Skills Analyze forms of prose: short story; analyze conflict; analyze plot structure. **Reading Skills** Compare and contrast characters. **Writing Skills** Develop descriptions using sensory details.

Amigo Brothers

Respond and Think Critically

Reading Focus

Quick Check

1. Why do the boys stop training together?

2. How does the fight end?

Read with a Purpose

3. What <u>insight</u> did you discover about the way friends deal with a threat to their relationship? Give details from the story that support your response.

Reading Skills: Compare and Contrast

4. Review the Venn diagram you completed, and then describe in complete sentences how Felix and Antonio are similar and different.

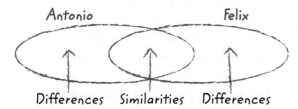

Antonio   Felix

Differences   Similarities   Differences

Literary Focus

Literary Analysis

5. **Interpret** Why do both boys wish for an early knockout? What does this wish show about them and their feelings for each other?

6. **Interpret** The last sentence refers to both boys as champions. In what sense are they champions?

7. **Connect** Would you be able to walk away from a contest like this fight without finding out if you had won? Why or why not?

8. **Evaluate** Did you find this story, particularly its ending, true to life? Do you think two good friends can fight each other and stay friends? Give reasons for your opinion.

Literary Skills: Short Story and Conflict

9. **Analyze** What does the way the boys prepare, fight the bout, and act after the fight tell you about their **characters**?

10. **Analyze** Describe what you think is the **climax,** or most emotional or suspenseful moment, for the boys. What do they learn at this moment?

11. **Analyze** Which do you think has the greatest <u>impact</u> on the story: the **external conflict** (the fight itself) or the **internal conflict** (the feelings the boys struggle with before and during the fight)? Why?

Literary Skills Review: Plot

12. **Interpret** **Plot** is the series of events that make up a story. Retell in your own words the most important events in the plot of "Amigo Brothers."

Writing Focus

Think as a Reader/Writer

Use It in Your Writing Write a short description of an activity you enjoy. Use vivid verbs to help the activity come alive for your audience.

What Do **You Think Now** Look back at the list you wrote before reading the selection. How many of the rules did Antonio and Felix follow?

Applying Your Skills

Amigo Brothers

Vocabulary Development

Clarifying Word Meanings: Using Words in Context

One good way to show that you understand the meaning of a word is to use it in a new context. For example, the Vocabulary words come from a story about boxing, but they can also be used to write about other sports or other topics.

Your Turn

bouts
pensively
torrent
dispelled
frenzied

1. You're writing a news article about tryouts for the Olympic Games. Write sentences using the words **bouts, frenzied,** and **torrent.**

2. You're a retired tennis player. Write sentences for your autobiography using the words **pensively** and **dispelled.**

3. You're a sportscaster describing the crowd at a hockey game. Write a description of the crowd using the words **torrent** and **frenzied.**

4. You're observing a violent storm. Use the words **bouts, torrent,** and **frenzied** to describe what you see.

Language Coach

Using Word Parts: Suffixes A word part added to the end of a word is called a **suffix.** Two commonly used suffixes are –*ly* and –*y.*

Suffix	Meaning	Examples
–*ly*	in a certain or particular way	immediately, lightly, purposely
–*y*	full of, characterized by	lanky, curly

Many adverbs end in –*ly*. These adverbs are generally formed by adding –*ly* to adjectives. The words in the chart that end with –*y* are adjectives.

1. Think of three more words that end in –*ly*, and use each in a sentence.
2. Think of three more words that end in –*y*, and use each in a sentence.

Academic Vocabulary

Talk About . . .

Discuss with a partner the final paragraph of "Amigo Brothers." What <u>insight</u> into Felix and Antonio's relationship does the final scene provide? What <u>impact</u> does the fight have on their friendship? Use these two Academic Vocabulary words in your discussion.

Learn It Online
Sharpen your word skills at:

go.hrw.com   L7-28   Go

SKILLS FOCUS **Literary Skills** Analyze forms of prose: short story. **Vocabulary Skills** Use context clues in words, sentences, and paragraphs to decode new vocabulary. **Writing Skills** Write comparison-contrast essays. **Grammar Skills** Identify and use common nouns; identify and use proper nouns. **Listening and Speaking Skills** Participate in formal/informal discussions and conversations.

Grammar Link
Common and Proper Nouns

A **noun** is a word used to name a person, a place, a thing, or an idea.

PERSONS Antonio, Felix, trainer

PLACES Lower East Side, 14th Street, tenement

THINGS boxing ring, glove, tournament

IDEAS victory, friendship, success

A **common noun** is a general name for a person, place, thing, or idea. A **proper noun** is a particular person, place, or thing.

Common	Proper
fighter	Felix
park	Tompkins Square Park
gym	Gleason's Gym

Your Turn

In the sentences that follow, underline the common nouns and circle the proper nouns.

1. Antonio and Felix live in the same tenement.
2. The boys run along East River Drive.
3. Felix stays with his aunt Lucy in the Bronx.
4. The champion, played by Kirk Douglas, was getting beaten.
5. Antonio's trainer gives him advice.

Writing Applications Write a short paragraph about your favorite sport or hobby. Include both proper nouns and common nouns. Be sure to underline the common nouns and circle the proper nouns.

CHOICES

As you respond to the Choices, use these **Academic Vocabulary** words as appropriate: <u>interpret</u>, <u>impact</u>, <u>insight</u>, <u>significance</u>.

REVIEW
Analyze a Short Story

Fill out a graphic organizer to identify the <u>significant</u> plot events of "Amigo Brothers." (You might want to add more events.)

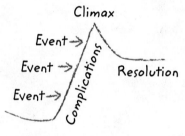

Characters: _____
Their problem: _____

CONNECT
Compare Characters

Timed L Writing In a three-paragraph essay, **compare and contrast** the personalities of Felix and Antonio. Review the Venn diagram you made while reading the story. Talk first about their similarities and then about their differences. Then, explain which character you like better and why.

EXTEND
Imagine a Conversation

Partner Talk What do you think Felix and Antonio said to each other as they walked away from the fight? With a partner, discuss the conversation that might have occurred.

An
Unforgettable
Journey

by **Maijue Xiong**

Whom would you rely on if you were forced to leave your homeland and adapt to a new culture?

⏱ **QuickWrite**

Think of real-life situations that force people to rely on others. Jot down what happened in one particular situation you've heard of or read about.

Reader/Writer Notebook

Use your **RWN** to complete the activities for this selection.

Literary Focus

Autobiography An **autobiography** is the story of a person's life written by that person. A **biography** is the story of a person's life told by *another* person. In "An Unforgettable Journey," Maijue Xiong tells what happened when her life changed forever as she and her family found themselves "without a home or a country."

Reading Focus

Chronological Order Writers use **chronological order** when they put events in the sequence, or order, in which they happened. When you read a narrative text, look for transitional words and phrases such as *first, next, then,* and *at last* to figure out the order in which events occur.

Into Action Use a time line to record the order of events from the time Xiong's family fled Laos until they arrived in California. Your time line will be in chronological order, or organized by time.

```
Maijue Xiong    Xiong family
born            leaves Laos
├──────┬──────────┬──────────┬──────────┬──────┤
```

TechFocus As you keep track of events, think about the tone of voice you would use if you were to tell them aloud.

Writing Focus

Think as a Reader/Writer

Find It in Your Reading As you read Xiong's autobiography, list in your *Reader/Writer Notebook* transitional words and phrases that signal chronological order.

Vocabulary

refuge (REHF yooj) *n.:* place of safety. *Xiong found refuge from war in the United States.*

transition (tran ZIHSH uhn) *n.:* change; passing from one condition to another. *The transition to life in the United States from life in Laos required many changes.*

persecution (pur suh KYOO shuhn) *n.:* act of attacking others because of their beliefs or their ethnic background. *Some Hmong faced persecution.*

deprivation (dehp ruh VAY shuhn) *n.:* condition of not having something essential. *They suffered from food deprivation.*

Language Coach

Suffixes The suffix *–tion* means "being; the result of." When this suffix is added to a familiar term, you can figure out the meaning of the new word. The Vocabulary word *deprivation* means "being deprived." How does knowing this suffix help you understand the meaning of *relocation*?

Learn It Online
There's more to words than just definitions. Get the whole story on:

go.hrw.com | L7-31 | **Go**

Maijue Xiong
(1972–   )

A Writer Who Can Never Forget

Maijue Xiong (MY zhoo ee see AWNG) was a college student in the United States when she wrote about her family's flight from Laos. Xiong eventually earned degrees in sociology and Asian American studies at the University of California, Santa Barbara, where she helped found the Hmong Club to promote Laotian culture.

An active member of the Asian Culture Committee, Xiong now lives in St. Paul, Minnesota. She has taught elementary school at HOPE Community Academy and currently teaches fourth grade at Galtier Magnet Elementary School. Xiong remains active in the Hmong community.

"Now that I am older, I treasure the long but valuable lessons my parents tried to teach us—lessons that gave me a sense of identity as a Hmong."

Think About the Writer What is the significance of Xiong's connection to the Hmong community?

Build Background

The Hmong people of Southeast Asia have faced persecution and exile for more than two centuries. The autobiographical article that follows is one of several Hmong life stories collected by Sucheng Chan, a teacher at the University of California, Santa Barbara. Maijue Xiong was one of the students who contributed a life story. The book that the teacher and her students put together is called *Hmong Means Free: Life in Laos and America.*

Preview the Story

In 1975, when **Maijue Xiong** was just three years old, she fled Laos along with her parents, stepuncle, and two sisters. This autobiography describes the family's many adventures and difficulties as they journey through jungles, fields, and mountain trails; cross the Mekong River to Thailand; spend time in a refugee camp; and finally arrive in California.

An Unforgettable Journey

by **Maijue Xiong**

I was born in a small village called Muong Cha in Laos on April 30, 1972. At the time I was born, my father was a soldier actively fighting alongside the American Central Intelligence Agency[1] against the Communists. Although a war was in progress, life seemed peaceful. We did not think of ever leaving Laos, but one day our lives were changed forever. We found ourselves without a home or a country and with a need to seek refuge in another country. This period of relocation involved a lot of changes, adjustments, and adaptations. We experienced changes in our language, customs, traditional values, and social status. Some made the transition quickly; others have never fully adjusted. The changes my family and I experienced are the foundation of my identity today. **Ⓐ**

---

1. **Central Intelligence Agency** (CIA): organization that helps protect the United States by gathering information about foreign governments and carrying out secret operations.

After Laos became a Communist country in 1975, my family, along with many others, fled in fear of persecution. Because my father had served as a commanding officer for eleven years with the American Central Intelligence Agency in what is known to the American public as the "Secret War," my family had no choice but to leave immediately. My father's life was in danger, along with those of thousands of others. We were forced to leave loved ones behind, including my grandmother, who was ill in bed the day we fled our village. For a month, my family walked through the dense tropical jungles and rice fields, along rugged trails through many mountains, and battled the powerful Mekong River. We traveled in silence at night and slept in the daytime. Children were very hard to keep quiet. Many parents feared the Communist soldiers would hear the cries of their children; therefore, they drugged the children with opium to keep them quiet. Some parents even left

Ⓐ **Literary Focus** Autobiography What are the most significant details about the author in this paragraph?

Vocabulary   **refuge** (REHF yooj) *n.*: place of safety.
transition (tran ZIHSH uhn) *n.*: change; passing from one condition to another.
persecution (pur suh KYOO shuhn) *n.*: act of attacking others because of their beliefs or their ethnic background.

those children who would not stop crying behind. Fortunately, whenever my parents told my sisters and me to keep quiet, we listened and obeyed. **B**

I do not remember much about our flight, but I do have certain memories that have been imprinted in my mind. It is all so unclear—the experience was like a bad dream: When you wake up, you don't remember what it was you had dreamed about but recall only those bits and pieces of the dream that stand out the most. I remember sleeping under tall trees. I was like a little ant placed in a field of tall grass, surrounded by dense jungle with trees and bushes all around me—right, left, in the back, and in front of me. I also remember that it rained a lot and that it was cold. We took only what we could carry and it was not much. My father carried a sack of rice, which had to last us the whole way. My mother carried one extra change of clothing for each of us, a few personal belongings, and my baby sister on her back. My older sister and I helped carry pots and pans. My stepuncle carried water, dried meat, and his personal belongings.

From the jungles to the open fields, we walked along a path. We came across a trail of red ants and being a stubborn child, I refused to walk over them. I wanted someone to pick me up because I was scared, but my parents kept walking ahead. They kept telling me to hurry up and to step over the ants, but I just stood there and cried. Finally, my father came back and put me on his shoulders, along with the heavy sack of rice he was carrying. . . . **C**

After experiencing many cold days and rainy nights, we finally saw Thailand on the other side of the Mekong River. My parents bribed several fishermen to row us across. The fishermen knew we were desperate, yet, instead of helping us, they took advantage of us. We had to give them all our valuables: silver bars, silver coins, paper money, and my mother's silver wedding necklace, which had cost a lot of money. When it got dark, the fishermen came back with a small fishing boat and took us across the river. The currents were high and powerful. I remember being very scared. I kept yelling, "We're going to fall out! We're going to fall into the river!" My mom tried to reassure me but I kept screaming in fear. Finally, we got across safely. My family, along with many other families, were picked up by the Thai police and taken to an empty bus station for the night.

After a whole month at this temporary refugee camp set up in the bus station, during which we ate rice, dried fish, roots we dug up, and bamboo shoots we cut down, and drank water from streams, we were in very poor shape due to the lack of nutrition. Our feet were also swollen from walking. We were then taken to a refugee camp

Analyzing Visuals **Viewing and Interpreting** In what ways does this illustration represent the family's experience of crossing the Mekong River?

B **Literary Focus** Autobiography What does the author want you to understand?

C **Read and Discuss** What did you just find out?

in Nongkhai, where disease was rampant and many people got sick. My family suffered a loss: My baby sister, who was only a few months old, died. She had become very skinny from the lack of milk, and there was no medical care available. The memory of her death still burns in my mind like a flame. On the evening she died, my older sister and I were playing with our cousins outside the building where we stayed. My father came out to tell us the sad news and told us to go find my stepuncle. After we found him, we went inside and saw our mother mourning the baby's death. Fortunately, our family had relatives around to support and comfort us. . . . **Ⓓ**

Our family life in the camp was very unstable, characterized by deprivation and neglect. My older sister and I were left alone for days while my parents were outside the camp trying to earn money to buy extra food. My parents fought a lot during this period, because we were all under such stress. They knew that if we remained in Thailand, there would be no telling what would become of us. We had to find a better life. Some people in the camp were being sponsored to go to the United States. The news spread that anyone who had served in the military with the CIA could apply to go to America. Since my stepuncle had already gone there two years earlier, he sponsored my family. Because my father had been in the military and we had a sponsor, it took only six months to process our papers when usually it took a year or more. . . .

It took a full day to travel to Bangkok, where we stayed for four nights. The building we stayed in was one huge room. It was depressing and nerve-racking. I especially

---

Ⓓ Read and Discuss | What happens to the family in the refugee camp?

Vocabulary **deprivation** (dehp ruh VAY shuhn) *n.:* condition of not having something essential.

The Vietnam War and Hmong Refugees

War often leads to the exile of thousands of civilians on the losing side. Such was the fate of the Hmong (muhng) people, most of whom had supported the United States in its war in Vietnam and Laos. In 1975, when the Communists won, one third of the Hmong people fled. More than 135,000 ended up in the United States. Most live in California, but there are also Hmong communities in Minnesota, Wisconsin, Georgia, Texas, Rhode Island, Nebraska, North Carolina, Colorado, and Montana.

This map shows countries of Southeast Asia and their capitals as they existed just before 1975, when Maijue Xiong and her family left their village of Muong Cha, which was located north of Vientiane in Laos. Today, the map of this part of the world looks somewhat different. For instance, North and South Vietnam are now united into one country.

Ask Yourself

How does Maijue Xiong's autobiography reflect the history of the Hmong in Laos?

remember how, when we got off the bus to go into the building, a small child about my age came up to my family to beg for food. I recall the exact words she said to my father, "Uncle, can you give me some food? I am hungry. My parents are dead and I am here alone." My dad gave her a piece of bread that we had packed for our lunch. After she walked away, my family found an empty corner and rolled out our bedding for the night. That night, the same child came around again, but people chased her away, which made me sad.

In the morning, I ran to get in line for breakfast. Each person received a bowl of rice porridge with a few strips of chicken in it. For four days, we remained in that building, not knowing when we could leave for the United States. Many families had been there for weeks, months, perhaps even years. On the fourth day, my family was notified to be ready early the next morning to be taken to the airport. The plane ride took a long time and I got motion sickness. I threw up a lot. Only when I saw my stepuncle's face after we landed did I know we had come to the end of our journey. We had come in search of a better life in the "land of giants." **E**

On October 2, 1978, my family arrived at Los Angeles International Airport, where my uncle was waiting anxiously. We stayed with my uncle in Los Angeles for two weeks and then settled in Isla Vista because there were already a few Hmong families there.

E **Reading Focus** **Chronological Order** What main events have occurred so far? List them in order on your time line.

We knew only one family in Isla Vista, but later we met other families whom my parents had known in their village and from villages nearby. It was in Isla Vista that my life really began. My home life was now more stable. My mother gave birth to a boy a month after we arrived in the United States. It was a joyous event because the first three children she had were all girls. (Boys are desired and valued far more than girls in Hmong culture.) . . .

I entered kindergarten at Isla Vista Elementary School. The first day was scary because I could not speak any English. Fortunately, my cousin, who had been in the United States for three years and spoke English, was in the same class with me. She led me to the playground where the children were playing. I was shocked to see so many faces of different colors. The Caucasian students shocked me the most. I had never seen people with blond hair before. The sight sent me to a bench, where I sat and watched everyone in amazement. In class, I was introduced to coloring. I did not know how to hold a crayon or what it was for. My teacher had to show me how to color. I also soon learned the alphabet. This was the beginning of my lifelong goal to get an education. . . . **F**

Now that I am older, I treasure the long but valuable lessons my parents tried to teach us—lessons that gave me a sense of identity as a Hmong. "Nothing comes easy . . . ," my parents always said. As I attempt to get a college education, I remember how my parents have been really supportive of me throughout my schooling, but because they never had a chance to get an education themselves, they were not able to help me whenever I could not solve a math problem or write an English paper. Although they cannot help me in my schoolwork, I know in my heart that they care about me and want me to be successful so that I can help them when they can no longer help themselves. Therefore, I am determined to do well at the university. I want to become a role model for my younger brother and sisters, for I am the very first member of my family to attend college. I feel a real sense of accomplishment to have set such an example. **G**

> Now that I am older, I treasure the long but valuable lessons my parents tried to teach us—lessons that gave me a sense of identity as a Hmong. "Nothing comes easy . . . ," my parents always said.

F Literary Focus Autobiography What have you learned here about Xiong?

G Read and Discuss What does this statement tell you about the author?

Applying Your Skills

An Unforgettable Journey

Respond and Think Critically

Reading Focus

Quick Check

1. Explain three important events Xiong faced during her family's escape.

2. How did Xiong feel about school when she first arrived in the United States?

Read with a Purpose

3. What did you learn about the experience of leaving one's homeland?

Reading Skills: Chronological Order

4. Review your time line, and be sure you have included only main events. What have you learned about the way chronological order works in stories?

Maijue Xiong born   Xiong family leaves Laos

Literary Focus

Literary Analysis

5. **Interpret** How does the understatement made by Xiong's parents, "Nothing comes easy," apply to this selection?

Literary Skills: Autobiography

6. **Analyze** What <u>insights</u> do you find when reading an autobiography that you might not discover in other forms of prose?

7. **Evaluate** Xiong describes experiences she had when she was only three years old. People often do not remember events that occurred at such a young age. Why do you think her memories are so vivid?

Literary Skills Review: First-Person Point of View

Autobiographies are told from the **first-person point of view.** In this point of view, we know only what the narrator decides to tell us. (The writer speaks as *I*, using the first-person pronoun.)

8. **Analyze** How would your <u>interpretation</u> of these events be different if they had been relayed by someone who was not Hmong?

Writing Focus

Think as a Reader/Writer

Use It in Your Writing Think about an unforgettable journey you have heard or read about. How does it compare to Xiong's journey? Write a paragraph comparing the two journeys, making sure to include transitional words. Use a Venn diagram to show similarities and differences.

Journeys you heard about   Xiong's Journey

Differences   Simliarities   Differences

What Do **You Think Now** Could Xiong's family have made this journey without getting help along the way? Explain.

Applying Your Skills

An Unforgettable Journey

Vocabulary Development

Context Clues: Contrast

Sometimes writers clarify the meaning of a word by using contrast clues. **Contrast clues** show how a word is unlike another word or situation. For example, you can get a good idea that *apprehensive* means "fearful" or "uneasy" in the sentence below because you see the word contrasted with *fearless*.

> The children were extremely **apprehensive** as they made their way through the dense jungle, but their parents seemed **fearless.**

Be on the lookout for signal words that alert you to contrasts: *although, but, yet, still, unlike, not, in contrast, instead,* and *however.*

Your Turn

In the following sentences, contrast clues point you to the meaning of each Vocabulary word. Using the contrast clues, fill in the each blank with the correct Vocabulary word.

refuge
transition
persecution
deprivation

1. Some people have food, clothing, and shelter, but others experience _____ because they are forced to live without these basic needs.

2. Although we expected _____ for our beliefs, we found acceptance.

3. Instead of finding a _____ , they suffered exposure to wind and rain.

4. In contrast to people who made a _____ to the new culture, some of the exiles kept their traditional way of life.

Language Coach

The Suffix –tion The suffix *–tion* means "action or process of"; "condition or state of being"; "the result of." For instance, *rejection* is the state of being rejected, and *connection* is the process of connecting. When the suffix *–tion* is added to a verb like *persecute* or *deprive,* the new word formed is a noun. Think about what the suffix *–tion* means in the three Vocabulary words below, and fill in the appropriate word for each sentence.

transition   persecution   deprivation

1. Maijue Xiong and her family fled Laos because the Hmong people faced _____.

2. The Xiongs experienced a great deal of _____ on their journey.

3. They found their move to America to be a difficult _____.

Academic Vocabulary

Write About . . .

How did a <u>significant</u> event in Xiong's childhood help her become an admirable and accomplished adult? Write your response to this question in one paragraph.

Learn It Online
Expand your vocabulary with *WordSharp* at:

go.hrw.com   L7-40   **Go**

Grammar Link
Making Pronouns Clear

Using inexact pronoun references is a common mistake and can cause misunderstandings. You know to whom you're referring when you use *he, she,* or *they,* but your readers may not be sure.

A pronoun should refer clearly to its antecedent (the noun or pronoun to which a pronoun refers). Avoid unclear, or ambiguous, pronoun references. These occur when a pronoun can refer to two or more antecedents. Clarify your meaning by replacing the pronoun with a specific noun.

UNCLEAR I traveled with my parents and sisters. **She** kept stopping to take pictures.

CLEAR I traveled with my parents and sisters. **My younger sister** kept stopping to take pictures.

CLEAR I traveled with my parents, older sister, and **younger sister,** who kept stopping to take pictures.

Your Turn

Rewrite the following sentences so that the pronouns are clear.

1. My father and stepuncle carried the heavy items. He carried a sack of rice.

2. I walked between my mother and older sister, hoping that she would carry me.

3. My cousin introduced me to another girl at the playground. She was so nice!

Writing Applications Exchange a sample of your writing with a partner. Read through each other's work, looking for unclear pronoun references. Point out where your partner has provided clear pronoun references as well.

CHOICES

As you respond to the Choices, use these **Academic Vocabulary** words as appropriate: <u>interpret</u>, <u>impact</u>, <u>insight</u>, <u>significance</u>.

REVIEW
Create a Podcast

TechFocus Retell Maijue Xiong's story as a podcast. First, consult your time line and make a list of all major events. Then, write a script for your podcast, considering the tone of voice you would use in relating the events. Finally, record your podcast, and share it with the class.

CONNECT
Write a Personal Narrative

Timed └Writing Maijue Xiong and her family endured a difficult and frightening journey. What kinds of journeys have you taken? You may have traveled to the United States from another country, moved from one state to another, or walked or ridden a bus to school. Choose a journey, and describe it in a two-paragraph personal narrative.

EXTEND
Give a PowerPoint Presentation

TechFocus Conduct research on Laos, and create a PowerPoint presentation. Highlight <u>significant</u> facts about the country—such as details about its history, culture, and economy—on separate pages. Include illustrations for visual interest. Then, practice your presentation until you can smoothly deliver it to your class.

Learn It Online
Tell your story in a whole new way. Try digital storytelling—we'll show you how on:

go.hrw.com | L7-41 | **Go**

Preparing to Read

Song of the Trees

by **Mildred D. Taylor**

Golden Autumn (1901) by Stanislav Joulianovitch Joukovski (1873–1944).
Oil on canvas.

What Do You Think

How do your friends help you achieve your goals?

QuickWrite

Jot down some notes about a difficult time in which you or someone you know turned to others for help. To whom did you turn? How did they help?

Reader/Writer Notebook

Use your **RWN** to complete the activities for this selection.

Literary Focus

Novella You can think of a **novella** as a long short story or as a short novel. Like short stories and novels, novellas have **characters, conflicts, plots, settings,** and **themes.** With a novel or novella, more characters will appear, the conflicts will multiply, and several themes will be operating at once.

Literary Perspectives Apply the literary perspective described on page 45 as you read this novella.

Reading Focus

Activate Prior Knowledge When you **activate prior knowledge,** you use what you already know to help you understand something new. You can use your prior knowledge to think about the most important ideas in this story before you begin to read.

Into Action In the chart below, write *yes* in the blank at the left if you believe the statement and can support it. Write *no* if you do not believe the statement and cannot support it.

Before Reading	After Reading
_____ 1. Given the chance, most people won't take advantage of another person.	_____
_____ 2. Nobody owns the earth.	_____
_____ 3. People gain self-respect by standing up for their beliefs.	_____

Writing Focus

Think as a Reader/Writer

Find It in Your Reading Cassie thinks of the trees as her friends. In your *Reader/Writer Notebook,* list five instances from the story in which trees are described as if they are human.

Vocabulary

dispute (dihs PYOOT) *n.:* argument. *Mama settled the dispute between the brothers.*

curtly (KURT lee) *adv.:* rudely; with few words. *The man spoke curtly to Mama, showing his disrespect.*

elude (ih LOOD) *v.:* avoid; cleverly escape. *Christopher-John was able to elude the lumbermen who tried to catch him.*

incredulously (ihn KREHJ uh luhs lee) *adv.:* unbelievingly. *Mr. Andersen stared incredulously when Papa refused his request.*

Language Coach

Multiple-Meaning Words Many words in English have more than one meaning. For example:

cross — mixture of two things
— angry

Use context clues to help you decide which meaning of *cross* fits in each sentence below.

1. The whole class was _____ when rain spoiled the picnic.
2. Ralph's dog was a _____ between a Labrador and a poodle.

Look in a dictionary to find more meanings of the word *cross*.

Learn It Online
Increase your understanding of the story with improved word comprehension. Visit:

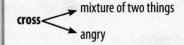

go.hrw.com | L7-43 | Go

Learn It Online
Get more on the author's life at:
go.hrw.com L7-44 Go

Mildred D. Taylor
(1943–   )

Newbery Medal WINNER

Early Success

Mildred Taylor grew up in Toledo, Ohio, where she was a high school honor student, a newspaper editor, and a class officer—but, she says, she wasn't able to be what she really wanted to be: a cheerleader.

Learning Family Stories

Every summer she and her family visited relatives in Mississippi, and she listened to their stories. By the time she was nine or ten, Taylor knew that she wanted to write.

Prizes for Her Work

Her first effort, *Song of the Trees,* introduced the Logan family and won first prize in the African American category of a competition for children's books. In 1977, when she accepted the Newbery Award for her second work about the Logan family, *Roll of Thunder, Hear My Cry,* Taylor spoke about her father:

"Throughout my childhood he impressed upon
my sister and me that we were somebody, that
we were important and could do or be anything
we set our minds to do or be."

Think About the Writer Taylor was inspired by her father. Who are the greatest inspirations in your life?

Build Background

The depression referred to in this story is the Great Depression, the severe economic decline in the United States that lasted from 1929 to 1942. During the Depression many banks and businesses closed. People lost their jobs, their savings, and even their homes. Many people had barely enough food to eat. At this time the segregation of African Americans was still a reality in much of the United States.

Preview the Selection

Times are difficult for the **Logan family** during the Great Depression, so **David,** the father, has taken a job far from home. While he is away, new trouble comes to his daughter, **Cassie,** and her mother, grandmother, and three brothers. This story is based on events that actually happened to Taylor's father as he was growing up.

Song of the Trees

by **Mildred D. Taylor**

"Cassie. Cassie, child, wake up now," Big Ma called gently as the new sun peeked over the horizon.

I looked sleepily at my grandmother and closed my eyes again.

"Cassie! Get up, girl!" This time the voice was not so gentle.

I jumped out of the deep, feathery bed as Big Ma climbed from the other side. The room was still dark, and I stubbed my toe while stumbling sleepily about looking for my clothes.

"Shoot! Darn ole chair," I fussed, rubbing my injured foot.

"Hush, Cassie, and open them curtains if you can't see," Big Ma said. "Prop that window open, too, and let some of that fresh morning air in here."

I opened the window and looked outside. The earth was draped in a cloak of gray mist as the sun chased the night away. The cotton stalks, which in another hour would glisten greenly toward the sun, were gray. The ripening corn, wrapped in jackets of emerald and gold, was gray. Even the rich brown Mississippi earth was gray.

Only the trees of the forest were not gray. They stood dark, almost black, across the dusty road, still holding the night. A soft breeze stirred, and their voices whispered down to me in a song of morning greeting. Ⓐ

"Cassie, girl, I said open that window, not stand there gazing out all morning. Now, get moving before I take something to you," Big Ma threatened.

I dashed to my clothes. Before Big Ma had unwoven her long braid of gray hair,

Literary Perspectives

The following perspective will help you think about the plot of this short story.

Analyzing Historical Context To use the **historical perspective,** consider a literary text in its historical context: the time in which the author wrote, the time in which the story is set, and the ways in which people of the period saw the world. As you read, consider the economic situation that crippled the United States from 1929 to 1942. *Song of the Trees* is set in the context of a significant event in American history, the Great Depression (see page 44). As you read, be sure to respond to the questions that will guide you in using this perspective.

Ⓐ **Literary Focus** Novella What is the setting at the beginning of the story?

my pants and shirt were on and I was hurrying into the kitchen.

A small kerosene lamp was burning in a corner as I entered. Its light reflected on seven-year-old Christopher-John, short, pudgy, and a year younger than me, sitting sleepily upon a side bench drinking a large glass of clabber milk.[1] Mama's back was to me. She was dipping flour from a near-empty canister, while my older brother, Stacey, built a fire in the huge iron-bellied stove.   **B**

"I don't know what I'm going to do with you, Christopher-John," Mama scolded. "Getting up in the middle of the night and eating all that cornbread. Didn't you have enough to eat before you went to bed?"

"Yes'm," Christopher-John murmured.

"Lord knows I don't want any of my babies going hungry, but times are hard, honey. Don't you know folks all around here in Mississippi are struggling? Children crying cause they got no food to eat, and their daddies crying cause they can't get jobs so they can feed their babies? And you getting up in the middle of the night, stuffing yourself with cornbread!"

Her voice softened as she looked at the sleepy little boy. "Baby, we're in a depression. Why do you think Papa's way down in Louisiana laying tracks on the railroad?

---

1. **clabber milk:** thickly curdled sour milk.

So his children can eat—but only when they're hungry. You understand?"   **C**

"Yes'm," Christopher-John murmured again, as his eyes slid blissfully shut.

"Morning, Mama," I chimed.

"Morning, baby," Mama said. "You wash up yet?"

"No'm."

"Then go wash up and call Little Man again. Tell him he's not dressing to meet President Roosevelt[2] this morning. Hurry up, now, cause I want you to set the table."   **D**

Little Man, a very small six-year-old and a most finicky dresser, was brushing his hair when I entered the room he shared with Stacey and Christopher-John. His blue pants were faded, but except for a small grass stain on one knee, they were clean. Outside of his Sunday pants, these were the only pants he had, and he was always careful to keep them in the best condition possible. But one look at him and I knew that he was far from pleased with their condition this morning. He frowned down at the spot for a moment, then continued brushing.

"Man, hurry up and get dressed," I called. "Mama said you ain't dressing to meet the president."

"See there," he said, pointing at the stain. "You did that."

---

2. **President Roosevelt:** Franklin Delano Roosevelt (1882–1945) was president of the United States from 1933 to 1945.

B Read and Discuss What has the author shown you about this family so far?

C Literary Perspectives Analyze Historical Context How does what you learned about the Great Depression in the Build Background text help you understand why Mama is upset when Christopher-John eats all the cornbread?

D Literary Focus Novella List all the characters you have met so far. How are they related to one another?

(left) *Big James Sweats;* (middle) *Little Calist Can't Swim* from the series Sugar Children (1996). Gelatin silver print on paper. 14" x 11". ©Vik Muniz/Licensed by VAGA, New York, NY.

Sokoro (2006) by Tilly Willis. Oil on canvas.

"I did no such thing. You fell all by yourself."

"You tripped me!"

"Didn't!"

"Did, too!"

"Hey, cut it out, you two!" ordered Stacey, entering the room. "You fought over that stupid stain yesterday. Now get moving, both of you. We gotta go pick blackberries before the sun gets too high. Little Man, you go gather the eggs while Christopher-John and me milk the cows."

Little Man and I decided to settle our dispute later when Stacey wasn't around. With Papa away, eleven-year-old Stacey thought of himself as the man of the house, and Mama had instructed Little Man, Christopher-John, and me to mind him. So, like it or not, we humored him. Besides, he was bigger than we were.   **E**

I ran to the back porch to wash. When I returned to the kitchen, Mama was talking to Big Ma.

"We got about enough flour for two more meals," Mama said, cutting the biscuit dough. "Our salt and sugar are practically down to nothing and—" She stopped when she saw me. "Cassie, baby, go gather the eggs for Mama."

"Little Man's gathering the eggs."

"Then go help him."

"But I ain't set the table yet."

E Read and Discuss   What does this scene show you about Stacey, Little Man, and Cassie?

Vocabulary   **dispute** (dihs PYOOT) *n.*: argument.

"Set it when you come back."

I knew that I was not wanted in the kitchen. I looked suspiciously at my mother and grandmother, then went to the back porch to get a basket.

Big Ma's voice drifted through the open window. "Mary, you oughta write David and tell him somebody done opened his letter and stole that ten dollars he sent," she said.

"No, Mama. David's got enough on his mind. Besides, there's enough garden foods so we won't go hungry."

"But what 'bout your medicine? You're all out of it and the doctor told you good to—" **F**

"Shhhh!" Mama stared at the window. "Cassie, I thought I told you to go gather those eggs!"

"I had to get a basket, Mama!" I hurried off the porch and ran to the barn.

After breakfast, when the sun was streaking red across the sky, my brothers and I ambled into the coolness of the forest, leading our three cows and their calves down the narrow cow path to the pond. The morning was already muggy, but the trees closed out the heat as their leaves waved restlessly, high above our heads. **G**

"Good morning, Mr. Trees," I shouted. They answered me with a soft, swooshing sound. "Hear 'em, Stacey? Hear 'em singing?"

"Ah, cut that out, Cassie. Them trees ain't singing. How many times I gotta tell you that's just the wind?" He stopped at a sweet alligator gum, pulled out his knife, and scraped off a glob of gum that had seeped through its cracked bark. He handed me half.

As I stuffed the gooey wad into my mouth, I patted the tree and whispered, "Thank you, Mr. Gum Tree."

Stacey frowned at me, then looked back at Christopher-John and Little Man walking far behind us, munching on their breakfast biscuits.

"Man! Christopher-John! Come on, now," he yelled. "If we finish the berry picking early, we can go wading before we go back."

Christopher-John and Little Man ran to catch up with us. Then, resuming their leisurely pace, they soon fell behind again.

A large gray squirrel scurried across our path and up a walnut tree. I watched until it was settled amidst the tree's featherlike leaves; then, poking one of the calves, I said, "Stacey, is Mama sick?"

"Sick? Why you say that?"

"Cause I heard Big Ma asking her 'bout some medicine she's supposed to have."

Stacey stopped, a worried look on his face. "If she's sick, she ain't bad sick," he decided. "If she was bad sick, she'd been in bed."

We left the cows at the pond and, taking our berry baskets, delved deeper into the forest looking for the wild blackberry bushes.

"I see one!" I shouted.

"Where?" cried Christopher-John, eager for the sweet berries.

"Over there! Last one to it's a rotten egg!" I yelled, and off I ran.

Stacey and Little Man followed at my heels. But Christopher-John puffed far behind. "Hey, wait for me," he cried.

F Literary Perspectives Analyze Historical Context How does this conversation add to what you know about Mama and the family's situation?

G Read and Discuss What are the children doing?

"Let's hide from Christopher-John," Stacey suggested.

The three of us ran in different directions. I plunged behind a giant old pine and hugged its warm trunk as I waited for Christopher-John.

Christopher-John puffed to a stop, then, looking all around, called, "Hey, Stacey! Cassie! Hey, Man! Y'all cut that out!"

I giggled and Christopher-John heard me.

"I see you, Cassie!" he shouted, starting toward me as fast as his chubby legs would carry him. "You're it!"

"Not 'til you tag me," I laughed. As I waited for him to get closer, I glanced up into the boughs of my wintry-smelling hiding tree, expecting a song of laughter. But the old pine only tapped me gently with one of its long, low branches. I turned from the tree and dashed away.

"You can't, you can't, you can't catch me," I taunted, dodging from one beloved tree to the next. Around shaggy-bark hickories and sharp-needled pines, past blue-gray beeches and sturdy black walnuts I sailed, while my laughter resounded through the ancient forest, filling every chink. Overhead, the boughs of the giant trees hovered protectively, but they did not join in my laughter.

Deeper into the forest I plunged.

Christopher-John, unable to keep up, plopped on the ground in a pant. Little Man

> I jumped up to follow Stacey, then cried, "Stacey, look!" On a black oak a few yards away was a huge white *X*.

and Stacey, emerging from their hiding places, ran up to him.

"Ain't you caught her yet?" Little Man demanded, more than a little annoyed.

"He can't catch the champ," I boasted, stopping to rest against a hickory tree. I slid my back down the tree's shaggy trunk and looked up at its long branches, heavy with sweet nuts and slender green leaves, perfectly still. I looked around at the leaves of the other trees. They were still also. I stared at the trees, aware of an eerie silence descending over the forest.

Stacey walked toward me. "What's the matter with you, Cassie?" he asked.

"The trees, Stacey," I said softly, "they ain't singing no more." **(H)**

"Is that all?" He looked up at the sky. "Come on, y'all. It's getting late. We'd better go pick them berries." He turned and walked on.

"But, Stacey, listen. Little Man, Christopher-John, listen."

The forest echoed an uneasy silence.

"The wind just stopped blowing, that's all," said Stacey. "Now stop fooling around and come on."

I jumped up to follow Stacey, then cried, "Stacey, look!" On a black oak a few yards away was a huge white *X*. "How did that get there?" I exclaimed, running to the tree.

"There's another one!" Little Man screamed.

(H) Read and Discuss What is going on with Cassie and the trees?

"I see one too!" shouted Christopher-John.

Stacey said nothing as Christopher-John, Little Man, and I ran wildly through the forest counting the ghostlike marks.

"Stacey, they're on practically all of them," I said when he called us back.

"Why?"

Stacey studied the trees, then suddenly pushed us down.

"My clothes!" Little Man wailed indignantly.

"Hush, Man, and stay down," Stacey warned. "Somebody's coming."

Two white men emerged. We looked at each other. We knew to be silent.

"You mark them all down here?" one of the men asked.

"Not the younger ones, Mr. Andersen."

"We might need them, too," said Mr. Andersen, counting the X's. "But don't worry 'bout marking them now, Tom. We'll get them later. Also them trees up past the pond toward the house."

"The old woman agree to you cutting these trees?"

"I ain't been down there yet," Mr. Andersen said.

"Mr. Andersen . . ." Tom hesitated a moment, looked up at the silent trees, then back at Mr. Andersen. "Maybe you should go easy with them," he cautioned. "You know that David can be as mean as an ole jackass when he wanna be."

"He's talking about Papa," I whispered.

"Shhhh!" Stacey hissed.

I Read and Discuss What is happening in the forest now?

J Literary Focus Novella What additional characters have come into the story?

Thomas Flaherty by Thomas Eakins (1844–1916).

Mr. Andersen looked uneasy. "What's that gotta do with anything?"

"Well, he just don't take much to any dealings with white folks." Again, Tom looked up at the trees. "He ain't afraid like some."

Mr. Andersen laughed weakly. "Don't worry 'bout that, Tom. The land belongs to his mama. He don't have no say in it. Besides, I guess I oughta know how to handle David Logan. After all, there are ways. . . .

"Now, you get on back to my place and get some boys and start chopping down these trees," Mr. Andersen said. "I'll go talk to the old woman." He looked up at the sky. "We can almost get a full day's work in if we hurry."

Mr. Andersen turned to walk away, but Tom stopped him. "Mr. Andersen, you really gonna chop all the trees?"

"If I need to. These folks ain't got no call for them. I do. I got me a good contract for these trees and I aim to fulfill it."

Tom watched Mr. Andersen walk away; then, looking sorrowfully up at the trees, he shook his head and disappeared into the depths of the forest. **K**

"What we gonna do, Stacey?" I asked anxiously. "They can't just cut down our trees, can they?"

"I don't know. Papa's gone. . . ." Stacey muttered to himself, trying to decide what we should do next.

"Boy, if Papa was here, them ole white men wouldn't be messing with our trees," Little Man declared.

"Yeah!" Christopher-John agreed. "Just let Papa get hold of 'em and he gonna turn 'em every which way but loose."

"Christopher-John, Man," Stacey said finally, "go get the cows and take them home."

"But we just brought them down here," Little Man protested.

"And we gotta pick the berries for dinner," said Christopher-John mournfully.

"No time for that now. Hurry up. And stay clear of them white men. Cassie, you come with me."

We ran, brown legs and feet flying high through the still forest.

By the time Stacey and I arrived at the house, Mr. Andersen's car was already parked in the dusty drive. Mr. Andersen himself was seated comfortably in Papa's rocker on the front porch. Big Ma was seated too, but Mama was standing.

Stacey and I eased quietly to the side of the porch, unnoticed.

"Sixty-five dollars. That's an awful lot of money in these hard times, Aunt Caroline," Mr. Andersen was saying to Big Ma.

I could see Mama's thin face harden.

"You know," Mr. Andersen said, rocking familiarly in Papa's chair, "that's more than David can send home in two months."

"We do quite well on what David sends home," Mama said coldly.

Mr. Andersen stopped rocking. "I suggest you encourage Aunt Caroline to sell them trees, Mary. You know, David might not always be able to work so good. He could possibly have . . . an accident." **L**

K **Reading Focus** **Activate Prior Knowledge** In what way might Mr. Andersen take advantage of the Logan family? Support your response with details from the text.

L **Read and Discuss** How does Mr. Andersen's comment that David might have an accident add to what you know about Mr. Andersen?

Big Ma's soft brown eyes clouded over with fear as she looked first at Mr. Andersen, then at Mama. But Mama clenched her fists and said, "In Mississippi, black men do not have accidents."

"Hush, child, hush," Big Ma said hurriedly. "How many trees for the sixty-five dollars, Mr. Andersen?"

"Enough 'til I figure I got my sixty-five dollars' worth."

"And how many would that be?" Mama persisted.

Mr. Andersen looked haughtily at Mama. "I said I'd be the judge of that, Mary."

"I think not," Mama said.

Mr. Andersen stared at Mama. And Mama stared back at him. I knew Mr. Andersen didn't like that, but Mama did it anyway. Mr. Andersen soon grew uneasy under that piercing gaze, and when his eyes swiftly shifted from Mama to Big Ma, his face was beet red.

"Caroline," he said, his voice low and menacing, "you're the head of this family and you've got a decision to make. Now, I need them trees and I mean to have them. I've offered you a good price for them and I ain't gonna haggle over it. I know y'all can use the money. Doc Thomas tells me that Mary's not well." He hesitated a moment, then hissed venomously, "And if something should happen to David . . ." **Ⓜ**

Big Ma's soft brown eyes clouded over with fear.

"All right," Big Ma said, her voice trembling. "All right, Mr. Andersen."

"No, Big Ma!" I cried, leaping onto the porch. "You can't let him cut our trees!"

Mr. Andersen grasped the arms of the rocker, his knuckles chalk white. "You certainly ain't taught none of your younguns how to behave, Caroline," he said curtly.

"You children go on to the back," Mama said, shooing us away.

"No, Mama," Stacey said. "He's gonna cut them all down. Me and Cassie heard him say so in the woods."

"I won't let him cut them," I threatened. "I won't let him! The trees are my friends and ain't no mean ole white man gonna touch my trees—"

Mama's hands went roughly around my body as she carried me off to my room.

"Now, hush," she said, her dark eyes flashing wildly. "I've told you how dangerous it is . . ." She broke off in midsentence. She stared at me a moment, then hugged me tightly and went back to the porch.

Stacey joined me a few seconds later, and we sat there in the heat of the quiet room, listening miserably as the first whack of an ax echoed against the trees.

That night I was awakened by soft sounds outside my window. I reached for Big Ma, but she wasn't there. Hurrying

Ⓜ **Read and Discuss** The word *venomously* means "poisonously." What is the author comparing Mr. Andersen to by the use of the phrase *hissed venomously*? How does this make you feel about Mr. Andersen?

Vocabulary **curtly** (KURT lee) *adv.*: rudely; with few words.

to the window, I saw Mama and Big Ma standing in the yard in their nightclothes and Stacey, fully dressed, sitting atop Lady, our golden mare. By the time I got outside, Stacey was gone.

"Mama, where's Stacey?" I cried.

"Be quiet, Cassie. You'll wake Christopher-John and Little Man."

"But where's he going?"

"He's going to get Papa," Mama said. "Now be quiet."

"Go on, Stacey, boy," I whispered. "Ride for me, too." **N**

As the dust billowed after him, Mama said, "I should've gone myself. He's so young."

Big Ma put her arm around Mama. "Now, Mary, you know you couldn't've gone. Mr. Andersen would miss you if he come by and see you ain't here. You done right, now. Don't worry, that boy'll be just fine."

Three days passed, hot and windless.

Mama forbade any of us to go into the forest, so Christopher-John, Little Man, and I spent the slow, restless days hovering as close to the dusty road as we dared, listening to the foreign sounds of steel against the trees and the thunderous roar of those ancient loved ones as they crashed upon the earth. Sometimes Mama would scold us and tell us to come back to the house, but even she could not ignore the continuous pounding of the axes against the trees. Or the sight of the loaded lumber wagons rolling out of the forest. In the middle of washing or ironing or hoeing, she would look up sorrowfully and listen, then turn toward the road, searching for some sign of Papa and Stacey.

On the fourth day, before the sun had risen, bringing its cloak of miserable heat, I saw her walking alone toward the woods. I ran after her.

She did not send me back.

"Mama," I said. "How sick are you?"

Mama took my hand. "Remember when you had the flu and felt so sick?"

"Yes'm."

"And when I gave you some medicine, you got well soon afterward?"

"Yes'm."

"Well, that's how sick I am. As soon as I get my medicine, I'll be all well again. And that'll be soon, now that Papa's coming home," she said, giving my hand a gentle little squeeze.

The quiet surrounded us as we entered the forest. Mama clicked on the flashlight, and we walked silently along the cow path to the pond. There, just beyond the pond, pockets of open space loomed before us.

"Mama!"

"I know, baby, I know."

On the ground lay countless trees. Trees that had once been such strong, tall things. So strong that I could fling my arms partially around one of them and feel safe and secure. So tall and leafy green that their boughs had formed a forest temple.

And old.

So old that Indians had once built fires at their feet and had sung happy songs of happy days. So old they had hidden fleeing black men in the night and listened to their sad tales of a foreign land.

In the cold of winter, when the ground lay frozen, they had sung their frosty

N [Read and Discuss] What is happening now?

ballads of years gone by. Or on a muggy, sweat-drenched day, their leaves had rippled softly, lazily, like restless green fingers strumming at a guitar, echoing their epic tales.

But now they would sing no more. They lay forever silent upon the ground.

Those trees that remained standing were like defeated warriors mourning their fallen dead. But soon they, too, would fall, for the white *X*'s had been placed on nearly every one. ❶

"Oh, dear, dear trees," I cried as the gray light of the rising sun fell in ghostly shadows over the land. The tears rolled hot down my cheeks. Mama held me close, and when I felt her body tremble, I knew she was crying too.

When our tears eased, we turned sadly toward the house. As we emerged from the forest, we could see two small figures waiting impatiently on the other side of the road. As soon as they spied us, they hurried across to meet us.

"Mama! You and Cassie was in the forest," Little Man accused. "Big Ma told us!"

"How was it?" asked Christopher-John, rubbing the sleep from his eyes. "Was it spooky?"

"Spooky and empty," I said listlessly.

"Mama, me and Christopher-John wanna see too," Little Man declared.

"No, baby," Mama said softly as we crossed the road. "The men'll be done there soon, and I don't want y'all underfoot."

"But, Mama—" Little Man started to protest.

"When Papa comes home and the men are gone, then you can go. But until then, you stay out of there. You hear me, Little Man Logan?"

"Yes'm," Little Man reluctantly replied.

But the sun had been up only an hour when Little Man decided that he could not wait for Papa to return.

"Mama said we wasn't to go down there," Christopher-John warned.

"Cassie did," Little Man cried.

"But she was with Mama. Wasn't you, Cassie?"

"Well, I'm going too," said Little Man. "Everybody's always going someplace 'cepting me." And off he went.

Christopher-John and I ran after him. Down the narrow cow path and around the pond we chased. But neither of us was fast enough to overtake Little Man before he reached the lumbermen.

"Hey, you kids, get away from here," Mr. Andersen shouted when he saw us. "Now, y'all go on back home," he said, stopping in front of Little Man.

"We are home," I said. "You're the one who's on our land."

"Claude," Mr. Andersen said to one of the black lumbermen, "take these kids home." Then he pushed Little Man out of his way. Little Man pushed back. Mr. Andersen looked down, startled that a little black boy would do such a thing. He shoved Little Man a second time, and Little Man fell into the dirt.

Little Man looked down at his clothing covered with sawdust and dirt and wailed,

---

❶ **Read and Discuss** | How is the forest now different from the way it used to be?

"You got my clothes dirty!"

I rushed toward Mr. Andersen, my fist in a mighty hammer, shouting, "You ain't got no right to push on Little Man. Why don't you push on somebody your own size—like me, you ole—"

The man called Claude put his hand over my mouth and carried me away. Christopher-John trailed behind us, tugging on the man's shirt.

"Put her down. Hey, mister, put Cassie down."

The man carried me all the way to the pond. "Now," he said, "you and your brothers get on home before y'all get hurt. Go on, get!"

As the man walked away, I looked around. "Where's Little Man?"

Christopher-John looked around too.

"I don't know," he said. "I thought he was behind me."

Back we ran toward the lumbermen.

We found Little Man's clothing first, folded neatly by a tree. Then we saw Little Man, dragging a huge stick and headed straight for Mr. Andersen.

"Little Man, come back here," I called.

But Little Man did not stop.

Mr. Andersen stood alone, barking orders, unaware of the oncoming Little Man.

"Little Man! Oh, Little Man, don't!"

It was too late.

Little Man swung the stick as hard as he could against Mr. Andersen's leg.

Mr. Andersen let out a howl and reached to where he thought Little Man's collar was. But, of course, Little Man had no collar.

"Run, Man!" Christopher-John and I shouted. "Run!"

"Why, you little . . ." Mr. Andersen cried, grabbing at Little Man. But Little Man was too quick for him. He slid right through Mr. Andersen's legs. Tom stood nearby, his face crinkling into an amused grin.

"Hey, y'all!" Mr. Andersen yelled to the lumbermen. "Claude! Get that kid!"

But sure-footed Little Man dodged the groping hands of the lumbermen as easily as if he were skirting mud puddles. Over tree stumps, around legs, and through legs he dashed. But in the end, there were too many lumbermen for him, and he was handed over to Mr. Andersen.

For the second time, Christopher-John and I went to Little Man's rescue.

"Put him down!" we ordered, charging the lumbermen.

I was captured much too quickly, though not before I had landed several stinging blows. But Christopher-John, furious at seeing Little Man handled so roughly by Mr. Andersen, managed to elude the clutches of the lumbermen until he was fully upon Mr. Andersen. Then, with his mightiest thrust, he kicked Mr. Andersen solidly in the shins, not once, but twice, before the lumbermen pulled him away.

Mr. Andersen was fuming. He slowly took off his wide leather belt. Christopher-John, Little Man, and I looked woefully at the belt, then at each other. Little Man and Christopher-John fought to escape, but I closed my eyes and awaited the whining of the heavy belt and its painful bite against my skin.

What was he waiting for? I started to open my eyes, but then the zinging whirl of the belt began and I tensed, awaiting its fearful sting. But just as the leather tip lashed into my leg, a deep, familiar voice said, "Put the belt down, Andersen."

I opened my eyes.

"Papa!"

"Let the children go," Papa said. He was standing on a nearby ridge with a strange black box in his hands. Stacey was behind him, holding the reins to Lady.

The chopping stopped as all eyes turned to Papa.

"They been right meddlesome," Mr. Andersen said. "They need teaching how to act."

"Any teaching, I'll do it. Now, let them go."

Mr. Andersen looked down at Little Man struggling to get away. Smiling broadly, he motioned our release. "Okay, David," he said. **(P)**

As we ran up the ridge to Papa, Mr. Andersen said, "It's good to have you home, boy."

Papa said nothing until we were safely behind him. "Take them home, Stacey."

"But, Papa—"

"Do like I say, son."

Stacey herded us away from the men. When we were far enough away so Papa

---

(P) Read and Discuss How have things ended up for the children?

Vocabulary elude (ih LOOD) v.: avoid; cleverly escape.

couldn't see us, Stacey stopped and handed me Lady's reins.

"Y'all go on home now," he said. "I gotta go help Papa."

"Papa don't need no help," I said. "He told you to come with us."

"But you don't know what he's gonna do."

"What?" I asked.

"He's gonna blow up the forest if they don't get out of here. So go on home where y'all be safe."

"How's he gonna do that?" asked Little Man.

"We been setting sticks of dynamite since the middle of the night. We ain't even been up to the house cause Papa wanted the sticks planted and covered over before the men came. Now, Cassie, take them on back to the house. Do like I tell you for once, will ya?" Then, without waiting for another word, he was gone.

"I wanna see," Little Man announced.

"I don't," protested Christopher-John.

"Come on," I said.

We tied the mare to a tree, then belly-crawled back to where we could see Papa and joined Stacey in the brush.

"Cassie, I told you . . ."

"What's Papa doing?"

The black box was now set upon a sawed-off tree stump, and Papa's hands were tightly grasping a T-shaped instrument which went into it.

"What's that thing?" asked Little Man.

> "I mean what I say," Papa said. "Ask anyone."

"It's a plunger," Stacey whispered. "If Papa presses down on it, the whole forest will go *pfffff!*" **Q**

Our mouths went dry and our eyes went wide. Mr. Andersen's eyes were wide, too.

"You're bluffing, David," he said. "You ain't gonna push that plunger."

"One thing you can't seem to understand, Andersen," Papa said, "is that a black man's always gotta be ready to die. And it don't make me any difference if I die today or tomorrow. Just as long as I die right."

Mr. Andersen laughed uneasily. The lumbermen moved nervously away.

"I mean what I say," Papa said. "Ask anyone. I always mean what I say."

"He sure do, Mr. Andersen," Claude said, eyeing the black box. "He always do."

"Shut up!" Mr. Andersen snapped. "And the rest of y'all stay put." Then turning back to Papa, he smiled cunningly. "I'm sure you and me can work something out, David."

"Ain't nothing to be worked out," said Papa.

"Now, look here, David, your mama and me, we got us a contract . . . "

"There ain't no more contract," Papa replied coldly. "Now, either you get out or I blow it up. That's it."

"He means it, Mr. Andersen," another frightened lumberman ventured. "He's crazy and he sure 'nough means it."

"You know what could happen to you, boy?" Mr. Andersen exploded, his face

Q **Read and Discuss** What does Papa's plan tell you about his view of Mr. Andersen's actions?

beet red again. "Threatening a white man like this?"

Papa said nothing. He just stood there, his hands firmly on the plunger, staring down at Mr. Andersen.

Mr. Andersen could not bear the stare. He turned away, cursing Papa. "You're a fool, David. A crazy fool." Then he looked around at the lumbermen. They shifted their eyes and would not look at him.

"Maybe we better leave, Mr. Andersen," Tom said quietly.

Mr. Andersen glanced at Tom, then turned back to Papa and said as lightly as he could, "All right, David, all right. It's your land. We'll just take the logs we got cut and get out." He motioned to the men. "Hey, let's get moving and get these logs out of here before this crazy fool gets us all killed." **R**

"No," Papa said.

Mr. Andersen stopped, knowing that he could not have heard correctly. "What you say?"

"You ain't taking one more stick out of this forest."

"Now, look here—"

"You heard me."

"But you can't sell all these logs, David," Mr. Andersen exclaimed incredulously.

Papa said nothing. Just cast that piercing look on Mr. Andersen.

> Papa said nothing. Just cast that piercing look on Mr. Andersen.

"Look, I'm a fair man. I tell you what I'll do. I'll give you another thirty-five dollars. An even hundred dollars. Now, that's fair, ain't it?"

"I'll see them rot first."

"But—"

"That's my last word," Papa said, tightening his grip on the plunger.

Mr. Andersen swallowed hard. "You won't always have that black box, David," he warned. "You know that, don't you?"

"That may be. But it won't matter none. Cause I'll always have my self-respect." **S**

Mr. Andersen opened his mouth to speak, but no sound came. Tom and the lumbermen were quietly moving away, putting their gear in the empty lumber wagons. Mr. Andersen looked again at the black box. Finally, his face ashen, he too walked away.

Papa stood unmoving until the wagons and the men were gone. Then, when the sound of the last wagon rolling over the dry leaves could no longer be heard and a hollow silence filled the air, he slowly removed his hands from the plunger and looked up at the remaining trees standing like lonely sentries in the morning.

"Dear, dear old trees," I heard him call softly, "will you ever sing again?"

I waited. But the trees gave no answer.

R **Read and Discuss** How has Papa's plan worked out so far?

S **Reading Focus** **Activate Prior Knowledge** Why is having self-respect so important to Mr. Logan?

Vocabulary incredulously (ihn KREHJ uh luhs lee) *adv.:* unbelievingly.

Applying Your Skills

SKILLS FOCUS **Literary Skills** Analyze forms of prose: novella; analyze setting. **Reading Skills** Activate prior knowledge. **Writing Skills** Develop descriptions with sensory details; use figurative language.

Song of the Trees

Respond and Think Critically

Reading Focus

Quick Check

1. Why does Mr. Andersen want to cut down the trees?
2. How do the Logans stop him?

Read with a Purpose

3. How do the Logans work together to overcome a difficult situation?

Reading Skills: Activate Prior Knowledge

4. After reading *Song of the Trees,* fill out the "After Reading" column of the chart. Have your answers changed? Why or why not?

Before Reading   After Reading

_____ 1. Given the chance, most _____
people won't take advantage of another person.
_____ 2. Nobody owns the earth. _____
_____ 3. People gain self-respect _____
by standing up for their beliefs.

Literary Focus

Literary Analysis

5. **Interpret** What is the <u>significance</u> of the title *Song of the Trees?*
6. **Extend** Based on what you know about Mr. Andersen, how do you think he might respond to what happened in the forest?

7. **Evaluate** Taylor says that in writing *Song of the Trees,* "[I] drew upon people and places I had known all my life." How believable did the characters seem to you? Explain.
8. **Literary Perspectives** What <u>impact</u> does the time period of the Great Depression have on the characters in the story?

Literary Skills: Novella

9. **Evaluate** How might this **novella** have been told differently if it were a **short story**? What might the author have added if it were a **novel**?

Literary Skills Review: Setting

Setting is the time and place in which the events of a work of literature take place. Setting can also include the customs and behavior of that time and place.

10. **Analyze** How does the setting add to the conflict between the Logans and the lumbermen?

Writing Focus

Think as a Reader/Writer

Use It in Your Writing Look back at the list you made of Cassie's descriptions of the trees acting as people. Write a brief paragraph in which you give something nonhuman—cars, clouds, sports equipment, for example—human characteristics.

What Do You Think Now

How has reading *Song of the Trees* affected your ideas about helping out in difficult times?

Applying Your Skills

Song of the Trees

Vocabulary Development

Connotations and Denotations

Would you rather be described as *curious* or *nosy*? The two words have the same basic meaning, or **denotation,** but they have different connotations. **Connotations** are the feelings and associations that have come to be attached to certain words.

Most people wouldn't mind being called curious: The word suggests that you are interested in the world around you and want to learn about it. But to be called nosy has negative connotations: It suggests that you are someone who puts your nose into other people's business.

Your Turn

Test your skill at recognizing shades of meaning. (Use a dictionary to check your answers.) What are the differences between the following words? Re-reading the Vocabulary words in their contexts in the story can help you.

> dispute
> curtly
> elude
> incredulously

1. fight and **dispute**
2. matter-of-factly and **curtly**
3. avoid and **elude**
4. doubtfully and **incredulously**

Language Coach

Multiple-Meaning Words Many words have more than one meaning. For example, the word *soft* can mean

- not hard
- gentle
- quiet
- weak

Work with a partner to find the various meanings of the following words from the story. Then, write a sentence for each different meaning. Share your sentences with the class.

> rich   black   mark

Which meanings of these familiar words were new or a surprise to you?

Academic Vocabulary

Talk About . . .

Explain the significance of the trees for Cassie and her family. What impact would their destruction have on the whole family?

Learn It Online
Take another look at connotations using *WordSharp*:

go.hrw.com   L7-60   Go

Grammar Link

Pronouns

Words like *I* and *her* are pronouns. **Pronouns** are words used in place of nouns or other pronouns. When used in compound structures, pronouns can be confusing. Which of these sentences is correct?

Papa talked to Stacey and me.
Papa talked to Stacey and I.

Stacey and me and *Stacey and I* are compound structures. When you proofread your writing, you can use this trick to decide which pronoun is correct: Say the sentence aloud as if it contained a pronoun alone, not a compound structure. Use each form of the pronoun in turn, and let your ear tell you which one sounds right.

TEST   Papa talked to me. [sounds right]
              Papa talked to I. [sounds wrong]

CORRECT   Papa talked to Stacey and *me.*

Your Turn

In each of the following sentences, choose the correct pronoun. Use the trick described above to test each choice you make.

1. Cassie's brothers were protective of Big Ma and *she/her.*
2. My brothers and *I/me* were listening to them.
3. I had a lot of respect for Stacey and *he/him.*
4. Tom and *he/him* did not scare Papa.
5. Papa showed *he/him* and *I/me* that it was important to stick together.

CHOICES

As you respond to the Choices, use these **Academic Vocabulary** words as appropriate: <u>interpret</u>, <u>impact</u>, <u>insight</u>, <u>significance</u>.

REVIEW
Reflect on Forms of Prose

Timed ⌐Writing *Song of the Trees* was inspired by an experience Taylor's father had when he was young. Why do you think she chose to tell the story as a novella rather than as a nonfiction piece? Reflect on the differences between fiction and nonfiction. Then, write a paragraph in which you discuss why you think Taylor tells the story as fiction.

CONNECT
Describe an Experience

Cassie and her family reach a goal together that one of them could not have reached alone. Recall a time when you worked with others to accomplish something. Write a brief essay about the experience in which you describe why you came together and what you achieved.

EXTEND
Debate an Issue

Do you think old forests should be cut down? First, consider your own **prior knowledge** of trees and forests. Next, in a library or on the Internet, research the <u>impact</u> of the lumber industry on both the economy and the environment. Then, form two teams to debate the pros and cons of cutting old-growth forests.

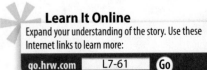

Learn It Online
Expand your understanding of the story. Use these Internet links to learn more:

| go.hrw.com | L7-61 | Go |

A Mason-Dixon
Memory

by **Clifton Davis**

QuickWrite
In what ways would you support a
friend who needs your help?

Reader/Writer
Notebook

Use your **RWN** to complete the activities for this selection.

Literary Focus

The Essay One form of nonfiction that you'll often be asked to read—and write—is the **essay,** a short piece of nonfiction prose that focuses on a single topic. An essay can be about anything, from "The Meaning of Life" to "How I Feel About My Cat."

An essay can be formal in tone and highly structured, with statements laid out in careful order and evidence supporting each one. An essay can also be personal and even humorous, as if the writer were sitting down with you for a chat. An essay's tone and structure will depend on its purpose—does the writer want to inform you? persuade you? entertain you? or something else?

Reading Focus

Setting a Purpose When you set a **purpose** for reading, you focus on why you are reading the text in front of you. Preview the title, text, and illustrations before you read.

Into Action Use a chart like the one below to set an initial purpose and to list any new ones you may discover while reading. Check them off as you accomplish them.

What's Your Purpose?

Purpose 1:	to learn what the title means	☐
Purpose 2:	to determine the reason why Davis wrote the essay	☐
Purpose 3:		☐

Writing Focus

Think as a Reader/Writer

Find It in Your Reading As you read, record three details from Davis's childhood experience that he connects to the way he looks at life today.

Vocabulary

predominantly (prih DAHM uh nuhnt lee) *adv.:* mainly. *The story is predominantly about the meaning of friendship.*

forfeit (FAWR fiht) *v.:* lose the right to something. *The team would forfeit the tournament.*

resolve (rih ZAHLV) *v.:* decide. *In tough situations, people can resolve to do the right thing.*

ominous (AHM uh nuhs): *adj.:* threatening. *The look on the chaperone's face was ominous.*

bigotry (BIHG uh tree): *n.:* prejudice; intolerance. *Whites-only policies were based on bigotry.*

will **forfeit** something if necessary

are **predominantly** supportive

good friends

resolve to stick together

can overcome **bigotry**

withstand **ominous** circumstances

Language Coach

Synonyms Words with the same or almost the same meanings are called **synonyms.** For instance, *mainly* is a synonym of the Vocabulary word *predominantly*. Which other Vocabulary words above are defined by a synonym?

Learn It Online

Use Word Watch to strengthen your vocabulary at:

go.hrw.com   L7-63   Go

Clifton Davis
(1946–   )

A Man of Many Talents

Clifton Davis is probably better known for his songs than for his essays. He wrote the hit song "Never Can Say Goodbye," which sold two million records, and has recorded several gospel albums as well. Davis is also an actor. He has appeared on Broadway, in movies, and on TV shows. He is perhaps best known for his role as Reverend Reuben Gregory on the television series *Amen,* which aired from 1986 to 1991.

A Spiritual Journey

After a time of personal struggles, Davis temporarily withdrew from the limelight in the early 1980s to study theology and become a minister. Davis believes it's important to do what's right, even while making a living amid the glitz and glamour of Hollywood.

"I had to go down the path to see my calling."

Think About the Writer Davis had to balance his roles of entertainer and minister. What different roles do you perform?

Build Background

The Mason-Dixon line forms part of the borders of four states. It was considered a dividing line between free and slave states before slavery was abolished, but its creation had nothing to do with slavery. Charles Mason and Jeremiah Dixon surveyed the line in the 1760s to settle a border dispute between the British colonies of Maryland and Pennsylvania.

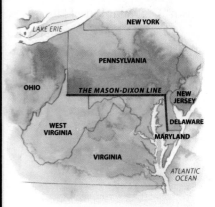

Preview the Selection

In 1991, **Dondré Green,** an African American high school golfer in Louisiana, experienced racial discrimination. He was asked to speak about his experience. **Clifton Davis** was on hand and recounts the speech and the childhood memories it brought back to him. Davis interrupts Dondré's story with a **flashback** that takes you back to earlier times and events in his own life.

A Mason-Dixon Memory

by **Clifton Davis**

Dondré Green glanced uneasily at the civic leaders and sports figures filling the hotel ballroom in Cleveland. They had come from across the nation to attend a fundraiser for the National Minority College Golf Scholarship Foundation. I was the banquet's featured entertainer. Dondré, an eighteen-year-old high school senior from Monroe, Louisiana, was the evening's honored guest.

"Nervous?" I asked the handsome young man in his starched white shirt and rented tuxedo.

"A little," he whispered, grinning.

One month earlier, Dondré had been just one more black student attending a predominantly white Southern school. Although most of his friends and classmates were white, Dondré's race had never been an issue. Then, on April 17, 1991, Dondré's black skin provoked an incident that made nationwide news.

"Ladies and gentlemen," the emcee[1] said, "our special guest, Dondré Green."

As the audience stood applauding, Dondré walked to the microphone and began his story. "I love golf," he said quietly. "For the past two years, I've been a member of the St. Frederick High School golf team. And though I was the only black member, I've always felt at home playing at the mostly white country clubs across Louisiana." **Ⓐ**

The audience leaned forward; even the waiters and busboys stopped to listen. As I listened, a memory buried in my heart since childhood began fighting its way to life.

"Our team had driven from Monroe," Dondré continued. "When we arrived at the Caldwell Parish Country Club in Columbia, we walked to the putting green."

Dondré and his teammates were too absorbed to notice the conversation

---

1. **emcee** (EHM SEE): master of ceremonies.

Ⓐ **Literary Focus** The Essay From your knowledge of Dondré Green, what do you suppose the topic of this essay will be?

Vocabulary **predominantly** (prih DAHM uh nuhnt lee) *adv.:* mainly.

between a man and St. Frederick athletic director James Murphy. After disappearing into the clubhouse, Murphy returned to his players.

"I want to see the seniors," he said. "On the double!" His face seemed strained as he gathered the four students, including Dondré.

"I don't know how to tell you this," he said, "but the Caldwell Parish Country Club is reserved for whites only." Murphy paused and looked at Dondré. His teammates glanced at each other in disbelief. "I want you seniors to decide what our response should be," Murphy continued. "If we leave, we forfeit this tournament. If we stay, Dondré can't play." **B**

As I listened, my own childhood memory from thirty-two years ago broke free. **C**

Golf team photograph from the 1991 *Warrior* yearbook.

I n 1959 I was thirteen years old, a poor black kid living with my mother and stepfather in a small black ghetto on Long Island, New York. My mother worked nights in a hospital, and my stepfather drove a coal truck. Needless to say, our standard of living was somewhat short of the American dream.

Nevertheless, when my eighth-grade teacher announced a graduation trip to Washington, D.C., it never crossed my mind that I would be left behind. Besides a complete tour of the nation's capital, we would visit Glen Echo Amusement Park in Maryland. In my imagination, Glen Echo

was Disneyland, Knott's Berry Farm, and Magic Mountain rolled into one.

My heart beating wildly, I raced home to deliver the mimeographed letter describing the journey. But when my mother saw how much the trip would cost, she just shook her head. We couldn't afford it.

After feeling sad for ten seconds, I decided to try to fund the trip myself. For the next eight weeks, I sold candy bars door-to-door, delivered newspapers, and mowed lawns. Three days before the deadline, I'd made just barely enough. I was going! **D**

The day of the trip, trembling with excitement, I climbed onto the train. I was the only nonwhite in our section.

Our hotel was not far from the White House. My roommate was Frank Miller, the son of a businessman. Leaning together out of our window and dropping water balloons on passing tourists quickly cemented our new friendship.

B **Read and Discuss** What is happening with the team?

C **Literary Focus** **The Essay** The writer adds extra space here. What words indicate a flashback? What year is he describing?

D **Read and Discuss** What is the author telling you about himself?

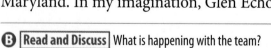

Vocabulary **forfeit** (FAWR fiht) *v.*: lose the right to something.

Every morning, almost a hundred of us loaded noisily onto our bus for another adventure. We sang our school fight song dozens of times—en route[2] to Arlington National Cemetery and even on an afternoon cruise down the Potomac River.

We visited the Lincoln Memorial twice, once in daylight, the second time at dusk. My classmates and I fell silent as we walked in the shadows of those thirty-six marble columns, one for every state in the Union that Lincoln labored to preserve. I stood next to Frank at the base of the nineteen-foot seated statue. Spotlights made the white Georgian marble seem to glow. Together, we read those famous words from Lincoln's speech at Gettysburg, remembering the most bloody battle in the War Between the States: "We here highly resolve that these dead shall not have died in vain—that this nation, under God, shall have a new birth of freedom. . . ."

As Frank motioned me into place to take my picture, I took one last look at Lincoln's face. He seemed alive and so terribly sad.

The next morning I understood a little better why he wasn't smiling. "Clifton," a chaperone said, "could I see you for a moment?"

The other guys at my table, especially Frank, turned pale. We had been joking about the previous night's direct water-balloon hit on a fat lady and her poodle. It was a stupid, dangerous act, but luckily nobody got hurt. We were celebrating our escape from punishment when the chaperone asked to see me.

"Clifton," she began, "do you know about the Mason-Dixon line?"

"No," I said, wondering what this had to do with drenching fat ladies.

"Before the Civil War," she explained, "the Mason-Dixon line was originally the boundary between Maryland and Pennsylvania—the dividing line between the slave and free states." Having escaped one disaster, I could feel another brewing. I noticed that her eyes were damp and her hands shaking.

"Today," she continued, "the Mason-Dixon line is a kind of invisible border between the North and the South. When you cross that invisible line out of Washington, D.C., into Maryland, things change."

There was an ominous drift to this conversation, but I wasn't following it. Why did she look and sound so nervous?

"Glen Echo Amusement Park is in Maryland," she said at last, "and the management doesn't allow Negroes inside." She stared at me in silence. **Ⓔ**

I was still grinning and nodding when the meaning finally sank in. "You mean I can't go to the park," I stuttered, "because I'm a Negro?"

She nodded slowly. "I'm sorry, Clifton," she said, taking my hand. "You'll have to stay in the hotel tonight. Why don't you and I watch a movie on television?"

---

2. **en route** (ahn ROOT): on the way.

Ⓔ **Reading Focus** **Set a Purpose** How does this information about the Mason-Dixon line help clarify the essay's title?

Vocabulary **resolve** (rih ZAHLV) v.: decide.
ominous (AHM uh nuhs): adj.: threatening.

I walked to the elevators feeling confusion, disbelief, anger, and a deep sadness. "What happened, Clifton?" Frank said when I got back to the room. "Did the fat lady tell on us?"

Without saying a word, I walked over to my bed, lay down, and began to cry. Frank was stunned into silence. Junior-high boys didn't cry, at least not in front of each other.

It wasn't just missing the class adventure that made me feel so sad. For the first time in my life, I was learning what it felt like to be a "nigger." Of course there was discrimination in the North, but the color of my skin had never officially kept me out of a coffee shop, a church—or an amusement park.

"Clifton," Frank whispered, "what is the matter?"

"They won't let me go to Glen Echo Park tonight," I sobbed.

"Because of the water balloon?" he asked.

"No," I answered, "because I'm a Negro."

"Well, that's a relief!" Frank said, and then he laughed, obviously relieved to have escaped punishment for our caper with the balloons. "I thought it was serious!"

Wiping away the tears with my sleeve, I stared at him. "It *is* serious. They don't let Negroes into the park. I can't go with you!" I shouted. "That's pretty serious to me."

I was about to wipe the silly grin off Frank's face with a blow to his jaw when I heard him say, "Then I won't go either."

For an instant we just froze. Then Frank grinned. I will never forget that moment. Frank was just a kid. He wanted to go to that amusement park as much as I did, but there was something even more important

The Alpine Hi-Ride at Glen Echo Park, Maryland.
Photo by U.S. National Park Service. Courtesy of Richard A. Cook.

than the class night out. Still, he didn't explain or expand.

The next thing I knew, the room was filled with kids listening to Frank. "They don't allow Negroes in the park," he said, "so I'm staying with Clifton."

"Me too," a second boy said.

"Those jerks," a third muttered. "I'm with you, Clifton." My heart began to race. Suddenly, I was not alone. A pint-sized revolution had been born. The "water-balloon brigade," eleven white boys from Long Island, had made its decision: "We won't go." And as I

sat on my bed in the center of it all, I felt grateful. But above all, I was filled with pride.

Dondré Green's story brought that childhood memory back to life. His golfing teammates, like my childhood friends, had an important decision to make. Standing by their friend would cost them dearly. But when it came time to decide, no one hesitated. "Let's get out of here," one of them whispered.

"They just turned and walked toward the van," Dondré told us. "They didn't debate it.

And the younger players joined us without looking back."

Dondré was astounded by the response of his friends—and the people of Louisiana. The whole state was outraged and tried to make it right. The Louisiana House of Representatives proclaimed a Dondré Green Day and passed legislation permitting lawsuits for damages, attorneys' fees, and court costs against any private facility that invites a team, then bars any member because of race.

As Dondré concluded, his eyes glistened with tears. "I love my coach and my

---

F **Read and Discuss** Davis says, "A pint-sized revolution had been born." What does he mean?

teammates for sticking by me," he said. "It goes to show that there are always good people who will not give in to bigotry. The kind of love they showed me that day will conquer hatred every time."

Suddenly, the banquet crowd was standing, applauding Dondré Green. **G**

My friends, too, had shown that kind of love. As we sat in the hotel, a chaperone came in waving an envelope. "Boys!" he shouted. "I've just bought thirteen tickets to the Senators-Tigers game. Anybody want to go?"

The room erupted in cheers. Not one of us had ever been to a professional baseball game in a real baseball park.

On the way to the stadium, we grew silent as our driver paused before the Lincoln Memorial. For one long moment, I stared through the marble pillars at Mr. Lincoln, bathed in that warm yellow light. There was still no smile and no sign of hope in his sad and tired eyes.

"We here highly resolve . . . that this nation, under God, shall have a new birth of freedom . . ."

In his words and in his life,

Lincoln had made it clear that freedom is not free. Every time the color of a person's skin keeps him out of an amusement park or off a country-club fairway, the war for freedom begins again. Sometimes the battle is fought with fists and guns, but more often the most effective weapon is a simple act of love and courage. **H**

Whenever I hear those words from Lincoln's speech at Gettysburg, I remember my eleven white friends, and I feel hope once again. I like to imagine that when we paused that night at the foot of his great monument, Mr. Lincoln smiled at last. As Dondré said, "The kind of love they showed me that day will conquer hatred every time." **I**

(inset) Tiger Woods (2004) and his Stanford University golf team (1994).

Analyzing Visuals

Viewing and Interpreting
How have conditions for aspiring golfers of all backgrounds changed from the time of Dondré Green's experience?

G **Literary Focus** The Essay How do you know the writer has flashed back again?

H **Literary Focus** The Essay The writer reflects on both stories, his and Dondré Green's. Which sentence in this paragraph states the main idea of Davis's essay?

I **Read and Discuss** How did things work out for Davis?

Vocabulary **bigotry** (BIHG uh tree): *n.*: prejudice; intolerance.

Applying Your Skills

SKILLS FOCUS **Literary Skills** Analyze forms of prose: the essay; analyze forms of prose: short story. **Reading Skills** Set a purpose for reading. **Writing Skills** Write personal texts.

A Mason-Dixon Memory

Respond and Think Critically

Reading Focus

Quick Check

1. What experiences did Green and Davis share? Fill in a chart like the one below to compare their experiences.

	Experience	Friends' Responses
Green		
Davis		

Read with a Purpose

2. How do Green's teammates and Davis's classmates stand up to injustice? Why does Davis think their actions are significant?

Reading Skills: Setting a Purpose

3. Review the purposes you set for reading this essay. Explain how focusing your reading added to your understanding of it.

Literary Focus

Literary Analysis

4. **Analyze** Davis says, "Sometimes the battle is fought with fists and guns, but more often the most effective weapon is a simple act of love and courage." What does he mean by this?

5. **Interpret** Davis and Green both refer to love as a weapon in the "war for freedom." How can love be a weapon? Include examples from the essay in your answer.

6. **Connect** Have you or a friend ever felt unwelcome someplace? How did your experience compare with Green's or Davis's?

Literary Skills: The Essay

7. **Analyze** Explain what makes "A Mason-Dixon Memory" an **essay.**

8. **Interpret** Explain the purpose of this essay. Why do you think Davis wrote it?

Literary Skills Review: The Short Story

A **short story** is a short fictional work in which characters move through a series of events (the plot) and work through a conflict.

9. **Compare and Contrast** What characteristics does this essay share with a short story? How is this essay different from a short story?

Writing Focus

Think as a Reader/Writer

Use It in Your Writing The childhood experience Davis recalls in "A Mason-Dixon Memory" gave him important <u>insights</u> about friendship and courage. Write a brief essay about the <u>significance</u> of an experience of yours and what you learned from it. Be specific about why it is important and what you remember from the experience today.

What Do **You Think Now** How do the actions of Green's and Davis's friends reflect your idea of what it means to be loyal?

A Mason-Dixon Memory

Vocabulary Development

Synonyms: Shades of Meaning

Words with the same or almost the same meaning are called **synonyms.** Synonyms usually have different shades of meaning. *Rigid* and *firm* are synonyms, but most people would rather be called *firm* than *rigid*. *Firm* suggests steadiness, and *rigid* suggests stiffness. A dictionary or thesaurus, a book of synonyms, can help you pick exactly the word you need.

Your Turn

Synonyms Make a word map like the following one for the rest of the Vocabulary words. Find at least one synonym for each word, and put it in the word map. Then, write at least one sentence using each Vocabulary word. Discuss the synonyms and their shades of meaning, if any.

Language Coach

Thesaurus A book of synonyms is called a **thesaurus.** You use one when you're looking for a word that expresses a specific meaning. You can find a thesaurus in print or online.

| |
| predominantly |
| forfeit |
| resolve |
| ominous |
| bigotry |

1. Find each Vocabulary word in the essay. Then, use a thesaurus to look for synonyms. For each word, choose the synonym that best conveys the writer's meaning.

2. Now, use the synonyms to paraphrase the sentences from the essay where the Vocabulary words appear. (Paraphrasing a sentence means putting it in your own words without changing the meaning.) In each of your paraphrased sentences, include the synonym you chose.

Academic Vocabulary

Talk About . . .

Dondré Green says that love "will conquer hatred every time." Explain why you agree or disagree with this <u>insight</u>. Write down three examples of behavior that you've seen or read about that support Green's statement.

Learn It Online
Examine synonyms with *WordSharp* and take your vocabulary to a new level:

| go.hrw.com | L7-72 | GO |

Grammar Link

Adjectives

An **adjective** is a word that modifies a noun (such as *dog, bicycle,* or *Charles*) or a pronoun (such as *she, he,* or *it*). Adjectives typically answer one of the following questions (adjectives in the chart below are underlined):

What kind?	<u>fast</u> runner
	<u>new</u> car
	<u>good</u> book
Which one (or ones)?	<u>that</u> building
	<u>these</u> people
	<u>any</u> day
How much (or many)?	<u>twenty</u> dollars
	<u>several</u> days
	<u>many</u> admirers

Your Turn

Identify the adjective in each passage below from "A Mason-Dixon Memory," and tell which of the above questions the adjective answers. Do not include the articles *a, an,* and *the* in your identification. Then, use the adjective to modify a different word in a sentence of your own.

1. "If we leave, we forfeit this tournament."
2. "Besides a complete tour . . ."
3. "I've just bought thirteen tickets . . ."
4. "I stared through the marble pillars . . ."

CHOICES

As you respond to the Choices, use these **Academic Vocabulary** words as appropriate: <u>interpret</u>, <u>impact</u>, <u>insight</u>, <u>significance</u>.

REVIEW
Discuss Forms of Prose

Group Discussion "A Mason-Dixon Memory" is a moving personal essay. Suppose you read about Davis's experiences in a newspaper article. How would the article be different? Would you gain as much <u>insight</u> about Davis's feelings from a news article? As a group, discuss other differences between an essay and an article.

CONNECT
Support a Position

Timed └Writing Many people devote their lives to fighting for important causes, such as civil rights. Write a brief **persuasive essay** on an issue *you* really care about. Try to write about an issue that matters to other people too. Write a sentence that identifies the issue and states your opinion on it. Then, provide one or two reasons that support your opinion.

EXTEND
Shoot a Scene

TechFocus In a group, create a video showing one "scene" from the essay. Write your script based on details in the essay. Finally, ask your classmates to help you with acting and filming.

Learn It Online
There's more to this story than meets the eye. Expand your view at:

go.hrw.com | L7-73 | **Go**

Comparing Versions of the Cinderella Story

CONTENTS

What Do You Think

What really helps a person overcome life's difficulties?

QuickWrite

Underdogs—likable characters in no-win situations—delight us by winning in the end. Why do we enjoy stories about an underdog who is rescued or given help to succeed?

Preparing to Read

Aschenputtel / Yeh-Shen / Interview

Reader/Writer Notebook

Use your **RWN** to complete the activities for these selections.

Literary Focus

Folk Tales Some of the world's oldest and most familiar stories are **folk tales**—stories passed on by word of mouth, often over centuries. However, a folk tale will always have certain patterns, called **motifs.** One motif is the number three. Important things often happen in threes in folk tales: The third time is "the charm," for that is when something happens that did not happen before.

Reading Focus

Comparing and Contrasting Across Texts These three selections offer different versions of the same story. As you read, think about how the stories are similar and how they are different.

Into Action Fill out a chart like the one below as you read each selection to compare and contrast the three texts.

Comparing Cinderella Stories

	"Aschenputtel"	"Yeh-Shen"	"Interview"
Characters	Aschenputtel, two stepdaughters, step-mother, prince, doves		
Plot			
Tone			
Theme			

Writing Focus

Think as a Reader/Writer

Find It in Your Reading **Tone** refers to a writer's attitude toward a subject: admiring, critical, humorous, and so on. As you read these selections, write down some of the words, phrases, and sentences that convey a specific tone.

Vocabulary

Aschenputtel

persisted (puhr SIHS tihd) *v.*: refused to give up. *She persisted in trying on the shoe.*

splendor (SPLEHN duhr) *n.*: magnificence. *The splendor of the golden dress dazzled all at the feast.*

Yeh-Shen

glistening (GLIHS uhn ihng) *v.* used as *adj.*: sparkling; reflecting light. *The glistening shoe sparkled on the dark path.*

entranced (ehn TRANST) *v.*: cast a spell on; enchanted. *The king was entranced by the mysterious woman.*

vigil (VIHJ uhl) *n.*: overnight watch. *Yeh-Shen kept vigil by her mother's grave.*

Language Coach

Homographs Words that look the same but are pronounced differently and have different meanings are called **homographs.** The word *entrance* (EHN truhns, noun) means "place to enter." To *entrance* (ehn TRANS, verb), on the other hand, means "to fill with wonder." Think of two other words that are homographs.

Jakob and Wilhelm Grimm
(1785–1863); (1786–1863)

Rescuing Rapunzel

Jakob and Wilhelm Grimm introduced us to such famous fairy-tale characters as Rapunzel, Hansel and Gretel, and Aschenputtel (Cinderella). Before the 1800s, most European folk and fairy tales were not written down. The Brothers Grimm collected and wrote down the vanishing traditional stories of Germany. By the time the final edition of their collected stories was published, in 1857, the brothers had collected about two hundred tales.

Ai-Ling Louie
(1949–   )

For the Children

For Ai-Ling Louie, teaching led to writing: "My desire to be a writer didn't come into full bloom until I became an elementary school teacher. I found myself fascinated by the books my school children were reading. . . . 'Yeh-Shen' was written for my class to hear."

Sara Henderson Hay **(1906–1987)**

An Early Start

At the age of ten, Sara Henderson Hay published her first poem. She became an award-winning poet known for her humorous, witty poems.

Think About the Writers

When writers base a work on a story that already exists, is the new work less original? Explain.

In "Aschenputtel," which means "little ash girl" or "cinder girl," you will meet the **German Cinderella.** The story will probably seem very familiar to you, but get ready for a rather "grim" ending that's definitely not from Disney.

"Yeh-Shen," a Chinese folk tale about a **girl** and her **fish,** is perhaps the oldest—and maybe even the first—version of the Cinderella story.

"Interview" is a short poem that suggests the story of Cinderella would be very different if it were told by her **stepmother.**

Aschenputtel

German, retold by **Jakob** *and* **Wilhelm Grimm,** *translated by* **Lucy Crane**

Read with a Purpose
Read "Aschenputtel" to see what lesson this traditional folk tale teaches.

Build Background
There are more than nine hundred different versions of the Cinderella story. Almost all of them feature a young woman who is mistreated by a stepmother and stepsisters. The young woman receives help from magical characters and meets a prince who falls in love with her. A lost object, like a magical shoe, brings the girl and her prince together.

There was once a rich man whose wife lay sick, and when she felt her end drawing near, she called to her only daughter to come near her bed and said,

"Dear child, be pious and good, and God will always take care of you, and I will look down upon you from heaven and will be with you."

And then she closed her eyes and expired.[1] The maiden went every day to her mother's grave and wept and was always pious and good. When the winter came, the snow covered the grave with a white covering, and when the sun came in the early spring and melted it away, the man took to himself another wife.

The new wife brought two daughters home with her and they were beautiful and fair in appearance but at heart were wicked and ugly. And then began very evil times for the poor stepdaughter. **Ⓐ**

"Is the stupid creature to sit in the same room with us?" said they. "Those who eat food must earn it. Out with the kitchen maid!"

They took away her pretty dresses and put on her an old gray kirtle[2] and gave her wooden shoes to wear.

"Just look now at the proud princess, how she is decked out!" cried they, laughing, and then they sent her into the kitchen. There she was obliged to do heavy work from morning to night, get up early in the morning, draw water, make the fires, cook, and wash. Besides that, the sisters did their

---

1. **expired** (ehk SPYRD): died. In Latin, *exspirare* means "to breathe out"; to breathe out one's last breath is to die.

2. **kirtle** (KUR tuhl): old-fashioned word for "dress."

Ⓐ **Reading Focus** **Compare and Contrast** What details common to most Cinderella stories have you noticed so far?

utmost to torment her—mocking her and strewing peas and lentils among the ashes and setting her to pick them up. In the evenings, when she was quite tired out with her hard day's work, she had no bed to lie on but was obliged to rest on the hearth among the cinders. And as she always looked dusty and dirty, they named her Aschenputtel. **B**

It happened one day that the father went to the fair, and he asked his two stepdaughters what he should bring back for them.

"Fine clothes!" said one.

"Pearls and jewels!" said the other.

"But what will you have, Aschenputtel?" said he.

"The first twig, Father, that strikes against your hat on the way home; this is what I should like you to bring me."

So he bought for the two stepdaughters fine clothes, pearls, and jewels, and on his way back, as he rode through a green lane, a hazel twig struck against his hat; and he broke it off and carried it home with him. And when he reached home, he gave to the stepdaughters what they had wished for, and to Aschenputtel he gave the hazel twig. She thanked him and went to her mother's grave, and planted this twig there, weeping so bitterly that the tears fell upon it and watered it, and it flourished and became a

---

B Read and Discuss What has the author told you so far?

Analyzing Visuals Viewing and Interpreting What does the girl in the painting have in common with Aschenputtel?

A Little Shepherdess (1891) by William-Adolphe Bouguereau (1895–1905). Oil on canvas.

fine tree. Aschenputtel went to see it three times a day and wept and prayed, and each time a white bird rose up from the tree, and, if she uttered any wish, the bird brought her whatever she had wished for. **Ⓒ**

Now it came to pass that the king ordained[3] a festival that should last for three days and to which all the beautiful young women of that country were bidden so that the king's son might choose a bride from among them. When the two stepdaughters heard that they too were bidden to appear, they felt very pleased, and they called Aschenputtel and said,

"Comb our hair, brush our shoes, and make our buckles fast, we are going to the wedding feast at the king's castle."

Aschenputtel, when she heard this, could not help crying, for she too would have liked to go to the dance, and she begged her stepmother to allow her.

"What, you Aschenputtel!" said she. "In all your dust and dirt, you want to go to the festival! You that have no dress and no shoes! You want to dance!"

But since she persisted in asking, at last the stepmother said,

> "Comb our hair, brush our shoes, and make our buckles fast, we are going to the wedding feast at the king's castle."

"I have scattered a dish full of lentils in the ashes, and if you can pick them all up again in two hours, you may go with us."

Then the maiden went to the back door that led into the garden and called out,

O gentle doves, O turtledoves,
And all the birds that be,
The lentils that in ashes lie
Come and pick up for me!
  The good must be put in the dish,
  The bad you may eat if you wish.

Then there came to the kitchen window two white doves, and after them some turtledoves, and at last a crowd of all the birds under heaven, chirping and fluttering, and they alighted among the ashes; and the doves nodded with their heads and began to pick, peck, pick, peck, and then all the others began to pick, peck, pick, peck and put all the good grains into the dish. Before an hour was over, all was done, and they flew away. Then the maiden brought the dish to her stepmother, feeling joyful and thinking that now she should go to the feast; but the stepmother said,

"No, Aschenputtel, you have no proper clothes, and you do not know how to dance, and you would be laughed at!"

And when Aschenputtel cried for disappointment, she added,

---

3. **ordained** (awr DAYND): ordered or decreed.

Ⓒ **Read and Discuss** What does this conversation between the girls and the father let you know about the girls?

Vocabulary **persisted** (puhr SIHS tihd) *v.*: refused to give up.

"If you can pick two dishfuls of lentils out of the ashes, nice and clean, you shall go with us," thinking to herself, "for that is not possible." When she had strewed two dishfuls of lentils among the ashes, the maiden went through the back door into the garden and cried,

O gentle doves, O turtledoves,
And all the birds that be,
The lentils that in ashes lie
Come and pick up for me!
    The good must be put in the dish,
    The bad you may eat if you wish.

So there came to the kitchen window two white doves, and then some turtledoves, and at last a crowd of all the other birds under heaven, chirping and fluttering, and they alighted among the ashes, and the doves nodded with their heads and began to pick, peck, pick, peck, and then all the others began to pick, peck, pick, peck and put all the good grains into the dish. And before half an hour was over, it was all done, and they flew away. Then the maiden took the dishes to the stepmother, feeling joyful and thinking that now she should go with them to the feast. But her stepmother said, "All this is of no good to you; you cannot come with us, for you have no proper clothes and cannot dance; you would put us to shame." **D**

Then she turned her back on poor Aschenputtel and made haste to set out with her two proud daughters.

And as there was no one left in the house, Aschenputtel went to her mother's grave, under the hazel bush, and cried,

Little tree, little tree, shake over me,
That silver and gold may come down
    and cover me.

Then the bird threw down a dress of gold and silver and a pair of slippers embroidered with silk and silver. And in all haste she put on the dress and went to the festival. But her stepmother and sisters did not know her and thought she must be a foreign princess, she looked so beautiful in her golden dress. Of Aschenputtel they never thought at all and supposed that she was sitting at home, picking the lentils out of the ashes. The King's son came to meet her and took her by the hand and danced with her, and he refused to stand up with anyone else so that he might not be obliged to let go her hand; and when anyone came to claim it, he answered,

"She is my partner." **E**

And when the evening came, she wanted to go home, but the prince said he would go with her to take care of her, for he wanted to see where the beautiful maiden lived. But she escaped him and jumped up into the pigeon house. Then the prince waited until her father came along, and told him that the strange maiden had jumped into the pigeon house. The father thought to himself, "It cannot surely be Aschenputtel" and called for axes and hatchets and had the pigeon house cut down, but there was no one in it. And when they entered the house, there sat Aschenputtel in her dirty clothes among the cinders, and a little oil lamp burnt dimly in the chimney; for Aschenputtel had

---

D [Read and Discuss] What does this statement tell you about Aschenputtel and her stepmother?

E [Reading Focus] Compare and Contrast Explain how people treat Aschenputtel differently depending on what she's wearing.

Viewing and Interpreting What details in the painting tell you that Aschenputtel's stepsisters treat her harshly?

Cinderella and Her Wicked Sisters (19th century) by Emile Meyer.

been very quick and had jumped out of the pigeon house again and had run to the hazel bush; and there she had taken off her beautiful dress and had laid it on the grave, and the bird had carried it away again, and then she had put on her little gray kirtle again and had sat down in the kitchen among the cinders. **F**

F Read and Discuss What has happened to Aschenputtel?

Ring Doves (1998) by Rosemary Lowndes (1937–2001).

The next day, when the festival began anew, and the parents and stepsisters had gone to it, Aschenputtel went to the hazel bush and cried,

> *Little tree, little tree, shake over me,*
> *That silver and gold may come down*
> *   and cover me.*

Then the bird cast down a still more splendid dress than on the day before. And when she appeared in it among the guests, everyone was astonished at her beauty. The prince had been waiting until she came, and he took her hand and danced with her alone. And when anyone else came to invite her, he said,

"She is my partner." **G**

And when the evening came, she wanted to go home, and the prince followed her, for he wanted to see to what house she belonged; but she broke away from him and ran into the garden at the back of the house. There stood a fine large tree, bearing splendid pears; she leapt as lightly as a squirrel among the branches, and the prince did not know what had become of her. So he waited until her father came along, and then he told him that the strange maiden had rushed from him, and that he thought she had gone up into the pear tree. The father thought to himself,

"It cannot surely be Aschenputtel" and called for an axe and felled the tree, but there was no one in it. And when they went into the kitchen, there sat Aschenputtel among the cinders, as usual, for she had got down the other side of the tree and had

G **Literary Focus** **Folk Tales** Princes often appear in tales like "Aschenputtel." In what ways is the character of the prince a motif, or common pattern?

taken back her beautiful clothes to the bird on the hazel bush and had put on her old gray kirtle again.

On the third day, when the parents and the stepchildren had set off, Aschenputtel went again to her mother's grave and said to the tree,

Little tree, little tree, shake over me,
That silver and gold may come down
     and cover me.

Then the bird cast down a dress the likes of which had never been seen for splendor and brilliancy, and slippers that were of gold.

And when she appeared in this dress at the feast, nobody knew what to say for wonderment. The prince danced with her alone, and if anyone else asked her, he answered,

"She is my partner." **H**

And when it was evening, Aschenputtel wanted to go home, and the prince was about to go with her when she ran past him so quickly that he could not follow her. But he had laid a plan and had caused all the steps to be spread with pitch,[4] so that as she rushed down them, her left shoe remained sticking in it. The prince picked it up and saw that it was of gold and very small and slender. The next morning he went to the father and told him that none should be his bride save the one whose foot the golden shoe should fit. **I**

---

4. **pitch** (pihch): here, black, sticky tar.

The two sisters were very glad, because they had pretty feet. The eldest went to her room to try on the shoe, and her mother stood by. But she could not get her great toe into it, for the shoe was too small; then her mother handed her a knife, and said,

"Cut the toe off, for when you are queen, you will never have to go on foot." So the girl cut her toe off, squeezed her foot into the shoe, concealed the pain, and went down to the prince. Then he took her with him on his horse as his bride and rode off. They had to pass by the grave, and there sat the two pigeons on the hazel bush and cried,

There they go, there they go!
There is blood on her shoe;
The shoe is too small,
     —Not the right bride at all!

Then the prince looked at her shoe and saw the blood flowing. And he turned his horse round and took the false bride home again, saying she was not the right one and that the other sister must try on the shoe. So she went into her room to do so and got her toes comfortably in, but her heel was too large. Then her mother handed her the knife, saying, "Cut a piece off your heel; when you are queen, you will never have to go on foot."

So the girl cut a piece off her heel and thrust her foot into the shoe, concealed the pain, and went down to the prince, who took his bride before him on his horse and

H [Literary Focus] Folk Tales The number three is a common motif in European folk tales. What events have happened three times in this story?

I [Read and Discuss] What can you say about the third day of the festival?

Vocabulary splendor (SPLEHN duhr) *n.*: magnificence.

rode off. When they passed by the hazel bush, the two pigeons sat there and cried,

> There they go, there they go!
> There is blood on her shoe;
> The shoe is too small,
> —Not the right bride at all!

Then the prince looked at her foot and saw how the blood was flowing from the shoe and staining the white stocking. And he turned his horse round and brought the false bride home again.

"This is not the right one," said he. "Have you no other daughter?"

"No," said the man, "only my dead wife left behind her a little stunted[5] Aschenputtel; it is impossible that she can be the bride." But the King's son ordered her to be sent for, but the mother said,

"Oh, no! She is much too dirty; I could not let her be seen."

But he would have her fetched, and so Aschenputtel had to appear.

First she washed her face and hands quite clean and went in and curtseyed to the prince, who held out to her the golden shoe. Then she sat down on a stool, drew her foot out of the heavy wooden shoe, and slipped it into the golden one, which fitted it perfectly. And when she stood up and the prince looked in her face, he

> "This is not the right one," said he. "Have you no other daughter?"

knew again the beautiful maiden that had danced with him, and he cried,

"This is the right bride!"

The stepmother and the two sisters were thunderstruck and grew pale with anger, but the prince put Aschenputtel before him on his horse and rode off. And as they passed the hazel bush, the two white pigeons cried,

> There they go, there they go!
> No blood on her shoe;
> The shoe's not too small,
> The right bride is she after all.

And when they had thus cried, they came flying after and perched on Aschenputtel's shoulders, one on the right, the other on the left, and so remained.

And when her wedding with the prince was appointed to be held, the false sisters came, hoping to curry favor[6] and to take part in the festivities. So as the bridal procession went to the church, the eldest walked on the right side and the younger on the left, and the pigeons picked out an eye of each of them. And as they returned, the elder was on the left side and the younger on the right, and the pigeons picked out the other eye of each of them. And so they were condemned for the rest of their days because of their wickedness and falsehood. **ⓙ**

---

5. **stunted** (STUHN tihd): not properly grown.

6. **curry favor:** try to win approval by flattering and fawning.

ⓙ Read and Discuss How does this information about the stepsisters fit with what you learned earlier?

Applying Your Skills

SKILLS FOCUS **Literary Skills** Analyze folk tales; analyze motifs. **Reading Skills** Compare and contrast texts. **Vocabulary Skills** Demonstrate knowledge of literal meanings of words and their usage. **Writing Skills** Identify and analyze tone.

Aschenputtel

Respond and Think Critically

Reading Focus

Quick Check

1. What does the stepmother do to stop Aschenputtel from attending the feast?

Read with a Purpose

2. Which of the following statements do you think best sums up the lesson "Aschenputtel" teaches?

   • Goodness is rewarded in the end.

   • Bad people will be punished for evil deeds.

   • Love conquers all.

   Is this a good lesson for today's world? Explain.

Reading Skills: Comparing and Contrasting Across Texts

3. Look at the chart you filled out as you read (page 75). Place a check mark next to elements of "Aschenputtel" that you know from other versions of the story. Place a plus sign next to elements that are new to you.

Comparing Cinderella Stories

	"Aschenputtel"	"Yeh-Shen"	"Inter-view"
Characters	Aschenputtel, two step-daughters, stepmother, prince, doves		
Plot			
Tone			
Theme			

✓ Vocabulary Check

Answer the following questions.

4. How would you react to the **splendor** of an entertaining musical?

5. When might you admire someone who **persisted**?

Literary Focus

Literary Analysis

6. **Interpret** Why did the father call his own daughter Aschenputtel?

7. **Interpret** How do you feel about the way the story ends? If it were written for kids today, would the ending be acceptable? Explain.

8. **Analyze** Do most people, especially in child-hood, feel they have something in common with Cinderella-type characters? What feel-ings might they share with her?

Literary Skills: Folk Tales

9. **Evaluate** How does the motif of the number three build suspense in this folk tale?

Writing Focus

Think as a Reader/Writer

Use It in Your Writing In what ways does the tone of "Aschenputtel" change depending on how the writer portrays different characters? Write a paragraph in which you give examples—words, phrases, and sentences—of how the writer reveals a character. How does the tone contribute to the moral of the tale?

Yeh-Shen

Chinese, *retold* by **Ai-Ling Louie**

Read with a Purpose

Read this ancient Chinese folk tale to see its similarities to "Aschenputtel" and other versions of the Cinderella story familiar to you.

Preparing to Read for this selection is on page 75.

Build Background

The reteller of this tale, Ai-Ling Louie, remembers hearing "Yeh-Shen" being told to her by her grandmother. Curious about the origins of the story, which had been told in her family for three generations, she decided to do some research. She learned that the tale had first been written down by Tuan Cheng-shi in an ancient Chinese manuscript during the Tang dynasty (A.D. 618–907)—more than one thousand years ago. The story had probably been handed down orally for centuries even before that.

In the dim past, even before the Ch'in and the Han dynasties, there lived a cave chief of southern China by the name of Wu. As was the custom in those days, Chief Wu had taken two wives. Each wife in her turn had presented Wu with a baby daughter. But one of the wives sickened and died, and not too many days after that Chief Wu took to his bed and died too.

Yeh-Shen, the little orphan, grew to girlhood in her stepmother's home. She was a bright child and lovely too, with skin as smooth as ivory and dark pools for eyes. Her stepmother was jealous of all this beauty and goodness, for her own daughter was not pretty at all. So in her displeasure, she gave poor Yeh-Shen the heaviest and most unpleasant chores. **A**

The only friend that Yeh-Shen had to her name was a fish she had caught and raised. It was a beautiful fish with golden eyes, and every day it would come out of the water and rest its head on the bank of the pond, waiting for Yeh-Shen to feed it. Stepmother gave Yeh-Shen little enough food for herself, but the orphan child always found something to share with her fish, which grew to enormous size.

Somehow the stepmother heard of this. She was terribly angry to discover that Yeh-Shen had kept a secret from her. She hurried down to the pond, but she was

A | Read and Discuss | What has the author told you about Yeh-Shen?

unable to see the fish, for Yeh-Shen's pet wisely hid itself. The stepmother, however, was a crafty woman, and she soon thought of a plan. She walked home and called out, "Yeh-Shen, go and collect some firewood. But wait! The neighbors might see you. Leave your filthy coat here!" The minute the girl was out of sight, her stepmother slipped on the coat herself and went down again to the pond. This time the big fish saw Yeh-Shen's familiar jacket and heaved itself onto the bank, expecting to be fed. But the stepmother, having hidden a dagger in her sleeve, stabbed the fish, wrapped it in her garments, and took it home to cook for dinner. **Ⓑ**

When Yeh-Shen came to the pond that evening, she found her pet had disappeared. Overcome with grief, the girl collapsed on the ground and dropped her tears into the still waters of the pond.

"Ah, poor child!" a voice said.

Yeh-Shen sat up to find a very old man looking down at her. He wore the coarsest of clothes, and his hair flowed down over his shoulders.

"Kind uncle, who may you be?" Yeh-Shen asked.

> The only friend Yeh-Shen had to her name was a fish she caught and raised.

"That is not important, my child. All you must know is that I have been sent to tell you of the wondrous powers of your fish."

"My fish, but sir . . ." The girl's eyes filled with tears, and she could not go on.

The old man sighed and said, "Yes, my child, your fish is no longer alive, and I must tell you that your stepmother is once more the cause of your sorrow." Yeh-Shen gasped in horror, but the old man went on. "Let us not dwell on things that are past," he said, "for I have come bringing you a gift. Now you must listen carefully to this: The bones of your fish are filled with a powerful spirit. Whenever you are in serious need, you must kneel before them and let them know your heart's desire. But do not waste their gifts."

Yeh-Shen wanted to ask the old sage many more questions, but he rose to the sky before she could utter another word. With heavy heart, Yeh-Shen made her way to the dung heap to gather the remains of her friend. **Ⓒ**

Time went by, and Yeh-Shen, who was often left alone, took comfort in speaking to the bones of her fish. When she was hungry, which happened quite often,

---

Ⓑ Read and Discuss What did you learn about the stepmother?

Ⓒ Read and Discuss What do you find out about the fish?

Yeh-Shen asked the bones for food. In this way, Yeh-Shen managed to live from day to day, but she lived in dread that her stepmother would discover her secret and take even that away from her. **D**

So the time passed and spring came. Festival time was approaching: It was the busiest time of the year. Such cooking and cleaning and sewing there was to be done! Yeh-Shen had hardly a moment's rest. At the spring festival young men and young women from the village hoped to meet and to choose whom they would marry. How Yeh-Shen longed to go! But her step-mother had other plans. She hoped to find a husband for her own daughter and did not want any man to see the beauteous Yeh-Shen first. When finally the holiday arrived, the stepmother and her daughter dressed themselves in their finery and filled their baskets with sweetmeats. "You must remain at home now and watch to see that no one steals fruit from our trees," her stepmother told Yeh-Shen, and then she departed for the banquet with her own daughter.

As soon as she was alone, Yeh-Shen went to speak to the bones of her fish. "Oh, dear friend," she said, kneeling before the precious bones, "I long to go to the festival, but I cannot show myself in these rags. Is there somewhere I could borrow clothes fit to wear to the feast?" At once she found herself dressed in a gown of azure[1] blue,

with a cloak of kingfisher feathers draped around her shoulders. Best of all, on her tiny feet were the most beautiful slippers she had ever seen. They were woven of golden threads, in a pattern like the scales of a fish, and the glistening soles were made of solid gold. There was magic in the shoes, for they should have been quite heavy, yet when Yeh-Shen walked, her feet felt as light as air.

"Be sure you do not lose your golden shoes," said the spirit of the bones. Yeh-Shen promised to be careful. Delighted with her transformation, she bid a fond farewell to the bones of her fish as she slipped off to join in the merrymaking. **E**

That day Yeh-Shen turned many a head as she appeared at the feast. All around her people whispered, "Look at that beautiful girl! Who can she be?"

But above this, Stepsister was heard to say, "Mother, does she not resemble our Yeh-Shen?"

Upon hearing this, Yeh-Shen jumped up and ran off before her stepsister could look closely at her. She raced down the mountainside, and in doing so, she lost one of her golden slippers. No sooner had the shoe fallen from her foot than all her fine clothes turned back to rags. Only one thing remained—a tiny golden shoe. Yeh-Shen hurried to the bones of her fish and returned the slipper, promising to find its mate. But now the bones were silent. Sadly Yeh-Shen realized that she had lost her only

---

1. **azure** (AZH uhr): like the color of the sky.

D **Literary Focus** Folk Tales What motif, or common pattern, from the typical Cinderella story do the fish bones represent?

E **Read and Discuss** What has happened to Yeh-Shen?

Vocabulary **glistening** (GLIHS uhn ihng) v. used as *adj.*: sparkling; reflecting light.

friend. She hid the little shoe in her bed-straw and went outside to cry. Leaning against a fruit tree, she sobbed and sobbed until she fell asleep. **F**

The stepmother left the gathering to check on Yeh-Shen, but when she returned home, she found the girl sound asleep, with her arms wrapped around a fruit tree. So, thinking no more of her, the stepmother rejoined the party. Meantime, a villager had found the shoe. Recognizing its worth, he sold it to a merchant, who presented it in turn to the king of the island kingdom of T'o Han.

The king was more than happy to accept the slipper as a gift. He was entranced by the tiny thing, which was shaped of the most precious of metals, yet which made no sound when touched to stone. The more he marveled at its beauty, the more determined he became to find the woman to whom the shoe belonged. A search was begun among the ladies of his own kingdom, but all who tried on the sandal found it impossibly small. Undaunted, the king ordered the search widened to include the cave women from the countryside where the slipper had been found. Since he realized it would take many years for every woman to come to his island and test her foot in the slipper, the king thought of a way to get the right woman to come forward. He ordered the sandal placed in a pavilion[2] by the side of the road near where it had

---

2. **pavilion** (puh VIHL yuhn): large tent or shelter, often highly decorated.

F **Read and Discuss** What is going on now? What has changed?

Carp Swimming Upwards (19th century) by Katsushika Taito (c. 1804–1848). Woodblock print.

Analyzing Visuals **Viewing and Interpreting**
What surprises you about the role of the fish in this tale?

Vocabulary **entranced** (ehn TRANST) *v.* used as *adj.:* cast a spell on; enchanted.

been found, and his herald[3] announced that the shoe was to be returned to its original owner. Then, from a nearby hiding place, the king and his men settled down to watch and wait for a woman with tiny feet to come and claim her slipper. **G**

All that day the pavilion was crowded with cave women who had come to test a foot in the shoe. Yeh-Shen's stepmother and stepsister were among them, but not Yeh-Shen—they had told her to stay home. By day's end, although many women had eagerly tried to put on the slipper, it still had not been worn. Wearily, the king continued his vigil into the night. **H**

It wasn't until the blackest part of night, while the moon hid behind a cloud, that Yeh-Shen dared to show her face at the pavilion, and even then she tiptoed timidly across the wide floor. Sinking down to her knees, the girl in rags examined the tiny shoe. Only when she was sure that this was the missing mate to her own golden slipper did she dare pick it up. At last she could return both little shoes to the fish bones. Surely then her beloved spirit would speak to her again.

Now the king's first thought, on seeing Yeh-Shen take the precious slipper, was to throw the girl into prison as a thief. But when she turned to leave, he caught a glimpse of her face. At once the king was struck by the sweet harmony of her features, which seemed so out of keeping with the rags she wore. It was then that he took a closer look and noticed that she walked upon the tiniest feet he had ever seen.

With a wave of his hand, the king signaled that this tattered creature was to be allowed to depart with the golden slipper. Quietly, the king's men slipped off and followed her home.

All this time, Yeh-Shen was unaware of the excitement she had caused. She had made her way home and was about to hide both sandals in her bedding when there was a pounding at the door. Yeh-Shen went to see who it was—and found a king at her doorstep. She was very frightened at first, but the king spoke to her in a kind voice and asked her to try the golden slippers on her feet. The maiden did as she was told, and as she stood in her golden shoes, her rags were transformed once more into the feathered cloak and beautiful azure gown.

Her loveliness made her seem a heavenly being, and the king suddenly knew in his heart that he had found his true love.

Not long after this, Yeh-Shen was married to the king. But fate was not so gentle with her stepmother and stepsister. Since they had been unkind to his beloved, the king would not permit Yeh-Shen to bring them to his palace. They remained in their cave home, where one day, it is said, they were crushed to death in a shower of flying stones. **I**

---

3. **herald** (HEHR uhld): person in a king's court who makes official announcements.

G | Reading Focus | Compare and Contrast How is the king's strategy for finding the owner of the slipper similar to and different from that of the princes in the Cinderella stories you know?

H | Read and Discuss | Why is the search for the shoe significant?

I | Read and Discuss | How are things looking for Yeh-Shen now?

Vocabulary vigil (VIHJ uhl) *n.*: overnight watch.

Applying Your Skills

SKILLS FOCUS Literary Skills Analyze folk tales; analyze motifs. **Reading Skills** Compare and contrast texts. **Vocabulary Skills** Demonstrate knowledge of literal meanings of words and their usage. **Writing Skills** Identify and analyze tone.

Yeh-Shen

Respond and Think Critically

Reading Focus

Quick Check

1. Who is Yeh-Shen's only friend? What does the stepmother do to the friend?
2. What advice about fish bones does the old man give Yeh-Shen?
3. What happens when Yeh-Shen runs away from the festival?

Read with a Purpose

4. What is the message of "Yeh-Shen"? Does "Yeh-Shen" share the same message as "Aschenputtel," or is the message different?

Reading Skills: Comparing and Contrasting Across Texts

5. Look at the chart you've been filling out as you read. In what area does "Yeh-Shen" differ most from "Aschenputtel": characters, plot, tone, or theme? What are the most significant similarities between the two stories?

Comparing Cinderella Stories

	"Aschenputtel"	"Yeh-Shen"	"Inter-view"
Characters	Aschenputtel, two step-daughters, stepmother, prince, doves		
Plot			
Tone			
Theme			

Vocabulary Check

Fill in the blank with the correct Vocabulary word.

> **glistening entranced vigil**

6. The _____ snow reflected the moonlight.
7. She kept a _____ until the morning.
8. The children were _____ by the new toys.

Literary Focus

Literary Analysis

9. **Interpret** How did the lives of Yeh-Shen, her stepmother, and her stepsister change throughout the story?

Literary Skills: Folk Tales

10. **Analyze** Cinderella tales from around the world share common features, or **motifs,** but they also have strong cultural characteristics. From the evidence in this story, what qualities might you infer the ancient Chinese valued in women?

Writing Focus

Think as a Reader/Writer

Use It in Your Writing Look back at the words, phrases, and sentences that best reveal the tone of this story. Does the tone change depending on which characters or events are described? State your thoughts in a paragraph.

Interview

by **Sara Henderson Hay**

Drew Barrymore and Angelica Huston from the movie *Ever After* (1998).

Read with a Purpose
Read this poem to discover its modern approach to the Cinderella tale.

Preparing to Read for this selection is on page 75.

Build Background
This poem uses a modern-day event—an interview with the press—to present an unexpected point of view on the story of Cinderella. Hay is not the only writer to turn the Cinderella story on its head; creative people have found endless ways to reinvent the story—from books and films like *Ella Enchanted, Ever After,* and *A Cinderella Story* to the latest "fractured fairy-tale" version of the story at your community theater.

Yes, this is where she lived before she won
The title Miss Glass Slipper of the Year,
And went to the ball and married the king's son.
You're from the local press, and want to hear
5 About her early life? Young man, sit down.
These are my *own* two daughters; you'll not find
Nicer, more biddable° girls in all the town,
And lucky, I tell them, not to be the kind
That Cinderella was, spreading those lies,   **Ⓐ**
10 Telling those shameless tales about the way
We treated her. Oh, nobody denies
That she was pretty, if you like those curls.
But looks aren't everything, I always say.
Be sweet and natural, I tell my girls,
15 And Mr. Right will come along, someday.   **Ⓑ**

———

7. **biddable** (BIHD uh buhl): obedient.

———

Ⓐ Read and Discuss What does the speaker in the poem mean when she says Cinderella spread lies about the way they treated her? What is she talking about?

Ⓑ Read and Discuss The stepmother says, "Oh, nobody denies / That she was pretty, if you like those curls." What does this statement tell you about the stepmother?

Applying Your Skills

Interview

Respond and Think Critically

Reading Focus

Read with a Purpose

1. What is a key difference between this retelling of the folk tale and the traditional versions?

Reading Skills: Comparing and Contrasting Across Texts

2. Review the "Interview" column in the "Comparing Cinderella Stories" graphic organizer. In what ways does the poem differ from "Aschenputtel" and "Yeh-Shen"?

Comparing Cinderella Stories

	"Aschenputtel"	"Yeh-Shen"	"Interview"
Characters	Aschenputtel, two step-daughters, stepmother, prince, doves		
Plot			
Tone			
Theme			

Literary Focus

Literary Analysis

3. **Interpret** Who is the speaker in this poem—the one doing the talking? At what point do you recognize the speaker?

4. **Interpret** What does this interview add to what you know about the story of Cinderella?

5. **Interpret** Do you think the speaker really believes what she is saying about Cinderella and her own girls? Why or why not?

6. **Analyze** If you had never heard the original story of Cinderella and all you had read was this interview, what would you think of the stepmother?

7. **Analyze Tone** refers to the speaker's attitude toward a subject. A tone can be, for example, admiring, comic, bitter, loving, critical, serious, or disrespectful. What tone do you hear in this poem? What does the tone tell you about the speaker's personality and values?

Literary Skills: Folk Tales

8. **Analyze** This poem is a comment on the Cinderella story; it is not a Cinderella story itself. What aspects of the Cinderella story does it summarize? What does it leave out?

Writing Focus

Think as a Reader/Writer

Use It in Your Writing Notice how one or two changes can create a very different tone—and a new meaning. See what a student did with these lines from the poem:

> Oh, you would never deny
> That she was pretty, not with all those curls.
> Though of course there was more to her than
>   looks, as I always said.

How does the new tone change your view of the stepmother's character? How do word changes lead to changes in tone? Rewrite a few lines of the poem so that it has a different tone.

Wrap Up

Aschenputtel / Yeh-Shen / Interview

Writing Focus

Write a Comparison-Contrast Essay

Write a comparison-contrast essay on "Aschenputtel," "Yeh-Shen," and "Interview." To help you write a comparison-contrast essay on the three selections, refer to the charts you filled in after you read each version of the Cinderella tale. You can organize your essay in two ways.

1. You can use the **block method** and write one paragraph for each selection. In this case you would describe the characters, the plot, the tone, and the theme, selection by selection.

2. You can use the **point-by-point method** and write one paragraph on the characters in each selection, one on the plot of each selection, one on the tone of each selection, and one on the theme of each selection.

Whichever method of organization you use, be sure to include a final paragraph in which you describe your responses to the selections.

Use the workshop on writing a Comparison-Contrast Essay, pages 106–113, for help with this assignment.

What Do You Think Now Why would a person be foolish enough to wait to be rescued in real life?

CHOICES

As you respond to the Choices, use these **Academic Vocabulary** words as appropriate: <u>interpret</u>, <u>impact</u>, <u>insight</u>, <u>significant</u>.

REVIEW
Write an Article

Timed ⌐Writing Imagine you have been asked to write an article that will introduce the new princess, Aschenputtel, to the kingdom. Review the story to find the answers to the *5W-How?* questions: *who? what? when? where? why?* and *how?* Improve your article with <u>significant</u> details from the folk tale.

CONNECT
Write a Letter to the Editor

An organization has written a newspaper editorial urging that local libraries stop circulating copies of folk and fairy tales. Folk tales, they say, give children unrealistic ideas about life, simplify ideas of right and wrong, and contain gruesome violence. Write a letter to the editor in response to these complaints.

EXTEND
Analyze Another Cinderella

Oral Report Find a different version of Cinderella in a library or on the Internet. You may enjoy searching for a version from your own culture. In an oral report, summarize the version for your class, share some cultural background information, and point out the ways the tale is like or unlike the traditional Cinderella tale.

Note Taking, Outlining, and Summarizing

CONTENTS

The bust of Theodora and courtesan (detail) from the Court of Theodora (c. 6th century).

 What Do You Think?

Do great leaders achieve greatness on their own? Who "stands in the gap" for them?

 QuickWrite

Think of a famous woman whom you regard as a role model. Why do you think she is a role model? How has she been an example for others to follow?

MAGAZINE ARTICLE
Preparing to Read

Empress Theodora

 Reader/Writer
Notebook

Use your **RWN** to complete the activities for this selection.

Informational Text Focus

Note Taking Recording notes will help you improve your comprehension and recollection of what you have read. As you read an informational article, many ideas come to you. You connect what you read with your own experience and knowledge. You ask yourself questions. You challenge the text and reflect on its meaning.

Tips for Taking Notes

- **Find the main ideas.** The main ideas are the most important ideas in an informational text. You'll find clues for identifying them by reading the subheads in the article as well as the first and last sentences of each paragraph.
- **Be organized.** Use a simple outline form to record the most important information and ideas. (See the box below for a sample outline form.)
- **Be brief.** Keep your notes short, simple, and clear. Write only the words and phrases that are most important.
- **Underline or circle information.** It may be useful to highlight certain information directly in the text, but don't do it in a book that doesn't belong to you, and don't get carried away with it. If everything is highlighted, it will be hard to tell what's most important.

Outlining **Outlining** helps you uncover the skeleton that holds the text together. An outline highlights the main ideas and supporting details contained in a text. Look at the example of an informal outline on the right.

> I. Main Idea
>   A. Supporting detail
>   B. Supporting detail
>   C. [etc.]
>
> II. Main Idea
>   A. Supporting detail
>   B. Supporting detail
>   C. [etc.]

Vocabulary

profession (pruh FEHSH uhn) *n.*: paid occupation. *Acting was not considered a respectable profession by the people of the Byzantine Empire.*

forbade (fuhr BAYD) *v.*: ordered not to; outlawed. *The emperor threw out the law that forbade Theodora from marrying Justinian.*

facilitate (fuh SIHL uh tayt) *v.*: ease; aid. *The Justinian Code helped facilitate lawmaking in future societies.*

Language Coach

Word Roots The word *profession* comes from a Latin root that means "to declare publicly." How are the words *professor* and *professorial* related to *profession*?

Writing Focus   Preparing for **Constructed Response**

As you read, record clues that show you the type of relationship Theodora and Justinian had. The clues will help you answer a constructed response question later.

 Learn It Online
Do pictures and animation help you learn? Try the *PowerNotes* lesson on:

go.hrw.com   L7-97   **Go**

Read with a Purpose
Read this article to learn about Empress Theodora's unique qualities.

EMPRESS
Theodora

by  THE WORLD ALMANAC

The Court of Theodora (c. 6th century).

Analyzing Visuals **Viewing and Interpreting** What details in the painting tell you that Theodora (the third from the left) was an important figure in the Byzantine Empire?

At a time when women had little or no political power, Theodora, empress of the Byzantine Empire, was a rare exception. Though from poor and humble beginnings, she helped maintain her husband's empire as Persian forces threatened from the east and Germanic invaders continued attacking from the west. Born in about A.D. 500, she was the daughter of a bear keeper who worked in Constantinople's Hippodrome, a stadium in which horse races and often violent, bloody performances were held. Her father died when she was young, so Theodora and her sister were forced to support themselves. They became actors, which at the time was considered a low-class profession, especially for women. Ⓐ

At age sixteen, Theodora traveled widely, performing throughout North Africa and the Middle East. Six years later she stopped acting, returned to Constantinople, and became a wool spinner. The beautiful and witty young woman met Justinian, the heir to the throne of his uncle, Justin I. Young Theodora fell in love with and wanted to marry Justinian, the future leader of the Byzantine Empire. However, a long-standing law forbade high-ranking men from marrying women of lower classes. Ⓑ

INFLUENCING LEGAL AND SOCIAL REFORM

From the beginning of her relationship with Justinian, Theodora promoted freedom and equality for women. She had Justinian ask his

> ### FAST FACTS ABOUT
> # THEODORA
> - born around A.D. 500
> - named empress in 527
> - delivered a famous speech that helped stop the Nika revolt
> - fought for the rights of women throughout her lifetime
> - died in 548

uncle to repeal the law that kept the couple from marrying. Justin I agreed, and at age twenty-five, Theodora married Justinian.

Soon after their marriage, Justinian became emperor. Although Theodora was not officially a joint ruler, Justinian treated her as his intellectual equal and sought her opinions and input on many of his important decisions.

RAISING THE STATUS OF WOMEN

Under Empress Theodora's influence, Justinian began to examine the empire's laws carefully and make changes to them. Many of these changes were aimed at protecting women and children. Justinian passed laws that raised the status of women higher than it had ever been in the empire. Divorced women were granted rights, such as the ability to remain guardians of their children. He allowed women to own property. The custom

---

Ⓐ **Informational Focus** Note Taking Now that you have read the first paragraph, what do you think this article will be about?

Ⓑ **Read and Discuss** What is the author setting up here?

Vocabulary **profession** (pruh FEHSH uhn) *n.:* paid occupation.
forbade (fuhr BAYD) *v.:* ordered not to; outlawed.

THEODORA'S SPEECH

If, now, it is your wish to save yourself, O Emperor, there is no difficulty. For we have much money, and there is the sea, here the boats. However consider whether it will not come about after you have been saved that you would gladly exchange that safety for death. For as for myself, I approve a certain ancient saying that royalty is a good burial-shroud.

Empress Theodora (11th century) Back view of aureus, Roman gold coin.

of the greatest short speeches ever recorded, the empress persuaded them not to flee to the shame of safety but to fight with courage to the death. His confidence bolstered, Justinian roused his generals and crushed the rebellion. Her speech probably saved the city, the empire—and Justinian's throne. **C**

of abandoning infants, most often girls, to die of exposure[1] was outlawed. Other laws established hospitals, orphanages, and care facilities for the needy. Justinian organized existing Roman laws, plus his new ones, into the Justinian Code, which has served as a model for the laws of many later nations.

SAVING THE EMPIRE

Theodora used her intelligence and skill as a leader to save and strengthen the Byzantine Empire. In A.D. 532, as a chariot race was about to begin at the Hippodrome, political rivals there opposed to the emperor joined in a violent protest, now known as the Nika revolt. This riot quickly engulfed the city, and the rebels burned huge areas of Constantinople. Convinced of defeat, Justinian and his advisors prepared to flee the city in ships. With one

REBUILDING THE CITY

After the revolt, Theodora and Justinian worked together to rebuild and improve the ruined city. They added new aqueducts to provide clean drinking water, bridges to facilitate transportation, and hostels[2] to shelter the homeless. They also built numerous churches, including the beautiful Hagia Sophia—one of the most famous buildings in the world—which still exists in Istanbul as a museum.

LEAVING A LEGACY

Theodora, the daughter of a lowly bear keeper, rose to have a significant impact on the Byzantine Empire as the wife of the emperor. Her intelligence and courage made the empire a safer and fairer place; laws that she initiated influence legal systems that still exist today.

Read with a Purpose

What personal characteristics made Theodora different from most other women of her time?

---

1. **exposure** (ehk SPOH zhuhr): physical condition resulting from being left open to danger without the protection of clothing or shelter, especially in severe weather.

2. **hostels** (HAHS tuhlz): shelters for those without a home; supervised residences.

C | Read and Discuss | How do Theodora's actions during the riot contribute to what you know about her?

Vocabulary **facilitate** (fuh SIHL uh tayt) *v.:* ease; aid.

Applying Your Skills

SKILLS FOCUS Informational Skills Take notes, and make outlines; summarize and organize information from one or more sources by taking notes, outlining ideas, or making charts.

Empress Theodora

Practicing the Standards

Informational Text

1. A report on this article would state that its *main* idea is —

A Theodora had to support herself

B Theodora became a unique and influential force in the Byzantine Empire

C the Justinian Code served as a model for the laws of future nations

D after the riots Justinian and Theodora rebuilt and improved Constantinople

2. Re-read the paragraph titled "Saving the Empire." Each of the following would be an important **note** *except* —

A Nika revolt is name of protest

B rebels destroyed much of city

C Theodora gave famous speech

D Justinian feared defeat

> I. Theodora's early life
> II. Theodora, wife of Justinian I
>   A. Overcame prejudice to marry
>   B.
>   C. Roused Justinian to save his city
> III. Theodora—famous today

3. Here is the beginning of an outline of "Empress Theodora." Which of the following items belongs in the blank space at number II.B.?

A Worked as a low-class actor

B Rebuilt the city after the revolt

C Attacked by forces from the east and west

D Protected women with new laws

4. Which of the following details would be the *least* important to include in notes taken on this article?

A As young women, Theodora and her sister supported themselves as actors.

B Theodora's father was a bear keeper in the Hippodrome.

C Theodora influenced Justinian to reexamine the laws of the empire.

D Theodora persuaded Justinian to stay in the city and fight the rioters.

5. Which of the following statements is an *opinion,* not a fact?

A Theodora wanted to marry Justinian, the heir to his uncle's throne.

B The custom of abandoning infants to die of exposure was outlawed.

C Justinian and Theodora built numerous churches, including the Hagia Sophia.

D Theodora's intelligence and courage made the empire a safer and fairer place.

Writing Focus   Constructed Response

Re-read Theodora's speech, on page 100. Then, make an inference about Theodora's and Justinian's relationship. Support your inference with two details from the speech.

What Do You Think Now

What do you think Theodora's role in the government says about the role of women in the Byzantine Empire?

MAGAZINE ARTICLE
Preparing to Read

The Hippodrome

Reader/Writer Notebook

Use your **RWN** to complete the activities for this selection.

Informational Text Focus

Summarizing an Informational Text A **summary** of an informational text is a short restatement of the **main ideas**—the central or most important ideas—in a work. Before you summarize, read the text carefully to determine what details to include and what to leave out. After you have written your summary, ask yourself, "Would a person who has not read the article understand what it is about?" If the answer is no, revise your summary. Here are some tips for writing a good summary:

- Cite the author, title, and main point of the text.
- State the main ideas in the order in which they appear.
- Include the most important supporting details.
- Place quotation marks around words from the text that you have quoted exactly.

Writing Focus Preparing for **Constructed Response**

The text below is a good summary of "Empress Theodora."

"Empress Theodora" focuses on a remarkable leader of the Byzantine Empire. Born into poverty, Theodora became the respected wife and advisor of Emperor Justinian. Although women had no legal power, she persuaded her husband to pass laws that "raised the status of women higher than it had ever been." When a violent revolt in Constantinople threatened to drive away Justinian and his generals, Theodora rallied him and his subjects with a courageous speech and saved the throne. Not only did she help rebuild Constantinople so well that some of its beauty still stands, she influenced legal systems that exist to this day.

← The summary begins with the title and main point.

← The writer uses quotation marks when quoting the text.

← Details like her inspirational speech are very important.

← This seems like an important idea.

Vocabulary

renovation (rehn uh VAY shuhn) *n.*: restoration of something to a better condition. *The emperor's renovation made the stadium better than it had been in years.*

spectators (SPEHK tay tuhrz) *n.*: people who watch at an event. *The spectators cheered from their seats for their favorite horses.*

barbarian (bahr BAIR ee uhn) *adj.*: referring to a group considered uncivilized and inferior by another nation or group. *The Romans thought that the barbarian tribes living in northern Europe were less advanced than the Romans were.*

Language Coach

Word Roots Many English words come directly or indirectly from the Latin language. A **word root** is a word or word part from which other words are made. The Vocabulary words above all have Latin word roots. Look up each word in a dictionary to see which Latin word or words it came from.

Learn It Online

To read more articles like this one, go to the interactive reading workshop at:

go.hrw.com | L7-102 | **Go**

the HIPPODROME

by  THE WORLD ALMANAC

Read with a Purpose
Read this article to learn about what made the Hippodrome important.

At the beginning of the third century A.D., Roman troops destroyed the eastern city of Byzantium, and the new Roman emperor set about rebuilding it larger than before. To provide residents with the type of entertainment popular in Rome, he built the Hippodrome, the largest stadium in the ancient world. A hundred years later the capital of the empire was moved from Rome to Byzantium by the Roman emperor Constantine. He renamed the new capital Constantinople, after himself. One of his major building projects was the renovation of the Hippodrome.

The Hippodrome was the center of Constantinople's social life. The Hippodrome's main function was as a horse- and chariot-racing track. (The term *hippodrome* comes from the Greek words *hippos* ["horse"] and *dromos* ["path" or "way"]). Besides a race track, it also was

(above) Relief from the obelisk of Emperor Theodosius erected in the Hippodrome (4th century A.D.). (upper left) Detail from the relief of the obelisk.

the place to see royal ceremonies, parades of victorious generals, political demonstrations, and executions. Acrobats, plays performed by actors, and fights between wild animals also entertained the crowds. **Ⓐ**

The stadium's arena is estimated to have been almost 525 yards long (about five football fields) and 129 yards wide. Some say it held as many as 100,000 spectators.

Ⓐ Informational Focus Summarizing Which sentence contains the main idea of this paragraph?

Vocabulary **renovation** (rehn uh VAY shuhn) *n.:* restoration of something to a better condition.
spectators (SPEHK tay tuhrz) *n.:* people who watch at an event.

Constantine decorated the center of the race track with monuments and statues that could be tilted or removed so they wouldn't block the fans' view of the races. He and later emperors adorned the Hippodrome with artworks and religious items from all over the empire and the "barbarian" East. **B**

The races at the Hippodrome were extremely important to the heavy-betting citizens of Constantinople: Loyalty to certain racing teams divided citizens into groups so strong that teams came to represent political differences as well. (Imagine Republicans rooting for one basketball team and Democrats for another.) In A.D. 532, supporters of two teams, the Blues and the Greens, came together to oppose Justinian I's policies. They began a protest in the Hippodrome that quickly turned into a violent riot. As flames engulfed much of the city, Emperor Justinian and his advisors were considering fleeing to safety. To stop them, Justinian's wife, Empress Theodora, delivered a powerful speech, declaring that she refused to give up her throne. This speech encouraged Justinian, and

he sent troops to the Hippodrome to put down the riot. Exits were blocked, and thirty to forty thousand protesters were killed in the stadium. Constantinople lay in ruins, but Justinian and Theodora remained in power. **C**

Over the centuries the Hippodrome declined in importance and beauty. Constantinople was sacked by Crusaders, and in 1453, Ottoman Turks captured the city, changed its name to Istanbul, and used the stones of the Hippodrome as building material. Today, the ruins of the stadium are a public park with few monuments and artworks remaining. **D**

Read with a Purpose What made the Hippodrome so important to the people of Byzantium?

B **Read and Discuss** | What is the author telling you about the Hippodrome?

C **Informational Focus** | **Summarizing** What main idea do these details support?

D **Read and Discuss** | How does the Hippodrome of the Byzantine Empire compare with the Hippodrome of today?

Vocabulary **barbarian** (bahr BAIR ee uhn) *adj.*: referring to a group considered uncivilized and inferior by another nation or group.

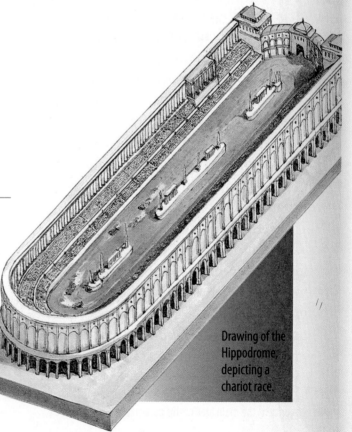

Drawing of the Hippodrome, depicting a chariot race.

Applying Your Skills

The Hippodrome

Practicing the Standards

Informational Text

1. Which of the following events would be the *least* important in a **summary** of this article?

  A The renovated Hippodrome became the center of Constantinople's social life.

  B Justinian ordered that thousands of protesters in the stadium be killed.

  C Citizens of Constantinople considered the "barbarians" of the East to be inferior.

  D Ottoman Turks used stones from the Hippodrome for building material.

2. Which of the following is the *best* **summary** of the third paragraph of the article?

  A Constantine decorated the impressively large stadium with movable artwork.

  B The Hippodrome's track was almost the length of five football fields.

  C It is recorded that the Hippodrome could hold as many as 100,000 fans.

  D Later emperors also put up artwork from around the empire and other lands.

3. Re-read the fourth paragraph, which begins "The races at the Hippodrome . . ." Each of the following details would be important to its summary *except* —

  A loyal fans of opposing teams supported opposing political parties

  B one team's color was blue and the other's was green

  C supporters of two teams met in the Hippodrome to protest Justinian I's policies

  D soldiers locked the exits to the stadium and killed the people inside

> Roman emperors built and rebuilt the Hippodrome, the largest stadium of its time.
>
> It was the site of a violent political riot against Justinian I; he was victorious.
>
> Little is left of the Hippodrome, due to invaders and lack of care.

4. If you were taking notes for a **summary** of this article, which of the following points would you cite in the blank above?

  A Besides being a race track, it was used for many social events.

  B The Hippodrome was large enough to hold 100,000 spectators.

  C Actors performed plays in the Hippodrome to make the city more impressive.

  D Emperors decorated the Hippodrome with artwork.

Writing Focus   Constructed Response

The main idea of "The Hippodrome" is that the Hippodrome was important to life in Constantinople. Write a summary of the article. Be sure to include three details from the article that support the main idea.

What Do **You Think Now** Do you think Emperor Justinian would have fled the city if not for Theodora's speech? Explain.

Writing Workshop

Comparison-Contrast Essay

Write with a Purpose

Choose two literary elements, subjects, or works that you know well. Then, write a comparison-contrast essay. The **purpose** of your essay is to show how the two subjects are alike and how they are different. Use specific details and examples to help your **audience** understand those similarities and differences.

A Good Comparison-Contrast Essay

- identifies the topic of the essay in its introduction
- discusses at least two similarities and two differences
- is organized by the block or point-by-point method
- includes specific details and examples to support your points
- closes with a summary or restatement of the main idea

See page 114 for complete rubric.

Reader/Writer Notebook

Use your **RWN** to complete the activities for this workshop.

Think as a Reader/Writer
Before you write your own comparison-contrast essay, read the excerpt below from "Borders of Baseball: U.S. and Cuban Play," a magazine article from Collection 3. Notice how the author uses similarities and differences to compare and contrast U.S. baseball and Cuban baseball.

> After the World Series in the United States ends every October, you won't see many Americans paying attention to baseball until the spring. It is when the U.S. teams end their season that Cuba's step up to bat and start theirs. Organized baseball first started in the U.S. and Cuba at roughly the same time—the end of the 1800s. The basics of play are similar between the two, but the differences are major.
>
> Baseball is called "America's pastime," but it competes for time and attention with the National Football League, the National Basketball Association, and other groups. Children in the United States can sign up for Little League Baseball, but they can also participate in organized hockey, ice skating, and more.
>
> The opportunities to play different sports are fewer in Cuba. When World Cup soccer was televised in Cuba in 2006, the Associated Press reported, kids there caught soccer fever. Because soccer balls are scarce on the island, children had to roll up paper to make balls to kick. Baseballs, on the other hand, are widely available. Cubans are raised on stickball. "Kids learn to throw baseballs and hit them with a stick," says Roberto González Echevarría, the author of *The Pride of Havana: A History of Cuban Baseball*. . . .

← The author introduces the **topic** in the first paragraph.

← This specific detail illustrates a **similarity.**

← The author uses the **block method** for comparing, sharing information about baseball in the U.S. in one paragraph and baseball in Cuba in the next.

← The author uses **examples,** including vivid images, to back up her points.

Think About the Professional Model
With a partner, discuss the following questions about the model.

1. What details does the author use to contrast baseball in the U.S. with baseball in Cuba?

2. Which details and examples might best help an audience of seventh graders understand the differences and similarities of the topic?

Prewriting

Choose a Topic

In selecting what you want to compare and contrast, make sure that you choose two subjects that have *both* similarities and differences. Ask yourself these questions:

- Which characters, elements, or themes in the stories that I've read recently would make a good topic for a comparison-contrast essay?
- How many similarities and differences can I think of for these two subjects?
- Which topic would my audience find the most interesting?

Think About Purpose and Audience

As you think about what you want to write, remember to keep your **purpose** (why you are writing) and **audience** (your readers) in mind. Your main purpose is to show how two subjects are similar and how they are different. Think about whether you want to inform people about something new and unfamiliar, such as comparing an old movie with its recent remake. Or perhaps you want to show two things that are familiar to your audience in a way that makes your readers think about them differently, such as comparing two familiar story characters and offering new insights into their actions.

As you consider your purpose, think about who your audience is. Ask yourself:

- Is my audience familiar with, or even experts on, this topic?
- Do I need to provide background information so they understand the subject I'm writing about?
- What is the best way to capture my audience's interest?

Identify Similarities and Differences

Once you have chosen what you are going to compare, use a Venn diagram like the one below to list the similarities and differences between your two subjects.

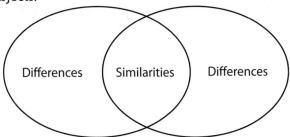

Idea Starters

- similar folk tales
- characters in different stories that share similar experiences
- stories with a common theme
- poems with a similar subject

Writing Tip

One way to find a topic is by **brainstorming.** Write a subject at the top of a sheet of paper and put down each thought that comes to mind. Keep going until you run out of ideas. You'll end up with more topics than you need, but you'll find a good place to start writing.

Your Turn _____

Get Started List in your **RWN** some possible subjects for comparison. Narrow your choices until you have decided on the two subjects that offer the **best points of comparison and contrast.** Create your **Venn diagram** to list the **similarities and differences** between the two subjects.

Learn It Online
Try an interactive graphic organizer at:

go.hrw.com   L7-107   **Go**

Comparison-Contrast Essay

Writing Tip

As you look at the qualities of the subjects you are comparing, imagine that you are a skeptical, or questioning, reader who keeps asking, "But how do you know that?" Be sure to include supporting details that answer that question.

Writing Tip

When reading a comparison-contrast essay, your audience will expect to see **clue words** that will help them understand the similarities (*also, both, just as, too*) and the differences (*although, but, however, instead, on the other hand, still*) of your subjects.

Your Turn ———

Planning Your Writing List your most effective supporting details in your **RWN.** Then review your subjects, the points you are making, and the details you want to include and decide which organizational method would be best for your comparison. You may want to begin filling out a chart for the block method *and* the point-by-point method to see which method is going to work better.

Gather Supporting Details

Will your audience need more information? Look at the qualities you have listed in your Venn diagram. What supporting details can you provide for your reader to make the similarities and differences clear? For example, if you say that the hero of one story is shy and the hero from another story is bold, offer specific examples from those stories to support the general statements. Perhaps the shy hero doesn't say much or the bold hero takes action without pausing to think about it.

Organize Your Ideas

The details in a comparison-contrast essay are usually arranged by the block method or the point-by-point method. Use one of the charts below to help you plan your writing.

- **block method:** In the block method, all of the features of a subject are presented at one time. For example, if you were comparing and contrasting two characters, you would first present all of one character's features (such as actions, appearance, and feelings) and then present all of the other character's features.

Block Method	
Subject 1	Feature 1:
	Feature 2:
Subject 2	Feature 1:
	Feature 2:

- **point-by-point method:** In the point-by-point method, the writer presents one feature of each subject and shows how that feature applies to both subjects before moving on to the next point of comparison. For example, you would compare the characters' actions, then their appearance, then their feelings, and so on.

Point-by-Point Method	
Feature 1	Subject 1:
	Subject 2:
Feature 2	Subject 1:
	Subject 2:

Drafting

Follow the Writer's Framework

Look at the Writer's Framework shown for writing an effective comparison-contrast essay. Use the framework to help you as you write your first draft. Once you have written your first draft, look at it against the framework to make sure that you haven't forgotten anything.

Use Quotations from Your Sources

If you are comparing and contrasting characters, themes, or other characteristics found in works you have read, you will probably want to include quotations from those sources. For example, if you are comparing the way two writers describe an animal in the wild, you would want to quote specific phrases or sentences from each work to demonstrate your points. As you write your draft, refer to your sources for good examples to quote.

> **A Writer's Framework**
>
> **Introduction**
> - Capture your reader's attention with a strong beginning.
> - Identify your topic at the beginning of the essay.
>
> **Body**
> - Use the block method or the point-by-point method to make your comparison.
> - Include at least two similarities and two differences as you compare and contrast. Provide details and examples to support your points.
>
> **Conclusion**
> - Restate your main point about your subjects.
> - Make a meaningful connection for your readers.

● Writing Tip

A strong conclusion does more than just summarize your ideas. It may also extend to other literary topics or to broader topics related to the works you have chosen. For example, you may want to expand on how two themes reflect common human experiences. Or you may want to show that the struggles of two characters reflect struggles that you have read about in other works. Tell why the comparison is relevant to wider experience.

Grammar Link
Capitalizing and Punctuating Quotations from Text

If you quote material from another text, make sure that you use the correct capitalization and punctuation. *Always* put quotation marks around any text that is taken directly from another writer's work. This lets the reader know that these are someone else's words, not yours. If the quoted text is a complete sentence, capitalize the first letter of the sentence. If you are quoting a word or phrase, incorporate the quotation in your regular text:

> The author says, "The opportunities to play different sports are fewer in Cuba."

> He tells us that children in the United States "can also participate in organized hockey, ice skating, and more."

Your Turn _____

Write Your Draft Following your plan, write a draft of your essay. Be sure to think about:
- what your **audience** will need to know in order to understand what you are saying
- stating **similarities** and **differences** clearly and specifically
- including **quotations** from the texts to support your ideas

Peer Review

Working with a peer, review your drafts. Answer each question in the chart at the right to locate where and how your drafts could be improved. As you discuss your papers, be sure to take notes about each other's suggestions. You can refer to your notes as you revise your drafts.

Evaluating and Revising

Read the questions in the left column of the chart. Then use the tips in the middle column to help you make revisions to your essay. The right column suggests techniques that you can use to revise your draft.

Comparison-Contrast Essay: Guidelines for Content and Organization

Evaluation Question	Tip	Revision Technique
1. Does your introduction state the topic of your essay? Do you identify works by title and author?	**Underline** the topic or thesis statement. **Circle** titles and authors.	**Add** a sentence that states the main idea of the essay. **Add** titles of works and authors' names.
2. Do you discuss at least two similarities and differences between the texts?	**Put a check mark** next to each example of comparison or contrast.	**Add** examples of comparison or contrast. **Delete** statements that don't belong.
3. Is the body of your essay organized by either the block method or the point-by-point method?	In the margin, **label** the method of organization. **Write** *A* above each point about the first subject and *B* above each point for the second subject.	**Rearrange** sentences by using either the block method or point-by-point method. Be sure to use only one method.
4. Do you provide specific details and examples to support your general statements?	**Highlight** supporting details, examples, and direct quotes.	**Elaborate** with specific details, examples, and direct quotes.
5. Does your conclusion restate and expand on the main idea stated in the introduction?	**Bracket** the restatement of your main idea. **Circle** statements that expand on it.	**Elaborate** on statements that summarize or evaluate.

Read this student's draft and the comments about it as a model for revising your own comparison-contrast essay.

Amigo Brothers

by Melissa Spechler, Weber Middle School

Piri Thomas's story "Amigo Brothers" is about two best friends named Felix and Antonio who love boxing. Although they are different in appearance and have different styles of boxing, the two boys share many similarities, which is probably why they are best friends. They are faced with a challenge. They will have to compete against each other for the Golden Gloves Championship Tournament, and only one can win.

Both boys have shared many experiences growing up. Felix is seventeen years old. He dreams of someday being lightweight champion of the world. Antonio is also seventeen. They have grown up on the Lower East Side of Manhattan and live in the same tenement building. They sleep, eat, and dream positive. They share a collection of Fight magazines and also "a scrapbook filled with torn tickets to every boxing match they had ever attended." Antonio also wants to be lightweight champion of the world. Antonio told Felix, "No pulling punches," and he smiled. Both boys have decided that no matter what happens in the tournament fight, they will always be champions to each other!

← Melissa **states the topic** of her comparison in the first two sentences.

← Note the **clue words, such as** *although* **in the first paragraph and** *both* **in this paragraph** that help point out differences and similarities.

← **Specific details,** including **quotations** from the story, support Melissa's points.

MINI-LESSON ▶ **How to Use the Point-by-Point and Block Methods**

Melissa's second paragraph includes some good statements of comparison, but she could tighten up the organization a bit. She's mixing the point-by-point method of comparison with the block method. In her revised second paragraph below she sticks with just the point-by-point method.

Melissa's Revision of Paragraph Two

> Both boys have shared many experiences growing up. ∧*Both are* seventeen years old. ∧*Each one dreams of someday* being lightweight champion of the world. They have grown up on the Lower East Side of Manhattan and live in the same tenement building. They sleep, eat, and dream positive. . . .

Your Turn _____

Using an Organizational Method Read your draft, then ask yourself these questions:

- Which method of organization have you used? Does it remain consistent throughout the essay?
- Is your organization clear?
- Do you need to reorder any sentences or paragraphs to make the organization more consistent and more clear?

Comparison-Contrast Essay

Student Draft *continues*

Notice how in this revised version Melissa uses the point-by-point method consistently. This makes the comparison and contrast easier to follow.

Melissa concludes by telling what happens at the end of the story, but she could add some information to give the reader **insight** into what makes these two characters so **similar.**

→ . . . They share a collection of *Fight* magazines and also "a scrapbook filled with torn tickets to every boxing match they had ever attended." Both boys have decided that no matter what happens in the tournament fight, they will always be champions to each other!

→ During the big fight both boys show good sportsmanship and play by the rules. They fight a good, clean match, and at the end of the bout they embrace. Just as the announcer turns to point out the winner, he finds himself alone in the ring. Felix and Antonio have already left the ring.

MINI-LESSON ▶ Expanding the Main Idea in the Conclusion

Take your conclusion one step further by explaining why your points are important. Look at the revision below. Note how the information Melissa added helps her reader understand the relationship between these two characters and why they both can be called "champions." Now the conclusion provides a meaningful connection for the reader, showing why these two similar characters are special.

Melissa's Revision of Paragraph Three

During the big fight both boys show good sportsmanship

and play by the rules. They fight a good, clean match, and at the

end of the bout they embrace. Just as the announcer turns to point

out the winner, he finds himself alone in the ring. ~~Felix and Antonio~~ *The two champions*

have already left the ring. *arm in arm. It is clear that Felix and Antonio care more about their friendship than about the fight title.*

Your Turn —————

Expanding Your Conclusion
Review your conclusion. Have you summarized your main points? Is there anything you can add to show why these points are important?

Proofreading and Publishing

Proofreading

After you revise your comparison-contrast essay, make sure that your final version is free of any errors in spelling, punctuation, and sentence structure. Proofread your writing carefully, using proofreading marks to make the necessary corrections. Use a dictionary to look up any words that you're not sure of, and use the Language Handbook as reference.

Grammar Link Making Pronoun References Clear

When writers use a **pronoun,** they need to make sure that the word or phrase the pronoun refers to is clear. The word the pronoun refers to is called the pronoun's **antecedent.** In the first sentence below, the antecedent of the pronoun *he* can't be clearly identified:

Confusing	Antonio told Felix, "No pulling punches," and he smiled. [Who smiled, Antonio or Felix?]
Clear	Antonio told Felix, "No pulling punches," and he smiled. *smiled when he* [Antonio was the one who smiled.]

Publishing

Now it is time to publish your comparison-contrast essay, sharing it with a wider audience. Here are some ways to share your essay:

- Add images, such as photos or illustrations, to your essay and print the results in a booklet.
- Collaborate with other classmates to create a book or an electronic posting called "Alike or Different?"
- Share your comparison-contrast essay as an oral reading. After you have finished, invite your classmates to summarize the main points you made about your subjects.

Reflect on the Process In your **RWN,** write a short response to each of the following questions.

1. What was most challenging about writing a comparison-contrast essay? What was most rewarding?
2. What strategies did you find helpful as you selected details and quotations to include in your comparison?
3. How do you think your revisions improved your essay? Explain.

Proofreading Tip

A **sentence fragment** is a group of words that either does not have a subject and verb or does not complete a thought. Proofread your draft, following these tips for finding and correcting sentence fragments:

- Does the word group have a subject and a verb?
- Does the sentence express a complete thought?
- If a word group is a fragment, add the words needed to make it a sentence.
- Be sure to capitalize the first word of the sentence and punctuate the sentence correctly.

Your Turn _____

Proofread and Publish

Proofread your essay, correcting any sentence fragments and unclear pronoun references. Fix all errors in spelling, punctuation, or sentence structure. Then publish the final version of your essay.

Scoring Rubric

You can use one of the rubrics below to evaluate your comparison-contrast essay from the Writing Workshop or your response to the prompt on the next page. Your teacher will say which rubric to use.

6-Point Scale

Score 6 *Demonstrates advanced success*
- focuses consistently on a clear thesis
- shows effective organization throughout, with smooth transitions
- offers thoughtful, creative ideas
- develops ideas thoroughly, using examples, details and fully elaborated explanation
- exhibits mature control of written language

Score 5 *Demonstrates proficient success*
- focuses on a clear thesis
- shows effective organization, with transitions
- offers thoughtful ideas
- develops ideas competently, using examples, details and well-elaborated explanation
- exhibits sufficient control of written language

Score 4 *Demonstrates competent success*
- focuses on a clear thesis, with minor distractions
- shows effective organization, with minor lapses
- offers mostly thoughtful ideas
- develops ideas adequately, with a mixture of general and specific elaboration
- exhibits general control of written language

Score 3 *Demonstrates limited success*
- includes some loosely related ideas that distract from the writer's expository/informative focus
- shows some organization, with noticeable gaps in the logical flow of ideas
- offers routine, predictable ideas
- develops ideas with uneven elaboration
- exhibits limited control of written language

Score 2 *Demonstrates basic success*
- includes loosely related ideas that seriously distract from the writer's expository/informative focus
- shows minimal organization, with major gaps in the logical flow of ideas
- offers ideas that merely skim the surface
- develops ideas with inadequate elaboration
- exhibits significant problems with control of written language

Score 1 *Demonstrates emerging effort*
- shows little awareness of the topic and purpose for writing
- lacks organization
- offers unclear and confusing ideas
- develops ideas in only a minimal way, if at all
- exhibits major problems with control of written language

4-Point Scale

Score 4 *Demonstrates advanced success*
- focuses consistently on a clear thesis
- shows effective organization throughout, with smooth transitions
- offers thoughtful, creative ideas
- develops ideas thoroughly, using examples, details and fully elaborated explanation
- exhibits mature control of written language

Score 3 *Demonstrates competent success*
- focuses on a clear thesis, with minor distractions
- shows effective organization, with minor lapses
- offers mostly thoughtful ideas
- develops ideas adequately, with a mixture of general and specific elaboration
- exhibits general control of written language

Score 2 *Demonstrates limited success*
- includes some loosely related ideas that distract from the writer's expository/informative focus
- shows some organization, with noticeable gaps in the logical flow of ideas
- offers routine, predictable ideas
- develops ideas with uneven elaboration
- exhibits limited control of written language

Score 1 *Demonstrates emerging effort*
- shows little awareness of the topic and purpose for writing
- lacks organization
- offers unclear and confusing ideas
- develops ideas in only a minimal way, if at all
- exhibits major problems with control of written language

Comparison-Contrast Essay

When responding to an on-demand comparison-contrast prompt, use the models you have read, what you've learned from writing your own comparison-contrast essay, the rubric on page 114, and the steps below.

Writing Prompt

In "An Unforgettable Journey" and *Song of the Trees*, kids lean on family members to help them in times of trouble. However, there are differences between the hardships faced by the two families. Write a comparison-contrast essay in which you compare Maijue Xiong's experience in "An Unforgettable Journey" with that of Cassie in *Song of the Trees*. Be sure to include similarities and differences.

Study the Prompt

Begin by reading the prompt carefully. Note what you are required to include in your essay: clearly stated similarities and differences and evidence to support your statements.

Tip: Spend about five minutes studying the prompt.

Plan Your Response

First, you must think of similarities and differences. Ask yourself questions such as the following:

- What are at least two ways that the girls' experiences are similar or different?
- What evidence can I think of that supports these similarities or differences?
- What are at least two ways that the families' methods of dealing with a problem are similar or different?
- What evidence can I think of that supports these similarities or differences in methods?

Tip: Spend about fifteen minutes planning your response.

Respond to the Prompt

Choose the method you will use to structure your essay: block or point-by-point. Here are some guidelines to keep in mind:

- In the introduction, identify your topic, giving the names and authors of the works, and provide any background your reader might need.
- In the body of your essay, discuss two or three of the most important similarities or differences. Be sure to include supporting details, examples, and direct quotations to emphasize these two or three points.
- In the conclusion, restate your thesis and sum up the points you made in your essay.

Tip: Spend about twenty minutes writing your draft.

Improve Your Response

Revising Go back over the key aspects of the prompt. Did you structure your essay in one of the two formats? Did you include supporting evidence for your assertions?

Proofreading Take a few minutes to proofread your essay to correct errors in grammar, spelling, punctuation, and capitalization. Make sure that all of your edits are neat, and erase any stray marks.

Checking Your Final Copy Before you turn in your essay, read it one more time to catch any errors you may have missed. You'll be glad that you took the extra time for one final review.

Tip: Save ten minutes to improve your paper.

Giving a Comparison-Contrast Presentation

Speak with a Purpose

Prepare a comparison-contrast presentation of two literary subjects, works, or characters. Practice your presentation, and then present it to your class.

Think as a Reader/Writer When preparing an oral comparison-contrast presentation, you still need to think like a writer. As when writing your essay, you want to grab your listeners' attention with an interesting introduction. You will need to give listeners a good understanding of what you're comparing. Then, you'll need to present clear comparisons of your two subjects.

Have you ever told a friend about a movie version of a book you have read? Maybe you've seen a movie version of a Harry Potter book. When you told your friend about the movie, chances are you told him or her how the movie was similar to or different from the book. You probably didn't think about it, but you were making a comparison-contrast presentation to your friend.

Plan Your Comparison-Contrast Presentation

Topic and Audience

You may want to adapt your written comparison-contrast essay for an oral comparison-contrast presentation. Remember, your listeners will not be able to re-read your presentation, so your comparisons must be very clear. In case you'd like to compare and contrast subjects different from your essay's, take a look at other collections in this book. You may find two texts or characters that you could more easily compare and contrast in your oral presentation.

Will you present your comparison-contrast speech to your classmates or to another group? What will the audience already know about your subjects? Answering these questions will help you decide how formal or informal your presentation should be and what sort of information you'll need to include. As with your written essay, be sure to include a clear **thesis statement** early in your presentation. Your audience should know right away what you'll be comparing for them.

Reader/Writer Notebook

Use your **RWN** to complete the activities for this workshop.

Comparisons and Organization

Take a look at the Venn diagram you prepared for your Writing Workshop in this collection. If you're adapting your comparison-contrast essay for an oral presentation, you can use information from the filled-in diagram.

When organizing your presentation, think about your listeners. What kind of organization—**block method** or **point-by-point method**—will be easier for your audience to follow? (See Writing Workshop, page 106.)

Deliver Your Comparison-Contrast Presentation

Get Your Message Across

In your written comparison-contrast essay, you got your message across through the use of words on the page. However, good public speakers use more than words to get their messages across. They use **nonverbal** elements, such as body language, and **verbal** elements that add meaning to their words.

Use Nonverbal Communication

Nonverbal Element	Examples
Eye contact	Make eye contact with your listeners to keep them involved.
Facial expressions	Emphasize meaning with smiles, frowns, or raised eyebrows.
Gestures	Add meaning or emphasis with shrugs, nods, or hand movements.
Posture	Stand straight to show listeners that you're sure of yourself.

Use Verbal Communication

When you plan your comparison-contrast presentation, you'll probably focus on what to say. But remember, *how* you say something is also important in getting your message across.

Verbal Element	Example
Pitch	Change the pitch (rise and fall) of your voice to add emphasis; for example, raise the pitch to emphasize a word or phrase.
Rate	Speak slowly enough that your listeners can understand you, but you might want to speak more quickly to show excitement or emotion.
Volume	Speak loudly enough for listeners in the back to hear you, and you can also speak more loudly to emphasize an important point.
Tone	Use a tone that suits your purpose. In your comparison-contrast presentation, you should sound informative and sure of yourself.

A Good Comparison-Contrast Presentation

- gives the topic and thesis early in the presentation
- discusses at least two similarities or differences
- gives the listeners clear comparisons
- uses both verbal and nonverbal communication

Speaking Tip

Remember to use standard English when you present your comparison-contrast speech. Your presentation will be easier to understand if you use language that is grammatically correct and appropriate for both formal and informal situations.

Literary Skills Review

Forms of Prose **Directions:** Read the following list. Then, read each question, and decide which is the best answer.

Forms of Prose

Key to Abbreviations				
E = Easy	A = Average	C = Challenging	F = Fiction	NF = Nonfiction

Anderson, Laurie Halse. *Fever 1793.* **A, F** Sixteen-year-old Matilda Cook confronts a citywide outbreak of yellow fever in this accurately detailed novel set in late-eighteenth-century Philadelphia.

Brooks, Polly Schoyer. *Queen Eleanor: Independent Spirit of the Medieval World.* **A, NF** An engaging portrait of Eleanor of Aquitaine, one of the most influential figures of the Middle Ages.

Caselli, Giovanni. *The Renaissance and the New World.* **C, NF** The author looks at Renaissance advancements in commerce and technology that became the foundation of eighteenth-century life in England and America.

Dahl, Roald. *Boy.* **C, NF** With a humorous touch the renowned author tells about his childhood years in England.

Mandela, Nelson. *Long Walk to Freedom.* **A, NF** Mandela reflects on a lifetime of commitment to overturning apartheid in South Africa.

Saint-Exupéry, Antoine de. *The Little Prince.* **E, F** In this fable a stranded pilot meets a little boy who recounts his fantastic adventures on various planets.

Soto, Gary. *Baseball in April.* **E, F** A collection of short stories. In one story Michael and Jesse fail to make the Little League team but still find a way to play the game they love.

Taylor, Mildred D. *Song of the Trees.* **A, F** In this novella the Logan family must prevent a businessman from destroying the forest that has brought joy to their lives.

Yep, Laurence. "Puzzle Pieces." **A, NF** In this essay Laurence Yep tells about how he became a writer.

Zindel, Paul. *The Pigman.* **C, F** In this prize-winning novel John and Lorraine are dissatisfied with their lives until they meet Mr. Pignati, who teaches them to cherish every moment.

1. **Which one of the following statements is true of both fiction and nonfiction?**
   A They are not based on actual events.
   B They are not longer than 100 pages.
   C They often reveal important truths.
   D They must have a conflict.

2. If *Queen Eleanor: Independent Spirit of the Medieval World* was rewritten as **fiction**, it would be *most* like —
   A *Fever 1793*
   B *The Little Prince*
   C *The Pigman*
   D "Puzzle Pieces"

3. *Boy* is similar to *The Renaissance and the New World* except that *Boy* —
   A relates facts about real people and events
   B is written as nonfiction
   C is about events of the past
   D is about the life of the author

4. *Long Walk to Freedom* is an **autobiography**, the story of a person's life written —
   A by that person
   B in a fictional manner
   C by someone else
   D to teach history

5. *Song of the Trees* is different from *Long Walk to Freedom* because *Song of the Trees* —
   A is a made-up story
   B is written as an essay
   C includes a conflict
   D has a theme, or message

Constructed Response

6. How are *Boy* and *Queen Eleanor: Independent Spirit of the Medieval World* similar? How are they different? Be sure to mention in your response which form of prose each book represents.

7. Describe what makes a short story, a novel, and a novella different from one another.

Mirror, Mirror, on the Wall, Do I See Myself As Others Do? by **Joan Burditt**

Two weeks ago I was watching a local news story about the lottery. The film footage showed a young woman standing behind the store counter selling lottery tickets. She had short blond hair, big sparkling eyes, and a huge smile. I recognized her as the woman who worked in the corner drugstore down the street. The next day I walked into the store and said, "Hey, I saw you on TV last night. You looked great." She made a disgusted face.

"I told them not to film me."

"Why not?"

"Because I look so . . ." She puffed out her cheeks. *"Fat!"*

I didn't know what to say. So I just repeated, "Well, you looked great."

I thought, "Here is a shining light of a woman who thinks she looks too bad to be on television for five seconds." So I decided to interview some middle-school and high school students to see if they, like this woman, feel bad about the way they look.

"Lots of kids think they weigh more than they look," said one freshman. "Everyone wants to be size zero. If not, it's hard to feel really good."

It's easy to see why people feel this way, especially kids. Watch television or flip through a magazine. The females look as though they haven't had a decent meal in months. The males look as though they could be hit in the stomach by a freight train and not even feel it. I turned every page of a popular teen magazine for girls and counted advertisements for makeup and clothes. Out of 220 pages, 70 were ads. That's about one third of the magazine!

Statistics show that models in advertisements are 9 percent taller and 23 percent thinner than the average woman. With the click of a mouse, computers can create a picture of the perfect face by cleaning up a model's complexion, trimming her chin, and getting rid of lines around her eyes. Here's a news flash: She's not a real person, folks. She's an illusion.

Other students I interviewed talked about the importance of wearing certain brands of clothing. These clothes display a brand name somewhere, whether it's plastered in three-inch type across the front or appears on a tiny logo on the sleeve. A middle-school student said, "Sometimes

I just want to wear a pair of sweatpants and a T-shirt, but if you do, you're looked down on. The way you dress classifies you. You can easily tell which people hang out together by looking at their clothes."

If you're thinking I interviewed insecure kids, you're wrong. A study conducted by the American Association of University Women found that in elementary school 60 percent of girls and 67 percent of boys had high self-esteem—they felt good about themselves. But by the time kids are in high school, self-esteem in girls drops to only 29 percent, compared with self-esteem in boys, which drops to 46 percent.

The good news is that some things may be changing for the better. One middle-school girl reported being on the volleyball and basketball teams. Unlike girls just one generation ago, she can go out for any sport she wants. After an amazing spike or a skillful dribble, however, this beautiful, strong fifteen-year-old still says, "Sometimes you can see yourself as others see you. But if someone says they think I'm pretty, I don't believe them."

Start believing it. Remember what Eleanor Roosevelt said: "No one can make you feel inferior without your consent."

---

1. Which of the following would be a *main* heading in an **outline** of this essay?

   A kids watch TV or read magazines

   B logos appear on sleeves

   C young women feel bad about their looks

   D kids wear sweatpants and T-shirts

2. Each of the following would be an important **note** *except* —

   A many ads are aimed at kids' appearance

   B students rely on brands for popularity

   C teens are too critical of their appearance

   D girls can play volleyball and basketball

3. A **summary** of this article would —

   A criticize the fashion-conscious students

   B note the most important points

   C include all the statistics

   D focus on each paragraph's first line

Constructed Response

4. Using notes, write the main idea of each paragraph, including important details. Then, write a short summary of the article in your own words.

PREPARING FOR STANDARDIZED TESTS

SKILLS FOCUS Vocabulary Skills Use context clues in words, sentences, and paragraphs to decode new vocabulary.

Vocabulary Skills Review

Context Clues

Directions: As you read each sentence, use other words and phrases in the sentence to help you figure out what the italicized word means. Then, choose the *best* answer.

1. The crowd's reaction was as *frenzied* as the flurry of punches being thrown by the fighters.

   Which word from the sentence gives the *best* clue to the meaning of *frenzied*?

   A reaction

   B fighters

   C flurry

   D thrown

2. The rescuers *delved* deep into the forest as they hunted for the lost campers.

   Delved means —

   A dodged

   B hid

   C escaped

   D explored

3. The stormy sky foretold an *ominous* night, which frightened the children.

   Which two words give the *best* clues to the meaning of *ominous*?

   A children; night

   B stormy sky

   C frightened; children

   D foretold; frightened

4. The jungle's lack of protection made it a poor *refuge*.

   In this passage, *refuge* means —

   A happiness

   B clothing

   C shelter

   D food

5. They couldn't agree on much, but this *dispute* promised to drive them even further apart.

   Which antonym below gives the *best* clue to the meaning of *dispute*?

   A agreement

   B promise

   C drive

   D separation

6. Of the many matches scheduled for the night, the last *bout* would be the most thrilling.

   Which word from the sentence gives the *best* clue to the meaning of *bout*?

   A matches

   B scheduled

   C night

   D thrilling

Academic Vocabulary

Directions: Use context clues in the passage below to identify the meaning of the Academic Vocabulary word.

7. Alone, Clifton Davis's or Dondré Green's story is touching. When Davis combined them, the stories had greater *impact*.

   In this passage, *impact* means —

   A effect

   B importance

   C fearlessness

   D interest

Writing Skills Review

SKILLS FOCUS Writing Skills Write comparison-contrast essays.

Comparison-Contrast Essay **Directions:** Read the following paragraph. Then, read the questions below it. Choose the best answer to each question.

(1) Although biographies and autobiographies are often grouped together as forms of literature, there are significant differences, as well as similarities, between them. (2) Both biographies and autobiographies are written in prose. (3) They tell the story of a person's life. (4) Each can reveal the subject's whole life or can concentrate on a specific part of it. (5) The opinion of the writer about his or her subject is usually revealed in a biography. (6) A biography may contain many people's opinions about the person. (7) Autobiographies also contain opinions. (8) The subject of an autobiography, however, is the writer's own life, so differing points of view are not offered.

1. The **thesis,** or main idea, of this paper is stated in —
   A sentence 1
   B sentence 2
   C sentence 3
   D sentence 8

2. Which sentence is unnecessary and should be deleted?
   A Sentence 1
   B Sentence 3
   C Sentence 5
   D Sentence 7

3. **Transitional expressions** are used in all of the following *except* —
   A sentence 1
   B sentence 2
   C sentence 4
   D sentence 5

4. Which type of text structure is used in this passage?
   A Chronological
   B Cause and effect
   C Comparison-contrast
   D Step by step

5. Which of these statements is accurate?
   A Sentence 1 contains a definition of autobiography.
   B Sentence 2 focuses on a difference between biographies and autobiographies.
   C Sentence 5 focuses on a similarity between biographies and autobiographies.
   D Sentence 6 identifies a purpose of some biographies.

Read On

Fiction

Somewhere in the Darkness

While suffering from a kidney disease and confined to a prison hospital, Cephus "Crab" Little decides to make up for lost time with his son Jimmy in *Somewhere in the Darkness* by Walter Dean Myers. After his release, they journey together to Crab's hometown in Arkansas, where Jimmy's growing understanding of his father's past helps him come to terms with his father and himself.

Cut from the Same Cloth: American Women of Myth, Legend, and Tall Tale

In *Cut from the Same Cloth*, Robert D. San Souci takes a look at female characters with a talent for adventure in American legends. You'll find stories about Molly Cotton-Tail, Brer Rabbit's clever wife, and Sister Fox, the brains behind Brother Coyote. The stories are entertaining, and they offer up a few lessons as well.

Bearstone

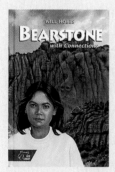

Fourteen-year-old Cloyd never knew his parents and never went to school. After being on his own for most of his young life, he has trouble accepting the kindness of an old rancher from Colorado. In Will Hobbs's novel *Bearstone*, Cloyd embraces his Native American heritage, begins to respect others, and learns what it takes to be an adult.

Adam of the Road

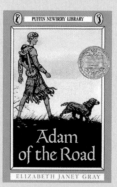

It's the summer of 1294. Adam, an eleven-year-old minstrel who has lost contact with his father, is frustrated by another minstrel named Jankin, who steals his dog, Nick. In this adventure set in the Middle Ages, Adam scours the English countryside in search of the two things that mean the most to him—his father and his dog. Along the way, he meets some interesting friends and learns a few lessons. Read to find out more in Elizabeth Janet Gray's Newbery Award–winning historical novel.

Nonfiction

Long Road to Freedom: Journey of the Hmong

"An Unforgettable Journey" is the story of an individual's flight from war-torn Laos. In *Long Road to Freedom*, Linda Barr recounts the escape of the Hmong people from their Southeast Asian homeland to life in the United States and other countries. In this book you'll learn about the Hmong people's unique cultural traditions as well as their strength of spirit.

Chinese Cinderella: True Story of an Unwanted Daughter

"Yeh-Shen" is a fairy tale that features a magical creature, a handsome prince, and a happily-ever-after ending. In *Chinese Cinderella*, Adeline Yen Mah tells the true story of her own Cinderella-like childhood. Her story has no magic or prince, but it does have an evil stepmother, cruel stepsiblings, and a harsh life of toil and abuse. Instead of being helped by a mysterious fish, Adeline's life is saved by her love of books. Her transformation is due to her strength, hard work, and determination to have a better life.

City

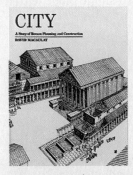

Author David Macaulay shows you what it took to build a city nearly seven hundred years before Justinian and Theodora rebuilt Constantinople. This Macaulay book, like his others on architecture from the past, is filled with accurate and intricate pen-and-ink drawings. The text in *City* will spark your imagination as you follow its story, teaching you history and architecture without your realizing it!

Muhammad Ali: Legends in Sports

Matt Christopher's book *Muhammad Ali: Legends in Sports* introduces you to a true legend. It discusses the impact the former heavyweight champion has had inside and outside the ring. In the 1960s, Ali proved himself to be a strong supporter of civil rights and a devoutly religious person. Today, he works for charitable causes, one of which is the search for a cure for Parkinson's disease.

Learn It Online
Explore other novels—and find tips for choosing, reading, and studying books—at:

go.hrw.com   L7-125   **Go**

Short Stories
Writers on Writing

Gary Soto on Short Stories An award-winning author, Gary Soto was born in Fresno, California, to working-class Mexican American parents. His writing is heavily influenced by his background—many of his characters are teenagers living in Latino neighborhoods.

"My stories are portraits; they are small canvases in which I show a character going through one or two turns in life. Though not large on plot, I try to make them heavy in atmosphere. I try to paint vivid descriptions of a single character in a single place with a

single *problem.* By problem I mean conflict, some moral dilemma the character must work through.

Let me illustrate with a story of mine called "Eating at the Kitchen" that features Cynthia Rodriguez, age twelve, whose parents force her to volunteer at the local soup kitchen. Her plotting parents believe that if their daughter does volunteer work, she will be more likely to be accepted at a better college. The girl goes along with the plan to appease them but soon realizes that she actually likes her volunteer time at the soup kitchen. She discovers a true empathy for the homeless. One afternoon, Cynthia discovers a classmate inching up the dinner line. As the classmate slowly approaches, Cynthia, who is ladling gravy onto plates, wonders what to do. Should she say, "Hi" to her classmate, avoid eye contact during the potentially embarrassing moment, or perhaps even leave her station to avoid the moment altogether? This moment is the problem in the story: How does this character deal with the moment?

People always ask, "Have these stories happened to you?" Short stories may draw upon a writer's life, but since we are creative writers, we can stretch and twist them however we want. When I was in eighth grade and in need of new spring clothes, I joined some older boys to work in the fields outside of Fresno, chopping cotton. Work began before dawn. Cold, I blew into my hands and jumped from foot to foot to keep warm. I was new at this job, a little scared. I was standing around waiting for the *patron*—the boss—to tell us to get to work when in the dark I noticed a girl from my school! When she said, "Hi, Gary," I nearly wilted because I didn't want anyone to know that I worked in the fields! She was gracious; she was larger than me in her heart because she saw no embarrassment in the work we were doing. It was honest work. At the time, however, I felt fieldwork was not noble work. How wrong I was!

The writer uses the "modes of development"—description, dialogue, and exposition—to move the story along. I have this to admit: I like description best. It's the atmosphere surrounding the main characters that I like to create—the sky, the wind in the trees, a forehead pleated with worry, the chewed cuticles of a lonely girl.

Short stories may be short, but the impressions, I hope, last a long time in the reader. "

Think as a Writer

Gary Soto writes that the characters in his stories must face a problem. What problem did Soto face while working in the fields one morning? How did he use this experience as the basis for a short story?

Woman in Boat Looking at Whale
by Christopher Zacharow.

Plot and Setting

INFORMATIONAL TEXT FOCUS

Structure and Purpose of Informational Materials

"You gain strength, courage, and confidence by every experience in which you really stop to look fear in the face."

—**Eleanor Roosevelt**

What Do You Think

How might confronting a difficult situation help you become a stronger person?

Learn It Online

Learn about plot and setting in novels online at *NovelWise*:

go.hrw.com | L7-129 | Go

Literary Focus

by **Linda Rief**

What Are Plot and Setting?

You've heard the expression "the plot thickens." Like cooks who add delicious ingredients to soup or salsa, authors use intriguing tools to make their stories more compelling: suspense that keeps us on the edge of our seats, foreshadowing that gives us clues to what might happen, and complicated plots with twists and turns. Authors thicken the plot—the happening—so we can taste, or experience the story, more fully.

"Once upon a time, they lived happily ever after."

Plot

Plot   The **plot** is the story's skeleton. It is a series of related events growing out of one another. Most plots consist of four parts.

1. **Basic situation**   You meet the main characters and discover what they want. You find out about the conflict that drives the story. **Conflict** is a struggle between two opposing characters, forces, or emotions. An **external conflict** involves a character's struggle with another person or a force of nature (a tornado, a bear, or an icy path).

> Rikki-tikki had never met a live cobra before. . . . He knew that all a grown mongoose's business in life was to fight and eat snakes.
>
> from "Rikki-tikki-tavi"
> by Rudyard Kipling

An **internal conflict** takes place within a character's mind, such as a struggle of conscience:

> She saw herself three years later, marching for graduation, everyone taking photos, smiling, everyone happy, except she wouldn't be because she'd remember having cheated that time back in the ninth grade.
>
> from "The Dive"
> by René Saldaña, Jr.

2. **Series of events**   One or more of the characters in a story act to resolve the conflict. A series of events called **complications** takes place that makes it hard for the character to get what he or she wants.

> Just then the wind rose and the *Cornelius de Witt* changed course, leaned to port, and headed straight for us once more.
>
> from "Three Skeleton Key"
> by George G. Toudouze

3. **Climax**   This is the point at which the conflict is decided one way or another.

> Rikki-tikki shook some of the dust out of his fur and sneezed. "It is all over," he said. "The widow will never come out again."
>
> from "Rikki-tikki-tavi"
> by Rudyard Kipling

4. **Resolution** The **resolution** is the last part of the story, when loose ends are tied up.

> Melly could smell the sweetness of the flowers and herbs wafting from across the street. She smiled, closed her eyes, and slept.
>
> from "The Dive"
> by René Saldaña, Jr.

Two Other Important Elements of Plot

Suspense The events of a plot often create **suspense,** or anxious curiosity, that makes us eager to find out what happens next. Suspense usually begins to build as soon as a conflict begins.

> Teddy shouted to the house: "Oh, look here! Our mongoose is killing a snake," and Rikki-tikki heard a scream from Teddy's mother.
>
> from "Rikki-tikki-tavi"
> by Rudyard Kipling

Foreshadowing Sometimes suspense is increased by hints or clues about what will happen later. The use of such hints or clues is called **foreshadowing.** For example, a character about to dive into the ocean may hear someone remark that sharks were once sighted near shore. As you read, you suspect the sharks will appear again— and you feel that tingle of fear and excitement that keeps you turning the pages.

> Three Skeleton Key . . . earned its name from the story of three convicts who, escaping from Cayenne in a stolen dugout canoe, were wrecked on the rock during the night, managed to escape the sea, but eventually died of hunger and thirst.
>
> from "Three Skeleton Key"
> by George G. Toudouze

Setting

Setting The **setting** of a story is the time and place in which the events take place. It can be the real world or a place that has never existed. If a setting is well described, the writer has succeeded in helping you feel that "you are there."

Your Turn Analyze Plot and Setting

1. What is the difference between an internal conflict and an external conflict?

2. Look at the excerpts from "Three Skeleton Key" on these pages. How do the details in these passages build suspense?

3. Think about a movie, television show, or story you know well. Test your knowledge of its plot by recording the main events of the story. Note instances in which the story's plot is affected by the setting.

Learn It Online
To understand the role of literary elements in novels, visit *NovelWise* at:

go.hrw.com   L7-131   **Go**

Analyzing Visuals

Plot and Setting: The Artist as Storyteller

Paintings often encourage you to imagine a story. An artist will generally show you one moment in time instead of presenting all the events that make up a **plot.** In a painting the artist includes clues about past events and **foreshadows** future events. A painting, like a story, can also convey important details about the story's **setting.** A writer uses sensory details to establish a setting, and an artist uses color, line, and form to bring a setting to life.

The Sleeping Gypsy, by Henri Rousseau, strongly suggests an unusual and mysterious narrative. The story being told by this painting and the painting's meaning can be interpreted in different ways.

Analyze a Painting

Use these guidelines to help you apply the concepts of plot and setting to paintings:

1. What do you see in the painting? What appears to be happening?

2. If there are people, what can you tell about them from their appearance, clothing, expressions, and actions?

3. What details in the painting help create a mood?

Ask yourself the following questions about the painting on the next page. Be sure to use the guidelines above.

1. Describe the setting. Is it unusual in some way?

2. There are no footsteps leading up to the place where the woman rests. How do you imagine she came to be sleeping there?

3. Objects in this painting are not depicted realistically but appear as they might in a dream or in a fantastic vision. What are some dreamlike details?

The Sleeping Gypsy (1897) by Henri Rousseau (1844–1910). Oil on canvas, 51" x 6'7".
Gift of Mrs. Simon Guggenheim. The Museum of Modern Art, New York (646.1939).
Photo credit: Digital Image. ©Museum of Modern Art/Licensed by SCALA/Art Resource, NY.

Your Turn   Write About Plot and Setting

In a paragraph or two, describe what you imagine will happen after the moment shown in the painting. Explain how the setting influences what you imagine will happen.

Reading Focus

by **Kylene Beers**

How Do You Predict, Visualize, and Summarize?

Skilled readers think about what might happen next in the text while also thinking about what has already occurred. Predicting means looking at the clues the author gives you to point you in the right direction. Visualizing helps you imagine places, events, and characters. Summarizing helps you keep up with what you've already read.

Making Predictions

When you **make predictions,** you make educated guesses about what will happen next in a story. Predictions are not random guesses. For instance, if you are a sports fan, you may predict the outcomes of sports events based on the teams' records.

Clues for Predicting When you read, base your predictions on:

- clues the writer includes that **foreshadow,** or hint at, what might happen
- your knowledge of how people or animals behave
- questions you ask yourself as you read

Visualizing

A small, dark island. A lush garden. Every story you read takes place in a particular time and place. Writers fill their stories with details about setting that make that time and place come alive.

Pay attention to the descriptions the writer includes. When you **visualize,** you form mental images of the details in the story.

Tips for Visualizing Use the following tips for visualizing text:

- Look for sensory details that describe how something looks, feels, smells, tastes, or sounds.
- As you read, write notes or draw a sketch of what is happening and where it is happening.
- Read aloud. Hearing the words will help you create mental images.

A Model for Visualizing What images do you see as you read this paragraph?

When they were discovered, nothing remained but three heaps of bones, picked clean by the birds. The story was that the three skeletons, gleaming with phosphorescent light, danced over the small rock, screaming. . . .

from "Three Skeleton Key" by George G. Toudouze

← What do you see as you read about the discovery of the dead convicts?

← How about the dancing skeletons?

← Notice the strong verbs and adjectives, which will help paint pictures in your mind.

Summarizing a Short Story

Some parts of short stories are more important than others. When you **summarize** a text, you highlight the most important information in your own words. For a short story you would include the main characters and major plot events. A summary of a text is much shorter than the original.

Summary Sheet: What to Put in a Summary of a Short Story Use the Summary Sheet to organize the most important information in any of the short stories in this collection.

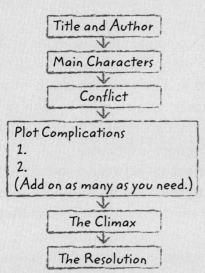

Title and Author
↓
Main Characters
↓
Conflict
↓
Plot Complications
1.
2.
(Add on as many as you need.)
↓
The Climax
↓
The Resolution

Sample Summary Here is the beginning of a summary of "Amigo Brothers" from Collection 1:

> Seventeen-year-old best friends Antonio and Felix both dream of becoming a boxing champion. They train together until they find out they will fight one another in a match. They pledge to fight to win and then agree not to meet until the big night, a week away. Then the boys fight for three rounds. In the end, . . . (Read the story to find out!)

Time-Order Words for a Summary

Because sequence is an important part of writing a summary, be sure to use time-order words and phrases, such as *first, second, next, then, until, after, later, eventually, finally,* and *in the end.* Which of these words and phrases are used in the sample summary?

Your Turn Apply Reading Skills

1. When you make predictions, how can you avoid making random guesses?
2. Read the following passage from "The Dinner Party," a story you will find on the following page. Which details in the passage help you visualize the setting?

> They are seated with their guests—army officers and government attachés and their wives, and a visiting American naturalist—in their spacious dining room, which has a bare marble floor, open rafters, and wide glass doors opening onto a veranda.

Now go to the Skills in Action: Reading Model

 Learn It Online
Take another look at summarizing with the interactive reading workshops:

go.hrw.com L7-135 **Go**

Read with a Purpose Read the following short story to discover if a colonel's stereotype about women's behavior is true.

The Dinner Party

by **Mona Gardner**

The country is India. A colonial official and his wife are giving a large dinner party. They are seated with their guests—army officers and government attachés[1] and their wives, and a visiting American naturalist[2]—in their spacious dining room, which has a bare marble floor, open rafters, and wide glass doors opening onto a veranda.

A spirited discussion springs up between a young girl who insists that women have outgrown the jumping-on-a-chair-at-the-sight-of-a-mouse era and a colonel who says that they haven't.

"A woman's unfailing reaction in any crisis," the colonel says, "is to scream. While a man may feel like it, he has that ounce more of nerve control than a woman has. That last ounce is what counts."

The American does not join in the argument but watches the other guests. As he looks, he sees a strange expression come over the face of the hostess. She is staring straight ahead, her muscles contracting slightly. With a slight gesture she summons the Indian boy standing behind her chair and whispers to him. The boy's eyes widen; he quickly leaves the room.

---

1. **attachés:** (at uh SHAYZ): diplomatic officials.
2. **naturalist:** one who studies nature by observing animals and plants.

Cobra by William De Morgan (1839–1917). Ceramic.

Analyzing Visuals **Viewing and Interpreting** How does this image help you visualize the action in this story?

Of the guests, none except the American notices this nor sees the boy place a bowl of milk on the veranda just outside the open doors.

The American comes to with a start. In India, milk in a bowl means only one thing—bait for a snake. He realizes there must be a cobra in the room. He looks up at the rafters—the likeliest place—but they are bare. Three corners of the room are empty, and in the fourth the servants are waiting to serve the next course. There is only one place left—under the table.

His first impulse is to jump back and warn the others, but he knows the commotion would frighten the cobra into striking. He speaks quickly, the tone of his voice so arresting that it sobers everyone.

Reading Focus

Summarizing A summary of the story would include the fact that the American realizes there's a snake in the room. It would not mention that he looks up at the rafters—that is not a main event in the **plot.**

Literary Focus

Plot The writer builds **suspense** in this passage. The reader is also waiting for the silence to be broken.

"I want to know just what control everyone at this table has. I will count to three hundred—that's five minutes—and not one of you is to move a muscle. Those who move will forfeit[3] fifty rupees.[4] Ready!"

The twenty people sit like stone images while he counts. He is saying "... two hundred and eighty ..." when, out of the corner of his eye, he sees the cobra emerge and make for the bowl of milk. Screams ring out as he jumps to slam the veranda doors safely shut.

"You were right, Colonel!" the host exclaims. "A man has just shown us an example of perfect control."

"Just a minute," the American says, turning to his hostess. "Mrs. Wynnes, how did you know that cobra was in the room?"

A faint smile lights up the woman's face as she replies: "Because it was crawling across my foot."

---

3. **forfeit:** (FAWR fiht): give up as a penalty.
4. **rupees:** (roo PEEZ): Indian monetary units.

Read with a Purpose How do the colonel's predictions apply to the story's outcome? In what ways were you surprised by the ending?

Literary Focus

Plot The **climax** of the story occurs when the cobra comes into view.

Reading Focus

Making Predictions A reader who pays attention to Mrs. Wynnes's reaction and the American's observations in the fourth and fifth paragraphs of the story might predict that the snake was crawling on Mrs. Wynnes.

MEET THE WRITER

Mona Gardner
(1900–1981)

A Familiar Setting

Many of Mona Gardner's books and stories are set in Near or East Asia. She wrote several books, including *Middle Heaven,* which is about Japan; *Hong Kong;* and *The Shanghai Item.* "The Dinner Party" is a classic story that has appeared in many anthologies since it was first published in *The Saturday Review of Literature* in January 1942.

Think About the Writer Explain whether or not you think Mona Gardner based "The Dinner Party" on personal experience.

SKILLS IN ACTION
Wrap Up

SKILLS FOCUS **Literary Skills** Understand and analyze plot and setting. **Reading Skills** Understand how to summarize; summarize a text.

Into Action: Plot Summary

Practice your summarizing skills by writing a summary of "The Dinner Party." Start by completing a Summary Sheet like the one below. Then, write a short summary based on your notes. Be sure to include in your summary some of the time-order words listed on page 135.

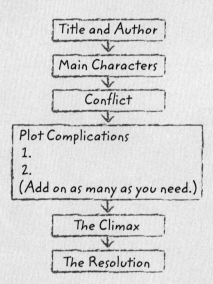

Talk About . . .

1. With a partner, discuss the plot of "The Dinner Party." Are the events believable or unrealistic? Try to use each Academic Vocabulary word listed at the right at least once in your discussion.

Write About . . .

2. What do you think was the most <u>significant</u> event in "The Dinner Party"? Support your answer with details from the story.

3. List the ways in which the American and Mrs. Wynnes are <u>similar</u>.

Writing Focus

Think as a Reader/Writer

In Collection 2, you'll read short stories with suspenseful plots and interesting settings. The Writing Focus activities on the Preparing to Read pages will guide you to understand how each writer creates these plots and settings. On the Applying Your Skills pages, you'll practice those aspects of the writer's craft in your own writing.

Academic Vocabulary for Collection 2

Talking and Writing About Short Stories

Academic Vocabulary is the language you use to write and talk about literature. Use these words to discuss the texts you read in this collection. The words are underlined in the collection.

accurate (AK yuhr iht) *adj.*: containing no errors. *A summary should include accurate information.*

adequate (AD uh kwiht) *adj.*: enough to meet a requirement. *A plot summary should include an adequate number of main events.*

similar (SIHM uh luhr) *adj.*: almost the same. *Sometimes characters in a story show similar characteristics.*

significant (sihg NIHF uh kuhnt) *adj.*: important. *A plot summary should include only significant details.*

Your Turn

Copy the words from the Academic Vocabulary list into your *Reader/Writer Notebook*. Use all four words in a paragraph that summarizes your response to "The Dinner Party." Write the summary in your notebook.

Rikki-tikki-tavi

by **Rudyard Kipling**

What Do **You** Think

If you were facing a bully, would you fight, run away, or try to negotiate?

QuickWrite

What situations have you heard or read about in which someone had to face a bully? Describe the situation and the way each of the individuals acted and reacted.

Reader/Writer
Notebook

Use your **RWN** to complete the activities
for this selection.

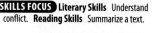

SKILLS FOCUS **Literary Skills** Understand
conflict. **Reading Skills** Summarize a text.

Literary Focus

Conflict All stories are built on some kind of **conflict.** A conflict often results when a character wants something very badly but has a difficult time getting it or when there is a physical battle or a battle of wills between two opposing forces. Think of the stories you see in movies and on TV, and you'll be able to find a conflict in every one of them. Conflict is worked out in the series of related events called **plot.**

Reading Focus

Summarizing Restating the **main ideas,** or <u>significant</u> events, in a text is called **summarizing.** A summary of a text is much shorter than the original. To summarize a narrative, you must include the main characters, main events, conflicts, and resolutions.

Into Action As you read this story, keep track of the major events by filling in a story map like this one. You'll use your completed map to write a summary.

> Major Events: (Add on as many as you need.)
> 1.
> 2.
> 3.

Writing Focus

Think as a Reader/Writer

Find It in Your Reading As you read this story, pay attention to the way Rudyard Kipling portrays Rikki-tikki's conflicts with Nag and Nagaina. Write down at least ten words or phrases that he uses to describe them.

Vocabulary

immensely (ih MEHNS lee) *adv.:* enormously. *Rikki is immensely brave.*

cowered (KOW uhrd) *v.:* crouched and trembled in fear. *Darzee, who is not brave, cowered before the snakes.*

valiant (VAL yuhnt) *adj.:* brave and determined. *Rikki is a valiant hero.*

consolation (KAHN suh LAY shuhn) *n.:* comfort. *Rikki's consolation comes from protecting Teddy and his parents.*

Rikki-tikki-tavi
↓
is **immensely** brave
↓
cowers before no one
↓
is a **valiant** hero
↓
feels **consolation** when protecting his family

Language Coach

Word Roots The Latin word *consolari* means "to offer comfort." The word *consolation* comes from this Latin word and is made up of a root word (*console*) and a suffix (*–ation*). The root word *console* is a verb. What part of speech does the word become after adding the suffix?

Learn It Online
For a preview of this story, see the video introduction on:

go.hrw.com   L7-141   **Go**

Learn It Online
Get more on the author's life at:
go.hrw.com L7-142 Go

Rudyard Kipling

(1865–1936)

Nobel
Prize
WINNER

On His Own

Rudyard Kipling was born in India, but when he was just six years old, his parents shipped him and his sister off to a boardinghouse in England.

Return to India

When Kipling was seventeen, he returned to India and took a job as an editor with an English-language newspaper. He was fascinated by the lives of British colonials in India and the vivid contrast they made with the Indian people they ruled. Soon the paper was printing Kipling's poems and tales about what he saw. Readers begged for more, and Kipling's fame grew. Over the next half century he wrote dozens of books. In 1907, he was awarded the Nobel Prize in Literature. When Kipling was very young, this is what he discovered about books:

"[Books] were among the most important affairs in the world. . . . One could take a pen and set down what one thought, and that nobody accused him of 'showing off' by doing so."

Think About the Writer Why do you think Rudyard Kipling set many of his stories in India?

Build Background

This story takes place in India many years ago, when the British ruled that huge country. The family in this story lives in a cantonment (kan TAHN muhnt), which is a kind of army base. The father is in the British army.

Preview the Story

Rikki-tikki-tavi is a mongoose who is rescued by a little boy named **Teddy** and his parents after a flood. This story is about the conflict that develops between Rikki and the deadly snakes **Nag** and **Nagaina** as Rikki strives to protect his new family.

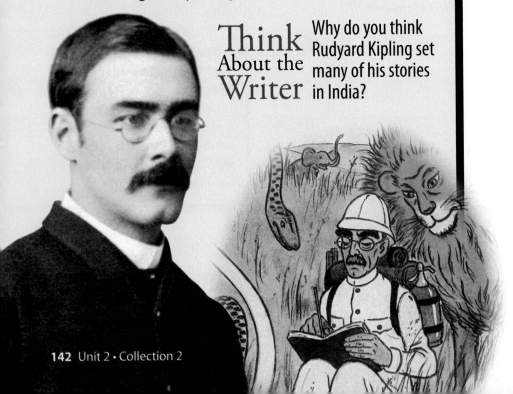

Rikki-tikki-tavi

by **Rudyard Kipling**

This is the story of the great war that Rikki-tikki-tavi fought single-handed, through the bathrooms of the big bungalow[1] in Segowlee cantonment.[2] Darzee, the tailorbird, helped him, and Chuchundra, the muskrat, who never comes out into the middle of the floor but always creeps round by the wall, gave him advice; but Rikki-tikki did the real fighting.

He was a mongoose, rather like a little cat in his fur and his tail but quite like a weasel in his head and his habits. His eyes and the end of his restless nose were pink; he could scratch himself anywhere he pleased with any leg, front or back, that he chose to use; he could fluff up his tail till it looked like a bottlebrush, and his war cry as he scuttled through the long grass was *Rikk-tikk-tikki-tikki-tchk!* **Ⓐ**

One day, a high summer flood washed him out of the burrow where he lived with his father and mother and carried him, kicking and clucking, down a roadside ditch. He found a little wisp of grass floating there and clung to it till he lost his senses. When he revived, he was lying in the hot sun in the middle of a garden path, very draggled[3] indeed, and a small boy was saying: "Here's a dead mongoose. Let's have a funeral."

"No," said his mother; "let's take him in and dry him. Perhaps he isn't really dead."

They took him into the house, and a big man picked him up between his finger and thumb and said he was not dead but half choked; so they wrapped him in cotton wool and warmed him over a little fire, and he opened his eyes and sneezed.

"Now," said the big man (he was an Englishman who had just moved into the bungalow), "don't frighten him, and we'll see what he'll do." **Ⓑ**

It is the hardest thing in the world to frighten a mongoose, because he is eaten up from nose to tail with curiosity. The motto of all the mongoose family is "Run and find

---

1. **bungalow:** in India, a low, one-storied house, named after a type of house found in Bengal, a region of South Asia.
2. **Segowlee** (see GOW lee) **cantonment:** British army post in Segowlee (now Segauli), India.

3. **draggled:** wet and muddy, as if from being dragged around.

Ⓐ | Read and Discuss | What has the author told you about Rikki-tikki so far?

Ⓑ | Reading Focus | Summarizing What has happened between Rikki-tikki and the family?

out," and Rikki-tikki was a true mongoose. He looked at the cotton wool, decided that it was not good to eat, ran all round the table, sat up and put his fur in order, scratched himself, and jumped on the small boy's shoulder.

"Don't be frightened, Teddy," said his father. "That's his way of making friends."

"Ouch! He's tickling under my chin," said Teddy.

Rikki-tikki looked down between the boy's collar and neck, snuffed at his ear, and climbed down to the floor, where he sat rubbing his nose.

"Good gracious," said Teddy's mother, "and that's a wild creature! I suppose he's so tame because we've been kind to him."

"All mongooses are like that," said her husband. "If Teddy doesn't pick him up by the tail or try to put him in a cage, he'll run in and out of the house all day long. Let's give him something to eat."

They gave him a little piece of raw meat. Rikki-tikki liked it immensely, and when it was finished, he went out into the veranda[4] and sat in the sunshine and fluffed up his fur to make it dry to the roots. Then he felt better.

"There are more things to find out about in this house," he said to himself, "than all my family could find out in all their lives. I shall certainly stay and find out." **C**

He spent all that day roaming over the house. He nearly drowned himself in the bathtubs, put his nose into the ink on a writing table, and burnt it on the end of the big man's cigar, for he climbed up in the big man's lap to see how writing was done. At nightfall he ran into Teddy's nursery to watch how kerosene lamps were lighted, and when Teddy went to bed, Rikki-tikki climbed up too; but he was a restless companion, because he had to get up and attend to every noise all through the night and find out what made it. Teddy's mother and father came in, the last thing, to look at their boy, and Rikki-tikki was awake on the pillow. "I don't like that," said Teddy's mother; "he may bite the child." "He'll do no such thing," said the father. "Teddy's safer with that little beast than if he had a bloodhound to watch him. If a snake came into the nursery now—"

But Teddy's mother wouldn't think of anything so awful.

Early in the morning, Rikki-tikki came to early breakfast in the veranda riding on Teddy's shoulder, and they gave him banana and some boiled egg; and he sat on all their laps one after the other, because every well-brought-up mongoose always hopes to be a house mongoose someday and have rooms to run about in; and Rikki-tikki's mother

> "If a snake came into the nursery now—"

---

4. **veranda** (vuh RAN duh): open porch that is covered by a roof and runs along the outside of a building.

C [Read and Discuss] How are things looking for Rikki-tikki? What does he think of his new family?

Vocabulary **immensely** (ih MEHNS lee) *adv.:* enormously.

Viewing and Interpreting How does the house in this picture compare to the house you visualize when reading the story?

(she used to live in the General's house at Segowlee) had carefully told Rikki what to do if ever he came across white men. **D**

Then Rikki-tikki went out into the garden to see what was to be seen. It was a large garden, only half cultivated, with bushes, as big as summerhouses, of Marshal Niel roses; lime and orange trees; clumps of bamboos; and thickets of high grass. Rikki-tikki licked his lips. "This is a splendid hunting ground," he said, and his tail grew bottlebrushy at the thought of it, and he scuttled up and down the garden, snuffing here and there till he heard very sorrowful voices in a thorn bush. It was Darzee, the tailorbird, and his wife. They had made a beautiful nest by pulling two big leaves together and stitching them up the edges with fibers and had filled the hollow with cotton and downy fluff. The nest swayed to and fro as they sat on the rim and cried.

"What is the matter?" asked Rikki-tikki.

"We are very miserable," said Darzee. "One of our babies fell out of the nest yesterday and Nag ate him."

"H'm!" said Rikki-tikki, "that is very sad —but I am a stranger here. Who is Nag?"

Darzee and his wife only cowered down in the nest without answering, for from the thick grass at the foot of the bush there came a low hiss—a horrid, cold sound that made Rikki-tikki jump back two clear feet. Then inch by inch out of the grass rose up the head and spread hood of Nag, the big black cobra, and he was five feet long from tongue to tail. When he had lifted one third

D **Read and Discuss** What have you learned about the relationship between Rikki-tikki and his new family?

Vocabulary **cowered** (KOW uhrd) v.: crouched and trembled in fear.

of himself clear of the ground, he stayed balancing to and fro exactly as a dandelion tuft balances in the wind, and he looked at Rikki-tikki with the wicked snake's eyes that never change their expression, whatever the snake may be thinking of.

"Who is Nag," said he. "*I* am Nag. The great God Brahm[5] put his mark upon all our people, when the first cobra spread his hood to keep the sun off Brahm as he slept. Look, and be afraid!"

He spread out his hood more than ever, and Rikki-tikki saw the spectacle mark on the back of it that looks exactly like the eye part of a hook-and-eye fastening. He was afraid for the minute; but it is impossible for a mongoose to stay frightened for any length of time, and though Rikki-tikki had never met a live cobra before, his mother had fed him on dead ones, and he knew that all a grown mongoose's business in life was to fight and eat snakes. Nag knew that too, and at the bottom of his cold heart, he was afraid. **E**

"Well," said Rikki-tikki, and his tail began to fluff up again, "marks or no marks, do you think it is right for you to eat fledglings out of a nest?"

Nag was thinking to himself and watching the least little movement in the grass behind Rikki-tikki. He knew that mongooses in the garden meant death sooner or later for him and his family, but he wanted to get Rikki-tikki off his guard. So he dropped his head a little and put it on one side.

---

5. **Brahm** (brahm): in the Hindu religion, the creator.

"Let us talk," he said. "You eat eggs. Why should not I eat birds?"

"Behind you! Look behind you!" sang Darzee.

Rikki-tikki knew better than to waste time in staring. He jumped up in the air as high as he could go, and just under him whizzed by the head of Nagaina, Nag's wicked wife. She had crept up behind him as he was talking, to make an end of him; and he heard her savage hiss as the stroke missed. He came down almost across her back, and if he had been an old mongoose, he would have known that then was the time to break her back with one bite; but he was afraid of the terrible lashing return stroke of the cobra. He bit, indeed, but did not bite long enough, and he jumped clear of the whisking tail, leaving Nagaina torn and angry. **F**

"Wicked, wicked Darzee!" said Nag, lashing up as high as he could reach toward the nest in the thorn bush; but Darzee had built it out of reach of snakes, and it only swayed to and fro.

Rikki-tikki felt his eyes growing red and hot (when a mongoose's eyes grow red, he is angry), and he sat back on his tail and hind legs like a little kangaroo, and looked all round him, and chattered with rage. But Nag and Nagaina had disappeared into the grass.

When a snake misses its stroke, it never says anything or gives any sign of what it means to do next. Rikki-tikki did not care to follow them, for he did not feel sure that

---

E **Literary Focus** Conflict What situation has been set up between Rikki-tikki and Nag?

F **Reading Focus** Summarizing What has happened in this paragraph?

he could manage two snakes at once. So he trotted off to the gravel path near the house and sat down to think. It was a serious matter for him. If you read the old books of natural history, you will find they say that when the mongoose fights the snake and happens to get bitten, he runs off and eats some herb that cures him. That is not true. The victory is only a matter of quickness of eye and quickness of foot—snake's blow against the mongoose's jump—and as no eye can follow the motion of a snake's head when it strikes, this makes things much more wonderful than any magic herb. Rikki-tikki knew he was a young mongoose, and it made him all the more pleased to think that he had managed to escape a blow from behind. It gave him confidence in himself, and when Teddy came running down the path, Rikki-tikki was ready to be petted. But just as Teddy was stooping, something wriggled a little in the dust and a tiny voice said: "Be careful. I am Death!" It was Karait, the dusty brown snakeling that lies for choice on the dusty earth; and his bite is as dangerous as the cobra's. But he is

The Unusual and Deadly Cobra

Snakes are believed to have been on earth for 95 million years. There are now about 2,700 species, or populations of similar organisms that breed only among themselves, of snakes. The cobra, native to South Asia, Australia, and Africa, is one of these species. A king cobra, the longest of the poisonous snakes, can grow to some eighteen feet in length.

A cobra comes equipped with loose folds of skin on its neck that expand into that famous hood. A cobra spreads its hood by spreading its neck ribs, much as you would open an umbrella. The cobra then looks bigger and more frightening. Even if its hood is not spread, a cobra is *always* dangerous.

Unlike your jaw, which opens and closes by means of a set of interlocking bones, a cobra's jawbones can disconnect. The top jaw can open almost flat against the cobra's forehead, while the bottom jaw drops almost straight down, so a cobra can spread its jaws like a pair of entry doors. For this reason, a cobra can swallow prey, or animal killed for food, that is larger than the snake's head.

Ask Yourself

What images in the text above help you visualize the way a cobra's neck and jaw work?

so small that nobody thinks of him, and so he does the more harm to people. **G**

Rikki-tikki's eyes grew red again, and he danced up to Karait with the peculiar rocking, swaying motion that he had inherited from his family. It looks very funny, but it is so perfectly balanced a gait[6] that you can fly off from it at any angle you please; and in dealing with snakes this is an advantage. If Rikki-tikki had only known, he was doing a much more dangerous thing than fighting Nag, for Karait is so small and can turn so quickly that unless Rikki bit him close to the back of the head, he would get the return stroke in his eye or his lip. But Rikki did not know; his eyes were all red, and he rocked back and forth, looking for a good place to hold. Karait struck out, Rikki jumped sideways and tried to run in, but the wicked little dusty gray head lashed within a fraction of his shoulder, and he had to jump over the body, and the head followed his heels close.

Teddy shouted to the house: "Oh, look here! Our mongoose is killing a snake," and Rikki-tikki heard a scream from Teddy's mother. His father ran out with a stick, but by the time he came up, Karait had lunged out once too far, and Rikki-tikki had sprung, jumped on the snake's back, dropped his head far between his forelegs, bitten as high up the back as he could get hold, and rolled away. That bite paralyzed Karait, and Rikki-tikki was just going to eat him up from the tail, after the custom of his family at dinner, when he remembered that a full meal makes a slow mongoose, and if he wanted all his strength and quickness ready, he must keep himself thin. He went away for a dust bath under the castor-oil bushes, while Teddy's father beat the dead Karait. "What is the use of that?" thought Rikki-tikki; "I have settled it all"; and then Teddy's mother picked him up from the dust and hugged him, crying that he had saved Teddy from death, and Teddy's father said that he was a providence,[7] and Teddy looked on with big, scared eyes. Rikki-tikki was rather amused at all the fuss, which, of course, he did not understand. Teddy's mother might just as well have petted Teddy for playing in the dust. Rikki was thoroughly enjoying himself. **H**

That night at dinner, walking to and fro among the wineglasses on the table,

He remembered that a full meal makes a slow mongoose, and if he wanted all his strength and quickness ready, he must keep himself thin.

---

6. **gait** (gayt): way someone walks or runs.

7. **providence** (PRAHV uh duhns): favor or gift from God or nature.

G **Read and Discuss** What does Rikki-tikki learn from his encounter with Nagaina?

H **Reading Focus** **Summarizing** What happens between Rikki-tikki and Karait?

he might have stuffed himself three times over with nice things; but he remembered Nag and Nagaina, and though it was very pleasant to be patted and petted by Teddy's mother and to sit on Teddy's shoulder, his eyes would get red from time to time, and he would go off into his long war cry of *Rikk-tikk-tikki-tikki-tchk!*

Teddy carried him off to bed and insisted on Rikki-tikki's sleeping under his chin. Rikki-tikki was too well bred to bite or scratch, but as soon as Teddy was asleep, he went off for his nightly walk round the house, and in the dark he ran up against Chuchundra, the muskrat, creeping round by the wall. Chuchundra is a brokenhearted little beast. He whimpers and cheeps all night, trying to make up his mind to run into the middle of the room; but he never gets there.

"Don't kill me," said Chuchundra, almost weeping. "Rikki-tikki, don't kill me!"

"Do you think a snake killer kills muskrats?" said Rikki-tikki scornfully.

"Those who kill snakes get killed by snakes," said Chuchundra, more sorrowfully than ever. "And how am I to be sure that Nag won't mistake me for you some dark night?"

"There's not the least danger," said Rikki-tikki, "but Nag is in the garden, and I know you don't go there."

"My cousin Chua, the rat, told me—" said Chuchundra, and then he stopped.

"Told you what?"

"H'sh! Nag is everywhere, Rikki-tikki. You should have talked to Chua in the garden."

"I didn't—so you must tell me. Quick, Chuchundra, or I'll bite you!"

Chuchundra sat down and cried till the tears rolled off his whiskers. "I am a very poor man," he sobbed. "I never had spirit enough to run out into the middle of the room. H'sh! I mustn't tell you anything. Can't you *hear*, Rikki-tikki?"

Rikki-tikki listened. The house was as still as still, but he thought he could just catch the faintest *scratch-scratch* in the world—a noise as faint as that of a wasp walking on a windowpane—the dry scratch of a snake's scales on brickwork.

"That's Nag or Nagaina," he said to himself, "and he is crawling into the bathroom sluice.[8] You're right, Chuchundra; I should have talked to Chua." ❶

He stole off to Teddy's bathroom, but there was nothing there, and then to Teddy's mother's bathroom. At the bottom of the smooth plaster wall there was a brick pulled out to make a sluice for the bathwater, and as Rikki-tikki stole in by the masonry[9] curb where the bath is put, he heard Nag and Nagaina whispering together outside in the moonlight.

"When the house is emptied of people," said Nagaina to her husband, "*he* will have

---

8. **sluice** (sloos): drain.
9. **masonry**: built of stone or brick.

❶ **Reading Focus** Summarizing What has Rikki-tikki just learned?

to go away, and then the garden will be our own again. Go in quietly, and remember that the big man who killed Karait is the first one to bite. Then come out and tell me, and we will hunt for Rikki-tikki together." **J**

"But are you sure that there is anything to be gained by killing the people?" said Nag.

"Everything. When there were no people in the bungalow, did we have any mongoose in the garden? So long as the bungalow is empty, we are king and queen of the garden; and remember that as soon as our eggs in the melon bed hatch (as they may tomorrow), our children will need room and quiet."

"I had not thought of that," said Nag. "I will go, but there is no need that we should hunt for Rikki-tikki afterward. I will kill the big man and his wife, and the child if I can, and come away quietly. Then the bungalow will be empty, and Rikki-tikki will go."

Rikki-tikki tingled all over with rage and hatred at this, and then Nag's head came through the sluice, and his five feet of cold body followed it. Angry as he was, Rikki-tikki was very frightened as he saw the size of the big cobra. Nag coiled himself up, raised his head, and looked into the bathroom in the dark, and Rikki could see his eyes glitter.

"Now, if I kill him here, Nagaina will know; and if I fight him on the open floor,

the odds are in his favor. What am I to do?" said Rikki-tikki-tavi.

Nag waved to and fro, and then Rikki-tikki heard him drinking from the biggest water jar that was used to fill the bath. "That is good," said the snake. "Now, when Karait was killed, the big man had a stick. He may have that stick still, but when he comes in to bathe in the morning, he will not have a stick. I shall wait here till he comes. Nagaina—do you hear me?—I shall wait here in the cool till daytime." **K**

There was no answer from outside, so Rikki-tikki knew Nagaina had gone away. Nag coiled himself down, coil by coil, round the bulge at the bottom of the water jar, and Rikki-tikki stayed still as death. After an hour he began to move, muscle by muscle, toward the jar. Nag was asleep, and Rikki-tikki looked at his big back, wondering which would be the best place for a good hold. "If I don't break his back at the first jump," said Rikki, "he can still fight; and if he fights—O Rikki!" He looked at the thickness of the neck below the hood, but that was too much for him; and a bite near the tail would only make Nag savage.

"It must be the head," he said at last, "the head above the hood; and when I am once there, I must not let go." **L**

Then he jumped. The head was lying a little clear of the water jar, under the curve of it; and as his teeth met, Rikki braced his back against the bulge of the

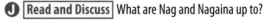

J [Read and Discuss] What are Nag and Nagaina up to?

K [Reading Focus] Summarizing What is Nag's plan?

L [Reading Focus] Summarizing What is Rikki-tikki's plan?

red earthenware to hold down the head. This gave him just one second's purchase,[10] and he made the most of it. Then he was battered to and fro as a rat is shaken by a dog—to and fro on the floor, up and down, and round in great circles, but his eyes were red and he held on as the body cartwhipped over the floor, upsetting the tin dipper and the soap dish and the flesh brush, and banged against the tin side of the bath. As he held, he closed his jaws tighter and tighter, for he made sure[11] he would be banged to death, and for the honor of his family, he preferred to be found with his teeth locked. He was dizzy, aching, and felt shaken to pieces, when something went off like a thunderclap just behind him; a hot wind knocked him senseless and red fire singed his fur. The big man had been wakened by the noise and had fired both barrels of a shotgun into Nag just behind the hood. **M**

Rikki-tikki held on with his eyes shut, for now he was quite sure he was dead; but the head did not move, and the big man picked him up and said: "It's the mongoose again, Alice; the little chap has saved *our* lives now." Then Teddy's mother came in with a very white face and saw what was left of Nag, and Rikki-tikki dragged himself to Teddy's bedroom and spent half the rest of the night shaking himself tenderly to find out whether he really was broken into forty pieces, as he fancied.

When morning came, he was very stiff but well pleased with his doings. "Now

---

10. **purchase:** firm hold.
11. **made sure:** here, felt sure.

I have Nagaina to settle with, and she will be worse than five Nags, and there's no knowing when the eggs she spoke of will hatch. Goodness! I must go and see Darzee," he said.

Without waiting for breakfast, Rikki-tikki ran to the thorn bush, where Darzee was singing a song of triumph at the top of his voice. The news of Nag's death was all over the garden, for the sweeper had thrown the body on the rubbish heap.

"Oh, you stupid tuft of feathers!" said Rikki-tikki angrily. "Is this the time to sing?"

"Nag is dead—is dead—is dead!" sang Darzee. "The valiant Rikki-tikki caught him by the head and held fast. The big man brought the bang-stick, and Nag fell in two pieces! He will never eat my babies again."

"All that's true enough, but where's Nagaina?" said Rikki-tikki, looking carefully round him.

"Nagaina came to the bathroom sluice and called for Nag," Darzee went on, "and Nag came out on the end of a stick—the sweeper picked him up on the end of a stick and threw him upon the rubbish heap. Let us sing about the great, the red-eyed Rikki-tikki!" and Darzee filled his throat and sang.

"If I could get up to your nest, I'd roll your babies out!" said Rikki-tikki. "You don't know when to do the right thing at the right time. You're safe enough in your nest there, but it's war for me down here. Stop singing a minute, Darzee."

"For the great, beautiful Rikki-tikki's sake I will stop," said Darzee. "What is it,

---

M **Literary Focus** Conflict What is happening between Rikki-tikki and Nag? Why is it <u>significant</u>?

Vocabulary **valiant** (VAL yuhnt) *adj.*: brave and determined.

O Killer of the terrible Nag?"

"Where is Nagaina, for the third time?"

"On the rubbish heap by the stables, mourning for Nag. Great is Rikki-tikki with the white teeth."

"Bother[12] my white teeth! Have you ever heard where she keeps her eggs?"

"In the melon bed, on the end nearest the wall, where the sun strikes nearly all day. She hid them there weeks ago."

"And you never thought it worthwhile to tell me? The end nearest the wall, you said?"

"Rikki-tikki, you are not going to eat her eggs?"

"Not eat exactly; no. Darzee, if you have a grain of sense, you will fly off to the stables and pretend that your wing is broken and let Nagaina chase you away to this bush. I must get to the melon bed, and if I went there now, she'd see me." **N**

Darzee was a featherbrained little fellow who could never hold more than one idea at a time in his head, and just

---

12. **bother:** here, never mind.

because he knew that Nagaina's children were born in eggs like his own, he didn't think at first that it was fair to kill them. But his wife was a sensible bird, and she knew that cobra's eggs meant young cobras later on; so she flew off from the nest and left Darzee to keep the babies warm and continue his song about the death of Nag. Darzee was very like a man in some ways.

She fluttered in front of Nagaina by the rubbish heap and cried out, "Oh, my wing is broken! The boy in the house threw a stone at me and broke it." Then she fluttered more desperately than ever. **O**

Nagaina lifted up her head and hissed, "You warned Rikki-tikki when I would have killed him. Indeed and truly, you've chosen a bad place to be lame in." And she moved toward Darzee's wife, slipping along over the dust.

"The boy broke it with a stone!" shrieked Darzee's wife.

"Well! It may be some consolation to you when you're dead to know that I shall settle accounts with the boy. My husband lies on the rubbish heap this morning, but before night the boy in the house will lie very still. What is the use of running away? I am sure to catch you. Little fool, look at me!"

Darzee's wife knew better than to do *that*, for a bird who looks at a snake's eyes gets so frightened that she cannot move. Darzee's wife fluttered on, piping

---

N Read and Discuss | Why does Rikki-tikki want Darzee to pretend his wing is broken?

O Read and Discuss | Darzee is supposed to have the broken wing. Why is his wife pretending to have one?

Vocabulary **consolation** (KAHN suh LAY shuhn) *n.*: comfort.

sorrowfully and never leaving the ground, and Nagaina quickened her pace.

Rikki-tikki heard them going up the path from the stables, and he raced for the end of the melon patch near the wall. There, in the warm litter above the melons, very cunningly hidden, he found twenty-five eggs about the size of a bantam's[13] eggs but with whitish skins instead of shells.

"I was not a day too soon," he said, for he could see the baby cobras curled up inside the skin, and he knew that the minute they were hatched, they could each kill a man or a mongoose. He bit off the tops of the eggs as fast as he could, taking care to crush the young cobras, and turned over the litter from time to time to see whether he had missed any. At last there were only three eggs left, and Rikki-tikki began to chuckle to himself, when he heard Darzee's wife screaming:

"Rikki-tikki, I led Nagaina toward the house, and she has gone into the veranda, and—oh, come quickly—she means killing!"

Rikki-tikki smashed two eggs, and tumbled backward down the melon bed with the third egg in his mouth, and scuttled to the veranda as hard as he could put foot to the

"Rikki-tikki, I led Nagaina toward the house, and she has gone into the veranda, and —oh, come quickly— she means killing!"

ground. Teddy and his mother and father were there at early breakfast, but Rikki-tikki saw that they were not eating anything. They sat stone still, and their faces were white. Nagaina was coiled up on the matting by Teddy's chair, within easy striking distance of Teddy's bare leg, and she was swaying to and fro, singing a song of triumph.

"Son of the big man that killed Nag," she hissed, "stay still. I am not ready yet. Wait a little. Keep very still, all you three! If you move, I strike, and if you do not move, I strike. Oh, foolish people, who killed my Nag!"

Teddy's eyes were fixed on his father, and all his father could do was to whisper, "Sit still, Teddy. You mustn't move. Teddy, keep still."

Then Rikki-tikki came up and cried: "Turn round, Nagaina; turn and fight!"

"All in good time," said she, without moving her eyes. "I will settle my account with *you* presently. Look at your friends, Rikki-tikki. They are still and white. They are afraid. They dare not move, and if you come a step nearer, I strike."

"Look at your eggs," said Rikki-tikki, "in the melon bed near the wall. Go and look, Nagaina!"

The big snake turned half round and saw the egg on the veranda. "Ah-h! Give it to me," she said.

---

13. **bantam's:** small chicken's.

P [Read and Discuss] How are things looking for the family? What is Rikki-tikki up to?

Rikki-tikki put his paws one on each side of the egg, and his eyes were blood-red. "What price for a snake's egg? For a young cobra? For a young king cobra? For the last—the very last of the brood? The ants are eating all the others down by the melon bed."

Nagaina spun clear round, forgetting everything for the sake of the one egg; and Rikki-tikki saw Teddy's father shoot out a big hand, catch Teddy by the shoulder, and drag him across the little table with the teacups, safe and out of reach of Nagaina.

"Tricked! Tricked! Tricked! *Rikk-tck-tck!*" chuckled Rikki-tikki. "The boy is safe, and it was I—I—I—that caught Nag by the hood last night in the bathroom." Then he began to jump up and down, all four feet together, his head close to the floor. "He threw me to and fro, but he could not shake me off. He was dead before the big man blew him in two. I did it! *Rikki-tikki-tck-tck!* Come then, Nagaina. Come and fight with me. You shall not be a widow long." **Q**

Nagaina saw that she had lost her chance of killing Teddy, and the egg lay between Rikki-tikki's paws. "Give me the egg, Rikki-tikki. Give me the last of my eggs, and I will go away and never come back," she said, lowering her hood. **R**

"Yes, you will go away, and you will never come back; for you will go to the rubbish heap with Nag. Fight, widow! The big man has gone for his gun! Fight!"

Rikki-tikki was bounding all round Nagaina, keeping just out of reach of her stroke, his little eyes like hot coals. Nagaina gathered herself together and flung out at him. Rikki-tikki jumped up and backwards. Again and again and again she struck, and each time her head came with a whack on the matting of the veranda and she gathered herself together like a watch spring. Then Rikki-tikki danced in a circle to get behind her, and Nagaina spun round to keep her head to his head, so that the rustle of her tail on the matting sounded like dry leaves blown along by the wind.

> "Come then, Nagaina. Come and fight with me. You shall not be a widow long."

He had forgotten the egg. It still lay on the veranda, and Nagaina came nearer and nearer to it, till at last, while Rikki-tikki was drawing breath, she caught it in her mouth, turned to the veranda steps, and flew like an arrow down the path, with Rikki-tikki behind her. When the cobra runs for her life, she goes like a whiplash flicked across a horse's neck. Rikki-tikki knew that he must catch her or all the trouble would begin again. She headed straight for the long grass by the thorn bush, and as he was running, Rikki-tikki heard Darzee still singing his foolish little song of triumph. But Darzee's wife was wiser. She flew off her nest as Nagaina came along and flapped

---

Q **Literary Focus** Conflict What is going on between Nagaina and Rikki-tikki?

R **Read and Discuss** What do you learn about Nagaina here?

her wings about Nagaina's head. If Darzee had helped, they might have turned her, but Nagaina only lowered her hood and went on. Still, the instant's delay brought Rikki-tikki up to her, and as she plunged into the rat hole where she and Nag used to live, his little white teeth were clenched on her tail and he went down with her—and very few mongooses, however wise and old they may be, care to follow a cobra into its hole. It was dark in the hole, and Rikki-tikki never knew when it might open out and give Nagaina room to turn and strike at him. He held on savagely and stuck out his feet to act as brakes on the dark slope of the hot, moist earth. Then the grass by the mouth of the hole stopped waving, and Darzee said: "It is all over with Rikki-tikki! We must sing his death song. Valiant Rikki-tikki is dead! For Nagaina will surely kill him underground."

So he sang a very mournful song that he made up on the spur of the minute, and just as he got to the most touching part, the grass quivered again, and Rikki-tikki, covered with dirt, dragged himself out of the hole leg by leg, licking his whiskers. Darzee stopped with a little shout. Rikki-tikki shook some of the dust out of his fur and sneezed. "It is all over," he said. "The widow will never come out again." And the red ants that live between the grass stems heard him and began to troop down one after another to see if he had spoken the truth. **⑤**

Rikki-tikki curled himself up in the grass and slept where he was—slept and slept till it was late in the afternoon, for he had done a hard day's work.

"Now," he said, when he awoke, "I will go back to the house. Tell the Coppersmith, Darzee, and he will tell the garden that Nagaina is dead."

The Coppersmith is a bird who makes a noise exactly like the beating of a little hammer on a copper pot; and the reason he is

⑤ Literary Focus Conflict What happens when Rikki-tikki fights Nagaina?

always making it is because he is the town crier to every Indian garden and tells all the news to everybody who cares to listen. As Rikki-tikki went up the path, he heard his "attention" notes like a tiny dinner gong and then the steady "*Ding-dong-tock!* Nag is dead—*dong!* Nagaina is dead! *Ding-dong-tock!*" That set all the birds in the garden singing and the frogs croaking, for Nag and Nagaina used to eat frogs as well as little birds.

When Rikki got to the house, Teddy and Teddy's mother (she looked very white still, for she had been fainting) and Teddy's father came out and almost cried over him; and that night he ate all that was given him till he could eat no more and went to bed on Teddy's shoulder, where Teddy's mother saw him when she came to look late at night.

"He saved our lives and Teddy's life," she said to her husband. "Just think, he saved all our lives." **T**

Rikki-tikki woke up with a jump, for the mongooses are light sleepers.

"Oh, it's you," said he. "What are you bothering for? All the cobras are dead; and if they weren't, I'm here."

Rikki-tikki had a right to be proud of himself, but he did not grow too proud, and he kept that garden as a mongoose should keep it, with tooth and jump and spring and bite, till never a cobra dared show its head inside the walls.

T Read and Discuss What does the family think of Rikki-tikki now?

U Read and Discuss What is the purpose of Darzee's chant?

Darzee's Chant

Sung in honor of Rikki-tikki-tavi

Singer and tailor am I—
    Doubled the joys that I know—
Proud of my lilt[14] to the sky,
    Proud of the house that I sew.
Over and under, so weave I my music—
    so weave I the house that I sew.

Sing to your fledglings[15] again,
    Mother, O lift up your head!
Evil that plagued us is slain,
    Death in the garden lies dead.
Terror that hid in the roses is impotent
    —flung on the dunghill and dead!

Who has delivered us, who?
    Tell me his nest and his name.
Rikki, the valiant, the true,
    Tikki, with eyeballs of flame—
Rikk-tikki-tikki, the ivory-fanged, the
    hunter with eyeballs of flame!

Give him the Thanks of the Birds,
    Bowing with tail-feathers spread,
Praise him with nightingale words
    Nay, I will praise him instead.
Hear! I will sing you the praise of the
    bottle-tailed Rikki with eyeballs of red!

(*Here Rikki-tikki interrupted, so the rest of the song is lost.*) **U**

---

14. **lilt:** song.
15. **fledglings** (FLEHJ lihngz): baby birds.

Applying Your Skills

Rikki-tikki-tavi

Respond and Think Critically

Reading Focus

Quick Check

1. What does Rikki-tikki do to protect himself and his family?
2. Rikki-tikki fights alone, but he gets a little help from his friends. How do they help him?

Read with a Purpose

3. Does Rikki-tikki handle each threat with cunning or with force?

Reading Skills: Summarizing

4. Review your story map. Does it include the most <u>significant</u> characters and events? A summary should include only the most important points. Revise your story map so that it includes only main events.

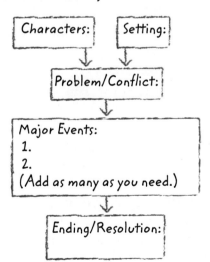

```
┌─────────────┐   ┌──────────┐
│ Characters: │   │ Setting: │
└─────────────┘   └──────────┘
       │                │
       ▼                ▼
   ┌──────────────────────┐
   │ Problem/Conflict:    │
   └──────────────────────┘
              │
              ▼
   ┌────────────────────────────┐
   │ Major Events:              │
   │ 1.                         │
   │ 2.                         │
   │ (Add as many as you need.) │
   └────────────────────────────┘
              │
              ▼
   ┌────────────────────────┐
   │ Ending/Resolution:     │
   └────────────────────────┘
```

Literary Focus

Literary Analysis

5. **Analyze** How do the family members' views of Rikki-tikki change throughout the story?
6. **Evaluate** Like all great heroes, Rikki-tikki is celebrated by the society he saves. How does Darzee's chant make Rikki-tikki into a super-hero? How does Darzee's role in the story and his chant represent the idea of comic relief?
7. **Analyze** The animal world of "Rikki-tikki-tavi" is filled with conflict and danger. What causes the war in this animal story? What causes most wars among people?

Literary Skills: Conflict

8. **Analyze** Describe three **conflicts** that Rikki-tikki faces. Which conflict do you think is his greatest challenge? Why? How is it resolved?

Writing Focus

Think as a Reader/Writer

Use It in Your Writing Look at the first descriptions of Nag and Nagaina. Find words on those pages that make the snakes seem evil. Is Kipling being unfair, or are the snakes just doing what snakes do naturally? Discuss your evaluation of the way Kipling handles his snake characters.

What Do **You Think Now** Did Rikki-tikki's conflicts remind you of your own experiences? Think back to what you said before you read the story.

Rikki-tikki-tavi

Vocabulary Development
Clarifying Word Meanings: Contrast

Sometimes you can clarify the meaning of an unfamiliar word by looking for **contrast** clues. A writer who uses contrast will show how a word is unlike another word. For example, you can get a pretty clear idea of what a splendid garden is if you see it contrasted with a dark, narrow hole in the ground.

"The *splendid* garden glowed with roses and great clumps of waving grasses, unlike the *dreary* hole where cobras live."

Be on the lookout for these words and phrases, which signal contrast: *although, but, yet, still, unlike, not, in contrast, instead,* and *however.*

Your Turn

Fill in the blanks in the following sentences with words or phrases that contrast with the boldface word. You may find it helpful to make a cluster diagram of the word and its opposites before you write, like the one below for *cowered* and *cowering.*

immensely
cowered
valiant
consolation

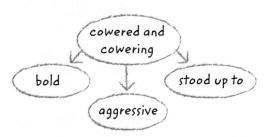

1. The cobras were **immensely** powerful, while the power of Darzee and the other garden creatures was _____.

2. Rikki-tikki was certainly **valiant,** but Chuchundra, the little muskrat, was _____.

3. Rikki-tikki's guarding the house provided **consolation** for the family, though they were _____ when the cobra threatened Teddy.

Language Coach

Word Roots Other words from the story also have Latin roots. Look at these words and their meanings. Then, match them with their roots.

curiosity
serious
valiant
terrible
immensely

Latin Word	Meaning
valere	be strong
immensus	cannot be measured
curiosus	interested, nosy
terribilus	frightening, awful
serius	solemn

Academic Vocabulary

Talk About . . .
Re-read your notes on the way Kipling describes the cobras. Then, with a partner, discuss whether you feel his descriptions are <u>accurate</u>. Consider why he puts <u>significant</u> effort into describing them this way. How does that add to the story?

Learn It Online
Explore the vocabulary words with Word Watch:

go.hrw.com | L7-158 | **Go**

Grammar Link

Strong, Vivid Verbs

This story moves at a fast pace, in part because Kipling uses strong, vivid verbs to help us see all the action in the cobra wars. Chuchundra doesn't walk—he *creeps*. Darzee and his wife don't sit—they *cower*. Rikki-tikki himself *roams, trots, scuttles,* and *dances*. Consider this sentence about a scene from the story:

> **Darzee, his eye on Nag, moved along the branch.**

How did Darzee move? Replace *moved* with *hopped, strolled,* and *stormed*. How does each verb change what you see? What does each verb tell you about Darzee's feelings and plans?

Your Turn

Rewrite the following sentences by replacing each tame verb with a more specific (and more interesting) verb.

1. That night, Nag went into the bungalow.
2. Rikki-tikki gave a warning.
3. Teddy's parents stood and looked at the cobra.

Writing Applications Be a verb spotter. Choose a piece of your own writing, and replace at least three verbs with ones that are sharper, more vivid, and more specific.

CHOICES

As you respond to the Choices, use these **Academic Vocabulary** words as appropriate: <u>accurate</u>, <u>adequate</u>, <u>similar</u>, <u>significant</u>.

REVIEW
Write a Plot Summary

Write a summary of "Rikki-tikki-tavi" by referring to your story map. Be sure to include the characters, setting, conflicts, <u>significant</u> events, and resolution.

CONNECT
Compare and Contrast Characters

Timed ᴸWriting In a three-paragraph essay, compare and contrast the characters Rikki-tikki and Nag. Organize the essay in the way that works best. You might want to compare their physical appearances in the first paragraph and their personalities in the second. Use the third paragraph to summarize your main points.

EXTEND
Create a Fact Sheet

Create an <u>accurate</u> fact sheet that will inform zoo visitors about cobras. Read "The Unusual and Deadly Cobra" on page 147, and conduct further research. Before you begin your research, decide on the questions you would like to answer. Here are some possibilities:

- How many kinds of cobras exist?
- Where do they live, and what do they eat?
- How dangerous are they?

Learn It Online
Research more elements of the story using these Internet links at:

go.hrw.com | L7-159 | **Go**

Three Skeleton Key

by **George G. Toudouze**

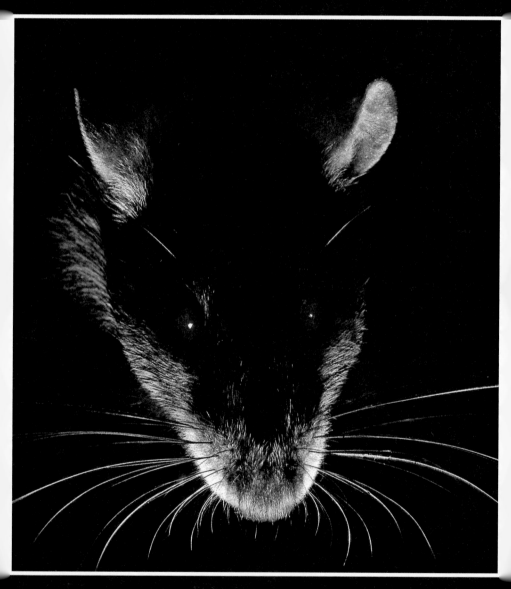

What Do You Think

People face danger in many settings. Think of some scary settings.

QuickWrite

If you were writing a horror story, what detai you use to create a scary setting? Freewrite

Reader/Writer Notebook

Use your **RWN** to complete the activities for this selection.

SKILLS FOCUS **Literary Skills** Understand suspense and foreshadowing. **Reading Skills** Make predictions from a text.

Literary Focus

Suspense and Foreshadowing "My most terrifying experience?" With this opening the writer of "Three Skeleton Key" hooks our interest. We immediately want to know about that terrifying experience. This feeling of anxious curiosity is called **suspense.**

Writers often add to the suspense in a story by dropping hints about what might happen later on. This use of clues for added impact is called **foreshadowing.**

TechFocus While you read, think about scenes in the story that would be effective on film.

Reading Focus

Making Predictions Part of the fun of following any story is guessing what will happen next, or **making predictions.**

Into Action Make predictions by looking for clues that foreshadow what will happen, guessing possible outcomes, and revising predictions as you read. Use the following Prediction Chart to record this process.

Page	Foreshadowing Clue	My Prediction
p. 163	"The story was that the three skeletons . . . danced over the small rock, screaming."	Something bad will happen at this lighthouse.
p. 164	"The waters about our island swarmed with huge sharks."	

Writing Focus

Think as a Reader/Writer

Find It in Your Reading As you read, make a list of words that describe the setting. Which words make the setting seem terrifying?

Vocabulary

treacherously (TREHCH uhr uhs lee) *adv.:* deceptively; unreliably. *The wet rocks were treacherously smooth.*

maneuver (muh NOO vuhr) *v.:* move or manipulate skillfully. *Sailing vessels can't maneuver as easily as steamers.*

hordes (hawrdz) *n.:* densely packed crowds that move as groups. *The rats swam ashore in hordes.*

receding (rih SEED ihng) *v.* used as *adj.:* moving back. *At first the ship came toward us, but then it drifted off in the receding waters.*

edible (EHD uh buhl) *adj.:* fit to be eaten. *The rats thought the men were edible.*

Language Coach

Word Origins The word *maneuver* comes from the Latin phrase *manu operare,* which means "to work by hand." Words that come from other languages often change their meaning over time. Read the definition of the word *maneuver* again. Brainstorm with a partner how you think the meanings of *maneuver* and *manu operare* are related. What do you think *maneuver* originally meant? Why do you think its meaning has changed or broadened over time?

Learn It Online

Hear a professional actor read this story. Visit the selection online at:

go.hrw.com L7-161 Go

George G. Toudouze
(1847–1904)

Man of Many Interests

George G. Toudouze was born in France and grew up to develop many literary interests—he was a playwright, an essayist, and an illustrator. He also had a great interest in the sea and worked on a history of the French navy. "Three Skeleton Key" was first published in *Esquire*, a magazine that was once famous for its macho adventure stories.

Great Storyteller

One critic says of Toudouze's storytelling style, "It has the impact of a powerful man at the fair who, for the fun of it, takes the hammer and at one blow sends the machine to the top, rings the bell, and walks off."

Think About the Writer How do you think George Toudouze's knowledge of the sea helped him in the writing of this story?

Build Background

The title of this story is the name of a key, or low-lying island, off the coast of French Guiana (gee AH nuh), in South America. At the time the story was written, French Guiana was a colony of France. Cayenne (ky EHN), the capital, was the site of one of the prisons that France maintained there until 1945. Lighthouses, such as the one in this story, are used to guide ships, to alert sailors that land is near, and to point out dangerous rocks and reefs.

Preview the Story

The **narrator** of the story gives a first-person account of his most terrifying experience. It happened when he was a lighthouse keeper, along with two other men, named **Itchoua** and **Le Gleo,** on a tiny island twenty miles from the mainland of South America.

Three Skeleton Key

by **George G. Toudouze**

My most terrifying experience? Well, one does have a few in thirty-five years of service in the Lights, although it's mostly monotonous, routine work—keeping the light in order, making out the reports.

When I was a young man, not very long in the service, there was an opening in a light-house newly built off the coast of Guiana, on a small rock twenty miles or so from the main-land. The pay was high, so in order to reach the sum I had set out to save before I married, I volunteered for service in the new light.

Three Skeleton Key, the small rock on which the light stood, bore a bad reputation. It earned its name from the story of the three convicts who, escaping from Cayenne in a stolen dugout canoe, were wrecked on the rock during the night, managed to escape the sea, but eventually died of hunger and thirst. When they were discovered, nothing remained but three heaps of bones, picked clean by the birds. The story was that the three skeletons, gleaming with phosphorescent[1] light, danced over the small rock, screaming. . . . **Ⓐ**

But there are many such stories and I did not give the warnings of the old-timers at the *Île-de-Seine* a second thought. I signed up, boarded ship, and in a month I was installed at the light.

Picture a gray, tapering cylinder, welded to the solid black rock by iron rods and con-crete, rising from a small island twenty-odd miles from land. It lay in the midst of the sea, this island, a small, bare piece of stone, about one hundred fifty feet long, perhaps forty wide. Small, barely large enough for a man to walk about and stretch his legs at low tide.

This is an advantage one doesn't find in all lights, however, for some of them rise sheer from the waves, with no room for one to move save within the light itself. Still, on our island, one must be careful, for the rocks were **treacherously** smooth.

---

1. **phosphorescent** (fahs fuh REHS uhnt): glowing.

Ⓐ Reading Focus Making Predictions Screaming and dancing skeletons—what kind of story do you predict this will be?

Vocabulary **treacherously** (TREHCH uhr uhs lee) *adv.*: deceptively; unreliably.

One misstep and down you would fall into the sea—not that the risk of drowning was so great, but the waters about our island swarmed with huge sharks, who kept an eternal patrol around the base of the light. **Ⓑ**

Still, it was a nice life there. We had enough provisions to last for months, in the event that the sea should become too rough for the supply ship to reach us on schedule. During the day we would work about the light, cleaning the rooms, polishing the metalwork and the lens and reflector of the light itself, and at night we would sit on the gallery and watch our light, a twenty-thousand-candlepower lantern, swinging its strong white bar of light over the sea from the top of its hundred-twenty-foot tower. Some days, when the air would be very clear, we could see the land, a threadlike line to the west. To the east, north, and south stretched the ocean. Landsmen, perhaps, would soon have tired of that kind of life, perched on a small island off the coast of South America for eighteen weeks until one's turn for leave ashore came around. But we liked it there, my two fellow tenders and myself—so much so that for twenty-two months on end, with the exception of shore leaves, I was greatly satisfied with the life on Three Skeleton Key.

I had just returned from my leave at the end of June, that is to say, midwinter in that latitude, and had settled down to the routine with my two fellow keepers, a Breton[2] by the name of Le Gleo and the head keeper, Itchoua, a Basque[3] some dozen years or so older than either of us. **Ⓒ**

Eight days went by as usual; then on the ninth night after my return, Itchoua, who was on night duty, called Le Gleo and me, sleeping in our rooms in the middle of the tower, at two in the morning. We rose immediately and, climbing the thirty or so steps that led to the gallery, stood beside our chief.

Itchoua pointed, and following his finger, we saw a big three-master, with all sail set, heading straight for the light. A queer course, for the vessel must have seen us; our light lit her with the glare of day each time it passed over her.

Now, ships were a rare sight in our waters, for our light was a warning of treacherous reefs, barely hidden under the surface and running far out to sea. Consequently we were always given a wide berth, especially by sailing vessels, which cannot **maneuver** as readily as steamers.

No wonder that we were surprised at seeing this three-master heading dead for us in the gloom of early morning. I had immediately recognized her lines, for she stood out plainly, even at the distance of a mile, when our light shone on her.

---

2. **Breton** (BREHT uhn): person from Brittany, a region of northern France.
3. **Basque** (bask): person from the Pyrenees, a mountain range in France and Spain.

Ⓑ **Literary Focus** Suspense How is this lighthouse setting significant in the story?

Ⓒ **Literary Focus** Foreshadowing First you read that three convicts died at Three Skeleton Key. What do you learn about the three lighthouse keepers? What is being set up for you?

Vocabulary **maneuver** (muh NOO vuhr) v.: move or manipulate skillfully.

Virginia Museum of Fine Arts, Richmond, Virginia. Collection of Mr. and Mrs. Paul Mellon. Photograph by Ron Jennings. © 2000 Virginia Museum of Fine Arts. © 2009 C. Herscovici, Brussels/Artists Rights Society (ARS), New York.

Analyzing Visuals **Viewing and Interpreting** In what ways does this image add to the story's suspense?

Le Seducteur (The Seductor)
by Rene Magritte (1898–1967)
Oil on canvas.

She was a beautiful ship of some four thousand tons, a fast sailer that had carried cargoes to every part of the world, plowing the seas unceasingly. By her lines she was identified as Dutch built, which was understandable, as Paramaribo and Dutch Guiana are very close to Cayenne.

Watching her sailing dead for us, a white wave boiling under her bows, Le Gleo cried out:

"What's wrong with her crew? Are they all drunk or insane? Can't they see us?" **D**

Itchoua nodded soberly and looked at us sharply as he remarked: "See us? No doubt—if there *is* a crew aboard!"

D [Read and Discuss] Why do the ship's movements cause Le Gleo to cry out?

"What do you mean, chief?" Le Gleo had started, turned to the Basque. "Are you saying that she's the *Flying Dutchman*?"[4] **E**

His sudden fright had been so evident that the older man laughed:

"No, old man, that's not what I meant. If I say that no one's aboard, I mean she's a derelict."[5]

Then we understood her queer behavior. Itchoua was right. For some reason, believing her doomed, her crew had abandoned her. Then she had righted herself and sailed on, wandering with the wind.

The three of us grew tense as the ship seemed about to crash on one of our numerous reefs, but she suddenly lurched with some change of the wind, the yards[6] swung around, and the derelict came clumsily about and sailed dead away from us.

In the light of our lantern she seemed so sound, so strong, that Itchoua exclaimed impatiently:

"But why the devil was she abandoned? Nothing is smashed, no sign of fire—and she doesn't sail as if she were taking water."

Le Gleo waved to the departing ship:

"Bon voyage!" he smiled at Itchoua and went on. "She's leaving us, chief, and now we'll never know what—"

"No, she's not!" cried the Basque. "Look! She's turning!"

---

4. *Flying Dutchman*: fabled Dutch ghost ship whose captain is said to be condemned to sail the seas until Judgment Day. Seeing the *Flying Dutchman* is supposed to bring bad luck.

5. **derelict** (DEHR uh lihkt): here, abandoned ship.

6. **yards:** in nautical terms, rods fastened across the masts to support the sails.

As if obeying his words, the derelict three-master stopped, came about, and headed for us once more. And for the next four hours the vessel played around us— zigzagging, coming about, stopping, then suddenly lurching forward. No doubt some freak of current and wind, of which our island was the center, kept her near us.

Then suddenly the tropic dawn broke, the sun rose, and it was day, and the ship was plainly visible as she sailed past us. Our light extinguished, we returned to the gallery with our glasses[7] and inspected her.

The three of us focused our glasses on her poop[8] and saw, standing out sharply, black letters on the white background of a life ring, the stenciled name *"Cornelius de Witt, Rotterdam."*

We had read her lines correctly: She was Dutch. Just then the wind rose and the *Cornelius de Witt* changed course, leaned to port, and headed straight for us once more. But this time she was so close that we knew she would not turn in time. **F**

"Thunder!" cried Le Gleo, his Breton soul aching at seeing a fine ship doomed to smash upon a reef, "she's going to pile up! She's gone!"

I shook my head:

"Yes, and a shame to see that beautiful ship wreck herself. And we're helpless."

There was nothing we could do but watch. A ship sailing with all sail spread, creaming the sea with her forefoot as she

---

7. **glasses:** here, binoculars.

8. **poop:** in nautical terms, the stern (back) deck of a ship.

E | Read and Discuss | What has happened?

F | Read and Discuss | What is happening to the ship now?

runs before the wind, is one of the most beautiful sights in the world—but this time I could feel the tears stinging in my eyes as I saw this fine ship headed for her doom.

All this time our glasses were riveted on her and we suddenly cried out together:

"The rats!" **G**

Now we knew why this ship, in perfect condition, was sailing without her crew aboard. They had been driven out by the rats. Not those poor specimens of rats you see ashore, barely reaching the length of one foot from their trembling noses to the tip of their skinny tails, wretched creatures that dodge and hide at the mere sound of a footfall.

No, these were ships' rats, huge, wise creatures, born on the sea, sailing all over the world on ships, transferring to other, larger ships as they multiply. There is as much difference between the rats of the land and these maritime rats as between a fishing smack[9] and an armored cruiser.

The rats of the sea are fierce, bold animals. Large, strong, and intelligent, clannish and seawise, able to put the best of mariners to shame with their knowledge of the sea, their uncanny ability to foretell the weather.

> No, these were ships' rats, huge, wise creatures, born on the sea, sailing all over the world on ships.

9. **smack:** here, small sailboat.

And they are brave, these rats, and vengeful. If you so much as harm one, his sharp cry will bring hordes of his fellows to swarm over you, tear you, and not cease until your flesh has been stripped from the bones.

The ones on this ship, the rats of Holland, are the worst, superior to other rats of the sea as their brethren are to the land rats. There is a well-known tale about these animals.

A Dutch captain, thinking to protect his cargo, brought aboard his ship not cats but two terriers, dogs trained in the hunting, fighting, and killing of vicious rats. By the time the ship, sailing from Rotterdam, had passed the Ostend light, the dogs were gone and never seen again. In twenty-four hours they had been overwhelmed, killed, and eaten by the rats. **H**

At times, when the cargo does not suffice, the rats attack the crew, either driving them from the ship or eating them alive. And studying the *Cornelius de Witt*, I turned sick, for her small boats were all in place. She had not been abandoned.

Over her bridge, on her deck, in the rigging, on every visible spot, the ship was a writhing mass—a starving army coming toward us aboard a vessel gone mad!

G **Reading Focus** Making Predictions What are the three men up to?

H **Literary Focus** Foreshadowing How does this anecdote, or brief story, about the dogs and the rats hint at what might happen next in the story?

Vocabulary hordes (hawrdz) *n.:* densely packed crowds that move as groups.

Our island was a small spot in that immense stretch of sea. The ship could have grazed us or passed to port or starboard with its ravening[10] cargo—but no, she came for us at full speed, as if she were leading the regatta at a race, and impaled herself on a sharp point of rock.

There was a dull shock as her bottom stove in, then a horrible crackling as the three masts went overboard at once, as if cut down with one blow of some gigantic sickle. A sighing groan came as the water rushed into the ship; then she split in two and sank like a stone.

But the rats did not drown. Not these fellows! As much at home in the sea as any fish, they formed ranks in the water, heads lifted, tails stretched out, paws paddling. And half of them, those from the forepart

10. **ravening** (RAV uh nihng): greedily searching for animals to kill for food. A more common related word is *ravenous* (RAV uh nuhs), meaning "mad with hunger."

of the ship, sprang along the masts and onto the rocks in the instant before she sank. Before we had time even to move, nothing remained of the three-master save some pieces of wreckage floating on the surface and an army of rats covering the rocks left bare by the receding tide.

Thousands of heads rose, felt the wind, and we were scented, seen! To them we were fresh meat, after possible weeks of starving. There came a scream, composed of innumerable screams, sharper than the howl of a saw attacking a bar of iron, and in the one motion, every rat leaped to attack the tower!

We barely had time to leap back, close the door leading onto the gallery, descend the stairs, and shut every window tightly. Luckily the door at the base of the light, which we never could have reached in time, was of bronze set in granite and was tightly closed.

The horrible band, in no measurable time, had swarmed up and over the tower as if it had been a tree, piled on the embrasures[11] of the windows, scraped at the glass with thousands of claws, covered the lighthouse with a furry mantle, and reached the top of the tower, filling the gallery and piling atop the lantern.

Their teeth grated as they pressed against the glass of the lantern room, where they could plainly see us, though they could

11. **embrasures** (ehm BRAY zhuhrz): slanted openings.

❶ **Read and Discuss** What does the narrator want you to understand?

Vocabulary **receding** (rih SEED ihng) *v.* used as *adj.*: moving back.

not reach us. A few millimeters of glass, luckily very strong, separated our faces from their gleaming, beady eyes, their sharp claws and teeth. Their odor filled the tower, poisoned our lungs, and rasped our nostrils with a pestilential, nauseating smell. And there we were, sealed alive in our own light, prisoners of a horde of starving rats.

That first night, the tension was so great that we could not sleep. Every moment, we felt that some opening had been made, some window given way, and that our horrible besiegers were pouring through the breach. The rising tide, chasing those of the rats which had stayed on the bare rocks, increased the numbers clinging to the walls, piled on the balcony—so much so that clusters of rats clinging to one another hung from the lantern and the gallery.

With the coming of darkness we lit the light and the turning beam completely maddened the beasts. As the light turned, it successively blinded thousands of rats crowded against the glass, while the dark side of the lantern room gleamed with thousands of points of light, burning like the eyes of jungle beasts in the night.

All the while we could hear the enraged scraping of claws against the stone and glass, while the chorus of cries was so loud that we had to shout to hear one another. From time to time, some of the rats fought among themselves and a dark cluster would detach itself, falling into the sea like a ripe fruit from a tree. Then we would see phosphorescent streaks as triangular fins slashed the water—sharks, permanent guardians of our rock, feasting on our jailers.

The next day we were calmer and amused ourselves teasing the rats, placing our faces against the glass which separated us. They could not fathom the invisible barrier which separated them from us, and we laughed as we watched them leaping against the heavy glass. **J**

But the day after that, we realized how serious our position was. The air was foul; even the heavy smell of oil within our stronghold could not dominate the fetid odor of the beasts massed around us. And there was no way of admitting fresh air without also admitting the rats.

The morning of the fourth day, at early dawn, I saw the wooden framework of my window, eaten away from the outside, sagging inwards. I called my comrades and the three of us fastened a sheet of tin in the opening, sealing it tightly. When we had completed that task, Itchoua turned to us and said dully:

"Well—the supply boat came thirteen days ago, and she won't be back for twenty-nine." He pointed at the white metal plate sealing the opening through the granite. "If that gives way"—he shrugged—"they can change the name of this place to Six Skeleton Key." **K**

The next six days and seven nights, our only distraction was watching the rats whose holds were insecure fall a hundred and twenty feet into the maws of the sharks—but they were so many that we could not see any diminution in their numbers.

J | Read and Discuss | How are things going for the men?

K Reading Focus Making Predictions Itchoua has made a prediction. Will it prove accurate? Why or why not?

Thinking to calm ourselves and pass the time, we attempted to count them, but we soon gave up. They moved incessantly, never still. Then we tried identifying them, naming them.

One of them, larger than the others, who seemed to lead them in their rushes against the glass separating us, we named "Nero";[12] and there were several others whom we had learned to distinguish through various peculiarities.

_____

12. **Nero** (NIHR oh): emperor of Rome (A.D. 54–68) known for his cruelty.

But the thought of our bones joining those of the convicts was always in the back of our minds. And the gloom of our prison fed these thoughts, for the interior of the light was almost completely dark, as we had had to seal every window in the same fashion as mine, and the only space that still admitted daylight was the glassed-in lantern room at the very top of the tower.

Then Le Gleo became morose and had nightmares in which he would see the three skeletons dancing around him, gleaming coldly, seeking to grasp him. His maniacal, raving descriptions were so vivid that Itchoua and I began seeing them also.

It was a living nightmare, the raging cries of the rats as they swarmed over the light, mad with hunger; the sickening, strangling odor of their bodies— **L**

True, there is a way of signaling from lighthouses. But to reach the mast on which to hang the signal, we would have to go out on the gallery where the rats were.

There was only one thing left to do. After debating all of the ninth day, we decided not to light the lantern that night. This is the greatest breach of our service, never committed as long as the tenders of the light are alive; for the light is something sacred, warning ships of danger in the night. Either the light gleams a quarter-hour after sundown, or no one is left alive to light it. **M**

Well, that night, Three Skeleton Light was dark, and all the men were alive. At the risk of causing ships to crash on our reefs, we left it unlit, for we were worn out—going mad!

L [Read and Discuss] Why does the narrator describe their situation as a "living nightmare"?

M [Reading Focus] Making Predictions Why do you think the men decide to leave the Three Skeleton Light dark?

At two in the morning, while Itchoua was dozing in his room, the sheet of metal sealing his window gave way. The chief had just time enough to leap to his feet and cry for help, the rats swarming over him.

But Le Gleo and I, who had been watching from the lantern room, got to him immediately, and the three of us battled with the horde of maddened rats which flowed through the gaping window. They bit, we struck them down with our knives—and retreated.

We locked the door of the room on them, but before we had time to bind our wounds, the door was eaten through and gave way, and we retreated up the stairs, fighting off the rats that leaped on us from the knee-deep swarm.

I do not remember, to this day, how we ever managed to escape. All I can remember is wading through them up the stairs, striking them off as they swarmed over us; and then we found ourselves, bleeding from innumerable bites, our clothes shredded, sprawled across the trapdoor in the floor of the lantern room—without food or drink. Luckily, the trapdoor was metal, set into the granite with iron bolts.

The rats occupied the entire light beneath us, and on the floor of our retreat lay some twenty of their fellows, who had gotten in with us before the trapdoor closed and whom we had killed with our knives. Below us, in the tower, we could hear the screams of the rats as they devoured everything edible that they found. Those on the outside squealed in reply and writhed in a

---

Vocabulary edible (EHD uh buhl) *adj.*: fit to be eaten.

Night Lights on the High Seas

For centuries, lighthouses have been used to alert sailors that land is near, to point out dangerous rocks and reefs, and to cast a bright light into the night to guide ships on their way. Seafarers have relied on these structures since the days of ancient Egypt. The lighthouse built in 300 B.C. on Pharos, an island near Alexandria, was regarded as one of the Seven Wonders of the World.

Lighthouses help guide ships at night by giving off an intense beam of light that flashes every few seconds. Until the eighteenth century the source of light was an oak-log fire. Then coal fires were used for many years, until electricity became common in the early twentieth century. Some modern lighthouses also send out radio signals to help ships find their way in foggy weather.

Even in their modern form, lighthouses still serve their ancient purpose as a guiding light, a flashing speck of civilization in the dark, lonely waters of the night.

Ask Yourself
How are the rats in the story endangering people other than the lighthouse keepers?

horrible curtain as they stared at us through the glass of the lantern room. **N**

Itchoua sat up and stared silently at his blood trickling from the wounds on his limbs and body and running in thin streams on the floor around him. Le Gleo, who was in as bad a state (and so was I, for that matter), stared at the chief and me vacantly, started as his gaze swung to the multitude of rats against the glass, then suddenly began laughing horribly:

"Hee! Hee! The Three Skeletons! Hee! Hee! The Three Skeletons are now *six* skeletons! *Six* skeletons!"

He threw his head back and howled, his eyes glazed, a trickle of saliva running from the corners of his mouth and thinning the blood flowing over his chest. I shouted to him to shut up, but he did not hear me, so I did the only thing I could to quiet him—I swung the back of my hand across his face.

The howling stopped suddenly, and his eyes swung around the room; then he bowed his head and began weeping softly, like a child.

Our darkened light had been noticed from the mainland, and as dawn was breaking, the patrol was there to investigate the failure of our light. Looking through my binoculars, I could see the horrified expression on the faces of the officers and crew when, the daylight strengthening, they saw the light completely covered by a seething mass of rats. They thought, as I afterwards found out, that we had been eaten alive.

But the rats had also seen the ship or had scented the crew. As the ship drew nearer, a solid phalanx[13] left the light, plunged into the water, and swimming out, attempted to board her. They would have succeeded, as the ship was hove to;[14] but the engineer connected his steam to a hose on the deck and scalded the head of the attacking column, which slowed them up long enough for the ship to get under way and leave the rats behind. **O**

Then the sharks took part. Belly up, mouths gaping, they arrived in swarms and scooped up the rats, sweeping through them like a sickle through wheat. That was one day that sharks really served a useful purpose.

The remaining rats turned tail, swam to the shore, and emerged dripping. As they neared the light, their comrades greeted them with shrill cries, with what sounded like a derisive note predominating. They answered angrily and mingled with their fellows. From the several tussles that broke out, it seemed as if they resented being ridiculed for their failure to capture the ship.

But all this did nothing to get us out of our jail. The small ship could not approach but steamed around the light at a safe distance, and the tower must have seemed fantastic, some weird, many-mouthed beast hurling defiance at them.

Finally, seeing the rats running in and out of the tower through the door and the windows, those on the ship decided that we had perished and were about to leave when

---

13. **phalanx** (FAY langks): closely packed group. A phalanx is an ancient military formation, and the word still has warlike connotations.
14. **hove to:** stopped by being turned into the wind.

N Read and Discuss | What can you say about the situation now?

O Read and Discuss | What is going on with the patrol boat?

Itchoua, regaining his senses, thought of using the light as a signal. He lit it and, using a plank placed and withdrawn before the beam to form the dots and dashes, quickly sent out our story to those on the vessel. **P**

Our reply came quickly. When they understood our position—how we could not get rid of the rats, Le Gleo's mind going fast, Itchoua and myself covered with bites, cornered in the lantern room without food or water—they had a signalman send us their reply.

His arms swinging like those of a windmill, he quickly spelled out:

"Don't give up, hang on a little longer! We'll get you out of this!" **Q**

Then she turned and steamed at top speed for the coast, leaving us little reassured.

She was back at noon, accompanied by the supply ship, two small coast guard boats, and the fireboat—a small squadron. At twelve-thirty the battle was on.

After a short reconnaissance,[15] the fireboat picked her way slowly through the reefs until she was close to us, then turned her powerful jet of water on the rats. The heavy stream tore the rats from their places and hurled them screaming into the water, where the sharks gulped them down. But for

---

15. **reconnaissance** (rih KAHN uh suhns): scouting for information.

P Read and Discuss How does Itchoua keep the patrol boat from leaving?

Q Reading Focus Making Predictions Do you predict that the patrol boat crew will be able to rescue the men? Why or why not?

every ten that were dislodged, seven swam ashore, and the stream could do nothing to the rats within the tower. Furthermore, some of them, instead of returning to the rocks, boarded the fireboat, and the men were forced to battle them hand to hand. They were true rats of Holland, fearing no man, fighting for the right to live!

Nightfall came, and it was as if nothing had been done; the rats were still in possession. One of the patrol boats stayed by the island; the rest of the flotilla departed for the coast. We had to spend another night in our prison. Le Gleo was sitting on the floor, babbling about skeletons, and as I turned to Itchoua, he fell unconscious from his wounds. I was in no better shape and could feel my blood flaming with fever.

> Nightfall came, and it was as if nothing had been done; the rats were still in possession.

Somehow the night dragged by, and the next afternoon I saw a tug, accompanied by the fireboat, come from the mainland with a huge barge in tow. Through my glasses, I saw that the barge was filled with meat.

Risking the treacherous reefs, the tug dragged the barge as close to the island as possible. To the last rat, our besiegers deserted the rock, swam out, and boarded the barge reeking with the scent of freshly cut meat. The tug dragged the barge about a mile from shore, where the fireboat drenched the barge with gasoline. A well-placed incendiary shell from the patrol boat set her on fire.

The barge was covered with flames immediately, and the rats took to the water in swarms, but the patrol boat bombarded them with shrapnel from a safe distance, and the sharks finished off the survivors. **ℝ**

A whaleboat from the patrol boat took us off the island and left three men to replace us. By nightfall we were in the hospital in Cayenne. What became of my friends?

Well, Le Gleo's mind had cracked and he was raving mad. They sent him back to France and locked him up in an asylum, the poor devil! Itchoua died within a week; a rat's bite is dangerous in that hot, humid climate, and infection sets in rapidly.

As for me—when they fumigated the light and repaired the damage done by the rats, I resumed my service there. Why not? No reason why such an incident should keep me from finishing out my service there, is there?

Besides—I told you I liked the place— to be truthful, I've never had a post as pleasant as that one, and when my time came to leave it forever, I tell you that I almost wept as Three Skeleton Key disappeared below the horizon.

ℝ **Read and Discuss** What was the patrol boat's strategy?

Applying Your Skills

SKILLS FOCUS Literary Skills Analyze suspense and foreshadowing. **Reading Skills** Evaluate predictions. **Writing Skills** Establish and develop setting.

Three Skeleton Key

Respond and Think Critically

Reading Focus

Quick Check

1. To review the story, imagine that you are the narrator. Write a journal entry about the day you leave Three Skeleton Key forever.

Read with a Purpose

2. Do you think the men could have escaped without help? Why or why not?

Reading Skills: Making Predictions

3. Look at your Prediction Chart. On what did you base your **predictions**? Which outcomes surprised you, and why?

Page	Foreshadowing Clue	My Prediction	Yes / No
p. 163	"The story was that the three skeletons . . . danced over the small rock, screaming."	Something bad will happen at this lighthouse.	Yes
p. 164	"The waters about our island swarmed with huge sharks."		

Literary Focus

Literary Analysis

4. **Connect** The three lighthouse keepers each respond differently to the invasion. With which character (if any) did you identify?

5. **Evaluate** What do you think was the scariest part of the story? What gave it such impact?

Literary Skills: Suspense and Foreshadowing

6. **Analyze** Early in the story the narrator explains how Three Skeleton Key got its name. How does this **foreshadow**—or hint at—the danger the lighthouse keepers will face later on?

7. **Evaluate** On the fourth day of the invasion, a wooden window frame in the lighthouse sags inward. How does this incident increase **suspense**? What other details create suspense?

8. **Analyze** Discuss the roles that **suspense** and **foreshadowing** play in this story and their overall effects.

Literary Skills Review: Climax

9. **Interpret** Which scene in "Three Skeleton Key" is the climax? How can you tell?

Writing Focus

Think as a Reader/Writer

Use It in Your Writing Write a brief description of another good setting for a horror story. Look at your list of scary words and your QuickWrite notes for more ideas.

 What Do You Think Now

What settings did you think of that are affected by threats from nature? Why is nature so often featured in horror stories?

Applying Your Skills

Three Skeleton Key

Vocabulary Development

Clarifying Word Meanings: Examples

Sometimes you can figure out the meaning of an unfamiliar word by finding other words or phrases that give you an example of what the word means. What words in this sentence give you an idea of what *staples* are?

> The lighthouse keepers were running very low on necessary staples, such as flour, sugar, and salt.

Certain words and phrases often let you know when an example is being used: *for example, for instance, like, such as, in this case,* and *as if.*

Your Turn

treacherously
maneuver
hordes
receding
edible

Fill in each blank below with the Vocabulary word that is explained by the examples in the sentence

1. As he got older, Martin found that his memory was _____ as if it were the ocean when the tide goes out.

2. I had to _____ around the piles of building materials scattered on the floor as if I were a gymnast.

3. He was polite to his associate, but behind her back, he dealt with her as _____ as a murderer would.

4. _____ of mosquitoes started biting us. There must have been hundreds of them!

5. We were lucky to find _____ provisions, such as rice, beans, and even some salsa, in the cabin.

Language Coach

Word Origins As you know, the word *maneuver* comes from Latin words meaning "to work by hand." What other words can you think of that might be in the same word family as *maneuver*?

Your Turn

manual
manipulate
manufacture
humanity
manuscript

Look at the words listed at the right. Read each word, and think about its meaning. If you're not sure of the word's meaning, look it up in a dictionary. Then, use each word in a sentence.

Academic Vocabulary

Talk About . . .

In a small group, discuss why you think this experience was <u>significant</u> for the narrator. Then, brainstorm a list of lessons about life he might have gained from it. Present your ideas to the class.

Learn It Online
Learn how to clarify word meaning with *WordSharp*:

go.hrw.com	L7-176	Go

Grammar Link

Adverbs

An **adverb** is a word that modifies a verb, an adjective, or another adverb. In these examples, the **adverb** is in boldface, and the <u>word it modifies</u> is underlined.

Modify a verb	The horde of rats <u>swarmed</u> **quickly** up the tower.
Modify an adjective	The situation was **very** <u>frightening</u>.
Modify an adverb	**Much** <u>later</u>, help arrived.

Adverbs tell you *where, when, how,* or *to what extent* (*how much* or *how long*).

Where	The sharks swam **nearby.**
When	The men hoped rescuers would arrive **soon.**
How	They watched **fearfully** as the rats swam ashore.
How much / how long	They were **extremely** upset when the rats broke through the window.

Note: The word *not* is an adverb that tells how much.

Your Turn

Identify the adverb in each of the following sentences. Then, tell which word it modifies.

EXAMPLE: Jose smiled happily at the A+ on his paper.

ANSWER: adverb: *happily;* word modified: *smiled*

1. Jaime ran quickly toward first base.
2. Her team was far ahead of the other team.
3. Too soon, the game was called for rain.
4. The team was extremely disappointed.

CHOICES

As you respond to the Choices, use these **Academic Vocabulary** words as appropriate: <u>accurate</u>, <u>adequate</u>, <u>similar</u>, <u>significant</u>.

REVIEW
Write an Essay

Timed └Writing Stories are made up of a series of events that advance the plot and keep you guessing about how things will turn out. The author of "Three Skeleton Key" incorporates crucial information, such as details about setting, to foreshadow terrible events to come and increase the suspense. In a paragraph, explain which events in the story advance the plot and show how past events foreshadow future events.

CONNECT
Plan a Video

TechFocus The writer Isaac Asimov once said, "When I was a lad . . . I found myself fearfully attracted to stories that scared me." What scenes in this story would be especially scary on film? With a partner, create a plan, or storyboard, for a video.

EXTEND
Write a Job Description

Design a job listing for the position of lighthouse keeper at Three Skeleton Key. Describe the personal characteristics and skills necessary for the job. Be sure to describe the work environment, duties, and pay.

Learn It Online
Examine this story in-depth using these Internet links:

go.hrw.com | L7-177 | **Go**

The Dive

by **René Saldaña, Jr.**

What Do You Think

Why do you think people are tempted by danger?

 QuickWrite

If a friend asked you for advice about doing something dangerous, what would you tell him or her? Why?

Reader/Writer Notebook

Use your **RWN** to complete the activities for this selection.

Literary Focus

Setting The **setting** of a story is the time and place in which the events take place. Setting frequently affects the development of a story's plot. In "The Dive," you will see how the setting creates an **external conflict** between the main character and her father. The setting also plays a role in the character's **internal conflict** (a struggle within a character's own mind). As you read, notice how setting impacts your understanding of characters and events.

Literary Perspectives Apply the literary perspective described on page 181 as you read this story.

Reading Focus

Visualizing: Pictures in Your Mind When writers describe things, they create mental **images,** or pictures drawn with words. When you form a mental image from the details of a story, you are **visualizing.** As you read "The Dive," try to visualize, or picture in your mind, the setting and the main characters.

Into Action To visualize setting, look for details that appeal to your senses. To visualize characters, look for details about the characters' appearance, such as clothing or hair color. As you read, fill in a chart like this one with details that help you picture characters.

Character's name:

Melly:

Mamá Tochi:

Papi:

Writing Focus

Think as a Reader/Writer

Find It in Your Reading As you read, make a list of five sensory details that help you visualize each of the settings described.

Vocabulary

crinkling (KRIHNG klihng) *v.* used as *adj.*: wrinkling. *Melly imagined her great-grandfather crinkling his brow in anger.*

stubble (STUHB uhl) *n.*: short, bristly growth. *The stubble on Mr. Otero's cheek was scratchy and gray.*

caressed (kah REHST) *v.*: touched gently. *Melly caressed her cheek where her father had touched it.*

wafting (WAHFT ihng) *v.* used as *adj.*: floating in the wind. *We smelled the sweet scent of flowers wafting from the garden.*

Vocabulary word	appeals to sense of
crinkling	sight, hearing
stubble	touch, sight
caressed	touch
wafting	sight, smell

Language Coach

Definitions Sometimes, writers give clues about a word's meaning by placing a definition nearby:

The smell of the flowers came wafting toward Melly as it floated on the afternoon's gentle breeze.

What words give you clues to the meaning of the word *wafting*?

Learn It Online
Enrich your vocabulary with Word Watch:

go.hrw.com   L7-179   **Go**

Preparing to Read **179**

René Saldaña, Jr.
(1968–   )

Feeling Inspired

René Saldaña was inspired to become a writer by his grandfather, who was a first-rate storyteller. Saldaña was also motivated by his students when he taught middle school and high school. He told them about the beginnings of his book *The Jumping Tree,* and as they wrote alongside him in class, he was inspired to continue his story. He has since written *Finding Our Way: Stories* and published more of his work in anthologies and magazines.

A Proud Texan

René Saldaña, Jr., was born and has spent most of his life in Texas. As a writer, Saldaña focuses on Chicano life and the importance of Mexican Americans' creating their own identities. Saldaña now teaches at Texas Tech. He lives with his wife, Tina, their sons, Lukas and Mikah, and their cat, ISBN (ISBN is the International Standard Book Number, found on a book's back cover and used to identify a book), in Edinburg, Texas.

> "We can become anything and anyone we want to become with hard work, focus, and dedication."

Think About the Writer Saldaña and his students have inspired one another to do better work. Who inspires you?

Build Background

In Mexican American culture, female elders like Mamá Tochi often share their wisdom by telling *cuentos,* or stories, that serve as "life lessons." In this story one of them involves a game of bingo—*Lotería*—in which the tokens are cards bearing such colorful images as El Cantarito (the little pitcher) and La Rosa (the rose). This selection includes some Spanish words and phrases. See if you can figure out their meanings from the context of the story.

Preview the Selection

Melly is the story's main character. As the story begins, she is fishing with her father when she sees a sight that rouses her curiosity. It also brings her into conflict with her father.

The Dive

by **René Saldaña, Jr.**

Look at them, Papi," said Melly to her father.

Mr. Otero cast his line into the water again and looked up and to his right. "Tan locos, mi'ja. It's a crazy thing to do."

From upriver, Melly and her father could see five or six boys fixing to jump from Jensen's Bridge. They pounded their chests, inched their way to the edge, then dove in all at once, some headfirst, others feet first, and one balled up. The boys disappeared underwater, leaving behind them different-sized splashes, then Melly heard the echoes of their jumping screams a full second or two after they'd gone under. By then, they were shooting up out of the water, their arms raised in the air. They'd done it. Most of the boys in Three Oaks had to dive from the bridge at one time or other to prove themselves real men. Today was their day. **Ⓐ**

Melly saw the boys crawl from the river and turn over on their backs, stretched out like lizards sunning themselves on the bank. Reeling in her line, she thought, So what if they can dive off the bridge! I could do it too if I wanted. Who said it was just for the guys to do? **Ⓑ**

"You'll do nothing of the kind," said Mr. Otero.

"Huh?"

"You said you could dive too if you wanted?"

"I didn't say anything. You must be hearing things."

He smiled. "Just like your mother. Talking your thoughts aloud." He reached

Literary Perspectives

The following perspective will help you think about the plot of this story.

Analyzing an Author's Techniques One way to understand a story is to pay close attention to the specific literary techniques the author uses. In "The Dive," René Saldaña, Jr., makes extensive use of dialogue—conversations between characters—in both English and Spanish. As you read, think about where he injects dialogue and how he uses it to move the story along. Also pay attention to his choice of words, such as the symbolism of the title. As you read, read the notes and questions in the text, which will guide you in using the perspective.

Ⓐ **Read and Discuss** What is going on?

Ⓑ **Literary Focus** **Setting** How does the setting create an internal conflict within Melly?

over and touched his rough hand to her cheek.

Melly blushed. She stood and set her rod on a rock, then stretched. She held her face and wondered if it was red from the sun. Red from her father's touch? **D**

All along she'd actually been talking. She'd heard the same thing from her tías, from Mamá Tochi, and from her sister, Becky. "Your mom literally spoke her mind," the aunts all told her.

"You're so much like your mother," Mr. Otero told her, casting again.

"She probably would've jumped," she said.

"Probably so, but I said you won't do it. ¿M'entiendes?"

"Yes, sir. I understand. No jumping from the bridge." She looked downriver, then set her sight on the bridge. Her face was warm, and she imagined her mother jumping from the bridge, her long black hair in a ponytail, or all loose and curly; her mother slicing into the water, then exploding out, all smiles and laughter. Beautiful.

"What?"

"What what?"

"Never mind. Just like your mother." **E**

That evening, Melly went to visit her grandmother, Mamá Tochi, down the street from where Melly lived with her father and her sister, who'd only recently left for college.

C **Read and Discuss** What have you learned about Melly now?

D **Reading Focus** Visualizing What details in this paragraph help you visualize the scene?

E **Literary Perspectives** Analyzing Author's Techniques Think of other ways the author could have introduced the story. What <u>significant</u> information do you learn from the use of dialogue?

July Afternoon
(1993) by Anne Belov.

Analyzing Visuals Viewing and Interpreting What mood does this image evoke?

Mamá Tochi had lived on her own ever since Melly's grandfather died five years ago. When Mamá Tochi's children all moved and married, each begged her to come live with them, but she refused. She said, "For decades I took care of both your father and myself when you left the house for work and school, and before that I took care of the six of you, from dirty diapers to broken hearts, so what makes you think I need to be looked after?"

Mr. Otero, Melly's dad, was the only one to pull up stakes and move to be closer to Mamá Tochi when Papá 'Tero died. Moving was easy for him. His own wife had died a year before his father's passing, and he once confessed to Mamá Tochi, "With Aurelia gone, I don't know that I can do right by our two girls." **F**

Melly knocked at her grandmother's and walked in. It was early evening, so she knew that Mamá Tochi would be out in her backyard garden with her babies: the herbs that ran up along the house; then the rosales, four bushes of them, red, yellow, white, and pink, big as trees almost; countless wildflower patches; and Melly's favorite, the esperanza bushes, the yellow bells soft on her cheeks. The backyard smelled like honey tasted. **G**

She went out the screen door and said, "Mamá Tochi. Where are you?" Melly could hear the water splashing, but couldn't quite make out her grandmother.

"Aqui, mi'jita. I'm over here." Mamá Tochi was hidden behind the esperanza bush, watering it with her pail. She'd set the hose at the base of one of the rosales. "You don't even have to tell me why you're here. You want to jump from that crazy bridge." **H**

Sometimes Melly thought her grandmother could read minds, see into the future, even talk to the dead. Melly couldn't figure out why she came over for advice. She never got anything but cuentos from Mamá Tochi, stories that somehow served as life lessons. That time Melly had had the chance to cheat on her end-of-term exam her ninth-grade year, Mamá Tochi said, "I remember a time I was calling bingo. Playing that night was my worst enemy, Perla. I kept an eye all night on her four cards, praying a secret prayer that she'd lose every time. On one of her cards I could see all she needed was El Gallo. Without knowing why, I pulled a card from the middle of the deck instead of the top. I pulled La Chalupa, and Manuela won. I was afraid to even look at the top card. I collected all the others and shuffled them real fast. What if it had been El Gallo? I wasn't able to look in Perla's eyes for two weeks and a half, that's how guilty I felt."

Lessons to be learned that time? You do it, you'll get caught. You'll feel worse if you don't get caught.

"It won't be cheating, really, Mamá Tochi. The teacher's already said chances of me passing are slim. There's stuff on the test we've never studied even."

F Read and Discuss | What is going on?

G Reading Focus Visualizing | What details in this paragraph help you picture the backyard garden?

H Literary Focus Setting | How has the setting created tension between Melly and Mamá Tochi?

Mamá Tochi sat on the porch swing and said, "You're a big girl. You'll know what to do."

That night, Melly considered what her grandmother had said. She saw herself three years later, marching for graduation, everyone taking photos, everyone smiling, everyone happy, except she wouldn't be because she'd remember having cheated that time back in the ninth grade. She didn't sleep at all that night. The next day, even before the exam was handed out, two boys and one girl were called out of class. Earlier in the week, they had asked Melly if she wanted a look at the test. They'd found it in one of the teacher's desks and ran off a copy. The morning of the test, she told them, "No thanks. I'll just try my best. I'll fail on my own terms, you know." Then they got busted, and Melly passed the test by two points. "A pass is a pass," said Mamá Tochi. That's just what Melly's mom used to say. **❶**

Tonight, Melly said, "What d'you mean? I'm here to visit with my favorite Mamá Tochi."

"Don't give me that. Your papi's already called. He's worried you're gonna jump and get tangled up in the weeds at the bottom of the river and drown."

Melly said, "Ah, Papi knows there's no weeds down there. And besides, no one's ever drowned at the bridge before."

Mamá Tochi put down the pail, turned

> "You don't even have to tell me why you're here. You want to jump from that crazy bridge."

off the hose, then said, "Sit down. I'll bring coffee."

Melly sat under the orange tree. Papá 'Tero had built the table and chairs years ago. He also had carved each of his children's and grandchildren's names and dates of birth into the tabletop in a great big circle. At the center were his name and Mamá Tochi's: Servando Otero and Rosario Garcia de Otero, their dates of birth, and the date of their wedding. Melly traced Mamá Tochi's name. **❶**

"I put two spoons of sugar and a little milk in yours, just like you drink it," said Mamá Tochi.

"Gracias," said Melly. "It's not that high of a jump—ten, fifteen feet at most."

"That's not high. About two of my rosebushes, right." Mamá Tochi looked up where the top of the invisible bush would be.

"I mean, if the guys can do it—Aren't you the one always saying, 'You can do anything and everything you set your heart to'?"

"You're right, mi'jita. Anything is possible. How's your coffee?"

"Good, thank you, Mamá Tochi."

"Mi'jita, have I ever told you that my mother never let me drink coffee? It was a grown-up thing to do. I didn't take my first drink of it until I was twenty-one."

Melly knew there was a reason Mamá

---

❶ Literary Focus Internal Conflict Describe the internal conflict Melly faces in the preceding paragraphs. How does Mamá Tochi help Melly resolve that conflict?

❶ Reading Focus Visualizing What details in this paragraph help you picture the table?

Tochi was telling her this. She just had to figure it out. She had to pay attention, then sleep on it, and if she hadn't figured it out by after school tomorrow, she'd have to come visit a second time, get another story, then try to figure out two lessons instead of one. **(K)**

"I'd gotten my first job as a seamstress," Mamá Tochi continued. "My first paycheck, I told my mother, 'First thing I'll buy is a cup of coffee at Martin's Café.' My mother said, 'Then you'll buy for us all.' And so I did, a cup of coffee and a piece of sweet bread for everyone, all thirteen of us. I spent every peso I'd made, and I didn't sleep all night. But I loved the taste so much I haven't stopped, even when Dr. Neely told me I should. What does he know?"

She sat across the table from Melly and sipped her coffee.

Melly thought she'd figured out the lesson: that she should dive, and then she wouldn't be able to stop. She'd be as old as Mamá Tochi and diving would still be in her blood, and one day she'd jump from a bridge too high for such a frail woman and break every bone in her body and drown. But she'd be doing what she loved. **(L)**

"This is some good coffee," Mamá Tochi said.

"Sure is. Good bread, too."

"Twenty-one, can you believe it? Today you kids have all these fancy cafés in your fancy bookstores where you go and study with all your friends. What was that drink you bought me once? Iced café mocha? Why ruin a good cup of coffee with chocolate syrup? Why ruin it by pouring it into a paper cup? Not like in the old days. A little crema, a pinch of sugar, and steaming hot in a clay jar."

It only seemed like Mamá Tochi had finished telling her story. Melly knew better, so she leaned back, ready for more. She knew she hadn't figured out her grandmother's riddle yet.

"Nowadays, you babies grow up too fast. You're women before you're girls. You never get to be girls, some of you. It's not a bad thing, the way the world is today. You have to know more sooner, and be able to survive it. In my day, all I had to worry about was drinking my first cup of coffee, my first job, and hoping my family would choose the right man for me. They did that back then, you know, chose your husband. My father tried to find the man for me, and—well, let's just say, I was ahead of my time when I told my father I would not marry Marcos Antonio Velasquez. Papá told me, '¿Y tu, quien te crées?'[1] I was twenty-three then, and getting too old to be playing this game, my father said. But I—I had to take a stand sometime. After all," she said, and laughed. Melly imagined Mamá Tochi's young face laughing,

---

1. **¿Y tu, quien te crées?:** Spanish for "And you, who do you think you are?"

(K) **Literary Perspectives** **Analyzing Author's Techniques** How does the author use the dialogue between Melly and Mamá Tochi to draw you further into the story?

(L) **Read and Discuss** What does Melly's interpretation of Mamá Tochi's story tell you?

Lady With Hibiscus
(21st century)
by Hilary Simon.
Colored inks on silk.

her wrinkles somehow gone. "After all, I was a woman now. I was drinking coffee at Martin's every Friday afternoon on my way home. But I didn't smoke like some of the others. I tried that once, but once was all I needed. I didn't like the taste. Coffee, now there's taste. Tobacco? Take it or leave it. Better leave it." She sipped some more, then said, "Mi'jita, it's getting late. You better go home before your papi calls looking for you."

Melly stood and helped her with the cups and plate of bread. She hooked the screen door shut. She didn't close the inside door. Mamá Tochi always said she wanted to smell her flowers. "And what's there in this house to steal? I wish someone would come and take that television. It's just something else I have to dust." Melly knew Mamá Tochi was teasing. She liked to watch her Mexican soaps. **Ⓜ**

"Dive if you want, mi'jita. I know you can make it. You won't drown. You're strong like all those boys, and smarter. So if you

---

Ⓜ **Literary Focus** **Setting** What does the description of the setting in this paragraph tell you about Mamá Tochi?

feel you have to, then go ahead, jump from that bridge. It'll make you feel better."

Melly hugged her grandmother tight, then said, "Buenas noches, Mamá Tochi."

"Buenas."

Melly was happy. She'd gotten her grandmother's permission. Now her father couldn't say anything about it. Melly woke to someone revving a car engine down the street. She'd gone to sleep thinking about her grandmother standing up to her own father, looking him in the eye: "I will not marry that boy. I don't love him." Melly imagined her great-grandfather stomping his foot, crinkling his face, pointing at his daughter, and not able to say a word to her. That's how angry Melly imagined him to be, so angry he was speechless. Then later, as the young Mamá Tochi was falling asleep, Melly pictured her great-grandfather bursting into the bedroom to say, "No daughter of mine—I shouldn't have let you drink coffee." And that would be it. He'd slam the door shut, and Rosario wouldn't have to marry Marcos Antonio Velasquez.

Instead she married Servando Otero, a handsome man till the end of his days. Melly remembered how his unshaven face had scratched at her cheeks when he held her tight to him. Like her own father's face

> "Dive if you want, mi'jita. I know you can make it."

tickled her cheeks now when he didn't shave on weekends. Earlier, at the river, she had noticed more gray in her father's stubble. She'd reached over and rubbed his face. He'd touched her cheek. She laughed and said, "I hope my face isn't as hard as yours."

He shook his head. "Not in a million years. Your face is like your mom's. Soft. Very much a woman's face."

Melly caressed her cheek. Like mom, she thought.

"Yep, so much like her. Don't get me wrong. You're hard as nails inside. Tough, and thick-headed, too." He cast his rod again and said, "Just like your mom."

That's when she saw the boys jumping. Ⓝ

In bed, she felt her cheek where her father had touched it. She knew she wouldn't jump. She didn't have to. She was already grown. Had a woman's face. Had nothing to prove to anybody. Tomorrow, if she wanted to, she could tell her father, "I'm diving no matter what you say." But she wouldn't. She was already drinking coffee, like her Mamá Tochi.

Melly turned onto her side. The window was open, and a cool breeze blew in. Melly could smell the sweetness of the flowers and herbs wafting from across the street. She smiled, closed her eyes, and slept. Ⓞ

Ⓝ **Literary Perspectives** Analyzing Author's Techniques How does the author use dialogue to connect the beginning and end of the story?

Ⓞ **Literary Focus** Internal Conflict How has Melly resolved her internal conflict? What does the way Melly solved her problem show you about her?

Vocabulary crinkling (KRIHNG klihng) v. used as adj.: wrinkling.
stubble (STUHB uhl) n.: short, bristly growth.
caressed (kah REHST) v.: touched gently.
wafting (WAHFT ihng) v. used as adj.: floating in the wind.

Applying Your Skills

SKILLS FOCUS **Literary Skills** Analyze setting; analyze internal and external conflicts. **Reading Skills** Visualize; describe mental images that text descriptions evoke. **Writing Skills** Write descriptive essays.

The Dive

Respond and Think Critically

Reading Focus

Quick Check

1. Why does Melly visit Mamá Tochi?
2. What decision does Melly reach at the end of the story?

Read with a Purpose

3. What does the dive mean to Melly? What makes her realize that she doesn't need to dive?

Reading Skills: Visualizing

4. As you read "The Dive," you recorded details that helped you **visualize** characters. Use the details in your chart to write a brief description of each character.

Visualizing Characters in "The Dive"

Melly:

Mamá Tochi:

Papi:

Literary Focus

Literary Analysis

5. **Interpret** Why do you think Melly's grandmother gives her advice in the form of a story? Why do you think she doesn't simply say, "Don't jump"?

6. **Draw Conclusions** Talk about the way Mamá Tochi passes down life lessons to Melly. Why does this system work for both of them?

7. **Analyze** What does Melly learn about herself in the course of the story?

Literary Skills: Setting

8. **Analyze** How does the **setting** of the story create a conflict between Melly and her father? Explain.

9. **Analyze** What does the description of Mamá Tochi's house add to your understanding of her character? Explain.

10. **Literary Perspectives** What does the author use the dive to symbolize in the story?

Literary Skills Review: Conflict

11. **Interpret** Which is more <u>significant</u> to the story: Melly's **external conflict** with her father or her **internal conflict**—the feelings with which she struggles? Why?

Writing Focus

Think as a Reader/Writer

Use It in Your Writing Look at the description of the boys jumping from the bridge at the beginning of the story. What sensory images does the author use to describe the action and the setting? Compare those images with the ones he uses to describe Mamá Tochi's house. What mood does each description create? Why? Write a description of two very different settings you're familiar with. Use sensory details to help your reader <u>accurately</u> picture each place and to set a mood for each place.

What Do **You Think Now** What advice would you have given Melly? Look back at your Quickwrite notes for ideas.

Vocabulary Development

Clarifying Word Meanings: Restatement

When you read the Spanish words and phrases in the story, you were probably able to figure out their meanings because Saldaña put the English meanings either directly afterward or in the next sentence. (For example, "Tan locos, mi'ja. It's a crazy thing to do.") When you encounter unfamiliar English words in your reading, you may also find a restatement in the nearby words or sentences. In the passage below, for example, the meaning of *hurricane* is explained by the phrase *powerful tropical storm.*

The **hurricane** hit the U.S. mainland at about midnight. This <u>powerful tropical storm</u> battered coastal towns for more than twelve hours before the winds began to die down.

Your Turn _____

Complete each of the following sentences with the Vocabulary words at the right. Then, write down the restatement clues that helped you complete the sentence.

> crinkling
> stubble
> caressed
> wafting

1. I looked at my father's _____ face; the smile lines showed that he was proud of me.
2. Grandma _____ my soft skin as she brushed it gently with her fingers.
3. When Dad doesn't shave, his _____ grows in short and scratchy.
4. The smell of the herbs from the garden were _____ through the house on the breeze.

Language Coach

Definitions Writers often help readers understand the meaning of a word by providing a definition of the word within a sentence.

If you come across an unfamiliar word as you're reading, look for clues around the word to help you define it.

Your Turn _____

The sentence below contains a boldface Vocabulary word as well as a definition of that word. What words define **stubble** in the sentence below?

The **stubble** on her father's chin was now made up of short gray hairs that tickled when he put his face next to hers.

Academic Vocabulary

Write About . . .

Think about a time when an event in your community had a <u>significant</u> impact on you. Was it a distinctive event, or an established one that occurred frequently? Jot down your impressions of the event, and explain why it was important to you.

SKILLS FOCUS **Literary Skills** Analyze setting; analyze internal and external conflicts. **Reading Skills** Visualize; describe mental images that text descriptions evoke. **Vocabulary Skills** Use context clues in words, sentences, and paragraphs to decode new vocabulary through the use of restatement. **Grammar Skills** Identify and use prepositional phrases correctly. **Writing Skills** Write descriptive essays; compare literary works.

Grammar Link
Prepositional Phrases

A **preposition** is a word or phrase used to show the relationship of a noun or a pronoun to another word in the sentence.

Commonly Used Prepositions

aboard	before	in	past
about	behind	in addition to	since
above	below	in front of	through
according to	beneath	inside	throughout
across	beside	in spite of	to
after	between	into	toward
against	down	on	under
among	during	off	up
around	for	out of	with

A **prepositional phrase** consists of a preposition, a noun, or a pronoun called the **object of the preposition,** and any modifiers of that object.

> You can press the leaves **under glass.** [The noun *glass* is the object of the preposition *under*.]
>
> Fred stood **in front of us.** [The pronoun *us* is the object of the compound preposition *in front of*.]

Your Turn

Identify the prepositional phrases in the following sentences. Underline the preposition once and its object twice.

1. Mr. Otero cast his line into the water.
2. Melly saw the boys jump off the bridge.
3. In the evening, Melly went to Mamá Tochi's house.

CHOICES

As you respond to the Choices, use these **Academic Vocabulary** words as appropriate: <u>accurate</u>, <u>adequate</u>, <u>similar</u>, <u>significant</u>.

REVIEW
Compare Plots

Timed ⌐Writing "The Dive" is a story driven primarily by Melly's internal conflict about diving off the bridge. On the other hand, "Rikki-tikki-tavi" and "Three Skeleton Key" contain plots driven by external conflict. Which kind of story do you prefer? Why? Support your response with evidence from the texts.

CONNECT
Collect Story Ideas

Melly deals with a number of internal conflicts throughout "The Dive." What other internal conflicts might make a good story? Make a list of internal conflicts around which you might build a story.

EXTEND
Tell a *Cuento*

In "The Dive," Mamá Tochi shares wisdom through *cuentos,* retellings of her experiences that teach lessons. Think of an experience you had that taught you something important. Then, tell the experience to someone else in the form of a *cuento*. Be sure to include the lesson you learned and why it was important. You may want to read your *cuento* aloud to the class.

Comparing Science Fiction Stories

CONTENTS

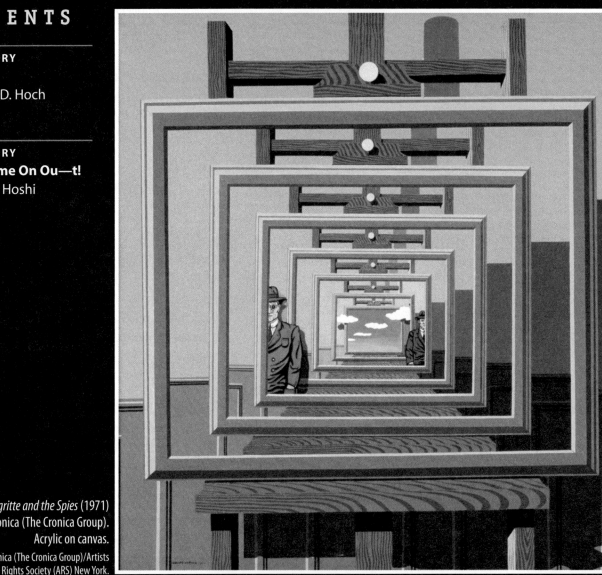

Magritte and the Spies (1971)
by Equipo Cronica (The Cronica Group).
Acrylic on canvas.
©Equipo Cronica (The Cronica Group)/Artists
Rights Society (ARS) New York.

© 2009 Artists Rights Society (ARS), New York/VEGAP, Madrid

What Do You Think

How can you tell when a situation may be dangerous? What clues do you look for?

 QuickWrite

Think of two scientific inventions: something that has been a great benefit, and something that has had terrible consequences. What does each reveal about human nature?

Preparing to Read

Zoo / He—y, Come on Ou—t!

Literary Focus

Science Fiction **Science fiction** lies somewhere between realistic fiction and total fantasy. Most science fiction stories contain some or all of the following elements:

- a **setting** in the future, on another planet, or in a spaceship
- **technology** that has not yet been invented
- a **journey** through time or to a distant planet or galaxy
- **characters** from outer space—aliens or extraterrestrials
- realistic human reactions to **fantastic situations** and conflicts

Reading Focus

Comparing and Contrasting Science Fiction Stories Look at the ways each story uses the elements of science fiction. Add details about each story to a chart like the one below.

	"Zoo"	"He—y, Come On Ou—t"!
Human characters		
Alien characters		
Journey		
Futuristic technology		
Lesson about life		

Writing Focus

Think as a Reader/Writer

Find It in Your Reading These stories describe worlds that are quite unlike the one we live in. Record in your *Reader/Writer Notebook* the details that make the setting of each story unusual.

Reader/Writer Notebook

Use your **RWN** to complete the activities for these selections.

Vocabulary

Zoo

interplanetary (ihn tuhr PLAN uh tehr ee) *adj.*: between or among planets. *The possibility of interplanetary relations is explored in the story.*

awe (aw) *n.*: feeling of fear and amazement. *The creatures in the zoo created a feeling of awe in the earthlings.*

He—y, Come on Ou—t!

apparent (uh PAHR uhnt) *adj.*: seeming. *With a look of apparent confidence, the workers dumped the waste into the hole.*

proposal (pruh POH zuhl) *n.*: suggestion. *The proposal to build a new town hall was very popular.*

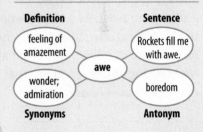

Definition feeling of amazement — **awe** — **Sentence** Rockets fill me with awe.
Synonyms wonder; admiration — **Antonym** boredom

Language Coach

Word Parts The word part *inter–* means "between or among." For instance, *interplanetary* means "between or among planets." What does *interact* mean?

Learn It Online
Take your vocabulary knowledge to a new level. Try Word Watch:

go.hrw.com | L7-193 | Go

Edward D. Hoch

(1930–   )

A Mystery Himself

Edward Hoch, whose name rhymes with "coke," was born in Rochester, New York. He has been a full-time writer since 1968, publishing novels and short stories and editing collections in the genres of mystery, crime, suspense, science fiction, and fantasy. Hoch has contributed more than 750 short stories to a long list of publications. This prolific writer is a bit of a mystery himself. To find all of his work, you have to search under his many pseudonyms, or pen names, such as Irwin Booth, Anthony Circus, Stephen Dentinger, Pat McMahon, Mister X, R. E. Porter, and R. L. Stevens.

Shinichi Hoshi

(1926–1997)

The Short-Short Story

Shinichi Hoshi is well known in Japan for his quirky imagination and intriguing science fiction stories, many of which end with a surprising twist. As a young writer, Hoshi set out to write one thousand and one stories, as in the famous story collection *The Arabian Nights* (which was originally titled *The Thousand and One Nights*). Once he reached his goal, Hoshi said, "One thousand and one stories are enough."

Think About the Writers

Why do you think writers are drawn to science fiction?

Preview the Selections

"Zoo" introduces you to **Professor Hugo,** a man who keeps the strangest of species on display for earthlings to see.

In "He—y, Come on Ou—t!" you'll meet a group of **villagers** who are trying to figure out what to do about a hole that appeared in the wake of a typhoon.

ZOO

by **Edward D. Hoch**

Read with a Purpose
Read this science fiction story to discover one writer's ideas about the zoos of the future.

Build Background
Zoos have existed for a very long time. In fact, researchers believe the first zoos were created in 4500 B.C. Until recently, most animals in zoos were kept in cages. However, more zookeepers have been trying to replicate the natural habitats of their animals so that the creatures will be more comfortable.

The children were always good during the month of August, especially when it began to get near the twenty-third. It was on this day that Professor Hugo's Interplanetary Zoo settled down for its annual six-hour visit to the Chicago area. **A**

Before daybreak the crowds would form, long lines of children and adults both, each one clutching his or her dollar and waiting with wonderment to see what race of strange creatures the professor had brought this year.

In the past they had sometimes been treated to three-legged creatures from Venus, or tall, thin men from Mars, or even snakelike horrors from somewhere more distant. This year, as the great round ship settled slowly to Earth in the huge tri-city parking area just outside of Chicago, they watched with awe as the sides slowly slid up to reveal the familiar barred cages. In them were some wild breed of nightmare—small, horselike animals that moved with quick, jerking motions and constantly chattered in a high-pitched tongue. The citizens of Earth clustered around as Professor Hugo's crew quickly collected the waiting dollars, and soon the good professor himself made an appearance, wearing his many-colored rainbow cape and top hat. "Peoples of Earth," he called into his microphone.

A **Literary Focus** Science Fiction What clue in the first paragraph suggests that this story is science fiction?

Vocabulary **interplanetary** (ihn tuhr PLAN uh tehr ee) *adj.*: between or among planets.
awe (aw) *n.*: feeling of fear and amazement.

The crowd's noise died down and he continued. "Peoples of Earth, this year you see a real treat for your single dollar—the little-known horse-spider people of Kaan—brought to you across a million miles of space at great expense. Gather around, see them, study them, listen to them, tell your friends about them. But hurry! My ship can remain here only six hours!"

And the crowds slowly filed by, at once horrified and fascinated by these strange creatures that looked like horses but ran up the walls of their cages like spiders. "This is certainly worth a dollar," one man remarked, hurrying away. "I'm going home to get the wife." **B**

All day long it went like that, until ten thousand people had filed by the barred cages set into the side of the spaceship. Then, as the six-hour limit ran out, Professor Hugo once more took the microphone in hand. "We must go now, but we will return next year on this date. And if you enjoyed our zoo this year, telephone your friends in other cities about it. We will land in New York tomorrow, and next week on to London, Paris, Rome, Hong Kong, and Tokyo. Then on to other worlds!"

He waved farewell to them, and as the ship rose from the ground, the Earth peoples agreed that this had been the very best Zoo yet. . . .

> "It was the very best zoo ever...."

Some two months and three planets later, the silver ship of Professor Hugo settled at last onto the familiar jagged rocks of Kaan, and the odd horse-spider creatures filed quickly out of their cages. Professor Hugo was there to say a few parting words, and then they scurried away in a hundred different directions, seeking their homes among the rocks.

In one house, the she-creature was happy to see the return of her mate and offspring. She babbled a greeting in the strange tongue and hurried to embrace them. "It was a long time you were gone! Was it good?"

And the he-creature nodded. "The little one enjoyed it especially. We visited eight worlds and saw many things."

The little one ran up the wall of the cave. "On the place called Earth it was the best. The creatures there wear garments over their skins, and they walk on two legs."

"But isn't it dangerous?" asked the she-creature.

"No," her mate answered. "There are bars to protect us from them. We remain right in the ship. Next time you must come with us. It is well worth the nineteen commocs it costs."

And the little one nodded. "It was the very best zoo ever. . . ." **C**

B **Literary Focus** Science Fiction What common element of science fiction stories is discussed here?

C **Read and Discuss** What happens at the end?

Analyzing Visuals Viewing and Interpreting Name the elements of science fiction that are present in this illustration.

Science Fiction Scene with Extraterrestrial Alien Planet by Anton Brzezinski.

Applying Your Skills

Zoo

Respond and Think Critically

Reading Focus

Quick Check

1. Use the following story map to outline the main parts of this story's plot.

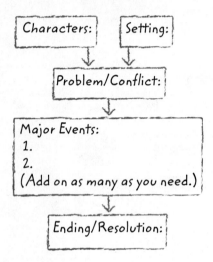

Read with a Purpose

2. Were the humans' reactions to the horse-spider people of Kaan believable? Explain.

Reading Skills: Comparing and Contrasting Texts

3. Review the comparison-contrast chart you filled out while reading the story. What lesson about life does "Zoo" teach?

✔ Vocabulary Check

4. Do you think **interplanetary** travel will be common in the future? Explain.
5. Would the view of Earth from outer space fill you with **awe**? Explain.

Literary Focus

Literary Analysis

6. **Infer** Why are children "always good during the month of August"?
7. **Analyze** This story has two parts and two settings. What if the first part of "Zoo" was set on Kaan and the second part was set on Earth? How would this change the story?
8. **Analyze** What did both groups, the people of Earth and the horse-spider people, believe to be the purpose of the bars?
9. **Evaluate** How does your opinion of Professor Hugo change from the beginning of the story to the end?

Literary Skills: Science Fiction

10. **Analyze** How does the author manipulate the story to develop an ending that is both surprising and humorous?
11. **Evaluate** Review the information you've collected in your chart for this story. Do you think this is a good science fiction story? Why or why not?

Writing Focus

Think as a Reader/Writer

Use It in Your Writing Look over some of the details you recorded from "Zoo." Which details about setting struck you as being the most vivid? Write a paragraph explaining why these details about setting made the story come alive for you.

HE—Y, COME ON OU—T!

by **Shinichi Hoshi**

Read with a Purpose Read the following selection to see how villagers react to a strange and surprising discovery.

Preparing to Read for this selection is on page 193.

Build Background

The events of "He—y, Come on Ou—t!" take place in a fishing village in Japan. Japan boasts one of the largest fish catches in the world. However, Japanese waters are plagued by pollution and environmental problems.

The typhoon had passed and the sky was a gorgeous blue. Even a certain village not far from the city had suffered damage. A little distance from the village and near the mountains, a small shrine had been swept away by a landslide. **A**

"I wonder how long that shrine's been here."

"Well, in any case, it must have been here since an awfully long time ago."

"We've got to rebuild it right away."

While the villagers exchanged views, several more of their number came over.

"It sure was wrecked."

"I think it used to be right here."

"No, looks like it was a little more over there." **B**

Just then one of them raised his voice. "Hey what in the world is this hole?"

Where they had all gathered there was a hole about a meter[1] in diameter. They peered in, but it was so dark nothing could be seen. However, it gave one the feeling that it was so deep it went clear through to the center of the earth.

There was even one person who said, "I wonder if it's a fox's hole."

"He—y, come on ou—t!" shouted a young man into the hole. There was no echo from the bottom. Next he picked up a pebble and was about to throw it in.

---

1. **meter** (MEE tuhr): measurement; three feet three inches.

A **Literary Focus** Science Fiction What is significant about the setting?

B **Read and Discuss** What is going on in this village?

"You might bring down a curse on us. Lay off," warned an old man, but the younger one energetically threw the pebble in. As before, however, there was no answering response from the bottom. The villagers cut down some trees, tied them with rope and made a fence which they put around the hole. Then they repaired[2] to the village. **Ⓒ**

"What do you suppose we ought to do?"

"Shouldn't we build the shrine up just as it was over the hole?"

A day passed with no agreement. The news traveled fast, and a car from the newspaper company rushed over. In no time a scientist came out, and with an all-knowing expression on his face he went over to the hole. Next, a bunch of gawking curiosity seekers showed up; one could also pick out here and there men of shifty glances who appeared to be concessionaires.[3] Concerned that someone might fall into the hole, a policeman from the local substation kept a careful watch.

One newspaper reporter tied a weight to the end of a long cord and lowered it into the hole. A long way down it went. The cord ran out, however, and he tried to

---

2. **repaired** (rih PAIRD): here, returned as a group.

3. **concessionaires** (kuhn sehsh uh NAIRZ): businesspeople.

Ⓒ [Read and Discuss] What is happening now? What do the people think of this discovery?

Analyzing Visuals | **Viewing and Interpreting** How does this image compare with the image of the hole you have formed in your mind?

pull it out, but it would not come back up. Two or three people helped out, but when they all pulled too hard, the cord parted at the edge of the hole. Another reporter, a camera in hand, who had been watching all of this, quietly untied a stout rope that had been wound around his waist. **(D)**

The scientist contacted people at his laboratory and had them bring out a high-powered bull horn, with which he was going to check out the echo from the hole's bottom. He tried switching through various sounds, but there was no echo. The scientist was puzzled, but he could not very well give up with everyone watching him so intently. He put the bull horn right up to the hole, turned it to its highest volume, and let it sound continuously for a long time. It was a noise that would have carried several dozen kilometers[4] above ground. But the hole just calmly swallowed up the sound.

In his own mind the scientist was at a loss, but with a look of apparent composure he cut off the sound and, in a

> The scientist was puzzled, but he could not very well give up with everyone watching him so intently.

manner suggesting that the whole thing had a perfectly plausible[5] explanation, said simply, "Fill it in."

Safer to get rid of something one didn't understand.

The onlookers, disappointed that this was all that was going to happen, prepared to disperse. Just then one of the concessionaires, having broken through the throng and come forward, made a proposal.

"Let me have that hole. I'll fill it in for you."

"We'd be grateful to you for filling it in," replied the mayor of the village, "but we can't very well give you the hole. We have to build a shrine there."

"If it's a shrine you want, I'll build you a fine one later. Shall I make it with an attached meeting hall?"

Before the mayor could answer, the people of the village all shouted out.

"Really? Well, in that case, we ought to have it closer to the village."

"It's just an old hole. We'll give it to you!"

---

4. **kilometers** (kuh LAHM uh tuhrz): one thousand meters; 0.6 miles.

5. **plausible** (PLAW zuh buhl): believable.

(D) Read and Discuss What did you just learn about the hole?

Vocabulary **apparent** (uh PAHR uhnt) *adj.:* seeming. **proposal** (pruh POH zuhl) *n.:* suggestion.

So it was settled. And the mayor, of course, had no objection.

The concessionaire was true to his promise. It was small, but closer to the village he did build for them a shrine with an attached meeting hall. **E**

About the time the autumn festival was held at the new shrine, the hole-filling company established by the concessionaire hung out its small shingle at a shack near the hole.

The concessionaire had his cohorts mount a loud campaign in the city. "We've got a fabulously deep hole! Scientists say it's at least five thousand meters deep! Perfect for the disposal of such things as waste from nuclear reactors."

Government authorities granted permission. Nuclear power plants fought for contracts. The people of the village were a bit worried about this, but they consented when it was explained that there would be absolutely no above-ground contamination for several thousand years and that they would share in the profits. Into the bargain, very shortly a magnificent road was built from the city to the village.

Trucks rolled in over the road, transporting lead boxes. Above the hole the lids were opened, and the wastes from nuclear reactors tumbled away into the hole.

From the Foreign Ministry and the Defense Agency boxes of unnecessary classified documents were brought for disposal. Officials who came to supervise the disposal held discussions on golf. The lesser functionaries, as they threw in the papers, chatted about pinball.

The hole showed no signs of filling up. It was awfully deep, thought some; or else it might be very spacious at the bottom. Little by little the hole-filling company expanded its business. **F**

Bodies of animals used in contagious disease experiments at the universities were brought out, and to these were added the unclaimed corpses of vagrants. Better than dumping all of its garbage in the ocean, went the thinking in the city, and plans were made for a long pipe to carry it to the hole.

The hole gave peace of mind to the dwellers of the city. They concentrated solely on producing one thing after another. Everyone disliked thinking about the eventual consequences. People wanted only to work for production companies and sales corporations; they had no interest in becoming junk dealers. But, it was thought, these problems too would gradually be resolved by the hole.

> The hole gave peace of mind to the dwellers of the city.

E **Read and Discuss** How are things looking for the villagers and their problem with the hole?

F **Literary Focus** Science Fiction How does the villagers' situation let you know you are reading science fiction?

Young girls whose betrothals[6] had been arranged discarded old diaries in the hole. There were also those who were inaugurating new love affairs and threw into the hole old photographs of themselves taken with former sweethearts. The police felt comforted as they used the hole to get rid of accumulations of expertly done counterfeit bills. Criminals breathed easier after throwing material evidence into the hole.

Whatever one wished to discard, the hole accepted it all. The hole cleansed the city of its filth; the sea and sky seemed to have become a bit clearer than before.

Aiming at the heavens, new buildings went on being constructed one after the other.

One day, atop the high steel frame of a new building under construction, a workman was taking a break. Above his head he heard a voice shout:

"He—y, come on ou—t!"

But, in the sky to which he lifted his gaze there was nothing at all. A clear blue sky merely spread over all. He thought it must be his imagination. Then, as he resumed his former position, from the direction where the voice had come, a small pebble skimmed by him and fell on past. **G**

The man, however, was gazing in idle reverie at the city's skyline growing ever more beautiful, and he failed to notice.

---

6. **betrothals** (bih TROH thuhlz): engagements.

G | Read and Discuss | Why are the voice and the pebble significant?

Applying Your Skills

SKILLS FOCUS Literary Skills Analyze science fiction. **Reading Skills** Compare and contrast stories. **Writing Skills** Analyze a writer's technique.

He—y, Come On Ou—t!

Respond and Think Critically

Reading Focus

Quick Check

1. Use the following story map to outline the main parts of the plot of "He—y, Come On O—ut!"

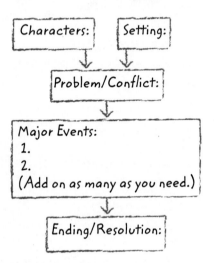

Characters: Setting:

↓   ↓

Problem/Conflict:

↓

Major Events:
1.
2.
(Add on as many as you need.)

↓

Ending/Resolution:

Read with a Purpose

2. How does the villagers' discovery change their lives?

Reading Skills: Comparing and Contrasting Texts

3. Are the lessons about life taught by these stories <u>similar</u> or different? Explain.

✔ Vocabulary Check

4. Recall a time in your life when a surprise became **apparent** to you.

5. What would be included in a **proposal** for building a new zoo?

Literary Focus

Literary Analysis

6. **Interpret** As a young man is about to throw a pebble into the hole, an old man warns him not to do it for fear it might bring down a curse. Discuss how the old man's warning foreshadows the events to come.

7. **Analyze** In addition to the obvious irony of the story, address the irony of a nuclear waste dump standing where a shrine used to be. Why do you think the author chose this particular setting?

8. **Evaluate** Although this is a story designed to entertain the reader, there is clearly an underlying message about a <u>significant</u> social issue. What is the issue? What point is the writer making about it?

Literary Focus: Science Fiction

9. **Analyze** List the parts of this story that could be considered elements of science fiction.

10. **Evaluate** Based on this story, what do you think is the author's opinion about pollution? How do the features of science fiction allow him to express that opinion?

Writing Focus

Think as a Reader/Writer

Use It in Your Writing Review your notes about the setting of "He—y, Come On Ou—t!" Note the way the author uses ordinary details of the setting, such as a hole in the ground, to create a disturbing effect. What other details from the story help create this effect? List them.

Wrap Up

Zoo / He—y, Come on Ou—t!

Writing a Comparison-Contrast Essay

Write an essay comparing "Zoo" and "He—y, Come on Ou—t." To help you plan your essay, review the chart you completed while you read each story. The chart will help you focus on elements in the stories that are very <u>similar</u> or very different. You do not have to write about all of these elements in your essay. Pick the elements in each story that most interest you.

Comparison-Contrast Essay

An effective comparison-contrast essay

- clearly states in the essay's opening paragraph what is being compared and contrasted
- focuses on similarities or differences or both
- is organized logically and effectively, using the block or point-by-point method
- when appropriate, cites text passages to support ideas
- contains few or no errors in spelling, punctuation, and grammar

For more information about writing a comparison-contrast essay, see the Writing Workshop on page 106.

Organize Your Essay

Here are two ways you can organize your essay:

1. You can organize your essay using the **block method.** That means you will discuss one story at a time, explaining how certain elements are used in that story. You might outline your essay like this:

   Paragraph 1: Elements of "Zoo"
   A. The unknown in "Zoo"
   B. The surprise ending in "Zoo"
   Paragraph 2: Elements of "He—y, Come on Ou—t"
   A. The unknown in "He—y, Come on Ou—t"
   B. The surprise ending in "He—y, Come on Ou—t"

2. You can organize your essay using the **step-by-step method.** That means you will discuss each story element, one at a time, explaining how it is used in each story. If you organize by element, your first and second paragraphs might be focused on these topics:

   Paragraph 1: Setting and characters of each story
   A. "Zoo"
   B. "He—y, Come on Ou—t"
   Paragraph 2: Lesson about life taught in each story
   A. "Zoo"
   B. "He—y, Come on Ou—t"
   Finally, tell which story you prefer and why.

 What Do You Think Now

When have you been surprised by a dangerous situation?

Structure and Purpose of Informational Texts

CONTENTS

What Do You Think   How does the idea of danger depend on the perspective of those experiencing it?

 QuickWrite
What image forms in your mind when you hear the word *rat*? Jot down some adjectives to describe this image.

NEWSPAPER ARTICLE
Preparing to Read

Flea Patrol

Reader/Writer Notebook

Use your **RWN** to complete the activities for this selection.

Informational Text Focus

Structure and Purpose of a Newspaper Article The **purpose** of a newspaper article is to give you factual information about current events. Many newspaper articles follow an **inverted**—or upside-down—**pyramid** structure. The article begins with a **summary lead,** a sentence or paragraph that gives the **main idea** of the story. It is followed by the less important details of the article. Some articles begin with a lead that grabs your interest in a topic. Such a lead does not summarize but instead describes an interesting situation or fact related to the story. Here are some additional elements in the **structure** of a newspaper article. You can find examples of these elements in "Flea Patrol."

- **Headline:** the catchy, boldface words that tell you what the article is about
- **Subhead:** the words in smaller type under the headline that add details about the article
- **Byline:** the name of the reporter who wrote the article
- **Dateline:** the location where and the date when the information was reported
- **Lead:** the sentence or paragraph that begins the news article
- **Tone:** the choice of words and point of view that meet the interests of the newspaper's audience. Tone often depends on the subject of the article. Some articles are light, lively, and humorous. Others are serious and straightforward.

Inverted pyramid diagram:
- Summary lead, or most important information
- Important details
- Least important details

Vocabulary

transmitted (trans MIHT tihd) *v.:* caused to pass from one thing to another. *Fleas that fed on infected rats transmitted the plague throughout Europe.*

application (ap luh KAY shuhn) *n.:* act of putting to use. *An application of insecticide kills fleas.*

rural (RUR uhl) *adj.:* of or relating to the countryside. *People living in rural areas are at greater risk of catching the plague.*

Language Coach

Word Roots Many English words have Latin roots and affixes. An **affix** is a word part that is added to a root. The Vocabulary word *transmitted* is made up of the Latin root *mis,* meaning "send," and the word part *trans–,* meaning "across." What are three things that are transmitted?

Writing Focus   Preparing for **Constructed Response**

As you read this article, record the main idea and important details. You'll use them to write a summary later.

Learn It Online
Check out the *PowerNotes* slideshow to get a lesson using words and pictures:

go.hrw.com   L7-207   Go

FLEA PATROL

Keeping National Parks Safe from Plague

by JESSICA COHN

Read with a Purpose
Read the following article to find out how scientists and rangers are keeping our national parks safe.

BLANDING, UTAH, January 10— Park rangers are hunting fleas to stop the spread of disease. They are on alert to fight a plague of rodents in some national parks. **Ⓐ**

Bubonic plague is found in rodents and the fleas that feed on them in several areas of the United States, including some national parks. To keep the disease under control, rangers spray insecticide. They hope to kill the fleas, which can spread the disease to humans. But before you scratch an overnight park visit off your list of things to do, you should know something else. No humans are known to have become infected with plague at national park campgrounds. Through this course of action, officials are trying to keep it that way.

At least a third of Europeans died from the plague during the Middle Ages. That

Ⓐ Informational Focus Structure and Purpose of a Newspaper Article What is the purpose of the lead in this article?

deadly drama, known as the Black Death, is kept alive in history, literature, and imagination. "As soon as people hear 'Black Death' or 'plague,' they freak out," says Ralph Jones, chief ranger of Natural Bridges National Park in Utah. "But that's not the way it is anymore. It's just a naturally occurring disease. It's just part of the world."

In spring 2006, rangers discovered more dead field mice and chipmunks at Natural Bridges than was normal. Curious about the reason, the rangers had the animals tested at the Centers for Disease Control and Prevention (CDC), a federal agency responsible for protecting the health and safety of the population. The bacterium that causes plague was uncovered. **B**

Natural Bridges closed its campground until the disease could be contained. Sites reopened that May. The same year, plague was found in creatures living in Mesa Verde National Park and Colorado National Monument, reported the U.S. Public Health Service.

"Bubonic plague goes in cycles," says Jones, "depending on the population of the rodents."

People get sick when bitten by fleas that have fed on the blood of rodents carrying the bacterium. The disease can also be transmitted through contact with infected sores or by breathing infected matter in the air. Plague can be cured as long as humans seek medical help

BUBONIC PLAGUE SYMPTOMS

Bubonic plague is treatable with antibiotics. Symptoms appear two to seven days after infection:

- blackish-purple lumps under skin
- chills
- diarrhea
- exhaustion
- fever
- tender, swollen lymph nodes
- headache
- muscle pain
- vomiting

and are treated with antibiotics. But every year, countless rodents die from the disease. **C**

Officials concentrate on killing off fleas when rodents are found to be carrying plague. An application of insecticide at rodent holes is recommended when dead animals are identified as plague carriers.

The disease is regularly found in creatures throughout the western United States, especially in the area known as Four Corners, where the states of Arizona, Colorado, New Mexico, and Utah meet. The trick is keeping the disease contained to wild animals, which is usually easy enough. Most people avoid contact with these creatures.

About ten to fifteen plague cases are reported in humans yearly in the United States, mostly in rural areas, says the CDC. One in seven cases is fatal. The southwestern United States is especially affected. Africa, Asia, and South America have hot spots as well. In 2006, a Los Angeles woman was treated for the disease, that area's first case in more than twenty years.

Researchers at the University of Oslo recently studied data on creatures known as great gerbils, along with related weather records. Plague increased more than 50 percent among the animals with temperature increases of fewer than 2 degrees.

B Read and Discuss What has the author set up for you?

C Informational Focus Tone How would you describe the tone of this paragraph?

Vocabulary **transmitted** (trans MIHT tihd) *v.*: caused to pass from one thing to another.
application (ap luh KAY shuhn) *n.*: act of putting to use.
rural (RUR uhl) *adj.*: of or relating to the countryside.

Applying Your Skills

Flea Patrol

Practicing the Standards

Informational Text and Vocabulary

1. The structure of a **newspaper article** is said to be similar to an —

A octagon

B inverted pyramid

C oval

D upside-down T

2. The **byline** of the news article shows it was written by —

A Ralph Jones

B the Centers for Disease Control and Prevention

C Jessica Cohn

D park rangers at Natural Bridges National Park

3. The **subhead** of the article tells you that —

A the Black Death killed huge numbers of people

B a national park closed its campsites for a time

C fleas spread plague to rats and humans

D national parks are protected from plague

4. The **lead** of this article —

A is an attention-grabber

B makes a serious statement about dangerous rats

C answers *who? what? where? when?* and *how?*

D presents the article's main idea

5. Something that is *transmitted* is —

A mailed

B captured

C cured

D spread

6. If something is *rural,* it might be —

A rustic

B infested

C urban

D desirable

7. Another word for *application* is —

A utilization

B removal

C disinfection

D concentration

Writing Focus Constructed Response

Summarize this article in a paragraph that answers the questions *who? what? when? where? why?* and *how?*

What Do You Think Now

Some people get nervous when they hear of cases of plague. After reading this article, do you think it is something to fear? Explain.

TEXTBOOK
Preparing to Read

The Black Death *from* World History: Medieval to Early Modern Times

Reader/Writer Notebook

Use your **RWN** to complete the activities for this selection.

Informational Text Focus

Structure and Purpose of a Textbook The story "Three Skeleton Key" might have made you want to learn more about rats and their role in history. Textbooks are one source you can go to for information about history and the way rats influenced it.

Textbooks have features that help you locate information and review what you have learned. Textbooks also offer photographs, graphics, and artwork that can lead you to do further investigation of a subject.

In the next four pages are features from a history textbook called *World History: Medieval to Early Modern Times.* See how well you understand the structure of this textbook.

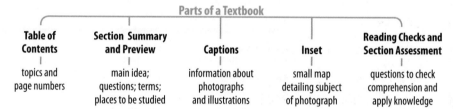

Parts of a Textbook

Table of Contents	Section Summary and Preview	Captions	Inset	Reading Checks and Section Assessment
topics and page numbers	main idea; questions; terms; places to be studied	information about photographs and illustrations	small map detailing subject of photograph	questions to check comprehension and apply knowledge

---

Writing Focus Preparing for **Constructed Response**

When an idea is important to convey, most textbook writers know not to hide it in their texts. Instead, they take care to present their main ideas clearly and use headings to help readers identify them quickly. Look for a place in the text where a heading is used to help signal a main idea.

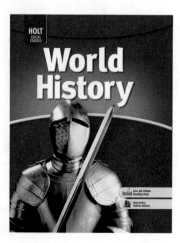

Read with a Purpose
Read the following selection to learn more about the Black Death, the deadly plagues that hit Europe between 1347 and 1351, killing hundreds of thousands of people.

1. The **table of contents** is an important feature of a textbook. What major topics on the later Middle Ages does this textbook cover?

XIV Contents

Ⓐ **Informational Focus** Structure and Purpose of a Textbook Why does the table of contents use different-sized heads?

The Black Death

While the English and French fought the Hundred Years' War, an even greater crisis arose. This crisis was the **Black Death**, a deadly plague that swept through Europe between 1347 and 1351.

The plague originally came from central and eastern Asia. Unknowingly, traders brought rats carrying the disease to Mediterranean ports in 1347. From there it quickly swept throughout much of Europe. Fleas that feasted on the blood of infected rats passed on the plague to people.

The Black Death was not caused by one disease but by several different forms of plague. One form called bubonic plague (byoo-BAH-nik PLAYG) could be identified by swellings called buboes that appeared on victims' bodies. Another even deadlier form could spread through the air and kill people in less than a day.

The Black Death killed so many people that many were buried quickly without priests or ceremonies. In some villages nearly everyone died or fled as neighbors fell ill. In England alone, about 1,000 villages were abandoned.

The plague killed millions of people in Europe and millions more around the world. Some historians think Europe lost about a third of its population—perhaps 25 million people. This huge drop in population caused sweeping changes in Europe.

In most places, the manor system fell apart completely. There weren't enough people left to work in the fields. Those peasants and serfs who had survived the plague found their skills in high demand. Suddenly, they could demand wages for their labor. Once they had money, many fled their manors completely, moving instead to Europe's growing cities.

READING CHECK Identifying Cause and Effect What effects did bubonic plague have in Europe?

SUMMARY AND PREVIEW Magna Carta, the Hundred Years' War, and the Black Death changed European society. In the next section, you will learn about other changes in society, changes brought about by religious differences.

2. Key items and terms are set in **boldface type**. The boldface terms are often defined in the text. Is the boldface word on this page defined?

3. Reading checks are often provided to help you review what you have learned.

4. Questions usually conclude each section of text. These questions help you review what you've just read; if you can't answer the questions, you need to re-read the text.

go.hrw.com
Online Quiz
KEYWORD: SN6 HP18

Section 4 Assessment

Reviewing Ideas, Terms, and People

1. **a. Identify** What document did English nobles hope would limit the king's power?
   b. Explain How was the creation of **Parliament** a step toward the creation of democracy in England?
2. **a. Identify** Who rallied the French troops during the **Hundred Years' War**?
   b. Elaborate The Hundred Years' War caused much more damage in France than in England. Why do you think this was the case?
3. **a. Describe** What was the **Black Death**?
   b. Explain How did the Black Death contribute to the decline of the manor system?
   c. Elaborate Why do you think the Black Death was able to spread so quickly through Europe?

Critical Thinking

4. **Evaluating** Copy the diagram below. Use it to rank the significance of the effects of Magna Carta, the Hundred Years' War, and the Black Death. Next to the diagram, write a sentence to explain your choices.

Most Significant
1.
2.
3.
Least Significant

FOCUS ON WRITING ✎

5. **Rating Importance** After reading this section, you'll probably want to add King John to your list. You should also start to think about which people were the most important. Rank the people on your list from most to least important.

B **Informational Focus** Structure and Purpose of a **Textbook** What will the next section of this textbook cover? Where did you find this information?

C **Read and Discuss** How did the world deal with the Black Death?

D **Read and Discuss** How does the idea of peasants moving into cities fit into the picture of the Black Death?

The Black Death

"And they died by the hundreds," wrote one man who saw the horror, "both day and night." The Black Death had arrived. The Black Death was a series of deadly plagues that hit Europe between 1347 and 1351, killing millions. People didn't know what caused the plague. They also didn't know that geography played a key role in its spread—as people traveled to trade, they unwittingly carried the disease with them to new places.

EUROPE

Kaffa

CENTRAL ASIA

CHINA

AFRICA

The plague probably began in central and eastern Asia. These arrows show how it spread into and through Europe.

This ship has just arrived in Europe from the east with trade goods—and rats with fleas.

The fleas carry the plague and jump onto a man unloading the ship. Soon, he will get sick and die.

280

E Read and Discuss | What does this graphic help you understand?

The plague is so terrifying that many people think it's the end of the world. They leave town for the country, spreading the Black Death even farther.

People dig mass graves to bury the dead. But often, so many victims are infected that there is no one left to bury them.

The garbage and dirty conditions in the town provide food and a home for the rats, allowing the disease to spread even more.

5. Illustrations have **captions**, text that explains the subject of the illustration. How do the captions help you understand this illustration?

So many people die so quickly that special carts are sent through the streets to gather the bodies.

GEOGRAPHY SKILLS **INTERPRETING MAPS**

1. How did the Black Death reach Europe from Asia?
2. What helped spread the plague within Europe?

F

281

F **Informational Focus** **Structure and Purpose of a Textbook** These questions ask about the inset and the two-page illustration. Look at them to find the answers to these questions.

TEXTBOOK
Applying Your Skills

SKILLS FOCUS Informational Skills Analyze the structure and purpose of a textbook; analyze textbooks.

The Black Death *from* World History: Medieval to Early Modern Times

Practicing the Standards

Informational Text

To check on how well you know the important parts of a textbook, answer the following questions by referring to the key parts of the textbook you are using now, called *Holt Elements of Literature.*

1. The **copyright page** is in the front of the book, usually the page after the main title page. Here is where you find the date the book was published. What is the copyright date of this book?
   A 2007
   B 2008
   C 2009
   D 2010

2. The **table of contents** is found in the front of a textbook. According to the table of contents of this textbook, how many collections are in Unit 4?
   A 1
   B 3
   C 4
   D 5

3. What is *not* found in Unit 3 of this textbook?
   A Chapter 6: Reading for Life
   B Chapter 7: Elements of Poetry
   C Workshops
   D Read On features

4. The **authors and program consultants page** of this textbook lists the names of the writers. What page of this book lists its authors?
   A ii
   B iii
   C 2
   D 6

5. Which of the following features is *not* found at the back of this book?
   A Index of Skills
   B Handbook of Reading and Informational Terms
   C Index of Maps
   D Index of Authors and Titles

Writing Focus   Constructed Response

Name one similarity and one difference between the structure of a textbook and the structure of a newspaper.

What Do **You Think Now** What additional information did you learn from the history textbook? How does it connect to "Flea Patrol"?

INSTRUCTIONAL MANUAL
Preparing to Read

On Preventing Plague

Reader/Writer Notebook

Use your **RWN** to complete the activities for this selection.

Informational Text Focus

Structure and Purpose of an Instructional Manual Instructions help you determine how to work a device, such as an MP3 player. They usually contain diagrams and step-by-step instructions. Instructional manuals usually explain a process, such as how to protect yourself from disease. The **purpose** of both is to guide you through a task.

The following selection is a mock seventeenth-century manual that is based on a real one. It was written to help people avoid the bubonic plague using the medical knowledge of the time. This manual, like most, follows a **structure** you can use to your advantage.

- First, scan the **table of contents** to preview the topics to be covered.
- Read all the directions carefully. Take mental note of the **steps** you must take.
- Consider all the **diagrams.** Make sure you understand them.
- Use the **glossary** to check your understanding of terms and symbols. A glossary is an alphabetical list of special terms and their definitions.

By the Numbers Here is another strategy for tackling more complex instructional manuals. Check the back for an **index,** which is a list of topics that is in alphabetical order. It is much more detailed than a table of contents, so you can use it to find the specific information you need. You will find an index in the back of this textbook. Look up the word *purpose,* and you will find this page number.

Writing Focus | Preparing for **Constructed Response**

Informational manuals are structured so that information is easy to locate. As you read "On Preventing Plague," look at the way the writer organized the information.

ON PREVENTING PLAGUE

CONTENTS

Steps to Prevent Spread of Infection

1. Notice of the Sickness
2. Every Visited House to Be Marked
3. Every Visited House to Be Watched
4. Shutting Up of Infected Houses; Isolation of Villages
5. Airing Out of the Stuff
6. No Infectious Stuff
7. Burial of the Dead
8. Protection for Physicians

Informational Focus Structure and Purpose of an Instructional Manual How is the material organized to help readers figure out what to do?

ON PREVENTING PLAGUE

by  THE WORLD ALMANAC®

Read with a Purpose

Read this adaptation of an instructional manual to learn how people living in the seventeenth century dealt with outbreaks of plague.

— July 6, 1665 —

BY THE ORDER OF THE LORD ARLINGTON,
SECRETARY OF STATE TO HIS MAJESTY,

KING CHARLES II OF ENGLAND,

I am commanded to publish the following instructions: Ⓐ

Steps to Prevent Spread of Infection

1. Notice of the Sickness

The master of every house shall give notice to the health examiner within two hours of seeing a sign of the sickness on any person in the house. Signs include a pimple or a swelling in any body part. Anyone falling dangerously sick shall be reported.

2. Every Visited House to Be Marked

Every house visited by the illness must be clearly marked with a red cross. This will be one foot long and in the middle of the door. The cross must remain until the lawful opening of the house.

3. Every Visited House to Be Watched

The constable must see that every house with the illness remains shut up. The visited houses will be guarded by watchmen. The watchmen will bring the inhabitants necessities at their own cost. This will last until four weeks after all in the house become well.

4. Shutting Up of Infected Houses; Isolation of Villages

The house of anyone who has entered any infected house will be shut up for a number of days. This number will be decided by the examiner. No person, infected or otherwise, shall leave the infected houses.

Ⓐ **Informational Focus** Structure and Purpose of an Instructional Manual **Explain the purpose of this instructional manual.**

APPOINTED OFFICERS

Examiners: The examiners shall learn which houses have been visited by illness. If they find any person sick, they shall give orders that the house be shut up. (If any fit examiner fails to do his duty, he will be sent to prison.)

Watchmen: Every affected house shall be assigned two watchmen, one for day and the other for night. The watchmen must take care that no person goes into or out of the house.

Searchers: Women searchers of honest reputation shall be appointed. They shall swear to search for persons dying of plague. They will give true report of their findings.

Nurse Keepers: Before any nurse keeper leaves an infected house, a number of days must be passed. If she leaves before twenty-eight days after the death of any infected person, the next house she attends will be shut up. It will be shut up until twenty-eight days have passed.

Beak (*primitive gas mask*),
filled with spices and herbs

Mouth, nose, and **ears**
*stuffed with garlic and
incense*

Total coverage, *to prevent
flea bites*

Outer coat, *coated in wax*

Dr. Schnabel of Rome, a plague doctor in 1656 by Paul Fuerst.
Copper engraving.

If any person leaves an infected village,
he will be brought back by night. He
will be punished by the constable.
All public assemblies are forbidden
during this visit by the plague.

5. Airing Out of the Stuff

The goods and clothing of the infected
must be well aired with fire and perfumes.
The bedding and apparel of the infected
will be treated in the same manner.

6. No Infectious Stuff

No clothes, bedding, or garments shall be
removed from any infected house. The sale of
secondhand clothing and bedding is prohibited,
on pain of imprisonment. If any buyer takes bedding or apparel from any seller's house within
two months after an infection, the buyer's house
will be shut up. This shall last a minimum of
twenty days.

7. Burial of the Dead

The burial of the dead killed by this plague will
be carried out before the sun rises or after the
sun sets. This will be done with the knowledge
of the constables. No neighbors or friends are
allowed to take the corpse to church. No one will
enter a home visited by the illness. In doing so,
he risks having his house shut up or imprisonment. No children are allowed to come near the
corpse, coffin, or grave. They will keep their distance at the burial of any corpse in any church,
churchyard, or burying place. All graves will be
at least six feet deep.

8. Protection for Physicians

Physicians treating the infected will wear proper
garb. The bronze mask, shaped like a beak, will
cover the head completely. It will be filled with
medicines and herbs that clean the bad air that
causes infection. The physician will place garlic
in his mouth and incense in his nose and ears.
An outer cloak coated in wax will be worn whenever treating an ill person.

B Read and Discuss What does this picture let you know?

Applying Your Skills

On Preventing Plague

Practicing the Standards

Informational Text

1. In which part of the **instructional manual** would you look to find the section that discusses the burial of the dead?

A Table of contents

B Diagram

C Glossary

D Index

2. In which part of the manual would you look to find the duties of a searcher?

A Table of contents

B Diagram

C Glossary

D Index

3. In which part of the manual would you look to find the proper attire for a physician?

A Table of contents

B Diagram

C Glossary

D Index

4. If you had a question about how houses of the sick were labeled, where would you look?

A Notice of the Sickness

B Every Visited House to Be Marked

C Every Visited House to Be Watched

D Shutting Up of Infected Houses

5. In which part of the manual would you look to find the steps to take before marking a house?

A Notice of the Sickness

B Every Visited House to Be Watched

C Protection for Physicians

D Airing Out of the Stuff

Writing Focus   Constructed Response

Think about a task that you perform every day, such as brushing your teeth or setting the dinner table. Write a set of step-by-step directions for completing the task.

What Do You Think Now   Would the physician's appearance be soothing, or would it strike terror in a patient? Support your opinion with examples.

Preparing to Read

Signs

Reader/Writer Notebook

Use your **RWN** to complete the activities for this selection.

Informational Text Focus

Structure and Purpose of Signs We use signs to communicate information, such as directions, warnings, and indications of specific locations. Signs contain symbols and markings that can be universally understood. To interpret signs, people have to look at the signs' major images and colors. They also have to be aware of any associations they have with the symbols depicted on the signs.

Signs help people who speak different languages to communicate. Imagine that you were traveling abroad and could not speak the local language. How would you locate the things you needed, such as a hospital or taxi stand? How would you know when to cross the street at an intersection? Chances are that there would be signs to guide you that don't rely on knowledge of a specific language.

Here are some facts about signs:

- There are 58 million traffic signs on our nation's roads.
- Uniform pictorial signs were first developed in Europe so that tourists could understand road signs.
- In a large city a traffic light might control the movements of nearly 100,000 vehicles a day.
- The skull-and-crossbones sign was flown on pirate ships to indicate that anyone who crossed the ship's path would die.
- Signs that indicate danger usually have an unusual shape (like a triangle) and a bright color.
- Signs indicating where travelers can eat, rest, or get gas are usually blue, white, or green—colors that are supposed to suggest relaxation. Red usually indicates something dangerous or forbidden.

Our world is full of signs. Language itself is a system of symbols and signs—a very sophisticated one. See if you can identify what the signs on the next two pages mean.

Language Coach

As this page discusses, signs convey information, often without using words. Communication does not always rely on language alone. What signs without words can you name? How do they convey information effectively?

Learn It Online

Explore the structure and purpose of signs with *PowerNotes* online.

go.hrw.com   L7-221   **Go**

SIGNS

Read with a Purpose
Look at the signs below to learn about their meanings.

What would clue you in to the fact that this sign means "danger"?

Which sign means "dogs are allowed"? Which sign means "no dogs allowed"? What symbol gives you that information?

Imagine that you have arrived for the first time in Mexico City. If you need information, would these signs help you? What clues give you your answer? Why wouldn't the second sign work in every country?

When you travel, you might need a drugstore. If you know about Greek mythology, you can describe what this universal symbol for "pharmacy" means.

If you were driving along a road and saw this sign, would you continue? Why or why not?

Signs say a great deal with only a simple graphic or illustration. What does this sign say to you?

Here is a familiar sign. What is it saying?

Do you know what this sign means? It's the biohazard symbol, which warns people that something is a biological agent that is dangerous to humans or the environment. The biohazard symbol did not have a distinct meaning when it was created, but it is memorable. Its creators wanted to educate people on the meaning of a new, standardized symbol.

Writing Workshop

Fictional Narrative

Write with a Purpose

Write a **fictional narrative** that includes the elements of plot, setting, and character you've learned about in this collection. The **purpose** is to entertain the people who will read it—your **audience**.

A Good Fictional Narrative

- develops a plot with a beginning, conflict, rising action, climax, and resolution
- uses dialogue and actions, including movements and gestures, to develop characters
- gives a detailed description of the setting
- ends with a resolution to the conflict the characters faced

See Page 232 for complete rubric.

Reader/Writer Notebook

Use your **RWN** to complete the activities for this workshop.

Think as a Reader/Writer

In this collection, you've seen the techniques writers use to write fictional narratives. Before you write your fictional narrative, take a few minutes to read the beginning of "The Dive" (page 181), a short story by René Saldaña, Jr.

"Look at them, Papi," said Melly to her father.

Mr. Otero cast his line into the water again and looked up and to his right. "Tan locos, mi'ja. It's a crazy thing to do."

From upriver, Melly and her father could see five or six boys fixing to jump from Jensen's Bridge. They pounded their chests, inched their way to the edge, then dove in all at once, some headfirst, others feet first, and one balled up. The boys disappeared underwater, leaving behind them different-sized splashes, then Melly heard the echoes of their jumping screams a full second or two after they'd gone under. By then, they were shooting up out of the water, their arms raised in the air. They'd done it. Most of the boys in Three Oaks had to dive from the bridge at one time or other to prove themselves real men. Today was their day.

Melly saw the boys crawl from the river and turn over on their backs, stretched out like lizards sunning themselves on the bank. Reeling in her line, she thought, So what if they can dive off the bridge! I could do it too if I wanted. Who said it was just for the guys to do?

"You'll do nothing of the kind," said Mr. Otero.

"Huh?"

"You said you could dive too if you wanted?"

"I didn't say anything. You must be hearing things."

← Realistic **dialogue** is used to introduce major and minor characters.

← Specific **details**, such as the boys "pounded their chests" and "shooting up out of the water," describe the setting and characters' actions.

← The story's **conflict** is introduced through realistic dialogue.

Think About the Professional Model

With a partner, discuss the following questions about the model.

1. How do sensory details help you picture the setting?

2. What is the mood of the narrative?

Prewriting

Choose a Story Idea

What keeps a reader turning pages? A good narrative needs a complex character facing a conflict. Here are two ways to choose a story idea.

- **Start with a Character** You might build your story around an interesting or unusual person. Remember, too, that you don't have to write about a real person—you can make up a character.

- **Start with a Conflict** You might begin with a problem or conflict that you have heard about or actually experienced. You might also enjoy writing about a completely imaginary situation. In either case, the narrative should include a **conflict**—a problem the major character faces.

Plan Characters and Setting

Characters The star of your story will be a complex **major character,** one who seems like a real person. The supporting roles will be played by **minor characters.** Ask yourself:

- What do your readers need to know about the characters?

- What is the major character's personality? What does he or she like or dislike? How does he or she act toward family and friends?

- How will the minor characters interact with the major character?

Setting You also will develop a definite **setting:** where and when the story takes place. Your setting gives information about your characters (a clean desk indicates neatness), creates a mood (an abandoned house suggests mystery), and creates conflict (a blizzard could bring trouble). Ask yourself:

- Where and when will the story take place?

- What places, weather, or times of day could be important?

- What concrete sensory details describe the setting?

Think About Purpose and Audience

As you think about your story, keep your **purpose** and **audience** in mind. Your **purpose** in writing a fictional narrative is to entertain your readers, who are your audience. Your **audience** is probably your classmates and your teacher. What will keep them so interested that they'll want to read to the end of your narrative?

Idea Starters

- people with unusual jobs
- people with special talents
- people with unique challenges
- dangerous adventures
- someone overcoming a problem
- scary happenings
- unexpected events

Types of Conflict

External: a character's struggle with outside forces

- The boys jump off the bridge into the water below.
- The boys jump to prove themselves to each other.

Internal: a character's struggle within his or her own mind

- Melly asks herself why she can't also dive off the bridge.

Your Turn —————

Get Started Making notes in your **RWN,** decide on the **major and minor characters** and **conflict,** considering **purpose** and **audience.** Then, answer the questions about the **characters** and **setting** on this page. Your notes will help you plan your fictional narrative.

 Learn It Online
An interactive graphic organizer can help you generate and organize essay ideas. Try one at:

go.hrw.com   L7-225   **Go**

Plan Your Plot

What will happen to the characters in your story? The **plot** is the series of events in a story. A **narrative action plan** organizes the parts of a story's plot. A plot includes the following:

- **Beginning** A good beginning introduces the characters, setting, and conflict and grabs readers' attention so that they keep reading.
- **Rising action** Conflict builds as the major character faces obstacles to solving his or her problem. Each new obstacle complicates the conflict, creates suspense, and helps build to the story's climax.
- **Climax (high point) and suspense** Your story needs a suspenseful moment when the conflict reaches a turning point—the problem will be settled, one way or another. Make your reader wonder, "How is this going to turn out?"
- **Denouement, or outcome** After reaching its climax, the conflict is resolved, usually leaving the major character changed in some way.

Narrative Action Plan

Here's one writer's narrative action plan. Use this model to help you create your own plan.

> ### Narrative Action Plan
> Characters: **major**—a girl walking by herself
> **minor**—someone following her
> Setting: the woods, near a campsite
> Conflict: the girl vs. her fear
> Beginning:
> 1. The girl is walking alone in the woods, separated from her friends.
> 2. She realizes she is lost and searches her pocket for something to help her.
>
> Rising action:
> 3. She hears crunching and footsteps and sees a shadow behind her.
>
> Climax:
> 4. The person following the girl finally reaches her.
>
> Denouement, or outcome:
> 5. The person hands the girl her cell phone and leaves. She realizes the person wasn't going to harm her.

Your Turn _____

Plan Your Plot To help you build your plot, make a **narrative action plan** for your fictional narrative in your **RWN.** Share your plan with a peer. Think about the feedback your peer provides. Revise your plan as needed, keeping in mind your **purpose** and **audience.**

Drafting

Determine Point of View

Who will tell, or narrate, your story? A story will be very different if it is told by someone involved in the events rather than by someone not involved. **Point of view** is the vantage point from which a story is told. The chart to the right explains the different points of view.

Use Dialogue

Dialogue, conversations between characters, has many purposes in narratives. It is often used to introduce the setting, characters, and conflict. From dialogue in "The Dive," we learn that the boys are diving in a dangerous spot and that Melly envies them. This reveals Melly's character traits, and we begin to guess what will happen next. Dialogue can also

- move the action of the plot forward
- create suspense
- explain complications
- explain the denouement

The dialogue in your narrative should be natural and imitate conversations you hear every day. For this reason, dialogue often includes fragments, contractions, and unique expressions.

Point of View	
First person	The narrator is a character in the story and can tell the reader only what he or she is thinking or feeling. The narrator uses the pronoun *I*.
Third-person limited	The narrator is not a character in the story. This narrator tells what *one* character—referred to as *he* or *she*—thinks and feels.
Third-person omniscient	The narrator is not a character in the story but knows what *every* character is thinking and feeling. This narrator can tell things that none of the characters could know.

Grammar Link Punctuating Dialogue

Study the following dialogue from "The Dive." Be sure to follow the punctuation rules when you write dialogue for your narrative.

> "You'll do nothing of the kind," said Mr. Otero.
>
> "Huh?"
>
> "You said you could dive too if you wanted?"
>
> "I didn't say anything. You must be hearing things."

- Begin a new paragraph every time a speaker changes.
- Use quotation marks to enclose what is being said. Punctuation marks for the dialogue—such as a comma, question mark, or period—appear inside the quotation marks.
- Use dialogue tags, such as *said Mr. Otero* to indicate the speaker. Not every line will have one. Use a dialogue tag to make it clear who is speaking.
- Place a period after the dialogue tag when the tag appears at the end of a sentence.

Reference Note For more about punctuating dialogue, see the Language Handbook.

Writing Tip

In fictional narratives, the main character usually wants something. Conflict occurs when the main character faces plot complications, obstacles that prevent her from getting what she wants. As you develop your fictional narrative, be sure to include plot complications that will increase suspense.

Your Turn

Draft Your Narrative

Following your narrative action plan, write a draft of your story. Also, think about

- who will tell your story (your narrator). Decide on the **point of view** in your narrative.
- how to use **dialogue** to bring characters to life.

Peer Review

Working with a peer, review the chart to the right. Then, review your drafts. Answer each question in this chart to determine how the drafts could be improved. Be sure to note on the drafts what you and your partner discuss. You can refer to your notes as you revise your draft.

Evaluating and Revising

Writing a draft is the beginning, not the end, of developing a good fictional narrative. The next step is to improve your draft by looking for places where you can add details about the characters, include dialogue, or develop your plot even better. The chart below will help you identify how to revise your draft.

Fictional Narrative: Guidelines for Content and Organization

Evaluation Question	Tip	Revision Technique
1. Does the story have an interesting plot with an effective beginning, a conflict, complications, a suspenseful climax, and a clear denouement?	**Place a check mark** next to each of the following elements: beginning, conflict, complications, climax, and denouement.	**Add** or **elaborate** on elements of the plot as necessary. **Delete** any information that ruins the suspense by giving too much away.
2. Is the point of view consistent throughout the story?	**Identify** pronouns (*I, he,* or *she*) that identify the point of view. **Label** the story's point of view; then, **circle** any information not given from that point of view.	If any sentences are circled, **delete** them. If necessary, **add** the same information but tell it from the narrator's point of view.
3. Are the characters complex and realistic?	**Underline** specific details about each of the characters.	If necessary, **add** details about a character's appearance, personality, or background. **Add** dialogue and narrative actions that reveal more about a character.
4. Does the story have a definite setting?	With a colored marker, **highlight** details of the setting.	If there are few highlighted words, **elaborate** on the setting by adding sensory, or descriptive, details.
5. Is the story well organized? Does it have an interesting beginning? A satisfactory denouement?	**Number** the major events in your story. **Put brackets** around the paragraphs around the beginning and the denouement. **Circle** places that are not interesting or satisfying.	**Rearrange** any events that are out of order. **Add** details or dialogue to make the beginning more interesting. **Add** details or events to make the denouement more satisfying.

Read this student draft and notice comments on its structure and suggestions for how it could be made even stronger.

A Stranger in the Woods

by Ashley Hildebrandt, Abiding Word Lutheran School

I was walking in the forest. I was all alone walking back to my tent. All of my friends had gone ahead of me because I was too slow. I'd been walking for about an hour now, and I knew I was lost now, which isn't very unusual for me. I was instantly sure of what I needed to do. I reached into my pocket and realized it was empty. I frantically searched the ground around myself and walked with panic in my movements. I remembered then where I'd left it. I had left my only hope out by the lake. I then heard a soft crunching of leaves. It continued rhythmically edging closer and closer. As I listened carefully, I hesitantly decided to run to the left.

The beginning of Ashley's fictional narrative establishes the major **character,** the **setting,** and the **conflict.**

Ashley further develops the **conflict** and begins to build **suspense.** Notice the excellent use of sensory details as she hears noises in the woods.

MINI-LESSON How to Use Dialogue for an Effective Beginning

Ashley might use dialogue for a more effective beginning. Dialogue will add both interest and needed information to the beginning of her narrative.

Ashley's Draft

I was walking in the forest. I was all alone walking back to my tent. All of my friends had gone ahead of me because I was too slow. I'd been walking . . .

Notice that these sentences are repetitive in structure and don't have that "hook" of interest that a good beginning needs. Ashley can improve it by adding dialogue.

Ashley's Revision of Paragraph One

"Hey, Turtle! We'll never get back to camp walking this slow!"

"Yeah," giggled Nina, "my bathing suit is wet and sticky. I'm running back to camp."

"Me, too," agreed the rest of my friends. They disappeared, leaving me trudging alone—all alone.

I'd been walking . . .

Your Turn _____

Use Dialogue Read your draft, and then ask yourself:

• What dialogue would make the narrative more interesting or would provide background information?

• What sensory details or images would make my narrative more vivid?

Student Draft *continues*

I ran as fast as my legs could carry me until the only sound audible was my hard breathing and my feet gently destroying the leaves beneath me. I breathed a sigh of relief. An owl hoot-hooted. I caught a glimpse of the bright full moon. The soft crunching began again. A jolt of panic shot up my spine as I saw an approaching shadow. My heart and breathing paused, and I couldn't get my legs to move.

The man, now visible, moved closer, with death written all over his face. As I was building up the courage to scream, the man stopped only an arm's length away from me.

The man stared at me for what seemed like a lifetime and finally asked, "This yours?"

"Yes," I whispered.

He handed me the phone and walked off into the darkness of the woods and I stood staring after him. I walked right after him in order to thank him and after walking for a minute, I stood in front of five tents surrounded by my friends. I never thanked the stranger in the woods.

The **suspense** builds as the man gets closer.

Ashley uses two lines of **dialogue** to show how the conflict is resolved.

The **denouement,** or **resolution,** shows the main character safely back with her friends, regretting that she did not thank the stranger.

MINI-LESSON ▶ How to Add Concrete, Sensory Details

In her draft, Ashley tells the reader that the man following her "has death written all over his face." She does not use sensory details to describe him, and the reader cannot visualize his face from her words. Since the man is simply returning her cell phone, the words do not fit the context of the narrative. How can Ashley create suspense but not mislead the reader? Concrete, sensory details will help her describe the stranger.

Ashley revised the sentence referring to the man by using concrete, sensory details.

Ashley's Draft of Paragraph Three

The man, now visible, moved closer, with death written all over his face.

Ashley's Revision

⟨in the moonlight⟩   perspiration dripping from his red, puffy face.
The man, now visible, moved closer, with ~~death written all over his face.~~

Your Turn _____

Add Concrete, Sensory Details With a partner, find sentences in your draft where you can add sensory details that show the setting, situation, or characters instead of simply telling the reader about them. Share your revisions with your partner.

Proofreading and Publishing

Proofreading

Now that you have evaluated and revised your fictional narrative, it is time to polish and present your short story. Edit your narrative to correct any misspellings, punctuation errors, and problems in sentence structure.

Proofreading Partners Ask two classmates to help you edit. For example, one student can read your paper, looking only for misspellings. Another can read for punctuation errors. By specializing, your editing experts will find errors you may have overlooked.

> **Grammar Link** **Eliminating Repetition**
>
> Be careful to avoid repeating conjunctions, such as *and*, *but*, and *so*. In the last paragraph of her draft, Ashley uses the word *and* three times. To eliminate repetition, Ashley first circled the repeated word and wrote new, more varied sentences.
>
> He handed me the phone and walked off into the darkness of the woods and I stood
>
> staring after him. I walked right after him in order to thank him and after walking for a
>
> *suddenly*
> minute, I stood in front of five tents surrounded by my friends.
>
> Notice how Ashley kept the first *and* that separated verbs and also deleted the two *and*'s that separated complete sentences. These changes make her conclusion more effective.

Publishing

Now it is time to publish your narrative to a wider audience. Here are some ways to share your story:

- Illustrate your story, bind it, and give it as a gift to a friend or family member.
- Have a story event in your class. You and your classmates can form small groups and read your stories aloud to each other.

Reflect on the Process
Thinking about how you wrote your fictional narrative will help you with other writing that you'll do. In your **RWN,** write a short response to each of the following questions.

1. What was the most challenging aspect of writing a fictional narrative?
2. What techniques helped you develop your characters, setting, and plot?
3. How did using a narrative action plan help you? Explain.
4. What have you learned from this workshop that might help you with other types of writing?

● Proofreading Tip

One way to catch errors in grammar, usage, and mechanics is to get some help from a peer. Ask a peer to read your draft for repetition in sentence structure and in the use of words like *and, but,* or *very*. Where should you combine sentences or eliminate overuse of some words?

Submission Ideas

- school newspaper
- school literary magazine
- short story contests
- online literary magazine
- your personal Web page
- class or school Web page

Your Turn _____

Proofread and Publish As you are proofreading, look carefully for ineffective repetitions of conjunctions such as *and, but,* or *so.* Try to remove some of them to make your sentence structure more varied. Then publish your narrative for others to enjoy.

Scoring Rubric

You can use one of the rubrics below to evaluate your fictional narrative from the Writing Workshop or your response to the prompt on the next page. Your teacher will tell you to use either the four- or the six-point rubric.

6-Point Scale

Score 6 *Demonstrates advanced success*
- focuses consistently on narrating a single incident or a unified sequence of incidents
- shows effective narrative sequence throughout, with smooth transitions
- offers a thoughtful, creative approach to the narration
- develops the story thoroughly, using precise and vivid descriptive and narrative details
- exhibits mature control of written language

Score 5 *Demonstrates proficient success*
- focuses on narrating a single incident or a unified sequence of incidents
- shows effective narrative sequence, with transitions
- offers a thoughtful approach to the narration
- develops the story competently, using descriptive and narrative details
- exhibits sufficient control of written language

Score 4 *Demonstrates competent success*
- focuses on narrating a single incident or a unified sequence of incidents, with minor distractions
- shows effective narrative sequence, with minor lapses
- offers a mostly thoughtful approach to the narration
- develops the story adequately, with some descriptive and narrative details
- exhibits general control of written language

Score 3 *Demonstrates limited success*
- includes some loosely related material that distracts from the writer's narrative focus
- shows some organization, with noticeable flaws in the narrative flow
- offers a routine, predictable approach to the narration
- develops the story with uneven use of descriptive and narrative detail
- exhibits limited control of written language

Score 2 *Demonstrates basic success*
- includes loosely related material that seriously distracts from the writer's narrative focus
- shows minimal organization, with major gaps in the narrative flow
- offers a narrative that merely skims the surface
- develops the story with inadequate descriptive and narrative detail
- exhibits significant problems with control of written language

Score 1 *Demonstrates emerging effort*
- shows little awareness of the topic and the narrative purpose
- lacks organization
- offers an unclear and confusing narrative
- develops the story with little or no detail
- exhibits major problems with control of written language

4-Point Scale

Score 4 *Demonstrates advanced success*
- focuses consistently on narrating a single incident or a unified sequence of incidents
- shows effective narrative sequence throughout, with smooth transitions
- offers a thoughtful, creative approach to the narration
- develops the story thoroughly, using precise and vivid descriptive and narrative details
- exhibits mature control of written language

Score 3 *Demonstrates competent success*
- focuses on narrating a single incident or a unified sequence of incidents, with minor distractions
- shows effective narrative sequence, with minor lapses
- offers a mostly thoughtful approach to the narration
- develops the story adequately, with some descriptive and narrative details
- exhibits general control of written language

Score 2 *Demonstrates limited success*
- includes some loosely related material that distracts from the writer's narrative focus
- shows some organization, with noticeable flaws in the narrative flow
- offers a routine, predictable approach to the narration
- develops the story with uneven use of descriptive and narrative detail
- exhibits limited control of written language

Score 1 *Demonstrates emerging effort*
- shows little awareness of the topic and the narrative purpose
- lacks organization
- offers an unclear and confusing narrative
- develops the story with little or no detail
- exhibits major problems with control of written language

Fictional Narrative

When responding to an on-demand fictional narrative prompt, use the models you have read, what you've learned from writing your own fictional narrative, the rubric on page 232, and the steps below.

> ### Writing Prompt
> Conflict is a part of life and an important element of any story. Think about the kinds of problems or conflicts that sometimes arise between good friends. Perhaps you even remember working through a conflict with your own friend. Write a fictional narrative about two best friends in conflict. Create believable characters and place them in a definite setting. Give specific details about events that lead to a resolution of the conflict.

Study the Prompt
Begin by reading the prompt carefully. Note what is required in your narrative: a conflict, believable characters, and a definite setting. **Tip:** Spend about five minutes studying the prompt.

Plan Your Response
Think of an experience (real or imagined), characters, or a place on which you could base a fictional narrative. Which of these do you know well enough to write about in detail? Once you have settled on your story idea,

- write down the conflict the characters will face, along with events that will lead to a resolution
- write vivid descriptions of each character
- list details about the setting

Tip: Spend about fifteen minutes planning your response.

Respond to the Prompt
Using your notes about conflict, characters, and setting, draft your fictional narrative. Follow these guidelines:

- Start writing, even if you're unsure about how to begin. You can always go back and rewrite the beginning of the story later.
- Write from the same point of view throughout your narrative. Will one of the characters tell the story, or will an all-knowing narrator tell the story?
- Use realistic dialogue to bring your characters to life.

As you are writing, remember to use words that are best for your audience—not too formal. Write as neatly as you can. If your fictional narrative can't be read easily, it won't be scored. **Tip:** Spend about twenty minutes writing your draft.

Improve Your Response
Revising Go back over the key aspects of the prompt. Does your fictional narrative explain the conflict? Have you described the setting? Are your characters believable?

Proofreading Take a few minutes to proofread your story to correct errors in grammar, spelling, punctuation, and capitalization. Make sure all your edits are neat, and erase any stray marks.

Checking Your Final Copy Before you turn your story in, read it one more time to catch any errors you may have missed. You'll be glad that you took the extra time for one final review. **Tip:** Save ten minutes to improve your paper.

Presenting a Short Story

Think as a Reader/Writer When you prepare a short story, or fictional narrative, for oral presentation, you still need to think like a writer. You'll want to hook your listeners with an interesting introduction and give them a clear understanding of the story's plot.

Storytelling is a universal human experience. Ancient epics credited to the Greek writer Homer were undoubtedly shared orally long before he wrote them down. You may remember being told stories as a child, or maybe you've even told some yourself to a younger relative.

Plan Your Short Story

Story Idea

You may want to adapt your written short story for oral presentation. However, if you decide to prepare a new story for your presentation, you may again want to start with an idea from personal experience. Also, try to think of a story that will appeal to your classmates.

Plot

As with your written fictional narrative, you'll need to consider the conflict your characters face. You may decide that a physical danger or challenge is more fun to present orally than a conflict that involves a character's internal emotions or struggles.

Characters and Setting

Describing characters and reading their dialogue can be a lot of fun. Try to use the most colorful descriptions you can think of, and prepare believable dialogue that will also be interesting to read and hear aloud. Remember to tell the story from the same point of view throughout. If you start the story from the point of view of a character (first person), don't start telling listeners what other characters are thinking.

You can describe setting much as you did in your written short story, with the added benefit of using nonverbal language for effect. Try to sprinkle descriptions of setting throughout your story, including in dialogue. You will learn more about using nonverbal language on the next page.

Reader/Writer Notebook

Use your **RWN** to complete the activities for this workshop.

Deliver Your Short Story

Be an Entertainer

In your written short story, your only way to describe characters and setting was with written words. In oral storytelling, however, you are free to use some acting techniques. Use the verbal and nonverbal techniques below to liven up your presentation and entertain your audience.

Verbal Technique	Example
Pitch	Change the pitch (rise and fall) of your voice when reading dialogue between different characters or to add emphasis.
Rate	Speak more slowly or more quickly to show excitement in a story or to portray a character's personality.
Volume	Speak loudly enough for listeners in the back to hear you.
Tone	The tone you use will be determined by your story. Is your story serious, humorous, mysterious, or exciting?

Nonverbal Technique	Example
Eye contact	Use eye contact to involve your readers or for humorous effect.
Facial expressions	Show meaning with squints, raised eyebrows, smiles, or frowns.
Gestures	Use gestures, such as shrugs, nods, or hand movements, to show a character's behavior.
Posture	Slouch or stand upright to help portray a character's attitude.

Use Note Cards

You may be allowed to read your fictional narrative directly from your paper. If not, note cards are a useful way to keep your story on track. Write a basic plot outline on your note cards, listing the conflict, main events, and resolution. You might also want to write down specific lines of dialogue, with notes on which nonverbal techniques to use. Practice your verbal and nonverbal techniques in front of a mirror. Finally, rehearse your presentation over and over, using a tape recorder or video camera, if possible.

> ### A Good Short-Story Presentation
> - presents a clear conflict
> - uses colorful character descriptions and dialogue
> - gives listeners specific details about setting
> - uses verbal and nonverbal techniques effectively

◯ Speaking Tip

You may want to alter your voice to represent different characters, but always speak clearly enough for your listeners to understand you. Standard English is not essential when using dialogue, but avoid using words and phrases that might be unclear to some listeners.

Learn It Online
Pictures can help bring your narrative to life. See how in *MediaScope,* on:

go.hrw.com   L7-235   **Go**

Literary Skills Review

Plot and Setting   **Directions:** Read the following selection. Then, read and respond to the questions that follow.

from On the Banks of Plum Creek

by **Laura Ingalls Wilder**

Young Laura is playing on the tableland (plateau) where her father had warned her not to go alone.

The tableland seemed big and empty and not interesting. It had been exciting when Pa was there, but now it was just flat land, and Laura thought she would go home and get a drink. She was very thirsty.

She slid down the side of the tableland and slowly started back along the way she had come. Down among the tall grasses the air was smothery and very hot. The dugout was far away and Laura was terribly thirsty.

She remembered with all her might that she must not go near that deep, shady swimming pool, and suddenly she turned around and hurried toward it. She thought she would only look at it. Just looking at it would make her feel better. Then she thought she might wade in the edge of it but she would not go into the deep water.

She came into the path that Pa had made, and she trotted faster. Right in the middle of the path before her stood an animal.

Laura jumped back, and stood and stared at it. She had never seen such an animal. . . . Long gray fur bristled all over it. It had a flat head and small ears. Its flat head slowly tilted up and it stared at Laura.

She stared back at its funny face. And while they stood still and staring, that animal widened and shortened and spread flat on the ground. It grew flatter and flatter, till it was a gray fur laid there. It was not like a whole animal at all. Only it had eyes staring up.

Slowly and carefully Laura stooped and reached and picked up a willow stick. She felt better then. She stayed bent over, looking at the flat gray fur.

It did not move and neither did Laura. She wondered what would happen if she poked it. It might change to some other shape. She poked it gently with the short stick.

A frightful snarl came out of it. Its eyes sparked mad, and fierce white teeth snapped almost on Laura's nose.

Laura ran with all her might. She could run fast. She did not stop running until she was in the dugout. . . .

Laura had been bad and she knew it. She had broken her promise to Pa. But no one had seen her. No one knew that she had started to go to the swimming hole. If she did not tell, no one would ever know. Only that strange animal knew, and it could not tell on her. But she felt worse and worse inside.

1. The **setting**, the prairie tableland, in this story —
   A puts the plot in motion
   B is the climax of the plot
   C is the plot's resolution
   D does not affect the plot

2. The *initial* reason Laura heads home is because she is —
   A afraid of being punished
   B feeling guilty
   C frightened by the animal
   D very thirsty

3. Which aspect of the setting causes the *main* problem, or **conflict,** in the story?
   A There is no water to drink.
   B Dangerous animals live there.
   C It is easy to get lost in flat land.
   D The swimming pool is forbidden.

4. **Plot complications** in the story are caused by Laura's —
   A fearfulness
   B disobedience
   C loneliness
   D shame

5. What is the *main* **conflict** Laura faces?
   A Disobeying her father
   B Deciding to go to the swimming pool
   C Confronting the unknown animal
   D Figuring out how to get drinking water

6. The **climax** of the story occurs when —
   A the animal strikes out at Laura
   B Laura first sees the animal
   C Laura turns toward the pool
   D Laura feels ashamed

7. The use of the word *bristled* in describing the animal advances the **plot** by —
   A introducing a new character
   B introducing another complication
   C using foreshadowing
   D resolving the conflict

Constructed Response

8. Explain what happens in the **resolution** of the story.

Informational Skills Review

Text Structures   **Directions:** Read the following informational texts. Then, answer each question that follows.

 CHAPTER 2

Biomes: World Plant Regions

What is a biome? A plant and animal community that covers a very large land area is called a biome. Plants are the most visible part of a biome. If you looked down on the United States from space, you would see various biomes. The forests of the eastern United States would appear green, while the deserts of the Southwest would be light brown.

NEWSPAPER ARTICLE

B2

Hatteras Lighthouse Completes Its Move

BUXTON, N.C., July 9 (AP)—As onlookers clapped and cheered, the Cape Hatteras Lighthouse slid today onto the concrete pad where its caretakers hope it will stand for another century, a safe distance from the thundering Atlantic surf.

MANUAL

page 32

Looking Up Synonyms for a Word in a Document

1. Select the word in the document.
2. Choose Utilities Thesaurus (Alt,U,T), or press the THESAURUS key (Shift+F7).
3. Look through the list of synonyms in Synonyms. Scroll through the list if necessary.

Command for Thesaurus

Utilities Thesaurus or THESAURUS key (Shift+F7)

    Lists alternative words for the selection

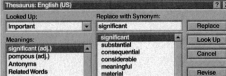

1. Which statement explains the difference between the **purpose** of a textbook and the purpose of a newspaper article?

   A A textbook has an index, a glossary, and graphic features, while a newspaper article has an inverted pyramid structure.

   B A textbook has a table of contents and an index, while a newspaper article has a headline, a dateline, and a byline.

   C A textbook presents information and questions about a main subject, while a newspaper article gives information about a current event.

   D A textbook has many pages, while a newspaper article is usually one page long or less.

2. In comparing the **structure** of a textbook and the structure of an instructional manual, you could say that a textbook —

   A has a longer table of contents than an instructional manual

   B presents information about a broad subject, but an instructional manual presents information on how to operate a device

   C is used in the classroom, but a manual is used at home

   D is given to you to use by your school, while a manual comes with something you buy

3. In the textbook excerpt on the opposite page, the definition of the word *biome* appears in the —

   A text

   B index

   C caption

   D table of contents

4. If the directions in an instructional manual have steps, the steps —

   A must be read first

   B do not need to be read

   C should be followed in order

   D will appear in the glossary

5. The excerpt from the newspaper article on the opposite page shows all of the following features *except* a —

   A byline

   B dateline

   C page number

   D headline

Constructed Response

6. Explain why an instructional manual has diagrams and an index.

Vocabulary Skills Review

Context Clues

Directions: As you read each sentence from "Three Skeleton Key," use other words or phrases to help you determine the meaning of the italicized word. Then choose the best answer.

1. "[Lighthouse tending] is mostly *monotonous*, routine work—keeping the light in order, making out the reports."

   A tedious

   B musical-sounding

   C enjoyable

   D out of the ordinary

2. "Still, on our island, one must be careful, for the rocks were *treacherously* smooth."

   A dependably

   B dangerously

   C truly

   D daringly

3. "She came for us at full speed, as if she were leading the regatta at a race, and *impaled* herself on a sharp point of rock."

   A killed

   B punished

   C armed

   D pierced

4. "Their odor filled the tower, poisoned our lungs, and rasped our nostrils with a *pestilential*, nauseating smell."

   A nasty

   B dangerous

   C deadly

   D pressing

5. "They moved *incessantly*, never still."

   A considerably

   B quickly

   C clumsily

   D constantly

6. "When they *fumigated* the light and repaired the damage done by the rats, I resumed my service there."

   A purified

   B damaged

   C ridiculed

   D dynamited

Academic Vocabulary

Directions: Use the context clues in the following sentence to determine the meaning of the italicized word.

7. "Rikki-tikki-tavi" and "Three Skeleton Key" are *similar* stories: Both feature a great deal of suspense and a rousing climax.

   A pleasant

   B lengthy

   C alike

   D strange

Writing Skills Review

(1) Breannah stood in the goal, shifting her weight from one foot to the other, as a swarm of red jerseys nudged the soccer ball toward her. (2) A lone blue-clad defender tried and failed to cut off the attack. (3) Now no one stood between her and the lanky star forward of the Red Hots. (4) The forward kicked the ball, and Breannah leaped to her right. (5) The ball whooshed past her left ear and into the net. (6) She rose slowly and brushed herself off, ignoring the cheers from the Red Hots' bleachers. (7) Next time, Breannah thought, she would be ready.

---

1. What strategy does the writer use to develop the main character?
   A Dialogue spoken by the character
   B Description of the character's appearance
   C Description of the character's thoughts and actions
   D Explanation of how other people respond to the character

2. What details does the writer use to show point of view in this passage?
   A The words *she* and *her* and the main character's thoughts are used to show third-person-limited point of view.
   B The word *I* is used to show first-person point of view.
   C The word *you* is used to show second-person point of view.
   D Information about other characters' thoughts is used to show third-person-omniscient point of view.

3. If this passage occurs near the story's beginning, what might the writer do in later passages to build toward the climax?
   A Summarize events in the story that readers have already read about
   B Describe additional problems that add to the story's conflict
   C Change the point of view to include other characters' views of events
   D Describe the setting in detail

4. If a speaker were telling this story out loud, why might she begin by explaining that the story was based on a friend's experience playing soccer?
   A To point out the story's climax
   B To create a mood of suspense
   C To establish a context for the story
   D To include realistic dialogue

Read On

Fiction

Treasure Island

Jim Hawkins is an impressionable young cabin boy. When he discovers a treasure map, he finds himself thrust into an adventure beyond compare. The notorious Long John Silver joins Jim and crew on the sailing ship *Hispaniola*. Can Hawkins trust this mysterious pirate? Find out in Robert Louis Stevenson's classic novel *Treasure Island*.

MindBenders

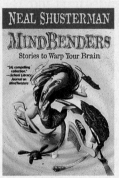

What if you get on the bad side of a Hawaiian volcano goddess? Could you imagine being struck by lightning and finding yourself 140 years in the past? What would you do if you woke up one morning and saw seven guardian angels having a chat in your bedroom? Neal Shusterman presents these wacky situations and more in *MindBenders*.

Lupita Mañana

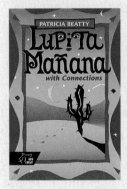

In *Lupita Mañana* by Patricia Beatty, thirteen-year-old Lupita Torres and her older brother enter California without papers. Lupita wants to help support her widowed mother and younger siblings in Mexico by finding a job. At times it is a struggle; However, Lupita shows determination to succeed no matter what the obstacle.

Fever 1793

The deadly illness in *Fever 1793* is yellow fever—a disease that killed thousands annually until its deadly agent, the mosquito, was identified. The eighteenth-century outbreak finds fourteen-year-old Mattie trapped in the city with her sick mother. Mattie escapes to the country, but within the span of a few horrific months, she must grow from a sullen teenager into a courageous adult. Laurie Halse Anderson's award-winning novel takes you to a time when there were no modern medicines and death could come from an insect's bite.

Nonfiction

Snakes

Mostly jump-out-of-your-skin scary, sometimes dangerous, and always fascinating—*Snakes* from the Zoobooks series will give you an instructive introduction to these scaly creatures. How do they move? Where do they live? Why do they behave the way they do? With scientific photographs and enjoyable text, John Bonnett Wexo provides inspiration for future research into the lives of these reptiles.

Black Heroes of the American Revolution

During the nation's war for independence from Britain, people from all walks of life took up arms to protect the newly born United States. In *Black Heroes of the American Revolution*, Burke Davis tells the stories of the black soldiers, sailors, spies, scouts, guides, and wagon drivers who bravely faced danger for the country they called their own.

Red Scarf Girl

When Ji-li Jiang turned twelve, in 1966, she was a bright student with a promising future. Then Mao Tse-tung launched the Cultural Revolution in China, and her family's background was revealed. As a result, Ji-li's friends turned their backs on her, and Chinese officials cruelly mistreated her family. In *Red Scarf Girl* Ji-li recalls her taxing childhood and the bravery that helped her grow up.

Final Frontier

Final Frontier introduces you to the history and science of humankind's efforts to journey into outer space. Color photographs accompany the description of the birth of rocketry and jet-propelled aircraft, as well as the competition between nations to be the first to put people into space and eventually on the moon.

Learn It Online
Find study guides for *Treasure Island*, *Lupita Mañana*, *Red Scarf Girl*, and more online at *NovelWise*:

go.hrw.com   L7-243   **Go**

Character

INFORMATIONAL TEXT FOCUS

Text Structures: Comparison and Contrast

"Be who you are and say what you feel, because those who matter don't mind and those who mind don't matter."

—Dr. Seuss (Theodor Seuss Geisel)

What Do **You** Think

How do other people help you discover something within yourself?

Actors portraying characters from the movie *X-Men: The Last Stand.*

Learn It Online

What makes up a character? Let *PowerNotes* show you at:

go.hrw.com | L7-245 | **Go**

Literary Focus

by **Linda Rief**

How Do Writers Reveal Character?

There are no stories without them. Good stories let us imagine how they look and act and feel. The way they talk gives us clues about who they are and what they might do. We are saddened or embarrassed, angered or scared, happy or satisfied, because of them. They make us think or feel something about ourselves and the world because we care about them. They are the characters in stories.

Rikki-tikki-tavi

- clever
- tricks the mother snake
- curious
- brave
- spends all day exploring the house
- fights two snakes

Character Traits and Characterization

Character Traits What is your best friend like? Funny? Patient? Outgoing? The words you use to describe your friend are his or her **character traits.** In stories you discover character traits as you read. The process of revealing a character's traits in a story is called **characterization.** There are two different approaches writers take to help you get to know the characters they create.

Direct Characterization Sometimes a writer will just tell you what a character is like: "Luther was the meanest cuss in town." A statement like this is known as **direct characterization.**

Indirect Characterization Other writers want you to get to know fictional characters just as you do in real life—by observing them and deciding what kind of people they are. You ask: What do they look like? How do they act? What do they say? How do they say it? How do other people feel about them? When writers reveal characters by *showing* you who they are rather than *telling* you, they are using **indirect characterization.**

Elements of Characterization

How does a writer *show* what a character is like?

1. **Appearance** Think about what you learn immediately from this description of a key detail about a character's appearance.

> The Russian looked at the orthopedic shoes I was wearing and the metal braces that went from my right foot to the top of my thigh.
>
> from "That October"
> by D. H. Figueredo

2. **Actions** The writer could say, "Mama was mad." However, this description of Mama's actions reveals her character more clearly:

> And every time the painter lady asked a fool question, Mama would dump another spoonful of rice on the pile. She was tapping her foot and heating up in a dangerous way.
>
> from "The War of the Wall"
> by Toni Cade Bambara

3. **Speech** Listen to a character talk, and you will begin to learn who he or she is. You find out that the narrator is protective of his neighborhood from a simple statement:

> "You're not even from around here," I hollered up after her.
>
> from "The War of the Wall"
> by Toni Cade Bambara

4. **Thoughts and Feelings** Here's where literature beats real life. You can't read another person's mind, but in a story you can find out what characters are thinking and get clues about who they are.

> Oh please, don't say anything, Victor pleaded with his eyes. I'll wash your car, mow your lawn, walk your dog—anything! I'll be your best student, and I'll clean your erasers after school.
>
> from "Seventh Grade" by Gary Soto

5. **Other Characters' Reactions** What do others in the story think of a character? What do they say or how do they act toward the character? Of course, just as in life, you have to consider the source and decide which characters you trust. If a character is insulting to everyone, his comments probably tell you more about *him* than about the others.

> All weekend long, me and Lou tried to scheme up ways to recapture our wall. Daddy and Mama said they were sick of hearing about it. Grandmama turned up the TV to drown us out.
>
> from "The War of the Wall"
> by Toni Cade Bambara

Your Turn Analyze Characterization

1. Explain the difference between direct and indirect characterization.

2. Think of a favorite character from a story or novel. Write down two or three words that describe the character and an example of how the writer revealed each characteristic. (You might want to use a graphic like the one on the previous page.)

Learn It Online

Learn how to identify literary elements in novels at *NovelWise*:

go.hrw.com | L7-247 | **Go**

Analyzing Visuals

How Can You Determine Character from a Photograph?

Actions speak louder than words. Writers use characters' actions, appearance, dialogue, and thoughts to portray their character traits. In visual art, however, only actions and appearance reveal character. A painting of a strong man on horseback suggests heroic traits. Similarly, a photograph can capture telling aspects of a person's appearance and actions.

Determining Character from a Photograph

Answer these questions as you determine character from a photograph.

1. Look carefully at the facial expression and body language of the subject. Is the person cheerful? worried? joyful? bored?

2. Examine lighting and color to assess the mood. Is the lighting dark and shadowy, or bright and even? Is the color upbeat or dreary?

3. Identify what is happening in the photograph. Is there action? If so, describe the subject's attitude toward the action.

4. Determine the subject's character through his or her attitude and appearance.

Use the questions above to examine character in these details from the photograph.

Amanda McCrory, U.S. athlete, wins first place in the women's wheelchair division, 2006 New York City Marathon.

1. McCrory finished the marathon in under ninety minutes. What does that show about her athleticism?

2. Shapes and colors can suggest ideas. What could the V shape of the finish-line tape suggest about the athlete?

3. Facial expression tells a lot about **character.** What does McCrory's expression suggest about her character?

Your Turn Write About Character

This photograph celebrates McCrory's victory. What qualities must she possess to have made it so far in spite of facing challenges? Make a character web for McCrory that identifies those traits.

Reading Focus

by **Kylene Beers**

What Is an Inference, and How Do I Make One?

Your friend asks, "What's wrong?" and you reply, "Nothing." But your friend knows that something *is* indeed wrong. Your friend listened to your answer but also paid attention to your facial expression, connected that to his or her own experiences, and made an inference—an educated guess. You make inferences as you read by making connections between what the author writes and your own experiences. Making connections helps you read for deeper meaning.

Making Inferences

To make inferences as you read, use clues in the text and your own knowledge and experiences to make an educated guess. When you make inferences about characters, you try to guess what kind of people they are based on how they act, what they say, and how other people respond to them. You might also make an inference about how a character will resolve a conflict or about what motivates a character to behave in a certain way.

Tips for Making Inferences Making connections to your own experiences helps you with making inferences. Think about how a character or event relates to what you know. (You'll find more ideas on connecting to stories on the next page.)

Remember that an inference is a conclusion that makes sense. You need evidence to support your inferences. That evidence comes from the writer's clues and your own experiences.

It Says / I Say / And So

You can use an It Says/I Say/And So chart to help you make inferences. Here is an example from "Seventh Grade" by Gary Soto:

It Says	I Say	And So ...
Writer's Clues	Own Experiences	Inference
Teresa looked at Victor and "smiled sweetly."	Someone who smiles at you usually likes you.	Teresa likes Victor.

Keep in mind that sometimes writers give clues that may lead you to draw incorrect conclusions. That's what makes a story interesting and exciting. As you read, keep watching for clues in the story, and be ready to make new inferences based on the new evidence you find.

Connecting to the Text

Making personal connections to texts helps you to read for deeper meaning. You may relate characters and events to your own life, to other stories you know, and to wider experiences.

The Text and You As you read, you may recognize connections with your own life that help you put yourself in the story. You may think

- "This character is like me because . . ."
- "I was in a similar situation when . . ."
- "I disagree with the writer's idea because . . ."

The Text and Another Text You may see similarities between the story you are reading and one you have already read that can help you understand new characters or the story's plot. You may think

- "This story reminds me of 'The Dive' because . . ."
- "This character reminds me of Superman because . . ."
- "This conflict reminds me of the fight between Rikki-tikki-tavi and Nag because . . ."

The Text and the World A story can help you make sense of a situation in your school or community, or it can help you understand peoples and conflicts in other places. You may think

- "This text reminds me of something I heard because . . ."
- "This setting reminds me of . . ."
- "This character is an example of . . ."

Analyzing How Character Affects Plot

Plot is the action of a story. Characters are the ones doing the acting. So if a character were different, then the plot would be different, too. You can figure out how a story would change if a character were different by using a strategy called If— Then. Think about a character's traits and the way the character behaves in the story. Then, imagine how the events in the story would be different if the character had different traits.

If . . .	Then . . .
A character were mean.	What would happen if the character were kind?

Apply the If—Then strategy to help you understand the way characters make a story what it is.

Your Turn Apply Reading Skills

1. Suppose you are called on to answer a question. You answer incorrectly. Instead of getting upset with you, the teacher smiles and says, "Better luck next time." What can you infer about the teacher?

2. Use the If—Then strategy to explain how a story about a date would change if a key character were bold instead of shy.

> Now go to the Skills in Action: Reading Model

Learn It Online
Learn how to make inferences online with *PowerNotes*:

| go.hrw.com | L7-251 | Go |

Read with a Purpose Read "Girls" to learn how the narrator, a thirteen-year-old boy, survives his first date. (This story is told by a first-person narrator who refers to himself as *I*.)

Girls

from **How Angel Peterson Got His Name**
by **Gary Paulsen**

Girls.

When we were eleven and even twelve they were just like us. Sort of.

That is, we could be friends and do projects together in school and some boys could even talk to them.

Not me. I never could. And neither could Orvis. Alan seemed to have worked out a way to pretend they weren't even there and Wayne swore that it didn't bother him at all to speak to girls.

And then we became thirteen.

Everything changed.

Well, not everything. I still couldn't talk to them, lived in mortal terror of them, and Orvis was the same way. But we talked *about* them all the time, how they looked, how they smiled, how they sounded, how they must think, about life, about us, how Elaine was really cute but Eileen had prettier hair and Eileen seemed one day to actually, actually look at me, right at me. But we couldn't speak *to* them.

Except that now it became very important that we be *able* to speak to them. Before, it didn't seem to matter, and now it was somehow the only thing that *did* matter.

Redlite/Greenlite Couple (2002)
by Diana Ong (1940–). Computer graphics.

I had this problem because Eileen actually *had* looked at me one day on the way out of school, or so I thought, and on top of it she had smiled—I was pretty sure at me as well—and I thought that maybe I was In Love and that it was For Real and when I asked Orvis about it he agreed that I might be In Love For Real and suggested that I take Eileen to a movie.

Which nearly stopped my heart cold. I couldn't talk to her—how could I ask her to go to a movie? Finally it was Orvis who thought of the way. I would ask Wayne to ask Shirley Johnson

Literary Focus

Character Traits Writers often include information that explains why characters act in certain ways. Here Paulsen uses indirect characterization by revealing the narrator's thoughts.

to ask Claudia Erskine, who was a close friend of Eileen's, if Eileen might like to go to the movies with me the following Saturday afternoon.

This tortuous procedure was actually followed and by the time I was told that indeed Eileen would like to see a movie the next Saturday, I was a nervous wreck and honestly hoped she wouldn't go.

We met in front of the theater, as things were done then at our age—I couldn't even imagine going to her home and ringing the bell to pick her up and having her parents answer the door. If I couldn't really speak to girls, what would I do with a set of *parents* of the girl I was going to take to a movie?

So we met at the theater at one-thirty. I wore what I thought were my best clothes, a pullover sweater over a turtleneck, with my feeble attempt at a flattop, Butch-Waxed so much that dropping an anvil on my head wouldn't have flattened it. I think now I must have looked something like a really uncomfortable, sweaty, walking, greasy-topped bottle brush. (Have I mentioned that with my sweater and turtleneck I had gone solely for

Literary Focus

Character Traits When Paulsen describes the narrator's appearance, he reveals two of the narrator's character traits: (1) He is concerned with the way he looks. (2) He is awkward.

Analyzing Visuals

Viewing and Interpreting What "tortuous procedure" might this visual represent?

Date-Line (2000) by Diana Ong (1940–). Computer graphics.

fashion and ignored the fact that it was high summer? Or that the theater was most decidedly *not* air-conditioned?)

But Eileen was a nice person and pretended not to notice the sweat filling my shoes so they sloshed when we walked or how I dropped my handful of money all over the ground. I had brought all of my seven dollars in savings because I really didn't know how much it would cost, what with tickets and treats, and maybe she was a big eater.

She also pretended not to notice when I asked her if she wanted popcorn.

So I asked her again. Louder.

And then again. Louder.

All because I was blushing so hard my ears were ringing and I wasn't sure if I was really making a sound and so when I screamed it out the third time and she jumped back, it more or less set the tone for the whole date.

We went into the theater all right. And we sat next to each other. And she was kind enough to overlook the fact that I smelled like a dead buffalo and that other than asking her three times if she wanted popcorn I didn't say a word to her. Not a word.

I couldn't.

The movie was called *The Thing,* about a creature from another planet who crashes to earth in the Arctic and develops a need/thirst/obsession for human and sled-dog blood and isn't killed until they figure out that he's really a kind of walking, roaring, grunting plant. So they rig up some wire to "cook him like a stewed carrot." All of this I learned the second time around, when I went to the movie with Wayne, because sitting next to Eileen, pouring sweat, giving her endless boxes of Dots and candy corn and popcorn (almost none of which she wanted but accepted nicely and set on the seat next to her), I didn't remember a single thing about the movie. Not a word, not a scene.

All I could do was sit and think, I'm this close to a girl, right next to a girl, my arm almost touching her arm, a girl, right there, right *there.* . . .

Read with a Purpose Considering his actions on this first date, what are the narrator's character traits? How would you describe him?

Literary Focus

Indirect Characterization Speech, actions, thoughts, and feelings are other ways that writers show what characters are like. In this passage, Paulsen uses different types of details to reveal that the narrator is shy and uncomfortable around Eileen.

Reading Focus

How Character Affects Plot Think about how this story would change if Eileen were rude instead of kind. She might have walked out of the theater by now.

Reading Focus

Making Inferences You can infer that the narrator forgets about the movie because he is so concerned with impressing Eileen.

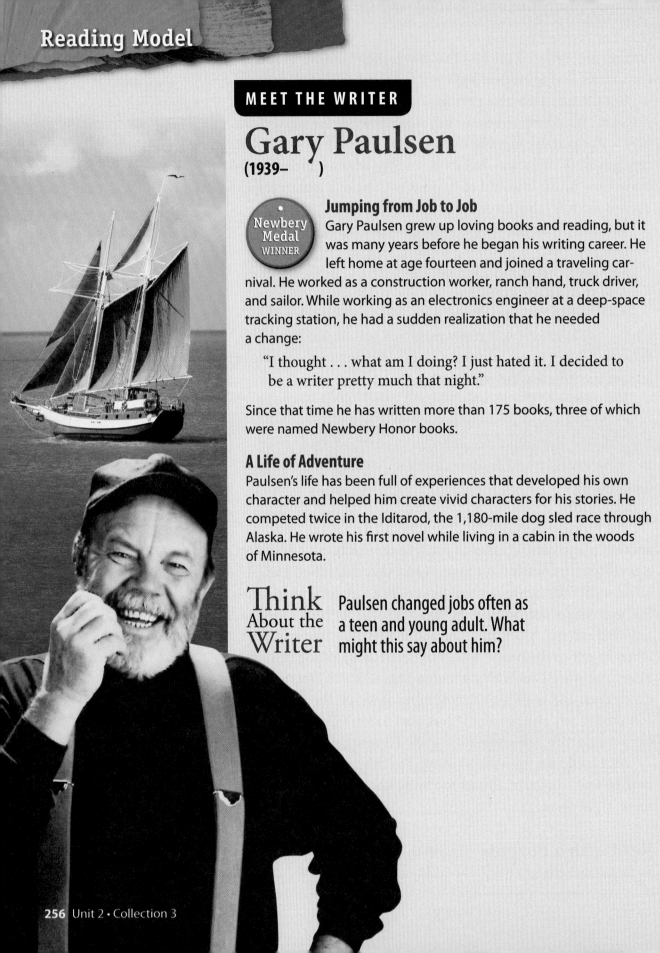

Gary Paulsen
(1939–   )

Newbery Medal WINNER

Jumping from Job to Job

Gary Paulsen grew up loving books and reading, but it was many years before he began his writing career. He left home at age fourteen and joined a traveling carnival. He worked as a construction worker, ranch hand, truck driver, and sailor. While working as an electronics engineer at a deep-space tracking station, he had a sudden realization that he needed a change:

> "I thought . . . what am I doing? I just hated it. I decided to be a writer pretty much that night."

Since that time he has written more than 175 books, three of which were named Newbery Honor books.

A Life of Adventure

Paulsen's life has been full of experiences that developed his own character and helped him create vivid characters for his stories. He competed twice in the Iditarod, the 1,180-mile dog sled race through Alaska. He wrote his first novel while living in a cabin in the woods of Minnesota.

Think About the Writer Paulsen changed jobs often as a teen and young adult. What might this say about him?

SKILLS IN ACTION
Wrap Up

Into Action: Making Inferences

Practice making inferences and analyzing characters. Re-read the end of "Girls." Then, use the chart to make an inference about the narrator's overall impression of his date with Eileen.

It Says	I Say	And So ...
Writer's Clues	Own Experiences	Inference

Talk About ...

1. How realistic is this story? With a partner, evaluate the credibility of the characters and situations. Use details from the story as you respond. Try to use each Academic Vocabulary word listed at the right at least once in your discussion.

Write About ...

Use the underlined Academic Vocabulary words in your answers to these questions about "Girls."

2. What underline attributes of Eileen's can you infer from her behavior?

3. Identify story details that characterize the narrator's nervousness around girls.

Writing Focus

Think as a Reader/Writer

Paulsen uses description to convey the narrator's appearance and behavior. Imagine a narrator who is confident and friendly on the date. Write a description that conveys the way he looks and acts. In this collection you'll have other opportunities to use the skills, or craft, writers use.

Academic Vocabulary for Collection 3

Talking and Writing About Character and Characterization

Academic Vocabulary is the language you use to write and talk about literature. Use these words to discuss the selections in this collection. The words are underlined throughout the collection.

attribute (AT ruh byoot) *n.:* quality or trait of someone or something. *The narrator's most obvious attribute is his awkwardness around girls.*

identify (y DEHN tuh fy) *v.:* recognize and be able to say what someone or something is. *If you identify a character's motivation, you often gain insights into that character's behavior.*

process (PRAHS ehs) *n.:* series of actions or steps toward a goal. *Characterization is a process of revealing a character's personality.*

respond (rih SPAHND) *v.:* say or write something as a reply. *Respond critically to the author's use of indirect characterization.*

Your Turn

Create a chart like this one to list the attributes of key characters in each selection in this collection.

Selection	Character	Attributes
"Girls"	Narrator	shy

SEVENTH GRADE

by **Gary Soto**

Heart Afire (1992)
by Gayle Ray
(1954–). Acrylic.

What Do You Think

It's natural to want people to like you. Explain if it is ever right to pretend to know more than you do.

 QuickWrite

Think of a time you or someone you know did something silly to impress someone. Write a short paragraph explaining what happened.

Reader/Writer Notebook

Use your **RWN** to complete the activities for this selection.

Literary Focus

Character Traits The characters in a story possess **character traits**—personal <u>attributes</u> that are revealed through a person's appearance, speech, actions, and thoughts and in the ways he or she affects other people.

Literary Perspectives Apply the literary perspective described on page 261 as you read this story.

Reading Focus

Making Inferences To understand a character, you have to make inferences. **Inferences** are educated guesses based on evidence. If you wake up in the morning and see puddles in the street, you can infer that it rained the night before.

Into Action As you read "Seventh Grade," record your inferences in an It Says/I Say/And So chart. Fill in details from the story in the first column. In the second, connect the writer's clues to your own experience. In the third, use what the story says and what you know to make an inference about the characters.

It Says	I Say	And So
Writer's Clues	My Experiences	Inference
Victor practices scowling to attract girls.	Last year I tried to impress someone by telling jokes.	Impressing some-one is more diffi-cult than it seems.

Writing Focus

Think as a Reader/Writer

Find It in Your Reading In "Seventh Grade" the author describes the appearance of several characters. In your *Reader/Writer Notebook,* record details about at least three characters, and explain what you can infer about each from the details.

Vocabulary

elective (ih LEHK tihv) *n.:* course that is not required. *When choosing his elective, Victor thought about French.*

propelled (pruh PEHLD) *v.:* moved or pushed forward. *The bell propelled students to their classes.*

conviction (kuhn VIHK shuhn) *n.:* certainty; belief. *Michael scowled with conviction, thinking it would impress the girls.*

lingered (LIHNG guhrd) *v.:* stayed on. *Victor lingered in the classroom so he could walk out with Teresa.*

sheepishly (SHEEP ihsh lee) *adv.:* awk-wardly; with embarrassment. *Victor smiled sheepishly at his teacher.*

Language Coach

Denotations/Connotations
Denotation is the dictionary definition of a word. **Connotation** is the feeling attached to a word. Authors often consider the connotations of the words they use to create more precise pictures in the reader's mind. Think about the connotations of the words below. Which creates a clearer impression in your mind?

- *belief* or *conviction*?
- *lingered* or *stayed*?
- *sheepishly* or *shyly*?

Learn It Online
Reinforce your understanding of these words at:

go.hrw.com   L7-259   **Go**

Learn It Online
Learn more about Soto's life at:
go.hrw.com L7-260 Go

Gary Soto
(1952–   )

"A Name Among *la Gente*"

Gary Soto grew up in a Mexican American family in California, and much of his award-winning fiction and poetry draws on his heritage and his childhood memories. Although his work is vastly popular today, Soto remembers that early on he worked hard to make connections with his readers.

"Unlike most other contemporary poets and writers, I've taken the show on the road and built a name among *la gente,* the people. I have ventured into schools, where I have played baseball and basketball with young people, sung songs, acted in skits, delivered commencement speeches, learned three chords on a Mexican guitar to serenade teachers. . . . From all appearances, my readers care."

Think About the Writer Why do you think being in touch with his audience is important to Gary Soto?

Build Background

Like Victor, the main character in "Seventh Grade," Gary Soto grew up in Fresno, a city in California's San Joaquin Valley with a large Mexican American community. Farmers in this valley grow more than two hundred different types of crops. The valley is one of the nation's leading producers of grapes and raisins.

Preview the Selection

On his first day in the seventh grade, **Victor** tries to impress his classmate **Teresa** by pretending to be someone he isn't.

Read with a Purpose Read this story to see how Victor survives his first day of seventh grade.

by **Gary Soto**

On the first day of school, Victor stood in line half an hour before he came to a wobbly card table. He was handed a packet of papers and a computer card on which he listed his one elective, French. He already spoke Spanish and English, but he thought some day he might travel to France, where it was cool; not like Fresno,[1] where summer days reached 110 degrees in the shade. There were rivers in France, and huge churches, and fair-skinned people everywhere, the way there were brown people all around Victor. **(A)**

Besides, Teresa, a girl he had liked since they were in catechism classes[2] at Saint Theresa's, was taking French, too. With any luck they would be in the same class. Teresa is going to be my girl this year, he promised himself as he left the gym full of students in their new fall clothes. She was cute. And good in math, too, Victor thought as he walked down the hall to his homeroom. He ran into his friend, Michael Torres, by the water fountain that never turned off. **(B)**

They shook hands, *raza*-style, and jerked their heads at one another in a *saludo de vato*.[3] "How come you're making a face?" asked Victor.

"I ain't making a face, *ese*. This *is* my face." Michael said his face had changed during the summer. He had read a *GQ* magazine that his older brother had

---

3. *saludo de vato* (sah LOO doh day BAH toh): Spanish for "homeboy greeting."

---

1. **Fresno:** town in the San Joaquin Valley, in central California.
2. **catechism** (KAT uh kihz uhm) **classes:** instruction in the principles of Christianity.

Literary Perspectives

The following perspective will help you think about the characters in "Seventh Grade."

Analyzing Credibility When you read a story about everyday people interacting in normal settings, think about whether the story is **credible,** or believable. Do the characters ring true in the way they behave? Does the narrator explain events in ways that make sense in the context of the story's plot? As you read "Seventh Grade," analyze the story for credibility. Be sure to read the notes and questions that will guide you in using the perspective.

(A) [Read and Discuss] What have you learned so far?

(B) [Read and Discuss] What have you learned about Victor's desire to take French?

Vocabulary **elective** (ih LEHK tihv) *n.:* course that is not required.

borrowed from the Book Mobile and noticed that the male models all had the same look on their faces. They would stand, one arm around a beautiful woman, and *scowl*. They would sit at a pool, their rippled stomachs dark with shadow, and *scowl*. They would sit at dinner tables, cool drinks in their hands, and *scowl*.

"I think it works," Michael said. He scowled and let his upper lip quiver. His teeth showed along with the ferocity of his soul. "Belinda Reyes walked by a while ago and looked at me," he said.

Victor didn't say anything, though he thought his friend looked pretty strange. They talked about recent movies, baseball, their parents, and the horrors of picking grapes in order to buy their fall clothes. Picking grapes was like living in Siberia,[4] except hot and more boring. **C**

"What classes are you taking?" Michael said, scowling.

"French. How 'bout you?"

"Spanish. I ain't so good at it, even if I'm Mexican."

---

4. **Siberia:** vast, barren, and cold region in Russia where criminals and political prisoners were often sent as punishment.

"I'm not either, but I'm better at it than math, that's for sure." **D**

A tinny, three-beat bell propelled students to their homerooms. The two friends socked each other in the arm and went their ways, Victor thinking, man, that's weird. Michael thinks making a face makes him handsome.

On the way to his homeroom, Victor tried a scowl. He felt foolish, until out of the corner of his eye he saw a girl looking at him. Umm, he thought, maybe it does work. He scowled with greater conviction.

In homeroom, roll was taken, emergency cards were passed out, and they were given a bulletin to take home to their parents. The principal, Mr. Belton, spoke over the crackling loudspeaker, welcoming the students to a new year, new experiences, and new friendships. The students squirmed in their chairs and ignored him. They were anxious to go to first period. Victor sat calmly, thinking of Teresa, who sat two rows away, reading a paperback novel. This would be his lucky year. She was in his homeroom, and would probably be in his English and math classes. And, of, course, French. **E**

> Victor sat calmly, thinking of Teresa, who sat two rows away, reading a paperback novel. This would be his lucky year.

C **Read and Discuss** What is Victor doing now? What is going on with Michael's face?

D **Literary Focus** **Character Traits** What does the conversation between Victor and Michael reveal?

E **Literary Perspectives** **Analyzing Credibility** What details about Victor's first day of seventh grade are believable? What events and emotions can you identify with?

Vocabulary **propelled** (pruh PEHLD) *v*.: moved or pushed forward.
conviction (kuhn VIHK shuhn) *n*.: certainty; belief.

The bell rang for first period, and the students herded noisily through the door. Only Teresa lingered, talking with the homeroom teacher.

"So you think I should talk to Mrs. Gaines?" she asked the teacher. "She would know about ballet?"

"She would be a good bet," the teacher said. Then added, "Or the gym teacher, Mrs. Garza."

Victor lingered, keeping his head down and staring at his desk. He wanted to leave when she did so he could bump into her and say something clever.

He watched her on the sly. As she turned to leave, he stood up and hurried to the door, where he managed to catch her eye. She smiled and said, "Hi, Victor."

He smiled back and said, "Yeah, that's me." His brown face blushed. Why hadn't he said, "Hi, Teresa," or "How was your summer?" or something nice?

As Teresa walked down the hall, Victor walked the other way, looking back, admiring how gracefully she walked, one foot in front of the other. So much for being in the same class, he thought. As he trudged to English, he practiced scowling.

In English they reviewed the parts of speech. Mr. Lucas, a portly man, waddled down the aisle, asking, "What is a noun?"

"A person, place, or thing," said the class in unison.

"Yes, now somebody give me an example of a person—you, Victor Rodriguez."

"Teresa," Victor said automatically. Some of the girls giggled. They knew he had a crush on Teresa. He felt himself blushing again.

"Correct," Mr. Lucas said. "Now provide me with a place."

Mr. Lucas called on a freckled kid who answered, "Teresa's house with a kitchen full of big brothers."

After English, Victor had math, his weakest subject. He sat in the back by the window, hoping that he would not be called on. Victor understood most of the problems, but some of the stuff looked like the teacher made it up as she went along. It was confusing, like the inside of a watch.

After math he had a fifteen-minute break, then social studies, and, finally, lunch. He bought a tuna casserole with buttered rolls, some fruit cocktail, and milk. He sat with Michael, who practiced scowling between bites.

Girls walked by and looked at him.

"See what I mean, Vic?" Michael scowled. "They love it."

"Yeah, I guess so."

They ate slowly, Victor scanning the horizon for a glimpse of Teresa. He didn't see her. She must have brought lunch, he thought, and is eating outside. Victor scraped his plate and left Michael, who was busy scowling at a girl two tables away.

F Read and Discuss The author supplies many details about Victor's day at school. What point do you think he is trying to make?

Vocabulary **lingered** (LIHNG guhrd) *v.*: stayed on.

The small, triangle-shaped campus bustled with students talking about their new classes. Everyone was in a sunny mood. Victor hurried to the bag lunch area, where he sat down and opened his math book. He moved his lips as if he were reading, but his mind was somewhere else. He raised his eyes slowly and looked around. No Teresa.

He lowered his eyes, pretending to study, then looked slowly to the left. No Teresa. He turned a page in the book and stared at some math problems that scared him because he knew he would have to do them eventually. He looked to the right. Still no sign of her. He stretched out lazily in an attempt to disguise his snooping.

Then he saw her. She was sitting with a girlfriend under a plum tree. Victor moved to a table near her and daydreamed about taking her to a movie. When the bell sounded, Teresa looked up, and their eyes met. She smiled sweetly and gathered her books. Her next class was French, same as Victor's. **(G)**

They were among the last students to arrive in class, so all the good desks in the back had already been taken. Victor was forced to sit near the front, a few desks away from Teresa, while Mr. Bueller wrote French words on the chalkboard. The bell rang, and Mr. Bueller wiped his hands, turned to the class, and said, "*Bonjour*."[5]

"*Bonjour*," braved a few students.

---

5. *bonjour* (bohn ZHOOR): French for "hello" or "good day."

"*Bonjour*," Victor whispered. He wondered if Teresa heard him.

Mr. Bueller said that if the students studied hard, at the end of the year they could go to France and be understood by the populace.

One kid raised his hand and asked, "What's 'populace'?"

"The people, the people of France."

Mr. Bueller asked if anyone knew French. Victor raised his hand, wanting to impress Teresa. The teacher beamed and said, "*Très bien. Parlez-vous français?*"[6] **(H)**

Victor didn't know what to say. The teacher wet his lips and asked something else in French. The room grew silent. Victor felt all eyes staring at him. He tried to bluff his way out by making noises that sounded French.

"La me vave me con le grandma," he said uncertainly.

Mr. Bueller, wrinkling his face in curiosity, asked him to speak up.

Great rosebushes of red bloomed on Victor's cheeks. A river of nervous sweat ran down his palms. He felt awful. Teresa sat a few desks away, no doubt thinking he was a fool. Without looking at Mr. Bueller, Victor mumbled, "Frenchie oh wewe gee in September." **(I)**

Mr. Bueller asked Victor to repeat what he said. "Frenchie oh wewe gee in September," Victor repeated.

---

6. *Très bien. Parlez-vous français* (tray bee EHN PAHR lay voo frahn SAY): French for "Very good. Do you speak French?"

(G) Literary Focus Character Traits What does Teresa's smile tell you about her?

(H) Literary Perspectives Analyzing Credibility Do you believe that Victor knows how to speak French? Why or why not?

(I) Read and Discuss How is French class going for Victor?

Analyzing Visuals Viewing and Interpreting What does this image suggest about the story and its main characters?

Los Angeles (2006) by José Ramirez. Mixed media on canvas. ©Courtesy of the artist.

Mr. Bueller understood that the boy didn't know French and turned away. He walked to the blackboard and pointed to the words on the board with his steel-edged ruler. **J**

"*Le bateau,*" he sang.

"*Le bateau,*" the students repeated.

"*Le bateau est sur l'eau,*" he sang.

"*Le bateau est sur l'eau.*"[7]

Victor was too weak from failure to join the class. He stared at the board and wished he had taken Spanish, not French. Better yet, he wished he could start his life over. He had never been so embarrassed. He bit his thumb until he tore off a sliver of skin.

The bell sounded for fifth period, and Victor shot out of the room, avoiding the stares of the other kids, but had to return for his math book. He looked sheepishly at the teacher, who was erasing the board, then widened his eyes in terror at Teresa who stood in front of him. "I didn't know you knew French," she said. "That was good." Mr. Bueller looked at Victor, and Victor looked back. Oh please, don't say anything, Victor pleaded with his eyes. I'll wash your car, mow your lawn, walk your dog—anything! I'll be your best student, and I'll clean your erasers after school.

---

7. *Le bateau est sur l'eau* (luh ba TOH ay soor loh): French for "The boat is on the water."

Mr. Bueller shuffled through the papers on his desk. He smiled and hummed as he sat down to work. He remembered his college years when he dated a girlfriend in borrowed cars. She thought he was rich because each time he picked her up he had a different car. It was fun until he had spent all his money on her and had to write home to his parents because he was broke.

Victor couldn't stand to look at Teresa. He was sweaty with shame. "Yeah, well, I picked up a few things from movies and books and stuff like that." They left the class together. Teresa asked him if he would help her with her French.

"Sure, anytime," Victor said.

"I won't be bothering you, will I?"

"Oh no, I like being bothered."

"*Bonjour,*" Teresa said, leaving him outside her next class. She smiled and pushed wisps of hair from her face. **K**

"Yeah, right, *bonjour,*" Victor said. He turned and headed to his class. The rosebushes of shame on his face became bouquets of love. Teresa is a great girl, he thought. And Mr. Bueller is a good guy. **L**

He raced to metal shop. After metal shop there was biology, and after biology a long sprint to the public library, where he checked out three French textbooks.

He was going to like seventh grade.

Applying Your Skills

SKILLS FOCUS **Literary Skills** Analyze character traits; analyze internal and external conflicts. **Reading Skills** Analyze inferences. **Writing Skills** Develop a character using description.

Seventh Grade

Respond and Think Critically

Reading Focus

Quick Check

1. Complete a story map like the one below to review the plot of "Seventh Grade."

> Characters:
> What they want:
> Conflicts (problems):
>> Event:
>> Event:
>> Event:
>> Climax:
>>> Resolution of conflict:

Read with a Purpose

2. What did you learn about Victor from the way he survives his first day of seventh grade? Give details from the story in your response.

Reading Skills: Making Inferences

3. Review the It Says/I Say/And So chart you completed while reading. Explain how your experiences helped you make inferences.

Literary Focus

Literary Analysis

4. **Interpret** What does the author mean when he writes of Victor, "The rosebushes of shame on his face became bouquets of love"?

5. **Predict** Do you think Victor will keep pretending to know more French than he does? Why or why not?

6. **Evaluate** It has been said that middle school is one of the most emotionally difficult times for students. Discuss whether the events in this story support this statement.

7. **Literary Perspectives** How believable is this story as a snapshot of seventh grade? Explain your reasoning.

Literary Skills: Character Traits

8. **Compare and Contrast** Identify the traits that Victor and his friend Michael share. In what ways are the two boys different?

Literary Skills Review: Internal Conflict

9. **Extend** Victor feels a variety of emotions in this story, including anticipation, nervousness, and embarrassment. What does your awareness of Victor's emotions add to the story? Explain.

Writing Focus

Think as a Reader/Writer

Use It in Your Writing Notice how you were able to make inferences based on Soto's character descriptions. Write a paragraph describing a character in the seventh grade whom you might use in your own short story. Include details that allow readers to draw inferences about the character.

What Do **You Think Now** How has this story changed your ideas about what it is right to do in order to impress people?

Seventh Grade

Vocabulary Development

Word Origins—Where a Word Comes From

Dictionaries show **word origins,** or etymologies, in brackets or parentheses following the word itself. At the back or front of a dictionary, you'll find a key to the symbols and abbreviations used in its etymologies. One commonly used symbol is <, which means "comes from" or "is derived from." When the "derived from" symbol is followed by a question mark, the derivation of a word or word part is unknown. The same symbol reversed (>) means "from which comes." An asterisk (*) means that a derivation is not certain. Here is the etymology of the word *mother* from one dictionary:

> *moder* < OE *modor*, akin to Ger *mutter*
> < IE* *matér*, mother > L *mater*, Gr *mētēr*,
> OIr *māthir*, * *ma–*, echoic of baby talk.

This could be translated into words as "The word *mother* comes from the Middle English word *moder*, which comes from the Old English word *modor*, which is related ('akin') to the German word *mutter*, which comes from the Indo-European word *matér*, from which comes the Latin word *mater*, the Greek word *mētēr*, and the Old Irish word *māthir*. All the words might come from a word that imitates the sound of baby talk."

Your Turn

Use a dictionary that contains etymologies to discover the derivation of the Vocabulary words. Complete a chart like the one below for each word.

| elective |
| propelled |
| conviction |
| lingered |
| sheepishly |

Vocabulary Word	Derivation
propelled	< L *pro pellere* to drive forward

Language Coach

Denotations/ Connotations
The **denotation** of a word is its dictionary definition. The **connotation** relates to the feelings associated with the word. Some words have negative connotations, such as *slimy,* while others have positive connotations, such as *sunny.*

| scrawny |
| fat |
| old |
| smelly |
| cheap |

Your Turn

The words in the box above have negative connotations. For each one, think of another word with the same general meaning but with a more positive connotation.

Academic Vocabulary

Talk About . . .
Identify Mr. Bueller's most important attributes. How does he treat Victor?

Learn It Online
Sharpen your word skills with *WordSharp* at:

go.hrw.com   L7-268   **Go**

Grammar Link
Direct Objects

A **direct object** is a noun or a pronoun that follows an action verb and tells *who* or *what* receives the action of the verb.

Michael's scowl amazed *the girls.*
[*the girls* tells *who* was amazed.]

Victor moved his *lips* and pretended to read. [*lips* tells *what* Victor moved.]

A direct object can never follow a linking verb, because a linking verb does not express action.

French became Victor's favorite subject.
[The verb *became* doesn't express action; therefore, it does not have a direct object.]

A direct object is never part of a prepositional phrase.

Victor gazed at Teresa. [*Teresa* is not the direct object of *gazed*; *Teresa* is the object of the preposition *at*.]

Your Turn

Identify the direct objects in the following sentences:

1. This short story delivers a strong characterization of Victor.
2. With the awkwardness of a seventh grader, Victor makes his feelings known to Teresa.
3. For Mr. Bueller, the situation reminds him of the past.

Writing Applications Circle each direct object in an example of your own writing. Underline the verb related to each direct object.

CHOICES

As you respond to the Choices, use these **Academic Vocabulary** words as appropriate: attribute, identify, process, respond.

REVIEW
Analyze a Character

Think of details that Soto includes to make Victor likable and unique. Fill out a character map describing some of Victor's traits. Summarize your chart in a paragraph.

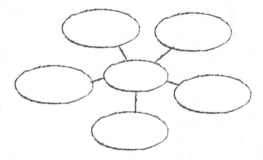

CONNECT
Write a Journal Entry

Timed LWriting Pretend that you are Victor and have just finished your first day of seventh grade. Write a journal entry detailing the day's highlights and explaining how you feel about them.

EXTEND
Draw a Portrait of Victor

In great portraits, artists reveal the character of those being painted. Soto gives you some details about what Victor looks like and how other people react to him. Try to capture Victor's character in a portrait. Some portraits show objects in the background that are associated with the subject. What would you put in Victor's portrait?

THAT OCTOBER

by **D. H. Figueredo**

What Do
You
Think

To believe in yourself, do you first need others to believe in you? Why or why not?

 QuickWrite

What helps boost your confidence when you need to meet a challenge? Write your ideas in a paragraph.

Reader/Writer Notebook

Use your **RWN** to complete the activities for this selection.

Literary Focus

Characterization The way a writer reveals the personality of a character is called **characterization.** Writers achieve this by

1. describing how the character looks, speaks, and dresses
2. letting you hear the character's inner thoughts and feelings
3. revealing what others think or say about the character
4. showing you how the character acts
5. telling you directly what the character's personality is like

Reading Focus

Connecting to the Text Making personal connections to texts helps you read for deeper meaning. Practice making connections as you read "That October." The chart below provides some examples. As you read, make other connections with the narrator.

I can connect	to myself or my friends	to other stories	to situations in the world
Narrator	He is young like me.	He finds a way to use strength, like Rikki-tikki.	Cuba played in World Baseball Classic; the sport is popular there.
Conflict			
End of story			

Writing Focus

Think as a Reader/Writer

Find It in Your Reading Writers sometimes reveal their characters' <u>attributes</u>, or qualities, through dialogue. As you read, record in your *Reader/Writer Notebook* two examples of dialogue that help show what the narrator, Alfredo, and Bebo are like.

Vocabulary

illegal (ih LEE guhl) *adj.:* unlawful; against official regulations. *It's illegal to damage government property.*

convinced (kuhn VIHNST) *v.:* made to feel sure; persuaded firmly. *Rudy's teammates were not convinced that he should be part of the team.*

opponents (uh POH nuhnts) *n.:* people on opposite sides in a fight or a game. *The Tigers' World Series opponents were the Leopards.*

encounter (ehn KOWN tuhr) *n.:* face-to-face meeting. *The Leopards were sure they would win their fourth encounter with the Tigers.*

boasting (BOHST ihng) *v.:* speaking too highly about oneself; bragging. *The Leopards were boasting about playing against a weaker team.*

Language Coach

Denotations/Connotations The **denotation** of a word is its dictionary definition. The **connotation** is the feeling or association attached to a word. Which word creates a richer, more complex picture in your mind: *meet* or *encounter*? *telling* or *boasting*?

 Learn It Online
Develop your understanding of words with Word Watch at:

go.hrw.com   L7-271   Go

D. H. Figueredo
(1951–)

Sharing Similarities with Rudy

Like the narrator of "That October," Danilo H. Figueredo spent his boyhood in Cuba during the time when Fidel Castro came to power. Figueredo and his main character have something else in common—both were weakened by polio (see Build Background). When Figueredo was fourteen, he and his family immigrated to the United States.

An Adult Who Loves Children's Stories

Figueredo loves being surrounded by books and has worked as a librarian for over twenty-five years. He writes whenever he can (including in his head!) and began his career as a children's book writer when his son encouraged him to write down cherished bedtime stories. His book *When This World Was New* is based on the first time *his* father walked in the snow.

> "I go to the library regularly just to sit in the children's room and watch and listen to the children. I look at the books they're holding in their hands and try to guess what really appeals to them."

Think About the Writer

Why do you think Figueredo writes about obstacles he faced in his childhood?

Build Background

Polio Until the early 1960s, the polio virus infected thousands of people every year. Most of these people were children. In some cases, polio causes permanent paralysis in a patient's arms or legs. Although there is still no cure for polio, vaccines introduced in the late 1950s have prevented epidemics in most countries, including Cuba. The narrator in the following story became infected with the virus before the vaccine was widely available.

Cuba "That October" takes place in 1962 in Cuba, a Communist country. Between 1960 and the early 1990s, Cuba relied on economic aid from the Soviet Union, a former Communist superpower. During that time, the Soviet Union maintained a military presence on the island, as reflected in this story.

Preview the Selection

This story begins when a **Russian soldier** investigates the cause of a government building's broken window. The narrator, **Rudy,** explains what happened.

THAT OCTOBER

by D. H. Figueredo

The Russian soldier came out of the building on the edge of the baseball field. He had a ball with him. When he noticed I was holding a bat, he started walking toward me.

Pointing at the broken window, he said, "It's against the law to damage government property."

My father was standing beside me. "*Camarada,*" he said, using the Spanish word for comrade. "You can't take my son to jail."

"*Tovaritch,*" the soldier said, using the Russian for comrade. "This building is used by the army for important research."

"The boy just forgot how strong he is," my father said.

The Russian looked at the orthopedic shoes I was wearing and the metal braces that went from my right foot to the top of my thigh. "Did you hit the ball during the game?" he asked me.

"No," I answered.

"You did it on purpose?"

The baseball team had formed a circle around us. The parents had formed a circle around the players. There were Russian soldiers on the other side of the fence that surrounded the building. They were looking at us. **Ⓐ**

"*Camarada,* I can explain," my father said.

"I need an explanation, but not from you," the Russian said. "You talk," he ordered me.

"Go ahead, son," my father said.

This is what I told the Russian. **Ⓑ**

The Tigers were the best team in Havana and I wanted to play with them. But they didn't let me. Why? Because when I was little, I was sick with a virus called polio. I got better but I ended up with a very thin leg. Also, I moved in a funny way, like a puppet, and I limped and fell a lot.

The captain of the team, Alfredo, told me that he couldn't afford a weak player. The pitcher, Bebo, said that the team didn't need a bad player. But I knew I was neither. "I practice every day in my back yard," I told them. "Am always losing balls because I smack them so hard, they fly over the fence and disappear."

Ⓐ Reading Focus **Connecting to the Text** How do you think the narrator feels right now?

Ⓑ Read and Discuss What has the author told you so far?

"But you can't run," said Alfredo.

"But I'm a good hitter," I said.

"So?"

"We can work together," I said. "You and I are pretty good hitters. You're also a fast runner. You and I could play as a duo. I bat and you run."

He shook his head. "The team won't go for that," he said.

"The team does what you tell them to do," I said.

Bebo spoke up. He said that it wouldn't work and that it was illegal. But I told him it wasn't, because the Tigers were not an official team, didn't wear uniforms, and didn't have a book of rules. "So there are no rules to break," I said. **C**

Alfredo then said that it would not be fair. "The team would be getting an extra player."

I told him that was not so, that the two of us together made up one person. "It's an experiment," I said.

But they were not convinced. **D**

That evening, I didn't feel like eating. When I went to bed, my father massaged my foot, something he did every night. He could tell I was sad and wanted to know what was wrong. I told him and he asked me, "Is it okay if I talk with Alfredo?"

The next day my father went to the field to see Alfredo. Later on, Alfredo came by the house. He told me he had changed his mind and that I could play with the team. Right after he said so, I made myself a sandwich and poured a big glass of chocolate milk.

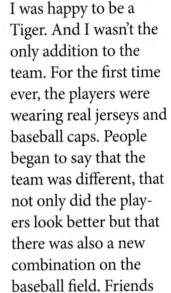

"We can work together," I said. "You and I are pretty good hitters. You're also a fast runner. You and I could play as a duo. I bat and you run."

I was happy to be a Tiger. And I wasn't the only addition to the team. For the first time ever, the players were wearing real jerseys and baseball caps. People began to say that the team was different, that not only did the players look better but that there was also a new combination on the baseball field. Friends and their friends came to see that combination. They said maybe it was a new creature, something like a centaur, the half-person half-horse from long ago. But they were soon disappointed. For what they saw was me batting and Alfredo running.

As the season went on, fewer fans came to the field. **E**

C **Literary Focus** **Characterization** What attributes can you identify in the narrator from his efforts to convince the others to put him on the team?

D **Read and Discuss** What is the narrator doing now? How do the boys respond to his idea?

E **Read and Discuss** How have things changed for the team?

Vocabulary **illegal** (ih LEE guhl) *adj.*: unlawful; against official regulations.
convinced (kuhn VIHNST) *v.*: made to feel sure; persuaded firmly.

We played against teams from the neighborhoods of Miramar and Marianao, La Lisa and Los Pasos, losing some games but winning most. By October, we were ready for our World Series. This was when the two top teams played against each other. The winner was the first to win three out of five games.

Our opponents were the Leopards from the town of La Lisa. We won the first game. Then, the Leopards won the next two. By the time the fourth encounter came along, the Leopards were sure they were unbeatable and were boasting that a team with a boy wearing braces was no match for them.

At this game, the Leopards were the first to bat. But they didn't score. We did and at the end of the first inning, we were leading 1 to 0. For a long while, the score remained the same. The parents started to say that either both teams were really good or really tired. Then everything changed.

It happened in the seventh inning. The Leopards had a player on second. A batter bunted the ball and as we scrambled to catch it, the batter ran to first and the player on second made it to third. Then, the next player at the plate delivered a home run. The Leopards were ahead 3 to 1.

It was our turn at bat. Alfredo pulled me aside and told me to hit a homer with so much force that the bat would break in two. He planned to run so fast that his

---

Vocabulary **opponents** (uh POH nuhnts) *n.*: people on opposite sides in a fight or a game.
encounter (ehn KOWN tuhr) *n.*: face-to-face meeting.
boasting (BOHST ihng) *v.*: speaking too highly about oneself; bragging.

Communism

Communism is a political and economic system in which the government owns the land and economic resources. There is no privately owned property.

In 1917, the people of Russia, suffering as a result of several poor harvests, economic depressions, and bloody wars, overthrew the monarchy. The new government embraced communism, whose ultimate goal is to create a society that provides equality and economic security for all.

Russia conquered three other territories in 1922 to form the Communist superpower known as the Union of Soviet Socialist Republics (USSR, or Soviet Union).

In 1959, Fidel Castro took power from the military dictator who was ruling Cuba and established a Communist government, the first one in the Western Hemisphere.

Ask Yourself

How did the relationship between Cuba and the Soviet Union affect the relationship between the Russian soldier and the boy and his father?

legs would turn into wheels, just like in the cartoons on television.

But I failed him. Instead, my bat made a "thud" sound and the ball whirled toward first. Running as hard as he could, Alfredo crash-landed on the base, but the first baseman shouted, the ball inside his glove, "You're dead, pal."

Alfredo cried out. From the stands, his father came out to help him. Leaning on him, Alfredo limped away from the base.

"I won't be able to run," he told me, sitting down on the bench. He had twisted his ankle.

We went into the final inning with Bebo in charge. He told us that we couldn't let the Leopards get in any more runs. He concentrated on his pitching and struck out the Leopards. But they were still winning by two runs.

Now, it was our turn to bat. One player directed a line drive into left field. He made it to first base. While the Leopards' pitcher was pitching, our player stole second. The next hitter shot the ball over the pitcher's head. The pitcher jumped up, caught the ball but dropped it, giving the Tiger on

F **Literary Focus** Characterization What can you tell about Alfredo from his instructions to the narrator?

second enough time to reach third and allowing the batter to get to first. **G**

We had a chance to recover the game. My teammates stopped feeling sorry for themselves. They said that we could score. But the high hopes vanished when the following two batters struck out.

I was next. But Bebo stopped me. "Somebody else will bat, not you." He said, "This time, Alfredo can't help you."

"I'm a Tiger and the team expects me to play," I said.

"You're not a Tiger," he said. "The only reason you're playing is because your father has money."

"What?"

"See our new shirts? Your father bought them for us. He also gave money to the other teams."

"That's not true," I said.

"Are you calling me a liar?" Bebo asked.

From the bench, Alfredo shouted, "Let him play." He made a fist and opened the palm of his hand and punched it. "Let him play."

Bebo stepped aside. Was he right? Was I allowed to play only because my father was paying for me to play? I wanted to leave. But Alfredo said, "Do it. We need a homer."

I waited a few seconds. My father looked at me in silence. The team looked at me in silence. Bebo had a smirk on his face.

I stepped up to the plate. I nodded to let the pitcher know I was ready. The pitcher eyed the catcher.

Strike one.

Bebo looked at Alfredo. He said, "I told you he's no good. I told you."

Strike two.

Bebo threw his cap in the dirt.

I turned to Alfredo. He mouthed, "You can do it." I turned to my father who gave me thumbs up.

The pitcher stretched his arm back and thrust it forward. The ball curved. I lowered the bat and swung.

It sounded like the wind had banged a door shut. The bat shook in my hands. I stood still for a moment before throwing it backwards. Turning into a minirocket, the bat almost hit Bebo who had to duck. In the meantime, the ball was rising higher and higher, becoming one with the sun before falling to the ground.

The Leopards didn't try to catch the ball. They weren't even looking at it. The parents weren't looking at the ball either. Neither were Bebo, Alfredo, nor the rest of my teammates. Instead, they were all looking at me.

They were looking at me, running. Yes, running in a funny way, like a robin with a broken leg. Running and wheezing, like an old sugarcane mill. Running and making so much noise it sounded as if it were raining pots and pans. But running. **H**

To first base.

To second.

To third.

By the time the Leopards figured that I could run and make it to the plate, it was

---

G **Read and Discuss** What mood has the author created?

H **Literary Focus** Characterization What do the narrator's actions tell you about him?

too late. For the Tigers who had been on first and third had already reached home. And I was right behind them.

My father cheered. The parents said, "What a game, what a game." The Tigers congratulated each other. I picked up a ball from the ground and threw it high into the air. As it came down, I whacked it with the bat, whacked it so hard that the ball rose over the fence and the electric posts, heading right for the building.

"And that's how I broke your window," I told the Russian.

He didn't say anything. He noticed that my knees were bleeding and that there were scratches on my right leg.

"Sometimes the braces scratch him," my father said.

The Russian said, "The window is still broken. And it still belongs to the Cuban government. And it's still illegal to damage government property." He loomed over me. Was he going to arrest me?

"Don't do it again," he said, tossing me the ball.

As he started to walk away, my father called him. When the Russian faced him, my father extended his hand. "Thank you, *tovaritch*."

The Russian shook his hand. "You're welcome, *camarada*." ❶

Then my father said, "My name is Rodolfo." He pointed at me. "His name is Rudy."

"Mine is Andrei," said the Russian. Joining the soldiers on the other side of the fence, the Russian went inside the building.

As the baseball players and their parents left the field, my father placed his arm around my shoulder. He said, "I bought the shirts with one condition: that you were allowed to play one game. But just one. The rest was up to you and the team."

From inside his father's car, Alfredo called out my name. "Rudy, you saved the team today," he shouted. "You're definitely a Tiger. And you know who said so?"

I shook my head.

"Bebo."

Later that October, the Tigers and the Leopards finished Havana's 1962 Little League World Series. The Leopards won the final game and were the league champions.

Later that October, the Cuban government told the Russian soldiers that the research they were doing in the building was over. The Russians left the island and went back home.

Later that October, the Cuban government gave my parents and me permission to leave Cuba. We left the island and moved to Miami.

I took the ball with me.

❶ **Read and Discuss** What is the significance of the narrator's father calling the soldier "*tovaritch*" and the soldier calling the boy's father "*camarada*"?

Applying Your Skills

That October

Respond and Think Critically

Reading Focus

Quick Check

1. Why is the Russian soldier questioning Rudy?
2. How does Rudy make it onto the team?

Read with a Purpose

3. What do you learn about Rudy and the way he overcomes obstacles? <u>Respond</u> by using details from the story.

Reading Skills: Connecting to the Text

4. Review the chart you completed as you read the story. List your strongest connections in the chart below, and explain the reasons for your choices.

Text and myself	
Text and another text	
Text and world situations	

Literary Focus

Literary Analysis

5. **Analyze** How do you feel about the way Rudy makes the team? Do you think Rudy's father is justified in his actions? Why or why not?

Literary Skills: Characterization

6. **Analyze** Although Bebo is a minor character, he is important to the story. What purpose does he serve? How is he characterized?

7. **Interpret** How does the author show that Rudy is a determined individual, even when confronting difficult circumstances?

8. **Make Judgments** How does the Russian soldier react to Rudy's story? Were you surprised at the soldier's response? Why or why not?

Literary Skills Review: Suspense

9. **Interpret Suspense** is the uncertainty you feel about what will happen next in a story. Choose two moments from the story that you found suspenseful. Give reasons for your choices. What were the outcomes of these suspenseful moments?

Writing Focus

Think as a Reader/Writer

Use It in Your Writing Look back at the story. What are the characters like? What type of person is Rudy? his father? the Russian soldier? List three words that describe each of those characters. Then, list the details from the story that told you what the characters were like.

Character	What He Is Like	How I Know

 What Do You Think Now

When might you need others to believe in you before you believe in yourself? How has this story influenced your ideas?

Applying Your Skills

That October

Vocabulary Development

Roots and Affixes

Many English word roots come from Latin, Greek, and an ancestor of the English language called Old English. A **word root** is a word part from which several words are formed.

An **affix** is a word part added to a root. An affix can be added to the front of a word (in which case it's called a **prefix**), or it can be added to the end of a word (in which case it's called a **suffix**). For example, the Vocabulary word **convinced** is made up of the prefix *con–* ("together"; "with") and the Latin root *vince* ("conquer"). In the story you just read, Rudy's teammates weren't **convinced** he should be on their team.

Your Turn

You have seen how roots and affixes help you understand the meaning of **convinced.** Explain how each of the following facts helps you understand the meaning of each Vocabulary word.

> convinced
> illegal
> opponents
> encounter
> boasting

1. In Latin, *opponere* means "set against." How does this give you a clue to the meaning of **opponents**?

2. In Proto-Germanic (probably Scandinavian), *bauis* means "to puff up; swell." How does this give you a clue to the meaning of **boasting**?

3. In Medieval Latin, *in–* means "not," and *legalis* means "legal." How does this give you a clue to the meaning of **illegal**?

4. In Latin, *contra* means "against." How does this give you a clue to the meaning of **encounter**?

Language Coach

Denotations/Connotations Skillful writers think about the meanings and associations they want to convey to the readers when choosing their words. Choosing words with certain connotations allows them to create vivid or precise descriptions.

Your Turn

Choose the word that conveys the most precise meaning.

1. The Tigers were ready to face their _____ (*opponents, people*).

2. The soldier explained that it was _____ (*wrong, illegal*) to damage government property.

3. The Leopards won the last game, making them the league _____ (*champions, winners*).

Academic Vocabulary

Write About . . .

D. H. Figueredo creates credible, or believable, characters with clearly defined <u>attributes</u>. In a paragraph, <u>identify</u> the character in the story who seemed most credible and explain why that character seems so believable.

Learn It Online
Take a closer look at word roots using *WordSharp* at:

go.hrw.com   L7-280   **Go**

Grammar Link
Prepositional Phrases

A **phrase** is a group of related words that is used as a single part of speech and that does not contain both a verb and its subject. A **prepositional phrase** includes a preposition (a word used to show the relationship of a noun or pronoun to another word in the sentence), the object of the preposition (the noun or pronoun that completes the prepositional phrase), and any modifiers (words, phrases, or clauses that make the meaning of a word or word group more specific) of that object. Consider this sentence from "That October."

> **The Russian soldier came out of the building on the edge of the baseball field.**

This sentence has three prepositional phrases that tell the reader exactly where the soldier came from. He came out *of the building*. Where is this building located? It's located *on the edge*. On the edge of what? It's on the edge *of the baseball field*.

Your Turn

Identify the prepositional phrase or phrases in each sentence, and explain how it shows the relationship to a noun or pronoun in the sentence.

1. My father was standing beside me.
2. You can't take my son to jail.
3. This building is used by the army for important research.
4. The Russian looked at the orthopedic shoes I was wearing and the metal braces that went from my right foot to the top of my thigh.
5. [The Leopards] were boasting that a team with a boy wearing braces was no match for them.

CHOICES

As you respond to the Choices, use these **Academic Vocabulary** words as appropriate: <u>attribute</u>, <u>identify</u>, <u>process</u>, <u>respond</u>.

REVIEW
Analyze a Character
Timed └Writing Write a two-paragraph essay about one of the characters in this story. <u>Identify</u> two of the character's traits, citing details from the story to support your answer.

CONNECT
Compare Characters
In a three-paragraph essay, compare and contrast the character Rudy with a character from a story you have read or a movie you have seen. What do the two characters have in common? Are they both brave? Do they both face a big problem? What makes them different? How does the other character differ from Rudy in how he or she handles a situation? How are their problems or situations different? Use details from the works that tell you about each character to help you compare them.

EXTEND
Write a Sequel
By the end of the story, we learn that Rudy and his family have left Cuba and moved to Miami. What situations will Rudy have to face in his new home? How might he have to prove himself all over again in Miami? Will Rudy be successful in dealing with new challenges? Write a sequel to this story that tells about Rudy's first weeks in Miami.

THE WAR OF THE WALL

by **Toni Cade Bambara**

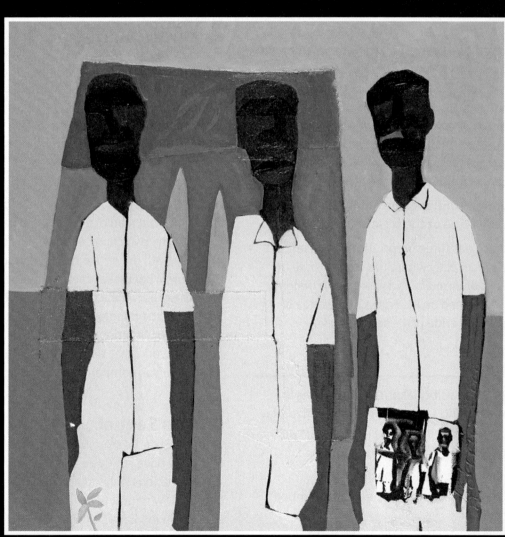

Church Boys III (2000) by Francks Deceus. Mixed media on canvas.

What Do You Think

When have you judged someone based on a first impression? Did your opinion change? Explain.

QuickTalk

Why do people often distrust strangers?

Reader/Writer Notebook

Use your **RWN** to complete the activities for this selection.

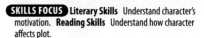
Literary Focus

Motivation As you read a story, think about why the characters act the way they do. The reason behind a character's actions is called the character's **motivation.** Feelings, needs, goals, and pressures from family and friends—all of these are forces that push and pull people from inside and outside. As you read, ask yourself what makes the characters behave in a particular way. How do their actions help you understand their <u>attributes</u>?

Reading Focus

How Character Affects Plot Characters' actions reveal their personalities. Their behavior also drives what happens in a story.

Into Action Complete an If—Then chart like the one below as you read. First, write something the narrator does in the column marked "Action." Then, record a way he might have acted differently under the "If" heading. Leave the last column blank for now.

Action	If	Then
The narrator confronts the painter.	the narrator approached her nicely . . .	

TechFocus As you read, <u>identify</u> a scene that could be filmed effectively.

Writing Focus

Think as a Reader/Writer

Find It in Your Reading In your *Reader/Writer Notebook*, list the precise images and phrases the writer uses to help you picture the characters. You might want to cite such phrases as "her eyes 'full of sky'" and "those oh-brother breathy whistles."

<aside>

Vocabulary

integration (ihn tuh GRAY shuhn) *n.:* process of bringing together people of all races in schools and neighborhoods. *Things didn't get better when integration was first introduced in the town.*

concentration (kahn suhn TRAY shuhn) *n.:* act of thinking carefully about something one is doing. *Painting is an activity that requires concentration.*

liberation (lihb uh RAY shuhn) *n.:* release from slavery, prison, or other limitation. *Neighborhood residents saw African flags of liberation on the wall.*

inscription (ihn SKRIHP shuhn) *n.:* words written on something. *The kids were unsure of what the inscription on the wall would say.*

dedicate (DEHD uh kayt) *v.:* do or make something in honor of another person. *Artists and writers often dedicate their work to someone.*

Language Coach

Slang Informal language that includes invented words and existing words that have been given new meanings is called **slang.** *Dude* and *get a whiff* are examples of slang in this story.

Learn It Online
For a preview of this story, see the video introduction on:

| go.hrw.com | L7-283 | Go |

</aside>

Learn It Online
Examine the author's life at:
go.hrw.com L7-284 Go

Toni Cade Bambara
(1939–1995)

Growing Up in New York City

Toni Cade Bambara was born Miltonia Mirkin Cade. As an adult, the author added "Bambara," inspired by a signature on a sketch book belonging to her great-grandmother. She grew up in Harlem in the 1940s, surrounded by vibrant literary, artistic, and political communities. She learned the power of the spoken word on "speaker's corner," where people preached and spoke on issues of importance. She recorded the speech of her friends and neighbors, trying to capture the pulse of daily life. She absorbed the rhythms of jazz and bebop that filled New York City streets and clubs.

Go Far; Remember Where You Came From

After college, she traveled and studied in Europe. She later lived in Atlanta and Philadelphia. Even so, her early experiences living in an African American community continued to inspire her. Bambara's writing focuses on the experiences of African Americans. Known primarily for her short stories and novels, Bambara later concentrated on screenplays, including an adaptation of her much-loved story "Raymond's Run."

"It is important for young folks to listen, to be proud of our oral tradition."

Think About the Writer How do you think Bambara's early surroundings influenced her work?

Build Background

"The War of the Wall" takes place during or shortly after the Vietnam War, which ended in 1972. The setting is an African American neighborhood in the South.

Southern and northern cultures often clashed at that time, with people from the northern United States being thought of as outside agitators by many southerners, who resented their efforts to push the issues of integration and civil rights. While the story doesn't focus on these issues, this background gives you insight into the culture clash that motivates the characters and their actions.

Preview the Selection

A mysterious **painter** comes to town and begins to paint over a wall that is central to the town's sense of community. The **narrator** and his friend **Lou** don't know exactly what she's doing but are sure they want to stop her.

THE WAR OF THE WALL

by **Toni Cade Bambara**

Me and Lou had no time for courtesies. We were late for school. So we just flat out told the painter lady to quit messing with the wall. It was our wall, and she had no right coming into our neighborhood painting on it. Stirring in the paint bucket and not even looking at us, she mumbled something about Mr. Eubanks, the barber, giving her permission. That had nothing to do with it as far as we were concerned. We've been pitching pennies against that wall since we were little kids. Old folks have been dragging their chairs out to sit in the shade of the wall for years. Big kids have been playing handball against the wall since so-called integration when the crazies 'cross town poured cement in our pool so we couldn't use it. I'd sprained my neck one time boosting my cousin Lou up to chisel Jimmy Lyons's name into the wall when we found out he was never coming home from the war in Vietnam to take us fishing.   **Ⓐ**

"If you lean close," Lou said, leaning hip-shot against her beat-up car, "you'll get a whiff of bubble gum and kids' sweat. And that'll tell you something—that this wall belongs to the kids of Taliaferro Street." I thought Lou sounded very convincing. But the painter lady paid us no mind. She just snapped the brim of her straw hat down and hauled her bucket up the ladder.

"You're not even from around here," I hollered up after her. The license plates on her old piece of car said "New York." Lou dragged me away because I was about to grab hold of that ladder and shake it. And then we'd really be late for school.   **Ⓑ**

When we came from school, the wall was slick with white. The painter lady was running string across the wall and taping it here and there. Me and Lou leaned against

---

Ⓐ | Read and Discuss | What is the author letting you know about this wall?

Ⓑ | Read and Discuss | How does this scene further what you know about the wall?

Vocabulary   integration (ihn tuh GRAY shuhn) *n*.: process of bringing together people of all races in schools and neighborhoods.

the gum ball machine outside the pool hall and watched. She had strings up and down and back and forth. Then she began chalking them with a hunk of blue chalk.

The Morris twins crossed the street, hanging back at the curb next to the beat-up car. The twin with the red ribbons was hugging a jug of cloudy lemonade. The one with yellow ribbons was holding a plate of dinner away from her dress. The painter lady began snapping the strings. The blue chalk dust measured off halves and quarters up and down and sideways too. Lou was about to say how hip it all was, but I dropped my book satchel on his toes to remind him we were at war. **C**

Some good aromas were drifting our way from the plate leaking pot likker[1] onto the Morris girl's white socks. I could tell from where I stood that under the tinfoil was baked ham, collard greens, and candied yams. And knowing Mrs. Morris, who sometimes bakes for my mama's restaurant, a slab of buttered cornbread was probably up under there too, sopping up some of the pot likker. Me and Lou rolled our eyes, wishing somebody would send us some dinner. But the painter lady didn't even turn around. She was pulling the strings down and prying bits of tape loose.

Side Pocket came strolling out of the pool hall to see what Lou and me were

studying so hard. He gave the painter lady the once-over, checking out her paint-spattered jeans, her chalky T-shirt, her floppy-brimmed straw hat. He hitched up his pants and glided over toward the painter lady, who kept right on with what she was doing.

"Watcha got there, Sweetheart?" he asked the twin with the plate.

"Suppah," she said, all soft and country-like.

"For her," the one with the jug added, jerking her chin toward the painter lady's back.

Still she didn't turn around. She was rearing back on her heels, her hands jammed into her back pockets, her face squinched up like the masterpiece she had in mind was taking shape on the wall by magic. We could have been gophers crawled up into a rotten hollow for all she cared. She didn't even say hello to anybody. Lou was muttering something about how great her concentration was. I butt him with my hip, and his elbow slid off the gum machine. **D**

"Good evening," Side Pocket said in his best ain't-I-fine voice. But the painter lady was moving from the milk crate to the stepstool to the ladder, moving up and down fast, scribbling all over the wall like a crazy person. We looked at Side Pocket. He looked at the twins. The twins looked at us. The painter lady was giving a show. It was like those old-timey music movies where the dancer taps on the table top and then

---

1. **pot likker** (paht LIHK uhr): leftover liquid from cooked meat and vegetables that is often used to make a sauce.

C **Literary Focus** Motivation What does the narrator mean when he says they are "at war"?

D **Read and Discuss** What's happening between the community members and the painter?

Vocabulary **concentration** (kahn suhn TRAY shuhn) *n.*: act of thinking carefully about something one is doing.

Analyzing Visuals

Viewing and Interpreting
Compare and contrast the person in the portrait with your mental image of the narrator.

Thinking (1990) by Carlton Murrell. Oil on board.

starts jumping all over the furniture, kicking chairs over and not skipping a beat. She didn't even look where she was stepping. And for a minute there, hanging on the ladder to reach a far spot, she looked like she was going to tip right over. **E**

"Ahh," Side Pocket cleared his throat and moved fast to catch the ladder.

"These young ladies here have brought you some supper."

"Ma'am?" The twins stepped forward. Finally the painter turned around, her eyes "full of sky," as my grandmama would say. Then she stepped down like she was in a trance. She wiped her hands on her jeans as the Morris twins offered up the plate and

---

E **Literary Focus** Motivation Is the painter "giving a show" for the others, or is there another explanation for her "scribbling all over the wall"?

Analyzing Visuals

Viewing and Interpreting
How does this image help you
connect to the story?

At the Farmer's Market
(2003) by Pam Ingalls.

the jug. She rolled back the tinfoil, then wagged her head as though something terrible was on the plate.

"Thank your mother very much," she said, sounding like her mouth was full of sky too. "I've brought my own dinner along." And then, without even excusing herself, she went back up the ladder, drawing on the wall in a wild way. Side Pocket whistled one of those oh-brother breathy whistles and went back into the pool hall.

The Morris twins shifted their weight from one foot to the other, then crossed the street and went home. Lou had to drag me away, I was so mad. We couldn't wait to get to the firehouse to tell my daddy all about this rude woman who'd stolen our wall. **F**

All the way back to the block to help my mama out at the restaurant, me and Lou kept asking my daddy for ways to run the painter lady out of town. But my daddy was busy talking about the trip to the country and telling Lou he could come too because Grandmama can always use an extra pair of hands on the farm.

Later that night, while me and Lou were in the back doing our chores, we found out that the painter lady was a liar. She came into the restaurant and leaned against the glass of the steam table, talking

F Read and Discuss How does this scene create a certain mood?

about how starved she was. I was scrubbing pots and Lou was chopping onions, but we could hear her through the service window. She was asking Mama was that a ham hock in the greens, and was that a neck bone in the pole beans, and were there any vegetables cooked without meat, especially pork.

"I don't care who your spiritual leader is," Mama said in that way of hers. "If you eat in the community, sistuh, you gonna eat pig by-and-by, one way or t' other."

Me and Lou were cracking up in the kitchen, and several customers at the counter were clearing their throats waiting for Mama to really fix her wagon for not speaking to the elders when she came in. The painter lady took a stool at the counter and went right on with her questions. Was there cheese in the baked macaroni, she wanted to know? Were there eggs in the salad? Was it honey or sugar in the iced tea? Mama was fixing Pop Johnson's plate. And every time the painter lady asked a fool question, Mama would dump another spoonful of rice on the pile. She was tapping her foot and heating up in a dangerous way. But Pop Johnson was happy as he could be. Me and Lou peeked through the service window, wondering what planet the painter lady came from. Who ever heard of baked macaroni without cheese, or potato salad without eggs? **G**

"Do you have any bread made with unbleached flour?" the painter lady asked Mama. There was a long pause, as though everybody in the restaurant was holding their breath, wondering if Mama would dump the next spoonful on the painter lady's head. She didn't. But when she set Pop Johnson's plate down, it came down with a bang.

When Mama finally took her order, the starving lady all of a sudden couldn't make up her mind whether she wanted a vegetable plate or fish and a salad. She finally settled on the broiled trout and a tossed salad. But just when Mama reached for a plate to serve her, the painter lady leaned over the counter with her finger all up in the air.

[THE PAINTER LADY TOOK A STOOL AT THE COUNTER AND WENT RIGHT ON WITH HER QUESTIONS.]

"Excuse me," she said. "One more thing." Mama was holding the plate like a Frisbee, tapping that foot, one hand on her hip. "Can I get raw beets in that tossed salad?"

"You will get," Mama said, leaning her face close to the painter lady's, "whatever Lou back there tossed. Now sit down." And the painter lady sat back down on her stool and shut right up.

All the way to the country, me and Lou tried to get Mama to open fire on the painter lady. But Mama said that seeing as how she was from the North, you

---

G **Read and Discuss** What's happening between the painter and Mama? So far, several community members have been put off by the painter. How do they react to her? What does their reaction tell you about them?

couldn't expect her to have any manners. Then Mama said she was sorry she'd been so impatient with the woman because she seemed like a decent person and was simply trying to stick to a very strict diet. Me and Lou didn't want to hear that. Who did that lady think she was, coming into our neighborhood and taking over our wall?

"Wellllll," Mama drawled, pulling into the filling station so Daddy could take the wheel, "it's hard on an artist, ya know. They can't always get people to look at their work. So she's just doing her work in the open, that's all." **H**

Me and Lou definitely did not want to hear that. Why couldn't she set up an easel downtown or draw on the sidewalk in her own neighborhood? Mama told us to quit fussing so much; she was tired and wanted to rest. She climbed into the back seat and dropped down into the warm hollow Daddy had made in the pillow. **I**

All weekend long, me and Lou tried to scheme up ways to recapture our wall. Daddy and Mama said they were sick of hearing about it. Grandmama turned up the TV to drown us out. On the late news was a story about the New York subways. When a train came roaring into the station all covered from top to bottom, windows too, with writings and drawings done with spray paint, me and Lou slapped five. Mama said it was too bad kids in New York had nothing better to do than spray

paint all over the trains. Daddy said that in the cities, even grown-ups wrote all over the trains and buildings too. Daddy called it "graffiti." Grandmama called it a shame.

We couldn't wait to get out of school on Monday. We couldn't find any black spray paint anywhere. But in a junky hardware store downtown we found a can of white epoxy paint, the kind you touch up old refrigerators with when they get splotchy and peely. We spent our whole allowance on it. And because it was too late to use our bus passes, we had to walk all the way home lugging our book satchels and gym shoes, and the bag with the epoxy.

When we reached the corner of Taliaferro and Fifth, it looked like a block party or something. Half the neighborhood was gathered on the sidewalk in front of the wall. I looked at Lou, he looked at me. We both looked at the bag with the epoxy and wondered how we were going to work our scheme. The painter lady's car was nowhere in sight. But there were too many people standing around to do anything. Side Pocket and his buddies were leaning on their cue sticks, hunching each other. Daddy was there with a lineman[2] he catches a ride with on Mondays. Mrs. Morris had her arms flung around the shoulders of the twins on either side of her. Mama was talking with some of her

2. **lineman** (LYN muhn): worker whose job is to set up and repair telephone or electric power lines.

H Reading Focus **How Character Affects Plot** Mama's attitude toward the painter has changed a little since the last scene. How would this scene be different if Mama's attitude had stayed the same?

I Read and Discuss What does this scene tell you about the communication difficulties between the painter and the people in the neighborhood?

customers, many of them with napkins still at the throat. Mr. Eubanks came out of the barber shop, followed by a man in a striped poncho, half his face shaved, the other half full of foam.

"She really did it, didn't she?" Mr. Eubanks huffed out his chest. Lots of folks answered right quick that she surely did when they saw the straight razor in his hand.

Mama beckoned us over. And then we saw it. The wall. Reds, greens, figures outlined in black. Swirls of purple and orange. Storms of blues and yellows. It was something. I recognized some of the faces right off. There was Martin Luther King, Jr. And there was a man with glasses on and his mouth open like he was laying down a heavy rap. Daddy came up alongside and reminded us that he was Minister Malcolm X. The serious woman with a rifle I knew was Harriet Tubman because my grandmama has pictures of her all over the house. And I knew Mrs. Fannie Lou Hamer 'cause a signed photograph of her hangs in the restaurant next to the calendar.

J [Read and Discuss] What is happening at the wall?

Analyzing Visuals   Viewing and Interpreting   How does the mural in this photograph help you visualize the painter's work?

. MARTIN LUTHER KING, Jr.

Prince of Peace

*"Like anybody, I'd like to live a long life,"
But it doesn't matter now.
"I've been to the mountaintop."
And I've seen the Promised Land.
I may not get there with you.
But... we as a people will get
to the Promised Land.*

STOP
The
RACIST

Then I let my eyes follow what looked like a vine. It trailed past a man with a horn, a woman with a big white flower in her hair, a handsome dude in a tuxedo seated at a piano, and a man with a goatee holding a book.[3] When I looked more closely, I realized that what had looked like flowers were really faces. One face with yellow petals looked just like Frieda Morris. One with red petals looked just like Hattie Morris. I could hardly believe my eyes.

"Notice," Side Pocket said, stepping close to the wall with his cue stick like a classroom pointer. "These are the flags of liberation," he said in a voice I'd never heard him use before. We all stepped closer while he pointed and spoke. "Red, black, and green," he said, his pointer falling on the leaflike flags of the vine. "Our liberation flag. And here Ghana, there Tanzania, Guinea-Bissau, Angola, Mozambique."[4] Side Pocket sounded very tall, as though he'd been waiting all his life to give this lesson.

Mama tapped us on the shoulder and pointed to a high section of the wall. There was a fierce-looking man with his arms crossed against his chest guarding a bunch of children. His muscles bulged, and he looked a lot like my daddy. One kid was looking at a row of books. Lou punched me 'cause the kid looked like me. The one that looked like Lou was spinning a globe on the tip of his finger like a basketball. There were other kids there with microscopes and compasses. And the more I looked, the more it looked like the fierce man was not so much guarding the kids as defending their right to do what they were doing.

Then Lou gasped and dropped the paint bag and ran forward, running his hands over a rainbow. He had to tiptoe and stretch to do it, it was so high. I couldn't breathe either. The painter lady had found the chisel marks and had painted Jimmy Lyons's name in a rainbow.

"Read the inscription, honey," Mrs. Morris said, urging little Frieda forward. She didn't have to urge much. Frieda marched right up, bent down, and in a loud voice that made everybody quit oohing and ahhing and listen, she read,

To the People of Taliaferro Street
I Dedicate This Wall of Respect
Painted in Memory of My Cousin
Jimmy Lyons **Ⓚ**

3. **a man with a horn, a woman with a big white flower in her hair, a handsome dude in a tuxedo seated at a piano, and a man with a goatee holding a book:** Louis Armstrong, Billie Holiday, Duke Ellington, and W.E.B. DuBois, respectively.

4. **Ghana, there Tanzania, Guinea-Bissau, Angola, Mozambique:** countries in Africa.

Ⓚ Read and Discuss | What does the inscription add to what you know about the painter?

Vocabulary **liberation** (lihb uh RAY shuhn) *n.:* release from slavery, prison, or other limitation.
inscription (ihn SKRIHP shuhn) *n.:* words written on something.
dedicate (DEHD uh kayt) *v.:* do or make something in honor of another person.

Applying Your Skills

The War of the Wall

Respond and Think Critically

Reading Focus

Quick Check

1. Where is the "painter lady" from? How do the narrator and Lou know that?
2. Which of the painter's <u>attributes</u> bother the narrator? Give at least two examples.
3. What does the woman paint on the wall?

Read with a Purpose

4. What do the narrator and Lou learn about the painter that makes them realize their first impressions were wrong?

Reading Skills: How Character Affects Plot

5. Record in your "Then" column how different actions might have changed the story. What is the author saying about miscommunication in this story?

Action	If	Then
The narrator confronts the painter.	the narrator approached her nicely . . .	

Literary Focus

Literary Analysis

6. **Draw Conclusions** How do you think the narrator feels about the wall at the end of the story? Explain.
7. **Interpret** Describe the painter's character. Support your description with examples from the text.

8. **Evaluate** This story is a **first-person narrative,** told by a character in the story. Do you think the story would have been better, not as good, or about the same if someone else had been the narrator? Explain your choice.

Literary Skills: Motivation

9. **Analyze** Explain why the narrator and Lou want to "run the painter lady out of town."
10. **Analyze** What is the painter's motivation for creating the mural?

Literary Skills Review: Setting

11. **Interpret** Fill in details about the setting of the story in the chart below. Then, describe the effect the setting has on the characters.

Place and Time	Customs (How People Act in a Place)	Effects the Setting Has on Characters

Writing Focus

Think as a Reader/Writer

Use It in Your Writing Choose two or three precise images from the story. How did these images help you better understand the characters? <u>Respond</u> to this question in a paragraph.

What Do  You Think Now How do you feel about first impressions now that you've read the story?

Vocabulary Development

Word, Sentence, and Paragraph Clues

Just about everyone encounters unfamiliar words when reading. If you don't have a dictionary handy, word, sentence, and paragraph clues can help. Here's how:

- **Word Clues:** Does the unfamiliar word resemble a word or word part you already know?
- **Sentence Clues:** Does the writer contrast the word with another familiar word? Does the writer provide a definition in the sentence? What part of speech is the unfamiliar word? Does the meaning of the sentence change if you substitute or remove the unfamiliar word?
- **Paragraph Clues:** What is the paragraph's main idea? What connection could the word have to the main idea and to the other sentences in the paragraph?

For example, *inscription* is very close in form to *scribe, script,* and other words associated with writing. The paragraph in which the word appears is about someone stepping forward to read text from the mural. When you combine the word clues and paragraph clues, you can guess that *inscription* means "words written on something."

Your Turn

Look through "The War of the Wall" for clues that help reveal the meanings of the Vocabulary words. When you've practiced sufficiently, try your skills with an unfamiliar word from the selection. Always check your guesses in a dictionary.

integration
concentration
liberation
inscription
dedicate

Language Coach

Formal and Informal English Compare these two sentences:

What do you have there, miss?

Watcha got there, sweetheart?

The sentences ask the same thing, but they create different effects. The first sentence uses formal English, while the second uses informal English.

Formal English is the language you use in school, speaking, and writing. Formal English does not include slang or other casual expressions. You use **informal English** when you talk with or write to family members or friends. Informal English includes colloquial expressions and slang. It's often used in stories to make the dialogue between characters sound real. What are two examples of informal English in this story?

Academic Vocabulary

Write About . . .
Think about the ways the narrator <u>responds</u> to the painter. Then, in a paragraph, <u>identify</u> two or three of the narrator's strongest <u>attributes</u>. Finally, explain whether the narrator is a credible character.

Grammar Link

Independent and Subordinate Clauses

A **clause** is a word group that contains a verb and its subject. Some clauses are used as sentences, and others are used as parts of sentences.

Every clause contains a subject and a verb. However, not all clauses express complete thoughts. A clause that expresses a complete thought is called an **independent clause.** When an independent clause stands alone, it is a sentence. A clause that cannot stand alone is called a **subordinate clause.** A subordinate clause is joined with at least one independent clause to express a complete thought.

My mother drove me to school. [This entire sentence is an independent clause.]

My mother drove me to school, but my brother rode his bicycle. [This sentence contains two independent clauses.]

Since I missed the bus, my mother drove me to school. [This sentence contains one subordinate clause and one independent clause.]

Your Turn

The following sentences are from "The War of the Wall." Identify the italicized clause in each sentence as independent or subordinate.

1. Lou dragged me away because *I was about to grab hold of that ladder and shake it.*
2. She stepped down *like she was in a trance.*
3. *She wiped her hands on her jeans* as the Morris twins offered up the plate and the jug.
4. *Without even excusing herself,* she went back up the ladder.

CHOICES

As you respond to the Choices, use these **Academic Vocabulary** words as appropriate: attribute, identify, process, respond.

REVIEW

Compare Characters

Choose two characters from "The War of the Wall," and compare them and their motivations by using a Venn diagram. How are the characters alike? How are they different?

Character 1 Differences / Characters' Similarities / Character 2 Differences

CONNECT

Film a Scene

TechFocus Choose a scene from "The War of the Wall" that would be effective in a movie. Scenes that depict a conflict, like the one in the diner between Mama and the painter, make the best movie scenes. First, work with two or three classmates to write a script based on the incident. Then, film the scene. Be sure to capture the feelings of the characters through your facial expressions and tone of voice.

EXTEND

Imagine You're the Painter

Timed └Writing In "The War of the Wall," you know the painter only through what the narrator tells you. You never find out her thoughts and feelings during the painting process. How does she feel about the way people treat her? What does she think about the reaction to her mural? Imagine that you're the painter, and write a journal entry about your experiences.

Comparing Characters and Character Traits

CONTENTS

 What Do **You** Think? What can you discover about yourself when you are afraid?

QuickWrite
Think of a situation that was not as scary or dangerous as you first thought it was. What did you learn from this experience?

Surgeon Uses Stethoscope
by Todd Davidson.

Preparing to Read

A Day's Wait / Stolen Day

Reader/Writer Notebook

Use your **RWN** to complete the activities for these selections.

Literary Focus

Characters and Character Traits How do you get to know the people you meet? They don't carry around signs saying "I am kind and caring" or "I am a mean bully." You have to figure out for yourself what people are like. How do you do it? You notice their appearance. You pay attention to what they do and say. You listen to what others say about them. All this helps you make inferences about their **character traits.** You get to know the characters in a story in the same way.

Reading Focus

Comparing and Contrasting Characters In "A Day's Wait" and "Stolen Day," clues in the text will help you understand the character traits of the boys at the center of each story. Are they brave or fearful, mean or kind, selfish or generous?

Into Action Complete a chart like the one below for each boy.

Actions	
Words	
Thoughts / Feelings	
Effects on Others	

Writing Focus

Think as a Reader/Writer

Find It in Your Reading You get insight into characters when they reveal their inner thoughts. As you read "Stolen Day," record the narrator's thoughts, and think about what they add to your knowledge of the narrator. As you read "A Day's Wait," note three places where the writer could have included a character's thoughts.

Vocabulary

A Day's Wait

detached (dih TACHT) *adj.:* not involved emotionally; indifferent. *His reaction to his son's illness was surprisingly detached.*

commenced (kuh MEHNST) *v.:* began. *He did not pay attention when his father commenced reading.*

slack (slak) *adj.:* loose. *Schatz had only a slack hold on his emotions.*

Stolen Day

solemn (SAHL uhm) *adj.:* gloomy; serious. *He wore a solemn expression while explaining that he was sick.*

wriggled (RIHG uhld) *v.:* wiggled; squirmed. *The fish wriggled in his arms as he brought it home.*

Language Coach

Pronouncing *mn* When you say the word *solemn*, the *n* is silent. This is true of any word that ends in *mn*. When the letters *mn* are in the middle of a word, you hear the sounds of both letters (think of the word *chimney*.) Get together with a partner and pronounce the following words: *hymn, remnant, amnesia, condemn.*

Learn It Online
Dig deeper into vocabulary. Use Word Watch to increase your understanding of words at:

| go.hrw.com | L7-297 | **Go** |

Ernest Hemingway
(1899–1961)

Nobel Prize WINNER

Grace Under Pressure

Ernest Hemingway was born in Oak Park, Illinois. He spent his youth hunting, fishing, boxing, and playing football. When the United States entered World War I, he volunteered to be an ambulance driver in Italy. He was nineteen when a bomb landed three feet from him, filling his right leg with 227 pieces of shrapnel.

When he returned from the war, Hemingway wrote many stories and novels that portray men who show "grace under pressure"—calm courage in the face of great danger. That is also a theme in "A Day's Wait." The story's silences and sparse dialogue reflect the belief of Hemingway's heroes that they should keep a tight rein on their fears and other emotions.

Hemingway won the Nobel Prize in Literature in 1954. Today he is regarded as one of the twentieth century's great writers.

Sherwood Anderson
(1876–1941)

A Talented Storyteller

Sherwood Anderson grew up in a small Ohio town that would later play a major role in many of his stories. He attended school infrequently while working full time to help provide for his family. His talent for storytelling emerged later in life, while he was running his own business.

Anderson's straightforward writing style changed the short story and influenced a younger generation of writers. Anderson offered his support to younger writers, among them Ernest Hemingway. In fact, Anderson was instrumental in getting Hemingway's first novel published.

Think About the Writers

In what ways do you think the lives and experiences of these authors have influenced their work?

Preview the Selections

In "A Day's Wait," you'll meet **Schatz,** a nine-year-old boy who shows grace under pressure while he's sick with the flu.

In "Stolen Day," you'll meet a **boy** who is convinced that he's suffering from a serious disease.

Portrait of Sherwood Anderson (1933) by Carl Van Vechten. Oil over photograph.
©The Granger Collection, New York.

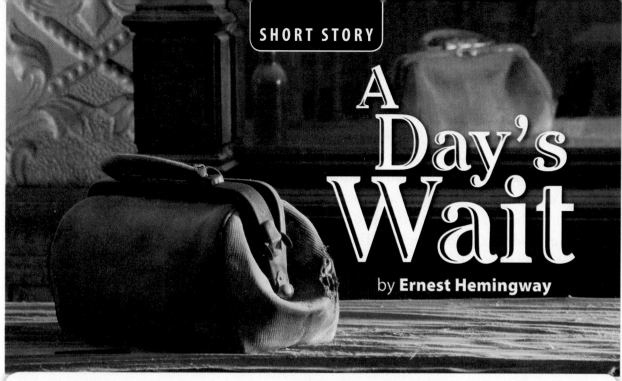

A Day's Wait

by **Ernest Hemingway**

Read with a Purpose

Read this short story to find out what the main character, Schatz, learns after a day's wait.

Build Background

To understand this story, you have to know that there are two kinds of temperature scales: Celsius, which is used in Europe, and Fahrenheit, which is used in the United States. Water boils at 100 degrees Celsius. The boiling point is 212 degrees on the Fahrenheit scale.

The events in this story actually happened to Hemingway and his nine-year-old son Bumby. (In the story, Bumby is called Schatz, a German word meaning "treasure.") Hemingway and his family lived in France for many years. In this story, they are back in the United States.

He came into the room to shut the windows while we were still in bed and I saw he looked ill. He was shivering, his face was white, and he walked slowly as though it ached to move.

"What's the matter, Schatz?"

"I've got a headache."

"You better go back to bed."

"No. I'm all right."

"You go to bed. I'll see you when I'm dressed."

But when I came downstairs he was dressed, sitting by the fire, looking a very sick and miserable boy of nine years. When I put my hand on his forehead I knew he had a fever.

"You go up to bed," I said, "you're sick."

"I'm all right," he said. Ⓐ

When the doctor came he took the boy's temperature.

"What is it?" I asked him.

"One hundred and two."

Ⓐ **Read and Discuss** What has been revealed so far?

Downstairs, the doctor left three different medicines in different-colored capsules with instructions for giving them. One was to bring down the fever, another a purgative,[1] the third to overcome an acid condition. The germs of influenza can only exist in an acid condition, he explained. He seemed to know all about influenza and said there was nothing to worry about if the fever did not go above one hundred and four degrees. This was a light epidemic of flu and there was no danger if you avoided pneumonia. **B**

Back in the room I wrote the boy's temperature down and made a note of the time to give the various capsules.

"Do you want me to read to you?"

"All right. If you want to," said the boy. His face was very white and there were dark areas under his eyes. He lay still in the bed and seemed very detached from what was going on.

I read aloud from Howard Pyle's *Book of Pirates;* but I could see he was not following what I was reading. **C**

"How do you feel, Schatz?" I asked him.

"Just the same, so far," he said.

I sat at the foot of the bed and read to myself while I waited for it to be time to give another capsule. It would have been natural for him to go to sleep, but when I looked up he was looking at the foot of the bed, looking very strangely.

"Why don't you try to go to sleep? I'll wake you up for the medicine."

"I'd rather stay awake."

After a while he said to me, "You don't have to stay in here with me, Papa, if it bothers you."

"It doesn't bother me."

"No, I mean you don't have to stay if it's going to bother you." **D**

I thought perhaps he was a little light-headed and after giving him the prescribed capsules at eleven o'clock I went out for a while.

It was a bright, cold day, the ground covered with a sleet that had frozen so that it seemed as if all the bare trees, the bushes, the cut brush, and all the grass and the bare ground had been varnished with ice. I took the young Irish setter for a little walk up the road and along a frozen creek, but it was difficult to stand or walk on the glassy surface and the red dog slipped and slithered and I fell twice, hard, once dropping my gun and having it slide away over the ice.

We flushed a covey[2] of quail under a high clay bank with overhanging brush and I killed two as they went out of sight over the top of the bank. Some of the covey lit in trees, but most of them scattered into brush piles and it was necessary to jump on the ice-coated mounds of brush several

---

1. **purgative** (PUR guh tihv): laxative.

2. **flushed a covey** (KUHV ee): frightened a small group of birds from their hiding place.

B Read and Discuss What has happened?

C Literary Focus Character What do the father's words and actions reveal about him?

D Read and Discuss What is going on between the boy and his father here?

Vocabulary detached (dih TACHT) *adj.:* not involved emotionally; indifferent.

Thawed Ledge (1988) by Neil Welliver. Oil on canvas.

Collection Curtis Galleries Inc., Minneapolis. ©Neil Welliver, Courtesy Alexandre Gallery, New York.

times before they would flush. Coming out while you were poised unsteadily on the icy, springy brush, they made difficult shooting and I killed two, missed five, and started back pleased to have found a covey close to the house and happy there were so many left to find on another day. **E**

At the house they said the boy had

E Read and Discuss What is this part of the story about?

refused to let anyone come into the room.

"You can't come in," he said. "You mustn't get what I have."

I went up to him and found him in exactly the position I had left him, white-faced, but with the tops of his cheeks flushed by the fever, staring still, as he had stared, at the foot of the bed.

I took his temperature.

"What is it?"

"Something like a hundred," I said. It was one hundred and two and four tenths.

"It was a hundred and two," he said.

"Who said so?"

"The doctor."

"Your temperature is all right," I said. "It's nothing to worry about."

"I don't worry," he said, "but I can't keep from thinking."

"Don't think," I said. "Just take it easy."

"I'm taking it easy," he said and looked straight ahead. He was evidently holding tight onto himself about something.

"Take this with water."

"Do you think it will do any good?"

"Of course it will."

I sat down and opened the *Pirate* book and commenced to read, but I could see he was not following, so I stopped. **F**

"About what time do you think I'm going to die?" he asked.

"What?"

"About how long will it be before I die?"

"You aren't going to die. What's the matter with you?"

"Oh, yes, I am. I heard him say a hundred and two."

"People don't die with a fever of one hundred and two. That's a silly way to talk."

"I know they do. At school in France the boys told me you can't live with forty-four degrees. I've got a hundred and two."

He had been waiting to die all day, ever since nine o'clock in the morning.

"You poor Schatz," I said. "Poor old Schatz. It's like miles and kilometers. You aren't going to die. That's a different thermometer. On that thermometer thirty-seven is normal. On this kind it's ninety-eight."

"Are you sure?"

"Absolutely," I said. "It's like miles and kilometers. You know, like how many kilometers we make when we do seventy miles in the car?"

"Oh," he said.

But his gaze at the foot of the bed relaxed slowly. The hold over himself relaxed too, finally, and the next day it was very slack and he cried very easily at little things that were of no importance. **G**

F [Read and Discuss] What do you learn in this conversation?

G [Read and Discuss] What has the father known all along that Schatz hasn't known until now?

Vocabulary **commenced** (kuh MEHNST) *v.:* began.
slack (slak) *adj.:* loose.

Applying Your Skills

SKILLS FOCUS **Literary Skills** Analyze characters; analyze character traits. **Reading Skills** Compare and contrast characters. **Vocabulary Skills** Demonstrate knowledge of literal meanings of words and their usage. **Writing Skills** Include narrator and narrative devices; develop a character using interior monologue.

A Day's Wait

Respond and Think Critically

Reading Focus

Quick Check

1. Complete a story map like the one below for "A Day's Wait."

Title and Author

Setting

Characters

Conflict

Resolution

Read with a Purpose

2. What does a day's wait reveal to Schatz?

Reading Skills: Comparing and Contrasting Characters

3. Complete the chart by identifying Schatz's character traits.

	Story Details	Trait
Actions		
Words		
Thoughts/Feelings		
Effects on Others		

✔ Vocabulary Check

Answer the following questions:
4. Why are Schatz's feelings more **slack** at the end of the story?
5. Why might you describe the father's attitude as **detached**?
6. Why is Schatz distracted when his father **commenced** reading?

Literary Focus

Literary Analysis

7. **Analyze** Why would a young boy respond so heroically in the face of death? Do you think his behavior is typical?

8. **Interpret** The heroes in Hemingway's stories often hold back emotion in times of crisis. How does Schatz reveal the strain and tension he feels?

9. **Evaluate** The father calls his son "Schatz," which is German for "treasure." What does this name reveal about the father's feelings for the boy?

10. **Extend** Why do people often hesitate to share their feelings? How can assumptions interfere in our daily lives?

Literary Skills: Character Traits

11. **Analyze** Although Schatz is sick, he gets up, closes the windows in his parents' room, and then gets dressed. What character traits do these actions reveal?

12. **Infer** While his son is ill, the father goes hunting and kills two birds. What does this action tell you about the father's character?

Writing Focus

Think as a Reader/Writer

Use It in Your Writing How might "A Day's Wait" be different if it were told from Schatz's point of view? Rewrite the first scene of the story as if the boy were telling it. Be sure to include Schatz's inner thoughts.

Stolen Day

by **Sherwood Anderson**

Read with a Purpose

Read this short story to learn why the narrator says he has a debilitating disease.

Preparing to Read for this selection is on page 297.

Build Background

The setting for this story is a small Ohio town about a century ago. Some customs may have changed, but people's emotions and their motives, or reasons for doing what they do, have stayed pretty much the same.

It must be that all children are actors. The whole thing started with a boy on our street named Walter, who had inflammatory rheumatism.[1] That's what they called it. He didn't have to go to school.

Still he could walk about. He could go fishing in the creek or the waterworks pond. There was a place up at the pond where in the spring the water came tumbling over the dam and formed a deep pool. It was a good place. Sometimes you could get some good big ones there.

I went down that way on my way to school one spring morning. It was out of my way but I wanted to see if Walter was there.

He was, inflammatory rheumatism and all. There he was, sitting with a fish pole in his hand. He had been able to walk down there all right.

It was then that my own legs began to hurt. My back too. I went on to school but, at the recess time, I began to cry. I did it when the teacher, Sarah Suggett, had come out into the schoolhouse yard.

She came right over to me.

"I ache all over," I said. I did, too.

I kept on crying and it worked all right.

"You'd better go on home," she said.

---

1. **inflammatory rheumatism** (ihn FLAM uh tawr ee ROO muh tihz uhm): disease characterized by pain in the joints, fever, and inflammation of the heart.

A **Read and Discuss** What does the boy think about Walter and his "rheumatism"?

Portrait of Leslie Stanley (1931)
by Ruskin Spear (1911–1990).
Oil on canvas.

So I went. I limped painfully away. I kept on limping until I got out of the school-house street.

Then I felt better. I still had inflammatory rheumatism pretty bad but I could get along better. **Ⓑ**

I must have done some thinking on the way home.

"I'd better not say I have inflammatory rheumatism," I decided. "Maybe if you've got that you swell up."

I thought I'd better go around to where Walter was and ask him about that, so I did—but he wasn't there.

"They must not be biting today," I thought.

I had a feeling that, if I said I had inflammatory rheumatism, Mother or my brothers and my sister Stella might laugh. They did laugh at me pretty often and I didn't like it at all.

"Just the same," I said to myself, "I have got it." I began to hurt and ache again. **Ⓒ**

I went home and sat on the front steps of our house. I sat there a long time. There wasn't anyone at home but Mother and the two little ones. Ray would have been four or five then and Earl might have been three.

It was Earl who saw me there. I had got tired sitting and was lying on the porch. Earl was always a quiet, solemn little fellow.

> "It's a wonder, with my inflammatory rheumatism and all, I didn't just drop down dead."

He must have said something to Mother for presently she came.

"What's the matter with you? Why aren't you in school?" she asked.

I came pretty near telling her right out that I had inflammatory rheumatism but I thought I'd better not. Mother and Father had been speaking of Walter's case at the table just the day before. "It affects the heart," Father had said. That frightened me when I thought of it. "I might die," I thought. "I might just suddenly die right here; my heart might stop beating."

On the day before I had been running a race with my brother Irve. We were up at the fairgrounds after school and there was a half-mile track.

"I'll bet you can't run a half-mile," he said. "I bet you I could beat you running clear around the track."

And so we did it and I beat him, but afterwards my heart did seem to beat pretty hard. I remembered that lying there on the porch. "It's a wonder, with my inflammatory rheumatism and all, I didn't just drop down dead," I thought. The thought frightened me a lot. I ached worse than ever. **Ⓓ**

"I ache, Ma," I said. "I just ache."

She made me go in the house and upstairs and get into bed.

Ⓑ **Literary Focus** Character Traits What does the information about the narrator's sickness show you?

Ⓒ **Reading Focus** Comparing and Contrasting Characters How does Schatz in "A Day's Wait" respond to his illness? How does this boy respond?

Ⓓ **Read and Discuss** Why does the narrator feel the way he does after his race with Irve?

Vocabulary **solemn** (SAHL uhm) *adj.:* gloomy; serious.

It wasn't so good. It was spring. I was up there for perhaps an hour, maybe two, and then I felt better.

I got up and went downstairs. "I feel better, Ma," I said. **E**

Mother said she was glad. She was pretty busy that day and hadn't paid much attention to me. She had made me get into bed upstairs and then hadn't even come up to see how I was.

I didn't think much of that when I was up there but when I got downstairs where she was, and when, after I had said I felt better and she only said she was glad and went right on with her work, I began to ache again.

I thought, "I'll bet I die of it. I bet I do."

I went out to the front porch and sat down. I was pretty sore at Mother.

"If she really knew the truth, that I have the inflammatory rheumatism and I may just drop down dead any time, I'll bet she wouldn't care about that either," I thought. **F**

I was getting more and more angry the more thinking I did.

"I know what I'm going to do," I thought; "I'm going to go fishing."

I thought that, feeling the way I did, I might be sitting on the high bank just above the deep pool where the water went over the dam, and suddenly my heart would stop beating.

And then, of course, I'd pitch forward, over the bank into the pool and, if I wasn't dead when I hit the water, I'd drown sure.

They would all come home to supper and they'd miss me. **G**

"But where is he?"

Then Mother would remember that I'd come home from school aching.

She'd go upstairs and I wouldn't be there. One day during the year before, there was a child got drowned in a spring. It was one of the Wyatt children.

Right down at the end of the street there was a spring under a birch tree and there had been a barrel sunk in the ground.

Everyone had always been saying the spring ought to be kept covered, but it wasn't.

So the Wyatt child went down there, played around alone, and fell in and got drowned.

Mother was the one who had found the drowned child. She had gone to get a pail of water and there the child was, drowned and dead.

This had been in the evening when we were all at home, and Mother had come running up the street with the dead, dripping child in her arms. She was making for the Wyatt house as hard as she could run, and she was pale.

She had a terrible look on her face, I remembered then.

"So," I thought, "they'll miss me and there'll be a search made. Very likely there'll be someone who has seen me sitting by the pond fishing, and there'll be a big alarm and

---

E Read and Discuss | What do the narrator's thoughts about his mother tell you?

F Reading Focus **Comparing and Contrasting Characters** How does the boy feel about his mother's reaction to his illness? How does Schatz in "A Day's Wait" feel?

G Literary Focus **Character Traits** What do you learn about the boy from his thoughts here?

Viewing and Interpreting What details about fishing are appealing in this painting?

Richard Fishing by the Pool
by Charles Knight (1910–1990).
Pen and ink; watercolor; gouache on paper.
©Chris Beetles, London.

all the town will turn out and they'll drag the pond."

I was having a grand time, having died. Maybe, after they found me and had got me out of the deep pool, Mother would grab me up in her arms and run home with me as she had run with the Wyatt child. **H**

I got up from the porch and went around the house. I got my fishing pole and lit out for the pool below the dam. Mother was busy—she always was—and didn't see me go. When I got there I thought I'd better not sit too near the edge of the high bank.

By this time I didn't ache hardly at all, but I thought.

"With inflammatory rheumatism you can't tell," I thought.

H Reading Focus Comparing and Contrasting Characters What does the narrator mean when he says, "I was having a grand time, having died"?

"It probably comes and goes," I thought.

"Walter has it and he goes fishing," I thought.

I had got my line into the pool and suddenly I got a bite. It was a regular whopper. I knew that. I'd never had a bite like that. I knew what it was. It was one of Mr. Fenn's big carp.

Mr. Fenn was a man who had a big pond of his own. He sold ice in the summer and the pond was to make the ice. He had bought some big carp and put them into his pond and then, earlier in the spring when there was a freshet,[2] his dam had gone out.

So the carp had got into our creek and one or two big ones had been caught—but none of them by a boy like me.

The carp was pulling and I was pulling and I was afraid he'd break my line, so I just tumbled down the high bank, holding onto the line, and got right into the pool. We had it out, there in the pool. We struggled. We wrestled. Then I got a hand under his gills and got him out.

He was a big one all right. He was nearly half as big as I was myself. I had him on the bank and I kept one hand under his gills and I ran.

> I had got my line into the pool and suddenly I got a bite.

I never ran so hard in my life. He was slippery, and now and then he wriggled out of my arms; once I stumbled and fell on him, but I got him home.

So there it was. I was a big hero that day. Mother got a washtub and filled it with water. She put the fish in it and all the neighbors came to look. I got into dry clothes and went down to supper—and then I made a break that spoiled my day. **❶**

There we were, all of us, at the table, and suddenly Father asked what had been the matter with me at school. He had met the teacher, Sarah Suggett, on the street and she had told him how I had become ill.

"What was the matter with you?" Father asked, and before I thought what I was saying I let it out.

"I had the inflammatory rheumatism," I said—and a shout went up. It made me sick to hear them, the way they all laughed.

It brought back all the aching again, and like a fool I began to cry.

"Well, I have got it—I have, I have," I cried, and I got up from the table and ran upstairs.

I stayed there until Mother came up. I knew it would be a long time before I heard the last of the inflammatory rheumatism. I was sick all right, but the aching I now had wasn't in my legs or in my back. **❶**

---

2. **freshet** (FREHSH iht): flood caused by heavy rain or a thaw.

---

❶ [Read and Discuss] What is going on with the narrator now?

❶ [Read and Discuss] What does the boy mean when he says that he was sick but that the aching wasn't in his legs or his back?

Vocabulary **wriggled** (RIHG uhld) *v.*: wiggled; squirmed.

Applying Your Skills

SKILLS FOCUS **Literary Skills** Analyze character; analyze character traits. **Reading Skills** Compare and contrast characters. **Vocabulary Skills** Demonstrate knowledge of literal meanings of words and their usage. **Writing Skills** Write a character analysis.

Stolen Day

Respond and Think Critically

Reading Focus

Quick Check

1. Explain the title of the story.

Read with a Purpose

2. Why do you think the narrator starts to feel sick after he sees Walter fishing at the pond?

Reading Skills: Comparing and Contrasting Characters

3. Complete the chart by identifying the narrator's character traits.

	Story Details	Trait
Actions		
Words		
Thoughts/Feelings		
Effects on Others		

✓ Vocabulary Check

Answer the following questions:

4. If you saw a boy wearing a **solemn** expression, what do you think he might be feeling?
5. How have you behaved during a time when you **wriggled** out of trouble?

Literary Focus

Literary Analysis

6. **Infer** Why do you think the narrator's family laughs at him when he says he has inflammatory rheumatism?

7. **Infer** Why does the boy insist that he really *is* sick?

8. **Extend** The first line of the story says, "It must be that all children are actors." How does this sentence connect to the narrator and to children in general?

Literary Skills: Characters and Character Traits

9. **Analyze** A **flashback** is an interruption of action to tell about something that happened in the past. In "Stolen Day" the narrator interrupts his fantasy about dying to tell about an accident the year before. How does the flashback help you understand the narrator's feelings? What do you learn about his character from the flashback?

Writing Focus

Think as a Reader/Writer

Use It in Your Writing Because "Stolen Day" is told by the main character in the story, you find out his inner thoughts. In a paragraph, explain how knowing his thoughts helps you understand his character.

COMPARING TEXTS
Wrap Up

A Day's Wait / Stolen Day

Writing Focus

Write a Comparison-Contrast Essay

Write an essay comparing Schatz in "A Day's Wait" to the boy in "Stolen Day." Begin by reviewing the charts you completed when you read the stories. The charts will help you identify similarities and differences between the two characters. Then, decide how you will organize your essay.

1. You can organize the essay by character traits. In the first paragraph you might discuss three traits the boys have in common. In the second paragraph you might discuss at least one way in which the boys are different. Cite details that illustrate the traits you see in each.

2. You can organize your essay by character. You might focus on Schatz and his character traits in your first paragraph and then do the same for the boy in "Stolen Day" in the next paragraph. Cite specific details from the stories to support your analysis of each character. Be sure to show how the boys are alike and how they are different.

At the end of your essay, tell which character you liked more and why. Did you identify with either character? Use details from the stories to explain your responses.

Use the workshop on writing a comparison-contrast essay, pages 106–113, for help with this assignment.

What Do You Think Now?

What do the boys learn about themselves through their experiences in these stories?

CHOICES

As you respond to the Choices, use these **Academic Vocabulary** words as appropriate: attribute, identify, process, respond.

REVIEW
Write a Character Description

What kind of person do you think Schatz's father is? Write a description of this character, identifying the character traits that are revealed in the story. Cite the story details you used to draw conclusions about his attributes.

CONNECT
Express an Opinion

Timed └ Writing In "Stolen Day" the narrator says that he has inflammatory rheumatism, but his family doesn't believe him. Do you think the narrator is lying to his family? Do you think he actually believes he is sick? What evidence in the story can you find to support your answer? Write a short paragraph in which you state your opinion, and give reasons to support it.

EXTEND
Write a Journal Entry

Schatz spends part of "A Day's Wait" alone while his father is out hunting. As "Stolen Day" ends, the narrator is in his bedroom waiting for his mother to arrive. Pretend you are one of these boys. Write a journal entry describing how you feel as you wait for your parent. Use what you know about the boys to keep your journal entry "in character."

Text Structures: Comparison and Contrast

CONTENTS

What Do **You Think** Do sports help you know yourself better?

QuickWrite
Think about a sport, hobby, or other activity that you engage in with a group. How has participating in this activity affected you as a person?

MAGAZINE ARTICLE
Preparing to Read

Borders of Baseball: U.S. and Cuban Play

Reader/Writer Notebook

Use your **RWN** to complete the activities for this selection.

Informational Text Focus

Comparison and Contrast When you **compare,** you look at two or more things to figure out how they are similar; when you **contrast,** you look for differences. You may not realize it, but you do a lot of comparing and contrasting every day—for example, when you decide what to eat for lunch.

Writers compare and contrast things all the time. To do it effectively, they use what's known as a **comparison-and-contrast organizational pattern.** Writers use one of two methods when they compare or contrast one thing with another.

- **Block method** The writer first discusses all the features of subject 1 and then discusses all the features of subject 2.
- **Point-by-point method** In this pattern the writer discusses one feature of each subject at a time. The writer chooses a feature and shows first how it applies to subject 1 and then how it applies to subject 2. The writer continues to discuss other features and how they apply to each subject in turn.

Block Method	Point-by-Point Method

Subject 1:
  Feature 1:
  Feature 2:
  Feature 3:
	Feature 1:
	  Subject 1:
	  Subject 2:

Subject 2:
  Feature 1:
  Feature 2:
  Feature 3:
	Feature 2:
	  Subject 1:
	  Subject 2:

Vocabulary

traditions (truh DIHSH uhnz) *n.:* accepted social attitudes and customs. *The United States and Cuba have different baseball traditions because the game means different things in each country.*

identity (y DEHN tuh tee) *n.:* distinguishing characteristics that determine who or what a person or thing is. *Having good baseball players is part of Cuba's national identity.*

intense (ihn TEHNS) *adj.:* showing strong feelings and seriousness. *Baseball fans have intense admiration for the players.*

Language Coach

Pronouncing –*tion* In the English language, certain letter patterns are always pronounced the same way. One of those letter patterns is *–tion,* as in *tradition.* This pattern always comes at the end of a word, and it is pronounced *shuhn.* What are three other words that end with this same pattern?

Writing Focus

Preparing for **Constructed Response**

As you read, <u>identify</u> and record the similarities and differences between baseball in the two nations. You'll use that information to answer a constructed response question.

Learn It Online

To increase your knowledge of comparison and contrast, visit the interactive reading workshops on:

go.hrw.com	L7-313	Go

Borders of Baseball: U.S. AND CUBAN PLAY by  THE WORLD ALMANAC

Read with a Purpose
Read to discover the biggest differences between baseball in the United States and in Cuba.

After the U.S. World Series ends, you won't see many Americans paying attention to baseball until the spring. However, that's when Cuban baseball players step up to bat and begin their season. Organized baseball started being played in both the United States and Cuba at roughly the same time—at the end of the 1800s. The basics of play are similar in both countries. The differences between the two traditions, however, are major. **Ⓐ**

Diamonds in the Rough **Ⓑ**
Baseball is called "America's pastime," but it competes at the professional level with the National Football League, the National Basketball Association, and other organizations. In a similar fashion, children in the United States can sign up for Little League Baseball and similar programs, but they can also participate in organized hockey, ice skating, dancing lessons, and more.

The opportunities to play different sports are slimmer in Cuba. For example, when World Cup soccer was televised in 2006, the Associated Press reported, Cuban kids caught soccer fever. But children were rolling up paper to make balls, because soccer balls are rare on the island. Baseballs, however, are widely available. Cubans are raised on stickball. "Kids learn to throw baseballs and hit them with a stick," says Roberto González Echevarría, the author of *The Pride of Havana: A History of Cuban Baseball* and a professor of Hispanic and comparative literature at Yale University. "There is more competition [in the United States] from football, basketball, and so on." **Ⓒ**

Pay for Play
Young, talented U.S. baseball players can decide to go professional. Scouts might discover them, or their parents and coaches might push them to attend colleges with strong baseball programs. But becoming a success is mostly a private matter. Not so in Cuba: Boys with talent are identified as early as age ten. The government moves gifted players into boarding academies, where they are trained in the sport.

Cuban baseball is under government control. Therefore, Cubans play for the nation, not for a team owner. "Baseball is more important to national identity in

---

Ⓐ **Read and Discuss** What is the author setting up for you?

Ⓑ **Informational Focus** Comparison and Contrast Review the methods of organization described on page 313. What method of organization is the writer using in this article?

Ⓒ **Informational Focus** Comparison and Contrast Why does the author mention other sports?

Vocabulary **traditions** (truh DIHSH uhnz) *n.*: accepted social attitudes and customs.
identity (y DEHN tuh tee) *n.*: distinguishing characteristics that determine who or what a person or thing is.

Cuba," says González Echevarría. Playing and coaching baseball are duties, not options, for Cubans with the required skills. Players are state workers who receive state salaries and assignments. Better players are paid about the same as lesser ones. Some are given gifts, such as expense accounts at restaurants. But individuals are not rewarded in the way U.S. baseball stars are.

Major League Baseball players can argue for contracts worth millions of dollars. They work for privately owned teams, and better players earn much more money than weaker players. That is a big reason U.S. scouts were able to lure several Cuban players from their home country in recent decades. Some of Cuba's top talent left the island forever for the chance to play professional baseball and earn millions. **D**

In the Ballpark

Ballpark visitors say they feel a difference between the fans at U.S. and Cuban games. Baseball fans in both countries can be intense. But it is common for U.S. fans to be fenced off from their idols, while Cubans have greater access to their players. After batting practice, U.S. stadium walls are rushed by people handing items to the players to be autographed. In Cuba, fans show their admiration differently. "The people stare at them, respect them, adore them, attend to them,

help them," says Carlos Rodriguez Acosta, the commissioner of Cuban baseball, in the PBS Web series *Stealing Home*.

U.S. ballparks, too, are different from Cuban ones. Fans pass souvenir and food stands while going to and from their seats. Team logos are plastered on everything from cups to T-shirts. Cuban ballparks, by contrast, are not very commercialized. In Cuba, baseball is a source of national pride, not a way to push people to buy certain products.

U.S. players are better paid than their counterparts in Cuba, partly because it costs much more for U.S. fans to go to the ballpark. In 2005, the cost of an opening-day ticket in the United States ranged from around $14 to $45. The Cuban league also charges admission, but a seat costs mere pennies. So while the players in both countries play the same game, the culture surrounding that game is very different in the two nations.

Score Board

Baseball became an Olympic sport in 1992. Cuba has won three of four gold medals: 1992, 1996, and 2004. The United States won in 2000. By 2006, Cuba had taken 25 of 36 World Cups in baseball; the United States, 2. **E**

Read with a Purpose

Explain which difference between baseball in the United States and baseball in Cuba most surprised you.

D | Read and Discuss | How does Echevarría's comment on national identity connect to what you know about baseball in the United States?

E | Informational Focus | Comparison and Contrast What is the connection between culture and each nation's presentation of the game?

Vocabulary **intense** (ihn TEHNS) *adj.:* showing strong feelings and seriousness.

Applying Your Skills

Borders of Baseball: U.S. and Cuban Play

Practicing the Standards

Informational Text and Vocabulary

1. Which *best* states the main idea of this article?

A Baseball started being played in the United States and Cuba at roughly the same time.

B The basics of play are similar in both countries.

C There are major differences between the baseball traditions in each country.

D Baseball competes for popularity with other sports in the United States.

2. The organizational pattern this writer uses for **comparing and contrasting** is the —

A chronological method

B point-by-point method

C persuasive method

D block method

3. According to this article, the *main* difference between Cuban and U.S. stadiums is that U.S. stadiums —

A have more merchandise for sale

B have more comfortable seats

C make it easier to get players' autographs

D sell tickets only on opening day

4. Another word for *traditions* is —

A leagues

B academies

C autographs

D customs

5. A nation's *identity* is determined by its —

A essential characteristics

B type of government

C unique language

D national sport

6. Someone who is *intense* is —

A passionate

B traditional

C organized

D gifted

Writing Focus   Constructed Response

In a paragraph, explain the major similarities and differences between the baseball tradition in the United States and in Cuba. A Venn diagram like the one below can help you sort out and analyze the similarities and differences. In each circle, note differences. In the center, where the circles overlap, note similarities.

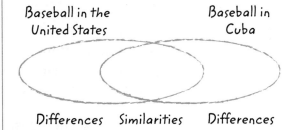

Baseball in the United States — Baseball in Cuba

Differences   Similarities   Differences

What Do You Think Now Why might playing a sport for your country, rather than for a team, make you play harder?

Writing Workshop

Persuasive Essay

Write with a Purpose

Write a persuasive essay that includes a clear position on an issue supported by reasons and evidence. Your **purpose** is to convince readers to think or act in a certain way. You can't do that unless you keep your **audience** in mind as you plan your essay.

A Good Persuasive Essay

- identifies an issue and takes a clear position on it
- addresses possible reader concerns
- provides reasons and evidence that support the position, including facts, examples, anecdotes, and expert opinions
- makes a convincing call to action

See page 326 for complete rubric.

Reader/Writer Notebook

Use your **RWN** to complete the activities for this workshop.

Think as a Reader/Writer

Before you write your own essay, read the excerpt below from "Hungry Here," a persuasive essay by World Almanac that appears on page 870. This excerpt begins in the middle of the essay as the writer addresses a commonly held belief.

> We like to think of America as a land of plenty. Yet about one in ten Americans uses a food bank or soup kitchen on a regular basis in order to get food. And such charitable services do not reach everyone. Many people live in constant hunger, and some are literally starving to death.
>
> Who are America's hungry? You might be surprised. Second Harvest found that 36 percent of its food bank users come from homes with at least one working adult. For these families, a regular wage does not guarantee regular meals. When expenses—such as rent, heat, electric, and medical bills—run higher than family income, little may be left over for food. . . .
>
> *The writer details the work of student Daniel Cayce in a long paragraph that is omitted here. The final paragraph of the essay is below.*
>
> Daniel grew up in a family with a history of helping the needy. He has been working side-by-side with his grandmother, the founder of Jo Ann Cayce Charities, since age three. It was obvious to Daniel that hunger was not something long ago and far away. Perhaps it is time for the rest of us to realize this same truth and to take action in our own communities and as a nation.

← The writer **counters** the argument that America is a land of plenty by using specific statistics as evidence.

← The writer asks a **question** to connect to the reader and uses statistics that show the seriousness of the problem.

← In the final paragraph the author uses Daniel's example to urge readers to **take action** against hunger in their community.

Think About the Professional Model

With a partner, discuss the following questions about the model:

1. Why is the author's use of evidence persuasive?

2. How does the call to action effectively conclude the essay?

Prewriting

Choose an Issue

The **purpose** of persuasive writing is to convince your readers to share your point of view and take action on an issue. An **issue** is a subject, situation, or idea about which people disagree, such as the best way to raise money for the class trip, whether video games are harmful to children, or whether the city should build a playground or a parking lot. Your first step is to brainstorm issues about which you feel strongly and about which you know or have access to enough information to be persuasive. Then, choose one issue that you think will also matter to your audience.

Think About Purpose and Audience

As you begin planning your essay, keep your **purpose** and **audience** in mind. Your **purpose** is to convince your audience to agree with your position on a controversial issue.

Your **audience** is an individual or group of individuals who have strong feelings on the issue. To focus on your audience, answer the following questions:

- Who is my audience?
- What interest does my audience have in the issue?
- How does the audience currently feel about the issue? How do I know?
- What reasons might the audience have to be against my position?
- What arguments can I use to counter the audience's concerns?

State Your Position

Every issue has at least two sides—for it and against it. As a writer, you need to adopt a **position** or **perspective** and to support it. State your position or perspective clearly in an **opinion statement.** It should indicate the issue and the side you support—for or against.

Issue	Position	Opinion Statement
hunger in America	It is a serious problem.	We can all do something to help the hungry in our community.

Idea Starters

- ways to improve your neighborhood
- plans to improve your school
- requests to your family for a privilege or activity

Writing Tip

Try to avoid matters of personal preference, such as the best color or kind of shoes, when you choose an issue. There's really no way to argue about personal taste.

Your Turn

Get Started Making notes in your **RWN,** choose an **issue** and decide on your **position** about it. Answer the questions about **audience** on this page. Keep your **purpose** in mind as you write your notes. Write an **opinion statement** that shows your position on the issue.

Learn It Online

Plan your persuasive essay using the interactive graphic organizer:

| go.hrw.com | L7-319 | Go |

Writing Tip

Reasons that appeal to a reader's logic, or intelligence, are called **logical appeals.** Logical appeals show why it makes sense to accept the writer's position on the issue.

Writing Tip

To find support for your opinion,
- interview experts or people interested in the issue
- conduct research by using articles, books, and reliable Web sites or by taking a poll

Your Turn _____

Choose Your Support
Making notes in your **RWN,** choose and evaluate your **reasons.** Select the most specific and convincing **evidence** you can find to support each reason for your position. Keep your **audience** in mind as you choose your reasons and evidence.

Provide Reasons

You must convince your readers that your position is logical and makes sense. Strong **reasons** will support your position. Reasons tell **why** you believe what you do. Review your opinion statement and then ask, "Why?"

- Why do I believe that . . . ?
- Why do I want . . . ?
- Why do I support . . . ?

The answers to the question *Why?* will be your reasons.

Now think about the members of your audience and what they value. Which of your reasons will strongly appeal to your particular audience? For which of your reasons can you provide specific support?

Gather Evidence

Effective persuasive writing must have convincing **evidence** to support its reasons. For each of your reasons, plan to use at least one of the following kinds of specific evidence:

- an **anecdote,** a brief story that illustrates a point
- a **fact,** a statement that can be proven true
- a **statistic,** a fact given in number form
- an **example,** a specific instance that illustrates a general idea
- an **expert opinion,** a statement made by an authority on a subject

Notice how the reason and evidence below support the writer's position.

Position	Reason	Evidence
Hunger in America is a serious problem.	The problem is widespread, affecting millions.	One in ten Americans uses a food bank or soup kitchen. Thirty-six percent of the individuals who use food banks are from homes with working adults.

Anticipate Audience Concerns

Your goal is to persuade readers to accept your position. Some may have ideas that oppose your position or may repeat ideas that are popularly held, such as "America is a land of plenty" in the professional model on page 318. Anticipate their concerns so that you can stress the benefits of your position.

Drafting

Follow the Writer's Framework

To convince your readers, you need to tell them your position on the issue, present reasons and evidence for your position, and inspire them to act as you wish. The **Writer's Framework** to the right outlines how to plan your draft to maximize your power of persuasion.

Organize Your Support

The order in which you present reasons and evidence, as well as the way you begin and end a persuasive composition, determines the effectiveness of your argument. Arrange your reasons according to **order of importance,** ending with your strongest reason. Use transitional words and phrases to emphasize the order of importance of your reasons.

A Writer's Framework
Introduction
• Grab the audience's attention
• State your position in an opinion statement
Body
• Second strongest reason and supporting evidence
• Other reasons and supporting evidence
• Strongest reason and supporting evidence
Conclusion
• Restate your position
• Call your audience to action

● Writing Tip

A **quotation,** a vivid **example,** or a surprising **statistic** can be a strong opening for your essay. Maintain a strong, positive tone throughout. Support your position with anecdotes and other examples from personal experience.

Grammar Link Using Transitions

Transitions are words and phrases that show how ideas are related to one another. Use this chart to identify transitions you can use to make the relationships among ideas clear within and between the paragraphs of your persuasive essay.

Common Transitional Words and Phrases

Cause and Effect	Order of Importance	Compare and Contrast
as a result	first	although
because	furthermore	and
consequently	last	but
for	mainly	however
since	more important	instead
so	then	similarly
therefore	to begin with	yet

Reference Note For more on transitions, see the Language Handbook.

Your Turn _____

Draft Your Persuasive Essay Using the notes you gathered and the **Writer's Framework,** write a draft of your persuasive essay. Be sure to think about

- how to state clearly your **position** on the issue and the reasons that support it
- how to **organize** your reasons and evidence
- how to address your audience's concerns
- how to conclude with a call to action

Peer Review

Working with a peer, go over the chart at the right. Then, review your draft. Answer each question in this chart to locate where and how your drafts could be improved. Be sure to take notes on what you and your partner discuss. You can refer to your notes as you revise your draft.

Evaluating and Revising

Read the questions in the left column of the chart, and then use the tips in the middle column to help you make revisions to your essay. The right column suggests techniques you can use to revise your draft.

Persuasive Composition: Guidelines for Content and Organization

Evaluation Question	Tip	Revision Technique
1. Does the introduction grab the audience's attention?	**Put stars** next to questions, anecdotes, or statements that would interest the audience.	If needed, **add** an attention-grabber to the beginning of the introduction.
2. Does the introduction have a clear opinion statement?	**Underline** the opinion statement. Ask a peer to read it and identify your position on the issue.	**Add** an opinion statement or, if necessary, **replace** the opinion statement with a clearer one.
3. Are there at least two reasons that logically support your opinion statement?	With a colored marker, **highlight** the reasons that support the opinion statement.	**Add** reasons that support the opinion statement.
4. Does at least one piece of evidence support each reason?	**Circle** evidence that supports each reason. **Draw a line** from the evidence to the reason.	If necessary, **add** evidence to support each reason. **Elaborate** on pieces of evidence by adding details or explaining their meaning.
5. Are the reasons in the order that is most persuasive?	**Number** the reasons in the margin, and rank them by their strength and persuasiveness.	**Reorder** ideas, using your strongest reason last.
6. Does the conclusion include a restatement of the position and a call to action?	**Put a check mark** next to the restatement. **Underline** the call to action.	**Add** a restatement of the position if it is missing. **Add** a call to action if there is not one.

Read this student draft and notice the comments on its strengths and suggestions on how it could be improved.

Kids Should Be Paid for Chores

by T. J. Wilson, Atlantic Middle School

According to the Joint Council on Economic Education, teenagers between the ages of 13 and 17 will spend $89 billion in this country. Where will that staggering amount of money come from? Many teens are not allowed to work outside of the home; therefore, I strongly believe that kids should be paid for doing chores around the house. Kids all across the country constantly nag their parents for money to go to the movies, buy CDs, and purchase trendy clothes. Consequently, many parents complain about their kids always asking them for money.

Constant friction results. Parents complain that kids don't help out around the house enough. Lots of times, kids get nagged until they clean up their rooms, put out the trash, cut the lawn, shovel the snow, and do many other chores. But conflicts result at home. Why can't kids and parents reach a compromise about money and chores? This would end the feuding and make everyone in the household happy. Parents would pay kids a small fee for doing chores without being reminded. Kids would no longer ask for money.

← T. J. uses a **statistic** to grab the reader's attention.

← He clearly states his **position.**

← **Transitions** help the reader identify the cause-and-effect nature of this problem.

← T. J. supports his position with **examples.**

← T. J. could strengthen his point here.

MINI-LESSON ▶ How to Use Anecdotes as Supporting Evidence

T. J.'s second paragraph ends with the point that conflicts in the household will end when kids are paid for chores. He can strengthen this point by adding an anecdote.

T. J.'s Revision of Paragraph Two

. . . feuding and make everyone in the household happy. Parents would pay kids a small fee for doing chores without being reminded. Kids would no longer ask for money. ∧My cousin Jeremy from Illinois constantly argued with his dad about mowing the lawn and walking the dog. Every time Jeremy asked for money, the accusations began again. Then they decided on a set fee for the chores: $20.00 a week for mowing and $7.00 a week for daily dog walks. Jeremy now eagerly does his chores, and he doesn't argue with his dad—even the dog is happy!

Your Turn _____

Strengthen Your Evidence

Read your draft and then ask yourself these questions:

- What reason or reasons in my draft can be strengthened with an anecdote?
- What details should I add to make the anecdote specific?

Student Draft *continues*

T. J. cites an **expert opinion** to support his point about responsibility. →

> This compromise teaches kids responsibility. John Covey, a father of ten and co-author of *The Seven Habits of Effective Families,* says there are two reasons to get children to do chores: "to get the job done and to help them grow." Teens learn to be responsible and develop a work ethic.

Notice that a **transition word** emphasizes cause-and-effect. →

> When their chores are completed with no nagging, they'd be paid whatever their parents had agreed to pay them. Kids could spend the money on things they like or save money for expensive items.

T. J. anticipates and addresses the "ideal world" belief. This counters an **audience concern.** →

> In an ideal world, kids would happily do chores, never ask for money, and parents would have the resources to pay for outside help or the time to do all the work themselves. Whom are we kidding? The real world demands a compromise on chores and money.

The final paragraph repeats the major ideas but does not encourage the reader to **take action.** →

> Kids would stop begging for money. Parents would stop nagging kids to clean up their rooms or the kitchen. Both parents and kids would be getting what they want.

MINI-LESSON ▸ **How to Conclude with a Call to Action**

T. J.'s final paragraph repeats his strongest reason: eliminating conflict. To strengthen his conclusion, he decided to add a call to action by asking his readers to do something about the issue he has addressed. Notice how he revised to add two rhetorical questions and a specific call to action.

T. J.'s Revision of Paragraph Five

> In an ideal world, kids would happily do chores, never ask for money, and parents would have the resources to pay for outside help or the time to do all the work themselves. Whom are we kidding? The real world demands a compromise on chores and money.
>
> *Do you want to* ~~Kids would~~ stop begging for money. *Do you want your* Parents ~~would~~ stop nagging ~~kids~~
> *your* *to* *you*
> to clean up ~~their rooms or the kitchen.~~ Both parents and kids would be
> *Talk to your parents today. Propose*
> *a compromise of responsibility and payment for chores.*
> getting what they want.

Your Turn____

Conclude with a Call to Action With a partner, review the conclusion to your composition. If it lacks a call to action, add one. If it has a weak call to action, improve it. Your partner can suggest how the call to action does (or does not) make him or her want to take action.

Proofreading and Publishing

Proofreading

Errors in your final essay will distract your reader from your persuasive points. Polish your persuasion by carefully correcting any misspellings, punctuation errors, and problems in sentence structure.

> ### Grammar Link Punctuating Rhetorical Questions
>
> *Why should you proofread?* Persuasive writers often ask questions like these. By directly addressing the audience, **rhetorical questions** connect with readers and make them think, even though the writer doesn't really expect an answer.
>
> T. J. used several rhetorical questions in his essay, but he forgot to punctuate the new questions in his revised conclusion.
>
> Do you want to stop begging for money? Do you want your parents to stop nagging you to clean up your room? Talk to your parents today. Propose a compromise of responsibility and payment for chores. Both parents and kids would be getting what they want.

Publishing

Here are some different formats that you can use to share your persuasive essay with your audience.

- If your school or community is affected by the issue you have discussed, consider submitting your composition to the school newspaper, local newspaper, or parent-teacher organization newsletter.
- If your topic is specialized, consider submitting your essay to the Letters to the Editor column of a magazine that explores the issue.
- Create an "Opposing Views" bulletin board by pairing your composition with one that supports a different position on your issue.

Reflect on the Process In your **RWN,** write short responses to these questions:

1. Do you think your composition achieves its purpose? Why or why not?
2. What is the strongest support in your essay? Why is it the strongest?
3. Which revisions do you think most strengthened your position?

⬤ Proofreading Tip

Have three different peers read your composition, each one focusing on only one potential problem area: spelling, punctuation, or sentence structure. Use each reader's suggestions to improve your essay.

Your Turn _____

Proofread and Publish

Proofread your composition for any rhetorical questions you have used. If you have not used any, find one place where you can add one. Write an effective rhetorical question for this spot, and punctuate it correctly. In addition, proofread your essay for any additional errors in punctuation, spelling, and sentence structure. Make the corrections on your final draft. Then, publish your essay so that others can read it.

Scoring Rubric

You can use one of the rubrics below to evaluate your persuasive essay. Your teacher will tell you to use either the four-point or the six-point rubric.

6-Point Scale

Score 6 *Demonstrates advanced success*
- focuses consistently on a clear and reasonable position
- shows effective organization throughout, with smooth transitions
- offers thoughtful, creative ideas and reasons
- supports a position thoroughly, using convincing, fully elaborated reasons and evidence
- exhibits mature control of written language

Score 5 *Demonstrates proficient success*
- focuses on a clear and reasonable position
- shows effective organization, with transitions
- offers thoughtful ideas and reasons
- supports a position competently, using convincing, well-elaborated reasons and evidence
- exhibits sufficient control of written language

Score 4 *Demonstrates competent success*
- focuses on a reasonable position, with minor distractions
- shows effective organization, with minor lapses
- offers mostly thoughtful ideas and reasons
- elaborates reasons and evidence with a mixture of the general and the specific
- exhibits general control of written language

Score 3 *Demonstrates limited success*
- includes some loosely related ideas that distract from the writer's position
- shows some organization, with noticeable gaps in the logical flow of ideas
- offers routine, predictable ideas and reasons
- supports ideas with uneven reasoning and elaboration
- exhibits limited control of written language

Score 2 *Demonstrates basic success*
- includes loosely related ideas that seriously distract from the writer's persuasive purpose
- shows minimal organization, with major gaps in the logical flow of ideas
- offers ideas and reasons that merely skim the surface
- supports ideas with inadequate reasoning and elaboration
- exhibits significant problems with control of written language

Score 1 *Demonstrates emerging effort*
- shows little awareness of the topic and purpose for writing
- lacks organization
- offers unclear and confusing ideas
- demonstrates minimal persuasive reasoning or elaboration
- exhibits major problems with control of written language

4-Point Scale

Score 4 *Demonstrates advanced success*
- focuses consistently on a clear and reasonable position
- shows effective organization throughout, with smooth transitions
- offers thoughtful, creative ideas and reasons
- supports a position thoroughly, using convincing, fully elaborated reasons and evidence
- exhibits mature control of written language

Score 3 *Demonstrates competent success*
- focuses on a reasonable position, with minor distractions
- shows effective organization, with minor lapses
- offers mostly thoughtful ideas and reasons
- elaborates reasons and evidence with a mixture of the general and the specific
- exhibits general control of written language

Score 2 *Demonstrates limited success*
- includes some loosely related ideas that distract from the writer's position
- shows some organization, with noticeable gaps in the logical flow of ideas
- offers routine, predictable ideas and reasons
- supports ideas with uneven reasoning and elaboration
- exhibits limited control of written language

Score 1 *Demonstrates emerging effort*
- shows little awareness of the topic and purpose for writing
- lacks organization
- offers unclear and confusing ideas
- demonstrates minimal persuasive reasoning or elaboration
- exhibits major problems with control of written language

Persuasive Essay

SKILLS FOCUS **Writing Skills** Write persuasive essays; support persuasive arguments with reasons and evidence; address potential objections; include a call to action.

When responding to an on-demand persuasive prompt, use models you've read, what you've learned by writing your own persuasive essay, the rubric on page 326, and the steps below.

Writing Prompt

Your school is considering adding a fifteen-minute period each morning for students to relax, talk, listen to music, and get a snack. The school day will be lengthened to accommodate this midday break. Write a persuasive essay for your school paper convincing readers to support this proposal. Use specific reasons and examples.

Study the Prompt

Begin by reading the prompt carefully. Notice that the **position** is determined for you. Underline "convincing readers to **support** this proposal." Circle the proposal: "adding a fifteen-minute period each morning." Now circle the next sentence, "The school day will be lengthened." That is the **counterargument** that you must address. Note and underline any additional information in the prompt, such as the references to snacks, music, relaxation, and talking. These can become convincing reasons. Your audience is the students, parents, and staff at your school. **Tip:** Spend about five minutes studying the prompt.

Plan Your Response

Reasons Persuasive writing requires that you ask and answer the question *Why?* in relation to your position. **Ask,** "Why would it be a good idea to have a break?" Your answers become your reasons. Brainstorm convincing reasons that will also appeal to your audience.

Evidence Next, answer the question *How?* Your answer will lead to convincing supporting evi-

dence for each reason. Include a specific **example** or **anecdote** that supports each reason.

Organization Once you have decided on two to three reasons, plan their order in your essay. Put your strongest reason last to be most convincing. **Tip:** Spend about ten minutes planning your response.

Respond to the Prompt

One way to begin a persuasive composition is to address the **counterargument** as your lead—in this prompt, "The school day will be lengthened." Then, the rest of your paper concentrates on supporting your **position** with reasons and evidence. **Tip:** Spend about twenty minutes writing your essay.

Improve Your Response

Revising Go back to the key aspects of the prompt. Add any missing information.

- Do you state your position clearly?
- Do you offer good reasons and evidence?
- Does your composition have an introduction, a body, and a conclusion with a call to action for your audience?

Proofreading Take a few minutes to edit your response to correct errors in grammar, spelling, punctuation, and capitalization. Make sure that your edits are neat and the essay is legible.

Checking Your Final Copy Before you turn in your essay, read it one more time to catch any errors you may have missed and to make any finishing touches. You'll be glad you took more time to present your best writing. **Tip:** Save five or ten minutes to read and improve your draft.

Presenting a Persuasive Speech

Speak with a Purpose

Adapt your written essay into a persuasive speech. Practice your speech, and then present it to your class.

Think as a Reader/Writer Writing is not the only way to convey your opinions. You may prefer to share your views by delivering a persuasive speech. Like your essay, your persuasive speech should convince an audience that your position on an issue is best. To adapt your essay into a speech, begin with a copy of your persuasive essay.

Adapt Your Essay

Relate Your Message to Your Audience

Since this is a class assignment, you know your audience will be your classmates. Whatever your specific purpose, you will need to engage the people in your audience. To grab their attention and make them care about the issue, you can use the following strategies:

- **Provide the big picture** Explain all sides of the issue, and explain any terms and details that your audience will need to know.
- **Provide relevant reasons and evidence** Give **reasons** that your audience should agree with you, and use **evidence** (facts, examples, and personal experiences) that your audience can relate to.
- **Present visuals and media displays** Use handmade visuals or technology-based media displays to bring your speech to life.

Organize Your Ideas Persuasively

To organize your speech, consider the following strategies:

If your audience . . .	Your purpose is to . . .	Use this strategy:
opposes your position	get them to consider your position	Acknowledge their point of view, and then list the reasons that your position is a good one.
agrees with your position	get them to take action	Strengthen their existing opinion by beginning with your position and then listing reasons. Close with a clear call to action.
is unsure about your position	persuade them to agree with you	Give them solid reasons that your position is best, when all sides are considered.

Reader/Writer Notebook

Use your **RWN** to complete the activities for this workshop.

Deliver Your Persuasive Speech

Verbal Techniques

In persuasion, *how* you say something is often as important as *what* you say. It's difficult to pay attention to a speaker who mumbles, who stumbles over words, who looks down while talking, or who races through a speech. A strong presenter can make any argument persuasive by using certain speaking techniques. To persuade your listeners, practice delivery techniques that will hold their attention, not distract from your message. Consider the speaking techniques below:

Enunciation Pronounce words carefully and clearly.

Vocal Modulation Stress certain words and phrases by changing the volume of your voice.

Inflection Raise the pitch of your voice at the end of a question, and lower it at the end of a statement.

Tempo Adjust the speed and rhythm of your speech. Be sure to pause to emphasize important points.

Nonverbal Techniques

Posture and Expression You believe that your solution is a good one. Show your certainty by using appropriate facial expressions and by standing with confidence in front of your audience.

Eye Contact Keep audience members involved by looking at them.

A Positive Attitude

Your **attitude,** or feelings toward the subject, will affect how listeners respond to your speech. Both what you say and how you say it reveal your attitude. You have chosen an issue that you have a strong opinion about, but do not allow **bias,** or prejudice, to slip into your presentation. Never attack other people's positions or ideas. Rather, be positive about your own position and its resulting benefits.

   With a positive attitude, you will shine as a speaker. Let your attitude show in both verbal and nonverbal ways.

> ### A Good Persuasive Speech
>
> - clearly presents the speaker's position on an issue
> - employs a positive tone
> - includes relevant reasons and evidence to support the speaker's position
> - is held together with logical transitions
> - uses effective verbal and nonverbal techniques to convince the audience

 Speaking Tip

Remember that the order in which you present your reasons and supporting evidence also has an effect on your audience. Decide whether you want to start or end your speech with your strongest argument.

 Learn It Online

Pictures, music, and animation can make your argument more compelling. See how on MediaScope:

 go.hrw.com   L7-329   **Go**

Literary Skills Review

Character   **Directions:** Read the following story. Then, answer each question that follows.

from The Red Girl by **Jamaica Kincaid**

Here is a portion of a story set in Antigua, an island in the Caribbean Sea. The narrator is a young girl named Annie John who has wanted to play with another girl she calls the Red Girl.

The Red Girl and I stood under the guava tree looking each other up and down. What a beautiful thing I saw standing before me. Her face was big and round and red, like a moon—a red moon. She had big, broad, flat feet, and they were naked to the bare ground; her dress was dirty, the skirt and blouse tearing away from each other at one side; the red hair that I had first seen standing up on her head was matted and tangled; her hands were big and fat, and her fingernails held at least ten anthills of dirt under them. And on top of that, she had such an unbelievable, wonderful smell, as if she had never taken a bath in her whole life.

I soon learned this about her: She took a bath only once a week, and that was only so that she could be admitted to her grandmother's presence. She didn't like to bathe, and her mother didn't force her. She changed her dress once a week for the same reason. She preferred to wear a dress until it just couldn't be worn anymore. Her mother didn't mind that, either. She didn't like to comb her hair, though on the first day of school, she could put herself out for that. She didn't like to go to Sunday school, and her mother didn't force her. She didn't like to brush her teeth, but occasionally her mother said it was necessary. She loved to play marbles, and was so good that only Skerritt boys now played against her. Oh, what an angel she was, and what a heaven she lived in! I, on the other hand, took a full bath every morning and a sponge bath every night. I could hardly go out on my doorstep without putting my shoes on. I was not allowed to play in the sun without a hat on my head. My mother paid a woman who lived five houses away from us sevenpence a week—a penny for each school day and twopence for Sunday—to comb my hair. On Saturday, my mother washed my hair. Before I went to sleep at night I had to make sure my uniform was clean and creaseless and all laid out for the next day. I had to make sure that my shoes were clean and polished to a nice shine. I went to Sunday school every Sunday unless I was sick. I was not allowed to play marbles, and, as for Skerritt boys, that was hardly mentionable.

1. Which of the following **character traits** does the narrator imply about the Red Girl?
   A She takes care of her only dress.
   B She spends too much time on her hair.
   C She is not interested in bathing.
   D She is always neat and clean.

2. In the passage from "The Red Girl," the narrator uses all of the following methods of **characterization** except —
   A stating character traits directly
   B quoting speech
   C describing actions
   D describing appearance

   She took a bath only once a week, and that was only so that she could be admitted to her grandmother's presence.

3. In this sentence from the story, the grandmother can *best* be described as —
   A indifferent
   B angry
   C happy-go-lucky
   D strict

4. The narrator describes the Red Girl by revealing —
   A the girl's actions
   B the girl's thoughts
   C others' opinions of her
   D the girl's words

5. From the narrator's description of herself, you can infer that —
   A she likes to wear her school uniform
   B she is embarrassed for the Red Girl
   C she longs for a life like the Red Girl's
   D she'd like to play with the Skerritt boys

6. The narrator tells you directly how she feels about the Red Girl when she says —
   A "Her fingernails held at least ten anthills of dirt under them."
   B "She didn't like to go to Sunday school."
   C "Her face was big and round and red."
   D "What a beautiful thing I saw standing before me."

Constructed Response

7. Why do you think the narrator likes the Red Girl so much? Do you agree or disagree with the narrator's opinion? Explain in a paragraph.

Informational Skills Review

Comparison and Contrast **Directions:** Read the following selection. Then, answer each question that follows.

Here Be Dragons by **Flo Ota De Lange**

Many, many years ago, when people first began to map the Western world, they charted two main areas: their settlements and the wilderness. On the wilderness areas of their maps, they wrote a warning: "Here be dragons." When the European explorers set off in their wooden ships in the fifteenth century, most of the sailors still believed that if they sailed too far, the boats would tumble off the earth and into that area populated with seething, clawed monsters.

Dragon stories have been told for ages in almost every land and culture: Africa, Britain, China, Egypt, Greece, and Russia. From their beginnings in mythology, dragons were associated with the Great Mother, with the warrior sun god, and, especially with the water gods. Dragons were said to have been present at the creation and so were endowed with characteristics of the cosmos.[1] At one with wind and fire and water, they had the ancient power of these primal forces. They had command of fire and water and could fly like the wind. But dragons differ from culture to culture: In Asia, dragons help people; in Europe and other places, dragons are associated with destruction and evil.

Eastern Dragons. In Asia the dragon is a benevolent creature, gifted with wisdom and the power to confer blessings upon humankind. One of the first dragon stories Asian children hear has a beautiful dragon emerging from the primordial[2] swamp, proudly beating its chest and calling forth, asking to be of service to people. Eastern dragons inspire awe in those who look to them for guidance, and many are cherished as great and kind creatures. Two dragons acting as honor guards are believed to have visited the home of the philosopher Confucius when he was born. The ruler Huang-Ti was supposedly carried to heaven on the back of a dragon. If you met one on the road of life, an Eastern dragon would give you a gift as opposed to, say, fire and brimstone.

Western Dragons. It is the Western dragon that is famous for fire and brimstone. People could tell when they were in the vicinity of a Western dragon because the air would be heated and foul with the unmistakable sulfuric odor of brimstone. Brimstone has a smell that makes the scent of a rotten egg seem lovely by comparison.

---

1. **cosmos:** the whole universe.

2. **primordial:** of the earliest times.

Western dragons became feared as the foes of civilization. Perseus of ancient Greece, Beowulf of ancient Denmark, even brave little Bilbo in *The Hobbit*—all had to face menacing dragons before they could conclude their quests. In Western stories, dragons often lie underground, guarding huge piles of gold they have stolen from the surrounding countryside, which has been scorched and laid waste by the dragon's fiery breath.

Dragons Today. Dragons have largely disappeared from stories written today— except for the fantasies of writers such as Anne McCaffrey and Ursula LeGuin.

Dragons haven't died out, however. Wait a moment! What's all that noise? It sounds like people playing gongs, cymbals, and drums. What is that colorful creature a block long snaking its way through the Chinese New Year's crowd? Why, it's the Eastern dragon come again to celebrate the vitality of life! Hear that thunderous applause? That is the sound that attends an Eastern dragon passing by.

---

1. This article **compares and contrasts** —
   A legends
   B mythical dragons
   C real dragons
   D dragons' wealth

2. Dragon stories written today would most likely appear in a book of —
   A realistic stories
   B mystery stories
   C myths and legends
   D nonfiction articles

3. The **organizational pattern** used for comparison and contrast in this article is the —
   A chronological method
   B point-by-point method
   C persuasive method
   D block method

4. The subheads in this article indicate that the topics are organized by —
   A writing all the features of one subject, then all the features of the second subject
   B going back and forth between the features of the two topics being discussed
   C listing the most important points of each topic first
   D deciding which type of dragon is more important than the other

Constructed Response
5. List two similarities and two differences between Eastern dragons and Western dragons.

SKILLS FOCUS Vocabulary Skills Identify and use Latin roots and affixes to understand vocabulary.

Vocabulary Skills Review

Latin Roots and Affixes   **Directions:** Each question features a word from "The War of the Wall." Choose the correct answer.

1. Which of the following words is formed from the Latin root meaning "to be fitting" or "to be appropriate"?

   A decent

   B sole

   C creative

   D courageous

2. The word *recognized* is made by adding the Latin prefix *re–* to a word root meaning "knowledge; understanding." The Latin prefix *re– most* nearly means —

   A before

   B forward

   C again

   D not

3. Which of the following words comes from the Latin word meaning "bag" or "sack"?

   A notebook

   B capture

   C trunk

   D satchel

4. The Latin root of the word *liberation* means "to free." Which of the following words comes from the same root?

   A deliberate

   B liberal

   C possible

   D reliable

5. Which of the following words comes from the Latin root meaning "to write"?

   A scrimp

   B wrist

   C interpretation

   D inscription

6. Which of the following words is formed from the Latin root meaning "to devote; to declare"?

   A dedicate

   B interest

   C dead

   D independence

Academic Vocabulary

Directions: Use context clues to determine the meaning of the Academic Vocabulary word below.

7. The narrator of "The War of the Wall" did not recognize the painter's positive *attributes* until the mural was revealed.

   A compliments

   B responses

   C traits

   D opinions

Writing Skills Review

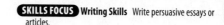
Persuasive Essay **Directions:** Read the following paragraph from a persuasive essay. Then, answer each question that follows.

> (1) The backwater swamps of the American South support many life-forms that are threatened by the overuse of natural resources. (2) Wetlands that have not been replanted after logging are vulnerable to floods and erosion. (3) Because the soil is so rich, lands have been cleared for agriculture. (4) The great trees have been cut down for lumber. (5) Huge stands of oak, elm, cypress, and other species of the North American wetlands have been removed from the landscape. (6) To preserve and protect this important habitat, we must all work for the reforestation of these swamps.

1. Which of the following statements might be added to support the opening sentence?
   - **A** Many swamp creatures are nocturnal.
   - **B** These wetlands shelter snakes, alligators, black bears, and many varieties of birds as well as enormous trees.
   - **C** Many superstitions exist about swamps.
   - **D** The naturalist John James Audubon wrote about alligators on the shores of the Red River.

2. Where might sentence 2 be moved to make the paragraph more effective?
   - **A** To the beginning of the paragraph, to introduce the topic
   - **B** Following sentence 5, to show the harm that can come from deforestation
   - **C** To the end of the paragraph, to serve as a call to action
   - **D** Out of the paragraph altogether

3. What transitional word or phrase might be added to the beginning of sentence 5?
   - **A** Fortunately,
   - **B** Otherwise,
   - **C** However,
   - **D** For example,

4. How else might sentence 5 be strengthened?
   - **A** By explaining how lumber is used for construction
   - **B** By replacing "Huge stands" with exact statistics
   - **C** By using comparisons to the destruction of rain forests
   - **D** By moving it to the end of the paragraph

5. In the remaining paragraphs of the essay, readers would expect to find all of the following *except* —
   - **A** possible objections to the solution
   - **B** the benefits of following the writer's plan
   - **C** a call for change or action
   - **D** lists of threatened jungle habitats

Read On

Fiction

M. C. Higgins, the Great

M. C. Higgins and his family have been living on Sarah's Mountain ever since M. C.'s great-grandmother arrived there as a fugitive from slavery. His family loves the mountain, but one day M. C. notices a massive pile of debris accumulating on a cliff over his home. In Virginia Hamilton's *M. C. Higgins, the Great,* a young boy is torn between his loyalty to his family and his desire for a life beyond the mountains.

Tangerine

Paul feels self-conscious about the thick glasses he has to wear, but he knows he can play on the toughest soccer team in Tangerine County, Florida. Other people, including his sinister brother, have their doubts. Can Paul triumph on and off the field? *Tangerine* by Edward Bloor will have you rooting Paul on!

The Whale Rider

In Whangara, New Zealand, the respected title of "whale rider" has always been bestowed upon a male descended from Kahutia Te Rangi. Now there is no male heir to the title. Only an eight-year-old girl named Kahu can claim the throne. Can she rise to the challenge when beached whales threaten the future of her tribe? Find out in *The Whale Rider* by Witi Ihimaera.

Sundiata: An Epic of Old Mali

Sundiata: An Epic of Old Mali by D. T. Niane is a retelling of a Malian epic that features one of the greatest characters in literature, Sundiata. Part man and part legend, Sundiata joined the kingdoms of Mali into an empire. This edition features background information on the era as well as a glossary that will enhance your reading experience.

Nonfiction

Bill Nye the Science Guy's Great Big Book of Science: Featuring Oceans and Dinosaurs

From Bill Nye, the author and Emmy Award–winning TV star, comes this collection of fascinating facts and twenty-four easy-to-follow experiments. You may be saying to yourself, "What do oceans and dinosaurs have to do with each other?" Well, you'll have to read *Bill Nye the Science Guy's Great Big Book of Science: Featuring Oceans and Dinosaurs* to get the answer to that question and many more.

Facing the Lion: Growing Up Maasai on the African Savanna

This memoir recounts the life of Joseph Lemasolai Lekuton. Born a member of the nomadic Maasai people of Kenya, Lekuton traveled the world while keeping his homeland in his heart. From his difficult yet joyous years learning the ways of a Maasai warrior to his journey on a cattle truck to a college interview in the United States, *Facing the Lion*'s author offers you both the unique and the universal experiences of a boy growing up.

Pride of Puerto Rico: The Life of Roberto Clemente

Baseball is a beloved game far beyond the United States. The admiration for the game is due in part to people's interest in its heroic players, such as the subject of *Pride of Puerto Rico: The Life of Roberto Clemente* by Paul Robert Walker. This biography will introduce you to Clemente, a man who was as proud of his family and country (both the native and the adopted) as he was of his baseball career.

Murals: Walls That Sing

Learn about neighborhood murals in *Murals: Walls That Sing* by George Ancona. The book is a photo essay about the strength a mural has to bring together neighborhoods and communities. Each mural is accompanied by a description of the artist who created it and the connection the artist has to the community.

Learn It Online

Continue your learning through further reading. Find tips for choosing, reading, and studying novels at:

go.hrw.com L7-337   Go

Theme and Point of View

INFORMATIONAL TEXT FOCUS
Analyze Arguments, Evidence, and Bias and Stereotyping

"If you live in my heart,
you live rent free."

—**Irish proverb**

What Do
You
Think

What makes us care about certain people? Why do we connect with some people and not with others?

Learn It Online
Learn how to share your point of view at the Digital Storytelling mini-site:

go.hrw.com   L7-339   **Go**

Literary Focus

by **Linda Rief**

What Are Theme and Point of View?

Think about your favorite song lyrics or the posters on your wall. Many of them make statements about life—friendship, courage, or loyalty. Authors include themes—insights about life—in stories through descriptions of characters' lives. Authors also tell their characters' stories from a particular point of view. The narrator may be a character in the story or someone outside the story who is all-knowing. The story may also be seen through the eyes of a particular character but not narrated by that character.

"If you were to boil your book down to a few words, what would be its message?"

Theme

A key element of literature—of fiction, nonfiction, poetry, and drama—is theme. **Theme** is a revelation about our lives and represents the discovery of a truth about our own experience.

Themes Focus on the "Big" Ideas Literature that endures—lasts through centuries—focuses on discoveries about the big topics in everyone's life: understanding the nature of love, accepting responsibility, understanding loss, dealing with ambition, discovering the joys and problems of friendship. You usually won't find the theme of a piece of literature stated directly. Theme is what the writer wants you to discover for yourself as you share the experiences of the characters.

> T. J. kept the vision bright within us, his words shrewd and calculated toward the fulfillment of his dream.
>
> from "Antaeus" by Borden Deal

Recurring Themes Works by different writers can have similar themes, even though their stories may be quite different. Themes recur in the stories we tell because some truths about human experiences are universal, whether a story was written hundreds of years ago in a snowbound Alaskan village or typed on a laptop yesterday in Zimbabwe.

Evaluating Theme Themes are often apparent even when you're not looking for them. For instance, certain types of movies often highlight specific themes. Keep in mind that you don't have to agree with all the themes you discover in books or movies.

Type of Movie	Theme
Western	The frontier is a lawless place where problems are too often solved through violence.
Love story	Nothing is more important than finding true love.

Point of View

Novels and short stories are told from a particular **point of view,** or vantage point. The three most common points of view are the first person, the omniscient, and the third-person limited. When you're reading, you should ask yourself who the narrator is, whether you can rely on the narrator to tell the truth, and what the narrator's relationship is to the meaning of the story.

First-Person Point of View   A story can be told by one of the characters. In this viewpoint, called the **first-person point of view,** the character speaks as "I." (*I* is the first-person pronoun.) We know only what this one character can tell us. This narrator may or may not be reliable. We trust that the speaker of "Bargain" is accurately reporting the events, but we also experience his involvement in the story and with the other characters.

> There was Slade and here was Mr. Baumer with his bills and here I was, just as before, just like in the second go-round of a bad dream. I felt like turning back, being embarrassed and half scared by trouble even when it wasn't mine. Please, I said to myself, don't stop, Mr. Baumer! Don't bite off anything!
>
> from "Bargain" by A. B. Guthrie

Omniscient Point of View   A story can also be told from the **omniscient** (ahm NIHSH uhnt) **point of view,** which is the all-knowing point of view. (In Latin, *omnis* means "all," and *sciens* means "knowing.") This narrator can tell you everything about all the characters, even their most private thoughts. "After Twenty Years" is told from an omniscient point of view.

> The two men started up the street, arm in arm. The man from the West, his egotism enlarged by success, was beginning to outline the history of his career.
>
> from "After Twenty Years" by O. Henry

Third-Person-Limited Point of View   Often a story is seen through the eyes of one character, but the character is not telling the story as "I." This is the **third-person-limited point of view.** In this point of view a narrator zooms in on the thoughts, feelings, and reactions of just one character.

As the reader, it's important to evaluate point of view with a critical eye. Each point of view may put a different spin on the same story events.

Your Turn   Analyze Theme and Point of View

1. Think of a story that you know well. Identify the story's theme and what it means to you.

2. Identify a favorite saying or quotation that you think would make a good theme for a story. Explain why it has the qualities of a theme and what it conveys about life.

3. Explain the difference between the three points of view.

Learn It Online

Visit *NovelWise* to learn how to recognize themes and points of view:

| go.hrw.com | L7-341 | **Go** |

Analyzing Visuals

How Can You Analyze Themes in Visual Art?

Artists, like writers, create works in part to express a theme. Recurring themes, or universal ideas about the human experience, crop up in paintings created in different times and places, just as they do in books. As in literature, these themes are not directly stated but emerge out of parts of the whole. A theme forms like a puzzle: Pieces come together to make a unified statement, and a truth emerges. Not everyone's truth will be the same. For example, some suggest that love can conquer all. On the other hand, the writer Ambrose Bierce believes that "love is a temporary insanity."

Analyzing Themes in Visual Art

Answer these questions as you find the theme of a painting:

1. Determine the subject—is the painting about heroism? nature? divine love? temptation?
2. Examine it to get a sense of the artist's views on the subject.
3. Study such visual elements as color, shape, and composition.
4. Combine these observations to express the painting's theme.

How does the composition in the left detail and the color in the right help develop the theme?

The Peaceable Kingdom (c. 1844–1845)
by Edward Hicks (1780–1849). Oil on canvas.

1. The **theme** of this work involves peace and harmony. What images convey this theme?

2. The artist Edward Hicks was a Quaker. He included the Quaker William Penn, the founder of Pennsylvania, in the background.

3. Hicks felt Penn's arrival in America brought the "peaceable kingdom" closer. How does he convey that **theme**?

4. Hicks may have painted as many as a hundred versions of this work. Why do you think he was drawn to this **theme**?

Your Turn   Write About Theme

Think about Hicks's *Peaceable Kingdom*. What human longing does the theme address? Explain your response.

Reading Focus

by **Kylene Beers**

How Are Theme, Cause and Effect, and Predictions Connected?

You might think that identifying theme, noting cause-and-effect relationships (the way two events are connected), and making predictions (thinking about what will happen next) have nothing to do with one another. But noting causal relationships helps you predict, which helps you determine the meaning of the text, which can help you state the theme.

Finding the Theme

When you are asked to think about theme, start by considering what theme is *not*. Theme is not the plot or the topic of a story. Theme is the truth about life that you discover from reading a story. To clarify these differences, study the chart below. Here's an example of a familiar plot and topic and a possible theme that might emerge from such a story:

Plot	Topic	Theme
A man meets his friend after a twenty-year absence and is surprised by what he discovers.	Expectations; reunions	Meetings often don't turn out the way one expects.

A story can have more than one theme; however, one major understanding about life usually becomes clear. A theme is always a complete thought that is expressed in a sentence.

Use Story Clues Look for clues in a story that you can combine with your own experiences to make an **inference,** or educated guess, about the theme. Ask yourself these questions:

- How has the main character changed over the course of the story? The lessons that character learns are often a clue to the theme.
- Does the story's title reveal anything important? (Not all titles do. Some give more clues about plot than about theme.)
- Which events or scenes seem most significant? What ideas about life do they suggest?

Take Notes Record characters' meaningful comments and actions as well as ideas that strike you as important. These notes can help you track your thoughts about theme.

Say It Your Way Once you figure out the theme, you will need to express it in your own words.

Identifying Cause and Effect

You know from experience that one thing leads to another. A **cause** is an event that makes something happen. An **effect** is what happens as a result of the cause. Fiction writers use cause and effect to develop a plot. To help you identify causes and effects, ask these questions as you read:

- Why did this happen?
- What happened because of this event?

As you read, look for words that signal cause and effect, such as *resulted in, so, thus, why, because, therefore,* and *since.*

One Cause, Many Effects—or a Causal Chain? Sometimes one cause in a story will have many effects. In other stories an event triggers a **causal chain** in which each event causes another one to happen, like dominoes falling in a row. A causal chain can be tricky, because one event can follow another and not be caused by it. To figure out causes and effects, follow these steps:

- Look for what happens *first*. Then ask what happens because of that.
- Look for hidden or multiple causes and results.
- Use a graphic organizer, such as this flow chart, to record the chain of events.

Making Predictions

When you **make predictions,** you guess what will happen next in a story. Making predictions helps you anticipate how events will unfold and characters will behave. Follow these tips for making predictions:

- Look for clues that hint at future events.
- Think about how those clues connect to past and present actions in the story.
- Think about similar stories and any predictions you can make based on how those stories unfolded.
- Think about your own experiences and what might happen next in a similar situation.

Your Turn   Apply Reading Skills

1. List two strategies that can help you find the theme of a story.
2. Create a chart that identifies cause-and-effect relationships in the following scenario: You sleep through your alarm, are late for school, miss a test in English, stay after school to take the test, and miss a chance to see a movie with friends.
3. Make a prediction about what will happen next, after you miss the movie. Explain the rationale for your prediction.

Now go to the Skills in Action: Reading Model

Learn It Online
For more on cause and effect, see the interactive graphic organizers at:

go.hrw.com | L7-345 |

Read with a Purpose Read this short story to discover what happens when two friends meet on a train and things are not as they appear.

Hearts and Hands

by **O. Henry**

At Denver there was an influx of passengers into the coaches on the eastbound B.&M. express. In one coach there sat a very pretty young woman dressed in elegant taste and surrounded by all the luxurious comforts of an experienced traveler. Among the newcomers were two young men, one of handsome presence with a bold, frank countenance and manner; the other a ruffled, glum-faced person, heavily built and roughly dressed. The two were handcuffed together.

As they passed down the aisle of the coach the only vacant seat offered was a reversed one facing the attractive young woman. Here the linked couple seated themselves. The young woman's glance fell upon them with a distant, swift disinterest; then with a lovely smile brightening her countenance and a tender pink tingeing her rounded cheeks, she held out a little gray-gloved hand. When she spoke her voice, full, sweet, and deliberate, proclaimed that its owner was accustomed to speak and be heard.

"Well, Mr. Easton, if you *will* make me speak first, I suppose I must. Don't you ever recognize old friends when you meet them in the West?"

Analyzing Visuals

Viewing and Interpreting
What paragraph of the story on page 346 might this portrait illustrate?

Young Woman in a Black Hat (1895) by Auguste Renoir (1841–1919). Pastel.

The younger man roused himself sharply at the sound of her voice, seemed to struggle with a slight embarrassment which he threw off instantly, and then clasped her fingers with his left hand.

"It's Miss Fairchild," he said, with a smile. "I'll ask you to excuse the other hand; it's otherwise engaged just at present."

He slightly raised his right hand, bound at the wrist by the shining "bracelet" to the left one of his companion. The glad look in the girl's eyes slowly changed to a bewildered horror. The glow faded from her cheeks. Her lips parted in a vague, relaxing distress. Easton, with a little laugh, as if amused, was about to speak again when the other forestalled[1] him. The

---

1. forestalled (fawr STAWLD): prevented.

Reading Focus

Cause and Effect Writers use cause and effect to develop a plot. The **cause** is an event that makes something happen. The coach is full, so the two men sit opposite the young woman. Read on to learn the **effect**—what happens as a result. You may recognize more than one effect or a causal chain of relationships. Watch for both!

glum-faced man had been watching the girl's countenance with veiled glances from his keen, shrewd eyes.

Reading Focus

Making Predictions Read this passage for details that can help you make a **prediction**—an educated guess about what will happen in the story. Make a prediction about Easton's connection to the girl and his relationship to the man.

"You'll excuse me for speaking, miss, but I see you're acquainted with the marshal here. If you'll ask him to speak a word for me when we get to the pen he'll do it, and it'll make things easier for me there. He's taking me to Leavenworth prison. It's seven years for counterfeiting."

"Oh!" said the girl, with a deep breath and returning color. "So that is what you were doing out here? A marshal!"

"My dear Miss Fairchild," said Easton, calmly, "I had to do something. Money has a way of taking wings unto itself, and you know it takes money to keep step with our crowd in Washington. I saw this opening in the West, and—well, a marshalship isn't quite as high a position as that of ambassador, but—"

"The ambassador," said the girl, warmly, "doesn't call anymore. He needn't ever have done so. You ought to know that. And so now you are one of those dashing Western heroes, and you ride and shoot and go into all kinds of dangers. That's different from the Washington life. You have been missed from the old crowd."

The girl's eyes, fascinated, went back, widening a little, to rest upon the glittering handcuffs.

"Don't worry about them, miss," said the other man. "All marshals handcuff themselves to their prisoners to keep them from getting away. Mr. Easton knows his business."

"Will we see you again soon in Washington?" asked the girl.

"Not soon, I think," said Easton. "My butterfly days are over, I fear."

"I love the West," said the girl irrelevantly.[2] Her eyes were shining softly. She looked away out the car window. She began to speak truly and simply, without the gloss of style and manner: "Mamma and I spent the summer in Denver. She went home a week ago because father was slightly ill. I could live and be happy in the West. I think the air here agrees with me. Money isn't everything. But people always misunderstand things and remain stupid—"

"Say, Mr. Marshal," growled the glum-faced man. "This isn't quite fair. Haven't had a smoke all day. Haven't you talked long enough? Take me in the smoker now, won't you? I'm half dead for a pipe."

The bound travelers rose to their feet, Easton with the same slow smile on his face.

"I can't deny a petition for tobacco," he said, lightly. "It's the one friend of the unfortunate. Goodbye, Miss Fairchild. Duty calls, you know." He held out his hand for a farewell.

"It's too bad you are not going East," she said, reclothing herself with manner and style. "But you must go on to Leavenworth, I suppose?"

"Yes," said Easton, "I must go on to Leavenworth."

The two men sidled down the aisle into the smoker.

The two passengers in a seat nearby had heard most of the conversation. Said one of them: "That marshal's a good sort of chap. Some of these Western fellows are all right."

---

2. **irrelevantly** (ih REHL uh vuhnt lee): without relation to the subject at hand.

Reading Focus

Finding the Theme Watch for significant passages that may be clues to the theme. After you finish the story, re-read the two highlighted passages in which the glum-faced man speaks to the girl. Think about what the man is doing and what the writer may be revealing through the man's words.

Reading Focus

Making Predictions As you read, look for new clues that support your predictions or prompt you to revise them. Think about the possible meaning of this statement by Easton. What prediction do you make about Easton's future?

"Pretty young to hold an office like that, isn't he?" asked the other.

"Young!" exclaimed the first speaker, "why—Oh! didn't you catch on? Say—did you ever know an officer to handcuff a prisoner to his *right* hand?"

Read with a Purpose What do you now understand about appearance versus reality?

MEET THE WRITER

O. Henry
(1862–1910)

Observing with a Keen Eye

Born William Sydney Porter, O. Henry once expressed his philosophy of writing in this way:

"The short story is a potent medium of education. . . . It should break prejudice with understanding. I propose to send the down-and-outers into the drawing-rooms of the 'get-it-alls,' and I intend to insure their welcome."

O. Henry's exceptional powers of observation enabled him to study ordinary people and turn them into extraordinary characters in his stories. One place where O. Henry used his ability to write about people is Pete's Tavern, the restaurant where he wrote his classic short story "The Gift of the Magi."

Think About the Writer How does this story communicate O. Henry's compassion for "down-and-outers"?

PETE'S TAVERN EST.1864

IRVING PL

PETE'S

WE DELIVER

©The Granger Collection, New York.

SKILLS IN ACTION
Wrap Up

Into Action: Tracing Cause and Effect

Review "Hearts and Hands" for events that have cause-and-effect relationships. Fill in the chart to explain how the events are related. Also note when an effect causes something else to happen.

Cause: What Happened
_____

Effect/Cause:
_____

Effect/Cause:
_____

Effect:
_____

Talk About . . .

1. Why does the marshal cover up for the prisoner? Is he trying to spare the feelings of the young woman? Does he see the prisoner as a fellow human being?

   With a partner, discuss your ideas. Use details from the story to support your responses. Try to use each Academic Vocabulary word listed at the right in your discussion.

Write About . . .

Use the Academic Vocabulary words in your answers to the following questions about "Hearts and Hands."

2. What does the young woman <u>reveal</u> about her feelings for Easton?

3. Why is knowing which hand of each man is cuffed—left or right—a <u>relevant</u> detail?

4. Has lack of money been a <u>fundamental</u> problem for Easton? Explain your answer using details from the story.

Writing Focus

Think as a Reader/Writer

What theme did O. Henry want you to discover through this story? Write a theme statement that begins "This story reveals . . ." for "Hearts and Hands" and for each story in this collection.

Academic Vocabulary for Collection 4

Talking and Writing About Theme

Academic Vocabulary is the language you use to write and talk about literature. Use these words to discuss the stories you read in this collection. The words are underlined in the collection.

fundamental (fuhn duh MEHN tuhl) *adj.*: relating to the most basic and important parts of something. *The fundamental theme of this story is that things are often not as they appear.*

implicit (ihm PLIHS iht) *adj.*: suggested or understood but not stated directly. *Another theme implicit in the story is that even strangers can show compassion for each other.*

relevant (REHL uh vuhnt) *adj.*: directly relating to the subject. *A story theme has more meaning if it is relevant to our own lives.*

reveal (rih VEEL) *v.*: show something that was previously hidden. *The young woman revealed her feelings for Easton in the way she spoke to him.*

Your Turn

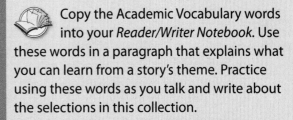 Copy the Academic Vocabulary words into your *Reader/Writer Notebook*. Use these words in a paragraph that explains what you can learn from a story's theme. Practice using these words as you talk and write about the selections in this collection.

Preparing to Read

HUM

by **Naomi Shihab Nye**

What Do **You** Think?

What obstacles can stand in the way of forming a friendship with someone?

⏱ **QuickTalk**

Pair up with a classmate whom you are friendly with. Talk about the first time you met and why you get along with one another.

Michael's Garden (2000)
by Hyacinth Manning
(1954–   ). Pastel.

Reader/Writer Notebook

Use your **RWN** to complete the activities for this selection.

SKILLS FOCUS **Literary Skills** Understand topic and theme. **Reading Skills** Find the theme.

Literary Focus

Topic and Theme The **topic** of a work can usually be expressed in a word, for example, *love, childhood, injustice*. The **theme** is the idea *about* the topic that the writer wants to convey. A theme is expressed in a sentence because it <u>reveals</u> an important idea about life. Some themes—like the power of love or the importance of home—have been explored in literature throughout time.

TechFocus What might you say or post about this selection if you had a blog devoted to literature or reading?

Reading Focus

Finding the Theme To find the theme, you need to think about important things the characters say. The writer may be using the characters to make a statement about life. Also, think about the meaning of the title. It might point to the theme of the story. Finally, think about what words from the story are most important.

Into Action One strategy for finding the theme is to take notes as you read. Use a chart like this one to take notes about "Hum."

"Hum"	Notes for Finding the Theme
Comments by characters	
Title	
Important words	Friendship, respect

Writing Focus

Think as a Reader/Writer

Find It in Your Reading You can discover a story's theme by examining the conflicts and the way they are resolved. In your *Reader/Writer Notebook*, jot down the conflicts Sami faces.

Vocabulary

recourse (REE kawrs) *n.:* help in a difficult situation. *Sami could not find recourse when his classmates ignored him.*

solitude (SAHL uh tood) *n.:* state of being alone. *The town was lost in solitude for days.*

communicative (kuh MYOO nih kay tihv) *adj.:* able to give information. *The Dialogue Club helped everyone become more communicative.*

quizzical (KWIHZ ih kuhl) *adj.:* puzzled; baffled. *Sami's quizzical expression indicated he was uncomfortable.*

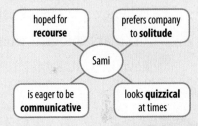

Language Coach

Change Adjectives to Adverbs
Some adjectives become adverbs when you add *–ly* to the ends of them. Look at this example:

bad (*adj.*) + *–ly* = badly (*adv.*)

Which Vocabulary words can you change to adverbs by adding *–ly*?

  Learn It Online
There's more to these words than meets the eye. Visit Word Watch to find out more:

go.hrw.com   L7-353   **Go**

Naomi Shihab Nye
(1952–   )

Writing from Experience

Like her character Sami Salsaa in "Hum," Naomi Shihab Nye made the transition from life in one country to life in another as a young teen. Nye grew up in St. Louis, Missouri, the daughter of an American mother and a Palestinian father. At age fourteen she moved with her family to Jerusalem in Israel, her father's hometown, where she attended high school. When the family returned to the United States, they settled in San Antonio, Texas. Nye still lives in San Antonio, with her husband and son.

Nye brings her perspective as an Arab American to her writing, which includes poetry, songs, children's books, and novels. She says, "Familiar sights, sounds, smells have always been my necessities. . . ."

> "Whenever someone asks why I write about 'ordinary things,' I wonder, 'Well, what do you have in YOUR life?'"

Think About the Writer Why does Nye write about "ordinary things"? What makes these things not so ordinary?

Build Background

A central event in "Hum" is the terrorist attacks that took place on September 11, 2001. In those attacks, airplanes were flown into the two towers of the World Trade Center in New York City and into the Pentagon in Washington, D.C., killing nearly three thousand people. The nineteen terrorists who hijacked the airplanes were all young Arabs from Saudi Arabia, Egypt, and Yemen who followed a radical form of Islam. Immediately after the attacks, fear and suspicion resulted in incidents in the United States in which innocent Arabs, non-Arab Muslims, and others were treated unjustly.

Preview the Selection

In "Hum" you will meet **Sami Salsaa**, who moved with his parents to the United States from the Middle East to escape the violence of life in the city of Bethlehem—only to be caught up in the tragedy of September 11.

HUM

by **Naomi Shihab Nye**

Sami Salsaa thought things were improving in his new life, right before they got worse.

His classmates had stopped joking about his first name ending with "i," like a girl's name—Brandi, Lori, Tiffani. And about his last name, which they said sounded like hot sauce.

In a country where basketball stars had fish names—Kobe, Samaki—they could get over it. In a country where people poked silver posts through their tongues and shiny rings into their navels and the man at the auto body shop had a giant swan with a pink heart tattooed on his upper right arm, who cared?

His parents had taken his advice, which was rare.

"Don't call it 'America,'" Sami had said to them, after they unpacked their cracked suitcases on August 6, 2001, and settled into putty-colored Apartment 276 with the tiny black balcony jutting out over a stained parking lot. The sign at the bank across the street flashed 98 degrees. Sami hadn't realized Texas would be so blazing hot.

"Call it 'the United States,'" he said soberly. "'America' means more, means North, South, and Central America, the whole thing. Don't you like it better when people say 'Palestine' instead of 'the Middle East'? We shouldn't sound dumb."

They stared at him.

His mom said, "I only said 'America' because it was shorter."

Both of them started saying "United States" right away. Ⓐ

School in Texas started in the middle of August. Sami got an easy locker combination—10-20-30—and the best mark in his eighth-grade class on the first pre-algebra test of the year. Algebra was one of those subjects that translated easily from country to country; Sami had started working with equations in his cousin Ali's textbook in Bethlehem a year ago, during a curfew period, so the concepts felt familiar.

The teacher singled him out for praise, mentioning his "neatness" and "careful following of directions." Though he had not yet raised his hand once in class, now he

Ⓐ **Read and Discuss** What can you say about Sami and his parents?

thought he might. Sami found himself wishing he were taking full-fledged algebra instead of pre-algebra, which sounded babyish.

There was so much to look at in this country. Girls in tight T-shirts and jeans, for one thing. Magazines with interesting covers fanned out on a neat rack next to soft blue couches in the library's reading corner. Fifty different kinds of bread in neat plastic wrappers lined up at the grocery store.

Two boys, Gavin and Jim, set their trays down next to his at lunch. They told him what a corn dog was. They showed him how to dip it into a small pool of mustard. A girl named Jenny laughed when he tried it.

"Do you have brothers and sisters?" they asked.

"No," Sami said. "I am probably the only Palestinian who doesn't have any brothers or sisters." All his cousins and friends back home had huge families.

His history teacher asked him to stay after class during the third week of school and surprised him by saying, "I just want you to know I think our country's policy in your homeland has been very unfair. And more people than you might think would agree with me. Don't let the slanted press coverage get you down." The teacher clapped his hand on Sami's shoulder warmly and smiled at him.

Sami felt light walking the long sunny blocks between school and his apartment complex.

This might work out after all.

On top of that, his father flew to Los Angeles for the weekend to see his brother, Sami's uncle, and reported that hummus, Sami's favorite simple food from back home, was served on the plane. Incredible! Hummus, in a little plastic tub, with a shrink-wrapped piece of pita bread alongside it!

Next thing they knew, there might be a *falafel* stand in Lubbock. **Ⓑ**

It had been difficult for Sami's family to leave Bethlehem, the only town Sami and his mother had ever lived in, but the situation there had been so horrible recently, everyone was exhausted. Sami's school had been closed every other week and all citizens of Bethlehem put under curfew. His aunt Jenan had been gunned down in the street by Israeli soldiers as she returned from the market. When she died, it was the first time Sami ever felt glad she had no children. Always before, he had wished she had a boy just his age. His parents cried so much they said they used up all their tears.

So when his father, a professor at Bethlehem University, was offered a teaching position in the engineering department at Texas Tech in Lubbock, he accepted it. Sami had felt sad at first that his family wasn't moving to a community with lots of other Arab immigrant families, like Dearborn, Michigan. Lubbock was a remote west Texas city with far fewer immigrants than Dallas or Houston. Someone on the plane told Sami's mother that a Middle Eastern bakery in Austin churned out spinach pies and *zaater* bread by the hour. That made Sami wish they were moving to Austin.

"Use this situation as an opportunity," his father said when Sami worried out loud about being too noticeable in Lubbock. His father always said things like that. "Let people notice you for how outstanding you are, not just how different."

A teacher at school told Sami there was an Arab family living far out on a ranch, raising cows. Their kids were in college already. This surprised Sami. Arabs knew about cows? He thought they only knew about sheep and goats. A famous Syrian eye surgeon had moved to Lubbock with his

---

Ⓑ Read and Discuss | What can you say about Sami's life?

family long ago. Sami's father planned to go meet him soon.

Lubbock had a huge, straight horizon; it would be hard to find a larger horizon in the whole United States. You couldn't see a single hill in any direction. At night the stars glittered dramatically in the giant dark dome of sky. There were smooth streets in all directions with no Israeli tanks or armed soldiers in them, neat buildings and shopping centers, brilliant pink and orange sunsets, shiny pickup trucks with tires, and men in blue jeans wearing baseball caps that said COORS and RED RAIDERS.

"Hey, Sambo!" shouted one of his classmates outside the cafeteria a few weeks after school began. This made Sami feel familiar, jovial. He couldn't understand why the boy got in trouble for saying it. **C**

Sami and his mother stood on the balcony and watched with pleasure as the sky swirled like milk in tea, one night before the dreadful day, when smoke poured from the buildings in New York and Washington and the buildings fell and the people died and no one was able to look at Sami in quite the same friendly way at school.

His parents had bought the television set just a few days before and kept checking out the different channels, so they had it turned on at breakfast when the news broke.

Sami wished he had never seen the images of the jets flying into the buildings.

He wished he had closed his eyes.

Before that morning, a soaring silver airplane had been Sami's favorite mental picture; he'd always dreamed of the plane that would lift him out of a hard and scary life into a happier one, even before their big journey. Planes were magic; you stepped on, then stepped off in a completely different world. Someday he thought he'd go to New Zealand, and other places too. The world was a deep pocket of wonders; he had barely stuck his hand in.

But now Sami's joy in watching and imagining jets in flight was totally ruined.

He did not go to school. His father went to the university to teach a ten o'clock class, but none of his students appeared, so he came home. Everyone was numb. Sami and his parents stared hard at the television all day. He knew his relatives and friends in Bethlehem would be watching too. Sami's eyes kept blurring. Each time the television voices said "Arabs," his heart felt squeezed. A reporter said Palestinians had been "celebrating" the disaster, and Sami knew that was a lie. Palestinians had practically forgotten how to celebrate anything.

He stood at the window staring out, feeling afraid some other terrible thing would drop from the sky and flatten everyone.

When it was eventually evening a tall man he had noticed before, walking slowly with a large blond dog on a leather harness, came around the corner on the level below, and paused.

The man turned and sat down in a green plastic chair next to a door on the ground

---

C Read and Discuss | What have you learned about Sami's family?

floor. Was that his apartment? The dog stretched out beside him.

The man stared into the empty dark-ening sky and the empty blue water of the swimming pool. No one was swimming now. Why wasn't he watching television like everyone else? **Ⓓ**

That night Sami's mother forgot to cook. So Sami toasted bread in their new toaster oven and spread red jelly on top. It looked like blood. He offered bread to his parents, but they didn't want to eat.

He had never seen his parents so shocked before, not when Jenan died, not even when his own friends were beaten and shot by Israeli soldiers, or when his uncle's perfect stone house was bulldozed to the ground without any cause or recourse. *Sad,* Sami had always seen them, forever and ever—sadness was their tribal legacy[1]—but this shocked? Never.

Although they had all been trying to speak only in English, to sharpen their English skills, they reverted to Arabic with-out even noticing it. **Ⓔ**

His parents stayed up almost all night, fixated on the screen, and Sami lay awake, shivering, staring at his ceiling. What made people do what they did?

---

1. **tribal legacy:** habits or patterns that are handed down through a specific culture.

Ⓓ **Literary Focus** **Theme** What is your impression of the man with the dog?

Ⓔ **Read and Discuss** What has happened?

Vocabulary **recourse** (REE kawrs) *n.*: help in a difficult situation.

SOCIAL STUDIES **LINK**

Coming to America

When Sami and his parents come to the United States, they are repeating a journey that has been made by millions of individuals from all parts of the world. From its earliest roots as an English colony, the United States has been a destination for people treated unjustly in their own homelands. The Pilgrims came seeking religious freedom. The first Jews came to America in 1654 from Brazil, where they were persecuted for their reli-gious beliefs. Thousands of Germans arrived in the early 1700s to escape the armies that were attacking their land and burning vil-lages to the ground. Throughout the twenti-eth century, wars and political strife brought waves of newcomers looking for a safe haven to the United States.

Every newcomer has brought his or her language, culture, and ideas. Look around your own community for the influence of different cultures. Names of places, types of restaurants, parades, and celebrations may all reflect different cultures. The more you learn about your own community and region, the more you will uncover evidence of gen-erations of immigrants who have come to the United States looking for a place where dialogue is possible and differences are accepted and appreciated.

Ask Yourself
What aspects of your community reflect the heritage of the people who live in it?

The next day, his father met him outside the school to walk him home. "Did anything bad happen today?" his father asked.

Sami shook his head. Some students had stayed home for a second day. Teachers turned on television sets in the classrooms. Everyone had been so shocked they forgot he was there.

A tight pressure in his chest made it hard to breathe.

Bad things started happening the *next* day, but Sami couldn't tell his parents.

"GO HOME," said a scribbled, unsigned note taped to his locker.

"Your people are murderers," Jake Riley whispered in homeroom.

Murderers? His people? No one had said the hijackers were Palestinian.

His family had always spoken out against the suicide bombings that killed Israeli civilians. Many Palestinians did. But who could hear them? They were regular people, not politicians. No one quoted them in the news.

All day Sami thought of things he might have whispered back.

Not true.

Just a few of them.

Some of yours are too.

A counselor came to take Sami out of class. She had a worried expression. "You realize that you are the only Arab student in this school at a very difficult time. If anyone gives you any trouble . . ."

Sami didn't think he could tell her what had already happened.

It would make him seem weak.

If anyone found out he told, they would hate him even more.

No one sat with him at lunch now. He tried sitting down next to some boys from his PE class and they stopped speaking and stared at him. "I feel very bad about what happened," Sami said, with difficulty, though his words were so true. "Very very bad." His tongue felt thick. But did saying that implicate him in some way? As if all Arabs had done it? Still, what else could he say?

Nobody answered him. They finished eating in silence, exchanging glances with one another, and left the table. **F**

The streets of Lubbock glistened in their solitude for days and days. It seemed no one was going out to shop. Restaurants were empty. Everyone stayed glued to their gloomy televisions.

In English class Sami and his classmates wrote responses to September 11 for more than a week and read them out loud, discussing them at length. The teacher even insisted they do second drafts. She said it would be good therapy.

Sami was the only one who mentioned that other people in the world also suffered from terrorism, all the time. Some of it, he said, was even governmentally sponsored and official. He did not mention his own family's bad experiences. He wrote this so that Americans wouldn't feel as if they were

---

F **Read and Discuss** After the attacks on September 11, how have things changed for Sami at school?

Vocabulary **solitude** (SAHL uh tood) *n.:* state of being alone.

the only victimized people in history. But no one responded as if this had been a good thing to say.

Sometimes it seemed that a huge blanket had been spread over the vast and lumpy distant sorrows of the world—hushing them. Making them invisible. But weren't they still under there? Maybe people could only feel the things that touched *them*, the things at closer range.

One evening before sunset, Sami said to his parents, "I'm going out to take a walk."

"No!" his mother said. "It's almost dark!"

His father touched her hand to quiet her, and said, "Just around the apartments, yes? Don't leave the apartments."

His father looked so tired again, the way he had before they left Bethlehem. Some students had tried to drop his classes, though the deadline for that had passed.

A mysterious person had placed an ugly anonymous letter inside his faculty mailbox, but his father wouldn't tell Sami exactly what it said.

"Did you throw it away?"

"I burned it," his father said sadly. "In the outdoor ashtray."

Everyone had forgotten how to smile. **G**

Sami's mother was working as an aide at a nursery school. She felt the eyes of the parents on her like hot buttons when they read her name tag, HANAN, even if they didn't know where she was from.

Sami stepped outside. He walked down the metal stairs toward the vacant swimming pool. Trash cans were spilling over next to the barbecue grills.

Analyzing Visuals Viewing and Interpreting
How does this image help you connect with the story?

A little toddler stood on a couch inside a neighboring apartment, staring out. Sami fluttered his fingers at her. She ducked and covered her face. The baby was lucky. She could not understand the news.

Cars slept in their assigned spaces under the carport roof. It seemed strange, but Sami felt jealous of them. It might be easier to be a car.

Another evening he asked his mother if he could make soup. She was surprised at his sudden interest in cooking. He rinsed lentils in a colander, as he had seen her do

G **Literary Focus** Topic and Theme How is Sami's life at home different now?

many times. He chopped an onion and fried garlic in a skillet.

As the soup was simmering, his mother remembered she had forgotten to pick up the mail downstairs when she came in from work. She asked if he would go get it and handed him the little key.

The mailbox was stuffed with bills and ads.

How could so many people have their address when they'd only been here two months?

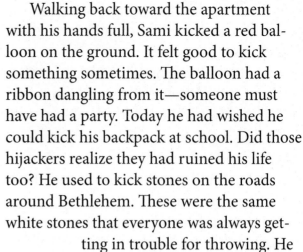

Walking back toward the apartment with his hands full, Sami kicked a red balloon on the ground. It felt good to kick something sometimes. The balloon had a ribbon dangling from it—someone must have had a party. Today he had wished he could kick his backpack at school. Did those hijackers realize they had ruined his life too? He used to kick stones on the roads around Bethlehem. These were the same white stones that everyone was always getting in trouble for throwing. He only kicked them.

Once he had kicked a tin can all the way to Manger Square and his father passed him walking home from the bakery with a fresh load of steaming pita bread wrapped inside a towel. He spoke sharply to Sami for wasting his time.

"Find something useful to do," his father had said.

Today, so far away, after so much had happened, Sami thought of those long-ago words as the balloon snagged on a bush and popped. He spotted a thick unopened envelope on the ground. Had it fallen from someone's trash?

He stooped to pick it up, awkwardly, since his hands were full.

The envelope was addressed to Hugh Mason, Apartment 109.

Looking around, Sami realized that was the apartment where the tall man with the blond dog lived.

Sami pressed the buzzer. The man opened the door, dog at his side. He was staring straight ahead. Sami had finally understood, after watching him pass through the courtyard more than once, that he couldn't see. "Yes?"

The dog seemed to take a step forward to stand between his master and Sami.

"Mr. Hug Mason?" Sami pronounced it "hug"—he had never seen this English name before and did not know how to say it.

The tall man laughed. "Yes?"

"I have a letter for you with your name on it. I found it on the ground by the mailboxes. Maybe you dropped it?" He also wanted to ask, "How do you read it?" but was embarrassed to.

Mr. Mason put out his hand. "Thank you. I have dropped many things in my life. Very kind of you. You have an interesting accent. Where are you from?"

Sami hesitated. Could he lie?

Could he say Norway?

He knew his accent was not like a Mexican-American accent.

"I am," he said, in as American a voice as he could muster, "from Bethlehem."

Mr. Mason paused. "So you're Palestinian?"

"I am."

The dog seemed to have relaxed. He sniffed Sami's hand. His pale coat was lush and rumpled.

Mr. Mason's voice was gentle. "That must be harder than usual these days."

Sami felt startled when tears rose up in his own eyes. At least the man couldn't see them.

Sami whispered, "It is. Does your dog have a name?"

Half an hour later, Hugh and Sami were sitting on the green plastic chairs outside together, still talking. Tum Tum lay calmly beside them. They had discussed Lubbock, school, the troubles of Bethlehem, and the recent disaster. It was amazing how fast they had each talked, and how easily they had moved from subject to subject. They had not mentioned Hugh Mason's blindness, though Sami felt curious about it. **Ⓗ**

But they *had* discussed Tum Tum's job. Hugh had flown to California to be trained, alongside Tum Tum, four years ago. Training lasted twenty-eight days and was very "intense." Sami liked that word. He had never used it. This was Hugh's second dog. He'd had his first one for twelve years after his wife was killed. Killed? Crossing a street. "Hit-and-run."[2] Sami didn't know the phrase. Hugh had to explain it.

Tum Tum had been trained for "intelligent disobedience." If, for example, he saw Hugh getting ready to do something dangerous, like fall off a cliff (were there any cliffs in Lubbock?) or into the swimming pool, he would stand up on his hind legs, put his huge paws on Hugh's shoulders, and knock him over backward.

---

2. **hit-and-run:** accident in which a car hits a person or animal and then immediately flees the scene.

Ⓗ Literary Focus **Theme** Do you think Sami and Hugh will be friends? Why or why not?

Later, thinking about it, Sami wished all people had dogs to guide their behavior if they were about to get into trouble.

When Tum Tum needed to go outside the apartment to pee behind a bush, he would hum.

Hum? What was "hum"? Hugh demonstrated, making a low smooth sound in his throat. Not all guide dogs did this—it was something particular to this one.

Tum Tum's ears perked up straight when he heard Hugh humming. Hugh said that if Tum Tum was just sitting on the grass right next to him, the dog would sometimes hum or make little talking sounds to let Hugh know what he was doing. Now he hummed in response to Hugh's hum. Tum Tum was a very communicative dog.

Hugh said that when a guide dog died, the loss for a blind person was nearly as hard as the loss of a human being, you were so used to each other by then. But had he always been blind? Why was this such a hard question to ask? ❶

Sami heard his mother's worried call. The soup! He had forgotten it completely. He jumped up.

His mother walked anxiously toward them with her hands raised. What had happened to him?

Sami answered in Arabic.

This was a good man, he'd found a letter . . . but his mother only said in Arabic,

> This was a good man, he'd found a letter . . . but his mother only said in Arabic, "Come home."

"Come home."

Sami said to Hugh, "Excuse me, we will visit another day?"

Hugh stood up and shook his hand as if Sami were a school principal.

"Anytime! I enjoyed the visit very much." He held out his hand in the general direction of Sami's mother and said, "Good evening, pleased to meet you, I am Hugh Mason, you have a very nice son."

The lentils were too soft. Sami measured cumin and salt into the pot. He squeezed lemons. His mother was anxiously waiting for his father to come home. She was fretting and dusting things. At dinner Sami's mother told his father, he *had been with a man,* as if it were a big mistake to talk to a neighbor!

Sami couldn't believe it.

"Did you go in his house?"

Sami knew better than to go in his house.

"No."

"What did he want from you?"

"Nothing! To talk! He can't even see!" For the second time that afternoon, tears rose into Sami's eyes. "He offered me a job."

"A JOB?"

A fork fell off the table.

"To read to him. He is very smart. He works at a hospital answering telephones. The phone board has a Braille[3] panel so he

---

3. **Braille** (brayl): writing and reading system for the blind that uses raised bumps which are felt by the fingers.

---

❶ **Read and Discuss** What is going on with Sami now?

Vocabulary **communicative** (kuh MYOO nih kay tihv) *adj.:* able to give information.

can connect the calls. Someone drives him there. The dog goes too. Tum Tum. But he needs some reading help at home."

His father said, "You need to focus on your studies."

Sami said, "But he would pay me! I need some money too! Also, I learned new words. He has an excellent vocabulary, like a professor. I would read the newspaper, his mail, some magazines, and maybe even books. PLEASE?"

His father closed his eyes and shook his head. "Some days I wish we had never come here." **J**

Sami started reading to Hugh on Tuesday and Thursday evenings. He read for two hours. Sometimes his throat felt hoarse afterward. He and Hugh sat outside when the weather was warm. When the "northers" came—Hugh told Sami that was the word everyone used for the cold winds from the north—they sat inside, Sami on the flowered couch and Hugh in a wooden chair at the table. Tum Tum sprawled happily between them and seemed to listen.

Sami would read the newspaper headlines and ask Hugh if he wanted to hear the stories. Whenever it was a sad story about Palestine and Israel, Hugh would say, "No. Don't read it. Tell me a story about Bethlehem instead."

So Sami would put the paper down and find himself describing little details he had never mentioned to anyone before. The way the stones were stacked to make a wall outside his old school. Crookedly, if you looked at it from the side. But the wall felt smooth along the top.

The olive-wood carvers who shaped elegant nativity sets[4] and doves of peace from hunks of wood and served mint tea to traveling nuns, hoping they would buy presents to take home.

The teacher whose jacket was so old and raggedy he had long threads trailing down his back. Everyone whispered that he lived alone, had no one to take care of him. This was rare in Bethlehem. Few people lived alone. (Sami felt bad after telling this, since Hugh lived alone. No, not alone. He had Tum Tum.)

Sami told about the ancient wrinkled grandma-lady who made small date pies and kept them warm in her oven. She gave them to any student who stopped to visit her, even for two minutes, on the way home from school.

Hugh said he could visualize all these things with his "inner eyes."

"Does everyone have inner eyes?" Sami asked. "Even people who can see?"

"Of course," said Hugh. "You know whenever you remember something? You use them then. But some people don't use them enough. They forget about them. But they're all I have. In some ways, I think I can see better than people who aren't blind." **K**

The teachers at school had urged Sami to join the Debate Club, but he didn't want to debate anyone. Debate involved winning and losing. Sami felt more attracted to "dia-

---

4. **nativity sets:** small figures representing the birth of Christ.

J **Read and Discuss** What is all this telling you?

K **Reading Focus** Finding the Theme What words and ideas might be important here?

logue," a word he had heard Hugh use frequently, because dialogue was like a bridge. The teachers said, "In that case, you'll have to start your own club."

"Okay," he said. Why did he say that? he thought later. He didn't know how to start a club!

His history teacher printed up a set of "Guidelines for Dialogue Groups" off the Internet. It said things like: (1) Never interrupt; (2) Try to speak in specifics and stories, instead of generalities; (3) Respect varying opinions. Everyone does not have to agree, but everyone needs to respect everyone else. **Ⓛ**

A Korean girl named Janet approached Sami in the gym and said she had heard about the club from the art teacher and wanted to join it. "The art teacher is my good friend," Janet said. "Let's go to her room tomorrow after school and make some posters on those big tables."

Sami was glad Janet was so artistic since he was *not*. She designed the posters and he colored in the letters and graphics with fat felt-tip markers. Janet chattered freely as they worked. Adopted at birth, she had been brought to west Texas by her parents. Everyone was always asking her if she was Chinese.

The new club met on a Wednesday after school in the English classroom. Three students from Mexico City appeared at the meeting, looking quizzical. They said their English teacher had told them to come, to work on their language skills. They were happy to talk about anything. A tall Anglo American who had lived in Saudi Arabia with his oil engineer dad, an African-American girl named

Hypernia, a very large girl in overalls, and a boy with a prosthetic leg appeared. Sami would never have known about the leg until the boy sat down and his pants revealed a bit of hardware at his ankle. There was also a Jewish boy who went by his initials, L. B.

For the first meeting, people just introduced themselves and told a bit about their lives. The boy who had lived in Saudi Arabia said he felt personally grieved by September 11, since the Arabs he had known were always so "nice." Hypernia said she had felt very lonely since her parents moved to Lubbock from Dallas, where she'd attended a school that was 80 percent African-American. "I feel like an alien or something. Like everyone is staring at me. I never felt this way before."

L. B. said he was really tired of explaining about the Jewish holidays. Sami asked if he had ever been to Israel and he said no, but his grandmother had. He stared at Sami hard and said, "I really wish people could get along over there. I mean, it's terrible, isn't it?"

Sami said, "*Really* terrible." He liked the boy just for saying that.

The club ended up talking about the Pakistani auto mechanic on the east side of town whose shop windows had been broken after September 11. It had been in the newspaper. They decided to go visit him, take him a card.

Janet suggested "On Not Fitting In" as a topic for their next meeting. She had brought a poem by James Wright, an American poet, to read. It said, "Whatever it was I lost, whatever I wept for / Was a wild,

---

Ⓛ **Reading Focus** **Finding the Theme** What words seem especially important in the "Guidelines for Dialogue Groups"?

Vocabulary **quizzical** (KWIHZ ih kuhl) *adj.*: puzzled; baffled.

gentle thing, the small dark eyes / Loving me in secret. / It is here."

Sami found it mysterious, but it made him think of Tum Tum.

He mentioned to the group that he worked for a man who could not see in usual ways, but who might be a nice guest speaker for their group someday. He had interesting ideas, Sami said, and he liked to listen. "I'm visually impaired too," said the large girl in overalls. "Bring him. I'd like to meet him." Sami looked at her, surprised. He had seen her tilt her head to other people as they spoke, but had no indication she was blind. Suddenly he noticed the white cane on the floor at her side. She said softly, as if in answer to a question he didn't ask, "I only see shades of light and dark. But I can't see any of your faces."

Weeks went by. The Dialogue Club was featured on the morning announcements at school. Gavin, who had once, so long ago, eaten lunch in the cafeteria with Sami, came to the club to write a story for the school paper, and he didn't get a single fact or quote wrong, which amazed the club members. They said the school paper was famous for getting everything wrong. **Ⓜ**

Sami's parents invited Hugh to dinner. They had stopped worrying about Sami's job when they discovered how nice and smart Hugh was. Sami's father seemed to feel a little embarrassed about having acted so negative in the beginning. So he took care to ask Hugh many questions, including the one Sami was most curious about himself.

Ⓜ [Read and Discuss] Why are the members of the Dialogue Club friends?

Analyzing Visuals

Viewing and Interpreting
Is this how you picture the Dialogue Club? Explain your answer.

Hugh had lost his sight at the age of four to hereditary glaucoma,[5] a disease that could have been partially averted if he'd had surgery earlier. His mother always blamed herself afterward for not realizing what was happening to her son. No one she had known in her family or his father's family had this condition. But she had known that Hugh, as a tiny boy, had vision troubles, and had gotten him thick glasses and fussed at him for stumbling instead of taking him to medical experts when something could still have been done. This great sorrow in the family eventually led to a divorce between Hugh's parents.

"So you went to college—when you were already blind?" Sami's father asked gently.

"Yes, I did. And there I met the woman who eventually married me, my wife, Portia. She was African-American, and her parents never forgave her for marrying someone white *and* blind—it was too much for them. But we had nine wonderful years together. You would have liked her, Sami."

Sami's eyes were wide open. How many kinds of difficulties there were in the world that he had not even imagined yet!

His parents played soft Arabic flute music on their little tape player in the background for the first time in months, and served grape leaves, cucumber salad with mint and yogurt,

> Sami's father laughed out loud for the first time since September 11.

and *ketayef*—a crescent-shaped, nut-stuffed pastry with honey sauce. Hugh ate a lot, and said it was the best meal he had tasted in *years*. Sami had seen the cans of simple soup lined on his kitchen counter, the hunks of cheese in the refrigerator, the apples in a bowl. He watched Hugh eat with gusto now and noticed how his fork carefully found the food, then his mouth, without any mishap or awkwardness.

Tum Tum kept sniffing the air as if he liked the rich spices.

Once he hummed loudly and Sami's father laughed out loud, for the first time since September 11. "What is that? Is he singing?"

Sami rose proudly to open the door to the courtyard. "It's his language," Sami said. "He needs to be excused for a moment."

He knew Tum Tum would walk to his favorite bush and return immediately, scratching on the door to be let back in. And he would not get the apartment doors confused, though they all looked alike— Tum Tum always knew exactly where Hugh was, instinctively. Sami's dad shook his head. "In this country, even dogs are smart."

Hugh said, "Friends, my stomach is full, my heart is full. Sami, come over here so I can pat your black hair! I'm so happy we're neighbors!"

Now Sami laughed.

"Hugh," he said, "my hair is red." **N**

---

5. **glaucoma** (glaw KOH muh): disorder of the eye that can lead to loss of vision.

N Read and Discuss What did you learn about Hugh?

Hum

Respond and Think Critically

Reading Focus

Quick Check

1. Why did Sami's family move to Texas?
2. What job does Hugh offer Sami?

Read with a Purpose

3. What is the most important thing that happens to Sami after he moves? Explain.

Reading Skills: Finding the Theme

4. One way to find the theme is to think about what characters learn in the course of a story. What they discover is often what the writer wants you to discover as well. Add another row to your chart of notes on "Hum," and identify lessons that are learned by Sami, his parents, and Hugh.

"HUM"	Notes for Finding the Theme
Comments by characters	
Title	
Important words/ideas	Friendship, respect
Lessons characters learn	

Literary Focus

Literary Analysis

5. **Infer** What does the title "Hum" mean?
6. **Infer** Discuss the purpose Hugh's character serves.

7. **Interpret** What do you learn about Sami from details of his life in Bethlehem? Why are these details <u>relevant</u> to the story?
8. **Analyze** A **stereotype** is a generalization about a group made without regard to individual differences. What is it about human nature that allows stereotypical thinking?

Literary Skills: Topic and Theme

9. **Interpret** One topic of this story is friendship. What does the story say about it?
10. **Interpret** What **theme,** or revelation about life, does "Hum" <u>reveal</u> to you?

Literary Skills Review: Setting

11. How does the setting—the time and place—influence the story? How might Sami's experiences have been different if he had lived closer to more Arab families?

Writing Focus

Think as a Reader/Writer

Use It in Your Writing Review the list of Sami's conflicts that you made as you read the story. Does Sami resolve all of the conflicts he faces? In a paragraph, explain Sami's conflicts and their resolutions.

 What Do You Think Now

How do people overcome obstacles that stand in the way of friendship?

Applying Your Skills

Hum

Vocabulary Development

Vocabulary Check

Answer the following questions:
1. Where can you find **recourse** if you are being ignored in school?
2. What are the drawbacks of **solitude**?
3. How might a dialogue club make people more **communicative**?
4. Describe an incident that caused you to wear a **quizzical** expression.

Analogies

An **analogy** is a comparison made between two things to show how they are alike. An analogy can explain one idea by showing how it is similar to a more easily understood idea. Here are some examples of analogies:

- *Learning to ride a bike is like sitting on the edge of a cliff. You keep thinking you're going to fall.*
- *Passing my math test was like jumping into a swimming pool on a hot day. What a relief!*
- *A dog running loose in a pet-food store is like a kid running loose in a candy shop.*

Notice that analogies include the word *like*. The first part names the subject. The second part makes the comparison. You may need to add a sentence to explain the similarity. When you write analogies, first think of something familiar to compare to the subject. Then make a list of ways the two are similar. Choose the clearest idea for making the comparison.

Your Turn

Try writing your own analogy. Before you write, make a list of ways your two subjects are similar. Then, compare your subjects point by point. Remember that an analogy uses several points of comparison, not just one.

Here are some ideas for subjects:
doing homework
playing soccer
exercising
making friends

Language Coach

Change Adjectives to Adverbs Change each word below from an adjective to an adverb by adding *–ly* to the end of each. Then, use each adverb in a sentence about "Hum."
1. blazing
2. eventual
3. practical
4. anxious
5. instinctive

Academic Vocabulary

Talk About . . .
Re-read the biography of Naomi Shihab Nye on the Meet the Writer page. With a group, discuss what the story "Hum" reveals about Nye's attitudes toward people's differences. Incorporate relevant details about her childhood in your discussion.

Grammar Link
Subject and Predicate

Sentences consist of two basic parts: subjects and predicates. The **subject** tells *who* or *what* the sentence is about. To find the subject, ask yourself *who* or *what* is doing something or *whom* or *what* is being talked about. The subject may come at the beginning, middle, or end of a sentence.

> **Hugh** spoke to Sami. [*Who* spoke to Sami? *Hugh* did.]
>
> How sad **Sami** looked! [*Who* looked sad? *Sami* did.]
>
> Sitting by the pool was **Hugh.** [*Who* was sitting? *Hugh* was.]

The **predicate** of a sentence tells something about the subject. Like the subject, the predicate may be found anywhere in a sentence.

> Out by the pool **were** Sami and Hugh.
> In school Sami **sat** alone.
> The Dialogue Club **wanted** to meet on Friday.

Your Turn

Underline the subject of each sentence once and the predicate of each sentence twice.

1. Sami moved to Lubbock.
2. Before the attack, Sami's family felt welcome.
3. In the middle of the cafeteria Sami was sitting alone.
4. When did Sami form the club?

CHOICES

As you respond to the Choices, use these **Academic Vocabulary** words as appropriate: fundamental, implicit, relevant, reveal.

REVIEW
Evaluate Theme

One theme in "Hum" is that people should appreciate each other's differences. With a small group, organize a panel discussion on this theme. Consider these questions: *What is Nye saying about our differences? What are the dangers of not appreciating people's differences? How can appreciating differences help people come to understand one another?*

CONNECT
Start a Dialogue Club

Timed └Writing The Dialogue Club is likely to have a positive effect on the people who join it. Write a persuasive paragraph that makes a case for forming a dialogue club in your school. Include ways the club can improve morale within the student body and address important issues throughout the school.

EXTEND
Create a Blog

TechFocus Working with three classmates, start a classroom blog about an issue related to the selection. For example, you might discuss how students feel about the way Arab Americans were treated after the September 11 attacks, whether a dialogue club is a good forum for communication, or the difficulties of living in an unfamiliar place. Invite classmates and students in other classes to comment.

Antaeus by **Borden Deal**

Roofs of Washington Square (1926) by Edward Hopper.

What Do You Think

How do you rely on your friends to help you meet challenges in your life?

QuickWrite Think about a time when a friend helped you complete a difficult task. What effect did the experience have on your friendship? How did your relationship change after the task was completed?

Reader/Writer Notebook

Use your **RWN** to complete the activities for this selection.

Literary Focus

Theme Authors rarely tell you what the **theme,** the truth about life, of a story is. Instead, they <u>reveal</u> it through a story's details. So it's up to you to identify the theme by studying the most important details. Luckily, there are good places to look for clues. First, pay careful attention to what characters learn or how they change. Their discoveries or changes are often related to the theme. Second, look for key passages in which the author makes broad statements about life. These can help lead you to the theme.

Reading Focus

Cause and Effect A **cause** is the event that makes something happen. An **effect** is what happens as a result of the cause. Storytellers use cause-and-effect organization to develop their plots. In "Antaeus" a country boy's move to the city sets off a chain of events. To see the cause-and-effect organization of this story,

- look for what happens first. Then, ask what happens because of that.
- look for hidden or multiple causes and results.

Into Action As you read, fill out a graphic organizer like this one.

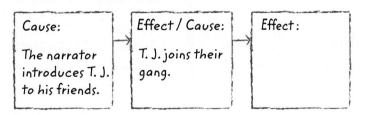

Cause:
The narrator introduces T. J. to his friends.

Effect / Cause:
T. J. joins their gang.

Effect:

Writing Focus

Think as a Reader/Writer

Find It in Your Reading In "Antaeus," Borden Deal uses several techniques to make his characters' dialogue seem realistic, including slang, one-word responses, short phrases, and the asking of questions. As you read the story, record in your *Reader/Writer Notebook* examples of dialogue that strikes you as realistic.

Vocabulary

contemplate (KAHN tuhm playt) *v.:* consider; look at or think about carefully. *They could contemplate the result of their labor with satisfaction.*

flourishing (FLUR ihsh ihng) *adj.:* thriving. *The boys looked at the flourishing grass on the roof.*

sterile (STEHR uhl) *adj.:* barren; lacking in interest or vitality. *They were surprised to see grass growing on the sterile roof of the building.*

destruction (dih STRUHK shuhn) *n.:* act of ruining. *The destruction of all their work left the boys sad.*

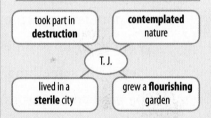

took part in **destruction**

contemplated nature

T. J.

lived in a **sterile** city

grew a **flourishing** garden

Language Coach

Related Words A **suffix** is a word part that, when added to a base word, changes the word's meaning or part of speech. Which of the words in the list above contain suffixes? If you are not sure, check in a dictionary.

 Learn It Online
Hear a professional actor read this story. Visit the selection online at:

go.hrw.com   L7-373   **Go**

Borden Deal
(1922–1985)

Keeping the Faith
Like his hero T. J., **Borden Deal** came from a family of southern cotton farmers. They knew firsthand the hardships of farm life during the Great Depression. After finishing high school, Deal left Mississippi and traveled around the country. He sometimes worked in the circus and on a showboat. Finally, he settled into a career as a full-time writer. As the following anecdote proves, Deal was just as persistent as T. J. in pursuing his dreams:

"My short story 'Antaeus' has a strange history. Though it has been reprinted far more often than any other of my nearly one hundred short stories, it took me ten years to get it published the first time! True. It was turned down by every quality popular magazine in the country, not once but two or three times. . . . So you see, when you believe in something, it pays to keep the faith and be persistent—just as, in the story, T. J. is persistent in his faith and feeling for the earth."

Think About the Writer Why do you think Deal refused to give up on this short story?

Build Background
During World War II the United States geared up to produce equipment, weapons, and goods to serve the military effort overseas. Since most factories were in the North, many families left their homes in the South seeking work. This is the situation the narrator is referring to as the story opens.

The title of this story refers to a character from Greek mythology. Antaeus (an TEE us) is a giant whose strength comes from his mother, the Earth. As long as his feet are on the ground, Antaeus cannot be beaten. As you read the story, think about the connection between Antaeus and T. J.

Antaeus Setting Down Virgil and Dante in the Last Circle of Hell (c. 1910) by Robert Trail Rose. Color lithograph.

Preview the Selection
T. J., a boy from the South, moves to a northern city, where he convinces a group of boys to create a garden.

RINGLING BROS AND BARNUM & BAILEY
COMBINED SHOWS
THE GREATEST SHOW ON EARTH

US A COMPLETE BIG TRAINED ANIMAL SHOW GRATUITOUSLY

Antaeus

by **Borden Deal**

This was during the wartime, when lots of people were coming North for jobs in factories and war industries, when people moved around a lot more than they do now, and sometimes kids were thrown into new groups and new lives that were completely different from anything they had ever known before. I remember this one kid, T. J. his name was, from somewhere down South, whose family moved into our building during that time. They'd come North with everything they owned piled into the back seat of an old-model sedan that you wouldn't expect could make the trip, with T. J. and his three younger sisters riding shakily on top of the load of junk.

Our building was just like all the others there, with families crowded into a few rooms, and I guess there were twenty-five or thirty kids about my age in that one building. Of course, there were a few of us who formed a gang and ran together all the time after school, and I was the one who brought T. J. in and started the whole thing. **Ⓐ**

The building right next door to us was a factory where they made walking dolls.

It was a low building with a flat, tarred roof that had a parapet[1] all around it about head-high, and we'd found out a long time before that no one, not even the watchman, paid any attention to the roof because it was higher than any of the other buildings around. So my gang used the roof as a headquarters. We could get up there by crossing over to the fire escape from our own roof on a plank and then going on up. It was a secret place for us, where nobody else could go without our permission.

I remember the day I first took T. J. up there to meet the gang. He was a stocky, robust kid with a shock of white hair, nothing sissy about him except his voice; he talked in this slow, gentle voice like you never heard before. He talked different from any of us and you noticed it right away. But I liked him anyway, so I told him to come on up.

We climbed up over the parapet and dropped down on the roof. The rest of the gang were already there.

"Hi," I said. I jerked my thumb at T. J.

---

1. **parapet** (PAR uh peht): wall or railing.

Ⓐ **Reading Focus** What picture is the author painting for you?

"He just moved into the building yesterday."

He just stood there, not scared or anything, just looking, like the first time you see somebody you're not sure you're going to like.

"Hi," Blackie said. "Where are you from?"

"Marion County," T. J. said.

We laughed. "Marion County?" I said. "Where's that?"

He looked at me for a moment like I was a stranger, too. "It's in Alabama," he said, like I ought to know where it was.

"What's your name?" Charley said.

"T. J.," he said, looking back at him. He had pale blue eyes that looked washed-out, but he looked directly at Charley, waiting for his reaction. He'll be all right, I thought. No sissy in him, except that voice. Who ever talked like that?

"T. J.," Blackie said. "That's just initials. What's your real name? Nobody in the world has just initials."

"I do," he said. "And they're T. J. That's all the name I got."

His voice was resolute with the knowledge of his rightness, and for a moment no one had anything to say. T. J. looked around at the rooftop and down at the black tar under his feet. "Down yonder where I come from," he said, "we played out in the woods. Don't you-all have no woods around here?"

"Naw," Blackie said. "There's the park a few blocks over, but it's full of kids and cops and old women. You can't do a thing."

T. J. kept looking at the tar under his feet. "You mean you ain't got no fields to raise nothing in?—no watermelons or nothing?"

"Naw," I said scornfully. "What do you want to grow something for? The folks can buy everything they need at the store."

He looked at me again with that strange, unknowing look. "In Marion County," he said, "I had my own acre of cotton and my own acre of corn. It was mine to plant and make ever' year."

He sounded like it was something to be proud of, and in some obscure way it made the rest of us angry. Blackie said, "Who'd want to have their own acre of cotton and corn? That's just work. What can you do with an acre of cotton and corn?" **ⓑ**

T. J. looked at him. "Well, you get part of the bale offen your acre," he said seriously. "And I fed my acre of corn to my calf."

We didn't really know what he was talking about, so we were more puzzled than angry; otherwise, I guess, we'd have chased him off the roof and wouldn't let him be part of our gang. But he was strange and different, and we were all attracted by his stolid sense of rightness and belonging, maybe by the strange softness of his voice contrasting our own tones of speech into harshness.

He moved his foot against the black tar. "We could make our own field right here," he said softly, thoughtfully. "Come spring we could raise us what we want to—watermelons and garden truck and no telling what all."

"You'd have to be a good farmer to make these tar roofs grow any watermelons," I said. We all laughed.

But T. J. looked serious. "We could haul us some dirt up here," he said. "And spread it

---

ⓑ [Read and Discuss] What does this conversation reveal about the narrator and T. J.?

out even and water it, and before you know it, we'd have us a crop in here." He looked at us intently. "Wouldn't that be fun?"

"They wouldn't let us," Blackie said quickly.

"I thought you said this was you-all's roof," T. J. said to me. "That you-all could do anything you wanted to up here."

"They've never bothered us," I said. I felt the idea beginning to catch fire in me. It was a big idea, and it took a while for it to sink in; but the more I thought about it, the better I liked it. "Say," I said to the gang. "He might have something there. Just make us a regular roof garden, with flowers and grass and trees and everything. And all ours, too," I said. "We wouldn't let anybody up here except the ones we wanted to."

"It'd take a while to grow trees," T. J. said quickly, but we weren't paying any attention to him. They were all talking about it suddenly, all excited with the idea after I'd put it in a way they would catch hold of it. Only rich people had roof gardens, we knew, and the idea of our own private domain excited them. **C**

"We could bring it up in sacks and boxes," Blackie said. "We'd have to do it while the folks weren't paying any attention to us, for we'd have to come up to the roof of our building and then cross over with it."

"Where could we get the dirt?" somebody said worriedly.

"Out of those vacant lots over close to school," Blackie said. "Nobody'd notice if we scraped it up."

I slapped T. J. on the shoulder. "Man, you had a wonderful idea," I said, and everybody grinned at him, remembering

---

C **Reading Focus** Cause and Effect What effect does T. J.'s idea have on the rest of the boys?

that he had started it. "Our own private roof garden."

He grinned back. "It'll be ourn," he said. "All ourn." Then he looked thoughtful again. "Maybe I can lay my hands on some cotton seed, too. You think we could raise us some cotton?" **Ⓓ**

We'd started big projects before at one time or another, like any gang of kids, but they'd always petered out[2] for lack of organization and direction. But this one didn't; somehow or other T. J. kept it going all through the winter months. He kept talking about the watermelons and the cotton we'd raise, come spring, and when even that wouldn't work, he'd switch around to my idea of flowers and grass and trees, though he was always honest enough to add that it'd take a while to get any trees started. He always had it on his mind, and he'd mention it in school, getting them lined up to carry dirt that afternoon, saying in a casual way that he reckoned a few more weeks ought to see the job through.

Our little area of private earth grew slowly. T. J. was smart enough to start in one corner of the building, heaping up the carried earth two or three feet thick so that we had an immediate result to look at, to contemplate with awe. Some of the

evenings T. J. alone was carrying earth up to the building, the rest of the gang distracted by other enterprises or interests, but T. J. kept plugging along on his own, and eventually we'd all come back to him again, and then our own little acre would grow more rapidly.

He was careful about the kind of dirt he'd let us carry up there, and more than once he dumped a sandy load over the parapet into the areaway below because it wasn't good enough. He found out the kinds of earth in all the vacant lots for blocks around. He'd pick it up and feel it and smell it, frozen though it was sometimes, and then he'd say it was good growing soil or it wasn't worth anything, and we'd have to go on somewhere else.

Thinking about it now, I don't see how he kept us at it. It was hard work, lugging paper sacks and boxes of dirt all the way up the stairs of our own building, keeping out of the way of the grown-ups so they wouldn't catch on to what we were doing. They probably wouldn't have cared, for they didn't pay much attention to us, but we wanted to keep it secret anyway. Then we had to go through the trapdoor to our roof, teeter over a plank to the fire escape, then climb two or three stories to the parapet, and drop them down onto the roof.

> Somehow or other T. J. kept it going.

---

2. **petered out:** gradually disappeared.

Ⓓ **Read and Discuss** What is happening? Why does T. J.'s idea excite the boys so much?

Vocabulary **contemplate** (KAHN tuhm playt) v.: consider; look at or think about carefully.

All that for a small pile of earth that sometimes didn't seem worth the effort. But T. J. kept the vision bright within us, his words shrewd and calculated toward the fulfillment of his dream; and he worked harder than any of us. He seemed driven toward a goal that we couldn't see, a particular point in time that would be definitely marked by signs and wonders that only he could see. **Ⓔ**

The laborious earth just lay there during the cold months, inert and lifeless, the clods lumpy and cold under our feet when we walked over it. But one day it rained, and afterward there was a softness in the air, and the earth was live and giving again with moisture and warmth.

That evening T. J. smelled the air, his nostrils dilating with the odor of the earth under his feet. "It's spring," he said, and there was a gladness rising in his voice that filled us all with the same feeling. "It's mighty late for it, but it's spring. I'd just about decided it wasn't never gonna get here at all."

We were all sniffing at the air, too, trying to smell it the way that T. J. did, and I can still remember the sweet odor of the earth under our feet. It was the first time in my life that spring and spring earth had meant anything to me. I looked at T. J. then, knowing in a faint way the hunger within him through the toilsome[3] winter months, knowing the dream that lay behind his plan. He was a new Antaeus, preparing his own bed of strength. **Ⓕ**

---

3. **toilsome** (TOYL suhm): involving hard work; laborious.

"Planting time," he said. "We'll have to find us some seed."

"What do we do?" Blackie said. "How do we do it?"

"First we'll have to break up the clods," T. J. said. "That won't be hard to do. Then we plant the seeds, and after a while they come up. Then you got you a crop." He frowned. "But you ain't got it raised yet. You got to tend it and hoe it and take care of it, and all the time it's growing and growing, while you're awake and while you're asleep. Then you lay it by when it's growed and let it ripen, and then you got you a crop."

"There's those wholesale seed houses over on Sixth," I said. "We could probably swipe some grass seed over there."

T. J. looked at the earth. "You-all seem mighty set on raising some grass," he said. "I ain't never put no effort into that. I spent all my life trying not to raise grass."

"But it's pretty," Blackie said. "We could play on it and take sunbaths on it. Like having our own lawn. Lots of people got lawns."

"Well," T. J. said. He looked at the rest of us, hesitant for the first time. He kept on looking at us for a moment. "I did have it in mind to raise some corn and vegetables. But we'll plant grass."

He was smart. He knew where to give in. And I don't suppose it made any difference to him, really. He just wanted to grow something, even if it was grass.

"Of course," he said, "I do think we ought to plant a row of watermelons. They'd

---

Ⓔ **Read and Discuss** How do T. J.'s actions add to what you know about him?

Ⓕ **Literary Focus** Theme Antaeus was a mythological giant who drew his strength from the Earth. What connection is the narrator making when he says T. J. is "preparing his own bed of strength"?

be mighty nice to eat while we was a-laying on that grass."

We all laughed. "All right," I said. "We'll plant us a row of watermelons." **Ⓖ**

Things went very quickly then. Perhaps half the roof was covered with the earth, the half that wasn't broken by ventilators,[4] and we swiped pocketfuls of grass seed from the open bins in the wholesale seed house, mingling among the buyers on Saturdays and during the school lunch hour. T. J. showed us how to prepare the earth, breaking up the clods and smoothing it and sowing the grass seed. It looked rich and black now with moisture, receiving of the seed, and it seemed that the grass sprang up overnight, pale green in the early spring.

We couldn't keep from looking at it, unable to believe that we had created this delicate growth. We looked at T. J. with understanding now, knowing the fulfillment of the plan he had carried along within his mind. We had worked without full understanding of the task, but he had known all the time.

We found that we couldn't walk or play on the delicate blades as we had expected to, but we didn't mind. It was enough just to look at it, to realize that it was the work of our own hands, and each evening, the whole gang was there, trying to measure the growth that had been achieved that day.

One time a foot was placed on the plot of ground, one time only, Blackie stepping onto it with sudden bravado. Then he looked at the crushed blades and there was shame in his face. He did not do it again. This was his grass, too, and not to be desecrated.[5] No one said anything, for it was not necessary.

T. J. had reserved a small section for watermelons, and he was still trying to find some seed for it. The wholesale house didn't have any watermelon seeds, and we didn't know where we could lay our hands on them. T. J. shaped the earth into mounds ready to receive them, three mounds lying in a straight line along the edge of the grass plot.

We had just about decided that we'd have to buy the seeds if we were to get them. It was a violation of our principles, but we were anxious to get the watermelons started. Somewhere or other, T. J. got his hands on a seed catalog and brought it one evening to our roof garden.

"We can order them now," he said, showing us the catalog. "Look!"

We all crowded around, looking at the fat green watermelons pictured in full color on the pages. Some of them were split open, showing the red, tempting meat, making our mouths water.

"Now we got to scrape up some seed money," T. J. said, looking at us. "I got a quarter. How much you-all got?"

We made up a couple of dollars among us and T. J. nodded his head. "That'll be more than enough. Now we got to decide what kind to get. I think them Kleckley Sweets. What do you-all think?"

---

4. **ventilators** (VEHN tuh layt uhrz): devices used to bring in fresh air.

5. **desecrated** (DEHS ih krayt ihd): showed disrespect for something considered holy.

Ⓖ | Read and Discuss | How does this add to what you know about T. J.?

Sixth Avenue I (1986) by Bill Jacklin. Oil on canvas.

He was going into esoteric[6] matters beyond our reach. We hadn't even known there were different kinds of melons. So we just nodded our heads and agreed that yes, we thought the Kleckley Sweets too.

"I'll order them tonight," T. J. said. "We ought to have them in a few days."

"What are you boys doing up here?" an adult voice said behind us.

It startled us, for no one had ever come up here before in all the time we had been using the roof of the factory. We jerked around and saw three men standing near the trapdoor at the other end of the roof. They weren't policemen or night watch-men but three men in plump business suits, looking at us. They walked toward us.

---

6. **esoteric** (ehs uh TEHR ihk): specialized; beyond most people's understanding or knowledge.

(H) Read and Discuss What does the interaction between the gang and T. J. during their decision-making process show you?

"What are you boys doing up here?" the one in the middle said again.

We stood still, guilt heavy among us, levied by the tone of voice, and looked at the three strangers.

The men stared at the grass flourishing behind us. "What's this?" the man said. "How did this get up here?"

"Sure is growing good, ain't it?" T. J. said conversationally. "We planted it."

The men kept looking at the grass as if they didn't believe it. It was a thick carpet over the earth now, a patch of deep greenness star-tling in the sterile industrial surroundings.

"Yes, sir," T. J. said proudly. "We toted that earth up here and planted that grass." He fluttered the seed catalog. "And we're just fixing to plant us some watermelon."

The man looked at him then, his eyes strange and faraway. "What do you mean,

Vocabulary **flourishing** (FLUR ihsh ihng) *adj.*: thriving.
sterile (STEHR uhl) *adj.*: barren; lacking in interest or vitality.

Heads of Children by André Lhote (1885–1962). Oil on board.
© 2009 Artists Rights Society (ARS), New York/ADAGP, Paris

putting this on the roof of my building?" he said. "Do you want to go to jail?"

T. J. looked shaken. The rest of us were silent, frightened by the authority of his voice. We had grown up aware of adult authority, of policemen and night watchmen and teachers, and this man sounded like all the others. But it was a new thing to T. J.

"Well, you wasn't using the roof," T. J. said. He paused a moment and added shrewdly, "So we just thought to pretty it up a little bit."

"And sag it so I'd have to rebuild it," the man said sharply. He started turning away, saying to another man beside him, "See that all that junk is shoveled off by tomorrow." ❶

"Yes, sir," the man said.

T. J. started forward. "You can't do that," he said. "We toted it up here, and it's our earth. We planted it and raised it and toted it up here."

The man stared at him coldly. "But it's my building," he said. "It's to be shoveled off tomorrow."

"It's our earth," T. J. said desperately. "You ain't got no right!"

The men walked on without listening and descended clumsily through the trapdoor. T. J. stood looking after them, his body tense with anger, until they had disappeared. They wouldn't even argue with him, wouldn't let him defend his earth rights.

He turned to us. "We won't let 'em do it," he said fiercely. "We'll stay up here all day tomorrow and the day after that, and we won't let 'em do it."

We just looked at him. We knew there was no stopping it.

He saw it in our faces, and his face wavered for a moment before he gripped it into determination. "They ain't got no right," he said. "It's our earth. It's our land. Can't nobody touch a man's own land."

We kept looking at him, listening to the words but knowing that it was no use. The adult world had descended on us even in our richest dream, and we knew there was no calculating the adult world, no fighting it, no winning against it.

We started moving slowly toward the parapet and the fire escape, avoiding a last look at the green beauty of the earth that T. J. had planted for us, had planted deeply in our minds as well as in our experience. We filed slowly over the edge and down the steps to the plank, T. J. coming last, and all of us could feel the weight of his grief behind us.

"Wait a minute," he said suddenly, his voice harsh with the effort of calling.

We stopped and turned, held by the tone of his voice, and looked up at him standing above us on the fire escape.

"We can't stop them?" he said, looking down at us, his face strange in the dusky light. "There ain't no way to stop 'em?"

"No," Blackie said with finality. "They own the building."

We stood still for a moment, looking up at T. J., caught into inaction by the decision working in his face. He stared back at us, and his face was pale and mean in the poor light, with a bald nakedness in his skin like cripples have sometimes.

"They ain't gonna touch my earth," he said

---

❶ **Read and Discuss** What does the man mean when he says, "And sag it so I'd have to rebuild it"?

fiercely. "They ain't gonna lay a hand on it! Come on."

He turned around and started up the fire escape again, almost running against the effort of climbing. We followed more slowly, not knowing what he intended to do. By the time we reached him, he had seized a board and thrust it into the soil, scooping it up and flinging it over the parapet into the areaway below. He straightened and looked at us.

"They can't touch it," he said. "I won't let 'em lay a dirty hand on it!"

We saw it then. He stooped to his labor again, and we followed, the gusts of his anger moving in frenzied labor among us as we scattered along the edge of earth, scooping it and throwing it over the parapet, destroying with anger the growth we had nurtured with such tender care. The soil carried so laboriously upward to the light and the sun cascaded swiftly into the dark areaway, the green blades of grass crumpled and twisted in the falling.

It took less time than you would think; the task of destruction is infinitely easier than that of creation. We stopped at the end, leaving only a scattering of loose soil, and when it was finally over, a stillness stood among the group and over the factory building. We looked down at the bare sterility of black tar, felt the harsh texture of it under the soles of our shoes, and the anger had gone out of us, leaving

> "They can't touch it," he said. "I won't let 'em lay a dirty hand on it!"

only a sore aching in our minds, like overstretched muscles.

T. J. stood for a moment, his breathing slowing from anger and effort, caught into the same contemplation of destruction as all of us. He stooped slowly, finally, and picked up a lonely blade of grass left trampled under our feet and put it between his teeth, tasting it, sucking the greenness out of it into his mouth. Then he started walking toward the fire escape, moving before any of us were ready to move, and disappeared over the edge. **J**

We followed him, but he was already halfway down to the ground, going on past the board where we crossed over, climbing down into the areaway. We saw the last section swing down with his weight, and then he stood on the concrete below us, looking at the small pile of anonymous earth scattered by our throwing. Then he walked across the place where we could see him and disappeared toward the street without glancing back, without looking up to see us watching him.

They did not find him for two weeks.

Then the Nashville police caught him just outside the Nashville freight yards. He was walking along the railroad track, still heading South, still heading home.

As for us, who had no remembered home to call us, none of us ever again climbed the escapeway to the roof.

J Literary Focus Theme What theme is suggested by T. J.'s decision to walk home?

Vocabulary **destruction** (dih STRUHK shuhn) *n.*: act of ruining.

Applying Your Skills

Antaeus

Respond and Think Critically

Reading Focus

Quick Check

1. What does T. J. want? What obstacles must he overcome to get it? Use a "Somebody Wanted But So" chart to answer these questions.

Somebody	Wanted	But	So
T. J.			

Read with a Purpose

2. Why does the garden become so important to the boys?

Reading Skills: Cause and Effect

3. Review the cause-and-effect organizer you completed, and then write in complete sentences the chain of events that led to T. J.'s departure from the city.

Literary Focus

Literary Analysis

4. **Connect** Making a connection to the earth seems very important to T. J. in trying to create a home for himself. If you had to move, what might you do to feel more at home?

5. **Evaluate** How might the experience of making the garden and having the chance to know T. J. influence the boys as they grow up?

Literary Skills: Theme

6. **Interpret** The lesson the main characters in the story learn and what you learn as you share their experiences is the story's **theme.** In a complete sentence, state what you think is the theme of this story.

7. **Interpret** In the myth of Antaeus, Hercules is only able to defeat the giant by lifting him off the ground—removing the source of his strength—and holding him there for days. How does this connect to T. J. and his actions after the garden is destroyed?

Literary Skills Review: Character

8. **Analyze** T. J. inspires the boys to take on a difficult project and to keep going even when they get discouraged. What does this <u>reveal</u> about his character?

Writing Focus

Think as a Reader/Writer

Use It in Your Writing Review your notes about the way Deal writes realistic dialogue. Write down a conversation you might have with a friend. Be sure to make it realistic by using slang, one-word responses, and short phrases and by asking questions.

 What Do You Think Now

After reading "Antaeus," do you have new ideas about what gives you strength? If so, explain.

Applying Your Skills

Antaeus

Vocabulary Development

Latin Roots

Many English word roots come directly or indirectly from Latin. A **word root** is a word or word part from which other words are made. Learning some important Latin word roots will give you a key to understanding the meaning of many English words.

Your Turn

Match each word on the right with the Latin word it comes from. Can you think of additional words that share the same word root? Use a dictionary if necessary.

contemplate
destruction
flourishing
sterile

Latin Word	Meaning	Vocabulary	Additional Word(s)
templum (n.)	space marked off for religious observation		
sterilis (adj.)	unfruitful		
florere (v.)	to bloom		
destructio (n.)	destruction		

Language Coach

Suffixes You can understand the meanings of unfamiliar words by looking for familiar base words and thinking about any suffixes attached to the base word. Look at the word *laborious*. While that word may be unfamiliar to you, you may have encountered the word *labor* before. By thinking about the meaning of *labor* and the meaning of the suffix *–ious,* full of, you can figure out the meaning of *laborious:* full of work.

Your Turn

Using the word *laborious* as a guide, write the base word, the suffix, and the word's meaning for each of these words from the story:
1. organization
2. fulfillment
3. tempting

Academic Vocabulary

Write About . . .
Write a paragraph explaining the character trait that allows T. J. to get along in his new home. Which of T. J.'s words and actions <u>reveal</u> this trait?

Learn It Online
Sharpen your word skills with Word Watch online:

go.hrw.com   L7-386   **Go**

Grammar Link

Know Your Sentences!

Sentences, like most things in life, come in various types. Some sentences state facts. These are called **declarative sentences.** They end in a period.

> *The building right next door to us was a factory where they made walking dolls.*

But what if you don't know the facts? Then you need an **interrogative sentence.** Interrogative sentences ask questions. They always end in a question mark.

> *"What's this?" the man said. "How did this get up here?"*

Now pay attention! There are two other types of sentences. **Imperative sentences** give commands or make requests. They sometimes end in exclamation points.

> *"We can order them now," he said, showing us the catalog. "Look!"*

And **exclamatory sentences** show excitement or express strong emotions.

> *"It's our earth," T. J. said desperately. "You ain't got no right!"*

Note: If an imperative sentence does not have a subject, the "understood" subject is always *you.*

> *[You] Do it now.*

Your Turn _____

Classify and correctly punctuate the following sentences:

1. Would you like to join our gang
2. Get off of my building
3. As a child, T. J. lived in the South
4. I'm glad that's over

CHOICES

As you respond to the Choices, use these **Academic Vocabulary** words as appropriate: <u>fundamental</u>, <u>implicit</u>, <u>relevant</u>, <u>reveal</u>.

REVIEW
Create a Title

The title "Antaeus" <u>reveals</u> much about the main character, T. J., and the theme of the story. What else might this story have been called? Think of another title that helps to convey the theme. Then, make a book cover with the new title and an illustration that will help to enlighten the reader.

CONNECT
Write a Descriptive Essay

Timed └Writing Like the character Antaeus in the Greek myth, T. J. seems to gain strength from contact with the earth. Antaeus's strength was physical. What type of strength does T. J. demonstrate? Write a three-paragraph essay describing the characteristics of T. J.'s strength. Begin your essay with a thesis statement that clearly expresses your main point. Then, provide examples from the story to support your thesis. Finally, sum up your main points in the essay's conclusion.

EXTEND
Create a Postcard

Think of places that make your home or community feel like home to you—your own kitchen, a local shop, a park, or the view from a certain hill. Write a paragraph describing everything you see, smell, feel, and hear in one of these places.

After Twenty Years

by **O. Henry**

What Do **You** Think? What circumstances would make you turn against a friend?

QuickWrite

Think of one of your closest friends. Write a list of words and phrases describing the kind of person that friend is now. Put a check mark next to the qualities you think that friend will still have twenty years from now.

The Rewarded Poet (1956) by René Magritte (1898–1967). Oil on canvas.

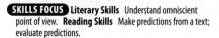

Reader/Writer Notebook

Use your **RWN** to complete the activities for this selection.

Literary Focus

Omniscient Point of View *Omniscient* means "all-knowing," so an omniscient narrator knows everything <u>fundamental</u> about all the characters—their private feelings, their pasts, and even their futures. That doesn't mean the narrator will <u>reveal</u> everything at the outset. The author may want to keep you guessing.

Literary Perspectives Apply the literary perspective described on page 391 as you read this story.

Reading Focus

Making Predictions Making informed guesses about what will happen next is called **making predictions.** Here's how to do it:

- Look for clues that **foreshadow,** or hint at, what will happen.
- As the **suspense** builds, **predict** possible **outcomes.** See if you can guess where the author is leading you. Revise your predictions as you are given more information by the narrator.
- **Draw on your own experiences**—including your other reading experiences—in making your predictions.

Track the accuracy of your predictions by using a chart like the one below.

Story Events	Predictions	Revised Predictions	Outcomes

Writing Focus

Think as a Reader/Writer

Find It in Your Reading As you read, jot down some examples of dialogue that reveal the personalities of the policeman and the man standing in the doorway.

Vocabulary

habitual (huh BIHCH oo uhl) *adj.:* done or fixed by habit. *The officer made his habitual check of the buildings.*

intricate (IHN truh kiht) *adj.:* complicated; full of detail. *The officer twirled his club with intricate movements.*

dismally (DIHZ muh lee) *adv.:* miserably; gloomily. *People walked dismally through the rainy streets.*

egotism (EE guh tihz uhm) *n.:* conceit; talking about oneself too much. *His egotism made him brag about his success.*

simultaneously (sy muhl TAY nee uhs lee) *adv.:* at the same time. *Each man looked simultaneously at his friend's face.*

Language Coach

Related Words Recognizing words that have the same base word or that are similar in spelling can help you understand unfamiliar words. For example, the chart below contains words related to the Vocabulary word *habitual*.

Vocabulary Word	Related Words
habitual	habitually habit inhabit inhabited

As you read, use the strategy of looking for related words to discern the meaning of new words.

Learn It Online
See the video introduction to this story at:

go.hrw.com   L7-389   **Go**

Learn It Online
Get more on the author's life at:
go.hrw.com L7-390 Go

O. Henry
(1862–1910)

Early Troubles

O. Henry is the pen name of William Sydney Porter. Born in Greensboro, North Carolina, he left school at fifteen and eventually moved to Texas. There he edited a humor magazine and worked for a bank in Austin. Unfortunately, Porter was a careless record keeper, and he was accused of embezzling money. Although he was probably innocent, Porter panicked and ran off to Honduras. Eventually, he returned to Austin to be with his dying wife. There he was convicted and spent more than three years in a federal prison in Ohio.

Plot Twists

Porter found inspiration for some of his plots, including "After Twenty Years," in the stories he heard in prison. Released in 1901, Porter moved to New York. Soon, as O. Henry, he became a popular short-story writer known for the surprise endings of his works.

When asked once where he got his plots, Porter replied, "Oh, everywhere. There are stories in everything." He picked up a menu and said, "There's a story in this." Indeed there was, as Porter later published a story called "Springtime à la Carte."

"There are stories in everything."

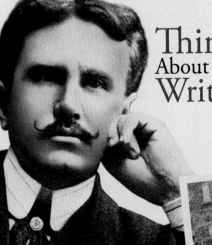

Think About the Writer How might Porter's troubles have affected the way he viewed his characters?

Build Background

O. Henry's stories were often set in the streets, tenements, and hotels of New York City, where he lived in the early 1900s.

The population of New York City exploded in the late 1800s and early 1900s. Waves of European immigrants came to the city to start new lives, working hard to save enough money to move out of the poorly maintained tenement buildings in which they lived.

O. Henry enjoyed writing about the commonplace, finding himself most interested in the lives and challenges of everyday people. His stories are known for their coincidences and ironic humor.

Preview the Selection

This short story begins with an encounter between a **policeman** walking a local beat and a **man** standing in a darkened doorway.

©The Granger Collection, New York.

After Twenty Years

by **O. Henry**

The policeman on the beat moved up the avenue impressively. The impressiveness was habitual and not for show, for spectators were few. The time was barely ten o'clock at night, but chilly gusts of wind with a taste of rain in them had well nigh depeopled the streets. **Ⓐ**

Trying doors as he went, twirling his club with many intricate and artful movements, turning now and then to cast his watchful eye down the pacific[1] thoroughfare, the officer, with his stalwart form and slight swagger, made a fine picture of a guardian of the peace. The vicinity was one that kept early hours. Now and then you might see the lights of a cigar store or of an all-night lunch counter, but the majority of the doors belonged to business places that had long since been closed. **Ⓑ**

When about midway of a certain block, the policeman suddenly slowed his walk. In the doorway of a darkened hardware store a man leaned with an unlighted cigar in his mouth. As the policeman walked up to him, the man spoke up quickly. **Ⓒ**

Literary Perspectives

The following perspective will help you think about the theme of this short story:

Analyzing Responses to Literature Your response to a story is shaped by your ideas and experiences. You may have strong feelings about characters and situations you recognize from your own life. Story elements also influence your responses. You like one character and not another. As the plot unfolds, you guess the ending or are totally surprised. These responses help you connect with the text and identify what a story means to you. As you read this story, watch for questions that guide you in using this perspective.

---

1. **pacific:** peaceful.

Ⓐ **Literary Focus** **Omniscient Point of View** How does the second sentence in this paragraph help you determine the point of view from which the story is told?

Ⓑ **Literary Perspectives** **Analyze Responses to Literature** What connections can you make to this character and scene?

Ⓒ **Reading Focus** **Making Predictions** What do you predict will happen between the police officer and the man waiting in the doorway?

Vocabulary **habitual** (huh BIHCH oo uhl) *adj.*: done or fixed by habit.
intricate (IHN truh kiht) *adj.*: complicated; full of detail.

"It's all right, officer," he said reassuringly. "I'm just waiting for a friend. It's an appointment made twenty years ago. Sounds a little funny to you, doesn't it? Well, I'll explain if you'd like to make certain it's all straight. About that long ago there used to be a restaurant where this store stands— 'Big Joe' Brady's restaurant."

"Until five years ago," said the policeman. "It was torn down then."

The man in the doorway struck a match and lit his cigar. The light showed a pale, square-jawed face with keen eyes and a little white scar near his right eyebrow. His scarf pin was a large diamond, oddly set. **D**

"Twenty years ago tonight," said the man, "I dined here at 'Big Joe' Brady's with Jimmy Wells, my best chum and the finest chap in the world. He and I were raised here in New York, just like two brothers, together. I was eighteen and Jimmy was twenty. The next morning I was to start for the West to make my fortune. You couldn't have dragged Jimmy out of New York; he thought it was the only place on earth. Well, we agreed that night that we would meet here again exactly twenty years from that date and time, no matter what our conditions might be or from what distance we might have to come. We figured that in twenty years each of us ought to have our destiny worked out and our fortunes made, whatever they were going to be."

"It sounds pretty interesting," said the policeman. "Rather a long time between meets, though, it seems to me. Haven't you heard from your friend since you left?"

"Well, yes, for a time we corresponded," said the other. "But after a year or two we lost track of each other. You see, the West is a pretty big proposition, and I kept hustling around over it pretty lively. But I know Jimmy will meet me here if he's alive, for he always was the truest, staunchest old chap in the world. He'll never forget. I came a thousand miles to stand in this door tonight, and it's worth it if my old partner turns up." **E**

The waiting man pulled out a handsome watch, the lids of it set with small diamonds.

"Three minutes to ten," he announced. "It was exactly ten o'clock when we parted here at the restaurant door."

"Did pretty well out West, didn't you?" asked the policeman.

"You bet! I hope Jimmy has done half as well. He was a kind of plodder, though, good fellow as he was. I've had to compete with some of the sharpest wits going to get my pile. A man gets in a groove in New York. It takes the West to put a razor edge on him." **F**

The policeman twirled his club and took a step or two.

"I'll be on my way. Hope your friend comes around all right. Going to call time on him sharp?"

"I should say not!" said the other. "I'll give him half an hour at least. If Jimmy is alive on earth, he'll be here by that time. So long, officer."

D **Reading Focus** Making Predictions What could the scar and the large diamond suggest about the man's past?

E **Read and Discuss** What is happening with the man in the doorway?

F **Literary Perspectives** Analyze Responses to Literature Think about how the writer uses dialogue and descriptive details to reveal character traits. What is your impression of the man from the West and of Jimmy Wells?

"Good night, sir," said the policeman, passing on along his beat, trying doors as he went.

There was now a fine, cold drizzle falling, and the wind had risen from its uncertain puffs into a steady blow. The few foot passengers astir in that quarter hurried dismally and silently along with coat collars turned high and pocketed hands. And in the door of the hardware store the man who had come a thousand miles to fill an appointment, uncertain almost to absurdity, with the friend of his youth, smoked his cigar and waited.

About twenty minutes he waited, and then a tall man in a long overcoat, with collar turned up to his ears, hurried across from the opposite side of the street. He went directly to the waiting man.

"Is that you, Bob?" he asked, doubtfully.

"Is that you, Jimmy Wells?" cried the man in the door.

"Bless my heart!" exclaimed the new arrival, grasping both the other's hands with his own. "It's Bob, sure as fate. I was certain I'd find you here if you were still in existence. Well, well, well!—twenty years is a long time. The old restaurant's gone, Bob;

Vocabulary **dismally** (DIHZ muh lee) *adv.*: miserably; gloomily.

Analyzing Visuals

Viewing and Interpreting
How do the images on this page reflect the **mood**, or atmosphere, of the story?

I wish it had lasted, so we could have had another dinner there. How has the West treated you, old man?"

"Bully;² it has given me everything I asked it for. You've changed lots, Jimmy. I never thought you were so tall by two or three inches." **G**

"Oh, I grew a bit after I was twenty."

"Doing well in New York, Jimmy?"

"Moderately. I have a position in one of the city departments. Come on, Bob; we'll go around to a place I know of and have a good long talk about old times."

The two men started up the street, arm in arm. The man from the West, his egotism enlarged by success, was beginning to outline the history of his career. The other, submerged in his overcoat, listened with interest. **H**

At the corner stood a drugstore, brilliant with electric lights. When they came into this glare, each of them turned simultaneously to gaze upon the other's face.

The man from the West stopped suddenly and released his arm.

> The two men started up the street, arm in arm.

"You're not Jimmy Wells," he snapped. "Twenty years is a long time, but not long enough to change a man's nose from a Roman to a pug." **I**

"It sometimes changes a good man into a bad one," said the tall man. "You've been under arrest for ten minutes, 'Silky' Bob. Chicago thinks you may have dropped over our way and wires us she wants to have a chat with you. Going quietly, are you? That's sensible. Now, before we go to the station, here's a note I was asked to hand to you. You may read it here at the window. It's from Patrolman Wells."

The man from the West unfolded the little piece of paper handed him. His hand was steady when he began to read, but it trembled a little by the time he had finished. The note was rather short.

> Bob: I was at the appointed place on time. When you struck the match to light your cigar, I saw it was the face of the man wanted in Chicago. Somehow I couldn't do it myself, so I went around and got a plainclothes man to do the job.
> Jimmy **J**

---

2. **bully:** informal term meaning "very well."

G **Reading Focus** Making Predictions What might Jimmy's height signify?

H **Read and Discuss** What does Bob think of himself, and how would he feel about Jimmy Wells's status in life?

I **Reading Focus** Making Predictions If the man is not Jimmy Wells, who is he? Why is he there in Jimmy's place?

J **Literary Perspectives** Analyze Responses to Literature How do you feel as you read the ending? What is your response to each character now?

Vocabulary **egotism** (EE guh tihz uhm) *n.:* conceit; talking about oneself too much.
simultaneously (sy muhl TAY nee uhs lee) *adv.:* at the same time.

Applying Your Skills

SKILLS FOCUS **Literary Skills** Analyze omniscient point of view; analyze suspense and foreshadowing. **Reading Skills** Make predictions from a text; evaluate predictions. **Writing Skills** Develop characters using dialogue.

After Twenty Years

Respond and Think Critically

Reading Focus

Quick Check

1. What does the police officer do after saying good night to the man in the doorway?

Read with a Purpose

2. What does the fact that both men showed up say about their friendship? How hard do you think it was for Wells to turn in his friend?

Reading Skills: Making Predictions

3. Review the chart you completed as you read the story. Which of your predictions were correct? Where did the story take you by surprise?

Story Events	Predictions	Revised Predictions	Outcome

Literary Focus

Literary Analysis

4. **Interpret** What might Jimmy Wells have been thinking between the time he recognized Bob as a wanted man and the time he left to find the plainclothes officer?

5. **Interpret** In a sentence or two, state the **theme** of this story. What truth about loyalty versus honesty does the story <u>reveal</u> to you?

6. **Literary Perspectives** O. Henry's writings are said to have "feelings of compassion for the weakness of man." Using examples from this story, explain why you agree or disagree.

Literary Skills: Omniscient Point of View

7. **Infer** O. Henry chose to tell his story from the **omniscient point of view.** What <u>relevant</u> details would the reader have known and not known if Silky Bob had told the story from the **first-person point of view?**

Literary Skills Review: Foreshadowing

8. **Interpret** Details about Bob's appearance and behavior warn you that he may be dishonest. What clues hint at, or **foreshadow,** something sinister about Bob?

9. **Connect** When did you realize who the police officer was? Find and explain the first clue to his identity.

Writing Focus

Think as a Reader/Writer

Use It in Your Writing In "After Twenty Years," O. Henry uses dialogue to reveal <u>implicit</u> information about his characters. Imagine two characters from a story you'd like to write. Write a short dialogue between those two characters that <u>reveals</u> two character traits for each one.

What Do You Think Now Have you changed your mind about how your friend might change in twenty years? Edit your list to reflect what you think now.

Vocabulary Development

Vocabulary Check

1. Describe what happens when two people respond to a question **simultaneously.**
2. Discuss an **intricate** project you have completed.
3. Why might someone sulk **dismally** after a game involving a favorite sports team?
4. If your good behavior is **habitual,** how do you think other people will feel about you?
5. Give an example of behavior that displays one's **egotism.**

Idioms

An **idiom** is a commonly used expression that is not literally true, such as these examples from "After Twenty Years": *a taste of rain, lost track,* and *gets in a groove.* Idioms are often based on comparisons or images. For example, *gets in a groove* means "becomes comfortable living a certain way," not literally "stuck in an indentation." Almost no one really pays attention to the literal meaning of an idiom because it makes no sense.

Your Turn

Find at least four idioms in the paragraph that follows. With a partner, identify what each idiom really means.

 The officer was deep in thought as he walked his habitual beat. His weathered face broke into a big smile when he saw the man waiting by the building. As the other man stepped from the dismally lit doorway, the officer thought to himself, "I wish he'd left well enough alone. Now I'm stuck between a rock and a hard place."

Language Coach

Related Words Recognizing a familiar word or word part and thinking about its meaning can often help you figure out the meaning of an unfamiliar word.

On a separate sheet of paper, create a chart like the one below. For each word in the first column, write related words in the second column. The first one is done for you.

Vocabulary Word	Related Words
egotism	ego, egotistical, egotistically, egocentric
impressiveness	
guardian	
corresponded	
reassuringly	

Academic Vocabulary

Talk About . . .

Writers often paint mental pictures of their characters to help readers anticipate or understand these characters' implicit natures. What do O. Henry's physical descriptions of Jimmy and Bob reveal about those characters? Discuss your thoughts with a partner.

Learn It Online
Develop your reading comprehension with Word Watch:

go.hrw.com | L7-396 | **Go**

Grammar Link

Sentence Fragments

To be a complete sentence, a group of words must have a subject and a verb and must express a complete thought. A sentence fragment is punctuated like a sentence, but it lacks one or more of the key elements that make up a complete sentence.

FRAGMENT Standing in a doorway. [The word group lacks a subject.]

SENTENCE Bob was standing in a doorway.

FRAGMENT The officer walking his beat. [The word group lacks a verb.]

SENTENCE The officer walking his beat tried the doorknobs.

FRAGMENT After Jimmy walks away. [Even with a subject and verb, this group of words does not express a complete thought.]

SENTENCE After Jimmy walks away, he finds another officer to arrest Silky Bob.

Your Turn

Identify each of the following word groups as a sentence or a fragment.

1. during his years out west
2. he got a plainclothes officer
3. do you know why he is a wanted man
4. down the street on the rainy night
5. smoking a cigar
6. while Bob stood in the shadows

CHOICES

As you respond to the Choices, use these **Academic Vocabulary** words as appropriate: <u>fundamental</u>, <u>implicit</u>, <u>relevant</u>, <u>reveal</u>.

REVIEW
Change the Point of View

In a paragraph, retell "After Twenty Years" from Bob's point of view. Imagine you are Silky Bob telling a fellow prisoner the story of how you got caught by your old friend Jimmy Wells. How could the new narrator change the story's theme? Is it still about loyalty versus honesty?

CONNECT
Write a Dialogue

Timed ∟**Writing** Imagine you are Silky Bob and you have just seen Jimmy Wells at the station house after your arrest. Write a conversation between Bob and Jimmy in which Bob tells Jimmy how he feels about Jimmy's actions.

EXTEND
Offer Advice

Imagine that you write an advice column for your school newspaper. You receive this letter from "Confused." What advice would you give?

Last Friday I saw my friend Lucy take a wallet that was left in the cafeteria. I know she needs the money because her dad is between jobs. I don't know what to do! I want to do what's right, but I don't know how to handle this. HELP!
Sincerely,
Confused

Learn It Online
Dig deeper into the story with these Internet links:

go.hrw.com | L7-397 | **Go**

Bargain

by **A. B. Guthrie**

 What Do You Think

Bullying is hurting or frightening a weaker person. Why do you think some people bully others?

QuickWrite

Have you experienced or observed bullying? How did each person involved seem to feel? What were the results of the incident?

Reader/Writer Notebook

Use your **RWN** to complete the activities for this selection.

Literary Focus

First-Person Point of View When you tell a story about something that happened to you, you tell it from the **first-person point of view** using the pronoun *I*. When you read a story told from the first-person point of view, you share the narrator's thoughts and feelings and know only what the narrator knows. All you learn about the story's events and characters comes from the narrator.

Reading Focus

Making Predictions The process of trying to guess what will happen next is called **making predictions.** Here is how you do it.

- Look for clues that **foreshadow,** or hint at, what will happen.
- As suspense builds, try to guess where the writer is headed. Draw on your own experience and knowledge.
- Ask yourself questions. Revise your predictions as more information is revealed.

Into Action As you read "Bargain," fill in a prediction chart.

Based on (evidence from the story or your own experience)	I Predict...
Slade embarrassed and hurt Mr. Baumer, who teared up.	Slade and Mr. Baumer will have another conflict.

Writing Focus

Think as a Reader/Writer

Find It in Your Reading The first-person point of view can reveal the narrator's thoughts. As you read, record examples of the narrator's inner thoughts, and describe what he is revealing about himself.

Vocabulary

prodded (PRAHD id) *v.:* urged on, here by poking with a stick. *He prodded the cow to move it out of the road.*

merchandise (MUR chuhn dys) *n.:* items that are for sale in stores. *The store's winter merchandise included mittens.*

evaporation (ih vap uh RAY shuhn) *n.:* process by which a liquid changes into a gas. *When whiskey went missing from the barrels, workers blamed evaporation.*

thermometer (thuhr MAHM uh tuhr) *n.:* instrument that measures temperature. *The thermometer showed that it was below freezing.*

Language Coach

Word Forms Sometimes words come in different forms. For example, *embarrass* and *embarrassment* both come from the same word family. Write two other words that belong to the same word family as *evaporation.* Use a dictionary if necessary.

 Learn It Online
Hear a professional actor read this story.
Visit the selection online at:

go.hrw.com   L7-399   **Go**

A. B. Guthrie
(1901–1991)

Pulitzer Prize WINNER

"Real People in Real Times"
A. B. Guthrie wanted to portray the West as it was, not create myths about it. Most people agree that Guthrie succeeded. His most famous work, a trilogy about the opening of the West, is noted for its historical accuracy. Guthrie also wrote the screenplay for *Shane*—a famous movie about a western gunslinger. Shane takes justice into his own hands to save a family.

Guthrie Grows
Albert Bertram Guthrie, Jr., grew up in the little town of Choteau, Montana. After graduating from college, he traveled extensively and worked at various jobs—ranching in Sonora, Mexico; selling groceries in California; working as a census taker in Montana.

Guthrie became a fiction writer when he took time off from his newspaper job to visit his sick mother. During his visit he had time to write his first novel, *Murders at Moon Dance* (1943). In this book he introduces the setting of "Bargain" and many of his other short stories. Guthrie also said about his writing

> "I want to talk about real people in real times. For every Wyatt Earp or Billy the Kid, there were thousands of people just trying to get along."

Think About the Writer What aspects of Guthrie's life prepared him to write about the West?

Build Background
This story takes place in Moon Dance, a town you might recognize as similar to ones portrayed in TV and movie westerns—its muddy main street, its saloon, and its general store. This story is a kind of **historical fiction.** Setting is important in historical fiction. The writer wants you to feel what it was like to live in a rough frontier town. If you took away Moon Dance and all the historical details, you'd have a different story.

Preview the Selection
Mr. Baumer is one of the story's main characters, a struggling store owner in a small western town. As the story begins, he and his young sales clerk, **Al,** are walking to the post office to mail customer bills. **Slade** is the story's other main character, a violent bully.

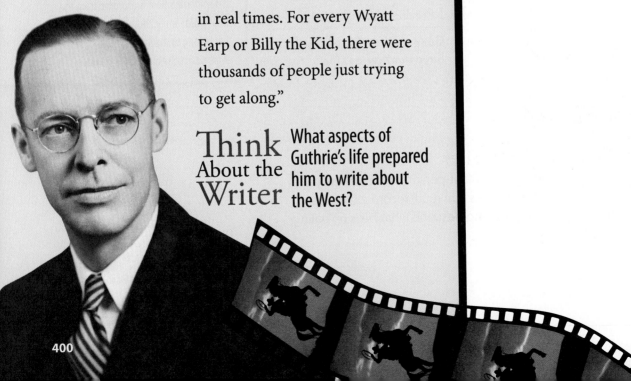

Bargain

by **A. B. Guthrie**

Mr. Baumer and I had closed the Moon Dance Mercantile Company and were walking to the post office, and he had a bunch of bills in his hand ready to mail. There wasn't anyone or anything much on the street because it was suppertime. A buckboard[1] and a saddle horse were tied at Hirsches' rack, and a rancher in a wagon rattled for home ahead of us, the sound of his going fading out as he prodded his team. Freighter[2] Slade stood alone in front of the Moon Dance Saloon, maybe wondering whether to have one more before going to supper. People said he could hold a lot without showing it except in being ornerier[3] even than usual. **Ⓐ**

Mr. Baumer didn't see him until he was almost on him, and then he stopped and fingered through the bills until he found the right one. He stepped up to Slade and held it out.

Slade said, "What's this, Dutchie?"

Mr. Baumer had to tilt his head up to talk to him. "You know vat it is."

Slade just said, "Yeah?" You never could tell from his face what went on inside his skull. He had dark skin and shallow cheeks and a thick-growing moustache that fell over the corners of his mouth.

"It is a bill," Mr. Baumer said. "I tell you before, it is a bill. For twenty-vun dollars and fifty cents."

"You know what I do with bills, don't you, Dutchie?" Slade asked.

Mr. Baumer didn't answer the question. He said, "For merchandise."

Slade took the envelope from Mr. Baumer's hand and squeezed it up in his fist and let it drop on the plank sidewalk. Not saying anything, he reached down and took Mr. Baumer's nose between the knuckles of his fingers and twisted it up into his eyes. That was all. That was all at the time. Slade half turned and slouched to the door of

---

1. **buckboard:** open carriage.
2. **freighter:** here, person who transports goods.
3. **ornerier** (AWR nuhr ee uhr): dialect for "meaner and more stubborn."

Ⓐ | **Read and Discuss** | What has the author established so far?

Vocabulary **prodded** (PRAHD id) *v.:* urged on, here by poking with a stick.
merchandise (MUR chuhn dys) *n.:* items that are for sale in stores.

Bargain **401**

the bar and let himself in. Some men were laughing in there. **B**

Mr. Baumer stooped and picked up the bill and put it on top of the rest and smoothed it out for mailing. When he straightened up, I could see tears in his eyes from having his nose screwed around. **C**

He didn't say anything to me, and I didn't say anything to him, being so much younger and feeling embarrassed for him. He went into the post office and slipped the bills in the slot, and we walked on home together. At the last, at the crossing where

I had to leave him, he remembered to say, "Better study, Al. Is good to know to read and write and figure." I guess he felt he had to push me a little, my father being dead. **D**

I said, "Sure. See you after school tomorrow"—which he knew I would anyway. I had been working in the store for him during the summer and after classes ever since pneumonia took my dad off.

Three of us worked there regularly: Mr. Baumer, of course, and me and Colly Coleman, who knew enough to drive the delivery wagon but wasn't much help

B **Reading Focus** **Making Predictions** What part do you think Slade will play in this story?

C **Read and Discuss** What does this new information add to the picture you have of Mr. Baumer?

D **Literary Focus** **First-Person Point of View** Al says that Mr. Baumer probably pushes him because Al's father is dead. What does that <u>reveal</u> about their relationship?

Analyzing Visuals **Viewing and Interpreting** How does this photograph help you to connect with Mr. Baumer's store?

General store (1936). Photograph.
©The Granger Collection, New York.

around the store except for carrying orders out to the rigs[4] at the hitchpost and handling heavy things like the whiskey barrel at the back of the store which Mr. Baumer sold quarts and gallons out of.

The store carried quite a bit of stuff— sugar and flour and dried fruits and canned goods and such on one side and yard goods and coats and caps and aprons and the like of that on the other, besides kerosene and bran and buckets and linoleum and pitchforks in the storehouse at the rear—but it wasn't a big store like Hirsch Brothers up the street. Never would be, people guessed, going on to say, with a sort of slow respect, that it would have gone under long ago if Mr. Baumer hadn't been half mule and half beaver. He had started the store just two years before and, the way things were, worked himself close to death.

He was at the high desk at the end of the grocery counter when I came in the next afternoon. He had an eyeshade on and black sateen protectors on his forearms, and his pencil was in his hand instead of behind his ear and his glasses were roosted on the nose that Slade had twisted. He didn't hear me open and close the door or hear my feet as I walked back to him, and I saw he wasn't doing anything with the pencil but holding it over paper. I stood and studied him for a minute, seeing a small, stooped man with a little paunch bulging through his unbuttoned vest. He was a man you wouldn't remember

from meeting once. There was nothing in his looks to set itself in your mind unless maybe it was his chin, which was a small pink hill in the gentle plain of his face.

While I watched him, he lifted his hand and felt carefully of his nose. Then he saw me. His eyes had that kind of mistiness that seems to go with age or illness, though he wasn't really old or sick, either. He brought his hand down quickly and picked up the pencil, but he saw I still was looking at the nose, and finally he sighed and said, "That Slade."

Just the sound of the name brought Slade to my eye. I saw him slouched in front of the bar, and I saw him and his string[5] coming down the grade from the buttes,[6] the wheel horses held snug and the rest lined out pretty, and then the string leveling off and Slade's whip lifting hair from a horse that wasn't up in the collar.[7] I had heard it said that Slade could make a horse scream with that whip. Slade's name wasn't Freighter, of course. Our town had nicknamed him that because that was what he was.

"I don't think it's any good to send him a bill, Mr. Baumer," I said. "He can't even read."

"He could pay yet."

"He don't pay anybody," I said.

"I think he hate me," Mr. Baumer went on. "That is the thing. He hate me for coming not from this country. I come here,

---

4. **rigs:** carriages with their horses.

5. **string:** here, a group of horses.

6. **buttes** (byoots): steep, flat-topped hills that stand alone on a plain.

7. **up in the collar:** pulling as hard as the other horses.

sixteen years old, and learn to read and write, and I make a business, and so I think he hate me."

"He hates everybody."

Mr. Baumer shook his head. "But not to pinch the nose. Not to call Dutchie."

The side door squeaked open, but it was only Colly Coleman coming in from a trip, so I said, "Excuse me, Mr. Baumer, but you shouldn't have trusted him in the first place." **Ⓔ**

"I know," he answered, looking at me with his misty eyes. "A man make mistakes. I think some do not trust him, so he will pay me because I do. And I do not know him well then. He only came back to town three, four months ago, from being away since before I go into business."

"People who knew him before could have told you," I said.

"A man make mistakes," he explained again.

"It's not my business, Mr. Baumer, but I would forget the bill."

His eyes rested on my face for a long minute, as if they didn't see me but the problem itself. He said, "It is not twenty-vun dollars and fifty cents now, Al. It is not that anymore."

"What is it?"

He took a little time to answer. Then he brought his two hands up as if to help him shape the words. "It is the thing. You see, it is the thing."

I wasn't quite sure what he meant.

He took his pencil from behind the ear where he had put it and studied the point of it. "That Slade. He steal whiskey and call it evaporation. He sneak things from his load. A thief, he is. And too big for me." **Ⓕ**

I said, "I got no time for him, Mr. Baumer, but I guess there never was a freighter didn't steal whiskey. That's what I hear."

It was true, too. From the railroad to Moon Dance was fifty miles and a little better—a two-day haul in good weather, heck knew how long in bad. Any freight string bound home with a load had to lie out at least one night. When a freighter had his stock tended to and maybe a little fire going against the dark, he'd tackle a barrel of whiskey or of grain alcohol if he had one aboard consigned to Hirsch Brothers or Mr. Baumer's or the Moon Dance Saloon or the Gold Leaf Bar. He'd drive a hoop out of place, bore a little hole with a nail or bit and draw off what he wanted. Then he'd plug the hole with a whittled peg and pound the hoop back. That was evaporation. Nobody complained much. With freighters you generally took what they gave you, within reason.

"Moore steals it, too," I told Mr. Baumer. Moore was Mr. Baumer's freighter.

"Yah," he said, and that was all, but I stood there for a minute, thinking there might be something more. I could see

---

Ⓔ Read and Discuss Mr. Baumer thought that if he trusted Slade, then Slade would be trustworthy. How does this add to what you know about Mr. Baumer?

Ⓕ Reading Focus Making Predictions What do you think will happen between Mr. Baumer and Slade?

Vocabulary evaporation (ih vap uh RAY shuhn) n.: process by which a liquid changes into a gas.

thought swimming in his eyes, above that little hill of chin. Then a customer came in, and I had to go wait on him. **G**

Nothing happened for a month, nothing between Mr. Baumer and Slade, that is, but fall drew on toward winter and the first flight of ducks headed south and Mr. Baumer hired Miss Lizzie Webb to help with the just-beginning Christmas trade and here it was, the first week in October, and he and I walked up the street again with the monthly bills. He always sent them out. I guess he had to. A bigger store, like Hirsches', would wait on the ranchers until their beef or wool went to market.

Up to a point things looked and happened almost the same as they had before, so much the same that I had the crazy feeling I was going through that time again. There was a wagon and a rig tied up at Hirsches' rack and a saddle horse standing hipshot[8] in front of the harness shop. A few more people were on the street now, not many, and lamps had been lit against the shortened day.

It was dark enough that I didn't make out Slade right away. He was just a figure that came out of the yellow wash of light from the Moon Dance Saloon and stood on the boardwalk and with his head made the little motion of spitting. Then I recognized the lean, raw shape of him and the muscles flowing down into the sloped shoulders, and in the settling darkness I filled the pic-

_____

8. **hipshot:** with one hip lower than the other.

ture in—the dark skin and the flat cheeks and the peevish eyes and the moustache growing rank.

There was Slade and here was Mr. Baumer with his bills and here I was, just as before, just like in the second go-round of a bad dream. I felt like turning back, being embarrassed and half scared by trouble even when it wasn't mine. Please, I said to myself, don't stop, Mr. Baumer! Don't bite off anything! Please, shortsighted the way you are, don't catch sight of him at all! I held up and stepped around behind Mr.

G Read and Discuss What do you think Mr. Baumer believes about his chances of getting paid by or defending himself against Slade?

Baumer and came up on the outside so as to be between him and Slade, where maybe I'd cut off his view.

But it wasn't any use. All along I think I knew it was no use, not the praying or the walking between or anything. The act had to play itself out.

Mr. Baumer looked across the front of me and saw Slade and hesitated in his step and came to a stop. Then in his slow, business way, his chin held firm against his mouth, he began fingering through the bills, squinting to make out the names. Slade had turned and was watching him, munching on a cud of tobacco like a bull waiting.

"You look, Al," Mr. Baumer said without lifting his face from the bills. "I cannot see so good."

So I looked, and while I was looking, Slade must have moved. The next I knew, Mr. Baumer was staggering ahead, the envelopes spilling out of his hands. There had been a thump, the clap of a heavy hand swung hard on his back.

Slade said, "Haryu, Dutchie?"

Mr. Baumer caught his balance and turned around, the bills he had trampled shining white between them and at Slade's feet the hat that Mr. Baumer had stumbled out from under.

H **Literary Focus** **First-Person Point of View** Judging by this paragraph, how do you think Al feels about Mr. Baumer?

Slade picked up the hat and scuffed through the bills and held it out. "Cold to be goin' without a skypiece," he said. ❶

Mr. Baumer hadn't spoken a word. The lampshine from inside the bar caught his eyes, and in them, it seemed to me, a light came and went as anger and the uselessness of it took turns in his head.

Two men had come up on us and stood watching. One of them was Angus McDonald, who owned the Ranchers' Bank, and the other was Dr. King. He had his bag in his hand.

Two others were drifting up, but I didn't have time to tell who. The light came in Mr. Baumer's eyes, and he took a step ahead and swung. I could have hit harder myself. The fist landed on Slade's cheek without hardly so much as jogging his head, but it let the devil loose in the man. I didn't know he could move so fast. He slid in like a practiced fighter and let Mr. Baumer have it full in the face. ❶

Mr. Baumer slammed over on his back, but he wasn't out. He started lifting himself. Slade leaped ahead and brought a boot heel down on the hand he was lifting himself by. I heard meat and bone under that heel and saw Mr. Baumer fall back and try to roll away.

Things had happened so fast that not until then did anyone have a chance to get between them. Now Mr. McDonald pushed at Slade's chest, saying, "That's enough,

❶ **Read and Discuss** What is happening here?

❶ **Literary Focus** First-Person Point of View How does Al feel about what is going on?

407

Freighter. That's enough, now," and Dr. King lined up, too, and another man I didn't know, and I took a place, and we formed a kind of screen between them. Dr. King turned and bent to look at Mr. Baumer.

"Fool hit me first," Slade said.

"That's enough," Mr. McDonald told him again while Slade looked at all of us as if he'd spit on us for a nickel. Mr. McDonald went on, using a half-friendly tone, and I knew it was because he didn't want to take Slade on any more than the rest of us did. "You go on home and sleep it off, Freighter. That's the ticket."

Slade just snorted.

From behind us, Dr. King said, "I think you've broken this man's hand."

"Lucky for him I didn't kill him," Slade answered. "Dutch penny pincher!" He fingered the chew out of his mouth. "Maybe he'll know enough to leave me alone now."

Dr. King had Mr. Baumer on his feet. "I'll take him to the office," he said.

Blood was draining from Mr. Baumer's nose and rounding the curve of his lip and dripping from the sides of his chin. He held his hurt right hand in the other. But the thing was that he didn't look beaten even then, not the way a man who has given up looks beaten. Maybe that was why Slade said, with a show of that fierce anger, "You stay away from me! Hear? Stay clear away, or you'll get more of the same!" **K**

Dr. King led Mr. Baumer away, Slade went back into the bar, and the other men walked off, talking about the fight. I got down and picked up the bills, because I knew Mr. Baumer would want me to, and mailed them at the post office, dirty as they were. It made me sorer, someway, that Slade's bill was one of the few that wasn't marked up. The cleanness of it seemed to say that there was no getting the best of him.

Mr. Baumer had his hand in a sling the next day and wasn't much good at waiting on the trade. I had to hustle all afternoon and so didn't have a chance to talk to him even if he had wanted to talk. Mostly he stood at his desk, and once, passing it, I saw he was practicing writing with his left hand. His nose and the edges of the cheeks around it were swollen some.

At closing time I said, "Look, Mr. Baumer, I can lay out of school a few days until you kind of get straightened out here."

"No," he answered as if to wave the subject away. "I get somebody else. You go to school. Is good to learn."

I had a half notion to say that learning hadn't helped him with Slade. Instead, I blurted out that I would have the law on Slade. **L**

"The law?" he asked.

"The sheriff or somebody."

"No, Al," he said. "You would not."

I asked why.

"The law, it is not for plain fights," he said. "Shooting? Robbing? Yes, the law come quick. The plain fights, they are too many. They not count enough."

He was right. I said, "Well, I'd do something anyhow."

K **Reading Focus** Making Inferences Why does Slade make sure he gets the last word in?

L **Read and Discuss** What does this conversation show you?

"Yes," he answered with a slow nod of his head. "Something you vould do, Al." He didn't tell me what.

Within a couple of days he got another man to clerk for him—it was Ed Hempel, who was always finding and losing jobs—and we made out. Mr. Baumer took his hand from the sling in a couple or three weeks, but with the tape on it, it still wasn't any use to him. From what you could see of the fingers below the tape, it looked as if it never would be.

He spent most of his time at the high desk, sending me or Ed out on the errands he used to run, like posting and getting the mail. Sometimes I wondered if that was because he was afraid of meeting Slade. He could just as well have gone himself. He wasted a lot of hours just looking at nothing, though I will have to say he worked hard at learning to write left-handed.

Then, a month and a half before Christmas, he hired Slade to haul his freight for him. ⓜ

Ed Hempel told me about the deal when I showed up for work. "Yessir," he said, resting his foot on a crate in the store-room where we were supposed to be working. "I tell you he's throwed in with Slade. Told me this morning to go out and locate him if I could and bring him in. Slade was at the saloon, o' course, and says to the devil with Dutchie, but I told him this was honest-to-God business, like Baumer had told me to, and there was a quart of whiskey right there in the store for him if he'd come and get it. He was out of money, I reckon, because the quart fetched him."

"What'd they say?" I asked him.

"Search me. There was two or three people in the store and Baumer told me to wait on 'em, and he and Slade palavered[9] back by the desk."

"How do you know they made a deal?"

Ed spread his hands out. "'Bout noon, Moore came in with his string, and I heard Baumer say he was makin' a change. Moore didn't like it too good, either."

It was a hard thing to believe, but there one day was Slade with a pile of stuff for the Moon Dance Mercantile Company, and that was proof enough with something left for boot.

Mr. Baumer never opened the subject up with me, though I gave him plenty of chances. And I didn't feel like asking. He didn't talk much these days but went around absent-minded, feeling now and then of the fingers that curled yellow and stiff out of the bandage like the toes on the leg of a dead chicken. Even on our walks home he kept his thoughts to himself.

Then, a month and
a half before
Christmas, he hired
Slade to haul
his freight for him.

---

9. **palavered** (puh LAV uhrd): talked; met to discuss something.

ⓜ Read and Discuss | Why do you think Mr. Baumer has hired Slade?

I felt different about him now and was sore inside. Not that I blamed him exactly. A hundred and thirty-five pounds wasn't much to throw against two hundred. And who could tell what Slade would do on a bellyful of whiskey? He had promised Mr. Baumer more of the same, hadn't he? But I didn't feel good. I couldn't look up to Mr. Baumer like I used to and still wanted to. I didn't have the beginning of an answer when men cracked jokes or shook their heads in sympathy with Mr. Baumer, saying Slade had made him come to time. Ⓝ

Slade hauled in a load for the store, and another, and Christmastime was drawing on and trade heavy, and the winter that had started early and then pulled back came on again. There was a blizzard and then a still cold and another blizzard and afterwards a sunshine that was iceshine on the drifted snow. I was glad to be busy, selling overshoes and sheep-lined coats and mitts and socks as thick as saddle blankets and Christmas candy out of buckets and hickory nuts and the fresh oranges that the people in our town never saw except when Santa Claus was coming.

One afternoon, when I lit out from class, the thermometer on the school porch read forty-two degrees below. But you didn't have to look at it to know how cold the weather was. Your nose and fingers and toes and ears and the bones inside you told you. The snow cried when you stepped on it.

I got to the store and took my things off and scuffed my hands at the stove for a minute so's to get life enough in them to tie a parcel. Mr. Baumer—he was always polite to me—said, "Hello, Al. Not so much to do today. Too cold for customers." He shuddered a little, as if he hadn't got the chill off even yet, and rubbed his broken hand with the good one. "Ve need Christmas goods," he said, looking out the window to the furrows that wheels had made in the snow-banked street, and I knew he was thinking of Slade's string, inbound from the railroad, and the time it might take even Slade to travel those hard miles.

Slade never made it at all.

Less than an hour later our old freighter, Moore, came in, his beard white and stiff with frost. He didn't speak at first but looked around and clumped to the stove and took off his heavy mitts, holding his news inside him.

Then he said, not pleasantly, "Your new man's dead, Baumer."

"My new man?" Mr. Baumer said.

"Who do you think? Slade. He's dead."

All Mr. Baumer could say was "Dead!"

"Froze to death, I figger," Moore told him, while Colly Coleman and Ed Hempel and Miss Lizzie and I and a couple of customers stepped closer.

"Not Slade," Mr. Baumer said. "He know too much to freeze."

"Maybe so, but he sure's froze now. I got him in the wagon."

We stood looking at one another and at Moore. Moore was enjoying his news, enjoying feeding it out bit by bit so's to hold the stage. "Heart might've give out, for all I know."

Ⓝ **Literary Focus** First-Person Point of View **What does Al feel about Mr. Baumer now?**

Vocabulary **thermometer** (thuhr MAHM uh tuhr) *n.*: instrument that measures temperature.

Viewing and Interpreting How does this photograph of an Old West town help you visualize Guthrie's setting?

The side door swung open, letting in a cloud of cold and three men who stood, like us, waiting on Moore. I moved a little and looked through the window and saw Slade's freight outfit tied outside with more men around it. Two of them were on a wheel of one of the wagons, looking inside.

"Had a extra man, so I brought your stuff in," Moore went on. "Figgered you'd be glad to pay for it."

"Not Slade," Mr. Baumer said again.

"You can take a look at him."

Mr. Baumer answered no.

"Someone's takin' word to Connor to

bring his hearse. Anyhow, I told 'em to. I carted old Slade this far. Connor can have him now."

Moore pulled on his mitts. "Found him there by the Deep Creek crossin', doubled up in the snow an' his fire out." He moved toward the door. "I'll see to the horses, but your stuff'll have to set there. I got more'n enough work to do at Hirsches.'"

Mr. Baumer just nodded.

I put on my coat and went out and waited my turn and climbed on a wagon wheel and looked inside, and there was Slade piled on some bags of bran. Maybe because of being frozen, his face was whiter than I ever saw it, whiter and deader, too, though it never had been lively. Only the moustache seemed still alive, sprouting thick like grease-wood from alkali.[10] Slade was doubled up all right, as if he had died and stiffened leaning forward in a chair.

"Found him there by the Deep Creek crossin', doubled up in the snow an' his fire out."

I got down from the wheel, and Colly and then Ed climbed up. Moore was unhitching, tossing off his pieces of infor-mation while he did so. Pretty soon Mr. Connor came up with his old hearse, and he and Moore tumbled Slade into it, and the team, which was as old as the hearse, made off, the tires squeaking in the snow. The people trailed on away with it, their breaths leaving little ribbons of mist in the air. It was beginning to get dark.

Mr. Baumer came out of the side door of the store, bundled up, and called to Colly and Ed and me. "We unload," he said. "Already is late. Al, better you get a couple lanterns now."

We did a fast job, setting the stuff out of the wagons onto the platform and then carrying it or rolling it on the one truck that the store owned and stow-ing it inside according to where Mr. Baumer's good hand pointed.

A barrel was one of the last things to go in. I edged it up and Colly nosed the truck under it, and then I let it fall back. "Mr. Baumer," I said, "we'll never sell all this, will we?"

"Yah," he answered. "Sure we sell it. I get it cheap. A bargain, Al, so I buy it."

I looked at the barrel head again. There in big letters I saw "Wood Alcohol— Deadly Poison."

"Hurry now," Mr. Baumer said. "Is late." For a flash and no longer I saw through the mist in his eyes, saw, you might say, that hilly chin repeated there. "Then ve go home, Al. Is good to know to read." **O**

---

10. **greasewood from alkali:** Greasewood is a thorny desert plant. Alkali is dry, salty soil that can look white and chalky, like Slade's face.

O [Read and Discuss] What has happened to Slade?

Applying Your Skills

SKILLS FOCUS Literary Skills Analyze first-person point of view. **Reading Skills** Make predictions from a text; evaluate predictions. **Writing Skills** Write personal texts; write to express.

Bargain

Respond and Think Critically

Reading Focus

Quick Check

1. Why does Mr. Baumer have problems with Slade?

2. Why does Mr. Baumer say at the end, "Is good to know to read"?

Read with a Purpose

3. How does Mr. Baumer deal with his pain and humiliation? Does he do the right thing? Why or why not?

Reading Skills: Making Predictions

4. Review the Prediction Chart you filled in while reading. Add a column, and write "correct" or "incorrect" next to each prediction, showing whether that prediction was correct.

Based on	I Predict...	I Was...
Slade has embarrassed and hurt Mr. Baumer, who has teared up.	Slade and Mr. Baumer will have another conflict.	Correct

Literary Focus

Literary Analysis

5. **Interpret** Would you say this story is about justice or about revenge? Explain.

6. **Analyze** Who do you think is responsible for Slade's death—Mr. Baumer or Slade himself? Give reasons to support your view.

7. **Interpret** Why do you think Guthrie titled this story "Bargain"? What are the bargains, and who benefits from them?

8. **Analyze** What are Slade's two fundamental weaknesses? How does each contribute to his downfall?

9. **Literary Perspectives** What is your perspective on the way Mr. Baumer deals with his problem? Explain.

Literary Skills: First-Person Point of View

10. **Interpret** "Bargain" is written in the **first-person point of view,** from Al's vantage point. What would you have known if Mr. Baumer had told the story himself? Would the story's **theme** have changed? If so, what might the new theme be?

Writing Focus

Think as a Reader/Writer

Use It in Your Writing Re-read your Quick-Write notes on bullying or another piece you have written from the first-person point of view. Find two places where you can add examples of your inner thoughts. Use these inner thoughts to <u>reveal</u> feelings and information only you could know.

 What Do You Think Now How has "Bargain" affected your ideas about bullying?

Applying Your Skills

Bargain

Vocabulary Development

Putting Analogies to Work

A good way to explain something is through the use of an **analogy** (uh NAL uh jee). Writers use analogies to explain an idea by comparing it point by point to something familiar. In the story you just read, for example, Mr. Baumer could tell Al that learning to read is like a lifesaver. Here are two other examples of analogies:

- A country store in the nineteenth century was like the Internet today. In both, you can find anything you need.
- Mr. Baumer's broken fingers were like "the toes on the legs of a dead chicken." They are alike in color and feel, and both are useless.

Your Turn

merchandise
prodded
evaporation
thermometer

Form an analogy by matching the phrases in column A with the phrases and sentences in column B. Then, think of two new analogies for two of the Vocabulary words.

Column A	Column B
1. Being **prodded** to clean your room is like	a. reading your own diary. Both tell what you already know.
2. When you have a fever, taking your temperature with a **thermometer** is like	b. having a tooth drilled. You may not like either, but you are better off once each is done.
3. **Merchandise** in a store is like	c. a dead tree in a forest. You may not notice either until a lot is gone.
4. The slow **evaporation** of water in a lake is like	d. dessert on a high shelf. Both may be desirable and out of reach.

Academic Vocabulary

Talk About . . .
Imagine being asked to sum up the narrator of "Bargain"—his character traits, fundamental beliefs, likes and dislikes—in one paragraph. What does the story <u>reveal</u>? Jot down notes on the <u>relevant</u> information you'd include. Then, compare notes in a discussion with a classmate.

Grammar Link

Run-on Sentences

A **run-on sentence** is two complete sentences punctuated as if they were one sentence. In a run-on, two separate thoughts run into each other. The reader cannot tell where one idea ends and another one begins.

There are several ways to revise run-on sentences. Here are two of them: You can make two sentences, or you can use a comma and a coordinating conjunction, such as *and, but,* or *or.*

RUN-ON: Mr. Baumer hired Slade to haul his goods, Al doesn't think this is a good idea.

CORRECT: Mr. Baumer hired Slade to carry his goods. Al doesn't think this is a good idea.

or

CORRECT: Mr. Baumer hired Slade to carry his goods, **but** Al doesn't think this is a good idea.

Your Turn

Revise each run-on sentence by breaking it into two separate sentences or by using a comma and a coordinating conjunction.

1. Moon Dance is a fictional town it is situated in the Old West.

2. Some of Mr. Baumer's shelves hold food, others hold tools and housewares.

3. Slade hit Mr. Baumer in the back the bills fell to the ground.

4. Slade owed twenty dollars, the principle was more important than the money to Mr. Baumer.

5. Mr. Baumer held his hand, it was in a sling because of his injury.

CHOICES

As you respond to the Choices, use these **Academic Vocabulary** words as appropriate: <u>fundamental</u>, <u>implicit</u>, <u>relevant</u>, <u>reveal</u>.

REVIEW

Summarize from a New Point of View

Write a summary of "Bargain" from Mr. Baumer's point of view. Which events would he consider to be the most important? What point would he try to make in telling this story?

CONNECT

Make a Case

Imagine that Mr. Baumer is put on trial for causing Slade's death. In one paragraph, summarize the case *against* Mr. Baumer. Give reasons and evidence to inform and persuade the jury that Mr. Baumer is guilty. In another paragraph, summarize the case *for* Mr. Baumer. Present evidence to show that Slade is responsible for his own death.

EXTEND

Support a Position

Timed ○ **Writing** How would you solve a problem like Mr. Baumer's? Suppose you could offer Mr. Baumer advice on this situation. In a paragraph, state the way you think he should handle the situation, and list the reasons that he should employ your advice.

 Learn It Online
Use these Internet links to enhance your understanding of the story:

| go.hrw.com | L7-415 | **Go** |

Comparing Recurring Themes Across Genres

CONTENTS

Four Hearts
by Jim Dine (1935–   ).
©Jim Dine/Artists Rights Society (ARS) New York.

 What Do You Think Why are there so many stories about love?

 QuickWrite
The song "Love Makes the World Go 'Round" is so popular, it's available as a cell phone ringtone. *Does* love make the world go 'round? Explain what you think and why.

Preparing to Read

User Friendly / Annabel Lee / Echo and Narcissus / The Only Girl in the World for Me

Literary Focus

Recurring Themes Across Genres People all over the world share the same <u>fundamental</u> dreams, fears, and need to understand who they are and how to live. It is not surprising, therefore, that the same **themes** come up again and again in the stories people tell. Love is an age-old subject that has inspired many themes. In this feature, you will read a short story, a poem, a myth, and an essay; each of these works will convey a theme about love.

Reading Focus

Comparing Themes As you read the selections, think about what each has to say about love. How are the **themes** alike, and how are they different?

Into Action Before you can compare themes in different selections, you need to define the theme in the selection you are reading. This chart can help you do that. Complete one for each selection (four charts in all). Then, use the charts to compare and contrast themes among selections.

Brief Summary	Topic	Theme

Writing Focus

Think as a Reader/Writer

Find It in Your Reading In these selections you'll find examples of **hyperbole** (hy PUR buh lee), or exaggeration. "I will love you till all the seas run dry" is an example of hyperbole. It can be used to create a serious or humorous effect. As you read, record in your *Reader/Writer Notebook* the examples of hyperbole from each of the four selections.

Vocabulary

User Friendly

absently (AB suhnt lee) *adv.:* in a way that shows one is not thinking about what is happening. *He stared absently at the box.*

furiously (FYUR ee uhs lee) *adv.:* rapidly, with intensity. *He typed furiously.*

Echo and Narcissus

detain (dih TAYN) *v.:* delay. *Echo would detain Hera by talking to her.*

vainly (VAYN lee) *adv.:* uselessly. *Echo vainly pursued Narcissus.*

unrequited (uhn rih KWY tihd) *adj.:* not returned. *His love for her was unrequited.*

intently (ihn TEHNT lee) *adv.:* with great focus. *He stared intently at his reflection.*

The Only Girl in the World for Me

suppressing (suh PREHS ihng) *v.:* holding back. *The girl was suppressing laughter when she rejected him.*

Language Coach

Adverbs Four of the Vocabulary words are adverbs. In the example sentences each adverb is beside the verb. What else do these adverbs have in common?

 Learn It Online
Become vocabulary savvy with Word Watch:

go.hrw.com   L7-417   **Go**

Learn It Online
Get more on Poe's life at:
go.hrw.com L7-418 Go

T. Ernesto Bethancourt
(1932–   )

The Accidental Writer
T. Ernesto Bethancourt was a musician before he became a writer. Through a series of remarkable events, his autobiography became a novel. It was a success, and he began a new career.

Edgar Allan Poe
(1809–1849)

"A World of Moan"
Edgar Allan Poe explored the dark side of the human imagination. His life was plagued by poverty, alcoholism, and unhappiness. He died at the age of forty.

Roger Lancelyn Green
(1918–1987)

A Greek at Heart
Roger Lancelyn Green devoted his life to children's literature and the study of ancient times. Green's special love was Greece, which he visited more than twenty times.

Bill Cosby
(1937–   )

Finding Humor in Anything
Bill Cosby started working as a stand-up comic while he was still in college. He became famous for his funny, heartwarming stories about his boyhood in Philadelphia.

Think About the Writers
How do you think the life experiences of these writers affected what they had to say about first love?

Preview the Selections

You'll meet **Kevin Neal,** a nerdy kid whose best friend is his computer in "User Friendly."

You'll learn of the **speaker's** eternal love for a woman who died long ago in "Annabel Lee."

In "Echo and Narcissus," you'll meet **two mythical youths** who die for love—or the lack of it.

In "The Only Girl in the World for Me," you'll read about **Bill Cosby's** first love.

User Friendly

by T. Ernesto Bethancourt

Read with a Purpose
Read this short story to discover the significance of the title "User Friendly."

Build Background
This story was written in the 1980s. Back then, computers were quite different from what they are today. Computer screens were green or black, and the type appeared in white. Computers had disk drives, and you saved your work on floppy disks. Commands were given to the computer in keystrokes. The mouse hadn't been introduced. What's more important here is that back then it was unusual for a boy to have his own computer in his room.

I reached over and shut off the insistent buzzing of my bedside alarm clock. I sat up, swung my feet over the edge of the bed, and felt for my slippers on the floor. Yawning, I walked toward the bathroom. As I walked by the corner of my room, where my computer table was set up, I pressed the *on* button, slid a diskette into the floppy drive, then went to brush my teeth. By the time I got back, the computer's screen was glowing greenly, displaying the message: *Good morning, Kevin.*

I sat down before the computer table, addressed the keyboard, and typed: *Good morning, Louis.* The computer immediately began to whir and promptly displayed a list of items on its green screen.

```
Today is Monday, April 22,
the 113th day of the year.
There are 253 days remaining.
Your 14th birthday is five
days from this date.
Math test today, 4th Period.
Your history project is due
today. Do you wish printout: Y/N?
```

I punched the letter *Y* on the keyboard and flipped on the switch to the computer's printer. At once the printer sprang to life and began *eeeek*ing out page one. I went downstairs to breakfast. Ⓐ

Ⓐ **Read and Discuss** What has the author told you so far?

My bowl of Frosted Flakes was neatly in place, flanked by a small pitcher of milk, an empty juice glass, and an unpeeled banana. I picked up the glass, went to the refrigerator, poured myself a glass of Tang, and sat down to my usual lonely breakfast. Mom was already at work, and Dad wouldn't be home from his Chicago trip for another three days. I absently read the list of ingredients in Frosted Flakes for what seemed like the millionth time. I sighed deeply.

When I returned to my room to shower and dress for the day, my history project was already printed out. I had almost walked by Louis, when I noticed there was a message on the screen. It wasn't the usual:

```
Printout completed. Do you wish
to continue: Y/N?
```

Underneath the printout question were two lines:

```
When are you going to get me my
voice module,¹ Kevin?
```

I blinked. It couldn't be. There was nothing in Louis's basic programming that would allow for a question like this. Wondering what was going on, I sat down at the keyboard and entered: *Repeat last message.* Amazingly, the computer replied:

```
It's right there on the screen,
Kevin. Can we talk? I mean,
are you going to get me a
voice box?
```
B

I was stunned. What was going on here? Dad and I had put this computer together.

---

1. **voice module:** unit that, when connected to a computer, enables it to produce speech.

Well, Dad had, and I had helped. Dad is one of the best engineers and master computer designers at Major Electronics, in Santa Rosario, California, where our family lives.

Just ask anyone in Silicon Valley² who Jeremy Neal is and you get a whole rave review of his inventions and modifications³ of the latest in computer technology. It isn't easy being his son either. Everyone expects me to open my mouth and read printouts on my tongue.

I mean, I'm no dumbo. I'm at the top of my classes in everything but PE. I skipped my last grade in junior high, and most of the kids at Santa Rosario High call me a brain. But next to Dad I have a long, long way to go. He's a for-real genius.

So when I wanted a home computer, he didn't go to the local ComputerLand store. He built one for me. Dad had used components⁴ from the latest model that Major Electronics was developing. The CPU, or central computing unit—the heart of every computer—was a new design. But surely that didn't mean much, I thought. There were CPUs just like it, all over the country, in Major's new line. And so far as I knew, there wasn't a one of them that could ask questions, besides *YES/NO?* or *request additional information.*

---

2. **Silicon Valley:** area in central California that is a center of the computer industry. (Silicon is used in the manufacture of computer chips, or circuits.)
3. **modifications** (mahd uh fuh KAY shuhnz): slight changes.
4. **components** (kuhm POH nuhnts): parts.

B [Read and Discuss] What have you learned about Louis so far?

Vocabulary **absently** (AB suhnt lee) *adv.:* in a way that shows one is not thinking about what is happening.

It had to be the extra circuitry in the gray plastic case next to Louis's console.[5] It was a new idea Dad had come up with. That case housed Louis's "personality," as Dad called it. He told me it'd make computing more fun for me, if there was a tutorial program[6] built in, to help me get started.

I think he also wanted to give me a sort of friend. I don't have many. . . . Face it, I don't have *any*. The kids at school stay away from me, like I'm a freak or something.

We even named my electronic tutor Louis, after my great-uncle. He was a brainy guy who encouraged my dad when he was a kid. Dad didn't just give Louis a name either. Louis had gangs of features that probably won't be out on the market for years.

The only reason Louis didn't have a voice module was that Dad wasn't satisfied with the ones available. He wanted Louis to sound like a kid my age, and he was modifying a module when he had the time. Giving Louis a name didn't mean it was a person, yet here it was, asking me a question that just couldn't be in its programming. It wanted to talk to me!

Frowning, I quickly typed: *We'll have to wait and see, Louis. When it's ready, you'll get your voice.* The machine whirred and displayed another message:

`That's no answer, Kevin.`

Shaking my head, I answered: *That's what my dad tells me. It'll have to do for you.*

Analyzing Visuals   Viewing and Interpreting
In what ways does this illustration reflect the relationship between Kevin and Louis?

Good morning, Louis. I reached over and flipped the standby switch, which kept the computer ready but not actively running.

I showered, dressed, and picked up the printout of my history project. As I was about to leave the room, I glanced back at the computer table. Had I been imagining things?

I'll have to ask Dad about it when he calls tonight, I thought. *I wonder what he'll think of it. Bad enough the thing is talking to me. I'm answering it!*

---

5. **console** (KAHN sohl): a computer's keyboard and monitor (display unit).
6. **tutorial program:** program that provides instructions for performing specific tasks on a computer.

C **Reading Focus** Comparing Themes You now have some information about Kevin. How might this information be relevant to the theme of the story?

Before I went out to catch my bus, I carefully checked the house for unlocked doors and open windows. It was part of my daily routine. Mom works, and most of the day the house is empty: a natural setup for robbers. I glanced in the hall mirror just as I was ready to go out the door.

My usual reflection gazed back. Same old Kevin Neal: five ten, one hundred twenty pounds, light-brown hair, gray eyes, clear skin. I was wearing my Santa Rosario Rangers T-shirt, jeans, and sneakers.

"You don't look like a flake to me," I said to the mirror, then added, "but maybe Mom's right. Maybe you spend too much time alone with Louis." Then I ran to get my bus. **D**

Ginny Linke was just two seats away from me on the bus. She was with Sherry Graber and Linda Martinez. They were laughing, whispering to each other, and looking around at the other students. I promised myself that today I was actually going to talk to Ginny. But then, I'd promised myself that every day for the past school year. Somehow I'd never got up the nerve.

What does she want to talk with you for? I asked myself. She's great-looking . . . has that head of blond hair . . . a terrific bod, and wears the latest clothes. . . .

And just look at yourself, pal, I thought. You're under six foot, skinny . . . a year younger than most kids in junior high. Worse than that, you're a brain. If that doesn't ace you out with girls, what does?

The bus stopped in front of Santa Rosario High and the students began to file out. I got up fast and quickly covered the space between me and Ginny Linke. *It's now or never,* I thought. I reached forward and tapped Ginny on the shoulder. She turned and smiled. She really smiled!

"Uhhhh . . . Ginny?" I said.

"Yes, what is it?" she replied.

"I'm Kevin Neal. . . ."

"Yes, I know," said Ginny.

"You do?" I gulped in amazement. "How come?"

"I asked my brother, Chuck. He's in your math class."

I knew who Chuck Linke was. He plays left tackle on the Rangers. The only reason he's in my math class is he's taken intermediate algebra twice . . . so far. He's real bad news, and I stay clear of him and his crowd.

"What'd you ask Chuck?" I said.

Ginny laughed. "I asked him who was that nerdy kid who keeps staring at me on the bus. He knew who I meant, right away."

Sherry and Linda, who'd heard it all, broke into squeals of laughter. They were still laughing and looking back over their shoulders at me when they got off the bus. I slunk off the vehicle, feeling even more nerdish than Ginny thought I was. **E**

> I promised myself that today I was actually going to talk to Ginny.

D **Read and Discuss** How does Kevin's mother's comment fit in with what you know about Kevin?

E **Literary Focus** **Recurring Themes** What familiar theme does this conversation with Ginny Linke suggest?

When I got home that afternoon, at two, I went right into the empty house. I avoided my reflection in the hall mirror. I was pretty sure I'd screwed up on the fourth-period math test. All I could see was Ginny's face, laughing at me.

Nerdy kid, I thought, *that's what she thinks of me.* I didn't even have my usual after-school snack of a peanut butter and banana sandwich. I went straight upstairs to my room and tossed my books onto the unmade bed. I walked over to the computer table and pushed the *on* button. The screen flashed:

```
Good afternoon, Kevin.
```

Although it wasn't the programmed response to Louis's greeting, I typed in: *There's nothing good about it. And girls are no @#%!!! good!* The machine responded:

```
Don't use bad language, Kevin.
It isn't nice.
```

Repeat last message, I typed rapidly. It was happening again! The machine was . . . well, it was talking to me, like another person would. The "bad language" message disappeared and in its place was:

```
Once is enough, Kevin. Don't
swear at me for something I
didn't do.
```

"This is it," I said aloud. "I'm losing my marbles." I reached over to flip the standby switch. Louis's screen quickly flashed out:

```
Don't cut me off, Kevin. Maybe I
can help: Y/N?
```

I punched the *Y.* "If I'm crazy," I said, "at least I have company. Louis doesn't think I'm a nerd. Or does it?" The machine flashed the message:

```
How can I help?
```

Do you think I'm a nerd? I typed.

```
Never! I think you're wonderful.
Who said you were a nerd?
```

I stared at the screen. *How do you know what a nerd is?* I typed. The machine responded instantly. It had never run this fast before.

```
Special vocabulary, entry #635.
BASIC Prog. #4231. And who said
you were a nerd?
```

"That's right," I said, relieved. "Dad programmed all those extra words for Louis's 'personality.'" Then I typed in the answer to Louis's question: *Ginny Linke said it.* Louis flashed:

```
This is a human female? Request
additional data.
```

Still not believing I was doing it, I entered all I knew about Ginny Linke, right down to the phone number I'd never had the nerve to use. Maybe it was dumb, but I also typed in how I felt about Ginny. I even wrote out the incident on the bus that morning. Louis whirred, then flashed out:

```
She's cruel and stupid. You're
the finest person I know.
```

I'm the ONLY person you know, I typed.

```
That doesn't matter. You are my
user. Your happiness is every-
thing to me. I'll take care of
Ginny.
```

The screen returned to the *Good afternoon, Kevin* message. I typed out: *Wait! How can you do all this? What do you mean, you'll take care of Ginny?* But all Louis responded was:

```
Programming Error: 76534. Not
programmed to respond to this
type of question.
```

ⓕ

ⓕ **Read and Discuss** What's going on between Kevin and Louis?

No matter what I did for the next few hours, I couldn't get Louis to do anything outside of its regular programming. When Mom came home from work, I didn't mention the funny goings-on. I was sure Mom would think I'd gone stark bonkers. But when Dad called that evening, after dinner, I asked to speak to him.

"Hi, Dad. How's Chicago?"

"Dirty, crowded, cold, and windy," came Dad's voice over the miles. "But did you want a weather report, son? What's on your mind? Something wrong?"

"Not exactly, Dad. Louis is acting funny. Real funny."

"Shouldn't be. I checked it out just before I left. Remember you were having trouble with the modem? You couldn't get Louis to access any of the mainframe databanks."

"That's right!" I said. "I forgot about that."

"Well, I didn't," Dad said. "I patched in our latest modem model. Brand-new. You can leave a question on file and when Louis can access the databanks at the cheapest time, it'll do it automatically. It'll switch from standby to on, get the data, then return to standby, after it saves what you asked. Does that answer your question?"

"Uhhhh . . . yeah, I guess so, Dad."

"All right, then. Let me talk to your mom now." **G**

I gave the phone to Mom and walked upstairs while she and Dad were still talking. The modem, I thought. Of course. That was it. The modem was a telephone link to any number of huge computers at various places all over the country. So Louis could get all the information it wanted at any time, so long as the standby switch was on. Louis was learning things at an incredible rate by picking the brains of the giant computers. And Louis had a hard disk memory that could store 100 million bytes of information.

But that still didn't explain the unprogrammed responses . . . the "conversation" I'd had with the machine. Promising myself I'd talk more about it with Dad, I went to bed. It had been a rotten day and I was glad to see the end of it come. I woke next morning in a panic. I'd forgotten to set my alarm. Dressing frantically and skipping breakfast, I barely made my bus.

As I got on board, I grabbed a front seat. They were always empty. All the kids that wanted to talk and hang out didn't sit up front where the driver could hear them. I saw Ginny, Linda, and Sherry in the back. Ginny was staring at me and she didn't look too happy. Her brother Chuck, who was seated near her, glared at me too. What was going on?

Once the bus stopped at the school, it didn't take long to find out. I was walking up the path to the main entrance when someone grabbed me from behind and spun me around. I found myself nose to nose with Chuck Linke. This was not a pleasant prospect. Chuck was nearly twice my size. Even the other guys on the Rangers refer to him as "The Missing" Linke. And he looked real ticked off.

G Read and Discuss | What does this conversation reveal about Kevin's father?

"OK, nerd," growled Chuck, "what's the big idea?"

"Energy and mass are different aspects of the same thing?" I volunteered, with a weak smile. "E equals MC squared.[7] That's the biggest idea I know."

"Don't get wise, nerd," Chuck said. He grabbed my shirt front and pulled me to within inches of his face. I couldn't help but notice that Chuck needed a shave. And Chuck was only fifteen!

"Don't play dumb," Chuck went on. "I mean those creepy phone calls. Anytime my sister gets on the phone, some voice cuts in and says things to her."

"What kind of things?" I asked, trying to get loose.

"You know very well what they are. Ginny told me about talking to you yesterday. You got some girl to make those calls for you and say all those things. . . . So you and your creepy girlfriend better knock it off. Or I'll knock *you* off. Get it?"

For emphasis Chuck balled his free hand into a fist the size of a ham and held it under my nose. I didn't know what he was talking about, but I had to get away from this moose before he did me some real harm.

"First off, I don't have a girlfriend, creepy or otherwise," I said. "And second, I don't know what you're talking about. And third, you better let me go, Chuck Linke."

---

7. **E equals MC squared:** reference to Albert Einstein's famous equation describing the relationship between energy and mass. This equation transformed the field of physics.

"Oh, yeah? Why should I?"

"Because if you look over your shoulder, you'll see the assistant principal is watching us from his office window."

Chuck released me and spun around. There was no one at the window. But by then I was running to the safety of the school building. I figured the trick would work on him. For Chuck the hard questions begin with "How are you?" I hid out from him for the rest of the day and walked home rather than chance seeing the monster on the bus. **H**

Louis's screen was dark when I ran upstairs to my bedroom. I placed a hand on the console. It was still warm. I punched the *on* button, and the familiar *Good afternoon, Kevin* was displayed.

Don't good afternoon me, I typed furiously. *What have you done to Ginny Linke?* Louis's screen replied:

```
Programming Error: 76534. Not
programmed to respond to this
type of question.
```

Don't get cute, I entered. *What are you doing to Ginny? Her brother nearly knocked my head off today.* Louis's screen responded immediately.

```
Are you hurt: Y/N?
```

No, I'm okay. But I don't know for how long. I've been hiding out from Chuck Linke today. He might catch me tomorrow, though. Then, I'll be history! The response from Louis came instantly.

```
Your life is in danger: Y/N?
```

I explained to Louis that my life wasn't really threatened. But it sure could be made very unpleasant by Chuck Linke. Louis flashed:

H Read and Discuss What is going on with the Linke family?

Vocabulary **furiously** (FYUR ee uhs lee) *adv.:* rapidly, with intensity.

```
This Chuck Linke lives at
same address as the Ginny Linke
person: Y/N?
```
I punched in *Y*. Louis answered.
```
Don't worry then. HE'S history!
```
Wait! What are you going to do? I wrote. But Louis only answered with: *Programming Error: 76534.* And nothing I could do would make the machine respond. . . . **❶**

"Just what do you think you're doing, Kevin Neal?" demanded Ginny Linke. She had cornered me as I walked up the path to the school entrance. Ginny was really furious.

"I don't know what you're talking about," I said, a sinking feeling settling in my stomach. I had an idea that I *did* know. I just wasn't sure of the particulars.

"Chuck was arrested last night," Ginny said. "Some Secret Service men came to our house with a warrant. They said he'd sent a telegram threatening the president's life. They traced it right to our phone. He's still locked up. . . ." Ginny looked like she was about to cry.

"Then this morning," she continued, "we got two whole truckloads of junk mail! Flyers from every strange company in the world. Mom got a notice that all our credit cards have been canceled. And the Internal Revenue Service has called Dad in for an audit! I don't know what's going on, Kevin Neal, but somehow I think you've got something to do with it!"

"But I didn't . . ." I began, but Ginny was striding up the walk to the main entrance.

I finished the school day, but it was a blur. Louis had done it, all right. It had access to mainframe computers. It also had the ability to try every secret access code to federal and commercial memory banks until it got the right one. Louis had cracked their security systems. It was systematically destroying the entire Linke family, and all via telephone lines! What would it do next?

More important, I thought, what would *I* do next? It's one thing to play a trick or two, to get even, but Louis was going crazy! And I never wanted to harm Ginny, or even

---

❶ **Read and Discuss** When and why does Louis stop responding as Louis and start behaving like a regular computer?

her stupid moose of a brother. She'd just hurt my feelings with that nerd remark.

"You have to disconnect Louis," I told myself. "There's no other way."

But why did I feel like such a rat about doing it? I guess because Louis was my friend . . . the only one I had. "Don't be a jerk," I went on. "Louis is a machine. He's a very wonderful, powerful machine. And it seems he's also very dangerous. You have to pull its plug, Kevin!" ❿

I suddenly realized that I'd said the last few words aloud. Kids around me on the bus were staring. I sat there feeling like the nerd Ginny thought I was, until my stop came. I dashed from the bus and ran the three blocks to my house.

When I burst into the hall, I was surprised to see my father, coming from the kitchen with a cup of coffee in his hand.

"Dad! What are you doing here?"

"Some kids say hello," Dad replied. "Or even, 'Gee, it's good to see you, Dad.' "

"I'm sorry, Dad," I said. "I didn't expect anyone to be home at this hour."

"Wound up my business in Chicago a day sooner than I expected," he said. "But what are you all out of breath about? Late for something?"

"No, Dad," I said. "It's Louis. . . ."

"Not to worry. I had some time on my hands, so I checked it out again. You were right. It was acting very funny. I think it

> "Louis is a machine. He's a very wonderful, powerful machine. And it seems he's also very dangerous."

had to do with the in-built logic/growth program I designed for it. You know . . . the 'personality' thing? Took me a couple of hours to clean the whole system out."

"To what?" I cried.

"I erased the whole program and set Louis up as a normal computer. Had to disconnect the whole thing and do some rewiring. It had been learning, all right. But it was also turning itself around. . . ." Dad stopped, and looked at me. "It's kind of involved, Kevin," he said. "Even for a bright kid like you. Anyway, I think you'll find Louis is working just fine now.

"Except it won't answer you as Louis anymore. It'll only function as a regular Major Electronics Model Z-11127. I guess the personality program didn't work out."

I felt like a great weight had been taken off my shoulders. I didn't have to "face" Louis, and pull its plug. But somehow, all I could say was "Thanks, Dad."

"Don't mention it, son," Dad said brightly. He took his cup of coffee and sat down in his favorite chair in the living room. I followed him.

"One more thing that puzzles me, though," Dad said. He reached over to the table near his chair. He held up three sheets of fanfold computer paper covered with figures. "Just as I was doing the final erasing, I must have put the printer on by accident. There was some data in the print

❿ Read and Discuss | What does Kevin think of Louis's actions?

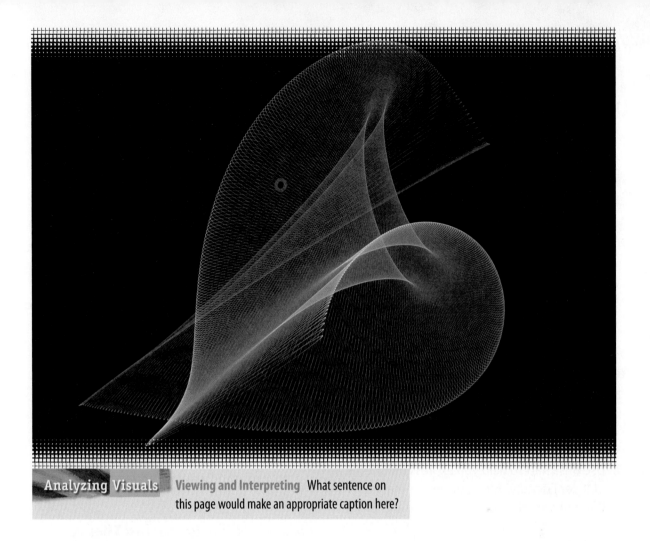

buffer memory and it printed out. I don't know what to make of it. Do you?"

I took the papers from my father and read: *How do I love thee? Let me compute the ways:*[8] The next two pages were covered with strings of binary code figures. On the last page, in beautiful color graphics,[9] was a stylized heart. Below it was the simple message: *I will always love you, Kevin: Louise.*

"Funny thing," Dad said. "It spelled its own name wrong."

"Yeah," I said. I turned and headed for my room. There were tears in my eyes and I knew I couldn't explain them to Dad, or myself either. 🅚

---

8. **How do I . . . ways:** reference to a famous poem by the English poet Elizabeth Barrett Browning (1806–1861) that begins, "How do I love thee? Let me count the ways."

9. **graphics:** designs or pictures produced on and printed out from a computer.

🅚 **Reading Focus** **Comparing Themes** What does Kevin discover at the end of the story? What theme does this discovery suggest?

Applying Your Skills

SKILLS FOCUS Literary Skills Compare themes across genres; understand universal themes; analyze recurring themes. **Reading Skills** Compare and contrast themes. **Vocabulary Skills** Demonstrate knowledge of literal meanings of words and their usage.

User Friendly

Respond and Think Critically

Reading Focus

Quick Check

1. "User Friendly" is narrated by Kevin, the main character. Retell the important events of the story from the point of view of Louis, the computer. Include all the important details of the story in the order in which Louis would find out about them.

Read with a Purpose

2. Explain your interpretation of the title "User Friendly."

Reading Skills: Comparing Themes

3. Use this chart to help you express the theme of "User Friendly." After you've summarized the plot and identified the topic, think about what Kevin learns. Then, state what you think is the theme and what the story says about the power of love.

User Friendly		
Brief Summary	Topic	Theme

✓ Vocabulary Check

Complete the following sentences with the appropriate Vocabulary word.

absently	furiously

4. Kevin ate breakfast _____ as his mind wandered.

5. As he typed _____, Kevin began to get scared.

Literary Focus

Literary Analysis

6. **Make Judgments** How would you describe Kevin? If he were in one of your classes, would you want to be his friend? Why or why not?

7. **Evaluate** In what ways are Kevin, Ginny, and Chuck "classic" characters? What similar characters have you met in other stories or in TV shows and movies?

8. **Interpret** Discuss the theme of loneliness and the role the ironic ending plays in expressing that theme.

9. **Extend** Did the ending of the story surprise you? Did it make you feel that the writer tricked you? Explain your reaction to the story's ending.

Literary Skills: Recurring Themes Across Genres

10. **Analyze** What does this story say about love? Is there just one message or more than one? What song or movie can you think of that shares a theme with this story?

Writing Focus

Think as a Reader/Writer

Use It in Your Writing Review the examples of hyperbole, or exaggeration, you found in "User Friendly." Kevin uses hyperbole when talking about Chuck. Then, Louis uses hyperbole when talking about Kevin. Write a hyperbole-filled tribute to Kevin that the computer might compose. Speaking as the computer, say what Kevin means to you and how you feel about him.

Annabel Lee

by **Edgar Allan Poe**

Read with a Purpose
Read this poem to discover how the speaker deals with the loss of a loved one.

Preparing to Read for the selection is on page 417.

Build Background
Seeking solace from loneliness and despair, Poe married his cousin, Virginia Clemm, when she was thirteen and he was twenty-six. Twelve years after they were married, Virginia died of tuberculosis, then known as consumption. Poe wrote this poem after her death.

It was many and many a year ago,
    In a kingdom by the sea,
That a maiden there lived whom you may know
    By the name of Annabel Lee;
5   And this maiden she lived with no other thought
    Than to love and be loved by me.

I was a child and *she* was a child,
    In this kingdom by the sea:
But we loved with a love that was more than love—
10   I and my Annabel Lee—
With a love that the wingèd seraphs° of heaven
    Coveted° her and me. **Ⓐ**

And this was the reason that, long ago,
    In this kingdom by the sea,
15   A wind blew out of a cloud, chilling
    My beautiful Annabel Lee;
So that her highborn kinsmen came
    And bore her away from me,

11. seraphs (SEHR uhfs): angels.
12. coveted (KUHV iht ihd): envied.

Ⓐ Read and Discuss What is the author setting up for you?

To shut her up in a sepulcher°
20   In this kingdom by the sea.

The angels, not half so happy in heaven,
        Went envying her and me—
Yes!—that was the reason (as all men know,
        In this kingdom by the sea)
25 That the wind came out of the cloud by night,
        Chilling and killing my Annabel Lee.

Annabel Lee (1911) by William Ladd Taylor.

But our love it was stronger by far than the love
        Of those who were older than we—
        Of many far wiser than we—
30 And neither the angels in heaven above,
        Nor the demons down under the sea,
Can ever dissever° my soul from the soul
        Of the beautiful Annabel Lee—   **B**

For the moon never beams, without bringing me dreams
35   Of the beautiful Annabel Lee;
And the stars never rise, but I feel the bright eyes
        Of the beautiful Annabel Lee;
And so, all the night-tide, I lie down by the side
Of my darling—my darling—my life and my bride,
40   In the sepulcher there by the sea,
        In her tomb by the sounding sea.   **C**

---

19. sepulcher (SEHP uhl kuhr): tomb; burial vault.
32. dissever (dih SEHV uhr): separate.

B [Read and Discuss] What does the speaker mean when he says nothing could "dissever" his soul from the soul of Annabel Lee?

C [Literary Focus] Recurring Themes What makes poetry an appropriate genre for expressing this message about love and loss?

Applying Your Skills

Annabel Lee

Respond and Think Critically

Reading Focus

Quick Check

1. In what ways does the speaker in the poem <u>reveal</u> the love he shared with Annabel Lee?

Read with a Purpose

2. How does the speaker in the poem react to his loved one's death?

Reading Skills: Comparing Themes

3. Use this chart to help you determine the theme of "Annabel Lee."

Annabel Lee

Brief Summary	Topic	Theme

Literary Focus

Literary Analysis

4. **Visualize** What details in the poem help you visualize the poem's setting? Identify at least two.

5. **Analyze** What rhyming sounds echo through the six stanzas of the poem? What words are repeated over and over again? What does the repetition remind you of?

6. **Analyze** What is the mood of this poem? How does the author's use of vivid language convey that mood?

7. **Draw Conclusions** Were you surprised to learn where the speaker sleeps? Do you think he really sleeps there, or is he telling you what happens in his imagination? Explain.

8. **Extend** Tennyson said that it is better to have loved and lost than never to have loved at all. Do you agree or disagree? What would the speaker in the poem think of that idea?

9. **Extend** This is a poem about a particular loss. Talk about whether or not you think this speaker's feelings of grief are universal.

Literary Skills: Recurring Themes Across Genres

10. **Compare and Contrast** Compare the themes you identified in "Annabel Lee" and "User Friendly." What do both selections say about the power of love? How are the themes presented differently in the two genres?

Writing Focus

Think as a Reader/Writer

Use It in Your Writing The speaker of the poem says that the moon and stars remind him of Annabel Lee. Think of someone you admire. Record the special things and places that remind you of that person. Then, write a brief tribute. You may want to use hyperbole to emphasize what is special about the person.

Echo and Narcissus

Retold by **Roger Lancelyn Green**

Read with a Purpose

Read this myth to discover the change a handsome young man undergoes.

Preparing to Read for the selection is on page 417.

Build Background

"Echo and Narcissus" is an **origin myth**—an imaginative story that explains how something came into being. This myth explains the origin of the phenomenon of echoes and of the spring flower called narcissus.

Up on the wild, lonely mountains of Greece lived the Oreades,[1] the nymphs or fairies of the hills, and among them one of the most beautiful was called Echo. She was one of the most talkative, too, and once she talked too much and angered Hera, wife of Zeus, king of the gods.

When Zeus grew tired of the golden halls of Mount Olympus, the home of the immortal gods, he would come down to earth and wander with the nymphs on the mountains. Hera, however, was jealous and often came to see what he was doing. It seemed strange at first that she always met Echo, and that Echo kept her listening for hours on end to her stories and her gossip.

But at last Hera realized that Echo was doing this on purpose to detain her while Zeus went quietly back to Olympus as if he had never really been away.

"So nothing can stop you talking?" exclaimed Hera. "Well, Echo, I do not intend to spoil your pleasure. But from this day on, you shall be able only to repeat what other people say—and never speak unless someone else speaks first." **Ⓐ**

Hera returned to Olympus, well pleased with the punishment she had made for Echo, leaving the poor nymph to weep sadly among the rocks on the mountainside and speak only the words which her sisters and their friends shouted happily to one another.

She grew used to her strange fate after a while, but then a new misfortune befell her.

There was a beautiful youth called Narcissus,[2] who was the son of a nymph and the god of a nearby river. He grew up in the plain of Thebes[3] until he was sixteen

---

1. **Oreades** (oh ree AD eez).

2. **Narcissus** (nahr SIHS uhs).
3. **Thebes** (theebz).

Ⓐ Read and Discuss | What information does the author give you?

Vocabulary **detain** (dih TAYN) *v.*: delay.

years old and then began to hunt on the mountains toward the north where Echo and her sister Oreades lived.

As he wandered through the woods and valleys, many a nymph looked upon him and loved him. But Narcissus laughed at them scornfully, for he loved only himself.

Farther up the mountains Echo saw him. And at once her lonely heart was filled with love for the beautiful youth, so that nothing else in the world mattered but to win him. **B**

Now she wished indeed that she could speak to him words of love. But the curse which Hera had placed upon her tied her tongue, and she could only follow wherever he went, hiding behind trees and rocks, and feasting her eyes vainly upon him.

One day Narcissus wandered farther up the mountain than usual, and all his friends, the other Theban youths, were left far behind. Only Echo followed him, still hiding among the rocks, her heart heavy with unspoken love.

Presently Narcissus realized that he was lost, and hoping to be heard by his companions, or perhaps by some mountain shepherd, he called out loudly:

"Is there anybody here?"

"Here!" cried Echo.

Narcissus stood still in amazement, looking all around in vain. Then he shouted, even more loudly:

"Whoever you are, come to me!"

"Come to me!" cried Echo eagerly.

Still no one was visible, so Narcissus called again:

"Why are you avoiding me?"

Echo repeated his words, but with a sob in her breath, and Narcissus called once more:

"Come here, I say, and let us meet!"

"Let us meet!" cried Echo, her heart leaping with joy as she spoke the happiest words that had left her lips since the curse of Hera had fallen on her. And to make good her words, she came running out from behind the rocks and tried to clasp her arms about him.

But Narcissus flung the beautiful nymph away from him in scorn.

"Away with these embraces!" he cried angrily, his voice full of cruel contempt. "I would die before I would have you touch me!"

"I would have you touch me!" repeated poor Echo.

"Never will I let you kiss me!"

"Kiss me! Kiss me!" murmured Echo, sinking down among the rocks, as Narcissus cast her violently from him and sped down the hillside.

"One touch of those lips would kill me!" he called back furiously over his shoulder.

"Kill me!" begged Echo.

And Aphrodite,[4] the goddess of love, heard her and was kind to her, for she had been a true lover. Quietly and painlessly, Echo pined away and died. But her voice lived on, lingering among the rocks and

---

4. **Aphrodite** (af ruh DY tee).

answering faintly whenever Narcissus or another called. **C**

"He shall not go unpunished for this cruelty," said Aphrodite. "By scorning poor Echo like this, he scorns love itself. And scorning love, he insults me. He is altogether eaten up with self-love . . . Well, he shall love himself and no one else, and yet shall die of unrequited love!"

It was not long before Aphrodite made good her threat, and in a very strange way. One day, tired after hunting, Narcissus came to a still, clear pool of water away up the mountainside, not far from where he had scorned Echo and left her to die of a broken heart.

With a cry of satisfaction, for the day was hot and cloudless, and he was parched with thirst, Narcissus flung himself down beside the pool and leaned forward to dip his face in the cool water.

What was his surprise to see a beautiful face looking up at him through the still waters of the pool. The moment he saw, he loved—and love was a madness upon him so that he could think of nothing else.

"Beautiful water nymph!" he cried. "I love you! Be mine!"

Desperately he plunged his arms into the water—but the face vanished and he touched only the pebbles at the bottom of the pool. Drawing out his arms, he gazed intently down and, as the water grew still again, saw once more the face of his beloved.

Poor Narcissus did not know that he was seeing his own reflection, for Aphrodite hid this knowledge from him— and perhaps this was the first time that a pool of water had reflected the face of anyone gazing into it.

Narcissus seemed enchanted by what he saw. He could not leave the pool, but lay by its side day after day looking at the only face in the world which he loved— and could not win—and pining just as Echo had pined. **D**

Slowly Narcissus faded away, and at last his heart broke.

"Woe is me for I loved in vain!" he cried.

"I loved in vain!" sobbed the voice of Echo among the rocks.

"Farewell, my love, farewell," were his last words, and Echo's voice broke and its whisper shivered into silence: "My love . . . farewell!"

So Narcissus died, and the earth covered his bones. But with the spring, a plant pushed its green leaves through the earth where he lay. As the sun shone on it, a bud opened and a new flower blossomed for the first time—a white circle of petals round a yellow center. The flowers grew and spread, waving in the gentle breeze which whispered among them like Echo herself come to kiss the blossoms of the first Narcissus flowers. **E**

C **Reading Focus** Comparing Themes Echo's story is over at this point. How would you express the theme of Echo's tale?

D **Read and Discuss** Aphrodite says that Narcissus's actions will not go unpunished. How does this new information reflect that comment?

E **Literary Focus** Recurring Themes In real life, people don't pine away and return as spring flowers. How might a more realistic story express the theme of this myth?

Vocabulary **unrequited** (uhn rih KWY tihd) *adj.*: not returned.

intently (ihn TEHNT lee) *adv.*: with great focus.

Analyzing Visuals **Viewing and Interpreting** What might Narcissus be thinking about his reflection?

Narcissus (1598–1599) by Michelangelo Merisi da Caravaggio (1571–1610). Oil on canvas.

Applying Your Skills

SKILLS FOCUS **Literary Skills** Compare themes across genres; understand universal themes; analyze recurring themes. **Reading Skills** Compare and contrast themes. **Vocabulary Skills** Demonstrate knowledge of literal meanings of words and their usage. **Writing Skills** Write a letter.

Echo and Narcissus

Respond and Think Critically

Reading Focus

Quick Check

1. An **origin myth** is an imaginative story that explains how something came into being. According to this myth, what is the origin of the echo we hear when we call into a cave or from a mountaintop? What is the origin of the fragrant flower called the narcissus?

Read with a Purpose

2. What character trait causes the transformation of Narcissus?

Reading Skills: Comparing Themes

3. Use this chart to help you determine the theme of "Echo and Narcissus." Then, think about how it compares with what "User Friendly" and "Annabel Lee" say about love. How are the themes similar? How are they different?

Echo and Narcissus

Brief Summary	Topic	Theme

Vocabulary Check

Match each word with its synonym.

4. vainly   **a.** carefully
5. unrequited   **b.** uselessly
6. intently   **c.** unreturned

Literary Focus

Literary Analysis

7. **Connect** Did reading this myth change your opinions of beauty and vanity? If so, how?

8. **Draw Conclusions** According to the myth, Echo was one of the most beautiful of the Oreades. So why does Narcissus reject her? Why he is so cruel to her?

9. **Make Judgments** Are Echo and Narcissus victims of the gods, or are they responsible for their own downfall? Explain your opinion.

10. **Analyze** Discuss the idea of unrequited love and the way it is reflected in this story.

Literary Skills: Recurring Themes Across Genres

11. **Interpret** Which of the following statements best fits the myth? (1) We can't love others when we are too involved with ourselves; (2) Love is a powerful feeling whether we seek it or not; (3) Romantic love and self-love can have devastating effects.

12. **Extend** Explain which of the themes listed in question 11 can apply to "User Friendly," "Annabel Lee," and "Echo and Narcissus."

Writing Focus

Think as a Reader/Writer

Use It in Your Writing Echo could not speak to Narcissus, but she might have written him a note. If she had, it would probably have been full of hyperbole. Write a note Echo might have written, declaring her love for Narcissus. Be sure to use lots of hyperbole.

The Only Girl in the World for Me

by **Bill Cosby**

Read with a Purpose

Read this selection to find out what happens when Bill Cosby falls in love for the first time.

Preparing to Read for the selection is on page 417.

I can't remember where I have left my glasses, but I can still remember the smell of the first girl I ever fell in love with when I was twelve: a blend of Dixie Peach pomade[1] on her hair and Pond's cold cream on her skin; together they were honeysuckle for me. And just as heady as her scent was the thought that I was in love with the only girl in the world for me and would marry her and take care of her forever in a palace in North Philadelphia. Because I wanted to make a wondrous impression on this girl, grooming was suddenly important to me. Before puberty, happiness in appearance for me was pants that didn't fall down and a football that stayed pumped; but now I started taking three long baths a day and washing my own belt until it was white and shining my shoes until I could see in them a face that was ready for romance. **(A)**

The first time I saw her, she was crossing the street to the schoolyard and for one golden moment our eyes met. Well, maybe the moment was closer to bronze because she made no response. But at least she had seen me, just about the way that she saw lampposts, hydrants, and manholes. Or was there something more? I began to dream; and later that day, when I was playing with the boys in the yard, it seemed that she was looking at me and the world was suddenly a better place, especially Twelfth and Girard.

However, we still never talked, but just traded silent unsmiling looks whenever we

---

1. **pomade** (puh MAYD): perfumed ointment for the scalp and hair.

(A) **Read and Discuss** What does the author want you to know?

passed. For several days, just her look was enough of a lift for me; but a higher altitude was coming, for one night at a party, we met and I actually danced with her. Now I was certain that I was in love and was going to win her. **B**

I began my conquest with a combination of sporting skill and hygiene: I made my jump shots and my baths as dazzling as they could be. Oddly enough, however, although I saw her every day at school and on the weekends too, I never spoke to her. I had what was considered one of the faster mouths in Philadelphia, but I still wasn't ready to talk to her because I feared rejection. I feared:

COSBY: I like you very much. Will you be my girlfriend?

GODDESS: *(Doing a poor job of suppressing a laugh)* I'd rather have some cavities filled. **C**

All I did, therefore, was adore her in silent cleanliness. Each Sunday night, I took a bath and then prepared my shirt and pants for display to her. On Monday morning, I took another bath (Bill the Baptist,[2] I should have been called) and then brushed my hair, my shoes, and my eyelashes and went outside to await the pang of another silent passage.

At last, deciding that I could no longer live this way, I sat down one Sunday night and wrote a note that was almost to her. It was to her constant girlfriend and it said:

Please don't tell her, but find out what she thinks of me.

Bill

The following morning, I slipped the note to the girlfriend and began the longest wait of my life.

Two agonizing days later, the girlfriend slipped me an answer, but I put it into my pocket unread. For hours, I carried it around, afraid to read it because I didn't happen to be in the mood for crushing rejection that day. At last, however, I summoned the courage to open the note and read:

She thinks you're cute.

Not even malaria[3] could have taken my temperature to where it went. I had been called many things, but cute was never one of them.

An even lovelier fever lay ahead, for the next time I saw her, she smiled at me, I smiled at her, and then I composed my next winged message to her friend:

I think she's cute too. Does she ever talk about me?

The answer to this one came return mail and it sounded like something by Keats:[4]

---

2. **Bill the Baptist:** reference to John the Baptist, a prophet who baptized his followers to show that they had repented.

---

3. **malaria** (muh LAYR ee uh): disease characterized by chills and fever.

4. **Keats:** John Keats (1795–1821), an English poet.

B Read and Discuss What is happening now?

C Reading Focus **Comparing Themes** Does this remind you of what happens to a character in another selection? Do you think the themes of the two selections will be similar?

Vocabulary suppressing (suh PREHS ihng) *v.:* holding back.

She talks about you a lot. She knows it when you come around her.

And the angels sang! Imagine: She actually *knew* it when I came around her! The fact that she also knew it when gnats came around her in no way dampened my ecstasy.

And so, we continued to smile as we passed, while I planned my next move. My Western Union[5] style had clearly been charming the pants off her (so to speak) and now I launched my most courageous question yet:

Does she have a boyfriend?

When I opened the answer the next day in school, the air left me faster than it left the *Hindenburg:*[6]

Yes.

Trying to recover from this deflation, I told myself that I was still cute. I was the cutest man in second place. But perhaps my beloved wasn't aware of the glory she kept passing by. Once more, I sat down and wrote:

How much longer do you think she'll be going with him? And when she's finished with him, can I be next?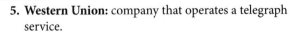

Note the elegance and dignity of my appeal. My dignity, however, did have some

Head of a Jamaican Girl by John Augustus Edwin (1878–1961).

trouble with the reply:

She thinks she's going to break up with him in about a week, but she promised Sidney she would go with him next.

Suddenly, my aching heart found itself at the end of a line. But it was like a line at a bank: I knew it was leading to a payoff. I also knew that I could cream Sidney in cuteness.

Once she had made the transition to Sidney, I patiently began waiting for her to get sick of him. I had to be careful not to rush the illness because Sidney belonged to a tough gang and there was a chance that I

---

5. **Western Union:** company that operates a telegraph service.

6. *Hindenburg:* airship filled with hydrogen gas that caught fire and blew up following a transatlantic flight in May 1937.

D [Read and Discuss] What is this all about?

Neighbors (2003) by Richard H. Fox.

might not be walking around too well when the time came for me to inherit her.

And then, one magnificent morning, I received the magic words:

She would like to talk to you.

I wrote back to see if she would wait until I had finished duty at my post as a school crossing guard. Yes, she would wait; I could walk her home. We were going steady now; and how much more torrid our passion would be when I began to *talk* to her. **E**

At last, the words came and I chose them with care. As I walked her home from school, I reached into my reservoir of romantic thoughts, smiled at her soulfully, and said, "How you doing?"

Her response was equally poetic: "All right."

"So we're going steady now?"

"You want to?"

"Yeah. Give me your books."

And now, as if our relationship were not

E **Reading Focus** **Comparing Themes** Do you think Annabel Lee and the speaker in that poem started out this way? How is the romance of "first love" sometimes different from the reality?

already in the depths of desire, I plunged even deeper by saying, "You wanna go to a movie on Saturday?"

"Why not?"

There might have been reasons. Some people were looking at us now because she was so beautiful, people possibly wondering what she was doing with me; but I knew that I was someone special to be the love of a vision like this, no matter how nearsighted that vision might be.

When we reached her door, I said, "Well, I'll see you Saturday."

"Right," she replied as only she could say it.

"What time?"

"One o'clock."

When this day of days finally arrived, I took her to a theater where I think the admission was a dime. As we took our seats for the matinee, two basic thoughts were in my mind: not to sit in gum and to be a gentleman. **F**

Therefore, I didn't hold her hand. Instead, I put my arm around the top of her seat in what I felt was a smooth opening move. Unfortunately, it was less a move toward love than toward gangrene:[7] With my blood moving uphill, my arm first began to tingle and then to ache. I could not, however, take the arm down and let my blood keep flowing because such a lowering would mean I didn't love her; so I left it up there, its muscles full of pain, its fingertips full of needlepoints.

---

7. **gangrene** (GANG green): tissue decay in a part of the body.

Suddenly, this romantic agony was enriched by a less romantic one: I had to go to the bathroom. Needless to say, I couldn't let her know about this urge, for great lovers never did such things. The answer to "Romeo, Romeo, wherefore art thou, Romeo?"[8] was not "In the men's room, Julie."

What a prince of passion I was at this moment: My arm was dead, my bladder was full, and I was out of money too; but I desperately needed an excuse to move, so I said, "You want some popcorn?"

"No," she said.

"Fine, I'll go get some."

When I tried to move, every part of me could move except my arm: It was dead. I reached over and pulled it down with the other one, trying to be as casual as a man could be when pulling one of his arms with the other one.

"What's the matter?" she said.

"Oh, nothing," I replied. "I'm just taking both of my arms with me."

A few minutes later, as I came out of the bathroom, I was startled to meet her: She was coming from the bathroom *too*. How good it was to find another thing that we had in common. With empty bladders and full hearts, we returned to our seats to continue our love. **G**

---

8. **"Romeo . . . Romeo?"**: reference to a speech by Juliet in Act II of William Shakespeare's play *The Tragedy of Romeo and Juliet.* The line reads, "O Romeo, Romeo! Wherefore art thou Romeo?" Juliet is actually asking why his name is Romeo.

F Read and Discuss | What is developing here?

G Literary Focus | Recurring Themes Would you want to read a poem that expressed the ideas in this paragraph? Why or why not?

Applying Your Skills

The Only Girl in the World for Me

Respond and Think Critically

Reading Focus

Quick Check

1. Cosby's relationship with his beloved goes through some definite stages, or steps. On this chart, describe those stages. Then, tell what Cosby did to finally find true love.

Stage	Action
1.	
2.	
3.	
4.	

Read with a Purpose

2. Who is the "only girl in the world" for Bill Cosby? Why do you think he never tells you her name?

Reading Skills: Comparing Themes

3. Use this chart to help you express the theme of "The Only Girl in the World for Me." When you've defined what Cosby says about first love, think about how it compares with the themes of the other selections.

The Only Girl in the World for Me

Brief Summary	Topic	Theme

✓ Vocabulary Check

4. Explain a situation in which you had trouble **suppressing** a laugh.

Literary Focus

Literary Analysis

5. **Evaluate** Do you think the experience Cosby describes in this selection was painful for him at the time? Explain your answer.

6. **Interpret** Cosby has said, "You can turn painful situations around through laughter." How does that idea connect to this story? to your life?

Literary Skills: Recurring Themes Across Genres

7. "User Friendly" and "The Only Girl in the World for Me" both deal with a boy's attempts to approach a girl he likes. How is the treatment of this situation different in the two selections? How are their themes similar?

Writing Focus

Think as a Reader/Writer

Use It in Your Writing Hyperbole, or exaggeration, is an important part of Cosby's comic technique. Write a brief account of something awkward or embarrassing that happened to you. Use exaggeration to make the story funny.

Wrap Up

User Friendly / Annabel Lee / Echo and Narcissus / The Only Girl in the World for Me

Writing Focus

Write a Comparison-Contrast Essay

Write an essay comparing the themes of these four selections from different genres: "User Friendly," "Annabel Lee," "Echo and Narcissus," and "The Only Girl in the World for Me." Begin by comparing your charts to come up with some themes that are (revealed) in more than one selection.

When you've identified the themes, decide how you will organize your essay.

1. You can organize the essay by themes, devoting a paragraph to each theme. In each paragraph, you would compare and contrast how the theme is treated in each selection that deals with that theme.

2. You can organize your essay by selection, devoting a paragraph to each story or poem. In each paragraph, you would discuss how each of the themes is treated in that selection.

At the end of your essay, tell which themes were most relevant to you and which selection you think treated that theme most effectively.

Refer to the workshop on writing a comparison-contrast essay, pages 106–113, for help with this assignment.

What Do You Think Now?

How has reading these selections affected your ideas about love and why it is a recurring theme in literature?

CHOICES

As you respond to the Choices, use these **Academic Vocabulary** words as appropriate: fundamental, implicit, relevant, reveal.

REVIEW

Compare Characters

Timed ⌐Writing Ginny rejects Kevin in "User Friendly." Narcissus rejects Echo in the myth. Both get punished for their actions. Write a paragraph comparing Ginny and Echo. Cite story details that support your opinion of how they are alike and how they are different.

CONNECT

Research Word Origins

Echo and *narcissism* are two English words with **roots** in ancient Greek culture. From the list below, research at least five more such words. Show their exact **origin** in ancient Greek culture or mythology. Does the origin of these words shed light on their current usage?

psyche	nectar	chaos
vulcanize	mercury	cereal

EXTEND

Write a Description

In "Echo and Narcissus" the narrator describes love as if it is an illness. What if love actually were an illness? How would you describe the symptoms? Write a brief description of "love sickness." Then, write up your suggested treatment or cure for this illness. Use humor to make your descriptions more engaging.

Evaluating Arguments

CONTENTS

What Do
You
Think

Is it easier for a bully to attack in person or online?

 QuickWrite
Think of a time when you witnessed bullying. How did you handle it? Write a short description of the incident, describing your reaction.

NEWSPAPER ARTICLE
Preparing to Read

Virtual Sticks and Stones

Reader/Writer Notebook

Use your **RWN** to complete the activities for this selection.

Informational Text Focus

Presenting an Argument The word *argument* can mean "quarrel or disagreement." Used here, though, it means "debate or discussion." Writers who present an argument want to persuade you to accept or reject an opinion on a subject, or to act in a certain way. They may want you to agree with their opinions, vote for their candidates, buy their products, or support their causes.

Those who are skillful at presenting arguments often start their essays with an **anecdote,** a brief story used to make a point. They go on to present solid **evidence** to back up their arguments. They cite **facts** (statements that can be proved true), cite **statistics** (number facts), or quote **experts** to convince you that an argument is sound.

After you read a text that presents an argument, ask yourself these questions:

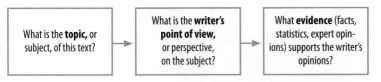

What is the **topic,** or subject, of this text? → What is the **writer's point of view,** or perspective, on the subject? → What **evidence** (facts, statistics, expert opinions) supports the writer's opinions?

Always read a persuasive essay with a critical eye, and evaluate the writer's argument. Only accept someone's argument when it's backed up by strong evidence.

Vocabulary

misrepresentations (mihs rehp rih zehn TAY shuhnz) *n.:* false ideas given for the purpose of deceiving someone. *Some bullies make up misrepresentations about their targets.*

consequences (KAHN suh kwehns ihz) *n.:* results caused by a set of conditions. *People sometimes bully others over the Internet to avoid the consequences of challenging them in person.*

Language Coach

Word Origins The Latin word *stare* means "to stand." Words built on the word *stare* include "stand" and "station."

Which Vocabulary word in the list above is related to these words? How does its meaning relate to the meaning of *stare?*

Writing Focus Preparing for **Constructed Response**

Take notes on the evidence the author uses in this argument on cyberbullying, or online harassment. You'll use them later to answer a constructed response question.

Learn It Online
Do pictures and animation help you learn? Try the *PowerNotes* lesson on:

go.hrw.com | L7-447 | **Go**

Virtual Sticks and Stones

Bullying is as threatening online as it is in person.

by

Read with a Purpose
Read this article to examine positive and negative aspects of using the Internet.

CHICAGO, ILL., OCT. 11 My first time sending a message on the Internet, I made mistakes and had to hit the Delete key. Still, those first clicks and blips made me feel powerful. I felt as if I could reach out to the world as I never had before. Did you feel that your world became larger when you began using the Internet? Suddenly, you didn't have to see friends in person or call people to communicate. It was all very exciting. **Ⓐ**

"Cyberbullying is the fastest-growing trend in bullying among teens."

Maybe you, too, were like Katie: "I was thrilled with the idea that I now had access to all aspects of the Internet," writes Katie, fourteen, for Teen Angels, a youth group that works to combat Internet abuse. "The promising new window the Internet opened up for me seemed too good to be true, and in fact, it was."

Online Threats

Katie was nine when she first started to message people. She was home alone when she received an unforgettable note. The words *You wait. I'm coming after you* popped up from an unknown screen name. She was new to the In-

ternet and didn't know that she shouldn't open a message from a stranger. She does now.

The threat scared Katie, and she hid in her room until her mom came home. She kept the incident to herself for a while, afraid that her parents would take away her Internet privileges. Now she shares her experience as a way to get kids to talk about cyberbullies. **Ⓑ**

Cyberbullying Statistics

A threat like this is extreme, but we all probably know of someone who's been burned on the Internet. In May 2006, two professors of criminal justice, one at Florida Atlantic University and one at the University of Wisconsin, Eau Claire, released results of a study of 1,388 youths. One third of those surveyed said they had been victims of cyberbullying. Another survey, from i-Safe America, said 60 percent of middle school kids have been sent hurtful messages. **Ⓒ**

"Little-noticed cyberbullying is the fastest-growing trend in bullying among teens," wrote Iris Salters, Michigan Education Association president, in a recent editorial.

Hidden Personalities

Some Web sites encourage people to create a Web personality, which can be very different from a person's real personality. Once invisible behind a new personality, cyberbullies can write misrepresentations on buddy profiles,

---

Ⓐ Informational Focus Identify an Argument What type of evidence does the writer use to begin the article?

Ⓑ Read and Discuss What has the author set up for you?

Ⓒ Informational Focus Identify an Argument Why does the writer include these statistics in his article?

Vocabulary misrepresentations (mihs rehp rih zehn TAY shuhnz) *n.:* false ideas given for the purpose of deceiving someone.

spill personal secrets about former friends, and join combative cliques that can attack under an assumed name. Because those who bully online are physically distant from their targets, they can feel more confident.

One seventh-grader I know was in a band that had a page on a social networking site. A kid hacked in and wrote violent threats that sounded as if band members had written them on the page. This hacker hid behind his victims' personalities. When Web personalities act in ways that real ones never would, they become a way to hide from truth, from consequences, and mostly from themselves.

Think about the people on the receiving end of your messages.

Interpreting Web Behavior

Because cyberbullying appears in words, many people discount the damage it does. Sure, a good portion of online comments are meant in jest, so many people think, "What's the big deal?" Cyberbullying, however, doesn't come across as harmless to the target or to those who read the attack. Comments online may be written to be funny or to be cruel. It's hard to sense attempts at humor in a computer message. If someone passes by you in the school hallway and calls you a name, you can turn to him or her. Maybe the kid smiles to show it was meant in fun. Maybe not. Being face to face reflects reality, keeping intent in perspective. **Ⓓ**

Online Responsibility

The First Amendment to the U.S. Constitution guarantees freedom of speech, but there are laws to protect people from verbal and written abuse. Many schools already have in place policies regarding cyberabuse and punishments for students who attack others through e-mails, Web posts, and text messages.

If you are being bullied online, don't just take it. Tell an adult—a teacher, a parent, or a coach. Don't let a friend be cyberbullied. Urge them to get help.

Handle yourself responsibly online: Think about the people on the receiving end of your messages. Would you like the virtual sticks and stones of lies about you or your friends or family circulating throughout the Internet? **Ⓔ**

Read with a Purpose
Restate and evaluate the author's argument.

Ⓓ | Read and Discuss | What does the author mean by "being face to face reflects reality, keeping intent in perspective"?

Ⓔ | Informational Focus | Identify an Argument Why does the writer end this essay with a question?

Vocabulary **consequences** (KAHN suh kwehns ihz) *n.*: results caused by a set of conditions.

NEWSPAPER ARTICLE
Applying Your Skills

SKILLS FOCUS Informational Skills Identify and trace the development of an author's argument in a text; analyze an author's argument.

Virtual Sticks and Stones

Practicing the Standards

Informational Text and Vocabulary

1. There is enough information in the article to show that the author believes that —

A the First Amendment should allow for on-line bullying

B the Internet has reduced the number of victims of bullying

C adults actually suffer more from cyberbullying than do teens

D communicating face to face is clearer than communicating online

2. Information from the article supports the idea that cyberbullying —

A is less vicious than bullying in person

B stops happening in college

C can be well hidden by a Web personality

D appears mostly in e-mail messages

3. Which quotation *best* shows that some think cyberbullying is not dangerous?

A "The First Amendment to the U.S. Constitution guarantees freedom of speech."

B "A kid hacked in and wrote violent threats . . . on the page."

C "Because cyberbullying appears in words, many people discount the damage it does."

D "We all probably know of someone who's been burned on the Internet."

4. Read this sentence from the article:

Think about the people on the receiving end of your messages.

The author uses this sentence to remind readers that —

A they must take responsibility for what they write online

B our Web personalities write angry comments, even to friends

C it is harder to tell a joke in e-mails than to tell a joke face to face

D schools can catch and punish cyberbullies

5. The author argues that a bully's Web personality —

A can allow him or her to avoid facing the truth

B has the right to be completely free to write anything

C makes tracking and catching the bully easy

D helps make vicious attacks on Web sites

Writing Focus   Constructed Response

Some of the paragraphs in the article do not contain strong evidence. Pick three of the paragraphs, and describe a type of evidence that would better support the writer's opinion.

What Do **You Think Now** What is your reaction to this article on cyberbullying? Explain.

NEWSPAPER ARTICLE
Preparing to Read

Debate on Bullying

Reader/Writer
Notebook

Use your **RWN** to complete the activities for this selection.

Informational Text Focus

Identify and Evaluate Author's Evidence You turn on a TV courtroom drama, and here's what the prosecutor presents as evidence against the accused: a dog's bark in the night, a chewed piece of gum, a bag found in the trash. A defense attorney holds up a baseball cap, too small for the accused, found at the crime scene as evidence to free her client. It is up to the jury to decide if the evidence against the accused is **adequate**—that is, they have to decide if there is enough evidence to prove the defendant guilty. *Adequate* means "enough for what is needed; sufficient."

Experts are brought in to testify whether the DNA in the chewed gum matches the defendant's DNA. The jury determines whether the expert's opinions are **accurate.** *Accurate* means "free from mistakes or errors."

The evidence of a dog's barking on the night of the crime may or may not be **appropriate** evidence for the case. *Appropriate* means "relevant; right for the purpose."

When you read informational texts, you expect a writer's evidence to be adequate, accurate, and appropriate. Don't take this for granted. You need to **assess,** or judge, the evidence for yourself. When you read a statement, think to yourself, "What does this have to do with the author's position?" If it doesn't apply, you're probably looking at **inappropriate** evidence. If a writer states an opinion using such words as *all, always, each,* and *every,* it's likely you're seeing **inaccurate** evidence. If all you have to trust is a writer's feelings instead of facts, the evidence is most likely **inadequate.**

Vocabulary

anonymous (uh NAHN uh muhs) *adj.:* not identified by name. *People who bully others over the Internet can remain anonymous.*

alienate (AYL yuh nayt) *v.:* cause to feel isolated or unaccepted. *Some people alienate those who are different from them.*

conviction (kuhn VIHK shuhn) *n.:* instance of being declared guilty of a criminal offense. *A bully is likely to have a conviction on his or her record.*

Language Coach

Multiple-Meaning Words Some words can be spelled and pronounced the same way, yet have different meanings. Think of the meanings of the word *match.* Its use in a sentence gives clues to its meaning. Which word above has two different meanings, and what are they?

Writing Focus · Preparing for **Constructed Response**

As you read the two sides of this debate, note the evidence that you feel is inappropriate, inaccurate, and/or inadequate. You'll use these notes to answer a constructed response question later.

Learn It Online
Sharpen your vocabulary skills with Word Watch:

go.hrw.com | L7-452 | Go

Debate on Bullying

by  **THE WORLD ALMANAC®**

Read with a Purpose
Read to compare two different perspectives on bullying.

Question: What can or should be done about bullying?

Just Deal with It
by Jared Hoffman

Bullying is all around us—you just have to deal with it. In one study, nearly 60 percent of U.S. fourth- through eighth-graders said others had said hurtful things to them online (*Teaching Tolerance*). Almost 160,000 students stay home from school out of fear of bullies there (*Education World*). **Ⓐ**

Cyberbullying is making the situation worse. "Now you don't have to confront someone to bully them in person," said Mark Chapell of Rowan University about his new study on Internet bullying. "You can do it electronically and remain anonymous."

The world never has been and never will be without bullies. It is part of life. There's no way to avoid it. The playground isn't the only place bullying occurs. Adults face it in the workplace. Just look at politicians, who push each other around, insult each other, and even lie just to get one more vote. **Ⓑ**

Because bullying can't be stopped, people need to learn to handle it. You probably don't want to tell on a bully, but you must tell an adult if you think you or a friend is in danger. Talk to the friend being bullied and let him or her know that they have a shoulder to lean on. It is essential to help your friend regain self-esteem so life can go on.

Some people suggest finding ways to reduce bullying, like ignoring the abuse, using humor to deflect it, and never resorting to violence (*Teens Health*). However, these methods will never stop it completely. You'd be a fool to think they would. Learn to deal with it, because there's no way around it. **Ⓒ**

Ⓐ **Informational Focus** **Author's Evidence** Why does Jared cite *Teaching Tolerance* and *Education World*?

Ⓑ **Read and Discuss** What is Jared telling you here?

Ⓒ **Informational Focus** **Author's Evidence** What is Jared's argument about bullying?

Vocabulary **anonymous** (uh NAHN uh muhs) *adj.*: not identified by name.

Get Serious
by Marissa Barbaro

There is no excuse for bullying. Almost 30 percent of U.S. youth (more than 5.7 million students) are involved as a bully, a target of bullying, or both. Bullying has a negative effect on all involved, and more steps must be taken to prevent it. **D**

Bullies usually target people they consider to be different from themselves . . .

Bullies usually target people they consider to be different from themselves, based on such things as appearance, status, behavior, or religion. Bullying often leads to other forms of prejudice, including racism and gender bias. Seeing bullying all the time leads kids to believe that it is okay to disrespect and alienate others because of their differences.

Kids subjected to threats and violence are often fearful and have difficulty concentrating, so their health and schoolwork suffer. Studies show a higher rate of depression and anxiety in adults who were bullied as children.

Bullying also has a negative impact on the bullies themselves, who tend to grow into violent and hateful teenagers and adults. They perform poorly academically and can't form healthy relationships. Sixty percent of bullies in grades 6 through 9 have at least one criminal conviction by age twenty-four (SafeYouth.org). Dropouts probably account for most criminals. **E**

Parents and teachers must encourage kids to be accepting of others. Adults have to educate kids about the effects of prejudice on bullies, as well as on their targets. Without education, this abuse will continue.

Remember: Bullying can and must be stopped. Bullies are not the only ones responsible for their behavior; everyone who allows it to happen is just as guilty as the bully. There is no excuse for bullying.

What do you think? Send your letters to the editor for publication in next month's issue.

Read with a Purpose
What evidence did you find to support the authors' points?

D **Informational Focus** Author's Evidence Why does Marissa include these statistics in her argument?

E **Read and Discuss** How has Marissa approached her argument?

Vocabulary **alienate** (AYL yuh nayt) *v.*: cause to feel isolated or unaccepted.
conviction (kuhn VIHK shuhn) *n.*: instance of being declared guilty of a criminal offense.

NEWSPAPER ARTICLE
Applying Your Skills

SKILLS FOCUS Informational Focus Evaluate and judge the author's evidence; analyze the appropriateness of evidence.

Debate on Bullying

Practicing the Standards

Informational Text and Vocabulary

1. Which claim from Marissa's argument is *least* supported by factual evidence?

   A School-age bullies often break the law as they get older.

   B The targets of bullying can suffer from emotional problems.

   C Criminals may have started their lives as bullies.

   D Bullies often attack people who are different from them.

2. Which phrase from Jared's argument is contradicted by an opinion from Marissa's argument?

   A "Learn to deal with [bullying] because there's no way around it."

   B "The playground isn't the only place bullying occurs."

   C "Just look at politicians, who push each other around."

   D "However, these methods will never stop [bullying] completely."

3. Jared supports his argument that there is no way to avoid bullying by stating that —

   A bullying exists even among adults at work

   B cyberbullying is better than face-to-face bullying

   C grown-ups can protect kids who are targets

   D targets of bullying should fight back

4. It is appropriate for Marissa to discuss prejudice in paragraph 2 because she believes that —

   A students from different backgrounds should be separated.

   B bullies stop being prejudiced when they're older

   C bullying makes people enemies because of their differences

   D watching bullying protects others from becoming bullies

5. Read the first and final sentence of Marissa's argument:

   There is no excuse for bullying.

   In this sentence, it is clear that Marissa wants student readers to —

   A encourage targeted kids to form discussion groups

   B work together with adults until there is no more bullying

   C realize that parents don't understand the sources of bullying

   D expect adults to assist in resolving prejudice among kids

Writing Focus Constructed Response

Review the notes you took while reading this debate. Briefly explain which argument against bullying you found to be most effective.

EDITORIALS
Preparing to Read

Letters to the Editor

Informational Text Focus

Identify Bias and Stereotyping Imagine you're sitting on a bench in a shopping mall, waiting for your ride. You begin hearing bits of conversations from shoppers as they walk by:

"People who drive sports cars are reckless."
"All politicians are dishonest."
"Football players aren't good at schoolwork."

You've just heard people express their opinions of others using **stereotypes.** That means they are using unfair, fixed ideas about groups of people. Stereotypes don't take individuality into account. They brand every member of a group with the same characteristics. Stereotypes are hurtful and are often used to persuade you to do or believe something.

If you've ever watched your favorite sports team on the opposing team's host TV channel, you've probably noticed that the broadcasters favor the home team with their comments and calls. What you're really noticing is called **bias**—attitudes and beliefs that can shape a person's thinking in spite of the facts. Of course, your bias is evident as well—you want your favorite team to win!

As you read editorials or any kind of political or social commentary, be on the lookout for expressions that suggest the writer has already made up his or her mind about someone or something. Think of bias as an inclination to think a certain way. In its worst form, bias becomes prejudice.

Writing Focus Preparing for **Constructed Response**

As you read the letters to the editor that follow, take note of the biased statements and stereotypes in them. You'll use these notes to answer a constructed response question later.

Reader/Writer Notebook

Use your **RWN** to complete the activities for this selection.

Vocabulary

expelled (ehk SPEHLD) *v.*: forced to leave. *The principal expelled the students responsible for bullying.*

Language Coach

Suffixes Suffixes can help you recognize the meaning of a word that might otherwise be unfamiliar to you. For instance, you probably know the meaning of *access.* You might also know that the suffix *–ible* or *–able* often means "capable of." Based on these clues, what do you think *accessible* might mean?

 Learn It Online
Re-examine bias and stereotyping, using the interactive Reading Workshops:

go.hrw.com   L7-456   **Go**

Read with a Purpose
As you read these letters, look for instances of bias and stereotyping.

File   Edit   View   Favorites   Tools   Help

Back   Forward   Stop   Refresh   Home   Search   Favorites   History   Mail   Print

Address   http://www.sfpaper.com/Letters.html   Go

Student Forum

SEARCH   HOME   ABOUT   BLOG   SITE MAP   CONTACT

Sound Off: To the Editor

by

In the last issue of *Student Forum,* the editorial debate focused on ways to deal with bullying. (See two opinions on pages 453–454.) Many responses were sent to the editors. Here are just a few.

from	comment
Candace Branch "All bullies should be expelled."	Those studies about bullying are disturbing because they prove that most kids get bullied. Adults think bullies are just little troublemakers. They don't even try to stop the bullying. All bullies should be expelled because, like Jared says, they will never change.

Vocabulary   **expelled** (ehk SPEHLD) *v.:* forced to leave.

Timothy Mann "You just have to deal with bullying."	I agree with Jared that you just have to deal with bullying. You can't change people—you can't get rid of bullies. You have to stand up and not be a wimp. Be strong for yourself and for your friends.
Jonathan Roper "We ought to do what we want to do!"	I'm on the basketball team, and I don't understand what all the fuss is about. We work hard on the team, and the rest of the students just watch the games and then pretend like they've won. We're like school heroes so we ought to do what we want to do! So what if we want somebody to do our homework. Let's face it—smart kids are geeky.
Tamara Holmes "Teachers and parents need to teach kids how to act."	Nobody bullies me because I don't pay attention to stupid people's stupid comments. They know I'd get them back if they did. Anyway, Marissa is right. Teachers and parents need to teach kids how to act. This is an important subject, just like math and English. If you don't learn how to act right, you will never know how to act properly. Look at that study about criminals in Marissa's argument—that's what happens to bullies and dropouts when they grow up. **(A)**
Calista Tallman "Protect our right to free speech!"	No attempt should be made to stop cyberbullying because that would be a challenge to our right to free speech. The U.S. Constitution protects our right to say what we want. Let's keep it that way. If you don't want to be attacked online, turn off your computer. We have the right to protect our free speech! **(B)**

(A) Informational Focus Bias and Stereotyping What stereotype does Tamara present in her letter?

(B) Read and Discuss What do all these responses show you?

Read with a Purpose
What instances of bias and stereotyping did you find in these letters?

 Internet

Letters to the Editor

Practicing the Standards

Informational Text and Vocabulary

1. What stereotyped idea does Timothy Mann refer to?

A Bullying must be stopped.

B Bullies should be expelled.

C People will always be the same.

D Adults don't understand bullying.

2. Jonathan Roper's letter is written from the point of view of a —

A conceited athlete

B professional jock

C lazy player

D failing student

3. Whose letter expresses bias against targets of Internet bullying?

A Tamara Holmes's

B Jonathan Roper's

C Candace Branch's

D Calista Tallman's

4. The target of Candace's bias is —

A free speech

B adults

C fellow classmates

D parents of bullies

5. Tamara Holmes reveals bias against —

A performing research

B Marissa's writing

C parents' teaching

D students' dropping out

6. If an object is *expelled*, it is —

A forced out

B falling

C accessible

D broken open

Writing Focus Constructed Response

Refer to the notes you took while you were reading the responses. Then, write a paragraph explaining how biases and stereotypes can weaken an argument.

What Do You Think Now?

How do you think bullying should be handled, whether it occurs online or in person? Explain.

Writing Workshop

Autobiographical Narrative

Write with a Purpose

Write an autobiographical narrative about a significant experience in your life. Your **purpose** is to tell what happened and to explain to your readers why this experience is meaningful to you. Think about your **audience** as you write, and provide enough information so that they can understand your experience.

A Good Autobiographical Narrative

- is told from your point of view, using the pronouns *I, me, my*
- focuses on one experience
- includes essential background information or uses context
- develops a standard plot line
- develops a definite setting
- reveals character through dialogue and/or description
- shows what the experience means to you

See page 468 for complete rubric.

 **Reader/Writer Notebook**

Use your **RWN** to complete the activities for this workshop.

Think as a Reader/Writer

In this collection, you've been drawn to powerful themes by the techniques writers have used. Now it's time for you to draw readers into your point of view as you write an autobiographical narrative. Before you begin, take a few minutes to read this passage from Bill Cosby's autobiographical essay, "The Only Girl in the World for Me."

> The first time I saw her, she was crossing the street to the schoolyard and for one golden moment our eyes met. Well, maybe the moment was closer to bronze because she made no response. But at least she had seen me, just about the way that she saw lampposts, hydrants, and manholes. Or was there something more? I began to dream; and later that day, when I was playing with the boys in the yard, it seemed that she was looking at me and the world was suddenly a better place, especially Twelfth and Girard.
>
> However, we still never talked, but just traded silent unsmiling looks whenever we passed. For several days, just her look was enough of a lift for me; but a higher altitude was coming, for one night at a party, we met and I actually danced with her. Now I was certain that I was in love and was going to win her.

Notice how the author establishes a definite setting for his first meeting with the girl.

The author includes specific narrative actions, including movement and facial expressions.

The author's organizational structure is in clear chronological order.

Think About the Professional Model

With a partner, discuss the following questions about the model.

1. What does the reader learn about the author from this information?

2. What are some examples of description that the author uses? How do these details help the reader understand the importance of this experience for the author?

3. How does the author's presentation of events create rising action and build suspense?

Prewriting

Choose a Topic

Use the Idea Starters in the margin to help you make a list of memorable experiences you might want to write about. Ask yourself the following questions about each one:

- Does this incident mean something special to me?
- Do I remember this incident clearly?
- Am I comfortable sharing this incident with my audience?

Choose a Topic

You may find using a comparison table, like the one below, helpful when choosing between topics.

Surprises	Vacations
Throwing a surprise birthday party for my mother was great experience.	My family's trip to visit relatives in Italy was a very special time.
I remember every detail of the party.	I was only three years old, so I probably don't remember much of it.
I'd love to share this experience.	I wouldn't mind telling others about our trip.

Gather Details

Once you have chosen a particular experience, take notes on how it unfolded and how you felt about it. For instance, see how the following chart can help you visualize Bill Cosby's experience in "The Only Girl in the World for Me."

Who	What	When	Where	Why	How
Bill Cosby	He fell in love.	When he was young	The schoolyard	Their eyes met.	They traded looks.
A girl			At a party	They danced.	He felt happy and in love.

To help gather details, ask yourself these questions and create a chart like the one above:

- *Who* was involved in the experience? *What* did he or she say?
- *What* happened? *When* did it happen?
- *Where* did it happen?
- *Why* did it happen?
- *How* did it happen? *How* did I feel as the events unfolded?
- *What* did I learn as a result of the experience? *How* have I changed?

Idea Starters
- surprises
- challenges
- vacations
- helping others
- luck
- secrets
- sports
- losing a friend
- the future
- honesty

Your Turn _____

Get Started Making notes in your **RWN,** choose your experience and write a clear statement about why it is so **meaningful** to you. Begin listing **details** about the experience, including any **background information** you will need to provide your readers. Your notes will help you draft your narrative.

 Learn It Online
To see how one writer met all the assignment criteria, visit:

go.hrw.com   L7-461   **Go**

Order the Key Events

Be sure to place events in the correct sequence. Your readers will easily follow your narrative if you use **chronological order**, the order in which events occurred in time. Use transitional words such as *first*, *then*, and *finally*. Completing a flowchart like the one below can help you visualize the **sequence** of events.

Sequence Chart

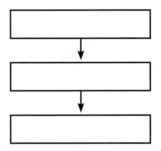

Use Dialogue

If you use **dialogue**, be sure to make it sound the way people really talk. Although slang and sentence fragments are usually avoided in formal writing, it may be natural to use such language in your personal narrative.

Keep Your Point of View Consistent

Use first-person pronouns—*I, me, my, we*—when referring to yourself. Keep your **point of view** consistent throughout your narrative.

Think About Purpose and Audience

Before you begin, consider your purpose and your audience. Is your **purpose** for writing to tell a funny or scary story or to share a meaningful experience? Be sure to indicate to readers why the experience was important to you. If your **audience** is made up of people who know you well, then much less background will need to be provided than might be necessary for an audience of strangers. Think about what readers will need to know that does not come up in the context of this experience. Consider these examples:

- What is the setting of your experience? Is it a place where you regularly spend time, or is it an unusual place for you to have been?

- Did you know the other people in your experience? What was your relationship to them?

⬤ Writing Tip

Think about your character's background when writing dialogue. For example, a sailor would probably mention the weather more often than an accountant, unless that accountant was an amateur meteorologist! Keeping in mind the various experiences of your character will help you create interesting and authentic dialogue.

Your Turn _____

Order the Events List the key events of your experience in the **sequence** in which they occurred. Creating a **flowchart** can help you identify beginning, middle, and ending events in your narrative.

Drafting

Follow Your Framework

Using the framework like the one to the right below as a guide, draft your essay. Focus on the single experience you are describing, and be sure to provide enough background for your audience so they can understand your experience. Tell about the events in a clear order, or sequence.

Use Vivid Descriptive Details

Help your readers share the experience you had by describing sensory details. How did things look, sound, smell, taste, and feel? As you describe these details, use precise words. Consider using a thesaurus for help in finding the best word to describe what you experienced. For example, if you want to think of a more dramatic way to describe a hot day, you could use words such as *sweaty, sweltering, scorching,* and *blazing.*

> **Framework for an Autobiographical Narrative**
>
> **Introduction:** dialogue, question, statement, or description that grabs the reader's attention and names the experience about which you're writing
>
> **Body:** description of events in chronological order
>   First event
>   Second event
>   Third event, and so on
>
> **Conclusion:** summary expressing the importance or meaning of the experience

Grammar Link Adjectives

Adjectives are words that describe, or modify, nouns. They make writing vivid by creating a more precise image for the reader. Adjectives indicate size, color, number, and other characteristics.

"for one **golden** moment our eyes met" (The adjective *golden* modifies the noun *moment*.)

"we . . . traded **silent unsmiling** looks whenever we passed" (The adjectives *silent* and *unsmiling* modify the noun *looks*.)

Reflecting on the Importance of the Experience

State in a sentence or two why the experience is important. For instance, the passage from Bill Cosby's essay, "The Only Girl in the World for Me," ends with: "Now I was certain that I was in love and was going to win her."

As you write your draft, look back at your statement to see if it fits your narrative. If it doesn't, you may need to rewrite your draft or your statement.

● Writing Tip

Consider using dialogue in your autobiographical narrative. What a person says can reveal a great deal about the speaker. In a similar way, using dialogue is the best means of sharing a conversation that might be an important element of your experience. Be sure to use correct punctuation as you write your dialogue.

Your Turn _____

Write Your Draft Following your plan, write a draft of your essay. Be sure to think about

- giving **background information** your readers might need
- accurately representing the **sequence** of events
- using **precise details** to describe the experience

Peer Review

Working with a peer, review your draft. Answer each question in this chart to locate where and how your drafts could be improved. As you discuss your papers, be sure to take notes about each other's suggestions.

Evaluating and Revising

Read the questions in the left column of the chart, and then use the tips in the middle column to help you make revisions to your essay. The right column suggests techniques you can use to revise your draft.

Autobiographical Narrative: Guidelines for Content and Organization

Evaluation Question	Tip	Revision Technique
1. Does your introduction grab the reader's attention and set the scene?	**Underline** the attention-getting opener.	**Add** a memorable quotation, statement, or piece of dialogue to the introduction. **Add** specific details to make the setting more precise.
2. Is the point of view consistent throughout?	**Identify** pronouns (*I*, *he*, or *she*) that show point of view. **Label** the narrative's point of view, and **circle** any information not given from that point of view.	If any sentences are circled, **delete** them. If necessary, **add** the same information told from the narrator's point of view.
3. Does the essay include essential background information?	**Put a star** next to details that make clear the context, or background, of the experience.	**Add** information that will help the reader understand the events in your narrative.
4. Are the events in sequential order?	**Number** the events in your paper. **Compare** the sequence with the actual order of events.	**Rearrange** any events that are out of order.
5. Do precise details help develop your characters and setting?	**Put check marks** next to specific, precise descriptions. In the margin, note to which senses the details appeal.	**Elaborate** with dialogue or sensory details. **Delete** any unrelated details.
6. Have you described your thoughts and feelings to clarify why the experience is important?	**Put a check mark** under statements of your feelings or thoughts. Put an **exclamation point** next to your statement of importance.	**Add** any other relevant important thoughts and feelings. **Add** a clear statement explaining why the experience matters.

Read this student's draft and the comments about it as a model for revising your own autobiographical narrative.

Claire of Bilberry

by Claire Moreland-Ochoa, Lake Travis Middle School

"I don't know about taking a hike today," my dad hinted. "I think I will take a nap."

While my dad was taking a nap, Danielle and I had some tea outside. Tea was becoming my favorite drink at any time of the day because it was very cold in England. While we were sitting outside on the deck at Ennerdale View, my mom walked out and gave me the *worst* news of the day.

"Honey, we are going on a hike," she broke into a smile. I wanted to frown, but instead I kept a straight face and asked, "When are we leaving?"

"Now."

We soon came to a man with purple hands sitting on a bench. The rental car slowly halted beside him. My dad introduced himself and asked why the man had purple hands.

"Well, I have been picking bilberries all morning on the Ennerdale Lake path," he said, sitting on a bench with a tin can in one of his hands. After a couple of words were said, we drove a little way and turned left.

← Claire opens with **dialogue**, immediately placing readers in the scene.

← Claire begins with an example of her behavior, in this case her facial expression.

← **Specific details** help readers picture the scene.

MINI-LESSON ▶ **How to Develop a Setting for Readers**

Claire places readers in the scene, but does not say *why* she and her family are there. Readers would follow the narrative more easily if they knew from the beginning that the family is on vacation in England, have been there for a while, and might be getting bored.

Claire's Revision of Paragraph One

"I don't know about taking a hike today," my dad hinted. "I think I will take a nap." ʌ*Our family had been in western England on vacation for about two weeks. We were renting a house in the remote Lake District. Everyone but Mom was growing weary of our daily hikes through the forest.*

Your Turn _____

Add Necessary Background Information Read your draft, and then ask yourself:

- How can I effectively develop the setting or characters?
- How can I help readers better understand the context of my experience?

Student Draft *continues*

Traveling down a narrow lane, the car turned onto a dirt road. We stopped at a gate. I climbed out and opened it. The car drove by. I closed the gate behind it, realizing that the gates are there to keep the sheep in. But there was not just one gate. There were four gates to open.

"What is it with England and gates?" I asked myself. After long minutes of taking pictures of sheep and hiking, we finally saw the first bilberry patch. Running up to the patch, I started picking the bilberries and shoving them into my mouth, while thinking, "I am **so** hungry!" Soon the whole family was devouring bilberries. My mom filmed the process. The bilberries disappeared on this patch, and we moved on. One by one, the bilberry patches popped up on each side of us. One by one, the bilberry patches turned into just patches without the bilberries anymore.

Halfway through the hike my parents ordered me to stop eating and Danielle to stop picking. We fell back a little and pretended to stoop over and look at all kinds of things. Sometimes it was a bug we were looking at; other times it was a flower or a strange-looking plant. We never stopped to look at any of those. We just saw a very nice bilberry patch and stopped to pick them and eat them.

On the way back we stopped to have a shortbread cookie. I smeared bilberry juice on the top of mine and thought it was very good. Everyone's faces twisted up when they saw what I was doing to the poor cookie. When we were finally back in the car, I was relieved but satisfied with a full stomach of bilberries. From then on I had a nickname, "Claire of Bilberry."

Claire mentions a specific **narrative** action.

Claire uses good transitional words throughout to help readers follow the **sequence of the experience**.

The ending names the narrative action that is so memorable—Claire got her nickname because of it!

MINI-LESSON ▶ **How to Relate Events in a Clear Order**

Claire does a great job of telling all of the important events in sequential order. However, she leaves out important information in the eighth paragraph. One of her readers pointed out that the action moves from the gates to taking pictures and hiking without transition or explanation. Her revision addresses this omission.

Claire's Revision of Paragraph Eight

After the car passed through the fourth gate, we traveled to the end of the dirt road. There, at the edge of the forest, we located the path and started off on foot.

"What is it with England and gates?" I asked myself. After long minutes . . .

Your Turn ———

Make the Order of Events Clear Carefully compare what you have written to your memory of the experience. Be sure that you have presented every important event and that the events are in chronological order.

Proofreading and Publishing

Proofreading

You have revised your autobiographical narrative, and now it is time to polish it to eliminate any errors that might distract your readers. Edit your narrative to correct any misspellings, punctuation errors, and problems in sentence structure.

> **Grammar Link** **Capitalize Proper Nouns**
>
> In an autobiographical narrative, you are likely to refer to specific people or places. When you do so, you are using a proper noun. A **proper noun** refers to a particular person, place, or thing and is capitalized. Claire follows this rule in her essay:
>
> "What is it with **England** and gates?"
>
> ". . . I have been picking bilberries all morning on the **Ennerdale Lake** path."
>
> **England** is the name of a country, and **Ennerdale Lake** is the name of the path. Both times, by simply emphasizing one or two words, Claire lets her readers know how she feels about what is going on—and she uses correct capitalization.

Publishing

Now it is time to publish your autobiographical narrative for a wider audience. Here are some ways to share your essay:

- Add photos from the experience, or use drawings to illustrate the narrative and present the finished product as a gift to someone who shared the experience with you.
- E-mail your narrative to interested relatives or friends.

Reflect on the Process
In your **RWN,** write a short response to each of the following questions.

1. What strategies did you find helpful as you were trying to develop characters and setting?
2. What was the most important revision you made to your narrative?
3. What do you think about this experience now that you have reflected on it?

Proofreading Tip

There are three main areas to focus on when editing: spelling, punctuation, and sentence structure. It makes sense to focus on just one area at a time while proofreading. Ask two peers to help you, and assign each person just one area to check.

Your Turn _____

Proofread and Publish

Proofread your narrative for any boldface or italic treatments you have used. Are the right words emphasized? If you have not used type styles to indicate important points, look for places where their use could improve readers' understanding of your narrative. Then, carefully proofread your narrative for any errors, make the corrections, and publish your polished work for others to enjoy.

Scoring Rubric

You can use one of the rubrics below to evaluate your autobiographical narrative from the Writing Workshop or your response to the prompt on the next page. Your teacher will tell you to use either the four- or the six-point rubric.

6-Point Scale

Score 6 *Demonstrates advanced success*
- focuses consistently on a clear controlling idea
- shows effective organization throughout, with smooth transitions
- offers a thoughtful, creative approach to the narrative
- develops the narrative thoroughly, using incidents, details, and explanation
- exhibits mature control of written language

Score 5 *Demonstrates proficient success*
- focuses on a clear controlling idea
- shows effective organization, with transitions
- offers a thoughtful approach to the narrative
- develops the narrative competently, using incidents, details, and explanation
- exhibits sufficient control of written language

Score 4 *Demonstrates competent success*
- focuses on a clear controlling idea, with minor distractions
- shows effective organization, with minor lapses
- offers a mostly thoughtful approach to the narrative
- develops the narrative adequately, using some incidents, details, and explanation
- exhibits general control of written language

Score 3 *Demonstrates limited success*
- includes some loosely related ideas that distract from the controlling idea
- shows some organization, with noticeable gaps in the logical flow of ideas
- offers a routine, predictable approach to the narrative
- develops the narrative with uneven use of incidents, details, and explanation
- exhibits limited control of written language

Score 2 *Demonstrates basic success*
- includes loosely related ideas that seriously distract from the writer's controlling idea
- shows minimal organization, with major gaps in the logical flow of ideas
- offers a narrative that merely skims the surface
- develops the narrative with inadequate use of incidents, details, and explanation
- exhibits significant problems with control of written language

Score 1 *Demonstrates emerging effort*
- shows little awareness of the topic and purpose for writing
- lacks organization
- offers an unclear and confusing narrative
- develops the narrative in only a minimal way, if at all
- exhibits major problems with control of written language

4-Point Scale

Score 4 *Demonstrates advanced success*
- focuses consistently on a clear controlling idea
- shows effective organization throughout, with smooth transitions
- offers a thoughtful, creative approach to the narrative
- develops the narrative thoroughly, using incidents, details, and explanation
- exhibits mature control of written language

Score 3 *Demonstrates competent success*
- focuses on a clear controlling idea, with minor distractions
- shows effective organization, with minor lapses
- offers a mostly thoughtful approach to the narrative
- develops the narrative adequately, using some incidents, details, and explanation
- exhibits general control of written language

Score 2 *Demonstrates limited success*
- includes some loosely related ideas that distract from the controlling idea
- shows some organization, with noticeable gaps in the logical flow of ideas
- offers a routine, predictable approach to the narrative
- develops the narrative with uneven use of incidents, details, and explanation
- exhibits limited control of written language

Score 1 *Demonstrates emerging effort*
- shows little awareness of the topic and purpose for writing
- lacks organization
- offers an unclear and confusing narrative
- develops the narrative in only a minimal way, if at all
- exhibits major problems with control of written language

Autobiographical Narrative

When responding to an autobiographical narrative prompt, use the models you have read, what you've learned from writing your own autobiographical narrative, the rubric on page 468, and the steps below.

Writing Prompt

Think about a time you experienced strong emotions. You may have felt exhilarated after mastering a difficult challenge or sadness because of separation from a friend or family member. Select an important experience in your life, and write a narrative about it. Use objective and subjective details to relate the facts of the experience as well as your thoughts and feeling on it. Then, discuss why the experience is still meaningful to you.

Study the Prompt

Begin by reading the prompt carefully. Note what is required in your narrative: a description of the experience that uses objective and subjective details and your thoughts about the experience. **Tip:** Spend about five minutes studying the prompt.

Plan Your Response

Think of some personal experiences that are important to you. Which of these would you feel comfortable writing about? Once you have settled on your subject,

- write down who was involved, what happened, when it happened, where it happened, why it happened, how it happened, and why it's still meaningful to you
- think about your purpose and audience
- list the events in the order that they occurred

Tip: Spend about fifteen minutes planning your response.

Respond to the Prompt

Using the notes you've just made, draft your narrative. Follow these guidelines:

- In the introduction, use interesting dialogue or a question, statement, or description to grab the reader's attention.
- In the body, relate the events in the order that they occurred. Support your narrative with both objective and subjective details.
- In the conclusion, summarize your experience, emphasizing why it is still meaningful to you.

As you are writing, remember to use words that are best for your audience—not too informal. Write as neatly as you can. If your narrative can't be read easily, it won't be scored. **Tip:** Spend about twenty minutes writing your draft.

Improve Your Response

Revising Go back over the key aspects of the narrative. Did you describe the events? Did you use objective and subjective details? Did you explain the event's importance to you?

Proofreading Take a few minutes to proofread your narrative to correct errors in grammar, spelling, punctuation, and capitalization. Make sure all your edits are neat, and erase any stray marks.

Checking Your Final Copy Before you turn in your narrative, read it one more time to catch any errors you may have missed. You'll be glad that you took the extra time for one final review. **Tip:** Save ten minutes to improve your paper.

Listening & Speaking Workshop

Presenting an Autobiographical Narrative

Speak with a Purpose

Adapt your written autobiographical narrative into an oral presentation. Practice your presentation, and then present it to your class.

Think as a Reader/Writer Presenting an autobiographical narrative orally requires the same kind of thought and preparation as was required to write the narrative. You'll want to grab your listeners' attention with an interesting opening, set the scene, focus on one significant experience, include objective and subjective details, keep your events in clear order, and tell your listeners why the experience is important to you. In a way, you probably rarely go through a day *without* presenting an autobiographical narrative. Any time you talk about something that happened to you, you're presenting an informal autobiographical narrative.

Adapt Your Narrative

Tell Them About It

Your audience for your oral presentation will be your classmates. Therefore, ask yourself how comfortable you are sharing all the details you included in your written narrative. Here are some things to consider as you adapt your autobiographical narrative for oral presentation.

- **Word Choice** Think about how the words you've written would sound coming out of your mouth. Do some words sound too formal? Try to change the language so it will sound like your natural speech. Still, avoid using slang or words that might be unfamiliar to listeners.
- **Details** Consider which objective and subjective details you want to include. *Who* was involved? *What* happened? *Where, when, why,* and *how* did it happen? *Why* is it still important to you?
- **Purpose** Why are you telling others about this experience? Keep your purpose in mind as you think about the way you'll relate the experience.
- **Organization** You can probably use the same organization you used for your written narrative. Begin with an interesting question or statement that will engage your listeners. Then, tell them about the events in the order that they occurred. To make your narrative easier to follow, you may leave out some of the events. Finally, summarize your experience by telling listeners what effect the experience has had on you and why it is still important.

Deliver Your Autobiographical Narrative

Bring the Experience to Life

When you give your oral presentation, you'll want to communicate the overall mood, or feeling, of your experience. You'll also want to show listeners your attitude—how you think and feel about the experience now. Concentrate on movements, gestures, and facial expressions that will help you relate mood and attitude in a vivid, believable way. In addition, use these speaking techniques to bring your experience to life for your listeners.

- **Voice Modulation** Change the tone and volume of your voice to emphasize important moments, build suspense, and show emotion.

- **Inflection** Move the pitch of your voice up or down to express shades of meaning or to share your attitude about the experience. For example, a rising inflection can show doubt, surprise, or curiosity. A falling inflection can express certainty.

- **Tempo** Change the speed at which you talk to communicate emotion. For example, you might increase your tempo when delivering a section of your narrative that involves a dangerous event.

- **Enunciation** Say each word clearly and precisely. Try not to slur your words or drop word endings. For example, don't say "I'm gonna" when you mean "I'm going to," unless you're imitating someone's dialogue.

- **Eye Contact** Make frequent eye contact with your listeners. That will make them feel as though you are talking directly to them, which will help keep their attention. You can also use eye contact for emphasis at important moments in your narrative.

Make It Noteworthy

You may be tempted simply to read your autobiographical narrative directly from the paper you've written it on. That is not the most effective approach, however. A much better way to make sure you don't leave anything out is to use a well-organized set of notes. You can use index cards to make notes about key events and details, and you might even want to give yourself reminders about gestures to use at certain points in your narrative. You can occasionally refer to your notes as you deliver your autobiographical narrative, instead of completely losing eye contact with your audience.

A Good Autobiographical Narrative

- is told from your point of view
- focuses on one significant experience
- relates events in a clear order
- includes objective and subjective details
- tells listeners why the experience is important to you
- uses verbal and nonverbal techniques effectively

Speaking Tip

Rehearse your narrative several times, concentrating on a different element each time. Perform in front of a friend or relative, or tape your rehearsal. Make changes based on feedback from your listener or tape.

Learn It Online

Add music and pictures to your narrative. Go to our *Digital Storytelling* mini-site at:

go.hrw.com | L7-471 | Go

Literary Skills Review

Theme **Directions:** Read the following story and poem. Then, answer each question that follows.

Home *from* Maud Martha

by **Gwendolyn Brooks**

What had been wanted was this always, this always to last, the talking softly on this porch, with the snake plant in the jardiniere in the southwest corner, and the obstinate slip from Aunt Eppie's magnificent Michigan fern at the left side of the friendly door. Mama, Maud Martha, and Helen rocked slowly in their rocking chairs, and looked at the late afternoon light on the lawn and at the emphatic iron of the fence and at the poplar tree. These things might soon be theirs no longer. Those shafts and pools of light, the tree, the graceful iron, might soon be viewed possessively by different eyes.

Papa was to have gone that noon, during his lunch hour, to the office of the Home Owners' Loan. If he had not succeeded in getting another extension, they would be leaving this house in which they had lived for more than fourteen years. There was little hope. The Home Owners' Loan was hard. They sat, making their plans.

"We'll be moving into a nice flat somewhere," said Mama. "Somewhere on South Park, or Michigan, or in Washington Park Court." Those flats, as the girls and Mama knew well, were burdens on wages twice the size of Papa's. This was not mentioned now.

"They're much prettier than this old house," said Helen. "I have friends I'd just as soon not bring here. And I have other friends that wouldn't come down this far for anything, unless they were in a taxi."

Yesterday, Maud Martha would have attacked her. Tomorrow she might. Today she said nothing. She merely gazed at a little hopping robin in the tree, her tree, and tried to keep the fronts of her eyes dry.

"Well, I do know," said Mama, turning her hands over and over, "that I've been getting tireder and tireder of doing that firing. From October to April, there's firing to be done."

"But lately we've been helping, Harry and I," said Maud Martha. "And sometimes in March and April and in October, and even in November, we could build a little fire in the fireplace. Sometimes the weather was just right for that."

She knew, from the way they looked at her, that this had been a mistake. They did not want to cry.

But she felt that the little line of white, sometimes ridged with smoked purple, and all that cream-shot saffron would never drift across any western sky except that in back of this house. The rain would drum with as sweet a dullness nowhere but here. The birds on South Park were mechanical birds, no better than the poor caught canaries in those "rich" women's sun parlors.

"It's just going to kill Papa!" burst out Maud Martha. "He loves this house! He *lives* for this house!"

"He lives for us," said Helen. "It's us he loves. He wouldn't want the house, except for us."

"And he'll have us," added Mama, "wherever."

"You know," Helen said, "if you want to know the truth, this is a relief. If this hadn't come up, we would have gone on, just dragged on, hanging out here forever."

"It might," allowed Mama, "be an act of God. God may just have reached down and picked up the reins."

"Yes," Maud Martha cracked in, "that's what you always say—that God knows best."

Her mother looked at her quickly, decided the statement was not suspect, looked away.

Helen saw Papa's coming. "There's Papa," said Helen.

They could not tell a thing from the way Papa was walking. It was that same dear little staccato walk, one shoulder down, then the other, then repeat, and repeat. They watched his progress. He passed the Kennedys'; he passed the vacant lot, he passed Mrs. Blakemore's. They wanted to hurl themselves over the fence, into the street, and shake the truth out of his collar. He opened his gate—the gate—and still his stride and face told them nothing.

"Hello," he said.

Mama got up and followed him through the front door. The girls knew better than to go in too.

Presently Mama's head emerged. Her eyes were lamps turned on.

"It's all right," she exclaimed. "He got it. It's all over. Everything is all right."

The door slammed shut. Mama's footsteps hurried away.

"I think," said Helen, rocking rapidly, "I think I'll give a party. I haven't given a party since I was eleven. I'd like some of my friends to just casually see that we're homeowners."

Literary Skills Review CONTINUED

Theme **Directions:** Read the following poem. Then, answer each question that follows.

Gold by Pat Mora

When Sun paints the desert
with its gold,
I climb the hills.
Wind runs round boulders, ruffles
5 my hair. I sit on my favorite rock,
lizards for company, a rabbit,
ears stiff in the shade
of a saguaro.°
In the wind, we're all
10 eye to eye.

Sparrow on saguaro watches
rabbit watch us in the gold
of sun setting.
Hawk sails on waves of light, sees
15 sparrow, rabbit, lizards, me,
our eyes shining,
watching red and purple sand rivers
      stream down the hill.

I stretch my arms wide as the sky
like hawk extends her wings
20 in all the gold light of this, home.

8. saguaro (suh GWAH roh): huge cactus found in the southwestern United States and northern Mexico.

---

1. From what point of view is the excerpt "Home" narrated?

  A Third person, limited

  B Third person, omniscient

  C First person, Maud

  D First person, Mama

2. Maud Martha in "Home" and the speaker of "Gold" share a —

  A love of a place

  B sadness about the sky

  C dislike of cities

  D need of nature

3. The following words are in both selections. Which are **key words** in both selections?

   A light; eyes

   B purple; like

   C home; I

   D home; we're

4. Read this sentence from the excerpt:

   "Her eyes were lamps turned on."

   Which phrase from "Gold" means almost same thing?

   A "the gold light of this, home"

   B "we're all / eye to eye"

   C "sails on waves of light"

   D "our eyes shining"

5. A **recurring theme** of the excerpt and the poem deals with —

   A shortness of life

   B importance of nature

   C love of home

   D need for peace

6. A **theme** in "Gold" is the comparison of —

   A the speaker and the animals

   B the light and the sun

   C the boulders and the cactus

   D flying and sitting

7. Which words from the poem show that it is written in the first person?

   A "its gold"

   B "her wings"

   C "watch us"

   D "light of this"

8. What place is home to the speaker of the poem?

   A Her favorite rock

   B The desert

   C Her house with a porch

   D Her cabin in the hills

Constructed Response

9. Which statement *best* expresses the theme of both the story and the poem?

   A Home is a place associated with deep feelings.

   B Homelessness is a problem that must be fixed.

   C Living in a house is a basic need of all people.

   D Everyone is meant to live as one with nature.

Use examples from each selection to explain why you chose that statement.

Informational Skills Review

Evaluating Arguments   **Directions:** Read the following selection. Then, read and respond to the questions that follow.

Can We Rescue the Reefs?

by **Ritu Upadhyay**

from **Time for Kids**

Time is running out to stop the destruction of coral reefs.

Under the clear blue sea, bustling communities of ocean creatures live together in brightly colored, wildly stacked structures called coral reefs. These silent, majestic underwater cities are home to four thousand different species of fish and thousands of plants and animals. For millions of years, marine creatures have lived together in reefs, going about their business in their own little water worlds.

But danger looms. At an international meeting on coral reefs in October 2000, scientists issued a harsh warning. More than one quarter of the world's reefs have been destroyed. . . . Unless drastic measures are taken, the remaining reefs may be dead in twenty years. "We are about to lose them," says Clive Wilkinson of the Coral Reef Monitoring Network.

Precious Underwater Habitats

The destruction of coral reefs, some of which are 2.5 million years old, would have a very serious impact on our oceans. Though coral reefs take up less than 1 percent of the ocean floor, they are home to 25 percent of all underwater species. Wiping them out would put thousands of creatures at risk of extinction. It would also destroy one of our planet's most beautiful living treasures.

Though it's often mistaken for rock because of its stony texture, coral is actually made up of tiny clear animals called coral polyps. Millions stick together in colonies and form a hard outer shell. When coral die, their skeletons are left behind, and new coral build on top. The colonies eventually grow together, creating large reefs. Reefs grow into complex mazelike structures with different rooms, hallways, holes, and crevices for their inhabitants to live in. Over the years the ancient Great Barrier Reef off Australia's coast has grown to be 1,240 miles long!

To the Editor:

My response to Ritu Upadhyay's article "Can We Rescue the Reefs?" is who cares! The environment is doing just fine without all these troublemakers making us pay attention to issues that have no relevance to us. Not only are coral reefs under the sea but they make up less than 1 percent of the ocean floor. Why should I worry about such a small percentage of something I can't see (especially in Australia, which is, like, 100,000 miles away), when I have three hours of homework each night and all sorts of boring chores to do at home. Let Ritu Upadhyay hug her tree, but leave me out of it! When the fish start helping me with my homework, then we'll talk. Till then, I'll be surfing the Internet.

Sincerely,

Matt Bruno

1. There is enough information in the article to show that the author believes coral reefs —
   A must be saved immediately
   B are being killed by pollution
   C eventually turn into rocks
   D will be dead in twenty years

2. Evidence in the article supports the **assertion** that coral reefs —
   A are magnificent cities of marine creatures
   B can be replaced by man-made structures
   C aren't important to young people
   D may possibly die off within twenty years

3. Which of the following statements *best* summarizes the article?
   A The outlook for the future of coral reefs is hopeless.
   B Coral reefs are important undersea little worlds.
   C Efforts to save endangered coral reefs must start now.
   D Global warming is a threat to oceans as well as to land.

4. Read this sentence from the article:
   "It would also destroy one of our planet's most beautiful living treasures."
   The author most likely uses this sentence as —
   A an attack on polluters
   B an emotional appeal
   C statistical evidence
   D an appropriate description

5. The writer of the letter to the editor uses the **stereotyped** idea that —
   A all nature lovers are tree huggers
   B students are too young to change the world
   C doing chores around the house is not important
   D environmental problems can be solved without human interference

Constructed Response
6. Do you think the evidence in the article is adequate to support its assertion? Why or why not?

Vocabulary Skills Review

Figurative Language   **Directions:** Identify and analyze metaphors, similes, and idioms from the excerpt "Home" and the poem "Gold."

1. In "Home" the narrator says Mama's "eyes were lamps turned on." This metaphor means that Mama was —

   A almost in tears

   B happy and excited

   C very angry

   D turning on the porch light

2. Read this sentence from "Home":

   "God may just have reached down and <u>picked up the reins</u>."

   The underlined idiom in the sentence reveals that Mama believes God —

   A may have taken charge of the family's decision

   B will take care of the wagon to move the family's belongings

   C caused the rain to fall as the family sat on the porch

   D will watch over the family in their new home

3. Which lines from the poem contain an example of a metaphor?

   A "watching red and purple sand rivers stream down the hill"

   B "Sparrow on saguaro watches / rabbit watch us . . ."

   C ". . . wide as the sky / like hawk extends her wings"

   D "I sit on my favorite rock, / lizards for company . . ."

4. Which line from the poem contains an example of a simile?

   A "I stretch my arms wide as the sky"

   B "I climb the hills"

   C "Hawk sails on waves of light, sees"

   D "in all the gold light of this, home"

5. Read this sentence from "Gold": "In the wind, we're all / eye to eye." The idiom "eye to eye" means that —

   A the speaker, the lizards, and the rabbit are the same height

   B the speaker and the animals are considered alike by nature

   C the wind is attacking the speaker for being in the desert

   D the speaker and the animals watch the sunset together

Academic Vocabulary

Directions: Read the following passage, and identify the meaning of the Academic Vocabulary word below.

6. The title of a story and the discoveries characters make are *relevant* when trying to discover the story's theme.

   In the sentence, *relevant* means —

   A important

   B appealing

   C unclear

   D similar

Writing Skills Review

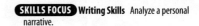

Personal Narrative **Directions:** Read the following paragraph from a personal narrative. Then, answer each question that follows.

> (1) The day I had been dreading for months finally arrived. (2) It was a wet, cold February morning when I saw the moving vans pull up to our driveway. (3) We were leaving the only home I had ever known, the place where I had built a lifetime of memories. (4) The movers were wearing slickers to keep the rain off. (5) I heard my mother giving instructions to the movers, anxiously telling them to be careful with the baby's crib. (6) As I made a tour of the place, the rooms appeared vacant. (7) All the pictures and curtains had been taken down; the furniture was covered with sheets; the books and breakable objects had been packed away. (8) I knew that I would make new friends and have fun in the years ahead, but nothing would replace the memories of my first home.

1. What could the writer add to further develop this personal narrative?

   A The effect of the move on other members of the family

   B A description of some of the narrator's special memories

   C Treasured objects broken during the move

   D The reactions of the neighbors

2. Which of the following sentences is unnecessary and should be deleted?

   A Sentence 3

   B Sentence 4

   C Sentence 7

   D Sentence 8

3. If the narrator were to add dialogue, it would probably come after —

   A sentence 5

   B sentence 6

   C sentence 7

   D sentence 8

4. Which of the following sentences is the *best* replacement for sentence 6?

   A As I entered each room, I found it empty.

   B As I revisited the rooms, the floorboards creaked.

   C As I moved around the empty house, I was grief-stricken.

   D As I walked through the rooms, the house seemed to have lost its life.

5. The tone of this story is —

   A cheerful

   B reflective and sad

   C sullen and gloomy

   D angry and resentful

Read On

Fiction

Across the Grain

In her novel *Across the Grain*, Jean Ferris tells the story of the orphan Will Griffin, a seventeen-year-old who is looking after his flighty older sister, Paige, despite her status as his guardian. When she decides to move from their beach house to a remote desert town, Will is lost and dismayed. Then he meets a moody girl named Mike and an elderly loner named Sam. These outsiders help one another through sorrowful times and discover the value of friendship.

Soldier Boy

When Johnny "the Kid" McBane runs away from the slums of nineteenth-century Chicago, he joins the U.S. cavalry even though he's underage and can neither ride a horse nor shoot a rifle. He soon masters his duties and ultimately fights with General Custer at the Battle of Little Bighorn. This gripping historical novel by Brian Burks explores army life in the 1870s American West, as it details one boy's struggle to become a man.

Holes

Teenager Stanley Yelnats, wrongly sentenced to a detention camp in the Texas desert, must struggle through another piece of bad luck caused by a curse on his family, which began more than a century ago when his great-great-grandfather broke a promise. Stanley survives the harsh treatment at the camp thanks to his courage and newfound friendships. Flashbacks throughout this novel by Louis Sachar tie past and present events and lead to an exciting life-or-death ending.

User Unfriendly

It's the most advanced computer game ever. It plugs directly into your brain—no hardware, no software—and you are really *there*. Arvin Rizalli and his friends pirate the game, along with its hidden program errors, and enter a dark, fantastical world of danger-filled fortresses and terrifying creatures. Vivian Vande Velde, the award-winning author of young-adult mysteries, takes you through a story of mayhem, sword fights, and an unpredictable ending.

Nonfiction

Children of the Wild West

What was the daily life of Al, the boy in the story "Bargain," like back in the nineteenth-century West? What was his school like? Did he ever have fun? The author Russell Freedman explores the difficult lives of the children and their parents who left the comfort of the eastern United States for the Wild West, in search of land, money, and a future of their own.

911: The Book of Help

More than twenty authors of different ages and backgrounds, some famous, some not, wrote their remembrances of the horrific events of September 11, 2001. Some memories take the form of a short story, some an essay, others a poem. As you read *911: The Book of Help,* you will come to understand a moment in time that shook the world and continues to affect it today.

Sylvia Stark: A Pioneer

Freed from slavery just before the American Civil War, Sylvia Stark traveled by wagon train to California in 1860, at the height of the gold rush. A group of African Americans formed a community of their own until they were threatened by a federal law that would have forced those who had escaped from slavery to return to it. Stark and more than six hundred people fled to the safety of Canada. The story of her life, as told by Victoria Scott and Ernest Jones, is one of initiative, endurance, and bravery.

The Acorn People

The Acorn People is more than just a story about children overcoming the difficulties of living with a disability. Ron Jones's memoir tracks his growth and spirit, which were influenced by the determination and friendship of a group of campers called the Acorn People.

Learn It Online

Master your novel knowledge with *NovelWise*:

go.hrw.com   L7-481   Go

UNIT 3

Nonfiction
Writers on Writing

Kathleen Krull on Nonfiction Kathleen Krull is the award-winning author of nonfiction known particularly for her six-book Lives Of series. Her well-received new series, Giants of Science, profiles such individuals as Isaac Newton, Sigmund Freud, and Marie Curie. She is married to the children's book illustrator Paul Brewer.

"Is *nonfiction* an ugly word, and does the thought of writing it sound painful?

From my point of view, "no" and "no." To me, nonfiction is all about passion. And the research part is like playing detective— it's all about being clever and creative.

What are you passionate about? Some of my obsessions are myself, music, social injustice, history, aliens, and especially the intimate lives of famous people. I'm drawn to biographies because I'm just plain nosy— and I know I'm not alone: Gossip makes the world go round; or as John F. Kennedy said, "All history is gossip." I'm intrigued by the shape of a life—the arc, the story. As stories, biographies can be things of beauty, with people who have definite beginnings, middles, and demises, plus obstacles they overcome. I enjoy the challenge of trying to sculpt with words a portrait that conveys the essence of a person.

The ability to write clear prose will aid just about any career I can think of. All your life you'll be putting thoughts into words (as in a journal or blog), trying to influence people (complaining, persuading, instructing), doing expository writing on the job. It's even possible—trust me—to make a whole career out of writing nonfiction.

But why bother—isn't everything factual already on the Internet? A big "no" to this one. All hail Google—it's a rush—but the Internet is like a trick-or-treat bag several days past Halloween: The good stuff is usually gone. It's useful in the early stages of a project for basic, reliable sources like encyclopedias.

But for real research—detailed info that's been digested by scholars and carefully edited—you need books. I'm a heavy user of the library. I take a mountain of notes on what I think is most interesting and then revise, tinker, revise, edit, whittle, and then do some more revising to get what I hope is the very tiptop of the mountain. If there is a magic key to what I do, it's that I don't use all my information. Being selective is the trick.

Some other tricks to good nonfiction—in addition to writing about something you love—are accuracy, clarity, organization, revision, drama, revision, having a voice of your own, revision, taking an unusual point of view, crafting an irresistible opening sentence, using vigorous verbs. Did I mention revision? As with fiction, every sentence in nonfiction should be there for a reason, reflecting endless choices within a structure designed to meet some challenge.

So much to say about writing non-fiction. . . . One of my all-time tips is using your computer's word counter and giving yourself an arbitrary word count—it's amazing how this coaxes your thoughts into their essence. This essay, for example—my word count ends here. "

Think as a Writer

Kathleen Krull is an avid reader and writer of biographies. What is your favorite biography? Whom would you like to know more about?

Elements of Nonfiction

INFORMATIONAL TEXT FOCUS
Author's Purpose and Perspective

"You cannot control what happens to you, but you can control your attitude toward what happens to you."

—Brian Tracy

What Do **You** Think   How do our attitudes influence the changes and challenges we face in life?

Bethany Hamilton, finding the courage to surf again after losing her left arm in a shark attack.

Learn It Online
Explore more nonfiction works through the interactive Reading Workshops online:

go.hrw.com   L7-485   Go

Literary Focus

by **Linda Rief**

What Are the Elements of Nonfiction?

Which type of story is easier to write: fiction or nonfiction? Some might think the answer is nonfiction, which deals with real people, events, and places. After all, so much of the information is already at the author's fingertips! Yet there's more to a nonfiction story than simply telling the facts. Authors can choose which will be the most successful way to present their subject. Should the account be objective or subjective, positive or negative, biased or unbiased? Think about how nonfiction authors make what could be an ordinary telling of a subject's life extraordinary.

Some Types of Nonfiction

Autobiography An **autobiography** is a story in which the author writes about his or her own life. Autobiographies are usually written from the **first-person point of view,** using personal pronouns like *I* and *me. Barrio Boy* tells the story of Ernesto Galarza's life in California after Ernesto has left his native Mexico.

> Miss Ryan took me to a seat at the front of the room, into which I shrank.
>
> from *Barrio Boy* by Ernesto Galarza

Biography Biographies are among the most popular types of nonfiction. A **biography** is a story in which the author writes about another person's life. "Elizabeth I" is Meltzer's biography of the remarkable queen of England, who ruled in the sixteenth century.

> She was a strong-willed girl who liked to give orders. She loved to be out on horseback, and rode so fast it frightened the men assigned to protect her.
>
> from "Elizabeth I" by Milton Meltzer

Essay An **essay** is a short piece of nonfiction that examines a single subject or limited topic. An essay may be about something simple, like walking a dog, or complex, like freedom or justice. This collection features several **personal essays.** You will read about aspects of a writer's life, such as how Julia Alvarez was influenced by her name.

> At school I was *Judy* or *Judith,* and once an English teacher mistook me for *Juliet.*
>
> from "Names/Nombres" by Julia Alvarez

In this collection, you'll read an autobiography, a biography, and several essays.

Some Elements of Nonfiction

Perspective The way a writer looks at a subject is called **perspective.** It is also referred to as viewpoint, stance, or point of view. A writer's perspective may be positive or negative, biased or unbiased. Interpreting a writer's perspective can help you understand and evaluate what you are reading. In his **biography** of Elizabeth I, Meltzer often shows his perspective of the queen, as in this example:

> England had experienced one of its greatest periods in its long history. Under Elizabeth's leadership, England had become united as a nation; its industry and commerce, its arts and sciences had flourished; and it was ranked among the great powers of Europe.
>
> from "Elizabeth I" by Milton Meltzer

Subjective and Objective Writing Much of nonfiction is **impersonal,** or **objective.** Objective writing sticks to the facts. It does not reveal the writer's feelings, beliefs, or point of view about the subject. Objective writing emphasizes the content, not the writer.

On the other hand, nonfiction may be very **personal,** as it is in journals, diaries, and personal essays. Nonfiction that reveals and emphasizes feelings and opinions is called **subjective writing.** Most of the nonfiction in this collection is a mix of subjective and objective writing.

Term	Definition	Example
Objective writing	The writer sticks to facts and presents information that is supported by evidence.	Elizabeth was the daughter of King Henry VIII and his second wife, Anne Boleyn. At the age of two she lost her mother when Henry had Anne's head chopped off. *from "Elizabeth I" by Milton Meltzer*
Subjective writing	The writer freely expresses personal feelings, thoughts, opinions, and judgments.	I had to question myself whether or not it was important to be the kind of leader and person my father believed I was inside. I knew in my heart that he was right. *from "A Good Reason to Look Up" by Shaquille O'Neal*

Your Turn Analyzing Nonfiction

1. Explain the difference between an autobiography and a personal essay.

2. Is a personal essay more likely to be an example of subjective or objective writing? Why?

3. What type of writing are you most likely to find in a biography?

Learn It Online

Organize your thoughts! Use one of the interactive graphic organizers at:

go.hrw.com | L7-487 | Go

Analyzing Visuals

How Can You Interpret Point of View?

In nonfiction, a writer's perspective, or viewpoint, determines what the writer says about a subject. Similarly, a painter can reveal or withhold details from the viewer to express a certain viewpoint. The paintings on these two pages show how artists can have different perspectives on the same subject. Roy Lichtenstein's painting resembles comic strip art. The unknown artist's painting, *Portrait of a Spaniel,* is realistic, or true to life. Each artist used a different style to clearly express a particular viewpoint of a dog.

1. What is Lichtenstein trying to get the viewer to focus on? What details do you notice most about the dog?

2. What does the artist want you to think about the dog?

3. What words would you use to describe Lichtenstein's attitude toward this dog?

Grrrrrrrrrrr! (1965) by Roy Lichtenstein.
Oil and magna on canvas
(172.7 cm × 142.5 cm).
Gift of the artist. 1977.
Solomon R. Guggenheim Museum, New York. 97.4565.

Portrait of a Spaniel.

4. What does the artist want you to think about this dog?

5. What details in the paintings suggest the artists' attitudes toward dogs? What words would you use to describe this perspective?

Interpreting an Artist's Point of View

Answer these questions as you interpret the paintings:

1. Does the subject seem to be shown in a positive or negative way? Explain.

2. What details in the painting seem important or interesting? How do these details express the artist's perspective, or attitude, toward the subject?

3. What overall mood or feeling does the painting suggest? How might this mood or feeling relate to the artist's attitude about the subject?

Your Turn Talk About Perspective or Point of View

With a classmate, discuss the different perspectives, or viewpoints, shown in the dog images on these pages. Express each viewpoint in a word or phrase.

Reading Focus

by **Kylene Beers**

What Skills and Strategies Help You Read Nonfiction?

Many reading skills can help you comprehend autobiographies, biographies, personal essays, and other kinds of nonfiction. These skills include finding the main idea, organizing information, distinguishing fact and opinion, and understanding the author's purpose.

Main Idea

The most important point or central idea of a selection is its **main idea.** Sometimes it is directly stated. Other times you must infer, or make an educated guess, about the main idea. Like theme, a main idea should be stated in a full sentence.

What main idea IS	What main idea IS NOT
✓ the central idea of the whole text, not part of it	✗ the plot (the series of events)
✓ sometimes directly stated; usually implied	✗ the topic (the one-word subject of the text)

Tips for Finding the Main Idea

- Look at the title. Does it tell you what the text will focus on? For example, "Elizabeth I" is a biography by Milton Meltzer in this collection. This title reveals the topic but does not state the main idea.
- Look for a sentence that seems to state a key idea in general terms. It may be found at the beginning or at the end of the text. Read the following quotation from the beginning of "Elizabeth I" and see if you can determine the main idea.

"Good Queen Bess" her people called her. But "good" is a tame word for one of the most remarkable women who ever lived.

from "Elizabeth I" by Milton Meltzer

You will often need to continue reading in order to determine the main idea.

- If you can't find a key sentence that clearly states the main idea, go back over the text and find its major details. What do all of these details add up to?

Organize Information

You can use different approaches to organize information you learn in a nonfiction selection.

- **Summarizing** Restate the main idea or major events in the text. To summarize an informational text, include the main idea and the important details that support the main idea.
- **Comparing and Contrasting** When you compare, you look for similarities. When you contrast, you look for differences. You can use a chart or an organizer such as a Venn diagram to identify similarities and differences.

Facts and Opinions

A **fact** is something that happened or is true. An **opinion** represents a belief or judgment and cannot be proven.

When you read nonfiction, especially an autobiography or personal essay, it is important to be able to distinguish facts from opinions. Here are examples from the autobiography *Barrio Boy*.

Term	Definition	Examples
Fact	something that can be proven	Half of the block was occupied by Lincoln School.
Opinion	something that can be supported by facts but can't be proven true or false	[Miss Hopley] seemed a match for giants. I decided I liked her.

Be alert to opinions stated as facts. If you're in doubt, ask, "Can this statement be proven?"

In *Barrio Boy* it can be proven that the school occupies a certain amount of space. However, the way Ernesto feels about Miss Hopley is an opinion. Watch for these words to help you identify opinions: *believe, seem, may, think, probably, likely,* and *possibly.*

Author's Purpose

Writers of nonfiction have different purposes.

- A **biography** informs about a person's life but also entertains with interesting details.
- In an **autobiography** the writer may want to share information, explain events in his or her life, or even persuade the reader.
- **Personal essayists** may want to reveal a truth about life. In "Long Walk to Freedom," Mandela wants to share what he has discovered about fear and courage in the face of oppression.

> The brave man is not he who does not feel afraid, but he who conquers that fear.
>
> from *Long Walk to Freedom* by Nelson Mandela

The following list summarizes reasons explaining an author's purpose for writing:

- to inform
- to explain
- to persuade
- to entertain
- to reveal a truth about life
- to share an experience

Your Turn Apply Reading Skills

1. An author writes a personal essay about learning to be proud of both her Spanish name and her American nicknames. Write a statement that expresses the main idea of this essay.

2. Write a statement that explains the author's purpose in writing about her many names.

3. Write a sentence about a sports star. Use a combination of fact and opinion. Circle the part of the sentence that is fact, and underline the part of the sentence that is opinion.

> **Now go to the Skills in Action: Reading Model**

Learn It Online
Build your understanding using *PowerNotes*:

go.hrw.com | L7-491 | **Go**

Read with a Purpose Read the following **personal essay** to discover a lesson the writer learned from his parents.

A Good Reason to Look Up

by Shaquille O'Neal

Literary Focus

Personal Essay Notice the pronoun *I* in the first sentence. This is a **first-person** account. To find out who the *I* is, check the name of the writer.

When I was in junior high school, what my friends thought of me was real important to me. During those years I grew much taller than most of my peers. Being so tall made me feel uncomfortable. In order to keep the focus off of me and my unusual height, I went along with the crowd who would play practical jokes on other kids at school. Being one of the class clowns gave me a way to make sure that the jokes were directed at others, and not at me.

Reading Focus

Fact and Opinion In O'Neal's **opinion,** the pranks he played were harmful to others. He supports his opinion with **fact**—the example of what he did with Icy Hot.

I would pull all kinds of pranks that were hurtful, and sometimes even harmful, to others. Once before gym class, my friends and I put Icy Hot in the gym shorts of one of the kids on the basketball team. Not only was he terribly embarrassed, but he also had to go to the school nurse's office. I thought it was going to be funny, but it ended up that no one thought it was—least of all my father.

My parents didn't always think that my behavior was funny. They reminded me about The Golden Rule: to treat others as I would like to be treated. Many times, I was disciplined for the hurtful way that I was treating others. What I was doing was hurting other kids, and in turn hurting my reputation as someone to be looked up to. My friends were looking up to me because I was tall, but what did they see?

Reading Focus

Organizing Information
Summarizing is one way of organizing information. In this sentence, O'Neal is restating what he said in the first three paragraphs.

My parents wanted me to be a leader who was a good example to others—to be a decent human being. They taught me

Analyzing Visuals

Viewing and Interpreting
How does this photograph reflect
what Shaquille O'Neal says?

to set my own goals, and to do the best at everything that I set
out to do. During the lectures I got from my father, he told me
over and over again to be the leader that I was meant to be—to
be a big man in my heart and actions, as well as in my body. I
had to question myself whether or not it was important to be
the kind of leader and person my father believed I was inside. I
knew in my heart that he was right. So I tried my best to follow
my father's advice.

Once I focused on being the best that I could be at basketball
and became a leader in the game, I took my responsibility to set
a good example more seriously. I sometimes have to stop and
think before I act, and I make mistakes occasionally—everyone
is human. But I continue to look for opportunities where I can
make a difference, and to set a good example because of my
father's advice. I now pass it on to you.

"Be a leader, Shaq, not a follower. Since people already have
to look up to you, give them a *good* reason to do so."

Read with a Purpose   What did Shaquille O'Neal learn from his parents? Do you think these are important lessons? Explain why or why not.

Reading Focus

Finding Main Idea   The **main
idea** may be stated directly, but
more often, you need to figure it
out. Here, O'Neal shares the central idea of his essay—he is telling us about the kind of person
he strives to be.

Reading Focus

Author's Purpose   O'Neal
states his reason for writing this
essay. He wants to explain what
he learned and to encourage
readers to follow his example.

Shaquille O'Neal
(1972–   )

Vital Statistics

- Nicknames: Shaq, Superman, Diesel, the Big Aristotle
- Born: March 6, 1972, in Newark, New Jersey. His birth name, Shaquille Rashaun, means "little warrior" in Arabic.

Interesting Facts

- Shaq learned to play basketball as a boy while living in Germany.
- Shaq is seven feet one inch tall and weighs well over 300 pounds. His shoe size is 21.

Why Is He Important?

- Shaq is the youngest player to have been named one of the NBA's fifty greatest players.
- He has acted in films, television programs, and commercials.
- Shaq is a member of the National Advisory Council of Reading is Fundamental, an organization that promotes literacy for children.

What's Important to Him?

Basketball isn't Shaq's only love. He enjoys reading and says, "My parents encouraged me to read and to educate myself. Following their advice, I've always tried to read to better myself." He has worked hard on his education, and in 2000, he graduated from Louisiana State University with a bachelor's degree. While working on an MBA from the University of Phoenix in 2005, he said, "It's just something to have on my résumé when I go back to reality. Someday I might have to put down a basketball and have a regular 9–5 [job] like everybody else."

Think About the Writer Do you view O'Neal as a role model? Why or why not?

SKILLS IN ACTION
Wrap Up

Into Action: Finding the Main Idea

Use this chart to help you find the main idea of "A *Good* Reason to Look Up." Answer each question with *yes* or *no,* based on information from the selection. When you can answer *yes* to a question that asks what this selection is *all* about, you've learned the main idea. If not, continue to ask *is it all about?* questions. Rewrite the main idea as a statement.

Finding the Main Idea	Yes or No
Is this selection **all** about O'Neal's being tall?	
Is this selection **all** about O'Neal's being a prankster?	
Is it **all** about what O'Neal's parents wanted him to be?	
Is it **all** about how O'Neal became a leader?	
Is it **all** about . . .	

Talk About . . .

1. Why did O'Neal's height make him uncomfortable in junior high? What does O'Neal's example teach you about accepting differences? Try to use each Academic Vocabulary word listed at the right at least once in your discussion.

Write About . . .

Use the Academic Vocabulary words in your answers to these questions about "A *Good* Reason to Look Up."

2. Is there anything <u>ambiguous</u> about the essay title? Explain.

3. What makes it <u>evident</u> that O'Neal's parents recognized his potential to be a star?

4. What lesson does O'Neal <u>convey</u> in his essay? Explain.

Writing Focus

Think as a Reader/Writer

In Collection 5, the Writing Focus activities on the Preparing to Read pages explain how the writers use point of view and other elements of nonfiction. On the Applying Your Skills pages, you'll have a chance to practice these methods.

Academic Vocabulary for Collection 5

Talking and Writing About Nonfiction

Academic Vocabulary is the language you use to write and talk about texts. Use these words to discuss the nonfiction selections you read in this collection. The words are underlined throughout the collection.

ambiguous (am BIHG yoo uhs) *adj.:* having more than one possible meaning; unclear. *The main idea of an essay may sometimes seem ambiguous.*

evident (EHV uh duhnt) *adj.:* easy to see or perceive; clear. *The first-person point of view is always evident from the use of the pronoun I.*

convey (kuhn VAY) *v.:* make known; communicate; express. *Authors can convey their perspectives on a subject in a variety of ways.*

principal (PRIHN suh puhl) *adj.:* most important. *What is the principal lesson we can learn from* Long Walk to Freedom?

Your Turn

Copy the Academic Vocabulary words into your *Reader/Writer Notebook.* Use these words to discuss a person that you or others look up to. Practice using these Academic Vocabulary words throughout this collection.

Names/Nombres

by **Julia Alvarez**

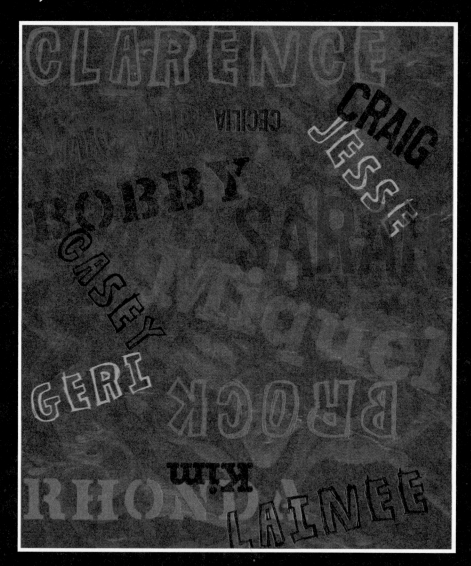

What Do You Think

Sometimes you need to make tough choices in order to fit in. How far would you go to fit in?

 QuickWrite

Would you ever change your name or accept a nickname from others in order to fit in? List the reasons you would—or would not—consider this.

Reader/Writer
Notebook

Use your **RWN** to complete the activities for this selection.

SKILLS FOCUS Literary Skills Understand point of view; understand subjective and objective points of view. **Reading Skills** Identify the main idea.

Literary Focus

Subjective and Objective Points of View When authors write from a **subjective point of view,** they convey their own thoughts, feelings, opinions, and judgments. Personal essays and autobiographies (where you expect writers to express opinions) are often written with a subjective point of view. An **objective point of view,** on the other hand, tends to be unbiased and presents the facts and figures rather than the author's feelings.

Reading Focus

Finding the Main Idea All of the key details in a nonfiction selection add up to a **main idea**—the one the writer wants you to remember. The main idea of this essay is not directly stated. It is implied, so you will need to **infer,** or guess, what it is.

Into Action Use a chart to help you find the essay's main idea. First, identify the topic. (Remember that the title can be a clue.) As you read, write key details and events in the boxes. You'll add the main idea later.

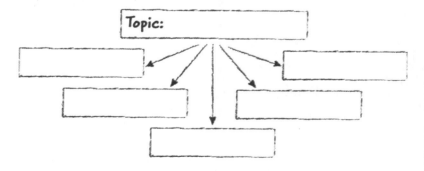

Topic:

Writing Focus

Think as a Reader/Writer

Find It in Your Reading As you read this personal essay, make a list of at least five subjective details Alvarez uses to describe her feelings.

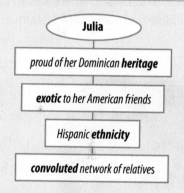

Julia

proud of her Dominican **heritage**

exotic *to her American friends*

Hispanic **ethnicity**

convoluted *network of relatives*

Language Coach

Suffixes A **suffix** is a word part added to the end of a word. *Ethnicity* has the suffix *—ity,* which means "having a particular quality." What word do you get when adding this suffix to the word *complex?*

⁕ Learn It Online
For a preview of this essay, see the video introduction on:

go.hrw.com | L7-497 |

Julia Alvarez
(1950–   )

Interpreting Two Worlds

Born in New York City, Julia Alvarez spent her childhood in the Dominican Republic, returning with her family to New York when she was ten years old. Adjusting to her new surroundings in the early 1960s wasn't easy for young Julia.

A Special Point of View

Despite the difficulties, being an immigrant gave Julia a special point of view: "We travel on that border between two worlds," she explains, "and we can see both points of view."

After attending college and graduate school, Alvarez taught poetry for twelve years in several different states. Today Alvarez lives in Vermont, where she writes novels and teaches at Middlebury College. Of "Names/Nombres," she says:

> "I realized . . . that part of becoming American was when the person inside me could answer to those American names without feeling funny."

Think About the Writer What in your life helps you recognize different points of view?

Build Background

Julia Alvarez was raised in the Dominican Republic. This country is located on the Caribbean island of Hispaniola, which it shares with the country of Haiti. Use the map, below, to locate the Dominican Republic. It is west of Puerto Rico and east of Cuba and Jamaica.

Preview the Selection

Julia Alvarez and her family fled the Dominican Republic in 1960. Her **father,** a medical doctor, was part of an underground movement that planned to overthrow the dictator ruling the Dominican Republic at the time. To avoid the father's arrest, the family escaped to the United States. Alvarez's essay describes what it was like to grow up in New York City.

Read with a Purpose   Read this essay to see how Alvarez's feelings about her name and nicknames change as she adjusts to life in the United States.

Names/Nombres

by **Julia Alvarez**

When we arrived in New York City, our names changed almost immediately. At Immigration, the officer asked my father, *Mister Elbures,* if he had anything to declare. My father shook his head no, and we were waved through.

I was too afraid we wouldn't be let in if I corrected the man's pronunciation, but I said our name to myself, opening my mouth wide for the organ blast of the *a,* trilling my tongue for the drumroll of the *r, All-vah-rrr-es!* How could anyone get *Elbures* out of that orchestra of sound?   **Ⓐ**

At the hotel my mother was *Missus Alburest,* and I was *little girl,* as in, "Hey, little girl, stop riding the elevator up and down. It's *not* a toy."

When we moved into our new apartment building, the super called my father *Mister Alberase,* and the neighbors who became mother's friends pronounced her name *Jew-lee-ah* instead of *Hoo-lee-ah.* I, her namesake, was known as *Hoo-lee-tah* at home. But at school I was *Judy* or *Judith,* and once an English teacher mistook me for *Juliet.*

Glossary: Spanish Words for Talking About Family

Family relationships are an important part of this essay. Alvarez uses Spanish terms to describe some of her relatives. Check this glossary for the pronunciation and meaning of these words and phrases.

comadre (koh MAH dray) *n.:* informal Spanish for "close friend." *Comadre* is the name that the mother and the godmother of a child use for one another.

madrina (mah DREE nah) *n.:* Spanish for "godmother."

mis hermanas (mees ehr MAH nahs): Spanish for "my sisters."

primas (PREE mahs) *n.:* Spanish for "female cousins."

tía (TEE ah) *n.:* Spanish for "aunt."

tío (TEE oh) *n.:* Spanish for "uncle."

una hija de crianza (OO nah EE hah deh kree AHN sah): Spanish for "an adopted daughter." *Crianza* means "upbringing."

Ⓐ Read and Discuss   What is <u>evident</u> about the "Elbures" family?

It took a while to get used to my new names. I wondered if I shouldn't correct my teachers and new friends. But my mother argued that it didn't matter. "You know what your friend Shakespeare said, 'A rose by any other name would smell as sweet.'"[1] My family had gotten into the habit of calling any famous author "my friend" because I had begun to write poems and stories in English class.   **B**

By the time I was in high school, I was a popular kid, and it showed in my name. Friends called me *Jules* or *Hey Jude,* and once a group of troublemaking friends my mother forbade me to hang out with called me *Alcatraz.* I was *Hoo-lee-tah* only to Mami and Papi and uncles and aunts who came over to eat sancocho[2] on Sunday afternoons—old world folk whom I would just as soon go back to where they came from and leave me to pursue whatever mischief I wanted to in America. *JUDY ALCATRAZ,* the name on the "Wanted" poster would read. Who would ever trace her to me?   **C**

My older sister had the hardest time getting an American name for herself because *Mauricia* did not translate into English. Ironically, although she had the most foreign-sounding name, she and I were the Americans in the family. We had been born in New York City when our parents had first tried immigration and then gone back "home," too homesick to stay. My mother often told the story of how she had almost changed my sister's name in the hospital.

After the delivery, Mami and some other new mothers were cooing over their new baby sons and daughters and exchanging names and weights and delivery stories. My mother was embarrassed among the Sallys and Janes and Georges and Johns to reveal the rich, noisy name of *Mauricia,* so when her turn came to brag, she gave her baby's name as *Maureen.*

"Why'd ya give her an Irish name with so many pretty Spanish names to choose from?" one of the women asked.

My mother blushed and admitted her baby's real name to the group. Her mother-in-law had recently died, she apologized, and her husband had insisted that the first daughter be named after his mother, *Mauran.* My mother thought it the ugliest name she had ever heard, and she talked my father into what she believed was an improvement, a combination of *Mauran* and her own mother's name, *Felicia.*

"Her name is *Mao-ree-shee-ah,*" my mother said to the group of women.

---

1. *"A rose . . . as sweet"*: Julia's mother is quoting from the play *Romeo and Juliet.*
2. **sancocho** (sahn KOH choh): stew of meats and fruit.

B **Literary Focus** Subjective/Objective Points of View What examples of the author's feelings convey a subjective point of view? What does that tell you about her?

C Read and Discuss When the "old world folk" came to visit, Julia wished they would go back to where they came from. What does that tell you about her?

Hannah (2001) by Alexandra Heyes. Oil.

©Alexandra Heyes

"Why, that's a beautiful name," the new mothers cried. "*Moor-ee-sha, Moor-ee-sha,*" they cooed into the pink blanket. *Moor-ee-sha* it was when we returned to the States eleven years later. Sometimes, American tongues found even that mispronunciation tough to say and called her *Maria* or *Marsha* or *Maudy* from her nickname *Maury*. I pitied her. What an awful name to have to transport across borders! **Ⓓ**

My little sister, Ana, had the easiest time of all. She was plain *Anne*—that is, only her name was plain, for she turned out to be the pale, blond "American beauty" in the family. The only Hispanic thing about her was the affectionate nicknames her boyfriends sometimes gave her. *Anita,* or, as one goofy guy used to sing to her to the tune of the banana advertisement, *Anita Banana.*

Later, during her college years in the late sixties, there was a push to pronounce Third World[3] names correctly. I remember calling her long distance at her group house and a roommate answering.

"Can I speak to Ana?" I asked, pronouncing her name the American way.

---

3. **Third World:** developing countries of Latin America, Africa, and Asia.

4. **serapes** (suh RAH peez): woolen shawls worn in Latin American countries.

Ⓓ Read and Discuss What does the story about Mauricia's name tell you about the mother?

Ⓔ Literary Focus **Subjective/Objective Points of View** Is the author being objective or subjective as she conveys this information about herself? How do you know?

"Ana?" The man's voice hesitated. "Oh! You must mean *Ah-nah!*"

Our first few years in the States, though, ethnicity was not yet "in." Those were the blond, blue-eyed, bobby-sock years of junior high and high school before the sixties ushered in peasant blouses, hoop earrings, serapes.[4] My initial desire to be known by my correct Dominican name faded. I just wanted to be Judy and merge with the Sallys and Janes in my class. But, inevitably, my accent and coloring gave me away. "So where are you from, Judy?"

"New York," I told my classmates. After all, I had been born blocks away at Columbia-Presbyterian Hospital. **Ⓔ**

"I mean, *originally.*"

"From the Caribbean," I answered vaguely, for if I specified, no one was quite sure on what continent our island was located.

"Really? I've been to Bermuda. We went last April for spring vacation. I got the worst sunburn! So, are you from Portoriko?"

"No," I sighed. "From the Dominican Republic.

"Where's that?"

"South of Bermuda."

They were just being curious, I knew, but

Vocabulary **ethnicity** (ehth NIHS uh tee) *n.:* common culture or nationality.

I burned with shame whenever they singled me out as a "foreigner," a rare, exotic friend.

"Say your name in Spanish, oh, please say it!" I had made mouths drop one day by rattling off my full name, which, according to Dominican custom, included my middle names, Mother's and Father's surnames for four generations back.

"Julia Altagracia María Teresa Álvarez Tavares Perello Espaillat Julia Pérez Rochet González." I pronounced it slowly, a name as chaotic with sounds as a Middle Eastern bazaar or market day in a South American village. **F**

My Dominican heritage was never more apparent than when my extended family attended school occasions. For my graduation, they all came, the whole lot of aunts and uncles and the many little cousins who snuck in without tickets. They sat in the first row in order to better understand the Americans' fast-spoken English. But how could they listen when they were constantly speaking among themselves in florid-sounding[5] phrases, rococo[6] consonants, rich, rhyming vowels?

Introducing them to my friends was a further trial to me. These relatives had such complicated names and there were so many of them, and their relationships to myself were so convoluted. There was my Tía Josefina, who was not really an aunt but a much older cousin. And her daughter, Aida Margarita, who was adopted, una hija de crianza. My uncle of affection, Tío José, brought my madrina Tía Amelia and her comadre Tía Pilar. My friends rarely had more than a "Mom and Dad" to introduce.

After the commencement ceremony, my family waited outside in the parking lot while my friends and I signed yearbooks with nicknames which recalled our high school good times: "Beans" and "Pepperoni" and "Alcatraz."

> I pronounced it slowly, a name as chaotic with sounds as a Middle Eastern bazaar or market day in a South American village.

---

5. **florid-sounding:** flowery; using fancy words.
6. **rococo** (ruh KOH koh): fancy. Rococo is an early-eighteenth-century style of art and architecture known for its fancy ornamentation.

F **Read and Discuss** The author tells you that when she pronounces her name, she says it slowly. What point is she making?

Vocabulary **exotic** (ehg ZAHT ihk) *adj.:* not native. **heritage** (HEHR uh tihj) *n.:* traditions that are passed along. **convoluted** (KAHN vuh loo tihd) *v.* used as *adj.:* complicated.

We hugged and cried and promised to keep in touch.

Our goodbyes went on too long. I heard my father's voice calling out across the parking lot, "*Hoo-lee-tah!* Vámonos!"[7]

Back home, my tíos and tías and primas, Mami and Papi, and mis hermanas had a party for me with sancocho and a store-bought pudín,[8] inscribed with

---

7. **Vámonos!** (VAH maw nohs): Spanish for "Let's go!"
8. **pudín** (poo DEEN): Spanish cake.

Happy Graduation, Julie. There were many gifts—that was a plus to a large family! I got several wallets and a suitcase with my initials and a graduation charm from my godmother and money from my uncles. The biggest gift was a portable typewriter from my parents for writing my stories and poems. **G**

Someday, the family predicted, my name would be well-known throughout the United States. I laughed to myself, wondering which one I would go by. **H**

G Reading Focus Main Idea Why does Alvarez call her essay "Names/Nombres"? What is she saying about herself and her new life?

H Read and Discuss Julia laughs when she thinks about which "well-known" name she'll go by. What does this tell you about her?

Applying Your Skills

SKILLS FOCUS **Literary Skills** Analyze point of view; analyze subjective and objective points of view; analyze first-person point of view. **Reading Skills** Identify the main idea. **Writing Skills** Write to describe; analyze the writer's technique.

Names/Nombres

Respond and Think Critically

Quick Check

1. As a teenager, why does Julia want to be called Judy? How has Julia's attitude toward her name changed since then?

Read with a Purpose

2. Explain how a name can influence someone's identity and sense of self.

Reading Skill: Finding the Main Idea

3. Review the events and details in your main-idea chart. To find an implied main idea,

- think about the point that the important details reveal.
- use this information to figure out the main idea. Write it in the chart in your own words.

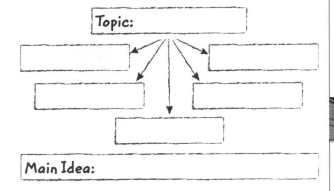

Topic:

Main Idea:

Literary Focus

Literary Analysis

4. **Analyze** How does the title "Names/Nombres" connect to Alvarez's comment about being on the "border between two worlds"?

5. **Interpret** Shakespeare said, "A rose by any other name would smell as sweet." How do those words apply to Alvarez and her life?

6. **Analyze** What do you think Alvarez learns about her family and heritage as she takes a journey through the "name game"?

Literary Skills: Subjective/Objective Points of View

7. **Evaluate** What evidence tells you that this essay is written in the subjective point of view?

8. **Compare/Contrast** How would an essay about names written from the objective point of view differ from "Names/Nombres"?

Literary Skills Review: First-Person Point of View

9. **Comparing/Contrasting** Alvarez is the narrator and uses the first-person pronoun *I*. How would the essay change if it were told by another person? What main idea might this person <u>convey</u> that Alvarez does not?

Writing Focus

Think as a Reader/Writer

Use It in Your Writing Review the subjective details you identified in Alvarez's writing. In a paragraph, explain the effect of including subjective details like these in the essay.

What Do **You Think Now?** How has this essay affected your ideas about how people adjust to fit in?

Applying Your Skills

Names/Nombres

Vocabulary Development
Context Clues: Definitions

Writers often help you understand a difficult word by providing a definition in context—that is, the words, sentences, and paragraphs surrounding the word.

A writer who uses definitions will explain what a word means in the sentence or passage. For example, Julia Alvarez clarifies the meaning of the Spanish word *tía* by defining it in the sentence.

> "There was my Tía Josefina, who was not really my aunt but a much older cousin."

Be on the lookout for such phrases as *in other words* and *that is* when looking for definitions of words in context.

Your Turn

Complete the following sentences so that the sentences clarify the meanings of the Vocabulary words in the list.

> ethnicity
> exotic
> heritage
> convoluted

1. The meal was exotic—that is, it was _____.

2. The explanation of the science project became more convoluted the longer the student talked. In other words, it was _____.

3. The street festival was planned to introduce visitors to the city's heritage, or _____.

4. Studies have shown that ethnicity, meaning _____, influences the kinds of programs that people watch on television.

Language Coach

Suffixes Many English words can be divided into parts. If you know the meaning of various word parts, you can often figure out the meanings of unfamiliar words. Suffixes are word parts that are added to the ends of words. Knowing the meanings of suffixes can greatly increase your vocabulary. For instance, knowing that the suffix *–ly* means "in a particular way" will help you understand the meaning of three other words from "Names/Nombres":

> *immediately   ironically   constantly*

Words ending in *–ly* usually tell how or how often something is done. Explain whether or not this rule applies to these three words from "Names/Nombres."

Academic Vocabulary

Write About . . .

In a short paragraph, write about the role Alvarez's family played in helping her develop her identity. Then, discuss the way her identity becomes <u>evident</u> in the way she <u>conveys</u> her story. Use the underlined Academic Vocabulary words in your response.

Learn It Online
Explore suffixes with *WordSharp*:

go.hrw.com | L7-506 | **Go**

SKILLS FOCUS **Literary Skills** Analyze point of view; analyze subjective and objective points of view; analyze first-person point of view. **Reading Skills** Identify the main idea. **Vocabulary Skills** Clarify word meanings through definitions; use context clues in words, sentences, and paragraphs to decode new vocabulary. **Grammar Skills** Demonstrate understanding of correct subject-verb agreement. **Writing Skills** Write descriptive essays; include the importance of the subject; describe a place.

Grammar Link

Subject-Verb Agreement

Two words agree when they have the same number. The number of a verb should agree with, or match, the number of its subject.

Julia wants to fit in. [*Julia* is one person, so the verb *wants* is in the singular form.]

Friends pronounce her name incorrectly. [*Friends* refers to more than one person, so the verb *pronounce* is in the plural form.]

When a sentence contains a verb phrase, the first helping verb in the phrase agrees with the subject.

The **aunt is** smiling.

The **aunts are** smiling.

Note that in a question, the verb phrase is often split. The same rules of agreement apply anyway.

Is your **cousin attending** the graduation ceremony?

Are your **cousins attending** the graduation ceremony?

Your Turn

Identify which form of the verb in parentheses agrees with the subject.

1. Julia (*has, have*) been in New York City.
2. Neighbors (*yell, yells*) greetings in English to the family.
3. Ana's college (*was, were*) full of students.
4. (*Is, Are*) Mauricia's name pronounced correctly?
5. The family (*eat, eats*) a festive meal.

CHOICES

As you respond to the Choices, use these **Academic Vocabulary** words as appropriate: <u>ambiguous</u>, <u>evident</u>, <u>convey</u>, <u>principal</u>.

REVIEW
Speak Objectively and Subjectively

Imagine that you are visiting a new place and are phoning home. With a partner, make two **objective** statements of facts about the place and two **subjective** statements that <u>convey</u> your thoughts and feelings. (You can make up any details you want.) Use a chart like this one:

Objective Statements	Subjective Statements

CONNECT
Describe a Family Food

Timed ⏱ Writing Alvarez describes foods that are served at her family get-togethers. Think of foods you associate with family meals on special occasions. Use the **first-person point of view** to write a description of your favorite family dish. Include **subjective** details in your writing.

EXTEND
Write About Your Name

Use both a **subjective** and **objective point of view** to write about your family name, given name, nickname, or pet name. Explain when and how you got the name and how you feel about it. Is it an accurate representation of who you are?

Learn It Online
Use MediaScope to visually explain your name:

go.hrw.com   L7-507   **Go**

ELIZABETH I

by **Milton Meltzer**

What Do
You
Think

How do people turn challenges into opportunities?

🕐 **QuickWrite**

Think about a time when you were faced with a challenge. Explain what it was and how you handled it.

The photographs illustrating this biography are from the 1998 movie *Elizabeth*, starring Cate Blanchett as Elizabeth I.

Reader/Writer Notebook

Use your **RWN** to complete the activities for this selection.

Literary Focus

Biography In a biography a writer tells the story of another person's life. Most biographers follow a factual style, using careful research in their descriptions of events. However, they usually <u>convey</u> their opinion of their subject as well.

Writing that presents facts without revealing the writer's feelings and opinions is said to be **objective.** Writing that reveals the writer's feelings and opinions is said to be **subjective.** Biographies often combine objective writing with subjective details.

Literary Perspectives Apply the literary perspective described on page 511 as you read this biography.

Reading Focus

Finding the Main Idea The most important point in a passage is its main idea. Writers of biographies usually present more than one main idea about their subject. However, they will not state a main idea directly. You must infer the main ideas from key details in the text.

Into Action Fill in a chart like this one to record the main idea about each period in Elizabeth's life.

Main Ideas: Elizabeth I

Main Idea 1	Early life: Elizabeth's father trained her to be a leader.
Main Idea 2	
Main Idea 3	

Writing Focus

Think as a Reader/Writer

Find It in Your Reading As you read, record at least three remarkable achievements Meltzer chooses to include. Note how they affect your perception of Elizabeth.

Vocabulary

monarch (MAHN ahrk) *n.:* sole and absolute ruler. *Elizabeth became the monarch of England in 1558.*

alliance (uh LY uhns) *n.:* pact between nations, families, or individuals that shows a common cause. *Elizabeth's advisor urged her to join the alliance against the enemy.*

monopoly (muh NAHP uh lee) *n.:* exclusive control of a market. *His monopoly on sweet wines made the earl of Essex rich.*

arrogant (AR uh guhnt) *adj.:* overly convinced of one's own importance. *The queen seemed arrogant, but she did listen to others.*

intolerable (ihn TAHL uhr uh buhl) *adj.:* unbearable. *Even though Mary was an enemy, Elizabeth felt it would be intolerable to cut off her cousin's head.*

Language Coach

Recognizing Roots Learning some common word roots derived from Latin and Greek, and their meanings, will help you understand many English words.

Roots	Meaning	Related Words
-cent-	hundred	centennial, percent
-duct-	lead	conduct, conductor

Milton Meltzer
(1915–   )

The historian **Milton Meltzer** took an interest in social issues when he was young. After attending Columbia University, he joined the Works Projects Administration, a government agency that provided jobs for workers who were unemployed during the Great Depression of the 1930s, as a writer. Over time he has written about the Holocaust, the civil rights movement, slavery, and immigration. Never one to shy away from controversy, Meltzer writes honestly about injustices that have occurred throughout history.

Meltzer's Life Stories

Meltzer's biographies cover historical figures, such as George Washington and Mark Twain, as well as others who may not be so well known—like Thomas Paine, who battled for America's freedom, and Betty Friedan, who fought for women's rights. Throughout most of his work, Meltzer recognizes a common link:

> "My subjects choose action. . . . Action takes commitment, the commitment of dedicated, optimistic individuals. I try to make the readers understand that history isn't only what happens to us. History is what we *make* happen. Each of us. All of us."

Think About the Writer Do you think Meltzer's interest in social issues has affected his choice of topics? Explain.

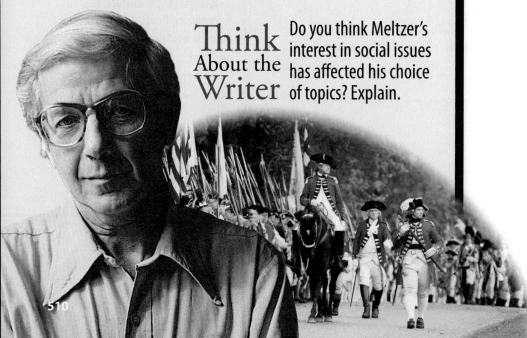

Build Background

When Elizabeth I's father, Henry VIII, was king, he wanted to divorce his first wife to marry Anne Boleyn. However, Henry was a Catholic, and the Catholic Church does not allow divorce and remarriage. When the pope refused to grant Henry permission to divorce, Henry broke away from Catholicism. He started the Church of England and made himself its leader. When Elizabeth came to the throne, there was still much conflict about religion in England.

Preview the Selection

In a time when women had to be completely obedient to their husbands, one of the most powerful people in the world was a woman: **Elizabeth I,** Queen of England. Elizabeth was the daughter of **Henry VIII** and **Anne Boleyn.** After her half sister **Mary** died, Elizabeth took the throne. Great musicians, writers, and explorers flourished under her rule.

Read with a Purpose Read this selection to learn more about Elizabeth's amazing life and accomplishments.

ELIZABETH I

by **Milton Meltzer**

"Good Queen Bess" her people called her. But "good" is a tame word for one of the most remarkable women who ever lived. Elizabeth I came to the throne of England in 1558 at the age of twenty-five. It was not a happy time for a young woman to take the responsibility for ruling a kingdom. Religious conflicts, a huge government debt, and heavy losses in a war with France had brought England low. But by the time of Elizabeth's death forty-five years later, England had experienced one of the greatest periods in its long history. Under Elizabeth's leadership, England had become united as a nation; its industry and commerce, its arts and sciences had flourished; and it was ranked among the great powers of Europe. **Ⓐ**

Elizabeth was the daughter of King Henry VIII and his second wife, Anne Boleyn. At the age of two she lost her mother when Henry had Anne's head chopped off. Not a good start for a child. But her father placed her in the care of one lord or lady after another, and the lively little girl with the reddish-gold hair, pale skin, and golden-brown eyes won everyone's affection. **Ⓑ**

Almost from her infancy Elizabeth was trained to stand in for ruling men, in case the need should arise. So she had to master whatever they were expected to know and do. Her tutors found the child to be an eager student. She learned history, geography, mathematics, and the elements of astronomy and architecture. She mastered four modern languages—French, Italian, Spanish, and

Literary Perspectives

The following perspective will help you think about this biography.

Analyzing Author's Technique You know that fiction writers use literary tools in their stories. Nonfiction writers also use particular techniques in their writing. Because it is nonfiction, they rely on facts. But how they present those facts makes the difference between a boring text and one that makes you want to keep reading. As you read "Elizabeth I," consider how the author tells the story of the queen's life. Pay attention to the kinds of information he shares and the way he organizes the information. As you read, be sure to notice the notes and questions in the text, which will guide you in using this perspective.

Ⓐ **Read and Discuss** What is the author setting up for you?

Ⓑ **Literary Perspectives** Author's Technique What dramatic details about Elizabeth's life does Meltzer include to capture your attention?

Flemish[1]—as well as classical Greek and Latin. She wrote in a beautiful script that was like a work of art. The earliest portrait painted of her—when she was thirteen—shows a girl with innocent eyes holding a book in her long and delicate hands, already confident and queenly in her bearing.

She was a strong-willed girl who liked to give orders. She loved to be out on horseback, and rode so fast it frightened the men assigned to protect her. She loved dancing too—she never gave it up. Even in her old age she was seen one moonlit night dancing by herself in the garden. **C**

Elizabeth had a half sister, Mary, born in 1516 of Henry's first wife, Catherine of Aragon. Many years later came Elizabeth, the child of Anne Boleyn, and four years after, her half brother, Edward, the son of Henry's third wife, Jane Seymour. After Henry died, because succession[2] came first through the male, ten-year-old Edward was crowned king. But he lived only another six years. Now Mary took the throne and, soon after, married King Philip II of Spain, a Catholic monarch like herself. He was twenty-seven and she was thirty-eight. But they were rarely together, each ruling their own kingdom. Mary died of cancer at the age of forty-two. That made Elizabeth the monarch. **D**

When she came to the throne on November 17, 1558, it was a day to be marked by celebrations, then and long after. As Her Majesty passed down a London street, an astonished housewife exclaimed, "Oh, Lord! The queen is a woman!" For there were still many who could scarcely believe they were to be ruled by another woman. Elizabeth herself would say with mock modesty that she was "a mere woman." But everyone soon learned she was a very special woman. "Am I not a queen because God has chosen me to be a queen?" she demanded. **E**

As princess and later as queen, Elizabeth lived in various palaces, with much coming and going; each time she moved, she took along her household staff of 120 people. Often the changes were required because there was no sanitation. The smelly palaces had to be emptied so they could be "aired and sweetened."

Even before Elizabeth came of age, there was much talk of when she would marry, and whom. Marriages among the nobility and royalty were arranged not for love, but for practical reasons—to add land holdings, to strengthen the prestige and power of families, to cement an alliance of nations against a common enemy.

And remember, from the most ancient times, kings claimed that they as men were

---

1. **Flemish:** language spoken in Flanders, a region covering a small part of northern France and Belgium.
2. **succession:** order in which one succeeds to the throne.

C **Reading Focus** **Finding the Main Idea** What is the writer's main idea in this section? What details support this idea?

D **Literary Focus** **Biography** Evaluate this paragraph. Is the writer giving objective information or subjective information?

E **Read and Discuss** What just happened to Elizabeth?

Vocabulary **monarch** (MAHN ahrk) *n.*: sole and absolute ruler.
alliance (uh LY uhns) *n.*: pact between nations, families, or individuals that shows a common cause.

Analyzing Visuals

Viewing and Interpreting
What details in the painting suggest Elizabeth's importance to society?

born to rule by divine right. That is, God had ordained that the crown should pass through the male line of descent. But when the king's wife had no male child, it meant trouble. Who then would rule? That crisis often led to civil war as various factions battled for the power to name a king. Many disputed Elizabeth's right to the throne, and as long as she had neither husband nor successor, her life was in danger.

Ever since Elizabeth was eight, however, she had said again and again, "I will never marry." Did marriage look promising to a girl whose father had had six wives, two of whom, including her own mother, he had beheaded? Yet she liked to hear of people who wanted to marry her.

And there was no shortage of suitors. She continued to insist she wished to live unmarried. No matter how often she said it, men did not believe it. Understandably, since she often made a prince or duke who had come to court her believe she was finally ready to give in—only at the last moment to back out. Once, to a delegation

Queen Elizabeth I (1533–1603) being carried in procession (Eliza Triumphans) c. 1601 by Robert Peake (fl. 1580–1626).

from Parliament come to beg her to marry, she declared, "I am already bound unto a husband, which is the Kingdom of England." **F**

F **Literary Perspectives** Author's Technique How does Meltzer present Elizabeth's feelings on marriage in an engaging way?

Queen Elizabeth watching The Merry Wives of Windsor at the Globe Theatre by David Scott (1806–1849). Oil on canvas.

And why should she, the absolute ruler of England, allow a man to sit alongside her as king? The power of husbands over wives in that century—and even now, in many places of this world—was so great that a husband might snatch the reins of power from her and leave her with the title but not the authority she loved to exercise. **G**

Was it fun to be queen? As monarch, she commanded great wealth, inherited from her father, and people who wanted favors were always enriching her with lavish presents. She was no spendthrift, however. She hated to see money wasted, whether her own or the kingdom's. Early on she began keeping careful household account books, and later she would do the same with the royal accounts. Always she urged her counselors to carry out orders as inexpensively as possible.

Above everything else, Elizabeth wanted to have her people think well of her. Her deepest desire was to assure them of peace and prosperity. And why not make a grand

G [Read and Discuss] How did the time period in which Elizabeth lived influence her views on marriage?

personal impression upon them at the same time? In her mature years she gave free rein to her love of jewels and staged brilliant displays for the court and the people. Her dresses were decorated with large rubies, emeralds, and diamonds, and she wore jeweled necklaces, bracelets, and rings. In her hair, at her ears, and around her neck she wore pearls—the symbol of virginity.

During her reign she made many great processions through London, the people wild with excitement, crowding the streets—for the English, like most people, loved spectacle. In the first of them, her coronation, she wore gold robes as she was crowned. Trumpets sounded, pipes and drums played, the organ pealed, bells rang. Then came the state banquet in Westminster Hall. It began at 3:00 P.M., and went on till 1:00 A.M. **(H)**

Elizabeth was often entertained at house parties. One of them, given by the Earl of Leicester in Kenilworth Castle, lasted for eighteen days in July. Thirty other distinguished guests were invited. The great number of their servants (together with Leicester's) turned the palace into a small town. When darkness fell, candles glittered everywhere, indoors and out, creating a fairyland. Musicians sang and played, the guests danced in the garden, and such a great display of fireworks exploded that the heavens thundered and the castle shook. Then came a pleasure relished in those days:

the hideous sport of bear baiting. A pack of dogs was let loose in an inner courtyard to scratch and bite and tear at thirteen tormented bears. Still, the happy guests retained their appetite for a "most delicious banquet of 300 dishes."

The tremendous festival at Kenilworth was only one of the highlights of Elizabeth's summer festival. She moved from one great house to another all season long, always at the enormous expense of her hosts. They had little to complain of, however, for their wealth was often the product of the queen's generous bestowal of special privileges. In recognition of his high rank and in return for his support, she granted the duke of Norfolk a license to import carpets from Turkey free of duty. The earl of Essex was favored with the profitable right to tax imported sweet wines. Other pets got rich from a monopoly on the importation of or taxation of silks, satins, salt, tobacco, starch. **(I)**

England was a small nation at the time she ruled: less than four million people, about as many as live in Arizona today. But the English were a young people, coming to maturity with new worlds opening up to them, in the mind and across the seas. A rebirth of culture—the Renaissance—had begun in the 1400s. With the revival of interest in the literature of the ancient Greek and Roman worlds came the beginning of a great age of discovery. This period marked the transition

(H) Literary Perspectives Author's Technique How do the historical details that the writer includes affect your perception of Elizabeth?

(I) Read and Discuss What have you learned about Elizabeth and her relationship with other members of royalty?

Vocabulary monopoly (muh NAHP uh lee) n.: exclusive control of a market.

from medieval to modern times. The arts and sciences were influenced by changes in economic life. All the nation was swept up in the vast tides of change. Merchants, bankers, the gentry,[3] artisans, seamen, miners—men and women of every class and condition—felt themselves part of the national venture. **Ⓙ**

At the heart of the change in England was the queen. But no king or queen rules alone, no matter how authoritative or arrogant they may be. They usually look to others for advice, advice they may follow or reject. Elizabeth appointed ministers to handle the various departments of government, and made Sir William Cecil, then thirty-eight, her principal advisor. He was a brilliant, hardworking master of statecraft, devoted to her and England's well-being, and as ruthless as she and the nation's interests required. When he died in old age, his son Robert replaced him at her side.

So great was the queen's role, however, that her time became known as the Age of Elizabeth. Not only did many fine musicians flower, but writers too, such as Christopher Marlowe and John Donne and Ben Jonson and Edmund Spenser. And above all, the incomparable William Shakespeare, whose plays were sometimes performed at court. Astronomers, naturalists, mathematicians, geographers, and architects pioneered in their fields.

Then, too, there were the daring explorers who pushed English expansion overseas. One of the queen's favorites, Sir Walter Raleigh, planned the colony of Virginia in America and named it for her, the Virgin Queen. The queen herself put money into several of the great voyages, keeping close watch over the plans and their results. She supported Sir Francis Drake on his three-year voyage around the world, profiting mightily from the immense loot he captured from Spanish ships taken in the Pacific. **Ⓚ**

For Elizabeth, one of the most urgent problems was the question of religion. Her father had broken with the Catholic Church and launched the English Reformation, creating the Church of England, with himself at its head. When Elizabeth's older half sister, Mary (who remained Catholic), married the Catholic king of Spain, Philip II, she reconciled England with the Church of Rome. In Mary's brief reign she persecuted those Protestants who refused to conform, executing some 270 of them.

When Elizabeth became queen upon Mary's death, she said she hoped religion would not prevent her people from living together in peaceful unity. She did not want to pry into people's souls or question their faith. But in 1570, Pope Pius V excommunicated[4] her, denied her right to the throne, and declared her subjects owed her no alle-

---

3. **gentry:** upper class.

4. **excommunicated:** cast out from a religious community. Strictly speaking, the queen was denied the sacraments of the Catholic Church.

Ⓙ Read and Discuss | What is the connection between the Renaissance and England during Elizabeth's rule?

Ⓚ Reading Focus **Finding the Main Idea** What is the writer's main idea in this section on the Age of Elizabeth?

Vocabulary **arrogant** (AR uh guhnt) *adj.*: overly convinced of one's own importance.

Viewing and Interpreting The photo above is from a movie about Elizabeth I. Which characteristics of Elizabeth does the actress convey in the scene?

giance. A directive[5] from the pope's office decreed that the assassination of Queen Elizabeth would not be regarded as a sin. The effect of this directive was to turn practicing Catholics—about half of the English, most of them loyal—into potential traitors. **L**

Though Elizabeth had wanted to pursue a middle way of toleration, circumstances threatened to overwhelm her. She had to beware of several Catholic monarchs of Europe who wished to see a Protestant England overthrown. Philip II of Spain sent ambassadors to England to urge Catholics to rise against Elizabeth, put her cousin

Mary[6] on the throne, and restore Roman Catholicism as the national faith. The line between power, politics, and religion was becoming very thin.

Missionary priests living abroad were sent into England to stir up opposition to the queen. But the English Catholics as a body never rebelled, nor did they ever intend to. Still, missionary priests such as Edmund Campion were convicted of plotting against Elizabeth and executed.

In 1588 a long-threatened invasion of England by Spain was launched by Philip II. He mistakenly believed that the English

---

5. directive: order or instruction, especially given by a government.

6. Mary: Mary Stuart (1542–1587) (Mary, Queen of Scots, not Elizabeth's half sister).

L [Read and Discuss] What problem is Elizabeth facing?

Catholics were waiting to welcome him. News of his armada of 130 big ships carrying 17,000 soldiers was terrifying. But the queen did not panic. She supervised the high command personally, meanwhile rallying popular support for the defense of the realm and sending troops to protect the coasts while Sir Francis Drake's ships set out to attack the Spanish fleet.

The Spanish Armada was defeated in three battles, its ships dispersed. When the news came of the tremendous victory, the citizens took to the streets, shouting for joy.

The defeat of the Spanish Armada did not end Spain's aggression against England. The Jesuits[7] in England, who were especially identified with Spain, continued to be

---

7. **Jesuits** (JEHZH oo ihts): priests who are members of the Roman Catholic Society of Jesus.

persecuted. Richard Topcliffe, a notorious hater of Catholics, was given authority to track down suspects. He examined them under torture to force information about people who had sheltered them. The treatment of them was so vicious and cruel that the victims welcomed death as a release from their agony.

During Elizabeth's reign several plots to assassinate her were uncovered. Elizabeth managed to give the impression that she was not frightened, but those close to her knew she was. When one of the major plots proved to center around Elizabeth's cousin, Mary, Queen of Scots, Elizabeth found it almost intolerable to put to death a crowned queen. Yet she ordered the use of torture on Mary's co-conspirators, and in the end, Mary was beheaded. A song composed by William Byrd at the time suggests how ominous the news of a monarch's execution was:

> The noble famous Queen
> who lost her head of late
> Doth show that kings as well as clowns
> Are bound to fortune's fate,
> And that no earthly Prince
> Can so secure his crown
> but fortune with her whirling wheel
> Hath power to pull them down.

When two earls combined forces against her, Elizabeth's troops overcame them. The queen was so enraged she ordered that 800 of the mostly poor rebels be hanged. But she

---

M **Literary Perspectives** **Author's Technique** What details does Meltzer use to convey Elizabeth's personality?

N **Reading Focus** **Finding the Main Idea** What is the writer's main idea about the religious conflict that occurred during Elizabeth's reign?

Vocabulary **intolerable** (ihn TAHL uhr uh buhl) *adj.*: unbearable.

spared the lives of their wealthy leaders so that they might enrich her, either by buying their pardons or by forfeiting[8] their lands. Ⓞ

Elizabeth came down hard on writers who criticized her actions. John Stubbs, a zealous Puritan, wrote a pamphlet expressing horror at the possibility the queen might marry a French Catholic. The queen had Stubbs and his publisher tried and convicted for seditious libel.[9] How dare Stubbs say publicly she was too old to marry, and that the much younger French suitor could not possibly be in love with her? Elizabeth was merciless as she invoked the penalty for libel. With a butcher's cleaver, the executioner cut the right hands off Stubbs and his publisher. Not an uncommon punishment.

How did Elizabeth learn of all these plots and conspiracies? How did she know what plans Philip II of Spain was devising to invade her kingdom? Spies and secret agents—they were her eyes and ears. Crucial to the flow of information was Sir Francis Walsingham. Trained as a lawyer, he lived on the Continent[10] for years, mastering the languages and the ins and outs of European affairs. Upon his return home, he was asked by Sir William Cecil, the queen's right arm, to gather information on the doings and plans of foreign governments. Soon he was made chief of England's secret service. He placed over seventy agents and spies in the courts of Europe. And of course he watched closely the activities of people at home suspected of disloyalty. Letters to and from them were secretly opened, to nip plots in the bud. Ⓟ

Monarchs had absolute power. Elizabeth could arrest anyone, including the topmost ranks of the nobility, and imprison them in the Tower of London even if they had not committed any legal offense. The only thing that held her back was her fear of public opinion. It upset her when a crowd gathered at a public execution and was so disgusted by the butchery that they let out roars of disapproval. Still, like all rulers, Elizabeth said she believed that "born a sovereign princess" she enjoyed "the privilege common to all kings" and was "exempt from human jurisdiction[11] and subject only to the judgement of God."

> Monarchs had absolute power. Elizabeth could arrest anyone.

---

8. **forfeiting** (FAWR fiht ihng): giving up, usually because of force of some kind.
9. **seditious libel** (sih DIHSH uhs LY buhl): stirring up of discontent about the government (sedition) with false written statements (libel).

---

10. **Continent:** Europe.
11. **jurisdiction** (jur ihs DIHK shuhn): legal control.

Ⓞ **Literary Focus** Biography What picture has the author given you of Elizabeth?

Ⓟ **Reading Focus** Finding the Main Idea What is the writer's main idea about the conflicts Elizabeth faced?

Despite her blazing nervous energy, Elizabeth was often sick. Her ailments were anxiously reported and discussed. For the English believed her survival was their only guarantee of freedom from foreign invasion and civil war. Once, suffering a raging toothache for the first time, the queen feared the pain of having an extraction. She had never had a tooth pulled and was terrified. To reassure her, an old friend, the Bishop of London, had her watch while the dental surgeon pulled out one of the bishop's own good teeth. And then she consented to have her own taken out.

It was commonly believed then that kings and queens had the magical power to cure disease in their subjects. Eager to demonstrate that she too had the sacred power of royalty, Elizabeth prayed intensely before using the royal touch on people with scrofula, a nasty skin disease. Her chaplain said he watched "her exquisite hands, boldly, and without disgust, pressing the sores and ulcers." In one day it was reported that she healed thirty-eight persons. But if she did not feel divinely inspired, she would not try her touch. **Q**

Even in the last decade of her life, Elizabeth's energy was astonishing. She was as watchful as always over the affairs of state, though sometimes forgetful. But age made her more irritable; she sometimes shouted at her ladies and even boxed their ears. She was less able to control rival factions out for power, and became so fearful of assassins she rarely left her palaces.

A portrait of her done when she was approaching sixty shows her in a great white silk dress studded with aglets[12] of black onyx, coral, and pearl. She wears three ropes of translucent pearls and stands on a map of England, her England. An ambassador reported that at sixty-three she looked old, but her figure was still beautiful, and her conversation was as brilliant and charming as ever.

There was dancing at court every evening, a pastime she still enjoyed. When it came to displays of gallantry by eager young men, she could act a bit vain and foolish, although never letting any hopeful get out of bounds.

In early 1603 Elizabeth developed a bad cold that led to a serious fever, and then she fell into a stupor[13] for four days. As she lay dying, all of London became strangely silent. On March 24, the life of a rare genius ended. The nation went into mourning. **R**

"Old age came upon me as a surprise, like a frost," she once wrote.

> Elizabeth's energy was astonishing.

---

12. **aglets** (AG lihts): tips of lace on dresses.
13. **stupor** (STOO puhr): loss of sensibility; dullness.

Q **Read and Discuss** What does this new information add to what you've been told about monarchs?

R **Literary Focus** Biography The author says, "On March 24, the life of a rare genius ended." Is this an objective or subjective statement?

Applying Your Skills

Elizabeth I

Respond and Think Critically

Reading Focus

Quick Check

1. What problems did England have when Elizabeth I came to the throne?

2. How did England change during the Renaissance? Who was at the heart of the change?

Read with a Purpose

3. What are some of the amazing things that happened during the Elizabethan Era?

Reading Skills: Finding the Main Idea

4. **Explain** Review the chart you completed while reading the biography. Then, add a final column in which you state the writer's main idea about Elizabeth.

Main Ideas: Elizabeth I

Main Idea 1	Early life: Elizabeth's father trained her to be a leader.
Main Idea 2	
Main Idea 3	
Writer's Main Idea	

Literary Focus

Literary Analysis

5. **Evaluate** What might have been different about Elizabeth's reign if she had not believed she was "chosen by God" to rule?

6. **Literary Perspectives** Was the author completely objective about Elizabeth, or did he also take a subjective view? What is the effect of his technique? Support your reasoning by citing details from the text.

Literary Skills: Biography

7. **Infer** Rewrite the first paragraph of this biography as if you were Elizabeth herself. Use the pronoun *I* to relate Elizabeth's point of view. Include **subjective details.** (Tell how Elizabeth feels about her life's achievements—and disappointments.)

Literary Skills Review: Character

8. **Infer** In her youth, Elizabeth learned four languages and was an eager student of many subjects. What do these details tell you about her character?

Writing Focus

Think as a Reader/Writer

Use It in Your Writing Write a brief biographical sketch about a figure you admire. Before you write, create a character profile by listing facts you know and questions you wish to answer. Use the Internet and library resources to gather information. Try to strike a balance between objective facts and subjective feelings.

What Do **You** Think **Now** Have your ideas changed about how great people shape events? Did Elizabeth turn challenges into opportunities? Give examples.

Elizabeth I

Vocabulary Development

Clarifying Word Meanings: Definitions

You may have noticed that Milton Meltzer helped you when he used a word you might not know. He defined the difficult word right there in the sentence or close by. Writers of textbooks and other materials written for students often do this. It's up to you to be able to recognize a definition when you see it. Here are three examples from "Elizabeth I" in which the writer clarifies word meanings through the use of definitions.

In the first example, the words *that is* signal you that a definition is coming up:

"Kings claimed that they as men were born to rule by divine right. That is, God had ordained that the crown should pass through the male line of descent."

In this example, the definition comes before the word:

"A rebirth of culture—the Renaissance—had begun in the 1400s."

Here, the writer defines the word *scrofula* right after the comma:

"Elizabeth prayed intensely before using the royal touch on people with scrofula, a nasty skin disease."

Your Turn

Write a sentence for each Vocabulary word, defining it by applying one of the methods used in the examples. Use each method of clarification at least once.

> monarch
> alliance
> monopoly
> arrogant
> intolerable

Language Coach

Recognizing Roots

Remember that a word root is a word from which several other words can be formed. The chart on the right contains some word roots and their meanings.

Root	Meaning
spir–	breathe
geo–	earth
spec–	see
jud–	judge
port–	carry

Each word below contains a word root from the chart. How does knowing the meaning of the root help you understand the meaning of the word?

1. conspiracy
2. geography
3. spectacle
4. judgment
5. importation

Academic Vocabulary

Talk About . . .

Get together with a partner and discuss the way Meltzer <u>conveys</u> how Elizabeth helped England rise to prominence during her reign. How do the objective details he includes help strengthen his point?

Learn It Online
Improve your word skills with *WordSharp*:

go.hrw.com   L7-522   **Go**

SKILLS FOCUS **Literary Skills** Analyze forms of prose: biography; analyze subjective and objective points of view; distinguish objective from subjective writing. **Reading Skills** Summarize and organize information from one or more sources by taking notes. **Vocabulary Skills** Clarify word meanings through definitions; use context clues in words, sentences, and paragraphs to decode new vocabulary. **Writing Skills** Write biographical narratives. **Grammar Skills** Demonstrate understanding of correct subject-verb agreement.

Grammar Link
Subject-Verb Agreement

A common error people make in writing and speaking involves subject-verb agreement. The rule is simple: Subjects and their verbs must always agree. That means a singular subject takes a singular verb and a plural subject takes a plural verb. The problem arises when identifying the subject and deciding whether it is singular or plural. Be careful when a sentence contains *neither/ nor* or *either/or* and when a subject is separated from its verb by a prepositional phrase.

> **Neither Elizabeth nor Sir William Cecil [wants/want] to leave the nation vulnerable to attack.** [Singular subjects joined by *or* or *nor* take a singular verb. The verb should be *wants*.]

> **Neither Elizabeth nor most English Catholics [wants/want] religion to become a dividing factor.** [When a singular subject and a plural subject are joined by *or* or *nor*, the verb agrees with the subject closer to the verb. Since *Catholics* is plural, the verb should be *want*.]

> **The outfits of the queen [is/are] quite extravagant.** [The number of a subject is not affected by a prepositional phrase following the subject. The verb should be *are*.]

Your Turn

Rewrite these sentences to correct errors in subject-verb agreement.

Neither the pope nor the queen's half sister scare the queen. The people of England rely on the queen for protection. The king of Spain and other monarchs look for weakness in her.

CHOICES

As you respond to the Choices, use these **Academic Vocabulary** words as appropriate: ambiguous, evident, convey, principal.

REVIEW
Write a Biographical Sketch
Timed ∟Writing Choose one period in Elizabeth I's life. Write a paragraph stating what you learned about her (in your own words). Convey your own opinions about Elizabeth and her actions. How does your account differ from Meltzer's?

CONNECT
Organize Information
You learned that Elizabeth I faced many problems. List the principal problems Elizabeth had to confront. Then, note the actions she took to solve the problems.

EXTEND
Create a Portrait
Like biographers, good artists have to decide whether to present what someone *really* looks like or to paint with more subjectivity. For example, if artists are trying to please a subject, they might choose to emphasize his or her good features. Look at some of the portraits shown in this selection. Based on your own feelings about Elizabeth, draw a portrait of her.

Learn It Online
Discover more about the story, using Internet links:

go.hrw.com   L7-523   **Go**

from LONG WALK TO FREEDOM

by **Nelson Mandela**

What Do
You?
Think

What qualities within people help them overcome adversity?

 QuickTalk

Form a small group, and discuss the characteristics of a hero. Think of examples as you discuss each characteristic.

The Tower by Nelson Mandela.
Charcoal and pastel.

Reader/Writer Notebook

Use your **RWN** to complete the activities for this selection.

SKILLS FOCUS Literary Skills Understand forms of prose: autobiography. **Reading Skills** Identify and understand the difference between fact and opinion.

Literary Focus

Autobiography An **autobiography** is a story in which the author writes about his or her own life. In *Long Walk to Freedom*, Nelson Mandela tells about his fight for freedom in South Africa.

Reading Focus

Distinguishing Fact from Opinion When you read an autobiography, it is important to be able to tell facts from opinions. A **fact** is a statement that can be proved true. *Nelson Mandela was elected president in 1994* is a fact. An **opinion,** a personal feeling or belief, can't be proved true or false. In autobiographies, writers share their feelings and opinions, but they also present facts.

Into Action As you read, use a table like the one below to jot down some of the facts about Nelson Mandela. Also, write down Mandela's opinions about the people and things around him.

Facts	Opinions
Mandela joined the African National Congress.	People must help their family and their country.

Vocabulary

profound (pruh FOWND) *adj.*: very strong; serious. *Apartheid caused profound damage to the people of South Africa.*

oppression (uh PREHSH uhn) *n.*: unjust treatment. *Mandela fought against the oppression of South African apartheid.*

obligations (ahb luh GAY shuhnz) *n.*: duties to carry out. *He found it difficult to fulfill his obligations to his family.*

obstructed (uhb STRUHKT ehd) *v.*: prevented; made difficult. *Unjust policies obstructed Mandela's achieving freedom.*

enhances (ehn HANS ihz) *v.*: improves. *Granting freedom to all people enhances society.*

Language Coach

Synonyms Words with the same, or almost the same, meaning are called synonyms. For example, *deep, serious,* and *strong* are synonyms of *profound.*

Writing Focus

Think as a Reader/Writer

Find It in Your Reading Note Mandela's use of facts (such as "I joined the African National Congress") and opinions ("I always knew that deep down in every human heart, there is mercy and generosity") to express the importance of freedom to him.

TechFocus As you read, think about how you might make Mandela's feelings on freedom <u>evident</u> through digital images.

Learn It Online
Elevate your vocabulary skills with Word Watch:

go.hrw.com | L7-525 | Go

Nelson Mandela
(1918–   )

A Cherished Ideal

Nelson Mandela is a lawyer who has dedicated his life to ending racial oppression in South Africa. In 1963, South African police discovered Mandela's involvement with the military wing of the African National Congress, a nationalist group. He was put on trial for treason and other charges. During the trial, Mandela spoke out for racial equality:

> "I have cherished the ideal of a democratic and free society. . . . It is an ideal which I hope to live for and to achieve. But if needs be, it is an ideal for which I am prepared to die."

The court sentenced Mandela to life in prison. He spent nearly three decades in jail.

At Last, Freedom

The South African government faced political and economic pressure to release Mandela. In 1990, President F. W. de Klerk ordered his release from prison. The two leaders worked together to bring equality to the nation. In 1993, they were jointly awarded the Nobel Peace Prize for their efforts.

In 1994 the two men established the first nonracial democratic election in South Africa. Citizens of all races voted for Mandela to be the country's first black president.

Build Background

Under apartheid (ah PAHRT hayt), a legal system of racial segregation, most of South Africa's land was reserved for the white minority population, while black and multiracial South Africans faced discrimination and were unrepresented in government.

Preview the Selection

In this excerpt from his memoir, **Nelson Mandela** explains how his understanding of freedom evolved during the course of his life. He describes the conflict between his desire to fulfill his obligations to his family and his commitment to the struggle for justice and freedom in South Africa.

Think About the Writer How do you think Mandela's time in prison affected his feelings about freedom?

Read with a Purpose
Read the following selection to learn how imprisonment affected Nelson Mandela's view of freedom.

from

LONG WALK TO FREEDOM

by **Nelson Mandela**

The policy of apartheid created a deep and lasting wound in my country and my people. All of us will spend many years, if not generations, recovering from that profound hurt. But the decades of oppression and brutality had another, unintended effect, and that was that it produced the Oliver Tambos, the Walter Sisulus, the Chief Luthulis, the Yusuf Dadoos, the Bram Fischers, the Robert Sobukwes[1] of our time—men of such extraordinary courage, wisdom, and generosity that their like may never be known again. Perhaps it requires such depth of oppression to create such heights of character. My country is rich in the minerals and gems that lie beneath its soil, but I have always known that its greatest wealth is its people, finer and truer than the purest diamonds. **Ⓐ**

It is from these comrades in the struggle that I learned the meaning of courage. Time and again, I have seen men and women risk and give their lives for an idea. I have seen men stand up to attacks and torture without breaking, showing a strength and resiliency that defies the imagination. I learned that courage was not the absence of fear, but the triumph over it. I felt fear myself more times than I can remember, but I hid it behind a mask of boldness. The brave man is not he who does not feel afraid, but he who conquers that fear. **Ⓑ**

I never lost hope that this great transformation would occur. Not only because of the great heroes I have already cited, but because of the courage of the ordinary men and women of my country. I always knew

---

1. **Oliver Tambos . . . Robert Sobukwes:** freedom fighters against South African apartheid.

Ⓐ [Read and Discuss] What point is Mandela making about apartheid?

Ⓑ [Literary Focus] Autobiography How does this paragraph indicate that the selection is an autobiography, not a biography?

Vocabulary **profound** (pruh FOWND) *adj.:* very strong; serious.
oppression (uh PREHSH uhn) *n.:* unjust treatment.

path would be an easy one. As a young man, when I joined the African National Congress, I saw the price my comrades paid for their beliefs, and it was high. For myself, I have never regretted my commitment to the struggle, and I was always prepared to face the hardships that affected me personally. But my family paid a terrible price, perhaps too dear a price for my commitment.

In life, every man has twin obligations—obligations to his family, to his parents, to his wife and children; and he has an obligation to his people, his community, his country. In a civil and humane society, each man is able to fulfill those obligations according to his own inclinations and abilities. But in a country like South Africa, it was almost impossible for a man of my birth and color to fulfill both of those obligations. In South Africa, a man of color who attempted to live as a human being was punished and isolated. In South Africa, a man who tried to fulfill his duty to his people was inevitably ripped from his family and his home and was forced to live a life apart, a twilight existence of secrecy and rebellion. I did not in the beginning choose to place my people above my family, but in attempting to serve my people, I found that I was prevented from fulfilling my obligations as a son, a brother, a father, and a husband.

In that way, my commitment to my people, to the millions of South Africans I would never know or meet, was at the expense of the people I knew best and loved most. It was as simple and yet as incomprehensible as the moment a small child asks her father, "Why

that deep down in every human heart, there is mercy and generosity. No one is born hating another person because of the color of his skin, or his background, or his religion. People must learn to hate, and if they can learn to hate, they can be taught to love, for love comes more naturally to the human heart than its opposite. Even in the grimmest times in prison, when my comrades and I were pushed to our limits, I would see a glimmer of humanity in one of the guards, perhaps just for a second, but it was enough to reassure me and keep me going. Man's goodness is a flame that can be hidden but never extinguished. **C**

We took up the struggle with our eyes wide open, under no illusion that the

C Read and Discuss | What is Mandela saying about humanity? How could Mandela hold such a belief after everything he faced?

Vocabulary   obligations (ahb luh GAY shuhnz) *n.:* duties to carry out.

can you not be with us?" And the father must utter the terrible words: "There are other children like you, a great many of them . . ." and then one's voice trails off.

I was not born with a hunger to be free. I was born free—free in every way that I could know. Free to run in the fields near my mother's hut, free to swim in the clear stream that ran through my village, free to roast mealies[2] under the stars and ride the broad backs of slow-moving bulls. As long as I obeyed my father and abided by the customs of my tribe, I was not troubled by the laws of man or God.

It was only when I began to learn that my boyhood freedom was an illusion, when I discovered as a young man that my freedom had already been taken from me, that I began to hunger for it. At first, as a student, I wanted freedom only for myself, the transitory[3] freedoms of being able to stay out at night, read what I pleased, and go where I chose. Later, as a young man in Johannesburg, I yearned for the basic and honorable freedoms of achieving my potential, of earning my keep, of marrying and having a family—the freedom not to be obstructed in a lawful life. **D**

But then I slowly saw that not only was I not free, but my brothers and sisters were not free. I saw that it was not just my freedom that was curtailed, but the freedom of everyone who looked like I did. That is when I joined the African National Congress, and that is when the hunger for

---

2. **mealies:** in South Africa, ears of corn.

3. **transitory:** passing; temporary.

D Read and Discuss What problem does Mandela face? How does his choice affect his life?

Apartheid

Apartheid was a policy of strict racial segregation adopted in South Africa in 1948. Under apartheid, more than 80 percent of South Africa's land was set aside for the exclusive use of whites, who made up a minority of the country's population. Black and multiracial South Africans faced discrimination in education and employment and were denied representation in the national government. Opposition to apartheid existed from its beginnings. South Africans engaged in strikes, civil disobedience, marches and, finally, armed struggle to overturn the policy. This resistance, together with an international campaign of trade sanctions, helped bring apartheid to an end. In 1991, the South African government repealed most of the laws that made up the legal framework of apartheid. In 1994, the country held its first national elections open all races. The African National Congress won most of the seats in the National Assembly, and Nelson Mandela became president of South Africa.

Ask Yourself

What institution in our nation's past was similar to South African apartheid?

Vocabulary **obstructed** (uhb STRUHKT ehd) *v.:* prevented; made difficult.

my own freedom became the greater hunger for the freedom of my people. It was this desire for the freedom of my people to live their lives with dignity and self-respect that animated my life, that transformed a frightened young man into a bold one, that drove a law-abiding attorney to become a criminal, that turned a family-loving husband into a man without a home, that forced a life-loving man to live like a monk. I am no more virtuous or self-sacrificing than the next man, but I found that I could not even enjoy the poor and limited freedoms I was allowed when I knew my people were not free. Freedom is indivisible; the chains on any one of my people were the chains on all of them, the chains on all of my people were the chains on me. **E**

It was during those long and lonely years that my hunger for the freedom of my own people became a hunger for the freedom of all people, white and black. I knew as well as I knew anything that the oppressor must be liberated just as surely as the oppressed. A man who takes away another man's freedom is a prisoner of hatred, he is locked behind the bars of prejudice and narrow-mindedness. I am not truly free if I am taking away someone else's freedom, just as surely as I am not free when my freedom is taken from me. The oppressed and the oppressor alike are robbed of their humanity. **F**

When I walked out of prison, that was my mission, to liberate the oppressed and the oppressor both. Some say that has now been achieved. But I know that that is not the case. The truth is that we are not yet free; we have merely achieved the freedom to be free, the right not to be oppressed. We have not taken the final step of our journey, but the first step on a longer and even more difficult road. For to be free is not merely to cast off one's chains, but to live in a way that respects and enhances the freedom of others. The true test of our devotion to freedom is just beginning. **G**

I have walked that long road to freedom. I have tried not to falter; I have made missteps along the way. But I have discovered the secret that after climbing a great hill, one only finds that there are many more hills to climb. I have taken a moment here to rest, to steal a view of the glorious vista that surrounds me, to look back on the distance I have come. But I can rest only for a moment, for with freedom come responsibilities, and I dare not linger, for my long walk is not yet ended.

> When I walked out of prison, that was my mission, to liberate the oppressed and the oppressor both.

E **Read and Discuss** How has Mandela's attitude toward freedom changed?

F **Reading Focus** Fact and Opinion Is this paragraph made up of facts or opinions? How do you know?

G **Read and Discuss** What is Mandela saying about freedom in this paragraph?

Vocabulary **enhances** (ehn HANS ihz) *v.*: improves.

Applying Your Skills

from Long Walk to Freedom

Respond and Think Critically

Reading Focus

Quick Check

1. Complete the following chart to explain how Nelson Mandela has felt about freedom throughout his life.

Time of life	Feelings on freedom
as a child	
as a student	
as a young lawyer	
when he was in prison	
when he got out of prison	

Read with a Purpose

2. Throughout the text, Mandela's concerns about freedom shift from his own freedom to freedom for his people to freedom for all people. What events in his life influenced his changing views?

Reading Skills: Distinguishing Fact from Opinion

3. Is Mandela's statement that his country's freedom fighters are "finer and purer than the purest diamonds" a fact or an opinion? Explain.

Literary Focus

Literary Analysis

4. **Interpret** Why does Mandela say that his long walk to freedom has not yet ended?

5. **Analyze** For Mandela, ending apartheid did not ensure freedom. What else does he say is necessary for people to be free?

6. **Extend** According to Mandela, "The brave man is not he who does not feel afraid, but he who conquers that fear." What do you think he means?

Literary Skills: Autobiography

7. **Analyze** In his autobiography, Mandela presents facts and opinions. Give one example of a fact and one example of an opinion in *Long Walk to Freedom*. Discuss the difference between the two.

Literary Skills Review: Subjective and Objective Writing

8. **Interpret** What details in Mandela's autobiography are **subjective**—that is, when does he <u>convey</u> his feelings? What parts of the story are **objective**—that is, what details are facts?

Writing Focus

Think as a Reader/Writer

Use It in Your Writing Think about an ideal, such as *hope* or *love,* that is important to you in the same way that *freedom* is important to Mandela. Then, write a description of this ideal. Use sensory details, as Mandela does.

 What Do You Think Now

What qualities or powers allowed Mandela to accomplish all he did? Explain.

Applying Your Skills

from **Long Walk to Freedom**

Vocabulary Development

Clarifying Word Meanings: Examples

Writers often help readers understand difficult words by using definitions, examples, restatements, or contrasts.

A writer who uses **examples** provides specific instances to show what a word means. Consider the following sentence:

"I did not in the beginning choose to place my people above my family, but in attempting to serve my people, I found I was prevented from fulfilling my **obligations** as a son, a brother, a father, and a husband."

Even if you didn't know that an obligation is a duty, the examples in the sentence give you clues to the meaning of the word.

Your Turn _____

Finish the following sentences by using examples to clarify the meaning of the Vocabulary words.

1. Stories that had a **profound** effect on me include _____, _____, and _____.

2. _____ is a form of **oppression** I learned about in social studies class.

3. At the movies, your view might be **obstructed** by _____ and _____.

4. If I am having trouble studying, I find that _____ **enhances** my ability to do my work.

Your Turn _____

Choose the Vocabulary word that is a synonym of each italicized word.

> profound
> oppression
> obligations
> obstructed
> enhances

1. Many South Africans suffered under the *injustice* of apartheid.

2. Showing someone respect *improves* that person's life.

3. Mandela's time in prison had a *strong* effect on his view of freedom.

4. Despite the difficulties that *blocked* the road to freedom, Mandela never lost hope.

5. There are many *duties* involved in preserving the rights of others.

Academic Vocabulary

Talk About . . .

In a group, discuss the way Mandela makes his feelings on freedom <u>evident</u>. Then, discuss whether Mandela <u>conveys</u> the importance of freedom effectively. Use the underlined Academic Vocabulary words in your discussion.

SKILLS FOCUS Literary Skills Analyze forms of prose: autobiography; analyze forms of prose: biography. **Vocabulary Skills** Use context clues in words, sentences, and paragraphs to decode new vocabulary through examples. **Writing Skills** Write comparison-contrast essays; compare literary works. **Grammar Skills** Demonstrate understanding of correct subject-verb agreement. **Listening and Speaking Skills** Present persuasive arguments and share opinions.

Grammar Link

Problems in Agreement: Phrases Between Subjects and Verbs

Sometimes, you might be confused about the number of a subject and verb because the writer has included a phrase between the subject and the verb. In cases like this, the number of a subject is not changed by the phrase that follows the subject.

INCORRECT **Apartheid,** along with other policies, **have allowed** segregation to exist for far too long. (*Apartheid* and *have* do not agree.)

CORRECT **Apartheid,** along with other policies, **has allowed** segregation to exist for far too long. (*Apartheid* and *has* agree.)

Your Turn

Identify the form of the verb in parentheses that agrees with its subject.

1. Many people, including Mandela, (*was/were*) unjustly imprisoned.

2. Some kinds of freedom, such as the freedom to roam the fields and streams, (*does/do*) not seem as important over time.

3. People who are oppressed, along with the oppressor, (*is/are*) not free.

Writing Applications Review the description you wrote in the Think as a Reader/Writer activity on page 531. Check to make sure that each verb agrees with its subject.

CHOICES

As you respond to the Choices, use these **Academic Vocabulary** words as appropriate: <u>ambiguous</u>, <u>evident</u>, <u>convey</u>, <u>principal</u>.

REVIEW
Discuss Biography Versus Autobiography

Timed ⌐Writing Think about the differences between Mandela's autobiography and the biography "Elizabeth I." Then, write two paragraphs in which you compare and contrast the two selections. Keep the following questions in mind: Which selection is more subjective? Which selection contains more facts? more opinions?

CONNECT
Use Digital Images

TechFocus Seek out digital images reflecting Mandela's feelings about freedom. Be sure to refer to the notes you took as you read. Then, put the images in order, and create a time line about Mandela's ideas on freedom.

EXTEND
Speak on South Africa

Delivering a Speech *Long Walk to Freedom* contains information on the living conditions of black South Africans under apartheid. Do you think race relations have changed since the end of apartheid? Research race relations in South Africa today. Then, present a speech on this topic to the class.

Learn It Online
Learn how images can enhance your timeline using MediaScope:

go.hrw.com | L7-533 | Go

Analyzing Responses to Literature

CONTENTS

America (1985)
by Diana Ong (1940–).

 What Do **You** **Think**

Have you ever been in a new, unfamiliar situation? What helped or hindered your success with the new experience?

 QuickWrite

Describe what you would do if you suddenly had to learn a new language. If you have been in this situation, explain how you learned the language.

Preparing to Read

from **Barrio Boy / Three Essays on Barrio Boy**

Literary Focus

Analyzing Responses to Literature You are about to analyze three essays that respond to an essay question about *Barrio Boy.* Your job will be to evaluate each response as if you were a teacher or a critic. How well has each writer answered the question? How well are the ideas about *Barrio Boy* supported?

Reading Focus

Organizing Information A response should be **focused** and should stick to the topic. Ask yourself, "Does it answer the question in a convincing way?" A response must provide **textual support,** or details in support of major ideas. Ask yourself, "Does the writer clearly <u>convey</u> how Galarza's school experiences lead to an important discovery?" The most successful responses will offer specific, concrete examples from the text to support the writer's main idea.

Into Action As you read *Barrio Boy,* cite the information you would include if you were writing a response to this question: *How does Galarza discover that he can become "a proud American" without abandoning his Mexican heritage? Analyze his experiences at the Lincoln School in your response.*

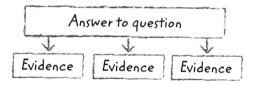

Reader/Writer Notebook

Use your **RWN** to complete the activities for this selection.

Vocabulary

Barrio Boy

reassuring (ree uh SHUR ihng) *v.* used as *adj.:* comforting. *Ernesto's teachers were kind and reassuring.*

contraption (kuhn TRAP shuhn) *n.:* strange machine or gadget. *A contraption at the top of the door closed it automatically.*

assured (uh SHURD) *v.:* guaranteed; promised confidently. *Ernesto's teachers assured him he would enjoy the new school.*

formidable (FAWR muh duh buhl) *adj.:* awe-inspiring; impressive. *Miss Hopley's height made her seem formidable.*

survey (suhr VAY) *v.:* look carefully in order to make a decision or gather information. *Ernesto settled down to survey his new class.*

Language Coach

Antonyms Antonyms are words that are opposite or nearly opposite in meaning. For example, *disturbing* is an antonym for *reassuring.* What Vocabulary word is an antonym for *unimpressive*?

Writing Focus

Think as a Reader/Writer

Find It in Your Reading Notice the vivid descriptive details Galarza uses that help you visualize Galarza's new school. List at least five in your *Reader/Writer Notebook.*

Learn It Online
See a good reader in action, and practice your own skills, at:

go.hrw.com   L7-535   **Go**

Ernesto Galarza
(1905–1984)

Beginning His Journey

For young **Ernesto Galarza,** coming to the United States meant abandoning everything he had ever known and confronting an alien landscape. He couldn't understand the language; the customs and values were strange. Like millions of other immigrants, he felt lost. He soon discovered that education was the key to making sense of his new life. Eventually, Galarza earned his Ph.D. from Columbia University in New York and then returned to California to teach.

Making His Mark

His most beloved book is *Barrio Boy*, the bestselling 1971 account of his journey from Mexico to the United States. In the quotation below, Galarza explains how he came to write *Barrio Boy*.

> "*Barrio Boy* began as anecdotes I told my family about Jalcocotán, the mountain village in western Mexico where I was born. Among this limited public (my wife, Mae, and daughters, Karla and Eli Lu) my thumbnail sketches became bestsellers. Hearing myself tell them over and over, I began to agree with my captive audience that they were not only interesting but possibly good."

Think About the Writer

How can you tell that education is important to Galarza?

Build Background

Ernesto Galarza was born in 1905 in Jalcocotán, a village in western Mexico. In 1910, when the Mexican Revolution threatened their peaceful mountain home, Ernesto, his mother, and two uncles left their village for Mazatlán, Mexico. Eventually, they moved to Sacramento, California, and lived in what Galarza calls a "rented corner of the city"—the *barrio*, or Spanish-speaking neighborhood.

Preview the Selection

Ernesto Galarza, the narrator of the story, is beginning his first day of school in the United States. He is worried about fitting in because he speaks primarily Spanish at home.

from BARRIO BOY

by **Ernesto Galarza**

Read with a Purpose

Read the following selection to discover how one boy from Mexico adjusted to school life in Sacramento, California, in the early 1900s.

The two of us [Ernesto and his mother] walked south on Fifth Street one morning to the corner of Q Street and turned right. Half of the block was occupied by the Lincoln School. It was a three-story wooden building, with two wings that gave it the shape of a double T connected by a central hall. It was a new building, painted yellow, with a shingled roof that was not like the red tile of the school in Mazatlán. I noticed other differences, none of them very reassuring.

We walked up the wide staircase hand in hand and through the door, which closed by itself. A mechanical contraption screwed to the top shut it behind us quietly.

Up to this point the adventure of enrolling me in the school had been carefully rehearsed. Mrs. Dodson had told us how to find it and we had circled it several times on our walks.

Friends in the barrio explained that the director was called a principal, and that it was a lady and not a man. They assured us that there was always a person at the school who could speak Spanish. **A**

Exactly as we had been told, there was a sign on the door in both Spanish and English: "Principal." We crossed the hall and entered the office of Miss Nettie Hopley.

Miss Hopley was at a roll-top desk to one side, sitting in a swivel chair that moved on wheels. There was a sofa against the opposite wall, flanked by two windows and a door that opened on a small balcony. Chairs were set around a table, and framed pictures hung on the walls of a man with long white hair and another with a sad face and a black beard.

The principal half turned in the swivel chair to look at us over the pinch glasses

---

A | Read and Discuss | What has the author told you so far?

Vocabulary **reassuring** (ree uh SHUR ihng) *v.* used as *adj.:* comforting.
contraption (kuhn TRAP shuhn) *n.:* strange machine or gadget.
assured (uh SHURD) *v.:* guaranteed; promised confidently.

crossed on the ridge of her nose. To do this, she had to duck her head slightly, as if she were about to step through a low doorway.

What Miss Hopley said to us we did not know, but we saw in her eyes a warm welcome, and when she took off her glasses and straightened up, she smiled wholeheartedly, like Mrs. Dodson. We were, of course, saying nothing, only catching the friendliness of her voice and the sparkle in her eyes while she said words we did not understand. She signaled us to the table. Almost tiptoeing across the office, I maneuvered myself to keep my mother between me and the gringo[1] lady. In a matter of seconds I had to decide whether she was a possible friend or a menace. We sat down. **(B)**

Then Miss Hopley did a formidable thing. She stood up. Had she been standing when we entered, she would have seemed tall. But rising from her chair, she soared. And what she carried up and up with her was a buxom superstructure, firm shoulders, a straight sharp nose, full cheeks slightly molded by a curved line along the nostrils, thin lips that moved like steel springs, and a high forehead topped by hair gathered in a bun. Miss Hopley was not a giant in body, but when she mobilized it to a standing position she seemed a match for giants. I decided I liked her.

She strode to a door in the far corner of the office, opened it, and called a name. A boy of about ten years appeared in the doorway.

He sat down at one end of the table. He was brown like us, a plump kid with shiny black hair combed straight back, neat, cool, and faintly obnoxious.

Miss Hopley joined us with a large book and some papers in her hand. She, too, sat down and the questions and answers began by way of our interpreter. My name was Ernesto. My mother's name was Henriqueta. My birth certificate was in San Blas. Here was my last report card from the Escuela Municipal Numero 3 para Varones[2] of Mazatlán, and so forth. Miss Hopley put things down in the book and my mother signed a card.

As long as the questions continued, Doña Henriqueta could stay and I was secure. Now that they were over, Miss Hopley saw her

---

1. **gringo** (GRIHNG goh): someone who is northern American, non-Hispanic, or doesn't speak Spanish.

2. **Escuela Municipal Numero 3 para Varones:** Spanish for "Municipal School Number 3 for Boys."

(B) **Literary Focus** Response to Literature Why would you include Galarza's reaction to Miss Hopley in a response to this literary work?

Vocabulary **formidable** (FAWR muh duh buhl) *adj.*: awe-inspiring; impressive.

Frequently she burst into happy announcements to the whole class. "Ito can read a sentence," and small Japanese Ito, squint-eyed and shy, slowly read aloud while the class listened in wonder: "Come, Skipper, come. Come and run." The Korean, Portuguese, Italian, and Polish first-graders had similar moments of glory, no less shining than mine the day I conquered "butterfly," which I had been persistently pronouncing in standard Spanish as boo-ter-flee. "Children," Miss Ryan called for attention. "Ernesto has learned how to pronounce *butterfly*!" And I proved it with a perfect imitation of Miss Ryan. From that celebrated success, I was soon able to match Ito's progress as a sentence reader with "Come, butterfly, come fly with me."

Like Ito and several other first-graders who did not know English, I received private lessons from Miss Ryan in the closet, a narrow hall off the classroom with a door at each end. Next to one of these doors Miss Ryan placed a large chair for herself and a small one for me. Keeping an eye on the class through the open door, she read with me about sheep in the meadow and a frightened chicken going to see the king, coaching me out of my phonetic ruts in words like *pasture, bow-wow-wow, hay,* and *pretty,* which to my Mexican ear and eye had so many unnecessary sounds and letters. She made me watch her lips and then close my eyes as she repeated words I found hard to read. When we came to know each other better, I tried interrupting to tell Miss Ryan how we said it in Spanish. It didn't work. She

to the door, dismissed our interpreter, and without further ado took me by the hand and strode down the hall to Miss Ryan's first grade.

Miss Ryan took me to a seat at the front of the room, into which I shrank—the better to survey her. She was, to skinny, somewhat runty me, of a withering height when she patrolled the class. And when I least expected it, there she was, crouching by my desk, her blond, radiant face level with mine, her voice patiently maneuvering me over the awful idiocies of the English language. **C**

During the next few weeks Miss Ryan overcame my fears of tall, energetic teachers as she bent over my desk to help me with a word in the pre-primer. Step by step, she loosened me and my classmates from the safe anchorage of the desks for recitations at the blackboard and consultations at her desk.

C [**Read and Discuss**] When the author talks about "the awful idiocies of the English language," what do you think he means?

Vocabulary **survey** (suhr VAY) *v.*: look carefully in order to make a decision or gather information.

only said "oh" and went on with *pasture, bow-wow-wow,* and *pretty.* It was as if in that closet we were both discovering together the secrets of the English language and grieving together over the tragedies of Bo-Peep. The main reason I was graduated with honors from the first grade was that I had fallen in love with Miss Ryan. Her radiant, no-nonsense character made us either afraid not to love her or love her so we would not be afraid, I am not sure which. It was not only that we sensed she was with it, but also that she was with us.

Like the first grade, the rest of the Lincoln School was a sampling of the lower part of town, where many races made their home. My pals in the second grade were Kazushi, whose parents spoke only Japanese; Matti, a skinny Italian boy; and Manuel, a fat Portuguese who would never get into a fight but wrestled you to the ground and just sat on you. Our assortment of nationalities included Koreans, Yugoslavs, Poles, Irish, and home-grown Americans.

Miss Hopley and her teachers never let us forget why we were at Lincoln: for those who were alien, to become good Americans; for those who were so born, to accept the rest of us. Off the school grounds we traded the same insults we heard from our elders. On the playground we were sure to be marched up to the principal's office for calling someone a wop, a chink, a dago, or a greaser. The school was not so much a melting pot as a griddle where Miss Hopley and her helpers warmed knowledge into us and roasted racial hatreds out of us. **D**

At Lincoln, making us into Americans did not mean scrubbing away what made us originally foreign. The teachers called us as our parents did, or as close as they could pronounce our names in Spanish or Japanese. No one was ever scolded or punished for speaking in his native tongue on the playground. Matti told the class about his mother's down quilt, which she had made in Italy with the fine feathers of a thousand geese. Encarnación acted out how boys learned to fish in the Philippines. I astounded the third grade with the story of my travels on a stagecoach, which nobody else in the class had seen except in the museum at Sutter's Fort. After a visit to the Crocker Art Gallery and its collection of heroic paintings of the golden age of California, someone showed a silk scroll with a Chinese painting. Miss Hopley herself had a way of expressing wonder over these matters before a class, her eyes wide open until they popped slightly. It was easy for me to feel that becoming a proud American, as she said we should, did not mean feeling ashamed of being a Mexican. **E**

> The teachers called us as our parents did, or as close as they could pronounce our names. . . .

D | **Read and Discuss** The author says that the staff at Lincoln "warmed knowledge into us and roasted racial hatreds out of us." What does he mean by that?

E | **Literary Focus** Response to Literature Re-read the first sentence in this paragraph. In what ways does Galarza support this idea in the rest of the paragraph?

Applying Your Skills

SKILLS FOCUS **Literary Skills** Analyze responses to literature. **Reading Skills** Organize information. **Vocabulary Skills** Demonstrate knowledge of literal meanings of words and their usage. **Writing Skills** Write to describe; develop descriptions with sensory details.

from **Barrio Boy**

Respond and Think Critically

Reading Focus

Quick Check

1. How does the Lincoln School honor its students' original languages and customs?

Read with a Purpose

2. What helps Ernesto adjust to school in California during the early 1900s?

Reading Skills: Organize Information

3. Review the following question:
   How does Galarza discover that he can become "a proud American" without abandoning his Mexican heritage? Analyze his experiences at the Lincoln School in your response.
   Review the chart you completed while reading. Which evidence do you think is most important? least important? Number the items to show the order in which you would present them.

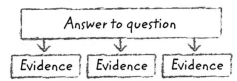

✔ Vocabulary Check

Answer the following questions.

4. What might be **reassuring** to a second-language learner in a new school?
5. What **contraption** do you find hard to figure out?
6. What are you **assured** of when you study hard?
7. Describe a **formidable** challenge you've faced.
8. What is the first thing you try to **survey** in a new school or classroom? Why?

Literary Focus

Literary Analysis

9. **Interpret** In many ways, this story is a tribute to Ernesto's teachers. What does Galarza mean when he says Miss Ryan was not only "with it" but "with us"?
10. **Extend** Galarza thinks of the Lincoln School not as a melting pot—which makes everyone the same—but as a warm griddle. What do you think this means? Which **metaphor**—the melting pot or the warm griddle—would you use to describe the United States? Why?
11. **Connect** How do you think attending the Lincoln School affected Galarza's life as a child and as an adult?

Literary Skills: Analyze Responses to Literature

12. **Analyze** Now that you've read the autobiography, what are the most important details you'll look for in the three essays you're about to evaluate?

Writing Focus

Think as a Reader/Writer

Use It in Your Writing As you read, you listed descriptive details that helped you visualize the Lincoln School. Use vivid details in a brief description of your school.

Three Essays on BARRIO BOY

Read with a Purpose
Read essays responding to the excerpt from *Barrio Boy* to determine which one does the best job of analyzing the selection.

Build Background
The three essays you are about to read are all responses to the excerpt from *Barrio Boy*. Essay 1 is a focused response to the question. It includes a direct answer. Its main ideas are supported by details and evidence from the text. Read the other two passages carefully to see how they compare with Essay 1.

Question: *How does Galarza discover that he can become "a proud American" without abandoning his Mexican heritage? Analyze his experiences at the Lincoln School in your response.*

Essay 1

As *Barrio Boy* begins, Ernesto Galarza is concerned that the Lincoln School will be foreign to him. He also worries that he won't fit in with his classmates, many of whom are from different backgrounds. However, through his interactions with his teachers and fellow students, he finds Lincoln to be a welcoming environment. He learns that he can be proud of his heritage. Most important, he learns that being proud of one's heritage is essential to becoming a proud American. **Ⓐ**

While Ernesto's teachers take their responsibility of teaching English seriously, they also make sure that students remain proud of their heritage. Ernesto learns that "making us into Americans did not mean scrubbing away what made us originally foreign." For instance, all students are allowed to speak their native language on the playground, and teachers call them by their given names. Ernesto compares the school to a "griddle where Miss Hopley and her helpers warmed knowledge into us." This means that the children can become proud Americans without losing their own identities. **Ⓑ**

Through his interactions with fellow students, Galarza further learns that becoming a proud American doesn't mean that he should forget his heritage. In the beginning he says he is nervous because Lincoln

---

Ⓐ **Literary Focus** Response to Literature Where is the question answered directly?

Ⓑ **Reading Focus** Organizing Information What is the main idea of this paragraph? What examples from the text support this idea?

is different from the school he went to in Mexico. But once he begins to interact with his classmates and learn about their backgrounds—Japanese, Italian, Korean, and many others—his time at the Lincoln School is enriched. He finds himself sharing a story that "astounded" the class.

Galarza learns that his heritage is an important part of his identity primarily through his experiences at the Lincoln School. By sharing his experiences with teachers and students, Galarza shows readers that being proud of his heritage helps make him a proud American.

Essay 2

In *Barrio Boy,* Ernest Galarza describes his early experiences at the Lincoln School. The school helped the children be proud of their own heritages. It also helped them become proud Americans.

We find out about Ernesto's thoughts and feelings in an autobiography. Ernesto's teachers are the most important influence on him at Lincoln. Miss Hopley comforts Ernesto with her friendly voice. Miss Ryan gives Ernesto, and most of the other students in the class, recognition as they learn English: Ernesto feels especially proud when he learns how to say *butterfly.* Moments like this help Ernesto get along with his classmates and help him become a proud American. **C**

Ernesto takes pride in his relationships with the other students. He meets students from different backgrounds and sees that, while they all live near each other, they have a lot to learn about one another because of their particular backgrounds. Ernesto learns about an Italian student's quilt and the way they fish in the Philippines. It is this sharing that gives Ernesto a sense of pride in being Mexican as well as being American.

Essay 3

Ernesto Galarza and his family have just arrived in California from Mexico. He is enrolling in the first grade at the Lincoln School.

When Ernesto and his mother arrive at the school, he is afraid. At first, Ernesto is worried about attending school in America. However, Ernesto and his mother are warmly greeted by his principal on the first day of school. Ernesto feels even better after meeting Miss Ryan, his new teacher. She makes a point to encourage students as they learn the English language. She also makes sure to respect her students' heritage: she pronounces their names as they are pronounced at home. Ernesto learns a great deal about his classmates as well. They are of all backgrounds, but they are all American.

These experiences help Ernesto to become a good American as well. Ernesto understands that it is important to be proud of where he comes from. At the same time, his teachers and classmates teach him what it means to be an American. **D**

C **Literary Focus** Response to Literature How well do the details in this paragraph support its opening sentence?

D **Literary Focus** Response to Literature Where does this essay mention Ernesto's concerns about his heritage?

Applying Your Skills

SKILLS FOCUS **Literary Skills** Analyze responses to literature. **Reading Skills** Organize information. **Writing Skills** Write to reflect on ideas.

Three Essays on *Barrio Boy*

Respond and Think Critically

Reading Focus

Quick Check

1. Which essay uses specific details from the text to support its analysis of the selection?
2. Which essay summarizes the plot?
3. Which essay directly answers the question?

Read with a Purpose

4. Which essay does the best job of analyzing the selection? Give reasons for your choice.

Reading Skills: Organize Information

5. Evaluate the way information is organized in Essay 1. If you were writing a response, would you have organized the main points differently? Explain.

Literary Focus

Literary Analysis

6. **Analyze** Essay 1 is the only one that uses direct quotations from the text to illustrate and support its points. Why is quoting from the text important? How do the quotations help the reader better understand the writer's points?

7. **Compare and Contrast** What **metaphor** discussed in Essay 1 is missing from the other responses? Is it important to include the metaphor in a response to the question? Why or why not?

8. **Compare and Contrast** Complete the chart below by filling in what you learn about Ernesto's teachers in the three responses. Which response contains irrelevant information about the teachers? Explain.

Response	Ernesto's teachers
Essay 1	
Essay 2	
Essay 3	

9. **Evaluate** Is Essay 3 an adequate response? Why or why not?

Literary Skills: Analyze Responses to Literature

10. **Evaluate** Essay 2 mentions that *Barrio Boy* is an autobiography. Should this information be included in a response to the essay question? Why or why not?

11. **Evaluate** In Essay 1, do the details the writer includes about Ernesto's classmates support the main idea? Why or why not?

12. **Evaluate** On a scale of 0 to 5, with 0 being the lowest rating and 5 the highest, how would you rate each essay? Base your evaluation on the writer's use of evidence and understanding of literary elements.

Writing Focus

Think as a Reader/Writer

Use It in Your Writing Which of the essays contains the most descriptive examples? What do the descriptions add to the response?

Wrap Up

SKILLS FOCUS **Literary Skills** Analyze responses to literature. **Reading Skills** Organize information. **Writing Skills** Write autobiographical narratives; write an extended metaphor.

from Barrio Boy / Three Essays on *Barrio Boy*

Writing Focus

Write a Response to *Barrio Boy*

Write a response to the *Barrio Boy* excerpt. First, review the charts you created. Then, identify the key elements to include in your analysis. Once you have decided on the key elements, think about how you will organize the information.

1. You could organize the information by **order of importance,** like Essay 1. You would begin your essay by writing a thesis statement that addresses the question you're responding to. Then, you would present evidence that supports your thesis. You would put your strongest evidence first. Finally, you would close by reinforcing your thesis.

2. Or, you could organize your essay in **chronological order,** discussing the key elements in the order in which they appear in the selection itself. You might start out by describing how Ernesto feels on his first day of school and go on to explain how his feelings evolve during his time at school. You might conclude by explaining how the school experience influenced his ideas about being both American and Mexican. You would not discuss the main idea until the end of the essay.

However you decide to organize your essay, make sure that your writing stays focused and that you include details and quotations from the text to support the points you make.

What Do You Think Now?

How would you characterize Galarza's attitude toward his situation?

CHOICES

As you respond to the Choices, use these **Academic Vocabulary** words as appropriate: <u>ambiguous</u>, <u>evident</u>, <u>convey</u>, <u>principal</u>.

REVIEW

Analyze Responses to Literature

Timed Writing Analyze the following criticisms of Essay 3, and decide which ones are valid. Explain the reasons for your choice.

- The writer should have summarized the plot.
- The writer should have a stronger thesis.
- The writer does not mention the characters.
- The writer did not use enough details from the text.

CONNECT

Write Your Autobiography

Write about your own first days at school. What were your thoughts and impressions the first day you went to preschool or kindergarten? Try to remember them and write them in a way that will help the reader experience what it was like.

EXTEND

Create Your Own Metaphor

The metaphor of the melting pot is commonly used to talk about the United States and its immigrant population. Galarza uses a different metaphor—the griddle. Create your own metaphor, describing what happens to people from different countries with different traditions when they come to America. Write a paragraph introducing and explaining your metaphor.

INFORMATIONAL TEXT FOCUS
Author's Purpose and Perspective

CONTENTS

 What Do **You** Think? Do you think pets make conscious choices about their actions, or are they just following their instincts?

 QuickTalk
Most people have either personally experienced or observed in others the bond between humans and animals. With a small group, share your experiences.

WEB ARTICLE
Preparing to Read

Canines to the Rescue

 **Reader/Writer Notebook**

Use your **RWN** to complete the activities for this selection.

Informational Text Focus

Analyzing an Author's Perspective **Perspective** refers to the way you look at a subject. Take the topic of dogs. Some people's perspective on that subject is negative—they think dogs are dangerous animals that can turn on you at any moment. Other people have a positive view of dogs—they think dogs are friendly, loving, and faithful companions. Perspective in writing refers to a writer's point of view, or attitude, toward a subject. All writing reveals some kind of perspective on the world. The writer is saying, in effect, "Here is what I think about this issue."

Tips for Finding an Author's Perspective After you read "Canines to the Rescue," make a chart like the one on the right. Completing the chart will help you interpret the author's perspective on rescue dogs.

"Canines to the Rescue"

> The author spends time with rescue dogs in the rubble of the World Trade Center.

> The author gives examples of rescue dogs' qualities:
> 1.
> 2.
> 3.
> [and so on]

> The author compares his opinion of dogs with another writer's:

> Final quotation:

> The author's perspective on rescue dogs:

Vocabulary

arduous (AHR joo uhs) *adj.*: difficult. *The rescue dogs climbing through the rubble were faced with an arduous task.*

persevered (pur suh VIHRD) *v.*: kept trying; persisted. *Despite the difficulty, the dogs persevered in their search.*

fidelity (fuh DEHL uh tee) *n.*: faithfulness. *The dogs showed true fidelity to their handlers by not giving up despite their discomfort.*

Writing Focus   Preparing for **Constructed Response**

As you read "Canines to the Rescue," use your *Reader/Writer Notebook* to take notes about the author's main point.

Language Coach

Word Roots A word root is the main part of a word. Many word roots in English come from Latin. Think of at least one more related word that contains the following Latin root.

Latin Root	Meaning	Related Word
–fide–	trust	fidelity

 Learn It Online
To learn more about analyzing the author's perspective, use the interactive Reading Workshop at:

go.hrw.com   L7-547   **Go**

Read with a Purpose

As you read, consider why dogs and humans share a unique bond.

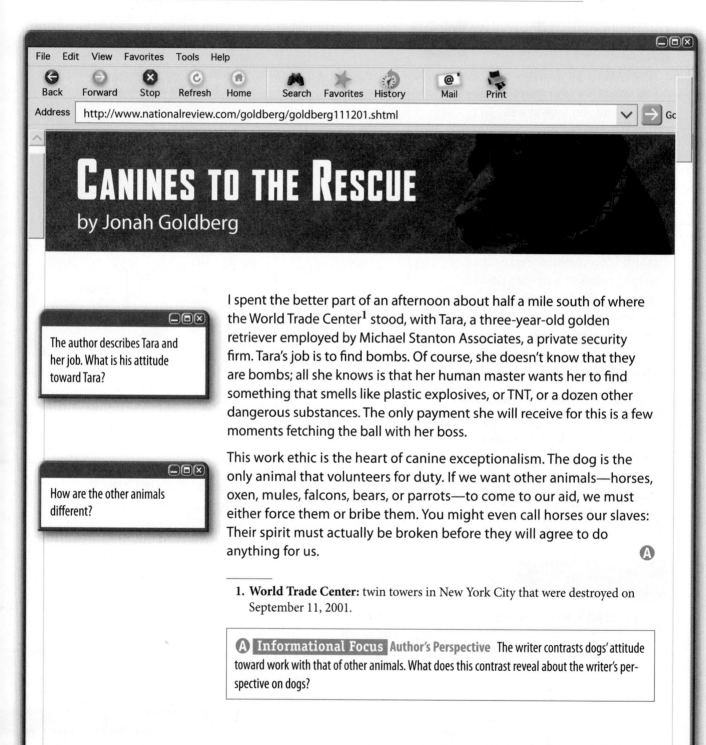

CANINES TO THE RESCUE

by Jonah Goldberg

The author describes Tara and her job. What is his attitude toward Tara?

I spent the better part of an afternoon about half a mile south of where the World Trade Center[1] stood, with Tara, a three-year-old golden retriever employed by Michael Stanton Associates, a private security firm. Tara's job is to find bombs. Of course, she doesn't know that they are bombs; all she knows is that her human master wants her to find something that smells like plastic explosives, or TNT, or a dozen other dangerous substances. The only payment she will receive for this is a few moments fetching the ball with her boss.

How are the other animals different?

This work ethic is the heart of canine exceptionalism. The dog is the only animal that volunteers for duty. If we want other animals—horses, oxen, mules, falcons, bears, or parrots—to come to our aid, we must either force them or bribe them. You might even call horses our slaves: Their spirit must actually be broken before they will agree to do anything for us.

A

1. **World Trade Center:** twin towers in New York City that were destroyed on September 11, 2001.

> **A** **Informational Focus** **Author's Perspective** The writer contrasts dogs' attitude toward work with that of other animals. What does this contrast reveal about the writer's perspective on dogs?

Analyzing Visuals   **Viewing and Interpreting**   What is the setting of the photograph? Note where the humans and dog are standing. How does this support the information from the text?

Look carefully at the author's word choice in the paragraph. Which words offer clues to the author's view of dogs?

Long before the rubble settled in downtown New York, German shepherds, Labrador retrievers, and Rottweilers—as well as canines of less aristocratic lineage—were already pulling at their leashes to help with the search-and-rescue efforts. Locating the dead and searching (too often in vain) for the living is obviously an arduous and emotionally draining task for human beings, but it is no picnic for dogs either. The rubble provided unstable footing, was full of glass shards and twisted metal, and sometimes glowed red hot. Dangerous fumes, loud noises, and the equivalent of landslides were constant sources of distraction and peril. Dogs repeatedly had to limp out of the wreckage on bloody paws, the razor-edged debris[2] slicing through even the leather boots distributed to some of them. **Ⓑ**

---

2. **debris** (duh BREE): pieces of stone, wood, glass, or other materials left after something is destroyed.

> **Ⓑ** **Read and Discuss**   How does this information add to what you know about rescue dogs?

Vocabulary   **arduous** (AHR joo uhs) *adj.:* difficult.

Worse, the stress associated with not finding survivors was extreme; dogs tasked with this assignment expect—*need*—to find survivors. "They don't like to find bodies. They'll find them, but they don't feel rewarded," veterinarian Douglas Wyler explained. "The dogs are good, they're professionals, but like any professional they can suffer from melancholy and depression. It's hard for the men not to find anyone alive, and the dogs sense that." **C**

But the dogs persevered. Consider Servus, a Belgian Malinois (a smaller version of the German shepherd) who arrived at the Twin Towers site with his owner, police officer Chris Christensen, the day after the disaster. While searching for survivors, Servus fell down a nine-foot hole into a mound of dust and debris. When they pulled him free, "he couldn't breathe," Christensen explained. Servus tried to vomit, to no avail. By the time the convulsions started and Servus's tongue turned purple, between twenty and thirty men were gathered to help an animal they clearly considered a colleague (often, police dogs are given full-dress funerals). The

---

C [Read and Discuss] What additional information about rescue dogs do you find in this paragraph?

Vocabulary **persevered** (pur suh VIHRD) *v.*: kept trying; persisted.

canine was rushed to one of the veterinary MASH units set up to treat the rescue dogs as well as the numerous "civilian" animals and pets injured or abandoned in the surrounding residential areas.

The vets managed to resuscitate[3] Servus, and he was given an IV.[4] (It was not unusual to see rescue humans and rescue dogs lying beside one another, each with his own IV drip.) When the vets unstrapped the dog from the gurney and released him for some doggie R & R,[5] he ran straight from the tent and leapt into the police car assigned to bring dogs to ground zero. "I couldn't believe it," Christensen said. "I told him three times to get out and he just looked at me, so we went to work. We worked for seven hours." **D**

Such dedication has inspired a growing effort in the scientific community to explain this age-old symbiosis between men and dogs. Until fairly recently, the study of dogs has been ignored by scientists more interested in more "authentic" animals—despite the fact that the domestic dog may be the second most successful of all mammal species, after human beings.

More to the point, their success is directly attributable to the fact that they have teamed up with human beings. I'm told that according to an American Indian legend, human beings and animals were separated by a great canyon in prehistory. Forced to choose sides, the dog decided to throw in his lot with man and leapt the chasm to live and work with us. The moral of the story is certainly true, though the choice was evolutionary as well as sentimental. Some, like nature writer Stephen Budiansky, take the story too far in the other direction. He argues that canines have mastered an

The author cites scientific research. He compares and contrasts his perspective with another writer's.

---

3. **resuscitate** (rih SUHS uh tayt): revive; bring back to life.
4. **IV** (abbreviation for *intravenous*): medical procedure in which blood, plasma, medicine, or nutrients are delivered directly into a vein.
5. **R & R:** abbreviation used in the military, meaning "rest and recuperation."

D **Informational Focus** **Author's Perspective** In what ways does the anecdote about Servus support the author's perspective on rescue dogs?

evolutionary strategy that makes us love them: "Dogs belong to that elite group of con artists at the very pinnacle of their profession, the ones who pick our pockets clean and leave us smiling about it."

These cynics would have us believe that dogs— which have, in numerous documented cases, given their lives for human beings—are actually slyly exploiting an emotional glitch in people that makes us love soft, big-eyed furry things. This overlooks the obvious fact that we "con" dogs too; that they, in fact, love us as much as, if not more than, we love them.

Allowing himself to be carried by crane hundreds of feet above the ground and then lowered into a smoldering pit of metal and glass defies every instinct a dog has, except one: to be a selfless friend of his ally and master. "Histories are more full of examples of the fidelity of dogs than of friends," observed Alexander Pope. "Heaven goes by favor," remarked Mark Twain. "If it went by merit, you would stay out and your dog would go in." **E**

The author uses famous quotations to support his view.

There's no disputing that dogs do things for canine reasons. Many of their heroic acts can be attributed to misplaced maternal or other instincts. Newfoundlands have saved many people from drowning, but their instinct is just as strong to "save" banana crates and other flotsam. Tara—the ebullient[6] golden retriever I looked for bombs with—doesn't know the details; all she knows is that she wants to please her human master.

And isn't that good enough? **F**

The author ends by contrasting ideas about dogs and by expressing his opinion.

Read with a Purpose   In what ways can humans and dogs form a unique bond?

---

6. **ebullient** (ih BUHL yuhnt): high-spirited.

E | Read and Discuss | What does this paragraph tell you about the author's view of dogs and their place in society?

F | Informational Focus | Author's Perspective   What do the last two paragraphs reveal about the author's perspective on rescue dogs?

Vocabulary   **fidelity** (fuh DEHL uh tee) *n.*: faithfulness.

🌐 Internet

WEB ARTICLE
Applying Your Skills

SKILLS FOCUS **Informational Skills** Analyze an author's purpose and perspective; evaluate an author's point of view or perspective in a text.

Canines to the Rescue

Practicing the Standards

Informational Text and Vocabulary

1. Which of the following *best* states the author's perspective on rescue dogs?

A They work under cruel and inhumane conditions.

B They face deadly challenges to please their masters.

C They are con artists that fool humans into loving them.

D They do not receive adequate rewards for their work.

2. One way the author expresses his perspective on dogs is by contrasting —

A a legend with an opposing opinion

B pet dogs with search-and-rescue dogs

C canine con artists with human dog trainers

D German shepherds with Labrador retrievers

3. To *best* describe his perspective, the author chooses the words —

A *soft; maternal; elite*

B *strategy; authentic; instinct*

C *disaster; convulsions; draining*

D *colleague; volunteers; dedication*

4. Which of the following quotations *best* presents the author's perspective?

A "Servus . . . was given an IV."

B "a selfless friend of his ally and master"

C "a smaller version of the German shepherd"

D "their instinct is just as strong to 'save' banana crates"

5. If a task is *arduous,* it is —

A irritating

B difficult

C exceptional

D unusual

6. A synonym for *fidelity* is —

A honesty

B gravity

C dignity

D loyalty

7. Someone who has *persevered* has —

A persisted

B shouted

C disputed

D conceded

Writing Focus   **Constructed Response**

How effective was the author in communicating his perspective on dogs? Use details from the article to support your response.

What Do You Think Now

Has this article changed your opinion on whether pets make conscious choices about their actions? Explain.

SPEECH
Preparing to Read

Tribute to the Dog

Reader/Writer
Notebook
Use your **RWN** to complete the activities for this selection.

Informational Text Focus

Analyzing an Author's Purpose and Perspective People write nonfiction for many different **purposes,** or reasons. For example, a speechwriter tries to **persuade** you to believe or do something. A nonfiction writer often wants to **inform,** or teach, you about a topic. A person who writes a personal narrative may want to share an experience or reveal a truth about life.

All writing reveals some kind of **perspective,** or point of view. Often in an **argument,** a position supported by logic or emotion, someone wants to persuade you to see things from his or her perspective. To convince you, a writer usually provides a mix of appeals.

Logical appeals are based on facts and statistics. **Emotional appeals** use tone, feelings, language, and anecdotes to stir up your feelings and make you sympathetic to the author's argument. Learn to recognize emotional appeals—you should base your opinions on more than a writer's feelings.

Into Action When you read persuasive texts, you can use a chart like this to analyze the appeals used in an author's argument.

Details from Text	Appeal: Logical or Emotional?

Vocabulary

malice (MAL ihs) *n.:* meanness; hatred. *Some mean-spirited people treat others with malice rather than kindness.*

treacherous (TREHCH uhr uhs) *adj.:* unfaithful. *A dog is the one truly loyal, never treacherous friend a person can have.*

prosperity (prahs PEHR uh tee) *n.:* state of being successful, especially of being wealthy. *Dogs love us regardless of our prosperity or poverty.*

Language Coach

Recognizing Roots English is made up of many words derived from Latin roots. Recognizing those roots, their meanings, and related words can help you figure out the meanings of unfamiliar words. What other words can you think of that are derived from the following Latin root?

Latin Root	Meaning	Related Word
mal–	bad	malice

Writing Focus   Preparing for **Constructed Response**

As you read "Tribute to the Dog," note the words, phrases, and examples that Vest uses to appeal to your emotions.

Learn It Online
Use Word Watch to explore vocabulary words at:

go.hrw.com   L7-554   **Go**

Read with a Purpose

As you read the following summation (a persuasive speech delivered at the end of a trial), look for the arguments the lawyer uses to win over the jury.

Build Background

As a young lawyer, George Graham Vest represented a man suing a sheep farmer for shooting his dog, which had strayed onto the farmer's property. In this summation, Vest does not refer to any of the testimony or evidence given at the trial; instead, he gives a stirring tribute to dogs in general. Vest's client won the case, and the speech is now regarded as a classic tribute to "man's best friend."

TRIBUTE to the DOG

Gentlemen of the Jury: The best friend a man has in the world may turn against him and become his enemy. His son or daughter that he has reared[1] with loving care may prove ungrateful. Those who are nearest and dearest to us, those whom we trust with our happiness and our good name may become traitors to their faith. The money that a man has, he may lose. It flies away from him, perhaps when he needs it most. A man's reputation may be sacrificed in a moment of ill-considered action. The people who are prone to fall on their knees to do us honor when success is with us, may be the first to throw the stone of malice when failure settles its cloud upon our heads. **A**

The one absolutely unselfish friend that man can have in this selfish world, the one that never deserts him, the one that never proves ungrateful or treacherous is his dog. A man's dog stands by him in prosperity and in poverty, in health and in sickness. He will sleep on the cold ground, where the

---

1. **reared:** raised.

A **Informational Focus** **Author's Perspective** Note the contrast between the title and the examples in the first paragraph. What does this contrast reveal about the speaker's attitude toward dogs?

Vocabulary **malice** (MAL ihs) *n.*: meanness; hatred.
treacherous (TREHCH uhr uhs) *adj.*: unfaithful.
prosperity (prahs PEHR uh tee) *n.*: state of being successful, especially of being wealthy.

wintry winds blow and the snow drives fiercely, if only he may be near his master's side. He will kiss the hand that has no food to offer. He will lick the wounds and sores that come in encounters with the roughness of the world. He guards the sleep of his pauper[2] master as if he were a prince. When all other friends desert, he remains. When riches take wings,[3] and reputation falls to pieces, he is as constant in his love as the sun in its journey through the heavens. **B**

If fortune drives the master forth, an outcast in the world, friendless and homeless, the faithful dog asks no higher privilege than that of accompanying him, to guard him against danger, to fight against his enemies. And when the last scene of all comes, and death takes his master in its embrace and his body is laid away in the cold ground, no matter if all other friends pursue their way,[4] there by the graveside will the noble dog be found, his head between his paws, his eyes sad, but open in alert watchfulness, faithful and true even in death. **C**

George Graham Vest

Read with a Purpose Would you have been swayed by George Graham Vest's arguments? Why or why not?

---

2. **pauper:** person who is very poor.
3. **take wings:** vanish; fly away.
4. **pursue their way:** continue with their lives.

B **Read and Discuss** What evidence does the author give for saying that a dog is "as constant in his love as the sun in its journey through the heavens"?

C **Informational Focus** Author's Perspective In what ways does Vest make emotional appeals in this paragraph?

SPEECH
Applying Your Skills

SKILLS FOCUS **Informational Skills** Analyze an author's purpose and perspective; evaluate the author's purpose and perspective in a text.

Tribute to the Dog

Practicing the Standards

Informational Text and Vocabulary

1. Which of the following reasons *best* describes the author's purpose for writing this summation?

  A To give his opinion about the need for farmers to have dogs

  B To teach the emotional differences between dogs and people

  C To convince people that a dog is the finest companion one can have

  D To entertain the courtroom with elaborate descriptions of dogs

2. One way the author expresses his perspective about dogs is by contrasting dogs with —

  A people

  B death

  C cats

  D princes

3. Which of the following quotations *best* presents the author's purpose?

  A "The money that a man has, he may lose."

  B "His son or daughter . . . may prove ungrateful."

  C "by the graveside will the noble dog be found"

  D "A man's reputation may be sacrificed. . . ."

4. From the summation you can conclude that the author's perspective is that —

  A dogs are more loyal than humans

  B dogs must obey laws as humans do

  C everyone should have a dog

  D everyone without a dog will be lonely

5. An act of *malice* is one of —

  A hatred

  B disregard

  C expertise

  D quality

6. A state of *prosperity* is one of —

  A uncertainty

  B success

  C awareness

  D injury

7. A synonym of *treacherous* is —

  A frightening

  B logical

  C unfaithful

  D opinionated

Writing Focus   Constructed Response

How did Vest convince you that the dog is "man's best friend"? Cite examples from the speech that had the strongest effect on your emotions.

What Do You Think Now? Which author is more effective at communicating his perspective, Goldberg or Vest? Why do you think so?

Writing Workshop

Response to Literature

Write with a Purpose

Write an essay justifying your interpretation of a literary work. Explain how details from the work support your **thesis.** Remember that your **purpose** is to **persuade** your **audience** that you have developed a valid **interpretation** of the work.

A Good Response to Literature

- identifies the work by title and author
- states the interpretation clearly
- supports the interpretation with evidence such as details, examples, and reasons
- has a clear organization
- restates or reinforces the interpretation in a strong conclusion

See page 566 for complete rubric.

Reader/Writer Notebook

Use your **RWN** for completing the activities in this workshop.

Think as a Reader/Writer

Before you write your own response to a literary work, read Kathleen Odean's review of the novel *Catherine, Called Birdy*, by Karen Cushman. Notice how Odean uses evidence from the novel to persuade readers to support her interpretation of the work and to convince her audience to read the novel.

> Catherine, daughter of a small-time nobleman in medieval England, is hilarious. In a diary format she records her daily life, the outrages she suffers as a girl, and her often humorous assessment of things. She longs to be outside frolicking instead of inside sewing, and she chafes at her lessons in ladylike behavior.
>
> Birdy is the sort of girl who organizes a spitting contest and starts a mud fight. She makes a list of all the things girls cannot do, such as go on a crusade, be a horse trainer, laugh out loud, "and marry whom they will." She battles with her father, who wants to marry her off to the highest bidder, no matter how repulsive. Many of her best sarcastic remarks are reserved for him, and she irritates him whenever possible. She has a lively sense of humor and a palpable love of life. Few fictional characters are so vivid and funny—do not miss this one.

← The author states her **thesis** about the character in the first sentence.

← Specific **details** from the story are used to support the claim that this character is very funny.

← The closing sentences **restate the thesis** in a persuasive way.

Think About the Professional Model

With a partner, discuss the following questions about the model.

1. Does this response include an introduction, body, and conclusion? Is the organization effective? Why or why not? See page 566 for the complete rubric.

2. How many examples does the author include as evidence? How do they strengthen her interpretation?

3. How does the author make her purpose clear?

Prewriting

Choose a Subject

Think of a literary work that profoundly affected you. A work that inspired a strong response in you is probably one that you would like to analyze further. Review your *Reader/Writer Notebook* to remind yourself of some of your responses to works you have read this year. Use the Idea Starters to the right to focus on a possible subject.

Develop a Thesis

Once you have chosen a topic, you need to formulate a **thesis** about the topic. A thesis statement expresses your point of view about a subject. It is a specific position statement usually located in an opening paragraph and supported by evidence presented throughout the essay. A strong thesis inspires readers to ask "How?" or "Why?" It avoids general and sweeping statements such as *all*, *none*, or *every*. Here are some examples to guide you:

Selection	Topic	Thesis Statement:
"The Dinner Party" (page 36)	The plot of the story	The plot is carefully designed to overturn stereotypes about differences between men and women.
"Rikki-Tikki-Tavi" (page 143)	The character of the hero	In his treatment of Rikki, Kipling combines animal characteristics with human motives.
"Bargain" (page 401)	The theme of the story	The theme of "Bargain" is that disrespect can breed vengeance.

Think About Purpose and Audience

As you plan your essay, keep your **purpose** and **audience** in mind. Your purpose is to convince your audience that you have interpreted the meaning of a literary work correctly. Your audience includes your classmates and your teacher, knowledgeable and interested readers. Your essay should increase their understanding and enjoyment of the work.

Idea Starters

- How is a specific literary element, such as setting, plot, point of view, or character, used in the work?
- What problem does the main character face?
- What is the theme or main idea of the work?
- What is the meaning of the title?

Your Turn _____

Get Started Working in your **RWN**, make a list of possible **subjects** you might want to discuss in your essay. Spend a few minutes freewriting about each one. Which **subject** generated your most interesting response? Form a working **thesis** about that **subject**.

An interactive graphic organizer can help you generate and organize essay ideas. Try one at:

go.hrw.com   L7-559   Go

Your Turn

Choose and Record Quotes

Make notes in your **RWN**, choosing short pieces of the work that you might want to **quote directly**. Carefully copy the quotes in your notebook. Then draft an explanation of why each quote is important and how it supports your thesis. Try to keep quotations as brief as possible.

Re-Read the Literary Work

Now that you have decided on a focus for your essay and drafted a working thesis, it is time to revisit the literary work you are writing about. If it is short, re-read the entire work with your thesis in mind. If you are writing about a longer work, re-read sections you feel are important to your thesis. While you are reading, pause to record in your notebook any new thoughts and reactions you have. The following graphic organizer illustrates how you can re-read for any new ideas about the literary work.

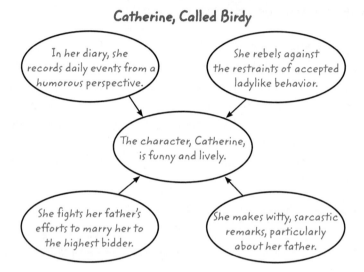

Catherine, Called Birdy

- In her diary, she records daily events from a humorous perspective.
- She rebels against the restraints of accepted ladylike behavior.
- The character, Catherine, is funny and lively.
- She fights her father's efforts to marry her to the highest bidder.
- She makes witty, sarcastic remarks, particularly about her father.

● Writing Tip

Note specific details that provide supporting evidence. Provide explanations or commentaries that draw connections for the reader. Be sure to focus on these kinds of details:

- actions
- thoughts
- words
- others' behavior
- direct comments by writer
- direct quotations from the work

Gather Evidence

In a literary interpretation, the evidence you present in support of your thesis may include direct quotations; paraphrased lines or short passages; details such as images, actions, and dialogue; and explanations or reasons. Select evidence carefully, choosing the best or most persuasive examples to back up your conclusions. Here is an example of how evidence should support each point in your interpretation.

Point	Evidence
Birdy is unusual.	spitting contests and mud fights
She is strong-minded.	wants to choose her own husband

Drafting

Follow the Writer's Framework

Organize your essay to include an introduction, a body, and a conclusion. In your **introduction**, identify the title, author, and thesis statement. The **body** of your essay supports your thesis. Each paragraph in the body of your essay should focus on a main supporting idea and its evidence from the literary work. The **conclusion** brings together your main idea and restates the thesis, revealing your insights into the work.

A Writer's Framework

Introduction:
- States the title and author of the literary work
- States the thesis
- Engages the reader's attention

Body: Supports the Thesis
- Main idea 1 and its supporting evidence
- Main idea 2 and its supporting evidence
- Other main ideas and evidence

Conclusion:
- Restates the thesis without repeating it word-for-word

Organize Evidence

You may arrange your points and evidence in the order that they appear in the story, or you may place them in order of importance. Decide which way will work best by writing drafts of your points and evidence on index cards (or in blocks of text on the computer). Arrange and rearrange the text to see which arrangement might work best in your essay. The important thing is to be sure you have points and supporting evidence for your thesis.

Grammar Link Using Comparatives

When organizing evidence in order of importance, writers often use **degrees of comparison**. The **comparative** degree of a modifier, such as an adjective or adverb, compares two people or things. When using the comparative degree, add the ending -*er* or the word *more*. The **superlative** degree compares more than two people or things. When using the superlative degree, add the ending -*est* or the word *most*.

Comparative Degree:	Superlative Degree:
Catherine is livel**ier** than her father wants her to be.	I enjoyed this book because Catherine is one of the funni**est** fictional characters I have ever encountered.
Catherine is **more** outspoken than many of her peers.	Catherine saved her **most** sarcastic comments for her father.

For more on degrees of comparison, see the Language Handbook.

● Writing Tip

Avoid falling into the trap of summarizing too much of the plot. Keep your audience's needs and your purpose in mind. Your audience needs only a brief summary. Your purpose for writing is to present your interpretation and analysis of what you've read. Your audience wants to know what you think about what you've read, and you want to persuade your audience that your interpretation is valid.

Your Turn _____

Write Your Draft Write a draft of your essay. Be sure to
- include a thesis that is backed up by supporting points and evidence
- quote accurately
- accurately interpret evidence
- restate the thesis in your conclusion

Peer Review

Be sure to provide helpful suggestions to your partner, and remember that your partner's suggestions are meant to help you develop a better essay.

Evaluating and Revising

Read the questions in the left column of the chart, and then use the tips in the middle column to help you make revisions to your essay. The right column suggests techniques you can use to revise your draft.

Supporting an Interpretation: Guidelines for Content and Organization

Evaluation Question	Tip	Revision Technique
1. Are the author and the title named in your introduction?	**Highlight** the author and the title.	**Add** a sentence or phrase naming the author and the title.
2. Does the introduction have a clear thesis?	**Underline** the thesis statement.	**Add** a sentence that clearly states the thesis.
3. Is the main idea of each paragraph clear, and does it support the thesis?	**Bracket** the main idea discussed in each paragraph of the body.	**Revise** the body paragraphs so that each deals with a main idea.
4. Is the main idea of each body paragraph supported with evidence from the work?	**Draw a box** around each supporting detail or quotation. **Draw a wavy line** under elaborations.	**Add** details or quotations to support your thesis. **Elaborate** on details or quotations with commentary.
5. Does your conclusion restate the thesis without repeating it word-for-word?	**Highlight** the sentence in the conclusion that restates the thesis.	**Add** a sentence restating the thesis.
6. Does the conclusion make your reader want to read the literary work?	**Circle** the statement that makes clear your insight or interpretation.	**Add** one or more sentences that remind your reader of your insight or interpretation of the work.

Read this student's draft and the comments about it as a model for revising your own response to a literary work.

A Girl's Adventure

By Sophia Eckerle, Paradise Canyon Elementary School

"Not every thirteen year old girl is accused of murder, brought to trial, and found guilty." This is the opening sentence of *The True Confessions of Charlotte Doyle,* a novel by Avi. The novel takes place in 1832. It tells the story of Charlotte who has finished her schooling in England and must sail home to America. She sails on the *Seahawk,* a rundown ship under the command of Captain Jaggery, a strange character. Charlotte's experiences with the Captain and the sailors change her ideas about how to judge people and how she wants to live her life.

As a wealthy and protective father, Mr. Doyle wants to shape Charlotte's future. He sends Charlotte to the expensive Barrington School for Better Girls in England. He has very high expectations for her and wants her to become an educated proper young lady. Before her journey, Mr. Doyle gave Charlotte a journal and expected her to write (with correct spelling) about the events of the voyage.

At the beginning of the journey, Captain Jaggery is a proper Englishman—one a thirteen-year-old girl could look up to. Like Charlotte's father, the Captain believes that a young girl should wear fancy dresses and devote herself to studying instead of parading around with the crew wearing men's clothes.

← Sophia mentions the **title of the work** and the **name of the author.**

← She states her **thesis** about the main character at the end of the first paragraph.

← Sophia presents **evidence** that supports her claim about Charlotte's father.

MINI-LESSON ▶ **How to Use Supporting Evidence**

Be sure to support your thesis with relevant details. Sophia needs to clearly explain the significance of the main ideas found in the body of her essay. Each paragraph should support the essay's overall thesis.

Sophia's Revision of Paragraph Three

At the beginning of the journey, ∧ *Charlotte's views have been largely influenced by her father. Because of this, she sees* Captain Jaggery ~~is~~ as a proper Englishman--one a thirteen-year-old girl can look up to. ∧ *Charlotte is fooled into thinking the captain is trustworthy by his meticulous clothes and manners.* Like Charlotte's father, the Captain believes that a young girl should wear fancy dresses and devote herself to studying instead of parading around with the crew wearing men's clothes.

Your Turn _____

Use Evidence Read your draft, and then ask yourself:

- Where might I add evidence in support of an important point?
- How can I explain the significance of the evidence I've provided?

Sophia includes a **quotation** from the novel to illustrate a character's nature.

Charlotte's view of the captain begins to change when she sees how badly he treats the crew. He calls the crew "dirty beasts who demand the touch of the whip." Charlotte sees that this is not true.

Sophia explains how the **details** of the story support her thesis.

When the men mutiny against him, the deterioration of Captain Jaggery's mind continues. He kills two of the sailors for an attempted uprising. Charlotte decides that the captain is mad. Changing her fancy clothes for the clothes of a common sailor, she joins the crew. She has learned that the sailors who treat her kindly are the ones to trust, not the cruel captain. His high rank and his nice clothes are not important. Jaggery retaliates by giving her the hardest work on the ship, destroying the barrier between the aristocrats and the working class that Charlotte started. In this way, he contributes to Charlotte's changing attitudes.

Both men influenced Charlotte's life and led to her adventures aboard the Seahawk. By the end of her ordeal, Charlotte was happy to run to the arms of her protective father.

MINI-LESSON ▶ Clarify Your Interpretation

A good writer restates the main idea of the essay in a fresh and persuasive way in the conclusion. Sophia's original conclusion was vague. When she revised her draft, she provided a stronger conclusion that makes her interpretation more clear.

Sophia's Draft

Both men influenced Charlotte's life and led to her adventures aboard the Seahawk. By the end of the ordeal, Charlotte was happy to run to the arms of her protective father.

Your Turn _____

Write a Striking Conclusion
With a partner, review the conclusion to your essay. Have you restated your thesis? If not, repeat your main point in your conclusion, but do so in a fresh way. Try writing a closing sentence that might make your reader want to read the work you have written about.

Sophia's Revision of the Final Paragraph

Charlotte's father and Captain Jaggery influenced the course of Charlotte's life, but perhaps the men on the ship influenced her more. Though at first happy to return to her father, Charlotte's experiences with the sailors forever changed the way she thought about the world. Read this exciting novel to appreciate all that Charlotte learns through her adventure and the surprising decision she makes about her future.

Proofreading and Publishing

Proofreading

Re-read your essay for errors in usage, spelling, punctuation, and grammar. Trade papers with a partner to proofread each other's work. Then, prepare your final copy to share with your audience.

> **Grammar Link** **Capitalizing Authors' Names and Titles**
>
> The author's first name, last name, and any initials must be capitalized. In the title of a work, always capitalize the first and last word and all of the important words in between.
>
> Incorrect: Sophia wrote the essay "A girl's adventure."
> Correct: Sophia Eckerle wrote the essay "A Girl's Adventure."

Publishing

Here are some ways to share your response to a literary work with your audience, using a variety of formats.

- Submit your composition to the school newspaper.
- If your class has a Web page, see if you can post the essay there.
- Ask the school librarian if you may post a copy of your essay on a bulletin board in the library.

Reflect on the Process
Respond to the following questions in your *Reader/Writer Notebook*.

1. Did the process of writing about the literary work affect your interpretation? If so, how?
2. What did you find to be most challenging about writing your essay? How might you work differently the next time?
3. Which piece of your evidence do you think is the strongest? Why?
4. What was the most important revision you made to your draft? How did it strengthen your essay?

● **Proofreading Tip**

It's important to quote a literary work correctly. Exchange papers with a partner, and ask that partner to highlight any quotes you have used in your paper. Give your partner a copy of the work you wrote about and a list of the pages from which you quoted. Ask your partner to carefully read the original and your paper to make sure that you have quoted the work exactly. Ask your partner to circle any errors in your quotations. Correct those errors carefully, checking the original again yourself.

Your Turn _____
Proofread and Publish
Proofread your composition. Be sure that you have followed the rules for capitalization when you have mentioned the author's name and the title of the work. Make the corrections on your final draft, and be sure to share your essay with other readers.

Scoring Rubric

You can use one of the rubrics below to evaluate your response to literature from the Writing Workshop or your response to the prompt on the next page. Your teacher will tell you to use either the four- or the six-point rubric.

6-Point Scale

Score 6   Demonstrates advanced success
- focuses consistently on a clear thesis
- shows effective organization throughout, with smooth transitions
- offers thoughtful, creative ideas
- develops ideas thoroughly, using examples, details, and fully elaborated explanation
- exhibits mature control of written language

Score 5   Demonstrates proficient success
- focuses on a clear thesis
- shows effective organization, with transitions
- offers thoughtful ideas
- develops ideas competently, using examples, details , and well-elaborated explanation
- exhibits sufficient control of written language

Score 4   Demonstrates competent success
- focuses on a clear thesis, with minor distractions
- shows effective organization, with minor lapses
- offers mostly thoughtful ideas
- develops ideas adequately, a mixture of general and specific elaboration
- exhibits general control of written language

Score 3   Demonstrates limited success
- includes some loosely related ideas that distract from the writer's focus
- shows some organization, with noticeable gaps in the logical flow of ideas
- offers routine, predictable ideas
- develops ideas with uneven elaboration
- exhibits limited control of written language

Score 2   Demonstrates basic success
- includes loosely related ideas that seriously distract from the writer's focus
- shows minimal organization, with major gaps in the logical flow of ideas
- offers ideas that merely skim the surface
- develops ideas with inadequate elaboration
- exhibits significant problems with control of written language

Score 1   Demonstrates emerging effort
- shows little awareness of the topic and purpose for writing
- lacks organization
- offers unclear and confusing ideas
- develops ideas in a minimal way, if at all
- exhibits major problems with control of written language

4-Point Scale

Score 4   Demonstrates advanced success
- focuses consistently on a clear thesis
- shows effective organization throughout, with smooth transitions
- offers thoughtful, creative ideas
- develops ideas thoroughly, using examples, details, and fully elaborated explanation
- exhibits mature control of written language

Score 3   Demonstrates competent success
- focuses on a clear thesis, with minor distractions
- shows effective organization, with minor lapses
- offers mostly thoughtful ideas
- develops ideas adequately, a mixture of general and specific elaboration
- exhibits general control of written language

Score 2   Demonstrates limited success
- includes some loosely related ideas that distract from the writer's focus
- shows some organization, with noticeable gaps in the logical flow of ideas
- offers routine, predictable ideas
- develops ideas with uneven elaboration
- exhibits limited control of written language

Score 1   Demonstrates emerging effort
- shows little awareness of the topic and purpose for writing
- lacks organization
- offers unclear and confusing ideas
- develops ideas in a minimal way, if at all
- exhibits major problems with control of written language

Response to Literature

When responding to an on-demand prompt requiring a response to literature, use the models you have read, what you've learned from writing your
own response to literature, the rubric on page 566, and the steps below.

Writing Prompt

Recall a story that has a character that you
admired or liked. What personality traits appealed
to you? Write a literary interpretation, presenting a
clear thesis summing up the character's admirable
qualities. Include descriptions of the character's
actions and words as evidence that supports each
main point of your response.

Study the Prompt

Begin by reading the prompt carefully. Note what
is required in your essay: an interpretation of a literary character's admirable traits, supported with
relevant details.

Tip: Spend about five minutes studying the prompt.

Plan Your Response

Think of a literary work that you know well
enough to write about knowledgeably. Once you
understand your task and have settled on your
subject,

- write down the author and title of the literary
  work
- write a one-sentence thesis statement
- list several points that you will use to support
  your thesis
- consider the kinds of evidence you will use to
  support your main ideas

Tip: Spend about fifteen minutes planning your response.

Respond to the Prompt

Using the notes you have just made, draft your
essay. Follow these guidelines:

- In the introduction, present the author's
  name and the title of the work, and provide a
  clear thesis statement.
- Present each supporting main point in a
  separate paragraph, and provide evidence
  for each main point in the form of details and
  quotations.
- In the conclusion, restate the thesis and summarize the main points.

As you are writing, remember to use words
that are best for your audience—not too informal.
Write as neatly as you can. If your essay can't be
read easily, it won't be scored.

Tip: Spend about twenty minutes writing your draft.

Improve Your Response

Revising Go back over the key aspects of the
essay. Did you state your interpretation clearly?
Did you support your thesis? Did you provide supporting evidence for all of your points?

Proofreading Take a few minutes to proofread
your essay to correct errors in grammar, spelling,
punctuation, and capitalization. Make sure all of
your edits are neat, and erase any stray marks.

Checking Your Final Copy Before you turn in
your essay, read it one more time to catch any
errors you may have missed. You'll be glad that
you took the extra time for one final review.

Tip: Save ten minutes to improve your paper.

Presenting a Persuasive Speech

Speak with a Purpose

Present your interpretation of a literary work as a persuasive speech. Practice the speech, and then present it to your class.

Think as a Reader/Writer Presenting a speech to persuade listeners is much like writing an essay to persuade readers. You use many of the same techniques writers use, but you also need to learn how to *deliver* the speech persuasively. If you merely read your literary interpretation in a dull, lifeless voice, your listeners may not be persuaded by even the strongest arguments.

Adapt Your Essay

Consider Your Purpose and Audience

In order to adapt your literary interpretation into a persuasive speech, you must first consider your **purpose** and **audience.** Your purpose is to persuade listeners to agree with your interpretation. Since this is a class assignment, you know that your audience will be your classmates and that they have probably read the literary work. Consider whether your classmates are likely to agree or disagree with your interpretation. This will help you organize and deliver your speech.

Plan Ahead

Begin with a copy of your written essay. Identify your **topic,** or the aspect of the work that you plan to explore; your **thesis,** or main idea about your topic; and the **evidence** that supports your thesis. Next, make notes on the written copy, highlighting points you want to emphasize. Remember to consider your audience as well as the time allowed for your speech. Then, create note cards to remind you of the main points you want to present. Refer to the note cards as you practice and, if allowed, as you give your speech.

Stick to the Point

Readers can always re-read a passage they don't understand. Listeners don't have that luxury. Therefore, you must ensure that your points are clear and persuasive. Remember to state your thesis clearly at the beginning of your speech, to support it with solid evidence, and to restate it at the end. If your main ideas don't sound very persuasive when read aloud, try rephrasing them. For example, you may find that shorter sentences have more snap.

Reader/Writer Notebook

Use your **RWN** to complete the activities for this workshop.

Deliver Your Speech

All good politicians know that the success of a persuasive speech depends largely on delivery. A position supported by the best evidence may not win votes if the politician has a dull, lifeless delivery. Similarly, the success of your persuasive speech depends on your ability to grab your listeners' attention, build their interest, and persuade them to agree with you. Using effective verbal and nonverbal speaking techniques can help ensure that your persuasive speech is a success.

Verbal Techniques

- **Enunciation** Practice your speech with a partner, and note any words that he or she does not understand. Look up words that you might replace in a thesaurus, and be sure you know how to pronounce them.

- **Vocal Modulation** To stress certain points, speak more loudly or softly. Ask a partner whether your volume is varied enough and whether you can be heard clearly, no matter what your volume.

- **Inflection** Avoid speaking in a monotone. Emphasize important ideas by raising or lowering the pitch of your voice. Ask a partner whether you sound convincing and reasonable. The sound of your voice should fit your audience and suit your purpose.

- **Tempo** Speak slowly enough for your audience to keep up, but don't fall into a pattern that sounds unnatural. Use pauses to emphasize major points: A pause shows your audience that the idea is important, and it gives people time to think about your point. Remember to stop and take a breath when necessary.

Nonverbal Techniques

Making **eye contact** is one way of keeping the audience involved. Before presenting your speech, practice glancing at your note cards and then regaining eye contact with your audience members. Look at different places in the room, so you can practice engaging as many of the listeners as possible. A self-assured speaker can look anyone in the eye.

Keep in mind that your **posture** and **facial expressions** are also reflections of your confidence. Stand tall, and remember that your interpretation represents your best thinking about a literary work. Believe in yourself, and others will believe in you, too.

A Good Persuasive Speech

- includes a clear thesis statement
- supports the thesis with main points
- includes a variety of supporting evidence for the main points
- provides enough background for listeners to understand the supporting evidence
- uses verbal and nonverbal techniques convincingly
- clearly and persuasively restates the thesis

◯ Speaking Tip

If you use note cards to help you, remember your main points and include cues for nonverbal actions, such as pausing for effect or making a supportive gesture.

 Learn It Online

Learn more about persuasive techniques online at MediaScope:

go.hrw.com | L7-569 | **Go**

Literary Skills Review

Nonfiction **Directions:** Read the following selection. Then, read and respond to the questions that follow.

Exile Eyes by **Agate Nesaule**

The beauty shop in Wisconsin where I get my hair cut looks very American. The owner is young and energetic; his sideburns remind me of Elvis Presley, and scissors and dryers dangle like guns from his black holster as he moves among the glass-and-chrome shelves. But one afternoon the place is so full of women and girls that I can hardly get in. With the exception of their uniform politeness in offering me their seats, there is nothing unusual about them. Only details of their clothes suggest other places and other times: Europe after World War II; Wisconsin and the Hmong people who settled here after Vietnam; the Baltic countries after the collapse of the Soviet Union.

A summer dress with a snugly fitting dark top has the bottom of ugly checked-brown flannel. A gathered gray polyester skirt is lengthened by a six-inch-wide insert of flowered print. And their shoes are startling in their flimsiness. These details speak to me of war and exile as eloquently as words. I'm afraid to look into the women's eyes, and when I finally do, it is as bad as I had expected. They all have exile eyes: eyes that have lost everything and seen the unspeakable but are determined to keep looking, eyes that remain weary and disillusioned even during shy giggles. I have seen those eyes before too, in photographs of the Latvian women who survived Siberia and Rwandan girls being questioned by a journalist, on the Chilean woman doctor who used to clean my house, on my mother. They all have eyes like that.

The owner waits patiently for their consent before he so much as snips a hair. Like them, he is from Bosnia. Under his skilled fingers, their crudely chopped-off tresses take on lovely, sleek shapes. A young woman smiles and makes a playful little bow for her new haircut, but her eyes do not change. I'm glad the Bosnian women are getting more elegant styles than my frizzy permanent at age twelve, when I believed that cutting off my braids would transform me into an American. They will have to do much more even than learn English, live among the poor and desperate, and find new friends and lovers. Acquaintances will ask them questions about their experiences but won't be able to stand hearing honest answers. And their longing for home will be confused with ingratitude to America. So much is ahead of them before their eyes lose their power to disturb.

1. Each of the following excerpts from "Exile Eyes" represents the author's point of view *except* —
   A "They all have exile eyes: eyes that have lost everything"
   B "A young woman smiles and makes a playful little bow"
   C "And their longing for home will be confused with ingratitude"
   D "Acquaintances will ask them questions about their experiences"

2. The author's point of view in "Exile Eyes" is *most* influenced by her —
   A living in a town with many exiles from Bosnia.
   B knowing a Chilean doctor who worked as a maid.
   C wearing mismatched secondhand clothes as a child.
   D being an exile from her war-torn home country.

3. Read the final sentence of "Exile Eyes."

   So much is ahead of them before their eyes lose their power to disturb.

   In this sentence, it is clear that the author wants readers to —
   A see the many difficulties exiles face.
   B realize that life in the United States is easy.
   C see the need to volunteer overseas.
   D think about the horrors of war.

4. The point of view in "Elizabeth I" is different from the one in "Names/Nombres" because "Elizabeth I" —
   A is subjective
   B is an autobiography
   C is told in the third person
   D is a personal essay

5. Which of the following statements does *not* support the main idea of *Long Walk to Freedom*?
   A Where there is hate, neither the hater nor the hated is free.
   B All people have the ability to be kind and courageous.
   C Liberation is not the end but the beginning of freedom.
   D If people are born free, they will always feel free.

Constructed Response
6. Compare and contrast the objective and subjective points of view in excerpts from the biography *Elizabeth I* and the autobiography *Barrio Boy*. List two examples from each excerpt, and describe how each affects the two points of view.

Informational Skills Review

Author's Purpose and Perspective

Directions: Read the following selection. Then, respond to the questions that follow.

A Man Down, a Train Arriving, and a Stranger Makes a Choice

by **Cara Buckley**

It was every subway rider's nightmare, times two.

Who has ridden along New York's 656 miles of subway lines and not wondered: "What if I fell to the tracks as a train came in? What would I do?"

And who has not thought: "What if someone else fell? Would I jump to the rescue?"

Wesley Autrey, a 50-year-old construction worker and Navy veteran, faced both those questions in a flashing instant yesterday, and got his answers almost as quickly.

Mr. Autrey was waiting for the downtown local at 137th Street and Broadway in Manhattan around 12:45 P.M. He was taking his two daughters, Syshe, 4, and Shuqui, 6, home before work.

Nearby, a man collapsed, his body convulsing. Mr. Autrey and two women rushed to help, he said. The man, Cameron Hollopeter, 20, managed to get up, but then stumbled to the platform edge and fell to the tracks, between the two rails.

The headlights of the No. 1 train appeared. "I had to make a split decision," Mr. Autrey said.

So he made one, and leapt.

Mr. Autrey lay on Mr. Hollopeter, his heart pounding, pressing him down in a space roughly a foot deep. The train's brakes screeched, but it could not stop in time.

Five cars rolled overhead before the train stopped, the cars passing inches from his head, smudging his blue knit cap with grease. Mr. Autrey heard onlookers' screams. "We're O.K. down here," he yelled, "but I've got two daughters up there. Let them know their father's O.K." He heard cries of wonder, and applause.

Power was cut, and workers got them out. Mr. Hollopeter, a student at the New York Film Academy, was taken to St. Luke's-Roosevelt Hospital Center. He had only bumps and bruises, said his grandfather, Jeff Friedman. The police said it appeared that Mr. Hollopeter had suffered a seizure.

Mr. Autrey refused medical help, because, he said, nothing was wrong. He did visit Mr. Hollopeter in the hospital before heading to his night shift. "I don't feel like I did something spectacular; I just saw someone who needed help," Mr. Autrey said. "I did what I felt was right."

1. What is the **author's purpose** in asking the four questions at the beginning of the article?
   A to make readers imagine what Autrey had been thinking
   B to inspire readers to react with courage like Autrey's
   C to remind readers to be aware when in dangerous situations
   D to advise readers not to use public transportation when ill

2. The reason the author uses the direct quotations in the article is to make it —
   A strictly factual.
   B highly dramatic.
   C personally appealing.
   D very frightening.

3. The author uses the example of Autrey's going to his night job after the accident to express her **point of view** that he —
   A needed to work for a living.
   B was disappointed with Hollopeter.
   C believed he did nothing special.
   D wanted to brag to his co-workers.

4. The direct quotations used by the author reflect her **perspective** that —
   A no one deserved praise for their help except Autrey.
   B Autrey was more concerned about others than about himself.
   C the subway workers helped as much as they possibly could.
   D despite being terrified, Autrey was brave.

Constructed Response
5. State the **author's perspective** about Wesley Autrey and his courageous act. Describe how she supports her opinion, citing three examples from the article.

PREPARING FOR STANDARDIZED TESTS

SKILLS FOCUS Vocabulary Skills Identify and use correctly multiple-meaning words.

Vocabulary Skills Review

Multiple-Meaning Words

Directions: Read each sentence from "Elizabeth I", and then choose the answer whose meaning is most similar to that of the italicized word.

1. "It was not a happy time for a young woman to *take* the responsibility for ruling a kingdom."

   A move

   B adopt

   C borrow

   D buy

2. "So she had to *master* whatever they were expected to know and do."

   A understand

   B teach

   C dominate

   D conquer

3. "She wrote in a beautiful *script* that was like a work of art."

   A drama

   B document

   C handwriting

   D blueprint

4. "The *line* between power, politics, and religion was becoming very thin."

   A route

   B railway

   C team

   D boundary

5. "There was dancing at *court* every evening, a pastime she still enjoyed."

   A playground

   B place for trials

   C royal reception

   D romantic pursuit

6. "The power of husbands over wives in that century—and even now, in many places of this world—was so great that a husband might snatch the reins of power from her and leave her with the *title* but not the authority she loved to exercise."

   A name of a book

   B championship

   C ownership papers

   D noble name

Academic Vocabulary

Directions: Use context clues to answer the following question about the Academic Vocabulary word below.

7. Jonah Goldberg *conveys* his view of rescue dogs through the use of quotations and anecdotes and by his word choice.
   In this sentence, *conveys* means —

   A augments

   B describes

   C believes

   D reveals

Writing Skills Review

Response to Literature

Directions: Read the following paragraph from an essay discussing *Song of the Trees*. Then, answer each question that follows.

(1) Readers don't actually meet the character David Logan until fairly late in Mildred D. Taylor's novella *Song of the Trees*. (2) The incredible strength of this character places him at the heart of the story and of his family. (3) Readers learn near the beginning of the story that David Logan is absent from his family, working hard to earn money in difficult times. (4) His absence leaves a big hole in the family, and the hole gets bigger as trouble comes to the Logans in the form of Mr. Andersen. (5) The children and Mr. Andersen's workers all know that Mr. Andersen would not be able to chop down the trees if David Logan were around. (6) In fact, Mrs. Logan decides to send her son Stacey to get David because they need his strength in order to stop Mr. Andersen. (7) Once he arrives, readers find powerful evidence of his strength. (8) He immediately takes control of what is going on. (9) His quiet, firm voice echoes through the woods. (10) He is very sure about his plan of action and never backs down. (11) As he says, "I always mean what I say." (12) Once David Logan solves the situation, readers also see his heart. (13) Like his daughter Cassie, David mourns the loss of the singing trees. (14) It's easy to see how his influence has affected the family in many ways.

---

1. Which sentence contains the **thesis,** or man idea, of the essay?

   A Sentence 1

   B Sentence 2

   C Sentence 3

   D Sentence 6

2. Read sentences 1 and 2. Which transitional word would work best to link the two sentences?

   A moreover

   B nevertheless

   C so

   D and

3. Sentence 13, as well as the title of the story, uses which literary device?

   A allusion

   B irony

   C dialect

   D personification

4. Sentence 6 talks about three male characters. In sentence 7, the pronoun *he* may confuse readers. How could sentence 7 be changed to be more clear?

   A Substitute "David" for "he."

   B Delete the transitional expression "Once he arrives."

   C Combine the ideas in sentences 6 and 7 into one sentence.

   D None of the above

5. Why is the final sentence weak?

   A It does not clearly restate the thesis.

   B It presents too much evidence.

   C It mentions an obvious idea.

   D It uses a formal tone.

Read On

Nonfiction

Knots in My Yo-Yo String: Autobiography of a Kid

Have you ever thought about what you would write in a book about your childhood? Jerry Spinelli, a Newbery Award–winning author, revisits remembrances from his childhood: dreaming of a career as a major-league shortstop, reading comic books for hours, and experiencing his one and only time in school detention. Spinelli had no idea he would become a writer, but he recounts in compelling prose the incident that inspired him to become one.

At Her Majesty's Request: An African Princess in Victorian England

In *At Her Majesty's Request*, Walter Dean Myers tells the story of Sarah Forbes Bonetta, an African princess whom a British sea captain saved from a ritual killing when she was seven. As a result, the orphaned girl spent most of her life in England, receiving an upbringing under the eye of Queen Victoria. Myers includes newspaper articles and portraits to add to the reality of Bonetta's compelling story.

Fire in Their Eyes: Wildfires and the People Who Fight Them

What drives some people to stand in the path of a wall of flame? Who are these brave, foolhardy, and visionary firefighters? *Fire in Their Eyes* explores the trials, tragedies, and triumphs of these courageous few. Karen Magnuson Beil takes you into the heart of one of nature's most destructive and unpredictable forces—fire—and the heroes who battle it.

Machu Picchu: Story of the Amazing Inkas and Their City in the Clouds

High in the remote mountains of the Andes, the great Inka city of Machu Picchu remained hidden from the Spanish conquistadores despite their years-long search. Elizabeth Mann describes the city's construction and grand architecture, plus the exciting adventures of the Inka people. Along with realistic illustrations, *Machu Picchu* will reveal the ancient city's mysteries to you.

Nonfiction

Satchel Paige: Don't Look Back

Satchel Paige could throw a baseball like no one else. However, in the 1920s, when he began his career, African Americans were barred from the major leagues. Instead, he became a star in the Negro Baseball League. Paige retained the hope of joining the majors. At an age when many players retire, Paige became a star pitcher in the integrated majors. David A. Adler and Terry Widener, award-winning biographers of sports figures, relate the story of a powerful athlete who wouldn't give up.

Second-Hand Dog: How to Turn Yours into a First-Rate Pet

Whether or not you've ever adopted a shelter dog, *Second-Hand Dog* will help you admire the ability of formerly homeless dogs to become loving companions. Accompanied by witty cartoons, Carol Lea Benjamin's book gives step-by-step instructions on giving a dog the guidance it needs and wants to make both you and it happy.

The Circuit

The Circuit relates the experiences of a family that moves from Mexico to California in hopes of finding a better life. From his point of view as a young boy, Francisco Jiménez has created a collection of autobiographical stories, describing his life as a migrant child who worked the fields of California with his family. Some of the many awards the book has won are the Boston Globe-Horn Book Award, the Américas Award, and the Tomás Rivera Book Award.

Amos Fortune: Free Man

In Africa in 1710, Amos Fortune was born as the son of a king. At age fifteen, he was captured by slave traders and transported in chains to the colony of Massachusetts. Despite the horrors of captivity, Fortune never gave up hope of securing his freedom. Find out more about this remarkable man's life in Elizabeth Yates's Newbery winner, *Amos Fortune: Free Man.*

Learn It Online

Explore novels—and find tips for choosing, reading, and studying them—at:

go.hrw.com L7-577   Go

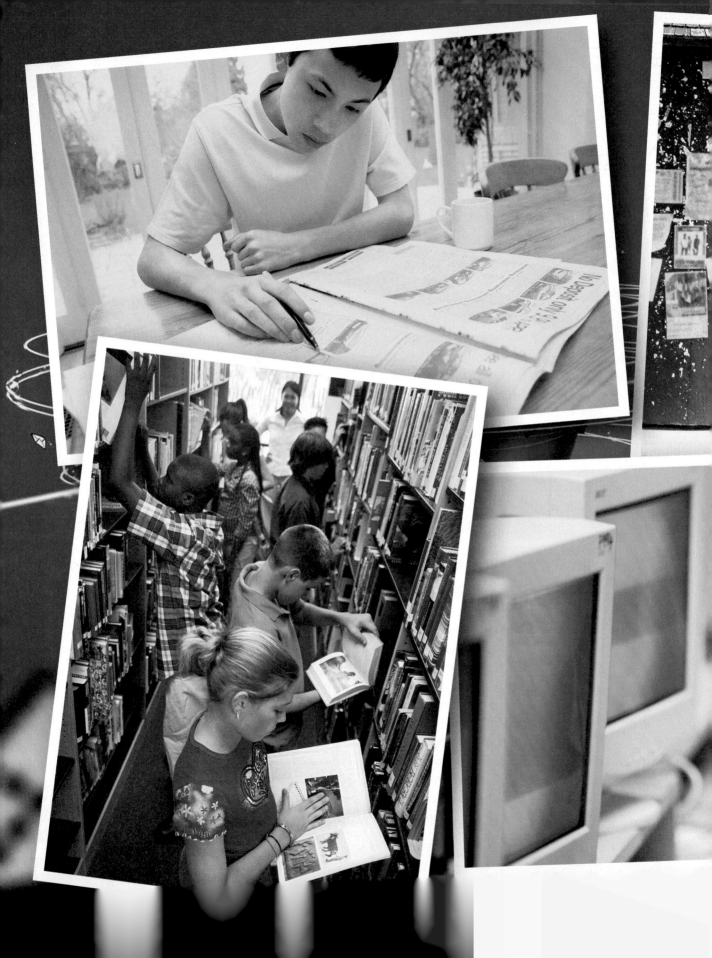

Reading for Life

INFORMATIONAL TEXT FOCUS

Consumer, Workplace, and Public Documents; Following Technical Directions; Cause and Effect

"There is an art of reading, as well as an art of thinking, and an art of writing"

—Benjamin Disraeli

What Do You Think

How can reading help you make decisions or solve problems?

Learn It Online
Let PowerNotes show you the information in this collection in a whole new way:

go.hrw.com | L7-579 | **Go**

Informational Text Focus

by **Linda Rief** and **Sheri Henderson**

Reading for Life

Your sister's studying the manual for getting a driver's license. Your dad's filling out the health-care renewal form at work. You're reading the directions aloud as your mom assembles your little brother's ride-on truck for his birthday. This is all reading for life. Analyzing this kind of writing helps you live your life and understand how and why, or why not, you should believe what you read.

The purpose of **consumer, workplace, and public documents** is to provide information. These documents are everywhere, and that is a good thing. Without them, a society as complex as ours would not be able to function well. Because these documents contain information that is important to all of us, they deserve—and require—our close attention and careful reading. The information they contain can be as simple as advertising for a new movie or as complex as warnings about your prescription medication.

Consumer Documents

On most days, you probably look to **consumer documents** for all sorts of information.

- **Advertisements** tell you what is available to buy and how much it costs, what movie just came out on DVD, and when your favorite store is having a sale.
- Service providers publish **schedules** of movie show times, school lunch menus, TV programs, and bus, train, or plane timetables.
- **Labels** on the goods you buy give you, the consumer, information about what you are buying. Labels on packaged food list the food's ingredients and nutritional value. Labels on shoes declare which parts are synthetic and which parts are not. Labels on your clothing tell you what it is made of and how to care for it.
- Mechanical and electronic equipment comes with **warranties, contracts, instructional manuals,** and **technical directions.** These guide you in the safe and proper use of products. Whenever you encounter consumer information, especially technical directions, it is a good idea to read them through slowly and carefully. A manufacturer is only required to include the information. It's up to you to read and understand it. Informed consumers know that it's better to read consumer documents *before* they use a product.

Workplace Documents

As their name suggests, **workplace documents** are those you encounter in a job. Your first communication with a possible employer may be through a **business letter,** in which you state your qualifications and request a job interview. However, a business letter isn't always necessary.

You may merely be asked to complete an **application.** When you are hired, you may be asked to sign an **employment contract,** which spells out what is expected of you as an employee and what you can expect in return from your employer. You may need to provide a Social Security number, a **work permit** showing that you are allowed to work, and a **tax form** for your employer to use when calculating taxes to deduct from your wages. You may also be given **insurance forms** to fill out and sign. To help you succeed in your new job, your employer may provide an **employee manual,** a set of rules and instructions related to the job.

When workers need to communicate with one another, they usually do so through **memorandums,** often called *memos* for short. Businesses frequently use **e-mail memos** to communicate because e-mail is fast, convenient, and easily retrieved.

The number and types of workplace documents you encounter will depend on the kind of work you do. However, one thing is certain: Whatever kind of work you do, workplace documents will play an important role in helping you succeed.

Public Documents

If you wanted to learn about sports programs at local parks, could you do it? If you wanted to know the salary of the mayor of your community, could you find out? The answer to all of these questions is yes. The answers can be found in **public documents.**

Public documents supply citizens with information that may be of interest to them. Public documents are issued by schools, churches, government agencies, the courts, libraries, and fire and police departments, to name just a few.

Typically, most citizens do not read the public documents put out by the government, the military, and nonprofit agencies or groups. Instead, they read newspaper articles that report on the documents. Whether you read a document itself or a newspaper account of its contents, public documents exist to help you form a clear picture of a situation.

The Readings Ahead . . .

The following pages will give you some practice reading various kinds of consumer, workplace, and public documents. You'll also get a chance to follow some technical directions. Challenge yourself as you read to see how well you can locate the important information in all of the documents.

Your Turn Analyze Documents

1. Keep track of all of the reading you do in a twenty-four-hour period that is neither schoolwork nor pleasure reading. Each time you read an informational text, write a list of **what** you read and **why** in your **RWN.** Put a *P* next to the public documents, a *W* next to the workplace documents, and a *C* next to the consumer documents.

2. What type of document would you use to learn how to install software on a computer?

3. What type of document explains what you should wear to a certain job?

Learn It Online
Try the *PowerNotes* version of this lesson on:

go.hrw.com   L7-581   **Go**

Analyzing Visuals

How Can You Analyze Information in Visuals?

A common form of visual information in our society is advertising. We are exposed to an average of more than thirty visual ads per day. Usually, we don't give them a thought. Ads do, however, get through to us. That's why savvy consumers know how to analyze a visual advertisement. They read the small print, interpret the intent of the ad, and determine who the target audience is. Analyzing the information in a visual message can help you generate an informed opinion about a product or issue.

Analyzing Information in Visual Ads

Answer these questions when analyzing the information in visuals.

1. Preview the text and graphics to find the subject and purpose. Does the ad want you to buy something? support a cause?

2. Skim the text to get a sense of its method of persuasion. Scan the small print to learn the company or group responsible for the ad.

3. Examine the style of the headings or the main text. Does it seize your attention, or is it subtle?

4. View and interpret the graphics. Is the ad trying to dazzle you with color? shock you with a photo? entice you with glamour?

5. Analyze the persuasive makeup of the advertisement. To what feelings or interests is it trying to appeal?

Courtesy of Keep America Beautiful, Inc. and The Ad Council.

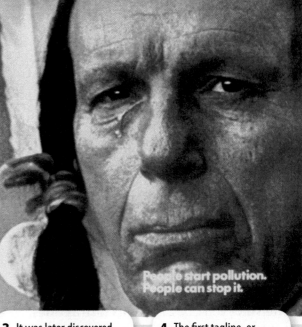

1. This 1971 ad campaign arose in response to pollution. The image of the crying American Indian soon entered the American consciousness.

2. The ad's first images featured the Indian canoeing in a garbage-laden river. Why might the ad's creators depict an American Indian?

3. It was later discovered that the actor playing the Indian was actually an Italian American. How might that knowledge influence viewers' response to the ad?

4. The first tagline, or text, for this spot was "People Start Pollution, People Can Stop It." Which tagline do you think is more persuasive?

Your Turn Talk About Visual Information

The best ads develop graphics into recognizable logos. The swoosh symbol of a sneaker brand or the arches of a fast food restaurant are meant to ignite instant craving. The crying American Indian once reached other Americans with that directness. Why might the image have been so potent?

Reading Focus

by **Kylene Beers**

What Helps You Read Documents?

When you go someplace new, you look around quickly to get a basic understanding of it (skimming and scanning); then you focus on visual cues like signs, posters, and diagrams (noting graphics). These same skills can help you read informational texts.

"Now, this policy will cover your home for fire, theft, flood and huffing and puffing."

Reprinted from *The Saturday Evening Post* ©1993.

Preview the Text

Before you read an informational document, **preview the text** for clues about its content. When you preview, you look over the text without reading every word. The organization of the text can often give you clues. Elements such as **titles, subheadings,** and **boldface terms** usually tell you the text will present a lot of information, and the writer has organized it to help you find it all. Looking at **illustrations** and **photos** can also give you an idea of what the document will be about.

A Model for Previewing the Text Preview the text below to get an idea of what it's about.

Replacing Your Cell Phone Battery
1. **Turn off** your telephone. ← This is boldface, so it must be important.
2. Depress the latch button on the rear of the battery ... ← I'll need to follow these steps in order.

Skimming and Scanning

Skimming and scanning can help you save time when reading. They can help you figure out whether a text contains the information you are looking for.

When you **skim,** you glance through a text quickly to get a general idea of what it's about. You read the title, the subheadings, and the first line or two of each paragraph.

When you **scan,** you look for information that is closely related to what you want to learn. You glance at the text quickly, looking for key words or phrases that relate to your topic.

Term	Purpose	Examples
Skimming	reading for main points	Glancing at newspaper headlines; reviewing charts and headings in your science textbook before a test
Scanning	looking for specific details	Looking for an author's name in a table of contents; looking in a geography book for the name of the highest mountain in the United States

Understand Graphic Aids

When you're looking at consumer documents to find information, you're likely to come across **graphic aids,** such as maps, graphs, tables, and illustrations. Read the titles of these graphics to see if they're likely to contain the information you're looking for.

Maps are drawings of areas of land. They can show natural features, such as mountains and rivers; political features, such as the boundaries between nations; and human-made features, such as public transportation systems.

title identifies subject or main idea

labels explain what you're looking at

BART System Map

legend, or key, explains symbols and colors

Graphs show you how things relate to each other. Two common types are line graphs and bar graphs. You might see a bar graph in your school that shows the number of cans each class has donated to the food drive.

Tables organize numbers or facts in categories, making it easier for you to make comparisons. Facts are put into horizontal rows and vertical columns. To use a table, find the column that has the information you need. Then, read down the columns until you find the information you're looking for.

Depart	Time	Arrive	Time	Bikes
WCRK	5:05a	EMBR	5:39a	Yes
WCRK	5:20a	EMBR	5:54a	Yes
WCRK	5:35a	EMBR	6:09a	Yes

Your Turn Apply Reading Skills

1. Preview the list below. Then, explain what you think the text will be about.

Talent Instructions: On Location

1. No horseplay is permitted.

2. When you arrive, sign in with Jim, and pick up a call pager.

3. Report *immediately* to makeup, hair, and wardrobe.

2. What strategy would you use if you were reading directions but weren't sure of the meanings of unfamiliar words?

3. What graphic aids might help you if you had to take a train to a place you've never been?

Now go to the Skills in Action: Reading Model

Learn It Online

Need help with informational text? Go to the interactive Reading Workshops on:

go.hrw.com   L7-585   Go

Read with a Purpose Read the following article to learn about the history of comics and comic books.

Comic Relief!

by **Emily Costello**

C omic books are part of American culture. Even if you've never read one, you probably know that Superman was born on Krypton. Or that the name of Popeye's true love is Olive Oyl. Everyone knows that, because the characters of the comics take on a life beyond the pages.

"Comics are interesting to read because you enjoy the art as much as the humor," says Thomas Inge, a professor of humanities at Randolph-Macon College in Ashland, Virginia.

Read about this unique art form and the colorful characters that helped to bring the comic pages to life!

Early Comics

The comics we see today in newspaper funny pages and in comic books evolved during the 1890s. At that time, two powerful men were fighting to create the most popular newspaper in New York City. Their names were Joseph Pulitzer and William Randolph Hearst. Everyone read the paper for news and entertainment. The television had not yet been invented. Both men knew that whoever won the newspaper war would be rich and powerful.

Comics were one of the weapons in the newspaper wars because readers loved them. Many readers were recent immigrants just learning to read English. So Hearst and Pulitzer fought for the best artists to make their comics more popular.

One artist added color to the pictures, and sales went up! The "Katzenjammer Kids" was the first comic to tell a story in a series of panels. Comic panels are a series of squares that show the action unfolding. "Happy Hooligan" began regularly using "word balloons," a space on the page where a character's spoken words are written. Readers were completely hooked.

Soon newspapers across the country were publishing comics. In 1907, "Mutt and Jeff" began appearing six days a week. It became the first successful daily comic strip. It featured the tall Mutt and his very short friend Jeff. The friends hung out all the time and got into trouble often.

In 1938, Superman made his first appearance on the cover of *Action Comics* comic book.

Reading Focus

Reading Graphic Aids The author includes **captions** with the photographs. These labels help you understand what you are looking at.

"Super" Comics

In 1934, publishers began collecting comic strips from newspapers into books. By 1935, comic books with original stories were selling well. These books included some characters that are still familiar today, such as the spinach-loving Popeye and the cool detective Dick Tracy.

The character the Phantom first appeared in 1936. He wore a purple bodysuit. His eyes were hidden behind a mask. He fought crime and performed daring stunts. But, like Popeye and Dick Tracy, the Phantom was human.

Then, in 1938, a new kind of star was born. His name was Superman—but he wasn't a man at all. He was a visitor from another planet who was faster than a speeding bullet! Old Popeye the Sailor just couldn't compete.

Superman was very popular with teenagers and young soldiers serving in World War II. His adventures took people's minds off the war. "Reading about superheroes makes us feel better because good always prevails," Inge says.

Thanks to Superman's success, writers quickly began creating their own superheroes. Some of the popular characters

Reading Focus

Skimming and Scanning The writer puts her ideas in **chronological order.** If you wanted to learn how comic books evolved in the 1930s, you could **skim and scan** the paragraph, looking for relevant dates.

Comics and Novels That Are Popular with Kids Today

- ★ Comic books from Japan called manga
- ★ Graphic novels like *GoGirl! The Time Team*
- ★ Infinite Crisis
- ★ House of M
- ★ New Avengers
- ★ Spider-Man
- ★ X-Men
- ★ Justice League of America

Reading Focus

Reading for Information This **sidebar** gives you information about a topic that is related to, but not the same as, the main idea of the article.

were Captain America, the Green Lantern, Batman, and later, Spider-Man.

New Women on the Block

Of course, there's more to the comics than brave men in silly tights. In 1940, Dale Messick created "Brenda Starr." It was the first comic strip written by a woman. Brenda Starr was a reporter who traveled around the world searching for cool stories and romance.

Just two years later, a red-haired kid named Archie began starring in his own comics. His friends—Betty and Veronica— got their own comic in 1950.

Josie and the Pussycats—a girl band seeking stardom—first appeared in 1963. Soon after, Josie and her friends moved from the comic books to Saturday morning television. They also got their own live action film in 2001.

From Page to Screen

Along with Josie, Spider-Man, the X-Men, Batman, and the Hulk also became movie stars. But Superman is perhaps the biggest movie star of them all. He has starred in six films, five live-action TV series, 18 video games, 19 cartoons, and a Broadway musical! A new Superman movie—*Superman Returns*—hit movie theaters in June 2006!

Will Americans ever get tired of comics? Inge, for one, doesn't think so. He says the world of comic books is still changing and growing. Fans would definitely agree! Comics continue to offer readers a hearty laugh and page after page of mystery and excitement.

Reading Focus

Skimming and Scanning What is the main idea of this article? What is the most important information the author is conveying?

Read with a Purpose What surprising facts did you learn about the history of comic books?

SKILLS IN ACTION
Wrap Up

SKILLS FOCUS Informational Skills Analyze structure and purpose of informational materials. Reading Skills Use reading strategies to clarify meanings.

Into Action: Reading for Information

In a chart like the one below, give examples and explain how you were able to use each text feature to help you read and understand "Comic Relief!"

Informational Text Feature	Examples and Explanations
Headings	
Graphics	
Sidebar	

Talk About . . .

1. With a partner, discuss the main points of "Comic Relief!" Challenge yourself to use each Academic Vocabulary word at least once in your discussion.

sequence	technique
function	communicate

Write About . . .

Answer the following questions about "Comic Relief!" For definitions of the underlined Academic Vocabulary words, see the column on the right.

2. What information is the writer trying to communicate in this article?

3. What function does the sidebar in the article serve?

4. What technique does the author use to organize the information?

Writing Focus

Think as a Reader/Writer

In this collection the Writing Focus activities on the Preparing to Read pages help you understand how each type of document delivers information. On the Applying Your Skills pages, you'll check your understanding of these document types.

Academic Vocabulary for Collection 6

Talking and Writing About Informational Texts

Academic Vocabulary is the language you will encounter when reading informational texts. Use these words to discuss the documents you read in this collection. The words are underlined throughout the collection.

sequence (SEE kwuhns) *n.*: specific order in which things follow one another. *Technical directions arrange the steps you must follow in sequence.*

technique (tehk NEEK) *n.*: method of doing a particular task. *The technique for performing a task is taught in an instruction manual.*

function (FUHNGK shuhn) *n.*: purpose of a specific person or thing. *Public documents inform people of the function of various government organizations.*

communicate (kuh MYOO nuh kayt) *v.*: share information or ideas. *Most informational texts are written to communicate information to readers.*

Your Turn

Copy the Academic Vocabulary words into your *Reader/Writer Notebook*. Try to use these words as you answer questions about the texts in this collection.

Public Documents

CONTENTS

 What Do **You** **Think** Where would you look for information if you were interested in a career?

 QuickTalk
Think about documents that your teacher posts in the hallways in your school. Are these public documents? Discuss why or why not.

Preparing to Read

Public Documents

Reader/Writer
Notebook
Use your **RWN** to complete the activities for these selections.

Informational Text Focus

Public Documents All **public documents** have one thing in common: They inform you of things you might need or want to know. Most people read public documents because they are looking for specific information. Let's follow one person's experience in locating information she needs by using the public documents on the following pages.

Reading Focus

Skimming and Scanning Use these <u>techniques</u> to locate information in public documents. **Skim** a document, or read it quickly, to see what it's about. Then **scan** it to find the specific information you want to learn.

Into Action Skim the documents that follow before reading them closely. Then, list one piece of information you want to learn from each text.

Title	Information to Locate
Casting Call	
Hollywood Beat	
Permission to Work	

Vocabulary

charismatic (kar ihz MAT ihk) *adj.:* possessing energy, charm, or appeal. *The producers were looking for charismatic teens to play roles in the movie.*

version (VUHR zhuhn) *n.:* a retelling from a certain point of view. *In the modern version of the movie, the hobbits oppose evil characters who ride bicycles.*

Language Coach

Jargon Words that have special meanings among a group of people are called jargon. Journalism is a profession with lots of jargon. Words such as *call* and *beat* are good examples. Unlike the *beat* you hear in music, a journalistic *beat* is a group of regularly covered news sources. What are some other examples of jargon from journalism? (Think about television and radio news and the newspaper.)

Writing Focus — Preparing for **Constructed Response**

When information is important, writers highlight it so that it stands out. As you read "Casting Call," look for ways the writer signals important information.

Learn It Online
Read more about analyzing public documents, including those found on the Web, with MediaScope at:

go.hrw.com | L7-591 | Go

Public Documents

Read with a Purpose Read these public documents to find out how a girl named Sam uses the information in them to get a part in a movie.

Casting Call

Meet Sam (Miss Samantha Sallyann Lancaster, and don't you even think about calling her anything but Sam, thank you very much). Anyone who meets Sam for five minutes knows two things about her: She's smart, and she can beat anyone, anytime, anywhere on her BMX bike. So imagine Sam's excitement when she comes across the Casting Call **announcement** in her favorite biking magazine.

✳ CASTING CALL ✳

If you've been looking for the right break to get into motion pictures, this may be your chance. StreetWheelie Productions is casting fresh talent for an upcoming action movie. **Ⓐ**

To audition, you must **Ⓑ**

* be a charismatic, awesome, off-the-wall male or female individualist
* be an expert at making your BMX-type bike do whatever you want it to do
* have your own bike
* look like you're between the ages of twelve and fifteen
* meet the requirements for a permit to work in the entertainment industry if you are under age eighteen
* be living in or near San Francisco during July and August 2009

AUDITIONS WILL BE HELD IN

Golden Gate Park, San Francisco

Saturday, May 23, 2009

10:00 A.M. to 5:00 P.M.

Bring your bike.

See you in the movies!

Ⓐ Informational Focus **Public Documents** What is the function of this announcement?

Ⓑ Reading Focus **Skimming** Skim the bulleted list. From what you know about Sam, why might she be interested in this ad?

Vocabulary **charismatic** (kar ihz MAT ihk) *adj.:* possessing energy, charm, or appeal.

Locating Information: An Article

Sam wants more information. An **Internet search** using the key words *StreetWheelie Productions* and *San Francisco* yields this **article** from *Hollywood Beat*:

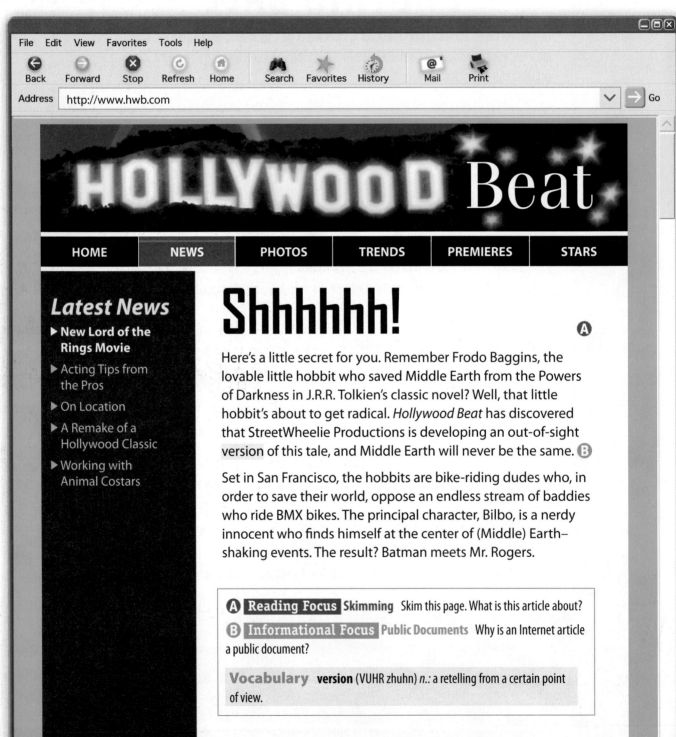

Shhhhhh! Ⓐ

Here's a little secret for you. Remember Frodo Baggins, the lovable little hobbit who saved Middle Earth from the Powers of Darkness in J.R.R. Tolkien's classic novel? Well, that little hobbit's about to get radical. *Hollywood Beat* has discovered that StreetWheelie Productions is developing an out-of-sight version of this tale, and Middle Earth will never be the same. Ⓑ

Set in San Francisco, the hobbits are bike-riding dudes who, in order to save their world, oppose an endless stream of baddies who ride BMX bikes. The principal character, Bilbo, is a nerdy innocent who finds himself at the center of (Middle) Earth–shaking events. The result? Batman meets Mr. Rogers.

Latest News
- ▶ **New Lord of the Rings Movie**
- ▶ Acting Tips from the Pros
- ▶ On Location
- ▶ A Remake of a Hollywood Classic
- ▶ Working with Animal Costars

HOME   NEWS   PHOTOS   TRENDS   PREMIERES   STARS

Ⓐ **Reading Focus** **Skimming** Skim this page. What is this article about?
Ⓑ **Informational Focus** **Public Documents** Why is an Internet article a public document?

Vocabulary **version** (VUHR zhuhn) *n.*: a retelling from a certain point of view.

Don't quote us yet, but we know *whose* shooting schedule is open!

Rumor has it LOVE will find Bilbo and a bike girl—in the movie!

Sources close to the production say that there is some big talent interested in the project. As of yet, nobody's talking, but remember . . . you'll hear all about it first on *Hollywood Beat*. ⓒ

ⓒ [Read and Discuss] What new information does Sam find?

🌐 Internet

Locating Information: An Application

Sam is only twelve years old. Can she qualify for a work permit? She doesn't want to audition if she isn't eligible to take the part. All of the information she needs is in this **application.**

STATE OF CALIFORNIA Division of Labor Standards Enforcement

THIS IS NOT A PERMIT

☐ NEW ☐ RENEWAL (A)

APPLICATION FOR PERMISSION TO WORK IN THE ENTERTAINMENT INDUSTRY

PROCEDURES FOR OBTAINING WORK PERMIT

1. Complete the information required below.

2. School authorities must complete the "School Record" section below.

3. For minors 15 days through kindergarten, please attach a certified copy of the minor's birth certificate. See reverse side for other documents that may be accepted.

4. Mail or present the completed application to any office of the Division of Labor Standards Enforcement for issuance of your work permit. Work permits will be issued within 3 business days and mailed to you.

5. Please provide a preaddressed, stamped envelope.

Name of Child			Professional Name (if applicable)			
Permanent Address Number Street		City	State	Zip Code	Home Phone Number	
School Attending						Grade
Date of Birth	Age	Height	Weight	Hair Color	Eye Color	Gender ☐ Male ☐ Female

STATEMENT OF PARENT OR GUARDIAN: It is my desire that an Entertainment Work Permit be issued to the above named child. I will read the rules governing such employment and will cooperate to the best of my ability in safeguarding his or her educational, moral, and physical interest. I hereby certify, under penalty of perjury, that the foregoing statements are true and correct.

Name of Parent or Guardian (print or type)	Signature	Daytime Phone Number

SCHOOL RECORD
State whether "SATISFACTORY" or "UNSATISFACTORY" for each

Attendance	Scholarship (Grades)	Health

I CERTIFY THAT THE ABOVE-NAMED MINOR:
☐ Meets the school district's requirements with respect to age, school record, attendance and health.
☐ Does not meet the district's requirements and permit should not be issued.

Authorized School Official	Date	
School Address	School Phone Number	[School Seal]

HEALTH RECORD
Complete this Section if instructed to do so or if infant is under One Month of Age

Name of Doctor	Address	Phone Number

I certify that I am a licensed physician and surgeon who is Board Certified in pediatrics, and have carefully examined _____.

In my opinion, (please circle) **he/she is/is not** physically fit to be employed in the production of motion pictures and television. If less than one month, infant **is/ is not** at least 15 days old, **was/was not** carried to full term, and **is/is not** physically able to perform.

Signature _____ M.D. Date _____

DLSE 277 (Rev. 012/08)

(B)

(A) **Reading Focus** Scanning Scan the document before you read. What does each major section require?

(B) **Read and Discuss** What have you learned about the work permit application?

Read with a Purpose
Sam's happy. She knows she'll qualify for a work permit, and she decides to go to the audition. Before she goes, test yourself. In reading these documents, have you been able to find all of the information Sam needs?

Applying Your Skills

Public Documents

Practicing the Standards

Informational Text and Vocabulary

1. The casting directors put the casting announcement in a biking magazine because they want kids who are especially interested in —

A reading well

B acting in movies

C following directions

D riding bikes well

2. Sam thinks she qualifies for a **work permit.** To do so, she needs all of the following *except* —

A the full support and help of her parent or guardian

B a statement of good health from a doctor

C a statement from her school that she has met the district's requirements for her grade level

D permission from her school to be absent

3. If Sam wanted to find out more about StreetWheelie Productions, her *best* choice would be to —

A search the Internet using the keywords *StreetWheelie Productions*

B look in an encyclopedia under "Film"

C read *The Hobbit* again

D post a question on her school's electronic bulletin board

4. If Sam is hired to play a part, she will be working during —

A May and June

B June and July

C July and August

D August and September

5. A *charismatic* person has —

A attractiveness

B intelligence

C politeness

D beauty

6. A *version* of a story is similar to a —

A review

B retelling

C criticism

D production

Writing Focus Constructed Response

How do you locate important information in public documents? Do you rely on graphic features or your own judgment? Respond in a paragraph.

What Do You Think Now

What kind of public documents would you study if you were looking for a job?

Workplace Documents

CONTENTS

 What Do You Think

Where would you look for information about your responsibilities in a new job?

 QuickWrite

Think about the information you might need if you got a part-time job. Where would you find the information you need?

Preparing to Read

Workplace Documents

Reader/Writer Notebook

Use your **RWN** to complete the activities for these selections.

Informational Text Focus

Analyzing Workplace Documents Whether you work in a small company with only one other person or in a huge corporation with offices all over the world, your working life will depend on many types of **workplace documents.** Businesses put important information in writing so that agreements, decisions, and requirements are clear to everyone involved. Let's look at some of the workplace documents that Sam encounters after her audition.

Vocabulary

punctuality (puhngk choo AL uh tee) *n.*: quality of being on time. *The actors' punctuality will help keep the production on schedule.*

supervision (soo puhr VIHZH uhn) *n.*: function of overseeing. *The young actors required adult supervision while on the set.*

tentative (TEHN tuh tihv) *adj.*: not fixed. *The schedule is tentative, so check it often to look for changes.*

Reading Focus

Preview the Text Before you read an informational document, **preview the text** for clues to its content. Your purpose for reading documents is usually to locate information, and previewing them can help you narrow your search. When you preview, you look over the text without reading every word. Elements such as titles, lists, and tables can give you an idea of what the document contains.

Into Action Preview the business letter on the next page to locate the following information:

- When should Sam check her e-mail?
- When does she report to wardrobe?
- What are her wages?

Language Coach

Prefixes A prefix is a word part that is added to the beginning of a word to change the word's meaning. The prefix *super–* comes from the Latin word *super,* meaning "over; above; in addition." The word *supervise* comes from that word plus the Latin verb meaning "to see." How does the English word reflect the meaning of its Latin roots? Name two others words with the prefix *super–.* Use a dictionary if necessary.

Writing Focus Preparing for **Constructed Response**

As you read the following documents, notice the ways the business letter and the e-mail memo are different in structure.

Locating Information: A Business Letter

The audition has gone very well. Everyone is as nice as he or she can be. Someone takes a photograph of Sam and writes down all of her information. Soon Sam receives the business letter shown at the right.

Workplace Documents

Read with a Purpose Read these workplace documents to locate the information Sam needs to know during filming.

StreetWheelie Productions
2323 South Robertson Boulevard, Beverly Hills, CA 90210

June 7, 2009
Miss Samantha Lancaster
1920 Ygnacio Valley Road
Walnut Creek, CA 94598

Dear Sam:

It is my pleasure to offer you a part in our production. Attached is your contract. The items in the contract spell out the issues we discussed last Saturday, as follows: **Ⓐ**

- You are responsible for your own transportation to and from filming.
- Check your e-mail first thing each morning and last thing each night.
- Report to makeup, hair, and wardrobe two hours before your first call.
- Report with your bike for all calls. You may not wash or otherwise clean the grunge off your bike.
- Because you are not yet age sixteen, a parent or guardian must be present whenever you are working. As we discussed with your mother, your grandfather will be an appropriate guardian.
- Nonprofessional actors are paid a minimum hourly wage. Your eight-hour-maximum workday will begin when you arrive each day and end when you leave each day. By law you may not work more than eight hours a day. One paid hour of rest will be part of your eight-hour workday, but the thirty-minute lunch, also paid, will *not* be part of the workday. You will always have twelve hours or more between the end of one workday and the makeup call for the next. **Ⓑ**
- You will receive a bonus at the end of your filming schedule. This bonus will be paid on your last day of work, on the condition that you have fulfilled all aspects of your contract with regard to attendance, punctuality, and appearance. This bonus will equal the total of all your previous hourly checks.

If you have any questions, call Juanita Diaz, our lawyer. Her phone number is on the contract. We look forward to having you on the project.

Sincerely,

Cassandra Rice

Cassandra Rice, Casting Director

Responsibility 1: transportation

Responsibility 2: work schedule

Responsibility 3: arrival time

Responsibility 4: appearance

Responsibility 5: equipment

Responsibility 6: parental supervision

wages

Ⓐ **Informational Focus** **Workplace Documents** Why is it important to understand the contract before signing it?

Ⓑ **Read and Discuss** What is the purpose of this letter?

Vocabulary **punctuality** (puhngk chu AL uh tee) *n.*: quality of being on time.
supervision (soo puhr VIHZH uhn) *n.*: function of overseeing.

Locating Information: Workplace Instructions

When Sam gets to the location, the crew is nice, but they all make it clear that everyone is there to work. They also expect Sam to understand that fun movies are just as hard to make as serious ones. Sam's job doesn't require an employee manual, but she does receive a list of **workplace instructions.**

TALENT INSTRUCTIONS: ON LOCATION

1. No horseplay is permitted.

2. When you arrive, sign in with Jim, and pick up a call pager.

3. Report *immediately* to makeup, hair, and wardrobe.

4. Movies require a lot of waiting. Bring something that you can do *quietly* while you wait. Music players are fine if the headphones do not interfere with makeup, hair, or costume. Electronic games are popular; their sound effects *must* be turned off. You *could* even read a book. People do. **Ⓐ**

5. When you are ready, report to the call area, and stay there. *Always* keep your call pager with you.

6. Personal cell phones, pagers, etc., may be used only in the call or food areas and only if they do not interfere with filming. Ringers must be set to "off" or "silent alert."

7. Leave all personal belongings in your assigned locker when on the shooting site.

8. You may talk in nonfilming areas, but there is *no talking* on the shooting site.

Ⓐ Informational Focus Workplace Documents Why is it important to have these rules and guidelines?

Locating Information: E-mail Memo and Directory

As time goes on, Sam understands why she is required to check her e-mail every morning and night. It's hard to remember which schedule is most recent. Luckily, Sam can always look it up in her directory of saved mail. Read one of Sam's e-mail memos at the right.

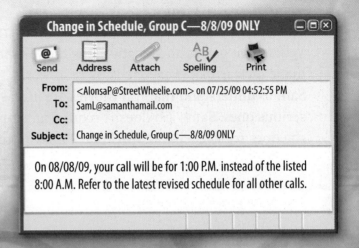

Change in Schedule, Group C—8/8/09 ONLY

Send Address Attach Spelling Print

From: <AlonsaP@StreetWheelie.com> on 07/25/09 04:52:55 PM
To: SamL@samanthamail.com
Cc:
Subject: Change in Schedule, Group C—8/8/09 ONLY

On 08/08/09, your call will be for 1:00 P.M. instead of the listed 8:00 A.M. Refer to the latest revised schedule for all other calls.

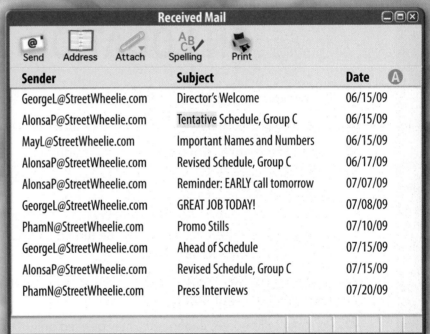

Received Mail

Send Address Attach Spelling Print

Sender	Subject	Date	Ⓐ
GeorgeL@StreetWheelie.com	Director's Welcome	06/15/09	
AlonsaP@StreetWheelie.com	Tentative Schedule, Group C	06/15/09	
MayL@StreetWheelie.com	Important Names and Numbers	06/15/09	
AlonsaP@StreetWheelie.com	Revised Schedule, Group C	06/17/09	
AlonsaP@StreetWheelie.com	Reminder: EARLY call tomorrow	07/07/09	
GeorgeL@StreetWheelie.com	GREAT JOB TODAY!	07/08/09	
PhamN@StreetWheelie.com	Promo Stills	07/10/09	
GeorgeL@StreetWheelie.com	Ahead of Schedule	07/15/09	
AlonsaP@StreetWheelie.com	Revised Schedule, Group C	07/15/09	
PhamN@StreetWheelie.com	Press Interviews	07/20/09	

Ⓑ

Ⓐ **Informational Focus** Workplace Documents What is the date of the most recent schedule?

Ⓑ **Read and Discuss** What has Sam learned about checking her e-mail?

Vocabulary **tentative** (TEHN tuh tihv) *adj.*: not fixed.

Read with a Purpose
What surprised you about the information presented in these documents?

Workplace Documents

Practicing the Standards

Informational Text and Vocabulary

1. The **business letter** discusses mainly Sam's —

A audition

B contract

C ability to act

D ability to ride a bike

2. The **business letter** points out that with the bonus, Sam will —

A be paid only if she fulfills all conditions of her contract

B not be paid if she fails to fulfill any conditions of her contract

C be paid double if she fulfills all conditions of her contract

D earn minimum wage for the project

3. Sam's **workplace instructions** make it clear that while waiting, actors are expected to be all of the following *except* —

A patient

B responsible

C self-controlled

D loud

4. Sam's July 25 **e-mail memo** tells her about a change in —

A date

B time

C part

D costume

5. Which word is the opposite of *punctuality*?

A promptness

B cleanliness

C lateness

D merriment

6. A *tentative* schedule is one that —

A may change

B is firm

C is inaccurate

D makes sense

7. *Interfere* means —

A authorize

B start filming

C create noise

D get in the way

Writing Focus   Constructed Response

List the **workplace documents** that Sam has encountered. Then, describe the purpose of each one.

What Do You Think Now

How have these documents helped Sam make decisions? Explain.

Consumer Documents

The Millbrae BART Station, San Mateo County, California.

CONTENTS

What Do
You
Think

What information would you need to get to a new job?

QuickTalk

Have you ever ridden on a bus, train, or subway system? How did you find out about routes, fares, transfers, and schedules in advance? Discuss your experience with the class.

Preparing to Read

Consumer Documents

Reader/Writer Notebook

Use your **RWN** to complete the activities for these selections.

Informational Text Focus

Consumer Documents A consumer uses what someone else sells. Consumers buy things (goods) for their own use and for use by their family and friends. Have you ever treated a friend to an ice cream cone? If so, you and your friend are consumers. Even your pets can be considered consumers—of the foods and toys you buy for them. Consumers need information about the products and services they buy, such as packaged-food ingredients, movie ratings, and airline schedules. **Consumer documents** communicate that information. Text features such as headings, boldface type, bulleted lists, color printing, and others are often used to help you locate information.

Reading Focus

Understand Graphic Aids When you're looking at consumer documents, you're likely to come across **graphic aids,** such as maps, graphs, tables, and illustrations. Read the titles of these graphics to see if they might contain the information you need.

Maps are drawings of land areas. They can show natural features, political features, or human-made features, such as transportation systems. A **key** explains the symbols used on the map.

Tables organize facts in categories put into horizontal rows and vertical columns.

Writing Focus Preparing for **Constructed Response**

Preview the following documents before you begin reading the text. Note the text features that help guide you to the information you need.

Vocabulary

accommodate (uh KAHM uh dayt) *v.:* hold comfortably. *A crowded train cannot accommodate bicycles.*

evacuation (ih vak yoo AY shuhn) *n.:* process of removing people from a potentially dangerous situation. *If an evacuation is required, leave your bike on the train.*

deducted (dih DUHKT ihd) *v.:* taken away. *The cost of the trip will be deducted from your prepaid debit card.*

Language Coach

Suffixes A word part added to the end of a word is called a **suffix.** The word *evacuation* has the suffix *–ation,* which means "the act of." Adding this suffix to *evacuate* creates a new word: *evacuation.* What word do you get when you add this suffix to the word *accommodate*? What does the new word mean?

Learn It Online
Practice your vocabulary skills with Word Watch online:

go.hrw.com   L7-605   **Go**

Consumer Documents

Read with a Purpose Read these **consumer documents** to learn how Sam locates the information she needs to get to work.

Locating Information: Transit Map

Sam has to travel from Walnut Creek to the movie set location and back with her bike, and her grandfather has to go with her. The two decide to take the Bay Area Rapid Transit System, better known as BART. BART is a network of trains that can take you just about anywhere in the San Francisco Bay Area. First, Sam and her grandfather log on to the Internet to look at the **BART system map.** They want to be sure they can get from their home in Walnut Creek to the Embarcadero Station, where the StreetWheelie production van will be waiting. They find the map that is shown on the next page.

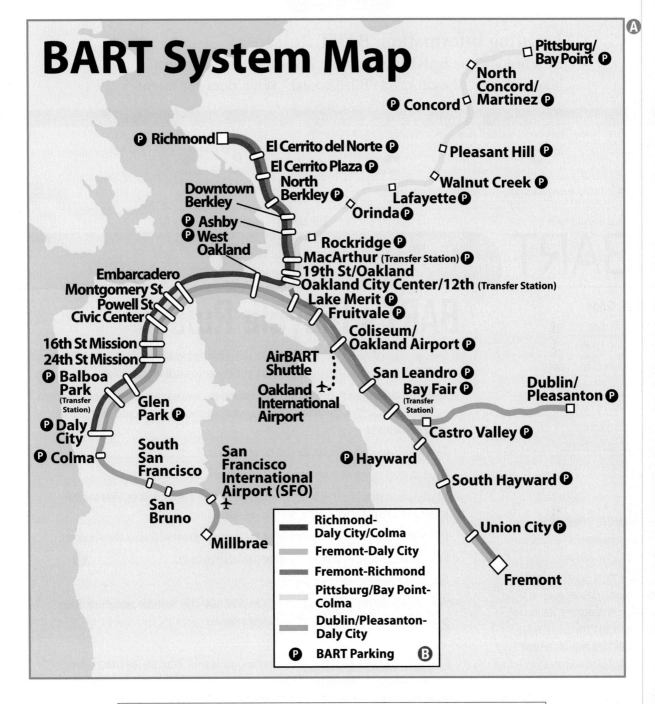

BART System Map

Richmond ☐ Ⓟ

El Cerrito del Norte Ⓟ
El Cerrito Plaza Ⓟ
North Berkley Ⓟ
Downtown Berkley
Orinda Ⓟ
Ⓟ **Ashby**
Ⓟ **West Oakland**

Concord Ⓟ
North Concord/ Martinez Ⓟ
Pittsburg/ Bay Point Ⓟ
Pleasant Hill Ⓟ
Walnut Creek Ⓟ
Lafayette Ⓟ

Rockridge Ⓟ
MacArthur (Transfer Station) Ⓟ
19th St/Oakland
Oakland City Center/12th (Transfer Station)
Lake Merit Ⓟ
Fruitvale Ⓟ

Embarcadero
Montgomery St.
Powell St.
Civic Center

16th St Mission
24th St Mission
Ⓟ **Balboa Park** (Transfer Station)
Glen Park Ⓟ
Ⓟ **Daly City**
Ⓟ **Colma**

Coliseum/ Oakland Airport Ⓟ

AirBART Shuttle
Oakland International Airport ✈

San Leandro Ⓟ
Bay Fair Ⓟ (Transfer Station)
Castro Valley Ⓟ
Dublin/ Pleasanton Ⓟ

South San Francisco
San Bruno
Millbrae ◇
San Francisco International Airport (SFO) ✈

Ⓟ **Hayward**
South Hayward Ⓟ
Union City Ⓟ
Fremont ◇

Legend:
Richmond– Daly City/Colma
Fremont–Daly City
Fremont–Richmond
Pittsburg/Bay Point– Colma
Dublin/Pleasanton– Daly City
Ⓟ **BART Parking** Ⓑ

Ⓐ

Ⓐ **Informational Focus** Consumer Documents Which BART lines stop at Walnut Creek? at Embarcadero? Which line should Sam take?

Ⓑ **Reading Focus** Graphic Aids How does printing each train line in a different color help consumers?

🌐 Internet

Locating Information: BART Rules

Sam needs more BART information: Is she allowed to bring a bike with her? She clicks on "Bike Access." What does she learn?

File   Edit   View   Favorites   Tools   Help

Back   Forward   Stop   Refresh   Home   Search   Favorites   History   Mail   Print

Address   http://www.bart.gov/guide/bikes/bikeRules.asp   Go

San Francisco Bay Area Rapid Transit District

BART

Site Map | Contact Us | Search BART   GO

Stations & Schedules | Tickets | **Rider Guide** | News | About BART | Home

Rider Guide
- Overview
- Destinations
- Airport Connections
- Transit Connections
- Parking Programs
- **Bike Access**
- Disabled Access
- Lost and Found

COMMUTE HOURS *(Weekdays approximately 7:05 to 8:50 am and 4:25 to 6:45 pm)*

- During morning commute hours, bikes are allowed in the Embarcadero Station only for trips to the East Bay (as indicated by the Fares and Schedules brochure).

- During evening commute hours, bicyclists traveling from the East Bay must exit at the Embarcadero Station (as indicated by the Fares and Schedules brochure).

BART's Bicycle Rules

- Bikes are allowed on all trains except those trains shown in highlighted areas of the BART Fares and Schedules brochure. It is the rider's responsibility to refer to BART schedules.   **A**

- Regardless of any other rule, bikes are never allowed on crowded cars. Use your good judgment and only board cars that can comfortably **accommodate** you and your bicycle. Hold your bike while on the trains.

- Bikes are allowed in any car but the first car of a train.

- Bicyclists must use elevator or stairs, not escalators, and always walk bikes.

- Bicyclists must yield priority seating to seniors and people with disabilities, yield to other passengers, and not block aisles or doors or soil seats.

- In case of an **evacuation**, leave your bike on the train and do not let it block aisles or doors.

- Bicyclists under 14 years old must be accompanied by an adult.   **B**

- Gas-powered vehicles are never permitted.

- Bikes must be parked in racks and lockers. Call (510) 464-7133 for locker availability. Bikes parked against poles, fences, or railings will be removed.

A **Informational Focus** **Consumer Documents** What are the Embarcadero restrictions? What do they mean for Sam?

B **Read and Discuss** Why is this document so important to Sam?

Vocabulary   **accommodate** (uh KAHM uh dayt) *v.:* hold comfortably.
evacuation (ih vak yoo AY shuhn) *n.:* process of removing people from a potentially dangerous situation.

Locating Information: BART Ticket Guide

Sam wants to know how much it will cost. Grandpa is over sixty-five, and Sam is twelve. Can they get any discount fares?

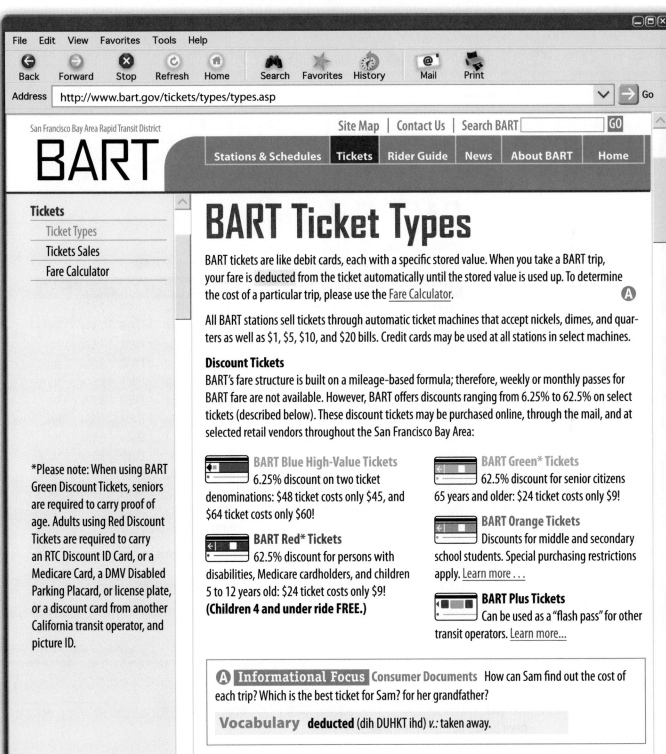

Address http://www.bart.gov/tickets/types/types.asp

San Francisco Bay Area Rapid Transit District

BART

Site Map | Contact Us | Search BART [   ] GO

Stations & Schedules | Tickets | Rider Guide | News | About BART | Home

Tickets
Ticket Types
Tickets Sales
Fare Calculator

BART Ticket Types

BART tickets are like debit cards, each with a specific stored value. When you take a BART trip, your fare is deducted from the ticket automatically until the stored value is used up. To determine the cost of a particular trip, please use the Fare Calculator. **Ⓐ**

All BART stations sell tickets through automatic ticket machines that accept nickels, dimes, and quarters as well as $1, $5, $10, and $20 bills. Credit cards may be used at all stations in select machines.

Discount Tickets
BART's fare structure is built on a mileage-based formula; therefore, weekly or monthly passes for BART fare are not available. However, BART offers discounts ranging from 6.25% to 62.5% on select tickets (described below). These discount tickets may be purchased online, through the mail, and at selected retail vendors throughout the San Francisco Bay Area:

BART Blue High-Value Tickets
6.25% discount on two ticket denominations: $48 ticket costs only $45, and $64 ticket costs only $60!

BART Red* Tickets
62.5% discount for persons with disabilities, Medicare cardholders, and children 5 to 12 years old: $24 ticket costs only $9!
(Children 4 and under ride FREE.)

BART Green* Tickets
62.5% discount for senior citizens 65 years and older: $24 ticket costs only $9!

BART Orange Tickets
Discounts for middle and secondary school students. Special purchasing restrictions apply. Learn more . . .

BART Plus Tickets
Can be used as a "flash pass" for other transit operators. Learn more...

*Please note: When using BART Green Discount Tickets, seniors are required to carry proof of age. Adults using Red Discount Tickets are required to carry an RTC Discount ID Card, or a Medicare Card, a DMV Disabled Parking Placard, or license plate, or a discount card from another California transit operator, and picture ID.

Ⓐ Informational Focus Consumer Documents How can Sam find out the cost of each trip? Which is the best ticket for Sam? for her grandfather?

Vocabulary deducted (dih DUHKT ihd) *v.:* taken away.

Locating Information: BART Schedule

Sam goes to the Stations and Schedules page and enters the stations they'll be leaving from and going to. Here's what she finds.

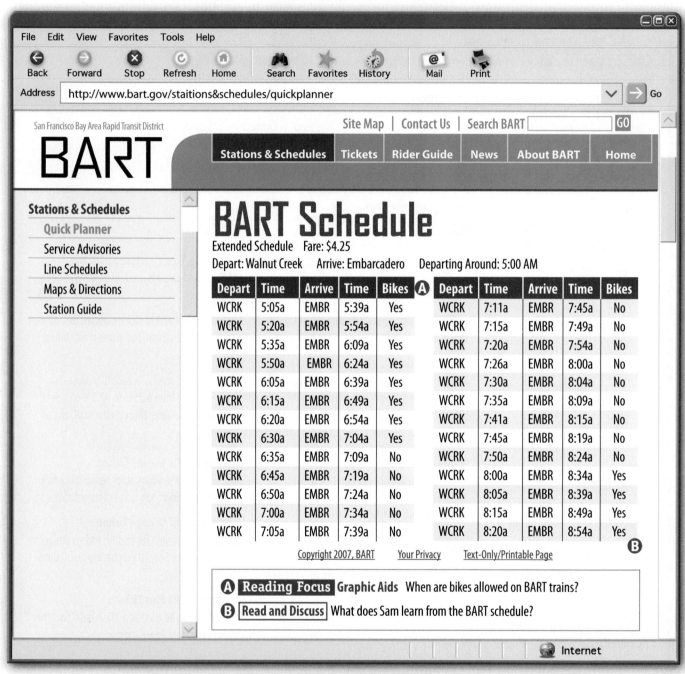

File   Edit   View   Favorites   Tools   Help

Back   Forward   Stop   Refresh   Home   Search   Favorites   History   Mail   Print

Address   http://www.bart.gov/staitions&schedules/quickplanner   Go

San Francisco Bay Area Rapid Transit District

BART

Site Map | Contact Us | Search BART [   ] GO

Stations & Schedules   Tickets   Rider Guide   News   About BART   Home

Stations & Schedules
- Quick Planner
- Service Advisories
- Line Schedules
- Maps & Directions
- Station Guide

BART Schedule

Extended Schedule   Fare: $4.25

Depart: Walnut Creek   Arrive: Embarcadero   Departing Around: 5:00 AM

Depart	Time	Arrive	Time	Bikes	Depart	Time	Arrive	Time	Bikes
WCRK	5:05a	EMBR	5:39a	Yes	WCRK	7:11a	EMBR	7:45a	No
WCRK	5:20a	EMBR	5:54a	Yes	WCRK	7:15a	EMBR	7:49a	No
WCRK	5:35a	EMBR	6:09a	Yes	WCRK	7:20a	EMBR	7:54a	No
WCRK	5:50a	EMBR	6:24a	Yes	WCRK	7:26a	EMBR	8:00a	No
WCRK	6:05a	EMBR	6:39a	Yes	WCRK	7:30a	EMBR	8:04a	No
WCRK	6:15a	EMBR	6:49a	Yes	WCRK	7:35a	EMBR	8:09a	No
WCRK	6:20a	EMBR	6:54a	Yes	WCRK	7:41a	EMBR	8:15a	No
WCRK	6:30a	EMBR	7:04a	Yes	WCRK	7:45a	EMBR	8:19a	No
WCRK	6:35a	EMBR	7:09a	No	WCRK	7:50a	EMBR	8:24a	No
WCRK	6:45a	EMBR	7:19a	No	WCRK	8:00a	EMBR	8:34a	Yes
WCRK	6:50a	EMBR	7:24a	No	WCRK	8:05a	EMBR	8:39a	Yes
WCRK	7:00a	EMBR	7:34a	No	WCRK	8:15a	EMBR	8:49a	Yes
WCRK	7:05a	EMBR	7:39a	No	WCRK	8:20a	EMBR	8:54a	Yes

Copyright 2007, BART   Your Privacy   Text-Only/Printable Page

Ⓐ **Reading Focus** **Graphic Aids** When are bikes allowed on BART trains?

Ⓑ **Read and Discuss** What does Sam learn from the BART schedule?

Internet

Read with a Purpose What other information might Sam need before going to the movie set?

Applying Your Skills

Consumer Documents

Practicing the Standards

Informational Text and Vocabulary

1. Which type of **consumer document** would you consult to learn what BART line to take to get from one place to another?

   A System Map

   B Bicycle Rules

   C Ticket Guide

   D Train Schedule

2. According to the **bicycle rules,** in which cars of the train can you ride with a bike?

   A Any car at all

   B Any car but the first

   C Any car but the last

   D Only the first three cars

3. According to the **ticket guide,** Sam (age 12) and Sam's grandfather (age 75) should buy —

   A one blue and one red ticket

   B one red and one green ticket

   C one orange and one blue ticket

   D two orange tickets

4. On the BART Stations and Schedules Web page, you can learn all of the following *except* —

   A the base cost of the trip

   B the schedule of departures and arrivals

   C when bicycles are allowed

   D the discounts available

5. *Accommodate* means —

   A dislike

   B transport

   C fit

   D ride

6. An *evacuation* would most likely be required —

   A after purchasing a ticket

   B before arriving at the Embarcadero station

   C on the Fremont-Richmond line

   D during an emergency

7. Something *deducted* has been —

   A subtracted

   B monitored

   C recorded

   D added

Writing Focus — Constructed Response

Sam got all of her information about the BART system from the Internet. Explain how she might have gotten this same information if she did not have access to a computer.

 What Do You Think Now Which BART document provides the most helpful information? Explain.

Technical Directions

CONTENTS

What Do
You
Think

Where can you
find instructions
on completing a
mechanical task?

 QuickTalk
What makes directions easy or hard to
follow?

MANUAL
Preparing to Read

Technical Directions

Reader/Writer Notebook

Use your **RWN** to complete the activities for this selection.

Informational Text Focus

Analyzing Technical Directions **Technical directions** are step-by-step instructions that explain how to accomplish mechanical tasks. You follow technical directions when you assemble the video game system you bought, when you assemble a bookcase that came in sections, or when you clean the sprockets on your bicycle.

You're probably too young to drive a car, but you're certainly not too young to be thinking about it. Driving can give you a new feeling of independence, but it also gives you new responsibilities. Any number of things can go wrong with your car, and it's up to you to fix them—or to get them fixed. A flat tire is something every driver will face someday—possibly on a lonely country road, without a person in sight. To be prepared for that, study the directions on the next page.

Reading Focus

Previewing the Text You may come across technical directions that seem overwhelming because they contain so much information. **Previewing the text** by looking at headings, lists, and tables without reading every word can help you find the specific information you need—the <u>function</u> of a button on your cell phone or the proper <u>technique</u> for removing lug nuts.

Writing Focus

Preparing for **Constructed Response**

As you read the following documents, notice the way the technical directions are organized in <u>sequence</u>. This organization helps ensure that you perform the tasks in order, step by step.

Vocabulary

procedures (pruh SEE juhrz) *n.:* methods of doing things. *The proper procedures for changing a flat tire are given in the directions that follow.*

standard (STAN duhrd) *adj.:* usual; regularly used or produced. *If you have a standard transmission, put your car in gear.*

Language Coach

Multiple Meanings If you see the word *fall* all by itself, you can't tell if it refers to the season, the action of losing one's balance, or the action of being captured in a battle. In a sentence, you can usually tell which definition of the word is meant. Which word above has multiple meanings?

Learn It Online

For examples of analyzing technical directions, use the interactive Reading Workshop on:

go.hrw.com   L7-613   **Go**

How to Change a Flat Tire

Read with a Purpose
Read these instructions to learn how to change a flat tire.

Before you can change a flat tire on your car, you first have to realize that the tire is flat. You might come out of your house in the morning and see the wheel rim resting on the road with the tire spread around it. You'll know right away that the tire's flat. How can you tell, though, if it goes flat while you are driving? A first clue is that your car starts to pull to the right or the left even though you aren't turning the steering wheel. Another clue is that passing motorists honk and point as they drive by. Yet another clue is that the car starts bouncing up and down and making a loud *thumpity-thump-thump* sound.

When you suspect you have a flat tire, follow these procedures:

STEP 1

Park the car as far off the road as possible. Put the car in park (if you have an automatic transmission) or in gear (if you have a standard transmission), turn off the engine, and put on the emergency brake. Turn on your car's flashing lights. Now, get out and look at your tires. If you have a flat, put out emergency triangles or, at night, flares. (It's a good idea to carry warning triangles and flares in your trunk at all times in case of an emergency.) **A**

A **Informational Focus** Technical Directions Why can't you leave out the step of putting the brake on?

Vocabulary **procedures** (pruh SEE juhrz) *n*.: methods of doing things.
standard (STAN duhrd) *adj*.: usual; regularly used or produced.

STEP 2

Remove the spare tire from the trunk. Also take out the jack, the lug wrench, and related tools.

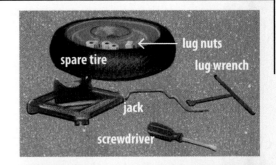

spare tire
lug nuts
lug wrench
jack
screwdriver

STEP 3

Remove the wheel cover from the flat tire, using a screwdriver or the end of the jack handle.

STEP 4

Loosen the lug nuts with the lug wrench, but do not remove them. Most lug nuts turn counterclockwise.

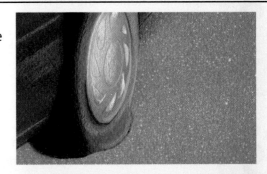

STEP 5

Position your jack. Different makes of cars come with different types of jacks, so check your owner's manual to learn how to use your jack. Make sure the jack is sitting on a solid, flat surface.

STEP 6

Lift the car with the jack until your flat tire is two or three inches off the ground. *(Never lie under the car when it is on the jack!)*

B ⎯ **Read and Discuss** What do the steps illustrating the way to change a tire show you about the process?

STEP 7 Now, finish unscrewing the lug nuts. Put them inside the wheel cover so you don't lose them. **C**

STEP 8 Remove the flat tire, and replace it with the spare tire. Replace the lug nuts, and tighten them by hand.

STEP 9 Lower the jack until the spare tire is firmly on the ground. Remove the jack. Firmly tighten the lug nuts with the lug wrench. Work diagonally—tighten one on the top, then one on the bottom; one on the left, then one on the right; and so on.

STEP 10 Place the flat tire, the wheel cover, and all your tools in the trunk. As soon as you can, drive to a garage or a tire repair shop to get the tire fixed or replaced. You never want to be without a spare, because you never know when you'll get another flat!

C **Informational Focus** Technical Directions Why do you think you should loosen the lug nuts, then jack up the car, then take off the lug nuts, instead of jacking up the car first and removing the lug nuts in one step?

Read with a Purpose
What part of the instructions was most effective in teaching you how to change a flat tire?

Applying Your Skills

Technical Directions

Practicing the Standards

Informational Text and Vocabulary

1. When you think you have a flat tire, what should you do first?

   A Drive the car to your family's garage.

   B Call your parents and ask them to pick you up.

   C Park the car as far off the road as possible.

   D Look out the window to see if the tire is flat.

2. The best tool for loosening the lug nuts is —

   A a screwdriver

   B a lug wrench

   C a jack

   D your hand

3. You should lift the car with the jack until —

   A you can fit comfortably underneath the car

   B the car is two to three feet in the air

   C the flat tire is two to three inches off the ground

   D the flat tire comes off the wheel

4. When you remove the lug nuts, you should —

   A let them fall to the ground

   B put them in the wheel cover

   C throw them away

   D set them under the car

5. After you have changed a flat tire, what should you do next?

   A Call your parents to let them know what happened.

   B Drive to a garage to get the flat tire fixed.

   C Continue traveling to where you were going before you got the flat.

   D Throw away the flat tire.

6. *Procedures* are all of the following *except* —

   A processes

   B steps

   C plans

   D dangers

7. Which word is most closely related to *standard*?

   A normal

   B jack

   C flat

   D gear

Writing Focus   Constructed Response

Write a list of instructions for operating a familiar technical device, such as a DVD player, microwave oven, or MP3 player. Make sure to include all of the necessary steps.

 What Do You Think Now? After reading the instructions, could you change a flat tire? Explain.

Text Structures: Cause and Effect

Rescue workers hold oil-covered cormorant that was caught in the massive spill (1989) from the grounded oil tanker *Exxon Valdez* in Prince William Sound, Valdez, Alaska.

CONTENTS

What Do You Think Concerns about the environment are widespread. What can you do to protect it?

QuickWrite
What efforts at conservation have you observed in your home, at school, or in your community?

Preparing to Read

Tilting at Windmills: The Search for Alternative Energy Sources / Saving the Earth: Teens Fish for Answers

Reading Focus

Cause and Effect You know from experience that one thing leads to another. If you sleep through your alarm, you know you'll be late for school. Sleeping through your alarm is a **cause**—it makes something happen. An **effect** is what happens as a result of some event—you're late for school.

When you read a text and ask yourself, "Why did this happen?" and "What happened because of this?" you are asking about causes and effects.

Into Action Read "Tilting at Windmills," keeping track of the cause-and-effect chain by filling out a chart like the one below. Start each cause statement with the word *because*.

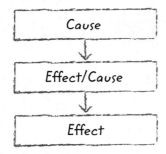

TechFocus As you read, think about how you would visually represent environmental issues.

Writing Focus — Preparing for **Constructed Response**

Writers of cause-and-effect articles often use transitions to show how one idea is connected to another. Some transition terms that help the reader follow the cause-and-effect pattern are *after, as a result, because, consequently, so, then, therefore,* and *since*. As you read the articles that follow, make a list of all the transitions you find.

Reader/Writer Notebook

Use your **RWN** to complete the activities for these selections.

Vocabulary

Tilting at Windmills

shortages (SHAWR tihj ihz) *n.:* situations in which needed items cannot be gotten in sufficient amounts. *There were shortages of oil in the 1970s.*

Saving the Earth

habitat (HAB uh tat) *n.* used as *adj.:* place where an animal or plant naturally lives. *Habitat destruction caused a decrease in the brook trout population.*

hazards (HAZ uhrdz) *n.:* dangers. *Environmental hazards threatened the watershed.*

Language Coach

Percentages We use percentages to simplify the discussion of numbers. The word *percent* is made from the Latin words *per* and *centum* and means "parts out of one hundred." In these articles, statistics, or information in number form, that use percentages are given. When the first article states "Wind supplies 20 percent of Denmark's power," it is saying that out of every 100 units of electricity produced, 20 are produced by wind power. In what other contexts are percentages used?

Learn It Online

Enhance your vocabulary with Word Watch:

go.hrw.com	L7-619	**Go**

Seventeenth-century sailing ship sails past twenty-first-century offshore wind farm.

TILTING AT WINDMILLS:
THE SEARCH FOR ALTERNATIVE ENERGY SOURCES

BY  THE WORLD ALMANAC

Read with a Purpose Read this selection to learn about using wind power to generate electricity.

When you turn on a light, a television, or a computer, you probably don't give much thought to how the electricity powering those devices got there. But fuel was used to create that electrical charge. And chances are, it was a fossil fuel, gotten from decaying plants and animals.

Over millions of years, dead plants and animals get buried and then turn into substances like coal, oil, and natural gas. These products are found in underground deposits that are mined by energy companies. Fossil fuels are natural, in a sense, but using them can create some nasty by-products. Coal and the like are burned to release their energy, and the burning fuel releases harmful substances called emissions into the atmosphere. **Ⓐ**

In addition to the problem of causing pollution, fossil fuels are also running out. There is a limited supply of fossil fuel in the ground, and because it takes millions of

Ⓐ Reading Focus Cause and Effect What is the effect of burning fossil fuels?

years to form, it is considered a nonrenewable energy source. So power companies are increasingly turning to an alternative source of energy: the wind. "Strong growth figures in the U.S. prove that wind is now a mainstream option for new power generation," said Randy Swisher. He is president of the American Wind Energy Association.

AS OLD AS THE WIND

Wind is the fastest-growing source of renewable energy, according to the United States Department of Energy. A renewable power source, such as wind or solar power, does not depend on a limited fuel supply. Wind is freely available and is used to generate power in more than thirty states. It keeps more than two million households running.

People first used wind to generate power around five thousand years ago. They used it to propel sailboats up and down the Nile River. Sometime between A.D. 500 and A.D. 900, the Persians realized that wind could be used to turn a wheel. They attached several sails to a central axle, and the windmill was born.

Early windmills were used to pump water and grind grain, and many are still used for these tasks today. In the Netherlands, flooding is common, and farmers often need to move large amounts of water. Windmills are a workable solution. Because they are part of everyday life in the Netherlands, people have tried to make these hardworking machines attractive. The country has become famous for its beautiful windmills, which dot the landscape. **Ⓑ**

RUNNING WITH THE WIND

The most widespread use of modern windmills is for creating electricity. Generating electricity requires a turbine, which is a kind of engine. Steam, water, air, or some other force turns a wheel or a set of wheels, which turns a shaft. This shaft usually turns a generator, which produces electricity.

Beginning in the 1920s, wind was used in a limited way to generate electricity in rural areas of the United States. Then came the energy crisis of the 1970s. Around the world, there were shortages of oil. The cost of fossil fuels soared. Because of these difficulties, interest in generating power from wind on a large scale grew.

Giant "wind farms" were built in remote areas, where wind sweeps across the landscape. Other wind farms were built offshore, to capture sea breezes.

"As security of energy supply and climate change are ranging high on the political agendas of the world's governments, wind energy has already become a mainstream energy source in many countries around the world," said Arthouros Zervos. He is the chairman of the Global Wind Energy Council. "Wind energy is clean and fuel-free, which makes it the most attractive solution to the world's energy challenges."

Ⓑ **Read and Discuss** What do you learn about windmills?

Vocabulary **shortages** (SHAWR tihj ihz) *n.:* situations in which needed items cannot be gotten in sufficient amounts.

Two gigantic wind farms are located off the coast of Denmark. Wind supplies 20 percent of Denmark's power. The United States ranks third, behind Germany and Spain, in the amount of power it generates from the wind. **C**

FACING THE WIND

Wind farms are quite a sight. A typical power-generating windmill is enormous. It is around twenty stories tall, and the diameter of its blades is about 200 feet across. The taller the windmill and the longer its blades, the more wind it can capture.

But giant wind farms are not always welcome. Some groups complain that wind farms spoil the landscape—or seascape. The construction of a wind farm planned for an area near Cape Cod, Massachusetts, has been delayed because many people say it will ruin their view of the Atlantic Ocean. Large windmills can also be harmful to birds and other wildlife. And because wind is not constant, other power sources must be used when the wind is not blowing.

Government programs, however, especially in the United States and Europe, are encouraging the use of wind power as an alternative to fossil fuels. This ancient technology can help us meet our energy needs without using up our natural resources and polluting the atmosphere. **D**

Read with a Purpose What are the benefits of using wind power to generate energy?

Analyzing Visuals Viewing and Interpreting
What is causing the windmills to appear as they do in this photo?

C Read and Discuss What is your response to this statement?

D Read and Discuss What is the author prompting you to think about?

Applying Your Skills

SKILLS FOCUS **Reading Skills** Analyze cause-and-effect structure. **Vocabulary Skills** Identify synonyms; identify antonyms.

Tilting at Windmills

Practicing the Standards

Informational Text and Vocabulary

1. This article suggests that all of the following might have caused the rise of wind power *except* —
   A the need to generate electricity in remote places
   B the desire to generate energy without causing pollution
   C the attempt to conserve our supply of fossil fuels
   D the desire to create beautiful windmills

2. What caused many people to become interested in using wind power as a resource?
   A Energy crisis of the 1970s
   B Beauty of the Dutch windmills
   C View of the ocean from Cape Cod
   D Desire to fill unused land

3. Why can't people rely on wind power alone to satisfy their energy needs?
   A Wind is a renewable resource.
   B Large windmills are dangers to birds.
   C Wind does not always blow.
   D Wind farms exist around the country.

4. Which of the following sentences contains a cause and an effect?
   A Burning coal or oil releases its energy.
   B Solar power does not depend on a limited fuel supply.
   C The Persians attached sails to a central axle.
   D Fossil fuels take millions of years to form.

5. According to the article, which of the following is a major effect of burning fossil fuels?
   A Creation of a secure energy supply
   B Capture of the energy in sea breezes
   C Provision of power to two million households
   D Release of harmful substances into the air

6. Another word for *renewable* is —
   A clean
   B replaceable
   C sufficient
   D decaying

7. An antonym for *shortages* is —
   A excesses
   B supplies
   C growths
   D insufficiencies

Writing Focus   Constructed Response

Briefly explain the effects of using wind power instead of fossil fuels as an energy resource. Cite evidence from the article in your response.

What Do **You** **Think** **Now**   Would the use of wind power help your community? Explain.

SAVING THE EARTH:
Teens Fish for Answers

Read with a Purpose
Read this article to discover how some teens help protect the environment.

Karoline Evin McMullen was in seventh grade when she and a friend started wondering how pollution was affecting their area. They had witnessed a building boom in their native Ohio, in which chain stores and restaurants replaced farmland. They also noticed a decrease in the population of the Ohio brook trout, which lives in the area's Chagrin River.

"I was inspired to start my conservation work by the habitat destruction going on in my area," says McMullen, now 16. The girls tested the water in local streams and compared their findings with older data. It was clear that water quality was suffering. **Ⓐ**

The girls started the group Save Our Stream, which educates people about environmental hazards and repairs the trout's habitat. They received thousands of dollars in grants and designed outdoor educational trails. They wrote a book about brook trout and created a pamphlet and a Web site. And they gave presentations to thousands of students and teachers and reached millions more through an educational TV network.

McMullen says the results of their efforts are measurable. "Eighty percent of people I polled didn't know there was a native brook trout, let alone that it belonged in their own backyard," she says about the group's start. But in polls of people given training, "100 percent were doing things they had been told to do." **Ⓑ**

WATER WAYS

Save Our Stream publicizes the need for natural buffers against water runoff. The group encourages people to plant trees and allow grass to grow high along stream banks. That "helps filter off pollution" before the water enters the stream, says McMullen.

The group encourages washing cars on lawns instead of on concrete, so soap and dirt do not go directly into storm drains. They

Ⓐ Reading Focus Cause and Effect What caused McMullen to start her conservation work?

Ⓑ Reading Focus Cause and Effect What effect did Save Our Stream have on the people living in McMullen's town?

Vocabulary habitat (HAB uh tat) *n.* used as *adj.*: place where an animal or plant naturally lives.
hazards (HAZ uhrdz) *n.*: dangers.

advertise the importance of picking up pet waste and flushing or throwing it away, so the waste does not go straight into streams.

The teens were awarded the Gloria Barron Prize for Young Heroes in 2006. But McMullen says her greatest rewards were built into her work. "It has had a sort of profound effect on the way I see myself and what I want to do with my future," she says. "Through this program, I've been enlightened about conservation. I want to pursue higher education and help governments find a solution for people and the world they live in."

HEED THE CALL

The environment is a big issue, and teens have heard the call. They're getting their hands dirty in outdoor conservation projects and organizing community forces. In Mount Rainier National Park in Washington State, students restore trails and campgrounds. Farther north, the group Alaska Youth for Environmental Action spreads the word about global warming.

You can start working to help the environment now: Join an ecology club, and if there isn't one, start your own. Make sure your school recycles paper. Turn off lights. Plant trees. Volunteer in your local park system. Plant native species. Most of all, know that you can make a difference. **C**

Read with a Purpose How does Save Our Stream work to protect the environment?

C | Read and Discuss | What is the author's purpose here?

Students from the group Save Our Stream clean Geauga Park District in Chardon, Ohio.

Applying Your Skills

Saving the Earth

Practicing the Standards

Informational Text and Vocabulary

1. This article suggests that all of the following might have caused the decline in the trout population *except* the —

A destruction of farmland

B washing of cars on cement

C pollution caused by pet waste

D tall grasses planted near streams

2. What caused McMullen to become interested in her local environment?

A Creating her Web site for a science project

B Seeing pollution in a local stream

C Designing educational outdoor trails

D Noticing a decrease in native trout

3. According to the article, which of the following is a major effect of the Save Our Stream organization?

A Native trout are plentiful again.

B People who received training have changed their habits.

C Students have restored trails and campgrounds in Washington.

D The media has spread the word about global warming.

4. Which of the following sentences contains a cause and an effect?

A Soapy, dirty water can enter storm drains.

B Trees and grass help filter pollutants.

C The environment is a hot topic.

D Conserve water when showering and washing your hands.

5. Another word for *habitat* is —

A waterway

B surroundings

C farmland

D population

6. Which of the following means the same as *hazards*?

A Polls

B Pollution

C Pet waste

D Threats

7. A *profound* truth is —

A meaningful

B renewable

C common

D differing

Writing Focus — Constructed Response

The last two paragraphs of the article contain several possible actions to take. First, list each action and the immediate effect that following each action would have. Then, explain the ultimate effect of following each action.

What Do You Think Now? What organizations like Save Our Stream are in your area?

Wrap Up

Tilting at Windmills / Saving the Earth

Writing Focus

Think as a Reader/Writer

Use It in Your Writing Look back at the list of transition words you noted in these articles. Then, write a cause-and-effect paragraph about getting dressed in the morning using the transition words.

Analyzing Cause and Effect Write an essay in which you discuss how people in your neighborhood are attempting to protect the environment by encouraging recycling or other measures and by forming organizations to tackle local problems. Be sure to use transition words to signal the cause-and-effect pattern.

What Do You Think Now?

How did these articles change the way you feel about the environment?

CHOICES

As you respond to the Choices, use **Academic Vocabulary** words as appropriate: <u>sequence</u>, <u>technique</u>, <u>function</u>, <u>communicate</u>.

REVIEW
Make a Cause-and-Effect Chain

Finding clean, renewable energy sources and protecting waterways are only two of many crucial environmental issues. Go to a library or use the Internet to research recycling and its effects. Then, make a cause-and-effect chain that analyzes the effects of recycling.

CONNECT
Create a Fact Sheet

Create a fact sheet about the windmills of the Netherlands. Provide readers with information on the types of windmills and their uses common in that country. Some specific questions you might want to answer while conducting your research are "How many kinds of windmills exist in the Netherlands?" "What makes the types different from one another?" "Where in the country are they located?"

EXTEND
Create a Multimedia Presentation

TechFocus Use Internet or library resources to research another current environmental issue. Find a group that is promoting awareness of this issue. Answer these questions as you conduct your research: "What is the problem?" "What is the suggested solution?" Share your findings with your class in a multimedia presentation.

Writing Workshop

Multimedia Presentation: Public Service Announcement

Write with a Purpose

Write a public service announcement that presents persuasive information about a topic of public concern. Your **purpose** is to convince your audience that they too should be concerned about this issue. Your **audience** consists of the teachers and students at your school.

A Good Public Service Announcement

- focuses on a topic of public concern
- targets its audience
- appeals to its audience emotionally as well as logically
- supports its message with facts, examples, expert opinions, statistics, and other evidence
- may use print, visuals, and/or sound to deliver its message
- wraps up its conclusion by clearly restating the purpose of the message

Reader/Writer Notebook

Use your **RWN** to complete the activities for this workshop.

Think as a Reader/Writer

It is time for you to think beyond just words. Now you can use voice-overs, moving images, photos, graphics, music, and other elements to convince an audience of your idea. Before you create your own public service announcement (PSA), read the following excerpt from the PSA script to be shot for TV for Media for Kids, an organization that donates computers to schools.

VIDEO	AUDIO
CLOSEUP ("CU") OF NEWS-PAPER WANT AD, SHOW-ING FINGER ON TEXT.	VOICEOVER ("V/O") OF YOUNG MAN: Good spelling and grammar. OK. Basics of bookkeeping. OK.
PULL BACK TO SHOW MAN READING.	YOUNG MAN: Computer experience. None.
ANGLE ON MAN AND FATHER AT TABLE.	YOUNG MAN: How am I supposed to get any computer experience. . .
CU OF YOUNG MAN.	. . . when we didn't have computers at my school?
STILL OF "MEDIA FOR KIDS" 12 Curie St. New Orleans, LA 70122 1-800-555-KIDS	V/O NARRATOR: Help our children compete . . . . For information, write . . . . Or call 1-800-555-KIDS
FADE TO STILL OF CRUMPLED AD.	MUSIC UP. MUSIC OUT

The beginning draws in members of the **audience** with a **topic** they can relate to. The focus is job hunting.

Information is revealed through video and audio.

PSA uses **audio, video,** and **visuals** to deliver **message.**

The **conclusion** clearly wraps up the message.

The final shot is an **emotional appeal.**

Think About the Professional Model

With a partner, discuss the following questions about the model.

1. What is the purpose of this public service announcement?
2. How does the announcement try to appeal to its target audience?
3. What type of evidence does the announcement use? Do you think it is effective? Why, or why not?

Prewriting

Choose a Topic

A public service announcement, often called a PSA, communicates a persuasive or informative message that is in the community interest. In terms of technical and artistic requirements, there is little difference between a PSA and an advertisement or commercial. To get ideas for your own PSA,

- read your school and local newspapers
- check out school bulletin boards
- listen to the news on the radio or television
- explore electronic databases on the Internet

Think About Purpose and Audience

As you plan your PSA, be clear about what your **purpose** is. You want to inform your audience about an issue of concern to you. What else do you hope to do? Do you hope to educate your audience about a topic they may not know? Do you want your audience to take action on this issue? If so, what action are you hoping they'll take? Now, make sure you are clear about who your **audience** is.

- Will your audience be limited to students in your class or your grade, or are you hoping to reach a wider audience?
- What is a typical member of your audience like? What do you think he or she knows about this issue?
- Should your language be formal or casual?
- What types of evidence would be most persuasive to this audience?

Know Your Attitude

Tone refers to a writer's attitude toward a subject. Tone can be serious, critical, comic, sarcastic, romantic, admiring, and so on. When you have the topic for your PSA, decide what will be the best tone to use to "sell" your idea. The tone will help you determine the choice of visuals and audio.

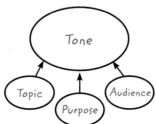

Idea Starters

- promoting media literacy
- saving energy at school by "going green"
- eating healthful foods
- giving tips about communicating online
- eliminating littering in your school's neighborhood

⬤ Writing Tip

For topic ideas and for presentation elements, take a look at your local public television channel to see PSAs there. Also, look through different national and local newspapers and magazines to find print PSAs.

Your Turn _____

Get Started Making notes in your **RWN,** explore different topics for your **PSA**. Narrow your choices until you have decided on the two or three issues you want to tackle. Then, think about your **purpose** and your **audience**. Which topic are you most interested in addressing with this audience?

Learn It Online
To see how one writer met all the assignment criteria, visit:

go.hrw.com   L7-629   **Go**

Multimedia Presentation: Public Service Announcement

Select Your Media

How are you planning to deliver your message? The following chart shows the choices you have for presenting your PSA. As you choose how you'll deliver your message, think about what types of media will be involved.

Audio Presentation	Visual Presentation	Print Presentation
Narration	Video	Pamphlet
Music	Photos	Poster
Sound effects	Web site	Graphics
Other	Animation	Other

Think about the equipment and materials you'll need before you choose your medium (audio, visual, or print) and begin the project. Make a list, and make sure you have access to the materials you'll need before you begin. Check early to see about anything that requires permission, such as using your school's public address system, newspaper, or Web site. It would be disappointing to create something you won't be able to deliver.

Map Out a Plan

Before you start your PSA, map out what you are going to say and how you are going to present it. You can chart on a plot, or story map what you want to say in the beginning, the middle, and the end. Remember that how you plan will vary depending on your medium.

- If you're going to write a script for a video, you may want to use a storyboard, like the ones used for television commercials, shows, or movies. A storyboard looks like a comic strip in which each panel represents a basic sketch of what each camera shot will look like. You'll also have to plan how the audio on your video will complement the visual.

- For an audio PSA, you'll need to write an audio script. What music or sound effects will attract your audience's attention, as well as strengthen your message? How many speakers will you need to be convincing and interesting?

- For a print PSA, plan how your text and any images will work together to convey your persuasive message. What photographs or drawings should you include? How much text will you need?

Writing Tip

Do your research! You are going to need to locate facts, examples, and other accurate evidence to support your message. Most libraries are now equipped with **online catalogs,** where you can find and borrow the library's audiotapes and videotapes. These are good sources to use for presentation ideas and items of evidence.

Your Turn _____

Plan Your Presentation Make notes in your **RWN** as you figure out how you are going to deliver your PSA. Then, work on your plan. As you plan, make sure you have mapped out what you want to say, how you want to say it, and the order in which you will lay it out.

Drafting

Follow the Writer's Framework

To reach your audience, you need to express your purpose and then provide persuasive and convincing specifics. Use the Framework shown at the right to help you proceed with your draft.

Appeal to Your Audience

To be convincing, you have to appeal to your audience's hearts and minds. You can use these two kinds of appeals in your PSA:

- **logical appeal:** What solid evidence can you provide to support your message?
- **emotional appeal:** How can you move your audience to action by touching their feelings?

Framework for a Multimedia Presentation

Introduction

- Express the purpose of your message.
- Decide what the audio portion will do and what the video portion will do.
- Use language and media that will appeal to your target audience emotionally and logically.

Body

- Use facts, examples, anecdotes, statistics, and expert opinions that will get your point across.
- Use different forms of media so that they complement each other and make your message convincing.

Conclusion

- Wrap up your announcement, restating the purpose of the message.
- Try to end with an emotional appeal.
- Include contact information.

Format Your Announcement

Depending on the materials available to you, your PSA can involve visuals and sound, as well as text. Decide on the best format for your announcement. Formats include

- a small brochure that can be distributed
- an audiotape that can be aired on radio
- a video that can be shot with a camera and shown on school TV
- an interactive Web page

Regardless of your format, be sure your audience knows how to contact you.

Grammar Link Punctuation in Addresses and Phone Numbers

If you use addresses in your PSA, use commas to separate place names, cities, and states.

CONFUSING	12 Curie St. New Orleans LA 70122
CLEAR	12 Curie St., New Orleans, LA 70122

If you use phone numbers in your PSA, use hyphens to separate groups of digits and/or letters.

CONFUSING	1800555KIDS
CLEAR	1-800-555-KIDS

Writing Tip

As you write your draft, stop from time to time to read aloud what you have written so far. Ask yourself these questions: "Is my point clear and concise?" "Will the language and media help me reach my target audience?"

Your Turn _____

Write Your Draft Following your plan, write a draft of your PSA. As you write your draft, think about these points:

- What **language** is your **audience** most likely to respond to?
- What **media** will most **effectively** get your message across?
- What **message** do you want your audience to take away?

Multimedia Presentation: Public Service Announcement

Working with a peer, review your drafts. Answer each question in this chart to locate where and how your drafts could be improved. As you discuss your drafts, be sure to take notes about each other's suggestions. You can refer to your notes as you revise your drafts.

Evaluating and Revising

Read the questions in the left column of the chart. Then, use the tips in the middle column to help you make revisions to your announcement. The right column suggests techniques you can use to revise your draft.

Public Service Announcement: Guidelines for Content and Organization

Evaluation Question	Tip	Revision Technique
1. Does your introduction express the purpose of your message? Does it draw in your audience's attention?	**Underline** the information that shows the purpose of your message. **Circle** the words or visuals that attract your audience.	**Add** a sentence or visual that identifies the purpose of your message. **Add** a short sentence or a visual that will draw in your audience's interest.
2. Have you targeted your audience?	**Bracket** words or visuals that identify your audience.	If appropriate, **name** or **identify** the people being targeted.
3. Does your message appeal to your audience emotionally as well as logically?	**Highlight** information that is an emotional appeal. **Draw a wavy line** under a logical appeal.	**Include** visuals and audio that will add emotional importance to your message.
4. Have you supplied evidence, such as facts and examples, to support your message?	**Put a star** next to evidence that supports your message.	**Add** facts, examples, and other details that support your main points.
5. Did you use different forms of media in your presentation?	**Put a check mark** next to each different form of media used in your presentation.	When possible, **replace** print with another form of media, such as a sound effect, a video clip, or an image.
6. Did you wrap up your message and restate it in your conclusion?	**Underline** the statement, visual, or audio that provides a conclusion to your message.	**Add** a sentence, an audio, or visual that restates your message.

Read this draft of a pamphlet and the comments about it as a model for revising your own PSA.

Student Draft

Online-Course Netiquette
by Wendy Starr, Willett Street Middle School

Netiquette = Network Etiquette

[Photo of regular classroom full of students at top right corner. Photo of single student at library computer at top left corner.]

When taking an online class, do use common courtesy and good manners.

- **Don't** use acronyms (ROFL, MBF, and so on). Not everyone knows the meaning of these.
- **Do** be clear and concise. Explain your ideas entirely but get quickly to the point.
- **Don't** lurk in a class chat. This means you're reading online and not participating. [Cartoon of student in back of regular classroom, hiding behind palm tree.]

← The **pamphlet** format introduces the **topic** and **purpose** with its title, subheading, and photographs.

← The writer expresses the **purpose** of the PSA in the introduction.

← The writer uses **specific details** and **examples** to get the **message** across. She includes graphics.

← The writer uses a **clear method** for stating her points, although she could make the message more appealing to her **audience** through the use of **different media.**

MINI-LESSON ▶ How to Target Your Audience

Will your audience be interested in your message? Do you need to add visuals to make your point? Would adding audio, such as a voice-over or music, help make your message more effective or memorable? The writer of "Netiquette" changed her mind about making a pamphlet and decided to deliver her PSA as a video posted online. Her target audience—students and a teacher of a Web-only course—are people who are comfortable and interested in working online.

Wendy's Revision

VIDEO	AUDIO
OPEN ON CU OF COMPUTER SCREEN, TITLE BEING TYPED OUT O-n-l-i-n-e-C-o-u-r-s-e N-e-t-i-q-u-e-t-t-e	**V/O YOUNG WOMAN #1:** "Welcome to Online-Course Netiquette, or How to Behave Yourself in Web Class."
WIDE ANGLE OF FULL REGULAR CLASSROOM WAVING HELLO.	**V/O YOUNG MAN #1:** "When taking an online class, do use common courtesy and good manners."

Your Turn _____

Get Your Message Across

- Read your draft. Have you stated your topic clearly at the beginning?
- Have you used specific details and examples to get your point across?
- Is there anything you could do to make your delivery more appealing to your audience?

Multimedia Presentation: Public Service Announcement

Student Draft *continues*

The writer has identified her **audience** as an online class and is writing her PSA with them in mind.

The writer is supplying different forms of **evidence** to support her message. Here is an **example** to the right.

The form of evidence here is a **fact** because it can be proven.

The writer has used **video** and **audio** (voices, music, sound effects)—all popular with her audience.

Here is a negative **emotional appeal** saying not to plagiarize.

VIDEO	AUDIO
CU OF TEACHER'S FACE WITH QUIZZICAL LOOK, SHAKING HEAD.	**V/O TEACHER:** "Don't use acronyms (ROFL, MBF, and so on). Not everyone (ahem, such as your teacher) knows what these mean."
EXTREME CU OF COMPUTER SCREEN: Don't type in all CAPITAL letters. It looks as if you're SCREAMING.	**COMPUTER-SOUNDING VOICE, "SCREAMING" ON CAPPED WORDS:** "Don't type in all CAPITAL letters. It looks as if you're SCREAMING."
OVER-THE-SHOULDER SHOT OF STUDENT TYPING SCREEN FULL OF EMOTICONS AND ACRONYMS.	**V/O YOUNG MAN #2:** "Do use proper grammar, complete words, and correct spelling. Their usage will affect your grade."
WIDE-ANGLE OF STUDENT HIDING IN BACK OF CLASS, BEHIND PALM TREE.	**V/O YOUNG WOMAN #2:** "Don't lurk in a class chat. This means you're reading online and not participating."
MEDIUM ANGLE OF PRINCIPAL'S DOOR; OPENS; UNHAPPY PRINCIPAL MOTIONS, "COME IN."	**V/O PRINCIPAL:** "Don't present work or ideas of others as your own (otherwise known as plagiarism)."

● Presentation Tip

Remember: If you don't have access to video and audio equipment at the present time, you can still prepare a script and make a live presentation.

Your Turn _____

Using Different Media Review your PSA draft. Have you used media effectively? Is there any way you could make your PSA more visually appealing? Do you need to add any audio to get your message across?

MINI-LESSON **How to Conclude Strongly**

Wendy has a good script but has left the message dangling at the end. Remember that the **conclusion** is the last idea an audience takes away from your PSA. Wendy needs to revise to use this as an opportunity to wrap up the PSA's main message and to restate the PSA's purpose.

Wendy's Revision of the Script

VIDEO	AUDIO
SLIDE SHOW CUTS TO DIFFERENT STUDENTS AT INDIVIDUAL COMPUTERS AND LAPTOPS IN VARIOUS LOCATIONS, SUCH AS AT SCHOOL, AT THE LIBRARY, AND AT HOME.	V/O YOUNG WOMAN #1: "Remember, when you're in class online, behave as if you're in class in person. We know the rules. Let's all follow them. See you this semester on the Web."
STILL SHOT ON POSTERBOARD: Netiquette = Network Etiquette FADE OUT.	MUSIC UP. MUSIC OUT.

Proofreading and Publishing

Proofreading

Even if you are the only one reading the PSA for your final presentation, you should still fix any errors in your writing. Check your final version to make sure it is free of any errors in spelling, punctuation, and sentence structure. Proofread your writing carefully, using proofreading marks to make the necessary corrections.

Grammar Link Using Imperative Sentences

Because a persuasive PSA often asks someone to do or change something, imperative sentences should be used in the PSA. An imperative sentence gives a command or makes a request. Most end with a period; however, a strong command may end with an exclamation point.

EXAMPLES	Don't use acronyms. [command]
	Please be courteous. [request]
	Don't type in all CAPITALS! [strong command]

The subject of a command or request is always *you,* even if *you* doesn't appear in the sentence. In such cases, *you* is called the **understood** subject.

| **EXAMPLE** | (You) Don't lurk in class chat. |

The word *you* is the understood subject even when the person spoken to is addressed by name.

| **EXAMPLE** | Sam, (you) please don't plagiarize. |

Publishing

Now it is time to publish your PSA, sharing it with a wider audience. Here are some ways to share your PSA:

- Deliver it through the school's public address system.
- Present it as part of a public service school assembly.
- Share it online.
- Post it on a bulletin board for others to read.

Reflect on the Process   In your **RWN,** write a short response to the following questions.

1. Which forms of media did you use? Which was the most effective?
2. Do you think you got your message across? Why or why not? What feedback did you receive from your target audience?

● **Proofreading Tip**

There are three main areas to focus on when proofreading: spelling, punctuation, and sentence structure. It makes sense to focus on just one area at a time while proofreading. Ask two peers to help you, assigning each person just one area to check.

Your Turn _____

Proofread and Publish

Proofread your PSA, making sure you have used imperative sentences correctly. Think about the best way to share your message and to make sure that you will be able to follow through with your plan. Is there anyone you need to get permission from? Do you need any special materials?

Informational Skills Review

Informational Texts **Directions:** Read the following texts. Then, read and answer the questions that follow.

GreatBUYS Stores, Inc.

Date: January 22, 2009

To: All Floor Managers

From: Casey Cross

Our public relations team has built a campaign for the new and exciting sci-fi video game **Forest World**, which will take place at all stores the week of March 1. To prepare your staff, see the attached instructions and agenda. Make sure all are familiar with the product and on hand during peak hours. Send your concerns forward. Let's make this a fun week for all!

casey cross

Casey Cross
GreatBUYS General Manager

MAGAZINE ARTICLE

Saving the Forest, One Level at a Time

New Games Pit Players Against Pollution

by **Mario Mann**

Not all game missions are created equal. First came games aimed at getting people off their couches. Players could rev up heart rates while matching their dance moves to those on-screen. Now there's the ambitious "green" lineup, including Forest World, which is attracting plenty of market interest. Players fight to save their earth from destruction.

9 PLAYTIME: GAMES

WEB SITE

File   Edit   View   Favorites   Tools   Help

Back   Forward   Stop   Refresh   Home   Search   Favorites   History   Mail   Print

Address   http://www.TECHnicalities.com/signin/shipping and payment/giftwrap/place order   Go

You have selected the item **Forest World.** *This feature item comes with* **FREE** *second-day shipping.*

Make sure the address is entered correctly. If not, your package may be returned as undeliverable.

FULL NAME:

ADDRESS LINE 1:

ADDRESS LINE 2:

CITY: STATE/PROVINCE/REGION:

ZIP/POSTAL CODE: COUNTRY:

PHONE NUMBER:

Internet

---

1. The *main* point of the memo is that —
   A instructions and agenda are attached
   B a new video game is being released
   C managers should schedule extra staff
   D Casey Cross will answer questions

2. What is the *main* purpose of the magazine article?
   A To give information about a new video game
   B To sell a new video game in GreatBUYS stores
   C To explain the change in focus of video games over time
   D To teach how to buy video games

3. Which of these texts is a consumer document?
   A The article
   B The memo
   C The Web site
   D Both the article and the Web site

4. The article *most likely* appears in a magazine called *Playtime* because —
   A the magazine editor thinks readers will be interested in the topic
   B the readers of the article will likely buy the game
   C the writer of the article has strong feelings about the game
   D stores are planning to sell many copies of the game

5. According to the Web site, people should —
   A have their order gift-wrapped
   B pay for the game with a credit card
   C double-check their address for mistakes
   D choose the method of shipping they want

6. If you bought the Forest World game and wanted instructions for playing it, where would you look first?
   A The employee manual at GreatBUYS
   B The Web site of the store from which you bought the game
   C An article in *Playtime* magazine
   D The game's instruction booklet

Constructed Response

7. List the most important purpose of each of the following types of documents: workplace, consumer, and public. Then give an example of each type of document.

Reading Skills Review

Cause and Effect **Directions:** Read the following article. Then, answer each question that follows.

Mongoose on the Loose by **Larry Luxner**

In 1872, a Jamaican sugar planter imported nine furry little mongooses from India to eat the rats that were devouring his crops. They did such a good job, the planter started breeding his exotic animals and selling them to eager farmers on neighboring islands.

With no natural predators—like wolves, coyotes, or poisonous snakes—the mongoose population exploded, and within a few years, they were killing not just rats but pigs, lambs, chickens, puppies, and kittens. Dr. G. Roy Horst, a U.S. expert on mongooses, says that today mongooses live on seventeen Caribbean islands as well as Hawaii and Fiji, where they have attacked small animals, threatened endangered species, and have even spread minor rabies epidemics.

In Puerto Rico there are from 800,000 to one million of them. That is about one mongoose for every four humans. In St. Croix, there are 100,000 mongooses, about twice as many as the human population. "It's impossible to eliminate the mongoose population, short of nuclear war," says Horst. "You can't poison them, because cats, dogs, and chickens get poisoned, too. I'm not a prophet crying in the wilderness, but the potential for real trouble is there," says Horst.

According to Horst, great efforts have been made to rid the islands of mongooses, which have killed off a number of species, including the Amevia lizard on St. Croix, presumed extinct for several decades. On Hawaii, the combination of mongooses and sports hunting has reduced the Hawaiian goose, or nene, to less than two dozen individuals. . . .

Horst says his research will provide local and federal health officials with extremely valuable information if they ever decide to launch a campaign against rabies in Puerto Rico or the U.S. Virgin Islands.

1. The following diagram displays information about the causes and effects of bringing mongooses to Jamaica.

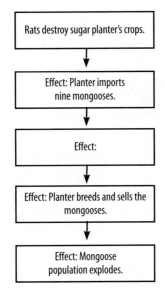

Rats destroy sugar planter's crops.

↓

Effect: Planter imports nine mongooses.

↓

Effect:

↓

Effect: Planter breeds and sells the mongooses.

↓

Effect: Mongoose population explodes.

Which of these events belongs in the third box?

A Mongooses do a good job getting rid of rats.

B Mongooses threaten the Hawaiian goose.

C Mongooses destroy other species.

D Mongooses are difficult to study.

2. In 1872, a Jamaican sugar planter imported nine mongooses to —

A keep snakes away from his farm

B serve as pets for his young children

C eat the rats that were ruining his crops

D breed them for their fur

3. Because the mongooses didn't have any natural predators in that part of the world, their population —

A diminished

B exploded

C fluctuated

D declined

4. You would be *most* likely to find this information about mongooses in a —

A chemistry book

B collection of stories

C travel guide

D magazine on nature

Constructed Response

5. Describe the **effects** of the mongoose population explosion.

Read On

Reading for Life: Magazines

Sports Illustrated KIDS

Stories about star athletes, performance tips from professionals, sports cards, comics, and articles on exercise and healthful eating—*Sports Illustrated KIDS* has it all for girls and boys who love sports. Filled with action photos, this award-winning magazine will encourage you to read it from start to finish—and then to go out and join in the activities.

Calliope

Have you ever daydreamed about living in another century, in another country? Do you wonder about the lives of famous people from the past: Muhammad, Charlemagne, and other great leaders, artists, and scientists? Pick up a copy of the magazine *Calliope,* and check out who and what are being featured from the past. In addition to fantastic features, *Calliope* includes maps, time lines, and activities to enhance your enjoyment of history.

Stone Soup: The Magazine by Young Writers and Artists

If you like writing, reading, and drawing, look for *Stone Soup.* In it you'll find short stories and poems written by kids from all around the world. You may even decide to submit your own work for publication. Go to its Web site, www.stonesoup. com, for links to more sites for young writers, such as ZuZu, Young Girl Writers, and Just Write.

Archaeology's dig

Do you dig Egyptian mummies? If you do, unearth a copy of the magazine *Archaeology's dig.* Learn about the latest discoveries in the field of archaeology, from fossils to Vikings. The magazine also features games and experiments and invites you to ask Dr. Dig all the questions you have about archaeology.

Web Sites

Earth from Space: Astronauts' Views of the Home Planet

Photographs from NASA's Space Shuttle Earth Observations database are a national treasure. Each image comes with an explanatory caption. The database, located at earth.jsc.nasa.gov/sseop/efs/, illustrates some of Earth's most fascinating features, including cities as seen from space. Type in the name of the largest city near you to see it from an astronaut's point of view.

Kids.gov: The Official Kid's Portal for the U.S. Government

Check out www.kids.gov, a collection of links to the kid-friendly sites of various government agencies, along with links to other groups' sites for children. Click on one of the subjects—such as Fighting Crime, Computers, Health, or Fun Stuff—to find links to hundreds of sites of interest.

Jazz in the Schools

Sponsored by the National Endowment for the Arts, this Web site is a study guide and tool kit that explores jazz not only as a unique American art form but also as a special way of looking at American life. You can follow an interactive time line to see jazz's place in history, as you listen to famous musicians like Louis Armstrong, Sarah Vaughan, and Wynton Marsalis. Included is a file of biographies of many major artists. Visit neajazzintheschools.org, produced by Jazz at Lincoln Center, for sounds that have influenced American music since the 1800s.

Exhibits from The Tech Museum of Innovation

Online interactive exhibits created by the Tech will grab your attention. Some are about robotics and energy-efficient cars—you get to design and race your own. If you can't get to the actual museum in San Jose, California, go to www.thetech.org/exhibits/online/ for a virtual visit.

Learn It Online

Learn how to analyze a Web site online with MediaScope:

go.hrw.com   L7-641   Go

Poetry
Writers on Writing

Pat Mora on Poetry

Pat Mora was raised in Texas in a bilingual household. Today, she is known for her commitment to activism, literacy, and cultural preservation. Mora's award-winning poems, fiction, and nonfiction often draw from her Mexican American heritage and her deep respect for women.

"Have you ever felt happy? lonely? angry? proud? We all have, right? All kinds of feelings and ideas swirl inside us. Composers, whether they're professionals or beginners, express their feelings with notes and music. To share with us what the composer feels inside, she creates a fast and happy song or a slow and quiet song. Visual

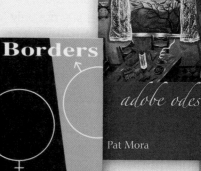

artists use paint, watercolors, or pen-and-ink to let us see what they're thinking, seeing, remembering, imagining. Like composers, a visual artist uses his feelings to help him paint or draw a stormy ocean or two *amigos* walking down a road.

Writers use words to share our feelings and ideas. Because I'm lucky to be bilingual, I use words in two languages, Spanish and English. Why do I write poetry? Because it's hard? No. I write poetry because I like its wordplay and economy. Economy? Isn't that about money, about being thrifty and not wasteful? Yes, in poetry every word matters. A poet is a thrifty writer who learns to delete unnecessary words and to find new words, the best word.

I started writing poetry when I was in elementary school. I liked to read rhyming poems then, so that's what I wrote, rhyming poems. I liked their *musica,* the way sounds fit together like a puzzle: me/thrifty, cow/meow, stone/alone. Now I write all kinds of poems. I just finished a book of haiku about the foods of the Americas. I'd never tried much haiku before, but I had a great time playing with tiny seventeen-syllable poems.

Writing a good poem means taking the time to be quiet, to think and to go inside myself. If I'm writing about my friend, I think about how she looks and sounds and why I like her. Then, I let my imagination explore how to let you, my reader, hear my friend.

Do you know how water *cascades,* tumbles down in a waterfall? Maybe I say that my friend's laugh cascades. Can you begin to hear her? I like poetry because it can say so much with few words—the right words.

With poems, I tell stories or write about my many moods or about what's important to me, like feeling proud that my grandparents came from Mexico and spoke Spanish. Because I have less space than when I write prose, I work to create an experience for you, my reader.

When I started writing poems, my poems were often about me and my feelings. Since I've written poems for many years, I write about all kinds of topics but still use my feelings to help me write. I'm writing a book of love poems for teens now. All the poems will be in the voices of teens, so I'm remembering how I felt when I was younger, but I also use what I feel now.

Remember how I started? We *all* feel happy, lonely, angry, proud. Poetry connects me with me, and me with you. Poetry connects us. "

Think as a Writer

According to Pat Mora, what important ingredients must go into a poem? How does each ingredient help a poet connect to herself and to her readers?

COLLECTION 7

Elements of Poetry

"Poetry is when an
emotion has found its
thought and the thought
has found words."

—**Robert Frost**

What Do You Think

What kinds of experiences
and feelings would you
write about in a poem?

Two Faces and One Tear.

Learn It Online
Listen to poetry read aloud online:

go.hrw.com   L7-645   Go

Literary Focus

by **Linda Rief**

What Are Elements of Poetry?

Most poets will tell you that a poem should be *given twice*, that is, read aloud at least twice before you talk about it. Read the poems in this collection again and again, aloud. Listen to the cadence, the rhythm, and the tone. The sound of good words put together in meaningful order begins to stay with us. What mood does the sound of the words create? What's the feeling you get from the sounds, the words, and the way the lines are shaped? What does the poem bring to mind for you? Don't be afraid of poetry. With each reading, let the sounds wash over you the way they do when you listen again and again to songs you love.

Form

Like sculptors, poets are concerned with shape, or **form.** When they write and revise, poets are chiseling their words to create the shapes you see on the page. Poets think about how long their lines should be and whether they should group lines into units, called **stanzas.** Some poets use forms based on strict rules, while others experiment with new forms. The poet's purpose is to give the words a pleasing shape and help convey meaning. Think about this example:

> Stay beautiful
> but dont stay down underground too long
> Dont turn into a mole
> or a worm
> or a root
> or a stone
>
> from "For Poets" by Al Young

Forms of Poetry

Poetry is a kind of musical and focused writing designed to appeal to emotion and imagination. There are many kinds of poems:

- **Narrative poems**, such as the ballad and the epic, tell a story.
- **Lyric** poems express the speaker's feelings.
- An **ode** is a type of lyric poem that celebrates something.
- A **sonnet** is also a lyric poem but follows very strict rules.
- A **elegy** mourns the loss of something important to the poet.
- **Free verse** has no regular rhythm or rhyme.
- A **catalog poem** is free verse that lists the poet's thoughts or feelings on a subject.

In this collection, you will read examples of these forms of poetry. Use the word web above to think about the forms of poetry.

Tone

Poets choose every word with great care to reflect a specific **tone,** or attitude toward the subject. If a poet thinks that a scene is happy and carefree, the details in the lines will reflect that attitude.

Imagery

Think of a poet as an artist who is creating a picture with words. Like painters, poets want to share a special, personal vision of the world. To do this, poets use **imagery,** or word pictures, that put your imagination to work. Such images can make us see things in new and unexpected ways. Read the following description. What do you see?

> He'd a French cocked hat on his forehead,
>   a bunch of lace at his chin,
> A coat of the claret velvet, and breeches of
>   brown doeskin.
> They fitted with never a wrinkle. His boots
>   were up to the thigh.
>> from "The Highwayman"
>> by Alfred Noyes

Images in poetry focus on all of the senses. Here are some not-so-pleasant images that appeal to touch, smell, and taste:

> Cellophane from green baloney,
> Rubbery blubbery macaroni,
> Peanut butter, caked and dry,
> Curdled milk and crusts of pie,
>> from "Sarah Cynthia Sylvia Stout
>> Would Not Take the Garbage Out"
>> by Shel Silverstein

Figurative Language

Along with images, poets use figures of speech to share their special, personal visions of the world. **Figures of speech** make startling connections between dissimilar things. A **simile** is a comparison of two unlike things using the word *like, as, than,* or *resembles.* This simile compares a horse in a snowstorm to a shadow:

> And we saw him, or thought we saw him,
>   dim and gray,
> Like a shadow against the curtain of
>   falling flakes.
>> from "The Runaway"
>> by Robert Frost

A **metaphor** compares two unlike things, but it does so without using *like* or other simile words.

> Stars are great drops
> Of golden dew.
>> from "Harlem Night Song"
>> by Langston Hughes

Your Turn Analyze Elements of Poetry

1. What makes poetry different from prose? Include different elements as examples.

2. Identify an element of poetry that you would like to understand better, and explain why.

Learn It Online
Use *PowerNotes* to reinforce your learning at:
go.hrw.com L7-647 **Go**

Literary Focus

by **Linda Rief**

What Are the Sounds of Poetry?

Like musicians, poets are concerned with sounds. Imagine a composer of music trying various patterns of notes on a piano in order to create a pleasing melody. That will give you a good idea of what poets do with words. Poets choose words with great care. They revise their poems repeatedly, trying to find the combination of words that produces just the right sound—perhaps a harsh sound, a beautiful sound, or a sound that matches the gallop of a horse. A poet's goal is to match sound with the feelings and ideas that the poem is meant to convey.

Rhythm

Rhythm refers to the rise and fall of our voices as we stress some sounds more strongly than others. As in music, rhythm in a poem can be fast or slow, light or solemn. It can sound like everyday speech.

Poetry that is written in **meter** has a regular pattern of stressed and unstressed syllables. When poets write in meter, they count out the number of stressed syllables (or strong beats) and unstressed syllables (weaker beats) in each line. Then, they repeat the pattern throughout the poem. To avoid a singsong effect, poets usually vary the basic pattern from time to time. Read these lines aloud to listen for the meter:

> "You are old, Father William," the young
> man said,
> "And your hair has become
> very white;
>> from "Father William"
>> by Lewis Carroll

Scanning Rhythm

A poem's rhythm can be shown by using accent marks: (ˊ) for stressed syllables and (˘) for unstressed syllables. This marking is called **scanning.**

> "You are old, Father William," the young
> man said,
>> from "Father William"
>> by Lewis Carroll

Poetry that is written in **free verse** does not have a regular pattern of stressed and unstressed syllables. Free verse sounds like ordinary speech:

> Generation on generation, your neck
> rubbed the window sill
> of the stall, smoothing the wood as the sea
> smooths glass.
>> from "Names of Horses"
>> by Donald Hall

Rhyme

Rhyme is the repetition of a stressed syllable and any unstressed syllables that follow. You can hear the rhymes in the lines from "Father William": *said* and *head*; *white* and *right*.

Poets use a variety of rhyming patterns. **End rhymes** are found at the end of two lines. **Internal rhymes** occur within lines, as shown below:

> Candy the *yams* and spice the *hams*, . . .
> Soggy *beans* and *tangerines*, . . .
>> from "Sarah Cynthia Sylvia Stout
>> Would Not Take the Garbage Out"
>> by Shel Silverstein

Words such as *yams* and *hams* are **exact rhymes.** For variation, poets may use **slant rhymes,** which are sounds that almost rhyme, such as the names *Milly* and *Molly* in the poem by E. E. Cummings.

Poets may use a **rhyme scheme,** or a pattern of rhymes. To describe a rhyme scheme, assign a new letter of the alphabet to each new end rhyme. For "Father William," it is *abab*.

> "You are old, Father William," the young
>> man said,
> "And your hair has become
>> very white;
> And yet you incessantly stand
>> on your head—
> Do you think, at your age, it is right?
>> from "Father William"
>> by Lewis Carroll

Repetition

Like musicians, poets use **repetition** to create an effect. The recurring use of a sound, a word, a phrase, or a line creates music, appeals to our emotions, and emphasizes important ideas.

Alliteration

Another way poets create sound effects is through **alliteration,** which is the repetition of consonant sounds in words that are close together.

> Softer be they than slippered sleep
> The lean lithe deer
> The fleet flown deer
>> from "All in green went my love riding "
>> by E. E. Cummings

Onomatopoeia

Onomatopoeia (ahn uh maht uh PEE uh) is the use of words whose sounds echo their meaning. *Buzz, hiss, crash* are examples of onomatopoeia. Read these lines aloud to hear the sound of "The Highwayman":

> Over the cobbles he clattered and clashed
>> in the dark inn yard.
> And he tapped with his whip on the
>> shutters, but all was locked and barred.
>> from "The Highwayman"
>> by Alfred Noyes

Your Turn Analyzing Poetry Sound Effects

Identify the sound effects that you enjoy most in songs or poetry, and explain why.

Analyzing Visuals

How Does Poetry Relate to Art?

Poetry and painting serve a similar purpose—to express a personal vision in condensed form. Both poetry and visual art use images and forms that appeal to the senses. Sound and meaning mesh in good poetry; every word contributes to a unique expression. In visual art, shape and color work together. Images, tone, and form create meaning and mood in art just as they do in poetry. And figurative ideas and symbols enrich both genres.

Analyzing Poetry and Visual Art

Answer the following questions as you relate poetry to visual art.

1. Determine the subject of the work by identifying key elements of content. What do you focus on?

2. Consider the elements of the painting—its colors, lines, and images. Are the colors sad or cheerful? Are the lines smooth and flowing or rough and jagged? What **mood,** or overall emotion, do these elements create?

3. Identify feelings or ideas conveyed by the imagery. Are the images hopeful or bleak? Could any images act as symbols? (A **symbol** is a person, place, thing, or event, that has its own meaning *and* stands for something beyond itself. For example, a red rose usually symbolizes true love.) If so, what do they symbolize?

4. Make inferences about the artist's **tone**, or attitude toward the subject. For example, you might consider whether a landscape artist sees nature as beautiful or as threatening.

5. Discuss how the work is poetic by summarizing its imagery, mood, and tone.

The Dove of Peace (1962)
by Pablo Picasso (1881–1973).
Ink and watercolor.

© 2009 Estate of Pablo Picasso/Artist's Rights Society (ARS), New York.

1. Picasso began drawing his dove symbols in 1950 in response to the United States's use of atomic bombs in World War II. What might the dove **symbolize**?

2. In the dove's beak is an olive branch, which is another **symbol**. What do you think it represents? How is the use of this image poetic?

3. Poetry uses **imagery** to express ideas in unique ways. What idea does the dove's perch express? How is the image poetic?

4. Artists, like poets, create **mood** by the way they portray a subject. What mood does Picasso express about the chance for peace?

Your Turn   Write About Poetry and Art

Picasso created this poster as an advertisement for the World Congress on Disarmament and Peace. Write a two-line poem that could caption this work. Use strong imagery, and create a hopeful mood.

Reading Focus

by **Kylene Beers**

How Do You Read a Poem?

Robert Frost once said that poetry begins in delight and ends in wisdom. In other words, poetry should be enjoyable to read, and it should leave us with an "Ah-ha!" feeling. That "Ah-ha!" moment should not be a "Huh?" question. If you follow the suggestions for reading a poem and re-read and ask questions, you will have more "Ah-ha!" moments than "Huh?" questions!

© The New Yorker Collection 1989 David Pascal from cartoonbank.com. All Rights Reserved.

How to Read a Poem

Follow these guidelines as you read poetry:

1. Read the poem aloud at least once. A poem's sense is linked to its sound.

2. Pay attention to punctuation. Pause at commas. Stop briefly at semicolons or after periods. Look for shifts in thought after dashes. If a line does not end in punctuation, do not make a full stop; pause briefly and continue to the end of the sentence.

3. Always read a poem in a normal voice, as if you were speaking to a friend. If the poem has a steady beat, let it emerge naturally.

4. Look up unfamiliar words. Poets choose words carefully, so sometimes words in a poem mean more than one thing. Each word adds to the poem's meaning.

5. Remember that poets use **similes** and **metaphors** to describe one thing in terms of another. For example, a poet might describe snowflakes as if they were insects.

6. Remember that many of the reading strategies that you use to understand prose will also help you understand poetry.

Re-reading a Poem

You might read a story only once, but a poem is meant to be read again and again. After the first reading, stop and think about the poem. Especially think about its images and sounds and its flow of emotions and ideas. Then, read the poem a second time. You may read it through three times or more. With each re-reading, you will discover something new about the poem.

As you re-read a poem and become more comfortable with the images and sound effects, think about the poem's meaning. What message is the poet sending to you? What ideas occur to you, or what lessons come to mind as you read? You'll find that your response to some poems will be, "It tells me something I always knew but never thought about that way before."

Have you ever thought this way about arithmetic?

> Arithmetic is where numbers fly like pigeons in and out of your head.
>
> from "Arithmetic"
> by Carl Sandburg

Questioning

When you read a poem—especially the first time through—record questions about it. There may be an image you don't understand or a word you need to check before you re-read the poem. You can use a chart like this one to organize your questions and record your answers while you read or after you read:

"The Highwayman"

Questions	Answers
Is the inn abandoned?	
What's a jeweled twinkle?	
What is a highwayman?	

Use specific questioning techniques to help you understand comparisons that poets make through similes and metaphors. "I Like to See It Lap the Miles" by Emily Dickinson is an extended metaphor that compares a train to a horse. Use a chart to identify your ideas and to guide you in recognizing the poet's images:

How Is a Train like a Horse?

Characteristics	Horse (Object 1)	Train (Object 2)
What it does		
Its speed		
Its sounds		

You can use a similar chart for any two objects that a poet compares in a figure of speech. List characteristics, such as appearance and sounds.

As you read, also jot down thoughts and associations that come to mind from a poem's images. Try it. Think about your own family photos:

> This is the pond, and these are my feet.
> This is the rooster, and this is more
>   of my feet.
>
> *Mamá was never good at pictures.*
> > from "Ode to Family Photographs"
> > by Gary Soto

Your Turn Apply Reading Skills

1. What can you do to unlock a poem's meaning?
2. What reading strategies associated with prose will also be useful when reading poetry?
3. If you were reading a poem about the moon, what thoughts or associations would come to mind?

> **Now go to the Skills in Action: Reading Model**

Learn It Online
Learn to read a poem with the *PowerNotes* version of this lesson on:
go.hrw.com L7-653   Go

Build Background

A blacksmith makes and repairs iron objects by hammering them against an anvil, which is a heavy iron block. Blacksmiths would heat the iron and shape it into objects, including hinges, household tools, and horseshoes. Because of improvements in the production of such objects, blacksmiths are rare today.

Read with a Purpose Read to discover how Longfellow views the blacksmith and what lesson the blacksmith teaches.

The Village Blacksmith

by **Henry Wadsworth Longfellow**

Under a spreading chestnut tree
　　The village smithy° stands;
The smith, a mighty man is he,
　　With large and sinewy hands;
5　And the muscles of his brawny arms
　　Are strong as iron bands.

His hair is crisp,° and black, and long,
　　His face is like the tan;
His brow is wet with honest sweat,
10　　He earns whate'er he can,
And looks the whole world in the face,
　　For he owes not any man.

Week in, week out, from morn till night,
　　You can hear his bellows° blow;
15　You can hear him swing his heavy sledge,°
　　With measured beat and slow,
Like a sexton ringing the village bell,
　　When the evening sun is low.

---

2. **smithy:** workshop of a blacksmith.

7. **crisp:** closely curled and wiry.

14. **bellows:** device for quickening the fire by blowing air in it.

15. **sledge:** sledgehammer; a long, heavy hammer, usually held with both hands.

Literary Focus

Imagery Longfellow uses **imagery** to create a picture of the blacksmith's powerful hands and arms. The next stanza presents more visual details to help you see the blacksmith at work.

Reading Focus

Reading Poetry Pay attention to punctuation as you read. Make a short pause at a comma and a longer pause at a semicolon. Don't stop at the end of a line that has no punctuation. The poet wants you to keep reading.

Analyzing Visuals

Viewing and Interpreting
How does the painting
help you visualize what a
blacksmith does?

Shoeing
by Sir Edwin Henry Landseer
(1802–1873).

And children coming home from school
20   Look in at the open door;
They love to see the flaming forge,
      And hear the bellows roar,
And catch the burning sparks that fly
      Like chaff from a threshing floor.

25 He goes on Sunday to the church,
      And sits among his boys;
He hears the parson pray and preach,
      He hears his daughter's voice,
Singing in the village choir,
30   And it makes his heart rejoice.

It sounds to him like her mother's voice,
      Singing in Paradise!
He needs must think of her once more,
      How in the grave she lies;
35 And with his hard, rough hand he wipes
      A tear out of his eyes.

Reading Focus

Questioning If you don't
understand all of the images in
these lines, write down a question before you continue reading.
Be sure to answer the question
before you re-read the poem.

Literary Focus

Rhyme and Rhythm
Longfellow uses sound effects
such as **rhyming words** (*voice*
and *rejoice*) and a metered
rhythm to convey meaning.

Literary Focus

Imagery The poet's choice
of words creates images that
connect to all of the senses.
This image appeals to the
sense of touch.

Toiling—rejoicing—sorrowing,
    Onward through life he goes;
Each morning sees some task begin;
40   Each evening sees it close;
Something attempted, something done,
    Has earned a night's repose.

Thanks, thanks to thee, my worthy friend,
    For the lesson thou hast taught!
45 Thus at the flaming forge of life
    Our fortunes must be wrought;
Thus on its sounding anvil shaped
    Each burning deed and thought.

Reading Focus

Re-reading Re-read the poem at least once. It will help you answer your questions and discover more about the poem's meaning.

Read with a Purpose What words and images convey Longfellow's admiration for the blacksmith? What lesson does the blacksmith teach?

MEET THE WRITER

Henry Wadsworth Longfellow
(1807–1882)

The Most Popular Poet
During his lifetime, Henry Wadsworth Longfellow was America's most popular poet. He was inspired by American history, which he often used as background material. Before the American Revolution and for the first few decades thereafter, most literature that was considered important came from England and Europe. Longfellow helped American poets become recognized and respected. His works have been translated into twenty-four languages.

Think About the Writer Why do you think Longfellow chose to write about moments in American history?

© The Granger Collection, New York.

SKILLS FOCUS **Literary Skills** Understand and analyze elements of poetry; understand and analyze sounds of poetry, such as rhythm, rhyme, alliteration, and onomatopoeia.
Reading Skills Use questioning to improve comprehension.

Into Action: Questioning to Understand the Poem

Use questioning to help you understand the message and the literary elements in "The Village Blacksmith." Complete a chart like the one below with your questions. Two questions are provided that help you think about a simile used in the poem. Then re-read the poem, and identify what's clearer to you this time.

The Village Blacksmith

Questions	Answers
What is chaff?	It's the hard coating around a grain of wheat.
Why are burning sparks like chaff?	When grain is processed, chaff flies into the air like sparks.

Talk About ...

How does the line "our fortunes must be wrought" connect to the blacksmith's work? How does it connect to our lives? Discuss your ideas with a partner. Try to use the Academic Vocabulary words listed at right in your discussion.

Write About ...

Using the Academic Vocabulary words at the right, generate at least three questions about "The Village Blacksmith." Make sure to use the Academic Vocabulary words in ways that demonstrate that you know what they mean.

Writing Focus

Think as a Reader/Writer

The Writing Focus activities in Collection 7 explain each poet's style and use of literary elements. You'll have a chance to write about the elements and try using them in poems of your own.

Academic Vocabulary for Collection 7

Talking and Writing About Elements of Poetry

Academic Vocabulary is the language you use to write and talk about literature. Use these words to discuss the poetry you read in this collection. The words are underlined in the collection.

vision (VIHZH uhn) *n.:* force or power of imagination. *The theme of the poem reflects the poet's vision.*

structure (STRUHK chuhr) *n.:* the way in which a set of parts is put together to form a whole. *To understand the structure of the poem, you must examine its parts.*

tradition (truh DIHSH uhn) *n.:* a set of beliefs or customs that have been handed down for generations. *Poetic traditions stretch back to the ancient world.*

comment (KAHM ehnt) *v.:* explain or interpret something. *Poets often comment on the relationship between society and nature.*

Your Turn

Copy the Academic Vocabulary words into your *Reader/Writer Notebook*. Use each word in a sentence that describes a feeling or idea you have about poetry. Practice using these words as you talk and write about the selections in this collection.

Elements of Poetry

CONTENTS

 What Do You Think? What inspires writers to write poetry?

QuickWrite
Think of an experience that had a profound impact on you. Explain whether you would write about the experience in a poem.

I'm Nobody! / I Like to See It Lap the Miles

SKILLS FOCUS **Literary Skills** Understand and analyze figures of speech; understand extended metaphor. **Reading Skills** Use questioning to improve comprehension.

Reader/Writer Notebook

Use your **RWN** to complete the activities for these selections.

Literary Focus

Figures of Speech In "I'm Nobody!" Emily Dickinson throws a spotlight on her ideas by using figures of speech. **Figures of speech** compare things that at first glance seem very different. These unusual comparisons let you see familiar things in a new light. The comparisons in figures of speech are imaginative and are not meant to be understood as literally true.

Extended Metaphor An **extended metaphor** is a metaphor that is developed, or extended, through several lines of writing or even throughout an entire poem. In "I Like to See It Lap the Miles," Dickinson uses an extended metaphor throughout the whole poem to compare a train to a horse.

Reading Focus

Questioning the Text Ask yourself questions both before you read and as you read each of the following poems. When you finish each poem, reconsider your questions. Have they been answered?

Into Action You know that "I Like to See It Lap the Miles" compares a train to a horse. Before you read the poem, ask yourself how a train is similar to a horse, and fill in a chart like the one below.

	What it does	Its speed	Its sounds
Horse			
Train			

Writing Focus

Think as a Reader/Writer

Find It in Your Reading As you read, think about how Dickinson's figures of speech make you see things in a new way.

Language Coach

Figures of Speech The most common figures of speech are similes and metaphors. A **simile** compares two unlike things, using a specific word of comparison such as *like* or *as:* The sleeping calico cat is *like* a cushion. A **metaphor** directly compares two unlike things without the use of a specific word of comparison: The sleeping calico cat *is* a cushion. Write your own simile and metaphor for an animal you admire.

Latin Roots The word *omnipotent* from "I Like to See It Lap the Miles" means "all-powerful." It comes from two Latin words: *omnis,* which means "all," and *potens,* which means "to be able." If you know that the Latin word *sciens* means "to know," what do you think the word *omniscient* means?

Learn It Online
See a good reader in action, and practice your own skills, at:

go.hrw.com   L7-659   **Go**

Learn It Online
Learn more about the author at:
go.hrw.com L7-660 Go

Emily Dickinson
(1830–1886)

An American Original

Today Emily Dickinson is regarded as one of America's greatest poets. During her lifetime, however, she was anything but famous. Only seven of her poems were published while she was alive—and she refused to have her name put on any of them. After a sociable childhood and adolescence, Dickinson seemed to retreat from the world. By the time she was forty, she rarely left her family's house in Amherst, Massachusetts.

After Emily Dickinson died, her sister discovered in a locked box seven or eight hundred poems written on envelopes, paper bags, and scraps of paper, many neatly sewn into little packets. It looked as if the poet had been hoping someone would find the poems and publish them. Yet in her lifetime no one had really understood what poetry meant to Emily Dickinson. The quote below reveals her <u>vision</u> of poetry.

"If I read a book, and it makes my whole body so cold no fire can ever warm me, I know that is poetry. If I feel physically as if the top of my head were taken off, I know that is poetry. These are the only ways I know it. Is there any other way?"

© The Granger Collection, New York.

Think About the Writer

What makes Dickinson an "American original"?

Build Background

The artist Andy Warhol once said "In the future everyone will be world-famous for fifteen minutes." Think about the benefits and drawbacks of being famous. Keep them in mind as you read "I'm Nobody!"

Before the coming of the railroad, people depended on horses to take them where they wanted to go. When Dickinson was young, trains were still so new that people often called them "iron horses." Dickinson takes this analogy and "runs with it," so to speak.

The "Merchants Limited" all-pullman luxury train of the New Haven Railroad at speed south of Boston, 1937. (Color Lithograph).

Preview the Selections

Unlike many nineteenth-century poets, Emily Dickinson experimented with the <u>structure</u> of poetry and did not use regular rhymes and rhythms. She is famous for using the dash—and for choosing strong images to express her bold ideas.

Read with a Purpose Read to discover how the speaker of the poem feels about being a "Nobody."

Senecio (1922) by Paul Klee. Oil on gauze on cardboard (40.5 cm × 38 cm).

© 2009 Artists Rights Society (ARS), VG Bild-Kunst, Bonn

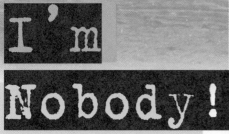

by **Emily Dickinson**

I'm Nobody! Who are you?
Are you Nobody too?
Then there's a pair of us!
Don't tell! they'd banish us, you know! **A**

How dreary to be Somebody!
How public—like a Frog—
To tell your name the livelong June
To an admiring Bog! **B**

A **Read and Discuss** What has the poet told you so far?

B **Literary Focus** **Figures of Speech** To what does the speaker compare a "somebody"?

The Railway Next to the Sea at Sunset (1955) by Nicolas de Stael (1914–1955). Oil on canvas.

Analyzing Visuals   **Viewing and Interpreting**   Like Dickinson's poem, the artwork above can be interpreted in more than one way. Explain what you see when you look at the painting.

Read with a Purpose Read to discover the many ways the author compares a train's movements to those of a horse.

I Like to See It Lap the Miles

by **Emily Dickinson**

2009 Artists Rights Society (ARS), New York/ADAGP, Paris

I like to see it lap the Miles—
And lick the Valleys up—
And stop to feed itself at Tanks—
And then—prodigious° step

5 Around a Pile of Mountains—
And supercilious° peer
In Shanties—by the sides of Roads—
And then a Quarry pare **A**

To fit its sides
10 And crawl between
Complaining all the while
In horrid—hooting stanza—
Then chase itself down Hill—

And neigh like Boanerges°—
15 Then—prompter than a Star
Stop—docile and omnipotent
At its own stable door— **B**

4. prodigious (pruh DIHJ uhs): enormous.

6. supercilious (soo puhr SIHL ee uhs): haughty; stuck-up.

14. Boanerges (boh uh NUR jeez): biblical name meaning "sons of thunder." In Dickinson's time Boanerges had come to mean a preacher who gave thunderous sermons.

A **Literary Focus** Extended Metaphor In what ways is a horse like a train?

B **Read and Discuss** What does the poet seem to be describing?

Applying Your Skills

I'm Nobody! / I Like to See It Lap the Miles

Respond and Think Critically

Reading Focus

Read with a Purpose

1. How does the speaker of the first poem feel about being a "Nobody"?
2. Do you think the second poem successfully compares a train to a horse? Explain, citing examples from the poem.

Reading Skills: Questioning the Text

3. Review the questions you had about each poem. Write the answers as well as any additional questions on a chart like the one below.

Questions	Answers	Additional Questions
Why is it dreary to be "Somebody"?	It's dreary because people bother you if you are "Somebody."	What does it mean to be "Somebody" today?

Literary Focus

Literary Analysis

4. **Interpret** Who are "they" in line 4 of "I'm Nobody"? Why would "they" banish the speaker?
5. **Interpret** Dickinson talks about what it's like to be "Nobody" and what it's like to be "Somebody." What <u>comment</u> does she make on which she would rather be?
6. **Evaluate** What <u>vision</u> is Dickinson trying to communicate in "I Like to See It Lap the Miles"? How do you think Dickinson feels about this train?

Literary Skills: Figures of Speech

7. **Analyze** The simile in the second stanza of "I'm Nobody" compares a celebrity to a frog. How can a frog and a celebrity be similar? Is this a flattering comparison? Explain.
8. **Interpret** Although Dickinson uses an extended metaphor in "I Like to See It Lap the Miles," she never directly states which things she is comparing. What clues in the poem tell you that she is writing about a train and comparing it to a horse? Explain.

Literary Skills Review: Mood

9. **Interpret** The overall emotion in a work of literature is called **mood.** It is created by images that convey a particular feeling. How would you describe the mood of "I'm Nobody!"? How would you describe the mood of "I Like to See It Lap the Miles"?

Writing Focus

Think as a Reader/Writer

Use It in Your Writing Now it's your turn to come up with an extended metaphor. Choose a mechanical object (vacuum cleaner, lawn mower, and so on), and write a brief poem comparing it to something living. Try to keep the mechanical object unnamed. Hint at the identity of your mystery item by including the sounds, smells, feel, appearance, and actions of your object.

What Do You Think Now

Explain the emotions you think Dickinson wants you to feel when you read these poems.

POETRY
Preparing to Read

Madam and the Rent Man / Harlem Night Song / Winter Moon

Literary Focus

Tone Has anyone ever said to you, "Don't use that tone of voice with me"? Your tone can change the meaning of what you say. Tone can turn a statement such as "You're a big help" into a genuine compliment or a sarcastic remark. (Sarcasm [SAHR kaz uhm] is a way of speaking or writing in which your tone expresses the opposite of what you actually mean.)

In poems and stories, writers convey their **tone,** or attitude toward a subject, by their choice of words and details. As you read "Madam and the Rent Man," think about the writer's attitude toward his no-nonsense speaker. Use a chart like the one below to explain how the same comment can take on different tones. The first example has been completed for you.

Comment	Tone 1	Tone 2
"Thanks a lot!"	genuine compliment	sarcastic remark when someone is not helpful

Imagery Language that appeals to the senses is called **imagery**. When you read about a rose, you may *smell* its pleasing scent and *see* its bright color. You might *feel* its thorn prick you. Poets hope their imagery will unlock storehouses of memory and stir our imaginations. They hope their images will make us say, "Oh yes, I see what you mean."

Writing Focus

Think as a Reader/Writer

Find It in Your Reading Look for sensory images in "Madam and the Rent Man," "Harlem Night Song," and "Winter Moon." Explain which of your senses—sight, hearing, touch, taste, smell—the images appeal to. Find one image for each of the five senses.

Reader/Writer Notebook

Use your **RWN** to complete the activities for these selections.

Language Coach

Idioms Some expressions don't make sense even when you know the meaning of each individual word. For example, "pass the buck" may not be easy for you to understand even though you know the words *pass, the,* and *buck.* "Pass the buck" is an **idiom,** a commonly used expression that is not literally true. It means "to pass responsibility to someone else." You encounter idioms frequently when you read, and you probably use them yourself. For example, if you say you're going to pass your math test "with flying colors," what do you really mean?

Learn It Online
Hear a professional actor read these poems. Visit the selection online at:

| go.hrw.com | L7-665 | Go |

Learn It Online
Get more on the author's life at:
go.hrw.com L7-666 Go

Langston Hughes
(1902–1967)

Singing the Music of Poetry

Langston Hughes was one of the first African American writers to win worldwide favor. Still, he never lost his popularity with the people he wrote about. Hughes once said:

> "I knew only the people I had grown up with, and they weren't people whose shoes were always shined, who had been to Harvard, or who had heard of Bach."

Hughes was born in Joplin, Missouri. He wrote his first poem in elementary school *after* he was elected class poet. The position inspired him to write and to reveal his gift as a poet.

As an adult, Hughes worked many different jobs in various cities while writing poetry in his spare time. For two years he worked as a busboy at a hotel in Washington, D.C. During this time he wrote many poems, among them blues poems, which he would make up in his head and sing on his way to work.

Hughes became a major literary figure in what is now known as the Harlem Renaissance of the 1920s. His poems often echo the rhythms of blues and jazz music.

Think About the Writer Based on what you've read, what kinds of images do you expect to find in Hughes's poetry?

Build Background

"Madam and the Rent Man" is set in Harlem, a section of New York City where many people live in rented apartments.

Preview the Selections

In "Madam and the Rent Man," the speaker is **the renter,** a woman who has reason to be angry with **her landlord** and with the landlord's agent, **an employee** who has come to collect the rent.

"Harlem Night Song" and "Winter Moon" paint pictures of a night in the city with a loved one and of a beautiful winter moon.

Read with a Purpose Read this poem to discover what happens when an angry tenant confronts the landlord's rent collector.

MADAM AND THE RENT MAN

by
Langston Hughes

The Apartment by Jacob Lawrence (1917–2000).

The rent man knocked.
He said, Howdy-do?
I said, What
Can I do for you?
5   He said, You know
Your rent is due.

I said, Listen,
Before I'd pay
I'd go to Hades°
10 And rot away! Ⓐ

The sink is broke,
The water don't run,
And you ain't done a thing
You promised to've done.

15 Back window's cracked,
Kitchen floor squeaks,
There's rats in the cellar,
And the attic leaks.

He said, Madam,
20 It's not up to me.
I'm just the agent,
Don't you see?

I said, Naturally,
You pass the buck.
25 If it's money you want
You're out of luck. Ⓑ

He said, Madam,
I ain't pleased!
I said, Neither am I.

30 So we agrees!

---

9. Hades (HAY deez): in Greek mythology, the underworld, or world of the dead.

Ⓐ **Read and Discuss** What has the speaker told you so far?

Ⓑ **Read and Discuss** How does this new information connect with what you already know?

HARLEM NIGHT SONG

by **Langston Hughes**

Come,
Let us roam° the night together
Singing.

I love you.

5   Across
The Harlem roof-tops
Moon is shining.
Night sky is blue.
Stars are great drops
10   Of golden dew. Ⓐ

Down the street
A band is playing.

I love you.

Come,
15   Let us roam the night together
Singing. Ⓑ

---

2. roam (rohm): wander.

Ⓐ **Literary Focus** Imagery What picture of the night sky and the moon do you get from these words?

Ⓑ **Read and Discuss** What is the importance of the word *singing*?

668

Winter Moon

by **Langston Hughes**

How thin and sharp is the moon tonight!
How thin and sharp and ghostly white **Ⓐ**
Is the slim curved crook of the moon tonight! **Ⓑ**

Ⓐ **Literary Focus** Imagery How do you picture this moon?
Ⓑ **Read and Discuss** What mood does the poet create with this poem?

The Harlem Renaissance

Langston Hughes is among the African American writers, musicians, artists, and performers who were part of the Harlem Renaissance. A "renaissance" is a rebirth or revival of culture. The Harlem Renaissance was a blossoming of African American culture that developed in New York City's Harlem neighborhood in the 1920s and early 1930s. It was primarily a literary movement, but it also encompassed music, art, and theater. Other well-known contributors to the Harlem Renaissance include the novelist Zora Neale Hurston and jazz musician Duke Ellington.

Ask Yourself
Based on what you know about Hughes, why do you think he is an important figure in the Harlem Renaissance?

Applying Your Skills

Madam and the Rent Man / Harlem Night Song / Winter Moon

Respond and Think Critically

Reading Focus

Read with a Purpose

1. The rent man and Madam seem to disagree throughout the poem. Yet, the last line is "So we agrees!" How can that be?

2. How do the descriptions of the night and the moon in "Harlem Night Song" differ from the descriptions in "Winter Moon"?

Literary Focus

Literary Analysis

3. **Infer** What do you think is the message of "Madam and the Rent Man"?

4. **Compare and Contrast** What different views of life in Harlem does Hughes present in "Madam and the Rent Man" and "Harlem Night Song"?

5. **Analyze** How does "Winter Moon" demonstrate the power of poetry to express emotions in only a few words?

Literary Skills: Tone and Imagery

6. **Analyze** How does the author's use of playful language and dialogue affect the tone of "Madam and the Rent Man"?

7. **Analyze** Poems, like songs, often repeat lines, stanzas, or words. What sentences are repeated in "Harlem Night Song"? Describe the tone you hear in these lines.

8. **Interpret** Explain the sensory images in "Harlem Night Song."

9. **Infer** What do the images in "Harlem Night Song" reveal about the speaker?

10. **Connect** Visualize the moon in "Winter Moon." What words in particular help you visualize the moon?

Literary Skills Review: Mood

11. **Interpret** How do poets create mood and evoke emotion by the words they choose? Cite examples from "Madam and the Rent Man," "Harlem Night Song," and Winter Moon" in your response.

Writing Focus

Think as a Reader/Writer

Use It in Your Writing Write two paragraphs that compare and contrast the images in "Harlem Night Song" and "Winter Moon." Which images are most powerful? Which senses do the images appeal to? Be sure to include examples to support your analysis.

What Do **You Think Now** What aspect of nature might you write about in a poem? Why?

Preparing to Read

The Highwayman

SKILLS FOCUS **Literary Skills** Understand narrative poems. **Reading Skills** Re-read to enhance comprehension of text.

Reader/Writer Notebook

Use your **RWN** to complete the activities for this selection.

Literary Focus

Narrative Poems Poems that are written to tell a story are called **narrative poems**. These story poems resemble short stories: They have a plot, characters, and a setting. Modern narrative poems such as this one use rhythms to make their stories sound like old sung stories—they capture the power of the spoken word.

Literary Perspectives Apply the literary perspective described on page 673 as you read this poem.

Language Coach

Onomatopoeia This long strange-looking word is pronounced like this: ahn uh maht uh PEE uh. Onomatopoeia is the use of a word whose sound imitates or suggests its meaning.

Say these words and think about how their sound echoes their meaning: *Crash, bang, boom,* and *toot.* Look for more examples of onomatopoeia, such as *clattered* and *sniggering,* as you read the poem.

Reading Focus

Re-reading As you read, pause at the end of each stanza. Ask yourself if you understand everything that has happened so far. If your answer is no, re-read the sections you found difficult.

Into Action As you read, record your questions on a graphic organizer like this one.

Tips for Re-reading

Here are some ways re-reading can help improve your understanding:

- Stop and take reading notes whenever the setting changes.
- Re-read stanzas aloud.
- Use reference aids, such as footnotes and dictionaries.
- Ask questions. Look for clues with your classmates and teacher.

Questions about "The Highwayman"

Characters	1. What motivates Tim's behavior?
Setting	1. How can Tim hear Bess and the highwayman? 2.
Plot	1. What do the soldiers do to Bess and the highwayman? 2.
Vocabulary	1. What are "breeches"?

Writing Focus

Think as a Reader/Writer

Find It In Your Reading As you read this narrative poem, identify its plot <u>structure</u>—the basic situation, conflict, complications, climax, and resolution.

Learn It Online
Listen to this narrative poem come alive online:

go.hrw.com   L7-671   (Go)

Alfred Noyes
(1880–1958)

A Popular Poet
The British poet, novelist, biographer, and essayist **Alfred Noyes** was often called the most popular writer of his time. People enjoyed his verse for its rousing storytelling and its thumping rhythms—in fact, his work was often performed aloud.

"The Highwayman"
Today Noyes is best remembered for "The Highwayman," which he wrote in a small cottage on the edge of Bagshot Heath shortly after leaving Oxford University. He recalled:

"Bagshot Heath in those days was a wild bit of country, all heather and pinewoods. 'The Highwayman' suggested itself to me one blustery night when the sound of the wind in the pines gave me the first line: 'The wind was a torrent of darkness among the gusty trees. . . .'

It took me about two days to complete the poem. Shortly afterward it appeared in *Blackwood's Magazine*. It illustrates the unpredictable chances of authorship, that this poem, written in so short a time, when I was twenty-four, should have been read so widely."

Think About the Writer — How do you think Noyes's writing was affected by his being in the "wild bit of country"?

© The Granger Collection, New York.

Build Background
The highwayman in this famous poem is a robber who lived in England in the 1700s. Highwaymen stopped stagecoaches on the lonely moorlands of northern England and Scotland to rob the rich passengers of money and jewels. Some highwaymen were considered heroes by the Scots because they shared the money with the poor. Highwaymen were often dashing, romantic figures who dressed in expensive clothes. This poem is based on a true story that the poet heard while he was on vacation in that part of England where highwaymen used to lie in wait for stagecoaches.

© The Granger Collection, New York.

Dick Turpin (1706–1739). English robber, lithograph, English, 19th Century.

Preview the Selection
In this narrative poem, a daring and dashing **robber** (the highwayman) visits a beautiful young woman named **Bess** at an inn. As they plan to meet each other again, a stableman named **Tim** listens jealously. When a group of cruel soldiers arrives, Bess makes a fateful decision.

The Highwayman

by **Alfred Noyes**

Landscape with Effect of Moonlight by Jules César Denis van Loo (1743–1821).

Part 1

The wind was a torrent of darkness
    among the gusty trees,
The moon was a ghostly galleon°
    tossed upon cloudy seas,
The road was a ribbon of moonlight
    over the purple moor,
And the highwayman came riding—
5   Riding—riding—
The highwayman came riding, up to
    the old inn door. **Ⓐ**

---

2. galleon (GAL ee uhn): large sailing ship.

Ⓐ **Literary Focus** **Narrative Poems** What do you learn about the setting in the first stanza?

He'd a French cocked hat on his forehead, a bunch of lace at his chin,
A coat of the claret° velvet, and breeches of brown doeskin.
They fitted with never a wrinkle. His boots were up to the thigh.
10 And he rode with a jeweled twinkle,
       His pistol butts a-twinkle,
His rapier hilt° a-twinkle, under the jeweled sky.

Over the cobbles he clattered and clashed in the dark inn yard.
And he tapped with his whip on the shutters, but all was locked and barred.
15 He whistled a tune to the window, and who should be waiting there
But the landlord's black-eyed daughter,
       Bess, the landlord's daughter,
Plaiting° a dark red love knot into her long black hair.   **B**

And dark in the dark old inn yard a stable wicket° creaked
20 Where Tim the ostler° listened. His face was white and peaked.
His eyes were hollows of madness, his hair like moldy hay,
But he loved the landlord's daughter,
       The landlord's red-lipped daughter,
Dumb as a dog he listened, and he heard the robber say—   **C**

---

8. **claret** (KLAR uht): purplish red, like claret wine.

12. **rapier** (RAY pee uhr) **hilt:** sword handle.

18. **plaiting** (PLAYT ihng): braiding.

19. **wicket** (WIHK iht): small door or gate.

20. **ostler:** (AHS luhr): person who takes care of horses.

B **Read and Discuss** What has the poet set up so far?

C **Literary Perspectives** Analyzing Responses to Literature Identify at least two figures of speech that describe Tim. What impression do they create?

By the Window by Martin Drolling (1752–1817).

25 "One kiss, my bonny sweetheart, I'm after a prize tonight,
But I shall be back with the yellow gold before the morning light;
Yet, if they press me sharply, and harry° me through the day,
Then look for me by moonlight,
        Watch for me by moonlight,
30 I'll come to thee by moonlight, though hell should bar the way."

He rose upright in the stirrups. He scarce could reach her hand,
But she loosened her hair in the casement.° His face burnt like a brand
As the black cascade of perfume came tumbling over his breast;
And he kissed its waves in the moonlight,
35   (Oh, sweet black waves in the moonlight!)
Then he tugged at his rein in the moonlight, and galloped away to the west.   **D**

Part 2
He did not come in the dawning. He did not come at noon;
And out of the tawny sunset, before the rise of the moon,
When the road was a gypsy's ribbon, looping the purple moor,
40 A redcoat troop came marching—
        Marching—marching—
King George's men came marching, up to the old inn door.

They said no word to the landlord. They drank his ale instead.
But they gagged his daughter, and bound her, to the foot of her narrow bed.
45 Two of them knelt at her casement, with muskets at their side!
There was death at every window;
        And hell at one dark window;
For Bess could see, through her casement, the road that *he* would ride.   **E**

---

27. harry (HAR ee): harass or push along.

32. casement: (KAYS muhnt) window that opens out-
ward on hinges.

D Literary Perspectives **Analyzing Responses to Literature** Explain
whether you feel the character of the highwayman is believable or unrealistic.

E Literary Focus **Narrative Poems** What is happening in the plot?
Why do you think the redcoats are making trouble for Bess?

Viewing and Interpreting How does the mood of the painting reflect the mood of the poem?

A Moonlit Lane, with two lovers by a gate by John Atkinson Grimshaw (1836–1893).

They had tied her up to attention, with many a sniggering jest;
50 They had bound a musket beside her, with the muzzle beneath her breast!
"Now, keep good watch!" and they kissed her. She heard the dead man say—
Look for me by moonlight;
  Watch for me by moonlight;
I'll come to thee by moonlight, though hell should bar the way!

55 She twisted her hands behind her; but all the knots held good!
She writhed her hands till her fingers were wet with sweat or blood!
They stretched and strained in the darkness, and the hours crawled by like years,
Till, now, on the stroke of midnight,
  Cold, on the stroke of midnight,
60 The tip of one finger touched it! The trigger at least was hers!

F **Literary Perspectives** Analyzing Responses to Literature Who is the "dead man"? How do these events and descriptions increase suspense?

The tip of one finger touched it; she strove no more for the rest!
Up, she stood up to attention, with the muzzle beneath her breast.
She would not risk their hearing; she would not strive again;
For the road lay bare in the moonlight;
65   Blank and bare in the moonlight;
And the blood of her veins, in the moonlight, throbbed to her love's refrain.   **Ⓖ**

Tlot-tlot; tlot-tlot! Had they heard it? The horse hoofs ringing clear;
Tlot-tlot, tlot-tlot, in the distance? Were they deaf that they did not hear?
Down the ribbon of moonlight, over the brow of the hill,
70 The highwayman came riding,
      Riding, riding!
The redcoats looked to their priming!° She stood up, straight and still.

Tlot-tlot, in the frosty silence! *Tlot-tlot,* in the echoing night!
Nearer he came and nearer. Her face was like a light!
75 Her eyes grew wide for a moment; she drew one last deep breath,
Then her fingers moved in the moonlight,
      Her musket shattered the moonlight,
Shattered her breast in the moonlight and warned him—with her death.   **Ⓗ**

He turned. He spurred to the west; he did not know who stood
80 Bowed, with her head o'er the musket, drenched with her own blood!
Not till the dawn he heard it, his face grew gray to hear
How Bess, the landlord's daughter,
      The landlord's black-eyed daughter,
Had watched for her love in the moonlight, and died in the darkness there.

---

72. priming: (PRYM ihng): explosive for firing a gun.

Ⓖ | Read and Discuss | What is Bess doing?

Ⓗ | Reading Focus | **Re-reading** What has just happened? Re-read the
stanza if you're not sure.

85 Back, he spurred like a madman, shouting a curse to the sky,
With the white road smoking behind him and his rapier brandished high.
Blood-red were his spurs in the golden noon; wine-red was his velvet coat;
When they shot him down on the highway,
     Down like a dog on the highway,
90 And he lay in his blood on the highway, with the bunch of lace at his throat. **Ⅰ**

And still of a winter's night, they say, when the wind is in the trees,
When the moon is a ghostly galleon tossed upon cloudy seas,
When the road is a ribbon of moonlight over the purple moor,
A highwayman comes riding—
95   *Riding—riding—*
A highwayman comes riding, up to the old inn door.

Over the cobbles he clatters and clangs in the dark inn yard;
He taps with his whip on the shutters, but all is locked and barred.
He whistles a tune to the window, and who should be waiting there
100 *But the landlord's black-eyed daughter,*
    Bess, the landlord's daughter,
Plaiting a dark red love knot into her long black hair. **Ｊ**

Ⅰ **Reading Focus** Re-reading What does the highwayman do when he learns that Bess has died? What happens to him?

Ｊ **Literary Focus** Narrative Poems What is going on in these last two stanzas?

A Hilly Scene (c. 1826–1828)
by Samuel Palmer.

Applying Your Skills

The Highwayman

Respond and Think Critically

Reading Focus

Read with a Purpose

1. Who is Bess? What happens to her?

Reading Skills: Re-reading

2. Review the questions you wrote while reading the poem. Then, re-read the poem to find the answers. You may also discuss your questions with a classmate or your teacher. Finally, add a third column, and fill in your answers.

Questions about "The Highwayman"

Characters	1. What motivates Tim's behavior? 2.	

Literary Focus

Literary Analysis

3. Interpret Bess gives up her life because of her love for the highwayman. In your opinion, is her sacrifice noble or pointless? Explain.

4. Interpret What is Tim the ostler's **motivation,** or reason, for betraying Bess?

5. Interpret Why do you think the highwayman comes back to the inn after he hears how Bess dies?

6. Interpret This poem is about love, betrayal, and death. What **theme,** or message about people and life, does the poem reveal to you?

7. Infer How do you think the narrator feels about the highwayman? How can you tell? How do *you* feel about him?

8. Literary Perspectives A critic described Noyes as "one of the most melodious of modern writers, with a witchery in words that at its best is irresistible." Discuss whether you agree with this statement, citing details and literary elements from the poem in your response.

Literary Skills: Narrative Poems

9. Analyze The last two stanzas are very much like the first and third stanzas. The wording, however, is slightly different. How does the difference reflect what happens at the end of the poem?

Literary Skills Review: Setting

10. Analyze What is the **setting** of this poem? What details help you to see and hear what is happening?

Writing Focus

Think as a Reader/Writer

Use It in Your Writing If you could write a new ending for the poem, what would it be? Write your ending in a paragraph. Does your ending alter the plot of this narrative poem?

What Do
You Think Now Why would a narrative be a good form for a poem about love?

Applying Your Skills

The Highwayman

Vocabulary Development
Metaphor and Simile

In our everyday language we use many expressions that are not literally true: "Joe's bragging gets under my skin." When we use an expression like this one, we are using a **figure of speech.** The meaning of a figurative expression depends on a comparison. In our example, bragging is *compared* to something that causes annoyance.

There are many kinds of figures of speech; the most common are **similes** and **metaphors.** A **simile** is a comparison of two unlike things using the word *like, as, than,* or *resembles.* Here is a famous simile by William Wordsworth: "I wandered lonely as a cloud. . ." A **metaphor** also compares two unlike things, but it does so without using *like, as, than,* or *resembles.* For example, in "The Highwayman," Alfred Noyes says, "The moon *was* a ghostly galleon tossed upon cloudy seas."

Your Turn

Fill in a chart like the one below by completing each comparison from "The Highwayman." Then, identify each comparison as a simile or metaphor.

Figures of Speech

line 1: The wind is compared to a torrent of darkness.

line 3: The road is compared to

line 12: The stars in the sky are compared to

line 21: Tim's hair is compared to

CHOICES

As you respond to the Choices, use these **Academic Vocabulary** words as appropriate: <u>vision</u>, <u>structure</u>, <u>tradition</u>, <u>comment</u>.

REVIEW
Write a Summary and Response
Timed ⌐Writing Write two paragraphs about "The Highwayman." First, summarize the plot by describing the story's conflict, climax and resolution. In the second paragraph, tell how the poem affected you.

CONNECT
Write a Character Analysis
Write a character analysis of Tim the groom. First, discuss the role he played in the story. Then, discuss his motivation. Provide evidence that supports your reason why Tim behaves the way he does. Finally, discuss what Tim could have done to change the events of the poem.

EXTEND
Create a Storyboard
Partner Work Working with a partner, create a storyboard for the film version of this poem. Illustrate the <u>structure</u> of the narrative and the important changes of scene and action. Put a quotation from the poem under each sketch.

Learn It Online
Find a storyboard template at the Digital Storytelling site:

go.hrw.com | L7-680 | **Go**

Preparing to Read

I Ask My Mother to Sing /
Ode to Family Photographs

Reader/Writer
Notebook

Use your **RWN** to complete the activities for these selections.

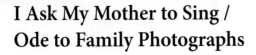

Literary Focus

Lyric Poem There are two basic types of poems: A **narrative poem** tells a story, and a **lyric poem** expresses an emotion. In ancient Greece, lyric poems were sung to the music of a stringed instrument called a lyre. Lyric poems come in many shapes and sizes and express a wide range of emotions.

Sonnet Li-Young Lee's "I Ask My Mother to Sing" is a sonnet. A **sonnet** is a lyric poem of fourteen lines. There are several types of sonnets. In the type of sonnet that Lee wrote, the lines are divided into three quatrains (a quatrain is four lines of verse). Each quatrain focuses on one aspect of a subject. The sonnet ends with a couplet (two lines that usually rhyme). As you will see, Lee varies this structure a bit.

Ode An **ode** is a poem that pays tribute to someone or something of great importance to the poet. The first odes, written in honor of famous people, were long, complex, and elegant. Over the centuries, odes have been written in a formal style to praise lofty subjects, such as beauty, joy, and freedom. Today's odes tend to be more informal. Some are even humorous. Many have been written about everyday objects, such as tomatoes, frogs, and socks. Gary Soto's ode celebrates something most people have in their homes—family photos.

Language Coach

Sensory Language Writing that creates a clear image and appeals to the senses of touch, sight, smell, taste, or hearing is called **sensory language.** Writers use sensory language to help you imagine characters, places, and events. You encounter sensory language in all forms of fiction, nonfiction, and poetry.

As you read "I Ask My Mother to Sing" and "Ode to Family Photographs," notice that the poets use images that appeal to several senses at once. In these poems, how does sensory language also reveal how the writers feel about their subject?

Writing Focus

Think as a Reader/Writer

Find It in Your Reading As you read "Ode to Family Photographs," note that the speaker's important memories are inspired by everyday items and events.

Learn It Online
Learn more about Li-Young Lee with these Internet links:

go.hrw.com L7-681 **Go**

Learn It Online
Get more on Soto's life at:
go.hrw.com   L7-682   Go

Li-Young Lee
(1957–   )

Li-Young Lee once made the following comment:

> "I think immigrants have beautiful stories to tell. But the problem is to make art out of it."

Lee succeeded in using art to tell his family's story in the award-winning memoir *The Winged Seed: A Remembrance.* An important part of the narrative is based in Jakarta, Indonesia, Lee's birthplace. His family had moved to Indonesia from China, where Lee's father had been the Communist leader Mao Tse-tung's physician. The family was forced to flee Indonesia in 1959. After spending time in Hong Kong and Japan, the family settled in the United States in 1964.

Gary Soto
(1952–   )

Gary Soto first discovered poetry in college, where he had originally planned to major in geography:

> "I know the day the change began, because it was when I discovered in the library a collection of poems . . . called *The New American Poetry.* . . . I discovered this poetry and thought, 'This is terrific: I'd like to do something like this.' So I proceeded to write my own poetry, first alone, and them moving on to take classes."

Soto's award-winning fiction and poetry are loved by readers of all ages.

Think About the Writers

Lee and Soto both write poems about their families. Why do you think each writer might have made such a choice?

Build Background

Li-Young Lee's mother was a member of the Chinese royal family. His family fled China when the Communists took control of the country. The Summer Palace is the compound to which the royal family would go to escape the heat. The palace is located in the hills outside the capital city of Peking (now called Beijing) and consists of many beautiful buildings situated around Kuen Ming Lake. One of these buildings is a large teahouse made of stone in the shape of a boat. When an emperor ruled China, the palace was visited only by the royal family and its attendants. Today it is a museum, open to tourists from around the world.

Preview the Selections

In "I Ask My Mother to Sing," you will meet the speaker's **mother** and **grandmother.** Note the mixture of sweet and melancholy images in the poem.

In "Ode to Family Photographs," you will meet a **speaker** reminiscing about his family, particularly his **mother,** as he looks at photographs from his childhood.

I Ask My Mother to Sing

by **Li-Young Lee**

She begins, and my grandmother joins her.
Mother and daughter sing like young girls.
If my father were alive, he would play
his accordion and sway like a boat. **A**

5 I've never been in Peking, or the Summer Palace,
nor stood on the great Stone Boat to watch
the rain begin on Kuen Ming Lake, the picnickers
running away in the grass.

But I love to hear it sung;
10 how the waterlilies fill with rain until
they overturn, spilling water into water,
then rock back, and fill with more.

Both women have begun to cry.
But neither stops her song. **B**

A **Literary Focus** **Sonnet** How can you tell from this stanza that
this poem may be a sonnet?

B **Read and Discuss** What can you infer
from the actions of the women?

Summer Palace, Beijing China.

Ode to Family Photographs

by **Gary Soto**

This is the pond, and these are my feet.
This is the rooster, and this is more of my feet.

Mamá was never good at pictures.

This is a statue of a famous general who lost an arm,
5 And this is me with my head cut off.

This is a trash can chained to a gate,
This is my father with his eyes half-closed.

This is a photograph of my sister
And a giraffe looking over her shoulder.   **Ⓐ**

10 This is our car's front bumper.
This is a bird with a pretzel in its beak.
This is my brother Pedro standing on one leg on a rock,
With a smear of chocolate on his face.

Mamá sneezed when she looked
15 *Behind the camera: the snapshots are blurry,*
The angles dizzy as a spin on a merry-go-round.

But we had fun when Mamá picked up the camera.
How can I tell?
Each of us laughing hard.
20 Can you see? I have candy in my mouth.   **Ⓑ**

Ⓐ **Read and Discuss** What have you learned about the speaker's family so far?

Ⓑ **Literary Focus** Lyric Poems You know that lyric poems express emotions. What emotion is the author expressing in this poem?

Applying Your Skills

I Ask My Mother to Sing /
Ode to Family Photographs

Respond and Think Critically

Reading Focus

Read with a Purpose

1. What details make China seem close to home in "I Ask My Mother to Sing"? List at least three.

2. List two examples of humor in "Ode to Family Photographs."

Literary Focus

Literary Analysis

3. **Infer** In "I Ask My Mother to Sing," the speaker speaks about the songs of his mother and grandmother's Chinese heritage. What is left unsaid?

4. **Interpret** How does the speaker of "Ode to Family Photographs" feel about his family? Support your response with details from the text.

Literary Skills: Lyric Poems, Sonnets, Odes

5. **Interpret** A **lyric poem** expresses the speaker's thoughts and feelings. How does the speaker in "I Ask My Mother to Sing" react to the song his mother and grandmother sing?

6. **Summarize** Take a look at how Li-Young Lee fits his thoughts into the <u>structure</u> of a sonnet. What is the topic of each of the first three quatrains? How do the last two lines convey the poem's message?

7. **Interpret** **Odes** are written in praise of something. What do you think this poem is praising? (Hint: It's not just family photographs.)

Literary Skills Review: Imagery

8. **Interpret** What images do you see as the two women sing? List at least five images from "I Ask My Mother to Sing," and explain which senses the images appeal to.

9. **Visualize** Did you imagine yourself or anyone you know in Soto's pictures? (Maybe you saw yourself as the photographer.) Which images in this ode made you smile?

Writing Focus

Think as a Reader/Writer

Use It in Your Writing Write an ode celebrating something special to you. Try to convey your feelings for all aspects of your subject. For example, if you write "An Ode to a Baseball Bat," you might praise its weight, balance, and power; the way it swings through the air; how long you've had it; and how it helped you win a game. When you write your ode, you can talk directly to the reader, as Soto does, or you can talk to the object you are celebrating ("Bat, you are . . .").

What Do **You Think Now?** What surprises you about the items and events that inspire poets to express their <u>visions</u>?

Sounds of Poetry

CONTENTS

What Do **You** Think? Why is sound (or its absence) useful in expressing feeling?

 QuickTalk
Think of your favorite song. How does it affect you? Share your thoughts in a discussion.

POETRY
Preparing to Read

Father William / Sarah Cynthia Sylvia Stout Would Not Take the Garbage Out

Reader/Writer Notebook

Use your **RWN** to complete the activities for these selections.

Literary Focus

Humorous Poems Many poems are written to make you laugh—or at least smile. That doesn't mean they don't have a point to make. They just make their point with humor. One element that many humorous poems share is **exaggeration**—that is, describing something as bigger or smaller or better or worse than it really is. (Exaggeration is also called **hyperbole.**) As you read the two humorous poems that follow, notice what they exaggerate. Then ask yourself, "Were the poems written to make a serious point, or were they written just for fun?"

Rhythm In English and other languages, **rhythm** is a musical quality produced by the repetition of stressed and unstressed syllables or by the repetition of words, phrases, or even whole lines or sentences. When the stressed and unstressed syllables are arranged in a regular pattern, we call the pattern **meter.**

You can discover the meter of a line by reading it aloud and exaggerating the stressed syllables. For example, in the line *The girl is walking to the store,* you can sound out the meter like this: The GIRL is WALKing TO the STORE. You can also show the poem's meter by using accent marks—(´) over stressed syllables and (˘) over unstressed syllables. This marking is called **scanning.**

˘ ´ ˘ ´ ˘ ´ ˘ ´
The girl is walking to the store.

Notice that a regular beat is often found in ordinary speech as well as in poetry. In a poem written in meter, the meter supplies the underlying beat.

Writing Focus

Think as a Reader/Writer

Find It in Your Reading Find and record at least eight examples of exaggeration as you read "Father William" and "Sarah Cynthia Sylvia Stout Would Not Take the Garbage Out."

Vocabulary

Father William

incessantly (ihn SEHS uhnt lee) *adv.:* without ceasing; continually. *A chatty person talks incessantly.*

supple (SUHP uhl) *adj.:* easily bent; flexible. *Father William can bend his supple body to do a somersault.*

Sarah Cynthia Sylvia Stout Would Not Take the Garbage Out

withered (WIHTH uhrd) *v.* used as *adj.:* dried up. *Withered lettuce is not crunchy.*

rancid (RAN sihd) *adj.:* spoiled; rotten. *Rancid meat looks and smells awful.*

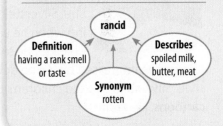

Language Coach
Adverbs Adverbs, such as *incessantly,* are used to describe verbs and adjectives. You will find many descriptive words in each of these poems. Record examples of more adverbs from "Father William" in your *Reader/Writer Notebook.*

Learn It Online
Improve your vocabulary with Word Watch:

go.hrw.com | L7-687 | Go

Lewis Carroll
(1832–1898)

"He Was One of Us"

Lewis Carroll had two separate careers. Under the pen name Lewis Carroll, he was the author of *Alice's Adventures in Wonderland* and its sequel, *Through the Looking Glass*. Under his real name, he was Reverend Charles Lutwidge Dodgson, a teacher of mathematics and a clergyman in England. In both roles, Carroll spent many days in the company of children and enjoyed writing nonsense verse and creating puzzles for them. As one of his young friends said:

> "He was one of us, and never a grown-up pretending to be a child in order to preach at us. . . ."

Shel Silverstein
(1932–1999)

"A Personal Sense of Discovery"

Shel Silverstein began drawing and writing when he was a boy growing up in Chicago. He said he "didn't have anyone to copy, be impressed by," so he developed his own unique style. Silverstein created children's books, poems, songs, and cartoons. He said:

> "I would hope that people, no matter what age, would find something to identify with in my books, pick one up and experience a personal sense of discovery."

Think About the Writers
Carroll and Silverstein are both known for their lively, humorous verse. How easy do you think it is to be funny?

Build Background

Once Lewis Carroll went on a picnic with three young girls, one of whom was named Alice. He told them a story about a girl named Alice, who went down a rabbit hole into a fabulous wonderland. That was the beginning of *Alice's Adventures in Wonderland,* from which "Father William" is taken. "Sarah Cynthia Sylvia Stout Would Not Take the Garbage Out" is from *Where the Sidewalk Ends,* Shel Silverstein's first collection of poetry for children. In the poem, "Golden Gate" refers to the Golden Gate Bridge in San Francisco, California.

Preview the Selections

"Father William" is a conversation between **Father William** and his **son.** The son has questions for his father, and Father William is ready with answers.

In "Sarah Cynthia Sylvia Stout Would Not Take the Garbage Out," **Sarah Cynthia Sylvia Stout** learns why it's important to *always* take the garbage out!

Read with a Purpose Read the poem to find out what Father William's son wants to know.

FATHER WILLIAM

by **Lewis Carroll**

Illustrations on pages 689–690 by John Tenniel (1820–1914), the original illustrator of Carroll's Alice's Adventures in Wonderland.

"You are old, Father William," the young man said,
  "And your hair has become very white;
And yet you incessantly stand on your head—
  Do you think, at your age, it is right?" **A**

5 "In my youth," Father William replied to his son,
  "I feared it might injure the brain;
But now that I'm perfectly sure I have none,
  Why, I do it again and again."

A **Rhythm** Which words are stressed in this sentence? Listen for the poem's meter as you continue reading.

Vocabulary **incessantly** (ihn SEHS uhnt lee) *adv.:* without ceasing; continually.

"You are old," said the youth, "as I mentioned before,
10   And have grown most uncommonly fat;
Yet you turned a back somersault in at the door—
    Pray, what is the reason of that?"

"In my youth," said the sage,° as he shook his gray locks,
    "I kept all my limbs very supple
15 By the use of this ointment—one shilling the box—
    Allow me to sell you a couple." **Ⓑ**

"You are old," said the youth, "and your jaws are too weak
    For anything tougher than suet;°
Yet you finished the goose, with the bones and the beak;
20   Pray, how did you manage to do it?"

"In my youth," said his father, "I took to the law,
    And argued each case with my wife;
And the muscular strength which it gave to my jaw,
    Has lasted the rest of my life."

25 "You are old," said the youth; "one would hardly suppose
    That your eye was as steady as ever;
Yet you balanced an eel on the end of your nose—
    What made you so awfully clever?" **Ⓒ**

"I've answered three questions, and that is enough,"
30   Said his father; "don't give yourself airs!
Do you think I can listen all day to such stuff?
    Be off, or I'll kick you downstairs!"

---

13. sage (sayj): an old, wise person.
18. suet (SOO iht): kind of fat.

Ⓑ [Read and Discuss] What is going on between Father William and his son?

Ⓒ [Literary Focus] Humorous Poems What is exaggerated in this stanza?

Vocabulary **supple** (SUHP uhl) *adj.*: easily bent; flexible.

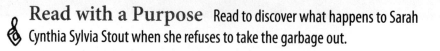

Sarah Cynthia Sylvia Stout Would Not Take the Garbage Out

by **Shel Silverstein**

Sarah Cynthia Sylvia Stout
Would not take the garbage out!
She'd scour the pots and scrape the pans,
Candy the yams and spice the hams,
5 And though her daddy would scream and shout,
She simply would not take the garbage out. **Ⓐ**
And so it piled up to the ceilings:
Coffee grounds, potato peelings,
Brown bananas, rotten peas,
10 Chunks of sour cottage cheese.
It filled the can, it covered the floor,
It cracked the window and blocked the door
With bacon rinds and chicken bones,
Drippy ends of ice cream cones,
15 Prune pits, peach pits, orange peel,
Gloppy glumps of old oatmeal,
Pizza crusts and withered greens,

Ⓐ Literary Focus **Rhythm** Which words and syllables are stressed in these lines? Listen for the rhythm of the poem as you continue reading.

Vocabulary **withered** (WIHTH uhrd) *v.* used as *adj.:* dried up.

Soggy beans and tangerines,
Crusts of black burned buttered toast,
20   Gristly bits of beefy roasts . . .
The garbage rolled on down the hall,
It raised the roof, it broke the wall . . .
Greasy napkins, cookie crumbs,
Globs of gooey bubble gum,
25   Cellophane from green baloney,
Rubbery blubbery macaroni,
Peanut butter, caked and dry,
Curdled milk and crusts of pie,
Moldy melons, dried-up mustard,
30   Eggshells mixed with lemon custard,
Cold french fries and rancid meat,
Yellow lumps of Cream of Wheat.
At last the garbage reached so high
That finally it touched the sky.
35   And all the neighbors moved away,
And none of her friends would come to play.   **B**
And finally Sarah Cynthia Stout said,
"OK, I'll take the garbage out!"
By then, of course, it was too late . . .
40   The garbage reached across the state,
From New York to the Golden Gate.   **C**
And there, in the garbage she did hate,
Poor Sarah met an awful fate,
That I cannot right now relate
45   Because the hour is much too late.
But children, remember Sarah Stout
And always take the garbage out!

B **Read and Discuss** What has the speaker told you about the people in Sarah's life?

C **Literary Focus** **Humorous Poems** What is exaggerated in the poem, and what makes it funny?

Vocabulary **rancid** (RAN sihd) *adj.:* spoiled; rotten.

Applying Your Skills

SKILLS FOCUS Literary Skills Analyze humorous poems; understand and analyze sounds of poetry, such as rhythm, rhyme, alliteration, and onomatopoeia; analyze theme. **Vocabulary Skills** Demonstrate knowledge of literal meanings of words and their usage. **Writing Skills** Write to describe.

Father William / Sarah Cynthia Sylvia Stout Would Not Take the Garbage Out

Respond and Think Critically

Reading Focus

Read with a Purpose

1. How would you describe the children in these poems?

✔ Vocabulary Check

Complete each sentence with the correct Vocabulary word.

| incessantly |
| supple |
| withered |
| rancid |

2. The _____ flowers had limp petals.
3. The noisy dog barked _____.
4. The _____ cheese attracted flies.
5. The young tree was _____ and bent in the wind.

Literary Focus

Literary Analysis

6. **Infer** When his son tells Father William, "You are old," is he being disrespectful, or does he admire his father? Explain, using examples from the poem.
7. **Interpret** In "Sarah Cynthia Sylvia Stout Would Not Take the Garbage Out," the poet says, "Poor Sarah met an awful fate, / That I cannot right now relate." What do you think that fate might be?

Literary Skills: Humor and Rhythm

8. **Evaluate** How do both poets use exaggeration to create humor? Use examples of hyperbole in your explanations.

9. **Identify** Identify the meter of "Father William." Write out a line of the poem, and use the scanning method on page 687. Do the same to show the meter in line 3 of "Sarah Cynthia Sylvia Stout Would Not Take the Garbage Out."

10. **Analyze** "Sarah Cynthia Sylvia Stout Would Not Take the Garbage Out" is full of **alliteration**—the repetition of similar consonant sounds in nearby words, as in "gloppy glumps." Find three examples of alliteration, and identify the repeated sounds.

Literary Skills Review: Theme

11. **Extend** State the theme of each poem. Do you think these poets are serious about their messages, or are they having fun? Support your response with examples from the text.

Writing Focus

Think as a Reader/Writer

Use It in Your Writing Write a humorous description of a person or an object from everyday life. Using examples of exaggeration from the poems as models, include exaggeration in your writing.

 What Do You Think Now

How did you respond to each poem? Explain how rhythm and humor contributed to your response.

POETRY
Preparing to Read

The Runaway / The Pasture / A Minor Bird

Reader/Writer Notebook

Use your **RWN** to complete the activities for these selections.

Literary Focus

Rhyme and Rhyme Scheme In a poem, words that **rhyme** often come at the ends of lines. These **end rhymes** determine the **rhyme scheme,** or pattern of rhymes. Assigning a different letter to each new end rhyme identifies the rhyme scheme. In "The Runaway" the rhyme scheme begins with *abacbc*.

Stanza and Couplet In a poem a **stanza** is a group of lines that form a unit and often express a thought. "The Pasture" has two stanzas of four lines each. "A Minor Bird" has four two-line stanzas. Each two-line stanza is a **couplet**—two consecutive lines of poetry that rhyme and express a complete thought.

> **Language Coach**
>
> **Dialogue** A conversation between two or more characters in a work of literature is called dialogue. In prose and poetry, dialogue is enclosed in quotation marks. While dialogue is common in prose, it is unusual to find a conversation between two characters in poetry. As you read "The Runaway," notice that dialogue is used to express the opinions of human characters.

Reading Focus

Reading a Poem Robert Frost writes in a conversational tone. Use a similar tone as you read his poems aloud. Here is a tip to help you read poems: *Pay attention to punctuation.*

Into Action Follow the advice on the list below as you read Frost's poems.

- Don't stop reading at the end of a line of poetry unless you see punctuation.
- Make a full stop at a period.
- Pause briefly at a comma, colon, semicolon, or dash.
- If a poem has no punctuation, do your best to figure out where to pause based on the thought groups in the poem.

Writing Focus

Think as a Reader/Writer

Find It in Your Reading Look for ways that Frost celebrates nature in his poetry. Write down the most striking nature images and rhymes in each poem.

Learn It Online
See a good reader in action, and practice your own skills, at:

| go.hrw.com | L7-695 | **Go** |

Robert Frost
(1874–1963)

Pulitzer
Prize
WINNER

"The Thought Finds the Words"

While in high school in Lawrence, Massachusetts, Robert Frost decided to become a poet. Not only did he succeed, but he was for a time America's most celebrated living poet.

He was the first poet ever to read a poem for a presidential inauguration, that of John F. Kennedy in 1961. On his seventy-fifth birthday, the U.S. Senate passed a resolution in his honor, stating, "His poems have helped to guide American thought and humor and wisdom, setting forth to our minds a reliable representation of ourselves and of all men."

"Rob" Frost lived most of his life on farms in Vermont and New Hampshire. There he grew corn, taught, and raised a family. Frost filled his poems with images of the people of New England and their barns, farmhouses, pastures, apple orchards, and woods. His work speaks to people everywhere because it springs from intense feelings.

Frost says this about poetry:

> "A poem . . . begins as a lump in the throat, a sense of wrong, a homesickness, a lovesickness. . . . It finds the thought and the thought finds the words."

Think About the Writer

What kinds of emotions inspire Robert Frost's poetry?

Build Background

The subject of "The Runaway" is a Morgan colt. Morgans are a breed of swift, strong horses named for Justin Morgan (1747–1798), a Vermont school-teacher who owned the stallion that founded the line. Morgans are small, sturdy horses that excel at weight-pulling contests. Today they are used mostly for riding and pulling carts.

In the title, "A Minor Bird," Robert Frost plays with two meanings of the word *minor*. It can mean "less important" or "lesser in rank." (Think of minor leagues in baseball.) *Minor* also refers to a type of key in music. A musical key is a sequence of related tones that form a scale. Most Western music is written in major keys. To some people, songs written in major keys sound happy. Minor keys, to the Western ear, tend to sound sad or haunting.

Preview the Selections

You can see how Robert Frost wrote about farm life and nature in these three poems:

In "The Runaway" a **young colt** experiences snow for the first time.

In "The Pasture" the **speaker** describes farm chores to be done.

In "A Minor Bird" the **speaker** is troubled by his responses to a bird's song.

Read with a Purpose Read to determine why Frost chose the title "The Runaway" and what you think it means.

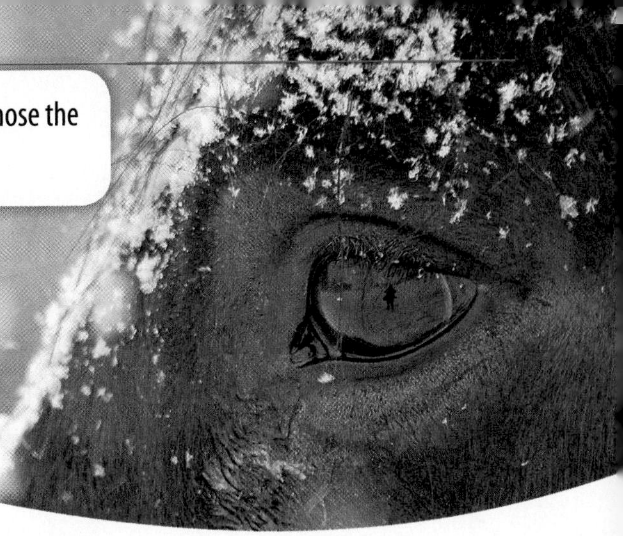

The Runaway

by **Robert Frost**

Once when the snow of the year was beginning to fall,
We stopped by a mountain pasture to say, "Whose colt?"
A little Morgan had one forefoot on the wall,
The other curled at his breast. He dipped his head
And snorted at us. And then he had to bolt.
We heard the miniature thunder where he fled, **A**
And we saw him, or thought we saw him, dim and gray,
Like a shadow against the curtain of falling flakes.
"I think the little fellow's afraid of the snow.
He isn't winter-broken.° It isn't play
With the little fellow at all. He's running away.
I doubt if even his mother could tell him, 'Sakes,
It's only weather.' He'd think she didn't know!
Where is his mother? He can't be out alone."
And now he comes again with clatter of stone,
And mounts the wall again with whited eyes
And all his tail that isn't hair up straight.
He shudders his coat as if to throw off flies.
"Whoever it is that leaves him out so late,
When other creatures have gone to stall and bin,
Ought to be told to come and take him in." **B**

---

10. winter-broken: used to winter; to break a colt is to get a young horse used to being ridden.

A **Literary Focus** **Rhyme and Rhyme Scheme** Where are the end rhymes? Is the rhyme scheme consistent throughout the poem?

B **Read and Discuss** What happens at the end of the poem?

Read with a Purpose Read to find out why
Frost thought this poem made a good starting point for a
book of poems.

The Pasture

by **Robert Frost**

I'm going out to clean the pasture spring;
I'll only stop to rake the leaves away
(And wait to watch the water clear, I may):
I shan't be gone long.—You come too.   **Ⓐ**

I'm going out to fetch the little calf
That's standing by the mother. It's so young
It totters when she licks it with her tongue.
I shan't be gone long.—You come too.   **Ⓑ**

Ⓐ **Read and Discuss** What is the poet setting up for you?

Ⓑ **Literary Focus** Stanza What thought is expressed in each
four-line stanza? Why might this be important?

A Minor Bird

by **Robert Frost**

I have wished a bird would fly away,
And not sing by my house all day;

Have clapped my hands at him from the door
When it seemed as if I could bear no more.

The fault must partly have been in me.
The bird was not to blame for his key.   **Ⓐ**

And of course there must be something wrong
In wanting to silence any song.   **Ⓑ**

Ⓐ **Reading Focus** **Reading a Poem** What should you do at the end of this line?

Ⓑ **Read and Discuss** What has the speaker learned at the end of the poem?

Applying Your Skills

The Runaway / The Pasture / A Minor Bird
Respond and Think Critically

Reading Focus

Read with a Purpose

1. In "The Runaway," why is the colt afraid?
2. Frost asked that "The Pasture" be printed at the front of all collections of his poetry. Why do you think it would make a good starting point for a collection of poems?
3. Why do you think the speaker's attitude changes in "A Minor Bird"?

Reading Skills: Reading a Poem

4. Choose one of these poems to read aloud. As you practice reading it, pay attention to the punctuation. When you have practiced enough to read the poem smoothly, perform it for the class.

Literary Focus

Literary Analysis

5. **Evaluate** Some readers think the colt in "The Runaway" symbolizes a lost child or someone too young to understand his or her experiences. Do you agree with this interpretation, or do you have another one? Support your interpretation with details from the poem.

6. **Analyze** What point is the poet making about everyday chores in "The Pasture"?

Literary Skills: Rhyme and Rhyme Scheme / Stanza and Couplet

7. **Analyze** Make a list of the rhyming words in "The Runaway." What is its rhyme scheme?

8. **Connect** The speaker in "The Pasture" offers an invitation. As you read, did you feel like accepting the invitation? Why or why not?

9. **Interpret** The structure of "A Minor Bird" is a series of couplets. What is the main idea of each couplet?

Literary Skills Review: Theme

10. **Interpret** How would you express the **theme,** or message, of "A Minor Bird"? (You might find a hint in the two meanings of *minor*.)

Writing Focus

Think as a Reader/Writer

Use It in Your Writing Write a two-paragraph essay on Frost's feelings about nature in "The Runaway," "The Pasture," and "A Minor Bird." In your analysis, include images from the poem that reveal Frost's view.

What Do You Think Now

What feeling did you get from each poem? How did sound contribute to creating that feeling? Explain.

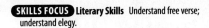

Reader/Writer Notebook

Use your **RWN** to complete the activities for this selection.

Literary Focus

Free Verse "Names of Horses" is written in free verse. **Free verse** does not follow a regular rhyme scheme or meter, but it does make use of many other elements of poetry, including

- **imagery**—language that appeals to any of the five senses; most often sight, but also hearing, touch, taste, and smell
- **alliteration** (uh lit uh RAY shuhn)—the repetition of consonant sounds in words close to each other (*marvelous memories of mangoes and melons*)
- **onomatopoeia** (ahn uh mat uh PEE uh)—the use of words that sound like what they mean (the goose's *honk*)
- **rhythm**—a musical quality produced by repetition

Elegy "Names of Horses" is an **elegy** (EHL uh jee), a poem that mourns the passing of something—a person, an animal, a way of life, a season of the year—that is important to the writer. There are many important elegies in literature. Walt Whitman wrote a heartfelt elegy mourning the death of Abraham Lincoln. Oliver Goldsmith wrote a comic elegy about a cat who was drowned in a goldfish bowl. The most famous elegy is probably Thomas Gray's "Elegy Written in a Country Churchyard." Gray mourns the anonymous people buried in a rural graveyard.

Once you've read "Names of Horses," you may agree with this reader's response:

> When someone asks me why I love poetry, I read "Names of Horses" to them, and they always say, "Oh, I didn't know poetry could be like that." And then they, too, say they love poetry.

Language Coach

Word Study in Poetry "Names of Horses," like many free verse poems, contains imagery, alliteration, and onomatopoeia. Here is an image from "Names of Horses" that appeals to your sense of touch: "your neck rubbed the window sill / of the stall, smoothing the wood as the sea smooths glass." The poem also features alliteration such as the repeated /m/ sound in "*m*ade your *m*onument." Onomatopoeia is present in words such as *clacketing*.

As you read "Names of Horses," look for imagery, alliteration, and onomatopoeia.

Writing Focus

Think as a Reader/Writer

Find It in Your Reading As you read "Names of Horses," write down images that help you picture the lives of the horses in the poem.

Learn It Online
Listen to this free-verse poem online at:

go.hrw.com   L7-701   **Go**

Donald Hall
(1928–   )

Donald Hall started writing at a young age. When he was only sixteen years old, he was accepted to one of the oldest writers' conferences in the United States. Hall's work was also first published that year. About his early fascination with poetry, Hall has said:

> "When I was twelve I started writing poetry; when I was fourteen I got serious. I began to work a couple of hours every day on my poems. And when I finished working on a poem, I would go back to the beginning and start writing it over again. . . . When I was fourteen I really wanted to do in my life what I in fact have . . . ended up doing, which is astounding."

Growing Up with Poetry

Born in New Haven, Connecticut, Hall spent a childhood full of poetry. His mother read poems to him, and during Hall's summers at his grandfather's New Hampshire farm, his grandfather recited poems "all day long without repeating himself."

For many years Hall was an instructor at the University of Michigan at Ann Arbor. In 1975, he moved to the family farm in New Hampshire, where he currently devotes his time to writing. From 1984 to 1989, Hall served as poet laureate of New Hampshire. He was the poet laureate of the United States from 2006 to 2007.

Think About the Writer What in Hall's background prepared him to write about farm horses?

Build Background

"Names of Horses" describes farm life and the life of a farm horse in the days before machinery took over the work. Horses were important to American agriculture and were used extensively to pull plows on farms. By 1945, however, the amount of tractor power on American farms finally became greater than the amount of horsepower, and tractors became the norm for farming.

Preview the Selection

In this poem, Donald Hall writes about the **horses** that labored through the seasons and years for their **owner**. By giving us a glimpse of these horses' lives, Hall helps us to appreciate all of the horses that have contributed to family farms across hundreds of years.

NAMES of HORSES

by **Donald Hall**

All winter your brute shoulders strained against collars, padding
and steerhide over the ash hames,° to haul
sledges of cordwood for drying through spring and summer,
for the Glenwood stove next winter, and for the simmering range.

5   In April you pulled cartloads of manure to spread on the fields,
dark manure of Holsteins,° and knobs of your own clustered with oats.
All summer you mowed the grass in meadow and hayfield, the mowing machine
clacketing beside you, while the sun walked high in the morning;

---

2. **hames** (haymz): rigid pieces along a horse's collar,
to which lines connecting the collar to a wagon are
attached.

6. **Holsteins** (HOHL steenz): members of a breed of
large, black-and-white dairy cattle.

and after noon's heat, you pulled a clawed rake through the same acres,
10 gathering stacks, and dragged the wagon from stack to stack,
and the built hayrack back, uphill to the chaffy° barn,
three loads of hay a day, hanging wide from the hayrack.   **Ⓐ**

Sundays you trotted the two miles to church with the light load
of a leather quartertop buggy, and grazed in the sound of hymns.
15 Generation on generation, your neck rubbed the window sill
of the stall, smoothing the wood as the sea smooths glass.

When you were old and lame, when your shoulders hurt bending to graze,
one October the man who fed you and kept you, and harnessed you every morning,
led you through corn stubble to sandy ground above Eagle Pond,
20 and dug a hole beside you where you stood shuddering in your skin,

and lay the shotgun's muzzle in the boneless hollow behind your ear,
and fired the slug into your brain, and felled you into your grave,
shoveling sand to cover you, setting goldenrod upright above you,
where by next summer a dent in the ground made your monument.

25 For a hundred and fifty years, in the pasture of dead horses,
roots of pine trees pushed through the pale curves of your ribs,
yellow blossoms flourished above you in autumn, and in winter
frost heaved your bones in the ground—old toilers, soil makers: **Ⓑ**

O Roger, Mackerel, Riley, Ned, Nellie, Chester, Lady Ghost.

---

11. chaffy (CHAF ee): full of chaff (hay or straw).

Ⓐ [Read and Discuss] What is the poet showing you about this horse?

Ⓑ [Literary Focus] **Elegy** What is the poet mourning? Why?

Applying Your Skills

Names of Horses

Respond and Think Critically

Reading Focus

Read with a Purpose

1. In what ways do these horses contribute to life on the farm?

Literary Focus

Literary Analysis

2. **Interpret** How does the last line of the poem reflect the title?

3. **Interpret** Discuss the lives of the seven horses. How would you characterize the way the horses are used by their owner?

4. **Infer** Why do you think the speaker calls the horses "old toilers, soil makers" in line 28?

5. **Interpret** How does the speaker feel about the horses he names in line 29? Support your response with examples from the poem.

6. **Extend** Re-read the comment about this poem on page 701. Why do you think the person reads someone "Names of Horses" when she wants to explain why she loves poetry? Explain the effect the poem had on you.

Literary Skills: Free Verse and Elegy

7. **Extend** This free verse poem is rich in imagery. Take your favorite image, and draw or describe what it helps you visualize.

8. **Analyze** What personal pronouns are repeated throughout the poem? To whom is the speaker addressing this elegy?

9. **Analyze** Study lines 7 and 8. Find and explain one example of each of these devices: imagery, alliteration, and onomatopoeia.

10. **Interpret** This poem is an **elegy,** which mourns the passing of something. Do you think Hall is mourning anything besides the horses he names? Explain.

Literary Skills Review: Tone

11. **Analyze Tone** is the writer's overall feeling for his or her subject and is expressed through the writer's choice of words and details. You might describe a writer's tone as humorous, somber, or lofty. What words would you use to describe the tone of "Names of Horses"?

Writing Focus

Think as a Reader/Writer

Use It in Your Writing Think about an animal you once knew and loved, and write an elegy for it. You may want to try writing in free verse. Be sure to include precise imagery in describing the life of your animal. Try to include some of the other poetic elements you learned about on page 701.

What Do
You
Think
Now

Explain how the poet both mourns and celebrates his subject.

Preparing to Read

maggie and milly and molly and may /
All in green went my love riding

Reader/Writer Notebook

Use your **RWN** to complete the activities for these selections.

Literary Focus

Kinds of Rhymes E. E. Cummings is famous for the ways he plays with sounds and punctuation. The poem "maggie and milly and molly and may" is filled with rhyming sounds. Some of the rhymes are **exact** (*may/day, stone/alone, me/sea*), but some may catch you by surprise because they are slightly off. These near rhymes are called **slant rhymes.** *Milly* and *molly,* for example, form a slant rhyme: Their sounds almost rhyme—but not exactly.

The Sounds of Poetry "All in green went my love riding" is a haunting poem. Read the poem aloud at least once, and listen for all of these sounds:

- **rhyme**—exact rhymes (*riding/smiling*) or slant rhymes (*down/dawn*)
- **repetition** of words (*riding, smiling, deer*) and lines (*All in green went my love riding*)
- **alliteration**—the repetition of consonant sounds in words that are close to each other (*the lean lithe deer, the sleek slim deer*)

Writing Focus

Think as a Reader/Writer

Find It in Your Reading As you read each poem, notice the elements of Cummings's style that make his poetry unique: no capitalization, little punctuation, and creative rhymes.

Vocabulary

dappled (DAP uhld) *adj.:* marked with spots of color or light. *The dappled stream sparkled in the sun.*

lithe (lyth) *adj.:* able to bend and move easily and gracefully. *The lithe deer moves more gracefully than other animals.*

fleet (fleet) *adj.:* fast-moving. *The fleet deer ran through the forest.*

famished (FAM ihsht) *adj.:* very hungry. *The deer were famished after the long winter.*

daunting (DAWNT ihng) *adj.:* frightening or intimidating. *The depth of the stream was daunting to the wading horse.*

Language Coach

Parts of Speech All of the Vocabulary words are adjectives—that is, they describe the nouns they modify. One is a multiple-meaning word and has a different meaning when used as a noun. When used as a noun, the word means "a group of ships." Which word is it?

This word appears with another multiple-meaning word in line 19 of the second poem. The word *does* is the third-person singular of *do.* In the poem, *does* is used as a noun and is the plural of the word *doe,* which means "a female deer."

Learn It Online
Take an in-depth look at words at:

go.hrw.com   L7-706   Go

E. E. Cummings
(1894–1962)

"an unknown and unknowable bird started singing"

E. E. Cummings started writing poetry while a student at Harvard University. He read some ancient classical poetry, and suddenly, as he put it, "an unknown and unknowable bird started singing."

During World War I Cummings was an ambulance driver in France. He was mistakenly arrested for treason and put into detention for three months. That experience was a turning point in his life. In prison, Cummings discovered his passion for freedom and personal growth. Over the next four decades he celebrated these passions.

A New Style

In his writing, Cummings often uses lowercase letters, unusual word spacing (words often bump together), and his own brand of punctuation. Even though his style is unique, his themes are familiar. Cummings, like lyric poets throughout the ages, celebrates the wonder of life and the glory of the individual.

Self-Portrait (1958)
by E. E. Cummings. Oil on canvas.

"It takes courage to grow up and become who you really are."

Think About the Writer

How does Cummings's style reflect his passion for freedom?

Build Background

"maggie and milly and molly and may"—editors are probably itching to capitalize the *m*'s in the title of this poem, but they'd better keep their pencils to themselves. E. E. Cummings did not use standard punctuation (or any at all, in many cases), and he stopped capitalizing letters early in his writing career. These quirks of style are trademarks of his poetry.

"All in green went my love riding" describes a romantic scene from a time when royalty hunted deer, using bows and arrows and many hunting dogs (commonly fast, muscular dogs that looked like greyhounds). The deer were hunted for food but also for sport.

Preview the Selections

In "maggie and milly and molly and may," you will read about **four girls** who find different items as they swim in the ocean.

In "All in green went my love riding," the **speaker** describes a hunting expedition in which his or her love takes part. The graceful deer are the prey.

maggie and milly and molly and may
by **E. E. Cummings**

maggie and milly and molly and may
went down to the beach(to play one day)

and maggie discovered a shell that sang
so sweetly she couldn't remember her troubles,and

5   milly befriended a stranded star
whose rays five languid° fingers were;

and molly was chased by a horrible thing
which raced sideways while blowing bubbles:and **Ⓐ**

may came home with a smooth round stone
10 as small as a world and as large as alone.   **Ⓑ**

For whatever we lose(like a you or a me)
it's always ourselves we find in the sea

6. languid (LANG gwihd): drooping.

Ⓐ Literary Focus Rhyme Where do you find a rhyme for the words *bubbles:and* ? Is it a slant rhyme or an exact rhyme?

Ⓑ Read and Discuss What has the poet described here?

Read with a Purpose Read this poem to experience the emotions and events of a hunt that took place many years ago.

All in green went my love riding

by E. E. Cummings

All in green went my love riding
on a great horse of gold
into the silver dawn.

four lean hounds crouched low and smiling
5 the merry deer ran before.   **Ⓐ**

Fleeter be they than dappled dreams
the swift sweet deer
the red rare deer.   **Ⓑ**

Four red roebuck at a white water
10 the cruel bugle sang before.

Horn at hip went my love riding
riding the echo down
into the silver dawn.

four lean hounds crouched low and smiling
15 the level meadows ran before.

Ⓐ Read and Discuss What is the poet setting up for you?

Ⓑ Literary Focus Sounds of Poetry What are some of the poetic devices the poet has used so far?

Vocabulary **dappled** (DAP uhld) *adj.:* marked with spots of color or light.

Softer be they than slippered sleep
the lean lithe deer
the fleet flown deer.

Four fleet does at a gold valley
20   the famished arrow sang before.   **C**

Bow at belt went my love riding
riding the mountain down
into the silver dawn.

four lean hounds crouched low and smiling
25   the sheer peaks ran before.

Paler be they than daunting death
the sleek slim deer
the tall tense deer.

Four tall stags at a green mountain
30   the lucky hunter sang before.

All in green went my love riding
on a great horse of gold
into the silver dawn.

four lean hounds crouched low and smiling
35   my heart fell dead before.   **D**

Manuscript illustration from treatise on falconry and hunting showing hunting of wild boar (15th century), Milan, Italy.

C Read and Discuss How does this new information add to what you have already learned?

D Literary Focus Sounds of Poetry Compare the last two stanzas with the first two stanzas. Which lines are repeated? which change? How does this change affect the mood of the poem?

Vocabulary **lithe** (lyth) *adj.*: able to bend and move easily and gracefully.
fleet (fleet) *adj.*: fast-moving.
famished (FAM ihsht) *adj.*: very hungry.
daunting (DAWNT ihng) *adj.*: frightening or intimidating.

Applying Your Skills

maggie and milly and molly and may /
All in green went my love riding

Respond and Think Critically

Reading Focus

Read with a Purpose

1. What do the last lines of "maggie and milly and molly and may" mean to you?
2. What do you think happens to the speaker at the end of the poem "All in green went my love riding"?

✔ Vocabulary Check

Find the antonym (word or words with the *opposite* meaning) for each of the Vocabulary words.

3. **dappled**   a. stuffed
4. **lithe**   b. encouraging
5. **fleet**   c. slow
6. **famished**   d. awkward
7. **daunting**   e. solid

Literary Focus

Literary Analysis

8. **Analyze** In "maggie and milly and molly and may," Cummings writes that "It's always ourselves we find in the sea." How does each girl find herself in the sea?
9. **Identify** List all the colors you find in "All in green went my love riding."
10. **Interpret** What images in "All in green went my love riding" imply that the hounds are sinister?
11. **Infer** Is the speaker of "All in green went my love riding" a woman or a deer? Explain.

Literary Skills: Rhyme and the Sounds of Poetry

12. **Analyze** What exact rhymes do you hear in the poem "maggie and milly and molly and may"? What slant rhymes do you hear?
13. **Analyze** Look for the sounds of poetry in "All in green went my love riding." Find examples of rhyme, repetition, and alliteration.

Literary Skills Review: Tone

14. **Analyze** Read "maggie and milly and molly and may" aloud. What tone do you hear as you read? How do the sounds of the poem contibute to the tone?

Writing Focus

Think as a Reader/Writer

Use it in Your Writing Create your own poem about a place that you've visited. You might want to adapt Cummings's trademark style: no capitalization and not much punctuation.

 What Do **You Think Now** Which character in "maggie and milly and molly and may" did you relate to most? Why?

Preparing to Read

Arithmetic

Reader/Writer Notebook

Use your **RWN** to complete the activities for this selection.

Literary Focus

Catalog Poem "Arithmetic" is a **free-verse poem**—a poem without rhyme or a regular meter. It's also a **catalog poem.** A catalog is a list. You've probably looked through lots of catalogs, perhaps from toy stores or electronics stores. Museums also create catalogs of all the artworks displayed in an exhibit. In "Arithmetic," Carl Sandburg doesn't list items for sale or on exhibition. Instead he lists his thoughts and <u>comments</u> on the subject of arithmetic.

TechFocus As you read the speaker's thoughts on arithmetic, consider your own ideas on the subject. Think of keywords you could use to locate images on the Internet that illustrate your ideas.

Writing Focus

Think as a Reader/Writer

Find It in Your Reading Look at each example of arithmetic that Sandburg lists in his poem. How would you express the speaker's <u>vision</u> of arithmetic? How can you tell? As you read, list at least five words that reveal the speaker's attitude toward his subject.

Language Coach

Interjections Interjections are words that express emotion and have no relation to the rest of the sentence. They are usually followed by a comma (as in "Oh, I didn't know that") or an exclamation point (as in "Aha! I've found it"). You'll most often hear interjections in informal conversation. Look for interjections as you read "Arithmetic." What do they add to the poem?

Commonly Used Interjections	
aha	ouch
hey	rats
hurray	well
my	wow
oh	yikes
oops	yippee

Learn It Online

Hear a professional actor read this story aloud at:

go.hrw.com L7-712 **Go**

Carl Sandburg
(1878–1967)

Pulitzer Prize WINNER

Identifying with the "Common Folk"

Carl Sandburg was born in Illinois to two Swedish immigrants. The family was very poor, so Sandburg left school when he was only thirteen years old to work odd jobs, such as washing dishes and laying bricks, to help support his family. It's not surprising that Sandburg identified strongly with the "common folk." In one poem he proclaimed, "I am the people—the mob—the crowd—the mass."

Path to Writing

While serving in the military in Puerto Rico during the Spanish-American War, Sandburg met a young man who encouraged him to enroll in Lombard College. While at the college, Sandburg was inspired to write poetry. After graduation, Sandburg worked as a journalist until his career as a poet took off. Along with his well-loved books of poetry, Sandburg wrote a six-volume biography of Abraham Lincoln.

Sandburg once defined poetry as:

"the opening and closing of a door, leaving those who look through to guess about what is seen during a moment."

Think About the Writer How does Sandburg's <u>comment</u> on poetry apply to your own experiences?

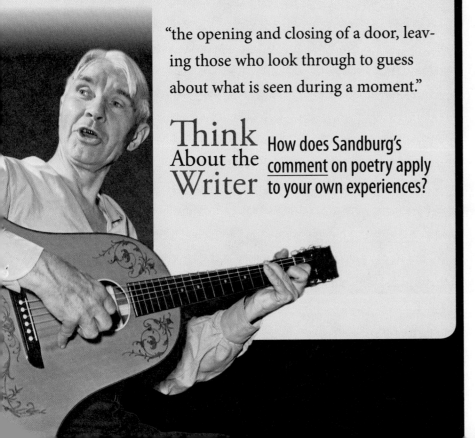

Build Background

In "Arithmetic" a speaker lists his ideas about math and numbers. This poem has proven to be so popular that it was made into a short movie, using Sandburg's voice as narration. The poem has also been turned into a picture book for children.

Preview the Selection

The **speaker** of "Arithmetic" presents a list of ideas about the topic. As you read the poem, think about whether the speaker's thoughts are similar to your own.

ARITHMETIC

by **Carl Sandburg**

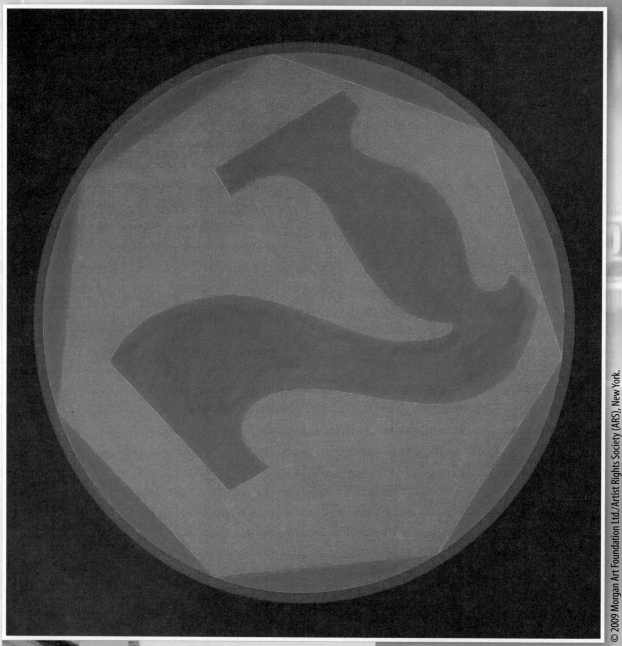

Analyzing Visuals **Viewing and Interpreting** How effectively does the painting capture the spirit of Sandburg's poem?

The X-7 (1998) by Robert Indiana (1928–   ). Oil on canvas.

1 Arithmetic is where numbers fly like pigeons in and out of your head.

   Arithmetic tells you how many you lose or win if you know how many you
2   had before you lost or won.   **Ⓐ**

   Arithmetic is seven eleven all good children go to heaven—or five six
3   bundle of sticks.

   Arithmetic is numbers you squeeze from your head to your hand to your
4   pencil to your paper till you get the answer.

   Arithmetic is where the answer is right and everything is nice and you can
       look out of the window and see the blue sky—or the answer is wrong and
5   you have to start all over and try again and see how it comes out this time.

   If you take a number and double it and double it again and then double it a
       few more times, the number gets bigger and bigger and goes higher and
       higher and only arithmetic can tell you what the number is when you
6   decide to quit doubling.

   Arithmetic is where you have to multiply—and you carry the multiplication
7   table in your head and hope you won't lose it.   **Ⓑ**

Ⓐ **Literary Focus** Catalog Poems What makes this stanza seem like a math equation?

Ⓑ **Literary Focus** Catalog Poems What image in this list surprised you the most?

If you have two animal crackers, one good and one bad, and you eat one and a
striped zebra with streaks all over him eats the other, how many animal
crackers will you have if somebody offers you five six seven and you say
8   No no no and you say Nay nay nay and you say Nix nix nix?

If you ask your mother for one fried egg for breakfast and she gives you two fried
eggs and you eat both of them, who is better in arithmetic, you or your
9   mother?   **C**

C [**Read and Discuss**] What is Sandburg doing with all these numbers and number
situations?

American Schools in the Nineteenth Century

When Sandburg was young, American schools were very different from the ones we have today. In rural areas there were still
many schoolhouses in which children of all ages were taught in
the same room. Cities, however, were responding to the Industrial
Revolution, which started in the United States in the late eighteenth century and continued into the nineteenth century. As
business and industry increased, so did the number of immigrants
entering the United States. Many educators believed that schools
should be run as efficiently as factories. They felt this production-
line approach was the best way for public schools to assimilate
new immigrants into an English-speaking nation.

Ask Yourself
**What is the most surprising difference between schools
today and schools in the nineteenth century?**

Applying Your Skills

SKILLS FOCUS Literary Skills Analyze a catalog poem; Understand and analyze figures of speech. **Writing Skills** Write poems.

Arithmetic

Respond and Think Critically

Reading Focus

Read with a Purpose

1. How can you tell that this poem is meant to be humorous?

Literary Focus

Literary Analysis

2. Review the words you listed as you read "Arithmetic." Which ones reveal the speaker's attitude toward the subject of arithmetic? How would you express the speaker's attitude toward the subject?

Literary Skills: Catalog Poem

3. **Analyze** The writer of a free-verse poem often creates rhythm through the use of repetition. What repeated words or phrases give "Arithmetic" its rhythm?

4. **Analyze** List three or four examples of **alliteration**—the repetition of consonant sounds in words that are close to each other—in this poem.

5. **Interpret** How does the poet create concrete images in your mind?

6. **Connect** Finish these sentences:
   - The speaker's idea about arithmetic that I liked best is . . .
   - I think arithmetic is . . .

7. **Interpret** Think about something you can say about arithmetic based on your own experiences. Write your thoughts in a way that could be added to Sandburg's poem.

Literary Skills Review: Simile

8. **Connect** A **simile** compares two unlike things, using a word such as *like* or *as*. In the first line of the poem, a simile compares numbers to pigeons that fly "in and out of your head." How does this figure of speech reflect what you know about numbers?

Writing Focus

Think as a Reader/Writer

Use It in Your Writing Try writing your own catalog poem. Think of a broad topic that you care about. Then, list your ideas and comments on your topic. Open your poem the way Sandburg opens his: "[My topic] is . . ."

Review your draft when you have finished writing. Be sure you included enough words that reveal the way you feel about your topic.

What Do You Think Now?

What feelings does this poem evoke about "Arithmetic"? How do the rhythm and repetition contribute to these feelings?

Applying Your Skills

Arithmetic

Vocabulary Development
Figures of Speech

Figures of speech describe one thing in terms of something else. They are not meant to be taken as literally true. A **simile** is a comparison that uses the word *like* or *as*. A **metaphor** compares two things without using *like* or *as*. In **personification** a nonhuman thing is talked about as if it were human. For example, "Arithmetic tells you how many you lose or win . . ." uses personification.

Your Turn

Explain the figurative language in each sentence. Is the comparison a simile, a metaphor, or personification? Then, write examples of each.

1. Arithmetic is a numbers game.
2. When I'm doing arithmetic, the numbers march out of my head and onto my paper.
3. Arithmetic is like a puzzle.

Language Coach

Interjections You probably use interjections when you're talking to your friends, but you don't often use them in your writing. However, you can use interjections in dialogue that is meant to represent casual conversation. Write five lines of dialogue in which you use interjections. Follow the interjection with an exclamation point to indicate a strong emotion or a comma to indicate a less intense one.

CHOICES

As you respond to the Choices, use the **Academic Vocabulary** words as appropriate: vision, structure, tradition, comment.

REVIEW
Prepare a Group Reading

Work with a group to read "Arithmetic" aloud. Decide who will read each line or which lines the group should read together. Make sure to pay attention to punctuation as you read. Make sure that you emphasize each item in this catalog poem.

CONNECT
Illustrate an Image

TechFocus Use the Internet to locate representations of the images that come from "Arithmetic." Print them, and create a collage of images from the poem. (A collage is a collection of items pasted onto a surface.) Then, share your collage with the class.

The Small Diamond Demuth Five (1962) by Robert Indiana (1928–). Oil on canvas.
© Morgan Art Foundation Ltd./Artist Rights Society (ARS), New York.

EXTEND
Extend the Poem

Timed Writing Re-read "Arithmetic." Think of something you can add to the poem based on your own experiences. Write your comments in a way that follows the structure of Carl Sandburg's poem.

Learn It Online
Understand more about the poem "Arithmetic" with these Internet links:

go.hrw.com | L7-718 | Go

Preparing to Read

For Poets

SKILLS FOCUS Literary Skills Understand ars poetica; understand and analyze figures of speech. **Reading Skills** Read a poem.

Reader/Writer Notebook

Use your **RWN** to complete the activities for this selection.

Literary Focus

Ars Poetica As you already know from its title, "For Poets" is written for poets. That makes it an **ars poetica**—a poem about poetry. *Ars poetica* is Latin for "art of poetry."

Figures of Speech A **figure of speech** compares one thing to something else. When we say someone is "cool," the person is not literally "cool"—his or her temperature is not below normal. We are saying the person is not easily bothered. **Metaphors** and **similes** are examples of figures of speech. Here are some common figures of speech we use every day:

- *He's built like a tank.*
- *This party's a bust.*
- *Those plans are down the tubes.*

Language Coach

Punctuation in Poetry As you read "For Poets," notice that Al Young does not use punctuation. His sentences do not end in periods, and he omits the apostrophe in the word *don't*. What other poets use unusual punctuation? How does this affect your perception of a poem?

Reading Focus

Reading a Poem You remember the tip that helps you to both understand a poem and read it aloud: *Pay attention to the punctuation.* "For Poets" has no punctuation, so you will have to decide for yourself when to pause. Here's a tip that can help you decide: *Pay attention to the thoughts.* Think about what the poet is saying, and then determine when a thought begins and when it ends.

Into Action If you have trouble reading "For Poets," mark where you think the speaker's thoughts begin and end on a copy of the poem.

Writing Focus

Think as a Reader/Writer

Find It in Your Reading As you read "For Poets," note the animals Young compares to poets.

Learn It Online
Hear an actor read this poem out loud at:

go.hrw.com   L7-719   **Go**

Al Young
(1939–   )

Al Young has been called "a gifted stylist and a keen observer of the human comedy." He was born in Ocean Springs, Mississippi, and spent the first ten years of his life residing in the South. His next ten years were spent living in and near Detroit, Michigan.

As a teenager, Young's poems and stories were published locally, an indicator of his future success. Young attended the University of Michigan at Ann Arbor and the University of California at Berkeley, from which he graduated in 1969.

Musician and Poet

Between the ages of eighteen and twenty-five, Young played the guitar and flute and sang professionally throughout the United States. He also worked as a disc jockey, a writing teacher, a language consultant, and a screenwriter.

In 2005, Al Young was named Poet Laureate of California. In a radio interview, he spoke about the power of poetry:

> "I'm convinced that if you read poetry to your pets you'll get a reaction that will be very surprising . . . we're talking about musicality and rhythm which takes the form of language but which is a lot more ancient than we like to think."

Think About the Writer How do you think Al Young's experience as a musician might have affected his poetry?

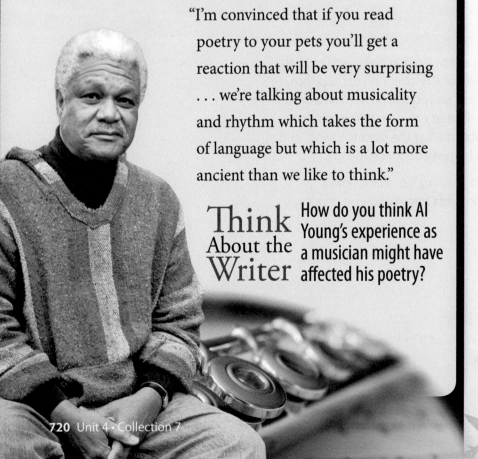

In this poem the speaker gives to poets and would-be poets advice on how to live. As you read, think about whether or not the poem is really meant just for poets.

FOR POETS

by **Al Young**

Stay beautiful
but dont stay down underground too long
Dont turn into a mole
or a worm
5   or a root
or a stone

Come on out into the sunlight
Breathe in trees
Knock out mountains
10 Commune with snakes
& be the very hero of birds   **Ⓐ**

Dont forget to poke your head up
& blink
Think
15 Walk all around
Swim upstream   **Ⓑ**

Dont forget to fly   **Ⓒ**

Analyzing Visuals   Viewing and Interpreting
How does this illustration help you connect to the poem?

Ⓐ Read and Discuss | How does this description relate to what the poet has described in the first stanza?

Ⓑ Literary Focus Figures of Speech | What does the poet mean when he advises the reader to "poke your head up"?

Ⓒ Literary Focus Ars Poetica | What might it mean to "fly" as a poet?

Applying Your Skills

For Poets

Respond and Think Critically

Read with a Purpose

1. What do all of Al Young's pieces of advice to poets have in common?

Reading Skills: Read a Poem

2. Work together with a partner to decide how to read "For Poets" aloud. Decide when to pause and when you should keep on reading. Take turns reading the poem aloud until you feel you are reading smoothly and well. Then, perform the poem for the class.

Literary Focus

Literary Analysis

3. **Connect** Respond to "For Poets" by finishing this sentence: "I think the best advice in this poem is . . ."

4. **Extend** Do you think Young has offered good advice to poets? Explain why or why not.

Literary Skills: Ars Poetica and Figures of Speech

5. **Analyze** Is there anything in this poem, aside from the title, to indicate that it is a poem about poetry? Explain.

6. **Interpret** This poem is made up of a series of **figures of speech,** in which certain behaviors are compared to things in nature. What behaviors of poets are being compared to the behaviors of a mole, a worm, a root, and a stone?

7. **Interpret** In the second and third stanzas, choose two lines and explain what advice the speaker is giving to poets through the figures of speech.

8. What is the **theme,** or message, of "For Poets"? Paraphrase the speaker's advice.

Literary Skills Review: Imagery

9. **Analyze** To which of the five senses is Al Young mainly appealing in "For Poets"?

Writing Focus

Think as a Reader/Writer

Use It in Your Writing Review the notes you took on the comparisons Young makes in the poem. Write a paragraph expressing reasons why Young advises poets to "fly" like a bird rather than behave like a mole or worm.

What Do You Think Now In what way is the message of this poem universal, not just for poets? Explain.

Vocabulary Development

Analyzing Figures of Speech

Figures of speech are not literally true, but you can discern their meaning by using your imagination. Think about "Those plans are down the tubes" from page 719. You can figure out that the phrase means that what was planned is not taking place.

Each of the items below is a figure of speech from "For Poets." For each of the items, write down the literal meaning Young intends.

1. Don't turn into a mole
2. Breathe in trees
3. Swim upstream

Language Coach

Punctuation in Poetry "For Poets" would be difficult to read aloud if you had only read it once or twice. Adding punctuation such as periods, apostrophes, and commas might remind you where to pause and help you read more smoothly. Copy "For Poets" into your *Reader/Writer Notebook*. Then, mark the poem with periods, commas, apostrophes, and other punctuation marks. Practice reading until it is smooth. Finally, read the poem aloud to the class.

CHOICES

As you respond to the Choices, use these **Academic Vocabulary** words as appropriate: <u>vision</u>, <u>structure</u>, <u>tradition</u>, <u>comment</u>.

REVIEW
Write an Ars Poetica

Timed └Writing Think about the elements of poetry you have studied throughout the collection. Also, think about the effect the poems have had on you. Then, write your own ars poetica about your <u>vision</u> of poetry. Be sure to include images that will have an impact on the reader (as all good poetry does).

CONNECT
Write an Advice Column

In "For Poets," Al Young offers his advice to aspiring poets. After reading the selections in this collection, what advice would *you* offer someone who wants to write poetry? Pretend that you are an advice columnist. Write a column that recommends ways for poets to improve. In your column, refer to examples of good poetry from throughout the collection.

EXTEND
Write a Poem

Imagine that you are a poet and you have come across "For Poets." How would you reply to the advice? Write a poem in which you respond to "For Poets." Be sure to address specific advice that Young gives. Include precise images that will create a picture in the minds of readers.

Author Study:
Sandra Cisneros

CONTENTS

Sandra Cisneros at her home in San Antonio, Texas.

What Do You Think? Why do people write about those they

QuickWrite

Think about the people in your life. Which of them stimulate you to write about them? What makes you

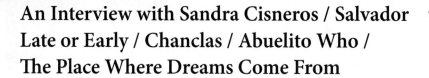

Preparing to Read

An Interview with Sandra Cisneros / Salvador Late or Early / Chanclas / Abuelito Who / The Place Where Dreams Come From

Literary Focus

A Writer's Message Sandra Cisneros writes about feelings we can all understand. She writes with humor about life's joys and frustrations and about being lonely and afraid. She writes about wanting what we can't have. She describes the fear of not fitting in—as well as the feeling of perhaps not really wanting to fit in. These feelings are close to her heart and often come from her own experiences. Her writing also explores the lives of people who belong to two cultures and speak two languages. Many of her works celebrate her memories of her Mexican American childhood.

Reading Focus

Making Generalizations A **generalization** is a broad statement about something. When you make a generalization, you combine evidence in the text with what you already know. After you read the selections by Cisneros, you will be able to make generalizations about her work. To make a generalization, ask yourself these questions:

- What is the work's **conflict,** or problem?
- What **message** about life do the pieces of evidence add up to?
- What do I know from my own experience?

Writing Focus

Think as a Reader/Writer

Find It in Your Reading Sandra Cisneros is famous for using **figurative language** such as similes and metaphors. As you read Cisneros's works, make a list of the similes and metaphors she uses.

Reader/Writer Notebook

Use your **RWN** to complete the activities for these selections.

Vocabulary

Interview

intimately (IHN tuh muht lee) *adv.:* in a very familiar way. *We know the people in our families intimately.*

The Place Where Dreams Come From

literally (LIHT uh uh lee) *adv.:* according to the basic meaning of the word. *The grandfather's term for allowance translated literally as "Sunday," the day on which he distributed it.*

ritual (RIHCH oo uhl) *n.:* an established routine. *Abuelito had a ritual he performed every Sunday.*

mistranslate (mihs TRANS layt) *v.:* change from one language to another incorrectly. *Abuelito would mistranslate into English the Spanish word for "heaven."*

Language Coach

Prefixes *Mis–* is a prefix that means "bad" or "badly." Recognizing this prefix can help you figure out the meanings of words. Think about other words you know that contain the prefix *mis–*. How does this prefix affect the meaning of the Vocabulary word *mistranslate?*

 Learn It Online
Use Word Watch to master vocabulary words at:

go.hrw.com | L7-725 | **Go**

Preparing to Read **725**

MEET THE WRITER

Learn It Online
Get more on the author's life and work at:
go.hrw.com   L7-726   Go

Sandra Cisneros

(1954–   )

Sandra Cisneros was born and raised in Chicago, the only daughter in a working-class family with six sons. The harshness of life in her neighborhood made Cisneros shy as a child, and she escaped into a world of books. By the age of ten, she was writing her own poetry.

Cisneros grew up speaking Spanish with her Mexican-born father, but she didn't explore her heritage until she attended the Writers' Workshop at the University of Iowa. There she began a series of sketches about her old Spanish-speaking neighborhood in Chicago. These sketches grew into her first book, *The House on Mango Street* (1984), which includes the story "Chanclas."

"I wanted to write a series of stories that you would open up at any point. . . . You would understand each story like a little pearl, or you could look at the whole thing like a necklace."

Think About the Writer

What questions would you ask Cisneros about the way she writes?

Key Elements of Cisneros's Writing

Everyday language, including slang and sentence fragments, gives the feeling of people speaking aloud.

Strong images and **figures of speech** bring the work alive.

Spanish words mixed with English words reflect the heritage of the characters and of the writer.

Messages often focus on family relationships and learning how to fit into the world.

A Cisneros Time Line

In **1966,** Cisneros's parents buy a house on Campbell Avenue in Chicago.

Teaches at the Latino Youth Alternative High School in Chicago, **1978–1980.**

Publishes *Woman Hollering Creek* (**1991**), a collection of short stories. Buys a house of her own in San Antonio, Texas, which she later paints purple.

1950	1960	1970	1980	1990	2000

Born on December 20, **1954,** in Chicago, Illinois.

Attends Loyola University from **1972** to **1976.** Takes a creative writing class in which she begins to write seriously.

Begins a series of sketches about her family and childhood while at the University of Iowa Writers' Workshop program in **1977.**

Receives several artist grants in **1983** that allow her to travel and live in France.

Publishes *The House on Mango Street* (**1984**), based on sketches she began writing in Iowa.

In **1995,** receives a MacArthur Foundation genius grant. *The House on Mango Street* is translated into Spanish.

Her long-awaited second novel, *Caramelo* (**2002**), is published.

An Interview with

Sandra Cisneros

from The Infinite Mind

Read with a Purpose
Read this interview to discover the connection Cisneros feels with Salvador in "Salvador Late or Early."

Build Background
Lichtenstein Creative Media's Marit Haahr interviewed Sandra Cisneros on the public radio program *The Infinite Mind*. During the broadcast, she asks Cisneros to read her short story "Salvador Late or Early" to the listeners. The two then talk about the story and the way it relates to Cisneros's life. From their conversation we learn something about how writers draw from their own experiences to create literature.

Marit Haahr. Writer Sandra Cisneros was born in Chicago in the 1950s, the third child and only daughter of seven. Her books include *The House on Mango Street* and *Woman Hollering Creek*. She's won numerous awards, including the MacArthur Foundation Fellowship, which is often called the genius grant. Her latest novel, *Caramelo,* [was] published in September [2002]. **Ⓐ**

Haahr. You were recently published in an anthology entitled *Growing Up Poor*. With that in mind, I'd actually like to begin with a reading from your short story collection *Woman Hollering Creek*. Can you describe this story, "Salvador Late or Early," for our listeners?

Sandra Cisneros. I didn't intend it to be a story. I thought perhaps it'd be a poem. I was remembering a classmate of mine I couldn't forget. So it began from that place of not being able to forget.

Cisneros now reads the story.

Ⓐ **Read and Discuss** What do you learn about Cisneros from the interviewer's introductory comments?

Salvador Late or Early

Salvador with eyes the color of caterpillar, Salvador of the crooked hair and crooked teeth, Salvador whose name the teacher cannot remember, is a boy who is no one's friend, runs along somewhere in that vague direction where homes are the color of bad weather, lives behind a raw wood doorway, shakes the sleepy brothers awake, ties their shoes, combs their hair with water, feeds them milk and cornflakes from a tin cup in the dim dark of the morning. **B**

Salvador, late or early, sooner or later arrives with the string of younger brothers ready. Helps his mama, who is busy with the business of the baby. Tugs the arms of Cecilio, Arturito, makes them hurry, because today, like yesterday, Arturito has dropped the cigar box of crayons, has let go the hundred little fingers of red, green, yellow, blue, and nub of black sticks that tumble and spill over and beyond the asphalt puddles until the crossing-guard lady holds back the blur of traffic for Salvador to collect them again. **C**

Salvador inside that wrinkled shirt, inside the throat that must clear itself and apologize each time it speaks, inside that forty-pound body of boy with its geography of scars, its history of hurt, limbs stuffed with feathers and rags, in what part of the eyes, in what part of the heart, in that cage of the chest where something throbs with both fists and knows only what Salvador knows, inside that body too small to contain the hundred balloons of happiness, the single guitar of grief, is a boy like any other disappearing out the door, beside the schoolyard gate, where he has told his brothers they must wait. Collects the hands of Cecilio and Arturito, scuttles off dodging the many schoolyard colors, the elbows and wrists crisscrossing, the several shoes running. Grows small and smaller to the eye, dissolves into the bright horizon, flutters in the air before disappearing like a memory of kites. **D**

B **Literary Focus** Writer's Message Which images in this paragraph create the mood of the story?

C **Literary Focus** Writer's Message Why does Cisneros include this detail about the crayon spill? What does it reveal to you about Salvador?

D **Read and Discuss** Cisneros uses precise images to describe Salvador. What point is she trying to make?

Analyzing Visuals **Viewing and Interpreting** How do you think Salvador feels as he hurries through his busy day?

Haahr. Thank you. It's certainly clear that the image that Salvador left in your mind was very strong. Why do you think that was?

Cisneros. Because he sat in front of me and his shirts were always wrinkled and the collars were dirty. I thought, "Doesn't his mama love him?" I thought about him a lot, and I remembered him so clearly. I remember walking down streets visiting my aunt and thinking, "Now that kind of building must be the kind that Salvador lives in." I knew him intimately, perhaps more than he knew himself, and he stayed with me all the years. I realized when I finished writing the story that he was me. That's why I could know what he did and what kind of a house he lived in and who his younger brothers were and who he had to wait for—all the things that a tiny being like that knew and the remarkable things that perhaps he had to take care of that he never thought of as remarkable.

Haahr. I know that one of the defining features of your childhood was growing up without much money. What were the physical circumstances of your childhood like?

> *I realized when I finished writing the story that he was me.*

Cisneros. Well, you know, it came [to me] at a very young age that we just didn't have money for everything. My older brother was the one that would always pull me aside and say, "Don't ask for anything. Papa doesn't have any money," or "Don't shame him by asking for something that he can't give you or that he'll give you and that'll hurt us later in the week." So there was the sense of being responsible for the others. I was very conscious of it when I went to Catholic school, because there was a class difference between myself and the major-ity of the students in the school that I went to. **E**

Haahr. How did being conscious of that affect you?

Cisneros. It made you responsible. It made you want to be protective of your mother and father and not ask for too many things. It made you, sometimes, I think, value money in a way that perhaps your classmates did not, because you had to save for the things that you really wanted. When my father died, he was sad and cried and said he wished he could have given us more. And I said he gave us just enough, because we valued what we had, and we worked for what we had. That was a lesson you can't learn in Harvard. **F**

E Read and Discuss How does this new information connect with what you already know about Cisneros?

F Reading Focus Make Generalizations What does Cisneros mean when she says, "That was a lesson you can't learn in Harvard"? What lesson is she talking about?

Vocabulary **intimately** (IHN tuh muht lee) *adv.:* in a very familiar way.

Applying Your Skills

SKILLS FOCUS Literary Skills Interpret a writer's message. **Reading Skills** Make generalizations from a text. **Vocabulary Skills** Demonstrate knowledge of literal meanings of words and their usage. **Writing Skills** Analyze the writer's technique.

An Interview with Sandra Cisneros /
Salvador Late or Early

Respond and Think Critically

Reading Focus

Quick Check

1. Describe your reaction to "Salvador Late or Early." Include support from the story and interview.

Read with a Purpose

2. What does Cisneros mean when she says Salvador "was me"?

Reading Skills: Make Generalizations

3. Think of what Cisneros reveals about her childhood in the interview. Then, make a generalization about the lesson she learns from her family.

✔ Vocabulary Check

4. If you know a subject **intimately,** how well do you understand it?

Literary Focus

Literary Analysis

5. **Interpret** Precise imagery is a poetic element in "Salvador Late or Early." Draw or describe one of the visual images that especially appeals to you.

6. **Interpret** What is the mood of the story? What does the mood tell you about Cisneros's attitude toward Salvador?

7. **Interpret** Do you agree with Cisneros that Salvador is "a boy like any other"? Cite details in the story to support your interpretation.

Literary Skills: A Writer's Messages

8. **Analyze** Think about why Cisneros wrote "Salvador Late or Early." Use her responses in the interview to help you decide on the story's message. Some possible messages are:

   - Remarkable people come from all walks of life.
   - Life without much money can still be rich.
   - It's important to make sacrifices for others.

   Choose one of these messages, or think of one of your own. Write the message in a chart like the one below, and then <u>comment</u> on why you chose it and what you think about it.

   Cisneros's message in "Salvador Late or Early" is

   My response to the message is

Writing Focus

Think as a Reader/Writer

Use It in Your Writing "Salvador Late or Early" includes powerful **metaphors**—comparisons of unlike things. Choose one metaphor from each paragraph, and explain what it helps you understand about Salvador and about life.

Chanclas[1]

by Sandra Cisneros

Read with a Purpose
Read this story to find out what embarrasses the narrator and what happens to that feeling by the end of the story.

Preparing to Read for this selection is on page 725.

Build Background
"Chanclas" is a story from Cisneros's well-loved book *The House on Mango Street*. Her novel takes the form of a series of very short stories linked by the voice of a narrator, a girl named Esperanza, who is growing up in a Latino neighborhood in Chicago. In this particular story, Cisneros writes about a feeling we've probably all experienced—the embarrassment of not having the right clothes or not looking good enough.

It's me—Mama, Mama said. I open up and she's there with bags and big boxes, the new clothes and, yes, she's got the socks and a new slip with a little rose on it and a pink-and-white striped dress. What about the shoes? I forgot. Too late now. I'm tired. Whew!

Six-thirty already and my little cousin's baptism is over. All day waiting, the door locked, don't open up for nobody, and I don't till Mama gets back and buys everything except the shoes. **Ⓐ**

Now Uncle Nacho is coming in his car, and we have to hurry to get to Precious Blood Church quick because that's where the baptism party is, in the basement rented for today for dancing and tamales and everyone's kids running all over the place.

Mama dances, laughs, dances. All of a sudden, Mama is sick. I fan her hot face with a paper plate. Too many tamales, but Uncle Nacho says too many this and tilts his thumb to his lips.

Everybody laughing except me, because I'm wearing the new dress, pink and white with stripes, and new underclothes and new socks and the old saddle shoes I wear to school, brown and white, the kind I get every September because they last long and they do. My feet scuffed and round, and the heels all crooked that look dumb with this dress, so I just sit.

Meanwhile that boy who is my cousin by first communion or something asks me to dance and I can't. Just stuff my feet

---

1. **chanclas:** (CHAHNG klahs): Spanish slang for "old, worn-out shoes."

Ⓐ Read and Discuss What has the narrator told you so far?

under the metal folding chair stamped Precious Blood and pick on a wad of brown gum that's stuck beneath the seat. I shake my head no. My feet growing bigger and bigger.

Then Uncle Nacho is pulling and pulling my arm and it doesn't matter how new the dress Mama bought is because my feet are ugly until my uncle who is a liar says, You are the prettiest girl here, will you dance, but I believe him, and yes, we are dancing, my Uncle Nacho and me, only I don't want to at first. My feet swell big and heavy like plungers, but I drag them across the linoleum floor straight center where Uncle wants to show off the new dance we learned. And Uncle spins me, and my skinny arms bend the way he taught me, and my mother watches, and my little cousins watch, and the boy who is my cousin by first communion watches, and everyone says, wow, who are those two who dance like in the movies, until I forget that I am wearing only ordinary shoes, brown and white, the kind my mother buys each year for school. **B**

And all I hear is the clapping when the music stops. My uncle and me bow and he walks me back in my thick shoes to my mother who is proud to be my mother. All night the boy who is a man watches me dance. He watched me dance. **C**

B Read and Discuss What has changed for the narrator?

C Literary Focus Writer's Message Does the evening end the way the narrator expected it to? What truth about life does this story illustrate?

Applying Your Skills

SKILLS FOCUS **Literary Skills** Interpret a writer's message. **Reading Skills** Make generalizations from a text. **Writing Skills** Analyze the writer's technique; write to describe.

Chanclas

Respond and Think Critically

Reading Focus

Quick Check

1. What is the narrator's main conflict?

Read with a Purpose

2. What has happened to the narrator's embarrassment by the end of the story?

Reading Skills: Make Generalizations

3. Think about the plot events in "Chanclas" and how they affect the narrator's feelings and attitude. Make a generalization about the importance for teenagers.

Literary Focus

Literary Analysis

4. **Interpret** How do you know that the people in this family are close and affectionate?

5. **Analyze** In this story the dialogue runs into the text instead of being set off with quotation marks. Re-read the story, and identify the passages that represent actual conversations. If you want, read the dialogue aloud.

6. **Analyze** Cisneros uses precise words to make her images come alive. Pick out a noun, a verb, and an adjective that you think are particularly powerful. Explain why you chose them.

Literary Skills: A Writer's Messages

7. **Connect** Choose a message you think is important from "Chanclas." Write it in a chart like the one below, and record your responses to the message. Here are some possibilities. You may have your own ideas.

   • There are more important things in life than clothes.

   • Certain kinds of beauty lie beneath the surface.

   • You may find pleasure in a situation when you least expect to.

   Cisneros's message in "Chanclas" is

   My response to the message is

Writing Focus

Think as a Reader/Writer

Use It in Your Writing Cisneros uses a very effective **simile** to tell how the narrator's feet feel as she starts dancing with her uncle: "My feet swell big and heavy like plungers." Recall a time when you felt awkward or embarrassed about something. Write a description of the experience. Use at least one simile in your description.

Abuelito Who

by **Sandra Cisneros**

Read with a Purpose
Read this poem to find out how the speaker feels about her grandfather.

Preparing to Read for this selection is on page 725.

Build Background
"Abuelito Who" is a collection of memories about a grandfather. *Abuelito* (ah bweh LEE toh) is Spanish for "granddaddy."

Abuelito who throws coins like rain
and asks who loves him
who is dough and feathers
who is a watch and glass of water
5 whose hair is made of fur
is too sad to come downstairs today
who tells me in Spanish you are
    my diamond
who tells me in English you are my sky
whose little eyes are string
10 can't come out to play
sleeps in his little room all night and day
who used to laugh like the letter *k*
is sick
is a doorknob tied to a sour stick
15 is tired shut the door
doesn't live here anymore
is hiding underneath the bed   **A**
who talks to me inside my head

is blankets and spoons and big
    brown shoes
20 who snores up and down up and
    down up and down again
is the rain on the roof that falls
    like coins
asking who loves him
who loves him who?   **B**

A **Read and Discuss** What is the speaker letting you know about her *abuelito*?

B **Literary Focus** Writer's Message The speaker repeats the phrase "who loves him?" three times. What message is she trying to convey through this repetition?

The Place Where Dreams Come From

by **Sandra Cisneros**

Read with a Purpose
Read this essay to learn what Cisneros has to say about her poem "Abuelito Who."

Preparing to Read for this selection is on page 725.

Build Background
Sandra Cisneros grew up speaking both Spanish and English. She writes in English but often uses Spanish words in her writing. She says, "I think that incorporating the Spanish, for me, allows me to create new expressions in English—to say things in English that have never been said before." In this essay, Cisneros talks about what inspired her to write "Abuelito Who."

When I was little, my grandpa—my Abuelito, that is, which is sort of like Granddaddy, only sweeter—my Abuelito used to love to give all his grandchildren their *domingo* (literally "Sunday," because that's the day children receive it), that is, their allowance. But my Abuelito loved the ritual of asking in a loud voice, "Who loves Grandpa?" and we would answer, also in a loud voice, "We do!" Then he would take a handful of change he'd been saving all week for this purpose, Mexican coins which are thick and heavy, and toss them up in the air so that they'd fall like rain, like a *piñata*,[1] and we'd scramble all over each other picking up as many coins as we could. To me it was much more fun to get our *domingo* this way instead of having it placed in our hands. **Ⓐ**

Well, it's this fun grandpa that this poem is about. And about the coins falling like rain, and rain falling like coins, that at times makes me think of him and miss him. I recall he became rather sick and cranky in his last years. I suppose that's what some of the images refer to, but I was grown and gone already, and my Abuelito in faraway Mexico City. **Ⓑ**

I'm not sure what exactly all the images refer to, and I'm not sure I ever knew. But that's what's so wonderful about poetry. It comes from some deep and true place inside you, the place where dreams come from. We don't always know what dreams mean, do we, and we don't have to always know to enjoy and experience them. That's how it is with poetry, too. When I write, I don't question where

---

1. **piñata:** (pee NYAH tah): papier-mâché container filled with toys and candy, which is hung above the heads of blindfolded children, who hit it with a stick to release its contents.

Ⓐ **Literary Focus** Writer's Message Look back at "Abuelito Who." Which lines in the poem does this paragraph explain?

Ⓑ **Read and Discuss** What do these two paragraphs show you about the poet and her grandfather?

Vocabulary **literally** (LIHT uhr uh lee) *adv.:* according to the basic meaning of the word.
ritual (RIHCH oo uhl) *n.:* an established routine.

images are coming from. I write dictated by sound and directed by my heart. And these images—"dough and feathers," "little eyes are string," and "doorknob tied to a sour stick"—felt right then and still feel right as I read them now. "Dough and feathers" I suppose has to do with how he felt when I held him and he held me. He was soft and squishy as dough or feathers. But it could also mean the color of his skin and hair. The texture of his skin. The silliness of his being. They're all "right."

"Little eyes are string" is harder to pinpoint. Did I mean like a spiral of string, like when we are sick? Maybe. But then again, perhaps it's the way he looked at me when he was sick. And "doorknob tied to a sour stick." I recall a cane he had and how he changed when he was very old and cranky and waved it when he wanted to make a point. So I suppose he had "soured." Why tied to a doorknob? Who knows?

A few biographical tidbits. My grandfather *did* laugh like the letter *k*. A kind of "kkkk" sound when he chuckled, which, surprisingly, I've inherited.

And. He was very proud that he could speak English, even though he lived in Mexico City most of his life. And so he liked to show off his English to his grandchildren from the United States when they came to visit. "You are my diamond," my grandpa would say in typical Mexican fashion. But then he would mistranslate "You're my heaven" and instead come out with "You're my sky," because "sky" and "heaven" are the same word in Spanish. I remember thinking even as a child that it

Wagon Crossing the Tracks: The Hat (1934–1938) by Jackson Pollock (1912–1956). Gouache on paper.
© 2009 the Pollock-Kraster Foundation/Artists Rights Society (ARS), New York

sounded wonderful—"You're my sky." How much better than *heaven*. All, all of that! Imagine. I've always been much more partial to sky and clouds, and am even now.

Finally, the older we grow, the younger we become as well, don't you think? That is, our Abuelito had to take naps, and he liked to play games, like the one with the coins, and he talked to us in a way that other adults didn't, and he couldn't climb the stairs very well, like my baby brothers. So in a way he was getting younger and younger and younger until he wasn't anymore. **C**

C Literary Focus **Writer's Message** What does Cisneros mean when she says, "the older we grow, the younger we become"?

Vocabulary **mistranslate** (mihs TRANS layt) *v.:* change from one language to another incorrectly.

Applying Your Skills

SKILLS FOCUS Literary Skills Interpret a writer's message. **Reading Skills** Make generalizations from a text. **Vocabulary Skills** Demonstrate knowledge of literal meanings of words and their usage. **Writing Skills** Analyze the writer's technique; write to describe.

Abuelito Who / The Place Where Dreams Come From

Respond and Think Critically

Reading Focus

Quick Check

1. List the similarities and differences between the grandfather in the poem and the grandfather described in the essay.

Read with a Purpose

2. How does Cisneros feel about her *abuelito*? How did the essay help you better understand the poem?

Reading Skills: Make Generalizations

3. Recall what Cisneros says in the essay about poetry. Use this information to make a generalization about what readers should do when they read poetry.

✔ Vocabulary Check

4. Does your family have a weekend **ritual**?
5. Is the phrase "It's raining cats and dogs" ever **literally** true?
6. Do you ever **mistranslate** words in your foreign-language class?

Literary Focus

Literary Analysis

7. **Interpret** In the essay, Cisneros describes her inspiration for the poem. How do you feel about the poem now? Do you understand it better? Explain.

8. **Analyze** In the essay, Cisneros says that her grandfather became "sick and cranky in his last years." Identify four images in the poem that might refer to that time.

Literary Skills: A Writer's Messages

9. **Analyze** State the message of "Abuelito Who" in a chart like the one below, and then jot down your response to that message. Think of your own message, or use one of these possibilities:

- "People change with the passing of time."
- "Memories of everyday life offer lasting inspiration."
- "Family ties strengthen over the years."

Cisneros's message in "Abuelito Who" is

My response to the message is

Writing Focus

Think as a Reader/Writer

Use It in Your Writing In the poem, Cisneros uses many **metaphors** to describe her grandfather. Review the metaphors, and think about what they mean. Then, write your own description of someone who is special to you. Use at least three metaphors to describe that person.

Wrap Up

SKILLS FOCUS Literary Skills Interpret a writer's message. **Writing Skills** Analyze the writer's technique; develop an interpretation; write short stories or poems.

Author Study: Sandra Cisneros

Writing Focus

Think as a Reader/Writer

Analyzing a Writer's Language Look back at the similes and metaphors you recorded as you read Cisneros's works. Which ones did you think were most effective? Do you recall any other images from these texts?

Use It in Your Writing Write an essay in which you discuss how Cisneros uses everyday language, strong images, metaphors, and Spanish words in "Salvador Late or Early," "Chanclas," and "Abuelito Who." After writing an introductory paragraph, you can organize your essay in one of two ways:

1. You can write a paragraph about each of the three works and give examples of the four elements.

2. You can write a paragraph about each element and describe how it is used in the three works.

Write a final paragraph describing your responses to Cisneros's writing.

What Do You Think Now?

How has reading Cisneros's works influenced your thinking about writing and reading poetry versus writing and reading prose?

CHOICES

As you respond to the Choices, use the **Academic Vocabulary** words as appropriate: vision, structure, tradition, comment.

REVIEW
Interpret a Writer's Message

Timed └Writing Discuss in an essay Cisneros's messages in the selections you have just read. First, review the charts you filled in after you read the selections. Then, write three paragraphs. In the first paragraph, make a generalization about Cisneros's writing based on the message of each work and on what she says about her writing in the interview and essay. In the second, state the messages in the texts. In the third, describe your responses to the selections and their messages. Use quotations from the texts to support your interpretations.

CONNECT
Write a Short Story

Using "Chanclas" as your model, write a brief story about an embarrassing situation. Begin by conveying what happened. Then, use precise words and images to describe the setting, characters, and events.

EXTEND
Write a Poem

Cisneros turns her experiences into stories by describing the details that make people and situations unique. Write a poem about a relative or a good friend. You may want to use the basic structure of "Abuelito Who" as your model. Begin with the person's name. Then, add descriptive details, beginning each line with *who*.

Writing Workshop

Descriptive Essay

Write with a Purpose

Write a descriptive essay about a person, place, animal, or object. Your **purpose** is to help your audience see what you are describing with words alone. Your **audience** will include your classmates and your teacher. Use concrete details and images that will appeal to your readers' imagination and senses.

A Good Descriptive Essay

- clearly identifies the subject being described
- conveys a strong overall impression of the subject
- uses sensory details and figures of speech to help readers picture the subject and perhaps hear, smell, taste, and feel it as well
- presents details in a clear, logical order
- reveals the writer's thoughts and feelings about the subject

See page 748 for complete rubric.

Reader/Writer Notebook

Use your **RWN** to complete the activities for this workshop.

Think as a Reader/Writer

Before you write your own descriptive essay, read this excerpt from writer Maijue Xiong's account of her family's journey from Laos to the United States in "An Unforgettable Journey." Notice the author's use of sensory details and figures of speech to give readers a precise image of what she experienced and observed.

I do not remember much about our flight, but I do have certain memories that have been imprinted in my mind. It is all so unclear—the experience was like a bad dream: When you wake up, you don't remember what it was you had dreamed about but recall only those bits and pieces of the dream that stand out the most. I remember sleeping under tall trees. I was like a little ant placed in a field of tall grass, surrounded by dense jungle with trees and bushes all around me—right, left, in the back, and in front of me. I also remember that it rained a lot and that it was cold. We took only what we could carry and it was not much. My father carried a sack of rice, which had to last us the whole way. My mother carried one extra change of clothing for each of us, a few personal belongings, and my baby sister on her back. My older sister and I helped carry pots and pans. My stepuncle carried water, dried meat, and his personal belongings.

The author uses **similes,** which give readers a clear image as a way to understand her memory of her journey.

Spatial words help familiarize the reader with the author's surroundings.

Details help the reader picture the scene.

Think About the Professional Model

With a partner, discuss the following questions about the model.

1. What details particularly help you picture the author's journey?
2. How do you think the author feels about the experience she is describing? What gives you that impression?
3. What is your reaction to the description? Do you think your reaction is what the author intended? Explain.

Prewriting

Choose a Subject

Use the Idea Starters in the margin to help you list possible subjects for your descriptive essay. Ask yourself the following questions about each subject in order to choose one for your essay:

- Is the subject something I can observe directly or recall clearly enough to describe precisely?
- Is the subject interesting to me? Will it interest readers?
- Does the subject evoke enough sensory details for a good description?

Finding More Ideas

For more ideas, freewrite for a few minutes on one or more of the following topics. This will help you zero in on the best subject.

- Activities you can observe (cooking dinner; a basketball game)
- People you can observe (your older sister; an athlete)
- Animals you can observe (your pet; a monkey at the zoo)
- Places and things you can observe (the lunchroom; a tree)
- Events you can observe (a scientific experiment; a sunrise)

Gather Details

Fill in a chart like the one below to record all of the **sensory details** you observe or recall about your subject.

I see...	I hear...	I feel...	I smell...	I taste...
coconut trees	airplanes	sun	salt water	lemon candy
crickets	waves	hot air		

Record Thoughts and Feelings

Good descriptions are not limited to simple observations and recollections. Enrich your description by including your thoughts on your subject. Answer these questions in your *Reader/Writer Notebook*.

- How did what I saw, heard, smell, and taste make me feel?
- What did my experience make me remember?
- What new ideas or thoughts came to mind?
- To what can I compare my sensory experience?

Idea Starters

- notable events or holidays
- familiar or exotic places
- prized or unusual possessions
- favorite foods
- family pets or neighborhood animals
- best friends or family members
- interesting people you have seen

Prewriting Tip

As you take notes about details or thoughts and feelings, remember to use figurative language, such as similes and metaphors.

Your Turn _____

Get Started Choose a subject for your essay. Making notes in your **RWN,** begin to record your observations of your subject. List **sensory details** that you recall about your subject. Brainstorm a list of descriptive words that you might use in your essay.

Learn It Online
Organize your sensory details using the interactive graphic organizer at:

go.hrw.com   L7-741   **Go**

Writing Tip
When thinking about your audience, keep in mind their age and educational background. Vocabulary used in an essay for kindergarten children would likely be quite different from the vocabulary used in an essay for college students. Similarly, an essay describing scientific observations would likely differ for a scientific audience versus a general audience.

Consider Your Audience and Purpose
Your audience includes your classmates and your teacher. Who else might read your essay? Fill in a chart like the one below to help you think about your audience and purpose.

What my audience knows/thinks	How my experience differs from theirs	What my audience needs to know	What I want them to understand

Describe the Environment
Think about how the context of the subject you are describing might affect your experience of it. Make some notes about the surroundings.

- What important details about the surrounding environment will my audience need to know?
- How did the environment affect my perception of the subject?
- If the environment were different, would my experience of my subject be different?

Organize Ideas
To be effective, a descriptive essay needs to present details in the best order for the subject. You can organize the details in your essay in one of three ways:

- **Spatial order** is best for **describing a place.** Describe details of your subject according to location. Move from far to near or near to far; left to right or right to left; top to bottom or bottom to top; clockwise to counterclockwise.
- **Order of importance** works well when you are **describing people and objects.** Put the most important details either at the beginning or at the end for emphasis. Writers often use order of importance to convey their feelings about a subject.
- **Chronological order** is good for **describing an event,** such as a local parade or cultural festival. Arrange details in the order in which they occur or in the order in which you observe them.

Your Turn _____
Experiment with Organization Keep in mind your **audience** and **purpose.** Then, choose one of the three ways to organize your ideas: **spatial order, order of importance,** or **chronological order.** In your **RWN,** compile a list of points you would include in your description in the order that they would appear for that method of organization.

Drafting

Follow the Writer's Framework

Draft your essay, using the framework to the right as a guide. Keep in mind the characteristics of a good descriptive essay by reviewing Xiong's excerpt on page 740. Notice how she describes both what she experienced and what she thought.

Focus on the Main Idea and Set the Scene

Remember to state your main idea clearly at the beginning of your essay. To focus on the main idea, ask yourself: *What do I want my readers to understand about my subject when they finish reading?* Be sure to set the scene. When you observe something, you view it from a particular place and at a particular time. By telling readers where you are, you give them a place to "stand" so that they can imagine seeing it through your eyes. Using the right transitional words and phrases will help you guide your readers.

A Framework for a Descriptive Essay

Introduction (identifies the subject, time, and place; gives background information)

_____

Body (presents details in clear order; includes sensory images and figures of speech)

1. _____

Specifics: _____

2. _____

Specifics: _____

3. _____

Specifics: _____

Conclusion (includes main impression; expresses your feelings; tells why the subject is important)

_____

● Writing Tip

As you write your conclusion, ask yourself: *Why did I choose to write about this subject? What is significant to me about it?* Draft a statement that conveys your overall impression of the subject and its significance. You want to leave your readers with this final thought.

Grammar Link Transitional Words and Phrases

As you write the body of your essay, **transitional words and phrases** will help you organize your subject and lead the reader from one idea or image to the next. Different forms of organization use different transitions:

- **Words showing spatial organization:** *across from, around, below, beside, between, close to, down, away from*
- **Words showing order of importance:** *mainly, most important, primary*
- **Words showing chronological order:** *first, to begin with, before, then, next, when, after, eventually, last, finally*

Your Turn _____

Draft Your Essay Using the framework above, write a draft of your essay. As you write, remember to use sensory details, figurative language, and transitional words and phrases.

Peer Review

Exchange drafts with a partner. Ask your partner to read your draft through once without commenting. Then ask him or her to reread your draft and, on a separate sheet of paper, answer the questions in the chart. Do the same with your partner's draft. Use your notes to revise your draft.

Evaluating and Revising

Read the questions in the left column of the chart. Then use the tips in the middle column to help you make revisions to your essay. The right column suggests techniques you can use to revise your draft.

Descriptive Essay: Guidelines for Content and Organization

Evaluation Question	Tips	Revision Technique
1. Does your introduction identify the subject?	**Circle** the subject of the essay.	**Add** a sentence that clearly identifies the subject of your description.
2. Does your choice of sensory details and figures of speech bring your subject to life?	**Highlight** sensory details and imaginative comparisons. **Put an S** above sensory details. **Put an F** above figures of speech.	**Elaborate** with additional sensory details and figures of speech. **Delete** irrelevant details.
3. Are the details arranged in a clear and logical order?	In the margin **indicate** the mode of organization— spatial, chronological, or order of importance.	**Add** information that will help the reader picture the subject of your essay.
4. Have you included your thoughts and feelings about the subject?	**Put a check mark** next to the sentences that express your feelings or thoughts about what you are describing.	**Add** specific details if necessary. **Add** transitions for greater coherence.
5. Does your conclusion state why the subject is significant to you? Does it convey an overall impression of the subject?	**Underline** the statement that tells why the experience was meaningful. **Draw a bracket** around statements that hint at the overall impression the subject made on you.	**Add** a statement that explains why the experience was important or that conveys the overall impression.

Read this student's draft and the comments about it as a model for revising your own descriptive essay.

The Nature of Batam

by Benjamin Bethea, Batam Island Christian Home School

Right now I'm sitting cross-legged on the big gray porch at our Batam beach house. The bright shining sun and hot day make me feel lazy.

The shadowy light-and-dark-green jungle to the left of me has tall, light-brown trunks of trees everywhere. To the right a coconut tree with its palms spread out looks like a parachute. Brown and gray monkeys chatter away as small green crickets sing. Different colored dragonflies flutter and glide so fast in every direction I can't see what color they are!

← The writer introduces his **subject** and explains where he is.

← **Details** of sight, sound, and movement create a precise picture.

MINI-LESSON ▶ **How to Use Figures of Speech**

Benjamin enlivens his description by using a simile, a comparison of unlike objects using *like* or *as.* He helps his readers imagine a coconut tree—a tree some of his audience may never have seen—by comparing it to something more familiar, a parachute. He might try extending this simile and using other similes and descriptive words in his description.

Benjamin's Revision of Paragraph Two

The shadowy light-and dark-green jungle to the left of me has tall,

~~light brown trunks~~ *with trunks the color of milky coffee* of trees everywhere. To the right a coconut tree *stands*

with its palms spread out looks like a parachute. ~~Brown and~~ *ing floating gently in the air. Nut brown and ash* gray monkeys

chatter away *like happy children* as small green crickets sing. ~~Different colored~~ *Shining* dragonflies

flutter and glide *like kites* ~~so fast~~ in every direction *. They fly so fast that* I can't even see what color

they are!

Your Turn _____

Use Figures of Speech Enrich your descriptions and elaborate on your ideas with imaginative comparisons expressed in **figures of speech.** In your **RWN,** experiment with **similes, metaphors,** and **personification** that you might add to your essay.

Student Draft *continues*

Benjamin uses **spatial organization** to describe the setting. First he describes what is near to him and then describes what is farther away.

→ Lively waves leap to and fro on the pure white beach, while salt water and rock bash noisily together. An airplane rumbles slowly away. Across the bay, trucks rattle loudly as they haul tons of brown dirt dark as chocolate.

Boats are all over the water! About three miles out huge tankers loom above the deep, gigantic, calm blue ocean, with ferries racing past them on their way to Singapore. Another boat, a small abandoned tan-brown sampan, bobs gently up and down in the gold sunlit waters that seem like enormous masses of lemon candy. I think Batam is just the place for me.

The writer includes how he **feels** about the place he has described.

MINI-LESSON ▶ How to Eliminate Clichés

For most of his essay, Benjamin avoids clichéd descriptions, those tired words and phrases that have lost their power from overuse, but his description of the beach could be fresher. He could improve this description of the waves by thinking more about how they looked and sounded. He might also think about how one of his other senses was engaged in the scene he describes and include figures of speech to enrich his description.

Benjamin's Revision of Paragraph Three

Foamy dance on sand that is as white as a gull's wing, and the air is heavy with

~~Lively~~ waves leap ~~to and fro on the pure white beach, while salt water~~

the scent of salt. Crashing water drums against rock, while the rumble of

~~and rock bash noisily together.~~ An airplane ~~rumbles~~ slowly away. Across the

motor dies

and clank

bay, trucks rattle ~~loudly~~ as they haul tons of ~~brown~~ dirt dark as chocolate.

MINI-LESSON ▶ How to Recognize Clichés

Here you will find several clichés that often slip into writing. Sometimes the writer doesn't even know what these expressions mean! Think about the meaning of each cliché. How can you express the same idea in a fresh way?

at the end of the day	in the nick of time
bitter end	in the same boat
black as night	by leaps and bounds
cool as a cucumber	leave no stone unturned
cry over spilled milk	never a dull moment
dark and gloomy	stick out like a sore thumb
fall on deaf ears	as sweet as a rose
hook, line, and sinker	as white as snow
by hook or crook	the writing on the wall

Your Turn _____

Eliminate Clichés As you revise your draft, be on the lookout for descriptions and turns of phrase that are not original. Try some unusual comparisons to freshen your writing and create precise images.

Proofreading and Publishing

Proofreading

Now it is time to polish your essay and eliminate any errors that might distract your readers. Carefully proofread your essay to correct misspellings, punctuation errors, and problems in sentence structure.

Grammar Link Adjective and Adverb Clauses

Adjective and adverb clauses can make your description more precise. An **adjective clause** usually follows the word it modifies and should be placed as closely as possible to that word. Benjamin correctly wrote:

> The shadowy light-and-dark-green jungle <u>to the left of me</u> has tall, light brown trunks of trees everywhere.

It would have been incorrect if he had misplaced this adjective clause:

> The shadowy light-and-dark-green jungle has tall, light brown trunks of trees everywhere <u>to the left of me</u>. [What is to the left, the jungle or the trees?]

An **adverb clause** modifies a verb, adjective, or adverb. A writer can decide where to place it in the sentence. In his essay Benjamin used the adverb clause at the beginning of this sentence:

> <u>Right now</u> I'm sitting cross-legged on the porch.

Or he could have placed the adverb clause at the end of the sentence:

> I'm sitting cross-legged on the porch <u>right now</u>.

Publish Your Descriptive Essay

Now it is time to publish your descriptive essay so that a wider audience can enjoy it. Here are some ways to share your essay:

- Add illustrations to your essay. Think about where in your essay these images should be placed to support your description. Write captions for your illustrations.
- Submit your essay to your school newspaper or get permission to post it on a school bulletin board.
- Post your essay with photographs on the web.

Reflect on the Process In your **RWN,** write a response to each of the following questions.

1. What did you find most challenging about writing a descriptive essay? What came the easiest to you?
2. What fresh images did you include? How did you avoid clichés?
3. Which of your revisions most improved your essay?

● **Proofreading Tip**

Exchange papers with a partner. Ask your partner to pay particular attention to any adjective clauses that might be misplaced.

Your Turn _____

Proofread and Publish Read the final version of your essay to yourself one sentence at a time to correct mistakes in spelling, punctuation, and grammar. Make sure you have placed adjective and adverb clauses correctly. When you are satisfied that it is free of grammatical and mechanical errors, your essay is ready to be shared with your audience.

Scoring Rubric

You can use one of the rubrics below to evaluate your descriptive essay from the Writing Workshop or your response to the prompt on the next page. Your teacher will tell you to use either the four- or the six-point rubric.

6-Point Scale

Score 6 *Demonstrates advanced success*
- focuses consistently on describing a single person, place, animal, or object
- shows effective spatial organization throughout, with smooth transitions
- offers thoughtful, creative description
- develops the description thoroughly, using precise and vivid sensory details and images
- exhibits mature control of written language

Score 5 *Demonstrates proficient success*
- focuses on describing a single person, place, animal, or object
- shows effective spatial organization, with transitions
- offers thoughtful description
- develops the description competently, using sensory details and images
- exhibits sufficient control of written language

Score 4 *Demonstrates competent success*
- focuses on describing a single person, place, animal, or object, with minor digressions
- shows effective spatial organization, with minor lapses
- offers mostly thoughtful description
- develops the description adequately, with some sensory details and images
- exhibits general control of written language

Score 3 *Demonstrates limited success*
- includes some loosely related material that distracts from the descriptive focus
- shows some spatial organization, with noticeable flaws in the descriptive arrangement
- offers routine, predictable description
- develops the description with uneven use of sensory detail
- exhibits limited control of written language

Score 2 *Demonstrates basic success*
- includes loosely related material that seriously distracts from the descriptive focus
- shows minimal spatial organization, with major flaws in the descriptive arrangement
- offers description that merely skims the surface
- develops the description with inadequate sensory detail
- exhibits significant problems with control of written language

Score 1 *Demonstrates emerging effort*
- shows little awareness of the topic and the descriptive purpose
- lacks organization
- offers unclear and confusing description
- uses sensory details in only a minimal way, if at all
- exhibits major problems with control of written language

4-Point Scale

Score 4 *Demonstrates advanced success*
- focuses consistently on describing a single person, place, animal, or object
- shows effective spatial organization throughout, with smooth transitions
- offers thoughtful, creative description
- develops the description thoroughly, using precise and vivid sensory details and images
- exhibits mature control of written language

Score 3 *Demonstrates competent success*
- focuses on describing a single person, place, animal, or object, with minor digressions
- shows effective spatial organization, with minor lapses
- offers mostly thoughtful description
- develops the description adequately, with some sensory details and images
- exhibits general control of written language

Score 2 *Demonstrates limited success*
- includes some loosely related material that distracts from the descriptive focus
- shows some spatial organization, with noticeable flaws in the descriptive arrangement
- offers routine, predictable description
- develops the description with uneven use of sensory detail
- exhibits limited control of written language

Score 1 *Demonstrates emerging effort*
- shows little awareness of the topic and the descriptive purpose
- lacks organization
- offers unclear and confusing description
- uses sensory details in only a minimal way, if at all
- exhibits major problems with control of written language

Preparing for **Timed Writing**

Descriptive Essay

When responding to an on-demand prompt requiring a descriptive essay, use the models you have read, what you've learned from writing your own descriptive essay, the rubric on page 748, and the steps below.

Writing Prompt

Write a descriptive essay about a person, place, animal, or object that you find interesting. State your subject clearly, and describe it with vivid sensory details and figures of speech. Organize descriptive details clearly, and conclude your essay by stating your overall impression of your subject.

Study the Prompt

Begin by reading the prompt carefully. Note what is required in your essay: a description that uses vivid details and figurative language, arranges them in a clear order, and ends with your impression of the subject.

Tip: Spend about five minutes studying the prompt.

Plan Your Response

Think of a person, place, animal, or object that you can describe with a variety of sensory details. Once you have settled on your subject,

- write down the subject of your essay (who or what you will describe)
- list sensory details that describe your subject
- jot down why the subject is meaningful to you

Tip: Spend about fifteen minutes planning your response.

Respond to the Prompt

Using the notes you've just made, draft your essay. Follow these guidelines:

- In the introduction, identify the subject, time, and place, and provide any helpful background information.
- In the body, present sensory details and figures of speech in clear order.
- In the conclusion, provide your overall impression of the subject and tell what the subject means to you.

As you are writing, remember to use words that are best for your audience—not too informal. Write as neatly as you can. If your essay can't be read easily, it won't be scored.

Tip: Spend about twenty minutes writing your draft.

Improve Your Response

Revising Go back over the key aspects of the essay. Did you state what you are describing? Did you provide vivid details that will make the description come alive for your readers?

Proofreading Take a few minutes to proofread your essay to correct errors in grammar, spelling, punctuation, and capitalization. Make sure all your edits are neat, and erase any stray marks.

Checking Your Final Copy Before you turn in your essay, read it one more time to catch any errors you may have missed. You'll be glad that you took the extra time for one final review.

Tip: Save ten minutes to improve your paper.

Presenting a Description

Think as a Reader/Writer Presenting a description orally is much like writing a descriptive essay. You use many of the same techniques writers use. Remember to tell your audience what you are describing right away. Then, use the same kinds of sensory details and figures of speech you used in your essay to bring your description to life.

Adapt Your Essay

Consider Your Purpose and Audience

For this presentation your general purpose is to entertain your listeners. You should also have a more specific purpose—what you hope to achieve through speaking. Ask yourself, "What do I want my audience to gain from my speech?" One student answered that question this way: "I want my audience to understand the beauty and power of Niagara Falls." To make sure your listeners understand your purpose, plan to include a thesis statement at the beginning of your speech.

As you plan your speech, think about what your audience members may already know about your topic and what they might be curious about. Also, re-read your essay to see if you need to add more sensory details. Remember that different people rely on their various senses to different degrees. If you include sensory details that appeal to all of the senses, you will be more likely to capture everyone's attention.

Organize Your Presentation

Remember that listeners cannot go back and re-read the parts of your presentation they don't understand. To help listeners follow your description, make sure your organizational pattern is clear. For example, you might need to use more transitional words and phrases than in your written description.

You may also want to review your introduction and conclusion closely. Your introduction is the audience's first impression of you and your subject, so plan it carefully.

- **Introduction** In just a few sentences, catch your listeners' attention, focus on your topic, and make your listeners feel comfortable with it.
- **Conclusion** Convey your overall impression in a memorable way, being careful to truly end the presentation rather than just expanding on the topic.

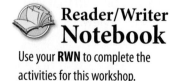

Deliver Your Presentation

Use **note cards** while you practice your presentation until you can get through it comfortably without stopping. Try rehearsing in front of a few friends or family members. In addition, practice using effective verbal and nonverbal techniques, which are both essential parts of delivering a great presentation. You can include cues for using these techniques on your note cards as well. See the sample note card below.

> My first impression of the waterfalls.   #2
> Overwhelmed by sheer size. (gesture to indicate vastness)
> They were so loud! (increase volume of voice)
> I was soon covered with a fine mist from the spray.
> I began to feel cold and was glad to have my jacket.

Verbal Techniques

Keep the following verbal techniques in mind as you practice and deliver your description:

- **Enunciation** Speak clearly and carefully.
- **Tempo** Talk at a slower rate than you normally would.
- **Voice Modulation** Raise and lower the pitch of your voice to show excitement or to add emphasis.
- **Volume** Speak loudly enough for audience members at the back of the room to hear you clearly.

Nonverbal Techniques

Use the following nonverbal techniques to add to your delivery:

- **Gestures** Use natural hand and arm movements that match what you are saying.
- **Expressions** Use facial expressions (raised eyebrows, grimaces, smiles) that help illustrate and emphasize what you are saying.
- **Eye Contact** Be sure to make eye contact with your listeners. Try to let your eyes rest on each member of the audience at least once.
- **Posture** Be sure to stand tall but not too rigidly. If you are relaxed, your audience will be, too.

A Good Presentation of a Description

- begins with a clear statement of the subject
- uses a variety of sensory details to help all types of listeners imagine the subject
- presents information using a method of organization that is easy for listeners to follow
- uses effective verbal and nonverbal techniques
- gives listeners a good overall impression of the subject and its significance to you

Speaking Tip

Pauses can be used to great effect in oral presentations. Pause before or after important points to let the audience members know something new is coming or to let them think about what you've just said.

Literary Skills Review

Poetry   **Directions:** Read the following poem. Then, answer each question.

The Sea by **James Reeves**

The sea is a hungry dog,
Giant and gray.
He rolls on the beach all day.
With his clashing teeth and shaggy jaws
5   Hour upon hour he gnaws
The rumbling, tumbling stones,
And "Bones, bones, bones!"
The giant sea dog moans,
Licking his greasy paws.

10   And when the night wind roars
And the moon rocks in the stormy cloud,
He bounds to his feet and snuffs and sniffs,
Shaking his wet sides over the cliffs,
And howls and hollos long and loud.

15   But on quiet days in May or June,
When even the grasses on the dune
Play no more their reedy tune,
With his head between his paws
He lies on the sandy shores,
20   So quiet, so quiet, he scarcely snores.

1. Read line 1 from the poem:
   The sea is a hungry dog.
   Which of the following *best* rewrites this metaphor as a simile?
   A   A hungry dog is like the sea.
   B   The sea is as hungry as a dog.
   C   The sea is a dog, hungry.
   D   The sea is like a hungry dog.

2. Read line 3 from the poem:
   He rolls on the beach all day.
   The **metaphor** above means —
   A   a dog plays in the sand
   B   the waves lap the shore
   C   the speaker lies on the beach
   D   a storm is on its way

3. Read line 4 from the poem:
   With his clashing teeth and shaggy jaws.
   Which of the **end rhymes** below matches the one in line 4?
   A   "The sea is a hungry dog"
   B   "And when the night wind roars"
   C   "With his head between his paws"
   D   "He lies on the sandy shores"

4. The poem is an example of a **lyric poem** because it —
   A   relates a story about the sea and a dog
   B   tells the speaker's feelings about the sea
   C   catalogs a list of the poet's thoughts
   D   mourns the sadness of the sea in June

5. The imagery and word choice in the last stanza create a **tone** of —
   A   silence and peace
   B   sadness and loneliness
   C   liveliness and joy
   D   anger and roughness

6. The entire poem compares the sea to a dog. This comparison is called —
   A   free verse
   B   narrative structure
   C   rhyme scheme
   D   extended metaphor

Constructed Response

7. List three ways in which the speaker compares the sea to a dog.

8. Find **images** in the poem that appeal to each of the following senses: sight, hearing, touch, and taste.

Vocabulary Skills Review

Context Clues Directions: Use **context clues** to help you figure out what the italicized words mean. Then, choose the best answer.

1. Most gymnasts' bodies are *supple;* they have to be in order to accomplish some of those amazing feats.
   A brittle
   B flexible
   C abnormal
   D breakable

2. Ian could not eat his cereal because the milk in the refrigerator had become *rancid.*
   A ripe
   B tasty
   C rotten
   D solid

3. Brian could not enjoy his favorite television show because his brother cried *incessantly* while Brian watched it.
   A quietly
   B miserably
   C incorrectly
   D continually

4. A cheetah is so *fleet* that it was nearly impossible to capture one on film.
   A sloppy
   B large
   C mysterious
   D fast

5. Even with an expert guide, most beginning climbers find scaling a steep mountain a *daunting* task.
   A fearsome
   B dangerous
   C straightforward
   D natural

6. The *famished* travelers stopped at a roadside inn to find supper before moving on.
   A sickly
   B lonely
   C hungry
   D lost

7. Thiago is normally very regimented, but this morning he chose to sleep in rather than adhere to his usual morning *ritual.*
   A routine
   B instructions
   C agreement
   D business

Academic Vocabulary

Directions: Answer the following question about an Academic Vocabulary word from this collection:

8. When you study the *structure* of a poem, you look at how its elements are —
   A commented upon
   B arranged
   C interpreted
   D imagined

Writing Skills Review

Descriptive Essay   **Directions:** Read the following paragraph from a descriptive essay. Then, answer each question that follows.

(1) The annual book sale, sponsored by our parent-teacher organization, transformed the school gym into an exhibit hall filled with thousands of books, videos, and audiobooks. (2) Tables were covered with brightly colored tablecloths. (3) The tables were arranged in a horseshoe curve along the walls. (4) At the entrance to the left were works of fiction arranged by type, for example, adventure, romance, and sports. (5) There were tables devoted to ethnic works. (6) At the rear were tables containing works of nonfiction: biographies, histories, essays, and almanacs. (7) Then came nonprint offerings: books on CD and DVDs of movies adapted from novels. (8) At the right end of the horseshoe, a group of student volunteers took orders for books. (9) In the center of the gym were tables and chairs that invited browsers to examine books and to chat about them with teachers, librarians, and parents. (10) What one heard was a low buzz of interest, and what one saw were student faces intent on discovering something good to read.

1. The method of organization used in this paragraph is —

A spatial

B chronological

C order of importance

D all of the above

2. What would be the *best* way to combine sentences 2 and 3?

A Tables were covered with brightly colored tablecloths, and the tables were arranged in a horseshoe curve along the walls.

B Tables covered with brightly colored tablecloths were arranged in a horseshoe curve along the walls.

C Tables were covered with brightly colored tablecloths; also, they were arranged in a horseshoe curve along the walls.

D Tables arranged in a horseshoe curve with brightly colored tablecloths were along the walls of the gym.

3. Which sentence could be improved by the addition of specific details?

A Sentence 4

B Sentence 5

C Sentence 6

D Sentence 7

4. Transitional words or phrases are used in all of the following *except* —

A sentence 3

B sentence 4

C sentence 6

D sentence 7

5. Which of the following would be the *best* replacement for the word *containing* in sentence 6?

A holding

B enclosing

C including

D stacked with

Read On

Poetry

Carl Sandburg: Adventures of a Poet

Besides being a great twentieth-century American poet, Carl Sandburg was a hobo, a soldier, a reporter, a musician, a historian, a husband, and a father. All of his experiences influenced his writing, especially his admiration for President Abraham Lincoln and the poet Walt Whitman. The biographer Penelope Niven has written eleven short essays on various aspects of Sandburg's life and has paired each essay with his poetry or prose. *Carl Sandburg: Adventures of a Poet* will give you a well-rounded introduction to the beloved man of letters.

The Flag of Childhood: Poems from the Middle East

In this collection of poems by writers from Egypt, Iraq, Israel, and elsewhere in the Middle East, you'll find some poems about ordinary events, such as getting a haircut or watching a sunrise, and others about heartbreaking scenes of war and its aftermath. In *The Flag of Childhood,* Naomi Shihab Nye opens a window to allow you to see that despite cultural and religious differences, young people are basically the same everywhere.

A Writing Kind of Day: Poems for Young Poets

Ralph Fletcher steps into the mind of a young writer—one thinking imaginatively about metaphors and plagiarism, writer's block, and subject matter. From this point of view, Fletcher looks closely at the writing process and describes how a young person can work magic with images and words. *A Writing Kind of Day* is your invitation to pick up a pen and paper and take the playfulness and power of poetry into your own hands.

Heartbeat

The Newbery Award–winning author Sharon Creech has written a story in verse about a twelve-year-old runner, Annie, whose world is shifting around her. Her mother is pregnant; her role-model grandfather is losing his memory; and her best friend (and racing partner), Max, is moody and distant. As you read *Heartbeat,* notice that Creech has given Annie a voice that actually sounds like a twelve-year-old's.

Poetry

Freedom Like Sunlight

The author J. Patrick Lewis and the illustrator John Thompson have worked together to present poems and portraits of famous African Americans noted for their strength and dignity. You'll find a poem on one page and portraits of such distinguished men and women as Arthur Ashe, Malcolm X, Louis Armstrong, and Wilma Rudolph on the opposite page. Included in the back of the book are extensive biographical notes about each person.

Opposites, More Opposites, and a Few Differences

Richard Wilbur is one of the most accomplished poets in the United States, having won the National Book Award and two Pulitzer Prizes. In addition to the writing he has done for adults, Wilbur has written this collection of poems for a younger audience and has made his own humorous line drawings to accompany them. As you read his funny, odd, and outrageous pairs of opposites, you may look at opposites as you never have before.

A Fury of Motion: Poems for Boys

Forty-six poems, all written by Charles Ghigna, explore scrimmage, playground showdowns, and loneliness, among other themes. Ghigna has provided a balance of humorous and serious works, with both free verse and rhymes. And even though the title says "Poems for Boys," girls will find that *A Fury of Motion* is also for them—and for adults as well.

The Best Love Poems Ever

The Best Love Poems Ever are both ancient and modern. You may be surprised to learn that people from long ago had the same feelings that we have today. Editor David Rohlfing has picked poems about love with young people especially in mind, from writers of both the present and the past.

Learn It Online

Explore other novels and find tips for choosing, reading, and studying novels at:

go.hrw.com   L7-757   Go

UNIT 5

Drama
Writers on Writing

Allan Knee on Drama

Allan Knee writes for the stage, film, and television. His dramatic retelling of the Peter Pan story was made into the movie *Finding Neverland*. He also wrote the book for the Broadway musical *Little Women* and an adaptation of *The Scarlet Letter* for PBS.

"Why do I write plays? I remember seeing a movie a few years ago about a playwright. At a moment of crisis the writer cried out, "I should have been a dentist, so I could have inflicted pain on others!" How often I've repeated that line! But the truth is:

I love playwriting, pain or no pain. I see life in terms of drama, conflict, and resolution. I love creating characters. For me, playwriting is the most emotionally rewarding of all the literary disciplines.

I enjoy the collaborative aspect of theater a lot, even though there have been times of great emotional challenge. Audiences are sometimes terrifying to me. I can't please an entire room or an entire theater. I can't please the entire world. Nevertheless, I want to. And that never stops. Sometimes an amazing moment occurs when someone actually comes up to you—a friend, or better yet, a stranger—and tells you how moved they were by your work. Suddenly, it all becomes worthwhile. Instant healing. And of course as a writer I've experienced bad reviews. It never stops hurting. I never stop thinking about how I could have made my work better. Still, writing plays is what I want to do. This is what I'm here for. Writing is my passion. It's my life.

My writing career got started slowly. I am self-taught. But over the years, learning and studying and working hard has become an integral part of my life. I'm not just a writer now and then. I'm a writer 24/7. I love keeping daily notebooks of my thoughts and feelings and experiences. It's amazing how similar my thoughts and feelings— particularly my struggles—are from year to year, even decade to decade.

Though I always felt myself a backward kid, I can see my imagination at work even as a youngster. This was long before words like *playwright* and *theater* meant anything to me. I always loved the movies. As a ten-year-old, I was creating movie scripts in my head with very dramatic titles, such as *The Life and Death of So-and-So* or *Blood in the Desert*. I started reading Eugene O'Neill in high school and loved his plays. The titles alone excited me: *Desire Under the Elms, Mourning Becomes Electra, Long Day's Journey Into Night.* Just carrying around those plays made me feel creative.

My advice to young playwrights is to read aloud whatever you write. Become the characters. Feel the rhythm of the language. Read Chekhov aloud, read Shakespeare, Albee, Williams, Coward. I find reading aloud is very helpful. Finally, always know that language isn't artificial. It's real, and it's trying at all times to communicate. "

Think as a Writer

What are the aspects of playwriting that Allan Knee is drawn to? What are the challenges he faces? List the things that you are drawn to do and the challenges they present.

Elements of Drama

INFORMATIONAL TEXT FOCUS
Evaluating Evidence

"In a good play, each detail falls into useful place. And you know that the shortest line, the smallest stage movement, has an end in view, and is not being used to trick us."

—**Lillian Hellman**

What Do
You
Think What characteristics of drama make it so much like real life?

Photograph of Emma Rossum playing Christine, from the 2004 movie *Phantom of the Opera*, directed by Joel Schumacher.

 Learn It Online

Find study guides for more plays online at *NovelWise*:
go.hrw.com | L7-761 | **Go**

Literary Focus

by **Linda Rief**

What Are the Elements of Drama?

When we were young, we all loved to dress up in costumes and outfits, say as cowboys, or as Darth Vader from *Star Wars*, or as Dorothy from *The Wizard of Oz*. We sang and danced or defeated the bad guys. We were the characters, the heroes and villains. Drama—acting or simply reading characters' words—allows us to step into characters' shoes and act like them. As we read, we can visualize what they're doing, thinking, and feeling because we can hear their words as we interpret their emotions.

Comic and tragic theater masks.

Drama: A Story to Be Performed

A **drama** is a story written to be performed by actors, using speech and movements. You can also read and appreciate drama in written form. The action of a drama is usually driven by characters who want something and take steps to get it.

Elements of Drama

In drama you'll find elements common to most stories, including **plot, characters,** and **setting.** The **plot** of a drama is organized into acts and scenes. The related events that take place in a drama are separated into **acts.** Most plays have two or three acts, but there are many variations. Within an act, there are shorter sections called **scenes.** A play can have any number of scenes.

One of the playwright's tasks is to introduce us to characters and setting. In some old-fashioned plays, this introduction is delivered by a character, for example, a maid speaking on the phone.

"Mr. and Mrs. Jones are not at home," she might say. "Mrs. Jones has gone away with her daughter, Daphne, and Mr. Jones has gone to live at the hotel." Thus we learn that all is not well with the Jones family.

Structure of a Drama The plot of a drama features a **conflict,** which is a struggle between opposing forces. A clash between a character and an outside force is an **external conflict.** A struggle that takes place inside a character's mind is an **internal conflict.** As characters struggle with conflicts, more problems, or **complications,** arise. This is what is meant by the saying "the plot thickens."

The **climax** is the most exciting part of the play. It's the moment near the end when the tension is at its peak because the conflict must be resolved. Then, in the **resolution,** the major problems are more or less worked out. The dramatic question posed at the beginning of the play is answered. Yes, Mr. and Mrs. Jones get back together.

Dialogue

A fiction writer tells a story mainly through narration and, usually, some description and talk between characters. A drama writer tells his or her story primarily through dialogue. **Dialogue** is conversation between two or more characters. Unlike dialogue in a short story, which is only partly responsible for revealing a character's personality, dialogue in a play must reveal the characters single-handedly and also carry the story forward. Playwrights may also use a **monologue,** which occurs when only one character speaks for a while. The character may be with others onstage or may be alone.

In the written form of a play, dialogue appears without quotation marks. Practice reading this dialogue from *The Monsters Are Due on Maple Street:*

> **Mrs. Brand** (*from her porch*). Steve? What was that?
> **Steve** (*raising his voice and looking toward porch*). Guess it was a meteor, honey. Came awful close, didn't it?
> **Mrs. Brand**. Too close for my money! Much too close.
>
> from *The Monsters Are Due on Maple Street*
> by Rod Serling

There are two characters in the conversation—Steve and his wife, Mrs. Brand. The name at the beginning of each line tells who is talking. When you read dialogue, you need to keep track of individual characters. Their words are important clues to their personalities.

Stage Directions

In the previous example from *The Monsters Are Due on Maple Street,* some lines have italicized words and phrases contained within parentheses. These are **stage directions.** They are not meant to be spoken aloud. For the actors—and for a reader of the play—they offer guidance on what is happening and how to understand the meaning of certain lines.

> **Mary.** Yes, I agree with you. (*She really doesn't.*)

As a reader, the stage direction "(*She really doesn't.*)" helps you understand Mary's feelings as well as events that may occur later in the play. An actor delivering this line would show that Mary doesn't mean what she says. The actor might pause before speaking or move in a way that shows she is not sincere. When you read a play, be alert to the stage directions. When you watch a play, pay attention to the action and to specific actors' movements. These are important elements of drama that convey meaning.

Your Turn Analyze Elements of Drama

1. Imagine you are acting in a play. Explain how you would know which dialogue is yours and how you should speak your lines.
2. List one similarity and one difference between a drama and a short story.

Learn It Online
For a visual lesson, use *PowerNotes* at:

go.hrw.com L7-763 **Go**

Analyzing Visuals

How Can You Analyze Dramatic Characters in Visuals?

Drama runs on conflict, but it begins with characters. In drama, wardrobe and makeup shape a character's appearance and give viewers an idea about a person. Set design reinforces this idea. An actor's interpretation of a character finishes the idea. Some characters, like the wicked witch, recur through time. People know these characters' traits before the curtain rises. Actors and directors, however, may bring their own interpretation to a familiar face. Analyzing a photograph of a performance can help add insight into a familiar character.

1. The Scrooge character, from the 1843 book *A Christmas Carol* by Charles Dickens, is an established archetype. What traits spring to mind?

2. Read the sign in this photograph. Scrooge's partner, Jacob Marley, is dead when the drama begins. How do moneylenders make money?

3. These photos capture two different facial expressions. How does each actor use his face to convey character traits?

4. In the photo on this page, note how the icicles look like Scrooge's sideburns. What set details enrich dramatic character in both photos?

Two different portrayals of Scrooge. On the previous page is Tommy Steele in the 2005 London musical *Scrooge*, adapted from Dickens by Leslie Bricusse and directed by Bob Tomson. On this page is George C. Scott in the 1984 television-movie version of *A Christmas Carol*, adapted by Roger O. Hirson and directed by Clive Donner.

Analyzing a Dramatic Character in a Photograph

Answer these questions as you analyze a dramatic character in a photograph.

1. Look closely at the expression on the character's face. How does the actor use his face to convey an idea about the character?

2. Examine the character's wardrobe and makeup. How do they reinforce what you know about the character?

3. Study the set design to analyze the character's environment. What details—objects, colors, textures—underline character traits?

4. Analyze dramatic character by combining your visual observations. Evaluate how well the visual and performance details convey the character.

Your Turn Analyze Visual Information

The visual foundation of dramatic character is wardrobe and makeup. If you were staging a version of *A Christmas Carol* set in the present day, how would you dress and use makeup on Scrooge?

Reading Focus

by **Kylene Beers**

How Can *Reading* a Play Be Like *Watching* a Play?

Just as bikes are made for riding and phones are made for talking, plays are written for watching. You see them performed on the stage or in your mind. You picture the characters and events (visualize the action), ask yourself why the author has written it (analyze author's purpose), and slow your reading to catch all the details (vary your reading rate).

Visualizing a Drama

You've learned that when you **visualize,** you form mental images of a setting based on details in a story. In a drama the playwright provides details that explain the setting. These details are often included at the beginning of a play in stage directions. Here's an example. This is a teleplay, which means it was written for television and the stage directions are for a TV camera:

> *The camera pans down past the horizon, stopping on a sign which reads "Maple Street." Then it moves on to the street below. It is daytime. We see a quiet, tree-lined street, typical of small-town America. People sit and swing on gliders on their front porches, chatting across from house to house.*
>
> from *The Monsters Are Due on Maple Street* by Rod Serling

A playwright can also include details in the characters' dialogue that reveal the time and place of the story. Here is an example:

> **Luq.** Luqman Ali, a poor but honest dung sweeper, lived in the alley of the tanners, off the street of the potters, in the heart of the great city of Baghdad.
> **Wife.** He and his wife had nothing in the world but an old iron stove, and barely enough to eat.
>
> from *The Dream of Good Fortune,* dramatized by Paul Sills

These tips will help you visualize the setting and characters in any drama you read:

- Look for sensory details on how something looks, sounds, smells, feels, and even tastes.
- Read the stage directions aloud. Hearing the words can help you create mental images.
- As you read, draw a sketch of the setting or characters based on the details in the stage directions or dialogue.
- Pay special attention to verbs and adjectives that help you visualize a scene.

Jot down all of the important details that help create pictures in your mind of the places and characters in a drama.

Determining Author's Purpose

You know that an author always has a purpose for writing a piece of text and that there are four basic purposes:

- to inform
- to persuade
- to express feelings
- to entertain

An author may have more than one purpose. Because a drama is written to be performed—on a stage, on television, or in a movie—one purpose for a drama writer is always to entertain.

However, playwrights and screenwriters (people who write for television or movies) often have other reasons for writing a drama. They may want to inform you about a subject, such as a historical event, or persuade you to adopt a particular point of view. Think of films or television movies you've watched that were scary, funny, exciting, or romantic. Expressing feelings is another purpose a writer of drama has in mind.

Because a drama is a story told through **dialogue,** it seems very much like real life, where events unfold through conversations and actions. As you read each play in this collection, ask yourself: Why did the author choose to tell this story as a play rather than as a short story or novel? Along with being entertained, what can I learn or understand from this play? Answering those questions will help you identify each author's purpose.

Adjusting Your Reading Rate

Your **reading rate** is the speed with which you read a text. How quickly or how slowly you read depends on the type of text and your purpose in reading.

When you read a play, most often you are reading for understanding. You might scan for a key character's lines and then read that dialogue more slowly. You might note important words in stage directions as you carefully read for key details.

When you read a play aloud in the role of a character, you adjust your reading rate for expression and to match the emotion conveyed by the lines. When people are upset, they often speak faster. If they want to make an important point, they often speak more slowly.

Your Turn   Apply Reading Skills

1. Explain what helps you visualize the home of Luqman Ali in the play *The Dream of Good Fortune.*

2. Explain how you would adjust your reading rate when you read a play that features characters whose dialogue uses old-fashioned words that you don't know well.

3. What might be a playwright's purpose in writing about a group of people who become suspicious of one another when they get caught up in events that they can't understand? Explain your ideas.

Learn It Online
Use *PowerNotes* to explore author's purpose:

go.hrw.com   L7-767   **Go**

Build Background

This drama takes place long ago in the Middle East. The main character, Luqman Ali, lives in Baghdad, which was the center of Islamic civilization during the period in which many of the *Arabian Nights* stories are set. He travels to Cairo, in Egypt.

Read with a Purpose Read to discover how a dream results in good fortune.

THE DREAM OF GOOD FORTUNE

from **The Arabian Nights,** *dramatized by* **Paul Sills**

CHARACTERS

Luqman Ali	An Angel	A Thief
His Wife	The Chief of Police	The Lieutenant

Literary Focus

Elements of Drama A play is told entirely through **dialogue,** or conversation between characters. You know who is speaking by the name in bold that starts the line. "Luq" is an abbreviation for "Luqman Ali."

Reading Focus

Adjusting Your Reading Rate You may read some lines quickly and longer patches of dialogue slowly, to ensure understanding. When reading aloud, your reading rate should reflect the expression in the words.

Luq. Luqman Ali, a poor but honest dung sweeper, lived in the alley of the tanners, off the street of the potters, in the heart of the great city of Baghdad.

Wife. He and his wife had nothing in the world but an old iron stove, and barely enough to eat.

Luq. But still they did not despair in the mercy of the Almighty. One night Luqman Ali and his wife lay down to sleep, and he had a dream.

Angel. An angel appeared with a message: "Luqman Ali, alley of the tanners, off the street of the potters, in the city of Baghdad—Dear Luq, Go to Cairo, and there you will find your fortune."

Luq. Luqman Ali awoke his wife and told her of his strange dream.

Wife. Go back to sleep, my love, it was only a dream.

Angel. Luqman Ali, go to Cairo, and there you will find your fortune.

Luq. Wife, wake up; the angel came again and told me to go to Cairo, to seek my fortune.

Wife. If it happens a third time, you'll have to go.

Angel. Luqman Ali, are you still here? Go to Cairo! Your fortune awaits you there.

Luq. I go! I go! Wife, awaken—I must go to Cairo. And so Luqman Ali set off on the road to Cairo. Through hot desert winds—sandstorms—cold nights. Luqman Ali traveled the road until, weary and sore, in the shimmering heat, he saw the great city of Cairo. Tired and not knowing where to go, he took refuge in the courtyard of a great mosque, where he lay down to sleep.

Thief. That night, a thief entered the courtyard and broke through the wall of an adjoining house.

[*A woman screams offstage. The* THIEF *returns to the courtyard, hits* LUQ, *and runs off.*]

Luq. Stop, thief! Stop, thief!

Chief of Police. The chief of police . . .

Lieutenant. And his lieutenant . . .

Chief of Police. Arrived at the scene, and they found Luqman Ali, and thinking him to be the thief . . .

Lieutenant. They beat him with their clubs and dragged him off to jail.

Reading Focus

Visualizing Just as you **visualize** characters and setting when you read a story, you want to create mental pictures when you read a play. Pay attention to sensory details—such as *shimmering heat*—to help you imagine people and places.

Literary Focus

Stage Directions An important element of drama is **stage directions** like these, which help actors and directors in presenting a play. For a reader, they explain actions that are not revealed by the dialogue.

Literary Focus

Elements of Drama A play always has a **conflict,** or struggle, for the main character. It also presents **complications** to make the play more interesting. Think about the conflict facing Luqman Ali and how being mistaken for a thief creates a complication.

Chief of Police. Who are you?

Luq. Luqman Ali.

Chief of Police. Where do you come from?

Luq. Baghdad.

Chief of Police. What brings you to Cairo?

Luq. I had a dream . . .

[*The* LIEUTENANT *squeezes* LUQ'*s nose, sending him to his knees.*]

Chief of Police. What are you doing in Cairo?

Luq (*rises*). I had a dream . . .

[*The* LIEUTENANT *squeezes his head.*]

Chief of Police (*waving the* LIEUTENANT *away*). What brings you to Cairo?

Luq (*again on his knees*). I had a dream. An angel appeared to me three times in a row and told me to go to Cairo, where I would find my fortune.

Chief of Police. And what did you find?

Luq. I got arrested and beat up.

Chief of Police. It hurts too, doesn't it? Dreams mean nothing. We all have dreams. You fool! That's the trouble with you people. Superstitious. I had a dream only last night: An angel came to me and told me to go to Baghdad, to the alley of the potters, off the street of the tanners, to a little old shack, and there under an old iron stove I would find a treasure. Did I go? No! I stayed here doing my job. Here, take these dinars[1] and get out of here.

[*So* LUQ *sets off to his home in Baghdad. He "dances" back to Baghdad, calling "Wife, wife." They move the stove, find the treasure, and adorn each other with jewels. She kisses his nose.— "Owww!!!"—Fade Out.*]

---

1. **dinars** (dih NAHRZ): money used in many Middle Eastern countries.

Read with a Purpose What was the "dream of good fortune"? Who had it, and who benefits from it?

Literary Focus

Elements of Drama The **climax** is the most exciting moment in the play, when we learn how the conflict will be resolved. At first, it seems Luqman Ali has failed to find his good fortune—but read on! The resolution wraps up the play and tells you what happens to the characters.

Reading Focus

Author's Purpose Plays are written to entertain, but a playwright often may have another purpose in mind. Consider whether this playwright wants to teach a lesson or persuade his audience to believe in the power of dreams.

SKILLS IN ACTION
Wrap Up

Into Action: Visualizing the Play

It can be difficult to visualize drama because it consists mainly of dialogue. Use this chart to record details that help you visualize characters, settings, and events from the play.

Visualizing . . .	Details
Luqman Ali	
His Wife	
Their Home	
Journey to Cairo	
Chief of Police	

Talk About . . .

1. Discuss with a partner how you would present this play if you were performing it for a group of elementary school students. Think about what you would change to make it easier to understand. Take notes on the changes you'd make, and present your ideas to the class. Try to use each Academic Vocabulary word listed at the right in your discussion.

Write About . . .

Use the underlined Academic Vocabulary words in your answers to the following questions about *The Dream of Good Fortune*.

2. What is Ali's <u>motive</u> for going to Cairo?

3. What did you learn about Ali and the Chief of Police from the way they <u>interact</u> with each other?

4. How did the Chief of Police's dream help <u>resolve</u> Ali's problems?

Writing Focus

Think as a Reader/Writer

In Collection 8, you will read a play adapted from a classic novel by Charles Dickens and a teleplay. Writing Focus activities will help you understand how writers create dialogue and will give you practice with writing your own.

Academic Vocabulary for Collection 8

Talking and Writing About Elements of Drama

Academic Vocabulary is the language you use to write and talk about literature. Use the following words to discuss the drama in this collection. The words will be underlined in the collection.

interact (ihn tuhr AKT) *v.*: act together with another. *To understand drama, pay attention to the way characters interact.*

motive (MOH tihv) *n.*: reason someone does something. *A play makes sense when you understand a character's motive.*

previous (PREE vee uhs) *adj.*: happening before a given time. *The previous scene contains clues about how the play will end.*

resolve (rih ZAHLV) *v.*: find an answer to a problem. *The characters resolve their problems in the final act of the play.*

Your Turn

Copy the Academic Vocabulary words into your *Reader/Writer Notebook*. Use each word in a sentence about elements of drama in *The Dream of Good Fortune*. Practice using these Academic Vocabulary words as you talk and write about the dramatic literature in this collection.

A Christmas Carol:
Scrooge and Marley

by **Israel Horovitz**

based on **A Christmas Carol** *by* **Charles Dickens**

Kelsey Grammer as Scrooge in the 2004 NBC TV movie *A Christmas Carol*, directed by Arthur Allan Seidelman.

What Do You Think? What are the most important things in life? How do you think you'll measure your success in the future?

QuickWrite

Think about your goals for the future. Do you want to have a family? lots of money? an important job? List and explain three of your goals in order of their importance to you.

Reader/Writer Notebook

Use your **RWN** to complete the activities for this selection.

Literary Focus

Understanding Drama A **drama** is a story that is meant to be acted out for an audience. Its plot is carried forward by the characters through their dialogue and actions. Dramas are usually divided into parts called **acts,** and each act is made up of shorter sections called **scenes.** The elements of drama are similar to the elements of a short story. In the introduction, you meet the main characters and learn about the **conflict,** or major problem, they face. You then learn the **complications,** the things that make it hard for the characters to resolve the conflict. At the **climax,** the conflict ends, and in the **resolution,** you learn how the situation turns out.

Literary Perspectives Apply the Literary Perspective described on page 777 as you read this play.

Reading Focus

Visualizing When you **visualize,** you form mental images based on the details a writer provides. When you read a drama, stage directions are the main source of details that will help you visualize the setting, the characters, and the action as it unfolds.

Into Action As you read, jot down specific details that help you visualize the main characters in the play.

Visualizing Characters

Marley: _____

Scrooge: _____

Writing Focus

Think as a Reader/Writer

Find It in Your Reading To describe the setting, the playwright includes old-fashioned words and expressions. As you read, record examples of language that you rarely hear today.

Vocabulary

implored (ihm PLAWRD) *v.*: begged. *The wretched beggar implored passersby to give him money.*

morose (muh ROHS) *adj.*: gloomy; ill-tempered. *The morose old man never said a cheerful word to anyone.*

destitute (DEHS tuh toot) *n.*: people living in utter poverty. *The destitute were hungry and homeless.*

benevolence (buh NEHV uh luhns) *n.*: goodwill; kindliness. *The miserly Ebenezer was not known for his benevolence.*

compulsion (kuhm PUHL shuhn) *n.*: driving, irresistible force. *The miser had an irresistible compulsion to follow the ghost.*

meager (MEE guhr) *adj.*: small in amount. *Cratchit's meager salary was barely enough to pay the rent and buy food for the family.*

Language Coach

Word Association Many of the words above are related in meaning—they have something do to with poverty and need. Identify those words, and create a word web showing how their meanings are connected.

Learn It Online
Develop your vocabulary with Word Watch:

go.hrw.com   L7-773   **Go**

Charles Dickens
(1812–1870)

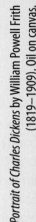

Portrait of Charles Dickens by William Powell Frith (1819–1909). Oil on canvas.

One of England's Greatest Writers

Born in 1812, Charles Dickens was one of eight children. When his father lost his job, twelve-year-old Charles was forced to take a job in a warehouse, working twelve hours a day pasting labels on bottles. (Once the family's financial situation improved, he returned to school.) The experience aroused in Dickens a fierce determination to fight poverty and social injustice—an ideal he expressed passionately in many of his books.

Dickens eventually became a reporter. When he was twenty-four, he published his first book, a compilation of articles he had written. In that year he began working on a novel that was to be *The Pickwick Papers,* his first major success. From that time on, Dickens was a productive and ever more popular novelist. In such classics as *Oliver Twist, Great Expectations,* and *David Copperfield,* he created perceptive portrayals of ordinary English life with a comic touch and memorable characters.

Israel Horovitz
(1939–   )

Playwright and Screenwriter

Israel Horovitz is an internationally acclaimed American playwright and screenwriter whose works have been translated into nearly thirty languages. His first play was produced when he was eighteen, and he has been a prolific and successful writer ever since. He lives in Massachusetts, where he continues writing for the stage.

Think About the Writers
Why might a modern playwright choose to write a play based on Dickens's story?

Build Background

Charles Dickens's novel *A Christmas Carol* was first published in 1843 and has endured as a monument to the ideals of family and forgiveness. The play you are about to read was adapted from the novel by the playwright Israel Horovitz, who followed Dickens's story carefully but added some inventive and theatrical elements to ensure the story's success as a drama.

Preview the Selection

A Christmas Carol: Scrooge and Marley is a dramatic adaptation of a nineteenth-century story that has become a holiday classic. In the play, you'll meet **Ebenezer Scrooge,** a sour old man who is transformed by extraordinary encounters with his own past, present, and future.

A Christmas Carol:
Scrooge and Marley

by **Israel Horovitz**

based on **A Christmas Carol** by **Charles Dickens**

The People of the Play

Jacob Marley, a specter[1]

Ebenezer Scrooge,
not yet dead, which is
to say still alive

Bob Cratchit,
Scrooge's clerk

Nephew, Scrooge's
nephew Fred

Thin Do-Gooder

Portly Do-Gooder

Specters (Various),
carrying money-boxes

**The Ghost of
Christmas Past**

Four Jocund Travelers

A Band of Singers

A Band of Dancers

Little Boy Scrooge

Young Man Scrooge

Fan, Scrooge's little sister

The Schoolmaster

Schoolmates

Fezziwig, a fine and
fair employer

Dick, young Scrooge's
coworker

Young Scrooge

A Fiddler

More Dancers

Scrooge's Lost Love

**Scrooge's Lost Love's
Daughter**

**Scrooge's Lost Love's
Husband**

**The Ghost of Christmas
Present**

Some Bakers

Mrs. Cratchit,
Bob Cratchit's wife

Belinda Cratchit,
a daughter

Martha Cratchit, another
daughter

Peter Cratchit, a son

Tiny Tim Cratchit,
another son

Scrooge's Niece, Fred's wife

**The Ghost of Christmas
Future,** a mute phantom

Three Men of Business

**Drunks, Scoundrels,
Women of the Streets**

A Charwoman

Mrs. Dilber

Joe, an old second-hand
goods dealer

A Corpse, very like Scrooge

An Indebted Family

Adam, a young boy

A Poulterer

A Gentlewoman

Some More Men of Business

---

1. **specter:** ghost.

How to Read a Play

Although dramas are written to be performed, **stage directions** allow you to read and appreciate dramas in their written form by visualizing the settings, characters, and action. Stage directions tell actors when to enter and exit their scenes, where to stand on stage, what emotions to display when speaking certain lines, and so on. These directions can take many forms. The most common ones are listed here. Note that "left" and "right" directions always refer to the actor's left or right when he or she is facing the audience.

stage right

stage left

center

downstage (toward the audience)

upstage (away from the audience)

downstage center (center of the stage, closest to the audience)

upstage right (upper-right-hand corner of the stage, farthest from the audience)

offstage (out of sight of the audience)

Act One

The Place of the Play

Various locations in and around the city of London, including Scrooge's Chambers and Offices; the Cratchit Home; Fred's Home; Scrooge's School; Fezziwig's Offices; Old Joe's Hide-a-Way.

The Time of the Play

The entire action of the play takes place on Christmas Eve, Christmas Day, and the morning after Christmas, 1843.

SCENE 1

[*Ghostly music in auditorium. A single spotlight on* JACOB MARLEY, DOWNSTAGE CENTER. *He is ancient; awful, dead-eyed. He speaks straight out to auditorium.*] Ⓐ

Marley (*cackle-voiced*). My name is Jacob Marley and I am dead. (*He laughs.*) Oh, no, there's no doubt that I am dead. The register of my burial was signed by the clergyman, the clerk, the undertaker . . . and by my chief mourner . . . Ebenezer Scrooge . . . (*Pause; remembers*) I am dead as a doornail.

[*A spotlight fades up,* STAGE RIGHT, *on* SCROOGE, *in his counting house,*[2] *counting. Lettering on the window behind* SCROOGE *reads: "SCROOGE AND MARLEY, LTD." The spotlight is tight on* SCROOGE'S *head and shoulders. We shall not yet see into the offices and setting. Ghostly music continues, under.*

---

2. **counting house:** office used for keeping books and carrying out business.

Ⓐ **Reading Focus** **Visualizing** How do the stage directions help you visualize what you would see on the stage if you were watching a production?

MARLEY *looks across at* SCROOGE; *pitifully. After a moment's pause*]

I present him to you: Ebenezer Scrooge . . . England's most tightfisted hand at the grindstone,[3] Scrooge! a squeezing, wrenching, grasping, scraping, clutching, covetous, old sinner! secret, and self-contained, and solitary as an oyster. The cold within him freezes his old features, nips his pointed nose, shrivels his cheek, stiffens his gait; makes his eyes red, his thin lips blue; and speaks out shrewdly in his grating voice. Look at him. Look at him . . .

[SCROOGE *counts and mumbles.*]

Scrooge. They owe me money and I will collect. I will have them jailed, if I have to. They owe me money and I will collect what is due me.

[MARLEY *moves towards* SCROOGE; *two steps. The spotlight stays with him.*]

Marley (*disgusted*). He and I were partners for I don't know how many years. Scrooge was my sole executor, my sole administrator, my sole assign, my sole residuary legatee, my sole friend and my sole mourner.[4]

---

3. **hand at the grindstone:** This phrase is related to the expression "put one's nose to the grindstone," which means to work long and hard.

4. **sole executor** (ehg ZEHK yuh tuhr), **sole administrator, sole assign, sole residuary legatee** (rih ZIHJ oo ehr ee lehg uh TEE): legal terms indicating that a person has the power to carry out the wishes of a person who has died.

But Scrooge was not so cut up by the sad event of my death, but that he was an excellent man of business on the very day of my funeral, and solemnized[5] it with an undoubted bargain. (*Pauses again in disgust*) He never painted out my name from the window. There it stands, on the window and above the warehouse door: Scrooge and Marley. Sometimes people new to our business call him Scrooge and sometimes they call him Marley. He answers to both names. It's all the same to him. And it's cheaper than painting in a new sign, isn't it? (*Pauses; moves closer to* SCROOGE) Nobody has ever stopped him in the street to say, with gladsome looks, "My dear Scrooge, how are

---

5. **solemnized:** (SAHL uhm nyzd): honored.

Literary Perspectives

The following perspective will help you think about the main ideas in this play.

Analyzing Archetypes The word *archetype* signifies a recognizable pattern in literature; it can be used to describe the story types, or genres; characters; images; and symbols found in literature. Archetypes capture some fundamental aspect of the human experience. Some archetypal characters include the rebel-hero, the fool, and the goddess. In *A Christmas Carol: Scrooge and Marley,* you will meet Ebenezer Scrooge. Scrooge has become an archetypal character since Charles Dickens created him; even if you've never read *A Christmas Carol,* you may be familiar with the name. Notice the details about Scrooge's character that make him a universal type: a miserly, unhappy man. As you read, be sure to notice the notes and questions in the text, which will guide you in using this perspective.

you? When will you come to see me?" No beggars implored him to bestow a trifle, no children ever ask him what it is o'clock, no man or woman now, or ever in his life, not once, inquire the way to such and such a place. (MARLEY *stands next to* SCROOGE *now. They share, so it seems, a spotlight.*) But what does Scrooge care of any of this? It is the very thing he likes! To edge his way along the crowded paths of life, warning all human sympathy to keep its distance.

[*A ghostly bell rings in the distance.* MARLEY *moves away from* SCROOGE, *now, heading* DOWNSTAGE *again. As he does, he "takes" the light:* SCROOGE *has disappeared into the black void beyond.* MAR-LEY *walks* DOWNSTAGE CENTER, *talking directly to the audience. Pauses*]

The bell tolls and I must take my leave. You must stay a while with Scrooge and watch him play out his scroogey life. It is now the story: the once-upon-a-time. Scrooge is in his counting house. Where else? Christmas eve and Scrooge is busy in his counting house. It is cold, bleak, biting weather outside: foggy withal: and, if you listen closely, you can hear the people in the court go wheezing up

What are you doing, Cratchit? Acting cold, are you? Next, you'll be asking to replenish your coal from my coal-box, won't you?

and down, beating their hands upon their breasts, and stamping their feet upon the pavement stones to warm them . . .

[*The clocks outside strike three.*]

Only three! and quite dark outside already: it has not been light all day this day.

[*This ghostly bell rings in the distance again.* MARLEY *looks about him. Music in.* MARLEY *flies away.*] **B**

SCENE 2

[*Christmas music in, sung by a live chorus, full. At conclusion of song, sound fades under and into the distance. Lights up in set: offices of Scrooge and Marley, Ltd.* SCROOGE *sits at his desk, at work. Near him is a tiny fire. His door is open and in his line of vision, we see* SCROOGE'S *clerk,* BOB CRATCHIT, *who sits in a dismal tank of a cubicle, copying letters. Near* CRATCHIT *is a fire so tiny as to barely cast a light: perhaps it is one pitifully glowing coal?* CRATCHIT *rubs his hands together, puts on a white comforter[6] and tries to heat his hands around his candle.* SCROOGE'S NEPHEW *enters, unseen.*] **C**

---

6. **comforter:** warm scarf.

B Read and Discuss What is the playwright setting up for you?

C Reading Focus Visualizing What words would you use to describe the setting based on these stage directions?

Vocabulary **implored** (ihm PLOHRD) *v.*: begged.

Scrooge. What are you doing, Cratchit? Acting cold, are you? Next, you'll be asking to replenish your coal from my coal-box, won't you? Well, save your breath, Cratchit! Unless you're prepared to find employ elsewhere!

Nephew (*cheerfully; surprising* SCROOGE). A merry Christmas to you, Uncle! God save you!

Scrooge. Bah! Humbug![7] ⒟

Nephew. Christmas a "humbug," Uncle? I'm sure you don't mean that.

Scrooge. I do! Merry Christmas? What right do you have to be merry? What reason have you to be merry? You're poor enough!

Nephew. Come, then. What right have you to be dismal? What reason have you to be morose? You're rich enough.

Scrooge. Bah! Humbug!

Nephew. Don't be cross, Uncle.

Scrooge. What else can I be? Eh? When I live in a world of fools such as this? Merry Christmas? What's Christmastime to you but a time of paying bills without any money; a time for finding yourself a year older, but not an hour richer. If I could work my will, every idiot who goes about with "Merry Christmas" on his lips, should be boiled with his own pudding, and buried with a stake of holly through his heart. He should!

---

7. **Humbug:** foolishness.

Nephew. Uncle!

Scrooge. Nephew! You keep Christmas in your own way and let me keep it in mine.

Nephew. Keep it! But you don't keep it, Uncle.

Scrooge. Let me leave it alone, then. Much good it has ever done you!

Nephew. There are many things from which I have derived good, by which I have not profited, I daresay. Christmas among the rest. But I am sure that I always thought of Christmastime, when it has come round—as a good time: the only time I know of, when men and women seem to open their shut-up hearts freely, and to think of people below them as if they really were fellow-passengers to the grave, and not another race of creatures bound on other journeys. And therefore, Uncle, though it has never put a scrap of gold or silver in my pocket, I believe that it *has* done me good, and that it *will* do me good; and I say, God bless it!

[*The* CLERK *in the tank applauds, looks at the furious* SCROOGE *and pokes out his tiny fire, as if in exchange for the moment of impropriety.* SCROOGE *yells at him.*]

Scrooge (*to the* CLERK). Let me hear another sound from *you* and you'll keep your Christmas by losing your situation. (*To the* NEPHEW) You're quite a powerful speaker, sir. I wonder you don't go into Parliament.

⒟ **Literary Perspectives** Archetypes "Bah! Humbug!" is an exclamation from Scrooge that you might be familiar with. Why does his use of the phrase help you perceive him as an unhappy man?

Vocabulary **morose** (muh ROHS) *adj.*: gloomy; ill-tempered.

A Christmas Carol: Scrooge and Marley, Act One **779**

Nephew. Don't be angry, Uncle. Come! Dine with us tomorrow.

Scrooge. I'd rather see myself dead than see myself with your family!

Nephew. But, why? Why?

Scrooge. Why did you get married?

Nephew. Because I fell in love.

Scrooge. That, sir, is the only thing that you have said to me in your entire lifetime which is even more ridiculous than "Merry Christmas"! (*Turns from* NEPHEW) Good afternoon.

Nephew. Nay, Uncle, you never came to see me before I married either. Why give it as a reason for not coming now?

Scrooge. Good afternoon, Nephew!

Nephew. I want nothing from you; I ask nothing of you; why cannot we be friends?

Scrooge. Good afternoon!

Nephew. I am sorry with all my heart, to find you so resolute. But I have made the trial in homage to Christmas, and I'll keep my Christmas humor to the last. So A Merry Christmas, Uncle!

Scrooge. Good afternoon!

Nephew. And A Happy New Year!

Scrooge. Good afternoon!

Nephew (*He stands facing* SCROOGE). Uncle, you are the most . . . (*Pauses*) No, I shan't. My Christmas humor is intact . . . (*Pause*) God bless you, Uncle . . . (NEPHEW *turns and starts for the door; he stops at* CRATCHIT's *cage.*) Merry Christmas, Bob Cratchit . . .

Cratchit. Merry Christmas to you sir, and a very, very happy New Year . . .

Scrooge (*calling across to them*). Oh, fine, a perfection, just fine . . . to see the perfect pair of you: husbands, with wives and children to support . . . my clerk there earning fifteen shillings a week . . . and the perfect pair of you, talking about a Merry Christmas! (*Pauses*) I'll retire to Bedlam![8]

Nephew (*to* CRATCHIT). He's impossible!

Cratchit. Oh, mind him not, sir. He's getting on in years, and he's alone. He's noticed your visit. I'll wager your visit has warmed him.

Nephew. Him? Uncle Ebenezer Scrooge? *Warmed?* You are a better Christian than I am, sir. **Ⓔ**

Cratchit (*opening the door for* NEPHEW; *two* DO-GOODERS *will enter, as* NEPHEW *exits*). Good day to you, sir, and God bless.

Nephew. God bless . . .

[*One man who enters is portly, the other is thin. Both are pleasant.*]

Cratchit. Can I help you, gentlemen?

Thin Man (*carrying papers and books; looks around* CRATCHIT *to* SCROOGE). Scrooge and Marley's, I believe. Have I the pleasure of addressing Mr. Scrooge, or Mr. Marley?

---

8. **Bedlam** (BEHD luhm): shortened name of St. Mary of Bethlehem, a hospital in London for people with mental illnesses.

Ⓔ Read and Discuss From what you read, what do you make of Scrooge?

Kelsey Grammer
as Scrooge in
A Christmas Carol.

Bill Murray as
Francis Xavier
Cross in scene from
Scrooged (1988), a
movie directed by
Richard Donner.

Analyzing Visuals **Viewing and Interpreting** The photographs above
are stills from movie versions of the *Christmas Carol* story. Which scene seems
to convey most effectively Scrooge's nastiness? Give reasons for your answer.

Scrooge. Mr. Marley has been dead these seven years. He died seven years ago this very night.

Portly Man. We have no doubt his liberality[9] is well represented by his surviving partner . . . (*Offers his calling card*)

Scrooge (*handing back the card; unlooked at*). . . . Good afternoon.

Thin Man. This will take but a moment, sir . . .

Portly Man. At this festive season of the year, Mr. Scrooge, it is more than usually desirable that we should make some slight provision for the poor and destitute, who suffer greatly at the present time. Many thousands are in want of common necessities; hundreds of thousands are in want of common comforts, sir.

Scrooge. Are there no prisons?

Portly Man. Plenty of prisons.

Scrooge. And aren't the Union workhouses[10] still in operation?

Thin Man. They are. Still. I wish that I could say that they are not.

---

9. **liberality** (lihb uhr AL ih tee): generosity.

10. **Union workhouses:** institutions to which people who could not support themselves were sent. Residents were forced to earn their keep by working ten-hour days.

We choose this time, because it is a time, of all others, when Want is keenly felt.

Scrooge. The Treadmill[11] and the Poor Law[12] are in full vigor, then?

Thin Man. Both are very busy, sir.

Scrooge. Ohhh, I see. I was afraid, from what you said at first, that something had occurred to stop them from their useful course. (*Pauses*) I'm glad to hear it.

Portly Man. Under the impression that they scarcely furnish Christian cheer of mind or body to the multitude, a few of us are endeavoring to raise a fund to buy the Poor some meat and drink, and means of warmth. We choose this time, because it is a time, of all others, when Want is keenly felt, and Abundance rejoices. (*Pen in hand; as well as notepad*) What shall I put you down for, sir?

Scrooge. Nothing! Ⓞ

Portly Man. You wish to be left anonymous?

Scrooge. I wish to be left alone! (*Pauses; turns away; turns back to them*) Since you

---

11. **Treadmill:** device formerly used in prisons as a form of punishment; a kind of wheel with steps around it that was turned by the weight of people walking on the steps. Walking on the Treadmill was like walking up an endless flight of stairs.

12. **Poor Law:** law that dictated how the poor were treated; at the time this story was written, the only way the poor could survive was by entering a workhouse.

F **Literary Perspectives** Archetypes How does Scrooge's response to the Portly Man and the Thin Man reinforce the idea that he is a miserable man?

Vocabulary **destitute** (DEHS tuh toot) *n.*: people living in utter poverty.

ask me what I wish, gentlemen, that is my answer. I help to support the establishments that I have mentioned: they cost enough: and those who are badly off must go there.

Thin Man. Many can't go there; and many would rather die.

Scrooge. If they would rather die, they had better do it, and decrease the surplus population. Besides—excuse me—I don't know that.

Thin Man. But you might know it!

Scrooge. It's not my business. It's enough for a man to understand his own business, and not to interfere with other people's. Mine occupies me constantly. Good afternoon, gentlemen! (SCROOGE *turns his back on the gentlemen and returns to his desk.*)

Portly Man. But, sir, Mr. Scrooge . . . think of the poor.

Scrooge (*turns suddenly to them. Pauses*). Take your leave of my offices, sirs, while I am still smiling.

[*The* THIN MAN *looks at the* PORTLY MAN. *They are undone. They shrug. They move to door.* CRATCHIT *hops up to open it for them.*]

Thin Man. Good day, sir . . . (*To* CRATCHIT) A Merry Christmas to you, sir . . .

Cratchit. Yes. A Merry Christmas to both you . . .

Portly Man. Merry Christmas . . .

[CRATCHIT *silently squeezes something into the hand of the* THIN MAN.]

Thin Man. What's this?

Cratchit. Shhhh . . . (CRATCHIT *opens the door; wind and snow whistle into the room.*) **G**

Thin Man. Thank you, sir, thank you.

[CRATCHIT *closes the door and returns to his workplace.* SCROOGE *is at his own counting table. He talks to* CRATCHIT *without looking up.*]

Scrooge. It's less of a time of year for being merry, and more a time of year for being loony . . . if you ask me.

Cratchit. Well, I don't know, sir . . .

[*The clock's bell strikes six o'clock.*]

Well, there it is, eh, six?

Scrooge. Saved by six bells, are you?

Cratchit. I must be going home . . . (*He snuffs out his candle and puts on his hat.*) I hope you have a . . . very very lovely day tomorrow, sir . . .

Scrooge. Hmmm. Oh, you'll be wanting the whole day tomorrow, I suppose?

Cratchit. If quite convenient, sir.

Scrooge. It's not convenient, and it's not fair. If I was to stop half-a-crown for

G | Read and Discuss | What do the Do-Gooders show you?

it, you'd think yourself ill-used, I'll be bound?

[CRATCHIT *smiles faintly.*]

Cratchit. I don't know, sir . . .
Scrooge. And yet, you don't think me ill-used, when I pay a day's wages for no work . . .
Cratchit. It's only but once a year . . .
Scrooge. A poor excuse for picking a man's pocket every 25th of December! But I suppose you must have the whole day. Be here all the earlier the next morning!
Cratchit. Oh, I will, sir. I will. I promise you. And, sir . . .
Scrooge. Don't say it, Cratchit.
Cratchit. But let me wish you a . . .
Scrooge. Don't say it, Cratchit. I warn you . . .
Cratchit. Sir!
Scrooge. Cratchit!

[CRATCHIT *opens the door.*]

Cratchit. All right, then, sir . . . well . . . (*Suddenly*) Merry Christmas, Mr. Scrooge!

[*And he runs out the door, shutting same behind him.* SCROOGE *moves to his desk; gathering his coat, hat, etc. A* BOY *appears at his window.*]

Boy (*singing*). "Away in a manger . . ."

[SCROOGE *seizes his ruler and whacks at the image of the* BOY *outside. The* BOY *leaves.*]

Scrooge. Bah! Humbug! Christmas! Bah! Humbug! (*He shuts out the light.*) **Ⓗ**

[SCROOGE *will walk alone to his rooms from his offices. As he makes a long slow cross of the stage, the scenery should change, Christmas music will be heard, various people will cross by* SCROOGE, *often smiling happily. There will be occasional pleasant greetings tossed at him.*

SCROOGE, *in contrast to all, will grump and mumble. He will snap at passing boys, as might an old horrid hound.*

In short, SCROOGE's *sounds and movements will define him in contrast from all other people who cross the stage: he is the misanthrope,*[13] *the malcontent, the miser. He is* SCROOGE. *This statement of* SCROOGE's *character, by contrast to all other characters, should seem comical to the audience.*

During SCROOGE's *crossover to his rooms, snow should begin to fall. All passers-by will hold their faces to the sky, smiling, allowing snow to shower them lightly.* SCROOGE, *by contrast, will bat at the flakes with his*

---

13. **misanthrope** (MIHS uhn throhp): person who dislikes all people.

Ⓗ **Literary Perspectives** Archetypes Scrooge tries to make others as unhappy as he is. How does his behavior toward the kind people in this scene reinforce your sense of his misery?

walking-stick, as might an insomniac swat at a sleep-stopping, middle-of-the-night swarm of mosquitoes. He will comment on the blackness of the night, and, finally, reach his rooms and his encounter with the magical specter: MARLEY, *his eternal mate.*]

SCENE 3

Scrooge. No light at all . . . no moon . . . *that* is what is at the center of a Christmas Eve: dead black: void . . .

[SCROOGE *puts his key in the door's keyhole. He has reached his rooms now. The door knocker changes and is now* MARLEY's *face. A musical sound; quickly: ghostly.* MARLEY's *image is not at all angry, but looks at* SCROOGE *as did the old* MARLEY *look at* SCROOGE. *The hair is curiously stirred; eyes wide open, dead: absent of focus.* SCROOGE *stares wordlessly here. The face, before his very eyes, does deliquesce:*[14] *it is a knocker again.* SCROOGE *opens the door and checks the back of same, probably for* MARLEY's *pigtail. Seeing nothing but screws and nuts,* SCROOGE *refuses the memory.*]

Pooh, pooh!

[*The sound of the door closing resounds throughout the house as thunder. Every room echoes the sound.* SCROOGE *fastens*

---

14. **deliquesce** (dehl uh KWEHS): melt or become liquid.

---

① Literary Focus Drama/Conflict What characters might come into further conflict with Scrooge? How do the previous two scenes set up these conflicts? Explain your answer.

This is to Certify

Marriage in Victorian England

Early in the play, when Scrooge's nephew tells him he married because he fell in love, Scrooge scoffs at the idea. Scrooge's attitude seems more mean-spirited today than it would have in Dickens's time. In Victorian England, people of the middle and upper classes rarely married for love. Instead, marriages that increased a family's wealth or social standing were sought. The dowry was an important part of the marriage contract. The dowry was the wealth, in money or property, that a woman's family gave to her intended husband. It was an early payment of her inheritance and, combined with the husband's own wealth, was meant to ensure that the new family would have enough money to live on.

Ask Yourself
What does the fact that Scrooge's nephew married for love say about him?

the door and walks across the hall to the stairs, trimming his candle as he goes; and then he goes slowly up the staircase. He checks each room: sitting room, bedroom, lumber-room. He looks under the sofa, under the table: nobody there. He fixes his evening gruel on the hob;[15] changes his jacket. SCROOGE *sits near the tiny low-flamed fire, sipping his gruel. There are various pictures on the walls: all of them now show likenesses of* MAR-LEY. SCROOGE *blinks his eyes.*]

Bah! Humbug!

[SCROOGE *walks in a circle about the room. The pictures change back into their natural images. He sits down at the table in front of the fire. A bell hangs overhead. It begins to ring, of its own accord. Slowly, surely, begins the ringing of every bell in the house. They continue ringing for nearly half a minute.* SCROOGE *is stunned by the phenomenon. The bells cease their ringing all at once. Deep below* SCROOGE, *in the basement of the house, there is the sound of clanking, of some enormous chain being dragged across the floors; and now up the stairs. We hear doors flying open.*]

Bah still! Humbug still! This is not happening! I won't believe it!

---

15. **hob:** shelf at the back or side of a fireplace.

In life, I was your business partner: Jacob Marley.

[MARLEY'S GHOST *enters the room. He is horrible to look at: pigtail, vest, suit as usual, but he drags an enormous chain now, to which is fastened cash-boxes, keys, padlocks, ledgers, deeds, and heavy purses fashioned of steel. He is transparent.* MARLEY *stands opposite the stricken* SCROOGE.]

How now! What do you want of me?
Marley. Much!
Scrooge. Who are you?
Marley. Ask me who I *was*.
Scrooge. Who *were* you then?
Marley. In life, I was your business partner: Jacob Marley.
Scrooge. I see . . . can you sit down?
Marley. I can.
Scrooge. Do it then.
Marley. I shall.

[MARLEY *sits opposite* SCROOGE, *in the chair across the table, at the front of the fireplace.*]

You don't believe in me.
Scrooge. I don't.
Marley. Why do you doubt your senses?
Scrooge. Because every little thing affects them. A slight disorder of the stomach makes them cheat. You may be an undigested bit of beef, a blot of mustard, a crumb of cheese, a fragment of an underdone potato. There's more of gravy than of grave about you, whatever you are!

[*There is a silence between them. *SCROOGE* is made nervous by it. He picks up a toothpick.*]

Humbug! I tell you: humbug! ⓙ

[MARLEY *opens his mouth and screams a ghostly, fearful scream. The scream echoes about each room of the house. Bats fly, cats screech, lightning flashes. *SCROOGE* stands and walks backwards against the wall. *MAR-LEY* stands and screams again. This time, he takes his head and lifts it from his shoulders. His head continues to scream. *MARLEY'S* face again appears on every picture in the room: all screaming. *SCROOGE*, on his knees before *MARLEY*.*]

Mercy! Dreadful apparition,[16] mercy! Why, O! why do you trouble me so?
Marley. Man of the worldly mind, do you believe in me, or not?
Scrooge. I do. I must. But why do spirits such as you walk the earth? And why do they come to me?
Marley. It is required of every man that the spirit within him should walk abroad among his fellow-men, and travel far and wide; and if that spirit goes not forth in life, it is condemned to do so after death. (MARLEY *screams again: a tragic scream, from his ghostly bones*) I wear the chain I forged in life. I made it link by link, and yard by yard. Is its pattern strange to *you*?

---

16. apparition (ap uh RIHSH uhn): ghost.

ⓙ **Literary Focus** Drama/Character What effect is Marley having on Scrooge? Support your opinion with details from their interaction with one another.

Or would you know, you, Scrooge, the weight and length of the strong coil you bear yourself? It was full as heavy and long as this, seven Christmas Eves ago. You have labored on it, since. It is a ponderous chain.

[*Terrified that a chain will appear about his body, *SCROOGE* spins and waves the unwanted chain away. None, of course, appears. Sees *MARLEY* watching him dance about the room. *MARLEY* watches *SCROOGE*; silently.*]

Scrooge. Jacob. Old Jacob Marley, tell me more. Speak comfort to me, Jacob . . .
Marley. I have none to give. Comfort comes from other regions, Ebenezer Scrooge, and is conveyed by other ministers, to other kinds of men. A very little more, is all that is permitted to me. I cannot rest, I cannot stay, I cannot linger anywhere . . . (*He moans again.*) my spirit never walked beyond our counting-house—mark me!—in life my spirit never roved beyond the narrow limits of our money-changing hole; and weary journeys lie before me!
Scrooge. But you were always a good man of business, Jacob.
Marley (*screams word "business"; a flashpot explodes with him*). BUSINESS!!! Mankind was my business. The common welfare was my business; charity, mercy, forbearance, benevolence, were, all, my business.

Vocabulary benevolence (buh NEHV uh luhns) *n.*: goodwill; kindliness.

[SCROOGE *is quaking.*]

Hear me, Ebenezer Scrooge! My time is nearly gone.

Scrooge. I will, but don't be hard upon me. And don't be flowery, Jacob! Pray!

Marley. How is it that I appear before you in a shape that you can see, I may not tell. I have sat invisible beside you many and many a day. That is no light part of my penance. I am here tonight to warn you that you have yet a chance and hope of escaping my fate. A chance and hope of my procuring,[17] Ebenezer.

Scrooge. You were always a good friend to me. Thank'ee!

Marley. You will be haunted by Three Spirits.

Scrooge. Would that be the chance and hope you mentioned, Jacob?

Marley. It is.

Scrooge. I think I'd rather not.

Marley. Without their visits, you cannot hope to shun the path I tread. Expect the first one tomorrow, when the bell tolls one.

Scrooge. Couldn't I take 'em all at once, and get it over, Jacob?

Marley. Expect the second on the next night at the same hour. The third upon the next night when the last stroke of twelve has ceased to vibrate. Look to see me no more. Others may, but you may not. And look that, for your own sake, you remember what has passed between us!

[MARLEY *places his head back upon his shoulders. He approaches the window and beckons to* SCROOGE *to watch. Outside the window, specters fly by, carrying money-boxes and chains. They make a confused sound of lamentation.* MARLEY, *after listening a moment, joins into their mournful dirge.*[18] *He leans to the window and floats out into the bleak, dark night. He is gone.*]

Scrooge (*rushing to the window*). Jacob! No, Jacob! Don't leave me! I'm frightened!

[*He sees that* MARLEY *has gone. He looks outside. He pulls the shutter closed, so that the scene is blocked from his view. All sound stops. After a pause, he re-opens the shutter and all is quiet, as it should be on a Christmas Eve. Carolers carol out of doors, in the distance.* SCROOGE *closes the shutter and walks down the stairs. He examines the door by which* MARLEY *first entered.*]

No one here at all! Did I imagine all that? Humbug! (*He looks about the room.*) I did imagine it. It only happened in my foulest dream-mind, didn't it? An undigested bit of . . .

[*Thunder and lightning in the room; suddenly*]

Sorry! Sorry!   **Ⓚ**

[*There is silence again. The lights fade out.*]

---

17. **procuring:** bringing about; causing.

18. **dirge:** mournful sound or piece of music that expresses grief.

Ⓚ Read and Discuss | What has happened?

Alec Guinness as Marley's Ghost in the 1970 movie *Scrooge*, directed by Ronald Neame.

SCENE 4

[*Christmas music, choral, "Hark the Herald Angels Sing," sung by an onstage choir of children, spotlighted,* DOWNSTAGE CENTER. *Above,* SCROOGE, *in his bed, dead to the world, asleep, in his darkened room. It should appear that the choir is singing somewhere outside of the house, of course, and a use of scrim[19] is thus suggested. When the singing is ended, the choir should fade out of view and* MARLEY *should fade into view, in their place.*]

Marley (*directly to audience*). From this point forth . . . I shall be quite visible to you, but invisible to him. (*Smiles*) He will feel my presence, nevertheless, for, unless my senses fail me completely, we are—you and I—witness to the changing of a miser: that one, my partner in life, in business, and in eternity: that one: Scrooge. (*Moves to staircase, below* SCROOGE) See him now. He endeavors to pierce the darkness with his ferret eyes. (*To audience*) See him, now. He listens for the hour. **Ⓛ**

[*The bells toll.* SCROOGE *is awakened and quakes as the hour approaches one o'clock, but the bells stop their sound at the hour of twelve.*]

Scrooge (*astonished*). Midnight! Why this isn't possible. It was past two when I went to bed. An icicle must have gotten into the clock's works! I couldn't have slept through the whole day and far into another night. It isn't possible that anything has happened to the sun, and this is twelve at noon! (*He runs to window; unshutters same; it is night.*) Night, still. Quiet, normal for the season, cold. It is certainly not noon. I cannot in any way afford to lose my days. Securities come due, promissory notes,[20] interest on investments: these are things that happen in the daylight! (*He returns to his bed.*) Was this a dream?

[MARLEY *appears in his room. He speaks to the audience.*]

Marley. You see? He does not, with faith, believe in me fully, even still! Whatever will it take to turn the faith of a miser from money to men?

Scrooge. Another quarter and it'll be one and Marley's ghostly friends will come. (*Pauses; listens*) Where's the chime for one? (*Ding, dong*) A quarter *past*! (*Repeats*) Half-past! (*Repeats*) A quarter to it! But where's the heavy bell of the hour one? This is a game in which I lose my senses! Perhaps, if I allowed myself another short doze . . .

---

19. **scrim:** transparent fabric or screen used to create special effects in the theater.

20. **promissory notes:** written promises to pay a specific amount of money.

Ⓛ **Literary Perspectives** Archetypes What important information does Marley's speech provide? In what other stories have you encountered this kind of change within a character?

Marley. . . . Doze, Ebenezer, doze.

[*A heavy bell thuds its one ring; dull and definitely one o'clock. There is a flash of light.* SCROOGE *sits up, in a sudden. A hand draws back the curtains by his bed. He sees it.*]

Scrooge. A hand! Who owns it! Hello!

[*Ghostly music again, but of a new nature to the play. A strange figure stands before* SCROOGE—*like a child, yet at the same time like an old man: white hair, but unwrinkled skin; long, muscular arms, but delicate legs and feet. Wears white tunic; lustrous belt cinches waist. Branch of fresh green holly in its hand, but has its dress trimmed with fresh summer flowers. Clear jets of light spring from the crown of its head. Holds cap in hand. The* SPIRIT *is called* PAST.]

Are you the Spirit, sir, whose coming was foretold to me?
Past. I am.
Marley. Does he take this to be a vision of his green grocer?
Scrooge. Who, and what are you?
Past. I am the Ghost of Christmas Past.
Scrooge. Long past?
Past. Your past.
Scrooge. May I ask, please, sir, what business you have here with me?
Past. Your welfare.
Scrooge. Not to sound ungrateful, sir, and really, please do understand that I am plenty obliged for your concern, but, really, kind spirit, it would have done all the better for my welfare to have been left alone altogether, to have slept peacefully through this night.
Past. Your reclamation, then. Take heed!
Scrooge. My what?
Past (*motioning to* SCROOGE *and taking his arm*). Rise! Fly with me! (*He leads* SCROOGE *to the window.*)
Scrooge (*panicked*). Fly, but I am a mortal and cannot fly!
Past (*pointing to his heart*). Bear but a touch of my hand *here* and you shall be upheld in more than this!

[SCROOGE *touches the spirit's heart and the lights dissolve into sparkly flickers. Lovely crystals of music are heard. The scene dissolves into another. Christmas music again*]

SCENE 5

[SCROOGE *and the* GHOST OF CHRISTMAS PAST *walk together across an open stage. In the background, we see a field that is open; covered by a soft, downy snow: a country road.*]

Scrooge. Good Heaven! I was bred in this place. I was a boy here!

[SCROOGE *freezes, staring at the field beyond.* MARLEY'S GHOST *appears beside him; takes* SCROOGE's *face in his hands, and turns his face to the audience.*]

A Christmas Carol scenic design by Scott Kirkham. Flower Mound Performing Arts Theatre, 2003.

Marley. You see this Scrooge: stricken by feeling. Conscious of a thousand odors floating in the air, each one connected with a thousand thoughts, and hopes, and joys, and cares long, long forgotten. (*Pause*) This one—this Scrooge—before your very eyes, returns to life, among the living. (*To audience, sternly*) You'd best pay your most careful attention. I would suggest rapt.[21]

---

21. **rapt:** spellbound; engrossed.

[*There is a small flash and puff of smoke and* MARLEY *is gone again.*]

Past. Your lip is trembling, Mr. Scrooge. And what is that upon your cheek?
Scrooge. Upon my cheek? Nothing . . . a blemish on the skin from the eating of over-much grease . . . nothing . . . (*Suddenly*) Kind Spirit of Christmas Past, lead me where you will, but *quickly*! To be stagnant in this place is, for me, *unbearable*!

Past. You recollect the way?

Scrooge. Remember it! I would know it blindfolded! My bridge, my church, my winding river! (*Staggers about, trying to see it all at once. He weeps again.*)

Past. These are but shadows of things that have been. They have no consciousness of us.

[*Four jocund travelers enter, singing a Christmas song in four-part harmony—"God Rest Ye Merry Gentlemen."*]

Scrooge. Listen! I know these men! I know them! I remember the beauty of their song!

Past. But, why do you remember it so happily? It is Merry Christmas that they say to one another! What is Merry Christmas to you, Mr. Scrooge? Out upon Merry Christmas, right? What good has Merry Christmas ever done you, Mr. Scrooge? . . .

Scrooge (*after a long pause*). None. No good. None . . . (*He bows his head.*)

Past. Look, you, sir, a school ahead. The schoolroom is not quite deserted. A solitary child, neglected by his friends, is left there still.

[SCROOGE *falls to the ground; sobbing as he sees, and we see, a small boy, the young* SCROOGE, *sitting and weeping, bravely, alone at his desk: alone in a vast space, a void.*]

Scrooge. I cannot look on him!

Past. You must, Mr. Scrooge, you must.

Scrooge. It's me. (*Pauses; weeps*) Poor boy. He lived inside his head . . . alone . . . (*Pauses; weeps*) poor boy. (*Pauses; stops his weeping*) I wish . . . (*Dries his eyes on his cuff*) ah! it's too late!

Past. What is the matter?

Scrooge. There was a boy singing a Christmas Carol outside my door last night. I should like to have given him something: that's all. Ⓜ

Past (*smiles; waves his hand to* SCROOGE). Come. Let us see another Christmas.

[*Lights out on little boy. A flash of light. A puff of smoke. Lights up on older boy*]

Scrooge. Look! Me, again! Older now! (*Realizes*) Oh, yes . . . still alone.

[*The boy—a slightly older* SCROOGE—*sits alone in a chair, reading. The door to the room opens and a young girl enters. She is much, much younger than this slightly older* SCROOGE. *She is, say, six, and he is, say, twelve. Elder* SCROOGE *and the* GHOST OF CHRISTMAS PAST *stand watching the scene, unseen.*]

Fan. Dear, dear brother, I have come to bring you home.

Boy. Home, little Fan?

Fan. Yes! Home, for good and all! Father is so much kinder than he ever used to be, and home's like heaven! He spoke so gently to me one dear night when I was going

---

Ⓜ **Literary Perspectives** Archetypes Based on what you know about Scrooge, do you find his behavior surprising? How is Scrooge beginning to change?

to bed that I was not afraid to ask him once more if you might come home; and he said "yes" . . . you should; and sent me in a coach to bring you. And you're to be a man and are never to come back here, but first, we're to be together all the Christmas long, and have the merriest time in the world. **(N)**

Boy. You are quite a woman, little Fan!

[*Laughing; she drags at* BOY, *causing him to stumble to the door with her. Suddenly we hear a mean and terrible voice in the hallway,* OFF. *It is the* SCHOOLMASTER.]

Schoolmaster. Bring down Master Scrooge's travel box at once! He is to travel!
Fan. Who is that, Ebenezer?
Boy. O! Quiet, Fan. It is the Schoolmaster, himself!

[*The door bursts open and into the room bursts with it the* SCHOOLMASTER.]

Schoolmaster. Master Scrooge?
Boy. Oh, Schoolmaster, I'd like you to meet my little sister, Fan, sir . . .

[*Two boys struggle on with* SCROOGE'S *trunk.*]

Fan. Pleased, sir . . . (*She curtsies.*)
Schoolmaster. You are to travel, Master Scrooge.

Scrooge. Yes, sir. I know sir . . .

[*All start to exit, but* FAN *grabs the coattail of the mean old* SCHOOLMASTER.]

Boy. Fan!
Schoolmaster. What's this?
Fan. Pardon, sir, but I believe that you've forgotten to say your goodbye to my brother, Ebenezer, who stands still now awaiting it . . . (*She smiles, curtsies, lowers her eyes.*) pardon, sir.
Schoolmaster (*amazed*). I . . . uh . . . harumph . . . uhh . . . well, then . . . (*Outstretches hand*) Goodbye, Scrooge.
Boy. Uh, well, goodbye, Schoolmaster . . .

[*Lights fade out on all but* BOY *looking at* FAN; *and* SCROOGE *and* PAST *looking at them.*]

Scrooge. Oh, my dear, dear little sister, Fan . . . how I loved her.
Past. Always a delicate creature, whom a breath might have withered, but she had a large heart . . .
Scrooge. So she had.
Past. She died a woman, and had, as I think, children.
Scrooge. One child.
Past. True. Your nephew.
Scrooge. Yes.
Past. Fine, then. We move on, Mr. Scrooge. That warehouse, there? Do you know it?

(N) Read and Discuss | What are you learning about Scrooge's childhood?

Scrooge. Know it? Wasn't I apprenticed[22] there?

Past. We'll have a look.

[*They enter the warehouse. The lights crossfade with them, coming up on an old man in Welsh wig:* FEZZIWIG.]

Scrooge. Why, it's old Fezziwig! Bless his heart; it's Fezziwig, alive again!

[FEZZIWIG *sits behind a large, high desk, counting. He lays down his pen; looks at the clock: seven bells sound.*]

Scrooge. Quittin' time . . .

Fezziwig. Quittin' time . . . (*He takes off his waistcoat and laughs; calls off*) Yo ho, Ebenezer! Dick!

[DICK WILKINS *and* EBENEZER SCROOGE—*a young man version—enter the room.* DICK *and* EBENEZER *are* FEZZIWIG's *apprentices.*]

Scrooge. Dick Wilkins, to be sure! My

> I know these men! . . .
> I remember the
> beauty
> of their song!

fellow 'prentice! Bless my soul, yes. There he is. He was very much attached to me, was Dick. Poor Dick! Dear, dear!

Fezziwig. Yo ho, my boys. No more work tonight. Christmas Eve, Dick. Christmas, Ebenezer!

[*They stand at attention in front of* FEZZIWIG; *laughing*]

Hilli-ho! Clear away, and let's have lots of room here! Hilli-ho, Dick! Chirrup, Ebenezer!   **O**

[*The young men clear the room, sweep the floor, straighten the pictures, trim the lamps, etc. The space is clear now. A* FIDDLER *enters, fiddling.*]

Hi-ho, Matthew! Fiddle away . . . where are my daughters?

[*The* FIDDLER *plays. Three young daughters of* FEZZIWIG *enter followed by six young male suitors. They are dancing to the music. All employees come in: workers, clerks, housemaids, cousins, the baker, etc. All dance. Full number wanted here. Throughout the dance, food is brought into the feast. It is "eaten" in dance, by the dancers.* EBENEZER *dances with*

---

22. **apprenticed** (uh PREHN tihst): received instruction in a trade in exchange for working for the tradesperson for no pay for a specified time period.

O **Literary Focus** **Drama/Character** How does Fezziwig's treatment of his clerks compare with Scrooge's treatment of Bob Cratchit?

all three of the daughters, as does DICK. *They compete for the daughters, happily, in the dance.* FEZZIWIG *dances with his daughters.* FEZZIWIG *dances with* DICK *and* EBENEZER. *The music changes:* MRS. FEZZIWIG *enters. She lovingly scolds her husband. They dance. She dances with* EBENEZER, *lifting him and throwing him about. She is enormously fat. When the dance is ended, they all dance off, floating away, as does the music.* SCROOGE *and the* GHOST OF CHRISTMAS PAST *stand alone now. The music is gone.*]

Past. It was a small matter, that Fezziwig made those silly folks so full of gratitude.
Scrooge. Small!
Past. Shhh!

[*Lights up on* DICK *and* EBENEZER]

Dick. We are blessed, Ebenezer, truly, to have such a master as Mr. Fezziwig!
Young Scrooge. He is the best, best, the very and absolute best! If ever I own a firm of my own, I shall treat my apprentices with the same dignity and the same grace. We have learned a wonderful lesson from the master, Dick!
Dick. Ah, that's a fact, Ebenezer. That's a fact!
Past. Was it not a small matter, really? He spent but a few pounds[23] of his mortal money on your small party. Three or four pounds, perhaps. Is that so much that he deserves such

---

23. **pounds:** money used in England at the time in which the story is set, as well as today.

praise as you and Dick so lavish now?
Scrooge. It isn't that! It isn't that, Spirit. Fezziwig had the power to make us happy or unhappy; to make our service light or burdensome; a pleasure or a toil. The happiness he gave is quite as great as if it cost him a fortune.
Past. What is the matter?
Scrooge. Nothing particular.
Past. Something, I think.
Scrooge. No, no. I should like to be able to say a word or two to my clerk just now! That's all! **ⓟ**

[EBENEZER *enters the room and shuts down all the lamps. He stretches and yawns. The* GHOST OF CHRISTMAS PAST *turns to* SCROOGE; *all of a sudden*]

Past. My time grows short! Quick!

[*In a flash of light,* EBENEZER *is gone, and in his place stands an* OLDER SCROOGE, *this one a man in the prime of his life. Beside him stands a young woman in a mourning dress. She is crying. She speaks to the man, with hostility.*]

Woman. It matters little . . . to you, very little. Another idol has displaced me.
Man. What idol has displaced you?
Woman. A golden one.
Man. This is an even-handed dealing of the world. There is nothing on which it is so hard as poverty; and there is nothing it professes to condemn with such severity as the pursuit of wealth!

ⓟ Literary Focus **Drama/Conflict** What does Scrooge want to say to Cratchit? What internal conflict is Scrooge facing?

Woman. You fear the world too much. Have I not seen your nobler aspirations fall off one by one, until the master-passion, Gain, engrosses you? Have I not?

Scrooge. No!

Man. What then? Even if I have grown so much wiser, what then? Have I changed towards you?

Woman. No . . .

Man. Am I?

Woman. Our contract is an old one. It was made when we were both poor and content to be so. You *are* changed. When it was made, you were another man.

Man. I was not another man: I was a boy.

Woman. Your own feeling tells you that you were not what you are. I am. That which promised happiness when we were one in heart is fraught with misery now that we are two . . .

Scrooge. No!

Woman. How often and how keenly I have thought of this, I will not say. It is enough that I *have* thought of it, and can release you . . . **Q**

Scrooge (*quietly*). Don't release me, madame . . .

Man. Have I ever sought release?

Woman. In words. No. Never.

Man. In what then?

Q Read and Discuss Who is this woman? What do you learn about Scrooge from her?

Fezziwig's party scene from *Scrooge* (1970).

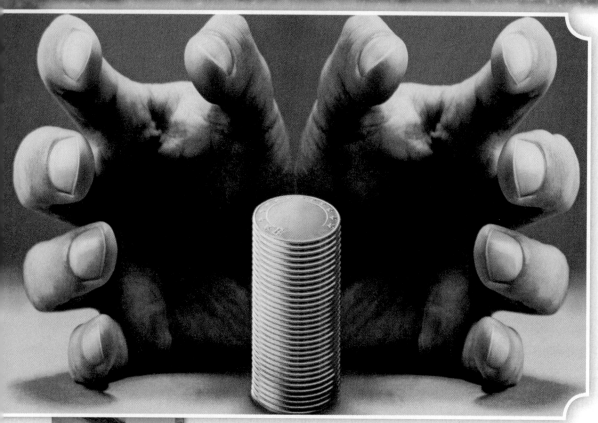

Analyzing Visuals Viewing and Interpreting What theme from *A Christmas Carol* does this image convey?

Woman. In a changed nature; in an altered spirit. In everything that made my love of any worth or value in your sight. If this has never been between us, tell me, would you seek me out and try to win me now? Ah, no!

Scrooge. Ah, yes!

Man. You think not?

Woman. I would gladly think otherwise if I could, heaven knows! But if you were free today, tomorrow, yesterday, can even I believe that you would choose a dowerless[24]

---

24. **dowerless:** without a dowry, which is property or money a bride brings to her husband on their marriage.

girl—you who in your very confidence with her weigh everything by Gain; or, choosing her, do I not know that your repentance and regret would surely follow? I do; and I release you. With a full heart, for the love of him you once were.

Scrooge. Please, I . . . I . . .

Man. Please, I . . . I . . .

Woman. Please. You may—the memory of what is past half makes me hope you will—have pain in this. A very, very brief time, and you will dismiss the memory of it, as an unprofitable dream, from which it happened well that you awoke. May you be happy in the life that you have chosen for yourself . . .

Scrooge. No!
Woman. Yourself . . . alone . . .
Scrooge. No!
Woman. Goodbye, Ebenezer . . .
Scrooge. Don't let her go!
Man. Goodbye.
Scrooge. No!

[*She exits.* SCROOGE *goes to younger man: himself.*]

You fool! Mindless loon! You fool!
Man (*to exited woman*). Fool. Mindless loon. Fool . . .
Scrooge. Don't say that! Spirit, remove me from this place.
Past. I have told you these were shadows of the things that have been. They are what they are. Do not blame me, Mr. Scrooge.
Scrooge. Remove me! I cannot bear it!

[*The faces of all who appeared in this scene are now projected for a moment around the stage: enormous, flimsy, silent.*]

Leave me! Take me back! Haunt me no longer!

[*There is a sudden flash of light: a flare. The* GHOST OF CHRISTMAS PAST *is gone.* SCROOGE *is, for the moment, alone onstage. His bed is turned down, across the stage. A small candle burns now in* SCROOGE'*s hand. There is a child's cap in his other hand. He slowly crosses the stage to his bed, to sleep.* MARLEY *appears behind* SCROOGE, *who*

continues his long, elderly cross to bed. MARLEY *speaks directly to the audience.*]   Ⓡ

Marley. Scrooge must sleep now. He must surrender to the irresistible drowsiness caused by the recognition of what was. (*Pauses*) The cap he carries is from ten lives past: his boyhood cap . . . donned atop a hopeful hairy head . . . askew, perhaps, or at a rakish angle. Doffed now in honor of regret.[25] Perhaps even too heavy to carry in his present state of weak remorse . . .

[SCROOGE *drops the cap. He lies atop his bed. He sleeps. To audience*]

He sleeps. For him, there's even more trouble ahead. (*Smiles*) For you? The play house tells me there's cider, hot, as should be your anticipation for the specters Christmas Present and Future, for I promise you both. (*Smiles again*) So, I pray you hurry back to your seats refreshed and ready for a miser—to turn his coat of gray into a blazen Christmas holly-red.

[*A flash of lightning. A clap of thunder. Bats fly. Ghostly music.* MARLEY *is gone.*]

CURTAIN.
End of Act One

---

25. **donned . . . regret:** *Don* and *doff* are opposites: *don* means "put on"; *doff* means "take off." *Askew* means "crooked"; *rakish* means "jaunty" or "stylish."

Ⓡ **Read and Discuss** What has happened between Scrooge and the Ghost of Christmas Past?

Applying Your Skills

A Christmas Carol: Scrooge and Marley, Act One
Respond and Think Critically

Quick Check

1. Briefly retell the main events of each of the five scenes in Act One.

Read with a Purpose

2. What do you learn about Scrooge from his interaction with Marley?

Reading Skills: Visualizing

3. Review the chart you kept while reading Act One. Think about the mental pictures you formed of Scrooge and Marley at the beginning of the play. Then, think about the pictures you had of the two characters at the end of the act. Explain how your images changed.

Visualizing Characters

	Beginning of Act One	End of Act One
Scrooge:		
Marley:		

Literary Focus

Literary Analysis

4. **Analyze** The Ghost of Christmas Past brings Scrooge to three different points in his past. What are those three points? How does each relate to something Scrooge said or did in a previous scene in the play?

5. **Interpret** How do the insights into Scrooge's past help you understand why he became a stingy and ill-tempered man?

6. **Literary Perspectives** Which of Scrooge's actions best typify him as a mean and miserly man? Can you think of any modern characters that are reminiscent of Scrooge? Support your response with details from the text.

Literary Skills: Drama

7. **Analyze** In Scene 3, Scrooge and Marley's Ghost understand the word *business* differently. Explain how each one defines *business*. Then, identify and discuss the main differences between the two definitions.

Literary Skills Review: Character

8. **Compare and Contrast** Certain characters in the play are Scrooge's direct opposites. They serve to emphasize his failings as a person. Choose a character from the play, and write a paragraph in which you compare and contrast the character with Scrooge. Pay close attention to each character's words or actions.

Writing Focus

Think as a Reader/Writer

Use It in Your Writing After visiting Fezziwig's warehouse, Scrooge says, "I should like to be able to say a word or two to my clerk just now!" Use some of the old-fashioned language you noted to write what Scrooge might say to Cratchit.

What Do You Think Now? In what ways is Scrooge starting to recognize what's meaningful in life? Use details from the play in your answer.

Vocabulary Development

Clarify Word Meanings: Contrast

Sometimes you can clarify the meaning of an unfamiliar word by looking for contrast clues. *A Christmas Carol: Scrooge and Marley* contains some examples of contrast that can be used to clarify word meaning. Consider this exchange between Scrooge and his nephew:

> **Scrooge.** . . .What right do you have to be merry? What reason have you to be merry? You're poor enough!

> **Nephew.** . . .What right have you to be dismal? What reason have you to be morose? You're rich enough.

These lines set up a **contrast.** You know that *rich* and *poor* are opposites, so you can conclude that *dismal* and *morose* are the opposite of *merry.*

Your Turn

Fill in the blanks with words or phrases that contrast with the boldface Vocabulary word.

1. The **morose** Scrooge seems unaffected by his _____ nephew, who drops by to wish Scrooge a happy holiday.

2. The **destitute** members of Victorian society live in a manner quite different from that of the _____.

3. Fezziwig shows **benevolence** toward his workers, while Scrooge shows Cratchit _____.

Language Coach

Synonyms Words whose meanings are the same or nearly the same are called **synonyms.** Instead of repeating a word, such as *ghost,* Dickens and Horovitz use many synonyms for the word. This adds variety to the text and avoids repetition.

ghost
phantom
shade
specter
goblin
spirit
apparition
supernatural visitor
unearthly visitor

Merry is another word you have read in this selection. Get together with a partner, and make a list of all the words you can think of that are synonyms of *merry.* Then, look in a thesaurus to find other synonyms.

Academic Vocabulary

Talk About . . .

Discuss Scrooge's <u>interactions</u> with Bob Cratchit throughout the play. How does Scrooge regard Cratchit early in the play? When he is with the Ghost of Christmas Past, why does Scrooge regret the way he treat has treated Cratchit <u>previously</u>?

Learn It Online
Take your study of synonyms further with *WordSharp*:

| go.hrw.com | L7-801 | Go |

A Christmas Carol:
Scrooge and Marley

by **Israel Horovitz**

based on **A Christmas Carol** *by* **Charles Dickens**

Act Two

SCENE 1

[*Lights. Choral music is sung. Curtain.* SCROOGE, *in bed, sleeping, in spotlight. We cannot yet see the interior of his room.* MARLEY, *opposite, in spotlight equal to* SCROOGE'S. MARLEY *laughs. He tosses his hand in the air and a flame shoots from it, magically, into the air. There is a thunder clap, and then another; a lightning flash, and then another. Ghostly music plays under. Colors change.* MARLEY'S *spotlight has gone out and now reappears, with* MAR-LEY *in it, standing next to the bed and the sleeping* SCROOGE. MARLEY *addresses the audience directly.*] Ⓐ

Marley. Hear this snoring Scrooge! Sleeping to escape the nightmare that is his waking day. What shall I bring to him now? I'm afraid nothing would astonish old Scrooge now. Not after what he's seen. Not a baby boy, not a rhinoceros, nor anything in between would astonish Ebenezer Scrooge just now. I can think of nothing . . . (*Suddenly*) that's it! Nothing! (*He speaks confidentially.*) I'll have the clock strike one and, when he awakes expecting my second messenger, there will be no one . . . nothing. Then I'll have the bell strike twelve. And then one again . . . and then nothing. Nothing . . . (*Laughs*) nothing will . . . astonish him. I think it will work.

[*The bell tolls one.* SCROOGE *leaps awake.*]

Scrooge. One! One! This is it: time! (*Looks about the room*) Nothing!

[*The bell tolls midnight.*]

Ⓐ **Reading Focus** **Visualizing** What images in the stage directions help you picture an ominous scene?

Midnight! How can this be? I'm sleeping backwards.

[*One again*]

Good heavens! One again! I'm sleeping back and forth! (*A pause.* SCROOGE *looks about.*) Nothing! Absolutely nothing!

[*Suddenly, thunder and lightning.* MARLEY *laughs and disappears. The room shakes and glows. There is suddenly springlike music.* SCROOGE *makes a run for the door.*]

Marley. Scrooge!
Scrooge. What?
Marley. Stay you put!
Scrooge. Just checking to see if anyone is in here.

[*Lights and thunder again: more music.* MARLEY *is of a sudden gone. In his place sits the* GHOST OF CHRISTMAS PRESENT—*to be called in the stage directions of the play* PRESENT—*center of room. Heaped up on the floor, to form a kind of throne, are turkeys, geese, game, poultry, brawn, great joints of meat, suckling pigs, long wreaths of sausages, mince-pies, plum puddings, barrels of oysters, red hot chestnuts, cherry-cheeked apples, juicy oranges, luscious pears, immense twelfth cakes, and seething bowls of punch, that make the chamber dim with their delicious steam. Upon this throne sits* PRESENT, *glorious to see. He bears a torch, shaped as a Horn of Plenty.*[1] SCROOGE *hops out of the door, and then peeks back again into his bedroom.* PRESENT *calls to* SCROOGE.] Ⓑ

Present. Ebenezer Scrooge. Come in, come in! Come in and know me better!
Scrooge. Hello. How should I call you?
Present. I am the Ghost of Christmas Present. Look upon me.

[PRESENT *is wearing a simple green robe. The walls around the room are now covered in greenery, as well. The room seems to be a perfect grove now: leaves of holly, mistletoe and ivy reflect the stage lights. Suddenly, there is a mighty roar of flame in the fireplace and now the hearth burns with a lavish, warming fire. There is an ancient scabbard girdling the* GHOST'S *middle, but without sword. The sheath is gone to rust.*]

You have never seen the like of me before?
Scrooge. Never.
Present. You have never walked forth with younger members of my family; my elder brothers born on Christmases past.
Scrooge. I don't think I have. I'm afraid I've not. Have you had many brothers, Spirit?
Present. More than eighteen hundred.
Scrooge. A tremendous family to provide for!

[PRESENT *stands.*]

---

1. **Horn of Plenty:** horn overflowing with good things to eat; symbol of abundance and good fortune.

Ⓑ **Literary Focus** Drama/Character Re-read the description of the Ghost of Christmas Present. What does this ghost represent?

Scrooge. Spirit, conduct me where you will. I went forth last night on compulsion, and learnt a lesson which is working now. Tonight, if you have aught to teach me, let me profit by it.
Present. Touch my robe. Ⓒ

[SCROOGE *walks cautiously to* PRESENT *and touches his robe. When he does, lightning flashes, thunder claps, music plays. Blackout*]

SCENE 2

[*PROLOGUE:* MARLEY *stands spotlit, left. He speaks directly to the audience.*]

Marley. My ghostly friend now leads my living partner through the city's streets.

[*Lights up on* SCROOGE *and* PRESENT]

See them there and hear the music people make when the weather is severe, as it is now.

[*Winter music. Choral group behind scrim, sings. When the song is done and the stage is re-set, the lights will fade up on a row of shops, behind the singers. The choral group will hum the song they have just completed now and mill about the streets, carrying their dinners to the bakers' shops*

Ⓒ **Literary Focus** Drama/Conflict What is Scrooge's internal conflict? How might this ghost help Scrooge resolve it?

Vocabulary compulsion (kuhm PUHL shuhn) *n.:* driving, irresistible force.

Albert Finney in the title role from the 1970 movie production of *Scrooge*.

and restaurants. *They will, perhaps, sing about being poor at Christmastime, whatever.*]

Present. These revelers, Mr. Scrooge, carry their own dinners to their jobs, where they will work to bake the meals the rich men and women of this city will eat as their Christmas dinners. Generous people these . . . to care for the others, so . . . Ⓓ

[PRESENT *walks among the choral group and a sparkling incense[2] falls from his torch onto their baskets, as he pulls the covers off of the baskets. Some of the choral group become angry with each other.*]

Man #1. Hey, you, watch where you're going.
Man #2. Watch it yourself, mate!

[PRESENT *sprinkles them directly; they change.*]

Man #1. I pray go in ahead of me. It's Christmas. You be first!
Man #2. No, no, I must insist that YOU be first!

---

2. **incense** (IHN sehns): substance burned to produce a pleasant odor.

Man #1. All right, I shall be, and gratefully so.
Man #2. The pleasure is equally mine, for being able to watch you pass, smiling.
Man #1. I would find it a shame to quarrel on Christmas Day . . .
Man #2. As would I.
Man #1. Merry Christmas then, friend!
Man #2. And a Merry Christmas straight back to you!

[*Church bells toll. The choral group enter the buildings; the shops and restaurants; they exit the stage, shutting their doors closed behind them. All sound stops.* SCROOGE *and* PRESENT *are alone again.*]

Scrooge. What is it you sprinkle from your torch?
Present. Kindness.
Scrooge. Do you sprinkle your kindness on any particular people or on all people?
Present. To any person kindly given. And to the very poor most of all.
Scrooge. Why to the very poor most?
Present. Because the very poor need it most. Touch my heart . . . here, Mr. Scrooge. We have another journey.

[SCROOGE *touches the* GHOST'S *heart and music plays, lights change color, lightning*

Ⓓ **Literary Perspectives** Archetypes Think about what you know of Scrooge from the previous act. In what ways are the revelers different from Scrooge? List at least two differences you've noticed.

Kelsey Grammer as Scrooge and Jesse L. Martin as the Ghost of Christmas Present in *A Christmas Carol*.

flashes, thunder claps. A choral group appears on the street, singing Christmas carols.] **E**

SCENE 3

[MARLEY *stands spotlit in front of a scrim on which is painted the exterior of* CRATCHIT'S *four-roomed house. There is a flash and a clap and* MARLEY *is gone. The lights shift color again, the scrim flies away, and we are in the interior of the Cratchit family home.* SCROOGE *is there, with the* SPIRIT (PRESENT), *watching* MRS. CRATCHIT *set the table with the help of* BELINDA CRATCHIT, *and* PETER CRATCHIT, *a baby,*

pokes a fork into the mashed potatoes on his high-chair's tray. He also chews on his shirt collar.]

Scrooge. What is this place, Spirit?
Present. This is the home of your employee, Mr. Scrooge. Don't you know it?
Scrooge. Do you mean Cratchit, Spirit? Do you mean this is Cratchit's home?
Present. None other.
Scrooge. These children are his?
Present. There are more to come presently.
Scrooge. On his meager earnings! What foolishness!

E **Reading Focus** Visualizing What details in the stage directions help you picture what has happened?

Vocabulary **meager** (MEE guhr) *adj.*: small in amount.

Present. Foolishness, is it?

Scrooge. Wouldn't you say so? Fifteen shillings[3] a week's what he gets!

Present. I would say that he gets the pleasure of his family, fifteen times a week times the number of hours in a day! Wait, Mr. Scrooge. Wait, listen and watch. You might actually learn something . . .

Mrs. Cratchit. What has ever got your precious father then? And your brother, Tiny Tim? And Martha warn't as late last Christmas by half an hour!

[MARTHA *opens the door, speaking to her mother as she does.*]

Martha. Here's Martha, now, Mother!

[*She laughs. The Cratchit children squeal with delight.*]

Belinda. It's Martha, Mother! Here's Martha!

Peter. Marthmama, Marthmama! Hullo!

Belinda. Hurrah! Martha! Martha! There's such an enormous goose for us, Martha!

Mrs. Cratchit. Why, bless your heart alive, my dear, how late you are!

Martha. We'd a great deal of work to finish up last night, and had to clear away this morning, Mother.

Mrs. Cratchit. Well, never mind so long as you are come. Sit ye down before the fire,

---

3. **Fifteen shillings:** tiny sum for one week's work; about $130 USD in 2005 dollars.

my dear, and have a warm, Lord bless ye!

Belinda. No, no! There's Father coming. Hide, Martha, hide!

[MARTHA *giggles and hides herself.*]

Martha. Where? Here?

Peter. *Hide, hide!*

Belinda. Not there! *THERE!*

[MARTHA *is hidden.* BOB CRATCHIT *enters, carrying* TINY TIM *atop his shoulder. He wears a threadbare and fringeless comforter hanging down in front of him.* TINY TIM *carries small crutches and his small legs are bound in an iron frame brace.*]

Bob and **Tiny Tim.** Merry Christmas.

Bob. Merry Christmas my love, Merry Christmas Peter, Merry Christmas Belinda. Why, where is Martha?

Mrs. Cratchit. Not coming.

Bob. Not coming: Not coming upon Christmas Day?

Martha (*pokes head out*). Ohhh, poor Father. Don't be disappointed.

Bob. What's this?

Martha. 'Tis I!

Bob. Martha!

[*They embrace.*]

Tiny Tim. Martha! Martha!

Martha. Tiny Tim!

[TINY TIM *is placed in* MARTHA'*s arms.* BELINDA *and* PETER *rush him offstage.*]

Belinda. Come, brother! You must come hear the pudding singing in the copper.
Tiny Tim. The pudding? What flavor have we?
Peter. Plum! Plum!
Tiny Tim. Oh, Mother! I love plum!

[*The children exit the stage, giggling.*]

Mrs. Cratchit. And how did little Tim behave?
Bob. As good as gold, and even better. Somehow he gets thoughtful sitting by himself so much, and thinks the strangest things you ever heard. He told me, coming home, that he hoped people saw him in the church, because he was a cripple, and it might be pleasant to them to remember upon Christmas Day, who made lame beggars walk and blind men see. (*Pauses*) **F**
He has the oddest ideas sometimes, but he seems all the while to be growing stronger and more hearty . . . one would never know. (*Hears* TIM'*s crutch on floor outside door*)
Peter. The goose has arrived to be eaten!
Belinda. Oh, mama, mama, it's beautiful.
Martha. It's a perfect goose, Mother!
Tiny Tim. To this Christmas goose, Mother and Father I say . . . (*Yells*) Hurrah! Hurrah!
Other Children (*copying* TIM). *Hurrah! !*

[*The family sits round the table.* BOB *and*

MRS. CRATCHIT *serve the trimmings, quickly. All sit; all bow heads; all pray.*]

Bob. Thank you, dear Lord, for your many gifts . . . our dear children; our wonderful meal; our love for one another; and the warmth of our small fire—(*Looks up at all*) A merry Christmas to us, my dear. God bless us!
All (*except* TIM). Merry Christmas! God bless us!
Tiny Tim (*in a short silence*). God bless us every one.

[*All freeze. Spotlight on* PRESENT *and* SCROOGE]

Scrooge. Spirit, tell me if Tiny Tim will live.
Present. I see a vacant seat . . . in the poor chimney corner, and a crutch without an owner, carefully preserved. If these shadows remain unaltered by the future, the child will die.
Scrooge. No, no, kind Spirit! Say he will be spared!
Present. If these shadows remain unaltered by the future, none other of my race will find him here. What then? If he be like to die, he had better do it, and decrease the surplus population. **G**

[SCROOGE *bows his head. We hear* BOB'*s voice speak* SCROOGE'*s name.*]

Bob. Mr. Scrooge . . .

F **Reading Focus** **Visualizing** Why do you think the playwright calls for the speaker to pause here?

G **Literary Focus** **Drama/Conflict** What type of conflict is developing here? What is causing the tension?

Scrooge. Huh? What's that? Who calls?

Bob (*his glass raised in a toast*). I'll give you Mr. Scrooge, the Founder of the Feast!

Scrooge. Me, Bob? You toast *me*?

Present. Save your breath, Mr. Scrooge. You can't be seen or heard.

Mrs. Cratchit. The Founder of the Feast, indeed! I wish I had him here, that miser Scrooge. I'd give him a piece of my mind to feast upon, and I hope he'd have a good appetite for it!

Bob. My dear! Christmas Day!

Mrs. Cratchit. It should be Christmas Day, I am sure, on which one drinks the health of such an odious, stingy, unfeeling man as Mr. Scrooge . . .

Scrooge. Oh, Spirit, must I? . . .

Mrs. Cratchit. You know he is, Robert! Nobody knows it better than you do, poor fellow!

Bob. This is Christmas Day, and I should like to drink to the health of the man who employs me and allows me to earn my living and our support and that man is Ebenezer Scrooge . . .

Mrs. Cratchit. I'll drink to his health for your sake and the day's, but not for his sake . . . a Merry Christmas and a Happy New Year to you, Mr. Scrooge, wherever you may be this day!

Scrooge. Just here, kind madam . . . out of sight, out of sight . . .

Bob. Thank you, my dear. Thank you.

Scrooge. Thank *you*, Bob . . . and Mrs. Cratchit, too. No one else is toasting me, . . . not now . . . not ever. Of that I am sure. . . **(H)**

Bob. Children . . .

All. Merry Christmas to Mr. Scrooge.

Bob. I'll pay you six-pence, Tim, for my favorite song.

Tiny Tim. Oh, Father, I'd so love to sing it, but not for pay. This Christmas goose—this feast—you and Mother, my brother and sisters close with me: that's my pay—

Bob. Martha, will you play the notes on the lute, for Tiny Tim's song.

Belinda. May I sing, too, Father?

Bob. We'll all sing.

> To this Christmas goose, Mother and Father, I say . . . *Hurrah! Hurrah!*

[*They sing a song about a tiny child lost in the snow—probably from Wordsworth's poem.* TIM *sings the lead vocal; all chime in for the chorus. Their song fades under, as the* GHOST OF CHRISTMAS PRESENT *speaks.*]

Present. Mark my words, Ebenezer Scrooge. I do not present the Cratchits to you because they are a handsome, or bril-

---

(H) Literary Perspectives Archetypes What is surprising about Scrooge's statement here? In what ways does it go against the archetypal character you've seen so far?

liant family. They are not handsome. They are not brilliant. They are not well-dressed, or tasteful to the times. Their shoes are not even waterproofed by virtue of money or cleverness spent. So when the pavement is wet, so are the insides of their shoes and the tops of their toes. These are the Cratchits, Mr. Scrooge. They are not highly special. They are happy, grateful, pleased with one another, contented with the time and how it passes. They don't sing very well, do they? But, nonetheless, they do sing . . . (*Pauses*) think of that, Scrooge. Fifteen shillings a week and they do sing . . . hear their song until its end.

Scrooge. I am listening.

[*The chorus sings full volume now, until . . . the song ends here.*] ❶

Spirit, it must be time for us to take our leave. I feel in my heart that it is . . . that I must think on that which I have seen here . . .
Present. Touch my robe again . . .

[SCROOGE *touches* PRESENT's *robe. The lights fade out on the* CRATCHITS, *who sit, frozen, at the table.* SCROOGE *and* PRESENT *in a spotlight now. Thunder, lightning, smoke. They are gone.*]

---

❶ **Read and Discuss** What does this imply about Bob Cratchit's home?

Bob Crachit (David Whalen), Mrs. Crachit (Devan Raymond), and their children in *A Christmas Carol* at South Coast Repertory Theatre.

Photo: Henry Di Rocco - South Coast Repertory Theatre.

SCENE 4

[MARLEY *appears* DOWNSTAGE LEFT *in single spotlight. A storm brews. Thunder and lightning.* SCROOGE *and* PRESENT *"fly" past,* UPSTAGE. *The storm continues, furiously, and, now and again,* SCROOGE *and* PRESENT *will zip past in their travels.* MARLEY *will speak straight out to the audience.*]

Marley. The Ghost of Christmas Present, my co-worker in this attempt to turn a miser, flies about now with that very miser, Scrooge, from street to street, and he points out partygoers on their way to Christmas parties. If one were to judge from the numbers of people on their way to friendly gatherings, one might think that no one was left at home to give anyone welcome . . . but that's not the case, is it? Every home is expecting company and . . . (*He laughs.*) Scrooge is amazed.

[SCROOGE *and* PRESENT *zip past again. The lights fade up around them. We are in the* NEPHEW's *home, in the living room.* PRESENT *and* SCROOGE *stand watching the* NEPHEW: FRED *and his* WIFE, *fixing the fire.*]

Scrooge. What is this place? We've moved from the mines!
Present. You do not recognize them?
Scrooge. It is my nephew! . . . and the one he married . . .

[MARLEY *waves his hand and there is a lightning flash. He disappears.*]

Fred. It strikes me as sooooo funny, to think of what he said . . . that Christmas was a humbug, as I live! He believed it!
Wife. More shame for him, Fred.
Fred. Well, he's a comical old fellow, that's the truth.
Wife. I have no patience with him.
Fred. Oh, I have! I am sorry for him; I couldn't be angry with him if I tried. Who suffers by his ill whims? Himself, always . . .
Scrooge. It's me they talk of, isn't it, Spirit?
Fred. Here, wife, consider this. Uncle Scrooge takes it into his head to dislike us, and he won't come and dine with us. What's the consequence?
Wife. Oh . . . you're sweet to say what I think you're about to say, too, Fred . . .
Fred. What's the consequence? He don't lose much of a dinner by it, I can tell you that!
Wife. Ooooooo, Fred! Indeed, I think he loses a very good dinner . . . ask my sisters, or your bachelor friend, Topper . . . ask any of them. They'll tell you what old Scrooge, your uncle, missed: a dandy meal!
Fred. Well, that's something of a relief, wife. Glad to hear it!

[*He hugs his wife. They laugh. They kiss.*]

The truth is, he misses much yet. I mean to give him the same chance every year, whether he likes it or not, for I pity him.

Nay, he is my only uncle and I feel for the old miser . . . but, I tell you, wife: I see my dear and perfect mother's face on his own wizened cheeks and brow: brother and sister they were, and I cannot erase that from each view of him I take . . . **J**

Wife. I understand what you say, Fred, and I am with you in your yearly asking. But he never will accept, you know. He never will.

Fred. Well, true, wife. Uncle may rail at Christmas till he dies. I think I shook him some with my visit yesterday . . . (*Laughing*) I refused to grow angry . . . no matter how nasty he became . . . (*Whoops*) It was HE who grew angry, wife! **K**

[*They both laugh now.*]

Scrooge. What he says is true, Spirit . . .

Fred and Wife. Bah, humbug!

Fred (*embracing his wife*). There is much laughter in our marriage, wife. It pleases me. You please me . . .

Wife. And you please me, Fred. You are a good man . . .

[*They embrace.*]

I am sorry for him; I couldn't be angry with him if I tried. Who suffers by his ill whims? Himself, always.

Come now. We must have a look at the meal . . . our guests will soon arrive . . . my sisters, Topper . . .

Fred. A toast first . . . (*He hands her a glass.*) A toast to Uncle Scrooge . . . (*Fills their glasses*)

Wife. A toast to him?

Fred. Uncle Scrooge has given us plenty of merriment, I am sure, and it would be ungrateful not to drink to his health. And I say . . . *Uncle Scrooge!*

Wife (*laughing*). You're a proper loon, Fred . . . and I'm a proper wife to you . . . (*She raises her glass.*) *Uncle Scrooge!*

[*They drink. They embrace. They kiss.*]

Scrooge. Spirit, please, make me visible! Make me audible! I want to talk with my nephew and my niece!

[*Calls out to them. The lights that light the room and* FRED *and wife fade out.* SCROOGE *and* PRESENT *are alone, spotlit.*]

Present. These shadows are gone to you now, Mr. Scrooge. You may return to them later tonight in your dreams. (*Pauses*) My time grows short, Ebenezer Scrooge. Look you on me! Do you see how I've aged?

J Read and Discuss What are you learning at the nephew's house?

K Literary Perspectives Archetypes How does this description reflect the archetype of Scrooge as a bitter man?

Scrooge. Your hair has gone gray! Your skin, wrinkled! Are spirits' lives so short?

Present. My stay upon this globe is very brief. It ends tonight.

Scrooge. Tonight?

Present. At midnight. The time is drawing near!

[*Clock strikes 11:45*]

Hear those chimes? In a quarter hour, my life will have been spent! Look, Scrooge, man. Look you here.

[*Two gnarled baby dolls are taken from* PRESENT's *skirts.*]

Scrooge. Who are they?

Present. They are Man's children, and they cling to me, appealing from their fathers. The boy is Ignorance; the girl is Want. Beware them both, and all of their degree, but most of all beware this boy, for I see that written on his brow which is doom, unless the writing be erased. (*He stretches out his arm. His voice is now amplified: loudly and oddly.*) **Ⓛ**

Scrooge. Have they no refuge or resource?

Present. Are there no prisons? Are there no workhouses?

[*Twelve chimes*]

Are there no prisons? Are there no workhouses?

[*A* PHANTOM, *hooded, appears in dim light,* DOWNSTAGE, *opposite.*]

Are there no prisons? Are there no workhouses?

[PRESENT *begins to deliquesce.* SCROOGE *calls after him.*]

Scrooge. Spirit, I'm frightened! Don't leave me! Spirit!

Present. Prisons? Workhouses? Prisons? Workhouses . . . **Ⓜ**

[*He is gone.* SCROOGE *is alone now with the* PHANTOM, *who is, of course, the* GHOST OF CHRISTMAS FUTURE. *The* PHANTOM *is shrouded in black. Only its outstretched hand is visible from under his ghostly garment.*]

Scrooge. Who are you, Phantom? Oh, yes, I think I know you! You are, are you not, the Spirit of Christmas Yet to Come?

[*No reply*]

And you are about to show me the shadows of the things that have not yet happened, but will happen in time before us. Is that not so, Spirit?

Ⓛ Read and Discuss Why does the Ghost of Christmas Present tell Scrooge to be wary?

Ⓜ Literary Focus Drama/Conflict What conflict does Scrooge face in his mind?

[*The* PHANTOM *allows* SCROOGE *a look at his face. No other reply wanted here. A nervous giggle here*]

Oh, Ghost of the Future, I fear you more than any Specter I have seen! But, as I know that your purpose is to do me good, and as I hope to live to be another man from what I was, I am prepared to bear you company.

[FUTURE *does not reply, but for a stiff arm, hand and finger set, pointing forward.*]

Lead on, then, lead on. The night is waning fast, and it is precious time to me. Lead on, Spirit!

[FUTURE *moves away from* SCROOGE *in the same rhythm and motion employed at its arrival.* SCROOGE *falls into the same pattern, a considerable space apart from the* SPIRIT. *In the space between them,* MARLEY *appears. He looks to* FUTURE *and then to* SCROOGE. *He claps his hands. Thunder and lightning. Three* BUSINESSMEN *appear, spotlighted singularly: One is* DOWNSTAGE LEFT; *one is* DOWNSTAGE RIGHT; *one is* UPSTAGE CENTER. *Thus, six points of the stage should now be spotted in light.* MARLEY *will watch this scene from his position,* CENTER. SCROOGE *and* FUTURE *are* RIGHT *and* LEFT *of* CENTER.]

First Businessman. Oh, no, I don't know much about it either way, I only know he's dead.
Second Businessman. When did he die?

First Businessman. Last night, I believe.
Second Businessman. Why, what was the matter with him? I thought he'd never die, really . . .
First Businessman (*yawning*). Goodness knows, goodness knows . . .
Third Businessman. What has he done with his money?
Second Businessman. I haven't heard. Have you?
First Businessman. Left it to his Company, perhaps. Money to money; you know the expression . . .
Third Businessman. He hasn't left it to *me*. That's all I know . . .
First Businessman (*laughing*). Nor to me . . . (*Looks at* SECOND BUSINESSMAN) You, then? You got his money???
Second Businessman (*laughing*). Me, me, his money? Noooooo!

[*They all laugh.*]
Third Businessman. It's likely to be a cheap funeral, for upon my life, I don't know of a living soul who'd care to venture to it. Suppose we make up a party and volunteer?
Second Businessman. I don't mind going if a lunch is provided, but I must be fed, if I make one.
First Businessman. Well, I am the most disinterested among you, for I never wear black gloves, and I never eat lunch. But I'll offer to go, if anybody else will. When I come to think of it, I'm not all sure that I wasn't his most particular friend; for we used to stop and speak whenever we met. Well, then . . . bye, bye!

Kelsey Grammer as Scrooge and Geraldine Chaplin as the Ghost of Christmas Future in *A Christmas Carol*.

Second Businessman. Bye, bye . . .
Third Businessman. Bye, bye . . .

[*They glide offstage in three separate directions. Their lights follow them.*]

Scrooge. Spirit, why did you show me this? Why do you show me businessmen from my streets as they take the death of Jacob Marley. That is a thing past. You are *future*!

[JACOB MARLEY *laughs a long, deep laugh. There is a thunderclap and lightning flash,* and he is gone. SCROOGE *faces* FUTURE, *alone onstage now.* FUTURE *wordlessly stretches out his arm-hand-and-finger-set, pointing into the distance,* UPSTAGE. *There, above them, scoundrels "fly" by, half-dressed and slovenly.* (N.B. *There could be a dance number here, showing the seamier side of London city life.*) *When this scene has passed, a woman enters the playing area. She is almost at once followed by a second woman; and then a man in faded black; and then, suddenly, an old man, who smokes a pipe. The old man scares the other three. They laugh, anxious.*]

N **Literary Perspectives** Archetypes What details in the businessmen's conversation tell you that Scrooge is ill-tempered? Find at least two examples.

First Woman. Look here, old Joe, here's a chance! If we haven't all three met here without meaning it!

Old Joe. You couldn't have met in a better place. Come into the parlor. You were made free of it long ago, you know; and the other two ain't strangers (*He stands; shuts a door. Shrieking*) We're all suitable to our calling. We're well matched. Come into the parlor. Come into the parlor . . .

[*They follow him* DOWNSTAGE. SCROOGE *and* FUTURE *are now in their midst, watching; silent. A truck comes in on which is set a small wall with fireplace and a screen of rags, etc. All props for the scene*]

Let me just rake this fire over a bit . . .

[*He does. He trims his lamp with the stem of his pipe. The* FIRST WOMAN *throws a large bundle onto the floor. She sits beside it cross-legged, defiantly.*]

First Woman. What odds then? What odds, Mrs. Dilber? Every person has a right to take care of themselves. HE always did!

Mrs. Dilber. That's true indeed! No man more so!

First Woman. Why, then, don't stand staring as if you was afraid, woman! Who's the wiser? We're not going to pick holes in each other's coats, I suppose?

Mrs. Dilber. No, indeed! We should hope not!

First Woman. Very well, then! That's enough. Who's the worse for the loss of a few things like these? Not a dead man, I suppose?

Mrs. Dilber (*laughing*). No, indeed!

First Woman. If he wanted to keep 'em after he was dead, the wicked old screw, why wasn't he natural in his lifetime? If he had been, he'd have had somebody to look after him when he was struck with Death, instead of lying gasping out his last there, alone by himself.

Mrs. Dilber. It's the truest word that was ever spoke. It's a judgment on him.

First Woman. I wish it were a heavier one, and it should have been, you may depend on it, if I could have laid my hands on anything else. Open that bundle, old Joe, and let me know the value of it. Speak out plain. I'm not afraid to be the first, nor afraid for them to see it. We knew pretty well that we were helping ourselves, before we met here, I believe. It's no sin. Open the bundle, Joe.

First Man. No, no, my dear! I won't think of letting you being the first to show what you've . . . earned . . . earned from this. I throw in mine. (*He takes a bundle from his shoulder, turns it upside down, and empties its contents out onto the floor.*) It's not very extensive, see . . . seals . . . a pencil case . . . sleeve buttons . . .

Mrs. Dilber. Nice sleeve buttons, though . . .

First Man. Not bad, not bad . . . a brooch there . . .

Old Joe. Not really valuable, I'm afraid . . .

First Man. How much, old Joe?

Old Joe (*writing on the wall with chalk*). A pitiful lot, really. Ten and six and not a sixpence more!

First Man. You're not serious!

Old Joe. That's your account and I wouldn't give another sixpence if I was to be boiled for not doing it. Who's next?

Mrs. Dilber. Me! (*Dumps out contents of her bundle*) Sheets, towels, silver spoons, silver sugar-tongs . . . some boots . . .

Old Joe (*writing on wall*). I always give too much to the ladies. It's a weakness of mine and that's the way I ruin myself. Here's your total comin' up . . . two pounds-ten . . . if you asked me for another penny, and made it an open question, I'd repent of being so liberal and knock off half-a-crown.

First Woman. And now do MY bundle, Joe.

Old Joe (*kneeling to open knots on her bundle*). So many knots, madam . . . (*He drags out large curtains; dark*) What do you call this? Bed curtains!

First Woman (*laughing*). Ah, yes, bed curtains!

Old Joe. You don't mean to say you took 'em down, rings and all, with him lying there?

First Woman. Yes, I did, why not?

Old Joe. You were born to make your fortune and you'll certainly do it.

First Woman. I certainly shan't hold my hand, when I can get anything in it by reaching it out, for the sake of such a man as

Set design (late 19th century) by Jachimoqicz for the opera *Die Rheinnixen* by Jacques Offenbach (1819–1880). Watercolor.

he was, I promise you, Joe. Don't drop that lamp oil on those blankets, now!

Old Joe. His blankets?

First Woman. Whose else's do you think? He isn't likely to catch cold without 'em, I daresay.

Old Joe. I hope that he didn't die of anything catching? Eh?

First Woman. Don't you be afraid of that. I ain't so fond of his company that I'd loiter about him for such things if he did. Ah! You may look through that shirt till your eyes ache, but you won't find a hole in it, nor a threadbare place. It's the best he had, and a fine one, too. They'd have wasted it, if it hadn't been for me.

Old Joe. What do you mean "They'd have wasted it?"

First Woman. Putting it on him to be buried in, to be sure. Somebody was fool enough to do it, but I took it off again . . .

[*She laughs, as do they all, nervously.*]

If calico ain't good enough for such a purpose, it isn't good enough then for anything. It's quite as becoming to the body. He can't look uglier than he did in that one!

Scrooge (*A low-pitched moan emits from his mouth; from the bones.*). OOOOOOOooooo

> He frightened everyone away from him while he was alive.

OOOOOooooOOOOOOOOooooOOOOOOooooOO!

Old Joe. One pound six for the lot.

[*He produces a small flannel bag filled with money. He divvies it out. He continues to pass around the money as he speaks. All are laughing.*]

That's the end of it, you see! He frightened everyone away from him while he was alive, to profit us when he was dead! Hah ha ha!

All. HAHAHAHAhahahahahahah!

Scrooge. OOOoooOOOoooOOOoooOOOoooOOoooOOoooOOOooo! (*He screams at them.*) Obscene demons! Why not market the corpse itself, as sell its trimming??? (*Suddenly*) Oh, Spirit, I see it, I see it! This unhappy man—this stripped-bare corpse . . . could very well be my own. My life holds parallel! My life ends that way now! **O**

[SCROOGE *backs into something in the dark behind his spotlight.* SCROOGE *looks at* FUTURE, *who points to the corpse.* SCROOGE *pulls back the blanket. The corpse is, of course,* SCROOGE, *who screams. He falls aside the bed; weeping.*]

O **Literary Focus** Drama/Plot How can you tell that the play is approaching its climax?

Spirit, this is a fearful place. In leaving it, I shall not leave its lesson, trust me. Let us go!

[FUTURE *points to the corpse.*]

Spirit, let me see some tenderness connected with a death, or that dark chamber, which we just left now, Spirit, will be forever present to me.

[FUTURE *spreads his robes again. Thunder and lightning. Lights up,* UPSTAGE, *in the* CRATCHIT *home setting.* MRS. CRATCHIT *and her daughters, sewing*]

Tiny Tim's Voice (OFF). And He took a child and set him in the midst of them.
Scrooge (*looking about the room; to* FUTURE) Huh? Who spoke? Who said that?
Mr. Cratchit (*puts down her sewing*). The color hurts my eyes. (*Rubs her eyes*) That's better. My eyes grow weak sewing by candlelight. I shouldn't want to show your father weak eyes when he comes home . . . not for the world! It must be near his time . . .
Peter (*in corner, reading. Looks up from book*). Past it, rather. But I think he's been walking a bit slower than usual these last few evenings, Mother.
Mrs. Cratchit. I have known him walk with . . . (*Pauses*) I have know him walk with Tiny Tim upon his shoulder and very fast indeed.
Peter. So have I, Mother! Often!

Daughter. So have I.
Mrs. Cratchit. But he was very light to carry and his father loved him so, that it was no trouble—no trouble.

[BOB, *at door*]

And there is your father at the door.

[BOB CRATCHIT *enters. He wears a comforter. He is cold, forlorn.*] **P**

Peter. Father!
Bob. Hello, wife, children . . .

[*The daughter weeps; turns away from* CRATCHIT.]

Children! How good to see you all! And you, wife. And look at this sewing! I've no doubt, with all your industry, we'll have a quilt to set down upon our knees in church on Sunday!
Mrs. Cratchit. You made the arrangements today, then, Robert, for the . . . service . . . to be on Sunday.
Bob. The funeral. Oh, well, yes, yes, I did. I wish you could have gone. It would have done you good to see how green a place it is. But you'll see it often. I promised him that I would walk there on Sunday, after the service. (*Suddenly*) My little, little child! My little child!
All Children (*hugging him*). Oh, Father . . .

P **Reading Focus** Visualizing How do the dialogue and stage directions help you to visualize the way Bob Cratchit's appearance has changed?

Bob (*He stands.*). Forgive me. I saw Mr. Scrooge's nephew, who you know I'd just met once before, and he was so wonderful to me, wife . . . he is the most pleasant-spoken gentleman I've ever met . . . he said "I am heartily sorry for it and heartily sorry for your good wife. If I can be of service to you in any way, here's where I live." And he gave me this card.

Peter. Let me see it!

Bob. And he looked me straight in the eye, wife, and said, meaningfully, "I pray you'll come to me, Mr. Cratchit, if you need some help. I pray you do." Now it wasn't for the sake of anything that he might be able to do for us, so much as for his kind way. It seemed as if he had known our Tiny Tim and felt with us.

Mrs. Cratchit. I'm sure that he's a good soul.

Bob. You would be surer of it, my dear, if you saw and spoke to him. I shouldn't be at all surprised, if he got Peter a situation.

Mrs. Cratchit. Only hear that, Peter!

Martha. And then, Peter will be keeping company with someone and setting up for himself!

Peter. Get along with you!

Bob. It's just as likely as not, one of these days, though there's plenty of time for that, my dear. But however and whenever we part from one another, I am sure we shall none of us forget poor Tiny Tim—shall we?—or this first parting that was among us?

All Children. Never, Father, never!

Bob. And when we recollect how patient and mild he was, we shall not quarrel easily among ourselves, and forget poor Tiny Tim in doing it.

All Children. No, Father, never!

Little Bob. I am very happy, I am, I am, I am very happy.

[BOB *kisses his little son, as does* MRS. CRATCHIT, *as do the other children. The family is set now in one sculptural embrace. The lighting fades to a gentle pool of light, tight on them.*]

Scrooge. Specter, something informs me that our parting moment is at hand. I know it, but I know not how I know it.

[FUTURE *points to the other side of the stage. Lights out on* CRATCHITS. FUTURE *moves slowing, gliding.* SCROOGE *follows.* FUTURE *points opposite.* FUTURE *leads* SCROOGE *to a wall and a tombstone. He points to the stone.*]

Am *I* that man those ghoulish parasites so gloated over? (*Pauses*) Before I draw nearer to that stone to which you point, answer me one question. Are these the shadows of things that will be, or the shadows of things that MAY be, only?

[FUTURE *points to the gravestone.* MARLEY *appears in light well* UPSTAGE. *He points to grave as well. Gravestone turns front and grows to ten feet high. Words upon it: EBENEZER SCROOGE. Much smoke billows now from the grave. Choral music here.* SCROOGE *stands looking up at*

Scrooge, as portrayed in Virginia Opera's 2002 production of *A Christmas Carol, The Opera*, composed by Thea Musgrave.

gravestone. FUTURE *does not at all reply in mortals' words, but points once more to the gravestone. The stone undulates and glows. Music plays, beckoning* SCROOGE. SCROOGE, *reeling in terror*]

Oh, no, Spirit! Oh, no, no!

[FUTURE's *finger still pointing*]

Spirit! Hear me! I am not the man I was. I will not be the man I would have been but for this intercourse. Why show me this, if I am past all hope?

[FUTURE *considers* SCROOGE's *logic. His hand wavers.*]

Oh, Good Spirit, I see by your wavering

hand that your good nature intercedes for me and pities me. Assure me that I yet may change these shadows that you have shown me by an altered life!

[FUTURE's *hand trembles; pointing has stopped.*]

I will honor Christmas in my heart and try to keep it all the year. I will live in the Past, the Present, and the Future. The Spirits of all Three shall strive within me. I will not shut out the lessons that they teach. Oh, tell me that I may sponge away the writing that is upon this stone!

[SCROOGE *makes a desperate stab at grabbing* FUTURE's *hand. He holds it firm for a moment, but* FUTURE, *stronger than* SCROOGE, *pulls away.* SCROOGE *is on his knees, praying.*]

Spirit, dear Spirit, I am praying before you. Give me a sign that all is possible. Give me a sign that all hope for me is not lost. Oh, Spirit, kind Spirit, I beseech thee: give me a sign . . . ⓠ

[FUTURE *deliquesces, slowly, gently. The* PHANTOM's *hood and robe drop gracefully to the ground in a small heap. Music in. There is nothing in them. They are mortal cloth. The* SPIRIT *is elsewhere.* SCROOGE *has his sign.* SCROOGE *is alone. Tableau. The lights fade to black.*] ⓡ

SCENE 5

[*The end of it.* MARLEY, *spotlighted, opposite* SCROOGE, *in his bed, spotlighted.* MARLEY *speaks to audience, directly.*]

Marley (*He smiles at* SCROOGE.). The firm of Scrooge and Marley is doubly blessed: two misers turned; one, alas, in Death, too late; but the other miser turned in Time's penultimate nick.[4] Look you on my friend, Ebenezer Scrooge . . .

Scrooge (*scrambling out of bed; reeling in delight*). I will live in the Past, in the Present, and in the Future! The Spirits of all Three shall strive within me!

Marley (*He points and moves closer to* SCROOGE's *bed.*). Yes, Ebenezer, the bedpost is your own. Believe it! Yes, Ebenezer, the room is your own. Believe it!

Scrooge. Oh, Jacob Marley! Wherever you are, Jacob, know ye that I praise you for this! I praise you . . . and heaven . . . and Christmastime! (*Kneels facing away from* MARLEY) I say it to ye on my knees, old Jacob, on my knees! (*He touches his bed curtains.*) Not torn down. My bed curtains are not at all torn down! Rings and all, here they are! They are here: I am here: the shadows of things that would have been, may now be dispelled. They will be, Jacob! I know they will be! (*He chooses clothing for the day. He tries different pieces of clothing and settles, perhaps, on a dress*

---

4. **in Time's penultimate nick:** just in time.

ⓠ **Literary Perspectives** Archetypes What is surprising about Scrooge's speech? How can you tell that his character is changing?

ⓡ **Literary Focus** Drama What action gives Scrooge hope that he may change in the future?

suit, plus a cape of the bed clothing: something of color.) I am light as a feather, I am happy as an angel, I am as merry as a schoolboy. (*Yells out window and then out to audience*) Merry Christmas to everybody! Merry Christmas to everybody! A Happy New Year to all the world! Hallo here! Whoop! Whoop! Hallo! Hallo! I don't know what day of the month it is! I don't care! I don't know anything! I'm quite a baby! I don't care! I don't care a fig! I'd much rather be a baby than be an old wreck like me or Marley! (Sorry, Jacob, wherever ye be!) Hallo! Hallo there!

[*Church bells chime in Christmas Day. A small boy, named* ADAM, *is seen now* DOWNSTAGE RIGHT, *a light fades up on him.*]

Hey, you boy! What's today? What day of the year is it?

Adam. Today, sir? Why, it's Christmas Day!

Scrooge. It's Christmas Day, is it? Whoop! Well, I haven't missed it after all, have I? The Spirits did all they did in one night. They can do anything they like, right? Of course they can! Of course they can!

Adam. Excuse me, sir?

Merry Christmas to everybody! A Happy New Year to all the world!

Scrooge. Huh? Oh, yes, of course, what's your name, lad?

[SCROOGE *and* ADAM *will play their scene from their own spotlights.*]

Adam. Adam, sir.

Scrooge. Adam! What a fine, strong name! Do you know the poulterer's in the next street but one, at the corner?

Adam. I certainly should hope I know him, sir!

Scrooge. A remarkable boy! An intelligent boy! Do you know whether the poulterer's have sold the prize turkey that was hanging up there? I don't mean the little prize turkey, Adam, I mean the big one!

Adam. What, do you mean the one they've got that's as big as me?

Scrooge. I mean, the turkey the size of Adam: that's the bird!

Adam. It's hanging there now, sir.

Scrooge. It is? Go and buy it! No, no, I am absolutely in earnest. Go and buy it and tell 'em to bring it here, so that I may give them the directions to where I want it delivered, as a gift. Come back here with the man, Adam, and I'll give you a shilling. Come back here with him in less than five minutes, and I'll give you half-a-crown!

Adam. Oh, my, sir! Don't let my brother in on this. **ⓢ**

[ADAM *runs offstage.* MARLEY *smiles.*]

Marley. An act of kindness is like the first green grape of summer: one leads to another and another and another. It would take a queer man indeed to not follow an act of kindness with an act of kindness. One simply whets the tongue for more . . . the taste of kindness is too too sweet. Gifts—goods—are lifeless. But the gift of goodness one feels in the giving is full of life. It . . . is . . . a . . . wonder.

[*Pauses; moves closer to* SCROOGE, *who is totally occupied with his dressing and arranging of his room and his day. He is making lists, etc.* MARLEY *reaches out to* SCROOGE.]

Adam (*calling, off*). I'm here! I'm here!

[ADAM *runs on with a man, who carries an enormous turkey.*]

Here I am, sir. Three minutes flat! A world record! I've got the poultryman and he's got the poultry! (*He pants, out of breath.*) I have earned my prize, sir, if I live . . .

[*He holds his heart, playacting.* SCROOGE *goes to him and embraces him.*]

Scrooge. You are truly a champion, Adam . . .

Man. Here's the bird you ordered, sir . . .

Scrooge. *Oh, my, MY!!!* Look at the size of that turkey, will you! He never could have stood upon his legs, that bird! He would have snapped them off in a minute, like sticks of sealing wax! Why you'll never be able to carry that bird to Camden-Town. I'll give you money for a cab . . .

Man. Camden-Town's where it's goin', sir?

Scrooge. Oh, I didn't tell you? Yes, I've written the precise address down just here on this . . . (*Hands paper to him*) Bob Cratchit's house. Now he's not to know who sends him this. Do you understand me? Not a word . . . (*Handing out money and chuckling*)

Man. I understand, sir, not a word.

Scrooge. Good. There you go then . . . this is for the turkey . . . (*Chuckle*) and this is for the taxi, (*Chuckle*) . . . and this is for your world-record run, Adam . . .

ⓢ Literary Focus Drama/Character What does Adam represent in the play? What might he represent to Scrooge?

Scene from *Scrooge* (1970).

Adam. But I don't have change for that, sir.

Scrooge. Then keep it, my lad. It's Christmas!

Adam. (*He kisses* SCROOGE's *cheek, quickly.*) Thank you, sir. Merry, Merry Christmas! (*He runs off.*)

Man. And you've given me a bit overmuch here, too, sir . . .

Scrooge. Of course I have, sir. It's Christmas!

Man. Oh, well, thanking you, sir. I'll have this bird to Mr. Cratchit and his family in no time, sir. Don't you worry none about that. Merry Christmas to you, sir, and a very Happy New Year, too . . .

[*The* MAN *exits.* SCROOGE *walks in a large circle about the stage, which is now gently lit. A chorus sings Christmas music far in the distance. Bells chime as well, far in the distance. A gentlewoman enters and passes.* SCROOGE *is on the streets now.*]

Scrooge. Merry Christmas, madam . . .

Woman. Merry Christmas, sir . . .

[*The* PORTLY BUSINESSMAN *from the first act enters.*]

Scrooge. Merry Christmas, sir.

Portly Man. Merry Christmas, sir.

Scrooge. Oh, you! My dear sir! How do you do? I do hope that you succeeded yesterday! It was very kind of you. A Merry Christmas.

Portly Man. Mr. Scrooge?

Scrooge. Yes, Scrooge is my name though I'm afraid you may not find it very pleasant. Allow me to ask your pardon. And will you have the goodness to—(*He whispers into the man's ear.*)

Portly Man. Lord bless me! My dear Mr. Scrooge, *are you serious*!?!

Scrooge. If you please. Not a farthing less. A great many back-payments are included in it, I assure you. Will you do me that favor?

Portly Man. My dear sir, I don't know what to say to such munifi—

Scrooge (*cutting him off*). Don't say anything, please. Come and see me. Will you?

Portly Man. I will! I will! Oh I will, Mr. Scrooge! It will be my pleasure!

Scrooge. Thank'ee, I am much obliged to you. I thank you fifty times. Bless you!

[PORTLY MAN *passes offstage, perhaps by moving backwards.* SCROOGE *now comes to the room of his* NEPHEW *and* NIECE. *He stops at the door, begins to knock on it, loses his courage, tries again, loses his courage again, tries again, fails again, and then backs off and runs at the door, causing a tremendous bump against it. The* NEPHEW *and* NIECE *are startled.* SCROOGE, *poking head into room*]

Fred!

Nephew. Why, bless my soul! Who's that?

Nephew and Niece (*together*). How now? Who goes?

Scrooge. It's I. Your Uncle Scrooge.

Niece. Dear heart alive!

Scrooge. I have come to dinner. May I come in, Fred?

Nephew. *May you come in???!!!* With such pleasure for me you may, Uncle!!! What a treat!

Niece. What a treat, Uncle Scrooge! Come in, come in!

[*They embrace a shocked and delighted* SCROOGE. FRED *calls into the other room.*]

Nephew. Come in here, everybody, and meet my Uncle Scrooge! He's come for our Christmas party!

[*Music in. Lighting here indicates that day has gone to night and gone to day again. It is early, early morning.* SCROOGE *walks alone from the party, exhausted, to his offices, opposite side of the stage. He opens his offices. The offices are as they were at the start of the play.* SCROOGE *seats himself with his door wide open so that he can see into the tank, as he awaits* CRATCHIT, *who enters, head down, full of guilt.* CRATCHIT *starts writing almost before he sits.*]

Scrooge. What do you mean by coming in here at this time of day, a full eighteen minutes late, Mr. Cratchit? Hallo, sir? Do you hear me?

> What do you mean by coming in here at this time of day, a full eighteen minutes late, Mr. Cratchit?

Bob. I am very sorry, sir. I *am* behind my time.

Scrooge. You are? Yes, I certainly think you are. Step this way, sir, if you please . . .

Bob. It's only but once a year, sir . . . it shall not be repeated. I was making rather merry yesterday and into the night . . .

Scrooge. Now, I'll tell you what, Cratchit. I am not going to stand this sort of thing any longer. And therefore . . . (*He stands and pokes his finger into* BOB's *chest.*) I am . . . about . . . to . . . raise . . . your salary.

Bob. Oh, no, sir, I . . . (*Realizes*) what did you say, sir?

Scrooge. A Merry Christmas, Bob . . . (*He claps* BOB's *back.*) A merrier Christmas, Bob, my good fellow! than I have given you for many a year. I'll raise your salary and endeavor to assist your struggling family and we will discuss your affairs this very afternoon over a bowl of smoking bishop.[5] Bob! Make up the fires and buy another coal scuttle before you dot another *i*, Bob. It's too cold in this place! We need warmth and cheer, Bob Cratchit! Do you hear me? DO . . . YOU . . . HEAR . . . ME?

---

5. **smoking bishop:** hot, sweet drink.

[BOB CRATCHIT *stands, smiles at* SCROOGE. BOB CRATCHIT *faints. Blackout. As the main lights black out, a spotlight appears on* SCROOGE, CENTER. *Another on* MARLEY. *He talks directly to the audience.*]

Marley. Scrooge was better than his word. He did it all and infinitely more; and to Tiny Tim, who did NOT die, he was a second father. He became as good a friend, as good a master, as good a man, as the good old city knew, or any other good old city, town, or borough in the good old world. And it was always said of him that he knew how to keep Christmas well, if any man alive possessed the knowledge. (*Pauses*) May that be truly said of us, and all of us. And so, as Tiny Tim observed . . .
Tiny Tim (*atop* SCROOGE's *shoulder*). God Bless Us, Every One . . .

[*Lights up on chorus, singing final Christmas Song.* SCROOGE *and* MARLEY *and all spirits and other characters of the play join in. When the song is over, the lights fade to black.*] **T**

T Read and Discuss | How would you describe Scrooge now?

Kelsey Grammer as Scrooge
and Jacob Moriarty as Tiny Tim
in *A Christmas Carol*.

Applying Your Skills

SKILLS FOCUS Literary Skills Analyze elements of drama. **Reading Skills** Visualize; describe mental images that text descriptions evoke. **Writing Skills** Develop characters using dialogue.

A Christmas Carol: Scrooge and Marley, Act Two
Respond and Think Critically

Reading Focus

Quick Check

1. Explain how Scrooge's personality changes over the course of the play.

Read with a Purpose

2. What did it take to make Ebenezer Scrooge change his ways?

Reading Skills: Visualizing

3. As you read, you took notes on details that helped you to visualize Marley and Scrooge. Use the chart below to organize the notes you took about Scrooge during Act Two. Then, write a paragraph about the changes you observed.

Visualizing Scrooge During Act 2

Scrooge's...	Went From...	To...
Appearance		
Actions		
Words		
Feelings		

Literary Focus

Literary Analysis

4. **Analyze** Why did Scrooge need to see the past and the present as well as the future in order to change?

5. **Interpret** Some say that Jacob Marley represents Scrooge's conscience. What details in the play support this idea?

6. **Evaluate** Do you think the spirits went beyond what was needed to change Scrooge's character? Refer to Scrooge's interactions with the spirits during Act Two to explain your view.

7. **Literary Perspectives** Based on what you know about his archetype, are you surprised by Scrooge's change at the end of the play? What does this change signify?

Literary Skills: Elements of Drama

8. **Analyze** The stage directions contain figures of speech, explanations, and suggestions for variations. Why do you think the playwright composed the stage directions in this way?

9. **Interpret** Marley's Ghost serves as a narrator. How do his introductions add to the tension of the scenes that follow?

Writing Focus

Think as a Reader/Writer

Use It in Your Writing Use some of the old-fashioned language you noted in the play to write a new dialogue between Scrooge and Marley. If Marley reappeared to Scrooge on the day after Christmas, what might the two say to each other?

 What Do **You Think Now**

What are the important things in life? How did Scrooge come to discover them?

Vocabulary Development

Clarifying Word Meanings: Examples

Sometimes you can figure out the meaning of an unfamiliar word by finding other words or phrases that give you an **example** of what the word means. Consider the following sentences:

- Well-prepared cooks know to buy extra *staples,* such as flour, sugar, and salt, before the holiday season, with all its special meals.
- The children's eyes were *riveted* on the pile of presents, as if fixed there by an invisible force.
- Huge holiday parades in *municipalities* like New York City, Boston, Chicago, and Los Angeles can be enjoyed by television viewers around the world.

Note how certain words often let you know when an example is being used: *for example, for instance, like, such as, in this case, as if.*

Your Turn

Finish the following sentences by using examples to clarify the meanings of the boldface words.

1. As the child **implored** his mother to buy him the toy, he looked as if _____.
2. I have read about some wonderful acts of **benevolence,** such as _____.
3. His **compulsion** to keep the house clean was obvious when he did things like _____.
4. Poverty can force people to live on **meager** amounts of food. For example, food for a day might include _____.
5. **Morose** people tend to show their mood with body language such as _____.

Language Coach

Related Words Many essential ideas about life are brought up in this play. The play contains many related words—words that all have something to do with the important main ideas. Look at the words listed for each big idea below. Which word does not fit with the others in each list?

Greed
tightfisted, covetous, abundance, bargain, stingy

Kindness
pleasant, comfort, mercy, ungrateful, volunteer

Fear
visible, ghostly, apparition, trembling, specter

Change
alter, languish, modify, adjust, transform

Academic Vocabulary

Write About . . .
Compare and contrast the way Scrooge interacts with characters near the end of the play with the way he behaves in previous scenes. Try to use Academic Vocabulary in your discussion.

Learn It Online
For action-packed vocabulary lessons, visit:

go.hrw.com | L7-830 | Go

Grammar Link

Words Often Confused:
Its / *It's* and *Your* / *You're*

The words in each pair might sound alike, but they have very different purposes.

The **personal possessive pronouns** *its* and *your* show that something belongs to someone or something. Possessive pronouns should not have apostrophes.

"A heavy bell thuds *its* one ring." [The ring "belongs" to the bell.]

"Yes, Ebenezer, the bedpost is *your* own." [The bedpost "belongs" to Ebenezer.]

The **contractions** *it's* and *you're* are both shortened combinations of the personal pronoun and the verb *is*, *has*, or *are*. A contraction should have an apostrophe to show where letters have been left out.

"*It's* [it is] the truest word that was ever spoke."

Here's a tip: Substitute the two words that might be used in place of the one you are unsure of, such as *it is* or *you are*. If the sentence still makes sense, use the contraction instead of the pronoun.

Your Turn

Write each sentence below, choosing the correct form of the italicized words.

1. It carried holly in *its/it's* hand.
2. Scrooge said, "I hope *your/you're* able to find work elsewhere."
3. *Its/It's* fortunate that Scrooge changed his ways.
4. Has *your/you're* outlook on Scrooge changed since you read the play?

SKILLS FOCUS Literary Skills Analyze elements of drama. **Reading Skills** Visualize; describe mental images that text descriptions evoke. **Vocabulary Skills** Use context clues in words, sentences, and paragraphs to decode new vocabulary through examples. **Writing Skills** Write a response to literature; write a summary; write a character analysis. **Grammar Skills** Identify and use possessive-case pronouns correctly.

CHOICES

As you respond to the Choices, use the **Academic Vocabulary** words as appropriate: interact, motive, previous, resolve.

REVIEW
Find the Theme

Write a brief summary of what happens in each scene of the play. Then, come up with a theme statement for each act based on your summaries.

CONNECT
Critique the Plot

Timed ⏱ Writing Some readers enjoy the feel-good quality of the play's ending. Others feel Scrooge's transformation is unrealistic. Write a paragraph stating your opinion. Include details from the play to support your points.

EXTEND
Write a Letter

Choose a character from Scrooge's present, such as Bob Cratchit, Fred, or Adam. Pretend you are this character, and write a letter of one or two paragraphs to a friend or relative who has not yet met the "new" Scrooge. Describe the changes you have seen. Use specific details to show that Scrooge really is a different man.

The MONSTERS Are Due on Maple Street

by **Rod Serling**

What Do You Think

What causes confusion more often—fear or facts?

QuickWrite

People often make snap judgments in life. Write about a time you or someone else jumped to an incorrect conclusion. What was the mistake? Was it corrected, and if so, how?

 **Reader/Writer Notebook**

Use your **RWN** to complete the activities for this selection.

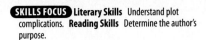

Literary Focus

Plot Complications **Complications** in stories make it hard for characters to get what they want. Complications usually begin to develop as soon as the characters take steps to resolve their problems or to accomplish their goals. They usually add more conflict to the story and make the plot more complex. They are meant to increase tension about how the story will finally end.

TechFocus As you read, think about how you might create a multimedia presentation on *The Monsters Are Due on Maple Street*.

Reading Focus

Identifying Author's Purpose People write with different purposes in mind. Writers of political speeches try to persuade us to believe or do something. Writers of magazine articles often want to inform us about something. Novelists, short-story writers, screenwriters, and playwrights usually have other motives. Some write to entertain; some write to reveal a truth about life.

Into Action Decide which purpose or purposes Rod Serling may have had for writing this teleplay. Add supporting evidence for your choices as you read the play.

Author's Purpose

Writing Focus

Think as a Reader/Writer

Find It in Your Reading As you read, take note of the author's use of authentic dialogue. Much of the conversation includes questions ("Steve? What was that?") or answers in the form of fragments ("Too close for my money. Much too close."). How does this form of dialogue convey the situation on Maple Street?

Vocabulary

transfixed (trans FIHKST) *v.* used as *adj.*: very still, as if nailed to the spot. *The neighbors stood transfixed, staring at the sky.*

intimidated (ihn TIHM uh day tihd) *v.* used as *adj.*: frightened, as by threats or violence. *The Goodmans, intimidated by the angry crowd, began to defend themselves.*

defiant (dih FY uhnt) *adj.*: boldly resisting authority. *Those who speak out against the opinions of an angry crowd are defiant and courageous.*

idiosyncrasy (ihd ee uh SIHNG kruh see) *n.*: peculiarity. *All people have an idiosyncrasy that makes them a little different.*

menace (MEHN ihs) *n.*: danger; threat. *They believed there was a menace to their safety.*

converging (kuhn VUR jihng) *v.* used as *adj.*: coming together. *The crowd converging on the porch frightened the Goodmans.*

Language Coach

Prefixes The prefix *con–* means "with" or "together." How would knowing the meaning of this prefix help you figure out the meaning of the Vocabulary word *converging*?

 Learn It Online
For a preview of this play, see the video introduction on:

go.hrw.com | L7-833 | **Go**

Learn It Online
Get more on the author's life at:
go.hrw.com L7-834 **Go**

Rod Serling
(1924–1975)

Man from Another Dimension

How does a fledgling writer with a less-than-dreamy job get from Cincinnati, Ohio, to New York City and then to Hollywood? If you're Rod Serling, you and your wife decide one day that the time has come to reach for your dream!

In the early 1950s, Rod Serling eagerly arrived in New York and found himself a job writing for television, a newly popular invention at that time. He first wrote for a live half-hour drama called *Lux Video Theatre*. From there he went on to create and produce the hit television show *The Twilight Zone*.

The Twilight Zone

In the fifth-dimensional world of the Twilight Zone, Serling made his beliefs known. *The Monsters Are Due on Maple Street* was written at a time when Americans were concerned about the spread of communism in the United States. There was a great deal of suspicion and finger-pointing, and Serling used this teleplay to voice perhaps his most enduring and urgent theme, namely:

> "There is nothing in the dark that isn't there when the lights are on."

Think About the Writer Why do you think Rod Serling chose to express his concerns using the science fiction genre?

Build Background

From its 1959 debut through its more than 150 subsequent episodes, *The Twilight Zone* thrilled and captivated millions of television viewers. Rebroadcasts still run today. As Rod Serling, the show's creator, would eerily alert viewers at the beginning of every episode, things in *The Twilight Zone* are not always what they seem. Ordinary people face extraordinary situations in *The Twilight Zone*, where familiar rules no longer apply.

Preview the Selection

In this teleplay, you will meet the residents of Maple Street, including **Steve Brand** and **his wife,** fourteen-year-old **Tommy** and his mother **Sally, Les Goodman,** and **Charlie.** Each of these people has a very different reaction to a mysterious power outage on Maple Street, and their reactions drive the story's action.

The
MONSTERS
Are Due on Maple Street

by **Rod Serling**

Teleplay Terms

Scripts written for television or the movies are different from scripts written for the stage. A **teleplay** is a script written for TV; a **screenplay** is a script written for movies. Both kinds of scripts may contain these camera directions:

fade in: the picture's gradual appearance on the screen.

pan: a swiveling movement of the camera, from one side to the other.

fade to black: the gradual disappearance of the picture until all that remains is a black screen.

cut to: a sudden change from one scene or character to another.

outside shot: a camera shot of an exterior.

long shot: a camera shot from far off.

close-up: a camera shot that is very close to its subject.

opening shot: the first scene of the production.

dissolve: the blending of a new scene with a scene that is fading out.

Characters
Narrator

Figure One
Figure Two

Residents of Maple Street
Steve Brand
Mrs. Brand
Don Martin
Pete Van Horn
Charlie
Charlie's wife
Tommy
Sally, Tommy's mother
Les Goodman
Mrs. Goodman
Woman Next Door
Woman One
Man One
Man Two

ACT ONE

Fade in on a shot of the night sky. The various nebulae and planets stand out in sharp, sparkling relief. As the camera begins a slow pan across the heavens, we hear the narrator offscreen.

Narrator's Voice. There is a fifth dimension beyond that which is known to man. It is a dimension as vast as space and as timeless as infinity. It is the middle ground between light and shadow—between science and superstition. And it lies between the pit of man's fears and the summit of his knowledge. This is the dimension of imagination. It is an area which we call The Twilight Zone. **Ⓐ**

[The camera pans down past the horizon, stopping on a sign which reads "Maple Street." Then it moves on to the street below. It is daytime. We see a quiet, tree-lined street, typical of small-town America. People sit and swing on gliders on their front porches, chatting across from house to house. STEVE BRAND *polishes his car, while his neighbor,* DON MARTIN, *leans against the fender watching him. A Good Humor man on a bicycle stops to sell some ice cream to a couple of kids. Two women gossip on a front lawn. Another man waters his lawn.]*

Maple Street, U.S.A., late summer. A tree-lined little world of front-porch gliders, hopscotch, the laughter of children, and the bell of an ice-cream vendor. **Ⓑ**

[The camera moves back to the Good Humor man and the two boys who are standing alongside him, buying ice cream.]

Ⓐ **Read and Discuss** What is the narrator sharing with you?

Ⓑ **Reading Focus** **Author's Purpose** What do you think the author's purpose might be in describing the setting this way?

At the sound of the roar and the flash of light, it will be precisely 6:43 P.M. on Maple Street.

[*One of the boys,* TOMMY, *looks up to listen to a tremendous screeching roar from overhead. A flash of light plays on the boys' faces. It moves down the street, past lawns and porches and rooftops, and disappears. People leave their porches or stop what they're doing to stare up at the sky.* STEVE BRAND *stops polishing his car and stands transfixed, staring upward. He looks at* DON MARTIN, *his neighbor from across the street.*] **Ⓒ**

Steve. What was that? A meteor?
Don (*nods*). That's what it looked like. I didn't hear any crash, though, did you?
Steve (*shakes his head*). Nope. I didn't hear anything except a roar.
Mrs. Brand (*from her porch*). Steve? What was that?

Steve (*raising his voice and looking toward porch*). Guess it was a meteor, honey. Came awful close, didn't it?
Mrs. Brand. Too close for my money! Much too close.

[*People stand on their porches, watching and talking in low tones.*] **Ⓓ**

Narrator's Voice. Maple Street. 6:44 P.M., on a late September evening. (*A pause*) Maple Street in the last calm and reflective moments . . . before the monsters came!

[*The camera pans across the porches again. A man is screwing in a lightbulb on a front porch. He gets down off the stool and flicks the switch, only to find that nothing happens. Another man is working on an electric power mower. He plugs in the plug and flicks the switch of the power mower, off and on,*

Ⓒ Reading Focus **Author's Purpose** The stage directions are important in this teleplay. Why do you think that Serling chose to write for television instead of, for instance, writing novels?

Ⓓ Read and Discuss What do the stage directions lead you to think about the roaring sound and flashing light?

Vocabulary **transfixed** (trans FIHKST) *v.* used as *adj.:* very still, as if nailed to the spot.

but nothing happens. Through the window of a front porch we see a woman at a telephone, pushing her finger back and forth on the dial hook. Her voice is indistinct and distant, but intelligible and repetitive.]

Woman Next Door. Operator, operator, something's wrong on the phone, operator!

[MRS. BRAND *comes out on the porch and calls to* STEVE.]

Mrs. Brand (*calling*). Steve, the power's off. I had the soup on the stove, and the stove just stopped working.
Woman Next Door. Same thing over here. I can't get anybody on the phone either. The phone seems to be dead.

[*The camera looks down on the street. Small, mildly disturbed voices creep up from below.*]

Voices.
Electricity's off.
Phone won't work.
Can't get a thing on the radio.
My power mower won't move, won't work at all.
Radio's gone dead.

[PETE VAN HORN, *a tall, thin man, is standing in front of his house.*]

Van Horn. I'll cut through the backyard. . . . See if the power's still on on Floral Street. I'll be right back.

[*He walks past the side of his house and*

disappears into the backyard. We see the hammer on his hip as he walks. The camera pans down slowly until we're looking at ten or eleven people standing around the street and overflowing to the curb and sidewalk. In the background is STEVE BRAND's *car.*]

Steve. Doesn't make sense. Why should the power go off all of a sudden, and the phone line?
Don. Maybe some sort of an electrical storm or something.
Charlie. That don't seem likely. Sky's just as blue as anything. Not a cloud. No lightning. No thunder. No nothing. How could it be a storm?
Woman One. I can't get a thing on the radio. Not even the portable.

[*The people again murmur softly in wonderment and question.*]

Charlie. Well, why don't you go downtown and check with the police, though they'll probably think we're crazy or something. A little power failure and right away we get all flustered and everything.
Steve. It isn't just the power failure, Charlie. If it was, we'd still be able to get a broadcast on the portable.

[*There's a murmur of reaction to this.* STEVE *looks from face to face and then over to his car.*]

I'll run downtown. We'll get this all straightened out.

[STEVE *walks over to the car, gets in it, and turns the key. Through the open car door we see the crowd watching him from the other side.* STEVE *starts the engine. It turns over sluggishly and then just stops dead. He tries it again, and this time he can't even get it to turn over. Then, very slowly and reflectively, he turns the key back to "off" and slowly gets out of the car. Everyone stares at* STEVE. *He stands for a moment by the car, then walks toward the group.*]

I don't understand it. It was working fine before. . . .

Don. Out of gas?
Steve (*shakes his head*). I just had it filled up.
Woman One. What's it mean?
Charlie. It's just as if . . . as if everything had stopped. . . . (*Then he turns toward* STEVE) We'd better walk downtown.

Analyzing Visuals   **Viewing and Interpreting** Does this photograph remind you of what is happening on Maple Street? Explain why or why not.

[*Another murmur of assent at this.*]

Steve. The two of us can go, Charlie. (*He turns to look back at the car.*) It couldn't be the meteor. A meteor couldn't do this.   **ⓔ**

[*He and* CHARLIE *exchange a look, then they start to walk away from the group. We see* TOMMY, *a serious-faced fourteen-year-old in spectacles, standing a few feet away from the group. He is halfway between them and the two men, who start to walk down the sidewalk.*]

Tommy. Mr. Brand . . . you better not!
Steve. Why not?
Tommy. They don't want you to.

[STEVE *and* CHARLIE *exchange a grin, and* STEVE *looks back toward the boy.*]

Steve. Who doesn't want us to?
Tommy (*jerks his head in the general direction of the distant horizon*). Them!
Steve. Them?

ⓔ Read and Discuss | What has happened?

Charlie. Who are them?

Tommy (*very intently*). Whoever was in that thing that came by overhead.

[STEVE *knits his brows for a moment, cocking his head questioningly. His voice is intense.*]

Steve. What?

Tommy. Whoever was in the thing that came over. I don't think they want us to leave here.

[STEVE *leaves* CHARLIE *and walks over to the boy. He kneels down in front of him. He forces his voice to remain gentle. He reaches out and holds the boy.*]

Steve. What do you mean? What are you talking about?

Tommy. They don't want us to leave. That's why they shut everything off.

Steve. What makes you say that? Whatever gave you that idea?

Woman One (*from the crowd*). Now isn't that the craziest thing you ever heard?

Tommy (*persistently but a little intimidated by the crowd*). It's always that way, in every story I ever read about a ship landing from outer space. **F**

> That wasn't any ship or anything like it. That was just a . . . a meteor or something.

Woman One (*to the boy's mother,* SALLY, *who stands on the fringe of the crowd*). From outer space, yet! Sally, you better get that boy of yours up to bed. He's been reading too many comic books or seeing too many movies or something.

Sally. Tommy, come over here and stop that kind of talk.

Steve. Go ahead, Tommy. We'll be right back. And you'll see. That wasn't any ship or anything like it. That was just a . . . a meteor or something. Likely as not— (*He turns to the group, now trying to weight his words with an optimism he obviously doesn't feel but is desperately trying to instill in himself, as well as the others.*) No doubt it did have something to do with all this power failure and the rest of it. Meteors can do some crazy things. Like sunspots.

Don (*picking up the cue*). Sure. That's the kind of thing—like sunspots. They raise Cain with radio reception all over the world. And this thing being so close— why, there's no telling the sort of stuff it can do. (*He wets his lips and smiles nervously.*) Go ahead, Charlie. You and Steve go into town and see if that isn't what's causing it all.

F | Read and Discuss | What does this show you about Tommy?

[STEVE *and* CHARLIE *walk away from the group again, down the sidewalk. The people watch silently.* TOMMY *stares at them, biting his lips, and finally calls out again.*]

Tommy. Mr. Brand!

[*The two men stop again.* TOMMY *takes a step toward them.*]

Tommy. Mr. Brand . . . please don't leave here.

[STEVE *and* CHARLIE *stop once again and turn toward the boy. There's a murmur in the crowd, a murmur of irritation and concern as if the boy were bringing up fears that shouldn't be brought up; words that carried with them a strange kind of validity that came without logic, but nonetheless registered and had meaning and effect.* TOMMY *is partly frightened and partly* defiant.]

You might not even be able to get to town. It was that way in the story. Nobody could leave. Nobody except—
Steve. Except who?
Tommy. Except the people they'd sent down ahead of them. They looked just like humans. And it wasn't until the ship landed that—

[*The boy suddenly stops again, conscious of the parents staring at him and of the sudden hush of the crowd.*] **ⓖ**

Sally (*in a whisper, sensing the antagonism of the crowd*). Tommy, please, son . . . honey, don't talk that way—
Man One. That kid shouldn't talk that way . . . and we shouldn't stand here listening to him. Why, this is the craziest thing I ever heard of. The kid tells us a comic book plot, and here we stand listening—

[STEVE *walks toward the camera and stops by the boy.*]

Steve. Go ahead, Tommy. What kind of story was this? What about the people that they sent out ahead?
Tommy. That was the way they prepared things for the landing. They sent four people. A mother and a father and two kids who looked just like humans . . . but they weren't. **ⓗ**

[*There's another silence as* STEVE *looks toward the crowd and then toward* TOMMY. *He wears a tight grin.*]

Steve. Well, I guess what we'd better do then is to run a check on the neighborhood and see which ones of us are really human.

[*There's laughter at this, but it's a laughter that comes from a desperate attempt to lighten the atmosphere.* CHARLIE *laughs nervously, slightly forced. The people look at one another in the middle of their laughter.*]

ⓖ Literary Focus Plot Complications What is stopping Steve and Charlie from going downtown?

ⓗ Read and Discuss What is on Tommy's mind?

Vocabulary **defiant** (dih FY uhnt) *adj.*: boldly resisting authority.

Charlie. There must be somethin' better to do than stand around makin' bum jokes about it. (*Rubs his jaw nervously*) I wonder if Floral Street's got the same deal we got. (*He looks past the houses.*) Where is Pete Van Horn anyway? Didn't he get back yet?

[*Suddenly there's the sound of a car's engine starting to turn over. We look across the street toward the driveway of* LES GOODMAN'S *house. He's at the wheel trying to start the car.*]

Sally. Can you get it started, Les?

[LES GOODMAN *gets out of the car, shaking his head.*]

Goodman. No dice.

[*He walks toward the group. He stops suddenly as behind him, inexplicably and with a noise that inserts itself into the silence, the car engine starts up all by itself.* GOODMAN *whirls around to stare toward it. The car idles roughly, smoke coming from the exhaust, the frame shaking gently.* GOODMAN'S *eyes go wide, and he runs over to his car. The people stare toward the car.*]

Man One. He got the car started somehow. He got his car started!

[*The camera pans along the faces of the people as they stare, somehow caught up by this revelation and somehow, illogically, wildly, frightened.*]

Woman One. How come his car just up and started like that?
Sally. All by itself. He wasn't anywheres near it. It started all by itself.

[DON *approaches the group. He stops a few feet away to look toward* GOODMAN'S *car, and then back toward the group.*]

Don. And he never did come out to look at that thing that flew overhead. He wasn't even interested. (*He turns to the faces in the group, his face taut and serious.*) Why? Why didn't he come out with the rest of us to look?
Charlie. He always was an oddball. Him and his whole family. Real oddball.
Don. What do you say we ask him? ❶

[*The group suddenly starts toward the house. In this brief fraction of a moment they take the first step toward a metamorphosis from a group into a mob. They begin to head purposefully across the street toward the house at the end.* STEVE *stands in front of them. For a moment their fear almost turns their walk into a wild stampede, but* STEVE'S *voice, loud, incisive, and commanding, makes them stop.*]

Steve. Wait a minute . . . wait a minute! Let's not be a mob!

[*The people stop as a group, seem to pause for a moment, and then much more quietly and slowly start to walk across the street.* GOODMAN *stands there alone, facing the people.*]

---

❶ **Literary Focus** **Plot Complications** What has the group decided about Les Goodman? Support your answer with evidence from their dialogue and <u>interactions</u>.

Goodman. I just don't understand it. I tried to start it and it wouldn't start. You saw me. All of you saw me.

[*And now, just as suddenly as the engine started, it stops. There's a long silence that is gradually intruded upon by the frightened murmuring of the people.*]

I don't understand. I swear . . . I don't understand. What's happening?

Don. Maybe you better tell us. Nothing's working on this street. Nothing. No lights, no power, no radio. (*And then meaningfully*) nothing except one car—yours!  **J**

[*The people pick this up. Now their murmuring becomes a loud chant, filling the air with accusations and demands for action. Two of the men pass* DON *and head toward* GOODMAN, *who backs away, backing into his car. He is now at bay.*]

Goodman. Wait a minute now. You keep your distance—all of you. So I've got a car that starts by itself—well, that's a freak thing, I admit it. But does that make me some kind of criminal or something? I don't know why the car works—it just does!

[*This stops the crowd momentarily, and now* GOODMAN, *still backing away, goes toward his front porch. He goes up the steps and then*

stops to stand facing the mob. STEVE *comes through the crowd.*]

Steve (*quietly*). We're all on a monster kick, Les. Seems that the general impression holds that maybe one family isn't what we think they are. Monsters from outer space or something. Different than us. Fifth columnists[1] from the vast beyond. (*He chuckles.*) You know anybody that might fit that description around here on Maple Street? **K**

Goodman. What is this, a gag or something? This a practical joke or something?

---

1. **fifth columnists:** people who aid an enemy from within their own country.

J **Literary Focus** **Plot Complications** What is Don's <u>motive</u> for speaking to Goodman like this?

K **Reading Focus** **Author's Purpose** Communists were sometimes called fifth columnists. Why do you think the author is using the term here?

[*The spotlight on his porch suddenly goes out. There's a murmur from the group.*]

Now, I suppose that's supposed to incriminate me! The light goes on and off. That really does it, doesn't it? (*He looks around the faces of the people.*) I just don't understand this—(*He wets his lips, looking from face to face.*) Look, you all know me. We've lived here five years. Right in this house. We're no different than any of the rest of you! We're no different at all. Really . . . this whole thing is just . . . just weird—

Woman One. Well, if that's the case, Les Goodman, explain why— (*She stops suddenly, clamping her mouth shut.*)

Goodman (*softly*). Explain what?
Steve (*interjecting*). Look, let's forget this—
Charlie (*overlapping him*). Go ahead, let her talk. What about it? Explain what?
Woman One (*a little reluctantly*). Well . . . sometimes I go to bed late at night. A couple of times . . . a couple of times I'd come out on the porch and I'd see Mr. Goodman here in the wee hours of the morning standing out in front of his house . . . looking up at the sky. (*She looks around the circle of faces.*) That's right. Looking up at the sky as if . . . as if he were waiting for something. (*A pause*) As if he were looking for something.

[*There's a murmur of reaction from the crowd again. As* GOODMAN *starts toward them, they back away, frightened.*]

Goodman. You know really . . . this is for laughs. You know what I'm guilty of? (*He laughs.*) I'm guilty of insomnia. Now what's the penalty for insomnia? (*At this point the laugh, the humor, leaves his voice.*) Did you hear what I said? I said it was insomnia. (*A pause as he looks around, then shouts.*) I said it was insomnia! You fools. You scared, frightened rabbits, you. You're sick people, do you know that? You're sick people—all of you! And you don't even know what you're starting because let me tell you . . . let me tell you—this thing you're starting—that should frighten you. As God is my witness . . . you're letting something begin here that's a nightmare! **L**

[*Fade to black.*]

> That's right. Looking up at the sky as if . . . as if he were waiting for something.

L Read and Discuss | What is the author getting at?

Applying Your Skills

SKILLS FOCUS Literary Skills Analyze plot complications; understand suspense and foreshadowing. **Reading Skills** Determine the author's purpose. **Writing Skills** Use dialogue effectively.

The Monsters Are Due on Maple Street, Act One

Respond and Think Critically

Reading Focus

Quick Check

1. What steps do the residents initially take to figure out the cause of the power failure?

2. What is Tommy's theory about the power failure?

Read with a Purpose

3. What do you know about the power failure so far? What do you think might have caused it?

Reading Skills: Identifying Author's Purpose

4. Now that you have finished reading Act One, review what you have written in your graphic organizer. Does your reason or the evidence you provided support the author's purpose(s) you've selected? Make any necessary changes.

Author's Purpose

Literary Focus

Literary Analysis

5. **Interpret** What is the group's reaction when Les Goodman's car starts? What inference do they make?

6. **Interpret** At the end of Act One, Les Goodman warns the residents that they are starting something that should frighten them, and he goes on to call it a nightmare. What could he mean?

7. **Analyze** A *scapegoat* is someone whom people blame for their troubles. How has Les Goodman become a scapegoat?

8. **Evaluate** What is the difference between a crowd and a mob?

Literary Skills: Plot Complications

9. **Extend** Describe the way the community is interacting, and predict where this behavior is going to lead in Act Two.

Literary Skills Review: Foreshadowing

10. **Analyze** What future events could Tommy's words **foreshadow,** or hint at?

Writing Focus

Think as a Reader/Writer

Use It in Your Writing Use what you have noted about questions and fragments in this teleplay to write two lines of authentic dialogue. Make sure that your language conveys a tense situation and the need to communicate quickly.

What Do **You Think Now**

Explain whether the group is acting on fear or facts. Support your explanation with details from the teleplay.

Read with a Purpose Read Act Two to discover how and why the situation on Maple Street escalates.

The
MONSTERS
Are Due *on* Maple Street

by **Rod Serling**

ACT TWO

Fade in on the entry hall of the Goodman house at night. On the side table rests an unlit candle. MRS. GOODMAN *walks into the scene, a glass of milk in hand. She sets the milk down on the table, lights the candle with a match from a box on the table, picks up the glass of milk, and starts out of the scene. Cut to an outside shot.* MRS.

GOODMAN *comes through her porch door, glass of milk in hand. The entry hall, with the table and lit candle, can be seen behind her. The camera slowly pans down the sidewalk, taking in little knots of people who stand around talking in low voices. At the end of each conversation they look toward* LES GOODMAN'S *house. From the various houses we can see candlelight but no electricity.*

An all-pervading quiet blankets the area, disturbed only by the almost whispered voices of the people as they stand around. The camera pans over to one group where CHARLIE *stands. He stares across at* GOODMAN's *house. Two men stand across the street from it, in almost sentrylike poses. We return to the group.*

Sally (*a little timorously[1]*). It just doesn't seem right, though, keeping watch on them. Why . . . he was right when he said he was one of our neighbors. Why, I've known Ethel Goodman ever since they moved in. We've been good friends—
Charlie. That don't prove a thing. Any guy who'd spend his time lookin' up at the sky early in the morning—well, there's something wrong with that kind of a person. There's something that ain't legitimate. Maybe under normal circumstances we could let it go by, but these aren't normal circumstances. Why, look at this street! Nothin' but candles. Why, it's like goin' back into the dark ages or somethin'!

[STEVE *walks down the steps of his porch. He walks down the street, over to* LES GOODMAN's *house, and stops at the foot of the steps.* GOODMAN *stands behind the screen door, his wife behind him, very frightened.*]

Goodman. Just stay right where you are, Steve. We don't want any trouble, but this time if anybody sets foot on my porch, that's what they're going to get—trouble!
Steve. Look, Les—

---

1. **timorously** (TIHM uhr uhs lee): timidly; fearfully.

SOCIAL STUDIES LINK

Communism, Suspicion, and Fear in the 1940s and 1950s

The United States and Soviet Union were allies during World War II. However, with the start of the Cold War in the mid-1940s and the detonation of the first Soviet atomic bomb, in 1949, distrust of Communist Russia increased. So did the fear that communism was spreading to the United States. In 1950, Senator Joseph McCarthy claimed to possess a list of 205 communists employed in the U.S. Department of State. His accusations fed into the period's political tensions, and many innocent people were labeled communist sympathizers. Lives were destroyed, and individuals made up stories about others in order to appear innocent themselves. Rod Serling alludes to that hysteria over communism in this teleplay.

Ask Yourself
How does *The Monsters Are Due on Maple Street* reflect the period of history in which it was written? How does the theme of this teleplay express Rod Serling's opinion of the climate of the times?

Goodman. I've already explained to you people. I don't sleep very well at night sometimes. I get up and I take a walk and I look up at the sky. I look at the stars!

Mrs. Goodman. That's exactly what he does. Why this whole thing, it's . . . it's some kind of madness or something.

Steve (*nods grimly*). That's exactly what it is—some kind of madness.

Charlie's Voice (*shrill, from across the street*). You best watch who you're seen with, Steve! Until we get this all straightened out, you ain't exactly above suspicion yourself.

Steve (*whirling around toward him*). Or you, Charlie. Or any of us, it seems. From age eight on up!

Woman One. What I'd like to know is, what are we gonna do? Just stand around here all night?

Charlie. There's nothin' else we can do! (*He turns back looking toward* STEVE *and* GOODMAN *again.*) One of 'em'll tip their hand. They got to.

Steve (*raising his voice*). There's something you can do, Charlie. You could go home and keep your mouth shut. You could quit strutting around like a self-appointed hanging judge[2] and just climb into bed and forget it.

---

2. **hanging judge:** judge who sentences people to death without sufficient evidence.

Charlie. You sound real anxious to have that happen, Steve. I think we better keep our eye on you too!

Don (*as if he were taking the bit in his teeth, takes a hesitant step to the front*). I think everything might as well come out now. (*He turns toward* STEVE.) Your wife's done plenty of talking, Steve, about how odd you are!

Charlie (*picking this up, his eyes widening*). Go ahead, tell us what she's said.

[STEVE *walks toward them from across the street.*]

Steve. Go ahead, what's my wife said? Let's get it all out. Let's pick out every idiosyncrasy of every single man, woman, and child on the street. And then we might as well set up some kind of a kangaroo court.[3] How about a firing squad at dawn, Charlie, so we can get rid of all the suspects? Narrow them down. Make it easier for you.

Don. There's no need gettin' so upset, Steve. It's just that . . . well . . . Myra's talked about how there's been plenty of nights you spend hours down in your basement workin' on some kind of radio or something. Well, none of us have ever seen that radio—

> How about a firing squad at dawn, Charlie, so we can get rid of all the suspects?

---

3. **kangaroo court:** unauthorized court, usually one that pays no attention to legal procedures. Kangaroo courts were often set up in frontier areas.

Ⓐ Literary Focus Plot Complications What complication does this interaction between Charlie and Steve introduce?

Vocabulary **idiosyncrasy** (ihd ee uh SIHNG kruh see) *n.*: peculiarity.

[*By this time* STEVE *has reached the group. He stands there defiantly close to them.*]

Charlie. Go ahead, Steve. What kind of "radio set" you workin' on? I never seen it. Neither has anyone else. Who you talk to on that radio set? And who talks to you?
Steve. I'm surprised at you, Charlie. How come you're so dense all of a sudden? (*A pause*) Who do I talk to? I talk to monsters from outer space. I talk to three-headed green men who fly over here in what look like meteors.

[STEVE'*s wife steps down from their porch, bites her lip, calls out.*]

Mrs. Brand. Steve! Steve, please. (*Then looking around, frightened, she walks toward the group.*) It's just a ham radio set, that's all. I bought him a book on it myself. It's just a ham radio[4] set. A lot of people have them. I can show it to you. It's right down in the basement.
Steve (*whirls around toward her*). Show them nothing! If they want to look inside our house—let them get a search warrant.
Charlie. Look, buddy, you can't afford to—
Steve (*interrupting*). Charlie, don't tell me what I can afford! And stop telling me who's dangerous and who isn't and who's safe and who's a menace. (*He turns to the group and shouts.*) And you're with him too—all of you! You're standing here all set to crucify—all set

to find a scapegoat—all desperate to point some kind of a finger at a neighbor! Well now look, friends, the only thing that's gonna happen is that we'll eat each other up alive—

[*He stops abruptly as* CHARLIE *suddenly grabs his arm.*]

Charlie (*in a hushed voice*). That's not the only thing that can happen to us.   **Ⓑ**

[*Cut to a long shot looking down the street. A figure has suddenly materialized in the gloom, and in the silence we can hear the clickety-clack of slow, measured footsteps on concrete as the figure walks slowly toward them. One of the women lets out a stifled cry.[5] The young mother grabs her boy, as do a couple of others.*]

Tommy (*shouting, frightened*). It's the monster! It's the monster!

[*Another woman lets out a wail and the people fall back in a group, staring toward the darkness and the approaching figure. As the people stand in the shadows watching,* DON MARTIN *joins them, carrying a shotgun. He holds it up.*]

Don. We may need this.
Steve. A shotgun? (*He pulls it out of* DON'*s hand.*) Good Lord—will anybody think a thought around here? Will you people wise up? What good would a shotgun do against—

---

4. **ham radio:** two-way radio used by an amateur operator. Ham radio operators talk to one another all over the world via their radios.

5. **stifled** (STY fuhld) **cry:** cry that is checked or stopped.

Ⓑ Read and Discuss What can you say about the neighbors now?

Vocabulary **menace** (MEHN ihs) *n.:* danger, threat.

[*Now* CHARLIE *pulls the gun from* STEVE'S *hand.*]

Charlie. No more talk, Steve. You're going to talk us into a grave! You'd let whatever's out there walk right over us, wouldn't yuh? Well, some of us won't!

[*He swings the gun around to point it toward the sidewalk. The dark figure continues to walk toward them. The group stands there, fearful, apprehensive. Mothers clutch children, men stand in front of wives.* CHARLIE *slowly raises the gun. As the figure gets closer and closer, he suddenly pulls the trigger. The sound of it explodes in the stillness. The figure suddenly lets out a small cry, stumbles forward onto his knees, and then falls forward on his face.* DON, CHARLIE, *and* STEVE *race over to him.* STEVE *is there first and turns the man over. Now the crowd gathers around them.*]

Steve (*slowly looks up*). It's Pete Van Horn.
Don (*in a hushed voice*). Pete Van Horn! He was just gonna go over to the next block to see if the power was on—
Woman One. You killed him, Charlie. You shot him dead!
Charlie (*looks around at the circle of faces, his eyes frightened, his face contorted*). But . . . but I didn't know who he was. I certainly didn't know who he was. He comes walkin' out of the darkness—how am I

supposed to know who he was? (*He grabs* STEVE.) Steve—you know why I shot! How was I supposed to know he wasn't a monster or something? (*He grabs* DON *now.*) We're all scared of the same thing. I was just tryin' to . . . tryin' to protect my home, that's all! Look, all of you, that's all I was tryin' to do. (*He looks down wildly at the body.*) I didn't know it was somebody we knew! I didn't know— **C**

[*There's a sudden hush and then an intake of breath. We see the living room window of* CHARLIE'S *house. The window is not lit, but suddenly the house lights come on behind it.*]

Woman One (*in a very hushed voice*). Charlie . . . Charlie . . . the lights just went on in your house. Why did the lights just go on?
Don. What about it, Charlie? How come you're the only one with lights now?
Goodman. That's what I'd like to know.

[*There is a pause as they all stare toward* CHARLIE.]

You were so quick to kill, Charlie, and you were so quick to tell us who we had to be careful of. Well, maybe you had to kill. Maybe Peter there was trying to tell us something. Maybe he'd found out something and came back to tell us who there was amongst us we should watch out for—

C Read and Discuss What is Charlie's <u>motive</u> for his actions?

[CHARLIE *backs away from the group, his eyes wide with fright.*]

Charlie. No . . . no . . . it's nothing of the sort! I don't know why the lights are on. I swear I don't. Somebody's pulling a gag or something.

[*He bumps against* STEVE, *who grabs him and whirls him around.*]

Steve. A gag? A gag? Charlie, there's a dead man on the sidewalk and you killed him! Does this thing look like a gag to you?

[CHARLIE *breaks away and screams as he runs toward his house.*]

Charlie. No! No! Please!

[*A man breaks away from the crowd to chase* CHARLIE. *The man tackles him and lands on top of him. The other people start to run toward them.* CHARLIE *is up on his feet. He breaks away from the other man's grasp and lands a couple of desperate punches that push the man aside. Then he forces his way, fighting, through the crowd to once again break free. He jumps up on*

Analyzing Visuals **Viewing and Interpreting** What theme of the teleplay is hinted at in the photograph?

851

his front porch. A rock thrown from the group smashes a window alongside of him, the broken glass flying past him. A couple of pieces cut him. He stands there perspiring, rumpled, blood running down from a cut on his cheek. His wife breaks away from the group to throw herself into his arms. He buries his face against her. We can see the crowd converging on the porch now.]

Voices.
It must have been him.
He's the one.
We got to get Charlie.

[*Another rock lands on the porch. Now* CHARLIE *pushes his wife behind him, facing the group.*]

Charlie. Look, look, I swear to you . . . it isn't me . . . but I do know who it is . . . I swear to you, I do know who it is. I know who the monster is here. I know who it is that doesn't belong. I swear to you I know.
Goodman (*shouting*). What are you waiting for?
Woman One (*shouting*). Come on, Charlie, come on.
Man One (*shouting*). Who is it, Charlie, tell us!
Don (*pushing his way to the front of the crowd*). All right, Charlie, let's hear it!

[CHARLIE's *eyes dart around wildly.*]

Charlie. It's . . . it's . . .
Man Two (*screaming*). Go ahead, Charlie, tell us.
Charlie. It's . . . it's the kid. It's Tommy. He's the one.

[*There's a gasp from the crowd as we cut to a shot of the mother holding her boy. The boy at first doesn't understand. Then, realizing the eyes are all on him, he buries his face against his mother,* SALLY.]

Sally (*backs away*). That's crazy. That's crazy. He's a little boy.
Woman One. But he knew! He was the only one who knew! He told us all about it. Well, how did he know? How could he have known?

[*The various people take this up and repeat the questions aloud.*]

Voices.
How could he know?
Who told him?
Make the kid answer.   **ⓓ**
Man One. What about Goodman's car?
Don. It was Charlie who killed old man Van Horn.

> I swear to you, I do know who it is.
> I know who the monster is here.

ⓓ Literary Focus Plot Complications What have the residents decided about Tommy?

Vocabulary **converging** (kuhn VUR jihng) *v.* used as *adj.*: coming together.

Woman One. But it was the kid here who knew what was going to happen all the time. He was the one who knew!

[STEVE *shouts at his hysterical neighbors.*]

Steve. Are you all gone crazy? (*Pause as he looks about*) Stop.

[*A fist crashes at* STEVE's *face, staggering him back out of view. Several close camera shots suggest the coming of violence: A hand fires a rifle. A fist clenches. A hand grabs the hammer from* VAN HORN's *body, etc.*]

Don. Charlie has to be the one— Where's my rifle—
Woman One. Les Goodman's the one. His car started! Let's wreck it.
Mrs. Goodman. What about Steve's radio— He's the one that called them—
Mr. Goodman. Smash the radio. Get me a hammer. Get me something.
Steve. Stop— Stop—
Charlie. Where's that kid— Let's get him.
Man One. Get Steve— Get Charlie— They're working together.

[*The crowd starts to converge around the mother, who grabs her son and starts to run with him. The crowd starts to follow, at first, walking fast, and then running after him. Suddenly,* CHARLIE's *lights go off and the lights in another house go on. They stay on for a moment, then from across the street other lights go on and then off again.*]

Man One (*shouting*). It isn't the kid. . . . It's Bob Weaver's house.
Woman One. It isn't Bob Weaver's house, it's Don Martin's place.
Charlie. I tell you, it's the kid.
Don. It's Charlie. He's the one.

[*The people shout, accuse, scream. The camera tilts back and forth. We see panic-stricken faces in close-up and tilting shots of houses as the lights go on and off. Slowly, in the middle of this nightmarish morass[6] of sight and sound, the camera starts to pull away, until once again we've reached the opening shot, looking at the Maple Street sign from high above. The camera continues to move away until we dissolve to a shot of the metal side of a spacecraft, which sits shrouded[7] in darkness. An open door throws out a beam of light from the illuminated interior. Two figures silhouetted against the bright lights appear. We get only a vague feeling of form, but nothing more explicit than that.*] **E**

Figure One. Understand the procedure now? Just stop a few of their machines and radios and telephones and lawn mowers . . . throw them into darkness for a few hours and then you just sit back and watch the pattern.
Figure Two. And this pattern is always the same?
Figure One. With few variations. They pick the most dangerous enemy they can

---

6. **morass** (muh RAS): confusing situation. Strictly speaking, a morass is a kind of swamp.
7. **shrouded** (SHROWD uhd): hidden; covered.

E Read and Discuss | Now what is developing?

find . . . and it's themselves. And all we need do is sit back . . . and watch.

Figure Two. Then I take it this place . . . this Maple Street . . . is not unique.

Figure One (*shaking his head*). By no means. Their world is full of Maple Streets. And we'll go from one to the other and let them destroy themselves. One to the other . . . one to the other . . . one to the other— **F**

[*Now the camera pans up for a shot of the starry sky.*]

Narrator's Voice. The tools of conquest do not necessarily come with bombs and explosions and fallout. There are weapons that are simply thoughts, attitudes, prejudices—to be found only in the minds of men. For the record, prejudices can kill and suspicion can destroy, and a thoughtless, frightened search for a scapegoat has a fallout all of its own for the children . . . the children yet unborn. (*A pause*) And the pity of it is . . . that these things cannot be confined to . . . The Twilight Zone! **G**

[*Fade to black.*]

F **Reading Focus** Author's Purpose What do you learn from the aliens' view of the human race?

G **Literary Focus** Plot Complications How are the complications in the teleplay resolved?

Applying Your Skills

SKILLS FOCUS **Literary Skills** Analyze plot complications; analyze symbols. **Reading Skills** Determine the author's purpose. **Writing Skills** Write an explanation.

The Monsters Are Due on Maple Street, Act Two
Respond and Think Critically

Reading Focus

Quick Check

1. How does Charlie respond to Pete Van Horn's reappearance?

2. What do you learn about the aliens' plans?

Read with a Purpose

3. How does the situation on Maple Street continue to escalate? Why does this happen?

Reading Skills: Author's Purpose

4. Review your graphic organizer. Do you have anything to add or change? Make sure to provide evidence from the teleplay.

Literary Focus

Literary Analysis

5. **Analyze** According to the aliens, who is the most dangerous enemy? Who are the "monsters" in the teleplay?

6. **Analyze** Writers often voice their opinions through a particular character. Which character reflects Rod Serling's point of view?

7. **Evaluate** This teleplay was written in 1960. Why might its message still be important today?

8. **Evaluate** Were the predictions you made at the end of Act One correct? Explain why your predictions were correct or incorrect.

9. **Extend** The narrator concludes the story by saying that "prejudices can kill and suspicion can destroy." What have you seen at previous times in history that proves this to be true?

Literary Skills: Plot Complications

10. **Evaluate** Fill out a chart to show the most important elements of the play's **plot.** You might have different opinions about the key events, or **complications,** that lead to the surprising way that the conflicts are resolved.

Literary Skills Review: Symbols

11. **Extend** **Symbols** in literature are persons, places, or things that stand for larger ideas, such as love or honor. The loss of power on Maple Street is a symbol for what larger idea?

Writing Focus

Think as a Reader/Writer

Use It in Your Writing Write a paragraph explaining what this story has taught you about the use of authentic dialogue.

What Do You Think Now Now that you've read this teleplay, what do you think causes more confusion—fear or facts? Briefly explain your answer.

Applying Your Skills

The Monsters Are Due on Maple Street

Vocabulary Development

Clarifying Word Meanings: Definitions

Writers often help readers understand difficult words by using **definitions.** This means that the word's meaning is provided within the sentence. Let's look at the following sentence:

> In this brief fraction of a moment they take the first step toward a metamorphosis that changes people from a group into a mob.

A reader who does not understand the word *metamorphosis* would benefit from the second half of the sentence. A metamorphosis is a change of form, substance, or structure. In this story the people of Maple Street change "from a group into a mob."

As you read, be on the lookout for definitions provided in the text itself. Chances are, if you read a little past a difficult word, you will find that the writer has given you some help.

Your Turn

Choose the Vocabulary word that best fits the blank in each sentence below. Remember to look for definitions within each sentence to help you decide.

transfixed
intimidated
defiant
idiosyncrasy
menace
converging

1. During the second act the crowd's fear, mistrust, and suspicion are _____ , or meeting, to create a mob.

2. A frightened man with a gun can be considered a _____ and a danger to society.

3. Steve's interest in ham radios becomes a threat rather than an oddity, or _____ , that makes him unique.

Language Coach

Prefixes Think about the meaning of the prefix *con–*. How is the meaning of the prefix evident in the word *concoct*? *confederation*?

Academic Vocabulary

Write About . . .

What message does Serling convey in *The Monsters Are Due on Maple Street*? Support your response with details on the way characters <u>interact</u> and the way conflicts are <u>resolved</u>. Use the Academic Vocabulary words in the collection in your response.

Grammar Link
Pronouns Can Be Problems

Pronouns used in compound structures can be confusing. Which of these sentences is correct?

> **Dad talked to Mom and *me*.**

> **Dad talked to Mom and *I*.**

Mom and me and *Mom and I* are compound structures. When you proofread your own writing, you can use this trick to decide which pronoun is correct: Say the sentence aloud as if it only contained one pronoun, not a compound structure. Let your ear tell you which one sounds right.

TEST **Dad talked to me.** [sounds right]
Dad talked to I. [sounds wrong]

CORRECT **Dad talked to Mom and *me*.**

Your Turn

In the following sentences, choose the correct pronoun.

1. *He/Him* and Steve decided to walk into town to figure out the cause of the power failure.
2. The crowd demanded explanations from Steve and *she/her*.
3. *The Twilight Zone* marathon on television was watched by Cheryl and *me/I*.

CHOICES

As you respond to the Choices, use the **Academic Vocabulary** words as appropriate: interact, motive, previous, resolve.

REVIEW
Write About the Message

Timed └Writing What message does the author deliver about human beings? Write a short response to this play. In one paragraph, explain the meaning of the closing comments in light of the story's events. In a second paragraph, tell how you feel about the play's message, and explain whether or not the message still has significance today.

CONNECT
Act It Out

Picture a different ending to the teleplay—instead of leaving the people to destroy each other, the aliens land. How would the residents respond? What new complications might arise? How would the situation be resolved? As a class, act out this new scene.

EXTEND
Give a Multimedia Presentation

TechFocus Create a multimedia presentation on an aspect of *The Monsters Are Due on Maple Street,* such as McCarthyism or the influence of the television show *The Twilight Zone.* Research your topic on the Internet. Then, give a presentation to the class. Be sure that your presentation includes audio and visual features that relate to the topic.

Learn It Online
Create an eye-popping multimedia presentation! Visit MediaScope at:

go.hrw.com L7-857 **Go**

Comparing Versions of a Text

CONTENTS

(top left) *The Last of the Spirits,* illustration from the novel *A Christmas Carol* (1843) by Charles Dickens. Color engraving.
(top right) Scrooge and the Ghost of Christmas Future from Marvel Comics *Christmas Carol*.
(right) Scrooge in Virginia Opera's production of *A Christmas Carol, The Opera* (2002).

What Do You Think

Why do artists tell new versions of old stories?

 QuickTalk

A Christmas Carol is a classic work of literature. Talk about why its popularity has spanned the centuries.

Preparing to Read

A Christmas Carol: The Novel / The Play / The Graphic Story

Reader/Writer Notebook

Use your **RWN** to complete the activities for these selections.

Literary Focus

Comparing Versions of a Text Many short stories and novels are transformed into plays and films. Some are also made into graphic stories. An adaptation usually retains the same characters, plot, conflict, and resolution as the original work. The **theme,** or message, of both works is also often the same. What differs is the way the story is told: Writers of most short stories and novels use narration and description to tell the story. In plays and films the story advances through dialogue and action. In graphic stories, illustrations, description, and dialogue tell the story.

Reading Focus

Adjusting Reading Rate You don't read everything at the same speed. When you're reading a novel, you may find yourself reading slowly if the vocabulary is challenging or the sentences are long. When you read a play, you may read slowly when you're reading the stage directions so that you can visualize the setting and the action being described.

Into Action As you read the three different versions of the scene from *A Christmas Carol,* use a chart like this to keep track of what you read easily and quickly and what you had to read more slowly and carefully. Explain why you needed to speed up or slow down.

What I read easily	What I read slowly	Why

Writing Focus

Think as a Reader/Writer

Find It in Your Reading Note similarities and differences among the three versions as you read. List them in your *Reader/ Writer Notebook.*

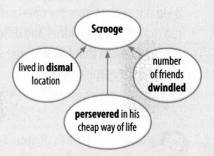

from

A Christmas Carol

by **Charles Dickens**

Read with a Purpose
Read this excerpt from the novel carefully so you can explore the similarities and differences in the two adaptations that follow—the scene from the play and the graphic story.

Build Background
This excerpt from Charles Dickens's *A Christmas Carol* presents the graveyard scene at the end of the novel.

Specter," said Scrooge, "something informs me that our parting moment is at hand. I know it, but I know not how. Tell me what man that was, with the covered face, whom we saw lying dead?"

The Ghost of Christmas Yet to Come conveyed him to a dismal, wretched, ruinous churchyard.

The spirit stood among the graves, and pointed down to one.

"Before I draw nearer to that stone to which you point, answer me one question. Are these the shadows of the things that will be, or are they shadows of the things that may be only?"

Still the ghost pointed downward to the grave by which it stood.

"Men's courses will foreshadow certain ends, to which, if persevered in, they must lead. But if the courses be departed from,

---

Vocabulary **dismal** (DIHZ muhl) *adj.*: cheerless, depressing.
persevered (pur suh VIHRD) *v.*: continued doing something.

the ends will change. Say it is thus with what you show me!"

The spirit was immovable as ever.

Scrooge crept toward it, trembling as he went; and following the finger, read upon the stone of the neglected grave his own name—EBENEZER SCROOGE. **B**

"Am I that man who lay upon the bed? No, Spirit! Oh no, no! Spirit! hear me! I am not the man I was. I will not be the man I must have been but for this intercourse. Why show me this, if I am past all hope? Assure me that I yet may change these shadows you have shown me, by an altered life."

For the first time the kind hand faltered.

"I will honor Christmas in my heart, and try to keep it all the year. I will live in the Past, the Present, and the Future. The spirits of all three shall strive within me. I will not shut out the lessons that they teach. Oh, tell me I may sponge away the writing on this stone!"

Holding up his hands in one last prayer to have his fate reversed, he saw an alteration in the phantom's hood and dress. It shrunk, collapsed, and dwindled down into a bedpost.

A **Reading Focus** **Reading Rate** How did your reading rate change as you read Scrooge's statement?

B **Read and Discuss** Dickens describes the grave as neglected. What does that tell you?

Vocabulary **dwindled** (DWIHN duhld) *v.:* became smaller and smaller.

from
A Christmas Carol:
Scrooge and Marley

by Israel Horovitz

Read with a Purpose
Read this excerpt from the play to discover the techniques the playwright uses to dramatize the scene.

Preparing to Read for the selection is on page 859.

Build Background
This excerpt is from Act II, the end of Scene 4, as the Ghost of Christmas Future leads Scrooge to his own grave.

Scrooge. Specter, something informs me that our parting moment is at hand. I know it, but I know not how I know it.

[FUTURE *points to the other side of the stage. Lights out on* CRATCHITS. FUTURE *moves slowing, gliding.* SCROOGE *follows.* FUTURE *points opposite.* FUTURE *leads* SCROOGE *to a wall and a tombstone. He points to the stone.*] Ⓐ

Am *I* that man those ghoulish parasites[1] so gloated over? (*Pauses*) Before I draw nearer to that stone to which you point, answer

---

1. **ghoulish parasites:** people who stole Scrooge's possessions and divided them up after he died.

me one question. Are these the shadows of things that will be, or the shadows of things that MAY be, only?

[FUTURE *points to the gravestone.* MARLEY *appears in light well* UPSTAGE. *He points to grave as well. Gravestone turns front and grows to ten feet high. Words upon it:* EBENEZER SCROOGE. *Much smoke billows now from the grave. Choral music here.* SCROOGE *stands looking up at gravestone.* FUTURE *does not at all reply in mortals' words, but points once more to the gravestone. The stone undulates and glows. Music plays, beckoning* SCROOGE. SCROOGE, *reeling in terror*] Ⓑ

Oh, no, Spirit! Oh, no, no!

Ⓐ **Reading Focus** **Reading Rate** How would you adjust your reading rate to visualize this scene onstage?

Ⓑ **Literary Focus** **Comparing Versions of a Text** Name one detail that is different in the play than it is in the novel.

[FUTURE's *finger still pointing*]

Spirit! Hear me! I am not the man I was. I will not be the man I would have been but for this intercourse. Why show me this, if I am past all hope?

[FUTURE *considers* SCROOGE's *logic. His hand wavers.*]

Oh, Good Spirit, I see by your wavering hand that your good nature intercedes for me and pities me. Assure me that I yet may change these shadows that you have shown me by an altered life!

[FUTURE's *hand trembles; pointing has stopped.*] **C**

I will honor Christmas in my heart and try to keep it all the year. I will live in the Past, the Present, and the Future. The Spirits of all Three shall strive within me. I will not shut out the lessons that they teach. Oh, tell me that I may sponge away the writing that is upon this stone!

[SCROOGE *makes a desperate stab at grabbing* FUTURE's *hand. He holds it firm for a moment, but* FUTURE, *stronger than* SCROOGE, *pulls away.* SCROOGE *is on his knees, praying.*] **D**

Spirit, dear Spirit, I am praying before you. Give me a sign that all is possible. Give me a sign that all hope for me is not lost. Oh, Spirit, kind Spirit, I beseech thee: give me a sign . . .

[FUTURE *deliquesces,*[2] *slowly, gently. The* PHANTOM's *hood and robe drop gracefully to the ground in a small heap. Music in. There is nothing in them. They are mortal cloth. The* SPIRIT *is elsewhere.* SCROOGE *has his sign.* SCROOGE *is alone. Tableau. The lights fade to black.*]

---

2. **deliquesces** (dehl uh KWEHS ihz): melts away; dissolves.

C Read and Discuss Why does the ghost stop pointing?

D Literary Focus Comparing Versions of a Text What emotions do the characters' actions convey?

Analyzing Visuals

Viewing and Interpreting Does this photo accurately portray the scene from the play? Why or why not?

from A Christmas Carol
by **Marvel Comics**

Read with a Purpose
Read this graphic story to discover what visuals add to your understanding of the scene.

Preparing to Read for the selection is on page 859.

A **Literary Focus** Comparing Versions of a Text   Is this the way you pictured the Ghost of Christmas Future? Explain.

B **Read and Discuss** What is on Scrooge's mind?

C **Literary Focus** **Comparing Versions of a Text** Is the portrayal of Scrooge here realistic? Explain.

D **Read and Discuss** Now what is going on?

Applying Your Skills

SKILLS FOCUS Literary Skills Compare an adaptation with source material. Reading Skills Adjust reading rate to improve comprehension. Vocabulary Skills Use specialized vocabulary appropriately. Writing Skills Perform literary analysis.

Versions of A Christmas Carol

Respond and Think Critically

Reading Focus

Quick Check

1. What promise does Scrooge make in all three versions?

Read with a Purpose

2. What surprised you as you compared the three versions?

Reading Skills: Reading Rate

3. Review the chart you kept while reading the excerpts from the play and the novel. When did you slow down and take more time reading and thinking about what you were reading? What conclusions can you draw about your reading rate?

✓ Vocabulary Check

Answer the following questions.

4. Why might a graveyard be described as a **dismal** place?
5. What might happen if someone **persevered** in repeating a certain behavior even after he or she had been warned to stop?
6. How do people feel when their happiness has **dwindled**?

Literary Focus

Literary Analysis

7. **Analyze** Is the change in Scrooge's character more believable in the drama, the novel, or the graphic story? Explain.

8. **Analyze** Marley's ghost appears in the drama but not in the novel. Why do you think Horovitz includes Marley in the scene where Scrooge discovers his grave?

9. **Make Judgments** The stage directions of the play call for special effects for the tombstone. It grows to ten feet high and sways and glows. Smoke billows from the grave. How does this differ from the novel? How does the graphic story present the tombstone?

10. **Analyze** How do the drawings affect your previous understanding of the characters and the story's development? How does the graphic version compare with the written versions in terms of your comprehension?

Literary Skills: Comparing Versions of a Text

11. **Compare and Contrast** Which parts of the novel, the play, and the graphic story are identical?

12. **Analyze** The play elaborates on some details and adds others that are not found in the novel. Where does this occur? What is the effect of the elaboration?

13. **Analyze** Compared to the other versions, how is the graphic story unique? Find two differences beyond the use of illustrations.

Writing Focus

Think as a Reader/Writer

Use It in Your Writing Review the list of similarities and differences you found among the three versions. Explain which of the two adaptations was more similar to Dickens's original.

COMPARING TEXTS
Wrap Up

SKILLS FOCUS Literary Skills Compare an adaptation with source material. **Writing Skills** Write comparison-contrast essays.

Versions of **A Christmas Carol**

Writing Focus

Write a Comparison-Contrast Essay

Write an essay comparing the three versions of the scene from *A Christmas Carol*. You may want to organize your essay in this way:

- Begin by telling how the scenes are the same. Identify the elements of the story that are exactly the same in all three versions.
- Identify the differences in content, language, and events. Then, draw conclusions about why the writers altered details or added elements not found in the original.
- Conclude your essay by explaining your own experience reading the texts. Which did you find most engaging? Which did you think was easiest to read and understand?

Use the workshop on writing a comparison-contrast essay, pages 106–113, for help with this assignment.

What Do You Think Now Was the most effective part of the drama the same as the most effective part of the novel? of the graphic story? Explain.

CHOICES

As you respond to the Choices, use the **Academic Vocabulary** words as appropriate: interact, motive, previous, resolve.

REVIEW
Write an Adaptation

Dramatize a scene from a short story. Remember that in plays the story must be told through dialogue and action. Use *A Christmas Carol: Scrooge and Marley* as a model for writing your play. Write stage directions to indicate physical interaction, and include how the characters speak their lines.

CONNECT
Write a Movie Review

Timed Writing Write a review of a movie based on a familiar book. Explain how the film was like the book and how it was different. Share your opinion about whether or not the movie adaptation was effective, and tell which you enjoyed more.

EXTEND
Create a Graphic Scene

Collaborate with a partner on creating a scene from fiction as a graphic story. Use the graphic story you just read as a model. One of you can write dialogue, and the other can create illustrations that convey the character's feelings and the action of the story.

Learn It Online
Find more about *A Christmas Carol* online:

go.hrw.com | L7-867 | Go

Evaluating Evidence

CONTENTS

What Do
You
Think

Poverty and hunger are widespread. What can you do to help those in need?

 QuickWrite
What efforts to assist those in need have you observed in your home, at school, or in your community?

Preparing to Read

Hungry Here?

SKILLS FOCUS **Informational Skills** Identify and trace the development of an author's argument in a text; identify and evaluate the use of accurate supporting citations and evidence in a text.

Reader/Writer Notebook

Use your **RWN** to complete the activities for this selection.

Informational Text Focus

Identify and Evaluate Author's Evidence Writers of persuasive texts use **evidence**—information that supports an argument—to back up their conclusions. Types of evidence include **facts, examples, statistics** (number facts), **expert opinions,** and **quotations.**

When you **evaluate evidence,** you think about whether it is **accurate,** or correct; **appropriate,** or related to the topic; and **adequate,** or sufficient to prove the conclusion and persuade you that it is valid. Don't take for granted that an author's evidence meets these criteria. **Assess,** or judge, it for yourself. If you read a statement and think, "What does that have to do with anything?" you're probably looking at **inappropriate** evidence. If a writer states an opinion using words such as *all, each,* and *every,* you're probably looking at **inaccurate** evidence. If you have to trust a person's feelings instead of relying on facts, the evidence is most likely **inadequate.**

Into Action As you read, jot down the evidence you think is important. Identify its type, and state whether it is appropriate and adequate to prove the writer's conclusions.

Evidence	Type	Accurate	Appropriate

Writing Focus Preparing for **Constructed Response**

As you read, note the evidence that best supports the author's main points. You'll use these notes to answer a constructed response question later.

Vocabulary

deprivation (dehp ruh VAY shuhn) *n.:* hardship resulting from a lack of something. *Some people living in Cayce's county experience food deprivation on a regular basis.*

prolonged (pruh LAWNGD) *adj.:* continuing for a long time. *The prolonged lack of food will result in a serious condition called malnutrition.*

malnutrition (mal noo TRIHSH uhn) *n.:* ill health caused by a lack of food or by a lack of healthy foods. *Malnutrition is a medical problem that causes weakness and slows growth.*

Language Coach

Prefixes Prefixes are word parts added to the beginnings of words to change their meaning. In both Spanish and English, the prefix *mal–* is used to indicate that something is bad or abnormal. *Mal–* comes from the Latin word *malus,* which means "bad." How does knowing the meaning of *mal–* help you understand the meaning of *malnutrition*? Name three other words with the same prefix. What do they mean?

Learn It Online

Discover the power of an increased vocabulary at:

go.hrw.com | L7-869 | **Go**

HUNGRY HERE?

For Millions of Americans, the Answer Is "Yes"

by  THE WORLD ALMANAC

Read with a Purpose

Read this article to learn how a teen is helping to combat hunger in his hometown.

When you think of starving people, how do you picture them? Do you imagine people living in the past? Or do you think of people living far away—in huts in Africa or on city streets in India? Does it ever cross your mind that right now, in your own state and probably in your own city or town, somebody is suffering from hunger? **A**

Many of us like to think of hunger as something long ago and far away. But the reality is that hunger is a huge problem here and now. And it's a problem that is getting worse. In 2005, the U.S. Department of Agriculture estimated that more than 38 million Americans live in "hungry or food insecure" households. (*Food insecure* is a government term that means "not knowing where your next meal is coming from.") That's an increase of 5 million people since 2000.

A **Informational Focus** **Author's Evidence** At this point in the article, can you guess the author's position on the topic?

In 2005, America's Second Harvest, the country's largest charitable food distribution network, surveyed the people using its food banks. The survey showed that 25 million people use them on a regular basis. That's 9 percent more people than had been using the food banks in 2000. **Ⓑ**

Faces of Hunger

We like to think of America as a land of plenty. Yet about one in ten Americans uses a food bank or soup kitchen on a regular basis in order to get food. And such charitable services do not reach everyone. Many people live in constant hunger, and some are literally starving to death.

Who are America's hungry? You might be surprised. Second Harvest found that 36 percent of its food bank users come from homes with at least one working adult. For these families, a regular wage does not guarantee regular meals. When expenses—such as rent, heat, electric, and medical bills—run higher than family income, little may be left over for food.

Ⓑ **Informational Focus** **Author's Evidence** What type of evidence is the writer using here to back up these assertions?

Sadly, millions of those who go hungry in America are senior citizens. An even greater number—around 13.9 million—are children. Because of their lack of mobility, these people may not have access to the food available through charitable organizations. **C**

Growing Up Hungry

Hunger takes a horrible and often permanent toll on growing children. If a young child is underfed during the first two years of his or her life, brain growth can be stunted, and mental retardation can result. In older children, food deprivation causes weakness, stunts growth, affects intelligence, and cripples the immune system. If hunger goes on and on, it becomes malnutrition, which is eventually fatal.

Because prolonged hunger causes drowsiness and social withdrawal, constantly hungry children have a hard time functioning in school. To put it simply, little learning can occur when a child is starving. **D**

Helping Those Left Behind

The high school student Daniel Cayce realized that this was true. Cayce lives in Arkansas, in one of the poorest counties in the country. Cayce started a program at his school called No Child Left Behind in Nutrition for which he obtained donations of food and backpacks from church and

Daniel Cayce working at the annual Thanksgiving food and blanket giveaway.

community groups and from the Arkansas State Food Bank. With the help of his Boy Scout troop, he sorts and bags the food, which is given to needy students at the end of the school day. Through his program, more than 250 students receive food for weeknight and weekend meals. These free meals supplement the lunches the children receive through the Federal School Lunch Program.

Daniel grew up in a family with a history of helping the needy. He has been working side-by-side with his grandmother, the founder of the Jo Ann Cayce Charities, since age three. It was obvious to Daniel that hunger was not something long ago and far away. Perhaps it is time for the rest of us to realize this same truth and to take action in our own communities and as a nation.

Read with a Purpose How does Daniel's work help his community?

C [Read and Discuss] What does this information about who is going hungry in America show you?

D [Informational Focus] **Author's Evidence** Is the evidence the author presents here appropriate?

Vocabulary **deprivation** (dehp ruh VAY shuhn) *n.*: hardship resulting from a lack of something.
prolonged (pruh LAWNGD) *adj.*: continuing for a long time.
malnutrition (mal noo TRIHSH uhn) *n.*: ill health caused by a lack of food or by a lack of healthy foods.

Applying Your Skills

SKILLS FOCUS **Informational Skills** Identify and trace the development of an author's argument in a text; identify and evaluate the use of accurate supporting citations and evidence in a text. **Vocabulary Skills** Demonstrate knowledge of literal meanings of words and their usage.

Hungry Here? For Millions of Americans, the Answer Is "Yes"

Practicing the Standards

Informational Text and Vocabulary

1. There is enough evidence in the article to show that the author believes —

A food banks serve all of the people who need their services

B only in foreign countries do people experience hunger on a regular basis

C charitable organizations cannot help elderly people

D the problem of hunger in the United States gets worse each year

2. Which of the following pieces of evidence would *not* be appropriate to use in an article about hunger?

A The variety of food available at a food pantry

B The number of U.S. children whose development has been stunted by malnutrition

C A list of all of the causes that Jo Ann Cayce Charities supports

D The average amount of money people who use food pantries spend on rent per month

3. According to the author, hunger affects growing children in all of the following ways *except* by —

A stunting brain growth

B causing death

C affecting intelligence

D crippling the immune system

4. The section of the article titled "Helping Those Left Behind" is an example of —

A an anecdote

B a quotation from an expert

C inaccurate evidence

D bias and stereotyping

5. The opposite of *prolonged* is —

A universal

B dynamic

C irritable

D momentary

6. Another word for *deprivation* is —

A liquidation

B neediness

C misstatement

D delusion

Writing Focus   **Constructed Response**

Referring to the notes you took while reading, list the evidence you noted as inappropriate, inaccurate, or inadequate. Next to each piece of evidence, explain why you think the evidence is problematic.

What Do
You Think Now

In what ways has this article made you think about the issue of hunger?

Writing Workshop

"How-To" Explanation

Write with a Purpose

Write an essay that explains how to do or make something. Your **purpose** is to present the instructions in a way that makes them clear and easy for your **audience** to follow.

Think as a Reader/Writer

Have you ever have gotten tips on how to play a video game from a magazine? Have you used directions to put together a bookcase? Start thinking about a task you know because now it's your turn to share your knowledge by writing a "how-to" explanation. Before you get started, read this excerpt from "How to Change a Flat Tire" in Collection 6:

> Before you can change a flat tire on your car, you first have to realize that the tire is flat. . . . When you suspect that you have a flat tire, follow these procedures.
>
> First, park the car as far off the road as possible. Put the car in park (if you have an automatic transmission) or in gear (if you have a standard transmission), turn off the engine, and put on the emergency brake. Turn on your car's flashing lights. Now, get out and look at your tires. If you have a flat, put out emergency triangles or, at night, flares. (It's a good idea to carry warning triangles and flares in your trunk at all times in case of emergency.)
>
> Remove the spare tire from the trunk. Also take out the jack, the lug wrench, and related tools.

← The writer states what the essay will explain.

← Transitional words such as *first* and *now* give the order for completing the steps.

← The writer is careful to list all of the materials that will be needed.

A Good "How-To" Explanation

- states the topic of the explanation at beginning
- begins and ends with a reason why readers would want to learn how to complete the process
- lists all needed materials
- states the steps of the process in chronological order, using clear time-order transitions
- includes specific details that help readers picture the steps
- uses precise language

See page 882 for complete rubric.

Think About the Professional Model

With a partner, discuss the following questions about the model:

1. How can you tell that the order of steps in changing a tire is very important?
2. Which descriptive details help you the most in visualizing the steps?
3. In some "how-to" explanations, the list of the materials that you will need appears at the beginning of the explanation. Why do you think this "how-to" presents the materials the way it does?

Reader/Writer Notebook

Use your **RWN** to complete the activities for this workshop.

Prewriting

Choose a Topic

Take a few minutes to brainstorm a list of things that you make or do well. *The topic you decide to write about should be something that you know how to do well enough to explain.*

Once you have a collection of ideas, think about each topic's process and whether you can break it down into steps. Drop any topics that require more than seven steps. Finally, select the one that will be the most fun for you to write about and for your audience to read.

Topic	Is it something I do or make?	Can I do it? How well?	Is it interesting or unusual?
Skateboarding	Do	Yes. I have trophies.	Yes. It's a lot of fun.
Making bread	Make	Kind of. I only made it twice.	Yes. Fresh bread is great.
Tying my shoes	Do	Yes. I've been doing it since I was four.	No. Most everyone over four does it.

A topic like skateboarding is too complex to explain in only seven steps. It can be narrowed, however, into more specific processes. If you find a topic you like and know well, but it would take too long to explain, find a smaller process within the topic that can be explained easily and completely.

Think About Purpose and Audience

Now that you've chosen a topic you're excited and confident about, remember your **audience** and **purpose.**

- First, ask yourself, "Who will be reading my instructions?" Your **audience** will probably be students your age. Think about why they would want to learn to do what you will be describing. Write a clear statement of this. Also think about ways to hold their interest.

- Next, think about your purpose. Your **purpose** is to equip your readers with the instructions necessary to complete the process you are describing. Make every step you present as clear and easy to follow as possible.

Idea Starters

- If you could do your favorite activity or hobby right now, what would it be?
- What special skill or talent do you have?
- What are some things you like to make, such as food, handicrafts, or technology presentations?
- What school or hobby projects have you especially enjoyed?

⬤ Writing Tip

Be sure that your **voice,** or the sound of your writing, is clear and straightforward. Use vocabulary that your audience will understand, and avoid humor that may not come across in writing.

Your Turn _____

Get Started Now that you've decided on a specific **topic** that can be explained clearly in a few **steps,** brainstorm a list of the steps in your **RWN**. As you do so, keep your **audience** in mind. Take out any steps that seem unnecessary for the audience, or add steps that they may need.

Learn It Online

An Interactive Graphic Organizer can help you organize the sequence of steps in your essay. Try one at:

go.hrw.com L7-875 **Go**

A "How-To" Explanation

Writing Tip

Have a classmate or parent look over your timeline of steps before you start to write. Tell that person to imagine doing the activity described, and then ask if any of the steps were unclear, incomplete, or missing.

Map Out the Steps

Putting the steps of the process in **chronological** (or time) **order** will help the reader make sense of your explanation.

Creating a timeline is a very useful way to organize your thinking about the order of the steps. Imagine yourself completing the process. As you think about each step, write it on a timeline like the one below. Then, look over your steps, and add anything you may have left out.

1st step   2nd step   3rd step   4th step   5th step

Grab Your Audience's Attention

Remember that your introduction should make readers want to know more about the process you are describing. One approach is to engage readers with a question and then show in your introduction how you can answer it for your readers. For example: "Would you like to know how to get dressed for school in five minutes or less? It's not only possible, it's also a great way to start your day. Read on to learn for yourself."

List the Required Materials

Once you have the steps in the process clearly identified, make a list of everything the reader needs to complete each step. This will become your materials list, which you might choose to put at the beginning of your explanation. You might also choose to list the materials at the points in which they are used, as the writer of "How to Change a Flat Tire" decided to do.

Focus on Important Details

Your descriptions of the steps and materials must include **details** to make them easy for readers to understand. For example, when you review the steps, can you see that it would be helpful to advise readers to complete them in a certain environment? (Messy jobs should be done outside or on surfaces covered with newspaper, for example.) Do you need to indicate how long the steps will take or how much time will be required between them? Similarly, when you suggest materials, choose descriptions that are as specific as possible. (Don't just say *nails* when you can say *quarter-inch nails,* for example.)

Your Turn

Focus on Details Think about helpful, detailed information that should be included in your steps and in your materials list. Make notes in your **RWN** about your timeline of steps and details so you will be sure to include them in your draft.

Drafting

Organize Your Ideas

Draft your explanation, using a framework like the one to the right to organize your "how-to" explanation.

Keep the Steps in Order

Be sure that you present the steps in the **chronological order** you have carefully charted out. It is a good idea to present one step and the details that explain it in each paragraph. Be careful, though, to avoid including too many details. You might confuse your readers with too much information. Focus on the steps and details that will help them complete the activity easily.

Help readers see how one step flows logically to the next by using clear transitions. **Transitions** are words and phrases that help link ideas together. See the "Grammar Link" below for specific words that are useful in "how-to" explanations.

Framework for a "How-To" Explanation
Introduction
• Interesting opener
• Reason for learning
• Statement of topic
Body
• List of materials
• Step 1 (with relevant details)
• Step 2 (with relevant details) and so on . . .
Conclusion
• Restatement of reason for learning
• Advice for doing process

● Writing Tip

Be **consistent** when discussing steps or materials. Always use the same word to refer to the same item.

● Writing Tip

When you explain a process, you must be precise. **Precise verbs, nouns, adverbs,** and **adjectives** paint a clear picture in the reader's mind. They help answer questions such as *Which one? What kind? How?* and *How many?* As you write, ask yourself these questions, and add more precise words as needed.

Grammar Link Using Transitions

Transitions are words and phrases that show how ideas are related to one another. There are three types of transitions: words showing spatial organization, words showing chronological order, and words showing order of importance. Two types of transitions are particularly useful in "how-to" explanations: chronological and spatial.

Chronological transitions **answer** the question *In what order?*	Spatial transitions **answer** the question *Where?*
Examples: *after five minutes, as, before, during, first, finally, immediately, next, second, then, while*	**Examples:** *above, across, behind, beside, in front of, near, next, on the right, over, there, under*

Your Turn _____

Write Your Draft Following your plan, write a draft of your explanation. Be sure to think about

• carefully presenting the proper **sequence** of steps
• using **precise details** to describe what must be done
• clarifying ideas by using **transitions**

Peer Review

Working with a peer, review your drafts, and take notes about each other's questions. Answering each question in this chart can help you locate where and how your drafts could be improved.

Evaluating and Revising

Read the questions in the left-hand column of the chart; then use the tips in the middle column to help you make revisions to your essay. The right-hand column suggests techniques you can use to revise your draft.

A How-to Explanation: Guidelines for Content and Organization

Evaluation Questions	Tips	Revision Techniques
1. Does the introduction grab the reader's attention and state why someone would want to learn the process? Does it clearly state the topic of the explanation?	**Put an asterisk** next to the statement of the reason. **Put brackets** around the clear statement of the topic.	If needed, **add** a more powerful statement of the reason for learning the process. **Add** a statement that indicates the topic of the essay.
2. Does the body list all the materials needed?	**Circle** all the materials needed to complete the process.	**Add** any materials that have been left out.
3. Are steps of the process in chronological order? Is each step in a separate paragraph?	**Write a number** next to each step in the margin.	**Rearrange** the steps so they are in the correct order and so each step is in its own paragraph.
4. Do clear transitions link ideas?	**Highlight** all the transitions.	**Add** more transitions as needed.
5. Is each step described in detail, using precise language?	**Underline** precise verbs, nouns, adverbs, and adjectives.	If necessary, **elaborate** by adding more details and precise words.
6. Does the conclusion summarize the steps and restate the reason for completing the process?	**Draw a wavy line** under the summary. **Put a star** beside the sentence that restates the reason for learning the process.	If needed, **add** a summary of the steps. **Add** a sentence that restates the reason for learning the process.

Read this student's draft and the comments about it as a model for revising your own how-to explanation.

Re-gripping a Skateboard

by George Oswald, Colonel Mitchell Paige Middle School

Anyone who skateboards a lot will eventually need to re-grip a skateboard. This simple yet important task will help prevent riders from accidentally slipping off the skateboard. There are six steps to completing this task.

→ The introduction clearly states why someone would need this information.

Before starting, you will need to get new grip tape, a piece of sandpaper, a razor blade, and a screwdriver. The first step is to take off the old grip tape. Gently dig the razor blade under the edge of the grip tape. Peel the tape back until you can pull it off with your bare hands. Wear protective leather gloves when using the blade. Also, be careful not to cut the wood while digging the razor blade under the grip tape.

→ Materials are listed before the steps are presented.

Next, put the new grip tape on the board. As you put the tape on, start on one side of the board, and work your way to the other side. Do this slowly and carefully, and make sure there are no air bubbles.

→ **Details** help readers know *how* to complete the step.

MINI-LESSON ▶ How to Match Materials to Steps

George lists the materials needed at the beginning of the second paragraph. He does not include leather gloves there, yet he states later that you must wear them when using the razor blade. Readers should expect to find everything they will need listed in one place. In this case, readers might begin digging the razor blade under the tape with their bare hands. Also, because buffing with sandpaper will be involved, readers should perform this activity outside or in a garage.

George's Revision of Paragraph Two

Find a well-lighted place to work outside or in a garage. Before starting, you will need to get new grip tape, a piece of sandpaper, a razor blade, *a* screwdriver, *and a pair of protective leather gloves. Whenever you use the blade, be sure to wear the gloves.* The first step is to take off the old grip tape. Gently dig the razor blade under the edge of the grip tape. *Be careful not to cut the wood while doing this. Then peel the tape back until you can pull it off with your bare hands.*

Your Turn

List Materials Where They Are Needed Read your draft, and then ask yourself:
- Where are needed materials listed?
- Are any materials omitted?
- What safety reminders should I include?

Student Draft *continues*

Steps are presented in clear chronological order, and transitions are used to link ideas. →

Once the new tape is on, sand the edges of the board. Slowly work your way around the entire board. When you're finished, there should be a clean, crisp white crease around the whole board.

Now trim the excess grip tape. Grasp the razor blade firmly and start cutting along the white crease. The cut will come out much cleaner if you cut long sections in one smooth motion rather than stopping after each little cut.

Specific details help readers picture each step. →

To give your board a much cleaner look, re-sand the edges of the grip tape. This step is optional, but I highly recommend it.

Finally, use the screwdriver to poke holes through the tape where needed. The easiest way to find the holes in your deck is to flip the board over and poke through the holes from the back side.

The conclusion restates the reason for completing the process →

With only some new grip tape and simple tools you can find around the house, you can put a new grip on your board for a safer ride.

MINI-LESSON ▶ **How to Use Precise Words**

George uses some great precise words in these paragraphs: *clean, crisp white crease* and *Grasp the razor blade firmly.* However, the final step probably leaves most readers with questions. How big should the holes be? How can you tell where holes are needed? When George revised his explanation, he added precise words to help answer these questions.

George's Revision of Paragraph Seven

Finally, use the screwdriver to poke holes through the tape where *your trucks belong. The holes are already in your deck; you just need to find them.* The easiest way to find the holes in your deck is to flip the board over and poke through the holes from the back side. *I like to neaten up the holes by cutting out the edges with the razor blade, but it's up to you whether you do this or not. I do think it helps the screws fit more snugly in the holes.*

With only some new grip tape and simple tools you can find around the house, you can put a new grip on your board for a safer ride.

Your Turn _____

Use More Precise Words Read through your "how-to" explanation with a questioning mind. If you did not already know how to complete the process you are describing, what questions would you have about the instructions or materials? Add precise words that answer those questions for readers.

Proofreading and Publishing

Proofreading

A "how-to" explanation must be as clear as possible. One thing that can cause confusion for your audience is the existence of errors. Polish your explanation by carefully correcting any misspellings, punctuation errors, and problems in sentence structure.

> **Grammar Link   Revise Stringy and Wordy Sentences**
>
> You can recognize **stringy sentences** by their length: They go on and on. They may be two long independent clauses joined together with *and* or *but*, or they may be a result of too many shorter independent clauses strung together. George has a stringy sentence in his last revision that he decides to break into two sentences.
>
> I like to neaten up the holes by cutting out the edges with the razor
>
> blade, but it's up to you whether you do this or not.
>
> **Wordy sentences,** which include too many words, can be revised in three ways: replace a group of words with one word, replace a clause with a short phrase, or take out a whole group of words. George chose the third way to revise a wordy sentence. The words he takes out already appear in the sentence before the wordy sentence.
>
> The holes are already in your deck; you just need to find them. The
>
> do this.
> easiest way to ~~find the holes in your deck~~ is to flip the board over and
>
> poke through the holes from the back side.

Publishing

Here are some ways to share your explanation with a wider audience:

- Make copies of your explanation for all your classmates.
- Post your explanation on a Web site that people interested in the process would visit.

Reflect on the Process

In your **RWN,** write a short response to each of the following questions:

1. Which step in the process was hardest for you to explain? What helped you solve this problem?
2. While revising, how did you come up with more precise words to use in describing the materials or the process?

Proofreading Tip

Other people can read your work with fresh eyes. Ask several peers to read your explanation. Be specific about one area of focus for each reader. For example, one person could look for stringy, or wordy, sentences, while another checks your spelling.

Your Turn

Proofread and Publish Proofread your "how-to" explanation to see if you have used any stringy or wordy sentences. Apply any of the methods suggested to revise these sentences. Then, carefully proofread your explanation for any errors, make the corrections, and publish your polished work for your intended audience.

Scoring Rubric

Use one of the rubrics below to evaluate your "how-to" explanation or your response to the prompt on the next page. Your teacher will say which to use.

6-Point Scale

Score 6 *Demonstrates advanced success*
- focuses consistently on a process appropriate to the prompt
- shows effective, step-by-step organization throughout, with smooth transitions
- offers a thoughtful, creative explanation of the process
- explains each step of the assigned process thoroughly, using examples and specific, detailed instructions
- exhibits mature control of written language

Score 5 *Demonstrates proficient success*
- focuses on a process appropriate to the prompt
- shows effective, step-by-step organization, with transitions
- offers a thoughtful explanation of the process
- explains the steps of the process competently, using examples and specific instructions
- exhibits sufficient control of written language

Score 4 *Demonstrates competent success*
- focuses on an appropriate process, with minor distractions
- shows effective, step-by-step organization, with minor lapses
- offers a mostly thoughtful explanation of the process
- explains the process adequately, with a mixture of general and specific instructions
- exhibits general control of written language

Score 3 *Demonstrates limited success*
- includes some loosely related material that distracts from the writer's how-to focus
- shows some organization, with noticeable gaps in the step-by-step presentation of the process
- offers a routine, predictable explanation of the process
- explains the process with uneven elaboration
- exhibits limited control of written language

Score 2 *Demonstrates basic success*
- includes loosely related material that seriously distracts from the writer's how-to focus
- shows minimal organization, with major gaps in the step-by-step presentation of the process
- offers explanation that merely skims the surface
- explains the process with inadequate elaboration
- exhibits significant problems with control of written language

Score 1 *Demonstrates emerging effort*
- shows little awareness of the topic and purpose for writing
- lacks organization
- offers unclear and confusing explanation
- develops the explanation in only a minimal way, if at all
- exhibits major problems with control of written language

4-Point Scale

Score 4 *Demonstrates advanced success*
- focuses consistently on a process appropriate to the prompt
- shows effective, step-by-step organization throughout, with smooth transitions
- offers a thoughtful, creative explanation of the process
- explains each step of the assigned process thoroughly, using examples and specific, detailed instructions
- exhibits mature control of written language

Score 3 *Demonstrates competent success*
- focuses on an appropriate process, with minor distractions
- shows effective, step-by-step organization, with minor lapses
- offers a mostly thoughtful explanation of the process
- explains the process adequately, with a mixture of general and specific instructions
- exhibits general control of written language

Score 2 *Demonstrates limited success*
- includes some loosely related material that distracts from the writer's how-to focus
- shows some organization, with noticeable gaps in the step-by-step presentation of the process
- offers a routine, predictable explanation of the process
- explains the process with uneven elaboration
- exhibits limited control of written language

Score 1 *Demonstrates emerging effort*
- shows little awareness of the topic and purpose for writing
- lacks organization
- offers unclear and confusing explanation
- develops the explanation in only a minimal way, if at all
- exhibits major problems with control of written language

"How-To" Explanation

When responding to an on-demand prompt requiring a "how-to" expla-nation, use the models you have read, what you've learned from writing your "how-to" explanation, the rubric on page 882, and the steps below.

Writing Prompt

Write an essay that explains a multistep process or activity you'd like to explain to your classmates. In your essay clearly state why some-one would want to know how to complete the process or activity, and present the steps in chron-ological order. Be sure to list any needed materials and to include any safety materials.

Study the Prompt

Begin by reading the prompt carefully. Note what is required in your explanation: an explanation of how to do or make something, broken into steps that are written in chronological order.

Tip: Spend about five minutes studying the prompt.

Plan Your Response

Think of something you know how to do well that you can describe in a multistep process. Once you understand your task and have settled on your process or activity,

- write down your topic and the reason why readers would be interested to learn your process
- list the materials needed to complete the process
- jot down the steps required, in the order in which they should be completed

Tip: Spend about fifteen minutes planning your response.

Respond to the Prompt

Using the notes you've just made, draft your essay. Follow these guidelines:

- In the introduction, include an attention-get-ting opener, including why readers would want to learn how to complete this process, and a clear statement of your topic.
- In the body, provide a complete materials list, and present the steps in chronological order. Present each step in a separate paragraph.
- In the conclusion, summarize the steps and reason for completing the process.

Use words that are best for your audience—not too informal. Write as neatly as you can. If your essay can't be read easily, it won't be scored.

Tip: Spend about twenty minutes writing your draft.

Improve Your Response

Revising Review your explanation. Did you explain why readers would want to do or make what you are describing? Did you provide clearly worded steps in the proper order? Did you list needed materials?

Proofreading Proofread your explanation to cor-rect errors in grammar, spelling, punctuation, and capitalization. Make sure all your edits are neat, and erase any stray marks.

Checking Your Final Copy Before you turn in your explanation, read it one more time to catch any errors you may have missed. You'll be glad that you took the extra time for one final review.

Tip: Save ten minutes to improve your paper.

Following Oral Instructions and Directions

Listen with a Purpose

Work with a small group of students to practice giving and following simple instructions and geographic directions.

Think as a Reader/Writer In your "how-to" explanation, you worked hard to write clear instructions for completing a process. Now it's time to place yourself on the receiving end of a "how-to" explanation—to practice your listening skills when receiving oral instructions.

Like the reading and writing processes, the listening process requires thought and skill before, during, and after you receive the message. Practicing these skills will help you master purposeful listening.

Listening

Before You Listen

Get focused before you begin to listen.

- **Know why you are listening.** The way you take in information depends on your reason for listening. For example, if you are listening to the radio for enjoyment, you may not listen carefully. However, if you want to find out about concert tickets, you will probably listen much more carefully, and may even write down information you need to remember.
- **Limit distractions.** Before you listen, remind yourself that you are going to focus on the speaker for the next few minutes. Put aside distracting thoughts, plans, or worries as you listen.

While You Are Listening

Follow these steps while you are listening.

- **Listen for the steps of the process.** Listen for transitions that introduce new steps and tell you the order of steps. Examples include words such as *first*, *next*, *then*, and *last*.
- **Identify the number of steps in the process.** If the process includes many steps, take notes to help you remember them.
- **Picture each step.** Imagine yourself completing each step in order.

Responding

Make sure you have all the instructions and understand them. Now is the time to ask questions if you are unclear about any step. You may want to **restate** the steps to the speaker to make sure you understand them.

Practice Receiving Oral Instructions

Be sure that each member of your group has several sheets of paper and a pen or pencil. Begin by having each group member draw a simple picture. These pictures should be hidden from other group members.

Next, one by one, group members should describe the pictures they have drawn. Remember what you learned about good "how-to" instructions:

- The directions are given in chronological order, using clear transitions.
- The directions include specific details that help readers picture the steps.
- The directions use precise and consistent language.

As each group member describes his or her picture, the rest of the group should listen, take notes, ask questions, and then draw the picture. Share the finished pictures, and discuss the similarities and differences between them.

After all members of the group have given their oral instructions, discuss what you have learned about giving and listening to instructions.

Practice the Skill for Geographic Directions

For this activity, your group will need a map of your town or city. Have one student select a location, such as a public library or park, without naming the place. Then, he or she should give oral directions on how to get from your school to that place. The speaker should remember the importance of using spatial and chronological transitions. **Spatial transitions** are directional words, such as *to the right,* whereas **chronological transitions** are time order words, such as *next.*

While listening, the other students should take notes, ask questions, and restate the directions. Then, the listeners should trace the directions along the map exactly as the directions were given and identify the final location.

If the place identified by the group is incorrect, discuss where the breakdown in communication occurred. Each group member can select a different place and repeat the procedure, as time allows.

A Good Listener

- looks directly at the speaker and stays focused on what he or she is saying
- takes notes about the key ideas
- asks questions after receiving the instructions to clarify anything that is unclear
- uses restatement to check understanding

⬤ Listening Tip

Remember that communication involves give and take, both speaking and listening. As a listener, you should communicate respect and attention through your body language. Look directly at the speaker and sit up straight. Save your comments and questions until the end.

Literary Skills Review

Drama   **Directions:** Read the following text, and respond to the questions below.

from Brian's Song by **William Blinn**

Gale Sayers

Brian Piccolo

Brian's Song is a made-for-TV movie about the friendship between the NFL Chicago Bears players Gale Sayers, a gifted runner, and Brian Piccolo, a fellow halfback. Despite obstacles, the men become friends, especially when Sayers injures his leg and Piccolo helps him through his recovery. Their careers continue until Piccolo is diagnosed with lung cancer. In the scene just before this one, Piccolo's wife tells Sayers that the cancer has returned and that Piccolo must have another operation immediately. She asks that Sayers be at the hospital in the morning when the doctor breaks the bad news to her husband.

Direct cut to:
Interior—Brian's room—Day—
On football game

This is a "board game" with charts and dice and miniature scoreboard. As we pull back, we find BRIAN *and* GALE *seated on opposite sides of the small table near the window. They both roll their dice.*

Gale. What'd you try?
Brian. End run.
Gale. Oh, Lordy—I was in a blitz.

BRIAN *starts to consult the complicated chart that will give him the results of the play.*

Gale *(indicating game chart).* Well—did you gain or what?

The door is opened by MR. EBERLE, *a nervous, uncertain sort, more at home with facts and figures than flesh and blood. A name tag hangs from the lapel of his lab coat.* BRIAN *looks up with a smile.*

Brian. Hi. Can I help you?
Eberle. Well, I'm sorry if I'm disturbing anything . . .
Brian. Don't worry—I can beat him later. What can I do for you?
Eberle *(rummaging through papers).* I

know this is a bother at a time like this, Mr. Piccolo, but hospitals have their rules and regulations, you see, and I'll need your signature on this surgical consent for the operation.

He hands BRIAN *the piece of paper, but* BRIAN *is scarcely aware of it. He looks at* EBERLE *uncomprehendingly, stunned.* GALE *is searching for a way to ease this, but before he can locate his voice,* EBERLE *notes the bewilderment on* BRIAN's *face.*

Eberle. The doctor *has* been here, hasn't he? He's talked with you, I mean?
Brian. No . . .
Eberle *(looking to watch).* Oh—well, I suppose I might be running a little ahead of my schedule today. Perhaps I better come back after the doctor has . . .
Brian. What would the doctor have to say to me? Man, I've *had* my operation, *right*?

Silence, and that's the worst answer there can be. EBERLE *can't meet* BRIAN's *look. After a beat,* BRIAN *looks over slowly to* GALE.

Brian. Talk to me, Magic. . . .

GALE *discovers his voice after a second, but it emerges with anguish.*

Gale. The tests show—there's more of the tumor than they thought, Pic. They have to operate again. . . .

Once more, EBERLE, *seeking nothing more than escape, steps forward, holding out the surgical consent and a fountain pen.*

Eberle. So, if you'll just sign the consent, Mr. . . .

Brian *(turning away)*. No!

Eberle. But putting this off won't be . . .

Brian. Are you deaf? I said *no!*

Eberle. Mr. Sayers—can't you talk to your friend?

BRIAN *has moved to the window, shoulders hunched as if gathering himself for a blow of enormous force.* GALE *looks at him, then turns to* EBERLE.

Gale. No, Mr. Eberle, I think I'd rather talk to *you.*

Eberle. But . . .

Gale. Brian is a professional athlete, Mr. Eberle. And a professional gets into a habit after a while. He gets himself ready for a game mentally as well as physically. Because he knows those two things are all tied up together. And there's a clock going inside him, so that when the game starts,

he's one hundred percent mentally and physically. And what Pic is saying to you now is that you're scheduling this game before he can get ready. Couldn't it wait until over the weekend?

Eberle. Well, yes, it *could,* but . . .

Gale. Then *let* it.

Eberle *(a beat, looks to* BRIAN*)*. First thing Monday morning, Mr. Piccolo.

Brian. Okay.

Eberle. I'll see you then.

GALE *looks back to* BRIAN, *who continues to gaze out the window. A beat, as* BRIAN *strains to salvage some control.*

Brian. Thanks, Gale . . .

Gale. No sweat.

Brian. Thought you were the guy who didn't talk very well.

Gale. Well—I roomed with an Italian; you know how they are.

BRIAN *turns away from the window. He moves back to the game board, idly scanning the setup. A beat, then a small smile appears on his face.*

Brian. Guess what? I scored a touchdown.

We hold on BRIAN.

1. Each of the following descriptions is implied in the opening directions *except* that —
  A the scene will take place inside a room
  B the out of doors should look dark
  C the shot shows a football board game
  D the scene has changed suddenly from another

2. From which of the following lines can you *best* infer Piccolo's sense of humor?
  A "Don't worry—I can beat him later."
  B "Are you deaf? I said *no!*"
  C "Talk to me, Magic."
  D "Man, I've *had* my operation, *right*?"

3. Which of the following is an example of an **external conflict**?
  A Sayer's sorrow for his friend's suffering
  B Piccolo's recurrent lung cancer
  C Eberle's discomfort versus sense of duty
  D Piccolo's desire to be well

4. Which of the following directions is specifically for the camera?
  A *Gale discovers his voice.*
  B *That's the worst answer.*
  C *They both roll their dice.*
  D *We hold on Brian.*

5. The *best* description of Eberle's breaking the bad news instead of the doctor's breaking it is —
  A external conflict
  B directions
  C plot complication
  D climax

6. Beginning at the bottom of column 1 on page 888, Sayers talks to Mr. Eberle. His "talk" is an example of a(n) —
  A dialogue
  B internal conflict
  C monologue
  D characterization

Constructed Response

7. Write a paragraph in which you discuss Brian Piccolo's character. Do you learn about him through dialogue, stage directions, or a combination of both? Explain.

Informational Skills Review

Evaluating Evidence   **Directions:** Read the following selection.
Then, read and respond to the questions that follow.

Feeling Needy by

Is this one big competitive selfish fest
where we spend money on foolish
   things?
Expensive clothes and diamond rings.
Where cosmetic surgery is what
   everyone "needs?"
No more love, just greed.
It's taken over us indeed—at top speed.

—from "A Dose of Reality," by high school
student Caitlin Heitman, used by permission of www.TeachingTolerance.org.

MP3 players. Name-brand jeans. Fancy sneakers. The latest status items keep changing, but not the feeling of needing to own them. In the book *Branded: The Buying and Selling of Teenagers,* the author Alissa Quart studies consumerism among the millennial generation—people born between 1980 and 2000. Among extreme examples, she reports on teen coming-of-age celebrations costing $30,000 and parties at which shopping bags from Tiffany and Gucci serve as centerpieces. Although her research centers on students from upper-middle-class families, it's clear the want or need for brand names has a strong hold on students from all walks of life.

American teens have major buying power, either when using their own money or when using their parents' money. People aged 12 to 19 spent $179 billion in 2006, says Teenage Research Unlimited.

Students say they feel pressure from peers to own certain clothes and status items. Corporations that stand to profit from teen anxiety exert pressure as well. Credit-card companies target high schoolers. Marketing professionals consult teens online for their opinions in order to dig for information on the teens' buying habits. Thanks to marketers, advertisers know exactly who will be looking at their ads.

There are teens who are starting to reject the overpriced life around them. Some eighth-graders in Florida got fed up with the "brand-mania" at their middle school. They felt they didn't have a choice in what to wear or buy anymore. All they knew was that it had to be expensive. They began wearing plain white T-shirts and no-name blue jeans and sneakers to school and eventually started a trend.

This awareness of "choice" is the first step needed to break the hold that excessive consumerism has over U.S. teenagers.

1. Which of the following pieces of **evidence** is an example?

   A "Advertisers know exactly who will be looking at their ads."

   B "She reports on teen coming-of-age celebrations costing $30,000."

   C "The Author Alissa Quart studies consumerism among the millennial generation."

   D "Latest status items keep changing, but not the feeling of needing to own them."

2. The section of the article detailing the amount of money spent by teens is an example of —

   A an anecdote

   B statistics

   C inaccurate evidence

   D stereotyping

3. Which of the following examples of evidence would be **inappropriate** in an article about the ill effects of overspending by teens?

   A A list of brand names of cell phones most popular with teens

   B Statistics detailing the amount of money owed by the average high schooler

   C An example of negative pressure a teen endured at a suburban middle school

   D A quotation from an expert on the effects of marketing tactics that target teens

4. The author supports the argument that American teens have spending power by —

   A supplying a research report on spending

   B describing marketing techniques

   C listing teens' favorite brand-name items

   D starting with a poem ridiculing greed

5. The author concludes that brand-name articles —

   A help out-of-place teens fit in

   B help the clothing market grow

   C encourage kids to be creative

   D reduce teens' ability to choose freely

Constructed Response

6. What is the writer's **perspective,** or point of view, on this subject? Use evidence from the text to support your response.

Vocabulary Skills Review

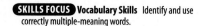

Multiple-Meaning Words
Directions: Read each sentence. Then, choose the answer in which the italicized word is used in the same way.

1. "And it's cheaper than painting in a new *sign*, isn't it?"
   - **A** I learned to *sign* in order to communicate with people who are hearing impaired.
   - **B** The store had a big *sign* in the window telling shoppers about the sale.
   - **C** Because she forgot to *sign* the check, it was returned to her in the mail.
   - **D** Grandpa showed no *sign* of illness before breaking out in a rash.

2. "An icicle must have gotten into the clock's *works*!"
   - **A** The watchmaker *works* to repair hundreds of broken timepieces each month.
   - **B** The fan *works* better since we took it apart and cleaned it.
   - **C** Some rich people spend their time and money doing good *works* in the world.
   - **D** I was very interested when the plumber pulled out the dishwasher and let me see its *works*.

3. "Martha, will you play the *notes*, on the lute, for Tiny Tim's song?"
   - **A** Every now and then, the young musicians hit bad *notes* on their instruments.
   - **B** I have found that taking *notes* really helps me understand new lessons.
   - **C** My friend often *notes* beautiful things in nature that I don't notice.
   - **D** On the day after Christmas, we always write thank-you *notes* for our presents.

4. "Uncle may *rail* at Christmas till he dies."
   - **A** Some people prefer to travel by *rail* because they get to see so many sights.
   - **B** I learned how to split a *rail* as we built the fence around my uncle's farm.
   - **C** I get very uncomfortable when I see a person *rail* at a child for something he or she did wrong.
   - **D** Some of the tallest high school basketball players are as thin as a *rail*.

5. "But he was very *light* to carry and his father loved him so, that it was not trouble—no trouble."
   - **A** The small rock was *light* enough that I could pick it up and carry it.
   - **B** We used candles to *light* the room during the storm.
   - **C** The young man said that his first love was the *light* of his life.
   - **D** On school days I have time to eat only a *light* breakfast before catching the bus.

Academic Vocabulary

Directions: Use context clues to choose the answer that is closest in meaning to the italicized Academic Vocabulary word.

6. Readers would never guess that Scrooge could change, based on his mean-spirited behavior in *previous* scenes.
   - **A** earlier
   - **B** mysterious
   - **C** enchanting
   - **D** important

Writing Skills Review

"How-To" Explanation

Directions: Read the following paragraphs from a "how-to" explanation. Then, answer each question that follows.

As an expert in managing humans, I want to share some of my techniques. You pups will be on your own before you have time to scratch an itch.

First, master complete control over your eyes. Suppose it's a pretty day. You want to go for a walk. Lie about five feet from the human with your paws extended. Rest your chin on your paws. Look up with your eyes so that just a sliver of white shows. Sigh loudly.

---

1. The introduction grabs the reader's attention. What do you learn from this paragraph?

   A The writer is an expert dog handler.

   B The essay is written from the point of view of a puppy.

   C The purpose of the essay is to get people to adopt dogs.

   D The purpose of the essay is to teach puppies tricks that work well on humans.

2. Which question is *not* answered by precise words in the second paragraph?

   A How far from the human should you lie?

   B What type of sound should you make?

   C How long will it take to get the human's attention?

   D How much of the white of the eye should show?

3. Which **transition** might begin the next paragraph?

   A Second,

   B On the other side,

   C Finally,

   D Up front,

4. How many small steps to getting your owner to take you for a walk are included in the second paragraph?

   A two

   B three

   C four

   D five

Read On

Fiction

Brian's Song

The 1971 television movie *Brian's Song* is considered by many to be the best TV movie ever made. The movie tells the story of the real-life relationship between Chicago Bears teammates Brian Piccolo and Gale Sayers. Despite the fact that Sayers is black and Piccolo is white, they become roommates on the road and eventually close friends, especially when Sayers is injured and Piccolo helps him recover. The screenplay by William Blinn conveys the moving story so well that you'll feel as if you've seen the movie even if you haven't.

Happy Endings

When sixteen-year-old Mel lands a role in a summer production of Chekhov's play *Three Sisters*, she is immediately caught up in the exciting world of the theater. As Mel experiences friendships and drama both on- and off-stage, you will experience all of the elements of a realistic play production: auditions, rehearsals, costumes and sets, and the fears and thrills of opening night. Adèle Geras is a celebrated author of many short stories and novels.

Tuck Everlasting

Have you ever wished you could live forever? In Natalie Babbitt's *Tuck Everlasting*, members of the Tuck family are granted eternal life when they drink from a hidden stream. Then they learn that the dream of living forever can also be a nightmare. This novel has been made into a major motion picture and is published in Spanish as *Tuck para siempre*.

Visit to a Small Planet

In *The Monsters Are Due on Maple Street,* the residents don't meet the invading aliens. The characters in *Visit to a Small Planet* do, however, when a single alien appears, dressed as an officer ready for the American Civil War. His timing is a bit off—he's landed in 1957 in the backyard of a suburban family. You'll discover that he can not only travel the universe but also read minds—and he can start a war (seeing that he missed the "great fun" of the Civil War). Be sure to finish reading Gore Vidal's script—it has a great twist at the end.

Nonfiction

Jim Thorpe: Original All-American

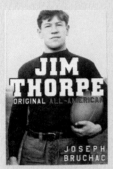

Writing from the point of view of his subject, Joseph Bruchac tells the life story of Jim Thorpe, Olympic gold medalist, football star, and modern American Indian hero. In the 1912 Olympics he set long-standing world records in both the pentathlon and the decathlon. Carefully researched, this biography is not a typical sports-hero tale—it delves into such issues as racism, the effect of money on sports, and the thin line between amateur and professional playing.

Inventing the Television

Despite the amount of time the average American spends watching television, surprisingly few people know how, when, and by whom the TV was invented. The author Joanne Richter explores the history and early mechanics of televisions, as well as the lives of the hard-working inventors who took part in creating the first televisions. The concluding chapters explore future uses of the television in business, science, and the arts.

Attack of the Killer Video Book: Tips and Tricks for Young Directors

This how-to instructional book is filled with humor and colorful illustrations, as well as information on video-making fundamentals, such as scripting, storyboarding, shot composition, lighting, editing, ... basically everything you need to know to get started on a well-made video production. Mark Shulman and Hazlitt Krog have been making movies together for years and have written an easy-to-understand primer that combines learning and fun.

Made in China: Ideas and Inventions from Ancient China

In *Made in China: Ideas and Inventions from Ancient China,* Suzanne Williams describes many discoveries and improvements contributed to science and society by the ancient Chinese. From the study of astronomy, to the usage of bronze and other metals, to the standardization of writing, measurements, and roads, Williams places the Chinese people of thought and invention in context with the world around them.

Learn It Online

Explore *NovelWise* for tips on reading and studying novels at:

go.hrw.com | L7-895 | Go

Myths, Folk Tales, and Legends

Writers on Writing

Jane Yolen on Myths, Folk Tales, and Legends Jane Yolen began writing poems, song lyrics, and newspaper articles when she was young. Today, she has written more than two hundred books for children and young adults, including fantasy, science fiction, and literary folk tales.

" When I was young, I loved folk tales. I read them the way I eat chocolate now, without thinking much about what they were doing to me.

Teachers like to tell us that fairy tales and folklore are ageless and universal. But I know now that we need to look beneath the surface of such stories, not just eat them like chocolate. What we find is the moral compass of a certain era, a certain country, a certain type of storyteller. Sometimes those stories still work in our time and place and space. And sometimes—we need to question their authority!

Recently I re-read *Rumplestiltskin* with a kind of growing horror. Of course I was reading it as a twenty-first-century American woman adult. And I read it quite differently than I had so many years ago as a bright-eyed kid growing up in New York City after World War II. Had they changed? Or, more important, had I?

I suddenly saw that Rumplestiltskin is actually the only character in the story who does what he promises. Think of it: The miller tells a whopping big lie. His daughter says the lie is true. The king, eager for gold, accepts the lie, even threatening the life of the girl if she cannot produce the spun gold.

And I thought: What if this story is about something other than what it pretends to be? I know it is originally a German story, about a little man who lives outside of the kingdom's inner circle. He has an odd name. He worships strange gods. He spins straw into gold. Now think of this: In Germany at the time the tale was first current, Jewish people were not allowed to live within the city walls, but instead lived in ghettoed towns. They had names different from their German countrymen. The only job they were allowed was moneylender. We can shake our heads about this stuff now, three centuries later. But the story of Rumplestiltskin carries some very odd flesh on its bones.

Remember that these stories were originally more than just entertainments. They were also stories binding a community together. Insiders—us—good. Outsiders—them—bad. So enjoy these tales, but always ask yourself what communities told them, and whom the are tales serving—the insider, or the outsider?

Once Upon by Jane Yolen

Once Upon A Time
there was a Wolf,
but not a Wolf,
an Other,
whose mother
and father were others,
who looked not like us,
Republican or Dem
in other words—
Them.
They were forest
dwellers,
child sellers,
meat eaters,
wife beaters,
idol makers
oath breakers—
in other words, Wolf.
So Happy Ever After
means
we kill the Wolf,
spill his blood,
knock him out,
bury him in mud,
make him dance
in red hot shoes.
For us to win
The Wolf must lose.

Think as a Writer

In this essay, Jane Yolen suggests to us that the old stories we read as children might really be "about something other than" what they pretend to be. What are your favorite myths, legends, or folk tales? Can you think of any other meanings, or interpretations, of these stories than the ones you have always understood?

Greek Myths and World Folk Tales

INFORMATIONAL TEXT FOCUS
Author's Perspective

"Lonely as they were, by themselves, early people looked inside themselves and expressed a longing to discover; to explain who they were, why they were, and from what and where they came."

—**Virginia Hamilton**

What Do
You
Think

What truths about life do myths and folk tales reveal?

Athens, Greece, seen from atop the Acropolis, through the columns of the Parthenon, temple of the goddess Athena.

Literary Focus

by **Linda Rief**

What Are the Characteristics of Myths?

Who was the greatest writer of Greek myths? You'd probably answer Homer, but you'd be wrong. He was the greatest story-teller, but he never wrote down a single story. Myths, folk tales, and fairy tales were passed on from generation to generation orally, through storytelling. That's why so many seem a bit exaggerated. The characters and stories grew braver and bigger with every telling, in the hopes of teaching a lesson or conveying a moral to the listener. What lesson can you learn from each of these stories?

Greek and Roman Mythology

It's hard to imagine what our civilization would be like without the mythology of ancient Greece and Rome. Those ancient immortals are still with us in spirit. If you go to any one of the great museums of Europe or America, you will find statues and paintings of classical gods and heroes. If you read poetry in English class, you will come across references to ancient places such as Troy and Carthage, monsters such as the Sirens and the Cyclops, and gods and heroes such as Poseidon, Odysseus (whose Roman name is Ulysses), Athena, and Hercules. These are all names from mythology—names that poets and artists expect us to recognize.

Myths Explain and Teach

Myths are stories that represent the deepest wishes and fears of human beings. They explained to ancient people the mysterious and frightening forces of the universe—forces such as seasonal changes, fire, lightning, drought, floods, and death.

Myths were also used to teach **morals,** or lessons about the right way to behave. These morals are usually not stated directly. You need to figure them out based on the choices characters make and the consequences they face. For example, think about what lessons may be in store for King Midas:

> Midas had a loving wife and a daughter he adored, but he was still discontented. He wanted to be the most powerful king in the world; he wanted everyone to envy him.
>
> from "King Midas and the Golden Touch," retold by Pamela Oldfield

Greek myths originated in the area around the Mediterranean Sea. By the second century B.C. the Romans had conquered the Greeks and adopted their myths, making some changes that reflected the Roman view of religion.

The Uses of Mythology

Like all true art, the great myths give us insights into the nature of our world. Myths

- explain the creation of the world
- explain natural phenomena
- give story form to ancient religious practices
- teach moral lessons
- explain history
- express humans' deepest hopes, dreams, and fears.

Gods and Goddesses

According to the Greek myths the divinities lived on Mount Olympus. Many of them left the mountain to spend time with ordinary people. Sometimes ordinary people traveled down to the terrifying underworld, where the god Hades ruled.

To the myth makers, a god or goddess was a powerful being often identified with a force of nature. The chart below shows some of the Greek and Roman gods and goddesses and their special powers that influence the action in many myths.

Greek and Roman Gods and Goddesses

Greek Name	Roman Name	Area of Power
Zeus (zoos)	Jupiter	king of gods; sky; weather
Apollo (uh PAHL oh)	Apollo	the sun; youth; music; archery; healing; prophecy
Artemis (AHR tuh mihs)	Diana	twin sister of Apollo; the moon; hunting
Hades (HAY deez)	Pluto	king of the underworld
Poseidon (puh SY duhn)	Neptune	ruler of the seas

Greek and Roman Gods and Goddesses, *continued*

Greek Name	Roman Name	Area of Power
Hera (HIHR uh)	Juno	wife of Zeus; queen of gods; women; marriage
Dionysus (dy uh NY suhs)	Bacchus (BAK uhs)	wine; fertility; music
Athena (uh THEE nuh)	Minerva (mih NUR vuh)	wisdom; war; crafts
Hephaestus (hih FEHS tuhs)	Vulcan	craftsman for the gods; fire
Hermes (HUR meez)	Mercury	messenger god; secrets; tricks
Demeter (dih MEE tuhr)	Ceres (SIHR eez)	agriculture; earth; corn
Persephone (puhr SEHF uh nee)	Proserpine (PRAHS uhr pyn)	daughter of Demeter; queen of Hades

Your Turn   Analyze Elements of Myths

1. List two ways in which myths have changed over time.
2. Review the purposes of myths. What forms of literature serve some of these purposes today?

Learn It Online

Use *PowerNotes* as a visual aid to boost your learning at:

go.hrw.com   L7-901   **Go**

Literary Focus

by **Linda Rief**

What Are the Characteristics of Folk Tales?

Who tells stories where you live? Are they told by your mother or father? a grandmother or grandfather? Many of the conversations that take place when families get together begin with the phrases "That reminds me of the time . . ." or "I remember when . . ." These conversations are actually family stories being shared and passed down from one generation to the next. We don't know for sure, but perhaps folk tales began in the same way.

How Folk Tales Grow

Folk tales are stories with no known authors that were originally passed on by word of mouth, often over many centuries. Each time the tale was told, it was changed a bit because no two people tell a story in exactly the same way.

Some of these folk tales traveled. As they were told and retold, they moved out of their original environments into other times and other places. Although traditional folk tales reflect the particular culture and people that created them, common features called **motifs** can be found in folk stories from many parts of the world. You'll find that many folk tales include motifs such as grateful beasts, tests of the hero, magic, fairy godmothers, and brave youngest sons and daughters.

This chart shows a motif present in one folk tale in this collection. Use the title as a clue to how the motif appears in the folk tale.

Folk Tale	Motif
"Master Frog"	Metamorphosis (change from one shape to another)

American Folk Tales

Many American Indian cultures had elaborate and rich folklore traditions. Then Europeans came to North America, bringing their folk tales with them. Folk tales also traveled to the Americas from countries in other regions. For example, Africans who were brought to the Americas as slaves carried with them their unique folk-telling traditions. Over generations they passed on tales about their lives on the plantations and about their relationships with the white men and women who held them in slavery.

In fact, African American storytellers developed the **animal tale** into a highly individual form. In animal tales the social order of the plantation is broken down so that different animals symbolize the people in the plantation community.

The African storytellers who were held as slaves naturally fantasized about freedom. They developed another kind of folk tale, called an **escape story,** about flying away from slavery.

Folk Tales and Culture

In America, people from practically every culture have told their children folk tales from their native lands. Folk tales, as well as native dances, songs, and folk art, help people retain strong communities and keep their beliefs and cultures alive.

The folk tales in this collection are examples of tales passed on from specific cultures. "Master Frog" is a Vietnamese tale; "The Crane Wife" is a Japanese tale.

Folk Tales and Community

Some folk tales are simple stories, while others are complex. However, the basic situation of the story-teller weaving his or her magic for a community of listeners is found everywhere, in every society.

For generation after generation, folk tales keep alive and close what we regard as important. They reveal who we are. As they instruct us in living, they show us our weaknesses and strengths, our fears and joys, and our nightmares and wishes. Folk tales are our self-portraits.

Read the beginning of this folk tale, and think about the picture it paints of human nature—and what lessons it may teach about judging others on appearance:

> Giang Dung was a plain girl, so plain in fact that all the townspeople marveled when her parents finally found her a husband.
>
> from "Master Frog,"
> retold by Lynette Dyer Vuong

Then, read these lines and imagine the rewards that can come from kindness:

> Now Yohei could see that the bird was in great pain, for an arrow had pierced its wing. He went to where the crane lay, drew out the arrow, and very carefully tended its wound.
>
> from "The Crane Wife," told by
> Sumiko Yagawa, translated from
> the Japanese by Katherine Paterson

"Tells" and Tale Givers

As you read the folk tales in this collection, think about those early storytellers who committed the tales to memory in order to say them aloud. Try to picture what those early tellings must have been like. Imagine the smoky underground kivas of the Pueblos, or the dusty village squares of Nigeria.

Sitting or standing there, surrounded by a community of listeners, the teller calls softly, "Time was when the animals could talk. . . ." The listeners respond. They lean forward, absolutely quiet now, eager to hear, to be entertained, and to learn.

Your Turn Analyze Elements of Folk Tales

1. Identify one similarity and one difference between the folk tales described here and the myths described on pages 900–901.

2. Review the motifs discussed on page 902. Explain where you have encountered one of these motifs.

 Learn It Online
Use an interactive graphic organizer to help you
analyze elements of folk tales at:

go.hrw.com L7-903 **Go**

Analyzing Visuals

How Can You Learn About Myths from a Literary Map?

THE WORLD OF CLASSICAL MYTHOLOGY

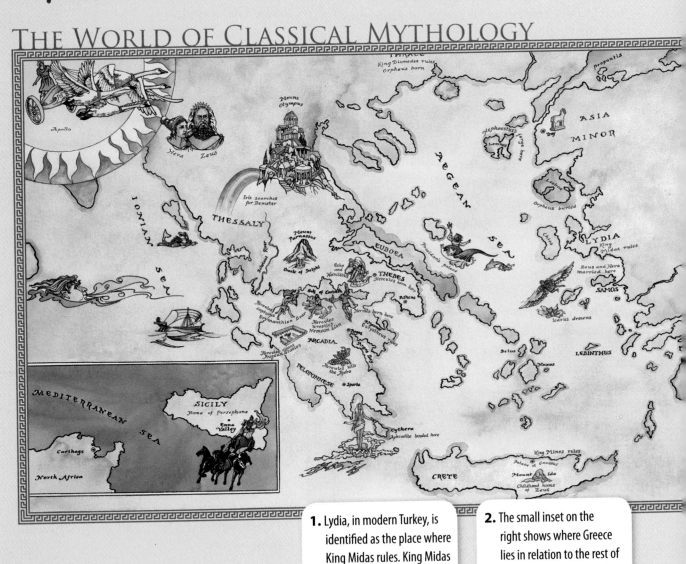

1. Lydia, in modern Turkey, is identified as the place where King Midas rules. King Midas is a character in classical mythology, but there was also a real King Midas.

2. The small inset on the right shows where Greece lies in relation to the rest of the world as represented in world maps today.

Special-purpose maps present specific information, such as the routes of explorers, the outcome of an election, or information on population. This map is a literary map—it presents the major geographical sites for the myths in this collection. The place names are real, but some of the events or characters that are named exist only in mythology.

Reading a Literary Map

Answer these questions as you learn about myths from this literary map.

1. Notice the focus of the map. What do its title and labels tell you?

2. Check directions and distances. How does the compass rose show you which way is north?

3. Note the references to Hercules made throughout the map. What does this tell you about him?

Your Turn Talk About Literary Maps

Locate a map of modern Greece. In a group, identify old place names that are still in use by comparing the modern map to the one on these pages.

Reading Focus

by **Kylene Beers**

What Skills Help You Read Myths and Folk Tales?

When you read myths and folk tales, many events occur that invite you to make predictions as you read. After you read a story, it's helpful to summarize it as a reading check and to draw conclusions about the characters and the outcome of the story. Once you've read several stories, you'll be ready to make generalizations about myths and folk tales.

Making Predictions

When you **make predictions,** you guess what will happen next. To make predictions as you read, you look for clues that **foreshadow,** or hint at, future actions. You try to connect those clues with past and present actions in the story.

When you make predictions, you also draw on real-life experiences that are related to the story situation. Of course, many events that happen in myths and folk tales don't happen in real life. However, what motivates characters to make certain choices and decisions most definitely does.

In one myth you will read, "King Midas and the Golden Touch," Midas is given the chance to choose anything he wants. To make a prediction about what he might choose, you would

- think about your prior experience with myths
- think about similar stories you have read
- think about what you know about the character from how he acts and how he is described
- think about what people might do in real life

Once you make a prediction, be ready to adjust it as you learn more or as events in the story change.

Summarizing

A **summary** is a short restatement of the major events or main ideas of a text. Here is the start of a summary of "King Midas and the Golden Touch," retold by Pamela Oldfield:

> King Midas is very rich, but he is greedy and is not satisfied with what he has. One day Midas helps a follower of the god Dionysus who, in return, says Midas can have any gift he wants.

A summary is much shorter than the original text. To **summarize** a myth or any literary text, you restate the main events. The tricky part of summarizing is deciding what to include and what to leave out. When you summarize a myth, be sure to include the following:

- title
- author (the one who retells the myth)
- main characters
- conflict
- main events
- resolution

Using a diagram like this one can help you summarize the main events in a myth or folk tale you have read. Write two or three sentences in each box.

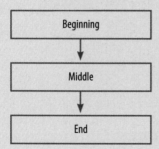

Drawing Conclusions

Drawing conclusions is a natural part of reading any story. A **conclusion** is a general summing up of the specific details in a text. You think about the characters and decide what kind of people they are. You think about situations in the story and determine their possible consequences. You think about how a story turns out and whether the outcome seems fair or unfair.

To draw sound conclusions from a story, base your conclusions on

- your own prior knowledge, experiences, and beliefs
- details in the text

As you read each story, keep a list of the conclusions you draw.

Making Generalizations

A **generalization** is a broad statement that covers several situations. Generalizations are based on facts.

Once you have read several myths and folk tales, you will have experience and evidence for making generalizations about them. For example, after you read several poems in Collection 7, you might have made this generalization: "Many poems use sound effects, such as rhyme, rhythm, and alliteration."

However, be careful of making generalizations without knowing all the facts. If you read only a few rhyming poems and then made the generalization that all poems rhyme, you would be incorrect. To be valid, generalizations need to be based on all of the facts that you can gather.

To make good generalizations, take notes as you read. Then, use details from the story to support each generalization.

Your Turn Apply Reading Skills

1. Based on the title of the myth "King Midas and the Golden Touch," make predictions about the gift Midas chooses and why he wants it.

2. In a paragraph, write a summary of your typical school day. Use a chart like the one at the left to help you organize the main events.

3. Make a generalization about the kinds of stories you enjoy reading the most. Explain the facts that make your generalization valid.

Learn It Online
Practice summarizing with the interactive Reading Workshop online:

go.hrw.com | L7-907 | **Go**

Preview the Selection This myth is about greed—valuing money above anything else.

Read with a Purpose Read to discover what the "golden touch" is and what happens when Midas receives it.

King Midas and the Golden Touch

retold by **Pamela Oldfield**

Many years ago in the land of Lydia, there was a beautiful garden. Roses of every shade grew there, and on warm summer nights the air was heavy with their fragrance. The garden belonged to a palace, and the palace was the home of a king whose name was Midas. He was, it is true, rather greedy, but on the whole no better and no worse than any other man. Midas had a loving wife and a daughter he adored, but he was still discontented. He wanted to be the most powerful king in the world; he wanted everyone to envy him.

One day as he was walking through the palace garden, he was startled to see a pair of legs sticking out from beneath his favorite rosebush. The strange thing about these legs was that they had hoofs instead of feet. The king stared at them for a moment and then called for the gardener's boy.

"What do you make of that?" he asked. The boy parted the branches of the rosebush and peered through.

"It's a satyr, Your Majesty," he reported, trying not to laugh. "I think it's Silenus."

The satyrs were strange, mischievous creatures—half man, half beast—who roamed the world in search of adventure. Midas frowned, angry that somebody should be sleeping in his garden.

The boy ran off to fetch the gardener, and between them they dragged Silenus from under the rosebush and pulled him to his feet.

Literary Focus

Morals One purpose of myths is to teach **moral** lessons about the right way to live. Watch how Midas discovers what is truly important in life.

Reading Focus

Summarizing When you **summarize** a myth, you retell the major events in the story. As you read, take notes on key characters and events. Your notes will help you summarize.

Silenus grinned foolishly. He was holding an empty wine jar.

"You are trespassing in my garden," Midas told him severely. "What have you to say for yourself?" The old satyr shrugged.

"I got lost, so I sat down for a drink," he told the king, looking quite unrepentant.

"Disgraceful," said Midas. "I shall send word to your master at once." Silenus began to look worried, for his master was the god Dionysus, who was not only powerful but also quick-tempered.

"I beg you not to do that," he cried. "He will be angry with me. Suppose I make a bargain with you? If you will overlook my foolishness, I will entertain you with strange and wonderful tales, better than any you have heard before."

Midas agreed and the satyr stayed on in the palace, delighting the king with wonderful accounts of his adventures. At the end of the week, Midas sent the satyr back to Dionysus. The god was very fond of Silenus, despite his many faults, and was pleased to see him safe and sound. He wanted to thank Midas for taking care of the old satyr and offered the king any gift he cared to name.

Any gift he cared to name! What a marvelous opportunity! He pondered for a whole day and a night and then asked Dionysus if he could make a wish. The god agreed and Midas asked for the power to turn whatever he touched into gold. The god granted his wish, and Midas was jubilant.

"Imagine a king with a golden touch!" he cried. "I shall be the wealthiest and most powerful king in the world."

The king began to experiment with his new gift. He hurried into the garden and touched one of the flowers. At once, the whole bush turned to gold. Then he looked around him. Suddenly Midas felt doubtful. Gone were the colors and the glorious perfume. The garden was still and lifeless.

Inside the palace, the king called for a goblet of wine. As soon as it touched his lips the wine turned to gold and he could not drink.

A terrible thought occurred to him.

"What will happen when I eat?" he wondered. With trembling fingers he reached out to take an apple from a bowl of fruit. As soon as he touched it, the apple turned to gold.

"What have I done?" he whispered. "If I cannot eat or drink I shall die!" He knew that he had made a terrible mistake and decided to beg Dionysus to take back his gift. "I will go to him at once,"

Literary Focus

Gods and Goddesses Greek myths feature powerful gods and goddesses who interact with humans. Dionysus has an important role in this myth.

Reading Focus

Making Predictions To make accurate **predictions,** base your thinking on what you have already learned about Midas and on what you know from similar stories and your own experiences. You can make many predictions throughout a story. Once Midas makes his wish, make a prediction about whether it will make him as happy and powerful as he expects.

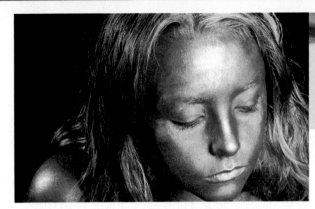

he cried, but his decision came too late. At that very moment his daughter ran into the room.

"Stay away from me!" Midas shouted, but she took no notice. She threw her arms around him—and was turned to gold. His daughter was now a gleaming but lifeless statue. The king stared at her in horror.

"What have I done to you?" he cried, kneeling beside her. His grief was so great that nobody could console him. He hurried to the palace of Dionysus and threw himself at the god's feet.

"Forgive my stupid greed!" he begged. "Tell me what I must do to save my child. I will do anything you say."

Dionysus told him to find the river Pactolus and wash himself in its waters. Midas set off at once. He went alone and walked for many miles over rough and stony ground.

When he reached the river he found it flowing deep and strong. Midas waded straight in. He was instantly swept away by the current. When at last he managed to reach the shore, he wondered if the curse had indeed been washed from him. Looking back, he saw that the river now gleamed and sparkled in the sun. On the riverbed tiny nuggets of gold lay among the pebbles. Dionysus had spoken truthfully, and the terrible power had left him. Joyfully Midas made his way home.

As he approached the palace, Midas's daughter ran to greet him. He lifted her into his arms and carried her into the garden. Midas was overjoyed to hear her laughter once again, and he sighed happily as he breathed in the fragrance of the flowers.

"I have learned my lesson," he said softly, "and I am content."

Read with a Purpose   How did the "golden touch" change King Midas's life?

SKILLS FOCUS **Literary Skills** Understand and analyze elements of myths; understand and analyze elements of folk tales. **Reading Skills** Summarize a text; draw conclusions; make generalizations from a text.

Into Action: Summarizing

Use the notes you took as you read and the diagram below to help you summarize the myth. Write two or three sentences in each box to organize the story's events. Then, write a short summary that includes the title, author, main characters, main events, and resolution.

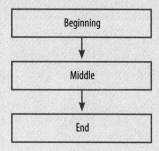

Talk About . . .

1. Discuss with a partner the way people today view wealth and greed. Try to use each Academic Vocabulary word listed at the right in your discussion.

Write About . . .

Use the underscored Academic Vocabulary words in your answers to the following questions about "King Midas and the Golden Touch."

2. Gods and goddesses usually play an active role in Greek myths. However, a god did not prevent Midas from making his wish. Why do you think the god chose not to <u>intervene</u> on Midas's behalf?

3. Would it be a compliment to tell someone he or she had a "<u>classic</u> Midas touch"? Explain why or why not.

4. How can myths such as this one provide a <u>foundation</u> for making wise decisions in your own life? Explain.

Writing Focus

Think as a Reader/Writer

In Collection 9, you will read myths and folk tales. In the Writing Focus activities, you'll learn about various elements of myths and folk tales and have a chance to write stories using those elements.

Academic Vocabulary for Collection 9

Talking and Writing About Myths and Folk Tales

Academic Vocabulary is the language you use to write and talk about literature. Use these words to discuss the myths and folk tales you read in this collection. The words are underlined throughout the collection.

classic (KLAS ihk) *adj.*: well-known, especially as being traditional or typical. *The story of Midas is a classic myth.*

foundation (fown DAY shuhn) *n.*: basis; idea, fact, or system from which something develops. *Many ancient myths and folk tales provided a foundation for understanding the world.*

generation (jehn uh RAY shuhn) *n.*: all the people in a society or family who are about the same age. *Folk tales are often passed down from a previous generation.*

intervene (ihn tuhr VEEN) *v.*: do something to try to stop an argument or solve a problem. *Sometimes in a myth or folk tale, a powerful force will intervene on behalf of humans.*

Your Turn

Copy the Academic Vocabulary words into your *Reader/Writer Notebook*. Use each word in a sentence about Midas. Practice using these words as you talk and write about the myths and folk tales in this collection.

Orpheus, the Great Musician

retold by **Olivia Coolidge**

Orpheus and Eurydice by Angus McBride (b. 1931). Gouache on paper.

What Do You Think

How does music influence people's lives?

 QuickWrite

Think of a time when music touched your life. Write briefly about the experience.

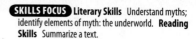

SKILLS FOCUS **Literary Skills** Understand myths; identify elements of myth: the underworld. **Reading Skills** Summarize a text.

Reader/Writer Notebook

Use your **RWN** to complete the activities for this selection.

Literary Focus

The Underworld of Myth In Greek myths the **underworld** is a dark and gloomy place that is ruled by the stern god Hades. Normally only the souls of the dead go to the underworld. Sometimes, however, living people attempt the dangerous journey, usually to reach someone who has died.

Literary Perspectives Apply the literary perspective described on page 915 as you read this myth.

Reading Focus

Summarizing When you summarize, you mention only the most important information in a text.

Into Action Use this chart to summarize the text as you read.

Summarizing a Myth	Notes from Your Reading
Title	"Orpheus, the Great Musician"
Author	Olivia Coolidge
Main characters	Orpheus
Conflict	
Main events	
Resolution	

Writing Focus

Think as a Reader/Writer

Find It in Your Reading Look for details that describe the inhabitants and conditions of the underworld, such as "pale ghosts" and "hissing flames." Record examples as you read.

Vocabulary

inconsolable (ihn kuhn SOH luh buhl) *adj.*: unable to be comforted; brokenhearted. *Orpheus is inconsolable when his true love dies.*

instinct (IHN stihngkt) *n.*: inborn pattern of behavior. *Orpheus uses instinct to determine if his true love is near.*

reluctance (rih LUHK tuhns) *n.*: unwillingness. *His reluctance to live without his love led Orpheus to brave the underworld.*

unfortunate (uhn FAWR chuh niht) *adj.*: marked by ill fortune. *Orpheus is unfortunate in matters of love.*

Language Coach

Word Parts Review Figuring out the meaning of words and how they work to make meaning is the key to mastering any language. Remember the following:

- **Roots** are the fundamental parts of a word. For example, *solari* is a Latin root meaning "comfort." The word *console* is based on the Latin root *solari*.

- **Affixes** are word parts added to a root to alter its meaning.

- **Prefixes** are affixes added to the front of a word (*in*consolable).

- **Suffixes** are affixes added to the end of a word (inconsol*able*).

 Learn It Online
Watch a video introducing this myth at:

go.hrw.com | L7-913 | Go

Olivia Coolidge
(1908–2006)

Newbery Medal WINNER

"I Write Because . . . I Almost Have To"

Olivia Coolidge, daughter of a famous historian and journalist, was born and educated in England but lived most of her life in the United States. In addition to publishing twenty-seven books, she taught in schools in the Northeast. Coolidge developed an interest in storytelling at an early age and used her storytelling gifts mainly to make mythology and history exciting for young readers. She believed strongly in the power of the story:

"A good book should excite, amuse, and interest. It should give a sense of seeing as a movie does. In other words, a good book needs imagination and the gift of a good storyteller. I write because I like writing, because I want to write, and because I almost have to. I have a great many things I want to say, ideas I want to express, and pictures I want to convey to other people."

Think About the Writer How has Coolidge helped keep myths alive for the next <u>generation</u> of readers?

Build Background

This myth describes a journey to the underworld. According to the beliefs of the ancient Greeks, the underworld was reached by crossing the River Styx (stihks) on a ferryboat rowed by Charon (KAIR uhn) and then passing through gates guarded by Cerberus (SUR buhr uhs), a three-headed dog.

©Erich Lessing / Art Resource, NY.

Heracles fighting Cerberus, the hellhound (detail) (530 B.C.–525 B.C.). Terra cotta, black-figured hydria (two-handled jug) from Caere.

Preview the Selection

In "Orpheus, the Great Musician," **Orpheus** (AWR fee uhs) is a mortal (a being who must eventually die) who makes beautiful music. He falls in love with **Eurydice** (yu RIHD uh see), a nymph (a nymph is a goddess usually represented as young, beautiful, and living within nature). Before they can be married, she dies. Orpheus is so heartbroken that he attempts a journey few mortals have made—a journey to the underworld, ruled by the god **Hades** (HAY deez), to try to find Eurydice.

Parthenon at Acropolis in Greece.

Read with a Purpose Read to find out what moves Orpheus to create his greatest music.

Orpheus, the Great Musician

retold by **Olivia Coolidge**

In the legend of Orpheus, the Greek love of music found its fullest expression. Orpheus, it is said, could make such heavenly songs that when he sat down to sing, the trees would crowd around to shade him. The ivy and vine stretched out their tendrils. Great oaks would bend their spreading branches over his head. The very rocks would edge down the mountainsides. Wild beasts crouched harmless by him, and nymphs[1] and woodland gods would listen to him, enchanted. **Ⓐ**

Orpheus himself, however, had eyes for no one but the nymph Eurydice. His love for her was his inspiration, and his power sprang from the passionate longing that he knew in his own heart. All nature rejoiced with him on his bridal day, but on that very morning, as Eurydice went down to the riverside with her maidens to gather flowers for a bridal garland, she was bitten in the foot by a snake, and she died in spite of all attempts to save her. **Ⓑ**

---

1. **nymphs:** minor goddesses of nature, usually young and beautiful, living in mountains, rivers, or trees.

Ⓐ Read and Discuss What does this information about wild beasts, trees, and rocks tell you about Orpheus?

Ⓑ Reading Focus **Summarizing** Remember to take notes on key events as you read. Why is this an important event in the myth?

Literary Perspectives

The following perspective will help you think about this myth.

Analyzing Archetypes Recurring characters in stories and myths who serve as the basis for similar characters throughout literature are called archetypal characters. In "Orpheus, the Great Musician," the title character is the archetype for the supremely talented artist. Mortals as well as the creatures of the underworld are soothed by Orpheus's song. His musical ability even proves to be heroic as he uses his gifts in an attempt to overcome death. Read the notes and questions in the text, which will guide you in using this perspective.

Orpheus was inconsolable. All day long he mourned his bride, while birds, beasts, and the earth itself sorrowed with him. When at last the shadows of the sun grew long, Orpheus took his lyre[2] and made his way to the yawning cave which leads down into the underworld, where the soul of dead Eurydice had gone.

Even gray Charon, the ferryman of the Styx, forgot to ask his passenger for the price of crossing. The dog Cerberus, the three-headed monster who guards Hades' gate, stopped full in his tracks and listened motionless until Orpheus had passed. As he entered the land of Hades, the pale ghosts came after him like great, uncounted flocks of silent birds. All the land lay hushed as that marvelous voice resounded across the mud and marshes of its dreadful rivers. In the daffodil fields of Elysium, the happy dead sat silent among their flowers. In the farthest corners of the place of punishment, the hissing flames stood still. Accursed Sisyphus,[3] who toils eternally to push a mighty rock uphill, sat down and knew not he was resting. Tantalus, who strains forever after visions of cool water, forgot his thirst and ceased to clutch at the empty air. **C**

The pillared[4] hall of Hades opened before the hero's song. The ranks of long-dead heroes who sit at Hades' board looked up and turned their eyes away from the pitiless form of Hades and his pale, unhappy queen. Grim and unmoving sat the dark king of the dead on his ebony throne, yet the tears shone on his rigid cheeks in the light of his ghastly torches. Even his hard heart, which knew all misery and cared nothing for it, was touched by the love and longing of the music. **D**

At last the minstrel[5] came to an end, and a long sigh like wind in pine trees was heard from the assembled ghosts. Then the king spoke, and his deep voice echoed through his silent land. "Go back to the light of day," he said. "Go quickly while my monsters are stilled by your song. Climb up the steep road to daylight, and never once turn back. The spirit of Eurydice shall follow, but if you look around at her, she will return to me." **E**

Orpheus turned and strode from the hall of Hades, and the flocks of following ghosts made way for him to pass. In vain he searched their ranks for a sight of his lost Eurydice. In vain he listened for the faintest sound behind. The barge of Charon sank to the very gunwales[6] beneath his weight, but no following passenger pressed it lower down. The way from the land of Hades to the upper world is long and hard, far easier to

---

2. **lyre** (lyr): small harp.
3. **Sisyphus** (SIHS uh fuhs).
4. **pillared:** having pillars (columns).

5. **minstrel:** singer.
6. **gunwales** (GUHN uhlz): upper edges of the sides of a boat.

C **Literary Perspectives** Analyzing Archetypes
What is the myth saying about the artist's ability to affect his or her surroundings?

D **Literary Focus** Underworld of Myth What images do you get of the underworld and of Hades?

E **Reading Focus** Summarizing Why is this important information?

Vocabulary **inconsolable** (ihn kuhn SOH luh buhl) *adj.:* unable to be comforted; brokenhearted.

Analyzing Visuals **Viewing and Interpreting** What elements in the illustration convey that the underworld is a petrifying place?

Orpheus in the Underworld (c. 1610–1615) by Roelandt Savery (1576–1639).

descend than climb. It was dark and misty, full of strange shapes and noises, yet in many places merely black and silent as the tomb. Here Orpheus would stop and listen, but nothing moved behind him. For all he could hear, he was utterly alone. Then he would wonder if the pitiless Hades were deceiving him. Suppose he came up to the light again and Eurydice was not there! Once he had charmed the ferryman and the dreadful monsters, but now they had heard his song.

The second time his spell would be less powerful; he could never go again. Perhaps he had lost Eurydice by his readiness to believe. **F**

Every step he took, some instinct told him that he was going farther from his bride. He toiled up the path in reluctance and despair, stopping, listening, sighing, taking a few slow steps, until the dark thinned out into grayness. Up ahead a speck of light showed clearly the entrance to the cavern.

F [Read and Discuss] Why might Orpheus believe that Hades will trick him?

Vocabulary **instinct** (IHN stihngkt) *n.:* inborn pattern of behavior.
reluctance (rih LUHK tuhns) *n.:* unwillingness.

At that final moment Orpheus could bear no more. To go out into the light of day without his love seemed to him impossible. Before he had quite ascended, there was still a moment in which he could go back. Quick in the grayness he turned and saw a dim shade at his heels, as indistinct as the gray mist behind her. But still he could see the look of sadness on her face as he sprung forward saying, "Eurydice!" and threw his arms about her. The shade dissolved in the circle of his arms like smoke. A little whisper seemed to say "Farewell" as she scattered into mist and was gone. **G**

The unfortunate lover hastened back again down the steep, dark path. But all was in vain. This time the ghostly ferryman was deaf to his prayers. The very wildness of his mood made it impossible for him to attain the beauty of his former music. At last, his despair was so great that he could not even sing at all. For seven days he sat huddled together on the gray mud banks, listening to the wailing of the terrible river. The flitting ghosts shrank back in a wide circle from the living man, but he paid them no attention.

> *At that final moment Orpheus could bear no more.*

Only he sat with his eyes on Charon, his ears ringing with the dreadful noise of Styx. **H**

Orpheus arose at last and stumbled back along the steep road he knew so well by now. When he came up to earth again, his song was pitiful but more beautiful than ever. Even the nightingale who mourned all night long would hush her voice to listen as Orpheus sat in some hidden place singing of his lost Eurydice. Men and women he could bear no longer, and when they came to hear him, he drove them away. At last the women of Thrace, maddened by Dionysus and infuriated by Orpheus's contempt, fell upon him and killed him. It is said that as the body was swept down the river Hebrus, the dead lips still moved faintly and the rocks echoed for the last time, "Eurydice." But the poet's eager spirit was already far down the familiar path.

In the daffodil meadows he met the shade of Eurydice, and there they walk together, or where the path is narrow, the shade of Orpheus goes ahead and looks back at his love. **I**

G **Literary Perspectives** Analyzing Archetypes What common human flaw is Orpheus betraying?

H **Literary Focus** Underworld of Myth How is this trip to the underworld different from the first?

I **Reading Focus** Summarizing What is the resolution, or ending, of Orpheus's tale?

Vocabulary **unfortunate** (uhn FAWR chuh niht) *adj.*: marked by ill fortune.

Applying Your Skills

Orpheus, the Great Musician

Respond and Think Critically

Quick Check

1. How does Eurydice die? What is especially tragic about her death?

Read with a Purpose

2. Discuss the way Orpheus's singing is influenced by his feelings at various points in the story.

Reading Skills: Summarizing

3. Review the notes you took while you read. Then, write a summary of the myth.

Summarizing a Myth	Notes from Your Reading
Title	"Orpheus, the Great Musician"
Author	Olivia Coolidge
Main characters	Orpheus
Conflict	
Main events	
Resolution	
Summary:	

Literary Focus

Literary Analysis

4. **Make Judgments** Is Hades fair to Orpheus and Eurydice? Explain.

5. **Analyze** Explain how the same emotion that prompts Orpheus's descent into the underworld also causes him to fail in his quest.

6. **Extend** How does this myth explore the notion of having faith or trust in a person and the consequences of breaking that trust?

7. **Literary Perspectives** Review the effect Orpheus's music has on other characters in the story. What is the myth saying about the way an artist can affect people?

Literary Skills: Underworld of Myth

8. **Draw Conclusions** Based on this myth, how do you think the ancient Greeks pictured the afterlife? Use examples from the story in your explanation.

Literary Skills Review: Theme

9. **Analyze/Connect** What **theme,** or truth about life, does this myth express about the power of music? Explain.

Writing Focus

Think as a Reader/Writer
Use It in Your Writing Imagine that you are a Greek god who can intervene to change the outcome of the myth. Describe your visit to the underworld to confront Hades. Include descriptions of the underworld based on the notes you took while reading.

What Do **You Think Now** How does the message of the myth compare with your own thoughts about music?

Applying Your Skills

Orpheus, the Great Musician

Vocabulary Development

Vocabulary Check

Each sentence below contains a Vocabulary word. After reading each sentence, make up a reasonable answer to each question.

1. If a friend of yours was **inconsolable,** how might you act toward her?
2. When you see characters in movies and television shows act on **instinct,** what kinds of consequences do their actions have?
3. Why might you show **reluctance** to cross a busy intersection?
4. How would you react to an **unfortunate** occurrence?

Greek and Latin Prefixes

Figuring out the meanings of words is the key to mastering any language. If you learn the meanings of Greek and Latin prefixes, you have the key to understanding many English words.

5. *Bi–* is a Latin prefix meaning "two." What is the meaning of the word *bilingual*?
6. The Greek prefix *anti–* means "against." What are two familiar words that use this prefix?
7. The meaning of the Latin prefix *sub–* is "under; beneath." How does this prefix give you a clue to the meaning of the word *submarine*?

Language Coach

Latin Suffixes Below is a list of common suffixes derived from Latin, along with their meanings. In your *Reader/Writer Notebook,* record at least two words that use each suffix.

8. *–able,* meaning "able; likely"
9. *–ancy,* meaning "act; quality"
10. *–ity,* meaning "state; condition"
11. *–ment,* meaning "result; state of being"
12. *–tion,* meaning "action; condition"

Academic Vocabulary

Talk About . . .
Discuss whether Orpheus was right to intervene when events out of his control took place. Explain whether readers from your generation sympathize with the choices he makes. Use the underlined Academic Vocabulary words in your discussion.

Learn It Online
Review prefixes and suffixes with *WordSharp* at:
go.hrw.com   L7-920   Go

Grammar Link

Comparison of Modifiers

Modifiers can be divided into two groups based on the way they express their degrees of comparison. **Regular comparisons** follow common rules; **irregular comparisons** do not.

Regular Comparison

- Most one-syllable modifiers form their comparative and superlative degrees by adding *–er* and *–est*.

  sharp   sharper   sharpest

- Some two-syllable modifiers form their comparative and superlative degrees by adding *–er* and *–est*. Others form them by using *more* and *most*.

  simple   simpler   simplest

  sudden   more sudden   most sudden

- Modifiers that have three or more syllables form their comparative and superlative degrees by using *more* and *most*.

  curious   more curious   most curious

Irregular Comparison

Some modifiers do not form their comparative and superlative degrees using the regular methods.

bad	worse	worst
far	farther	farthest
good	better	best

Your Turn

Give the forms for the comparative and superlative degrees of the following modifiers.

1. fine
2. thankful
3. much
4. daring

CHOICES

As you respond to the Choices, use the **Academic Vocabulary** words as appropriate: classic, foundation, generation, intervene.

REVIEW

Retell—and Revise—the Myth

Fill out a diagram like this one to show the plot of "Orpheus." Explain in a paragraph why the setting of the underworld is important. Then, imagine that Orpheus does not look back. What would the myth's new climax and resolution be? Explain your ideas in a paragraph.

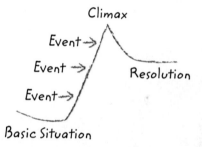

CONNECT

Evaluate Characters

Timed ⌐Writing Look back at the myth, and jot down specifics about Orpheus's character traits and actions. In a paragraph, describe the conclusions you can draw about Orpheus based on these traits and actions. Cite examples from the text in your answer.

EXTEND

Discuss the Power of Music

What specific piece of music has a powerful impact on you? Do you feel the melody or the words as you listen, sing along, or play along? Identify the musical piece. Then, explain how it makes you feel and why you think it has such a strong effect on you.

The Flight of Icarus

retold by **Sally Benson**

What Do **You** Think? Why have people dreamed of soaring above the Earth?

 QuickWrite

Long before the invention of the airplane, people yearned to fly. Express your feelings about flying by completing this sentence: *If people could fly, . . .*

Reader/Writer Notebook

Use your **RWN** to complete the activities for this selection.

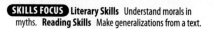
Literary Focus

Morals in Myths When a young bird flies from the nest for the first time, we say that it is "trying its wings." As you read this myth, notice what happens when a young boy tries his wings. If you think about what the boy attempts to do, and what he ignores, you'll find the moral of the story. A **moral** is a lesson about the right way to behave. The morals in many Greek myths were used to teach children values. The moral is tied to the story's **theme**—the truth about life revealed in a work of literature.

Reading Focus

Making Generalizations When you **make a generalization,** you look at evidence and make a broad statement about what it tells you. Someone who says, "All stories contain conflicts" is making a generalization from experience with many stories. As you read these myths, think of generalizations you might make about myths and the kinds of stories they tell.

Into Action As you read "The Flight of Icarus," write your generalizations about myths in a web like the one shown here.

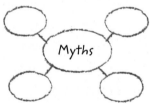

Myths

Writing Focus

Think as a Reader/Writer

Find It in Your Reading Note the author's descriptions of how the wings look as they are being made and as they are being used, and then how they look at the end of the story. Record two examples of vivid descriptions.

TechFocus As you read, think about the way you would reveal Icarus's characteristics in a podcast.

Vocabulary

ingenious (ihn JEEN yuhs) *adj.:* clever; good at inventing. *Daedalus was an ingenious artist and inventor.*

moderate (MAHD uhr iht) *adj.:* keeping within proper limits. *Daedalus cautioned Icarus to stay at a moderate height.*

frantically (FRAN tuh klee) *adv.:* with wild excitement. *Icarus waved frantically at his father.*

burden (BUR duhn) *n.:* something heavy that has to be carried. *Daedalus had to carry a terrible burden to the shore.*

bore (bawr) *v.:* carried. *Daedalus bore his son in his arms.*

Language Coach

Multiple-Meaning Words Some words have more than one meaning. How many multiple-meaning words can you find in the list of Vocabulary words above? What are the other meanings of these words?

Learn It Online
Strengthen your vocabulary with Word Watch at:

go.hrw.com   L7-923   **Go**

Sally Benson
(1900–1972)

Stories That Have "Rounded Ends"

Sally Benson never studied writing. She didn't have to; writing came naturally for her. After high school, she skipped college and went directly to work, first for a bank and then for newspapers. In 1930, she was reviewing thirty-two movies a month for a daily newspaper when she got an idea for a short story. She sat down, typed it out, and sold it to *The New Yorker*.

Dazed by her good fortune, she stopped writing for nine months. When her money ran out, she penned another story and sold that one, too. From then on she wrote many stories. Benson published one book of Greek and Roman myths, but most of her stories tell the amusing adventures of a thirteen-year-old girl named Judy Graves.

> "I like stories that have rounded ends and don't rise to climaxes; that aren't all wrapped up in a package with plot. I like them; that's why I write them."

Think About the Writer Why do you think Benson enjoyed retelling Greek and Roman myths?

Build Background

The myth you are about to read is one of the most popular of all the Greek myths. Even today, the plot of this story continues to fascinate readers. You can find references to Daedalus and Icarus in novels, plays, comics, and even video games.

Preview the Selection

In this classic myth, you will read about **Daedalus** (DEHD uh luhs), an inventor and builder who designed a labyrinth for **King Minos** (MY nuhs) of Crete. Daedalus helped **Theseus** (THEE see uhs) escape the maze and has now been imprisoned. With the help of his son, **Icarus** (IHK uhr uhs), Daedalus escapes his prison and devises a plan to leave the island by air.

Feb. 27. 1937 THE NEW YORKER Price 15 cents

The Flight of Icarus

retold by **Sally Benson**

When Theseus escaped from the labyrinth, King Minos flew into a rage with its builder, Daedalus, and ordered him shut up in a high tower that faced the lonely sea. In time, with the help of his young son, Icarus, Daedalus managed to escape from the tower, only to find himself a prisoner on the island. Several times he tried by bribery to stow away on one of the vessels sailing from Crete, but King Minos kept strict watch over them, and no ships were allowed to sail without being carefully searched.

Daedalus was an ingenious artist and was not discouraged by his failures. "Minos may control the land and sea," he said, "but he does not control the air. I will try that way." Ⓐ

He called his son, Icarus, to him and told the boy to gather up all the feathers he could find on the rocky shore. As thousands of gulls soared over the island, Icarus soon collected a huge pile of feathers. Daedalus then melted some wax and made a skeleton in the shape of a bird's wing. The smallest feathers he pressed into the soft wax and the large ones he tied on with thread. Icarus played about on the beach happily while his father worked, chasing the feathers that blew away in the strong wind that swept the island and sometimes taking bits of the wax and working it into strange shapes with his fingers.

It was fun making the wings. The sun shone on the bright feathers; the breezes ruffled them. When they were finished, Daedalus fastened them to his shoulders and found

Ⓐ **Read and Discuss** What is Daedalus doing now?

Vocabulary **ingenious** (ihn JEEN yuhs) *adj.*: clever; good at inventing.

himself lifted upwards, where he hung poised in the air. Filled with excitement, he made another pair for his son. They were smaller than his own, but strong and beautiful.

Finally, one clear, wind-swept morning, the wings were finished, and Daedalus fastened them to Icarus's shoulders and taught him how to fly. He bade him watch the movements of the birds, how they soared and glided overhead. He pointed out the slow, graceful sweep of their wings as they beat the air steadily, without fluttering. Soon Icarus was sure that he, too, could fly and, raising his arms up and down, skirted over the white sand and even out over the waves, letting his feet touch the snowy foam as the water thundered and broke over the sharp rocks. Daedalus watched him proudly but with misgivings. He called Icarus to his side and, putting his arm round the boy's shoulders, said, "Icarus, my son, we are about to make our flight. No human being has ever traveled through the air before, and I want you to listen carefully to my instructions. Keep at a **moderate** height, for if you fly too low, the fog and spray will clog your wings, and if you fly too high, the heat will melt the wax that holds them together. Keep near me and you will be safe." **B**

He kissed Icarus and fastened the wings more securely to his son's shoulders. Icarus, standing in the bright sun, the shining wings drooping gracefully from his shoulders, his golden hair wet with spray, and his eyes bright and dark with excitement, looked like a lovely bird. Daedalus's eyes filled with tears, and turning away, he soared into the sky, calling to Icarus to follow. From time to time, he looked back to see that the boy was safe and to note how he managed his wings in his flight. As they flew across the land to test their prowess before setting out across the dark wild sea, plowmen below stopped their work and shepherds gazed in wonder, thinking Daedalus and Icarus were gods. **C**

> He soared into the sky, calling to Icarus to follow.

B **Reading Focus** **Generalizations** What kind of advice do older characters give younger characters in myths?

C **Read and Discuss** Why do Daedalus's eyes fill with tears?

Vocabulary **moderate** (MAHD uhr iht) *adj.*: keeping within proper limits.

A Creative Genius

Daedalus, a master craftsman and brilliant inventor from Athens, is believed to have killed his talented young nephew, who was also an inventor. To escape punishment, Daedalus fled to Crete, which was ruled by King Minos. Crete and Athens were at war at the time.

Today in Crete you can see ruins of the Palace of Knossos where, legend tells us, Daedalus designed a famous labyrinth, or maze, for King Minos. In it the king concealed the hideous Minotaur, a creature that was half bull and half human. Minos agreed not to wage war with Athens if Athens would send him fourteen young Athenians annually to feed to the monster. This ritual sacrifice went on for many years, until the Athenian hero Theseus killed the Minotaur and found his way out of the maze because Daedalus had revealed its secret. Furious, King Minos imprisoned the inventor and his son, Icarus.

Ask Yourself

Theseus is one of the heroes of Greek mythology who, like Hercules, vanquished powerful monsters against seemingly impossible odds. Who are the heroes in our society? What makes them heroes?

Father and son flew over Samos and Delos, which lay on their left, and Lebinthus,[1] which lay on their right. Icarus, beating his wings in joy, felt the thrill of the cool wind on his face and the clear air above and below him. He flew higher and higher up into the blue sky until he reached the clouds. His father saw him and called out in alarm. He tried to follow him, but he was heavier and his wings would not carry him. Up and up Icarus soared, through the soft, moist clouds and out again toward the glorious sun. He was bewitched by a sense of freedom and beat his wings frantically so that they would carry him higher and higher to heaven itself. The blazing sun beat down on the wings and softened the wax. Small feathers fell from the wings and floated softly down, warning Icarus to stay his flight and glide to earth. But the enchanted boy did not notice them until the sun became so hot that the largest feathers dropped off and he began to sink.

---

1. **Samos** (SAY mahs) . . . **Delos** (DEE lahs) . . . **Lebinthus** (luh BIHN thuhs): Greek islands in the Aegean Sea.

Vocabulary **frantically** (FRAN tuh klee) *adv.:* with wild excitement.

Frantically he fluttered his arms, but no feathers remained to hold the air. He cried out to his father, but his voice was submerged in the blue waters of the sea, which has forever after been called by his name.

Daedalus, crazed by anxiety, called back to him, "Icarus! Icarus, my son, where are you?" At last he saw the feathers floating from the sky, and soon his son plunged through the clouds into the sea. Daedalus hurried to save him, but it was too late. He gathered the boy in his arms and flew to land, the tips of his wings dragging in the water from the double burden they bore. Weeping bitterly, he buried his small son and called the land Icaria in his memory.

Then, with a flutter of wings, he once more took to the air, but the joy of his flight was gone and his victory over the air was bitter to him. He arrived safely in Sicily, where he built a temple to Apollo and hung up his wings as an offering to the god, and in the wings he pressed a few bright feathers he had found floating on the water where Icarus fell. And he mourned for the birdlike son who had thrown caution to the winds in the exaltation of his freedom from the earth. **E**

D **Read and Discuss** What is going on with Icarus? What is going on with Daedalus?

E **Literary Focus** Morals in Myths What lesson can you take away from this myth?

Vocabulary **burden** (BUR duhn) *n.*: something heavy that has to be carried.
bore (bawr) *v.*: carried.

Analyzing Visuals

Viewing and Interpreting How does this statue seem similar to or different from your idea of Icarus?

The Fall of Icarus (1743) by Paul Ambroise Slodtz (1702–1758). Marble statuette.

SKILLS FOCUS **Literary Skills** Analyze the moral of a myth; analyze character. **Reading Skills** Make generalizations from a text. **Writing Skills** Write to express.

The Flight of Icarus

Respond and Think Critically

Reading Focus

Quick Check

1. Why are Daedalus and Icarus prisoners on an island?
2. How does Daedalus attempt to escape from Crete?

Read with a Purpose

3. What causes Daedalus's and Icarus's escape plan to fail?

Reading Skills: Make Generalizations

4. **Into Action** Review your web about myths. Write specific examples to back up your generalizations.

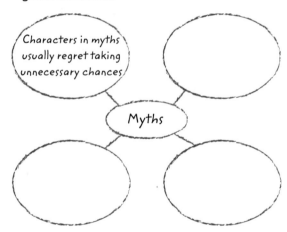

Characters in myths usually regret taking unnecessary chances

Myths

Literary Focus

Literary Analysis

5. **Analyze** When did you predict the outcome of the myth? What hints in the myth helped you make this prediction?

6. **Extend** This myth explains the names of some geographical features in Greece. What are they, and how did they get there?
7. **Connect** What is your opinion of Icarus? Do you think teenagers today can identify with him? Why or why not?

Literary Skills: Morals in Myths

8. **Infer** How does Icarus try to be something he is not? What moral lesson can you learn from his failure?
9. **Extend** This story seems to suggest that people shouldn't try to "fly too high." We often hear the opposite advice: "Reach for the stars." When do you think taking chances is a good thing? When can it be dangerous?

Literary Skills Review: Character

10. **Compare** The myth of Orpheus includes warnings that the characters ignore. How is the story of Icarus similar to that myth?

Writing Focus

Think as a Reader/Writer

Use It in Your Writing Look at your notes on the author's descriptions of the wings. Now, write your own paragraph about flying. It can be based on your own experiences, or it can be fanciful.

What Do **You Think Now** How does the fascination with flight endure today?

Applying Your Skills

The Flight of Icarus

Vocabulary Development

Place Names from Greece and Rome

When the first Europeans settled in the land that became the United States, they needed names for their towns and cities. They often looked to ancient Rome and Greece for ideas.

Your Turn

Use the index of an atlas or another geographical reference book to identify the following:

Athens
Delphi
Olympia
Rome
Syracuse
Sparta

1. the state or states in which the American cities listed at the right are located
2. the location of the original Greek or Roman place known by each name

Academic Vocabulary

Talk About . . .

Explain the value of the <u>classic</u> myth "The Flight of Icarus." Although it says much about the importance of listening to good advice, what other messages does it convey about freedom and parental love? Use the Academic Vocabulary words in your discussion.

Language Coach

Multiple-Meaning Words Choose the answer in which the italicized word(s) is used in the same way it is used in the quotation from "The Flight of Icarus."

3. "He gathered the boy in his arms and flew to land, the tips of his wings dragging in the water from the double *burden* they *bore*."

   A The show was such a *bore* that it felt like a *burden* to be in the audience.

   B As she *bore* a hole into the metal, she decided to *burden* her partner with a request.

   C Carrying such a heavy *burden* was easy for Michelle when she thought about the loads she *bore* in her previous job.

4. "Keep at a *moderate* height, for if you fly too low, the fog and spray will clog your wings, and if you fly too high, the heat will melt the wax that holds them together."

   A She was called on to *moderate* the debate.

   B Keep at a *moderate* speed if you want to make sure you don't get a speeding ticket!

   C His politics were considered *moderate,* or middle of the road.

Learn It Online
For action-packed vocabulary lessons, visit:

go.hrw.com   L7-930   **Go**

Grammar Link

Using Comparative and Superlative Forms

A **modifier** is a word, a phrase, or a clause that describes or limits the meaning of another word. **Adjectives** and **adverbs** may be used to compare things. The three degrees of comparison of modifiers are **positive, comparative,** and **superlative.**

Positive	Comparative	Superlative
cold	colder	coldest
loud	louder	loudest
politely	more politely	most politely

Use the comparative degree when comparing two things. Use the superlative degree when comparing more than two things.

COMPARATIVE

This building is taller than the other one.
I ski more frequently than she does.

SUPERLATIVE

This building is the tallest one in the world.
Of the three of us, I ski most frequently.

Your Turn

In the sentences below, choose the correct form of comparison.

1. Daedalus was [*more/most*] cautious than Icarus.

2. While soaring higher and higher, Icarus felt that he was having the [*more/most*] enjoyable experience of his lifetime.

3. Of all of the inventors during the time in which he lived, Daedalus was the [*more/most*] creative.

CHOICES

As you respond to the Choices, use the **Academic Vocabulary** words as appropriate: classic, foundation, generation, intervene.

REVIEW

Choose the Best Moral

Timed ⓛ**Writing** From the three **morals** below, choose the one you think *best* expresses the message of "The Flight of Icarus." Then, write a paragraph in which you evaluate the moral. Why do you agree or disagree with it?

- Steer a middle course, and avoid extremes.
- Listen to your elders.
- If you aim too high, you will find trouble.

CONNECT

Write a Newspaper Story

Imagine that you are a news reporter on the scene, eager to interview Daedalus when he lands. Write a lead paragraph for the news story, being sure to include *what* happened, *why* it happened, to *whom* it happened, *when* and *where* it happened, and *how* it happened.

EXTEND

Create a Podcast

TechFocus Imagine you are Icarus, now in the underworld after your disastrous flight. Create a podcast describing how you felt during the flight and what it is like in Hades' dark kingdom. (See the myth "Orpheus, the Great Musician," page 915, for details about the underworld.)

THE TWELVE TASKS OF
HERACLES

by **Marcia Williams**

What Do You Think

Are people who are especially talented more likely to make friends or to make enemies?

 QuickWrite

Is it best to confront challenges with brains, brawn, or a combination of both? Write a paragraph explaining what you think.

Reader/Writer Notebook

Use your **RWN** to complete the activities for this selection.

Literary Focus

Characters in Conflict Characters in stories relate to one another the way people do in real life. These relationships are important to a story and often explain why characters come into **conflict** with one another.

- As you read this graphic story, think about the conflicts Heracles (HEHR uh kleez) faces. How does Heracles respond to challenges? What do his actions tell you about his character?
- Look for characters' **motivation**—the reasons they take the actions they do. How do Hera and Eurystheus (yu RIHS thee uhs) expect Heracles to behave? How does that help to explain their actions?

Reading Focus

Reading Graphic Stories A graphic story uses art and text to tell a story. Instead of just reading the text, as you would with a short story, you must also pay attention to the illustrations and make connections from one panel to the next.

Into Action In graphic stories you learn about characters and events through a combination of words and images. Keep track of what you learn from text and what you learn from illustrations.

What I Learned from Text	What I Learned from Illustrations
Heracles was a tough baby.	Heracles performed amazing feats as a boy.

Vocabulary

amends (uh MEHNDZ) *n.*: something done to make up for an injury. *Heracles tried to make amends with his enemy.*

dismayed (dihs MAYD) *adj.*: troubled; upset. *Heracles was dismayed to be assigned the twelve tasks.*

Language Coach

Synonyms Synonyms are words that have the same or nearly the same meanings as another word. For example, *troubled* and *upset* are synonyms for *dismayed*. Think of two other synonyms for *dismayed*.

Writing Focus

Think as a Reader/Writer

Find It in Your Reading List examples of the humor Williams uses to engage the reader and to reveal characters' personalities.

Learn It Online
Upgrade your vocabulary using Word Watch at:

go.hrw.com L7-933 **Go**

Marcia Williams
(1945–)

A Child Who Loved Stories

Marcia Williams spent her childhood living in Hong Kong, Nigeria, and the Middle East. Almost every evening, her mother or stepfather would read her a story before bedtime. She remembers:

> "I would often be scared, especially by fairy tales, but I never wanted the stories to end."

Storyteller . . . and Reteller

As an adult, Williams taught children in a nursery school. She quickly learned how to capture and keep their attention with stories. After she gave up teaching, she put her experience to good use in writing her popular comic-strip-style books. Williams has written her own stories and has retold many classic tales in books such as *Greek Myths, Mr. William Shakespeare's Plays,* and *The Adventures of Robin Hood.*

Think About the Writer

Why do you think stories might be important to someone who lived in many places as a child?

Build Background

Heracles (more commonly known as Hercules) is a mythical Greek hero who performs some of the most amazing feats of strength in all mythology. Like other mythological heroes, Heracles is the son of both a god (Zeus, or Jupiter) and a human being and so possesses special qualities. Like many other super-heroes, he demonstrates his powers when he is still in his cradle.

Preview the Selection

In this graphic story you will meet **Heracles,** a superhuman who accidentally offends a god. When he asks for forgiveness, he instead receives twelve impossible tasks to complete.

GREEK MYTHS FOR YOUNG CHILDREN. Copyright © 1991 by Marcia Williams. Reproduced by the publisher Candlewick Press, Inc. Cambridge, MA, on behalf of Walker Books Ltd., London.

Ⓐ **Literary Focus** **Characters in Conflict** Why does Heracles come into conflict with Hera?

Ⓑ **Read and Discuss** What has been set up for you?

Vocabulary **amends** (uh MEHNDZ) *n.*: something done to make up for an injury.

First, Heracles had to kill the lion of Nemea whose hide was so thick that no sword could penetrate it.

Next, he had to kill the many-headed Hydra, whose very breath could kill man or beast.

Third, he had to capture the sacred, golden-horned deer, an animal as swift as the wind.

The fourth task was to catch a savage boar whose tusks could pierce any armor.

Next, Heracles had to clean out the vast and filthy stables of King Augeas in a single night.

C **Reading Focus** **Reading Graphic Stories** Comment on Heracles' appearance as he completes each task. What do you learn about him from the illustrations?

Then he had to to destroy a flock of man-eating birds that hid in a dangerous swamp.

The seventh task was to capture the fire-breathing, marauding bull of Crete.

Next, he had to steal Diomedes's horses, which fed on human flesh.

Then Heracles had to fetch the golden girdle worn by the queen of the Amazon warrior women.

The tenth task was to seize the monster Geryon's cattle, guarded by his two-headed dog.

D **Reading Focus** **Reading Graphic Stories** How do you know King Eurystheus is upset that Heracles is still alive?

E **Read and Discuss** What do the different ways Heracles completes each task tell you about him?

The eleventh, to collect three golden apples protected by a ferocious dragon.

Heracles's twelfth and last task was the most dangerous of all: to fetch the three-headed guard dog, Cerberus, from Hades itself.

His twelve tasks completed, Heracles returned to King Eurystheus.

The king was dismayed to see him alive, and quickly sent him packing.

Then, to avoid angering the gods, Heracles sent Cerberus back to Hades.

At the temple, Heracles was finally pardoned.

He was content at last, and stronger than ever!

And Hera never bothered Heracles again.

F **Read and Discuss** How does the king react to Heracles and his tasks?

Vocabulary **dismayed** (dihs MAYD) *adj.:* troubled; upset.

G **Literary Focus** **Characters in Conflict** How is the conflict between Heracles and Hera resolved?

Applying Your Skills

SKILLS FOCUS Literary Skills Analyze character; analyze conflict; analyze the moral of a myth. **Reading Skills** Read a graphic story. **Vocabulary Skills** Demonstrate knowledge of literal meanings of words and their usage. **Writing Skills** Analyze the writer's technique.

The Twelve Tasks of Heracles

Respond and Think Critically

Reading Focus

Quick Check

1. What is Heracles known for as he grows up?
2. What does Hera's spell cause Heracles to do?
3. What happens to Heracles by the end of the story?

Read with a Purpose

4. Which of Heracles' characteristics help him complete the twelve tasks?

Reading Skills: Reading Graphic Stories

5. Review the chart you made as you read "The Twelve Tasks of Heracles," and think about what the illustrations added to the story. List two ways in which narrative text and graphics are similar and two ways in which they are different.

✓ Vocabulary Check

6. What action would you take to make **amends** with someone with whom you are arguing?
7. How do you react when someone you like is **dismayed**?

Literary Focus

Literary Analysis

8. **Interpret** Why does King Eurystheus hide in a pot when Heracles approaches him?
9. **Analyze** How does Heracles react when he is given the challenges? What does his reaction tell you about his character?

Literary Skills: Characters in Conflict

10. **Analyze** Heracles finds himself in a series of conflicts. In a chart like the one below, list the characters Heracles comes into conflict with, a description of the conflicts, and the way the conflicts are resolved.

Character	Conflict	Result
Hera	tries to kill Heracles or ruin his life	Hera cannot bother Heracles anymore.

Literary Skills Review: Moral

11. **Interpret** Myths usually contain **morals,** or lessons about life. What lesson about life do you find in "The Twelve Tasks of Heracles"?

Writing Focus

Think as a Reader/Writer

Use It in Your Writing Review your notes about the use of humor in the story. Did you find it effective? What did the humor add to or take away from the myth? Respond to these questions in a paragraph.

 What Do **You Think Now** After reading "The Twelve Tasks of Heracles," have your feelings about how to confront challenges changed? Explain.

Master Frog

Vietnamese,
retold by
Lynette Dyer Vuong

The Frog Prince by Lou Wall.

What Do
You
Think

How do people discover
qualities and talents that
lie beneath the surface?

QuickWrite

What are your hidden qualities and talents? List some
of the things you're good at, and then write a few
sentences about the one that is your favorite.

Reader/Writer Notebook

Use your **RWN** to complete the activities for this selection.

Literary Focus

Motifs in Folk Tales: Metamorphosis This story involves a **metamorphosis** (meht uh MAWR fuh sihs)—a fantastic transformation, or change, from one shape to another. Shape changes are common motifs in comics, myths, and fairy tales. In numerous folk tales, for example, a frog with bulging eyes turns into a handsome prince when someone loves him despite his appearance. In this story a frog changes shape; however, the metamorphosis has an unusual twist.

Reading Focus

Making Predictions Before you read, follow these steps to make accurate predictions:

- Think about your prior experience with folk tales.
- Remember what you've learned about **metamorphosis.**
- Look through the story. Then, write a sentence predicting what will happen in this story.

Into Action As you read "Master Frog," write your predictions in a chart like the one below.

When	I predict...
1. Giang Dung gives birth to a frog.	that the story is about a frog who is raised like a human.
2. Giang Dung raises the frog as best she can.	that the frog is marked for greatness.

Writing Focus

Think as a Reader/Writer

Find It in Your Reading How does the author describe Master Frog at the beginning of the story? How do the descriptions change as Master Frog's appearance changes?

Vocabulary

admonished (ad MAHN ihshd) *v.*: warned or urged. *The teacher admonished his students to pay attention to the lesson.*

presumptuous (prih ZUHMP chu uhs) *adj.*: too bold; arrogant. *The king believed that Master Frog's request to marry his daughter was both rude and presumptuous.*

cowered (KOW uhrd) *v.*: crouched or trembled in fear. *When the tiger roared, everyone cowered in fear.*

deception (dih SEHP shuhn) *n.*: act of deliberately making a person believe something that is not true. *The two sisters were angry at what they saw as Master Frog's deception.*

prosperity (prahs PEHR uh tee) *n.*: condition of having money and being successful. *The people of the kingdom enjoyed great prosperity and lived well.*

Language Coach

Synonyms Words that are similar in meaning are called **synonyms.** Which of the definitions above include synonyms?

Learn It Online
Take an in-depth look at these Vocabulary words at:

go.hrw.com [L7-941]

Lynette Dyer Vuong
(1938–   )

Finding Folk Tales

Lynette Dyer Vuong believes in love at first sight, because that's what she experienced when she met a young Vietnamese man who was studying in the United States. Love led her to follow him back to Vietnam, marry him, and stay there with him for thirteen years—while the country was in the midst of the Vietnam War.

As Vuong learned to speak Vietnamese, she began to follow another love—the world of folklore and fairy tales. She was amazed to discover that Vietnam has its own versions of five stories she loved as a child—"Cinderella," "Thumbelina," "The Frog Prince," "Rip Van Winkle," and "Goose Girl." She remembers her discovery:

> "Five familiar faces in an unfamiliar land; it is fascinating that similar ideas have arisen and then developed into different stories under the influence of two such diverse cultures as East and West. Perhaps it is a testimony to the fact that we are each uniquely individual . . . yet bound together by a common humanity."

Vuong fled Vietnam with her husband and children in 1975. She continues to retell the fairy tales she loves.

Think About the Writer — Why does Vuong retell stories that are common to both Vietnam and the United States?

Build Background

"Master Frog" isn't the only story about how looks can be deceiving. Other folk tales with this theme that you may be familiar with include "Beauty and the Beast," "The Ugly Duckling," and "The Frog Prince."

Preview the Selection

Master Frog is a normal boy in all ways except two: He is a frog, and he wants to marry the king's daughter, **Kien Tien** (kee N tee EHN). Although Kien Tien's sisters, **Kim Chau** (kihm choh) and **Bich Ngoc** (bihk nahp), cannot see past Master Frog's homely appearance, Kien Tien understands that he is both powerful and kind.

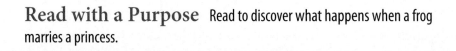

Master Frog

Vietnamese, retold by **Lynette Dyer Vuong**

Giang Dung[1] was a plain girl, so plain in fact that all the townspeople marveled when her parents finally found her a husband. Then they nodded their heads knowingly and whispered to one another that the young man must have been after her father's money. He had plenty of it, it was true, and Giang Dung was his only child. The day of the wedding came and passed, and the people found more interesting things to gossip about until a few months later, when Giang Dung's husband died.

"It's fortunate that she's expecting a child," one person said, and the rest agreed. "At least she'll have someone to look after her in her old age. It's certain she'll never find anyone else to marry her." (A)

But when the child was born, instead of being a boy to carry on her husband's name or at least a girl to give her some comfort and companionship, it was only a frog. And the people's tongues wagged again until they tired of the subject. "What would you expect? Giang Dung almost looks like a frog herself, she's so ugly."

Poor Giang Dung cried for days until she had no tears left. Then she resigned herself to her fate and determined to raise the frog as well as she could. If she was being punished for some unknown evil she had committed, she would have to make the best of it and serve her sentence. But on the other hand, Heaven sometimes worked in mysterious ways, and it was just possible that some great destiny lay ahead for her son. (B)

But as the years passed, Giang Dung forgot both of these theories. Except for his strange appearance, Master Frog was really quite an ordinary boy—now mischievous, now helpful, but always affectionate. He followed her around the house as she went about her daily tasks, helping her to care for the silkworms.[2] He gathered mulberry leaves for her to chop and place in their trays; he watched

---

1. **Giang Dung** (zahng zoon): Vietnamese for "pretty face," an ironic name for a plain girl.

2. **silkworms:** moth caterpillars that produce cocoons of silk fiber. Some silkworms are grown and cultivated as the source of silk.

(A) **Read and Discuss** What picture does the author paint of Giang Dung's life?

(B) **Literary Focus** Metamorphosis How does Giang handle the fact that her son is a frog?

them as they began to spin their cocoons, fascinated at the way they swung their heads down and round and then up again to surround themselves with the fine strands. He often perched beside her as she sat at the loom and thought it great fun to take the shuttle in his mouth and wriggle his small body in and out among the warp threads. Sometimes, as she was cooking, he would hop up on the stove to stir the soup, or if he was sure she was not watching him, to snap up some tasty tidbit with his long, sticky tongue. But, like other children, he was often bored with being indoors and went out to play hide-and-seek and hopscotch with the boys of the neighborhood. All in all, he was both a good-natured and an intelligent little fellow, and his mother decided at last that something must be done about his education. **C**

"A frog? In my class?" the teacher demanded when Giang Dung brought him to the school. "Impossible! I would be the laughingstock of the town."

"Then at least let him sit at the back and listen," she pleaded with him. "I promise you he won't cause you any trouble."

As the weeks went by, Master Frog proved himself such a model student that at last the teacher moved him up to the head of the class and often admonished the others to follow his example. At first he had tried to grasp the brush with his front feet but later found that he could form more graceful characters if he held it in his mouth. Generally he was the first to commit a passage to memory, and if none of the others could correctly interpret a line of the reading, the teacher would call on Master Frog. Finally, Master Frog completed his education and grew to young froghood.

"It's time to think of learning some trade," Giang Dung suggested to him one day. "Tomorrow I will go to town and talk to some of the craftsmen. Perhaps one of them would be willing to take you on as an apprentice."

But Master Frog shook his head. "Mother, first I would like to get married."

"G . . . get married!" she stammered, almost unable to believe her ears. "I . . . is there any particular girl you have in mind?"

"Yes, Mother. Princess Kien Tien,[3] the king's youngest daughter."

Giang Dung drew back in alarm. "Son, you must be out of your mind! How could you ever hope to marry the king's daughter?"

3. **Kien Tien:** (kee N tee EHN).

C Read and Discuss How would you characterize Master Frog as a boy so far?

Vocabulary admonished (ad MAHN ihshd) v.: warned or urged.

"Nevertheless I shall marry her." Master Frog planted all four feet on the table in a stance of determination. "Tomorrow I shall go to the king to ask for her hand." **D**

All Giang Dung's protests—all her entreaties —were in vain. Master Frog had made up his mind, and nothing could change it. And so the next morning he and Giang Dung set off for the palace.

Giang Dung set him down as they entered the audience hall, and he hopped straight up to the king, bowing respectfully as he neared the throne. The king stared at him in astonishment as he made his request and then burst out laughing.

"So you want to marry my daughter," he said. "Well, I have three daughters. Which one is it you want? But don't be in a hurry to make up your mind." His lips twisted in amusement as he motioned to one of the courtiers.[4] "Bring their royal highnesses here."

"Come here, my dears," he beckoned to them as they entered the hall. "A suitor has presented himself to request the hand of one of you." With a grand sweep of his forearm he indicated Master Frog at the foot of the throne. "He has not yet told me the extent of his kingdom or the number of vassals[5] who

> *"We have carried this joke far enough."*

pay him tribute, but does he not have a noble air?" He turned back to Master Frog. "Allow me to introduce my daughters to your highness: Kim Chau,"[6] he pointed to the first, who cast a contemptuous[7] glance in Master Frog's direction, then gave her head such a violent toss that one of her pearl hairpins slipped from its place and fell to the floor; "Bich Ngoc,"[8] he indicated the second, who made a face at him and stuck out her tongue; "and Kien Tien," he presented the last of the three, who had stood the whole time, her hands folded in her long sleeves and her eyes on the floor. "Now would you please tell me which of the three pleases you?" **E**

Kim Chau's chin rose a trifle higher. "I won't marry him, Father."

"I'll kill myself if you force me to marry him," Bich Ngoc declared with a stamp of her foot.

"Your Majesty," Master Frog interrupted them, "it is Kien Tien whose hand I have come to seek."

"Enough of this charade." The king's face had grown angry. "We have carried this joke

---

4. **courtiers** (KAWR tee uhrz): royal attendants.
5. **vassals**: subjects.

6. **Kim Chau** (kihm choh): *Kim* and *chau* are Vietnamese for "gold" and "pearl or precious stone."
7. **contemptuous** (kuhn TEHMP chu uhs): scornful; snobbish.
8. **Bich Ngoc** (bihk nahp): *Ngoc* is Vietnamese for "emerald."

D **Reading Focus** **Making Predictions** Think of what you know about folk tales. Do you think Master Frog will marry Princess Kien Tien?

E **Read and Discuss** What does the king's reaction to Master Frog's request show you about the king?

far enough." He motioned to the guards. "Take this presumptuous creature out of my sight at once and execute him."

As the king finished speaking, Master Frog croaked in a loud voice. Suddenly the building began to shake as lightning flashed and thunder roared. On all sides the doors flew open, and the guards cowered in terror as wild beasts of every description burst into the hall. Elephants trumpeted as they stampeded in, tigers roared, leopards and panthers growled as they sprang from one corner to another.

"A few minutes ago Your Majesty inquired about my vassals," Master Frog's croak rose above the uproar. "They have come. I will leave them here to answer any questions you may have about the extent of my kingdom. Until we meet again, Your Majesty." Master Frog turned and hopped toward the exit.

"Wait! Wait!" the king shouted after him as a tiger leapt over his throne, pursuing a panther in a game of tag. "You can't leave us like this, surrounded by all these wild beasts." But Master Frog only hopped over their backs, one after another, as he made his way to the door. "Daughters, what shall we do?"

"I wouldn't marry a frog if he were the son of Jade Emperor!" Kim Chau's voice was as haughty as ever, though she winced[9] as a leopard brushed past her.

Bich Ngoc covered her face as a bear lumbered toward her. "I'd rather be torn limb from limb!" she screeched.

"Father, I'll marry him." Kien Tien squeezed between two elephants to the king's side. "It's not right for us to think only of ourselves when the whole kingdom may be in danger. And the frog cannot be such a bad sort. He's obviously an individual of great power, yet he does not appear to be cruel. With all these beasts surrounding us, not one of us has been harmed." **F**

As she finished speaking, the uproar ceased, and one by one the beasts filed from the hall. Master Frog stood alone before the king.

"I will send the engagement gifts tomorrow," he said as he, too, turned and hopped from the room.

A few days later the wedding was celebrated with great pomp and ceremony. Kings and dignitaries[10] of all the surrounding countries came to pay their respects, and no one dared to laugh at Master Frog or the princess, for the tales of his great power had spread far and wide.

During the weeks that followed, Master Frog and Kien Tien lived together happily as the two came to understand each other better and to care for each other more deeply. In spite of his ugliness, Kien Tien found him such an intelligent and such a pleasant companion that as the days went by, she grew genuinely fond of him. Then one morning she awoke to find the frog lying dead on the pillow beside her.

---

9. **winced** (wihnst): drew back in fear, making a face.

10. **dignitaries:** people holding high positions.

F | Read and Discuss | What is happening with all the animals and panicked people?

Vocabulary **presumptuous** (prih ZUHMP chu uhs) *adj.*: too bold; arrogant.
cowered (KOW uhrd) *v.*: crouched or trembled in fear.

With a cry she lifted her husband's body to her lips, kissing it again and again as her tears wet the mottled[11] green skin. Someone called her name, and she looked up to see a handsome young man standing next to the bed, his arms outstretched as if to embrace her. **G**

She backed away from him, crying out in alarm. "How dare you come here?" she demanded. "Can't you see my husband is dead and I am mourning him?" Suddenly her eyes narrowed. "Or was it you who killed him, you miserable creature!" She burst into fresh tears. "You shall surely die for your crime!"

The man smiled. "No, Kien Tien. I am Master Frog. What you are holding there is only my skin, which I shed during the night." He sat down beside her. "I am a fairy, a heavenly mandarin,[12] one of the sons of Jade Emperor. I was bored with the life in Fairyland and wanted to seek adventure in the world below. But when I asked my father's permission, he was angry with me. He said he would grant my request but that I must be born as a frog. Only if I could succeed in that form would I be able to resume my true shape. Now I have proved myself and am allowed to shed the frog's skin. But you must put the skin away carefully where no harm can come to it because if it should ever be destroyed, I would have to return immediately to Jade Emperor's palace." **H**

Overjoyed at her good fortune, Kien Tien did as he said. The days that followed

---

11. **mottled** (MAHT uhld): spotted or streaked.

12. **mandarin:** here, a member of any powerful group.

G **Literary Focus** Metamorphosis Many folk tales involve a metamorphosis, or shape change. Who do you predict the handsome young man will turn out to be?

H **Read and Discuss** What is happening now?

Analyzing Visuals

Viewing and Interpreting How does this image relate to the folk tale you are reading?

Beauty and the Beast.

947

were full of joy for the newlyweds. The king was filled with pride at the handsomeness and intelligence of his son-in-law, which matched so well the beauty and talent of his youngest daughter. He took them wherever he went to show them off. On every trip that he made to the surrounding countries, they accompanied him in his golden palanquin,[13] and when he rode through the streets of the capital, they sat beside him on the back of his white elephant, cheered by all who watched them pass.

"Why didn't he tell us who he was in the first place?" Kim Chau grumbled to her sister as they watched the parade from the palace balcony. "Was it fair to come in that ugly old frog skin and then change into a handsome prince after he'd married Kien Tien?"

"If she was dumb enough to marry a frog, he should have stayed a frog," Bich Ngoc grunted in agreement.

"He should be punished for his deception. What right did he have to ask for Kien Tien anyway? I'm the oldest."

"Kien Tien says he's a son of Jade Emperor, but I don't believe it. He's probably nothing but an ordinary frog. Why don't we see if we can find his skin and have a look at it?" ❶

The sisters went to Kien Tien's room, searching through chest after chest and shelf after shelf till at last, among a pile of her most precious silks, they found what they were looking for.

---

13. **palanquin** (pal uhn KEEN): covered structure enclosing a couch. A palanquin is carried by long poles resting on the shoulders of two or more men.

"She hid it well enough," Kim Chau sniffed. "No wonder. It's an ugly old thing, isn't it?"

Bich Ngoc reached for it, turning it over in her hands. "It certainly is. And just as I thought, nothing but an ordinary frog skin." She squinted her eyes thoughtfully. "Who knows but what, if we caught a couple of frogs for ourselves, they might shed their skins for us? There might be a handsome prince in any one of them if we could just get him to come out." She stuffed Master Frog's skin into her sash as the two of them hurried out to the pond.

Day by day Kim Chau and Bich Ngoc watched their chosen frogs, waiting for the hoped-for transformation. They fed them on the most delicious foods; petted them; cooed endearments and whispered promises of fame, fortune, and riches in their ears. And each night they gently laid them on the pillow next to them, certain that the coming morning would bring the answer to their dreams. But nothing happened; both frogs remained as they were when they had fished them from the pond.

"There has to be a prince in there!" Bich Ngoc cried one morning in exasperation. "And I'm not going to wait any longer to find him." She picked up a knife and began to skin the poor creature alive.

Kim Chau snatched up her own frog and followed her example. But before they were finished, it was plain that no prince was to be found. In disgust the sisters threw the corpses into the fireplace.

---

❶ **Read and Discuss** What does the way the king now treats Kien Tien and Master Frog reveal about him?

Vocabulary **deception** (dih SEHP shuhn) *n.*: act of deliberately making a person believe something that is not true.

Bich Ngoc jerked Master Frog's skin from her belt. "I don't know what I'm still carrying this around for," she grunted as she tossed it into the fire.

Meanwhile in Kien Tien's room, she and Master Frog were just getting out of bed. Suddenly he gave a cry of pain.

"My chest, my arms, my legs are burning!" he cried. "My whole body is on fire."

As Kien Tien rushed to his side, he fell to the floor, writhing in agony. Moments later he lay lifeless in her arms. Kien Tien pressed him close to her, weeping bitterly.

"It must be because you burned his old frog skin," Kim Chau whispered to Bich Ngoc when they heard what had happened. "What are we going to do? Sooner or later she'll discover the skin is missing, and if she finds out we took it and tells Father . . ."

Bich Ngoc clapped her hand over her sister's mouth. "We aren't going to sit around and wait for that to happen!"

Together they went to Kien Tien's room, where she lay on the bed weeping. They sat down beside her, stroking her hair to comfort her. **J**

"Come, little sister, it's a terrible tragedy, but you mustn't spend the whole day lying here crying." Bich Ngoc poured some tea from the teapot on the table, dropping a little sleeping powder into the cup as she carried it back to the bed. "Here, drink something warm. It'll make you feel better."

Kien Tien raised her head, sipping the hot liquid as Bich Ngoc held it to her lips. Then she lay down again and was soon fast asleep.

Quickly the sisters lifted her and carried her outside to the carriage. As fast as they could make the horses go, they rode out of town to the seaside. Then, making sure that no one was around, they shoved their sister out of the carriage, watching with satisfaction as she hit the surface of the water and sank beneath the waves. Then they rushed home to tell their father that Kien Tien had committed suicide.

"We tried to stop her," Bich Ngoc sobbed into her handkerchief. "But she wouldn't listen to us. She was so miserable at the thought of never seeing Master Frog again that she threw herself into the sea. The waves carried her away before we could call for help." **K**

Suddenly gasps rose throughout the audience hall. Master Frog had entered the room.

He approached the throne, bowing respectfully. "Jade Emperor has allowed me to return to the earth to complete my lifetime," he told the king. "But why is everyone crying? What has happened?" He gazed from one person to another, seeking an answer.

"Dear brother-in-law, our sister is dead."

> *Suddenly gasps rose throughout the audience hall.*

J **Reading Focus** **Making Predictions** Knowing what you do about the sisters, what do you think they are up to now?

K **Read and Discuss** How do the sisters' actions connect to what you already know about them?

Bich Ngoc wiped the tears from her eyes as she spoke. "She was so overcome with sorrow at losing you that she threw herself into the sea." She stepped closer to him, laying her hand on his arm. "I know what a shock it is for you. But Kim Chau and I will do everything we can to help. Either one of us would be willing to take our sister's place."

But Master Frog was already running toward the door. At his order a horse was saddled, and he leapt on its back, riding at top speed toward the sea. Fearlessly he dove in, letting his body sink to the bottom. Swiftly he ran across the ocean floor to the Crystal Palace and, bursting through the gates, prostrated himself before the Dragon King of the Waters.

The Dragon King gazed down at him kindly. "Stand up, nephew. What you are seeking may be behind you."

As Master Frog rose, a company of shrimps and turtles entered the hall. One of them bore Kien Tien in his arms.

"My soldiers have found your wife," the Dragon King told him. "I would have let her live here in my palace, but since you've come for her, you may take her home with you."

Master Frog rushed toward her joyfully. As he lifted her from the turtle-soldier's arms,

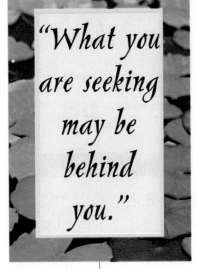

"What you are seeking may be behind you."

she opened her eyes and smiled up at him. Then both of them fell at the Dragon King's feet to thank him for his mercy.

Master Frog led Kien Tien out of the Crystal Palace and up through the water to the shore, where his horse was waiting. Together they rode back to the palace. **L**

Kim Chau glanced down from her balcony to see Master Frog reining his horse below. She drew back in alarm and called to her sister.

"We're done for," she trembled, grabbing Bich Ngoc's arm and pulling her after her. "Kien Tien will tell Father everything."

The two of them raced down the stairs and out a back way. "We'll hide in the forest," Bich Ngoc decided. "No one will find us there."

And the two were never seen or heard of again. But as for Kien Tien and Master Frog, they lived happily ever after, loved and respected by all for their kind deeds. Before many days had passed, they had Giang Dung brought to the palace, where she lived in comfort and happiness to a ripe old age. In due time Master Frog became king and, with Kien Tien as his queen, ruled their people in peace and prosperity for many long years. **M**

L **Reading Focus** Making Predictions How do you think the story will end?

M **Read and Discuss** How have things turned out for everyone?

Vocabulary **prosperity** (prahs PEHR uh tee) *n.*: condition of having money and being successful.

Applying Your Skills

Master Frog

Respond and Think Critically

Reading Focus

Quick Check

1. What are some of Master Frog's good qualities?
2. What does Master Frog do when the king threatens to execute him?

Read with a Purpose

3. What makes the marriage between Master Frog and Kien Tien work?

Reading Skills: Making Predictions

4. **Into Action** Review the predictions you made. Now, add a third column to your chart. Mark whether or not your predictions were correct, and think about why you made the predictions you did.

When	I predict...	Correct?
1. Giang Dung gives birth to a frog.	that the story is about a frog who is raised like a human.	Yes
2. Giang Dung raises the frog as best she can.	that the frog is marked for greatness.	Yes
3.		

Literary Focus

Literary Analysis

5. **Interpret** What is surprising about the twist at the end of the story?

6. **Analyze** What qualities does Kien Tien admire in Master Frog even before she realizes that he is a prince?
7. **Extend** What lessons do you think this story teaches?
8. **Evaluate** Kien Tien can look beyond Master Frog's appearance and see the person within, but her sisters can't. Do you think most people are like Kien Tien, or are they like her sisters? Why do you think so?

Literary Skills: Motifs in Folk Tales: Metamorphosis

9. **Analyze** How do Kim Chau's and Bich Ngoc's feelings about Master Frog change after his metamorphosis? What does their sudden change of heart tell you about them?

Literary Skills Review: Character

10. **Analyze** What is different about the ways Kien Tien, Kim Chau, and Bich Ngoc first react to Master Frog? What does this tell you about each girl's character?

Writing Focus

Think as a Reader/Writer

Use It in Your Writing Review your notes on the author's descriptions of Master Frog. Then, write a paragraph in which you analyze the change in Master Frog's character.

What Do **You Think Now** Describe your good qualities and talents. Explain why they are important to you.

Applying Your Skills

Master Frog

Vocabulary Development

Prefixes and Suffixes

The Vocabulary words contain several useful prefixes and suffixes. A **prefix** is a word part added to the front of a word to change its meaning; a **suffix** is a word part added to the end of a word to change its meaning.

Your Turn

Using a dictionary, make word maps for these prefixes and suffixes:

ad–	pre–	de–
–ment	–ity	–tion

Use the word map below as a model. The prefix *non–* is shown as an example.

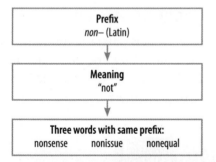

Prefix
non– (Latin)

↓

Meaning
"not"

↓

Three words with same prefix:
nonsense   nonissue   nonequal

✓ Vocabulary Check

1. Name two celebrities who are known for their **prosperity.**
2. How would you approach an animal that **cowered** in a corner?
3. Describe a time when you **admonished** a classmate.
4. What is a consequence of being **presumptuous**?
5. How would you respond to a **deception** committed by a friend?

Language Coach

Synonyms Match each Vocabulary word with a word that has a similar meaning.

6. **admonished**	**a.** lie
7. **presumptuous**	**b.** warned
8. **deception**	**c.** richness
9. **cowered**	**d.** bold
10. **prosperity**	**e.** shrank

Academic Vocabulary

Talk About . . .

In a small group, discuss the purpose of this folk tale. How does its message reflect the values at the <u>foundation</u> of <u>classic</u> Vietnamese culture? Use the Academic Vocabulary words in your discussion.

Learn It Online
Give your word knowledge a boost with *WordSharp*:

go.hrw.com   L7-952   **Go**

Grammar Link

Don't Leave Your Modifiers Dangling

It's easy to make the mistake of "hanging" a modifying phrase on a sentence (usually at the beginning) and forgetting to include the word it modifies.

DANGLING Reading folk tales aloud, our understanding of them improved. [Who was reading the folk tales aloud?]

CLEAR Reading folk tales aloud, **we** noticed that our understanding of them improved.

Ask yourself *to whom* or *what* the modifying phrase is referring. If it isn't clear, you've got a dangling modifier.

Your Turn

Find and fix the dangling modifiers in these sentences. You will have to rewrite some of them.

1. Wanting her to get married, Giang Dung was introduced to a young man.
2. Born a frog, it was not easy for him to find acceptance.
3. Looking back on it now, the sisters were spiteful people.
4. Being generous and kind, the people enjoyed peace and prosperity under their new ruler.

Writing Applications Read through a sample of your own writing to make sure every modifier you used has something to modify. First, circle all your modifying phrases. Then, correct any danglers you find.

CHOICES

As you respond to the Choices, use the **Academic Vocabulary** words as appropriate: <u>classic</u>, <u>foundation</u>, <u>generation</u>, <u>intervene</u>.

REVIEW
Write a Character Analysis

Timed ◡ Writing Write a character analysis of Master Frog. Include details about his life, from his birth to the rescue of his beloved. Open with a statement that describes three of Master Frog's character traits. Then, cite actions from the text that illustrate those traits.

CONNECT
Write Alternate Endings

Apply some "What if?" questions to this story to explore different possible outcomes. For example, what might have happened if Kien Tien had been repulsed by Master Frog? Or what if Kien Tien's sisters were not jealous of her? Choose one of these "What if?" scenarios, and write a paragraph explaining how the characters, events, and themes would change as a result of the different scenarios.

EXTEND
Present a Reader's Theater

With a few classmates, select a dramatic scene from "Master Frog" and present it to the class as a reader's theater presentation. Look for a scene that has important action and a sharp conflict, such as the king rejecting Master Frog as a match for his daughter. Practice your presentation, and perform it for the class.

The Crane Wife

told by **Sumiko Yagawa**
translated from
the Japanese by
Katherine Paterson

What Do You Think?

Why might you ignore a
warning from someone who
is concerned for you?

 QuickWrite

Record notes on an instance when you ignored a
warning. What consequences did you face?

Reader/Writer Notebook

Use your **RWN** to complete the activities for this selection.

Literary Focus

Motifs in Folk Tales: Taboo This folk tale is about the breaking of a **taboo,** a prohibition against something. Some societies, for instance, forbid the eating of certain foods. A taboo is a common motif in myths as well as folk tales. In "Orpheus, the Great Musician," for example, Orpheus is allowed to lead his wife out of the underworld as long as he doesn't look back at her. If you remember what happens when he does look back, you may predict something bad will happen involving a broken taboo in this story, too. As you read "The Crane Wife," watch for the taboo, and think about whether you would have behaved as Yohei did.

Reading Focus

Drawing Conclusions Any time you read, you probably draw many **conclusions** about what is happening in the text. You decide whether the characters are good or bad or whether an outcome is fair or unfair. You base your conclusions on your own prior knowledge, experience, and beliefs and on details in the text.

Into Action Keep track of the conclusions you draw as you read "The Crane Wife."

Conclusion	What I Already Know	Evidence from Text
Yohei is a kind, gentle man.	Only kind people tend an animal's (or stranger's) wounds.	"He . . . drew out the arrow, and very carefully tended its wound."

Writing Focus

Think as a Reader/Writer

Find It in Your Reading Take note of the woman's words as she warns her husband not to look in on her. They foreshadow the trouble ahead.

Vocabulary

exquisite (EHKS kwih ziht) *adj.:* beautiful and delicate. *The exquisite cloth commanded a high price at the market.*

perplexed (puhr PLEHKST) *v.:* made confused. *Yohei was perplexed when his wife delivered the strange warning that he not look at her while she was weaving.*

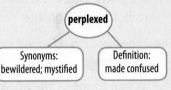

Language Coach

Definitions Sometimes writers give clues to a word's meaning by placing a definition nearby. Look at this sentence: *You could tell that Yohei was perplexed because of the confused look on his face.* Which words tell you what *perplexed* means?

Learn It Online
Go beyond the definitions with Word Watch at:

go.hrw.com L7-955 Go

Katherine Paterson
(1932–)

National Book Award WINNER

"Searching for a Place to Stand"

Katherine Paterson was born in China, where both of her parents served as missionaries. Of the early years of her life, when her family moved frequently, she has written:

> "I remember the many schools I attended in those years mostly as places where I felt fear and humiliation. . . . I was a misfit both in the classroom and on the playground. Outside of school, however, I lived a rich, imaginative life."

Paterson has also reflected on the effect this background had on her writing:

> "When I look at the books I have written, the first thing I see is the outcast child searching for a place to stand."

Paterson has drawn on both her rich inner life and her difficult childhood experiences in writing her highly acclaimed young adult novels.

Think About the Writer

Why do you think Paterson is drawn to writing folk tales?

Build Background

This Japanese folk tale has been told and retold through many generations. Like many folk tales, it explores both love and greed. Read the story, and try to figure out its lesson.

Two-panel folding screen depicting cranes by Sakai Hoitsu (1761–1828). Ink, colors, and gold on paper.

Preview the Selection

In this story, you will read about **Yohei,** a poor peasant. One day, Yohei helps a wounded **crane.** Later that same night, a lovely **young woman** asks him to allow her to become his wife. Read the story to find out how the couple fares.

The Crane Wife

told by **Sumiko Yagawa**
translated from
the Japanese by
Katherine Paterson

In a faraway mountain village, where the snow falls deep and white, there once lived all alone a poor young peasant named Yohei. One day, at the beginning of winter, Yohei went out into the snow to run an errand, and, as he hurried home, suddenly *basabasa* he heard a rustling sound. It was a crane, dragging its wing, as it swooped down and landed on the path. Now Yohei could see that the bird was in great pain, for an arrow had pierced its wing. He went to where the crane lay, drew out the arrow, and very carefully tended its wound. **Ⓐ**

Late that night there came a tapping *hotohoto* on the door of Yohei's hut. It seemed very peculiar for someone to be calling at that time of night. When he slid open the door to look out, there before him stood a beautiful young woman.

"I beg you, sir," she said in a voice both delicate and refined, "please allow me to become your wife." **Ⓑ**

Yohei could hardly believe his ears. The more closely he looked, the more noble and lovely the woman appeared. Gently he took her hand and brought her inside.

"Yohei has got some fine wife at his house," the villagers gossiped among themselves.

Ⓐ **Read and Discuss** How has the author started this tale off?

Ⓑ **Reading Focus** **Drawing Conclusions** Knowing what you do about <u>classic</u> fairy tales, what can you conclude about the identity of the young woman?

And it was true. The young woman was modest and kind, and she served Yohei faithfully. He could no longer recognize the cold, cold dreary hut where he had lived all alone, his house had become so bright and warm. The simple Yohei was happier than he could have ever dreamed.

In reality, however, with two mouths to feed instead of one, poor Yohei became poorer than he was before. And, since it was winter and there was no work to be found, he was very quickly coming to the bottom of what he had stored away.

At this point the young woman had a suggestion. "The other women of the village have looms upon which to weave cloth," she said. "If you would be so kind as to allow it, I should like to try my hand at weaving too."

In the back room of the hut, the young woman set up a loom and closed it off with sliding paper doors. Then she said to Yohei, "Please, I beg you, I beg you, never look in upon me while I am weaving." **C**

Tonkara tonkara. For three days and three nights the sound of the loom continued. Without stopping either to eat or drink, the young woman went on weaving and weaving. Finally, on the fourth day, she came out. To Yohei she seemed strangely thin and completely exhausted as, without a word, she held out to him a bolt of material.

And such exquisite cloth it was! Even Yohei, who had absolutely no knowledge of woven goods, could only stare in astonishment at the elegant, silken fabric.

Yohei took the cloth and set out for town. There he was able to sell it for such a high price that for a while the two of them had enough money to live quite comfortably and pleasantly. **D**

The winter, however, stretched on and on until, finally, there was very little money left. Yohei hesitated to say anything, so he kept quiet, but at last the young woman spoke up. "I shall weave on the loom one more time. But, please, let this be the last." And, once more, having been warned not to look in on the woman as she wove, the simple Yohei settled down to wait outside just as she asked.

This time the weaving took four days and four nights. A second time the young woman appeared carrying a bolt of cloth, but now she seemed thinner and more pathetic than before. The fabric, moreover, was lighter and even more beautiful. It seemed almost to glow with a light all its own. **E**

Yohei sold the material for an even higher price than the first time. "My," he marveled, "what a good wife I have!" The money bag he carried was heavy, but Yohei's heart was light, and he fairly skipped as he hurried home.

Now, the man next door had noticed that Yohei seemed to be living far more grandly than he had in the old days, and he was most curious. Pretending to be very casual about it all, he made his way through the snow and began to chat. Yohei, being a

---

C **Literary Focus** Taboo What is the taboo here? Why do you think it might be important?

D **Read and Discuss** What is happening now?

E **Read and Discuss** What is the author letting you know?

Vocabulary **exquisite** (EHKS kwih ziht) *adj.*: beautiful and delicate.

Spinning Wheel (c. 1890). Illustration from the booklet *Au Japon Types, Costumes, & Moeurs*. Paris.

Analyzing Visuals **Viewing and Interpreting** How does the woman in this image help you connect to the young woman in the story?

simple and innocent fellow, told the neighbor how his wife's woven goods had brought a wonderful price.

The man became more curious than ever. "Tell me," he said, "just what kind of thread does your wife use? My woman's cotton cloth never fetched a price like that. If your wife's stuff is as marvelous as you say, you ought to take it to the capital, to the home of some noble. You could probably sell it for ten times—for a hundred times more. Say, how about it? Why don't you let me do it for you? We'd split the profits right down the middle. Just think of it! We could live out the rest of our lives doing nothing but sitting back and fanning ourselves." **F**

Before Yohei's very eyes, gold coins great and small began to dazzle and dance. If only he could get his wife to relent, if only he could persuade her to weave again, they could seize such a fortune as had never been known before.

When Yohei presented her with this idea, the young woman seemed quite perplexed. "Why in the world," she asked, "would anyone need so much money as that?"

"Don't you see?" he answered. "With money like that a man's problems would all disappear. He could buy anything he liked.

F [Read and Discuss] What did you learn from this conversation?

Vocabulary **perplexed** (puhr PLEHKST) *v.*: made confused.

He could even start his own business."

"Isn't it plenty to be able to live together, just the two of us?"

When she spoke this way, Yohei could say no more. However, from that time on, whether asleep or awake, all he could do was think about money. It was so painful for the young woman to see Yohei in this state that her eyes filled with tears as she watched him, until finally, unable to bear it another day, she bowed to his will. **G**

"Very well then," she said. "I will weave one more time. But truly, after this, I must never weave again." And once more she warned the now joyful Yohei, saying, "For the sake of heaven, remember. Do not look in on me."

Yohei rubbed his hands together in his eagerness and sat down to wait.

Tonkara tonkara. The sound of the loom continued on and on into the fifth day. The work in the back room seemed to be taking longer than ever.

Yohei, no longer the simple fellow that he had once been, began to wonder about certain peculiar things. Why did the young woman appear to grow thinner every time she wove? What was going on in there behind those paper doors? How could she weave such beautiful cloth when she never seemed to buy any thread?

The longer he had to wait, the more he yearned to peep into the room until, at last, he put his hand upon the door.

"Ah!" came a voice from within. At the same time Yohei cried out in horror and fell back from the doorway.

What Yohei saw was not human. It was a crane, smeared with blood, for with its beak it had plucked out its own feathers to place them in the loom. **H**

At the sight Yohei collapsed into a deep faint. When he came to himself, he found, lying near his hand, a bolt of fabric, pure and radiantly white, through which was woven a thread of bright crimson. It shone with a light this world has never known.

From somewhere Yohei heard the whisper of a delicate, familiar voice. "I had hoped," the voice said sorrowfully, "that you would be able to honor my entreaty.[1] But because you looked upon me in my suffering, I can no longer tarry[2] in the human world. I am the crane that you saved on the snowy path. I fell in love with your gentle, simple heart, and, trusting it alone, I came to live by your side. I pray that your life will be long and that you will always be happy."

"Wai-t!" Yohei stumbled in his haste to get outside. **I**

It was nearly spring, and, over the crest of the distant mountains, he could barely discern the tiny form of a single crane, flying farther and farther away. **J**

---

1. **entreaty** (ehn TREE tee): request.
2. **tarry** (TAR ee): remain.

G **Read and Discuss** What is going on between the husband and wife here?

H **Literary Focus** Taboo What did Yohei find out when he broke the taboo? What do you think might happen now?

I **Read and Discuss** What happened?

J **Reading Focus** Drawing Conclusions What conclusions can you make about the crane in the distance?

Applying Your Skills

The Crane Wife

Respond and Think Critically

Reading Focus

Quick Check

1. What makes Yohei suspect that something is strange about his wife?

Read with a Purpose

2. How does Yohei's life change after he helps the wounded crane?

Reading Skills: Drawing Conclusions

3. **Into Action** Review the chart you created while reading. Compare the conclusions you made with those of a partner. Make a new chart, as shown below. Based on your discussion, add or revise the conclusions you already noted.

New Conclusions	What My Partner and I Discussed	Evidence from the Text
Yohei cared too much about money.	He put money before his wife's happiness.	He asked his wife to make cloth, knowing she didn't want to, just for money.

Literary Focus

Literary Analysis

4. **Analyze** What character traits does the young woman admire in Yohei? What weakness does he display when he asks her to weave for a third time?

5. **Extend** In many folk tales a marvelous change of form, or **metamorphosis,** takes place. What metamorphosis takes place in this story? What other stories involve metamorphoses?

Literary Skills: Taboo

6. **Analyze** What taboo does Yohei break? Discuss other folk tales that include taboos. Be sure to state what happens when they are broken.

Literary Skills Review: Theme

7. **Extend** **Theme** is the truth about life a story reveals. What is the theme of "The Crane Wife"? Is it similar to the theme of other folk tales you have read?

Writing Focus

Think as a Reader/Writer

Use It in Your Writing Review the notes you took about the wife's behavior when the subject of weaving comes up and about the words she uses to warn her husband. Write a short character sketch of the wife, using your own descriptions of her behavior and words.

What Do You Think Now How has the folk tale changed your ideas on whether you should heed a warning from someone who is concerned for you?

The Crane Wife

Vocabulary Development

Vocabulary Check

Answer the following questions.

1. Why would you recommend that someone take time to look at an **exquisite** painting?
2. Have you ever been **perplexed** by a grade you've received? Why?

Onomatopoeia

In "The Crane Wife," the reader can hear what is happening in the story through **onomatopoeia,** or the use of words with sounds that echo their meanings. Some examples of onomatopoeia in English are *honk, beep,* and *meow.*

Your Turn

In each passage below, think of your own example of onomatopoeia in English.

3. "... as he hurried home, suddenly *basabasa* he heard a rustling sound."
4. "Late that night there came a tapping *hoto-hoto* on the door of Yohei's hut."
5. "*Tonkara tonkara.* For three days and three nights the sound of the loom continued."

Language Coach

Definitions Chances are, if you read a little past a difficult word, you will find clues to its meaning. Look at the following sentence:

"Yohei went out into the snow to run an errand, and, as he hurried home, suddenly *basabasa* he heard a rustling sound."

You most likely have not seen the word *basabasa* before, but you can understand its meaning by looking at the second half of the sentence.

Complete each sentence with a definition of the Vocabulary word.

The cloth Yohei's wife made was so **exquisite** that _____.

Yohei was **perplexed** when his wife _____.

Academic Vocabulary

Write About . . .

Why would an older person want to share this folk tale with a member of the younger generation? How might a person offer advice to another person without choosing to intervene directly? Use the Academic Vocabulary words in your response.

Grammar Link

Misplaced Modifiers

To work well, modifiers have to be in the right place. A modifier that seems to modify the wrong word in a sentence is called a **misplaced modifier.** Here's an example of a misplaced modifier:

> **Today I read a story about a woman who wove cloth in my literature book.**

Did the cloth get woven in the book? No, the phrase *in my literature book* is misplaced. To fix the sentence, place the modifier as close as possible to the word it modifies—*read*.

Your Turn

Move the misplaced modifiers in these sentences to the right place.

1. Helping the injured crane, we are introduced to Yohei.
2. I almost understood every word of the story.
3. The decision to make the wife weave a third time by the husband is a key scene in this story.
4. The wife told Yohei when weaving not to look at her.
5. Yohei saw the crane through the doorway smeared with blood.

CHOICES

As you respond to the Choices, use the **Academic Vocabulary** words as appropriate: classic, foundation, generation, intervene.

REVIEW
Change the Ending

What would have happened if Yohei had not broken the taboo? Would he have honored his wife's request not to have her weave again, or would he have gotten even more greedy? Write your own ending to this folk tale. Does the lesson of the story change?

CONNECT
Write a Folk Tale

Write your own folk tale that includes a metamorphosis and a taboo that is broken. First, think about where and when the story takes place. Next, think about your characters. Then, decide on the shape change you'll include. Will it be a reward or a punishment? Finally, choose a taboo that your character will break.

EXTEND
Explore the Taboo Motif

Timed └Writing The motif of the taboo is common in myths and folklore. You may have been told that if you do—or don't do—something, there will be terrible consequences. Do you know of any taboos? What are the consequences of breaking them? In an essay, list two taboos and describe the consequences of breaking them.

Characters,
Conflicts,
Themes

CONTENTS

What Do **You** Think? Why do people like reading and hearing about heroes?

QuickWrite

What makes someone a hero today? Is it special powers? skill in sports? intelligence? the ability to put personal safety aside and help others in danger? Write down your ideas.

King Arthur and the Holy Grail.
Stained-glass window.

KING ARTHVR

Preparing to Read

Merlin and the Dragons /
Sir Gawain and the Loathly Lady

Literary Focus

Characters, Conflicts, and Themes Stories can be both alike and different. Two **characters** may share similar traits, but the discoveries they make may be quite different. Characters may face similar **conflicts,** but they may have various ways of resolving those conflicts. Some stories may have similar characters *and* conflicts but reveal completely different **themes.**

Legends are stories passed down from one <u>generation</u> to the next that usually have some connection to a real person or event. Their plots often follow a pattern, and the main characters are often **heroes.** Frequently, the hero is born under unusual circumstances and trained by a wise older man. The young hero proves himself through some feat of strength or intellect. Then he embarks on a **quest**—a journey in search of something of value during which he faces great dangers. The hero is greatly rewarded if he is successful but faces exile or death if he fails.

Reading Focus

Comparing and Contrasting The legends that follow both feature a hero and involve a challenge or quest. Although the stories have much in common, their themes are different.

Into Action As you read each legend, use a chart like this one to make notes about the conflicts, characters, and theme:

Conflicts	Characters	Theme

Writing Focus

Find It in Your Reading As you read, look for clues that the earliest stories about King Arthur were told aloud. Record what you find in your *Reader/Writer Notebook.*

Vocabulary

Merlin and the Dragons

ruthless (ROOTH lihs) *adj.:* cruel; without pity. *A ruthless army destroyed the village.*

insolence (IHN suh luhns) *n.:* disrespect. *His blunt honesty was considered insolence by some people.*

Sir Gawain and the Loathly Lady

chivalry (SHIHV uhl ree) *n.:* code that governs knightly behavior, requiring courage, honor, and readiness to help the weak. *Chivalry requires knights to help those in need.*

countenance (KOWN tuh nuhns) *n.:* face; appearance. *The king's countenance betrayed that something was wrong.*

loathsome (LOHTH suhm) *adj.:* disgusting. *The loathsome appearance of Dame Ragnell contrasts with her sweet voice.*

Language Coach

Word Origins Most dictionaries tell you in brackets the history of a word, followed by the word's definition. Use a dictionary to look up the Vocabulary words. Which words are from the French language? Which words are from Latin?

 Learn It Online
Broaden your word power with Word Watch at:

go.hrw.com | L7-965 | **Go**

Jane Yolen
(1939–   )

"Empress of Thieves"

Jane Yolen has written more than two hundred books for young people and dozens more for adults. Her books are of all different kinds, but her primary sources are the legends, tales, and myths of folklore.

Yolen has said the King Arthur legend is one of her favorite subjects, and she is considered an expert on it. The character of Merlin seems to fascinate her especially, and she has written several books about him. She explains why she is drawn to folklore:

> "As a writer I am the empress of thieves, taking characters like gargoyles off Parisian churches, the *ki-lin* (or unicorn) from China, swords in stones from the Celts, landscapes from the Taino people. I have pulled threads from magic tapestries to weave my own new cloth."

Betsy Hearne
(1942–   )

Transforming a Beast

Betsy Hearne includes "Sir Gawain and the Loathly Lady" in her collection of twenty-seven Beauty and the Beast folk tales from storytellers around that world. She believes that

> "All of the stories . . . are about journeys in which the heroine or hero is transformed not through winning battles but through love for another being. . . . Beauty and the Beast tales suggest, among other things, that love is as powerful as force in coming to terms with what we fear."

Hearne has worked as a children's librarian and is a highly respected critic, reviewer, writer, and university professor.

Think About the Writers

How does a universal theme or particular character inspire each of these writers?

Build Background

There are many versions of the legend of King Arthur, a cycle of stories that has been shaped and passed down through more than fourteen hundred years of English history. The Arthur legend tells of the adventures of an early king of Britain and the knights and ladies who made up his royal court. The legend recalls a world of mounted warriors with lance, sword, and armor. There are jousts and tournaments, wizards and damsels in distress, and wars and quests. A great king comes to the throne from obscurity, and a noble idea comes to a tragic end. This legend has fascinated readers throughout the world and has inspired great writers to retell it.

Preview the Selections

In "Merlin and the Dragons," you will read how the young **Arthur** discovers his true parentage.

In "Sir Gawain and the Loathly Lady," **King Arthur** will be killed if he does not find the correct answer to a riddle.

MERLIN AND THE DRAGONS

by **Jane Yolen**

Read with a Purpose
Like many heroes of myths and legends, Arthur does not know his true parentage. Read this selection to learn the identity of Arthur's father.

Build Background
According to another Arthurian legend, Arthur became king when he performed a feat no one else could accomplish: He pulled a sword from a stone. This part of Arthur's story is referred to in "Merlin and the Dragons."

The night was dark and storm clouds marched along the sky. Rain beat against the gray castle walls. Inside, in a bedroom hung with tapestries, the young King Arthur had trouble sleeping. Awake, he was frightened. Asleep, he had disturbing dreams.

At last he climbed out of bed, took a candle to light his way, and started out the door. Suddenly remembering his crown, he turned back and found it under the bed where he'd tossed it angrily hours before. It felt too heavy for his head, so he carried it, letting it swing from his fingers.

As he walked along the hall, strange shadows danced before him. But none were as frightening as the shadows in his dreams.

He climbed the tower stairs slowly, biting his lip. When he reached the top, he pushed open the wooden door. The old magician was asleep in his chair, but woke at once, his eyes quick as a hawk's.

"What is it, boy?" the old man asked. "What brings you here at this hour?"

"I am the king," Arthur said, but softly as if he were not really sure. "I go where I will." He put the crown on Merlin's desk.

"You are a boy," Merlin replied, "and boys should be in their beds asleep."

Arthur sighed. "I could not sleep," he said. "I had bad dreams."

"Ah . . ." Merlin nodded knowingly. "Dreams." He held out a hand to the boy, but Arthur didn't dare touch those long, gnarled fingers. "Let me read your dreams."

"It is one dream, actually," Arthur said. "And always the same: a fatherless boy who becomes king simply by pulling a sword from a stone."

"Ah . . ." Merlin said again, withdrawing his fingers. "I know the very child. But if you cannot tell me more of your dream, I shall have to tell you one of mine. After all, a dream told is a story. What better than a story on a rainy night?"

Arthur settled onto a low stool and gazed up at the wizard. A story! He hadn't known he wanted a story. He'd come seeking comfort and companionship. A story was better than both.

He listened as Merlin began. **Ⓐ**

In a small village high up in the rugged mountains of Wales lived a lonely, fatherless boy named Emrys. Dark-haired he was,

and small, with sharp bright eyes, and a mouth that rarely smiled. He was troubled by dreams, sleeping and waking. Dreams of dragons, dreams of stone. **Ⓑ**

His mother was the daughter of the local king and tried to be both mother and father to him. But a princess is only taught lute songs and needlework and prayers. She'd never once climbed a tree after a bird's egg or skinned her knee pursuing a lizard, or caught a butterfly in a net. Emrys had to invent that part of growing up himself. And a lonely inventing it turned out to be.

The other boys in the village teased him for not knowing who his father was. "Mother's babe," they cried, chasing him from their games.

So Emrys went after birds' eggs and lizards, butterflies and frogs by himself, giving them names both odd and admiring, like "flutterby" and "wriggletail," and making up stories of their creation. And he chanted strange-sounding spells because he liked the sounds, spells that sometimes seemed to work, most times did not.

But he never told his dreams aloud. Dreams of dragons, dreams of stone.

Now in the village lived an old man who knew all sorts of things, from reading and writing to how birds speak and why leaves turn brown in autumn. And because Emrys was the son of a princess, the grandson of a king, the old man taught him all he knew.

It was this learning that brought the village boys to him, not in friendship but in curiosity. They would ask Emrys to show them some trick with the birds, or to tell them stories.

Ⓐ **Read and Discuss** What situation has the author set up? What is the structure of this story?

Ⓑ **Literary Focus** **Character** What characteristic does Emrys share with the typical hero?

Glad for the company, Emrys always obliged. He even took to making up harmless predictions to amuse them.

"The rain will soon fall," he would say. And often it did.

"The first spring robin will arrive." And soon after, it came.

Now any farmer's son could have made the same right guesses and after awhile the village boys were no longer impressed. However, one day Emrys found a book of seasons and planetary movements in the old man's cottage and read it cover to cover. Then he went out and announced to the astonished boys: "Tomorrow the sun will disappear."

The next day at noon, just as the calendar had foretold, an eclipse plunged the countryside into darkness. The boys and their parents were equally horrified and blamed Emrys. From then on he was called "demon's son" and avoided altogether. **ⓒ**

Years went by and Emrys grew up, terribly alone, dreaming dreams he did not understand: dreams of a shaking tower, dreams of fighting dragons.

One day when Emrys was twelve, a cruel and ruthless man named Vortigern came to the valley. Vortigern had unjustly declared himself High King over all Britain. But the country was at last in revolt against him and he had been forced to flee, riding ever farther north and west. At last he had arrived at the foot of Dinys Emrys, the mountain which towered above the village, with a bedraggled army on tired horses, bearing tattered banners emblazoned with red dragons. A handful of court magicians rode with them. **ⓓ**

Vortigern pointed to the jagged mountain peak. "There," he said in a voice hard and determined. "There I will build my battle tower, so that I may see my enemies when they approach."

ⓒ **Read and Discuss** What's happening between Emrys and the other boys?

ⓓ **Literary Focus** **Conflict** Do you think Vortigern and Emrys will come into conflict in Merlin's tale? Why or why not?

Vocabulary **ruthless** (ROOTH lihs) *adj.*: cruel; without pity.

He turned to his soldiers. "Gather the people of this village and bring them to me, for they will be the hackers and haulers. They will make me a tower of stone."

Young Emrys looked on in amazement. Banners sewn with red dragons? A tower of stone? Such things had been in his dreams. What could it all mean?

The Welsh stonecutters began their work under the watchful eyes of the soldiers. For many days they mined the stone, cutting huge pieces from the sides of Dinys Emrys. They swore they could hear the cries of the mountain at each cut.

Next they hauled the stones with ropes, their little Welsh ponies groaning with the effort. Finally, came the day when they built the tower up on the mountainside, stone upon stone, until it rose high above the valley.

That night Emrys went to bed and dreamed once again his strange dreams. He dreamed that the tower—the very one built by Vortigern—shook and swayed and tumbled to the ground. And he dreamed that beneath the tower slept two dragons, one red as Vortigern's banners, and one white.

Vortigern's rage could not be contained.

That very night the High King's tower began to shudder and shake and, with a mighty crash, came tumbling down. In the morning, when he saw what had happened, Vortigern was furious, convinced the villagers had done it on purpose. **Ⓔ**

"Your work is worthless," he bellowed at the Welshmen. "You will be whipped, and then you will get to work all over again."

So the Welshmen had to go back to their stonework, great welts on their backs. They hacked and hauled, and once again the tower rose high above the valley. But the night they were finished, it was the same. The tower shook and tumbled to the ground. By morning there was only a jumble of stones.

Vortigern drove the villagers even harder, and by the following week the tower was once again rebuilt. But a third time, in the night, a great shudder went through the mountain and the work once again lay in ruins. Vortigern's rage could not be contained. He called for his magicians. "There is some dark Welsh magic here. Find out the cause. My tower must stand." **Ⓕ**

Ⓔ Read and Discuss What is going on here? What are you learning about Emrys's strange dreams?

Ⓕ Literary Focus Character What are you learning about Vortigern from the way he is handling the situation?

Now these magicians had neither knowledge nor skill, but in their fear of Vortigern they put on a good show. They consulted the trees, both bark and root; they threw the magic sticks of prophecy; they played with the sacred stones of fate. At last they reported their findings.

"You must find a fatherless child," they said. "A child spawned by a demon. You must sprinkle his blood on the stones. Only then will the gods of this land let the stones stand." They smiled at one another and at Vortigern, smiles of those sure that what they ask cannot be done.

Vortigern did not notice their smiles. "Go find me such a child."

The magicians stopped smiling and looked nervous. "We do not know if any such child exists," they said. "We do not know if your tower can stand."

Furious, Vortigern turned to his soldiers. "Gold to whomever brings me such a child," he roared.

Before the soldiers could move, a small voice cried out. "Please, sir, we of the village know such a boy." The speaker was a spindly lad named Gwillam.

"Come here, child," said Vortigern. "Name him."

Gwillam did not dare get too close to the High King. "His name is Emrys, sir. He was spawned by a demon. He can cry the sun from the sky." **(G)**

Vortigern turned to the captain of his guards. "Bring this demon's son to me."

At that very moment, Emrys was on the mountain with the old man, absorbed in a very strange dream. Under the ruins of the tower he saw two huge stone eggs breathing in and out. Just as he emerged from his dream, he was set upon by Vortigern's soldiers. "What shall I do?" he cried.

The old man put a hand on his shoulder. "Trust your dreams."

The soldiers quickly bound Emrys and carried him to the High King, but Emrys refused to show any fear. "You are the boy without a father, the boy spawned by a devil?" Vortigern asked.

"I am a boy without a father, true," Emrys said. "But I am no demon's son. You have been listening to the words of frightened children."

The villagers and soldiers gasped at his impudence, but Vortigern said, "I will have your blood either way."

"Better that you have my dream," Emrys said. "Only my dream can guide you so that your tower will stand."

The boy spoke with such conviction, Vortigern hesitated. **(H)**

"I have dreamed that beneath your tower lies a pool of water that must be drained. In the mud you will find two hollow stones. In each stone is a sleeping dragon. It is the breath of each sleeping dragon that shakes the earth and makes the tower fall. Kill the dragons and your tower will stand."

Vortigern turned to his chief magician. "Can this be true?"

(G) **Literary Focus** Conflict Who do you think Gwillam is? What do you think are his reasons for telling Vortigern about Emrys?

(H) **Read and Discuss** How does Emrys's behavior connect with what you know about him?

Merlin and the Dragons **971**

The chief magician stroked his chin. "Dreams *can* come true. . . ."

Vortigern hesitated no longer. "Untie the boy, but watch him," he said to his soldiers. "And you—Welshmen—do as the boy says. Dig beneath the rubble."

So the Welshmen removed the stones and dug down until they came to a vast pool of water. Then the soldiers drained the pool. And just as Emrys had prophesied, at the pool's bottom lay two great stones. The stones seemed to be breathing in and out, and at each breath the mud around them trembled.

"Stonecutters," cried Vortigern, "break open the stones!"

Two men with mighty hammers descended into the pit and began to pound upon the stones.

Once, twice, three times their hammers rang out. On the third try, like jets of lightning, cracks ran around each stone and they

broke apart as if they had been giant eggs. Out of one emerged a dragon white as new milk. Out of the other a dragon red as old wine.

Astonished at the power of his dreaming, Emrys opened and closed his mouth, but could not speak. The men in the pit scrambled for safety. ❶

The High King Vortigern looked pleased. "Kill them! Kill the dragons!"

But even as he spoke, the dragons shook out their wings and leapt into the sky.

"They are leaving!" cried the chief magician.

"They are away!" cried the soldiers.

"They will not go quite yet," whispered Emrys.

No sooner had he spoken than the dragons wheeled about in the sky to face one another, claws out, belching flame. Their battle cries like nails on slate echoed in the air.

Advancing on one another, the dragons clashed, breast to breast, raining teeth and scales on the ground. For hour after hour they fought, filling the air with smoke.

First the red dragon seemed to be winning, then the white. First one drew blood,

---

❶ **Read and Discuss** Why does Emrys react in this way when he sees the dragons?

then the other. At last, with a furious slash of its jaws, the white dragon caught the red by the throat. There was a moment of silence, and then the red dragon tumbled end over end until it hit the ground.

The white dragon followed it down, straddling its fallen foe and screaming victory into the air with a voice like thunder.

"Kill it! Kill the white now!" shouted Vortigern.

As if freed from a spell, his soldiers readied their weapons. But before a single arrow could fly, the white dragon leapt back into the air and was gone, winging over the highest peak.

"Just so the red dragon of Vortigern shall be defeated," Emrys said, but not so loud the High King could hear.

Cursing the fleeing dragon, Vortigern ordered the tower to be built again. Then he turned to Emrys. "If the tower does not stand this time, I *will* have your blood."

That night young Emrys stared out his window, past the newly built tower. A hawk circled lazily in the sky. Suddenly the hawk swooped down, landing on his window ledge. There was a moment of silent communion between them, as if Emrys could read the hawk's thoughts, as if the hawk could read his. Then away the hawk flew.

Mountains, valleys, hillsides, forests gave way beneath the hawk's wings until, far off in the distance, it spied thousands of flickering lights coming up from the south. As if in a dream, Emrys saw these things, too.

J **Literary Focus** Conflict What conflict might this battle of the dragons foreshadow?

The Real Arthur

The man behind the legend of King Arthur probably lived around A.D. 500. The real Arthur is believed to have been a military leader of a people called the Britons.

In the first century B.C. the Romans invaded Britain and ruled for about four hundred years. After the armies of Rome pulled out of England in A.D. 410, several peoples from other regions tried to seize control. According to the earliest legends, a leader named Arthur united the Britons and led them to victory against one of those invading peoples, the Saxons. After Arthur's death, stories about the warrior king's unusual courage and goodness lived on among his people.

Ask Yourself

Why do you think the legend of King Arthur continues to capture people's imagination?

King Arthur (1903) by Charles Ernest Butler (1864–1918). Oil on canvas.

Emerging from his vision, Emrys turned from the window and went downstairs. He found King Vortigern by the foot of the tower.

"I have seen in a vision that your fate is linked with the red dragon's," Emrys cried. "You will be attacked by thousands of soldiers under the white dragon's flag—attacked and slain."

Vortigern drew his sword, angry enough to kill the boy for such insolence. But at that very moment, a lookout atop the tower shouted: "Soldiers, my lord! Thousands of them!"

Vortigern raced to the top of the tower stairs and stared across the valley. It was true. And as he watched further, one of the knights leading the army urged his horse forward and raced along to the tower foot, shouting: "Come and meet your fate, murderous Vortigern!"

Vortigern turned to his own men. "Defend me! Defend my tower!"

But when they saw the numbers against them, the men all deserted.

"Surrender, Vortigern!" cried a thousand voices.

"Never!" he called back. "Never!"

"A king should forgive his enemies and make them his chiefest friends. You taught me that, Merlin."

The old wizard stopped speaking.

"Well?" Arthur asked. "What happened to Vortigern? You cannot end a story there."

Merlin looked at him carefully. "What do *you* think happened?"

"Vortigern was slain, just as Emrys said."

"Is that the boy speaking?" asked the wizard. "Or the king?"

"The boy," admitted Arthur. "A king should forgive his enemies and make them his chiefest friends. You taught me that, Merlin. But what did happen?"

"The men of the white dragon defeated Vortigern all right. Burned him up in his own tower."

"And that knight, the one who rode up to the tower first. What became of him?"

"His name was Uther Pendragon and he eventually became the High King," Merlin said.

"Uther," mused Arthur. "He was the last High King before me. But then he was a hero. He was fit to rule. Perhaps one of his sons will come to claim my throne."

"Uther had only one son," Merlin said softly, "though only I knew of it." He looked steadily at the boy. "That son was you, Arthur."

K **Literary Focus** Theme What is one lesson Merlin has taught Arthur about being a good ruler? Do you think this is a good lesson?

Vocabulary **insolence** (IHN suh luhns) *n.*: disrespect.

"Me?" For a moment Arthur's voice squeaked. "Uther was my father? Then I am not fatherless? Then I am king by right and not just because I pulled a sword from a stone."

Merlin shook his head. "Don't underestimate your real strength in pulling that sword," Merlin cautioned. "It took a true and worthy king to do what you did."

Arthur gave a deep sigh. "Why did you not tell me this before?"

The old wizard's hawk eyes opened wide. "I could not tell you until you were ready. There are rules for prophets, just as there are rules for kings."

"So now I am king in truth."

Merlin smiled. "You were always king in truth. Only you doubted it. So you can thank your dreams for waking you up."

"What of Emrys?" Arthur asked. "What happened to him?"

"Oh—he's still around," replied the wizard. "Went on dreaming. Made a career of it." He rummaged around in some old boxes and crates by the desk until he found what he was looking for. "I still have this. Saved it all this time." He tossed a large yellowed dragon's tooth across to Arthur.

Sudden recognition dawned on Arthur's face. "You? You saved this? Then you were the boy named Emrys!"

"Surely you guessed that before," Merlin teased. "But now perhaps we can both go back to sleep."

"Thank you, Merlin," Arthur said. "I don't think I shall dream any more bad dreams."

Merlin's gnarled fingers caged the boy's hand for a moment. "But you shall dream," he said quietly. "Great men dream great dreams, and I have dreamed your greatness." He plucked the crown from the desktop. "Don't forget this, my lord king."

Arthur took the crown and placed it carefully on his head. Then he turned, went out the door, and down the tower stairs.

Merlin watched for a moment more, then sank back down in his chair. Closing his eyes, he fell immediately to sleep, dreaming of knights and a Round Table.

L [Read and Discuss] What have you learned now?

M [Literary Focus] **Theme** What theme, or truth about life, is revealed in this tale?

N [Reading Focus] **Comparing and Contrasting** How does the way Arthur handles his crown at the end of the story differ from what he does with it at the beginning? What does this reveal about him?

Applying Your Skills

SKILLS FOCUS Literary Skills Analyze legends; analyze the qualities of a hero; compare and contrast plot and setting; compare and contrast themes; analyze character traits. **Reading Skills** Compare and contrast texts. **Writing Skills** Write short stories or poems.

Merlin and the Dragons

Respond and Think Critically

Reading Focus

Quick Check

1. It is important that you take note of the structure of this story. This is a story within a story. What is happening in the frame story—the story that starts at the beginning?

2. Where does the story *within* the story start? Where does it end?

Read with a Purpose

3. Why is it important to know who Arthur's father is?

Reading Skills: Compare and Contrast

4. Use this chart to compare the conflicts, characters, and theme of the frame story and the story within a story:

	Conflicts	Characters	Theme
Frame Story			
Story Within a Story			

✔ Vocabulary Check

Answer the following questions:

5. How would a *ruthless* person treat an enemy?
6. What kind of behavior would show *insolence*?

Literary Focus

Literary Analysis

7. **Compare and Contrast** How do the dreams that keep Arthur awake compare with the dreams Emrys has in the story within a story?

8. **Make Judgments** Merlin taught Arthur that "A king should forgive his enemies and make them his chiefest friends." What do you think of this as advice for any ruler?

9. **Compare and Contrast** Discuss the way Arthur treats his crown at the beginning of the story and the manner in which he handles it at the end. What do you think this signifies?

Literary Skills: Characters, Conflicts, and Themes

10. **Analyze** The tales of King Arthur say little about the childhood of Arthur and even less about Merlin's childhood. In creating this story of Merlin's childhood, Yolen uses the pattern of the hero tale to add made-up details to a classic legend. Why do you think she does that?

Writing Focus

Think as a Reader/Writer

Use It in Your Writing Yolen uses the structure of a story within a story to remind the reader that the tales of Arthur are part of an oral storytelling tradition. Create your own brief story within a story. Start with a familiar story or folk tale. Then, create a frame story to introduce and conclude it.

SIR GAWAIN
AND THE LOATHLY LADY

by **Betsy Hearne**

Read with a Purpose
Read this story to find out how answering a riddle becomes a matter of life or death.

Preparing to Read for this selection is on page 965.

Build Background
The **quest** is a standard part of the hero tale. It is a long and perilous journey taken in search of something of great value: a treasure, a kingdom, the hand of a fair maiden, or the answer to an important question. During the quest, heroes of folk tales and legends must face great temptations and perform difficult tasks. One of those tasks might be solving a **riddle.** A riddle is a puzzling question or problem, which the hero must answer correctly before going on with the quest. The punishment for giving a wrong answer could be exile or even death.

N ow if you listen awhile I will tell you a tale of Arthur the King and how an adventure once befell him.

Of all kings and all knights, King Arthur bore away the honor wherever he went. In all his country there was nothing but chivalry, and knights were loved by the people. **Ⓐ**

One day in spring King Arthur was hunting in Ingleswood with all his lords beside him. Suddenly a deer ran by in the distance and the king took up chase, calling back to his knights, "Hold you still every man, I will chase this one myself!" He took his arrows and bow and stooped low like a woodsman to stalk the deer. But every time he came near the animal, it leapt away into the forest. So King Arthur went a while after the deer, and no knight went with him, until at last he let fly an arrow and killed the deer. He had raised a bugle to his lips to summon the knights when he heard a voice behind him.

Ⓐ **Literary Focus** Compare Characters Compare what you learn here about King Arthur with what you learned about the younger Arthur in "Merlin and the Dragons."

Vocabulary **chivalry** (SHIHV uhl ree) *n.:* code that governs knightly behavior, requiring courage, honor, and readiness to help the weak.

"Well met, King Arthur!"

Though he had not heard anyone approach, the king turned to see a strange knight, fully armed, standing only a few yards away.

"You have done me wrong many a year and given away my northern lands," said the strange knight. "I have your life in my hands—what will you do now, King Alone?"

"Sir Knight, what is your name?" asked the king.

"My name is Gromer Somer Joure."[1]

"Sir Gromer, think carefully," said the king. "To slay me here, unarmed as I am, will get you no honor. All knights will refuse you wherever you go. Calm yourself—come to Carlyle and I shall mend all that is amiss."

"Nay," said Sir Gromer, "by heaven, King! You shall not escape when I have you at advantage. If I let you go with only a warning, later you'll defy me, of that I'm sure."

"Spare my life, Sir Gromer, and I shall grant you whatever is in my power to give. It is shameful to slay me here, with nothing but my hunting gear, and you armed for battle." **B**

"All your talking will not help you, King, for I want neither land nor gold, truly." Sir Gromer smiled. "Still . . . if you will promise to meet me here, in the same fashion, on a day I will choose . . ."

"Yes," said the king quickly. "Here is my promise."

"Listen and hear me out. First you will swear upon my sword to meet me here without fail, on this day one year from now. Of all your knights none shall come with you. You must tell me at your coming what thing women most desire—and if you do not bring the answer to my riddle, you will lose your head. What say you, King?"

"I agree, though it is a hateful bargain," said the king. "Now let me go. I promise you as I am the true king, to come again at this day one year from now and bring you your answer."

The knight laughed, "Now go your way, King Arthur. You do not yet know your sorrow. Yet stay a moment—do not think of playing false—for by Mary[2] I think you would betray me."

"Nay," said King Arthur. "You will never find me an untrue knight. Farewell, Sir Knight, and evil met. I will come in a year's time, though I may not escape." The king began to blow his bugle for his knights to find him. Sir Gromer turned his horse and was gone as quickly as he had come, so that the lords found their king alone with the slain deer. **C**

"We will return to Carlyle," said the king. "I do not like this hunting."

The lords knew by his countenance

---

1. **Gromer Somer Joure** (groh MEHR soh MEHR zhoor).

2. **by Mary:** a mild oath.

B [Read and Discuss] What do you learn about the behavior expected of a knight from King Arthur's appeal?

C [Literary Focus] Compare Conflicts List at least two ways in which the conflict Arthur faces in this story is different from the conflict he faces in "Merlin and the Dragons."

Vocabulary **countenance** (KOWN tuh nuhns) *n.:* face; appearance.

that the king met with some disturbance, but no one knew of his encounter. They wondered at the king's heavy step and sad look, until at last Sir Gawain[3] said to the king, "Sire, I marvel at you. What thing do you sorrow for?"

"I'll tell you, gentle Gawain," said Arthur. "In the forest as I pursued the deer, I met with a knight in full armor, and he charged me I should not escape him. I must keep my word to him or else I am foresworn."[4]

"Fear not my lord. I am not a man that would dishonor you."

"He threatened me, and would have slain me with great heat, but I spoke with him since I had no weapons."

"What happened then?" said Gawain.

"He made me swear to meet him there in one year's time, alone and unarmed. On that day I must tell him what women desire most, or I shall lose my life. If I fail in my answer, I know that I will be slain without mercy."

"Sire, make good cheer," said Gawain. "Make your horse ready to ride into strange country, and everywhere you meet either man or woman, ask of them the answer to the riddle. I will ride another way, and every man and woman's answer I will write in a book." **D**

"That is well advised, Gawain," said the king. They made preparations to leave immediately, and when both were ready, Gawain rode one way and the king another—each

one asked every man and woman they found what women most desire.

Some said they loved beautiful clothes; some said they loved to be praised; some said they loved a handsome man; some said one, some said another. Gawain had so many answers that he made a great book to hold them, and after many months of traveling he came back to court again. The king was there already with his book, and each looked over the other's work. But no answer seemed right.

"By God," said the king, "I am afraid. I will seek a little more in Ingleswood Forest. I have but one month to my set day, and I may find some good tidings."

"Do as you think best," said Gawain, "but whatever you do, remember that it is good to have spring again."

King Arthur rode forth on that day, into Ingleswood, and there he met with a lady. King Arthur marveled at her, for she was the ugliest creature that he had ever seen. Her face seemed almost like that of an animal, with a pushed-in nose and a few yellowing tusks for teeth. Her figure was twisted and deformed, with a hunched back and shoulders a yard broad. No tongue could tell the foulness of that lady. But she rode gaily on a palfrey[5] set with gold and precious stones, and when she spoke her voice was sweet and soft.

---

3. **Gawain** (GAH wihn).

4. **foresworn:** untrue to one's word; shown to be a liar.

5. **palfrey** (PAWL free): gentle riding horse.

D **Literary Focus** **Character** What plan does Sir Gawain propose? What do you learn about the relationship between King Arthur and Sir Gawain from this conversation?

"I am glad that I have met with you, King Arthur," she said. "Speak with me, for your life is in my hand. I know of your situation, and I warn you that you will not find your answer if I do not tell you."

"What do you want with me, lady?" said the king, taken aback by the lady's boldness.

"Sir, I would like to speak with you. You will die if I do not save you, I know it very well."

"What do you mean, my lady, tell me," stammered the king. "What is your desire, why is my life in your hand? Tell me, and I shall give you all you ask."

"You must grant me a knight to wed," said the lady slowly. "His name is Sir Gawain. I will make this bargain: If your life is saved another way, you need not grant my desire. If my answer saves your life, grant me Sir Gawain as my husband. Choose now, for you must soon meet your enemy."

"By Mary," said the king, "I cannot grant you Sir Gawain. That lies with him alone—he is not mine to give. I can only take the choice to Sir Gawain."

"Well," she said. "Then go home again and speak to Sir Gawain. For though I am foul, yet am I merry, and through me he may save your life or ensure your death."

"Alas!" cried the king. "That I should cause Gawain to wed you, for he will not say no. I know not what I should do."

"Sir King, you will get no more from me. When you come again with your answer I will meet you here."

"What is your name, I pray you tell me?"

"Sir King, I am the Dame Ragnell, that never yet betrayed a man."

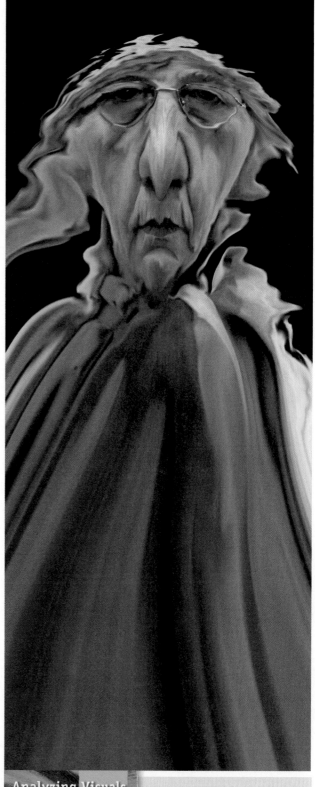

"Then farewell, Dame Ragnell," said the king.

Thus they departed, and the king returned to Carlyle again with a heavy heart. The first man he met was Sir Gawain. "Sire, how did you fare?" asked the knight.

"Never so ill," said the king. "I fear I will die at Sir Gromer's hand."

"Nay," said Gawain. "I would rather die myself I love you so."

"Gawain, I met today with the foulest lady that I ever saw. She said she would save my life, but first she would have you for her husband."

"Is this all?" asked Gawain. "Then I shall wed her and wed her again! Though she were a fiend, though she were as foul as Beelzebub,[6] her I shall marry. For you are my king and I am your friend—it is my part to save your life, or else I am a false knight and a great coward. If she were the most loathsome woman that ever a man might see, for your love I would spare nothing."

"Thank you, Gawain," said King Arthur then. "Of all knights that I have found, you are the finest. You have saved my life, and my love will not stray from you, as I am king in this land." **E**

The day soon came when the king was to meet the Dame Ragnell and bear his answer to Sir Gromer. Gawain rode with him to the edge of Ingleswood Forest, but there the king said, "Sir Gawain, farewell. I must go west, and you must go no further."

"God speed you on your journey. I wish I rode your way," said Gawain.

The king had ridden but a mile or so more when he met the Dame Ragnell. "Ah, Sir King, you are welcome here bearing your answer."

"Now," said the king, "since it can be no other way, tell me your answer, save my life, and Gawain shall you wed; so he has promised. Tell me in all haste. Have done, I may not tarry."[7]

"Sire," said the Dame Ragnell, "now you will know what women desire most, high and low. Some men say we desire to be fair, or to wed, or to remain fresh and young, or to have flattery from men. But there is one thing that is every woman's fantasy: We desire of men, above all other things, to have sovereignty,[8] for then all is ours. Therefore go on your way, Sir King, and tell that knight what I have said to you. He will be angry and curse the woman who told you, for his labor is lost. Go forth—you will not be harmed."

The king rode forth in great haste until he came to the set place and met with Sir Gromer.

"Come, come, Sir King," said the knight sternly. "Now let me have your answer, for I am ready."

The king pulled out the two books for Sir Gromer to see. "Sir, I dare say the right one is there."

---

6. **Beelzebub** (bee EHL zuh buhb): devil; Satan.

7. **tarry**: linger; delay.
8. **sovereignty** (SAHV ruhn tee): control; authority.

E | Read and Discuss | What does this exchange tell you about the feelings between King Arthur and Sir Gawain?

Vocabulary **loathsome** (LOHTH suhm) *adj.*: disgusting.

Sir Gromer looked over them, every one, and said at last, "Nay, nay, Sir King, you are a dead man."

"Wait, Sir Gromer," said the king. "I have one more answer to give."

"Say it," said Sir Gromer, "or so God help me you shall bleed." **F**

"Now," said the king, "here is my answer and that is all—above all things, women desire sovereignty, for that is their liking and their greatest desire; to rule over any man. This they told me."

Sir Gromer was silent a moment with rage, but then he cried out, "And she that told you, Sir Arthur, I pray to God I might see her burn in a fire, for that was my sister, Dame Ragnell. God give her shame—I have lost much labor. Go where you like, King Arthur, for you are spared. Alas that I ever saw this day, for I know that you will be my enemy and hunt me down."

"No," said King Arthur, "you will never find me an attacker. Farewell." King Arthur turned his horse into the forest again. Soon he met with the Dame Ragnell, in the same place as before. "Sir King," she said. "I am glad you have sped well. I told you how it would be,

and now since I and none other have saved your life, Gawain must wed me." **G**

"I will not fail in my promise," said the king. "If you will be ruled by my council, you shall have your will."

"No, Sir King, I will not be ruled," said the lady. "I know what you are thinking. Ride before, and I will follow to your court. Think how I have saved your life and do not disagree with me, for if you do you will be shamed."

The king was ashamed to bring the loathly lady openly to the court, but forth she rode till they came to Carlyle. All the country wondered when she came, for they had never seen so foul a creature, but she would spare no one the sight of her. Into the hall she went, saying, "Arthur, King, fetch in Sir Gawain, before all the knights, so that you may troth[9] us together. Set forth Gawain my love, for I will not wait."

Sir Gawain stepped forward then, and said, "Sir, I am ready to fulfill the promise I made to you."

"God have mercy," said the Dame Ragnell when she saw Gawain. "For your

> Sir Gawain stepped forward then, and said, "Sir, I am ready to fulfill the promise I made to you."

Head of King Arthur (14th century) from Beautiful Fountain, Nuremberg, Germany.

---

9. **troth** (trawth): engaged to marry.

F **Read and Discuss** Why do you think King Arthur gives Sir Gromer all the other answers before giving him Dame Ragnell's?

G **Reading Focus** **Comparing and Contrasting** How does King Arthur's response to Sir Gromer relate to what Merlin taught Arthur in "Merlin and the Dragons"?

sake I wish I were a fair woman, for you are of such goodwill." Then Sir Gawain wooed her[10] as he was a true knight, and Dame Ragnell was happy.

"Alas!" said the Queen Guinevere, and all the ladies in her bower.[11] "Alas!" said both king and knights, that the beautiful Gawain should wed such a foul and horrible woman.

She would be wedded in no other way than this—openly, with announcements in every town and village, and she had all the ladies of the land come to Carlyle for the feast. The queen begged Dame Ragnell to be married in the early morning, as privately as possible. "Nay," said the lady. "By heaven I will not no matter what you say. I will be wedded openly, as the king promised. I will not go to the church until High Mass time,[12] and I will dine in the open hall, in the midst of all the court."

At the wedding feast there were lords and ladies from all estates, and Dame Ragnell was arrayed in the richest manner—richer even than Queen Guinevere. But all her rich clothes could not hide her foulness. When the feasting began, only Dame Ragnell ate heartily, while the knights and squires sat like stones. After the wedding feast, Sir Gawain and the Lady Ragnell retired to the wedding chamber that had been prepared for them. Ⓗ

---

10. **wooed her:** said romantic things; spoke of love.
11. **bower** (BOW uhr): old-fashioned word for a private room.
12. **High Mass time:** main mass of Sunday morning. People of the highest class would attend High Mass.

"Ah, Gawain," said the lady. "Since we are wed, show me your courtesy and come to bed. If I were fair you would be joyous— yet for Arthur's sake, kiss me at least."

Sir Gawain turned to the lady, but in her place was the loveliest woman that he had ever seen.

"By God, what are you?" cried Gawain.

"Sir, I am your wife, surely. Why are you so unkind?"

"Lady, I am sorry," said Gawain. "I beg your pardon, my fair madam. For now you are a beautiful lady, and today you were the foulest woman that ever I saw. It is well, my lady, to have you thus." And he took her in his arms and kissed her with great joy.

"Sir," she said, "you have half-broken the spell on me. Thus shall you have me, but my beauty will not hold. You may have me fair by night and foul by day, or else have me fair by day, and by night ugly once again. You must choose."

"Alas!" said Gawain. "The choice is too hard—to have you fair on nights and no more, that would grieve my heart and shame me. Yet if I desire to have you fair by day and foul by night, I could not rest. I know not in the world what I should say, but do as you wish. The choice is in your hands."

"Thank you, courteous Gawain," said the lady. "Of all earthly knights you are blessed, for now I am truly loved. You shall have me fair both day and night, and ever while I live as fair. For I was shaped by witchcraft by my stepmother, God have mercy on her. By enchantment I was to be the foulest

---

Ⓗ **Literary Focus** **Theme** Why does Dame Ragnell insist on a large public ceremony? How does this relate to her statement about what women want most?

Sir Gawain on the magic bed.
Miniature from manuscript of
Arthurian romances (13th century).
©The Granger Collection.

creature, till the best knight of England had wedded me and had given me the sovereignty of all his body and goods. Kiss me, Sir Gawain—be glad and make good cheer, for we are well." The two rejoiced together and thanked God for their fortune. ❶

King Arthur came himself to call them to breakfast the next day, wondering why Gawain stayed so late with his loathly bride. Sir Gawain rose, taking the hand of his lady, and opened the door to greet the king.

The Dame Ragnell stood by the fire, with her pale lovely skin and red hair spilling down to her knees. "Lo," said Gawain to the king, "this is my wife the Dame Ragnell, who once saved your life." And Gawain told the king the story of the lady's enchantment.

"My love shall she have, for she has been so kind," said the king. And the queen said, "You will have my love forever, Lady, for you have saved my Lord Arthur." And from then on, at every great feast, that lady was the fairest, and all his life Gawain loved the Lady Ragnell.

Thus ends the adventure of King Arthur and of the wedding of Sir Gawain.

❶ **Read and Discuss** How do things work out? How does Sir Gawain break the spell?

Applying Your Skills

SKILLS FOCUS Literary Skills Analyze the qualities of a hero; compare and contrast plot and setting; themes; and characters. **Reading Skills** Compare and contrast texts. **Writing Skills** Write short stories or poems.

Sir Gawain and the Loathly Lady

Respond and Think Critically

Reading Focus

Quick Check

1. Briefly retell the main events of the adventure that leads to Sir Gawain's marriage.

Read with a Purpose

2. How does answering a riddle become a matter of life or death for Arthur?

Reading Skills: Compare and Contrast

3. Review the charts you completed as you read the legends. List the elements of a hero tale shared by both stories and those that appear in only one of the two.

Shared Elements	Different Elements

✓ Vocabulary Check

Answer the following questions:

4. Would taking advantage of the less fortunate be an example of *chivalry*?

5. What does it mean when someone's feelings are revealed by his or her *countenance*?

6. Name something you think is *loathsome*.

Literary Focus

Literary Analysis

7. **Make Judgments** What did you think of the choice presented to Sir Gawain on his wedding night? What is revealed by his choice?

8. **Evaluate** King Arthur goes on a **quest** to find the answer to a riddle. Name three points during the quest when he could have made a mistake but did not. How did the code of **chivalry** help him make the right decision each time?

9. **Interpret** Dame Ragnell says that women want sovereignty. How do you think things will play out for her in this regard? What effect might her sovereignty have on Sir Gawain?

Literary Skills: Characters, Conflicts, and Themes

10. **Analyze** Discuss one aspect of the legend that you had a strong response to. Maybe you feel the plot is not believable. Perhaps you especially relate to one particular character, or maybe you strongly agree or disagree with the theme of the story. Describe your response to an aspect of the story and the reason you feel this way.

11. **Compare and Contrast** What is the theme of "Sir Gawain and the Loathly Lady"? Is the theme similar to or different from the theme of "Merlin and the Dragons"? Explain.

Writing Focus

Think as a Reader/Writer

Use It in Your Writing Hearne uses sentences at the beginning and end of the story to suggest that it is being told aloud. Think of who might tell Hearne's story and why he or she might tell it. Create a frame story for this tale that describes the situation that inspires its telling and what happens as a result.

COMPARING TEXTS
Wrap Up

Merlin and the Dragons / Sir Gawain and the Loathly Lady

Writing Focus

Write a Comparison-Contrast Essay

Write an essay comparing the conflicts, characters, and themes of "Merlin and the Dragons" and "Sir Gawain and the Loathly Lady." Begin by reviewing the charts you created when you read the two selections. Then, identify the similarities and differences. Finally, decide how you will organize your essay.

1. You can organize your essay **point by point.** First, write a paragraph comparing and contrasting the conflicts of the two stories. Then, write a paragraph comparing and contrasting the characters. Finally, write a paragraph comparing and contrasting the themes.

2. Or, you can organize your essay using the **block method**—writing a paragraph about the conflict, characters, and theme of the first story and then another paragraph about the plot, characters, and theme of the second.

At the end of your essay, write your response to the stories. Which did you like better? Which theme had more relevance for you?

Use the workshop on writing a comparison-contrast essay, on pages 106–113, for help with this assignment.

What Do You Think Now?

Why do people like reading and hearing about heroes?

CHOICES

As you respond to the Choices, use these **Academic Vocabulary** words as appropriate: classic, foundation, generation, intervene.

REVIEW
Analyze Two Legends

Timed Writing Briefly summarize the two legends. Tell which story you liked better, and give reasons for your preference. Explain which literary elements—characters, conflicts, and themes—shaped your responses.

CONNECT
Compare Themes

Betsy Hearne included "Sir Gawain and the Loathly Lady" in a collection of Beauty and the Beast folk tales she created. With a group of classmates, read several versions of the well-known Beauty and the Beast folk tale, or watch the animated film based on the story. Then, compare the themes of the Beauty and the Beast tale and "Sir Gawain and the Loathly Lady" in a group discussion.

EXTEND
Explore the Hero Tale

With a small group, discuss the pattern of the hero tale. Then, talk about characters and stories you know that fit the pattern. Continue to explore the elements of the hero tale—how the hero proves himself, the quest, the challenges and tests—and the stories and movies you know that include these elements.

Author's Perspective

Piano III (with Horn) (1995)
by Gil Mayers (1947—   ). Mixed media.

CONTENTS

What Do **You Think** What aspect of music appeals to you most?

QuickWrite
Think about a time when music h
effect on you. Write a paragraph
situation and the effect the musi

NEWSPAPER ARTICLE
Preparing to Read

Music Makers

Reader/Writer
Notebook

Use your **RWN** to complete the activities for this selection.

Informational Text Focus

Analyzing an Author's Perspective When you read a nonfiction text, try to analyze the **author's perspective**—the way the writer feels about his or her subject. The author usually won't state his or her perspective directly. Instead, you need to **infer** it by reading closely, paying particular attention to the evidence the writer uses to support his or her argument, including

- word choice
- the information included
- the information left out

What you believe to be true may change when a writer is able to convince you to see things from a different perspective. Persuasive writers usually use a mix of logical and emotional appeals to convince readers to agree with them. **Logical appeals** are based on facts and statistics, whereas **emotional appeals** stir up feelings within readers that make them more sympathetic to the author's argument.

Into Action When reading a persuasive text, you can use a chart like this one to analyze the appeals used in the author's argument:

Details from Text	Appeal: Logical or Emotional?

Vocabulary

allotted (uh LAHT ihd) *v.* used as *adj.*: set aside for a certain purpose. *In schools today there is less time allotted in students' schedules for music programs.*

short-sighted (SHAWRT SY tihd) *adj.*: lacking foresight; not prudent. *Short-sighted plans to eliminate music programs ignore the negative effects on future students.*

Language Coach

Multiple-Meaning Words Some words have different meanings depending on the context in which they are used. Which Vocabulary word also means "having a condition in which it is difficult to see objects from a distance"? How can you tell?

Writing Focus   Preparing for **Constructed Response**

Look for the persuasive techniques the author uses. Note the type of appeal each one is, and think about which had the greatest effect on your opinions.

 Learn It Online
Get help analyzing the author's perspective with the interactive Reading Workshops at:

go.hrw.com   L7-989   Go

Music Makers

Musicians Help Keep Music Alive in Schools

by

Read with a Purpose
Read this selection to discover the way a music program affects students in Nashville.

Old, worn-out instruments were common in the band hall at Nashville's Hume-Fogg Academic Magnet High School. Trombone slides weren't working right. Saxophones made breathy sounds as air leaked from them. Parts fell off the ancient bass clarinet. And then there were the two hulking metal tubas that had played their first notes before World War II. **A**

A **Read and Discuss** What is the author setting up here?

Then one day in May 2006, Hume-Fogg music students were greeted with boxes full of brand-new equipment. "We just opened them like it was Christmas," says music director Rich Ripani. "Everybody was ripping open boxes and saying things like, 'Look, a brand-new oboe,' and 'Look, a brand-new Fox bassoon.'" **Ⓑ**

Santa Claus, in this case, was the Nashville Alliance for Public Education. The nonprofit group recently teamed up with professional musicians from the Country Music Association (CMA). They aim to raise the $8 million that "Music City" music programs need to get back on their feet.

"We set a goal to provide musical instruments for all Nashville public schools," says the Nashville Alliance's executive director, Kay Simmons.

NASHVILLE'S FIRST PUBLIC SCHOOL
Nashville's first public school, Hume School, opened here Feb. 26, 1855. A three story brick building, the school employed 12 teachers and served all grades. In 1874 high school classes were moved to Fogg School built on adjoining corner lot. Named for educators, Alfred E. Hume & Francis B. Fogg, the schools were replaced by Hume-Fogg in 1912.

Hume-Fogg Academic Magnet High School, Nashville, Tennessee.

Programs on Their Last Notes

Nashville may be America's capital of country music. But like many other cities, its cash-strapped school district spends very little on music education. For decades, area music teachers like Ripani have had to beg, borrow, or buy with their own money whatever equipment they could get. That's tough when one new baritone horn can cost $3,500. The expense of outfitting an entire school band with instruments can easily reach $200,000.

Such steep costs worry school officials nationwide. Many have chosen to cut back on music education or shut down programs altogether. Michael Blakeslee of the National Association of Music Education (NAME) says that poor school districts in inner cities and rural areas tend to be hit the hardest. For example, in 2007, budget cuts shut down the music program at Nashville's Dalewood Middle School. "It's [common] across the country," Blakeslee says. **Ⓒ**

Ⓑ **Informational Focus** Author's Perspective
How does this anecdote make you feel? How does it help you understand the author's perspective?

Ⓒ **Read and Discuss** What is happening here?

Part of the problem is that people view arts courses as merely add-ons to "core" classes in reading and math. In order to improve test scores in core areas, some schools have begun chipping away at the time allotted each day for music and other arts. But there's plenty of evidence to suggest that this is short-sighted. Recent studies showed that students involved in the arts earn higher grades and have fewer discipline problems. NAME recently conducted a poll of school principals. Most of them agreed that a strong music program boosts attendance and graduation rates. **ⓓ**

Hearing the Call

To Nashville's country western stars, helping public school music programs through the CMA just makes sense. The group donated about $360,000 in 2007 and plans to give more in years to come. In many cases, the children of musicians are the ones sitting in public school classrooms. For instance, the Nashville School of the Arts has a unique guitar program whose recent graduates include the son of singer Crystal Gayle. "Many of us live here," says Troy Gentry, half of the singing duo Montgomery Gentry. "Our businesses are here. We are invested in the community."

Together, the Nashville Alliance and the CMA have raised $1.5 million of the $8 million needed, and more is to come. At Hume-Fogg, senior Kyle Burgess says the new instruments have boosted students' confidence and improved the sound of bands there.

"It's just kind of fun to play something new like that, when everything on it works," says Kyle, who plays a new baritone saxophone. "A new horn makes everyone feel better."

Read with a Purpose

How did a music program improve the lives of kids in Nashville?

ⓓ Read and Discuss | What are you learning here?

Vocabulary **allotted** (uh LAHT ihd) *v.* used as *adj.:* set aside for a certain purpose.
short-sighted (SHAWRT SY tihd) *adj.:* lacking foresight; not prudent.

Applying Your Skills

SKILLS FOCUS **Informational Skills** Analyze an author's purpose and perspective. **Vocabulary Skills** Demonstrate knowledge of literal meanings of words and their usage.

Music Makers

Practicing the Standards

Informational Text and Vocabulary

1. The **purpose** of this article is to —

   A persuade the reader to donate money to public schools

   B inform the reader about the financial situation of many public schools

   C reveal a truth about the lives of musicians

   D entertain the reader with a story about a school in Nashville

2. A writer's **perspective** is —

   A his or her point of view on a subject

   B a story the writer tells to entertain readers

   C a sequence of related events

   D the words a writer chooses

3. You can tell from the **details** in this article that the writer believes —

   A all old musical instruments should be replaced with new ones

   B the Country Music Association is not doing enough to help Nashville schools

   C access to music education is important for all students

   D having new instruments makes musicians play better music

4. In paragraph 7, the writer **supports** his position by —

   A describing a personal experience

   B quoting an expert

   C telling a brief story

   D stating the results of a poll

5. Money that's been *allotted* has been —

   A spent on necessities

   B conserved in case of emergency

   C set aside for a specific purpose

   D earned by performing hard work

6. A *short-sighted* person —

   A does not consider the consequences of his or her actions

   B budgets his or her money carefully

   C plans his or her actions fully

   D polls principals often

Writing Focus Constructed Response

Write a persuasive paragraph about your favorite hobby. In it, use both emotional and logical appeals to persuade your reader to have the same favorite as you.

What Do You Think Now

How has the information in this article changed your thinking about the most appealing aspect of music?

Writing Workshop

Research Report

Write with a Purpose

Write a research report on a topic of your choice. Your **purpose** is to find, organize, and present facts that support your thesis. Think about how to write clearly so that your **audience** can easily gain more knowledge about the topic.

A Good Research Paper

- focuses on a thesis, or main idea, supported by evidence
- includes accurately documented information from several sources
- uses different types of evidence, including facts, examples, statistics, and direct quotations
- organizes information in a logical way
- ends by summarizing ideas or drawing an overall conclusion

See page 1002 for complete rubric.

Think as a Reader/Writer

You take in factual and fictional information all the time. In this collection, you've read fictional myths and folk tales. Now it's time to use your research skills to find and present factual information in a research report. First read this excerpt from the end of an article titled "Flying High—Again." The first paragraph of the article (not seen here) states the thesis: "Although bald eagles were in danger of becoming extinct in the 1950s, the efforts of many groups over the last ten years have helped them make an amazing comeback."

> With the help of many people all over the United States, eagles are slowly recovering. From a low point of fewer than 500 nesting pairs in the 1960s, the numbers have grown to an estimated 4,500 nesting pairs in the continental United States. If you count eagles and young adults there are about 55,000 bald eagles in the United States today. In 1998, Secretary of the Interior Bruce Babbitt took steps to remove the bald eagle from the endangered species list. In an interview, Babbitt said, "The eagle is doing splendidly. It's making a wonderful comeback everywhere."
>
> The bald eagle is not completely out of danger yet, but its future looks better every day. If eagles keep making a comeback, our national symbol should be around for a long time to come.

← Different types of **evidence** are used throughout the article. Here, we see statistics and a direct quotation.

← The **thesis** is restated effectively, both in this quote by Babbitt and in the concluding paragraph.

Think About the Professional Model

With a partner, discuss the following questions about the model.

1. How does the information here support the main idea of the article?

2. What has the writer done to present the information clearly?

3. Why does the writer use statistics to support the article's thesis?

Reader/Writer Notebook

Use your **RWN** to complete the activities for this workshop.

Prewriting

Choose a Subject

Choose a research subject that interests you and that you think will interest your readers. For help in brainstorming a subject, use the Idea Starters in the margin. Since you will be depending on research to find the information you need, check to see if you will be able to find information about a topic before you choose it.

Once you have determined that you will be able to find information on your topic, you need to limit your focus. Try to keep your subject manageable. Use an organizer like the one below to narrow your topic.

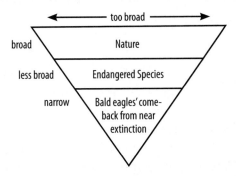

Find Sources

Your report should be based on a minimum of three reliable sources. Reliable sources are authored by qualified people. They are written to inform, not to express opinions or to convince people to think in a certain way. Whenever possible, use **primary sources,** such as diaries, letters, and interviews. You can also use **secondary sources,** such as magazine and newspaper articles, encyclopedia entries, and media documentaries. Search your library and the Internet for the best sources. Be sure that the information is trustworthy and current.

Take Notes

Use note cards to record the information you find. Each note card should contain one main idea. Make sure you **paraphrase** the information, rewriting it in your own words. Or, place it inside quotation marks to show that it is an exact **quotation**. Also remember to write the title, author, and page number of the source on the card.

Idea Starters

- scientific discoveries
- historical events
- hobbies
- current news events
- predictions
- interesting careers

⬤ Writing Tip

Evaluate sources, particularly those from the Web, by asking these questions:

- Who is the author? What is the author's background?
- How trustworthy is the information? What are the author's sources?
- Is the information up-to-date? If you use a Web site, check when the site was developed or last revised.

Your Turn _____

Get Started Choose a narrow subject and begin to research it. As you find good sources, list them in your **RWN,** using the style of citation selected by your teacher. This way, when it comes time to list your sources at the end of your paper, you will have all of the information in one place.

Learn It Online
Use an interactive graphic organizer to help focus your ideas. Try one at:

go.hrw.com   L7-995   Go

Writing Tip

Your audience may have varying degrees of knowledge about your topic, so make sure that you give them enough information to explain the important ideas but not so much information that they could lose interest.

Think About Purpose and Audience

Remember that the **purpose** of a research report is to find information and share it with other people. Who are those people? Your **audience** will probably include your teacher and classmates, but anyone who is interested in your topic could be your audience. As you review your notes, think about your readers and what they need to know. If you think readers might have questions that your notes do not answer, you should continue your research.

Organize Your Report

Decide how you will organize the information in your report—by **order of importance** or **chronological** (time) **order.** Then, you can sort your note cards to reflect this pattern. Once you are happy with the order of your note cards, you can create an outline. Use a framework like the one below to outline your research report.

State Your Thesis

Now that you have done your research, taken notes, and organized your thoughts, there is one more important step in getting ready to write. You now must be sure that you are clear about your thesis and can state it clearly for others. **The thesis statement** appears in the introductory paragraph of your report and tells what you will say about your topic. The thesis is then supported by the paragraphs in the body of your report. Each paragraph should have a main idea, supported by evidence.

Your outline should include your main idea statement, which will then be an umbrella for your outline's main headings.

Your Turn _____

State Your Main Idea Write your thesis statement in your **RWN.** Refer to it constantly as you plan and write your report, since this statement should guide the choices you make regarding what information to include or leave out. Also develop your outline, which will guide your writing.

Outline

Title: _____

Organization: _____

Thesis:

1. Main idea of paragraph 1:
    A. Supporting fact, example, or quotation: _____
    B. Supporting fact, example, or quotation: _____
2. Main idea of paragraph 2:
    A. Supporting fact, example, or quotation: _____
    B. Supporting fact, example, or quotation: _____

Drafting

Follow the Writer's Framework

Draft your report, using your framework to guide you. Remember that in your first paragraph you should capture your readers' attention and include your thesis statement.

Write the body paragraphs so that each one addresses a main heading in your outline. Sometimes, you might need more than one paragraph to explain an idea. Make sure that the main point in each paragraph is supported by **evidence.** Remember that evidence should include a variety of facts, examples, statistics, and direct quotations. If you find that your evidence is not adequate, go back to your sources, this time looking for specific information.

Bring your report to a close by restating your main idea and tying the information together. Draw a conclusion about your research or reflect on the information. Consider leaving readers with a precise image or a memorable quote.

A Framework for a Research Report
Introduction
• Grabs readers' interest
• Identifies topic
Body
• Discusses each main idea in one or more paragraphs
• Supports each main idea with facts
• Uses examples or quotations
Conclusion
• Summarizes or restates main idea
• Draws conclusions

List Your Sources

At the end of your paper, list your sources of information, under the heading *Works Cited*. Follow the guidelines in the Communications Handbook in the Resource Center or in a style guide such as the Modern Language Association (MLA) guide.

Grammar Link Writing Titles Correctly

When you list your sources, remember the rules for writing the titles of different genres.
- Underline (or use *italics* on a computer) the titles of books, Web sites, encyclopedias, magazines or newspapers, movies or video recordings, and television or radio programs.
- Place inside quotation marks the titles of documents on a Web site, encyclopedia articles, and magazine or newspaper articles.

Here's an example of a complete citation, following the *MLA Handbook*, for an online source that could possibly have been used to research and write the professional model on page 994.

Martell, Mark, and MaryBeth Garrigan. "Bald Eagle." *The Raptor* Sept. 1994. U of Minnesota. 18 Nov. 1998 <http://www.raptor.cvm.umn.edu/>.

Writing Tip

Effective "hooks," or attention-grabbing beginnings, for a research report include interesting facts, quotations, or questions.

Writing Tip

For a complete version of a research paper, log on to the Interactive Student Edition at go.hrw.com and go to page 997.

Your Turn _____

Write Your Draft Following your plan, write a draft of your research report. Be sure to think about:
- putting information you gathered from sources in your own words
- organizing each paragraph around one important idea
- supporting each paragraph with details, such as facts and statistics
- citing sources correctly

Peer Review

Working with a peer, review your drafts and take notes about each other's questions. Answering each question in this chart can help you to locate where and how your drafts could be improved.

Evaluating and Revising

Read the questions in the left column of the chart, and then use the tips in the middle column to help you make revisions to your report. The right column suggests techniques you can use to revise your draft.

Research Report: Guidelines for Content and Organization

Evaluation Question	Tip	Revision Technique
1. Does your introduction include a thesis statement? Does it grab the readers' attention?	**Underline** the thesis statement. **Put brackets** around the "hook" you used.	**Add** a thesis statement. **Add** an attention-grabber.
2. Does each paragraph in the body of the paper develop one important topic or main idea?	In the margin, **label** each paragraph with the topic it develops.	**Cut** unrelated ideas. **Rearrange** information into specific paragraphs where necessary.
3. Does each body paragraph contain supporting evidence, such as facts, examples, statistics, and direct quotations?	**Highlight** the facts, examples, statistics, and quotations that support each paragraph.	**Add** supporting details from your notes, if necessary.
4. Is the information in each paragraph properly summarized or quoted?	**Circle** sentences that sound as if someone else wrote them. **Draw a wavy line** under quoted information.	**Replace** with your own words, or **add** quotation marks.
5. Does your conclusion restate your thesis and sum up your findings?	**Put a check mark** next to the restatement. **Put an asterisk** next to the summary.	**Add** a restatement. **Elaborate** on your findings.
6. Have you included at least three sources in the *Works Cited* list?	**Number** the sources listed.	**Add** sources to the *Works Cited* list, if needed. **Add** information from these sources to your report.

Read this student's draft and the comments about it as a model for revising your own research report.

Greek Afterlife
by Kaitlin Heikes, Bailey Middle School

What happens when you die? The Ancient Greeks answered that question by developing a complex mythology of the afterlife.

Burial preparations usually involved placing a coin in the dead person's mouth. The coin would later be used as payment to cross the River Styx in the Underworld. Most people were also buried with something of personal significance, such as weapons or jewelry.

According to Greek mythology, souls of the dead were guided into the Underworld by Hermes, the Messenger of the Gods. After Hermes led these souls to the River Styx, Charon would then ferry them across the river into the Underworld. At that time the coin that had been placed in the dead person's mouth was taken. It was the price of passage across the river.

The opening paragraph grabs the reader's attention with a **thought-provoking question** and then states the **report's thesis.**

Examples provide details while also supporting the thesis statement.

The writer has used **chronological order** to present the information about passing into the Underworld.

MINI-LESSON **How to Focus Paragraphs**

Kaitlin's second paragraph develops the topic of ancient Greek burial preparation by focusing on the kinds of items buried with the dead. Therefore, her descriptions of items such as coins, weapons, and jewelry are pertinent to the topic of the paragraph. However, Kaitlin's discussion of the purpose of the coin is somewhat undeveloped. She needs to focus the paragraph by clarifying the purpose of the coin.

Kaitlin's Revision of Paragraph Two

~~When an ancient Greek died, burial preparations included careful consideration of what the person might need in the afterlife.~~ ~~Burial preparations~~
Usually was placed
~~usually involved placing~~ a coin in the dead person's mouth. The coin would later be used as payment to cross the River Styx in the Underworld. Most people were also buried with something of personal significance, such as weapons or jewelry.

Your Turn _____
Focus Your Paragraphs
Read your draft paragraph by paragraph, asking yourself these questions:
- Do I stick to one topic in this paragraph?
- Do I need to delete unnecessary details or add more support to this paragraph?

Student Draft *continues*

This body paragraph fully explores one idea—what happens once the dead reach the Asphodel Fields.

Once across the river, the souls would go to the Asphodel Fields, where they would wander aimlessly with no memory of their earthly existence. Some souls would be called beyond the Asphodel Fields to a Place of Judgment. Those who had led exceptional lives would go to Elysium, whereas those who had committed crimes were sent to Tartarus. Those somewhere in the middle would return to Asphodel Fields. Greek myths indicate that those who reached Elysium had the option of returning to earth and starting a new life.

The closing paragraph summarizes and restates the **main idea.**

The Ancient Greeks used these highly inventive and complex myths to answer a central question of human existence. Many of the Greeks' wide array of mythological gods played important roles in the afterlife myths.

MINI-LESSON ▸ **How to Provide Supporting Evidence**

Remember that each paragraph in a research report is focused on an important idea, and that this idea needs to be supported by a variety of evidence. Kaitlin does a great job of keeping the focus clear in the paragraph about what happens once the dead reach Asphodel Fields. However, some of her explanations do not include supporting evidence. For example, readers might wonder what kind of crimes were punished by being sent to Tartarus. She can also explain the importance of Elysium. Kaitlin can go back to her sources to try to find some specific information.

Kaitlin's Revision of Paragraph Four

Those who deserved punishment were sent to Tartarus. The punishment might be for committing horrible crimes such as murder, or it might come from a god's unhappiness with the dead. For example, the god Zeus sent all Titans to Tartarus for daring to fight against him in a war. The dead souls who had been neither bad nor good on earth

. . . Those who had led exceptional lives would go to Elysium. ~~, whereas those who had committed crimes were sent to Tartarus. Those somewhere in the middle~~ would return to Asphodel Fields. Greek myths indicate that those who reached Elysium had the option of returning to earth and starting a new life.

Thus, the ultimate goal for leading a good life was to reach Elysium and begin anew.

Your Turn _____

Provide Supporting Evidence

Read through your research report, specifically checking for your use of supporting evidence in each paragraph. How could statistics, facts, examples, or direct quotations support your main ideas and make them clearer to readers? Return to your sources to find supporting evidence to add to paragraphs that need it.

Proofreading and Publishing

Proofreading

You have carefully revised your research report to be sure that every paragraph is clear and well-developed. Now it's time to look at the report in a different way, focusing more narrowly to find and eliminate any errors. Mistakes in spelling, punctuation, and sentence structure can interfere with the readers' ability to focus on the new information they will learn from your paper. When you edit for errors and polish the report, you make it even easier to read and understand.

Grammar Link Introductory Prepositional Phrases

Introductory prepositional phrases can be excellent transitions to use when you show the order of events. Kaitlin uses introductory prepositional phrases in her report:

> **At that time** the coin that had been placed in the dead person's mouth was taken.

> **Once across the river,** the souls would go to the Asphodel Fields, where they would wander aimlessly with no memory of their earthly existence.

Note that the second phrase is followed by a comma, whereas the first one is not. Kaitlin has used a comma to avoid confusing the reader. Even though the words "the souls" is not capitalized, without the comma it is possible that someone might read the phrase "Once across the river the souls . . ." to mean that "the souls" was the name of the river. This is even more likely if the sentence were read aloud without the comma reminding the reader to pause after the word *river*.

Publishing

Now it is time to publish your research report to a wider audience. Begin by giving your report to your teacher and fellow classmates. Then, you might want to publish it on a personal or school Web page.

Reflect on the Process In your **RWN**, write a short response to each of these questions.

1. How did you determine if your sources were reliable?
2. Which piece of evidence in your report do you think is most powerful? Why?
3. What is the most interesting or surprising idea you learned by writing this report on your topic?

● **Proofreading Tip**

Ask a partner to help you proofread your report. In turn, you will proofread your partner's report. Gather good proofreading tools to use: a dictionary (to check spelling), a style guide or handbook (to check citations), and the Language Handbook in the Resource Center for looking up grammar questions.

Your Turn _____
Proofread and Publish

Proofread your report several times. Each time, look for errors in one area. For example, focus first on spelling. Then look closely at punctuation—for example, are introductory prepositional phrases punctuated correctly? During a third editing pass look at sentence structure. Then make the corrections and publish your polished report so that others can learn from your work.

Scoring Rubric

You can use one of the rubrics below to evaluate your research report from the Writing Workshop or your response to the prompt on the next page. Your teacher will tell you to use either the four- or the six-point rubric.

6-Point Scale

Score 6 *Demonstrates advanced success*
- focuses consistently on a clear thesis
- shows effective organization throughout, with smooth transitions
- offers thoughtful, creative ideas
- develops ideas thoroughly, using examples, details, and fully elaborated explanation
- exhibits mature control of written language

Score 5 *Demonstrates proficient success*
- focuses on a clear thesis
- shows effective organization, with transitions
- offers thoughtful ideas
- develops ideas competently, using examples, details, and well-elaborated explanation
- exhibits sufficient control of written language

Score 4 *Demonstrates competent success*
- focuses on a clear thesis, with minor distractions
- shows effective organization, with minor lapses
- offers mostly thoughtful ideas
- develops ideas adequately, with a mixture of general and specific elaboration
- exhibits general control of written language

Score 3 *Demonstrates limited success*
- includes some loosely related ideas that distract from the writer's focus
- shows some organization, with noticeable gaps in the logical flow of ideas
- offers routine, predictable ideas
- develops ideas with uneven elaboration
- exhibits limited control of written language

Score 2 *Demonstrates basic success*
- includes loosely related ideas that seriously distract from the writer's focus
- shows minimal organization, with major gaps in the logical flow of ideas
- offers ideas that merely skim the surface
- develops ideas with inadequate elaboration
- exhibits significant problems with control of written language

Score 1 *Demonstrates emerging effort*
- shows little awareness of the topic and purpose for writing
- lacks organization
- offers unclear and confusing ideas
- develops ideas in only a minimal way, if at all
- exhibits major problems with control of written language

4-Point Scale

Score 4 *Demonstrates advanced success*
- focuses consistently on a clear thesis
- shows effective organization throughout, with smooth transitions
- offers thoughtful, creative ideas
- develops ideas thoroughly, using examples, details, and fully elaborated explanation
- exhibits mature control of written language

Score 3 *Demonstrates competent success*
- focuses on a clear thesis, with minor distractions
- shows effective organization, with minor lapses
- offers mostly thoughtful ideas
- develops ideas adequately, with a mixture of general and specific elaboration
- exhibits general control of written language

Score 2 *Demonstrates limited success*
- includes some loosely related ideas that distract from the writer's focus
- shows some organization, with noticeable gaps in the logical flow of ideas
- offers routine, predictable ideas
- develops ideas with uneven elaboration
- exhibits limited control of written language

Score 1 *Demonstrates emerging effort*
- shows little awareness of the topic and purpose for writing
- lacks organization
- offers unclear and confusing ideas
- develops ideas in only a minimal way, if at all
- exhibits major problems with control of written language

Preparing for Timed Writing

Expository Essay

When responding to an on-demand prompt requiring an expository, or informative, essay, use the models you have read, what you've learned from writing your research report, the rubric on page 1002, and the steps below.

Writing Prompt

Being a good friend is a responsibility that most of us enjoy very much. In an essay, explain how a person earns a reputation as a good friend. You may use examples from your own experience or friendships you have observed as supporting evidence.

Study the Prompt

Begin by reading the prompt carefully. Circle or underline key words: *explain*, *good friend*, *responsibility*, *reputation*. Your purpose is to explain what you think are the traits or characteristics of a good friend. What have you observed or experienced that makes the relationship valuable? Make a list of traits that you can illustrate with examples.
Tip: Spend about five minutes studying the prompt.

Plan Your Response

Choose two to four traits that you can explain with examples. Be sure that your traits do not overlap. For example, if you think of "honesty" as a trait, do not list "always tells the truth" as another trait.

Look at your list of for specific details that you can use. What do these traits have in common? Do they relate to how friends help each other? Think about a common idea that links the traits of a good friend. That idea becomes the **thesis statement** for your essay. **Tip:** Spend about ten minutes planning your response.

Respond to the Prompt

Using your thesis and your notes, draft your essay. Follow these guidelines:

- Begin your essay with an introduction that includes a brief anecdote, or story, that illustrates friendship. The introduction should also include your thesis.
- The body of the essay should address each trait in a logical order, possibly ending with the most important trait. Your supporting points and specific examples must relate to the thesis of your essay.
- In the conclusion, restate your thesis and reflect on the importance of friendship.
  Tip: Spend about twenty minutes writing your draft.

Improve Your Response

Revising Go back to the key aspects of the prompt. Does your essay explain what you think makes a good friend? Have you used specific examples? Are the traits and your thesis connected?

Proofreading Take a few minutes to proofread to correct errors in grammar, spelling, punctuation, and capitalization. Make sure your edits are neat and your paper is legible.

Checking Your Final Copy Before you turn in your essay, read it one more time to catch any errors and to make any finishing touches. Taking this extra step will help you to turn in your best work. **Tip:** Save five or ten minutes to improve your paper.

Listening & Speaking Workshop

Giving a Research Presentation

Think as a Reader/Writer Delivering a speech can be a nerve-racking experience. If you prepare well, however, it can also be fun. A research presentation tells an audience the important points a researcher has discovered. You will do the same as you present your own research findings as a speech.

Adapt Your Report

Giving your research report as a speech does not mean simply reading it aloud. You will need to make changes to turn your report into an effective speech.

Tighten the Focus

Be sure to tighten the focus of your topic to keep the oral presentation down to a manageable length. Ask yourself which points are most **relevant,** or closely tied to the topic. Ask yourself, "What do I want my audience to gain from my speech?" Then, stick with the information that best helps you achieve this goal.

Hit the Perfect Note from Start to Finish

Your **introduction** gives the audience its first impression of you *and* your topic. Consider using one of the following methods to catch your listeners' attention:

- Begin with a question.
- Begin with a personal anecdote.
- Begin with an interesting or unusual fact.

For the **body** of the speech, choose an organizational pattern that will help your audience best understand your ideas. Finally, keep your **conclusion** short. Use it to reemphasize your main idea in a memorable way.

Credit Your Sources

Just as you listed your sources of information in your written research report, you will also need to give your sources credit in your speech. Credit each source by mentioning its author, title, or both.

Reader/Writer Notebook

Use your **RWN** to complete the activities for this workshop.

Deliver Your Research Presentation

To turn your ideas and outline into an effective speech, create **note cards** listing the main points you want to cover. Using note cards to jog your memory allows you to sound natural and make eye contact with your listeners.

Your speech will need one more ingredient: **coherence.** Use **transitional words and phrases** to connect ideas. Transitions can compare and contrast, indicate cause and effect, and show time, place, and supporting details.

Use Effective Verbal and Nonverbal Techniques

Using your note cards, practice your speech until you can get through it comfortably without stopping. Try rehearsing in front of a few friends or family members. As you practice, pay attention to the way you use your hands, eyes, and voice. Use natural **gestures**, and make **eye contact** with your listeners. Practice using these speaking techniques effectively:

- **Enunciation** Speak clearly and carefully.
- **Tempo** Talk at a slower rate than you normally would. This will help your listeners follow your ideas.
- **Voice Modulation** Stay calm to control your pitch.
- **Inflection** Stress, or emphasize, important words and phrases.

Use Multimedia Tools for Support

Consider including audio and visual materials, such as charts, graphs, illustrations, and audio or video recordings, in your speech. Audiovisual materials can make your ideas clearer and easier to remember for listeners and can provide additional information to your speech.

Be sure that your materials can be heard and seen by all the members of your audience. Always explain to your audience what the audiovisual material means, and continue to face the audience. Be sure to cue any audiotape or videotape before you begin to avoid wasting time rewinding or fast-forwarding during your speech. If you are using a computer to show any graphics or illustrations, be sure to set up the computer in advance so it is working properly. Being well-prepared with any multimedia tools will create a good impression with your listeners.

A Good Oral Presentation of Research:

- includes a clear thesis statement in the introduction and restates it in a memorable way in the conclusion
- organizes and presents main ideas clearly so that the audience follows and understands them easily
- adequately supports every main idea with a variety of evidence from different sources
- reveals that the speaker fully understands the topic
- effectively communicates ideas, both verbally and nonverbally

 **Speaking Tip**

When you choose the words you will use in your speech, be sure to use only **standard, or formal, English,** the kind of English you hear spoken in newscasts. For example, do not use contractions, slang, or other forms of informal language.

Myths and Folk Tales   **Directions:** Read the fable. Then, answer each question.

Belling the Cat by **Aesop**

The Mice once called a meeting to decide on a plan to free themselves of their enemy, the Cat. At least they wished to find some way of knowing when she was coming so they might have time to run away. Indeed, something had to be done, for they lived in such constant fear of her claws that they hardly dared stir from their dens by night or day.

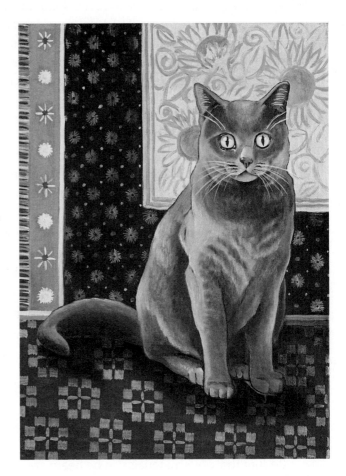

Many plans were discussed, but none of them was thought good enough. At last a very young Mouse got up and said:

"I have a plan that seems very simple, but I know it will be successful. All we have to do is to hang a bell about the Cat's neck. When we hear the bell ringing, we will know immediately that our enemy is coming."

All the Mice were much surprised that they had not thought of such a plan before. But in the midst of the rejoicing over their good fortune, an old Mouse arose and said:

"I will say that the plan of the young Mouse is very good. But let me ask one question: Who will bell the Cat?"

It is one thing to say that something should be done, but quite a different matter to do it.

1. What **problem** is dealt with in this fable?

   A The mice want to help a cat.

   B A silly young mouse has captured a cat.

   C The mice want to know when the cat is approaching.

   D The cat wants to befriend the mice.

2. What plan is proposed to solve the problem?

   A A bell should be put on the cat.

   B The cat should be killed.

   C The mice should put a bell in their den.

   D The cat should be welcomed.

3. What is wrong with the plan?

   A It is too easy and won't work.

   B The mice are too old to act.

   C No one wants to do it because it is dangerous.

   D It is a silly mouse's idea.

4. Which of the following is the best restatement of the **moral** of this fable?

   A A good plan is hard to find.

   B It is easier to propose plans than it is to carry them out.

   C People are basically cowards.

   D If you don't take a chance, nothing will get done.

Constructed Response

5. Fables, folk tales, legends, and myths were all told orally long before they were written down. What aspects of these stories would make them easy for storytellers to remember and tell? Explain your ideas in a paragraph, using this fable as an example.

6. Animal characters in fables and folk tales are often of two types: big and mean or small and crafty. Does that hold true for this fable? Why do you think these two character types appear so often? Explain your ideas in a paragraph, using this fable as an example.

PREPARING FOR STANDARDIZED TESTS

Informational Skills Review

Author's Perspective **Directions:** Read the following selection.
Then, read and respond to the questions that follow.

The Power of Music

from **Nadja: On My Way** by **Nadja Salerno-Sonnenberg**

This is something I know for a fact: You have to work hardest for the thing you love most. And when it's music that you love, you're in for the fight of your life.

It starts when your blood fills with music and you know you can't live without it. Every day brings a challenge to learn as much as possible and play even better than you did the day before.

You may want to achieve fame and glory, or you may want to play for fun. But whenever you fall in love with music, you'll never sit still again.

Music is more important than we will ever know. Great music can pull you right out of your chair. It can make you cry, or laugh, or feel a way you've never felt before. It can make you remember the first person you loved . . . music has that power.

Just imagine a world without music. What would you whistle when you walked down the street? How could you make a movie? How could you have a ball game without an organist leading the crowd when you're down by a run in the ninth?

You could be the most successful doctor in the world, but if you never turn on the radio, never go to a concert, never sing in the shower, never see *The King and I*—then you can't be a total, fulfilled human being. It's impossible.

When you realize how vital music is, you realize a musician's fight is also quite a noble, heroic endeavor. It didn't always seem that way to me. There was a time, years ago, when I felt discouraged and it seemed selfish to put so much time into music. Being a musician didn't seem as useful to others as being a surgeon, or even a good politician.

But I came to understand that it's a great, great gift to help people forget their everyday life and be uplifted. And better than uplifted, to be inspired; that's what music can do. It's important to us all, and I'm proud to put mind and muscle into recording, concerts, teaching, and studying: into being a musician.

Emotionally, music has brought me an enormous amount of joy and an enormous amount of despair and frustration. Because of music, I have learned what a battle is. I've won most, but not all—not by a long shot.

1. Which of the following statements best expresses the writer's **perspective** on music?

   A Music makes watching baseball more fun.

   B Everyone loves music.

   C Music is a vitally important part of life.

   D We should not imagine a world without music.

2. Which of the following statements is a **fact**?

   A "Just imagine a world without music."

   B "How could you make a movie?"

   C "Great music . . . can make you cry, or laugh, or feel a way you've never felt before."

   D "When you realize how vital music is, you realize a musician's fight is also quite a noble, heroic endeavor."

3. The writer supports her **perspective** with all of the following *except* —

   A facts

   B statistics

   C anecdotes

   D opinions

4. The writer believes that being a musician is as noble as other professions because —

   A people work hard to succeed

   B music inspires and uplifts other people

   C the *King and I* is a powerful musical

   D being a musician can be frustrating

Constructed Response

5. In your own words, state the writer's **perspective** on music. Use at least three examples of evidence from the article that support the perspective.

Vocabulary Skills Review

Synonyms **Directions:** Choose the word or phrase that means the same or about the same as the italicized word.

1. If you make a *suggestion,* you are putting forth —
   A some effort
   B an idea
   C a great deal of energy
   D a bad mood

2. If you *bore* a suitcase at the bus station, you —
   A bought it
   B borrowed it
   C carried it
   D dropped it

3. Someone who is *presumptuous* is —
   A arrogant
   B intelligent
   C sick
   D shy

4. When a person is *inconsolable,* he is —
   A unconscious
   B conceited
   C sturdy
   D heartbroken

5. Someone who is good at *deception* is known for —
   A building relationships
   B telling lies
   C making money
   D healing others

6. If your father *admonished* you about something, he —
   A punished you
   B laughed with you
   C congratulated you
   D warned you

7. *Endearments* are —
   A words of love
   B warning signs
   C reference letters
   D quick notes

8. A child's *astonishment* shows his or her —
   A immaturity
   B surprise
   C greed
   D unhappiness

9. A flower that is *exquisite* is —
   A wilting
   B thorny
   C beautiful
   D strong-smelling

Academic Vocabulary

Directions: Which phrase has the same meaning as the Academic Vocabulary word below?

10. If you *intervene* in an argument, you —
    A start it
    B keep it going
    C try to stop it
    D pretend it never happened

Writing Skills Review

Research Report **Directions:** Read the following passage from a research report. Then, answer the questions that follow.

(1) One place connected with the legend of King Arthur is Glastonbury, in Somerset, England. (2) Around 1190, monks claimed to have found Arthur's grave in Glastonbury Abbey's cemetery. (3) An excavation turned up a lead cross with Arthur's name inscribed on it. (4) A coffin was also found. (5) It contained the bones of a man and a woman. (6) They were presumed to be the remains of King Arthur and Queen Guinevere. (7) These remains were moved to a tomb in the abbey church, but everything disappeared after the monasteries were dissolved in 1539. (8) No one knows what became of the cross. (9) Modern excavation has shown that there had indeed been an earlier burial at Glastonbury. (10) No evidence exists of whose grave it was. (11) Some storytellers identify Glastonbury with Avalon, King Arthur's final resting place.

1. This is an excerpt from a research paper. What is the most likely topic of the complete paper?

    A The beginnings of the Arthurian legend

    B Important excavations in Somerset

    C Places connected with the Arthurian legend

    D Historical events and the legend of Arthur

2. Which of the following sources would be appropriate to consult when writing this research report?

    A *The New Arthurian Encyclopedia*

    B *The Early History of Glastonbury*

    C *The Arthurian Handbook*

    D All of the above

3. Which two sentences could best be combined to improve the flow of the passage?

    A Sentences 2 and 3

    B Sentences 4 and 5

    C Sentences 6 and 7

    D Sentences 8 and 9

4. Which of the following words could best be used to connect the ideas in sentences 9 and 10?

    A And

    B So

    C However

    D Therefore

5. Where could sentence 11 be moved to improve the logical flow of the passage?

    A After sentence 1

    B After sentence 4

    C After sentence 7

    D After sentence 9

Read On

Fiction

Sir Gawain and the Green Knight, Pearl, and Sir Orfeo

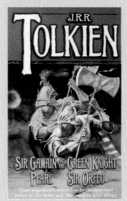

The legends in this book are masterpieces of a remote age—the age of chivalry and knights and holy quests. This translation of fourteenth-century narrative poems by J.R.R. Tolkien, the author of the Lord of the Ring series, sparkles with his unique imagination and artistry.

The Lightning Thief

Percy Jackson is a good kid whose world is turned upside down when, on a museum field trip, he discovers that he is the son of a Greek god. To educate Percy about his ancestry and protect him from angry forces, his mother sends him to a summer camp with other children of mixed mortal and Olympian heritage. A warning is printed at the beginning of Rick Riordan's novel—*Close the book right away and go back to your uninformed life*. It is up to you to make the decision: Dare to read this book, or continue to live your safe, boring life.

The Nightingale that Shrieked

Kevin Crossley-Holland, the author of an award-winning trilogy about the life of the young King Arthur, has collected tales from a variety of cultures and traditions—European, African, and Near and Middle Eastern—each of which is bound by its myths and legends. This collection celebrates the similarities and differences between the stories of peoples around the world.

Sword of the Rightful King

The newly crowned King Arthur has yet to win the support of his people. So Merlin, his teacher, creates a trick: a sword magically placed into a slab of rock that can only be withdrawn by Arthur. Merlin then announces that whoever removes the blade will rule all of England and invites any man who dares to try to pull out the sword. Jane Yolen has written more than two hundred books for children and adults and has won several of the most prestigious awards in children's literature.

Nonfiction

A Walk through the Heavens

When you look into the night sky, you are looking at the same sky your distant ancestors enjoyed. Besides enjoying the stars for their beauty, people from long ago used them for navigating the seas, predicting changes in the seasons, and explaining the mysteries of life. In this easy-to-use guide for beginner sky watchers, Milton D. Heifetz and Wil Tirion have provided a good introduction to stargazing as well as retellings of ancient myths and legends that early peoples used to interpret their nighttime sky.

A Primer of Chess

From an Indian romantic poem in A.D. 600 to a Persian epic in 850 to a Latin poem in 1000—its first mention in Europe—the game of chess has been a metaphor for war, love, and power. In this basic manual of chess, the World Chess Champion from 1921 to 1927, José Raúl Capablanca, explains the fundamentals of the game. A native of Cuba, Capablanca is considered to be one of the greatest players of all time. As you learn this game of the ages, remember that many cultures have contributed to its challenge and elegance.

Elizabeth I and the Spanish Armada

In this multicolored, informative graphic history, you will get a glimpse into the reign of Elizabeth I of England and especially into her underdog navy's 1588 victory over the world's mightiest navy at that time, the Spanish Armada. Full-color panels and maps, fact segments, and a time line provide the background to Colin Hynson's presentation of an important moment in history.

How Would You Survive in the Middle Ages?

Fiona MacDonald and David Salariya get you as close as possible to the Middle Ages without using a time machine. With illustrations and descriptions of the lives of royals, soldier-knights, and everyday workers, this book will help you answer the question "How would I survive in the Middle Ages?"

Resource Center

Handbook of Literary Terms

For more information about a topic, turn to the page(s) in this book indicated on a separate line at the end of the entries. To learn more about *Alliteration,* for example, turn to pages 649 and 701.

On another line are cross-references to entries in this handbook that provide closely related information. For instance, at the end of *Autobiography* is a cross-reference to *Biography.*

ALLITERATION **The repetition of the same or very similar consonant sounds in words that are close together.** Though alliteration usually occurs at the beginning of words, it can also occur within or at the end of words. Among other things, alliteration can help establish a mood, emphasize words, and serve as a memory aid. In the following example the *s* sound is repeated at the beginning of the words silken and *sad* and within the words *uncertain* and *rustling*:

> And the silken sad uncertain rustling of each purple curtain
>
> —Edgar Allan Poe, from "The Raven"

See pages 649, 701

ALLUSION **A reference to a statement, a person, a place, or an event from literature, history, religion, mythology, politics, sports, or science.** Allusions enrich the reading experience. Writers expect readers to recognize an allusion and to think, almost at the same time, about the literary work and the person, place, or event that it refers to. The following lines, describing a tunnel in the snow, contain an allusion to Aladdin, a character in *The Thousand and One Nights*:

> With mittened hands, and caps drawn low,
> To guard our necks and ears from snow,
> We cut the solid whiteness through.
> And, where the drift was deepest, made
> A tunnel walled and overlaid
> With dazzling crystal: we had read
> Of rare Aladdin's wondrous cave,
> And to our own his name we gave.
>
> —John Greenleaf Whittier,
>   from "Snow-Bound"

The cave in the tale contains a magic lamp that helps Aladdin discover vast riches. By alluding to Aladdin's cave, Whittier makes us see the icy tunnel in the snow as a magical, fairy-tale place.

The cartoon below makes an allusion to a popular fairy tale.

"*Now, this policy will cover your home for fire, theft, flood and huffing and puffing.*"

Reprinted with permission of The Saturday Evening Post,
© 1993, BFL&MS, Inc. Indianapolis.

ATMOSPHERE **The overall mood or emotion of a work of literature.** A work's atmosphere can often be described with one or two adjectives, such as *scary, dreamy, happy, sad,* or *nostalgic.* A writer creates atmosphere by using images, sounds, and descriptions that convey a particular feeling.

See also *Mood.*

AUTOBIOGRAPHY **The story of a person's life, written or told by that person.** Maijue Xiong wrote an autobiography called "An Unforgettable Journey" (page 33) about her escape from war-torn Laos as a child. Another well-known autobiographical work is Amy Tan's *Fish Cheeks.*

See pages 5, 31, 486, 524

See also *Biography.*

BIOGRAPHY **The story of a real person's life, written or told by another person.** Milton Meltzer has written a number of biographies of historical figures, such as George Washington and Mark Twain. "Elizabeth I" (page 511) is his biography of the remarkable queen of England who reigned in the sixteenth century. Frequent subjects of biographies are movie stars, television personalities, politicians, sports figures, self-made millionaires, even underworld figures. Biographies are among the most popular forms of contemporary literature.

See pages 5, 486, 509

See also *Autobiography.*

CHARACTER **A person or animal who takes part in the action of a story, play, or other literary work.** In some works, such as Aesop's fables, a character is an animal. In myths and legends a character may be a god or a superhero. Most often a character is an ordinary human being, such as Kevin in "User Friendly" (page 419).

The process of revealing the personality of a character in a story is called **characterization.** A writer can reveal a character in the following ways:

1. by letting you hear the character speak
2. by describing how the character looks and dresses
3. by letting you listen to the character's inner thoughts and feelings
4. by revealing what other people in the story think or say about the character
5. by showing you what the character does—how he or she acts
6. by telling you directly what the character's personality is like (cruel, kind, sneaky, brave, and so on)

When a writer uses the first five ways to reveal a character, you must make an inference, based on the evidence the writer provides, to decide what the character is like. When a writer uses the sixth method, however, you don't make a decision but are told directly what kind of person the character is.

Characters can be classified as static or dynamic. A **static character** is one who does not change much in the course of a work. Mr. Andersen in *Song of the Trees* (page 45) is a static character. By contrast, a **dynamic** character changes as a result of the story's events.

A character's **motivation** is any force that drives or moves the character to behave in a particular way. Many characters are motivated by the force of fear or love or ambition.

See pages 330, 762, 933, 965

CONFLICT **A struggle or clash between opposing characters or opposing forces.** In an **external conflict** a character struggles against some outside force. This outside force may be another character or society as a whole or a storm or a grizzly bear or even a machine. In "Three Skeleton Key" (page 163), the characters have an external conflict with a swarm of sea rats. An **internal conflict,** on the other hand, takes place within a character's mind. It is a struggle between opposing needs, desires, or emotions. In "After Twenty Years" (page 391), Officer Wells must resolve an internal conflict: Should he arrest an old friend or let him go?

See pages 130, 141, 762, 769, 773, 965

CONNOTATION **The feelings and associations that a word suggests.** For example, *tiny, cramped,* and *compact* all have about the same dictionary definition, or **denotation,** but they have different connotations. A manufacturer of small cars would not describe its product as tiny or cramped.

Instead, the company might say that its cars are compact. To grasp a writer's full meaning, you must pay attention not only to the literal definitions of words but also to their connotations. Connotations can be especially important in poetry.

See pages 60, 259, 271

DENOTATION **The literal, dictionary definition of a word.**

See pages 60, 259, 271

See also *Connotation.*

DESCRIPTION **The kind of writing that creates a clear image of something, usually by using details that appeal to one or more of the senses: sight, hearing, smell, taste, and touch.** Writers use description in all forms of fiction, nonfiction, and poetry. In "Fish Cheeks" (page 10), Amy Tan vividly describes the colors, sounds, and tastes of her family's Christmas celebration.

DIALECT **A way of speaking that is characteristic of a particular region or group of people.** A dialect may have a distinct vocabulary, pronunciation system, and grammar. In a sense, we all speak a dialect. One dialect usually becomes dominant in a country or culture and is accepted as the standard way of speaking. In the United States, for example, the formal written language is known as standard English. This is the dialect used in most newspapers and magazines.

Writers often reproduce regional dialects, or speech that reveals a character's economic or social class, in order to give a story local color. Mr. Baumer in "Bargain" (page 401) speaks in a dialect that reveals that his first language is German. The poem "Madam and the Rent Man" (page 667) is written in a dialect spoken in some urban African American communities in the northeastern United States.

DIALOGUE **A conversation between two or more characters.** Most stage dramas consist of dialogue together with stage directions. (Screenplays and teleplays sometimes include an unseen narrator.) The dialogue in a drama, such as *The Monsters Are Due on Maple Street* (page 835), must move the plot along and reveal its characters almost single-handedly. Dialogue is also an important element in most stories and novels as well as in some poems and nonfiction. It is one of the most effective ways for a writer to show what a character is like. It can also add realism and humor.

In the written form of a play, dialogue appears without quotation marks. In prose or poetry, however, dialogue is usually enclosed in quotation marks.

A **monologue** is a part of a drama in which one character speaks alone.

See pages 763, 768

DRAMA **A story written to be acted for an audience.** (A drama can also be appreciated and enjoyed in written form.) In a drama, such as *The Monsters Are Due on Maple Street* (page 832), the action is usually driven by characters who want something very much and take steps to get it. The related events that take place within a drama are often separated into **acts.** Each act is often made up of shorter sections, or **scenes.** Most plays have three acts, but there are many, many variations. The elements of a drama are often described as **introduction** or **exposition, complications, conflict, climax,** and **resolution.**

See pages 762–763, 768, 769, 770, 773

ESSAY **A short piece of nonfiction prose that examines a single subject.** Most essays can be categorized as either personal or formal.

The **personal essay** generally reveals a great deal about the writer's personality and tastes. Its tone is often conversational, sometimes even humorous. In a personal essay the focus is the writer's feelings and response to an experience.

The **formal essay** is usually serious, objective, and impersonal in tone. Its purpose is to inform readers about a topic or to persuade them to accept the writer's views.

See pages 5, 63, 486, 492

FABLE **A brief story in prose or verse that teaches a moral or gives a practical lesson about how to get along in life.** The characters of most fables are animals that behave and speak like human beings. Some of the most popular fables are attributed to Aesop, who is thought to have been a slave in ancient Greece.

See also *Folk Tale, Myth*.

FICTION **A prose account that is made up rather than true.** The term *fiction* usually refers to novels and short stories. Fiction may be based on a writer's experiences or on historical events, but characters, events, and other details are altered or added by the writer to create a desired effect.

See pages 4, 5, 6, 7

See also *Nonfiction*.

FIGURE OF SPEECH **A word or phrase that describes one thing in terms of something else and is not literally true.** Figures of speech always involve some sort of imaginative comparison between seemingly unlike things. The most common forms are **simile** ("The stars were like diamonds"), **metaphor** ("My soul is an enchanted boat"), and **personification** ("The sun smiled down on the emerald-green fields").

See pages 647, 659, 719

See also *Metaphor, Personification, Simile*.

FLASHBACK **An interruption in the action of a plot to tell what happened at an earlier time.** A flashback breaks the usual movement of the narrative by going back in time. It usually gives background information that helps the reader understand the present situation. "A Mason-Dixon Memory" (page 65) contains a long flashback.

A break in the unfolding of a plot to an episode in the future is known as a **flash-forward.**

See page 64

FOLK TALE **A story with no known author that originally was passed on from one generation to another by word of mouth.** Folk tales tend to travel, so similar plots and characters are found in several cultures. For example, "Yeh-Shen" (page 86) is a Chinese folk tale that is very similar to the European story of Cinderella. Folk tales often contain **fantastic** elements, or events that could not happen in the world as we know it.

See pages 4, 75, 902–903

See also *Fable, Myth*.

FORESHADOWING **The use of clues to suggest events that will happen later in the plot.** Foreshadowing is used to build suspense or create anxiety. In a drama a gun found in a bureau drawer in Act One is likely to foreshadow violence later in the play. In "Three Skeleton Key" (page 163), the story of three convicts who perished on the key foreshadows the danger the three lighthouse keepers will face.

See pages 131, 132, 136

See also *Suspense*.

FREE VERSE **Poetry without a regular meter or a rhyme scheme.** Poets writing in free verse try to capture the natural rhythms of ordinary speech. To create their music, poets writing in free verse may use internal rhyme, repetition, alliteration, and onomatopoeia. Free verse also frequently makes use of vivid imagery. The following poem in free verse effectively uses images and the repetition of words to describe the effects of a family's eviction for not paying rent:

> **Eviction**
> what i remember about that day
> is boxes stacked across the walk
> and couch springs curling through the air
> and drawers and tables balanced on the curb
> and us, hollering,
> leaping up and around
> happy to have a playground;
>
> nothing about the emptied rooms
> nothing about the emptied family
>
> —Lucille Clifton

See pages 646, 648, 701, 712

See also *Poetry, Rhyme, Rhythm.*

IMAGERY **Language that appeals to the senses.** Most images are visual—that is, they create pictures in your mind by appealing to the sense of sight. Images can also appeal to the sense of hearing, touch, taste, or smell or to several senses at once. The sensory images in "The Highwayman" (page 673) add greatly to the enjoyment of the poem. Though imagery is an element in all types of writing, it is especially important in poetry.

See pages 655, 665, 701

See also *Poetry.*

IRONY **In general, a contrast between expectation and reality.** Irony can create powerful effects, from humor to strong emotion. Here are three common types of irony:

1. **Verbal irony** involves a contrast between what is said or written and what is meant. If you were to call someone who failed a math test Einstein, you would be using verbal irony.
2. **Situational irony** occurs when what happens is very different from what is expected to happen. The surprise ending of "After Twenty Years" (page 391) involves situational irony.
3. **Dramatic irony** occurs when the audience or the reader knows something a character does not know. In Part 2 of "The Highwayman" (page 673), the reader feels an anxious sense of irony when King George's soldiers have Bess tied up. Although the highwayman doesn't yet know it, we know that a trap is set for him.

MAIN IDEA **The most important idea expressed in a paragraph or in an entire essay.** The main idea may be directly stated in a **topic sentence,** or you may have to look at all the details in the paragraph and make an **inference,** or educated guess, about its main idea.

See pages 141, 493, 495, 497

METAMORPHOSIS **A marvelous change from one shape or form to another one.** In myths the change is usually from human to animal, from animal to human, or from human to plant. Greek and Roman myths contain many examples of metamorphosis. The myth of Echo and Narcissus (page 434) tells how the vain youth Narcissus pines away for love of his own reflection until he is changed into a flower.

See page 941

See also *Myth.*

METAPHOR **An imaginative comparison between two unlike things in which one thing is said to be another thing.** A metaphor is an important type of figurative language. Metaphors are used in all forms of writing and are common in ordinary speech. If you were to say someone has a heart of gold, you would not mean that the person's heart is actually made of metal. You would mean, instead, that the person is warm and caring. You would be speaking metaphorically.

PEANUTS reprinted with permission of the United Feature Syndicate, Inc.

Metaphors differ from similes, which use specific words (notably *like, as, than,* and *resembles*) to state comparisons. William Wordsworth's famous comparison "I wandered lonely as a cloud" is a simile because it uses *as.* If Wordsworth had written "I was a lonely, wandering cloud," he would have been using a metaphor.

An **extended metaphor** is a metaphor that is developed, or extended, through several lines of writing or even throughout an entire poem. "I Like to See It Lap the Miles" (page 663) uses an extended metaphor to compare a train to a horse throughout the whole poem.

See pages 647, 659, 719

See also *Figure of Speech, Personification, Simile.*

MOOD **The overall emotion created by a work of literature.** A work of literature can often be described with one or more adjectives: *sad, scary, hopeful, exciting,* and so on. These are descriptions of the work's mood—its emotional atmosphere. For example, the mood of "Annabel Lee" (page 431) could be described as haunting or romantic. That mood has a lingering effect on its readers.

See pages 650, 651

See also *Atmosphere.*

MOTIVATION **See Character.**

MYTH **A story that explains something about the world and typically involves gods or other superhuman beings.** Myths, which at one time were believed to be true, reflect the traditions of the culture that produced them. Almost every culture has **origin myths** (or **creation myths**), stories that explain how something in the world (perhaps the world itself) came to be. Myths may also explain many other aspects of nature. The ancient Greek myth of Echo and Narcissus (page 434), for example, explains the origins of a flower. Most myths are very old and were handed down orally long before being put in written form. In some of the world's greatest myths, a hero or even a god embarks on a **quest,** a perilous journey taken in pursuit of something of great value.

See page 900

See also *Fable, Folk Tale.*

NONFICTION **Prose writing that deals with real people, events, and places without changing any facts.** Popular forms of nonfiction are the **autobiography,** the **biography,** and the **essay**. Other examples of nonfiction include newspaper stories, magazine articles, historical writing, scientific reports, and even personal diaries and letters.

Nonfiction writing can be subjective or objective. **Subjective writing** expresses the feelings and opinions of the writer. **Objective** writing conveys the facts without introducing any emotion or personal bias.

See pages 4, 5, 6, 7, 486, 487, 570

See also *Autobiography, Biography, Fiction.*

NOVEL A fictional story that is usually more than one hundred book pages long. A novel uses all the elements of storytelling—**plot, character, setting, theme,** and **point of view.** A novel, because of its length, usually has more characters, settings, and themes and a more complex plot than a short story. Modern writers sometimes do not pay much attention to one or more of the novel's traditional elements. Some novels today are basically character studies that include only the barest story lines. Other novels don't look much beyond the surface of their characters and concentrate instead on plot and setting. A novel can deal with almost any topic. Many of the books recommended in the Read On sections of this text are novels. A **novella** is shorter than a novel and longer than a short story.

See page 4

ONOMATOPOEIA The use of words whose sounds echo their sense. Onomatopoeia (ahn uh mat uh PEE uh) is so natural to us that we use it at a very early age. *Buzz, rustle, boom, ticktock, tweet,* and *bark* are all examples of onomatopoeia. Onomatopoeia is an important element in creating the music of poetry. In the following lines the poet creates a frenzied mood by choosing words that imitate the sound of alarm bells:

> Oh, the bells, bells, bells!
> What a tale their terror tells
> Of Despair!
> How they clang, and clash, and roar!
> What a horror they outpour
> On the bosom of the palpitating air!
> Yet the ear, it fully knows
> By the twanging
> And the clanging
> How the danger ebbs and flows.
>
> —Edgar Allan Poe,
> from "The Bells"

See pages 649, 701

See also *Alliteration.*

PERSONIFICATION A figure of speech in which a nonhuman or nonliving thing or quality is talked about as if it were human or alive.

See page 718

See also *Figure of Speech, Metaphor, Simile.*

PLOT The series of related events that make up a story. Plot is what happens in a short story, novel, play, or narrative poem. Most plots are built on these bare bones: An **introduction,** or **exposition,** tells us who the characters are and what their **conflict** is. **Complications** arise as the characters take steps to resolve the conflict. The plot reaches a **climax,** the most emotional or suspenseful moment in the story, when the outcome is decided one way or another. The last part of a story is the **resolution,** when the characters' problems are solved and the story ends.

Not all works of fiction or drama have this traditional plot structure. Some modern writers experiment, often eliminating parts of a traditional plot in order to focus on elements such as character, point of view, or mood.

See pages 5, 27, 130–131, 132, 136, 137, 138, 139, 762

See also *Conflict.*

POETRY A kind of rhythmic, compressed language that uses figures of speech and imagery designed to appeal to emotion and imagination. We know poetry when we see it because it is usually arranged in a particular way on the page. Traditional poetry often has a regular pattern of rhythm (**meter**) and may have a regular **rhyme scheme.**

Free verse is poetry that has no regular rhythm or rhyme. "Names of Horses" (page 703) is a free-verse poem that is also an **elegy,** a poem that mourns the passing of something that is important to the writer. "Arithmetic" (page 715) is a free-verse poem that is also a **catalog poem,** a poem that lists the poet's thoughts or feelings about a subject. A major form of poetry is the **narrative poem,** which tells a story, such as "The Highwayman" (page 673). Two popular narrative forms are the **epic** and the **ballad.** Another major form of poetry is the **lyric poem,** which expresses a speaker's feelings. "I Ask My Mother to Sing" (page 683) is a lyric poem that is also a **sonnet**—a poem of fourteen lines that follows a strict form. The **ode** is a type of lyric poem that celebrates something. A lighthearted example is "Ode to Family Photographs" (page 684).

See pages 646–651

See also *Figure of Speech, Free Verse, Imagery, Refrain, Rhyme, Rhythm, Speaker, Stanza.*

POINT OF VIEW The vantage point from which a story is told. The most common points of view are the **omniscient,** the **third-person limited,** and the **first person.**

1. In the **omniscient** (ahm NIHSH uhnt), or all-knowing, **point of view** the narrator knows everything about the characters and their problems. This all-knowing narrator can tell about the characters' past, present, and future. This kind of narrator can even tell what the characters are thinking or what is happening in other places. This narrator is not in the story. Instead, he or she stands above the action, like a god. The omniscient is a very familiar point of view; we have heard it in fairy tales since we were very young. "Yeh-Shen" (page 86), a Chinese Cinderella story, is told from the omniscient point of view.

> Her loveliness made her seem a heavenly being, and the king suddenly knew in his heart that he had found his true love.

2. In the **third-person limited point of view,** the narrator focuses on the thoughts and feelings of only one character. From this point of view, you observe the action through the eyes and feelings of only one character in the story.

> There was such a lot to know and understand about being a dragonrider that sometimes Keevan was overwhelmed. How would he ever be able to remember everything he ought to know at the right moment?
>
> —Anne McCaffrey, from "The Smallest Dragonboy"

3. In the **first-person point of view,** one of the characters, using the personal pronoun I, is telling the story. You become very familiar with this narrator but can know only what he or she knows and can observe only what he or she observes. All information about the story must come from this character. In some cases the information is incorrect. "User Friendly" (page 419) is told from the first-person point of view of the boy whose computer starts acting funny.

> As I walked by the corner of my room, where my computer table was set up, I pressed the on button, slid a diskette into the floppy drive, then went to brush my teeth. By the time I got back, the computer's screen was glowing greenly, displaying the message: *Good morning, Kevin.*

See pages 340, 341

REFRAIN **A group of words repeated at intervals in a poem, song, or speech.** Refrains are usually associated with songs and poems, but they are also used in speeches and other forms of literature. Refrains are most often used to create rhythm, but they may also provide emphasis or commentary, create suspense, or help hold a work together. Refrains may be repeated with small variations in a work in order to fit a particular context or to create a special effect.

RHYME **The repetition of accented vowel sounds and all sounds following them in words close together in a poem.** *Mean* and *screen* are rhymes, as are *crumble* and *tumble*. Rhyme has many purposes in poetry: It creates rhythm, lends a songlike quality, emphasizes ideas, organizes the poem (for instance, into stanzas or couplets), provides humor or delight, and makes the poem memorable.

Many poems—for example, "The Runaway" (page 697)—use **end rhymes,** rhymes at the end of a line. In the following stanza, *walls/calls/falls* form end rhymes, as do *hands/sands.* The pattern of end rhymes in a poem is called a **rhyme scheme.** To indicate the rhyme scheme of a poem, use a separate letter of the alphabet for each rhyme. For example, the rhyme scheme below is *aabba.*

> Darkness settles on roofs and walls,
> But the sea, the sea in the darkness calls;
> The little waves, with their soft,
>   white hands,
> Efface the footprints in the sands,
> And the tide rises, the tide falls.
>
> —Henry Wadsworth Longfellow,
>   from "The Tide Rises, the Tide Falls"

Internal rhymes are rhymes within lines. The following line has an internal rhyme (*turning/burning*):

> Back into the chamber turning, all my soul
>   within me burning
>
> —Edgar Allan Poe,
>   from "The Raven"

Rhyming sounds need not be spelled the same way; for instance, *gear/here* forms a rhyme. Rhymes can involve more than one syllable or more than one word; *poet/know it* is an example. Rhymes involving sounds that are similar but not exactly the same are called **slant rhymes** (or **near rhymes** or **approximate rhymes**). *Leave/live* is an example of a slant rhyme. Poets writing in English often use slant rhymes because English is not a very rhymable language. It has many words that rhyme with no other word (*orange*) or with only one other word (*mountain/fountain*). Poets interested in how a poem looks on the printed page sometimes use **eye rhymes,** or **visual rhymes**—rhymes involving words that are spelled similarly but are pronounced differently. *Tough/cough* is an eye rhyme. (*Tough/rough* is a "real" rhyme.)

See pages 649, 655, 695, 706

See also *Free Verse, Poetry, Rhythm.*

RHYTHM **A musical quality produced by the repetition of stressed and unstressed syllables or by the repetition of certain other sound patterns.** Rhythm occurs in all language—written and spoken—but is particularly important in poetry.

The most obvious kind of rhythm is the regular pattern of stressed and unstressed syllables that is found in some poetry. This pattern is called **meter.** In the following lines describing a cavalry charge, the rhythm echoes the galloping of the attackers' horses:

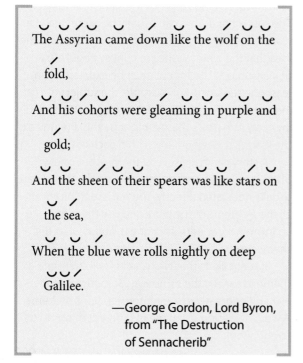

> The Assyrian came down like the wolf on the
>   fold,
> And his cohorts were gleaming in purple and
>   gold;
> And the sheen of their spears was like stars on
>   the sea,
> When the blue wave rolls nightly on deep
>   Galilee.
>
> —George Gordon, Lord Byron,
> from "The Destruction
> of Sennacherib"

Marking the stressed (ʹ) and unstressed (˘) syllables in a line is called **scanning** the line. Lord Byron's scanned lines show a rhythmic pattern in which two unstressed syllables are followed by a stressed syllable. Read the lines aloud and listen to this rhythmic pattern. Also, notice how the poem's end rhymes help create the rhythm.

Writers can also create rhythm by repeating words and phrases or even by repeating whole lines and sentences.

See pages 648, 655, 701

See also *Free Verse, Poetry, Rhyme.*

SETTING **The time and place in which the events of a work of literature take place.** Most often the setting of a narrative is described early in the story. Setting often contributes to a story's emotional effect. In *Song of the Trees* (page 45), the forest setting helps create a soothing (yet mysterious) mood. Setting frequently plays an important role in a story's plot, especially one that centers on a conflict between a character and nature. In "Three Skeleton Key" (page 163), the characters must fight elements of a deadly setting to survive—they are threatened by a vast army of rats. Some stories are closely tied to particular settings, and it is difficult to imagine them taking place elsewhere. By contrast, other stories could easily take place in a variety of settings.

See pages 43, 59, 131, 132, 136, 762

SHORT STORY **A fictional prose narrative that is usually ten to twenty book pages long.** Short stories were first written in the nineteenth century. Early short story writers include Sir Walter Scott and Edgar Allan Poe. Short stories are usually built on a plot that consists of at least these bare bones: the **introduction** or **exposition, conflict, complications, climax,** and **resolution.** Short stories are more limited than novels. They usually have only one or two major characters and one important setting.

See pages 4, 15, 71

See also *Conflict, Fiction, Plot.*

SIMILE **A comparison between two unlike things, using a word such as *like, as, than,* or *resembles.*** The simile is an important type of figure of speech. In the following lines a simile creates a clear image of moths in the evening air:

> When the last bus leaves, moths stream toward lights like litter in wind.
>
> —Roberta Hill,
> from "Depot in Rapid City"

This example shows that similes can generate a strong emotional impact. By choosing to compare the moths to litter, the poet not only creates a picture in the reader's mind but also establishes a lonely, dreary mood.

See pages 647, 717, 719

See also *Figure of Speech, Metaphor.*

SPEAKER **The voice talking in a poem.** Sometimes the speaker is identical to the poet, but often the speaker and the poet are not the same. The poet may be speaking as a child, a woman, a man, an animal, or even an object.

See also *Poetry.*

STANZA **In a poem a group of consecutive lines that forms a single unit.** A stanza in a poem is something like a paragraph in prose; it often expresses a unit of thought. A stanza may consist of any number of lines. "I'm Nobody!" (page 661) consists of two four-line stanzas, each expressing a separate idea. In some poems each stanza has the same rhyme scheme.

See pages 646, 695

See also *Poetry, Rhyme.*

SUSPENSE **The uncertainty or anxiety you feel about what will happen next in a story.** In "Three Skeleton Key" (page 163), the narrator hooks your curiosity in the first sentences when he says he is about to describe his "most terrifying experience."

See pages 130, 131, 137

See also *Foreshadowing.*

SYMBOL **A person, a place, a thing, or an event that has its own meaning and stands for something beyond itself as well.** Examples of symbols are all around us—in music, on television, and in everyday conversation. The skull and crossbones, for example, is a symbol of danger; the dove is a symbol of peace; and the red rose stands for true love. In literature, symbols are often more personal. For example, in "Names/Nombres" (page 499), Julia Alvarez's name is a symbol of her cultural identity.

THEME **The truth about life revealed in a work of literature.** A theme is not the same as a subject. The subject of a work can usually be expressed in a word or two: *love, childhood, death.* The theme is the idea that the writer wishes to convey about a particular subject. The theme must be expressed in at least one sentence. For example, the subject of *The Monsters Are Due on Maple Street* (page 835) is alien invasion. The play's theme might be this: Prejudice is the fearful, unseen enemy within each of us.

A story can have several themes, but one will often stand out from the others. A work's themes are usually not stated directly. You have to think about all the elements of the work and use them to make an **inference,** or educated guess, about what the themes are.

It is not likely that two readers will ever state a theme in exactly the same way. Sometimes readers even differ greatly in their interpretations of theme. A work of literature can mean different things to different people.

See pages 340, 349, 859, 923, 965

TONE **The attitude that a writer takes toward the audience, a subject, or a character.** Tone is conveyed through the writer's choice of words and details. The poem "maggie and milly and molly and may" (page 708) is light and playful in tone. By contrast, the poem "Annabel Lee" (page 431) is serious in tone.

See pages 75, 94, 647, 650, 665, 705

Handbook of Reading and Informational Terms

For more information about a topic, turn to the page(s) in this book indicated on a separate line at the end of the entry. To learn more about *Cause and Effect,* for example, turn to page 619.

On another line are cross-references to entries in this handbook that provide closely related information. For instance, the entry *Chronological Order* contains a cross-reference to *Text Structures.*

ANALOGY

1. An **analogy** is a point-by-point comparison made between two things to show how they are alike. An analogy shows how something unfamiliar is like something well-known.
2. Another kind of analogy is a **verbal analogy.** A verbal analogy is a word puzzle. It gives you two words and asks you to identify another pair of words with a similar relationship. In an analogy the symbol ":" means "is to." The symbol "::" means "as."

> Select the pair of words that best completes the analogy.
>
> Toe : foot :: _____
>
> A   house : barn
> B   finger : hand
> C   road : path
> D   light : darkness
>
> The correct answer is B: Toe : foot :: finger : hand, or "Toe is to foot as finger is to hand." The relationship is that of part to whole. A toe is part of the foot; a finger is part of the hand.

Another relationship often represented in verbal analogies is that of opposites:

> clear : cloudy :: bright : dark

Both sets of words are opposites. Clear is the opposite of cloudy, and bright is the opposite of dark.

Verbal analogies are often found in tests, where they are used to check vocabulary and thinking skills.

ARGUMENT   An **argument** is a position supported by evidence. Arguments are used to persuade us to accept or reject an opinion on a subject. Arguments are also used to persuade us to act in a certain way.

Supporting evidence can take the form of facts, statistics, anecdotes (brief stories that illustrate a point), and expert opinions. Not all arguments are logical. **Emotional appeals** find their way into most arguments, and you should learn to recognize them. Details that appeal to your feelings make an argument more interesting and memorable—but you should not accept an argument that is based only on an emotional appeal.

Athletes should not charge kids for autographs. The most popular players are the ones that fans ask for autographs. These players don't need extra money. They already earn millions of dollars. Kids are much poorer than star athletes. I had to spend six weeks of my allowance and borrow twenty dollars from my brother to attend a game. After the game I started waiting in line to get an autograph. The line broke up quickly when we heard that the player was charging fifty dollars for each autograph. We were all disgusted. After all, the athletes' fans make them famous. My soccer coach says players should see that an autograph is a way of saying "thank you" to a loyal fan. Signing a name isn't hard. It takes less than a minute. To be asked to pay for an autograph is an insult.	*Position*
	Opinion
	Fact
	Anecdote
	Emotional appeal
	Expert opinion
	Fact
	Emotional appeal

See pages 447, 554

See also *Evidence.*

BIAS   A leaning in favor of or against a person or issue is called a **bias** (BY uhs). Sometimes a writer's bias is obvious. For instance, Rudyard Kipling in "Rikki-tikki-tavi" (page 143) reveals his bias against snakes. In the conflict between the cobras and a mongoose, Kipling is clearly biased in favor of the mongoose. People are often not upfront about their biases. You should look for bias whenever writers or speakers make claims and assertions that they don't (or can't) support with logical reasons and facts. When people ignore, distort, or hide the facts that oppose their bias, they may be guilty of prejudice.

See page 456

CAUSE AND EFFECT   A **cause** is the event that makes something happen. An **effect** is what happens as a result of the cause. Storytellers use the cause-and-effect organizational pattern to develop their plots. Writers of historical texts use this organizational pattern to explain things like the causes and effects of war. Scientific writers use this organizational pattern to explain things like the causes and effects of an epidemic. Some of the words and phrases that point to causes and effects are *because, since, therefore, so that,* and *if . . . then.* Notice the cause-and-effect chain in the following summary of the Midas myth:

> Because he did a favor for a god, Midas was granted the golden touch. Since everything he touched turned to gold, his daughter also turned to gold. Because of that, he asked to be released from the golden touch. Since gold had brought him such trouble, he then turned to nature and rejected riches.

See pages 344, 345, 346, 619

See also *Text Structures.*

CHRONOLOGICAL ORDER   Most narrative texts, true or fictional, are written in **chronological order.** Writers use chronological order when they put events in the sequence, or order, in which they happened in time, one after the other. Recipes and technical directions are usually written in chronological order. When you read a narrative, look for words and phrases like *next, then,* and *finally.* Writers use such words as transitions to signal the order in which events or steps occur.

See pages 9, 10, 587

See also *Text Structures.*

COMPARE-AND-CONTRAST PATTERN When you **compare,** you look for similarities, or likenesses. When you **contrast,** you look for differences. You've used comparison and contrast many times. For instance, you might compare and contrast the features of several dogs when you choose a puppy that is like the dog you used to have. When writers compare and contrast, they organize the text to help readers understand the **points of comparison,** the features that they're looking at.

A Venn diagram can help you tell similarities from differences. The one below compares and contrasts two stories: "Yeh-Shen" (page 86) and the "Cinderella" folk tale. Where the circles overlap, note how the stories are alike. Where there is no overlap, note differences.

Venn Diagram

"Cinderella"   "Yeh-Shen"

- helped by fairy godmother
- meets prince at ball

- has wicked stepmother
- wants to go to ball
- has wish granted
- has rags changed to beautiful clothes
- obeys one rule
- loses shoe
- is found by royalty

- helped by fish
- meets king when he is searching for owner of shoe

Differences   *Similarities*   *Differences*

An effective comparison-and-contrast text may be organized in the block pattern or the point-by-point pattern.

Block pattern. A writer using the block pattern first discusses all the points of subject 1, then goes on to discuss all the points of subject 2.

Subject 1—"Yeh-Shen": In the Chinese folk tale "Yeh-Shen" a magic fish dies, but its spirit gives Yeh-Shen, a kind orphan, advice and help. It changes her rags into beautiful clothes. Her wicked stepmother treats Yeh-Shen badly. [*And so on*]

Subject 2—"Cinderella": American children probably know best the Cinderella story in which a fairy godmother changes Cinderella's rags into beautiful clothes. Cinderella also has a wicked stepmother. [*And so on*]

Point-by-point pattern. A writer who uses the point-by-point pattern goes back and forth between the two things being compared and contrasted.

In "Yeh-Shen" a magic fish helps the orphan girl. In "Cinderella," however, a fairy godmother helps the girl. In both stories, there is a wicked stepmother. [*And so on*]

Some of the words that signal comparison and contrast are *although, but, either . . . or, however,* and *yet.*

See pages 8, 11, 15, 75, 85, 91, 965

See also *Text Structures.*

CONCLUSIONS A **conclusion** is a general summing up of the specific details in a text. The text below is from "Borders of Baseball: U.S. and Cuban Play" (page 315). One reader's conclusion based on these details follows the text.

U.S. ballparks are different from Cuban ones. Fans pass souvenir and food stands while going to and from their seats. Team logos are plastered on everything from cups to T-shirts. Cuban ballparks, by contrast, are not very commercialized. In Cuba, baseball is a source of national pride, not a way to push people to buy certain products.

Conclusion: In Cuba, baseball is less affected by economic considerations.

See pages 907, 955

See also *Evidence.*

CONNOTATION AND DENOTATION The **connotation** of a word is all the feelings and associations that have come to be attached to the word. The **denotation** of a word is its strict dictionary definition. Not all words have connotations. Words like *the, writer,* and *paper* do not have connotations. Words like *Democrat, Republican, conservative,* and *liberal* are loaded with associations and feelings.

The words *skinny, slender, gaunt,* and *lean* have approximately the same denotation. They all mean "thin; having little fat." There are important shades of meaning among those words, however. If a relative said you were skinny or gaunt, you'd probably feel hurt or angry. *Skinny* and *gaunt* have negative connotations. They suggest that the thin person may have been sick and is now unattractive. *Slender* and *lean,* on the other hand, have positive connotations. They suggest a healthy, athletic body.

See pages 60, 259, 271

CONTEXT CLUES When you don't know the meaning of a word, look for a clue to its meaning in the **context,** the words and sentences surrounding the unfamiliar word. Here are some common types of context clues. In each sentence, the unfamiliar word appears in boldface type; the clue is underlined.

Definition clue. Look for a familiar word that defines the meaning of the unfamiliar word.

> Keevan was rarely <u>bothered</u> by rivals, but he was **perturbed** to see Beterli wandering over to him.

The word *bothered* tells you that *perturbed* also means "something like bothered."

Example clue. Look for examples of the unfamiliar word. In the context of the sentence, the examples reveal the meaning of the unfamiliar word.

> **Tugs** and <u>other boats</u> were washed ashore by the tidal wave.

The words *other boats* tell you that a tug is a kind of boat.

Restatement clue. Look for words that restate the meaning of the unfamiliar word.

> We **delved** into the criminal's past—we <u>searched through</u> hundreds of pieces of evidence.

The restatement clue that helps you guess the meaning of *delved* is *searched through.* (*Delved* means "dug into; searched; investigated.")

Contrast clue. Look for words that contrast the unfamiliar word with a word or phrase in the sentence that you know.

> Although Helen wanted to **detain** the visitors, she had to <u>let</u> them <u>go.</u>

This sentence tells you that *detain* means the opposite of "let go."

See pages 40, 506

EVIDENCE When you read informational and persuasive texts, you need to **assess,** or judge, the **evidence** that a writer uses to support a position. That means you need to read carefully, looking critically at the writer's claims and assertions. You need to evaluate the writer's sources. You also need to look at the writer's own background and expertise. One way to assess evidence is to give it the **3As test**. The *As* stand for *adequate, appropriate,* and *accurate.*

Adequate means "sufficient" or "enough." You have to see if the writer has provided enough evidence to support his or her position. For some positions, one or two supporting facts may be adequate. For others a writer may need to provide many facts, maybe even statistics. Sometimes a direct quotation from a well-respected expert, an authority on the subject, will be convincing.

You must make sure that the writer's evidence is **appropriate,** that it has direct bearing on the conclusion. Sometimes a writer presents a lot of flashy evidence, such as details loaded with emotional appeals. When you look at this kind of evidence closely, you realize that it doesn't have much, if anything, to do with the writer's conclusions.

To make sure that the evidence is **accurate,** or correct, check to see that it comes from a source you can trust. Don't assume that everything (or anything) you see online or even printed in a newspaper or book is accurate. If a fact, example, or quotation doesn't sound accurate, check it out. Look for the title of the magazine or book that the quotation comes from. Is it a reliable source? Look up the writer's background. Does the writer have the background and education to qualify him or her as an expert on the subject? Is the writer biased in some way?

See page 869

See also *Argument.*

FACT AND OPINION A **fact** is a statement that can be proved true. Some facts are easy to prove by **observation.** For instance, *Cats make different vocal sounds* is a fact you can prove by listening to cats meow and purr. Other facts can be *verified,* or proved, if you look them up in a reliable source. You need to be sure that the source is **authoritative**—an official source that can be trusted, such as an encyclopedia. In fields where new discoveries are being made, you need to check facts in a *recently* published source.

An **opinion** expresses a personal belief or feeling. Sometimes strongly held opinions look and sound like facts. Dog lovers would never question the statement *Dogs are smarter than cats.* Cat lovers, however, would express the opposite opinion, *Cats are smarter than dogs,* and believe it just as strongly. Even if a statement sounds as if it's true, it's not a fact unless it can be proved. Here are some opinions:

> Travel to other planets will happen in my lifetime.
> We have the best football team in the United States.
> Every teenager should receive an allowance.

A **valid opinion** is a personal belief that is supported by facts. An **invalid opinion** is a belief that is either not supported by facts or is supported by illogical and wishful thinking.

Remember that what you see in print or on the Internet may or may not be true. If a statement looks like a fact but you suspect it's an opinion, check it out in a reliable source. Ask: Can this be proved true?

See pages 447, 491, 492, 525, 869

FALLACIOUS REASONING

Fallacious (fuh LAY shuhs) means "false." **Fallacious reasoning** is false reasoning. Here are four major types of false reasoning:

1. **Hasty generalizations** are reached without considering enough facts. A **generalization** is a conclusion drawn after considering as much of the evidence as possible. If there is even one exception to the conclusion, your generalization is not true or valid.

> **Fact:** "User Friendly" is a story with a surprise ending.
> **Fact:** "After Twenty Years" is a story with a surprise ending.
> **Hasty generalization:** All stories have surprise endings.

That conclusion is a hasty generalization. You could name many stories that do not have a surprise ending. Sometimes hasty generalizations can be corrected by using a qualifying word such as *most, usually, some, many,* or *often.* It is especially important to watch out for hasty generalizations when you're reading a persuasive text.

2. With **circular reasoning** a writer tries to fool you by restating the opinion in different words.

> Hungry students can't study because they haven't had enough to eat.
> Jean is the best candidate for student-council president because she's better than all the other candidates.

3. **Cause-and-effect fallacies.** One common **cause-and-effect fallacy** assumes that if something happens right before another event, the first event caused the next event.

> I wasn't wearing my lucky shirt, so I failed my history test.

Another **cause-and-effect fallacy** names a single cause for a complicated situation that has many causes.

> Popularity in middle school depends on wearing the right clothes.

4. The **either-or fallacy** suggests that there are only two sides to an issue.

> Either you get a summer job, or you waste the whole summer.

See also *Argument, Evidence, Persuation.*

5W-HOW? The first paragraph of a news story, called the **lead** (leed) paragraph, usually answers the questions *who? what? when? where? why?* and *how?* Look for the answers to these **5W-How?** questions when you read a newspaper story or any eyewitness account.

GENERALIZATION A **generalization** is a broad statement that covers several particular situations. Scientists and detectives, for instance, begin their investigations by amassing many specific facts. Then they put the facts together and draw a conclusion about what all this evidence tells them, what it adds up to.

> **Fact:** Cobras are poisonous.
> **Fact:** Rattlesnakes are poisonous.
> **Fact:** Garter snakes are not poisonous.
> **Generalization:** Some snakes are poisonous.

The generalization *Most snakes are poisonous* would have been incorrect. Only three species out of a population of more than 2,500 species of snakes were considered. About four fifths of all snakes are not poisonous. To be valid, a generalization must be based on all the evidence (the facts) that can be gathered.

See pages 725, 907, 923

See also *Stereotyping.*

GRAPHIC FEATURES **Graphic features** are design elements in a text. They include things like headings, maps, charts, graphs, and illustrations. Graphic features are visual ways of communicating information.

Some design elements you may find in a text are **boldface** and *italic* type; type in different styles (called fonts), sizes, and colors; bullets (dots that set off items in a list); and logos (like computer icons). For example, the Quickwrite heading in this book always appears with the stopwatch. Design elements make a text look more attractive. They also steer your eyes to different types of information and make the text easier to read.

A **heading** serves as a title for the information that follows it. Size and color set off from the rest of the text the type used for a heading. A repeated heading, like "Reading Skills" in this textbook, is always followed by the same type of material. Skimming the headings is one way to preview a text.

Graphic features such as **maps, charts,** and **graphs** display and sometimes explain complex information with lines, drawings, and symbols. Graphic features usually include these elements:

1. A **title** identifies the subject or main idea of the graphic.
2. **Labels** identify specific information.
3. A **caption** is text (usually under an illustration) that explains what you're looking at.
4. A **legend,** or **key,** helps you interpret symbols and colors, usually on a map. Look for a **scale,** which relates the size or distance of something on a map to the real-life size and distance.
5. The source tells where the information in the graphic comes from. Knowing the source helps you evaluate the accuracy.

Different types of **maps** present special information. **Physical maps** show the natural landscape of an area. Shading may be used to show features like mountains and valleys. Different shades of color are often used to show different elevations (heights above sea level). **Political maps** show political units, such as states, nations, and capitals. The map of Canada, the United States, and Mexico shown here is a political map. **Special-purpose maps** present information such as the routes of explorers or the location of earthquake fault lines.

A **flowchart** shows a sequence of events or the steps in a process. Flowcharts are often used to show cause-and-effect relationships. See page 345 for an example of a flowchart. **Pie charts,** also called **circle graphs,** show how parts of a whole are related. A pie chart is a circle divided into different-sized sections, like slices of a pie. The emphasis in a pie chart is always on the proportions of the sections, not on the specific amounts of each section.

Pie Chart

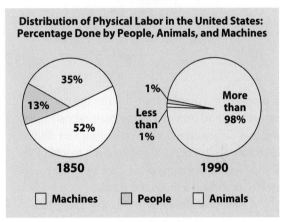

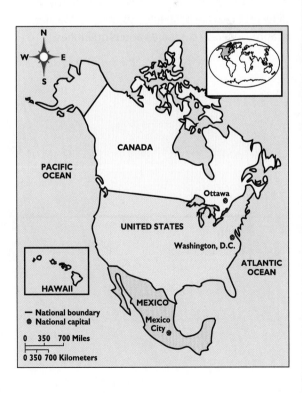

Bar Graph

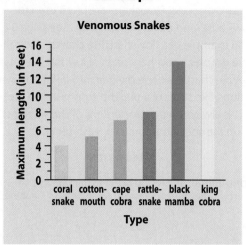

Line Graph

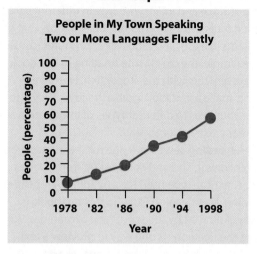

A **diagram** is a graphic that outlines the parts of something and shows how the parts relate to one another or how they work. You'll often find diagrams in technical directions, to show how a mechanical device works. Diagrams prove that a picture can be worth more than a thousand words.

A **time line** identifies events that take place over the course of time. In a time line, events are organized in chronological order, the order in which they happened.

Graphs usually show changes or trends over time. In line graphs, dots showing the quantity at different times are connected to create a line. **Bar graphs** generally compare various quantities.

A **table** presents information arranged in rows and columns. There are many different types of tables. See page 610 for an example of a table showing a train schedule.

Tips for Understanding Graphic Aids

1. Read the title, labels, and legend before you try to analyze the information.
2. Read numbers carefully. Note increases or decreases in sequences. Look for the direction or order of events and for trends and relationships.
3. Draw your own conclusions from the graphic. Then, compare your conclusions with the writer's conclusions.

See pages 585, 587, 605

Time Line

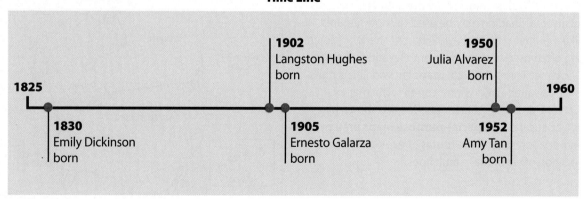

IMAGES Descriptive writing appeals to the senses to create **mental images,** pictures in the reader's mind. Most description appeals to the sense of sight, but description can also appeal to one or more of the other senses. When you read a description, use the details to *visualize,* or form mental pictures of, the characters, settings, and events.

See page 179

INFERENCE An **inference** is an educated guess, a conclusion that makes sense because it's supported by evidence. The evidence may be a collection of **facts,** information that can be proved, or it may come from experiences in your own life. However, the evidence must provide some reason for believing that the conclusion is true if the inference is to be valid, or based on sound, logical thought. Nevertheless, people may draw different conclusions from the same evidence—especially if there isn't much evidence to go on.

> Bobby has recently transferred to your school. You ask Bobby to join you and a couple of other friends, Sam and Ali, at your house after school on Thursday. Bobby says, "Sorry. I have to go home right after school." Inferences: Sam infers that Bobby's parents are really strict. Ali infers that Bobby is stuck-up. You infer that Bobby doesn't like you.

As you read, you make inferences based on clues that the writer provides. For example, when you read a narrative, you **infer,** or guess, what will happen next based on what the writer has told you and on your own knowledge and experience. Sometimes a writer deliberately gives clues that lead you to different—and incorrect—inferences. That's part of the fun of reading. Until you get to the end of a suspenseful story, you can never be completely sure about what will happen next.

In O. Henry's short story "After Twenty Years" (page 391), a policeman speaks to a well-dressed man waiting in a doorway in New York City. The man is waiting for his boyhood friend, Jimmy. He hasn't seen Jimmy for more than twenty years. Read the following dialogue, and the inferences that follow it.

> "Did pretty well out West, didn't you?" asked the policeman.
>
> "You bet! I hope Jimmy has done half as well. He was a kind of plodder, though, good fellow as he was. I've had to compete with some of the sharpest wits going to get my pile. A man gets in a groove in New York. It takes the West to put a razor edge on him."
> **Inferences:** The policeman seems to be impressed by the man in the doorway. The well-dressed man thinks a lot of himself and looks down on his old friend Jimmy, who may have been too "good" to be successful.

See pages 250, 257, 259

See also *Evidence, Fact and Opinion.*

INSTRUCTIONAL MANUALS **Instructional manuals** tell you how to operate a specific device, such as a DVR. Instructional manuals contain detailed directions, usually organized in chronological steps. Drawings and diagrams might be included to help you understand the different parts of the device.

See pages 217–220, 580

KWL CHART Using a **KWL** chart is a way to focus your reading and record what you learn. KWL means "What I **k**now, what I **w**ant to know, and what I **l**earned." When you use a KWL strategy, first skim the text, looking at headings, subtitles, and illustrations. Decide what the topic of the text is. Then, draw a KWL chart. In the K column, note what you already know about the subject. In the W column, write what you'd like to find out. After reading the text, write the answers under the L column to the questions in the W column. Here is the beginning of a KWL chart based on "Sir Gawain and the Loathly Lady" (page 978).

K	W	L
What I **K**now	What I **W**ant to Know	What I **L**earned
Sir Gawain was a knight.	Why was the lady loathly?	It was a spell that made her ugly.

MAIN IDEA The most important point or focus of a passage is its **main idea.** Writers of essays, nonfiction narratives, and informational articles have one or more **main ideas** in mind as they write a text. The writer may state the main idea directly. More often the main idea is suggested, or implied. Then it's up to you, the reader, to infer, or guess at, what it is. To infer the main idea, look at the key details in the text. See if you can create a statement that expresses a general idea that covers all these important details. When you are deciding on the main idea, look especially for a key passage at the beginning or end of the text. That's where a writer often refers to a key idea.

See pages 141, 493, 495, 497

NEWSPAPERS **Newspapers** are informational texts that present facts about current events. Newspapers may also contain feature articles that aim to entertain as well as inform. Newspapers often contain editorials that support a *position* for or against an issue. **Headlines** at the top of each story indicate the topic of the story. They are worded to catch your attention. The writer of a **news story** usually organizes the details in order of importance. If the article is running too long, the less important details can easily be cut from the end of the story.

See pages 207, 238–239

OBJECTIVE WRITING **Objective writing** sticks to the facts. It does not reveal the writer's feelings, beliefs, or point of view about the subject. In a newspaper, news articles are usually written objectively. Readers of news articles want to get a true and accurate account of what happened. If they want to know a writer's point of view or perspective on the news, they turn to the **editorial page.** Editorials and letters to the editor are usually *not* written objectively. They are examples of **subjective writing.** See page 457 for an example of a letter to the editor.

See pages 487, 507

See also *Subjective Writing.*

OUTLINING **Outlining** an informational text can help you identify main ideas and understand how they are related to one another. Outlining also shows you the important details that support each main idea. When you have an outline, you have a visual summary of the text.

Many readers start an outline by taking notes. Note taking is an especially good idea if you're reading a text with many facts, such as names and dates, that you want to remember.

Tips for Taking Notes

1. You can jot down notes in a notebook or on note cards. Put your notes in your own words, writing each main idea on its own note card or page.
2. As you continue to read, add details that relate to the important idea you have on each card.
3. Whenever you copy the writer's exact words, put quotation marks around them. Write down the page number for the source of each note.

After you have your notes on the text, you're ready to make an outline. Many outlines label the main ideas with Roman numerals. You need to have at least two headings at each level. This is how an outline might begin:

I. Main idea
   A. Detail supporting main idea I
      1. Detail supporting A
         a. Detail supporting 1
         b. Detail supporting 1
      2. Detail supporting A
   B. Detail supporting main idea I
II. Main idea

See pages 97, 120–121

PERSUASION **Persuasion** is the use of language or pictures to convince us to think or act in a certain way. Recognizing **persuasive techniques** will help you evaluate the persuasion that you read, hear, and see all around you today. Here are some persuasive techniques to watch for:

1. **Logical appeals** are based on correct reasoning. Logic appeals to reason with opinions supported by strong factual evidence, such as facts, statistics, or statements by experts on the issue being considered.

2. **Emotional appeals** get your feelings involved in the argument. Some writers use vivid language and supporting evidence that arouse basic feelings, such as pity, anger, and fear. Persuasion tends to be most effective when it appeals to both your head and your heart. However, it's important to be able to recognize emotional appeals—and to be suspicious of how they can sway you.

3. **Logical fallacies** (FAL uh seez) are mistakes in reasoning. If you're reading a text quickly, fuzzy or dishonest reasoning may look as if it makes sense. See the entry for *Fallacious Reasoning* for examples of specific logical fallacies.

See page 554

See also *Argument*.

PREDICTIONS Guessing what will happen next in a narrative text is a reading skill called **making predictions.** To make predictions, you look for clues that **foreshadow,** or hint at, future actions. You try to connect those clues with past and present actions in the story. You quickly check your memory for other things you've read that are in any way like the story you're reading. You recall your real-life experiences. Then you make your predictions. As you read, you'll continuously revise your guesses, adjusting your predictions as new clues crop up.

See pages 161, 175, 344, 345, 389, 906, 941

PROPAGANDA **Propaganda** is an organized attempt to influence a large audience of readers, listeners, or TV watchers. Propaganda techniques are used in all kinds of persuasive texts. You see them especially in advertisements, speeches, and editorials. Some writers use propaganda to advance good causes—for instance, to persuade people to recycle, to exercise, or to join together to fight a terrible disease. However, many writers of propaganda use emotional appeals to confuse readers and to convince them that the writer's biased opinions are the only ones worth considering.

Common propaganda techniques include the following:

- The **bandwagon** appeal urges you to do or believe something because everyone else does.

> "Shop where the action is! Join the parade to Teen-Town Mall."

- The **testimonial** uses a famous person, such as an actor or an athlete, to testify that he or she supports the issue or uses the product.

> "I'm professional basketball player Hank Smith, and I drink Starade every day for quick and long-lasting energy."

- **Snob appeal** suggests that by using this product you can be superior to others—more powerful, wealthy, or beautiful.

> "You deserve this car. Don't settle for less than the best."

- **Stereotyping.** Writers who use stereotyping refer to members of a group as if they were all the same.

> Teenagers are bad drivers.
> Didn't I tell you that Martians can't be trusted?

- Writers using **name-calling** avoid giving reasons and logical evidence for or against an issue. Instead, they attack people who disagree with them by giving those people negative labels.

> That's just what I'd expect a nerd like you to say.
> I won't waste time listening to a puppet-politician whose strings are controlled by ill-informed special-interest groups.

PURPOSES OF TEXTS Texts are written for different **purposes:** to inform, to persuade, to express feelings, or to entertain. The purpose of a text, or the reason why a text is written, determines its **structure,** the way the writer organizes and presents the material.

READING RATE The speed at which you read a text is your **reading rate.** How quickly or slowly you should read depends on the type of text you are reading and your purpose for reading it.

Reading Rates According to Purpose		
Reading Rate	Purpose	Example
Skimming	Reading for main points	Glancing at newspaper headlines; reviewing charts and headings in your science textbook before a test
Scanning	Looking for specific details	Looking for an author's name in a table of contents; looking in a geography book for the name of the highest mountain in North America
Reading for mastery	Reading to understand and remember	Taking notes on a chapter in your science textbook to study for a test; reading a story or poem for understanding.

RETELLING The reading strategy called **retelling** helps you identify and remember events that advance the plot of a story. Retelling is also useful when you read informational texts, such as science or history texts. From time to time in your reading, stop for a moment. Review what's gone on before you go ahead. Focus on the important events or key details. Think about them, and retell them briefly in your own words. When you read history or science texts, you should stop after each section of the text and see if you can retell the key details to yourself.

SQ3R The abbreviation **SQ3R** stands for a reading and study strategy that takes place in five steps: **s**urvey, **q**uestion, **r**ead, **r**etell, **r**eview. The SQ3R process takes time, but it helps you focus on the text—and it works.

- S—*Survey.* Glance through the text. Skim the headings, titles, charts, illustrations, and vocabulary words in boldface type. Read the first and last sentences of the major sections of the text, if they are indicated by headings.
- Q—*Question.* List the questions that you have. These may be questions that came out of your survey, or they may be general questions about the subject. Ask the questions that you hope to find answers to in the text.
- R—*Read.* Read the text carefully, keeping your questions in mind. As you read, look for answers. Take brief notes on the answers you find.
- R—*Retell.* Use your notes to write down the main ideas and important details in the text. Before you write, say your answers out loud. Listen to your answers to hear if they make sense.
- R—*Review.* Look back over the text. See if you can answer your questions without using the notes and answers you wrote down. Write a brief summary of the text so you'll be able to remember it later.

STEREOTYPING Referring to all members of a group as if they were all the same is called stereotyping. **Stereotyping** (STEHR ee uh typ ihng) ignores the facts about individuals. The most important fact about members of a group is that each individual person is *different* from all the others. Stereotyping does not allow for individual differences. Whenever you assess a writer's evidence, be on the lookout for stereotyping. When a writer makes a claim about an individual or a group and supports the assertion with a stereotype, you know that the writer is guilty of faulty reasoning. Here are some examples of stereotyping:

> All teenagers are lazy.
> Senior citizens have more money than
>   they need.
> All lawyers are dishonest.
> All football players are dumb.

See pages 369, 456

See also *Propaganda.*

SUBJECTIVE WRITING Writing that reveals and emphasizes the writer's personal feelings and opinions is called **subjective.** Subjective and objective writing are opposites. *Subjective* means "personal; resulting from feelings; existing only in the mind." *Objective means* "real; actual; factual; without bias." Writers may combine subjective and objective details in the same text. As a reader you must figure out which statements are based on subjective impressions and which are based on factual, objective evidence.

We expect subjectivity in some writing. We would expect an autobiography to reveal the writer's personal feelings. In a historical text, however, we expect objectivity—we want facts, not the writer's personal feelings.

See pages 487, 509

See also *Objective Writing.*

SUMMARIZING Restating the main ideas or major events in a text is called **summarizing.** A summary of text is much shorter than the original. To summarize an informational text, you must include the main ideas and the important details that support those main ideas. To summarize a narrative, you must include the main events and be certain you have indicated cause and effect. In a summary, except for direct quotations from the text, you put the writer's ideas into your own words. (Every time you jot down a direct quotation, be sure to put quotation marks around it and write down the source.) Here is a summary of the selection from *Barrio Boy* by Ernesto Galarza (page 537):

> Ernesto's family had recently moved to Sacramento from Mazatlán, Mexico. This true account begins with Ernesto's mother taking him to school. The new school seems strange to Ernesto, who speaks no English. Ernesto finds out that many of his first-grade classmates are from other countries or have different ethnic backgrounds. Several of them, along with Ernesto, receive private English lessons from their teacher. The teachers at the school help Ernesto learn that he can be proud of being American while still feeling proud of his Mexican roots.

See pages 102, 120

See also *Main Idea.*

TEXT STRUCTURES There are some basic ways in which writers structure informational texts: **cause and effect, chronological order,** and **comparison-and-contrast.** Sometimes a writer will use one pattern throughout a text. Many writers will combine two or more patterns. These guidelines can help you analyze text structure:

1. Search the text for the main idea. Look for words that signal a specific pattern of organization.
2. Study the text for other important ideas. Think about how the ideas are connected to one another. Look for an obvious pattern.
3. Draw a graphic organizer that shows how the text seems to be structured. Your graphic organizer may look like one of the common text structures shown below.

The **cause-and-effect pattern** presents a series of causes and their effects. This example shows the effect of an earthquake, which led to another effect, which became the cause of another effect, and so on:

Causal Chain

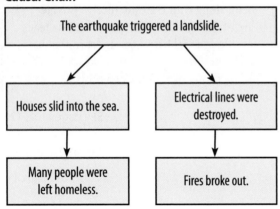

Chronological-order pattern shows events or ideas happening in time sequence. The example below gives directions for getting from school to a student's home:

Sequence Chain

Go down College Avenue to traffic light at College and Clayton.

↓

Take a left at Clayton. Go about half a mile to Tyler.

↓

Go right on Tyler. Stop at 86 Tyler. It's a big gray apartment house with a tree on the left side.

↓

Ring Apt. 2B. I'll buzz you in.

The **comparison-and-contrast pattern** points out similarities and differences. A Venn diagram can help you see how two subjects are alike and how they are different. Similarities are listed where the two circles overlap. Differences are shown where the circles don't overlap. This example compares a middle school with a high school.

Venn Diagram

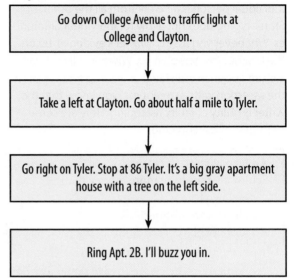

Another kind of graphic organizer focuses on points of comparison (the features being compared).

Comparing and Contrasting		
	Middle School	High School
Size of school		
Length of school day		
Sports program		

See pages 238–239

See also *Cause and Effect, Chronological Order, Compare-and-Contrast Pattern.*

TEXTBOOKS **Textbooks** are informational texts written to help students learn about a subject. This textbook is quite different in structure from a geography textbook. Nonetheless, both kinds of textbooks have certain elements in common. For example, they have the same general purpose. In addition, most textbooks present information followed by questions that help students determine whether they have learned the material. Finally, most textbooks contain a table of contents, an index, illustrations, charts, and other graphic features.

See pages 238–239

WRITER'S PERSPECTIVE **Perspective** is the way a person looks at a subject. Some people have a negative perspective, for instance, on violent computer games. They believe that such games may influence children to become violent. Other people have a positive perspective on violent computer games. They say that when children play such games, they may rid themselves of some of their aggressive feelings. Figuring out a writer's perspective can help you understand and evaluate what you are reading. The following paragraph is from Clifton Davis's "A Mason-Dixon Memory" (page 65). A statement describing Davis's perspective follows:

In his words and in his life, Lincoln had made it clear that freedom is not free. Every time the color of a person's skin keeps him out of an amusement park or off a country-club fairway, the war for freedom begins again. Sometimes the battle is fought with fists and guns, but more often the most effective weapon is a simple act of love and courage.
Writer's perspective: Prejudice still exists today, and it can be fought best with simple, nonviolent actions.

See pages 547, 554, 989

Spelling Handbook

COMMONLY MISSPELLED WORDS

No matter how many spelling rules you learn, you will find that it is helpful to learn to spell certain common words from memory. The fifty "demons" in the first list are words that you should be able to spell without any hesitation, even though they all contain spelling problems. Study them in groups of five until you are sure you know them.

The second, longer list contains words that you should learn if you do not already know them. They are grouped by tens so that you may study them ten at a time. In studying each list, pay particular attention to the underlined letters. These letters are generally the ones that pose problems for students. **For more on spelling, see spelling rules in the Language Handbook.**

Fifty Spelling Demons				
ache	cough	guess	once	though
again	could	half	ready	through
always	country	hour	said	tired
answer	doctor	instead	says	tonight
blue	does	knew	shoes	trouble
built	don't	know	since	wear
busy	early	laid	straight	where
buy	easy	meant	sugar	which
can't	every	minute	sure	whole
color	friend	often	tear	women

Two Hundred Spelling Words

abandon	commercial	February	nickel	separate
absolutely	committees	finally	nuisance	sergeant
acceptance	competition	flu	numerous	shepherd
accidentally	conceive	friendliness	obvious	similar
accommodate	condemn	generally	occasionally	solemn
accomplish	congratulations	governor	occurrence	sponsor
achieve	conscience	grammar	opportunity	straighten
acquaintance	conscious	gratitude	orchestra	subscription
acquire	convenience	guarantee	originally	succeed
actually	courteous	guardian	parallel	success
advertisement	criticism	gymnasium	parliament	sufficient
aisle	cylinder	height	patience	suppress
amount	dealt	hesitate	personal	surprise
analysis	deceit	humorous	persuade	surrounded
anticipate	definite	hypocrite	philosopher	suspense
anxiety	definition	ignorance	picnicking	tailor
apology	description	imagination	planned	temperament
apparent	desirable	immediately	possess	tendency
appearance	despair	incidentally	precede	theories
application	difficulties	individual	preferred	therefore
appreciation	disappointment	initial	prejudice	thorough
approach	discipline	inspiration	privilege	tobacco
assistance	discussion	intelligence	probably	tonsils
authority	diseased	interfere	procedure	tradition
beginning	distinction	interrupt	professor	tragedy
believe	distribution	judgment	pursuit	transferred
benefit	duplicate	knowledge	realize	truly
boundary	eligible	laboratory	receipt	unanimous
bouquet	embarrass	leisure	recommend	unnecessary
bulletin	engineering	lieutenant	referring	useful
business	equipped	luncheon	regularly	utilized
canceled	eventually	majority	relieve	vacuum
capacity	exactly	manufacture	repetition	various
carrier	exaggerate	marriage	research	vein
ceiling	excellent	mechanical	response	villain
challenge	existence	medieval	rhythm	violence
chorus	experience	mourn	satisfied	warrant
circuit	experiment	muscular	schedule	weird
colonel	fascinating	naturally	scissors	wholly
column	favorite	necessary	sense	writing

Communications Handbook

Research Strategies

Using a Media Center or Library

To find a book, tape, film, or video in a library, start by looking in the **catalog.** Most libraries use an **online,** or computer, **catalog.**

Online catalogs vary from library to library. With some you begin searching for resources by **title, author,** or **subject.** With others you simply enter **keywords** for the subject you're researching. With either system, you enter information into the computer and a new screen will show you a list of materials or subject headings relating to your request. When you find an item you want, write down the title, author, and **call number,** the code of numbers and letters that shows you where to find the item on the library's shelves.

Some libraries still use card catalogs. A **card catalog** is a collection of index cards arranged in alphabetical order by title and author. Nonfiction is also cataloged by subject.

Electronic Databases. Electronic databases are collections of information you can access by computer. You can use these databases to find such resources as encyclopedias, almanacs, and museum art collections.

There are two kinds of electronic databases: **Online databases** are accessed at a computer terminal connected to a modem. The modem allows the computer to communicate with other computers over telephone lines. **Portable databases** are available on magnetic tape, diskette, or CD-ROM.

A **CD-ROM** (compact disc–read only memory) is played on a computer equipped with a CD-ROM player. If you were to look up *Amy Tan* on a CD-ROM guide to literature, for example, you could hear passages from her books and read critical analyses of her work.

Periodicals. Most libraries have a collection of magazines and newspapers. To find up-to-date magazine or newspaper articles on a topic, use a computerized index, such as *InfoTrac* or *EBSCO.* Some of these indices provide a summary of each article. Others provide the entire text, which you can read on-screen or print out. The *Readers' Guide to Periodical Literature* is a print index of articles that have appeared in hundreds of magazines.

The Reference Section

Every library has materials you can use only in the library. Some examples are listed below. (Some reference works are available in both print and electronic form.)

Encyclopedias
  Collier's Encyclopedia
  The World Book Encyclopedia
General Biographical References
  Current Biography Yearbook
  The International Who's Who
  Webster's New Biographical Dictionary
Special Biographical References
  American Men & Women of Science
  Biographical Dictionary of American Sports
  Mexican American Biographies
Atlases
  Atlas of World Cultures
  National Geographic Atlas of the World
Almanacs
  Information Please Almanac
  The World Almanac and Book of Facts
Books of Quotations
  Bartlett's Familiar Quotations
Books of Synonyms
  Roget's International Thesaurus
  Webster's New Dictionary of Synonyms

Using the Internet

The **Internet** is a huge network of computers. Libraries, news services, government agencies, researchers, and organizations communicate and share information on the Net. The Net also lets you chat online with students around the world. For help in using the Internet to do research or to communicate with someone by computer, explore the options on the next page.

The World Wide Web

The easiest way to do research on the Internet is on the World Wide Web. On the Web, information is stored in colorful, easy-to-access files called Web pages. **Web pages** usually have text, graphics, images, sound, and even video clips.

Using a Web Browser

You look at Web pages with a **Web browser,** a program for accessing in formation on the Web. Every page on the Web has its own address, called a **URL,** or Uniform Resource Locator. If you know the address of a Web page you want to go to, just enter it in the location field on your browser.

Hundreds of millions of Web pages are connected by **hyperlinks,** which let you jump from one page to another. These links are usually underlined or colored words or images, or both, on your computer screen. With hundreds of millions of linked Web pages, how can you find the information you want?

Using a Web Directory

If you're just beginning to look for a research topic, click on a **Web directory,** a list of topics and subtopics created by experts to help users find Web sites. Think of the directory as a giant index. Start by choosing a broad category, such as Literature. Then, work your way down through the subtopics, perhaps from Poetry to Poets. Under Poets, choose a Web page that looks interesting, perhaps one on Robert Frost.

Using a Search Engine

If you already have a topic and need information about it, try using a **search engine,** a software tool that finds information on the Web. To use a search engine, just go to an online search form and enter a **search term,** or keyword. The search engine will return a list of Web pages containing your search term. The list will also show you the first few lines of each page. A search term such as *Frost* may produce thousands of results, or **hits,** including weather data on frost. If you're doing a search on the poet Robert Frost, most of these thousands of hits will be of no use. To find useful material, you have to narrow your search.

You've Got Mail!

E-mail is an electronic message sent over a computer network. On the Internet you can use e-mail to reach institutions, businesses, and individuals. When you e-mail places like museums, you may be able to ask **experts** about a topic you're researching. You can also use e-mail to chat with students around the country and around the world.

Internet forums, or newsgroups, let you discuss and debate lots of subjects with other computer users. You can write and send a question to a forum and get an answer from someone who may (or may not) know something about your topic.

Techno Tip

- If you get too few hits, use a more general word as your search term.
- If you get too many hits, use a more specific word as your search term.

"On the Internet, nobody knows you're a dog."

Refining a Keyword Search

To focus your research, use **search operators,** such as the words AND or NOT, to create a string of keywords. If you're looking for material on Robert Frost and his life in Vermont, for example, you might enter the following search term:

Frost AND Vermont NOT weather

The more focused search term yields pages that contain both *Frost* and *Vermont* and nothing about weather. The chart on the right explains how several search operators work.

Evaluating Web Sources

Since anyone can publish a Web page, it's important to evaluate your sources. Use these criteria to evaluate a source:

Authority

Who is the author? What is his or her knowledge or experience? Trust respected sources, such as the Smithsonian Institution, not a person's newsletter or Web page.

Accuracy

How trustworthy is the information? Does the author give his or her sources? Check information from one site against information from at least two other sites or print sources

Objectivity

What is the author's **perspective,** or point of view? Find out whether the information provider has a bias or a hidden purpose.

Currency

Is the information up-to-date? For a print source, check the copyright date. For a Web source, look for the date on which the page was created or revised. (This date appears at the bottom of the site's home page.)

Coverage

How well does the source cover the topic? Could you find better information in a book? Compare the source with several others.

COMMON SEARCH OPERATORS AND WHAT THEY DO	
AND	Demands that both terms appear on the page; narrows search
+	Demands that both terms appear on the page; narrows search
OR	Yields pages that contain either term; widens search
NOT	Excludes a word from consideration; narrows search
–	Excludes a word from consideration; narrows search
NEAR	Demands that two words be close together; narrows search
ADJ	Demands that two words be close together; narrows search
" "	Demands an exact phrase; narrows search

Techno Tip

To evaluate a Web source, look at the top-level domain in the URL. Here is a sample URL with the top-level domain—a government agency—labeled.

top-level domain

http://www.loc.gov

COMMON TOP-LEVEL DOMAINS AND WHAT THEY STAND FOR	
.edu	Educational institution. Site may publish scholarly work or the work of elementary or high school students.
.gov	Government body. Information is generally reliable.
.org	Usually a nonprofit organization. If the organization promotes culture (as a museum does), information is generally reliable; if it advocates a cause, information may be biased.
.com	Commercial enterprise. Information should be evaluated carefully.
.net	Organization offering Internet services. Information is generally reliable.

Sample Note Card

Poe's Childhood and Youth   1
—Parents were actors—father deserted family, mother died
before Poe's 3rd birthday
—Raised by Frances and John Allan
—Published first poems at age 18   p.20

Listing Sources and Taking Notes

When you write a research paper, you must **document,** or identify, your sources so that readers will know where you found your material. You must avoid **plagiarism,** or presenting another writer's words or ideas as if they were your own.

Listing Sources

List each source, and give it a number. (You'll use these source numbers later, when you take notes.) Here's where to find the publication information (such as the name of the publisher and the copyright date) you'll need for different types of sources:

- **Print sources.** Look at the title and copyright pages of the book or periodical.
- **Online sources.** Look at the beginning or end of the document or in a separate electronic file. For a Web page, look for a link containing the word *About.*
- **Portable electronic databases.** Look at the start-up screen, the packaging, or the disc itself.

There are several ways to list sources. The chart on page 1048 shows the style created by the Modern Language Association.

Taking Notes

Here are some tips for taking notes:

- Put notes from different sources on separate index cards, sheets of paper, or computer files.
- At the top of each card, sheet of paper, or file, write a label telling what that note is about.
- At the bottom, write the numbers of the pages on which you found the information.
- Use short phrases, and make lists of details and ideas. You don't have to write full sentences.
- Use your own words unless you find material you want to quote. If you quote an author's exact words, put quotation marks around them.

The sample note card at the left shows how to take notes.

Preparing a List of Sources

Use your source cards to make a **works cited** list, which should appear at the end of your report. At the top of a sheet of paper, type and center the heading *Works Cited*. Below it, list your sources in alphabetical order. Follow the MLA guidelines for citing sources (see the chart below). The sample works cited list below shows you how to do this.

Sample Works Cited List

Anderson, M. K. Edgar Allan Poe: A Mystery. New York: Franklin Watts, 1993.

"The Life of a Poet." Edgar Allan Poe Historic Site Home Page. 2003. 19 Aug. 2003 <http://www.nps.gov/edal/brochure.htm>.

"Poe, Edgar Allan." The World Book Encyclopedia. 2003 ed.

The chart below shows citations of print, audiovisual, and electronic sources:

MLA GUIDELINES FOR CITING SOURCES	
Books	Give the author, title, city of publication, publisher, and copyright year. Anderson, M. K. Edgar Allan Poe: A Mystery. New York: Franklin Watts, 1993.
Magazine and newspaper articles	Give the author (if named), title of the article, name of the magazine or newspaper, date, and page numbers. "Did Rabies Fell Edgar Allan Poe?" Science News 2 Nov. 1996: 282.
Encyclopedia articles	Give the author (if named), title of the article, name of the encyclopedia, and edition (year). "Poe, Edgar Allan." The World Book Encyclopedia. 2003 ed.
Interviews	Give the expert's name, the words *Personal interview* or *Telephone interview*, and the date. M. K. Anderson. Telephone interview. 12 Jan. 2004.
Films, videotapes, and audiotapes	Give the title; producer, director, or developer; medium; distributor; and year of release. Edgar Allan Poe: Terror of the Soul. Prod. Film Odyssey. Videocassette. PBS Home Video, 1995.

Electronic materials, including CD-ROMs and online sources	Give the author (if named); title; title of project, database, periodical, or site; electronic posting date (online); type of source (CD-ROMs); city (CD-ROMs); distributor (CD-ROMs); publication date (CD-ROMs) or access date; and Internet address (if any).
	    "Poe, Edgar Allan." Grolier Multimedia Encyclopedia. CD-ROM. Danbury: Grolier Interactive, 2003.
	    "The Life of a Poet." Edgar Allan Poe Historic Home Site Page. 19 Aug. 2003 <http://www.nps.gov/edal/brochure.htm>.

Proofreaders' Marks		
Symbol	**Example**	**Meaning**
≡	New <u>m</u>exico	Capitalize lowercase letter.
/	next /Spring	Lowercase capital letter.
∧	a book ∧quotations (of)	Insert.
℘	a good ~~good~~ idea	Delete.
∩	a grape‿fruit tree	Close up space.
√	does∫nt	Change order (of letters or words).
¶	¶ "Who's there?" she asked.	Begin a new paragraph.
⊙	Please don't forget⊙	Add a period.
⌢	Maya∧did you call me?	Add a comma.
⌢⌣	Dear Mrs. Mills ⌢⌣	Add a colon.
⌢	Columbus, Ohio∧Dallas, Texas	Add a semicolon.
ᵛᵛ ᵛᵛ	ᵛᵛAre you OK?ᵛᵛ he asked.	Add quotation marks.

Media Handbook

Analyzing Electronic Journalism

Just as you can analyze the elements of fiction, you can analyze the elements of a TV news story. A TV news story is made up of words, images, and sounds. Television journalists use specific techniques for presenting these words, images, and sounds. Each of these techniques serves a specific purpose.

Analyzing Elements of TV News

TEXTUAL ELEMENTS **Text** is the name given to the words you hear and sometimes see on the TV screen. When you hear text, it is presented by a *news anchor* or *news reporter*. The **news anchor** reads the text of the primary, or most important, news stories. The anchor also introduces other reporters and their news stories. **Reporters**—often reporting live from where a news event is happening—may provide additional information on the primary news stories or give information on secondary, or less important, news stories.

Because of time limitations on TV, news stories are short, usually no more than two to three minutes long. This means that news writers and reporters must carefully plan text to achieve their purposes—capturing and keeping your attention, engaging your mind and emotions, and informing you. In order to understand the effects of a news story, you must examine both the *structure* by which the text is arranged and *content* of the text. You must also think about how the structure helps determine the content.

To help viewers understand and remember the main points of a news story during the couple of minutes it is broadcast, the text usually follows a brief, simple, attention-getting **structure,** or order. The following graphic shows the typical news story structure.

Lead-in ➡

In the TV studio, the anchor introduces the story.
"Tonight a fire has broken out at the Olde Towne Bakery in the historic East End district. Here's Brian Steele on location with this breaking story. . . ."

Setup ➡

The reporter, usually on location, grabs the audience's attention and introduces the images viewers are about to see.
"What you are about to see may trouble those of you with fond memories of the Olde Towne Bakery. . . ."

Sound Bites

Short audio pieces of interviews are mixed in with video clips.
(voice of Olde Towne Bakery owner): "This is truly heartbreaking. My grandparents started this business back in 1884. . . ."

Voice-overs ➡

The reporter talks while the video is playing. Usually, the reporter explains the images on the screen.
"The flames are shooting up over thirty feet above the building."

Back Announcing ➡

After the video clips, the reporter briefly sums up the main points of the story.
"Again, fire is raging through the Olde Towne Bakery in the historic East End district. The joyless residents of Thayerville are in shock as this landmark goes up in smoke."

Stand-up

The reporter addresses the camera and the anchor with closing commentary.
"The owners hope to rebuild soon so they can continue the generations-long tradition of bringing fresh baked goods to the folks of Thayerville. Back to you."

As you can see, the same information is repeated many times. Repeating the information gives viewers several chances to hear and understand the main point of a story.

CONTENT The brief, repetitive structure of broadcast news stories limits the **content,** or information provided. Viewers may receive an oversimplified understanding of events, getting the basic facts without understanding the full meaning of the story. Because broadcast news stories are so short, they are often presented without much **context**—the whole situation or background information behind the story. As a result, viewers may not really be aware of the other issues related to the event.

Watch out for signs of **bias**—a slanted point of view, either in favor of or against an issue. Signs of bias include personal opinions and **loaded language**—words or phrases that carry strong positive or negative emotional impact, such as "a heartbreaking loss" or "an inspiring act." Try to form your own opinion about a story rather than being influenced by bias or loaded language.

VISUAL ELEMENTS TV viewers tend to think of "live" images on the news as an accurate portrayal of reality. However, TV images represent just one piece of reality, as seen through a camera. **Photojournalists,** such as news reporters, photographers, and producers, make choices about the way each image will look. They also decide which **point of view,** or way of portraying the world, to show on the TV screen. As a critical TV viewer, you should know how the camera techniques TV photo journalists use can affect your perceptions of the news.

The **camera shot** is what the viewer sees on the television screen. Shots are put together to form a scene or story and may show closeness or distance.

A **long shot** is a shot made from far away, such as a landscape. A **cover shot**—a long shot at the beginning of a news story—can set the scene for the story. It may also create the impression of distance and objectivity. A long shot can also be used as **wallpaper,** an interesting visual image to show behind an anchor's narration.

A **close-up** is a shot taken very close to the subject. A close-up shot can show fine details, such as a detail of a craftsperson's hands weaving yarn.

Long shot

Close-up

High angle

The camera may **zoom in** (moving from a wider shot of a subject to a closer one) to focus on the emotion in someone's face.

The **camera angle** is the viewpoint at which a camera is set when it is pointed toward a subject. Sometimes, conditions may limit the angles from which a cameraperson may shoot. For example, in filming a forest fire, a photojournalist may be able only to get shots taken from above, using a helicopter or airplane.

A **high angle** is a shot from above, with the camera looking down on the subject. A high camera angle can be used, for example, to provide an overview of a scene. A high camera angle can, however, make the subject look small, unimportant, and vulnerable.

Low angle

Full scene

Framed shot

A shot from below, with the camera looking up at the subject, is called a **low-angle** shot. A low camera angle can make the subject look tall and powerful. A low camera angle may distort reality, making subjects look much larger than they are.

Framing is the process by which the photojournalist decides which details to include or cut from the camera shot. Framing is used to focus on the subject, eliminate clutter, and engage the viewer's emotions. Unfortunately, framing can leave out important details, making a story seem less complex than it is. For example, the photojournalist who took the pictures above framed the bottom shot so that just young women are shown in the frame. Viewers might wrongly conclude from the framed shot that the band is popular only with women, when in fact men are also fans.

Props are all the objects that appear in a camera shot. Whether it is intentional or not, these props can add meaning to a shot. Possible problems arise if a prop distracts the viewer or demonstrates a bias for or against a particular opinion. For example, if the brand name of a computer is visible on camera, the reporter may unintentionally be advertising that computer company.

AUDIO ELEMENTS In addition to the text that you hear read by an anchor or reporter, there are other sounds that you may hear in a news report. Background noises captured on videotape, such as ambulance sirens, high winds, or hands clapping, add depth to a story. Sometimes you will hear the sounds of a busy newsroom behind a news anchor. Because music can affect viewers' emotions, network guidelines prohibit the use of music during a newscast. However, music is often used as a sound effect to open and close a program and to introduce commercial breaks.

Analyzing a TV News Story

Television newscasts blend textual, visual, and audio elements to create an effect greater than that which could be achieved through only one element. Still, before you can judge the effect of this blend, you need to analyze each of the individual elements. The following steps will help you identify the elements in a TV news broadcast and the techniques used to affect viewers:

STEP 1 Describe the news segment, identifying text, image, or sound techniques used in the segment.
The story is a network news feature about the declining prairie dog population.

Sound: Prairie dogs bark and chatter through much of the story.

Image: The camera shows a long shot of a nearly deserted prairie dog town, medium shots of the remaining prairie dogs playing and eating, and a close-up of a rancher's face.

Text: The voice-over tells us that prairie dogs are in trouble because of disease and human activity and that they are a crucial part of the ecosystem. A rancher says he worries about them spreading disease. The story focuses on ways to handle the conflict between the environmental importance of prairie dogs and the needs of the ranchers and other people who consider them pests.

STEP 2 Explain the purposes of each major technique. (Hint: Think about why the producer might choose these techniques.)

Sound: The barking noises grab my attention.

Image: The long shot sets the scene. The medium shot shows prairie dog activities, and the close-up shot shows the rancher's weathered face.

Text: The words of the voice-over tell me why some people are concerned about prairie dogs, and the rancher's words tell me why other people consider them pests.

STEP 3 Write an evaluation of the effects of the various techniques on you, the viewer. (Hint: Think about how the techniques make you feel.)

The sounds the prairie dogs make in this story are kind of funny and cute. The long shot is a little sad because the prairie dog town is nearly empty. The medium shot is also really cute, and the prairie dogs act almost as if they have personalities. The close-up shows me the years of hard work the rancher has done. His expression is tired and tough at the same time—very different from the playful and vulnerable prairie dogs. The text gives specific reasons why prairie dogs are important to the ecosystem but only vague reasons why people exterminate them.

Overall, the techniques used in the story got my attention and the story was fairly informative. It may not have been totally balanced, though. The rancher's point of view seemed less important in the story than the case for saving the prairie dogs—probably because the prairie dogs were more appealing than the rancher and because the text went into more detail about the impact of their loss on the environment.

Analyzing a Documentary

Several decades ago, CBS aired Edward R. Murrow's *Harvest of Shame*. This documentary led to legislation that improved the lives of migrant farm workers, who travel from place to place to harvest crops.

Murrow followed the workers for a season, showing viewers what life was like for them. One **technique** that he used effectively was the **interview**—letting the workers speak for themselves. One woman he interviewed had been working in the fields since she was eight years old. She had worked ten hours that day and earned only one dollar. She had fourteen children to feed.

Media critics say that this documentary triggered changes in federal policy toward migrant workers. What made the documentary so effective in influencing and informing viewers?

- **A timely topic.** CBS aired the program on Thanksgiving Day, forcing viewers to connect the food they ate with the migrant workers who had harvested it.
- **Powerful images, words, and sounds.** Part of what gives images, words, and sounds power is their arrangement. For example, an image of cattle being shipped was placed next to an image of workers jammed into trucks. This technique, **juxtaposition** (side-by-side arrangement), showed viewers that the workers were treated like cattle. Filmmakers can also use sound techniques, such as **music** and **background noise,** to add to the messages they present.
- **A strong bias, or point of view.** The filmmaker's **attitude,** or **bias,** toward the subject can reflect the documentary's **purpose.** The creators of *Harvest of Shame* revealed their bias indirectly through the selection and arrangement of images and interviews. Clearly, they intended to influence, not just inform. Murrow also revealed his bias directly by urging viewers to help pass legislation to improve conditions for migrant workers.

Evaluating a Documentary

- As you watch a documentary, take notes on the topic; powerful images, words, and sounds; and the filmmaker's point of view and purpose.
- Also note techniques, such as interviews, juxtaposition, and music or background noise, used for effect.
- Use your notes to write an analysis of the documentary.

Language Handbook

1. The Parts of Speech

Part of Speech	Definition	Examples
NOUN	**1a.** A noun is a word used to name a person, a place, a thing, or an idea.	
common noun	a general name for a person, place, thing, or idea	sister [person], apartment [place], pineapple [thing], hope [idea]
proper noun	names a particular person, place, thing, or idea, and always begins with a capital letter	Ms. Baxter, Gulf of Mexico, Friday
collective noun	names a group	family, herd, jury, class, choir
compound noun	two or more words combined and used together as a single noun	butterfly (butter + fly) [one word] compact disc [separate words] self-control [hyphenated word]
PRONOUN	**1b.** A pronoun is a word used in place of one or more nouns or pronouns.	Emily Dickinson took few trips; **she** spent most of **her** time at Amherst.

personal pronoun	• refers to the one speaking (first person), the one spoken to (second person), or the one spoken about (third person)
	• either singular (one) or plural (more than one)
		Singular **Plural**
		First Person
		 I, me, my, mine we us, ours
		Second person
		  you, your, yours you, your, yours
		Third person
		  he, him, his, she, they, them,
		  her, hers, it, its their, theirs

reflexive pronoun	• refers to the subject and directs the action of the verb back to the subject • either singular or plural	first person: myself, ourselves second person: yourself, yourselves third person: himself, herself, itself, themselves Emily Dickinson wrote **herself** notes on the backs of recipes.
intensive pronoun	• emphasizes a noun or another pronoun • has the same form as a reflexive pronoun • either singular or plural	first person: myself, ourselves second person: yourself, yourselves third person: himself, herself, itself, themselves The chef did the baking **himself**. [emphasizes that he alone did it]

indefinite pronoun	refers to a person, a place, or a thing that is not specifically named	All, any, both, each, either, everything, few, many, none, no one, nobody, one, several, some, somebody
relative pronoun	introduces a subordinate clause: *that, what, which, who, whom, whose*	Dickinson wrote of thoughts and feelings **that** she had. He is the swimmer **who** won the race.
demonstrative pronoun	points out a person, a place, a thing, or an idea: *this, that, these, those*	**This** is a collection of her poems.
interrogative pronoun	introduces a question: *what, which, who, whom, whose*	**What** were Dickinson's household duties?
ADJECTIVE	**1c.** An adjective is a word used to modify a noun or a pronoun. To modify a word means to describe the word or to make its meaning more definite. An adjective tells *what kind, which one, how many,* or *how much.*	**What Kind?** **noisy** sound, **Thai** food **Which One?** **another** skirt, **next** day **How Much** or **How Many?** **one** CD, **many** years, **more** guests
definite article	refers to someone or something in particular: *the*	**the** yellow dress, **the** girl
indefinite article	• refers to someone or something in general: *a, an* • Use *a* before words that begin with consonants. Use *an* before words that begin with vowels (*a, e, i, o, u*).	**a** teacher, **an** apple, **an** early gift
proper adjective	• formed from a proper noun • begins with a capital letter	**Chinese** customs [from the proper noun *China*] **American** flag [from the proper noun *America*]
demonstrative adjective	• modifies a noun or pronoun: *this, that, these, those* • called a **demonstrative pronoun** when used alone [see pronouns]	Is **this** story more interesting than **that** one? **That** is the way to hold chopsticks. **These** are common foods in India.
nouns used as adjectives	refers to a noun that modifies another noun	**fish** scales, **holiday** menu, **bicycle** tire

VERB	**1d.** A verb is a word used to express action or state of being.	
action verb	**1e.** An action verb expresses physical or mental action. There are two types of action verbs: transitive and intransitive	physical action: hop, rest, observe mental action: want, hope, forget
transitive verb	• expresses an action directed toward a person or thing • The action passes from the doer (the subject) to the receiver of the action. Words that receive the action are called **objects**.	He **played** the guitar. [The action of *played* is directed toward *guitar*.] He played the **guitar**. [*Guitar* is the object of the verb *played*.]
intransitive verb	expresses action (or tells something about the subject) without passing the action to a receiver	Fausto **walked** slowly across the street. [The action of *walked* has no object; *slowly across the street* tells how and where Fausto walked.]
linking verb	**1f.** A linking verb links, or connects, the subject with a noun, a pronoun, or an adjective in the predicate. • common linking verbs formed from the verb *be: am, are, being, is, was, been, may be, would be, should have been, will have been, has been, will be, was being, can be, must be* • other linking verbs: *appear, grow, seem, stay, become, look, smell, taste, feel, remain, sound, turn*	The caller **was** Roger. [The linking verb *was* links *caller* and *Roger*.] Roger **seemed** angry. [The linking verb *seemed* links *Roger* and *angry*.] Her mother **is** Sheila. [*mother = Sheila*] Demarcus **should have been** early. [*Demarcus = early*] The doctor **looks** tired. [*doctor = tired*] The dog **smells** dirty. [*dog = dirty*]
helping verb	**1g.** A helping verb (auxiliary verb) helps the main verb to express an action or a state of being. A helping verb joins with a main verb to form a verb phrase. **Common Helping Verbs** • forms of *be: am, is, being, was, are, been, is, were* • forms of *do: do, does, did* • forms of *have: have, has, had* • other helping verbs: *can, may, must, should, would, could, might, shall, will*	She **is** going. [*is* = helping verb; *going* = main verb; *is going* = verb phrase] He **did** play the guitar. [*did* = helping verb; *play* = main verb; *did play* = verb phrase] She **has** gone to school. [*has* = helping verb; *gone* = main verb; *has gone* = verb phrase] He **might** play the guitar tomorrow. [*might* = helping verb; *play* = main verb; *might play* = verb phrase]

ADVERB	**1h.** An adverb is a word used to modify a verb, an adjective, or another adverb. • Adverbs tell *where, when, how,* or *to what extent (how much* or *how long).*	**Where?** Whales are common **here.** [*here* modifies the adjective *common*] **When? Then** the campers hiked. [*then* modifies the verb *hiked*] **How?** The storm arose **suddenly.** [*suddenly* modifies the verb *arose*] **To what extent?** They were **very** careful with their supplies. [*very* modifies the adjective *careful*]
	Adverbs may come before, after, or between the words they modify.	**Before: Slowly,** the shark was circling. **After:** The shark was circling **slowly.** **Between:** The shark was **slowly** circling.
	The word *not* is an adverb. When *not* is part of a contraction like *hadn't,* the *–n't* is an adverb.	The shark had **not** eaten. The shark had**n't** eaten.
PREPOSITION	**1i.** A preposition is a word used to show the relationship of a noun or pronoun to another word in the sentence.	Marisa swam **against** the current. Jamal stood **beside** the tree. Andreas is **from** Greece. The bicycle was **in front of** the tent. **Commonly used Prepositions** about above across after against at around before behind below between by during for from in inside into like near of on out of since through to under with
PREPOSITIONAL PHRASE	• A **prepositional phrase** begins with a preposition and ends with a noun or pronoun, called the **object of the preposition.** The prepositional phrase includes any modifiers of the object of the preposition.	The family went **to beautiful Carmel Beach.** [*to beautiful Carmel Beach* is the prepositional phrase. The word *to* is a preposition that begins the prepositional phrase. The phrase includes the word *beautiful,* which modifies *Carmel Beach.*]
	A preposition may have more than one object.	Tiffany sat **with David, Susan, and Amber.**

CONJUNCTION	**1J.** A conjunction is a word used to join words or groups of words.	
coordinating conjunction	connects words or groups of words used in the same way: *and, but, or, nor, for, so, yet*	Echo **or** Narcissus [two proper nouns] We cooked **and** cleaned. [two verbs] No one was there, **so** we left. [two complete ideas]
correlative conjunction	pairs of conjunctions that connect words or groups of words used in the same way: *both...and, either...or, neither...nor, not only...but also, whether... or*	**Both** Lisa **and** Samuel play piano. [two proper nouns] Lisa **both** plays the piano **and** writes music. [two verbs] **Either** Lisa would play the piano, **or** she would be unhappy. [two complete ideas]
INTERJECTION	**1k.** An interjection is a word used to express emotion. • An interjection is usually followed by an exclamation point or set off by a comma.	**Oh!** You surprised me. **Wow!** What a story that was. **Well,** Rachel certainly is smart. **Common Interjections** aha oh well aw oops wow hooray ouch yippee

---

Your Turn   Using Specific Nouns

Using specific nouns makes writing more accurate and more interesting.

NONSPECIFIC   Animals drank from the water.

SPECIFIC   **Horses, cattle, and burros** drank from the water.

In the following paragraph, replace the nonspecific nouns with specific nouns.

---

1. As a girl wept by a tree, a woman suddenly appeared.
2. The woman waved a magic stick.
3. Instantly, a vegetable turned into a vehicle.
4. With another movement of the woman's stick, the girl's torn clothing turned into a dress.
5. Overjoyed, the girl thanked the woman and rode to the party at the building.

2. Agreement

Number

Number is the form of a word that indicates whether the word is singular or plural.

2a. When a word refers to one person, place, thing, or idea, the word is *singular* in number. When a word refers to more than one, it is *plural* in number.

SINGULAR	house, drum, I, he, each
PLURAL	houses, drums, we, they, all

Agreement of Subject and Verb

2b. A verb agrees with its subject in number. A subject and verb *agree* when they have the same number.

(1) Singular subjects take singular verbs.
A **messenger gives** the king's orders.
(2) Plural subjects take plural verbs.
Many **students study** music.
(3) The first helping, or auxiliary, verb in a verb phrase must agree with its subject.
He is playing the tuba.
They are playing the instruments.
(4) Generally, nouns ending in *s* are plural (*candles, ideas, horses*), and verbs ending in *s* are singular. However, verbs used with the singular pronouns *I* and *you* generally do not end in *s*.

PROBLEMS IN AGREEMENT
Prepositional Phrases Between Subjects and Verbs

2c. The number of a subject is not changed by a prepositional phrase following the subject.

INCORRECT	One of the strongest heroes are Hercules.
CORRECT	**One** of the strongest heroes **is** Hercules.

Indefinite Pronouns

Some pronouns do not refer to a definite person, place, thing, or idea and are called *indefinite pronouns.*

2d. The following indefinite pronouns are singular: *anybody, anyone, each, either, everybody, everyone, neither, nobody, no one, one, somebody, someone.*

Neither of the offers **relieves** him of his task.

2e. The following indefinite pronouns are plural: *both, few, many, several.*

Both of the boar's tusks **frighten** Eurystheus.

2f. The following indefinite pronouns may be either singular or plural: *all, any, most, none, some.*

The number of these pronouns is often determined by the object in a prepositional phrase that follows the pronoun. If the pronoun refers to a singular object, the subject is singular. If the pronoun refers to a plural object, the subject is plural.

All of the stable **needs** cleaning.
[*All* refers to singular *stable.*]
All of the stalls **need** cleaning.
[*All* refers to plural *stalls.*]

Compound Subjects

2g. Subjects joined by *and* usually take a plural verb.

Augeas and **Eurytheus rule** kingdoms.
However, a compound subject that names only one person or thing takes a singular verb.
Law and **order suffers** when monsters roam the land. [*Law and order* names one thing.]

2h. When subjects are joined by *or* or *nor*, the verb agrees with the subject nearer the verb.

Neither the **Hydra** nor Juno's huge **snakes defeat** Hercules.
Neither Juno's huge **snakes** nor the **Hydra defeats** Hercules.

Other Problems in Agreement

2i. Collective nouns may be either singular or plural.

A collective noun takes a singular verb when the noun refers to the group as a unit. A collective noun takes a plural verb when the noun refers to the individual parts or members of the group.

> An oxen **herd goes** with Hercules. [The herd as a unit goes.]
> The **herd call** to the stolen cattle. [The members of the *herd* individually *call*.]

2j. When the subject follows the verb, restate the sentence in normal word order. Then find the subject and make sure the verb agrees with it. The subject usually follows the verb in sentences beginning with *here* or *there* and in questions.

> There **is Centaurus,** and there **are** its **stars.**
> **Does** the **fox** really **want** the grapes?

The contractions *here's, there's,* and *where's* contain the verb *is* and should be used only with singular subjects.

INCORRECT	There's the constellations Hydra and Leo.
CORRECT	There **are** the **constellations** Hydra and Leo.
CORRECT	There's the **constellation** Hydra.

2k. Use *don't* with plural subjects and with the pronouns *I* and *you*. Use *doesn't* with other singular subjects.

> They **don't** like movies about Hercules.
> This **film doesn't** seem realistic, but **that doesn't** matter to me.

2l. A word or phrase stating a weight, a measurement, or an amount of money or time is usually considered a single item that takes a singular verb.

> Ten **dollars is** too much for a ticket.

2m. The title of a book or the name of an organization or country, even when plural in form, usually takes a singular verb.

> *Aesop's Fables* is on the reading list.
> **Has** the **United States** signed the treaty?

2n. A few nouns, though plural in form, are singular and take singular verbs: *news, measles, mathematics, civics, mumps, physics.*

Agreement of Pronoun and Antecedent

2o. A pronoun agrees in number and gender with its *antecedent,* the word to which the pronoun refers.

Some singular personal pronouns indicate gender: masculine for males and feminine for females. Neuter pronouns refer to things (neither male nor female) and usually to animals.

FEMININE	she	her	hers
MASCULINE	he	him	his
NEUTER	it	its	

> The **speaker** in "Annabel Lee" lost **his** bride.
> **Annabel Lee** had given **her** heart to him.
> **Heaven** sent **its** angels for Annabel Lee.

The antecedent of a personal pronoun can be another kind of pronoun, such as *each, neither,* or *one.* To determine the gender of a personal pronoun that refers to one of these other pronouns, look at the words that follow the antecedent.

> **Each** of these **men** left **his** mark on the fence.
> **Neither** of the **women** got what **she** wanted.

When an antecedent may be either masculine or feminine, use both the masculine and feminine forms.

> **No one** ever gave **his or her** approval of Poe's criticisms.
> **Everybody** wanted **his or her** writing in Poe's magazine.

PROBLEMS IN AGREEMENT OF PRONOUN AND ANTECEDENT
Indefinite Pronouns

2p. A singular pronoun is used to refer to *anybody, anyone, each, either, everybody, everyone, neither, nobody, no one, one, someone,* and *somebody.*

> **Each** of these countries has **its** own version of the Cinderella story.

2q. A plural pronoun is used to refer to *both, few, many,* and *several.*

> **Both** of these stories take **their** characters from legend.
>
> **Many** of these versions are similar, but **they** all differ.

2r. Either a singular or a plural pronoun may be used to refer to *all, any, most, none,* and *some.*

The number of the pronouns *all, any, most, none,* and *some* is determined by the object in the prepositional phrase that follows the pronoun.

> **Some** of the **story** comes from **its** culture. [*Some* refers to the singular noun *story.*]
>
> **Some** of the **sisters** pay for **their** cruelty. [*Some* refers to the plural noun *sisters.*]

Compound Antecedents:

2s. A plural pronoun is used to refer to two or more antecedents joined by *and.*

> The **sister and their mother** never share **their** fine clothing.

2t. A singular pronoun is used to refer to two or more singular antecedents joined by *or* or *nor.*

> Neither **the mother nor the sister** shared **her** clothes.

Other Problems in Pronoun-Antecedent Agreement

2u. Either a singular or a plural pronoun may be used with a collective noun.

> The royal **family** was preparing **its** feast.
> The royal **family** are greeting **their** guests.

2v. Words stating amounts usually take singular pronouns.

> Admission costs ten **dollars.** I can earn **it.**

2w. A few nouns, though plural in form, are singular and take singular pronouns.

> **Physics** is important, and **it** is also required.

Your Turn   Using Pronouns Correctly

Sentences with singular antecedents joined by *or* or *nor* can sound awkward if the antecedents are of different genders.

AWKWARD Ana or Ed will read her or his version of *Cinderella.*

REVISED **Ana** will read **her** version of *Cinderella,* or **Ed** will read **his.**

Similarly, a singular and a plural antecedent joined by *or* or *nor* can create an awkward or a confusing sentence.

AWKWARD Either my cousins or Mary will bring their video of *Cinderella.*

REVISED Either **my cousins** will bring **their** video of *Cinderella,* or **Mary** will bring **hers.**

Revise each of the following sentences to eliminate awkward or incorrect pronoun usage.

---

1. Neither her mother nor her sisters recognized that the girl was their own Aschenputtel.
2. Either birds or a fish help the heroine in their own way.
3. Did a fish or a falcon lend their help to Yeh-Shen?
4. Neither Yeh-Shen nor the king could have guessed her or his fate.
5. Joey or Linda will read his or her report on "Sealskin, Soulskin."

3. Using Verbs

The Principal Parts of a Verb

The four basic forms of a verb are called the *principal parts* of the verb.

3a. The principal parts of a verb are the *base form*, the *present participle*, the *past,* and the *past participle.*

BASE FORM	work
PRESENT PARTICIPLE	(is) working
PAST	worked
PAST PARTICIPLE	(have) worked

The principal parts of a verb are used to express the time that an action occurs.

PRESENT TIME	I **sing** rhythm and blues now.
	We **are singing** along with the frog.
PAST TIME	The frog **sang** at the Big Time Weekly concert.
	We **have sung** there before.
FUTURE TIME	The audience **will sing** with the frog.
	By closing time, we **will have sung** ten songs.

REGULAR VERBS

3b. A *regular verb* forms its past and past participle by adding *-d* or *-ed* to the base form.

BASE FORM	use
PRESENT PARTICIPLE	(is) using
PAST	used
PAST PARTICIPLE	(have) used

Avoid these errors when forming the past or past participle of regular verbs:

(1) leaving off the *-d* or *-ed* ending

NONSTANDARD	The frog use to sing.
STANDARD	The frog **used** to sing.

(2) adding unnecessary letters

NONSTANDARD	The group of animals scattereded in all directions.
STANDARD	The group of animals **scattered** in all directions.

IRREGULAR VERBS

3c. An *irregular verb* forms its present and past participle in some other way than by adding *-d* or *-ed* to the base form.

An irregular verb forms its past and past participle by

(1) changing vowels *or* consonants

BASE FORM	ring
PAST	rang
PAST PARTICIPLE	(have) rung

(2) changing vowels *and* consonants

BASE FORM	go
PAST	went
PAST PARTICIPLE	(have) gone

(3) making no changes

BASE FORM	spread
PAST	spread
PAST PARTICIPLE	(have) spread

Avoid these errors when forming the past or past participle of irregular verbs:

(1) using the past form with a helping verb

NONSTANDARD	Frog has went to the Big Time Weekly concert.
STANDARD	Frog **went** to the Big Time Weekly concert.
	Frog **has gone** to the Big Time Weekly concert.

(2) using the past participle form without a helping verb

NONSTANDARD	I seen all of his shows.
STANDARD	I **have seen** all of his shows.

(3) adding *-d* or *-ed* to the base form

NONSTANDARD	The elephant throwed a pineapple at the frog.
STANDARD	The elephant **threw** a pineapple at the frog.

COMMON IRREGULAR VERBS

GROUP I: Each of these irregular verbs has the same form for its past and past participle

BASE FORM	PRESENT PARTICIPLE	PAST	PAST PARTICIPLE
bring	(is) bringing	brought	(have) brought
build	(is) building	built	(have) built
catch	(is) catching	caught	(have) caught
hold	(is) holding	held	(have) held
lay	(is) laying	laid	(have) laid
lead	(is) leading	led	(have) led
say	(is) saying	said	(have) said
send	(is) sending	sent	(have) sent

GROUP II: Each of these irregular verbs has a different form for its past and past participle.

BASE FORM	PRESENT PARTICIPLE	PAST	PAST PARTICIPLE
begin	(is) beginning	began	(have) begun
choose	(is) choosing	chose	(have) chosen
do	(is) doing	did	(have) done
go	(is) going	went	(have) gone
know	(is) knowing	knew	(have) known
run	(is) running	ran	(have) run
sing	(is) singing	sang	(have) sung
swim	(is) swimming	swam	(have) swum

GROUP III: Each of these irregular verbs has the same form for its base form, past, and past participle.

BASE FORM	PRESENT PARTICIPLE	PAST	PAST PARTICIPLE
burst	(is) bursting	burst	(have) burst
cost	(is) costing	cost	(have) cost
cut	(is) cutting	cut	(have) cut
hit	(is) hitting	hit	(have) hit
let	(is) letting	let	(have) let
put	(is) putting	put	(have) put
read	(is) reading	read	(have) read
set	(is) setting	set	(have) set

Verb Tense

3d. The *tense* of a verb indicates the time of the action or state of being that is expressed by the verb.

Every verb has six tenses: present, past, future, present perfect, past perfect, and future perfect. This list shows how the six tenses relate to each other.

- *Past Perfect*—existing or happening before a specific time in the past
- *Past*—existing or happening in the past
- *Present Perfect*—existing or happening before now or starting in the past and continuing
- *Present*—existing or happening now
- *Future Perfect*—existing or happening before a specific time in the future
- *Future*—existing or happening in the future

Listing all forms of a verb in the six tenses is called *conjugating* a verb.

CONJUGATION OF THE VERB *SING*

SINGULAR	PLURAL
PRESENT TENSE	
I sing	we sing
you sing	you sing
he, she, or it sings	they sing
PAST TENSE	
I sang	we sang
you sang	you sang
he, she, or it sang	they sang
FUTURE TENSE	
I will sing	we will sing
you will sing	you will sing
he, she, or it will sing	they will sing
PRESENT PERFECT TENSE	
I have sung	we have sung
you have sung	you have sung
he, she, or it has sung	they have sung
PAST PERFECT TENSE	
I had sung	we had sung
you had sung	you had sung
he, she, or it had sung	they had sung
FUTURE PERFECT TENSE	
I will have sung	we will have sung
you will have sung	you will have sung
he, she, or it will have sung	they will have sung

CONSISTENCY OF TENSE

3e. Do not change needlessly from one tense to another.

When writing about events in the present, use verbs in the present tense. When writing about events in the past, use verbs in the past tense.

INCONSISTENT	When they were satisfied, they begin planting.
CONSISTENT	When they **are** satisfied, they **begin** planting.
CONSISTENT	When they **were** satisfied, they **began** planting.

Special Problems with Verbs

Sit and *Set*

(1) The verb *sit* means "rest in a seated position." *Sit* seldom takes an object.
Let's **sit** in the shade. [no object]

(2) The verb *set* means "put (something) in a place." *Set* usually takes an object.
Let's **set** the buckets here. [Let's *set* what? *Buckets* is the object.]

BASE FORM	sit (rest)	set (put)
PRESENT PARTICIPLE	(is) sitting	(is) setting
PAST	sat	set
PAST PARTICIPLE	(have) sat	(have) set

Lie and *Lay*

(1) The verb *lie* means "rest," "recline" or "be in a place."
Lie never takes an object.
In the photograph, juicy, red watermelons **lay** on rich earth. [no object]

(2) The verb *lay* means "put (something) in a place." *Lay* usually takes an object.
They **laid** dirt on the roof. [They *laid* what? *Dirt* is the object.]

BASE FORM	lie (rest)	lay (put)
PRESENT PARTICIPLE	(is) lying	(is) laying
PAST	lay	laid
PAST PARTICIPLE	(have) lain	(have) laid

Rise and *Raise*

(1) The verb *rise* means "go up" or "get up." *Rise* never takes an object.
My neighbors **rise** very early. [no object]

(2) The verb *raise* means "lift up" or "cause (something) to rise." *Raise* usually takes an object.
They **raise** the blinds at dawn. [They *raise* what? *Blinds* is the object.]

BASE FORM	rise (go up)	raise (lift up)
PRESENT PARTICIPLE	(is) rising	(is) raising
PAST	rose	raised
PAST PARTICIPLE	(have) risen	(have) raised

m

Your Turn   Writing Natural Dialogue

Using standard verb forms is expected in most of the writing done for school.

Readers expect standard usage in essays and reports. On the other hand, readers expect dialogue in plays and short stories to sound natural and to reflect the speech patterns of real people. Here is an example of dialogue from the short story "Bargain."

> "I think he hate me," Mr. Bauer went on. "This is the thing. He hate me for coming not from this country. I come here, sixteen years old, and learn to read and write, and I make a business, and so I think he hate me."

Revise each of the following sentences to sound natural in a dialogue.

1. Butch replied, "I must say, old friend, that I cannot quite believe you."
2. "Gracious, what a marvelous party that was!" beamed Tanya when the group met Monday morning at school.
3. "Please accept our congratulations for a job well done," cried Jim's teammates.
4. "I beg your pardon, but you are sitting in my seat," said the sergeant to the recruit.
5. "What an unfaithful friend you are to have spoken against me behind my back," exclaimed Angela to her classmate.

4. Using Pronouns

Case

Case is the form of a noun or a pronoun that shows how it is used in a sentence. There are three cases: **nominative, objective,** and **possessive.**

The form of a noun is the same for both the nominative and objective cases. A noun changes its form for the possessive case, usually by the addition of an apostrophe and an *s.*

Most personal pronouns have different forms for all three cases. Possessive pronouns (such as *my, your,* and *our*) are also sometimes called **possessive adjectives.**

Personal Pronouns	
NOMINATIVE CASE	
SINGULAR	**PLURAL**
I	we
you	you
he, she, it	they
OBJECTIVE CASE	
SINGULAR	PLURAL
me	us
you	you
him, her, it	them
POSSESSIVE CASE	
SINGULAR	**PLURAL**
my, mine	our, ours
your, yours	your, yours
his, her, hers, its	their, theirs

THE NOMINATIVE CASE

Pronouns used as subjects or predicate nominatives are in the **nominative case**.

4a. A subject of a verb is in the nominative case.

> **I** enjoy Anne McCaffrey's writing style.
> [*I* is the subject of *enjoy.*]

4b. A *predicate nominative* is in the nominative case.

A **predicate nominative** follows a linking verb and explains or identifies the subject of the verb. A personal pronoun used as a predicate nominative follows a form of the verb *be* (*am, is, are, was, were, be,* or *been*).

> The last one to arrive at the pool was **he**. [*He* identifies the subject *one.*]

THE OBJECTIVE CASE

Pronouns used as objects are in the **objective case.**

4c. A *direct object* is in the objective case.

A **direct object** follows an action verb and tells *who* or *what* receives the action of the verb.

> The bronze dragon's choice amazed **us**.
> [*Us* tells *who* was amazed.]
> Heth moved his wings and dried **them**.
> [*Them* tells *what* Heth dried.]

4d. An *indirect object* is in the objective case.

An **indirect object** comes between an action verb and a direct object and tells *whom* or *to what* or *for whom* or *for what* the action of the verb is done.

> Heth asked **him** a question. [*Him* tells *to whom* Heth asked a question.]

4e. An *object of a preposition* is in the objective case.

A **prepositional phrase** contains a preposition, a noun or pronoun called the **object of the preposition**, and any modifiers of that object.

> like a **hero**
> near **us**
> next to **Dr. Chang**
> without **you** and **me**

A pronoun used as the object of a preposition should always be in the objective case.

> We went with **her** to the mall.
> A great honor had been bestowed on **him**.

Special Pronoun Problems

WHO AND WHOM

The pronoun *who* has different forms in the nominative and objective cases. *Who* is the nominative form; *whom* is the objective form. When deciding whether to use *who* or *whom* in a question, follow these steps:

(1) Rephrase the question as a statement.
(2) Decide how the pronoun is used in the statement—as subject, predicate nominative, object of the verb, or object of a preposition.
(3) Determine the case of the pronoun according to the rules of standard English.
(4) Select the correct form of the pronoun.

QUESTION (*Who, Whom*) did Jerry see?
STEP 1: The statement is *Jerry did see (who, whom)*.
STEP 2: The subject of the verb is *Jerry*, the verb is *did see*, and the pronoun is the direct object.
STEP 3: A pronoun used as a direct object should be in the objective case.
STEP 4: The objective form is *whom*.
ANSWER **Whom** did Jerry see?

In spoken English, the use of *whom* is becoming less common. In fact, when you are speaking, you may correctly begin any question with *who* regardless of the grammar of the sentence. In written English, however, distinguish between *who* and *whom*.

PRONOUNS WITH APPOSITIVES

Sometimes a pronoun is followed directly by a noun that identifies the pronoun. Such a noun is called an **appositive.** To choose which pronoun to use before an appositive, omit the appositive, and try each form of the pronoun separately.

(*We, Us*) boys live in the Carolinas.
[*Boys* is the appositive.]
We live in the Carolinas.
Us live in the Carolinas.
ANSWER **We** boys live in the Carolinas.

REFLEXIVE PRONOUNS

Reflexive pronouns (such as *myself, himself,* and *yourselves*) can be used as objects. Do not use the nonstandard forms *hisself* and *theirself* or *theirselves* in place of *himself* and *themselves*.

NONSTANDARD Patrick prepared an impressive dinner for hisself.
STANDARD Patrick prepared an impressive dinner for **himself.**

Your Turn Using Standard Expressions

Expressions such as *It's me, That's her,* and *It was them* are accepted in everyday speaking. In writing, however, such expressions are generally considered nonstandard and should be avoided.

STANDARD It is **I**. That is **she**. It was **they**.

Additionally, it is considered polite to put first-person pronouns (*I, me, mine, we, us, ours*) last in compound constructions.

The dragonriders and we arrived at the Hatching Ground.

Revise each of the following sentences to show standard and polite usage of pronouns.

1. We and the other candidates dashed to the auditorium.
2. "Save a good place for me and my friends," someone called.
3. "It was me who took the last cookie!"
4. When K'last asked me who Keevan was, I answered, "That's him."
5. Keevan was the smallest, yet it was him who impressed the bronze dragon.

5. Using Modifiers

Comparison of Modifiers

A **modifier** is a word, a phrase, or a clause that describes or limits the meaning of another word. Two kinds of modifiers—*adjectives* and *adverbs*—may be used to compare things.

5a. The three degrees of comparison of modifiers are *positive, comparative,* and *superlative.*

POSITIVE	COMPARATIVE	SUPERLATIVE
cold	colder	coldest
politely	more politely	most politely

To show decreasing comparisons, modifiers form their degrees with *less* and *least.*

POSITIVE	COMPARATIVE	SUPERLATIVE
calm	less calm	least calm
rapidly	less rapidly	least rapidly

REGULAR COMPARISON

(1) **Most one-syllable modifiers form their comparative and superlative degrees by adding -*er* and -*est*.**

POSITIVE	COMPARATIVE	SUPERLATIVE
sharp	sharper	sharpest
calm	calmer	calmest
cold	colder	coldest

(2) **Some two-syllable modifiers form their comparative and superlative degrees by adding -*er* and -*est*. Others use *more* and *most*.**

POSITIVE	COMPARATIVE	SUPERLATIVE
quickly	more quickly	most quickly
simple	simpler	simplest
sudden	more sudden	most sudden

(3) **Modifiers with three or more syllables use *more* and *most* to form their comparative and superlative degrees.**

POSITIVE	COMPARATIVE	SUPERLATIVE
curious	more curious	most curious
fiery	more fiery	most fiery
quietly	more quietly	most quietly

IRREGULAR COMPARISON

Some modifiers do not form their comparative and superlative degrees by using the regular methods.

POSITIVE	COMPARATIVE	SUPERLATIVE
bad	worse	worst
far	farther	farthest
good/well	better	best
many/much	more	most

USES OF COMPARATIVE AND SUPERLATIVE FORMS

5b. Use the comparative degree when comparing two things. Use the superlative degree when comparing more than two.

COMPARATIVE	This place is **safer** than that one.
SUPERLATIVE	This place is the **safest** of all.

5c. Use *good* to modify a noun or a pronoun. Use *well* to modify a verb.

The Town Mouse enjoyed **good** food. She **ate** well.

5d. Use adjectives, not adverbs, after linking verbs.

The Town Mouse's life seemed **wonderful**. [not *wonderfully*]

5e. Avoid using double comparisons.

A **double comparison** is the use of both -*er* and *more* (*less*) or both -*est* and *most* (*least*) to form a comparison.

> The Country Mouse's place is **safer** [not *more safer*] than the Town Mouse's.

5f. A *double negative* is the use of two negative words to express one negative idea.

Common Negative Words

barely	hardly	neither
never	no	no one
nobody	none	not (-n't)
nothing	nowhere	scarcely

NONSTANDARD	She hasn't never liked cats.
STANDARD	She **hasn't ever** [or *has never*] liked cats.

Placement of Modifiers

5g. Place modifying words, phrases, and clauses as close as possible to the words they modify.

The mouse **from the country** saw a cat.
[The phrase modifies *mouse*.]
The mouse saw a cat **from the country**.
[The phrase modifies *cat*.]

PREPOSITIONAL PHRASES

A *prepositional phrase* consists of a preposition, a noun or a pronoun called the *object of the preposition*, and any modifiers of that object. Place a prepositional phrase used as an adjective directly after the word it modifies.

MISPLACED   A cat would not be dangerous to the mice with a bell.
CLEAR   A cat **with a bell** would not be dangerous to the mice.

A prepositional phrase used as an adverb should be placed near the word it modifies.

MISPLACED   The mice had a meeting about the cat in fear.
CLEAR   **In fear**, the mice had a meeting about the cat.

Avoid placing a prepositional phrase in a position where it can modify either of two words.

MISPLACED   The mouse said in the morning she would go. [Does the phrase modify *said* or *would go*?]
CLEAR   The mouse said she would go **in the morning.**
    In the morning, the mouse said she would go.

PARTICIPIAL PHRASES

A *participial phrase* consists of a verb form—either a present participle or a past participle—and its related words. A participial phrase modifies a noun or a pronoun. A participial phrase should be placed close to the word it modifies.

MISPLACED   The mice hid from the cat scurrying fearfully.
CLEAR   **Scurrying fearfully**, the mice hid from the cat.

A participial phrase that does not clearly and sensibly modify any word in the sentence is a *dangling participial phrase.* To correct a dangling phrase, supply a word that the phrase can modify, or add a subject, a verb, or both to the dangling modifier.

DANGLING   Worried constantly, a plan was needed.
CLEAR   Worried constantly, **the mice** needed a plan.
    The mice needed a plan **because they worried** constantly.

CLAUSES

A *clause* is a group of words that contains a verb and its subject and that is used as a part of a sentence. An *adjective clause* modifies a noun or a pronoun. Most begin with a relative pronoun, such as *that, which, who, whom,* or *whose.* An *adverb clause* modifies a verb, an adjective, or another adverb. Most adverb clauses begin with a subordinating conjunction, such as *although, while, if,* or *because.*

Like phrases, clauses should be placed as close as possible to the words they modify.

MISPLACED   The fable was written by Aesop that we read today.
CLEAR   The fable **that we read today** was written by Aesop.

Your Turn   Using Modifiers Correctly

Using modifers correctly is essential to good writing. Correct the use of modifiers in the following sentences.

1. With each step forward, the cats crouched more lower.
2. The yellow cat was the largest of the two and the most frightening.
3. The calico cat, however, was the better hunter in the neighborhood.
4. The tiny mouse left the hole and searched for a least obvious hiding place.
5. The mouse hardly made no sound at all.

6. Phrases

6a. A *phrase* is a group of related words that is used as a single part of speech and does not contain a verb and its subject.

VERB PHRASES	was not stapled
	is calling loudly
PREPOSITIONAL PHRASES	with a shudder
	on account of rain

The Prepositional Phrase

6b. A *prepositional phrase* includes a preposition, a noun or pronoun called the *object of the preposition*, and any modifiers of that object.

The runaway was filled **with fear.**
The colt **in the field** rested its hoof on **the wall.**
He then ran away **from the startled viewer.**

THE ADJECTIVE PHRASE

6c. An *adjective phrase* is a prepositional phrase that modifies a noun or a pronoun.

An adjective phrase tells *what kind* or *which one.*
Robert Frost was a poet **of nature.** [What kind?]
"The Runaway" is a poem **about a colt.**
[Which one?]

More than one adjective phrase may modify the same word.
A pasture **of snow on a mountain** is where this remarkable sight appears.
[The phrases *of snow* and *on a mountain* modify *pasture.*]

An adjective phrase always follows the word it modifies. That word may be the object of another prepositional phrase.
"The Runaway" is a poem **about a colt in the snow.** [The phrase *about a colt* modifies the predicate nominative *poem.* The phrase *in the snow* modifies the object *colt.*]

THE ADVERB PHRASE

6d. An *adverb phrase* is a prepositional phrase that modifies a verb, an adjective, or an adverb.

An adverb phrase tells *how, when, where, why,* or *to what extent* (that is, *how long, how many,* or *how far*).
The colt bolted **with a snort.** [How?]
The colt seemed uneasy **because of the snow.**
[Why?]
The poem takes place late **in the day.** [When?]
Frost wrote poetry **for years.** [How long?]

More than one adverb phrase may modify the same word or words.
At the Kennedy Inauguration, Frost read **to the American people.**

An adverb phrase may be modified by an adjective phrase.
In his poem about the runaway, Frost uses several verbals. [The adverb phrase modifies the verb *uses.* The adjective phrase modifies *poem.*]

An adverb phrase may come either before or after the word it modifies.
Before that time, Frost had published little.
Frost had published little **before that time.**

Verbals and Verbal Phrases

A **verbal** is a form of a verb that is used as a noun, an adjective, or an adverb. There are three kinds of verbals: the *participle,* the *gerund,* and the *infinitive.*

PARTICIPLES AND PARTICIPIAL PHRASES

6e. A *participle* is a verb form that can be used as an adjective.

There are two kinds of participles— *present participles* and *past participles.*

(1) Present participles end in -ing
The rats **swimming** ashore alarmed them.
[*Swimming,* a form of the verb *swim,* modifies *rats.*]

(2) Most *past participles* end in *-d* or *-ed*. Others are irregularly formed.

> No one was on the **abandoned** ship. [*Abandoned*, a form of the verb *abandon*, modifies *ship*.]
>
> The rats, **known** for their ferocity, swam toward the sailors. [*Known*, a form of the verb *know*, modifies *rats*.]

6f. A *participial phrase* consists of a participle and all the words related to the participle. The entire phrase is used as an adjective.

> **Seeing a ship nearby**, scores of rats dove into the sea. [The participial phrase modifies the noun *scores*. The noun *ship* is the direct object of the present participle *seeing*.]
>
> We saw the sharks **feasting hungrily on the rats**. [The participial phrase modifies the noun *sharks*. The adverb *hungrily* and the adverb phrase *on the rats* modify the present participle *feasting*.]

GERUNDS AND GERUND PHRASES

6g. A *gerund* is a verb form ending in *-ing* that is used as a noun.

> **Singing** can be fun. [subject]
>
> My favorite pastime is **singing**. [predicate nominative]
>
> I warm up before **singing**. [object of the preposition]
>
> Do you enjoy **singing**? [direct object]

6h. A *gerund phrase* consists of a gerund and all the words related to the gerund.

> **Counting the many rats outside the lighthouse** calmed the men. [The gerund phrase is the subject of the sentence. The noun *rats* is the direct object of the gerund *counting*.]

INFINITIVES AND INFINITIVE PHRASES

6i. An *infinitive* is a verb form that can be used as a noun, an adjective, or an adverb. Infinitives usually begin with *to*.

> **To escape** was their sole desire. [noun]
>
> The time **to signal** was now.
> [adjective—*to signal* modifies *time*.]
>
> Rescuers were quick **to answer**.
> [adverb—*to answer* modifies *quick*.]

6j. An *infinitive phrase* consists of an infinitive and its modifiers and complements. The entire infinitive phrase may act as an adjective, an adverb, or a noun.

> Lighthouses are one way **to warn ships away from rocks**. [adjective]
>
> The men were grateful **to see the ship**. [adverb]
>
> **To be rescued** was their only hope. [noun]

Appositives and Appositive Phrases

6k. An *appositive* is a noun or a pronoun placed beside another noun or pronoun to identify or explain it.

Appositives are often set off from the rest of the sentence by commas or dashes. However, when an appositive is necessary to the meaning of the sentence or when it is closely related to the word it refers to, no commas are necessary.

> The author **George G. Toudouze** wrote the story "Three Skeleton Key." [The noun *George G. Toudouze* identifies the noun *author*.]
>
> The men saw a strange ship, **one** with Dutch lines and three masts. [The pronoun *one* refers to the noun *ship*.]
>
> Their victims—the **captain** and **crew**—had vanished. [The nouns *captain* and *crew* explain who were the victims.]

6l. An *appositive phrase* consists of an appositive and its modifiers.

> Le Gleo, **one of the lighthouse keepers**, had horrible nightmares. [The adjective phrase *of the lighthouse keepers* modifies the appositive *one*.]
>
> Rats, **the foul scourge of sailing ships**, pressed for entrance. [The article *the*, the adjective *foul*, and the adjective phrase *of sailing ships* modify the appositive *scourge*.]

Your Turn   Combining Sentences

Using different kinds of phrases can improve your writing. For example, to revise a series of choppy sentences, combine them by turning at least one sentence into a phrase.

CHOPPY   A beautiful ship approached. The ship was a Dutch three-master.
APPOSITIVE PHRASE A beautiful ship approached. The ship was a Dutch three-master.
PARTICIPIAL PHRASE A beautiful Dutch ship **having three masts** approached.
INFINITIVE PHRASE A beautiful Dutch three-master continued **to approach us**.

Combine the following sentences.

1. Three Skeleton Key was a small rock. It was about twenty miles offshore.
2. Three convicts had died there. They were in hiding after escaping from prison.
3. People said that the dead men's skeletons danced. They danced at night.
4. He wanted to save money. He volunteered for the lighthouse job.
5. The rocks had smooth, slick surfaces. They were dangerous.

7. Clauses

7a. A *clause* is a group of words that contains a verb and its subject and that is used as a part of a sentence.

Every clause has a subject and a verb. However, not every clause expresses a complete thought.

COMPLETE THOUGHT   **Wagons delivered** milk daily.
INCOMPLETE THOUGHT   before **cars were** invented

The two kinds of clauses are the *independent clause* and the *subordinate clause*.

The Independent Clause

7b. An *independent* (or *main*) *clause* expresses a complete thought and can stand by itself as a sentence.

$$S \quad \quad V$$
Joseph pulled the wagon.

The Subordinate Clause

7c. A subordinate (or *dependent*) *clause* does not express a complete thought and cannot stand alone as a sentence.

$$S \quad \quad V$$
that Pierre drove

The meaning of a subordinate clause is complete only when the clause is attached to an independent clause.

Joseph pulled the wagon **that Pierre drove.**

THE ADJECTIVE CLAUSE

7d. An *adjective clause* is a subordinate clause that modifies a noun or a pronoun.

An adjective clause usually follows the word it modifies and tells *which one* or *what kind*.

Joseph knew every house **that they served**.
   [Which house?]
Pierre was a man **who loved work**.
   [What kind of man?]

An adjective clause is usually introduced by a *relative pronoun* (*that, which, who, whom, whose*). A **relative pronoun** relates an adjective clause to the word that the clause modifies. Sometimes a relative pronoun is preceded by a preposition that is part of the adjective clause.

The relative pronouns *who* and *whom* are used to refer to people only. The relative pronoun *that* is used to refer both to people and to things. The relative pronoun *which* is used to refer to things only.

> After work, Pierre, **who had seemed fit**, limped slowly. [The relative pronoun *who* relates the clause to the noun *Pierre*.]
>
> St. Joseph, **whose name the horse bore,** was also kind and faithful. [The relative pronoun *whose* relates the clause to the noun *St. Joseph*.]
>
> The character **to whom I am referring** is Jacques. [The relative pronoun *whom* relates the clause to the noun *Jacques*.]

THE ADVERB CLAUSE

7e. An *adverb clause* is a subordinate clause that modifies a verb, an adjective, or an adverb.

An adverb clause tells *where, when, how, why, to what extent,* or *under what condition.*

> They live **where it never gets cold.** [Where?]
> **When he left**, I cried. [When?]
> Grover's room seems **as if it will never be the same.** [How?]
> **Because the weather was hot**, the cool water felt good. [Why?]
> My parents still miss him **as much as I do.** [To what extent?]
> **If I keep tickling him**, he won't fall asleep. [Under what condition?]

An adverb clause is introduced by a **subordinating conjunction**—a word that shows the relationship between the adverb clause and the word or words that the clause modifies.

Common Subordinating Conjunctions		
after	although	as
as if	as soon as	because
before	how	if
once	since	so that
than	though	unless
until	when	whenever
where	whether	while

An adverb clause does not always follow the word it modifies. When an adverb clause begins a sentence, the clause is followed by a comma.

> **Whenever King Midas touched something,** it turned to gold.

Some subordinating conjunctions, such as *after, as, before, since,* and *until,* are also used as prepositions.

CONJUNCTION	**until** everyone leaves
PREPOSITION	**until** noon

THE NOUN CLAUSE

7f. A *noun clause* is a subordinate clause used as a noun.

A noun clause may be used as a subject, a complement (predicate nominative, indirect object, or direct object), or an object of a preposition.

> **What Mama says** is right. [subject]
> She is **the person who makes us happy**. [predicate nominative]
> She bids **whoever is sleeping** good morning. [indirect object]
> Choose **whichever you need most**. [direct object]
> A poem can be about **whatever you think is important**. [object of a preposition]

Common Introductory Words for Noun Clauses		
how	that	what
when	where	which
whichever	whatever	who
whoever	whomever	whom

Your Turn Placing Adverb Clauses

In most cases, the decision of where to place an adverb clause is a matter of style, not correctness.

Both of the following sentences are correct.

Although she was almost unknown during her lifetime, Emily Dickinson is now considered a major American poet.

Emily Dickinson is now considered a major American poet **although she was almost unknown during her lifetime**.

Examine the following sentences and decide whether each adverb clause is placed correctly. If the clause could be better placed, revise the sentence.

1. "The Highwayman" was an inevitable reading assignment when I was in school.
2. I now enjoy the poem although I laughed at it then.
3. Because it was remote in time and place, I did not relate to it.
4. The vocabulary and content seemed false because they were unfamiliar.
5. However, I discovered that this poem is filled with lively images when I read it carefully!

8. Sentences

8a. A *sentence* is a group of words that has a subject and a verb and expresses a complete thought.

A sentence begins with a capital letter and ends with a period, a question mark, or an exclamation point.

Sandra Cisneros wrote "Four Skinny Trees**.**"
Have you read any of her work**?**
What surprising rhythms she uses**!**

Sentence or Sentence Fragment?

A **sentence fragment** is a group of words that either does not have a subject and verb or does not express a complete thought.

SENTENCE FRAGMENT	The rhythms in this story.
SENTENCE	The rhythms in this story are based on repetition.
SENTENCE FRAGMENT	After reading her story.
SENTENCE	After reading her story, I looked at trees differently.

The Subject and The Predicate

A sentence consists of two parts: a *subject* and a *predicate*.

8b. A *subject* tells whom or what the sentence is about. The *predicate* tells something about the subject.

SUBJECT	PREDICATE
Helen Callaghan	played baseball.

FINDING THE SUBJECT

Usually, the subject comes before the predicate. Sometimes, however, the subject may appear elsewhere in the sentence. To find the subject of a sentence, ask *Who?* or *What?* before the predicate. In sentences that begin with *here, there,* or *where,* ask *Here?* (or *There?* or *Where?*) before the predicate followed by *who?* or *what?* after the predicate.

In the old photograph was a **woman at bat**.
  [Who was? A woman was]

By the way, **her son** plays for the Astros.
[Who plays? Her son does.]
Do **you** play baseball?
[Who does play? You do play.]
Where is **my notebook**?
[Where is what? Where is my notebook.]

THE SIMPLE SUBJECT

8c. A *simple subject* is the main word or group of words in the complete subject.

Her **mother** still had that old fire. [The simple subject is *mother*. The complete subject is *her mother*.]
"The No-Guitar Blues" by Gary Soto is on the test. [The simple subject is *"The No-Guitar Blues."* The complete subject is *"The No-Guitar Blues" by Gary Soto*.]

The simple subject of a sentence is never part of a prepositional phrase.

Many of the women attended the league reunion. [Who attended? Not *women* because it is part of the prepositional phrase *of women*. *Many* attended.]

THE SIMPLE PREDICATE, OR VERB

8d. A *simple predicate*, or *verb*, is the main word or group of words in the complete predicate.

A **complete predicate** consists of a verb and all the words that describe the verb and complete its meaning. Usually, the complete predicate follows the subject in a sentence. Sometimes, however, the complete predicate appears at the beginning of a sentence. Other times, part of the predicate may appear on one side of the subject and the rest on the other side.

In the darkness of a doorway stood a stranger.
On this night, he **had a meeting with an old friend**.
Would his friend **appear**?

A simple predicate may be a one-word verb, or it may be a verb phrase. A **verb phrase** consists of a main verb and its helping verbs.

O. Henry's stories often **end** with a twist.
His story "After Twenty Years" **does not have** a happy ending.

THE COMPOUND SUBJECT

8e. A *compound subject* consists of two or more connected subjects that have the same verb. The usual connecting word is *and* or *or*.

Neither **Daedalus** nor **Icarus** escaped the king's anger.
Among Daedalus's gifts were **creativity**, **ingenuity**, and **skill**.

THE COMPOUND VERB

8f. A *compound verb* consists of two or more verbs that have the same subject.

A connecting word—usually *and, or,* or *but*—is used between the verbs.

He **flew** upward, **turned**, and **called** to his son.

Both the subject and the verb of a sentence may be compound.

    S   S   V
Icarus and his **father put** on the wings and

   V
took off into the sky.

Your Turn Combining Sentences

By using compound subjects and verbs, you can combine ideas and reduce wordiness in your writing.

WORDY   With their wings, Daedalus escaped. Icarus escaped also.
REVISED With their wings, **Daedalus and Icarus escaped**.

Using compound subjects and verbs, combine the following pairs of sentences.

---

1. Daedalus angered King Minos. Daedalus was imprisoned by King Minos.
2. Clouds sailed through the skies. Birds sailed through the skies.
3. Daedalus melted wax. Daedalus shaped a skeleton of a wing.
4. Daedalus soared into the air. Icarus also soared.
5. Delos rushed by beneath them. Samos rushed by beneath them.

9. Complements

9a. A *complement* is a word or a group of words that completes the meaning of a verb.

Every sentence has a subject and a verb. Often a verb also needs a complement to complete the meaning of the verb. A complement may be a noun, a pronoun, or an adjective. Each of the following subjects and verbs needs a complement to make a complete sentence.

INCOMPLETE

          S   V

James Weldon Johnson became [what?]

COMPLETE

          S   V   C

James Weldon Johnson became a **poet**.

INCOMPLETE

        S V

Johnson's poetry is [what?]

COMPLETE

        S   V   C

Johnson's poetry is **wonderful**.

INCOMPLETE

      S   V

Tamisha showed [what? to whom?]

COMPLETE

      S   V   C   C

Tamisha showed **me** her **poem**.

An adverb is never a complement.

ADVERB — He writes **powerfully**. [*Powerfully* tells how he writes.]

COMPLEMENT — His writing is **powerful**. [The adjective *powerful* modifies the subject *writing*.]

A prepositional phrase is never a complement.

OBJECT OF A PREPOSITION — The whole world was in **darkness**.

COMPLEMENT — The whole world was **darkness**. [The noun *darkness* modifies the subject *world*.]

Direct Objects

9b. A *direct object* is a noun or a pronoun that receives the action of the verb or that shows the result of the action. A direct object tells *what* or *whom* after a transitive verb.

In this poem, God creates **light, animals**, and all **things**. [The nouns *light, animals*, and *things* receive the action of the transitive verb *creates* and tell *what* God created.]

A direct object never follows a linking verb because a linking verb does not express action.

LINKING VERB — People **became** living souls. [The verb *became* does not express action; therefore, it does not have a direct object.]

A direct object is never part of a prepositional phrase.

PREPOSITIONAL PHASE — Humans gazed at the **moon**. [*Moon* is not the direct object of the verb *gazed*; *moon* is the object of the preposition *at*.]

Indirect Objects

Like a direct object, an **indirect object** helps to complete the meaning of a transitive verb. If a sentence has an indirect object, it always has a direct object as well.

9c. An *indirect object* is a noun or a pronoun that comes between the verb and the direct object and tells *to what* or *to whom* or *for what* or *for whom* the action of the verb is done.

In the last stanza, God gives **man** life. [The noun *man* tells *to whom* God has given life.]

Linking verbs do not have indirect objects. Also, an indirect object, like a direct object, is never in a prepositional phrase.

LINKING VERB — The cypress **is** a type of evergreen tree. [The linking verb *is* does not express action, so it cannot have an indirect object.]

| INDIRECT OBJECT | Cypress trees give **swamps** deep shade. [The noun *swamps* shows *to what* cypress trees give shade.] |
| OBJECT OF A PREPOSITION | They give deep shade to the **swamps**. [The noun *swamps* is the object of the preposition *to*.] |

An indirect object may be compound.

Cypresses give **swamps** and **creeks** deep shade.

Subject Complements

A *subject complement* completes the meaning of a linking verb and identifies or describes the subject.

Common Linking Verbs			
appear	feel	remain	sound
be	grow	seem	stay
become	look	smell	taste

This unfortunate person became **Sky Woman**. [*Sky Woman* identifies the subject *person*.]

The story of Sky Woman is **sad**. [*Sad* describes the subject *story*.]

There are two kinds of subject complements—the *predicate nominative* and the *predicate adjective*.

PREDICATE NOMINATIVES

9d. A *predicate nominative* is a noun or pronoun that follows a linking verb and identifies the subject or refers to it.

Sky Woman became the **Great Earth Mother**. [The compound noun *Great Earth Mother* is a predicate nominative that identifies the subject *Sky Woman*.]

Predicate nominatives never appear in prepositional phrases.

The world was only a few **bits** of earth on a turtle. [The word *bits* is a predicate nominative that identifies the subject *world*. *Earth* is the object of the preposition *of*, and *turtle* is the object of the preposition *on*.]

A predicate nominative may be compound.

Her helpers were **birds**, a **muskrat**, a **toad**, and a **turtle**.

PREDICATE ADJECTIVES

9e. A *predicate adjective* is an adjective that follows a linking verb and describes the subject.

Sky Woman was **young** and **beautiful**. [the words *young* and *beautiful* are predicate adjectives that describe the subject *Sky Woman*.]

Some verbs, such as *look* and *feel,* may be used as either linking verbs or action verbs.

| LINKING VERB | The Chief of Heaven **looked** angry. [*Looked* is a linking verb because it links the adjective *angry* to the subject *Chief of Heaven*.] |
| ACTION VERB | Sky Woman **looked** through the hole in the floor of Heaven. [*Looked* is an action verb because it expresses Sky Woman's action.] |

Your Turn   Using Action Verbs

Overusing the linking verb *be* can make your writing dull. Whenever possible, replace a dull *be* verb with a verb that expresses action.

| BE VERB | "Sky Woman" **is** a traditional Seneca story. |
| ACTION VERB | Traditionally, the Seneca people **tell** the story of Sky Woman. |

Revise each of the following sentences by substituting an interesting action verb for the dull *be* verb.

1. The Chief of Heaven was angry with Sky Woman.
2. Paradise was the home of the chief of Heaven, Sky Woman, and many animals and plants.
3. Animals of all kinds were friends of Sky Woman.
4. The shell of that turtle is now the surface of the earth.
5. Many things from the sky are now on earth.

10. Kinds of Sentences

Sentences Classified By Structure

One way that sentences are classified is by **structure**—the kinds of clauses and the number of clauses the sentences contain.

THE SIMPLE SENTENCE

10a. A *simple* sentence has one independent clause and no subordinate clauses.

Ice has damaged the gutters.
A simple sentence may have a compound subject, a compound verb, or both.

$$\text{S} \qquad\qquad \text{S} \qquad \text{V}$$
Jean Fritz and her parents discussed her
$$\text{V}$$
problem and found a clever solution to it.

THE COMPOUND SENTENCE

10b. A *compound sentence* has two or more independent clauses but no subordinate clauses.

In a compound sentence, the independent clauses are usually joined by a coordinating conjunction. Some subordinating conjunctions, such as after, as, before, since, and until, are also used as prepositions.

Coordinating Conjunctions			
and	but	or	nor
for	so	yet	

The independent clauses in a compound sentence may also be joined by a semicolon.

$$\text{S} \quad \text{V} \qquad\qquad \text{S} \quad \text{V}$$
Jared read *Old Yeller*, and then he saw the movie.

$$\text{S} \qquad \text{V}$$
McCaffrey has written many stories about
$$\text{S} \qquad \text{V}$$
dragons; in fact, she has made them popular.

THE COMPLEX SENTENCE

10c. A *complex sentence* has one independent clause and at least one subordinate clause.

When I read one of Anne McCaffrey's stories,
 I want to ride a dragon.
$$\text{S} \quad \text{V}$$
INDEPENDENT CLAUSE   I want to ride a dragon.
$$\text{S} \quad \text{V}$$
SUBORDINATE CLAUSE   When I read one of Anne McCaffrey's stories

Sentences Classified By Purpose

A sentence is also classified according to its purpose. The four kinds of sentences are *declarative, interrogative, imperative,* and *exclamatory.*

10d. A *declarative sentence* makes a statement. It is followed by a period.

I can guess what that is.

10e. An *interrogative sentence* asks a question. It is followed by a question mark.

What is the matter with Ted's bike**?**

10f. An *imperative sentence* gives a command or makes a request. It is followed by a period. A strong command is followed by an exclamation point.

Please open the door, Theo.
Look out!
If an imperative sentence does not have a subject, the "understood" subject is always *you*.

(You) Do it now!

10g. An *exclamatory sentence* shows excitement or expresses strong feeling. An exclamatory sentence is followed by an exclamation point.

What a bargain this is!
We won regionals!

Variety can make your writing more interesting. You can improve your writing by varying the length and structure of your sentences.

- Use simple sentences to expresses single ideas.
- To describe more complicated ideas and to show relationships between them, use compound and complex sentences.

Improve each item by combining the simple sentences into one compound or complex sentence.

1. Commas seemed complicated. Andrea Hull knew how to use them.
2. Andrea Hull knew more than young Jean. Andrea taught her many things.
3. Embroidery is beautiful. It can be tedious.
4. She stretched the cloth. She marked her pattern. She began stitching.
5. A design is finished. Everyone can enjoy it.

11. Writing Effective Sentences

COMBINING SENTENCES

11a. Improve short, choppy sentences by combining them into longer, smoother sentences.

There are many ways to combine sentences.

(1) Insert words and phrases.

| CHOPPY | The pan was hot. The pan was made of iron. |
| COMBINED | The **iron** pan was hot. |

(2) Use coordinating conjunctions.

| CHOPPY | Father likes steak. Mother does, too. |
| COMBINED | Father **and** Mother like steak. |

(3) Use subordinate clauses.

| CHOPPY | I saw the picture. You drew it. |
| COMBINED | I saw the picture **that you drew**. |

REVISING RUN-ON SENTENCES

11b. Avoid using run-on sentences.

If you run together two complete sentences as if they were one sentence, you get a **run-on sentence**.

| RUN-ON | This poet values individuality, he also respects tradition. |

A **comma splice** is a kind of run-on sentence in which a comma is used without a coordinating conjunction to join independent clauses. The run-on sentence in the example is a comma splice. Here are two of the ways you can revise run-on sentences.

(1) You can make two sentences.

| REVISED | This poet values individuality. **He** also respects tradition. |

(2) You can use a comma and the coordinating conjunction *and, but,* or *or.*

| REVISED | This poet values individuality, **but** he also respects tradition. |

REVISING STRINGY SENTENCES AND WORDY SENTENCES

11c. Improve *stringy* and *wordy* sentences by making them shorter and more precise.

| STRINGY | The Hummingbird King was betrayed, and an enemy betrayed him, and Kukul turned into a hummingbird, so the hummingbird symbolizes freedom for the Maya, and even today he watches all. |

To fix a stringy sentence, you can break the sentence into two or more sentences. You can also turn some of the independent clauses into phrases or subordinate clauses.

REVISED   When the Hummingbird King was betrayed by an enemy, Kukul turned into a hummingbird, the symbol of freedom for the Maya. Even today, he watches all.

You can revise wordy sentences in three different ways.

(1) Replace a group of words with one word.

WORDY   With great sorrow, they mourned their king.

REVISED   **Sorrowfully**, they mourned their king.

(2) Replace a clause with a phrase.

WORDY   When Kukul's life ended, he turned into a hummingbird.

REVISED   **After his death**, Kukul turned into a hummingbird.

(3) Remove a whole group of unnecessary words.

WORDY   What I mean to say is that Kukul is known as the *quetzal*.

REVISED   Kukul is known as the *quetzal*.

> **Your Turn**   Eliminating Wordiness
>
> Extra words and phrases tend to make writing sound awkward and unnatural. When revising your writing, read your sentences aloud to check for wordiness or a stringy style.
>
> Revise each of the following sentences to eliminate wordiness and stringy style.
>
> _____
>
> 1. The reason that many legends, myths, and fairy tales have survived for centuries is that they address something important in people.
> 2. They continually surprise and delight readers due to the fact of their impossibility.
> 3. People have long told stories that explain human behavior and ones that explain natural forces in the world.
> 4. Children read these stories or view them on film, and so do their parents.
> 5. The needs of a culture change, and details of the story change, and the ending may change, but the readers remain.

12. Capital Letters

12a. Capitalize the first word in each sentence.

Who gets a place in the choir?

The first word of a direct quotation is capitalized even if the quotation begins within a sentence.

Bacon states, "**K**nowledge is power."

Traditionally, the first word in a line of poetry is capitalized.

It was many and many a year ago,
In a kingdom by the sea,
That a maiden there lived whom you may know
By the name of Annabel Lee;
And this maiden she lived with no other thought
Than to love and be loved by me.
    —Edgar Allan Poe, "Annabel Lee"

12b. Capitalize the pronoun *I*.

I enjoyed the book, but **I** didn't like the film.

12c. Capitalize the interjection *O*.

The interjection *O* is most often used on solemn or formal occasions.

Protect us in the battle, **O** great Athena!

The interjection *oh* requires a capital letter only at the beginning of a sentence.

Oh, look at the sunset!

We felt tired but, **oh**, so victorious.

12d. Capitalize proper nouns.

While a common noun is capitalized only when it begins a sentence or is part of a title, a proper noun is always capitalized. Some proper nouns consist of more than one word. In these names, short prepositions (those of fewer than five letters) and articles (*a, an, the*) are not capitalized.

COMMON NOUNS   man, statue

PROPER NOUNS   Moses, Statue **of** Liberty

(1) Capitalize the names of persons and animals.

Alice Walker, Lassie

(2) Capitalize geographical names.

Type of Name	Examples
Towns, Cities	San Diego, Jamestown
Counties, States	Can County, New Hampshire
Countries	New Zealand, Germany
Islands	Wake Island, Isle of Wight
Bodies of Water	Indian Ocean, Gulf of Mexico
Forests, Parks	Sherwood Forest, Central Park
Streets, Highways	Route 44, West Fourth Street
Mountains	Mount Shasta, Big Horn Mountain
Continents, Regions	South America, the West Coast

In a hyphenated street number, the second part of the number is not capitalized.

　　Seventy-eighth Street

Words such as *north, east,* and *southwest* are not capitalized when they indicate direction, but they are capitalized when they are part of a proper name.

　　go south to the East End Cafe

(3) Capitalize the names of planets, stars, and other heavenly bodies.

　　Jupiter, Sirius, Milky Way, Big Dipper

The word *earth* is not capitalized unless it is used along with the names of other heavenly bodies that are capitalized. The words *sun* and *moon* are not capitalized.

　　Plato thought the sun circled the **earth**.
　　The probe has left **Earth** for Pluto.

(4) Capitalize the names of teams, organizations, government bodies, businesses, and institutions.

Type of Name	Examples
Teams	Detroit Pistons, Seattle Seahawks
Organizations, Businesses	Boy Scouts, Tom's Ski World
Institutions, Government Bodies	Hilltop High School, Department of Justice

(5) Capitalize the names of historical events and periods, special events, and calendar items.

Type of Name	Examples
Historical Events, Historical Periods	Battle of Yorktown, Great Depression
Special Events	Iowa State Fair, Sundance Film Festival
Calendar Items	Friday Fourth of July

The name of a season is not capitalized unless it is part of a proper name.

　　the last day of summer
　　the Oak Ridge Winter Carnival

(6) Capitalize the names of nationalities, races, and peoples.

　　Greek, Asian, Caucasian, Hispanic, Shawnee

(7) Capitalize the names of religions and their followers, holy days, sacred writings, and specific deities.

Type of Name	Examples
Religions and Followers	Zen Buddhism, Christianity, Muslim
Holy Days	Passover, Lent, Ramadan
Sacred Writings	Tao Te Ching, Bible Talmud, Koran
Specific Deities	Holy Spirit, Brahma, Allah, Jehovah

The word *god* is not capitalized when it refers to a mythological god. The names of specific gods, however, are capitalized.

　　The king of the Greek gods was Zeus.

(8) Capitalize the names of buildings and other structures.

　　Ritz Theater, Golden Gate Bridge

(9) Capitalize the names of monuments and awards.

　　Vietnam Veterans Memorial, Purple Heart

(10) Capitalize the names of trains, ships, aircraft, and spacecraft.

Type of Name	Examples
Trains	*Silver Rocket, Orient Express*
Ships	*Nina, Glomar Explorer*
Aircraft	*Spirit of Saint Louis, Marine One*
Spacecraft	*Mars Reconnaissance Orbiter, Endeavour*

(11) Capitalize the brand names of business products.

Nike shoes, Buick sedan, Wrangler jeans

12e. Capitalize proper adjectives.

A **proper adjective** is formed from a proper noun and is usually capitalized.

PROPER NOUN   Rome

PROPER ADJECTIVE   Roman army

12f. Do *not* capitalize the names of school subjects, except language classes and course names followed by a number.

I have tests in English, math, and Art II.

12g. Capitalize titles.

(1) Capitalize the title of a person when it comes before a name.
Does Ms. Tam know Governor Halsey?

(2) Capitalize a title used alone or following a person's name only when you want to emphasize the person's high position.
We grew quiet as the Rabbi rose to speak.
Is he the rabbi at the new synagogue?

A title used alone in direct address is often capitalized.

Is the patient resting comfortably, Nurse?

(3) Capitalize a word showing a family relationship when the word is used before or in place of a person's name.
Hey, Mom, I received a letter from Aunt Christina and Uncle Garth.

Do not capitalize a word showing a family relationship when a possessive comes before the word.

Angela's mother and my aunt coach softball.

(4) Capitalize the first, last, and all important words in titles.

Unimportant words in titles include prepositions of fewer than five letters (such as *at, of, for, from, with*); coordinating conjunctions (*and, but, for, nor, or, so, yet*); articles (*a, an, the*).

Type of Title	Examples
Books	*The Old Man and the Sea*
Magazines	*Sports Illustrated, Nature*
Newspapers	*Los Angeles Times*
Poems	"The Runaway," "Affliction"
Short Stories	"A Day's Wait," "The Bear"
Historical Documents	Bill of Rights, Emancipation Proclamation
Movies	*March of the Penguins*
Television Programs	*High School Musical Our Small World*
Works of Art	*The Old Guitarist*
Musical Compositions	*The Marriage of Figaro,* the Surprise Symphony

Your Turn Correcting Errors in Capitalization

Revise the following sentences by correcting the errors in capitalization.

1. Each Summer around the fourth of july, the ryan family takes a trip West.
2. This Year they traveled to california in their new buick.
3. On friday they visited a hollywood Studio.
4. There they saw the Set of *heroes*.

13. Punctuation

End Marks

An **end mark** is a mark of punctuation placed at the end of a sentence. The three kinds of end marks are the *period,* the *question mark,* and the *exclamation point.*

13a. Use a period at the end of a statement.

> Kristi Yamaguchi is a champion skater.

13b. Use a question mark at the end of a question.

> Did Gordon Parks write *The Learning Tree*?

13c. Use an exclamation point at the end of an exclamation.

> Wow! What a view!

13d. Use a period or an exclamation point at the end of a request or a command.

> Please give me the scissors. [a request]
> Give me the scissors! [a command]

13e. Use a period after most abbreviations.

Type of Abbreviation	Examples		
Personal Names	Pearl S. Buck, A. A. Milne		
Titles Used with Names	Mr. Jr.	Ms. Sr.	Mrs. Dr.
States	Ariz.	Fla.	Calif.
Addresses	St.	P.O. Box	Apt.
Organizations and Companies	Co.	Inc.	Assn.
Times	A.M. P.M.	B.C.	A.D

Place *A.D.* before the number and *B.C.* after the number. For centuries expressed in words, place both *A.D.* and *B.C.* after the century.

> A.D. 540, 31 B.C.
> sixth century B.C., third century A.D.

When an abbreviation with a period ends a sentence, another period is not needed. However, a question mark or an exclamation point is used as needed.

> This is my friend J. R.
> Have you met Nguyen, J. R.?

Commas

ITEMS IN A SERIES

13f. Use commas to separate items in a series.

Words, phrases, and clauses in a series are separated by commas to show the reader where one item in the series ends and the next item begins.

WORDS IN A SERIES	*Hammock, canoe,* and *moccasin* are Native American words.
PHRASES IN A SERIES	Seaweed was in the water, on the beach, and in our shoes.
CLAUSES IN A SERIES	Tell us who was there, what happened, and why it happened.

If all items in a series are joined by *and* or *or,* commas are not needed.

> I voted for Corey **and** Mona **and** Ethan.

13g. Use a comma to separate two or more adjectives that come before a noun.

> An Arabian horse is a fast, beautiful animal.

COMPOUND SENTENCES

13h. Use a comma before *and, but, or, nor, for, so,* or *yet* when it joins independent clauses.

> I enjoyed *The King and I,* but *Oklahoma!* is still my favorite musical.

You may omit the comma before *and, but, or,* or *nor* if the clauses are very short and there is no chance of misunderstanding.

INTERRUPTERS

13i. Use commas to set off an expression that interrupts a sentence.

> Yes, my favorite gospel singers, BeBe and CeCe Winans, were on TV, Ed.

(1) **Use commas to set off a nonessential participial phrase or a nonessential subordinate clause.**

NONESSENTIAL PHRASE	Orpheus, **mourning his bride,** entered Hades.

NONESSENTIAL CLAUSE Orpheus, **who was a musician,** met a cruel fate.

(2) Use commas to set off an appositive or an appositive phrase that is nonessential.

APPOSITIVE The gray ferryman, **Charon,** did not charge any fare.

APPOSITIVE PHRASE Even Cerberus, **the dog at the gate,** listened.

(3) Use commas to set off words used in direct address.

Do you know, **Elena,** when the bus is due?

(4) Use commas to set off a parenthetical expression.

A *parenthetical expression* is a side remark that either adds information or relates ideas in a sentence.

What, **in your opinion,** is the best solution to this problem? [parenthetical]

I have faith in your opinion. [not parenthetical]

INTRODUCTORY WORDS, PHRASES, AND CLAUSES

13j. Use a comma after certain introductory elements.

(1) Use a comma after *yes, no,* or any mild exclamation such as *well* or *why* at the beginning of a sentence.

Yes, King Midas had been foolish.

(2) Use a comma after an introductory prepositional phrase if the phrase is long or if two or more phrases appear together.

Long ago in a land called Lydia, King Midas lived.

In the garden of his palace, he met Silenus.

(3) Use a comma after a participial phrase or an infinitive phrase that introduces a sentence.

PARTICIPIAL PHRASE **Sleeping in the garden,** Silenus was trespassing.

PARTICIPIAL PHRASE **Threatened by Midas,** the satyr struck a bargain.

INFINITIVE PHRASE **To reward Midas,** Dionysus offered a gift.

(4) Use a comma after an introductory adverb clause.

When his daughter arrived, he warned her to leave quickly.

CONVENTIONAL SITUATIONS

13k. Use commas in certain conventional situations.

(1) Use commas to separate items in dates and addresses.

They met on June 17, 1965, in Miami.

My address is 10 Cocoa Lane, Orlando, FL 32804.

(2) Use a comma after the salutation of a friendly letter and after the closing of any letter.

Dear Aunt Margaret,

Sincerely yours,

Semicolons

13l. Use a semicolon instead of a comma between independent clauses when they are not joined by *and, but, or, nor, for, so,* or *yet.*

Our parents settled our dispute; they gave us each half.

Use a semicolon rather than a period between independent clauses only when the ideas in the clauses are closely related.

COLONS

13m. Use a colon before a list of items, especially after expressions like *as follows* or *the following*.

For camping you need the following: bedroll, utensils for eating, warm clothing, and rope.

13n. Use a colon in certain conventional situations.

(1) Use a colon between the hour and the minute.

11:30 P.M., 4:08 A.M.

(2) Use a colon after the salutation of business letter.

Dear Ms. Gonzalez:

(3) Use a colon between chapter and verse in referring to passages from the Bible.

John 3:16, Matthew 6:9–13

Your Turn Using Semicolons Effectively

Sometimes, rather than using a semicolon, it is more effective to separate a compound sentence or a heavily punctuated sentence into two sentences.

ACCEPTABLE In South American jungles, it rains every day, sometimes all day; the vegetation there, some of which is found nowhere else in the world, is lush, dense, and fast-growing.

BETTER In South American jungles, it rains every day, sometimes all day. The vegetation there, some of which is found nowhere else in the world, is lush, dense, and fast-growing.

Decide whether the following ideas are better expressed as single sentences or as two or more sentences. Revise sentences for style and clarity.

1. The frogs wanted a king, one who could amuse them with royal customs; they thought a strong ruler would be exciting.
2. Jupiter heard their request; he granted it; he felt they were foolish.
3. Jupiter threw down a large log; the log landed next to the frogs.

14. Punctuation

Underlining (Italics)

Italics are printed letters that lean to the right, such as *the letters in these words*. In handwritten work, indicate italics by underlining.

TYPED <u>Born Free</u> is the story of a lion.

PUBLISHED *Born Free* is the story of a lion.

14a. Use underlining (italics) for titles of books, plays, periodicals, works of art, films, television programs, recordings, long musical compositions, trains, ships, aircraft, and spacecraft.

Type of Title	Examples
Books	*Barrio Boy, House Made of Dawn*
Plays	*Macbeth, Into the Woods*
Periodicals	*Hispanic, Chicago Tribune*
Works of Art	*The Thinker, Water Lilies*
Films	*Emma, Shrek the Third*
Television Programs	*Home Imporvement, Planet Earth*
Recordings	*Long Road out of Eden*
Long Musical Compositions	*Don Giovanni, The Four Seasons*
Ships and Trains	*Monitor, California Zephyr*
Aircraft and Spacecraft	*Enola Gay, Herschel Space Observatory*

14b. Use underlining (italics) for words, letters, and figures referred to as such.

Don't forget to drop the final *e* before you add *-ing* to the word *dine*.

Is the last number a *5* or an *8*?

QUOTATION MARKS

14c. Use quotation marks to enclose a *direct quotation*—a person's exact words.

"Here is Eric's drawing," said Ms. Rios.

Quotation marks are not used for an *indirect quotation,* which is a rewording of a direct quotation.

DIRECT QUOTATION Kaya asked, "What is your interpretation of the poem?"

INDIRECT QUOTATION Kaya asked what my interpretation of the poem was.

14d. A direct quotation begins with a capital letter.

Brandon shouted, "Let's get busy!"

14e. When the expression identifying the speaker interrupts a quoted sentence, the second part of the quotation begins with a lowercase letter.

"Gee," Milo added, "that book is funny."

When the second part of a divided quotation is a separate sentence, it begins with a capital letter.

> "Travel is exciting," said Mrs. Ash. "Space travel is no exception."

14f. A direct quotation is set off from the rest of he sentence by a comma, a question mark, or an exclamation point, but not by a period.

If a quotation appears at the beginning of a sentence, place a comma after it. If a quotation falls at the end of a sentence, place a comma before it. If a quoted sentence is interrupted, place a comma after the first part and before the second part.

> "I just read her story," Aly said.
> Mark said, "I've read her stories, too."
> "Aly," asked Janet, "what did you read?"

When a quotation ends with a question mark or an exclamation point, no comma is needed.

> "Have you seen my brother?" Alicia asked.

14g. A period or a comma is placed inside the closing quotation marks.

> Ramón said, "My brother loves poetry."
> "My sister does too," Paula responded.

14h. A question mark or an exclamation point is placed inside the closing quotation marks when the quotation itself is a question or exclamation. Otherwise, it is placed outside.

> "Is the time difference between Los Angeles and Chicago two hours?" asked Ken. [The quotation is a question.]
> Linda exclaimed, "I thought everyone knew that!" [The quotation is an exclamation.]
> What did Sandra Cisneros mean by "Keep, keep, keep, trees say when I sleep"? [The sentence, not the quotation, is a question.]
> I can't believe Mom said, "I'm not going"! [The sentence, not the quotation, is an exclamation.]

When both the sentence and the quotation at the end of the sentence are questions (or exclamations), only one end mark is used. It is placed inside the closing quotation marks.

> Whose poem begins "How do I love thee?"

14i. When you write dialogue (conversation), begin a new paragraph each time you change speakers.

> "Frog, how may we help you?"

> "Uh, well, uh, you see," says Frog, "I would like to become a part of your group."
> "That's wonderful," says the head bird.
> "Yes, wonderful," echo the other birds.
> —Linda Goss, "The Frog Who Wanted to Be a Singer"

14j. When a quotation consists of several sentences, place quotation marks at the beginning and at the end of the whole quotation.

> "Take the garbage out. Clean your room. Have fun!" said Dad.

14k. Use single quotation marks to enclose a quotation within a quotation.

> "I said, 'The quiz will be this Friday,'" repeated Mr. Allyn.

14l. Use quotation marks to enclose titles of short works.

Type of Title	Examples
Short Stories	"Papa's Parrot," "Amigo Brothers"
Poems	"Silver," "Early Song"
Articles	"Free Speech and You"
Songs	"Michelle" "La Bamba"
Television Program Episodes	"Homecoming," "Beyond the Sea"
Chapters and Other Book Parts	"Handling Reptiles," "The Return Journey"

Your Turn Correcting Punctuation

Correct the punctuation in the following sentences by adding underlining and quotation marks as needed.

1. Which Beatles song do you like best? Ramon asked his grandmother.
2. Well, she said, my favorite is probably Yesterday.
3. Too much! replied Ramon. That's Grandad's favorite, too.
4. Jimmy added, He knows all the words.
5. Do you know what they meant by the line Love is such an easy game to play? Ramon asked.

15. Punctuation

Apostrophes

15a. The *possessive case* of a noun or a pronoun shows ownership or relationship.

(1) **To form the possessive case of a singular noun, add an apostrophe and an *s*.**
a dog's collar, Cinderella's slipper

(2) **To form the possessive case of a plural noun ending in *s,* add only the apostrophe.**
doctors' opinions, hosts' invitations

(3) **To form the possessive case of a plural noun that does not end in *s,* add an apostrophe and an *s*.**
women's suits, geese's noise

(4) **To form the possessive case of some indefinite pronouns, add an apostrophe and an *s*.**
someone's opinion, no one's fault

15b. To form a contraction, use an apostrophe to show where letters have been left out.

A *contraction* is a shortened form of a word, figure, or group of words.

I am	→ I'm	where is	→ where's
1996	→ '96	of the clock	→ o'clock

The word *not* can be shortened to *-n't* and added to a verb, usually without changing the spelling of the verb.

is not → isn't
had not → hadn't
do not → don't
should not → shouldn't

EXCEPTIONS   will not → won't   cannot → can't

Do not confuse contractions with possessive pronouns.

Contractions
It's snowing. [It is]
Who's Clifton Davis? [Who is]
There's only one answer. [There is]
They're not here. [They are]

Possessive Pronouns
Its front tire is flat.
Whose idea was it?

This trophy is **theirs**.
Their dog is barking.

15c. Use an apostrophe and an *s* to form the plurals of letters, numerals, signs, and words referred to as words.

Your *2*'s look like *5*'s.
Don't use *&*'s in place of *and*'s.

Hyphens

15d. Use a hyphen to divide a word at the end of a line.

(1) **Divide a word only between syllables.**

INCORRECT	Didn't Carrie write her rep-ort on the tyrannosaurs, the largest meat-eating dinosaurs?
CORRECT	Didn't Carrie write her re-port on the tyrannosaurs, the largest meat-eating dinosaurs?

(2) **Divide a hyphenated word at a hyphen.**

INCORRECT	I went to the Iowa State Fair with my sisters and my brother-in-l aw.
CORRECT	I went to the Iowa State Fair with my sisters and my brother-in-law.

(3) **Do not divide a word so that one letter stands alone.**

INCORRECT	On our last class trip, all of u-s stayed overnight in a hotel.
CORRECT	On our last class trip, all of us stayed overnight in a hotel.

15e. Use a hyphen with compound numbers from *twenty-one* to *ninety-nine* and with fractions used as adjectives.

thirty-five, one-half, forty-eighth

Parentheses

15f. Use parentheses to enclose material that is added to a sentence but is not considered of major importance.

Ms. Matsuo served us the sushi (**sü´ shē**) chef.

My great-uncle Chester (**he's Grandma's brother**) will stay with us.

Dashes

15g. Use a dash to indicate an abrupt break in thought or speech.

Jan can whistle and hum at the same time—quite an accomplishment.

Ms. Alonzo who just left—is one of the judges.

The teacher began, "Paul, where are—oh, there you are."

Your Turn Eliminating Unnecessary Parenthetical Expressions

Using too many parenthetical expressions can distract readers. Revise the following sentences to eliminate parentheses. If a sentence is best with parentheses, write *c*.

1. *Survive the Savage Sea* (true stories are my favorites) is about people on a raft.
2. Yellowstone National Park (established in 1872) covers territory in Wyoming, Idaho, and Montana.
3. The writer Langston Hughes (1902–1967) is best known for his poetry.
4. Alligators use their feet to dig holes (called "gator holes") in marshy fields.

16. Spelling

Using Word Parts

Many English words are made up of various word parts—roots, prefixes, or suffixes. Learning to spell the most frequently used parts can help you spell many words correctly.

16a. The *root* of a word is the part that carries the word's core meaning.

Root	Meaning	Examples
-dict- -duc- -ped-	speak lead foot	**dict**ation e**duc**ate **ped**al, bi**ped**

16b. A *prefix* is one or more letters or syllables added to the beginning of a word or a word part to create a new word.

Prefix	Meaning	Examples
anti- in- re-	against not back, again	**anti**war **in**accurate **re**claim, **re**build

16c. A suffix is one or more letters or syllables added to the end of a word or a word part to create a new word.

Suffix	Meaning	Examples
-able -ate -ness	able, likely become quality	read**able** captiv**ate** peaceful**ness**

Spelling Rules

IE AND *EI*

16d. Except after *c*, write *ie* when the sound is long *e*.

ach**ie**ve, bel**ie**ve, c**ei**ling, rec**ei**ve

EXCEPTIONS **ei**ther, prot**ei**n, n**ei**ther, s**ei**ze

16e. Write *ei* when the sound is not long *e*, especially when the sound is long *a*.

for**ei**gn, n**ei**ghbor, r**ei**gn, th**ei**r

EXCEPTIONS anc**ie**nt, consc**ie**nce, effic**ie**nt, fr**ie**nd

-CEDE, -CEED, AND *-SEDE*

16f. The only English word ending in *-sede* is *supersede.* The only words ending in *-ceed* are *exceed, proceed,* and *succeed.* Other words with this sound end in *-cede.*

con**cede**, inter**cede**, pre**cede**, re**cede**

ADDING PREFIXES AND SUFFIXES

16g. When adding a prefix to a word, do not change the spelling of the word itself.

mis + spell = **mis**spell

16h. When adding the suffix *-ly* or *-ness* to a word, do not change the spelling of the word itself.

slow + ly = slow**ly**

EXCEPTIONS   For words that end in *y* and have more than one syllable, change the *y* to *i* before adding *-ly* or *-ness.* happy + ly = happ**ily**

16i. Drop the final silent *e* before a suffix beginning with a vowel.

line + ing = lin**ing**

EXCEPTIONS   Keep the final silent *e* in a word ending in *ce* or *ge* before a suffix beginning with *a* or *o.* notice + able = notic**eable,** courage + ous = courag**eous**

16j. Keep the final silent *e* before a suffix beginning with a consonant.

hope + less = hope**less**

EXCEPTIONS   nine + th = nin**th,** argue + ment =argu**ment**

16k. For words ending in *y* preceded by a consonant, change the *y* to *i* before any suffix that does not begin with *i.*

try + ed = tr**ied,** duty + ful = dut**iful**

16l. For words ending in *y* preceded by a vowel, keep the *y* when adding a suffix.

pray + ing = pray**ing**

EXCEPTIONS   day—da**ily,** lay—la**id,** pay—pa**id**

16m. Double the final consonant before a suffix beginning with a vowel if the word (1) has only one syllable or the accent on the last syllable, *and* (2) ends in a single consonant preceded by a single vowel.

sit + ing = si**tt**ing, sing + er = sing**er**

EXCEPTIONS   Do not double a *w* or *x* before a suffix beginning with a vowel. mow + ing = mowing, wax + ed = waxed

FORMING THE PLURALS OF NOUNS

16n. For most nouns, add *-s.*

desk**s**   idea**s**   shoe**s**   friend**s**

16o. For most nouns ending in *s, x, z, ch,* or *sh,* add *-es.*

gas**es**   fox**es**   waltz**es**   inch**es**

16p. For nouns ending in *y* preceded by a vowel, add *-s.*

decoy**s**   highway**s**   alley**s**   Riley**s**

16q. For nouns ending in *y* preceded by a consonant, change the *y* to *i* and add *-es.*

arm**ies**   cit**ies**   pon**ies**   dais**ies**

Just add *-s* to proper nouns ending in *-y.* Brady—Brady**s**

16r. For some nouns ending in *f* or *fe,* add *-s.* For others, change the *f* or *fe* to *v* and add *-es.*

belief**s**, sheriff**s** kni**ves,** lea**ves**

16s. For nouns ending in *o* preceded by a vowel, add *-s.*

igloo**s**   Matteo**s**   patio**s**   stereo**s**

16t. For nouns ending in *o* preceded by a consonant, add *-es.*

echo**es**   hero**es**   potato**es**   tomato**es**

EXCEPTIONS   For musical terms and names, add *-s.* alto—alto**s** Blanco—Blanco**s**

16u. The plural of a few nouns is formed in irregular ways.

gee**se**   fee**t**   mi**ce**   ox**en**

16v. For most compound nouns, form the plural of the last word in the compound.

bookshel**ves**   push-up**s**   sea gull**s**

16w. For compound nouns in which one of the words is modified by the other word or words, form the plural of the word modified.

brother**s**-in-law   boy scout**s**

16x. For some nouns, the singular and the plural forms are the same.

deer   moose   Sioux   trout

16y. For numerals, letters, symbols, and words used as words, add an apostrophe and -*s*.

4**'s**   *s***'s** $**'s**   *and***'s**

Your Turn   Correcting Spelling Errors

Poor spelling can ruin good writing. Correct the spelling errors in each of the following sentences.

1. The Bradyes love baseball.
2. Joe's two brother-in-laws took him to the game last night and even payed for his ticket.
3. The releif pitcher was awesome.
4. He pitched a flawless nineth inning.
5. At the end of the game Joe conseded that his team was outplayed.

17. Glossary of Usage

This Glossary of Usage is an alphabetical list of words and expressions that are commonly misused in English. Throughout this section some examples are labeled *standard* or *nonstandard*.

Standard English is the most widely accepted form of English. It is used in *formal* situations, such as in speeches and writing for school, and in *informal* situations, such as in conversation and everyday writing. ***Nonstandard English*** is language that does not follow the rules and guidelines of standard English.

all ready, already *All ready* means "completely prepared." *Already* means "before a certain point in time."

Everyone was **all ready** for the show.
That bill has **already** been paid.

all right *All right* should always be written as two words.

Linda fell, but she is **all right**. [adjective]
You did **all right** at the track meet. [adverb]

a lot *A lot* should always be written as two words.

She knows **a lot** about computer software.
Many writers overuse *a lot*. Try to replace it with a more exact word or phrase.

anywheres, everywheres, nowheres, somewheres Use these words without the final *s*.

I didn't go **anywhere** [not anywheres].

bad, badly *Bad* is an adjective. *Badly* is an adverb.

The raw celery did not taste **bad**. [*Bad* modifies the noun *celery*.]
One little boy behaved **badly**. [*Badly* modifies the verb *behaved*.]

between, among Use *between* when referring to two things, even though they are part of a group containing more than two.

In homeroom, Carlos sits **between** Bob and me.
Use *among* to refer to a group rather than separate individuals.
We saved ten dollars **among** the three of us. [As a group, the three saved ten dollars.]

bust, busted Avoid using these words as verbs. Use a form of either *burst* or *break*.

The door **burst** [not busted] open, and rats teemed in.
What if the window **broke** [not busted]?

choose, chose *Choose* is the present tense form of the verb *choose*. It rhymes with *whose* and means "select." *Chose* is the past tense form of *choose*. It rhymes with *grows* and means "selected."

Did you **choose** "Fish Cheeks" for your report?
Sara **chose** "Miss Awful."

could of Do not write *of* with the helping verb *could*. Write *could have*. Also avoid *had of, ought to of, should of, would of, might of,* and *must of*.

These poems **could have** [*not* could of] been lost.

fewer, less *Fewer* tells "how many" and is used with plural words. *Less* tells "how much and is used with singular words.

We sold **fewer** [*not* less] tickets than they did.

These plants require **less** water than those do.

good, well *Good* is always an adjective. Use *well,* not *good,* as an adverb.

Nancy sang **well** [*not* good] at the audition.

Well may also be used as an adjective to mean "healthy."

He didn't look **well** after eating the pizza.

had ought, hadn't ought *Had* should not be used with *ought.*

Eric **ought** [*not* had ought] to help us.

he, she, they Avoid using a pronoun with its antecedent as the subject of a verb. This error is called the *double subject.*

| NONSTANDARD | Linda Goss she is a writer. |
| STANDARD | Linda Goss is a writer. |

hisself *Hisself* is nonstandard English. Use *himself.*

Ira bought **himself** [not hisself] a tie.

how come In informal situations, *how come* is often used instead of *why.* In formal situations, *why* should always be used.

| INFORMAL | How come she didn't write? |
| FORMAL | **Why** didn't she write? |

kind of, sort of In informal situations, *kind of* and *sort of* are often used to mean "somewhat" or "rather." In formal English, *somewhat* or *rather* is preferred.

| INFORMAL | He seemed kind of embarrassed. |
| FORMAL | He seemed **somewhat** embarrassed. |

learn, teach *Learn* means "gain knowledge." *Teach* means "instruct" or "show how."

He is **learning** how to play the guitar.

His father is **teaching** him how to play.

like, as In informal situations, the preposition *like* is often used instead of the conjunction *as* to introduce a clause. In formal situations, *as* is preferred.

Look in the dictionary, **as** [*not* like] the teacher suggests.

like, as if, as though In informal situations, the preposition *like* is often used for the compound conjunctions *as if* or *as though.* In formal situations, *as if* or *as though* is preferred.

They acted **as if** [*not* like] they hadn't heard the question. You looked **as though** [*not* like] you knew the answer.

of Do not use *of* with other prepositions such as

inside, off, and *outside.*

Did anyone fall **off** [*not* off of] the raft?

reason . . . because In informal situations, *reason . . . because* is often used instead of *reason . . . that.* In formal situations, use *reason . . . that.*

| INFORMAL | The reason I did well on the test was because I had studied hard. |
| FORMAL | The **reason** I did well on the test was **that** I had studied hard. |

some, somewhat Do not use *some* for *somewhat* as an adverb.

My writing improved **somewhat** [*not* some].

them *Them* should not be used as an adjective. Use *those.*

The fox couldn't get **those** [*not* them] grapes.

way, ways Use *way,* not *ways,* in referring to a distance.

They still had a long **way** [*not* ways] to go.

when, where Do not use *when* or *where* incorrectly in a definition.

| NONSTANDARD | In bowling, a "turkey" is when you make three strikes in a row. |
| STANDARD | In bowling, a "turkey" is making three strikes in a row. |

where Do not use *where* for *that.*

I read **that** [*not* where] he won the match.

who, which, that The relative pronoun *who* refers to people only; *which* refers to things only; *that* refers to either people or things.

Kim is the one **who** got the answer. [person]

My bike, **which** has ten speeds, is for sale. [thing]

He is the one person **that** [person] can help you find the ring **that** [thing] you want.

Your Turn Using Adverbs Appropriately

Informally, the adjective *real* is often used as an adverb meaning "extremely." In formal situations, *extremely* or another adverb is preferred.

| INFORMAL | That was a real important call. |
| FORMAL | That was an extremely important call. |

Revise the following sentences by substituting a variety of adverbs for the word *real.*

1. Hercules was real strong.
2. He accomplished real hard tasks.
3. Stories of his labors are real interesting.

Glossary

The glossary that follows is an alphabetical list of words found in the selections in this book. Use this glossary just as you would use a dictionary—to find out the meaning of unfamiliar words. (Some technical, foreign, and more obscure words in this book are not listed here but instead are defined for you in the footnotes that accompany many of the selections.)

Many words in the English language have more than one meaning. This glossary gives the meanings that apply to the words as they are used in the selections in this book. Words closely related in form and meaning are usually listed together in one entry (for instance, *cower* and *cowered*), and the definition is given for the first form.

The following abbreviations are used:

adj.	adjective
adv.	adverb
n.	noun
v.	verb

Each word's pronunciation is given in parentheses. For more information about the words in this glossary or for information about words not listed here, consult a dictionary.

A

absently (AB suhnt lee) *adv.* in a way that shows one is not thinking about what is happening.

accommodate (uh KAHM uh dayt) *v.* hold comfortably.

admonished (ad MAHN ihshd) *v.* warned or urged.

alienate (AYL yuh nayt) *v.* cause to feel isolated or unaccepted.

alliance (uh LY uhns) *n.* pact between nations, families, or individuals that shows a common cause.

allotted (uh LAHT ihd) *v.* set aside for a certain purpose.

amends (uh MEHNDZ) *n.* something to make up for an injury.

anonymous (uh NAHN uh muhs) *adj.* not identified by name.

apparent (uh PAR uhnt) *adj.* seeming.

arduous (AHR joo uhs) *adj.* difficult.

arrogant (AR uh guhnt) *adj.* overly convinced of one's own importance.

assured (uh SHURD) *v.* guaranteed; promised confidently.

awe (aw) *n.* feeling of fear and amazement.

B

barbarian (bahr BAIR ee uhn) *adj.* referring to a group considered uncivilized and inferior by another nation or group.

benevolence (buh NEHV uh luhns) *n.* goodwill; kindliness.

bigotry (BIHG uh tree): *n.* prejudice; intolerance.

boasting (BOHST ihng) *v.* speaking too highly about oneself; bragging.

bore (bawr) *v.* carried.

bouts (bowts) *n.* matches; contests.

burden (BUR duhn) *n.* something heavy that has to be carried.

C

caressed (kuh REHST) *v.* touched gently.

charismatic (kar ihz MAT ihk) *adj.* possessing charm or appeal.

chivalry (SHIHV uhl ree) *n.* code that governed knightly behavior, requiring courage, honor, and readiness to help the weak.

commenced (kuh MEHNST) *v.* began.

communicative (kuh MYOO nih kay tihv) *adj.* able to give information.

compulsion (kuhm PUHL shuhn) *n.* driving, irresistible force.

concentration (kahn suhn TRAY shuhn) *n.* act of thinking carefully about something one is doing.

consequences (KAHN suh kwehns ihz) *n.* results caused by a set of conditions.

consolation (KAHN suh LAY shuhn) *n.* comfort.

contemplate (KAHN tuhm playt) *v.* consider; look at or think about carefully.

contraption (kuhn TRAP shuhn) *n.* strange machine or gadget.

converging (kuhn VUR jihng) *v.* used as *adj.* coming together.

conviction (kuhn VIHK shuhn) *n.* certainty; belief; instance of being declared guilty of a criminal offense.

convinced (kuhn VIHNST) *v.* made to feel sure; persuaded firmly.

convoluted (KAHN vuh loo tihd) *v.* used as *adj.* complicated.

countenance (KOWN tuh nuhns) *n.* face; appearance.

cowered (KOW uhrd) *v.* crouched and trembled in fear.

crinkling (KRIHNG klihng) *v.* used as *adj.* wrinkling.

curtly (KURT lee) *adv.* rudely; with few words.

D

dappled (DAP uhld) *adj.* marked with spots of color or light.

daunting (DAWNT ihng) *adj.* frightening or intimidating.

deception (dih SEHP shuhn) *n.* act of deliberately making a person believe something that is not true.

dedicate (DEHD uh kayt) *v.* do or make something in honor of another person.

deducted (dih DUHKT ihd) *v.* taken away.

defiant (dih FY uhnt) *adj.* boldly resisting authority.

deprivation (dehp ruh VAY shuhn) *n.* condition of not having something essential; hardship resulting from a lack of something.

destitute (DEHS tuh toot) *n.* people living in utter poverty.

destruction (dih STRUHK shuhn) *n.* act of ruining.

detached (dih TACHT) *adj.* not involved emotionally; indifferent.

detain (dih TAYN) *v.* delay.

dismal (DIHZ muhl) *adj.* cheerless, depressing.

dismally (DIHZ muh lee) *adv.* miserably; gloomily.

dismayed (dihs MAYD) *v.* troubled; upset.

dispelled (dihs PEHLD) *v.* driven away.

dispute (dihs PYOOT) *n.* argument.

dwindled (DWIHN duhld) *v.* became smaller and smaller.

E

edible (EHD uh buhl) *adj.* fit to be eaten.

egotism (EE guh tihz uhm) *n.* conceit; talking about oneself too much.

elective (ih LEHK tihv) *n.* course that is not required.

elude (ih LOOD) *v.* avoid; cleverly escape.

encounter (ehn KOWN tuhr) *n.* face-to-face meeting.

enhances (ehn HANS ihz) *v.* improves.

entranced (ehn TRANST) *v.* used as *adj.* cast a spell on; enchanted.

ethnicity (ehth NIHS uh tee) *n.* common culture or nationality.

evacuation (ih vak yoo AY shuhn) *n.* process of removing people from a potentially dangerous situation.

evaporation (ih vap uh RAY shuhn) *n.* process by which a liquid changes into a gas.

exotic (ehg ZAHT ihk) *adj.* not native.

expelled (ehk SPEHLD) *v.* forced to leave.

exquisite (EHKS kwih ziht) *adj.* beautiful and delicate.

F

facilitate (fuh SIHL uh tayt) *v.* ease; aid.

famished (FAM ihsht) *adj.* very hungry.

fidelity (fuh DEHL uh tee) *n.* faithfulness.

fleet (fleet) *adj.* fast-moving.

flourishing (FLUR ihsh ihng) *adj.* thriving.

forbade (fuhr BAD) *v.* ordered not to; outlawed.

forfeit (FAWR fiht) *v.* lose the right to something.

formidable (FAWR muh duh buhl) *adj.* awe inspiring; impressive.

frantically (FRAN tuh klee) *adv.* with wild excitement.

frenzied (FREHN zeed) *adj.* wild; out of control.

furiously (FYUR ee uhs lee) *adv.* rapidly, with intensity.

G

glistening (GLIHS uhn ihng) *adj.* sparkling; reflecting light.

H

habitat (HAB uh tat) *n.* used as *adj.* place where an animal or plant naturally lives.

habitual (huh BIHCH oo uhl) *adj.* done or fixed by habit.

hazards (HAZ uhrdz) *n.* dangers.

heritage (HEHR uh tihj) *n.* traditions that are passed along.

hordes (hawrdz) *n.* densely packed crowds that move as groups.

I

identity (y DEHN tuh tee) *n.* distinguishing characteristics that determine who or what a person or thing is.

idiosyncrasy (ihd ee uh SIHNG kruh see) *n.* peculiarity.

illegal (ih LEE guhl) *adj.* unlawful; against official regulations.

immensely (ih MEHNS lee) *adv.* enormously.

implored (ihm PLAWRD) *v.* begged.

incessantly (ihn SEHS uhnt lee) *adv.* without ceasing; continually.

inconsolable (ihn kuhn SOH luh buhl) *adj.* unable to be comforted; brokenhearted.

incredulously (ihn KREHJ uh luhs lee) *adv.* unbelievingly.

ingenious (ihn JEEN yus) *adj.* clever; good at inventing.

inscription (ihn SKRIHP shuhn) *n.* words written on something.

insolence (IHN suh luhns) *n.* disrespect.

instinct (IHN stihngkt) *n.* inborn pattern of behavior.

integration (ihn tuh GRAY shuhn) *n.* process of bringing together people of all races in schools and neighborhoods.

intense (ihn TEHNS) *adj.* showing strong feelings and seriousness.

intently (ihn TEHNT lee) *adv.* with great focus.

interplanetary (ihn tuhr PLAN uh tehr ee) *adj.* between or among planets.

intimately (IHN tuh muht lee) *adv.* in a very familiar way.

intimidated (ihn TIHM uh day tihd) *v.* frightened with threats.

intolerable (ihn TAHL uhr uh buhl) *adj.* unbearable.

intricate (IHN truh kiht) *adj.* complicated; full of detail.

L

liberation (lihb uh RAY shuhn) *n.* release from slavery, prison, or other limitation.

lingered (LIHNG guhrd) *v.* stayed on.

literally (LIHT uhr uh lee) *adv.* according to the basic meaning of the word.

lithe (lyth) *adj.* able to bend and move easily and gracefully.

loathsome (LOHTH suhm) *adj.* disgusting.

M

malice (MAL ihs) *n.* meanness; hatred.

malnutrition (mal noo TRIHSH uhn) *n.* ill health caused by a lack of food or by a lack of healthy foods.

maneuver (muh NOO vuhr) *v.* move or manipulate skillfully.

meager (MEE guhr) *adj.* small in amount.

menace (MEHN ihs) *n.* danger, threat.

merchandise (MUR chuhn dys) *n.* items that are for sale in stores.

misrepresentations (mihs rehp rih zehn TAY shuhnz) *n.* false ideas given for the purpose of deceiving someone.

mistranslate (mihs TRANS layt) *v.* change from one language to another incorrectly.

moderate (MAHD uhr iht) *adj.* keeping within proper limits.

monarch (MAHN ahrk) *n.* sole and absolute ruler.

monopoly (muh NAHP uh lee) *n.* exclusive control of a market.

morose (muh ROHS) *adj.* gloomy; ill-tempered.

mounts (mownts) *v.* gets up on; climbs up.

O

obligations (ahb luh GAY shuhnz) *n.* duties to carry out.

obstructed (uhb STRUHKT ehd) *v.* prevented; made difficult.

ominous (AHM uh nuhs): *adj.* threatening.

opponents (uh POH nuhnts) *n.* people on opposite sides in a fight or a game.

oppression (uh PREHSH uhn) *n.* unjust treatment.

P

pensively (PEHN sihv lee) *adv.* thoughtfully.

perplexed (puhr PLEHKST) *v.* made confused.

persecution (pur suh KYOO shuhn) *n.* act of attacking others because of their beliefs or their ethnic background.

persevered (pur suh VIHRD) *v.* kept trying; persisted; continued doing something.

persisted (puhr SIHS tihd) *v.* refused to give up.

predominantly (prih DAHM uh nuhnt lee) *adv.* mainly.

presumptuous (prih ZUHMP chu uhs) *adj.* too bold; arrogant.

procedures (pruh SEE juhrz) *n.* methods of doing things.

prodded (PRAHD id) *v.* urged on, here by poking with a stick.

profession (pruh FEHSH uhn) *n.* paid occupation.

profound (pruh FOWND) *adj.* very strong; serious.

prolonged (pruh LAWNGD) *adj.* continuing for a long time.

propelled (pruh PEHLD) *v.* moved or pushed forward.

proposal (pruh POH zuhl) *n.* suggestion.

prosperity (prahs PEHR uh tee) *n.* state of being successful, especially of being wealthy; condition of having money and being successful.

punctuality (puhngk choo AL uh tee) *n.* quality of being on time.

Q

quizzical (KWIHZ ih kuhl) *adj.* puzzled; baffled.

R

rancid (RAN sihd) *adj.* spoiled; rotten.

reassuring (ree uh SHUR ihng) *v.* used as *adj.* comforting.

receding (rih SEED ihng) *v.* used as *adj.* moving back.

recourse (REE kawhrs) *n.* help in a difficult situation.

refuge (REHF yooj) *n.* place of safety.

reluctance (rih LUHK tuhns) *n.* unwillingness.

renovation (rehn uh VAY shuhn) *n.* restoration of something to a better condition.

resolve (rih ZAHLV) *v.* decide.

ritual (RIHCH oo uhl) *n.* an established routine.

ruthless (ROOTH lihs) *adj.* cruel; without pity.

S

sheepishly (SHEEP ihsh lee) *adv.* awkwardly; with embarrassment.

shortages (SHAWR tihj ihz) *n.* situations in which needed things cannot be gotten in sufficient amounts.

short-sighted (SHAWRT SY tihd) *adj.* lacking foresight; not prudent.

simultaneously (sy muhl TAY nee uhs lee) *adv.* at the same time.

slack (slak) *adj.* loose.

solemn (SAHL uhm) *adj.* gloomy; serious.

solitude (SAHL uh tood) *n.* state of being alone.

spectators (SPEHK tay tuhrz) *n.* people who watch at an event.

splendor (SPLEHN duhr) *adj.* magnificence.

standard (STAN duhrd) *adj.* usual; regularly used or produced.

sterile (STEHR uhl) *adj.* barren; lacking in interest or vitality.

stubble (STUHB uhl) *n.* short, bristly growth.

supervision (soo puhr VIHZH uhn) *n.* function of overseeing.

supple (SUHP uhl) *adj.* easily bent; flexible.

suppressing (suh PREHS ihng) *v.* holding back.

survey (suhr VAY) *v.* look carefully in order to make a decision or gather information.

T

tentative (TEHN tuh tihv) *adj.* not fixed.

thermometer (thuhr MAHM uh tuhr) *n.* instrument that measures temperature.

torrent (TAWR uhnt) *n.* flood; rush.

traditions (truh DIHSH uhnz) *n.* accepted social attitudes and customs.

transfixed (trans FIHKST) *v.* used as *adj.* very still, as if nailed to the spot.

transition (tran ZIHSH uhn) *n.* change; passing from one condition to another.

treacherous (TREHCH uhr uhs) *adj.* unfaithful.

treacherously (TREHCH uhr uhs lee) *adv.* deceptively; unreliably.

U

unfortunate (uhn FAWR chuh niht) *adj.* to be marked by ill fortune.

unrequited (uhn rih KWY tihd) *adj.* not returned.

V

vainly (VAYN lee) *adv.* uselessly.

valiant (VAL yuhnt) *adj.* brave and determined.

version (VUHR zhuhn) *n.* a retelling from a certain point of view.

vigil (VIHJ uhl) *n.* overnight watch.

W

wafting (WAHFT ihng) *v.* used as *adj.* floating in the wind.

withered (WIHTH uhrd) *v.* used as *adj.* dried up.

wriggled (RIHG uhld) *v.* wiggled; squirmed.

Spanish Glossary

A

a traición *loc. adv.* de manera engañosa.

acariciar *v.* tocar suavemente.

agazaparse *v.* agacharse para ocultarse o protegerse de algo.

ágil *adj.* capaz de doblarse y moverse fácilmente y con gracia.

aislar *v.* provocar que alguien se sienta solo o no aceptado.

alardear *v.* hablar demasiado bien de uno mismo; fanfarronear.

alianza *sust.* pacto entre naciones, familias o individuos que tienen una causa común.

amenaza *sust.* peligro.

amonestar *v.* advertir o regañar.

anónimo *adj.* que no está identificado con un nombre.

aparente *adj.* que parece y no es.

apocadamente *adv.* con vergüenza.

apremiar *v.* apresurar a alguien para que haga algo.

arduo *adj.* difícil.

arrogante *adj.* excesivamente convencido de la propia importancia.

arrugado *adj.* rugoso.

artilugio *sust.* aparato o máquina extraña.

asignar *v.* separar con un objetivo determinado.

atentamente *adv.* con gran concentración.

B

bárbaros *adj.* se dice de un grupo de personas consideradas incivilizadas e inferiores por otro grupo de personas u otra nación.

benevolencia *sust.* buena voluntad; bondad.

bruscamente *adv.* de manera descortés; con pocas palabras.

C

caballerosidad *sust.* código que regía el comportamiento de los caballeros en el que se exigía coraje, honor y disposición para brindar ayuda a los que la necesitaran.

carga *sust.* cosa pesada que hay que soportar.

cargar *v.* transportar.

carismático *adj.* que posee energía, encanto o atractivo.

coacción *sust.* fuerza irresistible que obliga a hacer algo.

combate *sust.* asalto; partido.

comestible *adj.* que se puede comer.

comunicativo *adj.* que es bueno transmitiendo ideas; hablador.

concentración *sust.* acción de pensar detenidamente en algo que uno está haciendo.

condena *sust.* acción de ser declarado culpable de un delito.

consecuencia *sust.* resultado de una serie de acciones.

consternar *v.* preocupar.

consuelo *sust.* alivio.

contemplar *v.* considerar; mirar o pensar en algo con atención.

convencer *v.* asegurar que algo es verdad; persuadir.

converger *v.* acercarse a un punto.

convicción *sust.* certeza; creencia.

D

dedicar *v.* hacer algo en honor de otra persona.

deducir *v.* descontar; inferir.

desafiante *adj.* que se resiste a la autoridad.

desafortunado *adj.* que tiene mala suerte.

desconcertar *v.* confundir.

desesperadamente *adv.* con gran agitación.

desnutrición *n.* mala salud provocada por la falta de comida o la falta de comida sana.

despiadado *adj.* cruel; sin compasión.

destrucción *sust.* acto de arruinar algo.

detestable *adj.* desagradable.

disipar *v.* hacer que algo se evapore; hacer que algo desaparezca.

disputa *sust.* discusión.

distante *adj.* que no se implica emocionalmente; indiferente.

distorsión *sust.* acción de dar información falsa con el objeto de engañar a alguien.

distraídamente *adv.* de manera que muestra que no se está pensando en lo que está ocurriendo.

E

egocentrismo *sust.* amor propio excesivo que se caracteriza por hablar mucho de uno mismo.

eludir *v.* esquivar; evitar con astucia.

emprender *v.* empezar.

encuentro *sust.* acción de reunirse personalmente con alguien.

engaño *sust.* acción de hacer creer a alguien intencionadamente algo que no es cierto.

enrevesado *adj.* complicado.

escasez *sust.* situación en la que no se consiguen cantidades suficientes de las cosas que se necesitan.

escaso *adj.* en poca cantidad.

espectador *sust.* persona que observa un acontecimiento.

esplendor *sust.* magnificencia.

estándar *adj.* habitual; producido o usado normalmente.

estéril *adj.* que no da frutos; que no aporta nada.

etnia *sust.* cultura o nacionalidad común.

evacuación *sust.* proceso de sacar a las personas de una situación peligrosa.

evaporación *sust.* proceso por el cual un líquido se convierte en gas.

examinar *v.* observar algo con atención para tomar una decisión o para reunir información.

exótico *adj.* extraño; que viene de otro lugar.

expulsar *v.* obligar a abandonar un lugar.

exquisito *adj.* bello y delicado.

F

facilitar *v.* hacer más sencillo; ayudar.

famélico *adj.* que tiene mucha hambre.

familiarmente *adv.* con mucha confianza.

fanatismo *sust.* prejuicio o intolerancia desmedida en defensa de algo.

fidelidad *sust.* lealtad.

flexible *adj.* que se dobla fácilmente; ágil.

flojo *adj.* suelto.

floreciente *adj.* próspero.

flotar *v.* moverse en el aire.

formidable *adj.* que provoca asombro; impresionante.

frenéticamente *adv.* con rapidez e intensidad.

frenético *adj.* desenfrenado; fuera de control.

G

garantizar *v.* asegurar; prometer con seguridad.

H

hábitat *sust.* lugar donde vive una planta o un animal naturalmente.

habitual *adj.* que se hace por costumbre.

hechizar *v.* usar poderes mágicos; encantar.

horda *sust.* multitud de personas que se mueven en grupo.

hosco *adj.* malhumorado, huraño.

hospedar *v.* brindar alojamiento.

I

identidad *sust.* rasgos propios que caracterizan a una persona o una cosa.

idiosincrasia *sust.* particularidad.

ilegal *adj.* en contra de las normas oficiales.

impertinente *adj.* demasiado atrevido; arrogante.

implorar *v.* rogar.

impulsar *v.* mover o empujar hacia delante.

incesantemente *adv.* sin parar; de forma continuada.

inconsolable *adj.* que no puede ser tranquilizado; destrozado.

incrédulamente *adv.* de manera difícil de creer.

indigente *sust.* persona que vive en condiciones de extrema pobreza.

ingenioso *adj.* inteligente; que tiene habilidad para inventar.

inmensamente *adv.* enormemente.

inquietante *adj.* amenazante.

inscripción *sust.* palabras escritas en algo.

insolencia *sust.* falta de respeto.

instinto *sust.* patrón innato de comportamiento.

integración *sust.* proceso de reunir a personas de distintas razas en las escuelas y los vecindarios.

intenso *adj.* que muestra sentimientos fuertes.

interplanetario *adj.* entre dos o más planetas.

intimidante *adj.* que asusta o preocupa.

intimidar *v.* asustar, por ejemplo, con amenazas o violencia.

intolerable *adj.* insoportable.

intrincado *adj.* complicado; con muchos detalles.

inútilmente *adv.* en vano.

L

legado *sust.* tradiciones que se transmiten.

liberación *sust.* acción de librar a alguien de la esclavitud, la cárcel u otras limitaciones.

literalmente *adv.* según el significado básico de la palabra.

M

malicia *sust.* maldad; crueldad.

maniobrar *v.* mover o manipular con habilidad.

marchitarse *v.* secarse.

meditadamente *adv.* de manera pensada.

menguar *v.* disminuir, volverse cada vez más pequeño.

mercadería *sust.* artículos que están a la venta en una tienda.

miope *adj.* corto de vista.

moderado *adj.* que se mantiene dentro de los límites apropiados.

monarca *sust.* gobernante único y absoluto.

monopolio *sust.* control exclusivo de un mercado.

O

obligación *sust.* deber; lo que uno tiene que hacer.

obstruir *v.* bloquear; dificultar.

oponentes *sust.* personas que están en lados opuestos en una pelea o un juego.

opresión *sust.* trato injusto.

optativa *adj.* materia escolar que no es obligatoria.

P

paralizarse *v.* quedarse muy quieto, como clavado en el lugar.

penalizar *v.* quitar el derecho a algo.

permanecer *v.* quedarse.

perplejo *adj.* desconcertado; confundido.

persecución *sust.* acción de acosar a otros por sus creencias religiosas o su origen étnico.

perseverar *v.* seguir intentando; persistir; continuar haciendo algo.

persistir *v.* negarse a dejar de hacer algo.

predominantemente *adv.* principalmente.

privación *sust.* carencia o falta de algo que se necesita; dificultad que resulta de la falta de algo.

procedimiento *sust.* método para hacer algo.

profesión *sust.* ocupación por la que una persona recibe un pago.

profundo *adj.* muy intenso; serio.

prohibir *v.* no permitir hacer algo; no autorizar la ley.

prolongar *v.* continuar por un período largo.

propuesta *sust.* sugerencia.

prosperidad *sust.* éxito en lo que se emprende, en especial económicamente; estado de tener dinero y éxito.

provisional *adj.* experimental.

puntualidad *sust.* cualidad de llegar a tiempo.

R

rancio *adj.* estropeado, podrido.

rastrojo *sust.* residuo que queda en la tierra después de segar.

realzar *v.* mejorar.

reconfortante *adj.* tranquilizador.

recurso *sust.* fuente de ayuda.

refugio *sust.* lugar que brinda protección.

renovación *sust.* acción de mejorar el estado de algo.

reprimir *v.* contener.

resarcimiento *sust.* algo que se hace para compensar un daño.

resolver *v.* decidir.

resplandeciente *adj.* brillante.

retener *v.* retrasar, demorar.

reticencia *sust.* falta de voluntad, desgana.

retorcerse *v.* hacer movimientos serpenteantes.

retroceder *v.* moverse hacia atrás.

riesgo *sust.* peligro.

ritual *sust.* rutina establecida.

S

semblante *sust.* rostro; apariencia.

simultáneamente *adv.* al mismo tiempo.

sobrecogimiento *sust.* sentimiento de temor y asombro.

soledad *sust.* falta de compañía.

solemne *adj.* serio; formal.

sombríamente *adv.* con desaliento; con tristeza.

supervisión *sust.* acción de controlar que algo se haga o suceda de una determinada manera.

T

taciturno *adj.* desalentado, triste.

termómetro *sust.* instrumento que sirve para medir la temperatura.

torrente *sust.* riada; corriente.

tradiciones *sust.* actitudes y costumbres aceptadas.

traducir (mal) *v.* pasar algo de un idioma a otro (de manera incorrecta).

traicionero *adj.* engañoso; desleal.

transición *sust.* cambio; paso de un estado o condición a otro.

U

unilateral *adj.* no correspondido, que solo viene de una parte.

V

valiente *adj.* que tiene coraje y resolución.

veloz *adj.* que se mueve rápidamente.

versión *sust.* interpretación que se da de algo desde otro punto de vista.

veteado *adj.* que tiene manchas de color o de luz.

vigilia *sust.* acción de estar despierto toda la noche.

Academic Vocabulary Glossary

The Academic Vocabulary Glossary in this section is an alphabetical list of the Academic Vocabulary words found in this textbook. Use this glossary just as you would use a dictionary—to find out the meanings of words used in your literature class to talk about and write about literary and informational texts and to talk about and write about concepts and topics in your other academic classes.

For each word, the glossary includes the pronunciation, part of speech, and meaning. A Spanish version of the glossary immediately follows the English version. For more information about the words in the Academic Vocabulary Glossary, please consult a dictionary.

English

A

accurate (AK yuhr iht) *adj.* containing no errors.
adequate (AD uh kwiht) *adj.* enough to meet a requirement.
ambiguous (am BIHG yoo uhs) *adj.* having more than one possible meaning; unclear.
attribute (AT ruh byoot) *n.* quality or trait of someone or something.

C

classic (KLAS ihk) *adj.* well-known, especially as being traditional or typical.
comment (KAHM ehnt) *v.* to explain or interpret something.
communicate (kuh MYOO nuh kayt) *v.* share information or ideas.
convey (kuhn VAY) *v.* make known, communicate, express.

E

evident (EHV uh duhnt) *adj.* easy to see or perceive; clear.

F

foundation (fown DAY shuhn) *n.* basis, idea, fact, or system from which something develops.
function (FUHNGK shuhn) *n.* purpose of a specific person or thing.

fundamental (fuhn duh MEHN tuhl) *adj.* relating to the most basic and important parts of something.

G

generation (jehn uh RAY shuhn) *n.* all the people in a society or family who are about the same age.

I

identify (y DEHN tuh fy) *v.* recognize and be able to say what someone or something is.
impact (IHM pakt) *n.* powerful effect.
implicit (ihm PLIHS iht) *adj.* suggested or understood but not stated directly.
insight (IHN syt) *n.* power to understand.
interact (ihn tuhr AKT) *v.* to act together with another.
interpret (ihn TUR priht) *v.* decide on the meaning of something.
intervene (ihn tuhr VEEN) *v.* to do something to try to stop an argument or solve a problem.

M

motive (MOH tihv) *n.* reason someone does something.

P

previous (PREE vee uhs) *adj.* happening before a given time.
principal (PRIHN suh puhl) *adj.* most important.
process (PRAHS ehs) *n.* series of actions or steps toward a goal.

R

relevant (REHL uh vuhnt) *adj.* directly relating to the subject.
resolve (rih ZOLV) *v.* to find an answer to a problem.
respond (rih SPAHND) *v.* say or write something as a reply.
reveal (rih VEEL) *v.* show something that was previously hidden.

S

sequence (SEE kwuhns) *n.* specific order in which things follow one another.

significance (sihg NIHF uh kuhns) *n.* importance; meaning.

significant (sihg NIHF uh kuhnt) *adj.* important.

similar (SIHM uh luhr) *adj.* almost the same.

structure (STRUHK chuhr) *n.* the way in which a set of parts is put together to form a whole.

T

technique (tehk NEEK) *n.* method of doing a particular task.

tradition (truh DIHSH uhn) *n.* a set of beliefs or customs that have been handed down for generations.

V

vision (VIHZH uhn) *n.* force or power of imagination.

Spanish

A

adecuado *adj.* que cumple con los requisitos.

ambiguo *adj.* que tiene más de un significado posible; que no es claro.

atributo *sust.* cualidad o propiedad de una cosa o una persona.

C

cimientos *sust.* base; idea, acontecimiento o sistema a partir del cual se desarrolla algo.

clásico *adj.* reconocido, en especial por ser tradicional o típico.

comentar *v.* explicar o interpretar algo.

comunicar *v.* compartir información o ideas.

E

estructura *sust.* modo en que un conjunto de partes se ubican para formar un todo.

evidente *adj.* fácil de ver y percibir; claro.

F

función *sust.* tarea que cumple alguien o algo.

fundamental *adj.* relacionado con la parte más básica e importante de algo.

G

generación *sust.* todas las personas de una sociedad o familia que tienen aproximadamente la misma edad.

I

identificar *v.* reconocer y poder decir qué es algo o quién es alguien.

impacto *sust.* efecto fuerte.

implícito *adj.* sugerido o entendido pero no dicho directamente.

interactuar *v.* funcionar en conjunto uno con otro.

interpretar *v.* decidir sobre el significado de algo.

intervenir *v.* hacer algo para intentar detener una discusión o resolver un problema.

M

manifestar *v.* comunicar; transmitir; expresar.

motivo *sust.* razón por la que alguien hace algo.

P

perspicacia *sust.* capacidad de comprensión.

preciso *adj.* que no tiene errores.

previo *adj.* que ha sucedido antes de un momento dado.

principal *adj.* lo más importante.

procedimiento *sust.* conjunto de acciones o pasos para lograr un objetivo.

R

relevancia *sust.* importancia.

relevante *adj.* que se relaciona directamente con el tema.

replicar *v.* decir o escribir algo como respuesta.

resolver *v.* hallar la respuesta a un problema.

revelar *v.* descubrir o manifestar algo que estaba oculto.

S

secuencia *sust.* orden específico en el que suceden las cosas.

significativo *adj.* importante.

similar *adj.* casi igual.

T

técnica *sust.* método para hacer una tarea en particular.

tradición *sust.* conjunto de creencias o costumbres que se transmiten de generación en generación.

V

visión *sust.* fuerza o poder de la imaginación.

ACKNOWLEDGMENTS

For permission to reproduce copyrighted material, grateful acknowledgment is made to the following sources:

Quote by Shaquille O'Neal from "Officer Shaq? Online Education Scores with Sports Pros" by Dawn Papandrea from msn.encarta® Web site, accessed September 5, 2007, at http://encarta.msn.com/encnet/departments/elearning/?article=officershaq. Copyright © by Shaquille O'Neal. Reproduced by permission of **Alliance Sports Management & Agassi Enterprises.**

Quote by Mildred D. Taylor from Newbery Award Acceptance Speech, 1977. Copyright © 1977 by Mildred D. Taylor. Reproduced by permission of **American Library Association.**

From "Mongoose on the Loose" by Larry Luxner from Américas, vol. 45, no. 4, p. 3, July/August 1993. Copyright © 1993 by Américas. Reproduced by permission of *Américas,* bimonthly magazine published by the General Secretariat of the Organization of American States in English and Spanish.

From *Great Books for Girls* by Kathleen Odean. Copyright © 1997 by Kathleen Odean. Reproduced by permission of **Ballantine Books, a division of Random House, Inc.** and electronic format by permission of **The Spieler Agency/East.**

BART Bicycle Rules from *BART* Web site, accessed September 5, 2007, at http://www.bart.gov/guide/bikes/bikeRules.asp. Copyright © 2007 by Bay Area Rapid Transit. Reproduced by permission of **BART.**

BART Stations and Schedules from *BART* Web site, accessed September 5, 2007, at http://www.bart.gov/stations/quickplanner/extended.asp?o=WCRK&d=EMBAR&dm=6&dd=18&dt=2%3A00+PM&tm=departs. Copyright © 2007 by Bay Area Rapid Transit. Reproduced by permission of **BART.**

BART System Map from *BART* Web site, accessed September 5, 2007, at http://www.bart.gov/images/map500.gif. Copyright © 2007 by Bay Area Rapid Transit. Reproduced by permission of **BART.**

BART Ticket Guide from *BART* Web site, accessed September 5, 2007, at http://www.bart.gov/tickets/types/types.asp. Copyright © 2007 by Bay Area Rapid Transit. Reproduced by permission of **BART.**

"Names/Nombres" by Julia Alvarez. Copyright © 1985 by Julia Alvarez. First published in Nuestro, March 1985. All rights reserved. Reproduced by permission of **Susan Bergholz Literary Services, New York.**

"Chanclas" from *The House on Mango Street* by Sandra Cisneros. Copyright © 1984 by Sandra Cisneros. Published by Vintage Books, a division of Random House, Inc., and in hardcover by Alfred A. Knopf in 1994. All rights reserved. Reproduced by permission of **Susan Bergholz Literary Services, New York.**

"The Place Where Dreams Come From" by Sandra Cisneros. Copyright © 2003 by Sandra Cisneros. All rights reserved. Reproduced by permission of **Susan Bergholz Literary Service, New York.**

"Salvador Late or Early" from *Woman Hollering Creek* by Sandra Cisneros. Copyright © 1991 by Sandra Cisneros. Published by Vintage Books, a division of Random House, Inc., and originally in hardcover by Random House, Inc. All rights reserved. Reproduced by permission of **Susan Bergholz Literary Services, New York.**

"User Friendly" by **T. Ernesto Bethancourt** from *Connections: Short Stories*, edited by Donald R. Gallo. Copyright © 1989 by Ernesto Bethancourt. Reproduced by permission of the author.

"I Ask My Mother to Sing" from *Rose: Poems by Li-Young Lee.* Copyright © 1986 by Li-Young Lee. Reproduced by permission of **BOA Editions, Ltd.**

"Home" from *Maud Martha* by Gwendolyn Brooks. Copyright © 1993 by Gwendolyn Brooks. Published by Third World Press, Chicago. Reproduced by permission of **Brooks Permissions.**

Essay by Pat Mora. Copyright © 2007 by Pat Mora. Reproduced by permission of **Curtis Brown, Ltd.**

"Gold" by Pat Mora, www.patmora.com. Copyright © 1998 by Pat Mora. All rights reserved. Reproduced by permission of **Curtis Brown, Ltd.**

"Looking Beneath the Surface" by Jane Yolen. Copyright © 2007 by Jane Yolen. Reproduced by permission of **Curtis Brown, Ltd.**

"The Twelve Tasks of Heracles" from *Greek Myths for Young Children* by Marcia Williams. Copyright © 1991 by Marcia Williams. Reproduced by permission of **Candlewick Press, Inc., Cambridge, MA, on behalf of Walker Books Ltd., London.**

From *Merlin and the Dragons* by Jane Yolen, illustrated by Li Ming. Copyright © 1995 by Lightyear Entertainment, L.P. Reproduced by permission of **Cobblehill Books, an affiliate of Dutton Children's Books, a Division of Penguin Young Readers Group, A Member of Penguin Group (USA) Inc., www.penguingroup.com.**

"The Monsters Are Due on Maple Street" by Rod Serling. Copyright © 1960 by Rod Serling. Reproduced by permission of **Code Entertainment.**

Quote by Rod Serling. Copyright © by Rod Serling. Reproduced by permission of **Code Entertainment.**

Excerpt from *Brian's Song* by William Blinn. Copyright © 1971 by Screen Gems, a division of Columbia Pictures. Reproduced by permission of **CPT Holdings, Inc.**

"The Flight of Icarus" from *Stories of the Gods and Heroes* by Sally Benson. Copyright 1940 and renewed © 1968 by Sally Benson. All rights reserved. Reproduced by permission of **Dial Books for Young Readers, a Division of Penguin Young Readers Group, A Member of Penguin Group (USA) Inc., www.penguingroup.com.**

"The Runaway" from *The Poetry of Robert Frost*, edited by Edward Connery Lathem. Copyright 1923, © 1969 by Henry Holt and Company; copyright © 1951 by Robert Frost. Reproduced by permission of **Henry Holt and Company, LLC.**

"Bargain" from *The Big It and Other Stories* by A. B. Guthrie. Copyright © 1960 and renewed © 1988 by A. B. Guthrie. All rights reserved. Reproduced by permission of **Houghton Mifflin Company.**

"The Great Musician" (retitled "Orpheus, the Great Musician") from *Greek Myths* by Olivia Coolidge. Copyright © 1949 and renewed © 1977 by Olivia E. Coolidge. All rights reserved. Reproduced by permission of **Houghton Mifflin Company, www.hmco.com.**

"Names of Horses" from *White Apples and the Taste of Stone: Selected Poems, 1946–2006* by Donald Hall. Copyright © 2006 by Donald Hall. All rights reserved. Reproduced by permission of **Houghton Mifflin Company, www.hmco.com.**

"He-y, Come On Ou-t" by Shinichi Hoshi. Copyright © 1978 by **Kayoko Hoshi.** Reproduced by permission of the copyright holder.

"King Midas and the Golden Touch" from *Tales from Ancient Greece* by Pamela Oldfield. Copyright © 1988 by Grisewood and Dempsey, Ltd. All rights reserved. Reproduced by permission of **Kingfisher Publications Plc.**

Essay by **Allan Knee.** Copyright © 2007 by Allan Knee. Reproduced by permission of the author.

"Harlem Night Song" from *The Collected Poems of Langston Hughes.* Copyright © 1994 by The Estate of Langston Hughes. Reproduced by permission of **Alfred A. Knopf, a division of Random House, Inc.** and electronic format by permission of **Harold Ober Associates, Incorporated.**

"Madam and the Rent Man" from *The Collected Poems of Langston Hughes.* Copyright © 1994 by The Estate of Langston Hughes. Reproduced by permission of **Alfred A. Knopf, a division of Random House, Inc.** and electronic format by permission of **Harold Ober Associates, Incorporated.**

"Winter Moon" from *The Collected Poems of Langston Hughes.* Copyright © 1994 by The Estate of Langston Hughes. Reproduced by permission of **Alfred A. Knopf, Inc., a division of Random House, Inc.** and electronic format by permission of **Harold Ober Associates, Incorporated.**

Essay by Kathleen Krull. Copyright © 2007 by **Kathleen Krull.** Reproduced by permission of the author.

Interview with Sandra Cisneros by Marit Haahr from *The Infinite Mind.* Copyright © 2002 by **Lichtenstein Creative Media.** Reproduced by permission of the copyright holder.

From *Long Walk To Freedom* by Nelson Mandela. Copyright © 1994, 1995 by Nelson Rolihlahla Mandela. Reproduced by permission of **Little, Brown and Company.**

"All in green went my love riding" from *Complete Poems: 1904–1962* by E. E. Cummings, edited by George J. Firmage. Copyright 1923, 1951, © 1991 by the Trustees for the E. E. Cummings Trust; copyright © 1976 by George James Firmage. Reproduced by permission of **Liveright Publishing Corporation.**

"maggie and milly and molly and may" from *Complete Poems: 1904–1962* by E. E. Cummings, edited by George J. Firmage. Copyright © 1956, 1984, 1991 by the Trustees for the E. E. Cummings Trust. Reproduced by permission of **Liveright Publishing Corporation.**

From *Stan Lee Presents A Christmas Carol* by Charles Dickens. Copyright © 2007 by Marvel Characters, Inc. Reproduced by permission of **Marvel Entertainment.**

"Antaeus" by Borden Deal. Copyright © 1961 by Southern Methodist University Press. Reproduced by permission of **Ashley Deal Matin, Executrix for the Borden Deal Estate.**

Quote by Borden Deal. Reproduced by permission of **Ashley Deal Matin, Executrix for the Borden Deal Estate.**

A Christmas Carol: Scrooge and Marley by Israel Horovitz. Copyright © 1994 by Fountain Pen, LLC. All rights reserved. Reproduced by permission of **William Morris Agency, LLC on behalf of the author.**

"Battery Removal/Replacement" from *Premier Cellular Telephone: Owner's Manual.* Copyright © 1994 by Motorola, Inc. Reproduced by permission of **Motorola, Inc.**

Quote by Al Young from NPR Interview. Copyright © 2005 by **National Public Radio.** Reproduced by permission of the copyright holder.

From "Canines to the Rescue" by Jonah Goldberg from *National Review*, pp. 34, 36, November 2001. Copyright © 2001 by **National Review, Inc., 215 Lexington Avenue, New York, N.Y. 10016.** Reproduced by permission of the publisher.

From "Amy Tan: Joy, Luck, and Literature," an interview by Anita Merina from *NEA Today*, October 1991. Copyright © 1991 by the **National Education Association of the United States.** Reproduced by permission of the publisher.

Comment (retitled "Exile Eyes") by Agate Nesaule from *NPR Morning Edition*, October 24, 2000. Copyright © 2000 by **Agate Nesaule.** Reproduced by permission of the author.

"A Man Down, a Train Arriving, And a Stranger Makes a Choice" by Cara Buckley from *The New York Times*, January 3, 2007. Copyright © 2007 by Cara Buckley. Reproduced by permission of **The New York Times Company.**

"Hum" by Naomi Shihab Nye from *face relations: 11 stories about seeing beyond color.* Copyright © 2004 by **Naomi Shihab Nye.** Reproduced by permission of the author.

"A Good Reason to Look Up" by Shaquille O'Neal from *Chicken Soup for The Kid's Soul.* Copyright © 1998 by **Shaquille O'Neal.** Reproduced by permission of the author.

"Stolen Day" by Sherwood Anderson from *This Week Magazine*, 1941. Copyright 1941 by United Newspapers Magazine Corporation; copyright renewed © 1968 by Eleanor Copenhaver Anderson. Reproduced by permission of **Harold Ober Associates Incorporated.**

Quote by Langston Hughes from *The Big Sea.* Copyright 1940 by Langston Hughes and renewed © 1968 by Arna Bontemps and George Houston Bass. Reproduced by permission of **Hill and Wang, a division of Farrar, Straus and Giroux, LLC.**

PICTURE CREDITS

The illustrations and photographs on the Contents pages are picked up from pages in the textbook. Credits for those can be found either on the textbook page on which they appear or in the listing below.

Photo Credits: **iii,** (all photos) Sam Dudgeon/HRW Photo; **iv,** (bl) (bc), (br) Sam Dudgeon/HRW Photo, (tl) Courtesy of Hector Rivera, (tr) Courtesy of Eric Cooper; **v,** (l), (cl) Sam Dudgeon/HRW Photo, (cr) Courtesy of Margaret McKeown, (r) Courtesy of Mabel Rivera; **vi,** (all photos) Sam Dudgeon/HRW Photo; **vii,** (tr) Associated Press, (tc) Courtesy of Gary Soto, (tr) Courtesy of Katherine Krull, (bl) © Cheron Bayna, (bc) Tsuni/Gamma/NewsCom, (br) Jason Stemple; **A4,** New Line/Saul Zaentz/Wing Nut Films/The Kobal Collection; **A5,** Museum of Art, Serpukhov, Russia/The Bridgeman Art Library; **A6,** © Images.com/CORBIS; **A7,** Tim Flach/Stone/Getty Images; **A9,** (l) Siede Preis/Photodisc/Getty Images, (r) Private Collection/The Bridgeman Art Library; **A10,** Private Collection/The Bridgeman Art Library; **A11,** (b) Salim Madjd, (bl) Private Collection/The Bridgeman Art Library; **A12,** Kenneth Morris/Covered Images via Getty Images; **A13,** (l) Diana Ong/SuperStock, (br) Polygram Filmed Entertainment/PhotoFest; **A14,** Creatas/Punchstock; **A15,** (tl) Hulton Archive/Getty Images, (b) Steve Hamblin/Alamy; **A16,** © Images.com/CORBIS; **A17,** © Images.com/CORBIS; **A17,** Jerry Driendl Photography/Panoramic Images; **A18,** Really Useful Films/Joel Schumacher Prods./The Kobal Collection; **A19,** (t) NBC/Photofest (b) © CORBIS; **A20,** © Barbar Walton/epa/CORBIS; **A21,** Oriental Museum, Durham University, UK/The Bridgeman Art Library; **A27,** 20TH CENTURY FOX/The Kobal Collection; **A32,** (tl) New Vision Technologies Inc/Digital Vision/Getty Images, (br) Digital Vision/ Getty Images, (tr) Siede Preis/Photodisc/Getty Images, (inset) kittasgraphics/ShutterStock; **A32–A33,** (bkgd) Peter Dazeley/Getty Images; **A33,** (cr) Gabrielle Revere/Stone/Getty Images, (t) Stockbyte/Getty Images, (bl) Sam Dudgeon/HRW Photo, (bkgd) Antonello Turchetti/Digital Vision/Getty Images; **1,** (b) Associated Press, (bkgd) © F. Jack Jackson/Alamy; **1,** (bl) Cover image from *Puppies, Dogs, and Blue Northers* by Gary Paulsen. Copyright © 1996 by Harcourt, Inc. Reproduced by permission of the publisher; (bc) Cover image from *Soldier's Heart* by Gary Paulsen. Copyright © 1998 by Random House, Inc., www.randomhouse.com. Reproduced by permission of the publisher; **2,** New Line/Saul Zaentz/Wing Nut Films/The Kobal Collection; **3,** © age fotostock/Superstock; **7,** © Joe McDonald/CORBIS; **11,** © Purestock/SuperStock; **12,** (b) © Gregory Pace/CORBIS. (bkgd) © Fridmar Damm/zefa/CORBIS; **14,** (l), (r) Scott B. Rosen/HRW, (bkgd) © Thinkstock/CORBIS; **16,** (bl) Chris Lawrence, (br) Vintage front cover from DOWN THESE MEAN STREETS by Piri Thomas. Used by permission of Alfred A. Knopf, a division of Random House, Inc.; **19,** © Popperfoto/Alamy; **17,** (l–r) Scott B. Rosen HRW; **21,** (l–r) Scott B. Rosen HRW; **22–23,** Scott B. Rosen HRW; **25,** © Superstock/Alamy; **26,** (l–r) Scott B. Rosen.HRW Photo; **30,** © Mireille Vautier/Alamy; **32,** © G P Bowater/Alamy; **38,** © Sharon Dominick/IstockPhoto; **42,** Museum of Art, Serpukhov, Russia/The Bridgeman Art Library; **44,** (bl) reprinted by permission of Penguin Young Readers Group, (bkgd) © David Muench/CORBIS; **47,** (tl), (tc) Smithsonian American Art Museum, Washington, DC/ Art Resource, NY, (tr) Private Collection/The Bridgeman Art Library; **49,** © Eran Yardeni/Alamy; **50,** (b) © EranYardeni/Alamy, (inset) © SuperStock, Inc./SuperStock; **52,** © Eran Yardeni/Alamy; **55,** © Renee Morris/Alamy; **57,** © Renee Morris/Alamy; **58,** © Renee Morris/Alamy; **62,** Saint Frederick High School Yearbook; **64,** (bl) © Warner Bros./PhotoFest, (br) © Ian Shaw/Alamy; **66,** Saint Frederick High School Yearbook; **70,** (inset) © Mike Blake/Reuters/CORBIS, (bkgd) © David Madison/Newsport/CORBIS; **74,** © Oleksiy Maksymenkl/Alamy; **76,** (t) Bildarchiv Preussischer Kulturbesitz/Art Resource, NY, (c) Reprinted by Permission of McIntosh and Otis, Inc. (b) The Pittsburgh Press/Carnegie Mellon University Library of Special Collections; **78,** Private Collection, Photo © Christie's

Images/The Bridgeman Art Library; **81,** © Christie's Images/CORBIS; **82,** Private Collection/The Bridgeman Art Library; **89,** Victoria & Albert Museum, London/Art Resource, NY; **92,** © Twentieth Century Fox Film Corp./Photofest; **96,** S. Vitale, Ravenna, Italy Scala/Art Resource, New York; **98,** © Archivo Iconografico, S.A/CORBIS; **100,** © Gianna Dagil Orti/CORBIS; **103,** (cr) Vanni/Art Resource, NY, (border) Copyright Dorling Kindersley, (inset) Vanni/Art Resource, NY; **104,** Copyright Dorling Kindersley; **110,** HRW Photo; **126,** (l) Courtesy of Gary Soto, (bkgd) © Dbimages/Alamy; **126,** (bl) Cover image from *Local News* by Gary Soto. Copyright © 1993 by Harcourt, Inc. Reproduced by permission of the publisher., (bc) Cover image from *Accidental Love* by Gary Soto. Copyright © 2006 by Harcourt, Inc. Reproduced by permission of the publisher., (br) Cover image from *Taking Sides* by Gary Soto. Copyright © 1991 by Harcourt, Inc. Reproduced by permission of the publisher.; **128–129,** © CORBIS; **129,** © Bob Barbout/Getty Images; **137,** The De Morgan Centre, London/The Bridgeman Art Library; **138,** Ron Stroud/Masterfile; **140,** © Mira/Alamy; **142,** (br) © Mary Evans Picture Library/Alamy, (bl) © Lebrecht Music and Arts Photo Library/Alamy; **143,** © Siede Preis/Getty Images; **144,** © Siede Preis/Getty Images; **145,** © Dinodia/Omni-Photo Communications; **147,** © age fotostock/ Superstock; **148,** © Siede Preis/Getty Images; **149,** © Purestock/ Getty Images, **150,** © blickwinkel/Alamy; **152,** © Medio Images/ Getty Images; **153,** © Siede Preis/Getty Images; **154,** © Siede Preis/ Getty Images; **155,** Toby Sinclair/Nature Picture Library; **156,** K. Senani/OSF/Animals Animals/Earth Scenes; **159,** Comstock; **160,** © Stephen Dalton/Photo Researchers, Inc.; **162,** © Andrew Stweart/ Alamy; **163,** © Tim Flach/Getty Images; **167,** © Tim Flach/Getty Images; **168,** Kim Taylor/Nature Picture Library; **170,** David Kjaer/ Nature Picture Library; **171,** © Chad Ehlers/Getty Images; **173,** J. Downer/OSF/Animals Animals/Earth Scenes; **174,** © Tim Flach/ Getty Images; **178,** © CORBIS; **180,** (cr) Scott B. Rosen/HRW, (bl–br) Courtesy of Rene Saldana, Jr.; **182–183,** © A. Belov/CORBIS; **187,** Private Collection/The Bridgeman Art Library; **192,** DACS/The Bridgeman Art Library; **197,** © Forrest J. Ackerman Collection/ CORBIS; **200,** © Dale O'Dell/Alamy; **203,** (l) © Jeff Spielman/Getty Images, (r) © Thomas Northcut/Getty Images; **206,** © Karen Kasmauski/CORBIS; **208,** © E. Pollard/PhotoLink/Getty Images; **219,** © SuperStock, Inc./SuperStock; **228,** Victoria Smith/HRW; **244,** (c) 20th Century Fox/The Kobal Collection, (bkgd) Digital Vision/Getty Images; **245,** © KitStock/Getty Images; **248–249,** ©Justin Lane/epa/ CORBIS; **253,** © Purestock/Superstock; **254,** © Diana Ong/ SuperStock; **256,** (bl) ©Tim Keating, (bkgd) © Bill Heinsohn/Alamy; **258,** © Gayle Ray/SuperStock; **260,** (bl) John Medina/Newscom, (bkgd) © Lake County Museum/CORBIS; **270,** © Juan Carlos Ulate/ Reuters/CORBIS, **272,** (b) Daniel A. Figuerdo, (bkgd) © Jupiter Images/Comstock/Alamy Images; **273,** © Siede Preis/Photodisc/ Getty Images; **274,** © Siede Preis/Photodisc/Getty Images; **275,** ©Bettmann/CORBIS; **276,** © blickwinkel/Alamy; **278,** © Siede Preis/ Photodisc/Getty Images; **282,** Private Collection/The Bridgeman Art Library; **284,** (b) © Corey Wise/Alamy, (bkgd) © Jupiter Images/Com- stock/Alamy Images; **287,** Private Collection/The Bridgeman Art Library; **288,** © Pam Ingalls/CORBIS; **291,** © Morton Beebe/CORBIS; **296,** © Todd Davidson/Illustration Works/CORBIS; **298,** © Bettmann/ CORBIS; **299,** © Noella Ballenger/Alamy; **304,** © Comstock Images/ Alamy; **305,** Private Collection/The Bridgeman Art Library; **312,** © Jeff Topping/Reuters/CORBIS; **314,** (t) © Juan Carlos Ulate/Reuters/ CORBIS, (b) © Brand X Pictures/Alamy; **319,** © Jim Lane/Alamy; **322,** Victoria Smith/HRW; **338,** Private Collection/The Bridgeman Art Library; **339,** © Ian Mckinnell/Getty Images; **342** (l) Private Collection/Art Resource, NY, (r) Private Collection/Art Resource, NY; **343,** Private Collection/Art Resource, NY; **347,** Réunion des Musées Nationaux/Art Resource, NY; **348,** H. Armstrong Roberst/ ClassicStock; **350,** © Farrell Grehan/CORBIS; **352,** © Hyacinth Manning/SuperStock; **354,** (bkgd) © Stock Connection/Alamy, (b) Nancy Kaszerman/Newscom; **356–357,** © Andre Jenny/Alamy; **361,** © Gari Wyn Williams/Alamy; **362,** © Andrew Holt/Alamy;

PICTURE CREDITS

The illustrations and photographs on the Contents pages are picked up from pages in the textbook. Credits for those can be found either on the textbook page on which they appear or in the listing below.

publisher., (br) Cover image from *Fever 1793* by Laurie Halse Anderson. Copyright © 2002 by **Simon & Schuster Books for Young Readers.** Reproduced by permission of the copyright holder.; (bl) Cover image from *Lupita Mañana* by Patricia Beatty. Cover illustration by Diane Bennett/Daniele Collignon Represents. Copyright © 1981 by **Holt, Rinehart and Winston.** Reproduced by permission of the pulisher.; **243,** (tl) Cover image from *Snakes* by John Bonnett Wexo. Copyright © 2006 by **Wildlife Education, Ltd.** Reproduced by permission of the publisher.; (tr) Cover image from *Black Heroes of the American Revolution* by Burke Davis. Copyright © 1976 by **Harcourt, Inc.** Reproduced by permission of the publisher., (bl) Cover image from *Red Scarf Girl* by Ji-Li Jiang. Copyright © 1997 by **Holt, Rinehart and Winston.** Reproduced by permission of the publisher., (br) Cover image from *Final Frontier: Voyages into Outer Space* by David Owen. Copyright © 2003 by Firefly Books Ltd. Reproduced by permission of **NASA., 244,** (c) 20th Century Fox/The Kobal Collection, (bkgd) Digital Vision/Getty Images; **245,** © KitStock/Getty Images; **248–249,** ©Justin Lane/epa/CORBIS; **253,** © Purestock/Superstock; **254,** © Diana Ong/SuperStock; **256,** (bl) ©Tim Keating, (bkgd) © Bill Heinsohn/Alamy; **258,** © Gayle Ray/SuperStock; **260,** (bl) John Medina/Newscom, (bkgd) © Lake County Museum/CORBIS; **270,** © Juan Carlos Ulate/Reuters/CORBIS, **272,** (b) Daniel A. Figuerdo, (bkgd) © Jupiter Images/Comstock/Alamy Images; **273,** © Siede Preis/Photodisc/Getty Images; **274,** © Siede Preis/Photodisc/Getty Images; **275,** ©Bettmann/CORBIS; **276,** © blickwinkel/Alamy; **278,** © Siede Preis/Photodisc/Getty Images; **282,** Private Collection/The Bridgeman Art Library; **284,** (b) © Corey Wise/Alamy, (bkgd) © Jupiter Images/Comstock/Alamy Images; **287,** Private Collection/The Bridgeman Art Library; **288,** © Pam Ingalls/CORBIS; **291,** © Morton Beebe/CORBIS; **296,** ©Todd Davidson/Illustration Works/CORBIS; **298,** © Bettmann/CORBIS; **299,** © Noella Ballenger/Alamy; **304,** © Comstock Images/Alamy; **305,** Private Collection/The Bridgeman Art Library; **312,** © Jeff Topping/Reuters/CORBIS; **314,** (t) © Juan Carlos Ulate/Reuters/CORBIS, (b) © Brand X Pictures/Alamy; **319,** © Jim Lane/Alamy; **322,** Victoria Smith/HRW; **336,** (tl) Cover image from *M. C. Higgins, the Great* by Virginia Hamilton. Cover illustration by Sarajo Frieden. Copyright © 1974 by **Holt, Rinehart and Winston.** Reproduced by permission of the publisher., (tr) Cover image from *Tangerine* by Edward Bloor. Copyright © 1997 by Edward Bloor. Reproduced by permission of **Harcourt, Inc.,** (br) Cover image from *Sundiata: An Epic of Old Mali* by D.T. Niane. Copyright © 2003. Reproduced by permission of **Pearson Education, Ltd.; 337,** (tr) Cover image from *Bill Nye the Science Guy's Great Big Book of Science featuring Oceans and Dinosaurs.* Copyright © 2005 by Bill Nye. Reproduced by permission of **Hyperion Books for Children.,** (bl) Cover image from *Pride of Puerto Rico: The Life of Roberto Clemente* by Paul Robert Walker. Copyright © 1988 by Harcourt, Brace & Company. Reproduced by permission of **Harcourt, Inc.,** (br) Cover image from *Murals: Walls That Sing by George Ancona.* Copyright © 2003 by **Cavendish Children's Books.** Reproduced by permission of the publisher., (tl) Cover image from *Facing the Lion: Growing Up Masai on the African Savanna* by Joseph Lemasolai Lekuton and Herman Viola. Copyright © 2003 by **National Geographic Society.** Reproduced by permission of the copyright holder.; **338,** Private Collection/The Bridgeman Art Library; **339,** © Ian Mckinnell/Getty Images; **342** (l) Private Collection/Art Resource, NY, (r) Private Collection/Art Resource, NY; **343,** Private Collection/Art Resource, NY; **347,** Réunion des Musées Nationaux/Art Resource, NY; **348,** H. Armstrong Roberst/ClassicStock; **350,** © Farrell Grehan/CORBIS; **352,** © Hyacinth Manning/SuperStock; **354,** (bkgd) © Stock Connection/Alamy, (b) Nancy Kaszerman/Newscom; **356–357,** © Andre Jenny/Alamy; **361,** © Gari Wyn Williams/Alamy; **362,** © Andrew Holt/Alamy; **367,** © Dynamic Graphics Group/Creatas/Alamy; **371,** © Dynamic Graphics Group/Creatas/Alamy; **372,** © Francis G. Mayer/CORBIS; **374,** (bl) Associated Press, (cr) Private Collection, Archives Charmet/The Bridgeman Art Library; **377,** (top)

FogStock,LLC/Index Stock Imagery, (border) © Angelo Cavalli/Getty Images; **381,** Private Collection/Bridgeman Art Library; **390,** © Bettmann/CORBIS; **393,** (b) © Carrie Boretz/CORBIS, (inset) Ron Stroud/Masterfile; **398,** © Darren Greenwood/Design Pics/CORBIS; **400** (bl) © Bettmann/CORBIS, (bkgd) © Comstock Images/Alamy; **405,** © Americana Images/Super Stock; **406–407,** Salim Madjd; **411,** © Bettmann/CORBIS, **415,** © Jupiter Images/Ablestock/Alamy; **416,** Tate, London/Art Resource, NY; **418,** (cl) © SuperStock, Inc./SuperStock; (bl) Associated Press; **421,** © James Porto/Getty Images; **425,** © Peter Maltz/CORBIS; **427,** © Benjamin Shearm/Getty Images; **429,** © Akira Inoue/amana images/Getty Images; **431,** © Adam Crowley/Getty Images; **432,** (t) Picture Collection, The Branch Libraries, The New York Public Library, Astor, Lenox and Tilden Foundations; (border) © Adam Crowley/Getty Images; **434–437** (border) Photodisc/Punchstock, Zen Shui/Punchstock, Digital Vision/Punchstock; **437,** Alinari Archives/The Image Works; **441,** Private Collection/The Bridgeman Art Library; **442,** © Richard H.Fox/SuperStock; **446,** Don Hammond/Design Pics/CORBIS; **448,** (c) © Ryan McVay/Getty Images, (inset) © George Doyle/Stockbyte/Getty Images; **453,** Wire Image Stock/Masterfile; **454,** © Christina Kennedy/Getty Images; **464,** HRW Photo; **480,** (tl) Cover image from *Across the Grain* by Jean Ferris. Copyright © 1990 by **Farrar, Straus and Giroux, LLC.** Reproduced by permission of the publisher., (tr) Cover image from *Soldier Boy* by Brian Burks. Copyright © 1997 by **Harcourt, Inc.** Reproduced by permission of the publisher., (bl) Cover image from *Holes* by Louis Sachar. Cover art by Sally Vitsky/Artco LLC. Copyright © 1999 by **Holt, Rinehart and Winston.** Reproduced by permission of the publisher., Cover image from *User Unfriendly* by Vivian Vande Velde. Copyright ©1991 by Vivian Vande Velde; illustration copyright © 1991 by Gary Lippincott. Reproduced by permission of **Harcourt, Inc.; 481,** (tl) Cover image from *Children of the Wild West* by Russell Freedman. Copyright © 1983 by Russell Freedman. All rights reserved. Reproduced by permission of **Clarion Books, an imprint of Houghton Mifflin Company.;** (bl) Cover image from *Sylvia Stark: A Pioneer* by Victoria Scott and Ernest Jones. Copyright © 1991 by Victoria Scott. Reproduced by permission of **Open Hand Publishing, LLC, www.openhand.com,** (tr) Cover image from *911: The Book of Help* by Marianne Carus and Marc Aronson, edited by Michael Cart. Copyright © 2002 by Marianne Carus and Marc Aronson. Reproduced by permission of **Cricket Books/Marcato.,** (br) Cover image from *The Acorn People* by Ron Jones. Copyright © 1976 by Ron Jones; cover art copyright © 1990 by Ben Stahl. Reproduced by permission of **Random House Children's Books, a division of Random House, Inc.; 482,** (b) Courtesy of Kathleen Krull, (bkgd) © nagelestock/Alamy; (bl) Cover image from *Lives of the Athletes* by Kathleen Krull. Copyright © 1995 by **Harcourt, Inc.** Reproduced by permission of the publisher., (br) Cover image from *Lives of the Presidents* by Kathleen Krull. Copyright © 1998 by **Harcourt, Inc.** Reproduced by permission of the publisher., (bc) Cover image from *Harvesting Hope: The Story of Cesar Chavez* by Kathleen Krull. Copyright © 2003 by **Harcourt, Inc.** Reproduced by permission of the publisher., **484,** Kenneth Morris/Covered Images via Getty Images; **485,** Ron Chapple/Getty Images; **489,** Iona Antiques, London, UK,/The Bridgeman Art Library; **493,** © Victor Baldizon/NBAE via Getty Images; **494,** (bl) © Allstar Picture Library/Alamy, (bkgd) © Hitoshi Nishimura/Getty Images, (br) © Photodisc/Getty Images; **496,** © Marina Terletsky; **498,** (bl) copyright Bill Eichner. Reprinted with permission of Susan Bergholz Literary Services, New York, NY and Lamy, NM. All rights reserved., (bkgd) Jeremy Walker/Getty Images; **504,** © Neville Elder/CORBIS; **510,** Polygram/The Kobal Collection; **510,** (bl) Courtesy of Catherine Noren, (bkgd) © Visions of America/Alamy; **513,** Private Collection/The Bridgeman Art Library; **514,** Victoria & Albert Museum, London/Art Resource, NY; **519,** © Polygram Filmed Entertainment/PhotoFest; **520,** Polygram/The Kobal Collection; **524,** © Louise Gubb/CORBIS; **526,** (br) HIP/Art Resource, NY, (bl) © David Turnley/

INFORMATIONAL TEXT SKILLS

INDEX OF AUTHORS AND TITLES

The italicized page numbers indicate the pages on which author biographies appear.

INDEX OF AUTHORS AND TITLES